W9-CYV-619

Organizational Behavior

A Practical, Problem-Solving Approach

Angelo Kinicki
Arizona State University

Mel Fugate
Southern Methodist University

Mc
Graw
Hill
Education

ORGANIZATIONAL BEHAVIOR: A PRACTICAL, PROBLEM-SOLVING APPROACH
International Edition 2016

Published by McGraw-Hill Education, 2 Penn Plaza, New York, NY 10121. Copyright © 2016 by McGraw-Hill Education. All rights reserved. No part of this publication may be reproduced or distributed in any form or by any means, or stored in a database or retrieval system, without the prior written consent of McGraw-Hill Education, including, but not limited to, in any network or other electronic storage or transmission, or broadcast for distance learning.

Some ancillaries, including electronic and print components, may not be available to customers outside the United States.

This book cannot be re-exported from the country to which it is sold by McGraw-Hill. This International Edition is not to be sold or purchased in North America and contains content that is different from its North American version.

10 09 08 07 06 05 04 03 02
20 19 18 17 16
CTP   MPM

All credits appearing on page or at the end of the book are considered to be an extension of the copyright page.

When ordering this title, use ISBN 978-981-4714-42-6 or MHID 981-4714-42-9

The Internet addresses listed in the text were accurate at the time of publication. The inclusion of a website does not indicate an endorsement by the authors or McGraw-Hill Education, and McGraw-Hill Education does not guarantee the accuracy of the information presented at these sites.

Printed in Singapore

www.mhhe.com

DEDICATION

To Bob Kreitner, my best friend and co-author for over 30 years. I love ya man.

— *Angelo*

I want to thank my sweet wife, Donna. Her support, understanding, and friendship are invaluable. I'm glad you're my wife.

— *Mel*

Angelo Kinicki is an award winning professor, author, and consultant. He is a Professor of Management and is the recipient of the Weatherup/Overby Chair in Leadership at the W.P. Carey School of Business, Arizona State University. He also is a Dean's Council of 100 Distinguished Scholar at the W. P. Carey School of Business. He joined the faculty in 1982, the year he received his doctorate in business administration from Kent State University.

Angelo is the recipient of six teaching awards from Arizona State University, where he teaches in its nationally ranked MBA and PhD programs. He also received several research awards, and was selected to serve on the editorial review boards for four scholarly journals. His current research interests focus on the dynamic relationships among leadership, organizational culture, organizational change, and individual, group, and organizational performance. Angelo has published over 98 articles in a variety of academic journals and is co-author of eight textbooks (30 including revisions) that are used by hundreds of universities around the world. Several of his books have been translated into multiple languages, and two of his books were awarded revisions of the year by The McGraw-Hill Company.

Angelo is a busy international consultant and is a principal at Kinicki and Associates. Inc., a management consulting firm that works with top management teams to create organizational change aimed at increasing organizational effectiveness and profitability. He has worked with many *Fortune* 500 firms as well as numerous entrepreneurial organizations in diverse industries. His expertise includes facilitating strategic/operational planning sessions, diagnosing the causes of organizational and work-unit problems, conducting organizational culture interventions, implementing performance management systems, designing and implementing performance appraisal systems, developing and administering surveys to assess employee attitudes, and leading management/executive education programs. He developed a 360^0 leadership feedback instrument called the Performance Management Leadership Survey (PMLS) that is used by companies throughout the World.

Angelo and his wife of 32 years Joyce have enjoyed living in the beautiful Arizona desert for 31 years. They are both natives of Cleveland, Ohio. They enjoy traveling, hiking, and spending time in the White Mountains with Gracie, their adorable golden retriever. Angelo also has a passion for golfing.

Mel Fugate is a professor and consultant. He is an associate professor of Management and Organizations in the Cox School of Business at Southern Methodist University. He teaches executive, MBA, and undergraduate courses. He has won six teaching awards across undergraduate and graduate levels. Prior to the Cox School he was a visiting assistant professor of Organizational Behavior at Tulane University's A.B. Freeman College of Business. He also has international teaching experience in the International MBA program at EM Lyon School of Management in Lyon, France. Prior to earning his Ph.D. in Business Administration and Management from Arizona State University, Mel performed consulting services in marketing and business development and was a sales representative and manager in the pharmaceutical industry. He also has a BS in engineering and business administration from Michigan State University.

Mel's primary research interests involve employee reactions to organizational change and transitions at work. This includes but is not limited to downsizings, mergers and acquisitions, restructurings, and plant closings. Another research stream involves the development of a dispositional perspective of employability and its implications for employee careers and behavior. Current interests also include the influence of leadership and organizational culture on performance and the influence of emotions on behavior at work. He has published in a number of premier management and applied psychology journals. His current consulting work includes many industries (e.g., healthcare, legal, energy, information technology, and financial services) and aims to enhance individual and organizational performance by utilizing a variety of practical, research-based tools.

Professor Fugate's research and comments have been featured in numerous media outlets: *The Wall Street Journal, The New York Times, Financial Times, FastCompany, Dallas Morning News*, CNN, Fox, ABC, and NBC.

Mel and his wife, Donna, are both very active and enjoy fitness, traveling, live music, and catering to their sweet Jack Russell Terrier, Mila.

Kinicki/Fugate: A Book Aimed at Helping Students Flourish Both Personally & Professionally

Organizational Behavior: A Practical Problem-Solving Approach is intended for use as a concepts book for the Organizational Behavior (OB) course at the undergraduate and MBA levels. We wrote this book because of our sincere belief that the application of knowledge about organizational behavior can help people flourish both personally and professionally.

Drawing on our combined 51 years of teaching organizational behavior along with our key strengths—12 teaching awards, success publishing scientific OB research, extensive management consulting and textbook writing—we have created a highly engaging, practical text based solidly on classic and contemporary OB research. To achieve this, we've integrated an informal and conversational writing style with a visually interesting magazine-like layout that **appeals to the preferences and learning styles of today's students**. This follows an approach successfully applied by Angelo Kinicki and Brian Williams's text *Management: A Practical Introduction*, 6th ed. Topics are broken down into **easily grasped, "bit-sized" portions, interspersed with frequent features that reinforce learning**. Our goal was to create a text that students enjoy reading and that will make a difference in their lives by providing them with practical tools that can be used at work, home, and school. If we have made learning about organizational behavior engaging, easy, and practical, we have accomplished our mission.

The text is organized according to the traditional flow from individual to group to organizational levels. Within each level we discuss the issues that today's students need to master to succeed, such as human and social capital, ethics, emotional intelligence, person–environment fit, critical thinking, problem solving, diversity, positive OB, social media, crucial conversations, influence, working with others and leadership.

While our book is unique in many ways, five features are especially notable:

1. A student-centric approach to learning
2. An explicitly applied and practical approach
3. An emphasis on problem solving
4. Imaginative writing for readability and engagement
5. Resources that work

FEATURE #1: A STUDENT-CENTRIC APPROACH TO LEARNING

Chapter openers are designed to frame chapter content and help students read with purpose. Each chapter begins with four to seven provocative, motivational **Major Questions** associated with the main topics of the chapter. These Major Questions are intended to help students answer the more fundamental questions "so what?" and "why does this matter to me?" for each major topic in the chapter. The Major Questions help students read with purpose and focus.

Instead of opening with a conversational vignette or short case like many texts, we open with **Winning at Work**, a feature which offers practical nuts-and-bolts or "how to" advice about issues that are important to students' personal and professional success.

> *"I think this [Major Question/ The Bigger Picture] is a great idea. Students want to have an idea of why it is important and what it means to them. This book will really speak to the Millennial generation."*
>
> **—Holly Schroth, University of California, Berkley**

winning at work

YOUR FUTURE

Imagine you are about to walk in the door and start your first full-time job. It's the job you've always wanted. Or if you are working now, imagine you've finally won the promotion you've worked so hard for, and you're about to enter your new office or work area on a new floor. Both cases are full of excitement—your professional life has so much promise!

Now take stock of your existing knowledge, skills, experiences, and common sense. Even with these assets, wouldn't you want to give yourself an even greater advantage and transform your knowledge and common sense into practical benefits at your job? After all, what value are your talents if you don't apply them?

This is why we study OB.

The Future
NEXT EXIT

WHERE EMPLOYERS SAY NEW HIRES FALL SHORT

Fortune published results from a Global Strategy Group study of 500 senior managers and executives. Only 65 percent of these business leaders found new employees "somewhat prepared" for success in business, while a significant percentage said new employees are "not prepared at all." Jeffrey Holmes, a principal at architectural firm Woods Bagot and sponsor of the survey, confirmed these findings and said: "Companies need people who can synthesize information and apply it to business problems. . . . There's less room for new hires who don't have that ability. Technical skill is not enough." This preference applies to both bachelors and masters students.[2]

KNOWLEDGE IS NOT ENOUGH

Expertise alone does not solve business problems. For decades, businesses have attributed their successes to the knowledge or technical expertise of their employees. The rationale was that if workers had the knowledge and necessary technical training, then results would automatically follow. But over time firms have realized that knowledge and training alone do not guarantee success. In recent years, business experts have called this disparity the *knowing-doing gap*.[1] The **knowing-doing gap** identifies the gap between what people know and what they actually do. For instance, everybody knows that treating people with respect is a good idea, but some managers don't always do this. Closing such gaps is an important element of your own success at school, work, and home. This also is a major focus of OB and this book.

THE LIMITS OF COMMON SENSE

You may feel that common sense will go a long way toward solving most business and career challenges. But you'd be wrong. If common sense were all that mattered, businesses would be more successful and all managers would be effective, while you and other new employees would consistently be happy and perform at your very best. However, this certainly isn't true of all employers and managers, and entry-level employees are often ill prepared and underperform.

EMPLOYERS WANT PROBLEM SOLVING AND CRITICAL THINKING

Regardless of your area of study, arguably the greatest benefit of your education is developing problem-solving and critical thinking skills. The Global Strategy Group survey of executives revealed that the most sought-after skills for all entry-level employees were problem solving (49%), collaboration (43%), and critical thinking (36%).[3] Building your skills in these areas is the overarching goal of this book.

FOR YOU   WHAT'S AHEAD IN THIS CHAPTER

You'll learn how OB can drive your job and career success. We'll explain why it's important that you and your employers invest in building both your human and social capital. We'll also explore how ethics are integral to long-term individual and organizational success and we'll introduce a problem-solving framework you can use in a wide variety of situations at school, work, and life more generally. But what really powers this book is our Integrative Framework for Understanding and Applying OB, which we introduce mid-chapter. This framework will help you organize and apply OB concepts and tools as you learn them.

---

major question

2.1   PERSONAL VALUES

MAJOR QUESTION

What role do values play in influencing my behavior?

THE BIGGER PICTURE

You may already have a good understanding of your personal values and the role they play in your life. In an organization, personal values contribute to workplace attitudes and behavior. So it's important to understand how the full range of potential human values impacts our attitudes and behavior at work. In the values model shown on the next page, see if you can locate yourself first, and then your friends or coworkers. From an OB perspective, you first need to understand personal values to understand, let alone influence, workplace attitudes.

Values are abstract ideals that guide one's thinking and behavior across all situations. They are strongly influenced by our religious or spiritual beliefs, the values of our parents, experiences during childhood, and events occurring throughout the communities and societies in which we live. Managers need to understand an employee's values because they encompass concepts, principles, or activities for which people are willing to work hard. All workers need an understanding of values to work effectively with others and manage themselves. Renowned researcher Shalom Schwartz created a theory of personal values that over time many managers and OB professionals have found especially useful for understanding the motivational impact of our values.

Examples include being proactive in the first 30 days of a new job, managing perceptions during employment interviews, nine daily habits that make people happy, negotiating a salary for a new job, multitasking and personal effectiveness, and leading meetings.

The Winning at Work feature is followed with **For You: What's Ahead in This Chapter,** that outlines the content to come in the chapter and why it is important to students' personal and professional lives. Chapters then are organized to cover each major question in turn, giving students bite-sized chunks of information. Each section begins with a recap of the **Major Question** and includes **The Bigger Picture**, which are intended to help students consider how the chapter content will be useful in their own professional and personal lives. The goal here is to go beyond the narrower demands of the course and show personal relevance.

Content portioning aids student interest and retention of information. Topics divide into easily grasped segments to make them more "digestible." Each section consists of a certain number of full pages. *Each new section starts on a new page.*

Other pedagogical devices in the chapter text also help students develop understanding:

- **Key terms** are highlighted and definitions boldfaced, to help students build their OB vocabulary.

- **Illustrations appear with relevant text discussion** so students can avoid the frustration of having to flip pages back and forth in order to study an important figure, table, or diagram described in the text.

- Frequent use of **bulleted lists and headings** helps students grasp the main concepts.

- Our consistent use of the **Integrative Framework for Understanding and Applying OB,** especially at the beginning and end of chapters, provides a structure to help students classify, organize, and apply the many OB concepts and theories that define the study of OB. We find that without some type of organizing structure, students experience information overload and fail to see how concepts are related, which in turn reduces their ability to apply their knowledge. The Integrative Framework

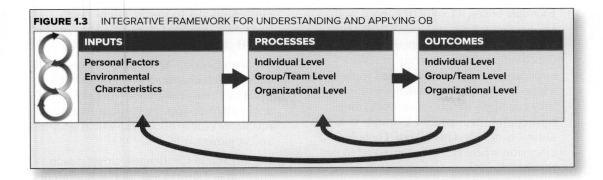

FIGURE 1.3 INTEGRATIVE FRAMEWORK FOR UNDERSTANDING AND APPLYING OB

INPUTS	PROCESSES	OUTCOMES
Personal Factors Environmental Characteristics	Individual Level Group/Team Level Organizational Level	Individual Level Group/Team Level Organizational Level

is introduced in Chapter 1, is consistently applied in every chapter, applied, and grows in detail and scope as additional topics are introduced.

- **Chapter summaries** pull much of this together and are organized around the Major Questions outlined at the beginning of each chapter.

FEATURE #2: AN EXPLICITLY APPLIED & PRACTICAL APPROACH

We want this book to be a "keeper" for students, a resource they retain and continue to use in order to effectively navigate issues in their jobs, careers, and personal lives. To achieve this goal, a central theme of Chapter 1 is to explain to students why OB matters in their professional and personal lives and how OB can help them develop higher-level soft skills such as problem solving, critical thinking, and teamwork that employers seek. The focus on application is reinforced in the following special features:

- **Winning at Work** opens each chapter and shows the personal, real-world importance of the coming chapter content.

- **Problem-Solving Applications** are box features that appear in every chapter (30 total). They describe actual problems facing real-world people and organizations. The feature always conclude with a **Your Call** extension, asking students to apply an easy 3-Stop Problem-Solving Approach, which we introduce in Chapter 1 and apply in every subsequent chapter to strengthen their problem-solving skills.

solving application

problem

Sodexo Encounters Diversity-Related Problems

Sodexo, one of the world's largest providers of food services and management, with nearly 420,000 employees in 80 countries, is a good example of a company that has attempted to effectively manage diversity. Sodexo has a deserved if well-groomed reputation for its diversity efforts, but the company's record is not perfect. Although the company was rated by DiversityInc in 2013 as the very best company for diversity based on its annual survey of 893 firms, Sodexo still is encountering diversity-related problems.[89]

Problems at Sodexo. Sodexo began its diversity program in 2002 in response to an anti-discrimination class-action lawsuit, brought by African-American employees who claimed they were not being promoted at the same rate as their white colleagues. The suit was eventually settled for $80 million in 2005. In 2010 NPR reported that "about a quarter of the company's managers are minorities, but only about 12 percent are black, which is not much of a change from five years ago, when the lawsuit was settled."[90]

Sodexo continues to have issues with labor and the law. Since the 2005 settlement, allegations of discrimination have continued, although often local in scope. The company has had other labor problems, with workers complaining about low wages. Also in 2010 Sodexo was called out by the Human Rights Watch in a 2010 report detailing the company's violations of workers' rights to unionize at several US

Executives from Sodexo speaking to employees.

locations. On the legal front Sodexo has fought isolated health code violations and charges of pocketing rebates from vendors to the detriment of several state clients.[91] In 2013 Sodexo agreed to pay $20 million in one such rebate fraud lawsuit brought by New York.[92]

YOUR CALL *Apply the 3-Stop Problem-Solving Approach.*

Stop 1: What is the problem in this case?

Stop 2: Identify the OB concepts or theories to use to solve the problem.

Stop 3: What would you do to correct this situation?

> *"Problem solving is what company leaders want to know that students can do. By incorporating this throughout the text you [provide] students multiple opportunities to learn and master this skill. . . . I am impressed with the clarity and process used to teach this skill."*
>
> —Brenda D. Bradford,
> **Missouri Baptist University**

- **Example boxes,** 44 vignettes about well-known companies and individuals taken from today's headlines, appear throughout the chapters to demonstrate practical application of OB concepts and tools. These Examples arm students with tools they can apply at school, at work, and throughout their careers. Example boxes always conclude with a **Your Thoughts?** extension where students are asked to put themselves in the situation and describe what they might do.

EXAMPLE Google Search: "How Can We Keep Talented Employees?"

While Google's talent is constantly being poached by its competitors, some employees simply quit, especially women. The company noticed that many women were leaving, or, more precisely, not returning after maternity leave. Some women of course choose to stay home after childbirth. However, Google realized that such employees were leaving at twice the average rate of all employees. It then explored the possibility that its policies might play a role.

THE INDUSTRY STANDARD Generally, the tech industry, Silicon Valley in particular, offers 12 weeks of paid time off for maternity leave and seven weeks for employees outside of California.

NEW PLAN Google's response was to offer five months of full pay and full benefits! Better still, new mothers can split the time and take some before the birth, some after, and some later still when the child is older.

NEW PLAN PLUS Seven weeks of "new-parent" leave is now offered to all of its employees around the world. This enables new mothers *and fathers* the opportunity to manage their time and new joy/baby.[5] Other companies expand these practices further still. Alston & Bird, an Atlanta-based law firm, provides employees $10,000 and 90 days of paid leave toward adoptions. Infertility issues are also covered by their health plan.[6]

YOUR THOUGHTS?

1. If you alone could make policies at Google (or where you work), what would you do to keep valuable employees?
2. How could you apply the contingency approach to make these and other policies more effective?
3. What else would you do?

- **Take-Away Applications—TAAPs** represent 42 opportunities throughout the text for students to apply the material and concepts immediately after reading them. TAAPs ask students to apply OB concepts to issues that affect their personal and professional success.

TAKE-AWAY APPLICATION—TAAP

Using Table 1.3:

1. Think of your most desired job. Now describe what you could do to develop your human *and* social capital to make you a more attractive job candidate.
2. Assume you graduate this year and are fortunate enough to get a job interview with your most desired employer. Explain in terms of human *and* social capital how you would promote or sell yourself in that interview.

- **Self-Assessments,** 57 research-based self-assessments integrated within the text,

allow students to immediately assess their own personal characteristics related to OB concepts being discussed.

- **Problem-Solving Application Cases** at the end of each chapter allow students to practice their problem-solving skills and apply chapter-specific content to actual problems confronting real-world people and organizations.
- **Legal/Ethical Challenges,** closing each chapter, are short cases that ask students to recommend a course of action when faced with business situations that fall into a "gray" area of legal or ethical conflicts.
- **Group Exercises** for each chapter enable students to engage in experiential activities aimed at applying chapter content.

FEATURE #3: AN EMPHASIS ON PROBLEM SOLVING

A simple **Problem-Solving Approach** is introduced in Chapter 1 and applied multiple times in every chapter throughout the book. The repeated application in every chapter helps students develop their problem-solving skills. Our problem-solving approach is described as a journey with three stops along the way: **Stop 1,** in which students define the problem; **Stop 2,** in which students use OB concepts to identify causes of the problem; and **Stop 3,** in which students apply their knowledge to generate (or even implement) a solution.

> *"Repeating the problem-solving approach in detail helps guide the students on the correct path to solving the problem in a methodical way . . . it encourages the students to become critical thinkers."*
>
> —**Kenneth Solano, Northeastern University**

> *"This is a great collection of self-assessments. I feel that it adds a lot to the student experience, provides rich fodder for class discussions, and makes the concepts relate specifically to students, and that has many advantages in learning and retention."*
>
> —**Laura Martin, Midwestern State University**

The **Integrative Framework for Understanding and Applying OB** is another tool to help students solve problems. Not only does it help students organize OB concepts and understand relationships among them, but it also assists in identifying problems, causes, and solutions.

Integrative Framework for Understanding and Applying OB

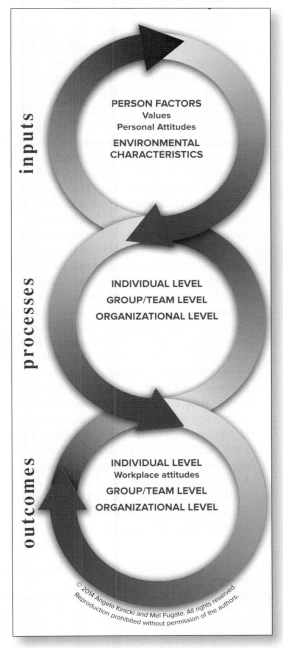

PERSON FACTORS
Values
Personal Attitudes
ENVIRONMENTAL
CHARACTERISTICS

inputs

INDIVIDUAL LEVEL
GROUP/TEAM LEVEL
ORGANIZATIONAL LEVEL

processes

INDIVIDUAL LEVEL
Workplace attitudes
GROUP/TEAM LEVEL
ORGANIZATIONAL LEVEL

outcomes

© 2014 Angelo Kinicki and Mel Fugate. All rights reserved. Reproduction prohibited without permission of the authors.

To build and reinforce students' problem-solving skills, we utilize a number of features in each chapter:

- The 30 **Problem-Solving Application** boxes, mentioned previously, appearing one or more times in each chapter, offer students the opportunity to solve problems facing real individuals, teams, and organizations.

- As mentioned above, each chapter concludes with a more in-depth **Problem-Solving Application Case.** These cases, which involve a host of companies including DISH, Google, Costco, Yahoo!, and McDonald's, enable students to hone the application of OB by trying to solve real problems with chapter-related content.

- A **Comprehensive Problem-Solving Application Case** on Zappos that spans multiple chapters allows students to exercise their growing problem-solving skills in a more complex context that involves multiple concepts and challenges across the three levels of OB (individual, team, and organizational).

FEATURE #4: IMAGINATIVE WRITING FOR READABILITY & ENGAGEMENT

Research shows that textbooks written in an **imaginative, people-oriented style significantly improve students' ability to retain information.** We use a number of journalistic devices to make the material as engaging as possible for students.

- Our use of a *conversational and informal tone* provides a casual and direct connection to the student. This tone removes barriers and draws students in to the content.

- We use *colorful facts, attention-grabbing quotes, biographical sketches, lively tag lines, and innovative illustrations* to get students' attention and enhance retention.

- Our *emphasis on practicality and application* extends to the Example boxes, Problem-Solving Application boxes, Take-Away Applications, and Self-Assessments, all of which help to keep students involved and make OB relevant.

- The text is animated by an *enticing and diverse photo program* of varying sizes and shapes to help illustrate concepts. Many photo captions end with a question to generate student interest.

"I like the idea of bite-sized chunks and applicability of the material . . . because student friendliness is one part readability, one part personal application, and two parts style."

—Dan Morrell, Middle Tennessee State University

FEATURE #5: RESOURCES THAT WORK

No matter the course you teach—on-campus, hybrid, or online courses—we set out to provide you with the most comprehensive set of resources to enhance your Organizational Behavior course.

McGraw-Hill *Connect Management*

Less managing . . . More teaching . . . Greater learning . . .

McGraw-Hill *Connect Management* is an online assignment and assessment solution that connects students with the tools and resources they need to achieve success. With *Connect Management,* students can engage with their coursework anytime, anywhere, enabling faster learning, more efficient studying, and higher retention of knowledge. It also offers faculty powerful tools that make managing assignments easier, so instructors can spend more time teaching.

Features

1. **SmartBook™**. Fueled by LearnSmart—SmartBook is the first and only adaptive reading experience available today. Distinguishing what students know from what they don't, and honing in on concepts they are most likely to forget, SmartBook personalizes content for each student in a continuously adapting reading experience. Reading is no longer a passive and linear experience, but an engaging and dynamic one where students are more likely to master and retain important concepts, coming to class better prepared. Valuable reports provide instructors insight as to how students are progressing through textbook content, useful for shaping in-class time or assessment. As a result of the adaptive reading experience found in SmartBook, students are more likely to retain knowledge, stay in class, and get better grades.

2. **Interactive Applications.** Interactive Applications offer a variety of automatically graded exercises that require students to apply key concepts. Whether the assignment includes a drag and drop, video case, sequence, or case analysis, these applications provide instant feedback and progress tracking for students and detailed results for the instructor.

3. **Interactive Self-Assessments.** Self-awareness is a fundamental aspect of personal or professional development. And because self-awareness is so important to students' professional and personal effectiveness, *Organizational Behavior* incorporates self-assessments unlike any other textbook in the market. *Multiple* SAs are incorporated in each chapter, which provides students with frequent opportunities *to make OB concepts come to life* by seeing how they apply to them personally. *Organizational Behavior* does this with 57 SAs spread across the chapters that help make OB real for students and show them how to apply concepts and theories as they learn them. These assessments are research-based and are drawn from notable journals in the field of OB, such as the *Journal of Applied Psychology, Journal of Management, Journal of Organizational Behavior, Personnel Psychology, Educational and Psychological Measurement,* and *Journal of Personality and Social Psychology.*

---

connect
SELF-ASSESSMENT 1.1   How Strong Is My Motivation to Manage?

Go to connect.mheducation.com and when finished respond to the following:

1. Does this instrument accurately assess your potential as a manager? Explain.
2. Which of the seven dimensions do you think is likely the best predictor of managerial success? Which is the least? Explain.
3. The instrument emphasizes competition with others in a win-lose mentality. Describe the pros and cons of this approach to management.

- Every SA is introduced in-text by explaining its benefits and practical relevance to the student. The intent is to motivate students to complete the assessments and appreciate their value.

- Each chapter contains an average of three self-assessments.

- Multiple-choice questions accompany each SA, which enable instructors to assure that students complete assigned assessments and understand how they illustrate the associated concepts and theories.

- Self-assessments are automatically scored in *Connect*.

- In addition to being housed in *Connect*, SA references are positioned near the concepts they illustrate in-text, with questions that focus on having students reflect on their scores; contemplate the implications for them at school, work, and home; and apply this new self-knowledge to their own lives. These questions were also written to be amenable to class discussion or personal development plan–type assignments.

- The Instructor's Manual includes guidance on how to interpret each SA and suggested avenues for class discussion and student application.

4. **Problem-Solving Application and Comprehensive Case.** While cases are common in the OB textbook market, *Organizational Behavior* takes a different approach. First, each chapter concludes with a Problem-Solving Application Case that is also available with assignable content in *Connect*. These cases are all based on real companies and people and explicitly focus on actual problems they confront. Students therefore have repeated opportunities to build their problem-solving skills, a key attribute sought by employers, while also applying the concepts and tools they learned in that particular chapter.

Second, *Organizational Behavior* has created a comprehensive case for *Connect* that includes assignable content. Unlike many additional or integrative cases used in other books, which are often based on fictitious people or organizations and illustrate only a handful of concepts, the case used in *Organizational Behavior* is an actual company—Zappos. Not only does the company have appeal to today's students, but it also was created using multiple sources to provide a truly comprehensive case. The intent is to offer students and their instructors a single case that spans all three levels of OB—individual, group/team, and organizational—and allows for the application of the many concepts and tools introduced throughout the book. We wrote this case to serve many potential purposes—a comprehensive final exam, team project, or complex problem-solving case.

Consistent with some of the major themes of our book, we selected and wrote cases that students will find both appealing and highly relevant opportunities to apply their OB knowledge.

5. **Manager's Hot Seat.** This interactive, video-based application puts students in the manager's hot seat; it builds critical-thinking and decision-making skills and allows students to apply concepts to real managerial challenges. Students watch as 21 real managers apply their years of experience when confronting unscripted issues such as bullying in the workplace, cyber loafing, globalization, intergenerational work conflicts, workplace violence, and leadership versus management.

VIDEO CASE 1: Office Romance: Groping for Answers

VIDEO CASE 2: Ethics: Let's Make a Fourth Quarter Deal

VIDEO CASE 3: Negotiation: Thawing the Salary Freeze

VIDEO CASE 4: Privacy: Burned by the Firewall?

VIDEO CASE 5: Whistle Blowing: Code Red or Red Ink?

VIDEO CASE 6: Change: More Pain Than Gain

VIDEO CASE 7: Partnership: The Unbalancing Act

VIDEO CASE 8: Cultural Differences: Let's Break a Deal

VIDEO CASE 9: Project Management: Steering the Committee

VIDEO CASE 10: Diversity: Mediating Morality

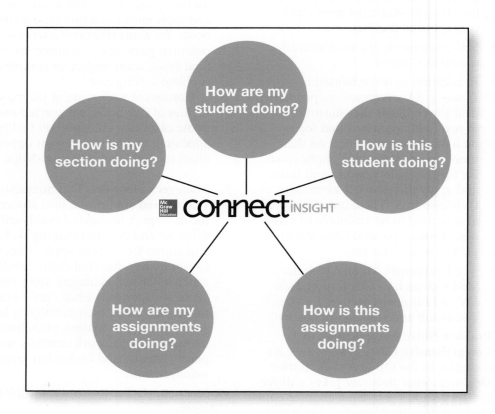

6. **Insight.** Insight plots students on a graph of core by time-spent, revealing, among other things, which students are trying but still not succeeding, suggesting that they might be the most responsive to help. Insight plots assignments on a graph of average student score by average time-spent, revealing, among other things, relatively difficult assignments and relatively easy assignments.

7. **Smart Grading.** When it comes to studying, time is precious. *Connect Management* helps students learn more efficiently by providing feedback and practice material when they need it, where they need it. When it comes to teaching, your time also is precious. The grading function enables you to . . .

- Have assignments scored automatically, giving students immediate feedback on their work and side-by-side comparisons with correct answers.

- Access and review each response; manually change grades or leave comments for students to review.

- Reinforce classroom concepts with practice tests and instant quizzes.

8. **Simple Assignment Management.** With *Connect Management,* creating assignments is easier than ever, so you can spend more time teaching and less time managing. The assignment management function enables you to . . .

   - Create and deliver assignments easily with selectable end-of-chapter questions and test bank items.
   - Streamline lesson planning, student progress reporting, and assignment grading to make classroom management more efficient than ever.
   - Go paperless with the eBook and online submission and grading of student assignments.

9. **Instructor Library.** The *Connect Management* Instructor Library is your repository for additional resources to improve student engagement in and out of class. You can select and use any asset that enhances your lecture. The *Connect Management* Instructor Library includes . . .

   - Instructor's Manual
   - PowerPoint files
   - Test Bank
   - Management Asset Gallery
   - eBook
   - Connect IM

10. **McGraw-Hill *Connect Plus Management.*** McGraw-Hill reinvents the textbook-learning experience for the modern student with *Connect Plus Management. Connect Plus* features the following:

    - An integrated eBook.
    - All *Connect* assignments and tools, which provide a dynamic link between your assignment and chapter content.
    - A powerful search function to pinpoint and connect key concepts in a snap.

For more information about *Connect,* go to **www.mcgrawhillconnect.com,** or contact your local McGraw-Hill sales representative.

Organizational Behavior Video Library DVDs

McGraw-Hill/Irwin offers the most comprehensive video support for the Organizational Behavior classroom through a course library video DVD. This discipline has a library volume DVD tailored to integrate and visually reinforce chapter concepts. The library volume DVD contains more than 55 clips! The rich video material, organized by topic, comes from sources such as PBS, NBC, BBC, SHRM, and McGraw-Hill. Video cases and video guides are provided for some clips.

Tegrity Campus

Lectures 24/7. Tegrity Campus is a service that makes class time available 24/7 by automatically capturing every lecture in a searchable format for students to review when they study and complete assignments. With a simple one-click start-and-stop process, you capture all computer screens and corresponding audio. Students can replay any part of any class with easy-to-use browser-based viewing on a PC or Mac.

Educators know that the more students can see, hear, and experience class resources, the better they learn. In fact, studies prove it. With Tegrity Campus, students quickly recall key moments by using Tegrity Campus's unique search feature. This search helps students efficiently find what they need, when they need it, across an entire semester of class recordings. Help turn all your students' study time into learning moments immediately supported by your lecture. Lecture Capture enables you to . . .

- Record and distribute your lecture with a click of a button.
- Record and index PowerPoint presentations and anything shown on your computer so it is easily searchable, frame by frame.
- Offer access to lectures anytime and anywhere by computer, iPod, or mobile device.
- Increase intent listening and class participation by easing students' concerns about note taking.

Lecture Capture will make it more likely you will see students' faces, not the tops of their heads.

To learn more about Tegrity, watch a two-minute Flash demo at **http://tegritycampus.mhhe.com**

Create

Craft your teaching resources to match the way you teach!

With McGraw-Hill Create, **www.mcgrawhillcreate.com**, you can easily rearrange chapters, combine material from other content sources, and quickly upload content you have written, like your course syllabus or teaching notes. Find the content you need in Create by searching through thousands of leading McGraw-Hill textbooks. Arrange your book to fit your teaching style. Create even allows you to personalize your book's appearance by selecting the cover and adding your name, school, and course information. Order a Create book and you'll receive a complimentary print review copy in three to five business days or a complimentary electronic review copy (eComp) via e-mail in about one hour. Go to **www.mcgrawhillcreate.com** today and register. Experience how McGraw-Hill Create empowers you to teach your students *your way.*

McGraw-Hill Higher Education and Blackboard have teamed up. What does this mean for you?

The **Best** of **Both Worlds**

1. **Your life simplified.** Now you and your students can access McGraw-Hill's Connect™ and Create™ right from within your Blackboard course—all with one single sign-on. Say goodbye to the days of logging in to multiple applications.

2. **Deep integration of content and tools.** Not only do you get single sign-on with Connect™ and Create™, you also get deep integration of McGraw-Hill content and content engines right in Blackboard. Whether you're choosing a book for your course or building Connect™ assignments, all the tools you need are right where you want them—inside of Blackboard.

3. **Seamless gradebooks.** Are you tired of keeping multiple gradebooks and manually synchronizing grades into Blackboard? We thought so. When a student completes an integrated Connect™ assignment, the grade for that assignment automatically (and instantly) feeds your Blackboard grade center.

4. **A solution for everyone.** Whether your institution is already using Blackboard or you just want to try Blackboard on your own, we have a solution for you. McGraw-Hill and Blackboard can now offer you easy access to industry-leading technology and content, whether your campus hosts it or we do. Be sure to ask your local McGraw-Hill representative for details.

INSTRUCTOR RESOURCES

Multiple high-quality, fully integrated resources are available to make your teaching life easier:

-   **The Instructors Manual (IM)** includes thorough coverage of each chapter. New in this edition, we offer two versions of the IM, for newer and experienced faculty. Included in both versions are the appropriate level of theory, recent application or company examples, teaching tips, PowerPoint references, critical discussion topics, and answers to end-of-chapter exercises.

-   **The PowerPoint (PPT)** slides provide comprehensive lecture notes, video links, and company examples not found in the textbook. There will be instructor media-enhanced slides as well as notes with outside application examples.

-   **The Test Bank** includes 100–150 questions per chapter, in a range of formats and with a greater-than-usual number of comprehension, critical-thinking, and application (or scenario-based) questions. It's tagged by learning objective, Bloom's Taxonomy levels, and AACSB compliance requirements.

-   **EZ Test**, McGraw-Hill's flexible and easy-to-use electronic testing program, allows instructors to create tests from book-specific items. It accommodates a wide range of question types, and instructors may add their own questions. Multiple versions of the test can be created, and any test can be exported for use with course management systems such as WebCT or BlackBoard.

- **EZ Test Online**, available at **www.eztestonline.com**, allows you to access the test bank virtually anywhere at any time, without installation, and to administer EZ Test–created exams and quizzes online, providing instant feedback for students.
- **The Online Learning Center (OLC)**, located at **www.mhhe.com/kfob1e**, offers downloadable resources for instructors. On the instructors' portion of the OLC, which is password-protected, instructors can access all of the teaching resources described above.

MCGRAW-HILL CUSTOMER CARE CONTACT INFORMATION

At McGraw-Hill, we understand that getting the most from new technology can be challenging. That's why our services don't stop after you purchase our products. You can e-mail our Product Specialists 24 hours a day, seven days a week, to get product training online. Or you can search our knowledge bank of Frequently Asked Questions on our support website. For Customer Support, call **800-331-5094,** e-mail **hmsupport@mcgraw-hill.com,** or visit **www.mhhe.com/support.** One of our Technical Support Analysts will be able to assist you in a timely fashion.

ASSURANCE OF LEARNING READY

Many educational institutions today are focused on the notion of assurance of learning, an important element of many accreditation standards. *Organizational Behavior* is designed specifically to support your assurance of learning initiatives with a simple yet powerful solution.

Each chapter in the book begins with a list of numbered learning objectives, which appear throughout the chapter as well as in the end-of-chapter assignments. Every Test Bank question for *Organizational Behavior* maps to a specific chapter learning objective in the textbook. Each Test Bank question also identifies topic area, level of difficulty, Bloom's Taxonomy level, and AACSB skill area. You can use our Test Bank software, EZ Test and EZ Test Online, or *Connect Management* to easily search for learning objectives that directly relate to the learning objectives for your course. You can then use the reporting features of EZ Test to aggregate student results in a similar fashion, making the collection and presentation of assurance of learning data simple and easy.

AACSB STATEMENT

McGraw-Hill/Irwin is a proud corporate member of AACSB International. Understanding the importance and value of AACSB accreditation, *Organizational Behavior* recognizes the curricula guidelines detailed in the AACSB standards for business accreditation by connecting selected questions in the Test Bank to the general knowledge and skill guidelines in the AACSB standards.

The statements contained in *Organizational Behavior* are provided only as a guide for the users of this textbook. The AACSB leaves content coverage and assessment within the purview of individual schools, the mission of the school, and the faculty. While *Organizational Behavior* and the teaching package make no claim of any specific AACSB qualification or evaluation, we have within *Organizational Behavior* labeled selected questions according to the general knowledge and skills areas.

Acknowledgements

We could not have completed this product without the help of a great number of people. It all began with the vision of our executive brand manager Michael Ablassmeir. He signed the project and assembled a fantastic team to work with us to craft a text that was unlike anything else in the market. Among our first-rate team at McGraw-Hill, we want to acknowledge key contributors: Ann Torbert's assistance was instrumental in structuring the editorial process and arriving at the text's vision and predicted appeal; Bill Teague, Jane Beck, Trina Hauger, and Andrea Scheive, developmental editors, helped us realize our vision and enhance that appeal; Elizabeth Trepkowski, executive marketing manager, for creative and proactive marketing; Harvey Yep, lead project manager, led the product through the production process; designer Keith McPherson; Lori Hancock, content licensing specialist; Terri Lawson for permission; and Danielle Clement, project manager, for managing the digital products.

We would also like to thank Mindy West, Arizona State University, for her work on the Instructor's Manual; Christine Mark, Lander

University, for PowerPoint slides; Eileen Hogan, Kutztown University, for the test bank; Floyd Ormsbee, Clarkson University, for his work on *Connect,* and Patrick Soleymani, George Mason University, for his work on creating self-assessment material for *Connect.*

Warmest thanks and appreciation go the individuals who provided valuable input during the development stages of this first edition, as follows:

James Bishop,
New Mexico State University, Las Cruces

Brenda D. Bradford,
Missouri Baptist University

Chris Bresnahan,
University of Southern California

Holly Buttner,
University of North Carolina, Greensboro

Dean Cleavenger,
University of Central Florida

Matthew Cronin,
George Mason University

Kristen DeTienne,
Brigham Young University

Ken Dunegan,
Cleveland State University

Steven M. Elias,
New Mexico State University

Aimee Ellis,
Ithaca College

John D. Fuehrer,
Baldwin Wallace University

Cynthia Gilliand,
University of Arizona

Early Godfrey,
Gardner Webb University

Roy Lynn Godkin,
Lamar University

Connie Golden,
Lakeland Community College

Wayne Hochwarter,
Florida State University

Madison Holloway,
Metropolitan State University of Denver

Kendra Ingram,
Texas A&M University Commerce

Hank Karp,
Hampton University

Michael Kosicek,
Indiana University of Pennsylvania

Caroline Leffall,
Bellevue College

Fengru Li,
Business School, University of Montana

Katie Liljequist,
Brigham Young University

Douglas Mahony,
Lehigh University

Laura Martin,
Midwestern State University

Douglas McCabe,
Georgetown University

Lorianne Mitchell,
East Tennessee State University

Dan Morrell,
Middle Tennessee State University

Paula Morrow,
Iowa State University

Dave Mull,
Columbia College, Columbia (MO)

Floyd Ormsbee,
Clarkson University

Bradley P. Owens,
State University of New York at Buffalo

Jeff Peterson,
Utah Valley State College

Don Powell,
University of North Texas

Gregory R. Quinet,
Southern Polytechnic State University

Jude Rathburn,
University of Wisconsin, Milwaukee

Herb Ricardo,
Indian River State College

Joe Rode,
Miami University, Oxford

Matt Rodgers,
The Ohio State University

Kristie Rogers,
University of Kansas

Christopher Roussin,
Suffolk University

Gordon Schmidt,
Indiana Purdue University, Ft. Wayne

Holly Schroth,
University of California

Kenneth Solano,
Northeastern University

Patrick Soleymani,
George Mason University

Dan Spencer,
University of Kansas

Judy Tolan,
University of Southern California

Brian Usilaner,
University of Maryland University College

Finally, we would like to thank our wives, Joyce and Donna, for being tough and caring "first customers" of our work. This book has been greatly enhanced by their input and reality testing. Thanks in large part to their love, moral support, and patience, this project was completed on schedule and it strengthened rather than strained a treasured possession—our friendship.

We hope you enjoy this textbook. Best wishes for happiness, health, and success!

Angelo Kinicki
Mel Fugate

"The Kinicki/ Fugate text is an excellent collection of learning tools that are current, interesting, and carefully constructed."

—Early Godfrey, Gardner Webb University

SELF-ASSESSMENT LIBRARY

Organizational Behavior:
A Practical, Problem-Solving Approach 1e

The following Self-Assessment list was created to help you navigate through the library of 94 available assessments. As noted earlier, 57 of these assessments have been integrated directly into the textbook. The first part of the table of contents shows you a chapter-by-chapter outline of the title for each of these assessments. This can help you to decide which of the in-text assessments you might like to use. The second part of this table of contents provides a listing of the additional 37 self-assessments in the Kinicki Self-Assessment Library. These additional self-assessments are categorized according to topic—individual, group/team, and organization. It is important to note that all 95 self-assessments are contained within *Connect,* making them assignable and gradable.

* Indicates assessments used in both books (Kinicki/Fugate—*Organizational Behavior: A Practical, Problem-Solving Approach,* 1e and Kinicki/Williams—*Management: A Practical Introduction,* 7e).

* Indicates assessments used in both books (Kinicki/Fugate—Organizational Behavior: A Practical Problem Solving Approach, 1e and Kinicki/Williams—Management: A Practical Introduction 7e).

Additional Assessments Found in Kinicki/Williams—*Management: A Practical Introduction, 7e*

WHAT ABOUT ME?

A. Learning About Your Personality

- Assessing Your Entrepreneurial Orientation
- Assessing Your Ethical Ideology
- Where Do You Stand on the Big Five Dimensions of Personality?
- What Is Your Level of Emotional Intelligence?
- How Adaptable Are You?

B. Your Values and Work Attitudes

- What Is Your Orientation Toward Theory X/Y?
- Assessing Your Consumer Ethnocentrism
- Assessing Your Stand on the GLOBE Dimensions
- Assessing Your Career Vision and Plan
- Assessing Your Financial Literacy
- Assessing Your Attitudes Toward Corporate Social Responsibility
- Is a Career in HR Right for You?
- Assessing Your Attitudes Toward Unions
- Assessing Your Satisfaction with Your University Experience

C. Your Motivation

- Assessing Your Intrinsic/Extrinsic Motivation
- Assessing Motives Associated With Self-Determination

WORKING IN GROUPS

A. Groups and Teams

- Assessing Your Attitudes toward Teamwork
- Assessing Your Team's Productive Energy
- Assessing Your Team's Level of Groupthink
- Assessing Your Team's Effectiveness

B. Communication Skills

- Assessing Your Listening Style
- Assessing Your Supportive and Defensive Communication Climate
- To What Extent Are You Using Online Social Networking at Work?

C. Conflict and Negotiations

- Assessing Your Conflict Management Style

D. Effective Leadership

- Assessing Your Motivation to Lead
- Assessing Your Global Manager Potential

ORGANIZATION LIFE

A. Culture, Socialization, and Mentoring

- Assessing the Four Basic Strategy Types
- To What Extent Is Your Organization Committed to Total Quality Management (TQM)?
- Assessing the Quality of Goal Setting within an Organization
- Assessing the Quality of HR Practices
- Assessing Your Job Fit
- Assessing the Innovation and Learning Perspective of the Balanced Scorecard

B. Organizational Design, Effectiveness, and Innovation

- Assessing Strategic Thinking
- Core Skills Required for Strategic Planning
- Assessing Obstacles to Strategic Execution
- Assessing Your Organizational Structure Preference

C. Managing Change and Stress

- Assessing Your Resistance to Change

brief contents

PART ONE
Individual Behavior   1

2 VALUES AND ATTITUDES

How Do They Affect Work-Related Outcomes?   38

3 INDIVIDUAL DIFFERENCES AND EMOTIONS

How Does Who I Am Affect My Performance?   72

PART TWO
Groups   253

8 GROUPS AND TEAMS
How Can Working with Others Increase Everybody's Performance?   254

9 COMMUNICATION IN THE DIGITAL AGE

How Can I Become a More Effective Communicator? 292

10 MANAGING CONFLICT AND NEGOTIATIONS

How Can These Skills Give Me an Advantage? 328

13 LEADERSHIP EFFECTIVENESS

What Does It Take to Be Effective? 438

PART THREE
Organizational Processes   477

14 ORGANIZATIONAL CULTURE, SOCIALIZATION, AND MENTORING

How Can I Use These Concepts for Competitive Advantage? 478

15 ORGANIZATIONAL DESIGN, EFFECTIVENESS, AND INNOVATION

How Can Understanding These Key Processes and Outcomes Help Me Succeed? 518

16 MANAGING CHANGE AND STRESS

How Can You Apply OB and Show What You've Learned?   556

Organizational Behavior

Behavior

A Practical, Problem-Solving Approach

Individual Behavior

1 MAKING OB WORK FOR ME

What Is OB and Why Is It Important?

inputs

PERSON FACTORS

ENVIRONMENTAL CHARACTERISTICS

processes

INDIVIDUAL LEVEL

GROUP/TEAM LEVEL

ORGANIZATIONAL LEVEL

outcomes

INDIVIDUAL LEVEL

GROUP/TEAM LEVEL

ORGANIZATIONAL LEVEL

MAJOR TOPICS I'LL LEARN AND QUESTIONS I SHOULD BE ABLE TO ANSWER

1.1 THE VALUE OF OB TO MY JOB AND CAREER

MAJOR QUESTION: *How can I use knowledge of OB to enhance my job performance and career?*

1.2 HUMAN AND SOCIAL CAPITAL

MAJOR QUESTION: *How can human and social capital affect my career opportunities and job performance?*

1.3 RIGHT VS. WRONG—ETHICS AND MY PERFORMANCE

MAJOR QUESTION: *Why do people fall into ethical lapses, even unwittingly, and what lessons can I learn from that?*

1.4 APPLYING OB TO SOLVE PROBLEMS

MAJOR QUESTION: *How can I apply OB in a practical way to increase my effectiveness?*

1.5 STRUCTURE AND RIGOR IN SOLVING PROBLEMS

MAJOR QUESTION: *How could I explain to a fellow student the practical relevance and power of OB to help solve problems?*

1.6 THE INTEGRATIVE FRAMEWORK FOR UNDERSTANDING AND APPLYING OB

MAJOR QUESTION: *How can the Integrative Framework help me understand and apply OB knowledge and tools—and improve my problem solving?*

© 2014 Angelo Kinicki and Mel Fugate. All rights reserved. Reproduction prohibited without permission of the authors.

winning at work

YOUR FUTURE

Imagine you are about to walk in the door and start your first full-time job. It's the job you've always wanted. Or if you are working now, imagine you've finally won the promotion you've worked so hard for, and you're about to enter your new office or work area on a new floor. Both cases are full of excitement—your professional life has so much promise!

Now take stock of your existing knowledge, skills, experiences, and common sense. Even with these assets, wouldn't you want to give yourself an even greater advantage and transform your knowledge and common sense into practical benefits at your job? After all, what value are your talents if you don't apply them?

This is why we study OB.

KNOWLEDGE IS NOT ENOUGH

Expertise alone does not solve business problems. For decades, businesses have attributed their successes to the knowledge or technical expertise of their employees. The rationale was that if workers had the knowledge and necessary technical training, then results would automatically follow. But over time firms have realized that knowledge and training alone do not guarantee success. In recent years, business experts have called this disparity the *knowing-doing gap*.[1] **The *knowing-doing gap* identifies the gap between what people know and what they actually do.** For instance, everybody knows that treating people with respect is a good idea, but some managers don't always do this. Closing such gaps is an important element of your own success at school, work, and home. This also is a major focus of OB and this book.

THE LIMITS OF COMMON SENSE

You may feel that common sense will go a long way toward solving most business and career challenges. But you'd be wrong. If common sense were all that mattered, businesses would be more successful and all managers would be effective, while you and other new employees would consistently be happy and perform at your very best. However, this certainly isn't true of all employers and managers, and entry-level employees are often ill prepared and underperform.

WHERE EMPLOYERS SAY NEW HIRES FALL SHORT

Fortune published results from a Global Strategy Group study of 500 senior managers and executives. Only 65 percent of these business leaders found new employees "somewhat prepared" for success in business, while a significant percentage said new employees are "not prepared at all." Jeffrey Holmes, a principal at architectural firm Woods Bagot and sponsor of the survey, confirmed these findings and said: "Companies need people who can synthesize information and apply it to business problems. . . . There's less room for new hires who don't have that ability. Technical skill is not enough." This preference applies to both bachelors and masters students.[2]

EMPLOYERS WANT PROBLEM SOLVING AND CRITICAL THINKING

Regardless of your area of study, arguably the greatest benefit of your education is developing problem-solving and critical thinking skills. The Global Strategy Group survey of executives revealed that the most sought-after skills for all entry-level employees were problem solving (49%), collaboration (43%), and critical thinking (36%).[3] Building your skills in these areas is the overarching goal of this book.

FOR YOU   WHAT'S AHEAD IN THIS CHAPTER

You'll learn how OB can drive your job and career success. We'll explain why it's important that you and your employers invest in building both your human and social capital. We'll also explore how ethics are integral to long-term individual and organizational success and we'll introduce a problem-solving framework you can use in a wide variety of situations at school, work, and life more generally. But what really powers this book is our Integrative Framework for Understanding and Applying OB, which we introduce mid-chapter. This framework will help you organize and apply OB concepts and tools as you learn them.

THE VALUE OF OB TO MY JOB AND CAREER

MAJOR QUESTION

How can I use knowledge of OB to enhance my job performance and career?

THE BIGGER PICTURE

Are you uncertain about the value of organizational behavior (OB) and how it fits into your curriculum, or even into your professional life? Use that uncertainty to judge how well this section makes the case for the value of OB. You'll see how OB knowledge and tools can enhance your personal job performance and career success. Look for the differences between what it takes to get hired versus promoted, and the importance of building your human and social capital. All of these topics affect your future.

The term *organizational behavior (OB)* describes an interdisciplinary field dedicated to understanding and managing people at work. This includes self-management. OB draws on research and practice from many disciplines to deal with how people behave at work, including:

- Anthropology
- Economics
- Ethics
- Management
- Organizational Theory
- Political Science
- Psychology
- Sociology
- Statistics
- Vocational Counseling

As you can see, OB is very much an applied discipline that draws from many sources; its value depends on its usefulness to your job and career. In that spirit, we wrote this book to make the material as applied and useful for you as possible.

Let's begin by looking at how OB compares to your other courses and explain the contingency perspective, which is the fundamental premise of contemporary OB.

How OB Fits into My Curriculum and Future Success

Consider how OB fits in with other courses in your curriculum. Organizational behavior is an academic designation focused on understanding and managing people at work. This includes managing yourself, as well as others, up, down, and sideways. But unlike jobs associated with functional disciplines (like accounting, marketing, and finance), you will not get a job in OB.

So then, what is the benefit to learning about and applying OB? The answer is that the effective application of OB is critical for your success in all fields and across disciplines. As you'll learn, technical knowledge associated with any given job is important, but what makes the difference is your ability to influence, get along with, and manage others. People skills! Applying OB knowledge and tools gives you job opportunities, sets you apart from your peers and competition, and contributes to your success. And an important part of your success is your ability to know which tools to use and under what circumstances. This is described as a contingency approach to managing people and is the foundation of contemporary OB.

A Contingency Perspective—The Contemporary Foundation of OB A *contingency approach* **calls for using OB concepts and tools as situationally appropriate, instead of trying to rely on "one best way."** This means there is no single best way to manage people, teams, and organizations. The best or most effective course of action instead depends on the situation. A particular management practice that worked today may not work tomorrow. What worked with one employee may not work with another.

This is why the contingency approach is so central to OB. It is both pragmatic and demanding. Pragmatically, the user of the approach is not looking for any single approved or canned response but the one that will work most appropriately. Demanding, because the user of the approach must often work to find that appropriate solution. We will expand on the contingency approach later in this chapter.

Harvard's Clayton Christensen puts it like this: "Many of the widely accepted principles of good management are only situationally appropriate."[4] In other words, don't use a hammer unless the job involves nails. You'll learn in Chapter 13, for instance, that there is no single best style of leadership. In this way, OB differs from many of your other courses in that answers are not always black and white, right or wrong, but instead the best answer (behavior) *depends on the situation*. The explicit consideration of the situation or environmental factors is fundamental to OB and is emphasized later in the chapter and throughout the book.

Accordingly, to be effective you need to do what is appropriate given the situation, rather than adhering to hard-and-fast rules. Organizational behavior specialists, and many effective managers, embrace the contingency approach because it helps them consider the many factors that influence behavior and performance within and among individuals, groups, and organizations. Whether you are a manager or employee, you need to consider many potential factors that can influence your performance and the performance of the people you may manage or affect. You also need to be aware of your own preferences or typical responses, and question them so as to do what the situation requires, rather than default to personal habit or organizational custom. Taking a broader, contingent perspective like this is a fundamental key to your success in the short and long term.

The following Example box illustrates how Google has applied the contingency approach and changed some of its benefits to more precisely meet employees' preferences for work–life balance and parenthood.

EXAMPLE Google Search: "How Can We Keep Talented Employees?"

While Google's talent is constantly being poached by its competitors, some employees simply quit, especially women. The company noticed that many women were leaving, or, more precisely, not returning after maternity leave. Some women of course choose to stay home after childbirth. However, Google realized that such employees were leaving at twice the average rate of all employees. It then explored the possibility that its policies might play a role.

THE INDUSTRY STANDARD Generally, the tech industry, Silicon Valley in particular, offers 12 weeks of paid time off for maternity leave and seven weeks for employees outside of California.

NEW PLAN Google's response was to offer five months of full pay and full benefits! Better still, new mothers can split the time and take some before the birth, some after, and some later still when the child is older.

NEW PLAN PLUS Seven weeks of "new-parent" leave is now offered to all of its employees around the world. This enables new mothers *and fathers* the opportunity to manage their time and new joy/baby.[5] Other companies expand these practices further still. Alston & Bird, an Atlanta-based law firm, provides employees $10,000 and 90 days of paid leave toward adoptions. Infertility issues are also covered by their health plan.[6]

YOUR THOUGHTS?

1. If you alone could make policies at Google (or where you work), what would you do to keep valuable employees?

2. How could you apply the contingency approach to make these and other policies more effective?

3. What else would you do?

Uncommon Sense   At first glance the contingency perspective may look like simple common sense. But it's different. It attempts to overcome the limits of common sense by not settling for traditional options if another solution may be more practical and effective. Similarly, understanding the Integrative Framework and 3-Stop Problem Solving Approach you'll learn about later provides more insight than common sense alone. The goal of OB is to give you *more* than common sense and instead enhance your understanding of situations at work and guide your behaviors.

Moreover, common sense has three main weaknesses that you need to consider and avoid.

- **Overreliance on hindsight.** Common sense excels in well-known scenarios with predictable outcomes. But much of modern business involves uncertainty and adapting to change. In other words, common sense is especially weak in responding to the unknown or unexpected. And because it focuses on the past, common sense lacks vision for the future.
- **Lack of rigor.** If we are comfortable with our commonsense response, we may not apply the effort required to find the real problem when considering possible causes. This will likely result in not choosing the optimal course of action or solution. If you lack rigor, then you are unlikely to measure the right predictors and outcomes when solving problems.
- **Lack of objectivity.** Common sense can be overly subjective and lack a basis in science. In such cases we are not always able to explain our reasoning to others, let alone apply it to new situations.

In *BusinessNewsDaily,* Microsoft researcher Duncan Watts says we love common sense because we prefer narrative. "You have a story that sounds right and there's nothing to contradict it." Watts contrasts a more effective approach, as outlined in his book *Everything Is Obvious Once You Know the Answer: How Common Sense Fails Us*. He advocates using a scientific approach. "The difference is we test the stories and modify them when they don't work," he says. "Storytelling is a useful starting point. The real question is what we do next."[7]

One way that OB moves beyond the limitations of common sense is by its systematic and science-based approach to understanding people and how they behave at work. OB therefore can make you more attractive to potential employers and more effective once employed. Let's explore this idea in more detail, beginning with the importance of possessing and developing both hard and soft skills.

Employers Want Both Hard and Soft Skills

Most of us know the difference between hard and soft skills.

- *Hard skills* **are the technical expertise and knowledge to do a particular task or job function,** such as financial analysis, accounting, or operations.
- *Soft skills* **relate to our human interactions and include both interpersonal skills and personal attributes.**

Employers are increasingly aware of the importance of soft skills. "People rise in organizations because of their hard skills and fall due to a dearth of soft skills."[8] Maybe that's why firms tend to weight soft skills so heavily when hiring for top positions. Recruiters rate interpersonal skills, cultural fit with the company, and leadership attributes as the top three selection criteria for MBA graduates.[9]

Experts agree: Anyone can take a course in C++, but it's not going to land you the job. . . . The most sought-after skill-sets for recruiters are becoming less and less about proficiency in specific [technical or job skills] and more about how you think . . . and work within the context of the team. Learning [the technical details or skills of a job] is the easy part. Having the mindset to apply it . . . [and social/psychological dexterity] are the critical skills.[10]

TABLE 1.1   FOUR SKILLS MOST DESIRED BY EMPLOYERS

SKILL	DESCRIPTION	THIS BOOK
1. Critical thinking	Using logic and reasoning to identify the strengths and weaknesses of alternative solutions, conclusions, or approaches to problems.	Fundamental to this book and woven throughout. We designed features and exercises to help you think critically and apply your OB knowledge and tools.
2. Problem solving	Identifying complex problems and reviewing related information to develop and evaluate options and implement solutions.	Our problem-solving approach is used throughout the book. We repeatedly ask you to apply your knowledge for solving problems at school, work, and life.
3. Judgment and decision making	Considering the relative costs and benefits of potential actions to choose the most appropriate ones.	Integral to problem solving and success. We integrate judgment and decision making in all problem-solving content and devote an entire chapter to these soft skills.
4. Active listening	Giving full attention to what other people are saying; taking time to understand the points being made; asking questions as appropriate and not interrupting.	Key success factor at work. We address this directly in the chapters on influencing others and leadership.

SOURCE: Adapted from M. Casserly, "The 10 Skills That Will Get You Hired in 2013," *Forbes,* December 12, 2012, http://www.forbes.com/sites/meghancasserly/ 2012/12/10/the-10-skills-that-will-get-you-a-job-in-2013/; and M. Robles, "Executive Perception of the Top 10 Skills Needed in Today's Workplace," *Business Communication Quarterly,* 2012, 453–65.

The above quote comes from a study by CareerBuilder on the most desired skills for the top 10 jobs in 2013. Table 1.1 shows the top four such skills, along with a brief explanation of how they are directly addressed in this book.

What do you notice about the top four items? Which are hard skills? None! Instead, all are soft skills, the skills you need to interact with, influence, and perform with others.

Soft skills are not job specific. **They are *portable skills,* more or less relevant in every job, at every level, and throughout your career.**[11] All of these and many more soft skills represent OB topics covered in this book, whether in the personal or inter-personal domain:

Personal attributes
(build goodwill and trust; demonstrate integrity)
- **Attitudes** (Chapter 2)
- **Personality** (Chapter 3)
- **Teamwork** (Chapter 8)
- **Leadership** (Chapter 13)

Interpersonal skills
(foster respectful interactions)
- **Active listening** (Chapters 12 and 13)
- **Positive attitudes** (Chapters 2 and 7)
- **Effective communication** (Chapter 9)

How OB Fits into My Career

Hard skills are of course important, as they give you credibility. For instance, accountants need to understand debits and credits; finance people, net present value; and both need to understand cash flows. However, to be competitive and give employers what they want, you need to develop your soft skills as well. In fact, certain kinds of soft skills *increase* in importance over one's career and help set you apart from your competition.[12] To highlight this point, think about the criteria used for hiring workers versus promoting them.

- **What It Takes to Get Hired.** Regardless of where you are in your career today, ask yourself: What criteria were used to hire you for your first job? What factors did your hiring manager consider? (If your first job is still ahead of you, what factors do you imagine are most important?) Most of you will identify things like education, grades, interpersonal skills, and experience. In short, for most jobs you are

An understanding of OB can give you extremely valuable knowledge and tools to help "sell" yourself during job interviews. Applying this OB knowledge can also enhance your chances for promotions.

selected for your technical skills, your ability to do the given job. Firms may assume you possess particular competencies needed to meet basic job responsibilities based on your education (say an accounting degree if you're going to be an auditor or a finance degree if you're going to be an analyst).

- **What It Takes to Get Promoted.** Now ask yourself, what criteria are being used for promotions? Of course, often performance in the current job will be a primary consideration. However, you and many other employees may fail to realize that your perceived ability to get things done through others and manage people will be another important deciding factor. If you and three of your coworkers are all vying for an open manager's job, likely all four of you perform at a high level. Therefore performance isn't the deciding factor. Instead, it is your perceived ability to directly or indirectly manage others!

Roxanne Hori, an associate dean at Northwestern University's Kellogg School of Management, echoes this argument: "Yes, your knowledge of the functional area you're pursuing is important. But to succeed longer term . . . having strong team skills and knowing how to build and manage relationships were seen as just as important." One executive she interviewed suggested that students "take as much organizational behavior coursework as possible . . . because as you move into leadership roles, the key skills that will determine your success will be around your ability to interact with others in a highly effective fashion."[13]

We make this point visually in Figure 1.1. It illustrates how technical or job-specific skills decline in importance as you move to levels of higher responsibility, while personal skills increase.

Performance Gives Me Credibility Performance matters because it gives you credibility with your peers and those you may manage. Just be aware that early in your career your bosses will be looking for more. They will evaluate your management potential, and their opinion affects your opportunities. So even in a line (non-management) position you need to know how to:

- Apply different motivational tools (Chapter 5)
- Provide constructive feedback (Chapter 6)
- Develop and lead productive teams (Chapters 8 and 13)
- Understand and manage organizational culture and change (Chapters 14 and 16)

Therefore, knowledge of OB is critical to your individual performance, your ability to work with and manage others, and your career success (promotions, pay raises, increased opportunities).

FIGURE 1.1 RELATIVE IMPORTANCE OF DIFFERENT SKILLS BASED ON JOB LEVEL

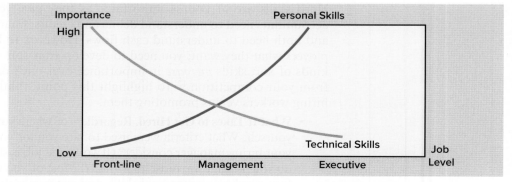

SOURCE: Adapted from M. Lombardo and R. Eichinger, *Preventing Derailment: What to Do Before It's Too Late* (Greensboro, NC: Center for Creative Leadership, 1989).

major question

MAJOR QUESTION

How can human and social capital affect my career opportunities and job performance?

THE BIGGER PICTURE

You've likely heard the expression—"It's not what you know, but who you know" that determines whether you get a particular job. We argue that both matter, and that you and your employers benefit from investing in what you know and who you know.

You may have older or retired relatives who worked the same job for all of their lives. But such "cradle-to-grave" careers are increasingly rare. The U.S. Bureau for Labor Statistics, examining a younger segment of the baby-boomer generation (born 1946–1964), finds that the average number of jobs was 11! Men had on average 11.4 jobs and women, 10.7. But we're not all average. Twenty-five percent had 15 or more jobs and 12 percent had zero to four. The same study revealed that changes continue into middle age, where 33 percent of employees held jobs for less than a year![14] It thus seems extremely unlikely you will experience a "cradle-to-grave" career with one company as in generations past. It therefore is extremely important that you continually develop your skills and your network. The first is part of your human capital and the second, part of your social capital.

Human and Social Capital as Investments

Just as individuals and companies invest in more traditional forms of capital (e.g., real estate, stocks, bonds, facilities, and equipment) to earn a positive future return, both employees and their employers invest in human and social capital with the intention of reaping future returns or benefits. This is good news to all of us, as we can continue to increase our value through such investments.

Human resource experts acknowledge this development, which is highlighted in the following comment: "In the modern knowledge-based and service-oriented economy, the success of many firms has shifted from acquisition of tangible (physical) resources to the accumulation of intangible (human) resources."[15]

In the ideal job environment, both employer and employee will invest in these two forms of capital, which is why we discuss them together. Table 1.2 lists some basic forms of human and social capital.

A Closer Look at Human Capital   Remember that ***human capital*** **is the productive potential of an individual's knowledge, skills, and experiences.** *Potential* is the operative word in this intentionally broad definition. A present or future employee with the right combination of knowledge, skills, experience, and motivation represents human capital with the potential to give the organization a competitive advantage. For that reason today's executives concern themselves with recruiting and retaining talented people, developing employees' skills, keeping them fully engaged, and preparing for the day when valuable people retire or leave for another employer.[16] Research also supports the benefits of human capital, such that employers who invest in employees' human capital by building their skills, purposefully motivating them, and providing opportunities also enjoy lower turnover and improved financial outcomes.[17]

TABLE 1.2 A BRIEF LIST OF VARIOUS FORMS OF HUMAN AND SOCIAL CAPITAL

HUMAN CAPITAL	SOCIAL CAPITAL
Education	Social relationships
Experience	Family relationships
Knowledge, skills, and abilities	Relationships within current employer
Vision	Relationships within industry
Confidence and self-esteem	Professional memberships
Initiative and entrepreneurship	Goodwill
Adaptability and flexibility	Trust
Readiness to learn	Status
Reputation	Support from others

SOURCE: Adapted in part from J. A. Felicio, E. Couto, and J. Caiado, "Human Capital and Social Capital in Entrepreneurs and Managers of Small and Medium Enterprises," *Journal of Business Economics and Management,* 2012, 395–420.

The topic of a firm's human capital arose when Tim Cook, for example, replaced Steve Jobs as the CEO of Apple. Many argue that it is not possible to actually replace Jobs, but Apple nevertheless needed a capable executive to replace the then-ailing icon. It helped that Cook had served as interim CEO three times previously when Jobs was dealing with cancer and was the chief of operations before taking the top spot full time. Add to that seven years of previous experience as senior and executive VP. And before Apple he also was a VP at Compaq computers (now part of Hewlett-Packard) and COO of Intelligent Electronics. Cook also worked in a paper mill and aluminum plant. Until Cook assumed the CEO role on a permanent basis in late 2011, few people knew who he was and even fewer recognized him or knew much about his background.[18]

The value of each employee's individual human capital (e.g., knowledge, skills, and experience) accumulates to produce a company's overall human capital.[19] Think of the massive human capital that exists for companies such as Apple and Google. No wonder so many other companies continually attempt to poach their talent!

A Closer Look at Social Capital Recall that *social capital* **is the productive potential resulting from relationships, goodwill, trust, and cooperative effort.** As described in Table 1.2, with social capital the focus shifts from the individual to social units (e.g., friends, family, company, group, club, or nation). Again, the word *potential* is key. But here the potential lies in your relationships with other people rather than in your own skills, abilities, and experience.

Author and speaker Joe Gerstandt said, "If you want more influence in your organizations, relationships will help you get there. . . . Having thousands of friends on Facebook isn't the solution . . . social capital is about quality not quantity."[20] Think of social capital as a means for leveraging or utilizing the knowledge, skills, experience, and relationships of people you know. We've all been told "network, network, network" and "it's not what you know but who you know." These common sayings support the importance of the relationships that make up your social capital.

What does Steve Jobs's successor's résumé need to look like? What human capital characteristics are needed? Tim Cook's résumé is quite varied and quite impressive. How well do you think his experience fits the needs of the CEO job at Apple?

Building social capital, by Identifying and building relationships with others, can improve your transition and performance at a new job.

Researchers and businesses continue to discover how social capital can improve operations. In a recent study in the journal *Human Relations*, Russell Korte and Shumin Lin looked at how new hires are brought up to speed. They found that when newly hired workers developed social capital with other team members in their work groups, there was a correlation with better job satisfaction and faster learning of their responsibilities and fitting in to the workplace culture. More than manager supervision, social capital was key to successful integration. Higher quality relationships with members of the work group translated into greater access to information and resources.[21]

Companies are starting to realize the business potential in their employees' relationships. The firm Ernst & Young (EY) gives preference in the selection process to candidates referred by existing employees. Riju Parakh, for example, submitted her résumé through normal channels. However, on the basis of the recommendation of a friend who works at EY, Riju's résumé was fast-tracked—separated from the "pile of thousands" and inserted into the interview process—resulting in her being hired within three weeks. She said, "You know how long this usually takes . . . it was miraculous." EY says employees now recommend approximately 45 percent of non–entry level hires—up from 28 percent in 2010.[22] Other companies provide incentives and rewards for such recommendations, all as means for identifying and attracting talent contained in employees' networks.

How to Build Human and Social Capital

How can you build these valuable assets? Table 1.3 provides several examples. You can also increase your human capital by building on strengths and overcoming weaknesses identified by completing the Self-Assessments in this book. Human capital can be either *specific* to your current job (e.g., knowledge of your company's products) or more *generic* and serve you across jobs (e.g., Series 7 certification to sell financial products). Social capital can be either *internal* or *external* to your current organization.

TABLE 1.3 WAYS OF BUILDING MY HUMAN AND SOCIAL CAPITAL

HUMAN CAPITAL	EXAMPLES AND PURPOSES
1. Training	Software certification to gain knowledge and skills to improve performance in current job
2. Work-based development opportunities	Job rotation (Chapter 5), shadowing, and cross-functional project teams (Chapter 8) to build your knowledge and your relationships
3. Learning activities outside of work	Fluency gained in a second language to increase opportunities within and outside of current employer
4. Career planning	Opportunities identified inside or outside of your current place of employment and assessing your strengths and weaknesses

SOCIAL CAPITAL	EXAMPLES AND PURPOSES
1. Internal	Mentoring relationship to provide guidance and opportunities (Chapter 13)
	Membership on a company softball team to build relationships outside of your work area
2. External	Conference attendance to meet people at other companies and learn of other job opportunities
	Join local, industry-specific organizations to identify new customers

building human & social capital

SOURCE: Derived from T. W. H. Ng and D. C. Feldman, "The Effects of Organizational Embeddedness on Development of Social and Human Capital," *Journal of Applied Psychology,* 2010, 696–712.

TAKE-AWAY APPLICATION—TAAP

Using Table 1.3:

1. Think of your most desired job. Now describe what you could do to develop your human *and* social capital to make you a more attractive job candidate.

2. Assume you graduate this year and are fortunate enough to get a job interview with your most desired employer. Explain in terms of human *and* social capital how you would promote or sell yourself in that interview.

Both forms of capital are extremely important. We therefore strongly encourage you to take initiative—build your own human and social capital *and* look for employers that also will make such investments in you!

How Self-Awareness Can Help You Build a Fulfilling Career

To have a successful career, you need to know who you are and what you want. Larry Bossidy (former CEO of Honeywell) and Ram Charan (world-renowned management expert) said it best in their book *Execution*: "When you know yourself, you are comfortable with your strengths and not crippled by your shortcomings. . . . Self-awareness gives you the capacity to learn from your mistakes as well as your successes. It enables you to keep growing."[23] They also argue that you need to know yourself in order to be authentic—real and not fake, the same on the outside as the inside. This is essential to influencing others (which we discuss in detail in Chapter 12). People don't trust fakes, and it is difficult to influence or manage others if they don't trust you.

As professors, consultants, and authors, we couldn't agree more. We are strong advocates of self-awareness, and to help you increase yours we include multiple Self-Assessments in every chapter. The Self-Assessments are an excellent way to learn about yourself, measure the extent to which you possess many of the OB topics we will discuss, and apply knowledge of both yourself and OB to school, work, and your personal lives. Put another way, the Self-Assessments are an interesting and especially effective way to make OB come alive and be practical for you. We therefore encourage you to go to the web, complete the assessments, and then answer the questions included in each of the Self-Assessment boxes.

Let's start with you learning about your motivation to manage others, considering the strong case we made that working with and through others is critical for your near and long-term success. First, realize that many employees never manage others. Sometimes this is by choice; other times it is because they shouldn't or never get the chance! But what about you? How motivated are you to manage others? Go to connect .mheducation.com and take this Self-Assessment to learn your motivation for managing others. What you learn might surprise you. Surprised or not, understanding more precisely your motivation to manage others can guide your course selection in college and your job choices in the marketplace.

connect

SELF-ASSESSMENT 1.1   How Strong Is My Motivation to Manage?

Go to connect.mheducation.com and when finished respond to the following:

1. Does this instrument accurately assess your potential as a manager? Explain.

2. Which of the seven dimensions do you think is likely the best predictor of managerial success? Which is the least? Explain.

3. The instrument emphasizes competition with others in a win-lose mentality. Describe the pros and cons of this approach to management.

major question

MAJOR QUESTION

Why do people fall into ethical lapses, even unwittingly, and what lessons can I learn from that?

THE BIGGER PICTURE

If you were asked, "Do you know right from wrong? Are you secure in your ethics?" you would likely answer "yes" to both questions. What's interesting is that most people who suffer ethical lapses also answer yes. OB can teach you about the drivers of unethical behavior, and in the process improve your awareness and enable you to reduce your risk. You'll learn that even though most unethical behavior is not illegal, it still causes tremendous damage to people and businesses. Fortunately, the OB concepts and tools you pick up through this course will help you recognize and navigate ethical challenges.

Ethics **is concerned with behavior—right versus wrong, good versus bad, and the many shades of gray in between.** We present ethics here at the start of your OB journey and weave it throughout the book for three key reasons.

1. **Employees are confronted with ethical challenges at all levels of organizations and throughout their careers.**
2. **Unethical behavior damages relationships, erodes trust, and thus makes it difficult to conduct business.**
3. **Unethical behavior also reduces cooperation, loyalty, and contribution, which of course hurts the performance of individuals, teams, and organizations.**

Ethics also gets priority because many OB topics have direct and substantial influence on the ethical conduct of individuals and organizations. Notably, reward systems (Chapter 6), decision making (Chapter 11), leader behavior (Chapter 13), and organizational culture (Chapter 14) all can powerfully affect ethical conduct at work. Let's begin by describing the legal implications, frequency, causes, and solutions of unethical behavior at school and work.

Cheating

In 2013, Lance Armstrong made alarming public confessions of blood doping and performance enhancing drug (PED) use during his cycling career (legal charges were ultimately filed). Not long after, many professional baseball players also were accused of PED use. Studies revealed that 87 percent of undergraduate business students admitted to cheating on exams![24] And research shows that pressure to perform starts early in life.

A survey of 787 youngsters ages 13 to 18 found that "44 percent of teens feel they're under strong pressure to succeed in school, no matter the cost. Of those, 81 percent believe the pressure will be the same or worse in the workplace."[25]

Anonymous surveys by the Josephson Institute of over 23,000 students from private and public high schools across the United States found 59 percent admitted cheating on a test in 2009 and 51 percent in 2011. Thirty-two percent reported plagiarizing

Some of Armstrong's actions will cause him legal troubles, but what effect will his cheating have on the sport of cycling? Other professional sports? What can be done to prevent cheating like Armstrong's?

via the Internet in 2011, down from 34 percent in 2009. The Institute noted that for the first time in a decade, "students are cheating, lying and stealing less than in previous years."[26] What do you think the incidence is at your school? Now let's explore other forms of unethical conduct and their legality, frequency, and solutions.

Ethical Lapses—Legality, Frequency, Causes, and Solutions

"The vast majority of managers mean to run ethical organizations, yet corporate corruption is widespread."[27] You likely recognize the names of some of the executives and scandals of the past few decades that bankrupted the companies they led, destroyed the lives of many employees, and caused enormous losses for investors and customers: Kenneth Lay and Jeff Skilling (Enron, 2001), Bernie Ebbers (WorldCom, 2002), and, of course, Bernie Madoff (Madoff Investment Securities LLC, 2009). None of these leaders acted alone.

To clarify, we are not indicting other employees—that is a matter for the courts. Our point is that each of these disgraced captains of industry led companies that in most cases employed thousands of other people. Surely these companies did not advertise for and hire thousands of criminally minded individuals to help the leaders in their criminal endeavors. The reality is that the degree of knowledge and involvement on the part of these other employees ranged from intense and detailed to little or none. So how does the work environment produce unethical conduct, sometimes on an extreme scale, from people who are otherwise good, well-intentioned, and on the right side of the law? Knowledge of OB helps you answer this question.

Unethical Does *Not* Mean Illegal   Forms of unethical conduct and the degree of its consequences vary greatly. At the extreme we have highly publicized criminal acts of now-jailed executives like those noted above, forcing losses on employees, investors, and other stakeholders (e.g., suppliers) that sometimes reach billions of dollars! While these examples filled the headlines, they are the exception. The truth is that very few unethical acts are illegal, most are not punished in any way, and even if illegal few are prosecuted.

This means you should *not* rely on the legal system to manage or assure ethical conduct at work. For instance, FoxConn, Apple Computer's number one supplier in China, has been in the spotlight for its highly publicized repugnant treatment of its 1.2 million Chinese employees—14-hour workdays, 6–7 days per week schedules, low wages, and retaliation for protesting.[28] American Airlines pilots provided another example in 2012 when they created widespread slowdowns in flights to pressure the company in negotiations with their union. American's on-time performance was 48 percent versus 77 percent for Southwest and 69 percent for Delta (on-time was 80 percent in the previous period). Such slowdowns had enormous costs and inconveniences for their thousands of customers.[29] The following Example box provides another notable instance of how widespread unethical behavior has resulted in virtually no legal consequences.

EXAMPLE Wrong? Absolutely! Illegal? Seemingly Not.

Unethical behavior is rarely illegal. The Wall Street meltdown of 2008–2009 that caused the Great Recession has produced very few prosecutions and virtually no convictions. The US Department of Justice and the Securities and Exchange Commission keep surprisingly little related data. Why? "I can tell you why you wouldn't keep the data," said economics and law professor William Black: "Because it would be really embarrassing." Of the more than 14,000 financial fraud cases during the period, only 17 involved CEOs and other executives, and only one of these was directly related to the financial crisis (a case against three Credit Suisse employees for inflating mortgage bond values). Eric Holder, the US Attorney General, said that the conduct that led to the crisis was "unethical and irresponsible." And "some of this behavior—while morally reprehensible—may not necessarily have been criminal."[30]

YOUR THOUGHTS?

1. What is your reaction?
2. If you think the executives (and perhaps other employees) of financial institutions should be punished, then describe what you think is appropriate.
3. Alternatively, if you think they should not be punished, then explain why.

Why Ethics Matter to Me and My Employer   Criminal or not, it is important to realize that unethical behavior negatively affects not only the offending employee but also his or her coworkers and employer. Unethical behavior by coworkers (e.g., company executives) can make you look bad and tarnish your career. SAC Capital Advisors, for example, is one of the most successful hedge funds in recent years. But the fund and its founder, Steven Cohen, were dogged throughout 2012–2013 by suspicions of potential insider trading. Their troubles were in part due to the fact that many traders with ties to SAC have been convicted or pled guilty to insider trading. Before any formal charges were made against the firm itself or its founder, clients withdrew nearly $2 billion in assets.[31] SAC investors ultimately withdrew even more money, over a billion dollars in fines were levied, and the fund was ordered to close.

To make this more personal, imagine you are interviewing for a job. How would you explain your past employment history if it included jobs at SAC, Enron, Countrywide, MF Global, or Madoff and Associates? While you certainly would find a way, it is safe to assume that you'd rather not have to make such explanations. Understanding ethics improves your job performance and increases your career opportunities and success. Research shows that "sustainable businesses are led by CEOs who take a people-centered, inclusive approach rather than a controlling, target-driven one. They are people who listen, who foster cultures in which employees are not scared to point out problems and in which staff feel they have a personal responsibility to enact corporate values, be they health and safety concerns or putting the client's interests first."[32]

Ethical Dilemmas   ***Ethical dilemmas* involve situations with two choices, neither of which resolves the situation in an ethically acceptable manner.** Such situations surround us at school and work. They highlight the fact that choosing among available options is not always a pure choice between right versus wrong. As a result, many ethical dilemmas place us in an uncomfortable position. An excellent example is those who are responsible for determining which employees are downsized. When Audi of North America decided to relocate a large percentage of its operations from one part of the United States to another, one of the finance managers was responsible for "working the numbers" on how many people would be invited to relocate, how many would be terminated, and what types of severance packages to offer and to whom.

All of this is necessary and, of course, is somebody's responsibility. The problem however was that many of these people were friends and colleagues of the person doing these analyses. In other words, she had the "hit list" for weeks and was unable to share this information with the others, even as they worked side-by-side, had lunch, and did things socially in the meantime.

EXAMPLE The Whistleblower's Dilemma

Whistleblowing often creates a particularly challenging type of ethical dilemma. People do wrong, bad, unethical, and even illegal things at work. And you and other employees may know that they did. The dilemma is what to do about it. Many times you're tempted to reveal the behavior to management or to the authorities—blow the whistle. This seems like the "right thing to do." Depending on the situation, you may even profit, but you might also pay.

WHISTLEBLOWING FOR PROFIT Dodd-Frank legislation and some regulatory agencies provide incentives for whistleblowers. Some can receive up to 30 percent of any settlement, if regulators collect over $1 million due to the infraction.[33] Bradley Birkenfeld, an ex-banker for UBS, was awarded $104 million for exposing how his bank helped US clients hide money in Swiss accounts. Cheryl Eckard was awarded $96 million for revealing manufacturing flaws in the production of some of Glaxo Smith Kline's pharmaceuticals.[34]

Sherron Watkins became famous as the whistleblower that helped undo Enron. She now earns a living speaking about her experience and ethics more generally, which pays far less than jobs in the energy sector.

THE COSTS As a VP at Chase Bank, Linda Almonte and her team were asked to review more than 20,000 past-due credit card accounts before they were sold to another company. "Almonte's team reported back to her that nearly 60 percent contained some sort of major error, including discrepancies about the amount or whether the court had indeed ruled for the bank. Concerned, Almonte went up the chain of command, flagging the errors and encouraging management to halt the sale. Instead, the bank fired Almonte and completed the deal."[35] Nobody would hire her, which ruined her professionally and financially. She and her family ultimately moved to another state, where they lived in a hotel while she continued to look for work.

WHAT'S THE LESSON? Don't underestimate the likelihood and costs of retaliation. Codes of ethics that forbid retaliation are just empty words if unethical people aren't held accountable. And a lack of accountability is the hallmark of corrupt organizations. "Doing the right thing" can be very costly.

YOUR THOUGHTS?

1. What can employers do to encourage and avoid punishing whistleblowers?
2. What can you do as an individual employee when you witness or become aware of unethical conduct?

What Causes Unethical Behavior? Harvard professor Max Bazerman and Ann Tenbrunsel of the University of Notre Dame have studied ethical and unethical conduct extensively. They concluded that while criminally minded people exist in the workplace, most are in fact good people with good intentions. Instead of ill-intent, Bazerman and Tenbrunsel contend that cognitive biases (see Chapter 4) and organizational practices "blind managers to unethical behavior, whether it is their own or

TABLE 1.4 CAUSES OF UNETHICAL BEHAVIOR AT WORK AND WHAT TO DO ABOUT IT

	ILL-CONCEIVED GOALS	MOTIVATED BLINDNESS	INDIRECT BLINDNESS	THE SLIPPERY SLOPE	OVERVALUING OUTCOMES
DESCRIPTION	We set goals and incentives to promote a desired behavior, but they encourage a negative one.	We overlook the unethical behavior of another when it's in our interest to remain ignorant.	We hold others less accountable for unethical behavior when it's carried out through third parties.	We are less able to see others' unethical behavior when it develops gradually.	We give a pass to unethical behavior if the outcome is good.
EXAMPLE	The pressure to maximize billable hours in accounting, consulting, and law firms leads to unconscious padding.	Baseball officials failed to notice they'd created conditions that encouraged steroid use.	A drug company deflects attention from a price increase by selling rights to another company, which imposes the increases.	Auditors may be more likely to accept a client firm's questionable financial statements if infractions have accrued over time.	A researcher whose fraudulent clinical trial saves lives is considered more ethical than one whose fraudulent trial leads to deaths.
REMEDY	Brainstorm unintended consequences when devising goals and incentives. Consider alternative goals that may be more important to reward.	Root out conflicts of interest. Simply being aware of them doesn't necessarily reduce their negative effect on decision making.	When handing off or outsourcing work, ask whether the assignment might invite unethical behavior and take ownership of the implications.	Be alert for even trivial ethical infractions and address them immediately. Investigate whether a change in behavior has occurred.	Examine both "good" and "bad" decisions for their ethical implications. Reward solid decision processes, not just good outcomes.

SOURCE: Reprinted by permission of *Harvard Business Review.* "Ethical Breakdowns: Good People Often Let Bad Things Happen" by M. Bazerman and A. Tenbrunsel, April 2011. Copyright © 2011 by the Harvard Business School Publishing Corporation; all rights reserved.

that of others."[36] Table 1.4, which summarizes their findings, outlines causes of unethical behavior and what can be done to address that behavior as employees and managers.

TAKE-AWAY APPLICATION—TAAP

1. Think of the three most common forms of unethical behavior at school or where you work. Be specific.
2. Using Table 1.4, determine what the likely causes are for each.
3. Describe one thing that can be done to prevent or remedy each of the three most common unethical behaviors you noted in question 1. Use Table 1.4 for ideas/suggestions.

What about Unethical Behavior in College and When Applying for Jobs? A study of graduate students, including MBAs, in the United States and Canada found that peer behavior was by far the strongest predictor of why students cheated, followed by severity of potential penalties, and certainty of being reported.[37] However, don't be too quick to blame it on your lying, cheating classmates. The same researchers acknowledge that there are many other potential reasons for cheating, such as the perceived fairness in grading. It also is possible that students see different degrees of cheating—for instance, in homework assignments versus exams.

As for job hunting, an analysis of 2.6 million job applicant background checks by ADP Screening and Selection Services revealed that "44 percent of applicants lied about their work histories, 41 percent lied about their education, and 23 percent falsified credentials or licenses."[38] Can you imagine being a recruiter? If you believe these numbers, then it is likely that half of the people you interview are lying to you about something! Like cheating in school, many potential reasons for unethical behavior at work exist, beyond those listed in Table 1.4, such as:

1. One's personal motivation to perform ("I must be number 1")
2. Pressure from a supervisor via unrealistic performance goals along with threats for underperforming
3. Reward systems that incentivize bad behavior
4. Employees' perception of no consequences for crossing the line[39]

Some of the most unethical people don't see themselves this way. The Enron executives, Ken Lay (until he died) and Jeff Skilling (to this day), emphatically claimed their innocence. And while a skeptic could find it hard to believe, they may truly believe this. We explore such self-serving bias in Chapter 4. Nevertheless, it will be helpful for you to learn more specifically about your own ethical tendencies. Some people view ethics in ideal terms, which means that ethical principles or standards apply universally across situations and time.

Others, however, take a relativistic view and believe that ethical standards are dependent on the situation. Take Self-Assessment 1.2 to learn about your own views. Knowing this will help you understand your view of ethics, as well as that of others.

---

connect

SELF-ASSESSMENT 1.2 **Assessing My Perspective on Ethics**

Go to connect.mheducation.com and when finished respond to the following:

1. Are your views more idealistic or more relativistic?
2. What do you think about students cheating on homework assignments in school? What about them cheating on exams?
3. Are your answers consistent with your score? Explain.
4. Given your score, and assuming you're a manager, what are the implications for how you would handle the unethical behavior of somebody you manage? What about the unethical behavior of your boss?

What Can I Do about It?   You, like most everybody else, have or will likely witness either questionable or even blatantly unethical conduct at work. And when this happens you'll likely think of many excuses for not confronting the unethical conduct. Excuses include the following: This is common practice, the incident is minor, it's not my responsibility to confront such issues, and loyal workers don't confront each other. While such rationalizations for not confronting unethical conduct are common, they have consequences for individuals, groups, and organizations. What can you do? Below are a few suggestions:

1. **It's Business; Treat It That Way.** Ethical issues are business issues, just like costs, revenues, and employee development. Therefore, collect data and present a convincing case against the unethical conduct just as you would to develop a new product or strategy.
2. **Accept that Confronting Ethical Concerns Is Part of *Your* Job.** Whether it is explicit in your job description or not, ethics is everybody's job. If you think something is questionable, then take action.

Edward Snowden blew the whistle on the NSA's monitoring of phone and Internet communications. His actions had a enormous impact on his own life, as well as policies and practices within and between companies, industries, and even countries!

3. **Challenge the Rationale.** Many issues occur despite actual policy against it. If this is the case, then ask: "If what you did is common practice or okay, then why do we have a policy forbidding it?" Alternatively, and no matter the rationale, you can ask: "Would you be willing to explain what you did and why in a meeting with our superiors or customers, or, better still, during an interview on the evening news?"

4. **Use Your Lack of Seniority or Status as an Asset.** While many employees unfortunately use their junior status to avoid confronting ethical issues, being junior can instead be an advantage. It enables you to raise issues by saying, "Because I'm new, I may have misunderstood something, but it seems to me that what you've done is out of bounds or could cause problems."

5. **Consider and Explain Long-Term Consequences.** Of course, many ethical issues are driven by temptations and benefits in the short term. It therefore can be helpful to frame and explain your views in terms of long-term consequences.

6. **Solutions—Not Just Complaints.** When confronting an issue, you will likely be perceived as more helpful and taken more seriously if you provide an alternative course or solution. Doing so will also make it more difficult for the offender to disregard your complaint.[40]

What Role Do Business Schools Play? To be clear, each of us as individuals is first and foremost responsible for our own ethical conduct. However, we also know that our conduct is shaped by the environment and people around us. Leaders have particular influence on the ethical policies, practices, and conduct of organizations. For instance, a recent study reported that 35 percent of all undergraduate degrees are in business, yet 75 percent of business schools do not require ethics courses![41] If ethics are so important, then this disparity begs the question: "Why?"

The researchers asked this question and investigated what role the deans, leaders of business schools, played in this striking disconnect. They found that the gender and academic background of the deans, along with the private-public nature of the school, predicted the likelihood of requiring ethics courses. Female deans with a background in management were most likely to require ethics courses, while men with economics and finance backgrounds were least likely. Private and religiously affiliated schools were more likely than publics.[42] What is the case at your school? Does it align with these findings?

APPLYING OB TO SOLVE PROBLEMS

MAJOR QUESTION

How can I apply OB in a practical way to increase my effectiveness?

THE BIGGER PICTURE

Now that you know that OB is not just common sense, the challenge is to find a way to organize and apply its many concepts and theories. In this section, we use the metaphor of taking a journey to explain how you can apply OB. The journey includes three stops: Stop 1—define the problem; Stop 2—identify potential causes using OB concepts; and Stop 3—make recommendations.

We all encounter problems in our lives. **A *problem* is a difference or gap between an actual and a desired situation.** Problems arise when our goals (desired outcomes) are not being met (actual situation). So it is important to carefully consider what your goal or desired outcome is in order to define the problem appropriately. In turn, ***problem solving* is a systematic process of closing these gaps.**

For example, Jeff Bezos, CEO and founder of Amazon, famously downplays the importance of meeting quarterly numbers to please Wall Street. Instead, Bezos

Military operations often involve extremely complex problems and coordinating the efforts of many individuals. This White House photo depicts President Obama and the national security team monitoring the raid of Osama bin Laden's compound. The decision and eventual action took place in the context of tremendous uncertainty and time pressure, and the outcome had (potentially) enormous consequences. Can you think of a problem you confronted that had similar characteristics?

If you view problem solving as a journey, like we suggest in this book, then you need to know where you are and where you want to go. From a problem solving perspective, you could view this distance as a problem, as it represents a gap between your current and desired location. Identifying and selecting route is another part of the journey and problem solving process.

defines his problem as delivering superior service to customers, today, tomorrow, and forever. His problem-solving efforts are thus more likely to focus on innovative products and delivery times than profit margins and earnings per share.

Problem-solving skills are increasingly important in today's complex world. Loren Gary, associate director at Harvard's Center for Public Leadership, echoes this conclusion: "The ability to identify the most important problems and devising imaginative responses to them is crucial to superior performance in the modern workplace, where workers at all levels of the organization are called upon to think critically, take ownership of problems, and make real-time decisions."[43] The understanding and application of OB knowledge and tools will help you do these very things.

To help you increase your personal performance and well-being at school, work, and home, we created an informal approach you can use today to apply OB tools and concepts to help you solve problems. It's simple, practical, and ready for you to use now.

A 3-Stop Journey

We compare problem solving in OB to taking a journey. You choose a destination. You plan your route and identify which roads you'll take and important stops along the way. Then you take the trip.

Basics of the 3-Stop Approach   Our applied approach to problem solving proposes three activities or stops along the way:

Stop 1: Define the Problem. The definition of the problem is closely linked to the desired outcome. Students and managers routinely make the same common mistake during Stop 1—they don't spend enough time defining the problem. One reason for this is that most people identify problems reactively—after the fact—which causes them to quickly jump to conclusions. People make snap judgments or assumptions that lead to selecting the wrong causes and solutions for the problem at hand. All of us would likely benefit from the comment of Albert Einstein. He said: "If I were given one hour to save the planet, I would spend 59 minutes defining the problem and one minute resolving it." Why don't we take Professor Einstein's advice?

Stop 2: Identify Potential Causes Using OB Concepts and Theories. So far, you already have OB concepts like the contingency perspective, human and social capital, and ethics—and many more are coming. The more options you have to choose from, the more likely you will identify the appropriate cause(s) and response

Stop 3: Make Recommendations and (if Appropriate) Take Action. In some workplace situations you will be making recommendations and in others you will also be implementing the recommendations. To be successful in Stop 3, it is necessary to define the problem appropriately and identify the likely causes.

How This Problem-Solving Approach Develops Throughout the Book   As we introduce more OB concepts and tools, this approach will become richer and more useful. After all, there are many useful approaches to solving problems. As your knowledge deepens, you'll see in Chapter 11 that this approach is an abbreviated version of the rational approach to decision making. Along the way you'll learn that the 3-Stop approach shows you how to effectively apply your OB knowledge to produce better performance for you, your team, and your organization.

Tools to Reinforce My Problem-Solving Skills

Because of the value of problem solving at school, work, and home, we created numerous opportunities for you to master this skill while applying OB. Each chapter, for instance, includes the following features:

- **Problem-Solving Applications**—A brief example or mini-case that presents a problem or challenge. You are asked to apply the 3-Stop approach to each.
- **Self-Assessments**—A validated instrument that allows students to immediately assess personal characteristics related to OB concepts, frequently with a personal problem-solving focus, and often followed by a Take-Away Application (TAAP) (see below).
- **Take-Away Applications (TAAPs)**—You are asked to apply what you just learned to your own life at school, at work, or socially.
- **End of Chapter Problem-Solving Application Case**—Full-length case that requires you to apply OB knowledge gained in that particular chapter to define the problem, determine the causes, and make recommendations.

How good are your problem-solving skills? To get you started, take Self-Assessment 1.3 to measure your problem-solving skills. It will help you understand:

- What types of things you consider.
- How you think about alternative solutions.
- Which approach you prefer.

This self-awareness will help you learn about OB and apply it to improve performance. (**Tip:** Take this assessment again at the end of the course to see if your skills have increased.)

---

connect

SELF-ASSESSMENT 1.3   **Thinking and Problem Solving**

Go to connect.mheducation.com and when finished respond to the following:

1. What do items 1–3 tell you about your ability to define problems?
2. Do your scores on items 4–6 match your perceptions of your ability to generate effective solutions?
3. Using the individual items, describe the pros and cons of your tendencies toward implementing solutions.

MAJOR QUESTION

How could I explain to a fellow student the practical relevance and power of OB to help solve problems?

THE BIGGER PICTURE

Have you ever felt the solution to a problem was just beyond your reach? That you knew what the solution was but somehow you didn't know it? Sometimes this is a matter of organizing or structuring the problem and its elements. In such situations OB can help. We show you some useful tools to help you organize and apply your OB knowledge as it grows throughout this book and course. These same tools can be applied to solve problems both more rigorously and effectively.

Your ability to understand and apply OB knowledge and concepts is made easier by categorizing or organizing them. The first and most fundamental distinction is between elements that reside within individuals, like you, and those that are in the environment.

The Person–Environment Distinction

OB concepts and theories can be classified into two broad categories: person factors and environmental characteristics. The person–environment distinction integrates these categories.

- **Person factors represent the infinite number of characteristics that give individuals their unique identities.** These characteristics combine to influence every aspect of your life. In your job and career, these elements influence your goals and aspirations, the plans you make to achieve them, how you execute such plans, and your ultimate level of achievement. (Part One of this book is devoted to person factors.)

This makes perfect sense, but as we all know in reality it isn't so simple. *Things get in the way,* and these "things" often are environmental characteristics.

- **Environmental characteristics consist of all the elements outside of ourselves that influence what we do, how we do it, and the ultimate results of our actions.** A potentially infinite number of environmental factors can either help or hinder you when trying to accomplish something (see the following Problem-Solving Application box). In either case, environmental characteristics are critically important to OB and your performance. Parts Two and Three of this book are devoted to such characteristics.

Hundreds, if not thousands, of studies have shown that many person–environment characteristics influence a host of important outcomes, such as job satisfaction, performance, and turnover. But this also begs the question—which is more important—the person or the situation?

Which Influences Behavior and Performance More—Person or Environmental Factors? Researchers and managers have debated the answer to this question for decades. Common versions of this debate revolve around the issues of "nature versus nurture" or whether "leaders are born or made." These issues will be addressed in

solving application

Technology: An Environmental Characteristic That Greatly Impacts My Performance

Technology is both helpful and detrimental to employee performance and well-being. To set the stage, consider that roughly two-thirds of all full-time workers own smartphones.[44]

What are the benefits? More and more companies are using smartphones to save time and money. At Rudolph & Sletten, for example, a contractor located in Redwood City, California, workers use blueprint software on their iPads. "The digitized documents partly replace hundreds of pages of construction blueprints that need to be updated so often that student interns handle the monotonous work." The company estimates that using digitized blueprints can save from $15,000 to $20,000 on a large building contract. This also leads to fewer construction errors because workers are using up-to-date blueprints. Coca-Cola Enterprises similarly uses mobile-centric devices to streamline the workday of its restaurant service

technicians. The company estimates that the technology saves about 30 minutes a day.[45]

So what's the downside of technology? More and more people report working more hours because they use their smartphones after hours. This is why roughly

two-thirds of US employees indicate that they work during vacations. "People are tired of always being plugged in," says Tanya Schevitz, a spokeswoman for the Jewish cultural think tank Reboot.

Do you get paid for this "overtime"? Another problem concerns the payment of overtime. According to the Fair Labor Standards Act, employees receive overtime pay for any time spent working beyond 40 hours in a week. This can create a problem if employees access their mobile devices after hours. For example, a court allowed a class-action lawsuit filed by a Chicago police officer. He claimed that employees were using their work-issued BlackBerrys for police work after leaving their shifts, and they were not paid for the time they used the device. "They're hourly wage earners," says the officer's lawyer. He concluded that "if you are going to make people work when they're not on duty, you've got to pay them."[46]

YOUR CALL *Let's use the 3-Stop approach:*

Stop 1: What problem is described in this example?

Stop 2: Identify two potential causes (be sure to link the causes to the problem you identified).

Stop 3: Make a recommendation aimed at the cause that you feel will improve or remove the problem.

Chapters 3 and 13, respectively, but the relative influence of person and environment characteristics on behavior and performance is fundamental to OB.

Many observers believe that some people are by their nature better suited than others to perform well at work ("born winners"). In contrast, others believe that some people are clearly better in *a given job or situation*. No particular person would outperform every other person in every possible job! Nobody is the best at everything. This common view is supported by research in psychology and OB. Notably, **the *interactional perspective* states that behavior is a function of interdependent person and environmental factors.** Put another way, environments present various types of rewards and opportunities that people achieve or realize with diverse knowledge, skills, abilities, and motivations. Furthermore, "different people may perceive similar situations in different ways and similar people may perceive different situations in the same way."[47]

People and Environments Are Dynamic   It is important to note that neither people nor environments are static. People change, situations change, and the two change each other. To illustrate:

- People bring their abilities, goals, and experiences to each and every situation, which often changes the situation.
- Conversely, because situations have unique characteristics, such as opportunities and rewards, they change people. What you value in a job will likely differ between now and the time you are trying to make a move to senior management.
- It also is true that the current job market and employer expectations differ from those at the height of the technology bubble in the late 1990s or at the depths of the Great Recession in 2007–2009. In the first scenario, you changed, and in the second the environment changed.
- Finally, your manager—an environmental characteristic—can change what you do, how you do it, and your effectiveness. You in turn can impact these same characteristics in your manager.

The bottom-line implication for OB and your work life is that knowledge of one without the other is insufficient. *You need to understand the interplay between both person and environmental characteristics to be an effective employee, and especially an effective manager.*

How Can I Use Person and Environmental Characteristics to Apply OB Knowledge?   It is helpful to classify what you learn about OB into two easily understood categories or buckets. This will assist you when trying to identify which OB concepts or theories are relevant to a particular problem because every new concept or theory you learn represents a possible cause of a problem. Consider the ever-common event of downsizing, also referred to as a reduction in force or RIF, rightsizing, reorganization, restructuring, trimming dead wood, elimination of redundancies, strategic realignment, or just cutting back.

Many companies restructure indiscriminately and cut large percentages of their employee ranks. Assume you and five of your coworkers, who all do the same job, are kicked off the island (downsized). You experienced the same event—all of you lost your jobs. Yet despite this it is likely that you and your coworker's reactions will vary. For instance, while personally you are not delighted about losing your job, you might not feel too bad given that you didn't like the job and were considering going to graduate school next year anyway. Two of your coworkers, however, may be devastated and depressed.

Nevertheless, because the event was the same for all of you (environmental characteristic), we can assume that the differences in everyone's reactions were due to things about you as individuals (person factors), such as other job opportunities, how much each of you likes the job you just lost, your savings versus debt, and whether you have kids, mortgages, or a working spouse. The person–environment distinction therefore provides a means for classifying OB concepts and theories into causes of behavior.

Levels—Individual, Group/Team, and Organization

Another lens through which OB sees the world relies on organizational levels. OB distinguishes among three: individual, group, and organizational. The distinction between levels is fundamental to OB. (Note that it even provides the structure for this book, with separate parts on each level.)

As an example of how being sensitive to these levels helps in considering real-world problems, consider the many reasons why people quit their jobs:

- Some people quit because their job just doesn't fulfill what they value, such as challenging and stimulating work (an individual-level input).
- Others quit because of conflicts with their boss or they have nothing in common with their coworkers (a group/team level process).
- A faulty reward system (an organizational-level process) that unfairly distributes raises, bonuses, and recognition is another common reason people quit.

Understanding and considering levels increases your problem-solving effectiveness.

Applying OB Concepts to Identify the Right Problem

Nothing causes more harm than solving for the wrong problem. If you don't define the problem accurately, then all subsequent problem-solving efforts are adversely affected. This happens because people end up focusing on a symptom or the wrong problem. It's like a doctor treating your fever with aspirin instead of diagnosing and treating an underlying infection that caused the fever.

The distinctions we've just discussed allow you to see the current situation with more clarity. To illustrate, assume that many people in your department at work are quitting. What could be the cause of the problem? Of course, the fact that people are quitting doesn't necessarily indicate a problem, but at the least it raises a red flag. Using the person–environment distinction allows you to consider unique individual factors as well as external factors that might be the source of the problem. And the structural levels of individual, group, and organization will allow you to look at each level for possible reasons.

For example, the reason for the turnover may become more apparent by applying these concepts as you look at the situation. Such considerations could include:

- **Person factors.** Do the people who quit share something in common? Is there anything in their personality that makes work difficult for them? What about their ages? Gender? Is the rate or level of turnover in your company greater than for your industry as a whole?
- **Environmental characteristics.** Have there been changes in the environment, such as a sudden increase in employment opportunities at better wages? Have the working conditions changed in any meaningful way?
- **Individual level.** Can you identify any change in how the company treats employees or what it expects of them?
- **Group/team level.** Have there been any changes or other causative factors in your work group, including your manager, that might make work less satisfactory? How does turnover in your group compare to other groups in the organization?
- **Organizational level.** Has the organization changed ownership, or rewritten company policies, or is it enforcing policies differently?

By going through such an exercise, you widen your focus and review a larger number of possible causes for the problem, increasing the likelihood you will identify the right problem.

MAJOR QUESTION

How can the Integrative Framework help me understand and apply OB knowledge and tools—and improve my problem solving?

THE BIGGER PICTURE

You're about to receive the single best tool for understanding and applying OB's many concepts and tools—the Integrative Framework for Understanding and Applying OB. The framework also helps tremendously in improving your problem-solving abilities at school, work, and home. In the final section, we give you some practical and effective guidance on how to choose among alternative solutions to problems.

We're now ready to assemble a basic version of the Integrative Framework. Figure 1.2 illustrates this framework, which we will use throughout the book to help you organize, understand, and apply your knowledge as you acquire it. The Integrative Framework is also a crucial part of our problem-solving approach.

A Basic Version of the Integrative Framework

To assemble our framework, we use the Systems Approach as our foundation. It includes inputs, processes, and outcomes. The person–environmental distinction acts as inputs. Processes and outcomes are organized into the three levels of OB—individual, group, and organization. This framework implies that person factors and environmental characteristics are the initial drivers of all outcomes that managers want to achieve. This is the case because inputs affect processes, and processes affect outcomes. And since events are dynamic and ongoing, many outcomes will in turn impact inputs and processes. See Figure 1.2.

> A recent study of 111 people over one week showed that taking time away from work led employees to feel rested (an outcome) and to [experience] higher levels of work engagement (a process). Such breaks also enabled them to recover better during the work day, and this reenergized them for their remaining work (an input).[48]

FIGURE 1.2   INTEGRATIVE FRAMEWORK FOR UNDERSTANDING AND APPLYING OB

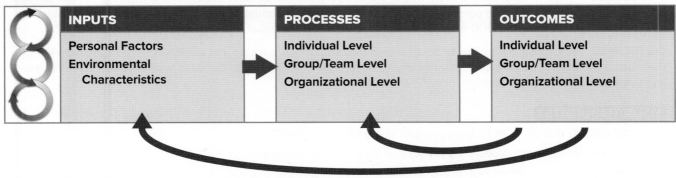

© 2014 by Angelo Kinicki and Mel Fugate. All rights reserved. Reproduction prohibited without express permission of the authors.

These time-sensitive relationships are shown as feedback loops in the Integrative Framework. Determining the causal relationships between inputs, processes, and outcomes often depends on a particular point in time—*an outcome at one point in time may be an input at another*.

As you work through this book you will notice that each chapter begins with a version of the Integrative Framework that helps introduce the concepts discussed in that particular chapter. Each chapter repeats the version of the framework at the end as part of the chapter review. If you take the cumulative effect of the content of each chapter, you'll end up with the fully articulated Integrative Framework. We provide you with a version of this at the end of the book, in the Epilogue, if you'd like to get a more complete picture. The same complete framework is a useful tool for preparing for a comprehensive final exam.

By definition frameworks are simplifications of reality; they necessarily exclude information. This means that the Integrative Framework at the end of the book will not show every OB concept that might impact employee behavior and performance. But the basic elements of the Framework will help you understand and apply any OB topic you encounter. The following Example box does an excellent job of illustrating the value of the Integrative Framework and its components. Be sure to answer the "Your Thoughts?" questions, as these will show you how to apply your new OB knowledge and tools.

EXAMPLE Life Is Sweeter on Mars

Whether it is the well-known candy (M&M's, Snickers, Lifesavers) or the similarly popular cat and dog foods (Whiskas and Pedigree), life is indeed sweet for the employees of Mars. The Integrative Framework can help us explain and understand why the 72,000 employees feel they have it so good, and why the company made the *Fortune* 100 Best Companies to Work For in 2013.

INPUTS The environment at Mars lacks the perks touted by many tech companies—no foosball tables, no free gourmet lunches, and no premier health clubs. More than this, some of their practices seem not just old school but prehistoric. For instance, all employees, including the president. have to punch a time clock each day and are docked 10 percent if late. However, what Mars may seem to lack in style it makes up for with its culture. President Paul S. Michaels explains how the company aligns its values and practices by asking: "Does it add value for the consumer to pay for marble floors and Picassos?" If it doesn't, then the company doesn't provide it. The employees seem to love the place and have very positive relationships at work, as many families have three generations working at Mars. The culture seems to be one big family, albeit one of cats, dogs, and candy. At one facility more than 200 employees bring their dogs to work each day. (Leash rules apply.) This family-type environment flows from the founding Mars family that still tightly controls the company, and it is built on the "Five Principles of Mars": quality, responsibility, mutuality, efficiency, and freedom. Employees not only recite but also live these principles.

PROCESSES While some practices seem frugal, the company reportedly awards bonuses of between 10 and 100 percent of employees' salaries. The company also invests heavily in the community via its Mars Volunteers and Mars Ambassadors programs. In 2011, 9,600 employees volunteered 37,000 hours at 290 organizations!

OUTCOMES Mars posts a very low turnover rate (5 percent), which is a sign that employees are highly satisfied with their jobs. And the fact that the company has managed to grow consistently for decades and remain private is compelling evidence for its financial performance.[49]

YOUR THOUGHTS?

1. What positive outcomes does Mars produce at the individual level?

2. What positive outcomes does Mars produce at the organizational level?

3. What inputs and processes help produce each of these outcomes?

Let's now consider the details of the Integrative Framework and apply it during Stop 2 of the 3-Stop approach to identify potential causes of a problem.

Using the Integrative Framework for Problem Solving

OB and problem solving go hand-in-hand. The concepts and tools you'll learn can be applied to understand and overcome challenges in many arenas of your life.

When confronted with a problem, we recommend tackling it using what we call the 3-Stop Problem Solving Approach. It is simple and widely applicable. Using the Integrative Framework makes the 3-Stop approach even more effective.

You can use the Integrative Framework at all three stops of the problem-solving journey to add rigor, intelligently apply your OB knowledge, and in turn improve your performance: Stop 1—make sure you are identifying the right problem; Stop 2—consider appropriate solutions; and Stop 3—select the solution that seems most appropriate.

Your ultimate problem-solving success will be determined by the effectiveness of your recommendation and resulting solution. So let's discuss this next.

Selecting a Solution and Taking Action (if appropriate)   Selecting solutions is both art and science. Some managers like to rely largely on intuition (discussed in Chapter 11) and experience. While these approaches can work, others use more analytical or systematic methods to select a solution.

> **EXAMPLE**   Intel has long been famous for its data-driven decision-making practices. When employees encounter and notify their managers of problems, it is common if not expected that managers automatically reply: "Call me when you've worked through your 7-step," referring to a companywide problem-solving process.

Intel's selection process is so entrenched that employees use a common PowerPoint template to fill in and ultimately present the relevant details of their proposed solutions. (Intel illustrates an organizational level–process approach that is similar to the rational approach to decision making we'll discuss in Chapter 11.)

Don't Forget to Consider Constraints   Pragmatically, most people lack the time, knowledge, or access to data to routinely follow such a rigorous procedure. Therefore, your ultimate selection most often requires you to consider various constraints—time, money, your own authority, and information—which can occur at different levels. We therefore close this chapter with some practical pointers on how to select the best solution among the alternatives you generated in Stop 2.

Applied Approaches to Selecting a Solution

You can save yourself time and grief with this practical advice (from renowned problem-solving professor and expert Russell Ackoff): First decide how complete of a response you are looking for. Do you want the problem to be *resolved, solved,* or *dissolved*?

- **Resolving** problems is arguably the most common form for managers and simply means choosing a satisfactory solution, one that works but is less than ideal. Putting on a bald and badly worn tire fixes a flat, but it certainly is less than ideal.
- **Solving** problems is the optimal or ideal response. For instance, you could buy a brand new, high-quality, full-size spare to keep in your trunk (not the typical "donut" or the "run-flats" that manufacturers frequently provide).

- **Dissolving** problems requires changing or eliminating the situation in which the problem occurs. Keeping with our example, the city you live in could build and utilize effective public transportation and thus remove the necessity of having cars (and tires) altogether.[50]

Making this decision then helps guide your choice among alternatives. It helps you determine what is needed, if it is realistic, and, accordingly, what level of effort and resources to use (e.g., money and time).

Basic Elements for Selecting an Effective Solution

After deciding whether to resolve, solve, or dissolve your identified problem, you then need to select the most effective solution. A problem-solving expert says: "The essence of successful problem solving is to be willing to consider real alternatives."[51] To help you choose among alternatives identified in Stop 2, we combed through the many books and articles written on the topic and distilled these three common elements:

1. **Selection criteria.** Determine the basis (criteria) for the decision, such as its effect on:
   - Bottom-line profits
   - You and classmates or coworkers
   - Reputation with customers or the community
   - Your own values
   - The ethical implications

2. **Consequences.** Consider the consequences of each alternative, especially the trade-offs between the pros and the cons, such as:
   - Who wins and who loses
   - Ideal vs. practical options
   - Perfection vs. excellence
   - Superior results vs. satisfactory results

3. **Choice process.** Decide who will be involved in choosing the solution. (If more than one person is involved, then you need to agree on the method. Will it be by vote? Public or secret? Unanimous or simple majority?):
   - You
   - Third party
   - Team

Whatever the case, it is important to consider the necessary resources, including which people will be key sources of support for (and resistance to) your ultimate selection. Consider who can help and who can hurt your efforts—"what's in it for them?"

Putting it all together, the OB knowledge and tools you'll learn in this book will help tremendously in selecting and implementing your "best" solution given the situation you face. Let's conclude with a brief scenario that will enable you to "test drive" your new tools.

A Practice Problem-Solving Scenario

You are approaching the summer before your senior year in college. Because of your financial situation, you must graduate next spring, which means you need to take 30 credit hours in the next 12 months (May of your junior year through the following June). With these facts in mind, you need to decide how you are going to spend your summer. You would like to study abroad (earns 6 credit hours), do an internship to improve your job prospects (assume you get paid for the internship), and, of course, you need to work part time and earn some money to pay tuition (you have to pay half and your parents pay half) and support your college student lifestyle. You are determined not to take any loans from anybody. Apply the 3-Stop Approach to solve your problem. After you work through this scenario on your own, then look at how we worked through the same scenario applying the 3-Stop Approach. (Don't skip ahead; try it yourself first.)

Apply the Problem-Solving Approach to OB

Stop 1: What is the problem?
- Identify the outcomes that are important in this case.
- Which of these outcomes are not being achieved in the case?
- Based on considering the above two questions, what is the most important problem in this case?

Stop 2: Use the material in this chapter to help you understand the problem in this case.
- What person factors are most relevant?
- What environmental characteristics are most important to consider?
- Do you need to consider any processes? Which ones?
- What concepts or tools discussed in this chapter are most relevant for solving the key problem in this case?

Stop 3: What are your recommendations for solving the problem?
- Review the material in the chapter that most pertains to your proposed solution and look for practical recommendations.
- Use any past OB knowledge or experience to generate recommendations.
- Outline your plan for solving the problem in this case.

We followed the same procedure and process to apply the 3-Stop Approach to this scenario. Our results are in ALL CAPS below. Compare our results to yours and identify sources of agreement and disagreement. Don't be surprised if yours differ. You may have defined the problem differently or you may have made different trade-offs. Besides, the authors were in school a long time ago. Internships were rare back then and few people studied abroad.

Authors' Application of the 3-Stop Approach

Stop 1: What is the problem? NEED TO DO SEVERAL THINGS AND STILL GRADUATE ON TIME. Desired state—graduate on time. Current state—several opportunities and needs between now and graduation.
- Identify the outcomes that are important in this case. GRADUATE ON TIME, IMPROVE JOB PROSPECTS, STUDY ABROAD, MAKE MONEY TO PAY BILLS
- Which of these outcomes are not being achieved in the case? GRADUATE ON TIME, IMPROVE JOB PROSPECTS, STUDY ABROAD, MAKE MONEY TO PAY BILLS
- Based on considering the above two questions, what is the most important problem in this case? GRADUATE ON TIME

Stop 2: Use the material in this chapter to help you understand the problem in this case.
- What person factors are most relevant? PERSONAL VALUES (e.g., education, fun, being responsible), FINANCIAL SITUATION, CAREER GOALS AND ASPIRATIONS
- What environmental characteristics are most important to consider? NUMBER OF CREDITS TO GRADUATE, CALENDAR OF WHEN CLASSES ARE OFFERED, STUDY ABROAD OPPORTUNITIES, INCOME OPPORTUNTIES DURING SCHOOL
- Do you need to consider any processes? Which ones? NO. WE'LL ASSUME YOU QUALIFY FOR THE STUDY ABROAD PROGRAM, YOU'RE NOT ON PROBATION AT SCHOOL, YOUR CLASSES ARE

AVAILABLE WHEN YOU WANT THEM, AND YOU'RE HIGHLY MOTIVATED

- What concepts or tools discussed in this chapter are most relevant for solving the key problem in this case? HUMAN CAPITAL (it is what qualifies you to study abroad and earn money during the year), ETHICS (we assume you won't steal or do anything illegal to earn income but not work), 3-STOP APPROACH, ELEMENTS OF SELECTING APPROPRIATE SOLUTIONS

Stop 3: What are your recommendations for solving the problem?
- A. DON'T DO STUDY ABROAD; DO INTERNSHIP, WORK, AND GO TO SCHOOL IN THE FALL
- B. DO STUDY ABROAD, TAKE REDUCED LOAD (study abroad was 6 hours) IN THE FALL AND FIND AN INTERNSHIP THEN, TAKE A FULL LOAD IN THE SPRING

- Review the material in the chapter that most pertains to your proposed solution and look for practical recommendations.
- Use any past OB knowledge or experience to generate recommendations.
- Outline your plan for solving the problem in this case. FINAL RECOMMENDATION: ALTERNATIVE B—DO THE STUDY ABROAD AND PURSUE INTERNSHIP IN THE FALL WHILE TAKING A REDUCED LOAD. THIS WILL MAKE YOU MORE VALUABLE TO PROSPECTIVE EMPLOYERS AND STILL ALLOW YOU TO GRADUATE ON TIME AND FINANCE YOUR LAVISH COLLEGE LIFESTYLE.

what did i learn?

You learned that OB is an interdisciplinary field that focuses on understanding and managing people at work. The same rich collection of OB tools and insights that can help you succeed at work can also help at school and at home. Your understanding of the practical value of OB knowledge was increased further with the Integrative Framework for Understanding and Applying OB and the 3-Stop Problem Solving Approach. Reinforce your learning with the chapter's Key Points listed below. Next, consolidate your learning using the Integrative Framework, shown in Figure 1.3. Then, challenge your mastery of the material by answering the chapter's Major Questions in your own words.

Key Points for Understanding Chapter 1

You learned the following key points.

1.1 THE VALUE OF OB TO MY JOB AND CAREER

- OB is an interdisciplinary and applied field that involves managing the behaviors of individuals, groups/teams, and organizations.
- The practical benefits of OB are based on the contingency approach, which says that the best or most effective approach requires one to apply the appropriate knowledge and tools to a given situation, rather than relying on one best way across all situations.
- OB is far more than common sense. Common sense has limits and inherent pitfalls that OB knowledge and tools help you avoid and overcome.
- OB helps you enhance your attractiveness to employers, as they want employees who have both hard and soft skills.

1.2 HUMAN AND SOCIAL CAPITAL

- Human and social capital are critically important aspects of your career success in the short and long term.
- Career success has two dimensions or types: objective and subjective.
- OB helps you increase your self-awareness and achieve your job and career goals.

1.3 RIGHT VS. WRONG—ETHICS AND YOUR PERFORMANCE

- Ethics is concerned with behavior—right vs. wrong, good vs. bad, and the many shades of gray in between. Unethical behavior thus has many forms and causes.
- The vast majority of unethical conduct at work is *not* illegal.
- Unethical conduct negatively affects the individual targets, the perpetrators, coworkers, and potentially entire organizations.
- Employees often encounter ethical dilemmas, or situations where none of the potential solutions are ethically acceptable.
- Whistleblowers are rarely protected and often suffer substantial emotional and professional costs.

1.4 APPLYING OB TO SOLVE PROBLEMS

- A problem is a difference or gap between a current and a desired situation.
- Problem solving is a systematic means for closing such differences or gaps.

FIGURE 1.3 INTEGRATIVE FRAMEWORK FOR UNDERSTANDING AND APPLYING OB

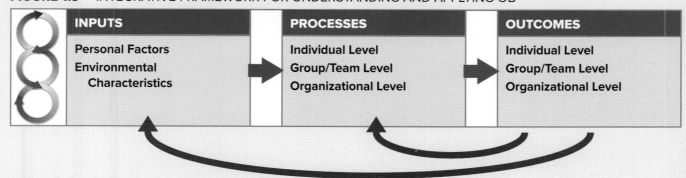

INPUTS	PROCESSES	OUTCOMES
Personal Factors	Individual Level	Individual Level
Environmental Characteristics	Group/Team Level	Group/Team Level
	Organizational Level	Organizational Level

© 2014 Angelo Kinicki and Mel Fugate. All rights reserved. Reproduction prohibited without permission of the authors.

- The 3-Stop Approach to Problem Solving involves defining the problem, using OB concepts and theories to understand the problem, and making recommendations and action plans to solve the problem.

1.5 STRUCTURE AND RIGOR IN SOLVING PROBLEMS

- The person–environment distinction is a fundamental way to organize, understand, and apply OB concepts.
- Person factors represent the vast number of characteristics that give individuals their unique identities.
- Environmental characteristics consist of all the elements outside of ourselves that influence what we do, how we do it, and the ultimate results of our actions.
- Workplace behavior occurs at three levels—individual, group/team, and organizational.

1.6 THE INTEGRATIVE FRAMEWORK FOR UNDERSTANDING AND APPLYING OB

- The Integrative Framework for OB is a tool that helps you to organize, understand, and apply your knowledge to solve problems.
- The systems approach is used to create the Integrative Framework for OB. Person and environment factors are inputs, and the processes and outcomes are organized into individual, group/team, and organizational levels.
- Apply the Integrative Framework to the 3-Stop Approach to Problem Solving to help you define problems, identify their causes, and generate recommendations.

The Integrative Framework for Chapter 1

In this chapter we introduced our first application of the Integrative Framework, showing the basic structure of inputs, processes, and outcomes (see Figure 1.3). The basic framework shown here will help you organize new concepts, theories, and tools as they are introduced, as well as help you retain and apply them. Accordingly, we'll use the Integrative Framework at the end of each chapter as an aid to review and apply what you've just learned.

If you want a preview of all that you'll learn, then take a quick look at the full Integrative Framework at the end of this book (in the Epilogue). We think you'll be quite impressed with how much you will have learned! In addition to its usefulness as a study aid, the Integrative Framework is a fundamental tool to use in the 3-Stop journey of problem solving. And beyond the course, the same framework can help you understand and manage behavior in many different organizational contexts (e.g., clubs, sports teams, and other social groups).

Challenge: Major Questions for Chapter 1

At the start of the chapter, we told you that after reading the chapter you should be able to answer the following major questions. Unless you can, have you really processed and internalized the lessons in the chapter? Refer to the Key Points, Figure 1.3, the chapter itself, and your notes to revisit and answer the following major questions:

1. How can I use knowledge of OB to enhance my job performance and career?
2. How can human and social capital affect my career opportunities and job performance?
3. Why do people engage in unethical behavior, even unwittingly, and what lessons can I learn from that?
4. How can I apply OB in a practical way to increase my effectiveness?
5. How could I explain to a fellow student the practical relevance and power of OB to help solve problems?
6. How does the Integrative Framework help me understand and apply OB knowledge and tools—and improve my problem solving?

The Cost of "Doing the Right Thing"

Apply the knowledge of OB presented in this chapter to the following case. Applying this knowledge should enable you to recommend realistic and effective solutions. As you read this case, please assume that you are the employee who is the target of the abuse and that, as the employee, you want to be treated fairly and with respect.

Background

If asked publically, you, like most people, would say that unethical behavior should be confronted—the perpetrators called out. This is what people believe *should* happen. But as you know, what people should do and what they actually do are often different. This is one reason why many organizations have codes of ethics that explicitly require those that simply witness or have knowledge of unethical conduct to come forward and make it known. (What do the Codes of Ethics at your school/employer say you are supposed to do if you have knowledge of unethical conduct?) The rationale is based on the assumption that if you are the target or victim of unethical conduct, then you are more likely to take action. But requiring others to take action is a means for making ethics everybody's responsibility.

Why Don't People Speak Up?

You undoubtedly agree that retaliating against somebody who speaks up—whether the actual target or only a witness—is wrong. Retaliation actually makes unethical behavior worse, as it punishes people for "doing the right thing" and rewards the wrongdoers. But it happens more often than you might think. True, legislation is in place to help protect some whistleblowers, but these laws are very specific (e.g., financial fraud) and do not apply to the vast majority of people and the vast majority of unethical conduct. Consider this hypothetical scenario to illustrate.

An employee at a brand management company in the southern United States was treated unfairly by the manager of his department. (Incidentally, fairness is a common element in ethics codes and often an explicit value in many organizations.) When he complained, the manager then built a coalition with two other senior employees and retaliated by trying to intimidate and undermine him for speaking out, such as giving him undesirable work assignments and schedules. The manager also purposefully damaged his reputation to other employees (e.g., labeled him a "troublemaker"), misrepresented him during his performance reviews, and blocked opportunities for him both inside and outside the organization. Because the actions were so blatantly unprofessional and unethical, and because they persisted over time, the targeted employee took the matter to the director (his manager's boss). The director did nothing.

Pursuing Accountability

The unethical treatment continued, which then motivated the employee to escalate the matter to the corporate level and pursue the formal grievance process. This process transferred his complaint to the vice president's (VP) office. The VP is responsible for all employee matters across the company including enforcing the company's code of ethics. The VP reviewed the case and said, "Life is unfair . . . deal with it. I will take no action." The mistreatment continued and resulted in the targeted employee filing a complaint of intimidation and retaliation with the Ethics Committee of the company, which was the only remaining option within the company's grievance process. He explained in his complaint the pattern of mistreatment and violations of the company's code of ethics.

Now It's Really Going to Cost You

To make matters worse, the targeted employee's director retaliated against him for filing his complaint! He reduced the scores on his performance review and cut his standard raise by more than 50 percent. The original and seemingly minor unethical matter of an infraction against fairness escalated into a matter that involved many people at many levels in the company. "Doing the right thing" had been very costly.

The Lesson?

Don't be too quick to think that retaliation of this sort is rare or that you are protected. Codes of ethics are just empty words if unethical people are not held accountable (e.g., colleagues, managers, directors, and executives).

Note: When answering the questions below, assume two things. First, you are the targeted employee in this case and you cannot quit. The market for your job is very constrained and being unemployed in not an option. Besides, your wife cannot leave her job for at least two years and you cannot make it on just her income. Second, also assume that you have no legal recourse. Remember what we said earlier in the chapter—most unethical behavior is not illegal. Legal remedies, even if available, have their own risks/costs. Given these two caveats, answer the following questions.

Apply the 3-Stop Problem Solving Approach to OB

Stop 1: What is the problem?

- Identify the outcomes that are important in this case.
- Which of these outcomes are not being achieved in the case?

- Based on considering the above two questions, what is the most important problem in this case?

Stop 2: Use the material in this chapter to help you understand the problem in this case.

- What person factors are most relevant?
- What environmental characteristics are most important to consider?
- Do you need to consider any processes? Which ones?
- What concepts or tools discussed in this chapter are most relevant for solving the key problem in this case?

Stop 3: What are your recommendations for solving the problem?

- Review the material in the chapter that most pertains to your proposed solution and look for practical recommendations.
- Use any of your existing OB knowledge or experience to generate recommendations.
- Outline your plan for solving the problem in this case.
- Be sure that your problem links to your causes, and that your recommendations address the causes and will solve the problem.

LEGAL/ETHICAL CHALLENGE

To Tell or Not to Tell?

Assume you are a nursing director for a nursing home. You've been working at your facility for a few short months when you learn that the company that owns the home has been improperly overbilling Medicare for the care and services provided to your residents. You bring this to the attention of the company's management. They do nothing. You then notify the appropriate authorities (you are now a whistleblower). For this, and a host of other reasons, you quit.

Several months later you are contacted by a headhunter, one you've worked with before. She convinces you to interview for a new position at another company. You agree to the interview and within days you are called in for an interview for a nursing director's job. Your interview happens to be a panel of 10, including the CEO, medical director, and other administrators. This panel will decide up or down whether you get the job.

One other important detail, this facility is just two miles down the road from the one you reported to the authorities before quitting. And nursing, like some other industries, tends to be a very close circle of people who often cross paths repeatedly in different jobs over time.

Your Response

What would you do about divulging information regarding your claim against your previous employer? Choose your answer from the options below. Be sure to explain and justify your choice.

1. Do not divulge the claim.
2. Wait until you learn the outcome of the interview, and if you don't get the offer, then you don't share the information.
3. Wait until you learn the outcome of the panel interview, and if you get the job offer, then tell the person who makes you the offer.
4. Tell all members of the panel during your interview.
5. Create and explain another course of action.

GROUP EXERCISE

Timeless Advice

Objectives

1. To get to know some of your fellow students.
2. To put the management of people into a lively and interesting historical context.
3. To begin to develop your teamwork skills.

Introduction

Your creative energy, willingness to see familiar things in unfamiliar ways, and ability to have fun while learning are keys to the success of this warm-up exercise. A 20-minute, small-group session will be followed by brief presentations and a general class discussion. Total time required is approximately 40–45 minutes.

Instructions

Your instructor will divide your class randomly into groups of four to six people each. Acting as a team, with everyone offering ideas and one person serving as official recorder, each team will be responsible for writing a one-page memo to your current class. The subject matter of your group's memo will be: "My advice for managing people today is . . ." The fun part of this exercise (and its creative element) involves writing the memo from the viewpoint of the person assigned to your group by your instructor.

Among the memo viewpoints your instructor may assign are the following:

1. Marissa Mayer (CEO of Yahoo).
2. An ancient Egyptian slave master (building the great pyramids).
3. Tony Hsieh (CEO of Zappos).
4. Reid Hoffman (cofounder of LinkedIn).
5. A contingency management theorist.
6. Alan Mulally (CEO of Ford Motor Company).
7. The CEO of Microsoft in the year 2030.
8. Bernie Madoff.
9. Others, as assigned by your instructor.

Using your imagination, make sure that everyone participates and tries to be true to any historical facts you've encountered. Attempt to be as specific and realistic as possible. Remember, the idea is to provide advice about managing people from another person's point of view, and, in some cases, at another point in time. Make sure to manage your 20-minute time limit. A recommended approach is to spend 2 to 3 minutes thinking about the exercise, putting it into perspective. Next, spend about 10 to 12 minutes brainstorming ideas. Be sure to have somebody record your ideas. Then, use the remaining time to write your one-page memo. Pick a spokesperson to read your group's memo to the class.

Questions for Discussion

1. What valuable lessons about managing people have you heard?
2. What have you learned about how *not* to manage people?
3. From the distant past to today, what significant shifts in the management of people seem to have taken place?
4. Where does the management of people appear to be headed?
5. All things considered, what mistakes are today's managers typically making when managing people?
6. How well did your group function as a "team"?

2 VALUES AND ATTITUDES

How Do They Affect Work-Related Outcomes?

inputs

PERSON FACTORS
Values
Personal Attitudes

ENVIRONMENTAL
CHARACTERISTICS

processes

INDIVIDUAL LEVEL

GROUP/TEAM LEVEL

ORGANIZATIONAL LEVEL

outcomes

INDIVIDUAL LEVEL
Workplace attitudes

GROUP/TEAM LEVEL

ORGANIZATIONAL LEVEL

© 2014 Angelo Kinicki and Mel Fugate. All rights reserved. Reproduction prohibited without permission of the authors.

MAJOR TOPICS I'LL LEARN AND QUESTIONS I SHOULD BE ABLE TO ANSWER

2.1 PERSONAL VALUES
MAJOR QUESTION: *What role do values play in influencing my behavior?*

2.2 PERSONAL ATTITUDES AND THEIR IMPACT ON BEHAVIOR AND OUTCOMES
MAJOR QUESTION: *How do personal attitudes affect workplace behavior and work-related outcomes?*

2.3 KEY WORKPLACE ATTITUDES
MAJOR QUESTION: *Why is it important for management to pay attention to workplace attitudes?*

2.4 THE CAUSES OF JOB SATISFACTION
MAJOR QUESTION: *How can changes in the workplace improve job satisfaction?*

2.5 MAJOR CORRELATES AND CONSEQUENCES OF JOB SATISFACTION
MAJOR QUESTION: *What work-related outcomes are associated with job satisfaction?*

INTEGRATIVE FRAMEWORK FOR UNDERSTANDING AND APPLYING OB

Values are a key input that affect important OB processes such as motivation and leadership styles, which in turn impact the outcome of indivdiual workplace attitudes. We cover these processes in later chapters.

LEARNING TO COMBAT BULLYING

Most folks think they left bullying back in the schoolyard. Sometimes they are wrong. Consider Carl Dessureault. He was a bus driver who was repeatedly harassed by coworkers because of his appearance being similar to a rapist. He was asked questions like "What's it like to rape women?" and "Who's your next victim?" Carl sought counseling, was put on antidepressants, and ultimately committed suicide.[1]

Bullying **is the repeated mistreatment of an individual or individuals by aggressive or unreasonable behavior, including persistent abuse and humiliation by verbal, nonverbal, psychological, or physical means.** We discuss bullying here as an example of a behavior that is partly driven by an individual's values.

FREQUENCY AND SOURCE OF BULLYING
Research conducted by the Workplace Bullying Institute estimates that 37 percent of the US workforce (approximately 54 million people) has been bullied. Interestingly, most bullies are bosses, and the majority are men (about 60 percent). Women also tend to be bullied more than men.

TYPES OF BULLYING BEHAVIOR
There are multiple forms of bullying behavior. They include physical aggression (like being pushed, pinched, or cornered), verbal aggression (name calling, the brunt of jokes, and threats), relational aggression (gossip and rumors, social isolation), and cyber-aggression (sending negative or derogatory images, text messages, or e-mail).[2]

CONSEQUENCES OF BULLYING
Targets or victims of bullying tend to experience stress-related health problems, which can lead to anxiety, panic attacks, depression, and suicide.[3] Bullied employees are less satisfied at work and are more likely to quit and exhibit counterproductive behaviors such as not putting in full effort and gossiping.[4]

COMBATING BULLYING
The first step is to document the event in writing, particularly if the bully is your boss. Be truthful and stick to the facts. Remember, the bully is likely going to deny your accusations. If the bullying is done via electronic means, smile because the bully is doing the work for you. Just keep a copy of the bullying messages.

With documentation in hand, contact either the bully's boss, a member of human resources, or your state's employee assistance program. Be sure to state what you want to occur in the future. Do you want someone to intervene? If yes, how? At a minimum, we recommend that you let people know that you want to be treated with dignity, respect, and fairness. You may want to request a transfer if the perpetrator is your boss and you are afraid of retaliation.

If you have no choice but to continue working with the bully in the short run, then try to avoid being alone with this person. Make sure someone is within earshot of any interactions. Bullies are more active when they are alone with their victims. You can also consider carrying a mechanical witness—smartphone audio or video function.

Resist the temptation to strike back. This can cost you your job or reputation. Finally, seek social support from family and friends. Discuss the issue and let off some steam. They also may provide useful tips.[5]

| FOR YOU | WHAT'S AHEAD IN THIS CHAPTER |

Now that you have new tools to make OB work for you—tools like the Integrative Framework and the 3-Stop Problem Solving Approach—you're ready to put them to work. With this chapter we start you on your OB journey by exploring how individual-level factors influence a host of important outcomes. Specifically, we explore how one of the most important of these individual-level factors, values, affects workplace attitudes and behavior. We will help you explore how your personal values affect your own workplace attitudes and behavior. We'll outfit you with OB concepts to understand key work-related attitudes—organizational commitment, employee engagement, and perceived organizational support—which lead to important outcomes at the individual and organizational levels. Before you're done, we hope you will understand the causes and consequences of job satisfaction, an important outcome for both employees and managers.

major question

What role do values play in influencing my behavior?

THE BIGGER PICTURE

You may already have a good understanding of your personal values and the role they play in your life. In an organization, personal values contribute to workplace attitudes and behavior. So it's important to understand how the full range of potential human values impacts our attitudes and behavior at work. In the values model shown on the next page, see if you can locate yourself first, and then your friends or coworkers. From an OB perspective, you first need to understand personal values to understand, let alone influence, workplace attitudes.

Values are abstract ideals that guide one's thinking and behavior across all situations. They are strongly influenced by our religious or spiritual beliefs, the values of our parents, experiences during childhood, and events occurring throughout the communities and societies in which we live. Managers need to understand an employee's values because they encompass concepts, principles, or activities for which people are willing to work hard. All workers need an understanding of values to work effectively with others and manage themselves. Renowned researcher Shalom Schwartz created a theory of personal values that over time many managers and OB professionals have found especially useful for understanding the motivational impact of our values.

Schwartz's Value Theory

Schwartz believes that values are motivational in that they "represent broad goals that apply across contexts and time."[6] For example, valuing achievement will likely result in your studying hard to get an A in this class. It could also drive you to compete against friends in a weekly golf game. Values also are relatively stable and can influence behavior outside of our awareness.

Schwartz proposed that 10 broad values guide behavior. (See Figure 2.1.) These values are categorized around two bipolar dimensions, which are described below.

FIRST BIPOLAR DIMENSION	
SELF-ENHANCEMENT	**SELF-TRANSCENDENCE**
Concern for the welfare and interests of others (universalism, benevolence).	Pursuit of one's own interests and relative success and dominance over others (power, achievement).
SECOND BIPOLAR DIMENSION	
OPENNESS TO CHANGE	**CONSERVATION**
Independence of thought, action, and feelings and readiness for change (self-direction, stimulation).	Order, self-restriction, preservation of the past, and resistance to change (security, conformity, tradition).

FIGURE 2.1 VALUES AND MOTIVES IN SCHWARTZ'S THEORY

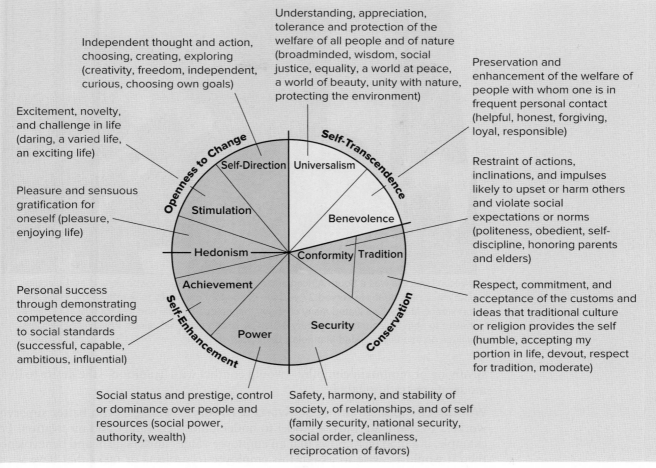

SOURCE: Graphic from S. H. Schwartz, "An Overview of the Schwartz Theory of Basic Values," *Online Readings in Psychology and Culture* 2(1), December 1, 2012, http://dx.doi .org/10.9707/2307-0919.1116. Reprinted with permission of the author. Definitions from A. Bardi and S. H. Schwartz, "Values and Behavior: Strength and Structure of Relations," *Personality & Social Psychology Bulletin,* October 2003, 1208. Reproduced with permission of Sage Publications, Inc. via Copyright Clearance Center.

Not only have these 10 values been found to predict behavior as outlined in the theory, but they also generalize across cultures.[7] The model in Figure 2.1 organizes values by showing the patterns of conflict and congruity among them. In general, adjacent values like self-direction and universalism are positively related, whereas values that are farther apart (like self-direction and power) are less strongly related. Taking this one step further, Schwartz proposes that values that are in opposing directions from the center conflict with each other.

In Figure 2.1, notice the unique treatment of several values. Tradition and conformity share a single wedge, supporting the same broad motivational goal. Conformity is toward the center because it does not conflict quite as much as tradition, which is toward the periphery, with their opposing values. See also how hedonism shares elements of both openness to change and self-enhancement. Values are identified in each section of the circle, with underlying motives for the values shown outside the circle. Schwartz noted that one set of values is in opposition to the other set, as suggested by the use of color.

Not all values are compatible. "One basis of the value structure is the fact that actions in pursuit of any value have consequences that conflict with some values but are congruent with others."[8] In the circular model, Schwartz positions values most in conflict the farthest apart and those most in congruity the closest together. For instance, Stimulation—the drive to live a stimulating life by engaging in activities like

Nelson Mandela was a South African anti-apartheid revolutionary who served as the country's first black president. He served 27 years in prison for conspiracy to overthow the state. As president, Mandella initiated many changes that helped people and the country at large. His desire to help his country was cleary driven by strong personal values. Which of Schwartz's values do you think guided Mandela's behavior?

skydiving or mountain climbing—would conflict with Tradition—the desire to live a moderate or traditional life.

Workplace Application of Schwartz's Theory   Managers can better supervise workers by using Schwartz's model to understand their values and motivation. For example, if a manager knows that an employee values universalism and benevolence, then it would be wise to assign this employee to projects or tasks that have social value. Managers can also use Figure 2.1 to reduce the chances of employees' experiencing conflict between their values and their work assignments, when options are available. If an employee values tradition and conformity over achievement, for example, then he or she will not be happy about being asked to work on a holiday or to miss a child's school play due to work.

Managers can also reduce employee turnover by trying to reduce the gap between an employee's values and the values that comprise the organization's culture. Organizational culture is discussed in Chapter 14. For example, if an employee wants security and tradition (two values that are part of the conservation motive), they will not be happy with a job that provides little direction and lots of changing job requirements (two values that are part of the openness to change motive).

connect

SELF-ASSESSMENT 2.1   **What Are My Core Values?**

Go to connect.mheducation.com and complete Self-Assessment 2.1. It measures the extent to which you subscribe to each of Schwartz's 10 values. Then answer the following questions:

1.   Rank the values from high to low; do you agree with the rank order?

2.   What are your top five values? Which of these do you think has the greatest impact on your personal goals?

3.   Do you think that you may want to focus more on any of the five lowest-rated values as you graduate from school and pursue a career? Explain.

Personal Application of Schwartz's Theory   This model can help you determine if your values are consistent with your goals and whether you are spending your time in a meaningful way. We illustrate this by having you first complete a Self-Assessment that measures Schwartz's 10 values and then incorporate the results into a Take-Away Application (TAAP).

TAKE-AWAY APPLICATION—TAAP

1. Identify the three most important goals in your life.

2. Now consider the extent to which your personal goals are aligned with the top five values identified in the Self-Assessment. Are your goals and values aligned?

3. For those values that are inconsistent with your goals, theory suggests that you need to either change your values or change your goals. Because values don't easily change, it typically is wise to change your goals. Identify what you might do to make your goals more aligned with your values.

The Dynamics of Values

In general, values are relatively stable across time and situations. This means that positive employee attitudes and motivation are greatest when the work environment is consistent with employee values. For example, outdoor gear retailer Recreational Equipment (REI) attempts to attract and motivate employees by letting them "use kayaks, skis, and other equipment for free [which they can buy new at a deep discount]."[9] The company does this because it believes that its employees are motivated to participate in outdoor activities. Starbucks represents another company that is trying to appeal to employees' values regarding education. The company created a partnership with Arizona State University in order to offer employees the chance to complete a bachelors degree online with full tuition reimbursement. Employees can choose from 40 different bachelors degrees.

REI and Starbucks are good examples of companies where attention to the input of values as a person factor could yield measurable positive outcomes such as low turnover, higher retention, increased employee engagement, and better customer satisfaction.

Values tend to vary across generations because they are influenced by events occurring during childhood. For example, our parents both lived through the depression that lasted through parts of the 1930s and 40s. This experience led them to value security and to be conservative with their money. They did not like debt, and they were against the use of credit cards. Do you know anyone with values like these? In contrast, the values held by baby boomers, people born between 1946 and 1964, are influenced by events like the assassination of President John Kennedy, the Vietnam War, and the shooting deaths of student protestors at Kent State University. In contrast, Gen Ys, people born between 1980 and 2001, tend to have different values than boomers because their values are influenced by events like September 11, wars in Iraq and Afghanistan, and the financial crisis of 2008. We discuss generational differences thoroughly in Chapter 4.

PERSONAL ATTITUDES AND THEIR IMPACT ON BEHAVIOR AND OUTCOMES

MAJOR QUESTION

How do personal attitudes affect workplace behavior and work-related outcomes?

THE BIGGER PICTURE

Closely related to values are personal attitudes. Like values, personal attitudes operate as an input in the Integrative Framework for Understanding and Applying OB. (In contrast, *workplace* attitudes are defined as outcomes in the Integrated Framework.) Starting from the personal, look for your own experiences in the OB view that personal attitudes have three components—affective, cognitive, and behavioral. Knowing these components brings you closer to understanding how and when personal attitudes affect behavior. Have you ever been stopped short by something that didn't seem to make sense? When personal attitudes collide with reality, the result is cognitive dissonance. From an OB perspective, your personal attitudes affect your behavior via your intentions.

In this section, we discuss the components of personal attitudes and examine the connection between personal attitudes and behavior.

Personal attitudes affect behavior at a different level than do values. While values represent *global* beliefs that influence behavior across *all* situations, personal attitudes relate only to behavior directed toward *specific* objects, persons, or situations. We can summarize the differences between the two as follows:

CONCEPT	SCOPE	INFLUENCE	AFFECTS BEHAVIOR
Personal Values	Global	Broad: All situations	Variously
Personal Attitudes	Specific	Targeted: Specifically	Via intentions

Attitudes represent our feelings or opinions about people, places, and objects, and range from positive to negative. They are important because they impact our behavior. For example, you are more likely to select chocolate ice cream over vanilla if you are more positively disposed toward chocolate. In contrast, **workplace attitudes** are an outcome of various OB-related processes, including leadership, a topic to be discussed in Chapter 13. In this chapter we reserve the term "workplace attitudes" for attitudes that have resulted from the interaction of various individual, group, and organizational processes. We examine the effects of workplace attitudes later in Section 2.3.

As predictors of likely behavior, attitudes attract serious attention. Hardly a day goes by without the popular media reporting the results of another effort to take the pulse of public opinion (attitudes). What do we think about the president and members of Congress, efforts to combat terrorism, the war on drugs, gun control, or taxes? Political consultants use this information to craft messages to nudge the public's attitudes toward the results they feel are favorable to their side. In the workplace, managers conduct attitude surveys to monitor workplace attitudes like job satisfaction and employee engagement, and to determine the causes of employee turnover.

For example, one study showed that seniors with a positive attitude about aging had better memory, had better hearing, and lived longer than those with negative attitudes.[10] In a work setting, workplace attitudes were positively related to performance and negatively to indicators of withdrawal—lateness, absenteeism, and turnover.[11]

Personal Attitudes: They Represent My Consistent Beliefs and Feelings about Specific Things

Consider a work example. If you have a positive attitude about your job (specifically, you like what you are doing), you would be more willing to extend yourself at work by working longer and harder: Working longer and harder is often referred to as "organizational citizenship behavior," a concept discussed later in this chapter. This example illustrates that attitudes propel us to act in a specific way in a specific context.

Values and attitudes generally, but not always, are in harmony. A manager who strongly values helpful behavior may have a negative attitude toward helping an unethical coworker.

We are more likely to purchase a car when we have positive attitudes toward it. These attitudes might pertain to make, model, color, price, and quality. What are your attitudes toward purchasing a white, used car? Which component of attitudes is most strongly impacting your overall attitude toward white, used cars?

The Three Components of Attitudes: Affective, Cognitive, and Behavioral   Our overall attitudes toward someone or something are a function of the combined influence of three components:

1. **The affective component—"I feel." The *affective component* of an attitude contains the feelings or emotions one has about a given object or situation.** For example, how do you *feel* about people who talk on their cell phones in restaurants? If you feel annoyed or angry with such people, you are experiencing negative affect or feelings toward people who talk on cell phones in restaurants.

2. **The cognitive component—"I believe." The *cognitive component* of an attitude reflects the beliefs or ideas one has about an object or situation.** What do you *think* about people who talk on cell phones in restaurants? Your ideas about such behavior represents the cognitive component of your attitude toward people talking on cell phones in restaurants.

3. **The behavioral component—"I intend." The *behavioral component* refers to how one intends or expects to act toward someone or something.** For example, how would you intend to respond to someone talking on a cell phone during dinner at a restaurant if this individual were sitting in close proximity to you and your guest?

All three components influence our behavior. You are unlikely to say anything to someone using a cell phone in a restaurant if you are not irritated by this behavior (affective), if

Social psychologist Leon Festinger

you believe cell phone use helps people to manage their lives (cognitive), and if you have no intention of confronting this individual (behavioral).

When Attitudes and Reality Collide: Consistency and Cognitive Dissonance

Have you ever been accused of being a hypocrite—saying one thing and then behaving differently? Like most people, you probably want to maintain consistency between your attitudes and your behavior.

But sometimes attitudes conflict with reality. Suppose that Samantha has a positive attitude about helping others. One day her boss asks her if she would work on a special project for an important new client—and it must get done in two months. The project represents significant revenue, and her boss even promises a one-time bonus for successfully completing the project on time. The rub is that two of her peers have also come to her seeking help on *their* project. Samantha feels that she is best suited to help them, given her past experience, but she feels pressured given the demands of her new assignment. While Samantha has some flexibility in how she uses her time, she doesn't want to miss the project deadline. Should she make time to help her peers or singularly focus on the special project? According to social psychologist Leon Festinger, this situation would create *cognitive dissonance*.

Cognitive dissonance **represents the psychological discomfort a person experiences when simultaneously holding two or more conflicting cognitions (ideas, beliefs, values, or emotions).**[12] Festinger was fascinated by how people are motivated to maintain consistency (and avoid dissonance) among their attitudes and beliefs, and how they resolve inconsistencies that drive cognitive dissonance. From observation, he theorized that if you are experiencing cognitive dissonance, or psychological tension, you can reduce it in one of three ways:

1. *Change your attitude or behavior or both.* Samantha could either (a) tell herself that she can't help her peers because the special project is too important for the company or (b) schedule extra time each day or week to help her peers.

2. *Belittle the importance of the inconsistent behavior.* Samantha could belittle (in the sense of "make small") the belief that she needs to help peers every time they ask for assistance.

3. *Find consonant elements that outweigh dissonant ones.* Samantha could tell herself that she can't help because the company needs the revenue and she needs the bonus.

Attitudes Affect Behavior via Intentions

Psychologist I. Ajzen and M. Fishbein further explored the rationale for why someone's attitudes and behavior could misalign. Based on this work, Ajzen developed and refined a model focusing on intentions as the key link between attitudes and planned behavior. See Figure 2.2.

Determinants of Intention

Figure 2.2 suggests how three key general motives predict or at least influence intention and behavior.

1. *Attitude toward the behavior.* The degree to which a person has a favorable or unfavorable evaluation or appraisal of the behavior in question.

2. *Subjective norm.* A social factor representing the perceived social pressure for or against the behavior.

3. *Perceived behavioral control.* The perceived ease or difficulty of performing the behavior, assumed to reflect past experience and anticipated obstacles.[13]

FIGURE 2.2   AJZEN'S THEORY OF PLANNED BEHAVIOR

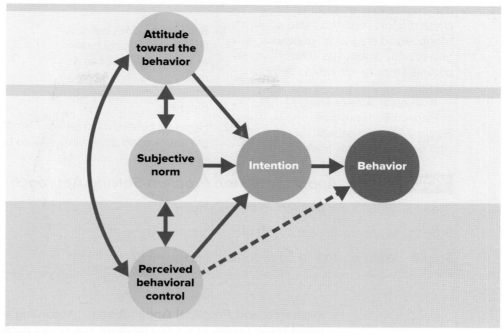

SOURCE: Reprinted from *Organizational Behavior and Human Decision Processes* , Vol. 50, No. 2, I. Arjzen, "The Theory of Planned Behavior," Copyright © 1991, with permission from Elsevier.

Putting the Theory into Practice   Theories are developed from observation and prove their usefulness in application. Let's demonstrate this with Ajzen's theory. Consider the behavior of patients lying to doctors and doctors lying to patients. See the Problem-Solving Application below. Read the example and answer the questions posed under "Your Call."

solving application

problem

Why Do Patients Lie to Doctors and Doctors Lie to Patients?

Doctors are cautious about what patients say. "It's a rule many residents learn in training. If a patient says he has four drinks a week, consider it eight. The same for cigarettes and illicit drugs, doctors say." Kevin Campbell, a cardiologist from North Carolina, noted that he had patients who claimed to have stopped smoking, yet smelled like cigarettes when they came in to his office. Why does this happen when lying can lead to the wrong diagnosis, wrong treatment, and wrong prescriptions?

    Some lie for fear of a bad diagnosis or hospitalization. Others

lie in order to get the preferred handicapped parking permit or mood-altering drugs. Doctors also note that some patients lie for more positive reasons, such as avoiding embarrassment or

disappointing the doctor. "Others worry about electronic medical records or information being communicated to employers, insurance companies, or the authorities." Parents also lie about their children when they believe that they will be judged.

    It works both ways. A recent survey of physicians revealed that 10 percent told patients things that were untrue. Fifty percent of these doctors "told patients something that was untrue in the previous year. More than half said they described a prognosis in a more positive manner than warranted, and about 20% admitted to not fully disclosing a mistake to a patient due to fears of litigation." Other doctors reported using a "generalized diagnosis" instead of a specific illness like schizophrenia so as to not alarm patients.[14]

If we apply Ajzen's Theory of Planned Behavior (see Figure 2.2) to the patient who underreports his drinking, we might analyze his behavior as follows:

1. Because he does not see his existing alcohol intake as problematic, he has no reservations about telling a white lie (attitude toward the behavior).
2. He might believe most people underreport their drinking behavior to doctors (subjective norm). One would not want to be labeled an alcoholic.
3. He sees little downside risk or difficulty in underreporting his intake (perceived behavioral control).

The result? The patient proceeds to lie to the doctor.

YOUR CALL *Apply the 3-Stop Problem-Solving Approach.*

Stop 1:   What is the problem in this example?

Stop 2:   What are the causes of the problem?

Stop 3:   What would you do to correct this situation?

Research and Practical Applications   According to the Ajzen model, someone's intention to engage in a given behavior is a strong predictor of that behavior. For example, if you want a quick way to determine whether a worker will quit his or her job, have an objective third party ask the worker if that is what the worker is intending. The answer is likely to be accurate. Research supports this conclusion[15] and the prediction that intentions are influenced by the three general motives in Ajzen's model.[16]

So if we want to change behavior we should look at intentions and how we might modify them by working on the three general motives shown in Figure 2.2. Managers may be able to influence behavioral change by doing or saying things that affect the three determinants of employees' intentions to exhibit a specific behavior: attitude toward the behavior, subjective norms, and perceived behavioral control. In your own life, if you want to exercise more, you should start by changing your intentions about exercising and your associated beliefs about exercising.

Let's consider another practical illustration that has happened to many of our students. It involves a lack of equal contribution among team members on class projects. Have you ever wanted a classmate to increase the quality of his/her work on a team project? If yes, Ajzen's model can be used to help you get the desired behavior. Start by trying to create a positive intention to contribute high-quality work. You might do this by telling the person that getting a good grade will increase everyone's chances of getting higher grades and a better job upon graduation (attitude toward the behavior). Next, role model the desired behavior by producing good work yourself and recognize others who do the same. This should increase the subjective norm about doing high-quality work. Finally, talk to the individual about any obstacles getting in the way of high-quality work and discuss solutions for overcoming them. We expect that this will increase the person's perceived behavioral control.

The Lever of Information   In the workplace, one of the simplest levers managers can use to change behavior is information. Management provides information to employees daily. Standard organizational information that can affect motivation includes:

- Reports on the organization's culture.
- Announcements of new training programs.
- News on key managers.
- Updates to human resource programs and policies.
- Announcements of new rewards of working for the company.

EXAMPLE Alston & Bird Engages Employees through Its Words and Deeds

Managing partners at the firm wanted to boost employee morale after the Great Recession in 2008–2009. Richard Hays, managing partner at the firm, decided that increased communication would help. "We started town hall meetings and initiated an online suggestion box," he says, "where employees could comment (or vent) about anything on their minds." He also spent more time in offices outside of Atlanta to communicate with geographically dispersed employees.

The company also tried to make the work environment more enjoyable by installing chair massages and employees' favorite coffee on all floors. To help employees manage work–life balance issues, it instituted on-site day care, offered on-site dining, and provided financial experts

Town hall meetings like this were used at Alston & Bird to increase communication with employees. Do you think such meetings are useful? Why?

once a quarter to assist employees in their short- and long-term financial planning. Hays concluded that these actions "convey a message to employees that you care."[17]

YOUR THOUGHTS?

1. What beliefs do you have about Alston & Bird?

2. What type of performance intentions would the company's actions help create?

3. Would you like to work at Alston & Bird?

All such messages reinforce certain beliefs, and managers may consciously use them to influence behavior. For example, if management wants to improve employee retention, it can provide information or implement policies that underscore the value of staying at the company.

Such efforts extend beyond perception into programs that can benefit the workplace. This is precisely what happened at Alston & Bird, an Atlanta law firm that was rated as the 40th best place to work by *Fortune* in 2014 (see Example box above). The company wanted to enhance employees' beliefs about the value of staying at the firm rather than taking a job elsewhere.

TAKE-AWAY APPLICATION—TAAP

1. Based on the theory of planned behavior, how might you improve your attitude about studying for this course?

2. How can you influence the social norms about studying for classes?

3. Assume you want to get a good job upon graduation. What does the theory of planned behavior suggest that you should start or continue doing?

KEY WORKPLACE ATTITUDES

MAJOR QUESTION

Why is it important for management to pay attention to workplace attitudes?

THE BIGGER PICTURE

Of the many workplace attitudes we might see as outcomes in the Integrative Framework for understanding and applying OB, researchers have identified a small number that are especially potent. These *key* attitudes allow you to track a limited number of workplace attitudes to gauge how the organization is doing. When you try to make sense of the workplace on either side of a manager's desk, these are the important attitudes to follow.

Savvy managers will track four key workplace attitudes:

1. Organizational commitment
2. Employee engagement
3. Perceived organizational support
4. Job satisfaction

That's because these attitudinal measures serve a dual purpose. First, they represent important outcomes that managers may be working to enhance directly. Second, they link to other significant outcomes that managers will want to improve where possible. For example, low job satisfaction and low employee engagement imply lower task performance and higher employee turnover.[18] This is why managers should track key workplace attitudes and understand their causes and consequences.

This section specifically examines the first three of these: organizational commitment, employee engagement, and perceived organizational support. We're saving job satisfaction, the most studied workplace attitude, for a later section of its own.

Organizational Commitment

OB researchers define commitment as "a force that binds an individual to a course of action of relevance to one or more targets."[19] This definition highlights how OB researchers link commitment to behavior and how workers can commit to multiple targets or entities. For example, an individual can be committed to his or her job, family, girl- or boyfriend, faith, friends, career, organization, and/or a variety of professional associations. Let us now consider the application of commitment to a work organization.

Organizational commitment reflects the extent to which an individual identifies with an organization and commits to its goals. Committed individuals tend to display two outcomes:

• Likely continuation of their employment with the organization.
• Greater motivation toward pursuing organizational goals and decisions.

What Drives Organizational Commitment? There are many factors we will encounter through this book, but let's start with something basic, like personal values. Organizational commitment exists to the degree that your personal values generally match the values that undergird a company's organizational culture. For example, if you value achievement and your employer rewards people for accomplishing goals, you are more likely to be committed to the company. This consistency is called person-culture fit and is discussed in Chapter 15.

Throughout this book we will cover other drivers of organizational commitment, in the course of discussing:

- Personality, Chapter 3.
- Meaningfulness, Chapters 5 and 7.
- Organizational climate, Chapter 7.
- Leader Behavior, Chapter 13.
- Organizational Culture, Chapter 14.

Finally, commitment depends on the quality of an employee's psychological contracts. **Psychological contracts represent an individual's perception about the terms and conditions of a reciprocal exchange between him- or herself and another party.** In a work environment, the psychological contract represents an employee's beliefs about what he or she is entitled to receive in return for what he or she provides to the organization. Research shows that an employer breach of the psychological contract is associated with lower organizational commitment, job satisfaction, and performance, and greater intentions to quit.[20]

How Can Managers Increase Employees' Commitment? To highlight how managers can increase employees' commitment, we review three general best practices and then discuss approaches used by Edward Jones, Cisco, and Google.

General Best Practices
- Hire people whose personal values align with the organization's.
- Make sure that management does not breach its psychological contracts.
- Explicitly and conscientiously enhance the level of trust throughout the organization.

Example Company: Edward Jones
- *Fortune*'s 4th best company to work for in 2014.
- Promotes close-knit culture.
- Does so across about 11,000 small offices.
- Hosts regular regional gatherings for ice skating, fishing tournaments, etc.
- Pulls about 44 percent of new hires from employee referrals.[21]

Example Company: Cisco
- CNN/*Fortune*'s third top-paying company in 2013 and 55th best company to work for in 2014.
- Great pay.
- Flextime. (**Flextime consists of giving employees flexible work hours that allow people to come and go at different times, as long as they work the normal number of hours.**) *Cisco Payoff:* "[T]he fact that I am given so much flexibility makes me want to go above and beyond," Cisco employee.
- Employees called into military service continue with full benefits for themselves and family.
- Employees called into military service receive additional pay to make up difference between Cisco pay and military pay.
- Employees called onto jury duty receive full pay while in jury for up to three months.[22]

Example Company: Google

- *Fortune*'s number 1 best company to work for in 2013 and 2014.
- Free electric cars to borrow for short jaunts.
- Microkitchens open 24/7 throughout campus.
- Hundreds of Google bikes on which to speed off to another building.
- Weekly group sitdowns with Google founders Larry Page and Sergey Brin.
- Free food in over 30 cafeterias.
- Drop-in free IT repair centers (with loaners).
- Community gardens.
- Free massages. Sleep pods.
- Free laundry rooms.
- Three wellness centers.
- Seven-acre sports complex, with roller hockey rink; courts for basketball, bocce, and shuffle-ball; and horseshoe pits.[23]

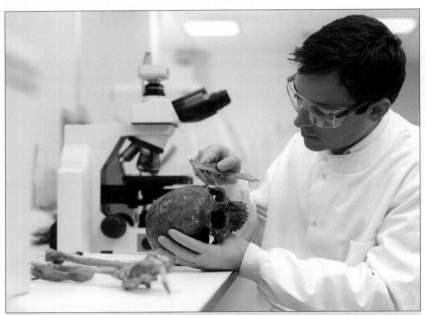

This employee looks highly engaged with his work. Note the attention and focus being used to measure aspects of this skull. Would you find this type of work meaningful?

Employee Engagement

A relatively new concept to the field of organizational behavior, *employee engagement* was defined in 1990 by William Kahn. Observing workers at a summer camp and an architecture firm, Kahn defined **employee engagement** as "the harnessing of organization members' selves to their work roles; in engagement, people employ and express themselves physically, cognitively, and emotionally during role performance."[24] The essence of this definition is the idea that engaged employees "give it their all" at work. Further study identified its components as four feelings:

- Urgency
- Being focused
- Intensity
- Enthusiasm[25]

Have you ever felt at work or school that time seems to fly by you? If yes, then you understand why academics, consultants, and managers want to understand how they can harness the power of employee engagement.

How Much of the US Workforce Is Actively Engaged? Our workforce appears to be operating above the global average. Consulting firm Aon Hewitt has tracked data on employee engagement around the globe for over 15 years on millions of employees. They released figures on North America (of which the United States is the largest component) as shown:[26]

AT WORK	WORLD	NORTH AMERICA
engaged HIGHLY OR MODERATELY	60%	63%

The US workforce leads several regions but is not riding highest. Latin America outpaces us. The other regions rank as follows:

AT WORK	EUROPE	ASIA PACIFIC	LATIN AMERICA
engaged HIGHLY OR MODERATELY	57%	58%	74%

What Contributes to Employee Engagement? Multiple views of employee engagement identify various factors.

Person Factors (discussed in more detail in Chapter 3)
- Positive or optimistic personalities
- Proactive personality
- Conscientiousness

Environmental Characteristics
- Job characteristics. These represent the motivating potential of the tasks we complete at work. For example, people are engaged when their work contains variety and when they receive timely feedback (discussed in Chapter 5).
- Leadership. People are more engaged when their manager is charismatic and when a positive, trusting relationship exists between managers and employees[27] (leadership is discussed in Chapter 13).
- Stressors. **Stressors are environmental characteristics that cause stress.** Finally, engagement is higher when employees are not confronted with a lot of stressors[28] (stress is discussed in Chapter 16).

What motivates employee engagement at the organizational level? Aon Hewitt, the global engagement consulting firm, identifies from 2012 data the top five engagement drivers for organizations in North America:

Organizational Level Factors
1. Career opportunities
2. Managing performance
3. Organization reputation
4. Communication
5. Recognition

Interestingly, only North America leaves pay out of the top five drivers.[29]

What Outcomes Are Associated with Employee Engagement? Consulting firms such as Gallup, Hewitt Associates, and Blessing White have been in the forefront of collecting proprietary data supporting the practical value of employee engagement. For example, Gallup estimates that when an organization's employees are highly engaged, it can achieve 12 percent higher customer satisfaction/loyalty, 18 percent more productivity, and 12 percent greater profitability.[30] Other recent academic studies similarly showed a positive relationship between employee engagement and employees' performance and physical and psychological well-being, and corporate-level financial performance and customer satisfaction.[31]

Now that you know engagement is correlated with performance at work, can you see the value of increasing your engagement for your school work? We created the following Self-Assessment to measure your level of engagement for your studies so that you can consider how to improve your performance in the classroom.

Mc Graw Hill Education **connect**

SELF-ASSESSMENT 2.2 **To What Extent Am I Engaged in My Studies?**

Do you think you learn more and get higher grades when you are engaged? Do you have any idea how you might increase your engagement with studying? If you answered yes and no, then you will find it valuable to go to connect.mheducation.com and take Assessment 2.2—it assesses your level of engagement with your school work. Then consider the following reflections:

1. Is your level of engagement what you expected?
2. How might you increase your level of engagement?
3. To what extent do your professors influence your level of engagement? How might they foster more engagement from you?

How Can I Increase Engagement?   As a manager you will have many opportunities to improve employee engagement, even if the lavish perks of the richest corporation are out of reach financially. One way is to make sure that the inputs in the Integrative Framework are positively oriented. Organizations do this by measuring, tracking, and responding to surveys of employee engagement.

> **EXAMPLE**   The Ritz-Carlton was able to significantly lower employee turnover (18 percent vs. an industry average of 158 percent) and increase both customer satisfaction and customer spending by following this recommendation.[32]

Other ideas include the creation of career and developmental opportunities for employees, recognizing people for good work, effectively communicating and listening, effective use of performance management practices (discussed in Chapter 6), allowing people to exercise during the work day, creating a physically attractive and stimulating work environment, and giving people meaningful work to do.[33]

solving application

Companies Foster Employee Engagement in Different Ways

problem

Here's a roundup of how several companies are working to improve worker engagement.

- **Red Bull.** Red Bull created a stimulating work environment in its Amsterdam office to engage its employees, according to a dispatch in *Bloomberg Businessweek*. "Employees who chug too much of the merchandise, from seven Red Bull–stocked fridges, can burn off excess energy in 'The Beast,' the half of the office dedicated to play. It includes an Xbox connected to a giant screen made up of four LG Flatron TVs." Employees really get jazzed at

Red Bull employees having fun at work.

5:30 on Fridays when they "stop answering their phones, and take turns DJ-ing as beer and wine are served."[34]

- **CHG Healthcare Services.** The CHG Learning & Development team is one of the company's main ways of fostering its corporate efforts "in putting people first, fostering a Return on Culture philosophy, and providing an opportunity to make a difference in people's lives," according to one industry write-up. CHG strives to create a people-driven culture by spending "significant training time developing new leaders on how to create a team of engaged employees." The CEO and top management team also travel around the United States twice a year to meet with employees and explain the company's strategies and update them on corporate performance.[35]

- **Duke Energy.** James Rogers, president and CEO of Duke Energy, uses "listening sessions" to enhance engagement. He regularly meets with groups of 90 to 100 managers and encourages them to raise any issues on their minds. He also asks these employees to anonymously grade his performance.[36]

YOUR CALL *Let's apply the 3-Stop Approach. While there may not seem to be a problem, because all three companies are doing interesting and potentially beneficial things, can you determine what common problem they are trying to head off or solve proactively?*

Stop 1: What is the implied problem in this example?

Stop 2: Which OB concepts are these managers using to explain the causes of the implied problem?

Stop 3: What other recommendations can you make?

Perceived Organizational Support

Perceived organizational support (POS) reflects the extent to which employees believe their organization values their contributions and genuinely cares about their well-being. Perceptions of support can be either positive or negative. For example, your POS would be negative if you worked for a bad boss and a company that did not provide good health benefits or career opportunities. It would more likely be positive if you worked for The Everett Clinic in Washington. The Clinic pays employees a $10,000 bonus for referring physicians, pays 100 percent of health expenses, and offers profit-sharing up to 5 percent of pay.[37]

How Does POS Impact Employees?   The basic idea is that people are willing to work hard and commit to their organizations when they believe that the company "truly" cares about their best interest. Quite simply, we are motivated by the *norm of reciprocity* when someone treats us well. The norm of reciprocity obliges the return of favorable treatment. This is why we are more likely to reciprocate with hard work and dedication when our employer treats us favorably. There is one caveat, however, for this to work. The favorable treatment must be voluntary as opposed to imposed by external constraints such as the government or unions. This is critical because voluntary actions demonstrate that the giver genuinely values and respects us.

Benefits of POS   The outcomes associated with POS include increased organizational commitment, job satisfaction, organizational citizenship behavior, and task performance. POS also is related to lower turnover.[38] How can managers foster POS?

POS can be increased by treating employees fairly, by avoiding political behavior, by providing job security, by giving people more autonomy, by reducing stressors in the work environment, and by eliminating abusive supervision.[39]

solving application

POS Can Be Positive or Negative

Salesforce.com CEO Marc Benioff.

Salesforce.com is a great example of a company that is supportive of its employees. The company showed its true colors when engineer John Greene got cancer—acute myeloid leukemia—at the age of 40. He had worked for the company for only one year. Initially, John only informed his boss and small team about his illness. This changed when he sent a systemwide message on the company intranet revealing that he needed a bone marrow transplant. CEO Marc Benioff called John within five minutes of the post and then made sure that John received the best care from the hospital. Marc also sent a follow-up message to all employees that said, "Salesforce employee John Greene has AML and needs a bone marrow transplant to survive. Are you a match?" Three hundred fifty people signed up with the match registry by morning. In turn, the company "covered insurance costs that Greene would have had to pay for himself. Its foundation made a $25,000 grant to the marrow registry in Greene's name." Greene is back at work and doing well. "The company was awesome," Greene said.[40]

Naiel Nassar, an Egyptian who became a US citizen in 1990, was the recipient of negative POS. Dr. Nassar was hired by the University of Texas Southwestern Medical Center as an assistant professor of infectious disease. Dr. Beth Levine, chief of the infectious disease program, "directed that Nassar begin billing for the services he provided to the HIV clinic. Nassar objected to the directive, arguing that his salary for clinical services was fully funded by a federal grant and stating that billing the patients therefore would be 'double dipping.' Nassar claimed that Levine then began to 'harass' him, making derogatory statements about his race and his Muslim religion, including one comment that Middle Easterners were 'lazy.' His allegations were supported by a clinical supervisor." Nassar later applied for another job, only to learn that "the medical center retaliated against him by blocking the offer."[41]

YOUR CALL *These examples illustrate very different workplace experiences. We'll focus on just one stop in our 3-Stop decision-making journey:*

Stop 2: What OB concepts or theories explain the causes of these different experiences?

THE CAUSES OF JOB SATISFACTION

MAJOR QUESTION

How can changes in the workplace improve job satisfaction?

THE BIGGER PICTURE

Job satisfaction is the most frequently studied outcome in the Integrative Framework. You will live with this outcome as an employee or manager. To help you understand job satisfaction better, the next section provides you with the five predominant models of job satisfaction. These models can help you to manage others and yourself, leading to an increased sense of satisfaction at work or school for you and others.

Job satisfaction essentially reflects the extent to which an individual likes his or her job. Formally defined, *job satisfaction* **is an affective or emotional response toward various facets of one's job.** This definition implies job satisfaction is not a unitary concept. Rather, a person can be relatively satisfied with one aspect of her or his job and dissatisfied with one or more other aspects.

Researchers at Cornell University developed the Job Descriptive Index (JDI) to assess satisfaction with the following job dimensions: work, pay, promotions, coworkers, and supervision.[42] In contrast, researchers at the University of Minnesota identified 20 different dimensions underlying job satisfaction. Several other surveys also provide assessments of employee job satisfaction. We use one of them in the following Self-Assessment to measure your level of job satisfaction for a current or past job. Are you curious where you stand? Taking this survey will make the rest of this chapter more meaningful and practical.

connect

SELF-ASSESSMENT 2.3 How Satisfied Are You with Your Present Job?

If you currently work, or have worked in the past, your boss should care about your level of job satisfaction because it is related to a host of important outcomes. More importantly, understanding your level of satisfaction will help you think about ways to improve your current job situation. If you would like to know more about your level of satisfaction, go to connect.mheducation.com and take Assessment 2.3, which assesses your level of job satisfaction for your current job. Then consider the following questions:

1. What is the relative satisfaction among the aspects of recognition, compensation, and supervision?

2. Which of these three aspects of satisfaction are most important to you? Explain.

3. What can you do to increase your level of satisfaction?

Source: Adapted from D.J. Weiss, R.V. Dawis, G.W. England and L.H. Lofquist, *Manual for the Minnesota Satisfaction Questionnaire,* Minneapolis: Industrial Relations Center, University of Minnesota, 1967. Used with permission.

Do you think job satisfaction across the country has been going up or down over the last few years? A national survey conducted by Gallup attempted to answer this question. The company conducted phone interviews between 2008 and 2011 with 61,889 people from all 50 states and the District of Columbia. Results revealed that 87.5 percent of Americans were satisfied with their jobs in 2011. While this was down from satisfaction levels in 2008 (89.4 percent), it was higher than the low of 86.9 percent in 2010. These results, which were supported by another national survey in 2012, suggest that American workers are highly motivated. The importance of this conclusion will become more apparent after you read the final section of this chapter. It focuses on the correlates and consequences of job satisfaction.[43]

At a Glance: Five Predominant Models of Job Satisfaction

While OB has developed numerous concepts to improve our understanding of job satisfaction, we can capture many of their insights by considering five predominant models, summarized as follows.

MODEL	HOW MANAGEMENT CAN BOOST JOB SATISFACTION
Need fulfillment	Understand and meet employees' needs.
Met expectations	Meet expectations of employees about what they will receive from the job.
Value attainment	Structure the job and its rewards to match employee values.
Equity	Monitor employees' perceptions of fairness and interact with them so they feel fairly treated.
Dispositional/genetic components	Hire employees with an appropriate disposition. (See qualifications below.)

Brief Review: Five Predominant Models of Job Satisfaction

For these models to make more sense, and provide further insight into the variety of methods for increasing employees' job satisfaction, we should look closer.

Need Fulfillment   Need fulfillment models propose that satisfaction is determined by the extent to which the characteristics of a job allow an individual to fulfill her or his needs. *Needs* **are physiological or psychological deficiencies that arouse behavior.** All of us have different needs, which means that managers need to learn about employees' needs if they want to increase employees' job satisfaction.

> **EXAMPLE**   A 2012 national survey of 600 individuals by the Society for Human Resource Management asked employees to choose the aspects of their job that were very important to their job satisfaction. Their top five choices were opportunities to use skills and abilities, job security, compensation, communication between employees and senior management, and the relationship with the immediate supervisor.[44] Are any of these aspects important to you?

Research generally supports the conclusion that need fulfillment is correlated with job satisfaction.[45]

Met Expectations   These models propose that satisfaction results from met expectations. *Met expectations* **represent the difference between what an individual expects to receive from a job, such as good pay and promotional opportunities, and**

what she or he actually receives. When expectations are greater than what is received, a person will be dissatisfied. In contrast, this model predicts that an individual will be satisfied when she or he attains outcomes above and beyond expectations. Research strongly supports the conclusion that met expectations are significantly related to job satisfaction.[46] Many companies use employee attitude or opinion surveys to assess employees' expectations and concerns, and then they plan how best to meet these expectations.

Value Attainment **The idea underlying *value attainment* is that satisfaction results from the perception that a job allows for fulfillment of an individual's important values.** In general, research consistently supports the prediction that value fulfillment relates positively to job satisfaction. Managers can thus enhance employee satisfaction by structuring the work environment and its associated rewards and recognition to reinforce employees' values.

Equity Equity theory, discussed in Chapter 5, builds on the notion that satisfaction ties to how "fairly" an individual is treated at work. Satisfaction results from one's perception that work outcomes, relative to inputs, compare favorably with a significant other's outcomes/inputs. Research has strongly supported the theory behind this model.[47] Managers thus are encouraged to monitor employees' fairness perceptions and to interact with employees in such a way that they feel equitably treated. Chapter 5 explores how this can be accomplished.

This diverse group of employees from Great Harvest Bread Company displays the company's products.

Dispositional/Genetic Components Ever notice that some coworkers or friends remain satisfied in situations where others always seem dissatisfied? This model posits that job satisfaction remains partly a function of both personal traits and genetic factors. Indeed, the model implies that stable individual differences at least match characteristics of the work environment in their impact on satisfaction.

Although few studies have tested these propositions in depth, a review of existing literature reveals a more nuanced understanding. Dispositional factors were significantly associated with only selected aspects of job satisfaction. Dispositions had stronger relationships with intrinsic aspects of a job (e.g., having autonomy) than with extrinsic aspects of work (e.g., receipt of rewards).[48] Genetic factors also were found to significantly predict life satisfaction, well-being, and general job satisfaction.[49] Overall, researchers estimate that 30 percent of an individual's job satisfaction is associated with dispositional and genetic components.[50]

> **EXAMPLE** Consider Pete and Laura Wakeman, founders of Great Harvest Bread Company. They have used this model of job satisfaction while running their company for more than 25 years. Pete sees it this way:
>
> Our hiring ads say clearly that we need people with "strong personal loves as important as their work." This is not a little thing. You can't have a great life unless you have a buffer of like-minded people all around you. . . . If you want a happy company, you can do it only by hiring naturally happy people . . . you can't really "make" people any way that they aren't already.[51]

Caveat: Although Pete and Laura's hiring approach is consistent with the dispositional and genetic model of job satisfaction, it raises legal and ethical concerns.

Hiring "like-minded" people could lead to discriminatory decisions. Managers must not discriminate on the basis of race, gender, religion, color, national origin, and age.

A Shorter Walk to Work

Now that we have looked at the predominant models of job satisfaction, let's highlight one element that allows people to balance their work and family lives. And that's the opportunity to telecommute. **Telecommuting allows employees to do all or some of their work from home, using advanced telecommunications technology and Internet tools to send work electronically from home to the office, and vice versa.**

- Roughly 24 percent of the US workforce telecommutes for at least part of the job.
- On average, telecommuters work six hours per week from home.
- Studies confirm telecommuting enhances productivity and retention, and decreases absenteeism.[52]

These positive statistics imply that the opportunity to telecommute could improve job satisfaction. Despite telecommuting's appeal, Yahoo! CEO Marissa Mayer decided to ban it for all employees—see the Problem-Solving Application below.

solving application

problem

Yahoo! CEO Marissa Mayer Bans Telecommuting

Yahoo!'s 14,500 employees were told that they could no longer telecommute after June 1, 2013. The company's head of Human Resources, Jackie Reses, said, "We need to be one Yahoo!, and that starts with physically being together." She defended the decision by stating, "Some of the best decisions and insights come from hallway and cafeteria discussion, meeting new people, and impromptu team meetings." Reses believes that telecommuting negatively impacts the company. "Speed and quality are often sacrificed when we work from home," Reses said.

Yahoo! CEO Marissa Mayer is the youngest leader of a Fortune 500 company and was hired from Google when she was five months pregnant. Mayer took two weeks off after having her child, and then installed a nursery next to her office. The company later decided to ban telecommuting, which provoked a wave of negative reactions among employees.[53]

While Reses may have a point about potential downsides to telecommuting, Yahoo! might have been better served by eliminating telecommuting for only those specific jobs that are better done at work than home.

YOUR CALL

Stop 1: What is the problem in this example?

Stop 2: What OB concepts explain Yahoo! employees' response to Mayer's decision?

Stop 3: If you were CEO, what would you recommend?

TAKE-AWAY APPLICATION—TAAP

Complete this activity by reviewing the results of your Self-Assessment of your job satisfaction you completed earlier in this section.

1. Which causes of job satisfaction are impacting your level of satisfaction?
2. Describe two things you might do to improve your job satisfaction.
3. If you could ask your boss or employer to change one thing to improve your job satisfaction, what would you suggest?

MAJOR CORRELATES AND CONSEQUENCES OF JOB SATISFACTION

major question

MAJOR QUESTION

What work-related outcomes are associated with job satisfaction?

THE BIGGER PICTURE

The documented relationship between job satisfaction and other positive organizational outcomes is good news. It means that employers have economic reasons for fostering job satisfaction to improve results. You're about to learn four key attitudinal and four key behavioral outcomes associated with this relationship.

Thousands of studies have examined the relationship between job satisfaction and other organizational variables. We consider a subset of the most important variables from the standpoint of managerial relevance. Eight key outcomes correlate to job satisfaction, four attitudinal and four behavioral. Job satisfaction has positive correlations to:

Attitudes

- Motivation
- Job involvement
- Withdrawal cognitions
- Perceived stress

Behavior

- Job performance
- Organizational citizenship behavior (OCB)
- Counterproductive work behavior (CWB)
- Turnover

Attitudinal Outcomes of Job Satisfaction

We examine four attitudinal outcomes of job satisfaction that are important to OB researchers and managers: motivation, job involvement, withdrawal cognitions, and perceived stress.

Motivation   Employee motivation, which is discussed in Chapter 5, represents a psychological process that arouses our interest in doing something, and it directs and guides our behavior. As you might expect, employee motivation positively correlates to job satisfaction. Managers can potentially enhance employees' motivation by using a host of techniques and recommendations that are discussed throughout this book.

Job Involvement   ***Job involvement* represents the extent to which an individual is personally involved with his or her work role.** Many years of research have demonstrated that job involvement is moderately related to job satisfaction.[54] Managers can foster satisfying work environments to fuel employees' job involvement.

Have you ever felt like this when studying for exams. Unfortunately, too much stress impairs our ability to perform at school or work.

Withdrawal Cognitions Although some people quit their jobs impulsively or in a fit of anger, most go through a process of thinking about whether or not they should quit. **Withdrawal cognitions encapsulate this thought process by representing an individual's overall thoughts and feelings about quitting.** What causes an individual to think about quitting his or her job? Job satisfaction is believed to be one of the most significant contributors.

EXAMPLE A study of managers, salespersons, and auto mechanics from a national automotive retail store chain demonstrated that job dissatisfaction caused employees to begin the process of thinking about quitting.[55] Results from this study imply that managers can indirectly help to reduce employee turnover by enhancing employee job satisfaction.

Perceived Stress Stress has negative effects on many different OB-related outcomes. For instance, stress is positively related to absenteeism, turnover, coronary heart disease, and viral infections. As expected, perceived stress has a strong, negative relationship to job satisfaction. Perceived stress also was found to be negatively associated with employee engagement. Managers should attempt to reduce the negative effects of stress by improving job satisfaction and by encouraging employees to detach from work during off-job time (i.e., stop thinking about work and "don't take it home with you").[56]

solving application

problem

What to Do about Bullying

Let's return to the issue of bullying with which we started this chapter and consider how you might have resolved the situation faced by Stuart McGregor. Stuart's goal was to be a chef, and he received a highly prestigious apprenticeship as a chef just before turning 17. Shortly after starting his apprenticeship, he experienced verbal abuse and colleagues began making innuendos about his sexuality. He was once given a large bag of peas by the kitchen managers and asked to count them.

Stuart was told by his colleagues that he was going to receive an award. Excitedly, he called his family and could not wait to receive the award later in the day. Unbeknownst to him, his peers broke into his car and stole the knob of his gearstick. They then wrapped it up and gave it to him as his "award" in front of the entire staff. Stuart was humiliated!

Stuart was regularly asked to perform tasks he did not know how to do, and then was ridiculed when he did them incorrectly. Shortly before the conclusion of the

apprenticeship period, Stuart was invited to go on a camping trip with his workmates. Sadly, the kitchen managers threatened Stuart with bodily harm if he went on the trip. Stuart was afraid for his safety and made excuses to avoid the trip.

Another employee ultimately complained about being bullied, and investigators questioned Stuart about his experience. Stuart denied being bullied, probably out of fear for his safety, fear of losing his job, or because he thought he could handle the situation.[57]

YOUR CALL *Let's apply the 3-Stop Approach.*

Stop 1: What is the problem in this case?

Stop 2: What OB concepts or theories help explain Stuart's situation and reaction?

Stop 3: What would you do if you were Stuart? What would you do as a manager of the restaurant?

Behavioral Outcomes of Job Satisfaction

Job satisfaction has a positive association with two constructive behavioral outcomes—job performance and organizational citizenship behavior (OCB). It also has a negative relationship with two potentially negative behaviors—counterproductive work behavior (CWB) and turnover. The following discussion is more practical when you consider that these individual-level outcomes in our Integrative Framework are driven by processes at the group and organizational level, which, further upstream, are influenced by environmental characteristics.

Job Performance   One of the biggest controversies within OB research centers on the relationship between job satisfaction and job performance. You might be surprised to learn that this is more complicated than it might first appear and that OB experts have identified at least eight different ways in which these variables are related. The good news (for you learning about this) is that the dominant theories are either that satisfaction causes performance or performance causes satisfaction.[58] But which causes which?

Which comes first, the performance or the satisfaction? A team of researchers recently attempted to resolve this controversy by analyzing data from 312 samples involving over 54,000 individuals.[59] They made two key findings:

- **Job satisfaction and performance were *moderately* related.** This is an important finding because it supports the belief that employee job satisfaction is a key workplace attitude that managers should consider when attempting to increase employees' job performance.

- **The relationship is complex.** In fact, the relationship between job satisfaction and performance is much more complex than originally thought. It is not that one directly influences the other or vice versa. Rather, researchers now believe **both variables indirectly influence each other** through a host of person factors and environmental characteristics contained in the Integrative Framework.

There is one additional consideration to keep in mind regarding the relationship between job satisfaction and job performance: measurement of performance. Researchers now believe that incomplete measures of individual-level performance understate the relationship between satisfaction and performance.

> **EXAMPLE**   If performance ratings used in past research did not reflect the actual interactions and interdependencies at work at the individual level, inaccurate measures of performance served to lower the reported correlations between satisfaction and performance.

To solve this problem, researchers examined the relationship between *aggregate* measures of job satisfaction and organizational performance. In support of these ideas, a team studied more than 5,000 business units. The result? The researchers uncovered significant positive relationships as shown:[60]

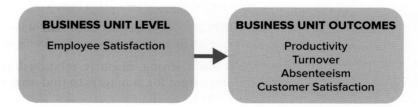

It thus appears managers indirectly or directly can positively affect a variety of important organizational-level outcomes such as job performance and customer satisfaction by increasing employee job satisfaction.

Organizational Citizenship Behavior   ***Organizational citizenship behavior (OCB)*** **is defined as "individual behavior that is discretionary, not directly or explicitly**

recognized by the formal reward system, and that in the aggregate promotes the effective functioning of the organization."[61] This definition highlights two key points:

- OCBs are voluntary.
- OCBs help work groups and the organization to effectively achieve goals.

Examples include such gestures as:

- Constructive statements about the department.
- Expression of personal interest in the work of others.
- Suggestions for improvement or training new people.
- Respect for the spirit as well as the letter of housekeeping rules.
- Care for organizational property, and punctuality and attendance well beyond standard or enforceable levels.[62]

Managers certainly would like employees to exhibit these behaviors, and research clearly supports the value of this outcome. OCBs have a moderately positive correlation with job satisfaction.[63] Moreover, OCBs are significantly related to both individual-level consequences (e.g., performance appraisal ratings, intentions to quit, absenteeism, and turnover) and organizational-level outcomes (e.g., productivity, efficiency, lower costs, customer satisfaction, and unit-level satisfaction and turnover).[64] These results are important for two reasons. First, exhibiting OCBs is likely to create positive impressions about you among your colleagues and manager. In turn, these impressions affect your ability to work with others, your manager's evaluation of your performance, and ultimately your promotability. Second, the aggregate amount of employees' OCBs affects important organizational outcomes. It thus is important for managers to foster an environment that promotes OCBs.

Counterproductive Work Behavior   You already know from personal experience and OB research that the absence of satisfaction may be associated with some types of undesirable behavior, such as low employee engagement and performance. In contrast to the helping nature of OCBs, **counterproductive work behavior (CWB) represents behavior that harms other employees, the organization as a whole, or organizational stakeholders such as customers and shareholders.** CWBs represent a particularly negative work-related outcome. Examples of CWBs include bullying, theft, gossiping, backstabbing, drug and alcohol abuse, destroying organizational property, violence, purposely doing bad or incorrect work, surfing the Internet for personal use, excessive socializing, tardiness, sabotage, and sexual harassment.[65]

> **EXAMPLE**   A Maryland man swiped 32 laptops from his nonprofit health-care employer and put them on eBay.

> **EXAMPLE**   A chief financial officer changed the color of the type on some spreadsheet data from black to white so as to render the fake numbers invisible while juicing the totals—and his bonus.

> **EXAMPLE**   One regional vice president for sales billed his corporate card $4,000 for Victoria's Secret lingerie—and not for his wife, either.[66]

CWB has a strong, negative relationship with job satisfaction. This means that it is important for managers to find ways to reduce CWB. This can be done in three key ways.

1. Organizations can limit CWBs by hiring individuals who are less prone to engage in this type of behavior. Cognitive ability is associated with many measures of success, so it is a logical quality to screen for in hiring decisions. Personality tests also may be relevant.

2. Organizations should ensure they are motivating desired behaviors and not CWBs, for example, by designing jobs that promote satisfaction and by preventing abusive supervision. A study of 265 restaurants, for example, found that CWBs were

greater in restaurants where employees reported abuse by supervisors and where managers had more employees to supervise.[67] CWBs in these restaurants were associated with lower profits and lower levels of customer satisfaction, so adequate staffing and management development could not only make employees' lives more pleasant but also improve the bottom line.

3. If an employee does engage in CWBs, the organization should respond quickly and appropriately, defining the specific behaviors that are unacceptable and the requirements for acceptable behavior.

Turnover   Consider the pros and cons of turnover. Yes, turnover can be a good thing when a low-performing person like George Costanza from the *Seinfeld* show quits or is fired. This situation enables managers to replace the Georges of the world with better or more diverse individuals or to realign the budget. In contrast, losing a good employee is bad because the organization loses valuable human and social capital (see Chapter 1), and it can be costly. Experts estimate that the cost of turnover for an hourly employee is roughly 20 percent of annual salary, whereas the cost is higher for professional employees needing specialized skills.[68]

Job satisfaction has a moderately strong, negative relationship with turnover. This finding suggests that managers are well served to reduce turnover by trying to enhance employees' job satisfaction. This recommendation is even more important for high performers.[69] For example, a survey of 20,000 high-potential employees indicated that 27 percent planned to find another job within a year.[70]

All of these considerations suggest several practical steps employers can take to tackle a turnover problem. Managers can reduce voluntary turnover if they:

1. Hire people who "fit" within the organization's culture. Person-culture fit is discussed in Chapter 14.
2. Spend time fostering employee engagement. Engaged employees are less likely to quit.
3. Provide effective onboarding.[71] **Onboarding programs help employees to integrate, assimilate, and transition to new jobs by making them familiar with corporate policies, procedures, culture, and politics by clarifying work-role expectations and responsibilities.**[72]
4. Recognize and reward high performers because they are more likely to quit than average performers.[73]

If more approaches are desired, revisit the five causes of job satisfaction we previously discussed (need fulfillment, met expectations, value attainment, equity, and dispositional/genetic components).

One Last Piece of Advice   On the topic of turnovers, consider the issue of flexible work schedules. Counter to Yahoo!'s decision to eliminate telecommuting in 2013, a recent survey of 637 employees demonstrated that 66 percent desired *greater* flexibility. This means that managers should consider the value of offering flexible work schedules to enhance job satisfaction and reduce turnover.

> **EXAMPLE**   This is exactly what State Street Corp., a multinational financial services firm with over 29,000 employees, has done. The company offers five different work schedules that allow employees increased flexibility in deciding when and where they work.[74]

TAKE-AWAY APPLICATION—TAAP

1. What are the three most important things you want from a job and its associated working conditions?
2. How can you determine if a future job opportunity offers these things?
3. Assume that you are in a job that is not meeting your needs and that you cannot quit. How would you improve your workplace attitudes in this situation?

what did i learn?

You learned that values and attitudes directly affect a variety of organizational outcomes. You saw how companies pay attention to employees' values and personal attitudes to align positively with improved performance results. You also saw how companies track the work attitude of job satisfaction because it positively correlates with other positive workplace attitudes (like motivation, job involvement, and reduced stress) and behavior (like job performance, OCB, and reduced CWB and turnover). Reinforce your learning with the chapter's Key Points listed below. Next, consolidate your learning using the Integrative Framework, shown in Figure 2.3. Then, challenge your mastery of the material by answering the chapter's Major Questions in your own words.

Key Points for Understanding Chapter 2

You learned the following key points.

2.1 PERSONAL VALUES

- Values are abstract ideals that guide your thinking and behavior across all situations.
- Schwartz proposed that 10 core values guide behavior across contexts and time (see Figure 2.1).
- The 10 core values relate to one of four themes: self-transcendence, conservation, self-enhancement, and openness to change (see Figure 2.1).
- Managers can use the Schwartz model to motivate employees and to reduce the chances of employees' experiencing conflict between their values and their work assignments.

2.2 PERSONAL ATTITUDES AND THEIR IMPACT ON BEHAVIOR AND OUTCOMES

- Attitudes represent your feelings or opinions about people, places, and objects, and range from positive to negative. Workplace attitudes are outcomes in the Integrative Framework of OB.
- Three components of attitudes are affective, cognitive, and behavioral.
- Cognitive dissonance represents the psychological discomfort an individual experiences when his or her attitudes or beliefs are incompatible with his or her behavior.
- Intentions are the key link between attitudes and behavior in Ajzen's model. Three determinants of the strength of an intention are one's attitude toward the behavior, subjective norms, and perceived behavioral control (see Figure 2.2).

2.3 KEY WORKPLACE ATTITUDES

- Organizational commitment reflects how strongly a person identifies with an organization and is committed to its goals. It is influenced by a host of factors in the Integrative Framework, including personality, leader behavior, organizational culture, meaningfulness, organizational climate, and psychological contracts.
- Employee engagement occurs when employees give it their all at work. It contains feelings of urgency, being focused, intensity, and enthusiasm.
- Employee engagement is influenced by a host of personal factors and environmental characteristics contained in the Integrative Framework.
- Perceived organizational support reflects the extent to which employees believe their organization values their contributions and genuinely cares about their well-being. Employees are happier and work harder when they feel supported.

2.4 THE CAUSES OF JOB SATISFACTION

- Job satisfaction is an affective or emotional response toward various facets of one's job. It is a key OB outcome.
- The five major causes of job satisfaction are need fulfillment, met expectations, value attainment, equity, and dispositional/genetic components.
- Telecommuting allows people to balance their work and family lives. It consists of using advanced telecommunication technology and Internet tools to send and receive work from home to work, and vice versa.

2.5 MAJOR CORRELATES AND CONSEQUENCES OF JOB SATISFACTION

- Job satisfaction has been correlated with many different attitudes and behaviors. It is significantly associated with the following attitudinal variables: motivation, job involvement, withdrawal cognitions, and perceived stress.
- Job satisfaction is significantly related to four key behavioral outcomes: job performance, organizational citizenship behavior, counterproductive work behavior, and turnover.

FIGURE 2.3 INTEGRATIVE FRAMEWORK FOR UNDERSTANDING AND APPLYING OB

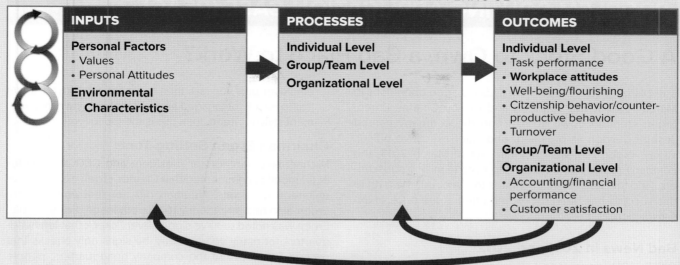

© 2014 Angelo Kinicki and Mel Fugate. All rights reserved. Reproduction prohibited without permission of the authors.

The Integrative Framework for Chapter 2

As shown in Figure 2.3, you learned how values and personal attitudes serve as inputs that lead to workplace attitudes as an outcome. In the figure, we boldface the term *workplace attitudes* so it will stand out among the other outcomes mentioned in passing in the chapter, at both the individual and organizational levels. In future chapters we will look at other of these outcomes in more detail, as well as other related processes that generate them.

Challenge: Major Questions for Chapter 2

At the start of the chapter, we told you that after reading the chapter you should be able to answer the following major questions. Unless you can, have you really processed and internalized the lessons in the chapter? Refer to the Key Points, Figure 2.3, the chapter itself, and your notes to revisit and answer the following major questions:

1. What role do values play in influencing my behavior?

2. How do personal attitudes affect workplace behavior and work-related outcomes?

3. Why is it important for management to pay attention to workplace attitudes?

4. How can changes in the workplace improve job satisfaction?

5. What work-related outcomes are associated with job satisfaction?

A Good Stock to Own, a Bad Place to Work?

The Dish Network Corporation (DISH) started operations in March 1996. It was founded and run by Charles Ergen. Ergen stepped down in 2011 and the company named Joseph Clayton as president and chief executive officer. Today, Ergen remains chairman. As of March 2013, the company provided satellite TV to over 14 million subscribers. And the stock price continues to climb. But the path to this success has been rocky, and often at the price of job satisfaction.

Bad News in 2011 and 2012

DISH's 2011 annual report revealed that the company "lost approximately 166,000 net subscribers" in 2011, compared "to a gain of approximately 33,000 net new subscribers during the same period in 2010." A 2012 *MSN Money* survey of 1,500 randomly chosen people also was used to assess the customer service provided by 150 companies in 15 industries. Ratings were obtained on a scale ranging from excellent, good, and fair, to poor. *MSN Money* then selected the 10 companies with the greatest percentage of "poor" ratings and designated them to the Hall of Shame. DISH was on that list.

The bad news did not stop here. In 2012 DISH was designated as the worst employer to work for by website *24/7 Wall St.* People at *24/7 Wall St.* tried to identify the worst place to work by reviewing comments posted at *Glassdoor.com,* an online service that allows employees to gossip about their employers and jobs. While not a scientific study, *24/7 Wall St.* identified a sample of 202 companies that had a minimum of 300 reviews. DISH had 346 former or current employees post comments about the company, and many were quite negative.

Complaints included long hours, limited paid holidays, and excessive mandatory overtime. One post stated, "You're part of a poisonous environment . . . go find a job where you can use your talents for good rather than evil." Other comments included, "You work all day all night. Your day starts from 6:45 am till 6 pm, or 10pm. You work every holiday that your day falls on." Here is another comment from a former employee who worked at the company for over 10 years, mainly as a Field Service Manager.

If you like being told "there's the door" every time you disagree with or question a policy's effectiveness or purpose and then offer viable solutions/ideas, then this is the job for you. If you want to be told to "just drink the Kool-Aid" and "just get on board" no matter the cost, then this is the job for you. If you like to work 60+ hours per week with no overtime pay (salaried employees), then this is the job for you. If you like to put your job first when your employer puts you last, then this is the job for you. If you like to be micromanaged and told that your own management style is wrong, then this is the job for you.

Chairman Ergen Setting Tone

Michael Neuman, former president and CEO at DISH for eight months, commented that Charles Ergen made a lot of unilateral decisions. Neuman did not feel empowered. Ergen also had a tendency to micromanage. For example, Ergen was noted to have signed every check that left headquarters for many years. Today, he signs only checks that exceed $100,000. At the company headquarters, people are supposed to start working at 9 a.m., and the company had employees use their badges to scan in when they arrived for work. Ergen was unhappy with this system because "some employees were taking advantage of the system by having others badge-in for them." He installed fingerprint scanners to stop this from happening. E-mails were sent to human resources when someone arrived late. A message might also be sent to the employee's boss and Ergen himself.

A few years ago Ergen became frustrated with employees who arrived late to work because of snow. He told employees at a quarterly meeting that they should stay at nearby hotels, at their expense, if the weather suggested a few inches of snow.

Current and former employees describe the culture in terms of values representing "condescension and distrust." DISH does not allow people to work from home, and employees do not get corporate credit cards. If you like flexibility at work, DISH is not the place for you. For many years, employees had to reimburse the company if they provided a tip greater than 15 percent for an expensed meal.

Ergen's style also pertains to how he treats Wall Street analysts and large investors. For example, Chris Marangi, a portfolio manager for a firm that holds 4 million shares, says, "DISH goes out of its way to be uncooperative." Despite visiting corporate headquarters many times, he has not met Ergen or other DISH executives. "They're probably the least transparent company of any I've ever dealt with," said Marangi.

Corporate Culture

Liz Ryan, founder of human workplace, wrote an article about the culture of DISH for *Huffington Post.* She commented on an interaction she had with a recruiter from DISH a few years ago while attending a networking event for human resource professionals. Liz approached the recruiter from DISH and asked, "Are you busy?" The recruiter said, "We're swamped. We have so many openings, we're going crazy." Liz then inquired about the types of employees DISH was looking to hire. The recruiter replied, "Hispanics." She wanted to hire Hispanics because "they don't complain about the pay." When Liz told her that you can't favor one ethnic or racial group more than another, the recruiter replied, "We'll hire anyone who's qualified, but we prefer to hire Hispanic people."

The company is also very litigious. The company has sued, or been sued by, so many companies that it has employed more than 100 law firms in 10 years. DISH once sued one of its own lawyers. The lawsuit resulted in a $40 million judgment against DISH.

DISH Network CEO Joe Clayton responded to the label of DISH being the worst company to work for as "ridiculous." What do you think? As noted earlier, the stock continues to climb and was up 30 percent just in 2012. The company has beaten earnings estimates five of the last eight quarters as of this writing.[75]

Apply the 3-Stop Problem-Solving Approach to OB

Stop 1: What is the problem?

- Use the Integrative Framework shown in Figure 2.3 to help identify the outcomes that are important in this case.

- Which of these outcomes are not being achieved in the case?

- Based on considering the above two questions, what is the most important problem in this case?

Stop 2: Use the Integrative Framework in Figure 2.3 to help identify the OB concepts or theories that help you to understand the problem in this case.

- What person factors are most relevant?

- What environmental characteristics are most important to consider?

- What concepts or theories discussed in Chapter 1 and in this chapter are most relevant for solving the key problem in this case?

Stop 3: What are your recommendations for solving the problem?

- Review the material in the chapter that most pertains to your proposed solution and look for practical recommendations.

- Use any past OB knowledge or experience to generate recommendations.

- Outline your plan for solving the problem in this case.

LEGAL/ETHICAL CHALLENGE

Social Media in the Hiring Process

This challenge focuses on your attitudes toward the use of social media in the hiring process.

Justin Bassett, a statistician in New York City, was interviewing for a job when the interviewer used the computer to search his Facebook page. The interviewer could not access Justin's private profile, so she asked for his login information. This practice is increasingly happening to job applicants.

How common is the practice of employers looking at information on Facebook profiles, Twitter accounts, and other available sites to learn about applicants? Probably enough to worry about. Annual surveys have shown results ranging from 10 percent to almost 70 percent in recent years. A July 2013 survey by CareerBuilder showed a slight increase:

> [N]early 39 percent of employers use social networking sites to research job candidates, up from 37 percent last year. Of those, 43 percent said they have found information that factored into their decision not to hire a candidate.[76]

Because many people set their profiles to private, employers have begun asking for passwords. Rather than asking for passwords, other companies ask applicants to friend someone at the company or to log into the site during the interview. The end result is the same; employers want to view applicants' private profiles.[77]

Addressing the Challenge

1. What would you do if an interviewer requested that you provide private login information? Be sure to explain or justify your answer.
   a. Don't provide the information. Private is private, and the employer has no right to view this information.
   b. If you want the job, provide the information.
   c. Withdraw your application. Who wants to work for a company that wants to see such private information?
   d. Invent other options.
2. What information about a person's values or attitudes might be gleaned from a Facebook page?
3. If you were running a company, would you want to review potential employees' social media pages? Why or why not?

The Paper Airplane Contest

Objectives

1. To examine the role of attitudes in completing a group-based task.
2. To determine the impact of job satisfaction, job involvement, and engagement on task performance.

Introduction

In this chapter, we discussed the impact of an individual's values and attitudes on a variety of outcomes such as performance and turnover. We did not consider, however, that these same concepts apply in the context of working on a team project. The purpose of this exercise is to examine the role of abilities and attitudes when working on a team project to build a paper airplane. The quality of the team's work will be assessed by measuring three aspects of your team's airplane: (1) how far it flies, (2) how far it flies with a payload, and (3) design characteristics.[78]

Instructions

Your instructor will divide the class into groups of three to six people. Each team should pick a team name. Once formed, begin to plan what type of plane you want to design and actually construct. Keep in mind that the quality of your work will be measured through the three criteria noted above. You will be provided with one 8.5-by-11-inch sheet of blank paper and adhesive tape. Try not to make mistakes, as you will not be given more than one piece of paper. Use these materials to construct one airplane.

Decorate your plane as you see fit. It is recommended that you decorate your plane before actually building it. Once all groups complete their work, a contest will be held to determine the best overall plane. There will be three rounds to complete this assessment. In the first round, each team will be asked to launch their plane and distance flown will be measured. The second round entails adding a payload—a paperclip—to your plane and then flying it once again. Distance flown will be measured. The final round entails a subjective evaluation by the entire class of the plane's design. Each team's overall performance will be assessed and posted.

Questions for Discussion

1. How did the group decide to design the plane?
2. Did the team consider each member's abilities when designing and flying the plane? Explain.
3. Were all team members equally involved in the task and equally satisfied with the team's final product? Discuss why or why not.
4. What did you notice or infer about the attitudes of each group member based on how he or she approached the group exercise?
5. How could the team have increased its members' job involvement, engagement, and task performance? Provide specific recommendations.
6. What values in the Schwartz model (discussed early in the chapter; see Figure 2.1) do you see as predicting successful participation in this group exercise?

3 INDIVIDUAL DIFFERENCES AND EMOTIONS

How Does Who I Am Affect My Performance?

inputs

PERSON FACTORS
Personality
Skills and abilities

ENVIRONMENTAL CHARACTERISTICS

processes

INDIVIDUAL LEVEL
Emotions

GROUP/TEAM LEVEL

ORGANIZATIONAL LEVEL

outcomes

INDIVIDUAL LEVEL

GROUP/TEAM LEVEL

ORGANIZATIONAL LEVEL

© 2014 Angelo Kinicki and Mel Fugate. All rights reserved. Reproduction prohibited without permission of the authors.

MAJOR TOPICS I'LL LEARN AND QUESTIONS I SHOULD BE ABLE TO ANSWER

3.1 THE DIFFERENCES MATTER
MAJOR QUESTION: *How does understanding the relative stability of individual differences benefit me?*

3.2 INTELLIGENCES: THERE IS MORE TO THE STORY THAN IQ
MAJOR QUESTION: *How do multiple intelligences affect my performance?*

3.3 PERSONALITY, OB, AND MY EFFECTIVENESS
MAJOR QUESTION: *How does my personality affect my performance?*

3.4 CORE SELF-EVALUATIONS: HOW MY SELF-EFFICACY, SELF-ESTEEM, LOCUS OF CONTROL, AND EMOTIONAL STABILITY AFFECT MY PERFORMANCE
MAJOR QUESTION: *How do self-evaluations affect my performance at work?*

3.5 THE VALUE OF BEING EMOTIONALLY INTELLIGENT
MAJOR QUESTION: *What is emotional intelligence and how does it help me?*

3.6 UNDERSTAND EMOTIONS TO INFLUENCE PERFORMANCE
MAJOR QUESTION: *How can understanding emotions make me more effective at work?*

3.7 PRACTICE, LUCK, AND SUCCESS
MAJOR QUESTION: *How can I be "deliberate" about success?*

INTEGRATIVE FRAMEWORK FOR UNDERSTANDING AND APPLYING OB

When you discuss individual differences among your friends, you might start by talking about your presonalities, or skills and abilities. We'll do the same. In the chapter that follows we will discuss these and other differences. We will also discuss emotions, which we consider a key individual level process in response to personal and environmental inputs. By the end of the chapter you will have a much greater understanding of how individual differences and emotions affect a host of outcomes at the individual and group levels of OB. You also will learn some practical tips on how to use this knowledge to improve your success at school, at work, and in your larger life.

winning at work

TO START FAST AND START RIGHT, BE PROACTIVE IN YOUR FIRST 30 DAYS

Shannon Deegan, director of People Operations at Google, said: "We tell employees, 'You own your career.' . . . If an employee loves part of a job yet wanted to do it on a different team, 'it's cool,' he says."[1] This is a loud endorsement for proactivity at work. And while you may never work for Google, you can still benefit from his advice. Being proactive is a benefit in many arenas of life and can be especially beneficial when starting a new job.

Don't count on your employer to do all the work in the early stages, or onboarding process, of a new job. We've listed seven recommendations to help you start fast and start right.

1. **Come Up with Your Elevator Pitch.** You only get one chance to make a first impression. So, before you start introducing yourself to everyone, figure out what you're going to say when you meet them.

2. **Understand Your Role and How You'll Be Evaluated.** The responsibilities of the job you were hired for could change by the time you start work. Reach out to your manager about what may have changed and make sure you have a clear understanding of your current role, responsibilities, and authority before you take on any projects.

3. **Learn the Business.** Before you can begin to contribute to an organization, you need to figure out how the company works. How does your company do business? What are its objectives?

4. **Interview Your Boss.** The key to being a successful new employee is helping your boss be successful. Find out what keeps your boss up at night and come up with creative ways to alleviate those worries.

5. **Be Ambitious, but Have Restraint.** You might be eager to start contributing right away and fixing everything you see wrong with the organization. That intention is good, but tread lightly. As a new hire you won't have the historical context about why a policy or process may or may not need fixing.

6. **Be Proactive about Your Onboarding.** One day of orientation and a meet and greet with your team may be the extent of your company's onboarding program. If so, be proactive with your managers about their

training plan and what you need to accomplish in your first three months on the job.[2]

7. **Problem Solve.** When problems arise, or seem likely, proactive people take action—they don't wait to be asked.

Such characteristics are even more important given that 38 percent of companies reported doing three days or less of onboarding or orienting new employees, 54 percent did little or no follow-up, and 67 percent collected little to no feedback from new employees.[3] The lesson: you are often on your own!

But proactivity continues to yield benefits. A study showed that the three most common traits of successful CEOs are persistence, efficiency, and proactivity.[4] Proactive people also tend to have more career success (as measured by promotions and raises), innovation, creativity, and entrepreneurship.[5]

SOURCE: From Jennifer King, "6 Things New Hires Should Do in the First 30 Days," SoftwareAdvice.com, http://blog.softwareadvice.com/articles/hr/new-hire-check-list-1071312/. Reprinted with permission.

FOR YOU — WHAT'S AHEAD IN THIS CHAPTER

You'll explore individual differences (IDs), which are the many attributes that distinguish all of us from one another. Understanding IDs is critical to the effective application of OB knowledge and tools. This is why we introduce IDs early in the book as an input in the Integrative Framework of OB. A more thorough understanding of IDs will help you manage these differences for your job and career success. For managers, recognition of such differences is fundamental to attracting, motivating, retaining, and improving the performance of others.

Your exploration of IDs begins with an explanation of the relative stability of these differences. Next, you'll delve into a subset of individual differences found to be particularly important in the work context and supported by research: (1) intelligence, (2) cognitive abilities, (3) personality, (4) core self-evaluations, (5) attitudes (covered in Chapter 2), and (6) emotions (including emotional intelligence). Knowledge of IDs enables you to more effectively solve problems and manage individual, group, and organizational outcomes at school, work, and home.

MAJOR QUESTION

How does understanding the relative stability of individual differences benefit me?

THE BIGGER PICTURE

You undoubtedly notice changes in your friends' behaviors when they are in different situations (in class vs. a tailgating party) or circumstances (cramming for an exam or coping with a new job). However, what you probably don't pay much attention to are the characteristics and behaviors that don't change. To help you understand and use this knowledge, you'll see that we arrange many individual attributes on a continuum of their relative stability.

At one extreme are relatively fixed traits (like intelligence), and at the other extreme are more flexible states (like emotions), with various trait-like and state-like characteristics in between. A sharper understanding of individual differences in this spot will help you manage these differences for your job and career success. For managers, recognition of such differences is fundamental to attracting, motivating, retaining, and improving the performance of others.

Individual differences (IDs) is a broad category used to collectively describe the vast number of attributes (for example, traits and behaviors) that describe you as a person. So what is it that makes us different? Is it our genetics or our environment? The answer is both. And while how you are raised, along with your experiences and opportunities, indeed helps shape who you are, a large volume of research on twins suggests that genetics matter more. But what is more important at work is recognizing the many attributes that make us who were are, regardless of whether these characteristics are due to genetics or how we are raised. Like the importance of dealing with diversity discussed in Chapter 2, effective employees and managers must understand and utilize the many individual differences possessed by those with whom we work. IDs therefore are fundamental to OB and your personal success at work, school, and the other arenas of your life. To help you understand and apply knowledge about IDs, we organize and discuss them according to Figure 3.1.

On the left-hand side of Figure 3.1 you'll notice that we arrange individual differences on a continuum from top to bottom. At the top are intelligence and mental abilities, which are relatively fixed. This means they are stable over time and across situations and difficult to change. At the bottom are attitudes (which we discussed in Chapter 2) and emotions, which are relatively flexible. Emotions change over time, from situation to situation, and can be altered more easily. The right-hand side of the figure previews some of the workplace outcomes we will encounter in the chapter.

The distinction between relatively fixed and flexible individual differences has great practical value for managers. Wise managers know they have little or no impact on fixed IDs. You can't change an employee's level of intelligence or remake an employee's personality.[6] But you can help employees manage their attitudes and emotions. For instance, many effective managers (and their employers) select employees based on positive, job-relevant, but relatively stable IDs. This enables managers to

major question

FIGURE 3.1 RELATIVE STABILITY OF INDIVIDUAL DIFFERENCES

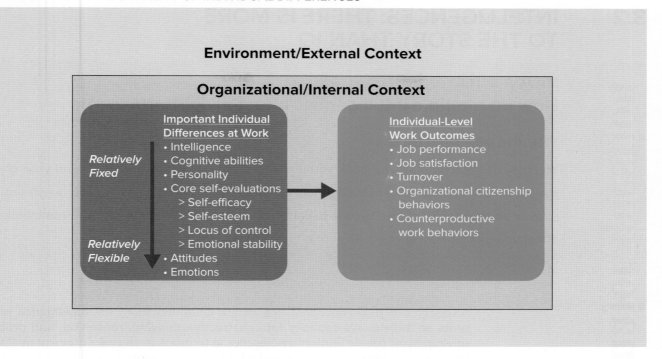

capitalize on the personal strengths that someone brings to a job because these stable strengths affect behavior and performance in most every work situation.[7] Intelligence and analytical abilities, for example, are beneficial in front of customers, in teams with coworkers, and working alone on a project.

In contrast, managers have more influence on relatively flexible IDs that influence individual-level work outcomes. This implies that managers are more likely to influence individual-level work outcomes, like performance and job satisfaction, by implementing different policies and practices that positively impact employees' core self-evaluations, attitudes, and emotions. For example, as a manager you'd likely be better off assigning employees who are open to experience (a dimensions of the Big Five personality framework you'll learn about later in this chapter) to jobs involving new products and new markets than employees with low levels of this attribute. Similarly, you could help build new employees' self-efficacy (another ID you'll learn about) for selling to tough customers if you role model how to do this effectively, give them experience presenting to "easy customers" first, and give them verbal encouragement before and constructive feedback after.

You will explore a number of related OB theories, concepts, and tools in Chapters 6 (performance management), 10 (conflict and negotiation), and 12 (power and influence) that you can use for this purpose.

INTELLIGENCES: THERE IS MORE TO THE STORY THAN IQ

MAJOR QUESTION

How do multiple intelligences affect my performance?

THE BIGGER PICTURE

You may be smarter than you think you are. You may already know your IQ, and your grades may also reflect intellectual intelligence. But you can be intelligent in other ways too. We explain various forms of intelligence because all are inputs to the Integrative Framework and affect your performance.

Although experts do not agree on a specific definition, many say **intelligence represents an individual's capacity for constructive thinking, reasoning, and problem solving.** Most people think of intelligence in terms of intelligence quotient or IQ, the famous score from tests taken as a child. Thus many people typically view intelligence and IQ as one, big attribute of brainpower. However, intelligence, intelligence testing (IQ), and related research are more complex. The concept of intelligence has expanded over the years and more often is thought of and discussed in terms of general mental abilities. Of course, people are different in terms of such abilities, but this isn't what is important at work. What is important is to understand intelligence or mental abilities so you can manage people more effectively. Put another way, the reason we highlight intelligence and mental abilities is because they are related to performance.[8] This section provides a brief overview of intelligence and mental abilities and then highlights practical implications.

Intelligence Matters . . . And We Have More Than We Think

Do you agree with the definition of intelligence above? Historically, intelligence was believed to be purely genetic—something passed from one generation to another—you're either born "smart" or you're not. Do you agree with this belief? What are the implications of believing that intelligence is a gift of birth? Regardless of your personal views, research has shown that intelligence, like personality, can be altered or modified in a number of ways.[9] Think about it. No matter who you are or your starting point (e.g., education or experience), if you engage in more constructive thinking, reasoning, and problem solving, you will get better at these. You'll be more intelligent. If you buy this argument, then after reading this book and studying OB you'll be more intelligent due to practicing critical thinking and problem solving. (As the authors, we'd certainly like to think so.) Unfortunately, however, research in children also shows that this is a two-way street. Your intellectual development can also be damaged or diminished by organic factors, such as drugs, alcohol, and poor nutrition.[10]

Do I Think I'm More Intelligent Than My Parents? If you answer, yes, to this question, then research might just support such a claim. A steady and significant rise in average intelligence among those in developed countries has been observed over the last 70 years. Why? Experts at an American Psychological Association conference

Dr. Evangelo Katsioulis reportedly has an IQ of 198—the highest in the world. He is a Greek psychiatrist and has degrees in philosophy, psychopharmacology, and research technology. Hall of Fame baseball player Reggie Jackson's is 160, the same as physicist Stephen Hawking and movie director Quentin Tarantino. People who score less than 70 are identified as intellectually disabled; over 130, gifted; and over 165, genius. Two-thirds of people score in the normal range of 85–115.

concluded, "Some combination of better schooling, improved socioeconomic status, healthier nutrition, and a more technologically complex society might account for the gains in IQ scores."[11] So, if you think you're smarter than your parents and your teachers, despite them saying you don't know important facts that they do, then you're probably right!

Multiple Intelligences (MI)   While many people think of intelligence in general terms, such as IQ, it is more common and practical to think in terms of multiple intelligences or intelligence for something specific. Howard Gardner, a professor at Harvard's Graduate School of Education, investigated this issue for years and summarized his findings in his 1983 book *Frames of Mind: The Theory of Multiple Intelligences.*[12] The eight different intelligences he identified include not only mental abilities but social and physical abilities and skills as well. See Table 3.1.

Practical Intelligence   We can draw practical benefits from Gardner's notion of multiple intelligences. For instance, Yale's Robert J. Sternberg applied Gardner's "naturalist intelligence" to the domain of leadership under the heading *practical intelligence.* He explains: " ***Practical intelligence*** **is the ability to solve everyday problems by utilizing knowledge gained from experience in order to purposefully adapt to, shape, and select environments.** It thus involves changing oneself to suit the

TABLE 3.1 GARDNER'S EIGHT INTELLIGENCES

TYPE OF INTELLIGENCE	EXAMPLE
Linguistic intelligence: potential to learn and use spoken and written languages.	If you are European, or at least traveled to Europe, then you could argue that the multilingual people born and raised there have developed much higher levels of linguistic intelligence than most people born and raised in the United States. The same holds true for parts of Africa and Asia and other pockets of the world.
Logical-mathematical intelligence: potential for deductive reasoning, problem analysis, and mathematical calculation.	Did this intelligence help or hurt you on your college entrance exam?
Musical intelligence: potential to appreciate, compose, and perform music.	Do you play the guitar? Have you heard Tony MacAlpine? He is widely considered to be a guitar virtuoso. If you were to measure this form of intelligence, then his musical intelligence score is likely high.
Bodily-kinesthetic intelligence: potential to use mind and body to coordinate physical movement.	LeBron James, besides being in the top 1% in terms of height, clearly has masterful control of his body compared to most any athlete, any size, any sport, and any level.
Spatial intelligence: potential to recognize and use patterns.	Fighter pilots are excellent examples.
Interpersonal intelligence: potential to understand, connect with, and effectively work with others.	Compare Jeff Bezos (CEO of Amazon) to Larry Ellison (CEO of Oracle). Critics see the first as approachable and friendly, the second as arrogant.
Intrapersonal intelligence: potential to understand and regulate oneself.	Any president of the United States. It requires incredible self-awareness and control to endure the constant criticism.
Naturalist intelligence: potential to live in harmony with one's environment.	The Dali Lama comes to mind. But for people more mainstream, John Mackey of Whole Foods and the late Ray Anderson of Interface, Inc. epitomize this form of intelligence.

environment (adaptation), changing the environment to suit oneself (shaping), or finding a new environment within which to work (selection). One uses these skills to (*a*) manage oneself, (*b*) manage others, and (*c*) manage tasks."[13]

Others believe the concept of multiple intelligences has important implications for employee selection, training, and performance. The implication is that one-size-fits-all training programs fall short when diversity of intelligences is taken into consideration. Near the end of this chapter, you will encounter the concept of *emotional intelligence,* which can be used for selection and other purposes. We look forward to breakthroughs in this area as the field of multiple intelligences attracts more OB researchers and practicing managers.

TAKE-AWAY APPLICATION—TAAP

Using the list of intelligences in Table 3.1 and discussed above,

1. Which do you think are your strongest? Weakest?
2. Which do you think are most important for this course? Your current, last, and most desired jobs?
3. Which do you think are least important?
4. Describe how you could use this knowledge to improve your performance in this class (and your job if you're working).

Practical Implications

Many people (e.g., educators and parents) have embraced multiple intelligences because it helps explain how a child could score poorly on a standard IQ test yet be obviously gifted in one or more ways (e.g., music, sports, or relationship building). It then follows that the concept of multiple intelligences underscores the need to help each child develop in his or her own unique way and at his or her own pace. Many people make the same arguments about college students and employees. Of course, everybody has strengths and weaknesses. But practically what is important is to identify intelligences relevant to the job, and then select, place, and develop individuals accordingly. What is your view? Do you see any value in intelligence tests at work? Why or why not?

Not Just Kid Stuff   The interest in improving intelligence now goes far beyond children and child development. Recently, companies such as Lumosity, Cogmed, and even Nintendo have touted and profited from the idea that adult intelligence can be increased. Either through games or training, subjects and customers have been shown to improve scores on IQ and other related tests. One piece of evidence to support their case is a study that showed a six-point boost on an IQ test. Researchers, however, recommend caution. They note that intelligence is still largely a fixed trait, and that improvements are modest and typically the result of intensive, long-term interventions. Psychology professor David Hambrick of Michigan State University put it this way: "Demonstrating that subjects are better on one reasoning test after cognitive training doesn't establish that they are smarter. It merely establishes that they're better on one reasoning test."[14] This seems to suggest that "pure intellectual heft is like someone who can bench-press a thousand pounds. But so what, if you don't know what to do with it?"[15]

Some Proof?   Regardless of your personal view on the practical value of intelligence at school or work, the following Example box offers a couple compelling endorsements for the importance of mental abilities and IQ.

EXAMPLE Smarts and Money

Intelligence in its various forms is important because of its link to performance. For example, a study of stock traders in Finland revealed that those with high IQs are more likely to: (1) sell losing stocks, (2) engage in tax-loss selling, and (3) hold stocks at 30-day highs—all desirable. Performance also was better than that for their low IQ counterparts, by as much as 2.2 percent per year.[16]

NFL—INTELLIGENCE TESTING?   Yes, not only does the National Football League have an employment test for players, but they've been using one since the 1970s! This began with the Dallas Cowboys using the popular Wonderlic test (50 questions with a 12-minute time limit). Now, many teams have developed and used their own. The belief is that test scores will help identify players who will get along with teammates, those who will make it to meetings on time, and how best to teach them the playbook (e.g., in written form, visual aids, or on-the-field demonstration).[17]

BE SMART AND PROTECT YOUR INVESTMENTS   Both financial advisors and professional football teams make multimillion-dollar investments—the former in stocks and the latter in football players. It seems that powerful people in both industries believe that intelligence matters.

YOUR THOUGHTS?

1. When interviewing financial advisors, would you compare IQs? If you were the coach, GM, or owner of a professional sports team, would you use intelligence testing? In each case, why or why not?

2. If you were a hiring manager for your company, how much weight would you give intellectual intelligence?

3. Would you require an IQ test? Explain your answers.

PERSONALITY, OB, AND MY EFFECTIVENESS

MAJOR QUESTION

How does my personality affect my performance?

THE BIGGER PICTURE

You probably feel you know yourself better than anyone else, but you're about to learn some tools to help you see how others see you. One such tool is the Big Five personality profile, which summarizes hundreds of personality traits into five categories. Another useful approach centers on *proactivity*. These tools will help you understand how you may be seen by others and understand the managerial implications of these characteristics. We explore these topics because personality is a fundamental driver of your behavior and performance at work, and it is an important input in the Integrative Framework of OB.

Personality is defined as the combination of stable physical, behavioral, and mental characteristics that give individuals their unique identities. These characteristics or traits—including how one looks, thinks, acts, and feels—are the product of interacting genetic and environmental influences and are stable over time and across situations and cultures.[18] Personality is a person input in the Integrative Framework.

There Is More to Personality Than Liking and Fit

You, like most people, may often think of personality in general "like/dislike" terms. For instance, if you're asked to describe your professor for this class you might say: "She is great. I love her personality." Or, if asked to describe your boss you might say: "He is a horrible individual, he is unethical, many of his colleagues won't associate with him, and he is widely disrespected and should be fired." Or if you are recruiting somebody for a job (or your fraternity/sorority) you might say: "I really like his/her personality . . . I think he/she will fit in great with the rest of us."

What Can I Do with "Like"? While "liking" and "fit" matter, these general and evaluative types of descriptions aren't very useful from a management standpoint. To be more specific, assume you are a manager at a company or an officer in a fraternity or sorority and are planning to recruit new employees or pledges. If you only think of personality in terms of (dis)like and fit, what type of guidance would you give to your recruiters? "Go find people you like and be sure they fit." Again, liking and fit of coworkers (or pledges) matter, but these are too general and too varied from one recruiter to the next. Moreover, because you like somebody doesn't mean you should hire that person, that he or she will perform well, or that he or she will be a good person to add to your house.

Jeff Bezos (top) and Steve Jobs (bottom) were ranked #1 and #2 top performing CEOs by *Harvard Business Review*. Jobs was not known to be especially likeable, whereas Bezos is seen as relatively friendly, down to earth, and approachable. The lesson—don't make too much of "likeable" personalities. If you started a company, you'd likely be delighted to have either Bezos or Jobs work for you!

Be Precise to Be Effective The challe... cise is part of what has motivated a tremend... research in psychology and OB regarding p... other words, to be effective at managing people... be more precise and specific (and scientific) abou... ity. As with other IDs discussed in this chapter and ... ...gn-out the book, what is needed are more precise definitions of what personality is and is not, how to measure it, and what effect it has on important processes and outcomes across levels of the Integrative Framework.

The Big Five Personality Dimensions

To meet this need, psychologists and researchers have distilled long and confusing lists of personality dimensions into what they call the ***Big Five Personality Dimensions.*** **These are five basic dimensions that simplify more complex models of personality: extraversion, agreeableness, conscientiousness, emotional stability, and openness to experience.**[19] See Table 3.2. For example, someone scoring high on extraversion would be an extrovert, that is, outgoing, talkative, sociable, and assertive. Someone scoring low on emotional stability would tend to be nervous, tense, angry, and worried.

A person's scores on the Big Five reveal a personality profile as unique as his or her fingerprints. Complete Self-Assessment 3.1 to discover your own Big Five profile. In the process you'll learn that there is more to personality than just being likeable or fitting in. This Self-Assessment will increase your self-awareness and illustrate some of the concepts we just described. Moreover, many companies use personality profiles for hiring and promotions. Your profile should provide some practical insights.

TABLE 3.2 CHARACTERISTICS OF PERSONS SCORING HIGH ON THE FIVE DIMENSIONS

The Big Five Personality Dimensions	Personality Dimension
1. Extraversion	Outgoing, talkative, sociable, assertive
2. Agreeableness	Trusting, good-natured, cooperative, softhearted
3. Conscientiousness	Dependable, responsible, achievement oriented, persistent
4. Emotional stability	Relaxed, secure, unworried
5. Openness to experience	Intellectual, imaginative, curious, broad-minded

SOURCE: Adapted from M. R. Barrick and M. K. Mount, "Autonomy as a Moderator of the Relationships between the Big Five Personality Dimensions and Job Performance," *Journal of Applied Psychology,* February 1993, 111–118.

Mc Graw Hill connect

SELF-ASSESSMENT 3.1 What Is My Big Five Personality Profile?

Go to connect.mheducation.com and take Self-Assessment 3.1 to learn your Big Five personality profile. Then answer the questions below.

1. What are your reactions? Do you agree with the scores on your Big Five profile?

2. Which dimension(s) is (are) your highest? In which situations would this be most beneficial?

3. Which one or two dimensions do you think are likely the best predictor of managerial success? Which is the least? Explain.

4. Given your profile, describe the implications for working in teams at school and/or work.

But one important question lingers: Are personality models unique to the culture in which they were developed? At least as far as the Big Five model goes, cross-cultural research evidence points in the direction of "no." Specifically, the Big Five personality structure held up very well in a study of women and men from Russia, Canada, Hong Kong, Poland, Germany, and Finland.[20] A comprehensive analysis of Big Five studies revealed: "To date, there is no compelling evidence that culture affects personality structure."[21]

Proactive Personality

A *proactive personality* is "someone who is relatively unconstrained by situational forces and who affects environmental change. Proactive people identify opportunities and act on them, show initiative, take action, and persevere until meaningful change occurs."[22] In short, people with proactive personalities are "hardwired" to change the status quo. It therefore is no surprise that this particular individual difference has received growing attention from both researchers and managers. Think about it. Companies, and their managers, routinely say they want employees who take initiative and are adaptable. Many argue that today's hypercompetitive and fast-changing workplace requires such characteristics. In support of these desired traits, research shows that those with proactive personalities positively influence many of the work outcomes shown in Figure 3.1 (and later in Figure 3.4). For example, proactivity is related to increased performance, satisfaction, affective organizational commitment (genuine desire to remain a member of an organization), and social networking.[23]

Proactive Managers What about your manager? Interesting recent work showed that the ideal scenario is for both you and your manager to be proactive. This results in a better fit and relationship between the two of you, and it also increases your level of job performance, job satisfaction, and affective commitment.[24] It also is important to know that the same study showed that the worst scenario in terms of performance was low proactivity for both you and your manager, followed by a highly proactive manager and a low proactivity follower. Thus proactivity is a highly valued characteristic in the eyes of employers. And being proactive has direct and indirect (via your manager) benefits for your performance. Given these facts, how proactive do you see yourself? How might you increase your proactivity? To help answer these questions, learn about your own proactivity, and explore some of potential benefits for you, complete Self-Assessment 3.2.

![Mc Graw Hill Education] **connect**

SELF-ASSESSMENT 3.2   **How Proactive Am I?**

Go to connect.mheducation.com and complete Self-Assessment 3.2. Compare your perceptions with your score, then answer the questions below. This knowledge can help you better understand and "sell" yourself in job interviews and at work.

1. Do you see a pattern between the questions on which you scored the highest? Lowest?

2. On those you scored the highest, what are the implications for your success in school? In other words, how can these aspects of your proactivity help you?

3. How can knowledge of your proactive personality score help you when you look for a job? Be specific.

Proactivity and Entrepreneurs   Successful entrepreneurs often exemplify the proactive personality. Consider Rachel Coleman, who founded Two Little Hands Productions after discovering that her baby daughter was severely hearing impaired. Her company produces DVDs that teach American Sign Language to children. When Coleman learned of her daughter's disability, she abandoned her career as a singer/songwriter, taught herself to sign, and began teaching children at local preschools. She and her sister made their first video just to teach others, but when the *Today Show* inquired, Coleman saw an opportunity and started building a business.[25]

Sal Khan's Khan Academy, now world famous, provides Internet-based learning for nearly every scholastic subject under the sun. Here's how it started. Khan, who has three graduate degrees, offered to help his cousin with one of her classes via the Internet. She learned, the word spread, and a company was born. Khan Academy now provides more than 4,000 different subject tutorials for free and has presented more than 240 million lessons.[26] Some other fascinating statistics, shown in Table 3.3, highlight other notable individual differences of entrepreneurs. How do you match up?

TABLE 3.3   TAKING THE MEASURE OF ENTREPRENEURS

40	Average and median age
95.1%	Have bachelor's degrees
47%	Have advanced degrees
71.5%	Come from middle-class backgrounds
<1%	Come from extremely rich or extremely poor backgrounds
70%	Used own savings as major source of funding
42.5%	Were firstborn
3.1	Average number of siblings
51.9%	First in family to start a business
69.9%	Married when they launched first business
59.7%	Had at least one child
73%	Think luck is an important factor in the success of their venture

SOURCE: "By the Numbers: Taking the Measure of Entrepreneurs," *The Wall Street Journal*, November 12, 2012.

In Table 3.3, it is worth noting that these are only averages, and if you do not possess these qualities you still can succeed as an entrepreneur. To help make this point, let's explore the link between personality and performance.

Personality and Performance

Instead of simply assuming personality affects performance, let's see what research has to say and how this can make you more effective. Let's begin with the Big Five, as knowledge of these stable personality dimensions could assist in selecting the right people and assigning them responsibilities that will set them up to win. To this end, a study involving more than 20,000 employees from many professions showed that *conscientiousness* had the strongest (most positive) effects on job performance and training performance. According to the researchers, "those individuals who exhibit traits associated with a strong sense of purpose, obligation, and persistence generally perform better than those who do not." They also tend to have higher job satisfaction.[27] Another expected finding: Extraversion (an outgoing personality) was associated with success for managers and salespeople. Extraversion also was a stronger predictor of job performance than agreeableness, across all professions. The researchers concluded, "It appears that being courteous, trusting, straightforward, and softhearted has a smaller impact on job performance than being talkative, active, and assertive."[28]

Besides increases in job performance, job satisfaction, and affective commitment (as discussed in Chapter 2), proactive personality also is linked to intentions to be entrepreneurial. This really should not be surprising, but it is helpful to know that scientific OB research substantiates this belief. Building on this, employees with proactive personalities are more likely to be more engaged (again, see Chapter 2) and creative at work.[29]

Mr. Ambani is India's richest man with much of his fortune coming from oil and gas. He is social, he and his wife throw extravagant parties, but at the same time he's reclusive. He did his first interview in more than a decade in early 2013 with Fareed Zakaria.

Personality Testing at Work

Personality testing as a tool for making decisions about hiring, training, and promotion is commonplace. A recent study by the Aberdeen Group, a human capital market research firm, found 53 percent of companies use some form of pre- and post-hiring assessments. Many of these are personality-type tests. According to the same study, 86 percent of "best in class" companies used assessments in the pre-hire stage.[30] However, despite their widespread use, a panel of industrial-organizational psychologists concluded that the typical personality test is not a valid predictor of job performance.[31] One reason might be that many test-takers don't describe themselves accurately but instead try to guess what answers the employer is looking for.

Another reason for the dismal results is that such tests are typically bought off the shelf and often given indiscriminately by people who aren't trained or qualified. And while rigorous research shows that personality actually is related to performance, the effects are small. Moreover, and more importantly perhaps, the fact is that personality tests are designed to measure personality, not what individual differences are needed to *perform at a high level in a particular job*. This means that managers need different and better ways to measure personality if they want to select employees based on performance-conducive personality traits. Managers are therefore wise to learn about personality and tools used to measure it before investing in and/or utilizing the data from such tests. Table 3.4 provides some insights.

TABLE 3.4 ADVICE AND WORDS OF CAUTION ABOUT PERSONALITY TESTING IN THE WORKPLACE

Researchers, test developers, and organizations that administer personality assessments offer the following suggestions for getting started with testing or for evaluating whether tests already in use are appropriate for forecasting job performance:
• Determine what you hope to accomplish. If you are looking to find the best fit between a job and applicant, analyze the aspects of the position that are most critical for it.
• Look for outside help to determine if a test exists or can be developed to screen applicants for the traits that best fit the position. Industrial psychologists, professional organizations, and a number of Internet sites provide resources.
• Insist that any test recommended by a consultant or vendor be validated scientifically for the specific purpose that you have defined. Vendors should be able to cite some independent, credible research supporting a test's correlation with job performance.
• Ask the test provider to document the legal basis for any assessment: Is it fair? Is it job-related? Is it biased against any racial or ethnic group? Does it violate an applicant's right to privacy under state or federal laws? Get legal advice to assure that a test does not adversely affect any protected class.
• Make sure that every staff member who will be administering tests or analyzing results is educated about how to do so properly and keeps results confidential. Use the scores on personality tests with other factors you believe are important to the job—such as skills and experience—to create a comprehensive evaluation of the merits of each candidate, and apply those criteria identically to each applicant.

SOURCE: From S. Bates, "Personality Counts," *HR Magazine,* February 2002, 34. Reprinted with permission of the Society for Human Resource Management (www.shrm.org), Alexandria, VA, publisher of *HR Magazine.* © SHRM.

There Is No "Ideal Employee" Personality

Given the complexity of today's work environments, the diversity of today's workforce, and recent research evidence, the quest for an ideal employee personality profile is sheer folly. Just as one shoe does not fit all people, one personality profile does not fit all job situations. Good management involves taking the time to get to know *each employee's unique combination* of personality traits, abilities, and potential and then creating a productive and satisfying person-job fit. In other words, a contingency approach to managing people is best (recall the discussion of contingency in Chapter 1).

3.4 CORE SELF-EVALUATIONS: HOW MY SELF-EFFICACY, SELF-ESTEEM, LOCUS OF CONTROL, AND EMOTIONAL STABILITY AFFECT MY PERFORMANCE

MAJOR QUESTION

How do self-evaluations affect my performance at work?

THE BIGGER PICTURE

You can significantly improve your self-awareness by understanding your core self-evaluations (CSEs). Such self-evaluations provide broad and useful ways to describe personality that comprise specific individual differences of self-efficacy, self-esteem, locus of control, and emotional stability. CSEs and their component dimensions are more flexible than IQ but more stable than emotions. Your knowledge of CSEs can improve your performance at work, throughout your career, and in your larger life space.

So far we've discussed both general and more narrow or specific individual differences (e.g., multiple intelligences). Knowledge and use of both general and specific approaches have benefits. A narrow concepts perspective enables you to more precisely *describe* individuals. Think about it: describing somebody in terms of musical intelligence or extraversion is more specific than using one's general personality. To illustrate, a narrow concepts approach would conclude that it is more insightful to say that Steve Vai, a phenomenal progressive rock guitarist and favorite of one of your authors, has incredible musical intelligence than to say that he is intelligent. In contrast, using a broader perspective can enable you to more effectively *predict* behavior—"the whole is greater than the sum of the parts." The rationale is that broader concepts provide a more comprehensive and practical account of an individual's behavior.[32] However, part of Vai's guitar-playing prowess likely is due to other factors beyond his musical intelligence. While there is no clear answer regarding the accuracy of these two approaches, researchers have identified a broad or general personality concept that has significant relationships with a host of individual-level work outcomes included in Figure 3.1 and the Integrative Framework. It is called *core self-evaluations (CSEs)*.

People with high core self-evaluations see themselves as

Steve Vai studied with Joe Satriani and attended the renowned Berklee College of Music in Boston. Early in his career he transcribed music and played for the legendary musician Frank Zappa. He is widely considered a virtuoso and would be expected to score very highly on musical intelligence. What other intelligences might influence his guitar playing, composing, and song writing?

major question

FIGURE 3.2 THE CORE SELF-EVALUATION AND ITS COMPONENTS

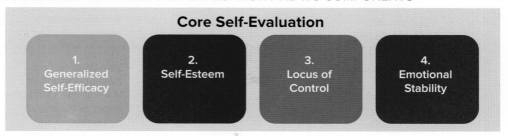

Core Self-Evaluation

| 1. Generalized Self-Efficacy | 2. Self-Esteem | 3. Locus of Control | 4. Emotional Stability |

capable and effective. *Core self-evaluations (CSEs)* **represent a broad personality trait comprised of four narrower and positive individual traits: (1) generalized self-efficacy, (2) self-esteem, (3) locus of control, and (4) emotional stability.** (See Figure 3.2.) This section discusses these component traits and highlights research and managerial implication for each separately. This is done because it is necessary to understand the component traits to comprehend CSEs and to fully appreciate the practical value. We conclude by comparing what we know about these individual traits with what research reveals about combining them into the broad concept of CSE.

Why should you care about CSEs? CSEs have desirable effects on outcomes such as increased job performance, job and life satisfaction, motivation, organizational citizenship behaviors, and better adjustment to international assignments.[33] They are related to reduced conflict (Chapter 10) and lower stress (Chapter 16). CSEs also have been studied in the executive suite. A study of 129 CEOs and top management teams showed that CEOs with high core self-evaluations had a positive influence on their organization's drive to take risks, innovate, and seek new opportunities. This effect was especially strong in dynamic business environments.[34] Now let's explore the component dimensions.

Self-Efficacy—"I Can Do That"

Have you noticed how those who are confident about their ability tend to succeed, while those who are preoccupied with failing tend to fail? At the heart of such performance differences is self-efficacy. *Self-efficacy* **is a person's belief about his or her chances of successfully accomplishing a specific task.**

Self-efficacy can be developed. Helpful nudges in the right direction from parents, role models, and mentors are central to the development of high self-efficacy. For example, a study of medical residents showed that guidance and social support from their mentors improved the resident's clinical self-efficacy.[35]

Sara Blakely, the founder of Spanx, epitomizes self-efficacy. Not only is she the youngest self-made female billionaire, but her path to the top contained more failures than successes. She failed to get into law school, worked at Disney World, did stand-up comedy, and sold fax machines all before designing, making, and selling her modern and fashionable girdles out of her apartment and car. Think of some of your own "failures" and how you responded. How did this build your efficacy?

Mechanisms of Self-Efficacy A detailed model of self-efficacy is shown in Figure 3.3. To apply this model, imagine you have been told to prepare and deliver a 10-minute talk to an OB class of 50 students on how to build self-efficacy. Part of your self-efficacy calculation would involve evaluating interaction between your personal capabilities and environmental characteristics, just as described in the Integrative Framework.

FIGURE 3.3 SELF-EFFICACY PAVES THE WAY FOR SUCCESS OR FAILURE

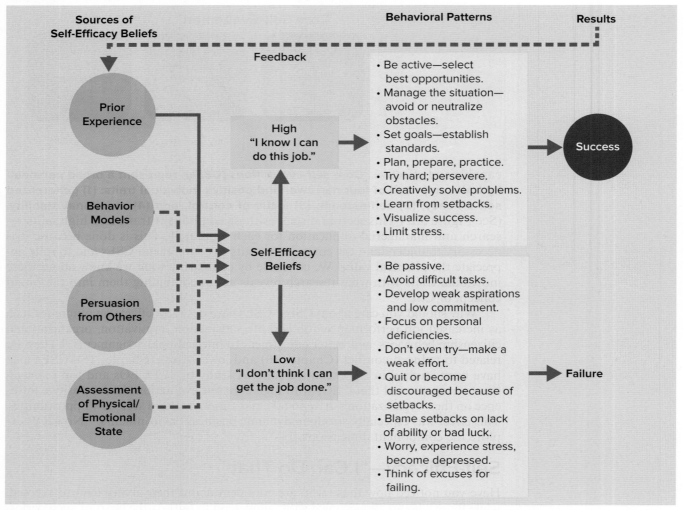

SOURCES: Adapted from discussion in A. Bandura, "Regulation of Cognitive Processes through Perceived Self-Efficacy," *Developmental Psychology,* September 1989, 729–735, and R. Wood and A. Bandura, "Social Cognitive Theory of Organizational Management," *Academy of Management Review,* July 1989, 361–84.

On the left-hand side of Figure 3.3, among the sources of self-efficacy beliefs, prior experience takes first position as the most potent of the four sources. This is why it connects to self-efficacy beliefs with a *solid* line. Past success in public speaking would boost your self-efficacy and bad experiences would diminish it. Other sources (behavior models, persuasion from others, and physical and emotional factors) might also affect your self-confidence. As weaker sources, they connect to beliefs with *dashed* lines in the figure. Your evaluation of the situation then would yield a self-efficacy belief—ranging from high to low expectations for success. Importantly, self-efficacy beliefs are not mere bravado; they are deep convictions supported by experience.

Moving to the *behavioral patterns* right-hand portion of Figure 3.3, we see how self-efficacy beliefs are acted out. In short, if you have high self-efficacy about giving your 10-minute speech, you will work harder, more creatively, and longer when preparing for your talk than would a low-self-efficacy classmate. Better performance would follow. People program themselves for success or failure by enacting their self-efficacy expectations. Positive or negative results subsequently become feedback for one's base of personal experience and future self-efficacy.

solving application

How Can I See My Own Blind Spots to Build Efficacy and Effectiveness?

A recent report on first-time leaders showed that 89 percent have blind spots, or areas in which they think they are capable but are not. There are many reasons for such disconnects, such as promoting technical experts who do not have management skill-sets, lack of training and preparation for managerial roles, and insufficient feedback to help reveal blind spots. All of the blind spots noted in this study are OB topics covered in this book.

A first step toward seeing your own blind spots would be to reflect on those that are most common. Here are the three most common

for technical experts who were recently promoted:

1. **Guiding Interactions.** Eighty-eight percent were "blind" in this area, which includes influencing meetings, conversations, and other communications in a productive manner to achieve objectives.

2. **Coaching for Improvement.** Sixty-nine percent were deficient in confronting and solving performance problems and developing others. These are skills that many organizations rarely practice, train, or develop.

3. **Delegation.** Sixty-eight percent are reluctant to let go of these responsibilities.

Other common blind spots are problem solving (34%) and influencing others (27%). The first was covered in Chapter 1 and the latter will be in Chapter 12. Whatever the case, blind spots set new leaders up to fail. To avoid this, you are urged to identify and "unveil" your blind spots. Beyond considering those that are generally common, you can complete the Self-Assessments throughout this book.[36] Another way is to seek feedback, a process that we discuss in detail in Chapter 6.

YOUR CALL

Stop 1: Review your Self-Assessments to date, and if you currently work, then consider soliciting feedback from coworkers to help identify any of your blind spots. Be sure to consider the common blind spots noted above. Then decide, what are two of your biggest blind spots?

Stop 2: Which OB concepts help you explain these blind spots?

Stop 3: How could you increase your efficacy in each? Be specific and use Figure 3.3 to help.

Managerial Implications Self-efficacy has been extensively studied in the workplace. The data support a number of recommendations. As a general rule, managers are encouraged to nurture self-efficacy in themselves and in others because it is related to improved job performance and job satisfaction (both are important individual-level outcomes). See Table 3.5 for more examples.

Self-Esteem—"Look in the Mirror"

Self-esteem is your general belief about your own self-worth. Personal achievements and praise tend to bolster one's self-esteem, while prolonged unemployment and destructive feedback tend to erode it. Self-esteem is measured by having people indicate their agreement or disagreement with both positive and negative statements about themselves. An example of a positive statement is, "I feel I am a person of worth, the equal of other people." An example of a negative statement is, "I feel I do not have much to be proud of." Those who agree with the positive statements and disagree with the negative statements have high self-esteem. They see themselves as worthwhile, capable, and accepted. People with low self-esteem view themselves in negative terms. They do not feel good about themselves and are hampered by self-doubts.[37]

Nationality, Life Span, and Gender Some have argued that self-esteem is largely a Western or even American concept. To address this allegation, researchers surveyed

TABLE 3.5   WAYS TO APPLY KNOWLEDGE OF SELF-EFFICACY AT WORK

APPLICATION	EXPLANATION
1. Job Design	Complex, challenging, and autonomous jobs tend to enhance perceived self-efficacy. Boring, tedious jobs generally do the opposite.
2. Training and Development	Employees' self-efficacy expectations for key tasks can be improved through guided experiences, mentoring, and role modeling.
3. Self-Management	Systematic self-management training involves enhancement of self-efficacy expectations.
4. Goal Setting and Quality Improvement	Goal difficulty needs to match the individual's perceived self-efficacy.[38] As self-efficacy and performance improve, goals and quality standards can be made more challenging.
5. Creativity	Supportive managerial actions can enhance the strong linkage between self-efficacy beliefs and workplace creativity.[39]
6. Coaching	Those with low self-efficacy and employees victimized by learned helplessness need lots of constructive pointers and positive feedback.[40]
7. Leadership	Leadership talent surfaces when top management gives high self-efficacy managers a chance to prove themselves under pressure.

more than 13,000 students from 31 countries. They found that self-esteem and life satisfaction were moderately related on a global basis. However, the relationship was stronger in individualistic cultures (e.g., United States, Canada, New Zealand, and the Netherlands) than in collectivist cultures (e.g., Korea, Kenya, and Japan). The reasoning is that individualistic cultures socialize people to focus more on themselves, while people in collectivist cultures "are socialized to fit into the community and to do their duty."[41]

Some notable practical recommendations:

- **Nationality**—Global managers need to remember to deemphasize self-esteem when doing business in collectivist ("we") cultures, as opposed to emphasizing it in individualistic ("me") cultures.
- **Life-Span**—You can expect your self-esteem to remain fairly stable over the course of your life, especially after age 30.
- **Gender**—Differences between men and women are small at best.

While this suggests that self-esteem is relatively consistent within cultures, over time, and for men and women, it begs the question: *Can it be improved?*

Can Self-Esteem Be Improved?   The short answer is "yes." So if your self-esteem is lower than you'd like now, then don't despair. For example, it has been shown that supportive clinical mentors improved medical residents' self-esteem.[42] But not everyone is convinced.

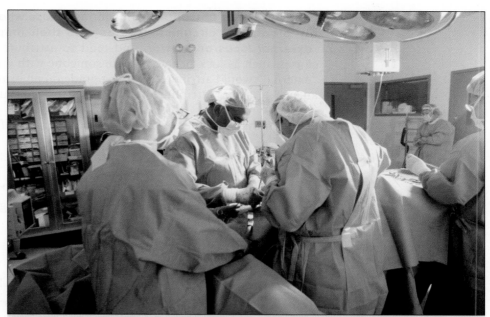

Many individual differences influence performance. Of those discussed so far in this chapter, which do you think are most important for surgeons? Would you rather have a surgeon with high self-efficacy or high self-esteem?

Improving Self-Esteem to Improve Performance

Case for: Researchers have found one method especially effective. "Low self-esteem can be raised more by having the person think of *desirable* characteristics *possessed* rather than of undesirable characteristics from which he or she is free."[43]

Case against: Some researchers believe performing at a high level boosts your self-esteem, and not the other way round. Therefore, they reason it's a mistake to focus on the self-esteem portion. We all know people who "talk big" but "deliver small," and thus seem to suffer from delusions of competency.

Our recommendation: Apply yourself to things that are important to you. If getting an A in your OB course affects your sense of self-worth, then you will be motivated to work harder and presumably perform better.

Locus of Control: Who's Responsible— Me or External Factors?

Locus of control is a relatively stable personality characteristic that describes how much personal responsibility you take for your behavior and its consequences. People tend to attribute the causes of their behavior primarily to either themselves or environmental factors.[44] (Recall our discussion of the person–environment distinction in Chapter 1.) Locus of control has two fundamental forms—internal and external.

Internal Locus of Control People who believe they control the events and consequences that affect their lives are said to possess an *internal locus of control.* For example, such a person tends to attribute positive outcomes to her or his own abilities. Similarly, an "internal" tends to blame negative events on personal shortcomings. Many entrepreneurs eventually succeed because their *internal* locus of control helps them overcome setbacks and disappointments.[45] They see themselves as masters of their own fate and not as simply lucky. Accordingly, those who willingly take high-stakes jobs in the face of adversity (e.g., scandal or bankruptcy) likely have a high internal locus.

External Locus of Control   In contrast, **those who believe their performance is the product of circumstances beyond their immediate control possess an _external locus of control_** and tend to attribute outcomes to environmental causes, such as luck or fate. Unlike someone with an internal locus of control, an "external" would attribute a passing grade on an exam to something external (e.g., an easy test) and attribute a failing grade to an unfair test or distractions at work.

Locus in the Workplace   Internals and externals differ greatly at work.

Internals

- Display greater work motivation
- Have stronger expectations that effort leads to performance
- Exhibit higher performance on tasks involving learning or problem solving, when performance leads to valued rewards
- Derive more job satisfaction from performance

Externals

- Demonstrate less motivation for performance when offered valued rewards
- Earn lower salaries and smaller salary increases
- Tend to be more anxious[46]

Emotional Stability

As described in our discussion of the Big Five and in Table 3.2, **individuals with high levels of _emotional stability_ tend to be relaxed, secure, unworried, and less likely to experience negative emotions under pressure.** In contrast, if you have low levels of emotional stability you are prone to anxiety and tend to view the world negatively. How is this knowledge useful at work? Employees with high levels of emotional stability have been found to have higher job performance, perform more organizational citizenship behaviors (OCBs—going above and beyond one's job responsibilities), and exhibit fewer counterproductive work behaviors (CWBs—undermining your own or others' work). Both OCBs and CWBs are discussed in Chapter 2, but all are individual-level outcomes illustrated in Figure 3.1 and the Integrative Framework. For an excellent illustration of emotional stability and how it impacts an individual's professional and personal lives, see the Example box on the following page about Morgan Stanley Chief Financial Officer Ruth Porat.

Three Practical Considerations Regarding CSEs

Before we leave CSEs, we'll briefly touch on three areas of interest:

- Is more of a CSE component always better?
- Is the whole of the CSE components greater than its parts?
- How can CSEs be used by managers?

Is More Always Better?   As with self-esteem, locus of control, and most other personality attributes, more emotional stability is not always better. Researchers found curvilinear, or inverted-U, relationships between emotional stability and outcomes. This suggests that as your emotional stability increases, so too will your job performance and OCBs, *but only to a point.*

   Effect on organizational citizenship behaviors (OCBs). As emotional stability continues to increase, OCBs decline. The reasoning is that as emotional stability increases you focus your attention on the task at hand and your coworkers. Typically, a good thing. However, at a certain level emotional stability becomes problematic, too much of a good thing, and you are likely to begin obsessing over details and lose sight

EXAMPLE A Female Wall Street Financial Chief Avoids the Pitfall That Stymied Others[47]

Ruth Porat is the current chief financial officer of Morgan Stanley and one of the most powerful women on Wall Street. She is not an accountant and has never worked in a finance department. However, she has effectively leveraged her Stanford economics degree and Wharton MBA. More impressive than this is that she has overcome many adversities during her rise to the corporate suite.

NOT A CRASH   She started in finance in 1987 at Morgan Stanley, just before the market crashed. She survived and a few years later moved on to Smith Barney, a move she immediately regretted and feared ruined her career. Obviously it didn't. In 1996 she made her way back to Morgan Stanley and eventually became a technology banker during the tech boom, and bust, of the late 1990s.

NOT A BUBBLE   Porat then transformed herself into a financial services banker and rode out the financial crisis of 2008–2010 and was named CFO of Morgan Stanley. Many of her colleagues on the Street cautioned her about her new role. They noted that the last two female CFOs for Wall Street firms—Erin Callan of Lehman and Sally Krawcheck of Citigroup—were casualties of the crisis. Worse still, Zoe Cruz, formerly a co-president at Morgan, also was kicked off the island.

NOT EVEN CANCER AND CHILDBIRTH   But once again Porat was undaunted. Despite also weathering two bouts of breast cancer in the 2000s, she stayed the career course. Her colleagues recognize her as one of the smartest, hardest working, and most unshakeable people with whom they have worked. She even made client calls in the delivery room during the birth of her first child. She also insisted on finishing a business presentation while lying on a conference room table, after throwing her back out!

Ruth Porat epitomizes emotional stability—relaxed, secure, and unworried!

YOUR THOUGHTS?

1. What are the advantages and disadvantages of such high levels of emotional stability at school and work?

2. Do you think such a personality characteristic is necessary to be a successful executive on Wall Street? How do your answers change (if they do) for a female executive?

3. How would you evaluate Porat on the other three CSE traits of self-efficacy, self-esteem, and locus of control?

The San Antonio Spurs once again beat the Miami Heat in the NBA Championship. This happened despite many people saying that Miami's top three players—James, Wade, and Bosh—are the best threesome in the league. Can you think of non-sports examples, where the whole is greater than the sum of the parts?

of the larger objectives and those with whom you work. The effect is similar for counterproductive work behaviors.

Effect on counterproductive work behaviors (CWBs). Emotional stability buffered or protected participants against stressors at work (e.g., trouble with their supervisors, unfair policies, and too much work), such that they were less bothered and thus less likely to act out (commit CWBs). But there was a tipping point when the stress became too much and emotional stability could not prevent employees from committing CWBs.

What is the lesson for you to take away? Emotional stability is an asset for many types of jobs, but it will only take you so far.

Is the Whole of CSE Greater Than Its Parts?   As shown in Figure 3.2, core self-evaluations are composed of self-esteem, self-efficacy, locus of control, and emotional stability. To clarify the value of a CSE as a whole versus its component traits, think of basketball as a metaphor.

Clearly a team outperforms any individual playing alone. Even the greatest player ever would have no chance against an entire team. The five greatest players ever, playing individually, still have no chance against an entire team. Individually they would never score! Thus the sum of their solo efforts would be zero.

However, if you assembled a *team* of the five greatest players (you can debate this with a classmate—the authors have their own picks), they would likely perform very well. We don't want to overemphasize the team concept that is addressed in detail in Chapter 8, but the combination of (talented) players in a team enables individual players to do things they couldn't otherwise do on their own. Moreover, history tells us that teams with the best individual players ("all-star teams") don't win every game. The fact that such teams lose shows that indeed the whole is greater than the sum of the parts—for their competitors! The sum of the all-stars is less than the sum of their lesser competitors, at least sometimes. CSE and its component traits are much the same. Core self-evaluation is the team and the traits are the individual players—the whole is greater than the sum of the parts.

How Can I Use CSEs? Especially in a managerial role, you can use knowledge of CSEs in many practical ways, such as:

- **Employee selection.** It is more efficient to select using CSE as one, broad personality characteristic rather than its four component traits. Doing so also enables managers and employers to take advantage of the many beneficial outcomes described above.

- **Training.** The training potential of CSEs is limited because most of its components are traitlike or relatively fixed (self-esteem, locus of control, and emotional stability). That said, self-efficacy is relatively more flexible than the other three components and thus can be enhanced as explained above. (Figure 3.3 is an excellent "how to" guide.)

Before moving on, we encourage you to assess your own core self-evaluations in Self-Assessment 3.3. Knowledge of your CSEs helps you understand other components of your personality beyond the Big Five discussed and assessed earlier. Awareness of your self-esteem, self-efficacy, locus, and emotional stability can help guide many aspects of your work life, such as what types of jobs to look for and what types of development opportunities may be most useful for you.

Mc Graw Hill Education connect

SELF-ASSESSMENT 3.3 How Positively Do I See Myself? *Measure Your Core Self-Evaluations and Find Out*

Go to connect.mheducation.com and take Self-Assessment 3.3 to learn your core self-evaluations. Once you know your score, then answer the questions below:

1. What is your CSE score? A score greater than 48 is high, between 36 and 48 moderate, and less than 36 low.

2. What are the implications for your performance in school? Work?

3. Now consider a scenario: You're on a three-member team for a project in this class. This project requires research, a paper, and a presentation. Your CSE score is high, one team member's is moderate, and the other's is low. Describe the potential implications for how the three of you will work together and your ultimate performance on the paper and presentation.

Let's continue our discussion of IDs and learn about emotional intelligence (EI) next. EI is an increasingly popular OB concept, one that is relatively more flexible than CSEs and the others discussed thus far.

THE VALUE OF BEING EMOTIONALLY INTELLIGENT

MAJOR QUESTION

What is emotional intelligence and how does it help me?

THE BIGGER PICTURE

You may have already seen how the smartest people are not always the best people for the job. Smart or not, everybody performs better if they have emotional intelligence. When you understand the concept of emotional intelligence from an OB perspective, you'll understand why it is an important person factor input in the Integrative Framework.

As we know, people deal with their emotions in many different ways, which is one reason why we are discussing them in the chapter on individual differences. For a long time many people simply considered how well you manage your emotions as a matter of maturity. However, since the mid-1990s researchers, consultants, and managers have increasingly described emotional maturity using the phrase *emotional intelligence (EI)*.

What Is Emotional Intelligence?

Emotional intelligence is the ability to monitor your own emotions and those of others, to discriminate among them, and to use this information to guide your thinking and actions. Referred to by some as EI (used in this book) and others as EQ, emotional intelligence is a mixture of personality and emotions and has four key components (see also Table 3.6):

1. Self-awareness
2. Self-management
3. Social awareness
4. Relationship management[48]

The first two constitute *personal competence* and the second two feed into *social competence*. Recall the discussion earlier in the chapter of inter- and intrapersonal intelligences described by Gardner. EI builds on this work, although scholars and consultants don't always acknowledge this history or similarity. That said, you might wonder: "Why another type of intelligence, and how is EI different from IQ?"

Those who developed the concept argue that traditional models of IQ are too narrow, failing to consider interpersonal competence. They also argue from a practical perspective that EI is more flexible than IQ and can be developed throughout your working life. If you recall, this is consistent with how we described things in Figure 3.1 and the practical benefits of relatively flexible IDs.

Benefits of EI

EI has been linked to better social relationships, well-being, and satisfaction across ages and contexts, including work. For instance, employees with high EI were

Christine Lagarde, head of the International Monetary Fund since 2011, illustrates the importance of EI for leaders. For instance, EI was essential in negotiating a solution to the Greek financial crisis, as many of the players had conflicting interests and intense emotions. Success required her not only to be aware of and able to manage her own emotions, but she also needed to accurately assess and respond to the emotions of many other European Union leaders.[49]

perceived more positively by co-workers and more effective as sellers (but not buyers) in negotiations. And while research results are mixed, EI also has implications for job performance and leadership:

Job Performance

- EI has been linked to higher sales and greater customer retention for both real estate and insurance sales representatives.[50]
- A study of executives found that *how* those with high EI produced results was rated positively by subordinates, but the actual results themselves were not related to EI.[51]

Leadership

- EI was positively related to leadership emergence, behavior, and effectiveness (all discussed in detail in Chapter 13).
- EI was not clearly related to job performance, satisfaction, and other outcomes.[52]

Take-aways. Considered together, the results of EI research are mixed. We therefore encourage you to proceed with caution, as every day there are more consulting companies selling EI programs and claiming EI is the silver bullet of performance. To date, the research just isn't clear. However, we also encourage you to identify and develop your own EI to realize the clear interpersonal benefits. Table 3.6 can serve as a guide.

TAKE-AWAY APPLICATION—TAAP

1. Using Table 3.6, evaluate and develop a plan to enhance your EI. What are your personal strengths and weaknesses in terms of both personal and social competence? Be honest.
2. Think of an example where your EI has helped you and an example where you would have benefited from greater EI.
3. Identify one aspect of personal competence from Table 3.6 and describe how you can improve it. Be specific.
4. Identify one aspect of social competence from Table 3.6 and describe how you can improve it. Be specific.

TABLE 3.6   DEVELOPING MY EMOTIONAL INTELLIGENCE

PERSONAL COMPETENCE	HOW WE MANAGE OURSELVES	
	CAPABILITY	**DESCRIPTION**
Self-Awareness	Emotional self-awareness	Reading one's own emotions and recognizing their impact; using "gut sense" to guide decisions
	Accurate self-assessment	Knowing one's strengths and limits
	Self-confidence	A sound sense of one's self-worth and capabilities
Self-Management	Emotional self-control	Keeping disruptive emotions and impulses under control
	Transparency	Displaying honesty and integrity; trustworthiness
	Adaptability	Flexibility in adapting to changing situations or overcoming obstacles
	Achievement	The drive to improve performance to meet inner standards of excellence
	Initiative	Readiness to act and seize opportunities
	Optimism	Seeing the upside in events

SOCIAL COMPETENCE	HOW WE MANAGE RELATIONSHIPS	
	CAPABILITY	**DESCRIPTION**
Social Awareness	Empathy	Sensing others' emotions, understanding their perspective, and taking active interest in their concerns
	Organizational awareness	Reading the currents, decision networks, and politics at the organizational level
	Service	Recognizing and meeting follower, client, or customer needs
Relationship Management	Inspirational leadership	Guiding and motivating with a compelling vision
	Influence	Wielding a range of tactics for persuasion
	Developing others	Bolstering others' abilities through feedback and guidance
	Change catalyst	Initiating, managing, and leading in a new direction
	Conflict management	Resolving disagreements
	Building bonds	Cultivating and maintaining a web of relationships
	Teamwork and collaboration	Cooperation and team building

SOURCE: Reprinted by permission of Harvard Business School Press. From *Primal Leadership: Realizing the Power of Emotional Intelligence* by D. Goleman, R. Bovatzis, and A. McKee, Boston, MA, 2002, p. 39. Copyright 2002 by the Harvard Business School Publishing Corporation; all rights reserved.

Now that you've learned about emotional intelligence, let's explore emotions themselves.

UNDERSTAND EMOTIONS TO INFLUENCE PERFORMANCE

major question

MAJOR QUESTION

How can understanding emotions make me more effective at work?

THE BIGGER PICTURE

Because you're human you have emotions. You won't be surprised then to learn that emotions are important both at work and as an individual-level process in the Integrative Framework of OB. You're about to learn the difference between felt versus displayed emotions and how emotions serve as an important means of communication with both ourselves and others. Most of your experiences elicit a mix of positive and negative emotions, and these emotions also are tightly related to your goals.

Historically, and still true today, many people believe that employees should check their emotions at the door when they come to work. The reality is that this is impossible. Like personality and the other IDs discussed thus far, emotions are an integral part of who we are as people, a fundamental part of the human experience, and therefore they are an essential part of our identity at work and influence how we perform. Given this reality, it is important to understand emotions and how they affect people so you can manage emotions *as a process* to benefit you, your team, and your employer. This will help make emotions a practical tool for you to use, rather than something to avoid, ignore, or suppress.

Emotions—We All Have Them, but What Are They?

Emotions are complex, relatively brief responses aimed at a particular target, such as a person, information, experience, event, or nonevent. They also change psychological and/or physiological states.[53] Importantly, researchers draw a distinction between *felt* and *displayed* emotions.[54] For example, if your boss screams at you when she's angry, you might feel threatened or fearful (felt emotion). You might keep your feelings to yourself or begin to cry (either response is the displayed emotion). The boss might feel alarmed (felt emotion) by your tears but could react constructively (displayed emotion) by asking if you'd like to talk about the situation when you feel calmer.

Emotions also motivate your behavior and are an important means for communicating with others. Think about it—a smile on your face signals that you're happy or pleased, while a scowl and a loud, forceful tone of voice may reflect anger. We also know that our emotions can and often do change moment to moment and thus are more flexible than the other IDs discussed thus far. As such, emotions have important implications for you at school, work, and every other social arena of your life.

Emotions as Positive or Negative Reactions to Goal Achievement

You'll notice from the definition that emotions can be thought of in terms of your goals.[55] Accordingly, positive and negative emotions can be distinguished in terms of goals.

- **Positive.** If your goal is to do well at school and you graduate on time and with honors, you are likely to experience common positive emotions, such as *joy, gratitude, pride, satisfaction, contentment, and relief.* The emotions are positive because *they are congruent* (or consistent) with your goal.

- **Negative.** Negative emotions are triggered by frustration and failure when pursuing one's goals. They are said to be goal incongruent. Common negative emotions are *anger, fright, anxiety, guilt, shame, sadness, envy, jealousy, and disgust.* Which of these are you likely to experience if you fail the final exam in a required course? Failing the exam would be incongruent with your goal of graduating on time with a good GPA. Typically, the more important the goal, the more intense the emotion.

- **Mixed.** Meeting or failing to meet our goals can also generate *mixed* emotions. Say you receive a well-earned promotion, which includes positives like more responsibility and pay—but only if you relocate to another state, which you don't want to do.

Besides Positive and Negative, Think Past vs. Future

To be sure, the negative-positive distinction matters—you're happy, you're sad. However, another characteristic of emotions can be especially useful for managers. Say you're a manager in a company that just downsized 15 percent of its employees. This is horrible for all those who lost their jobs, but let's focus on two fictitious employees who survived the cuts—Shelby and Jennifer. Both of them feel negatively about the job cuts, but in different ways.

Shelby. Her dominant emotion is anger. People are typically angry about things that happened (or didn't happen) in the past. This means that anger is a "backward-looking" or retrospective emotion.

Jennifer. Her dominant emotion is fear. People are typically fearful of things that might happen in the future. As such, fear is a "forward-looking" or prospective emotion.

Practical implications for managers. Knowing these emotions tells you that Shelby is likely most concerned with something that happened in the past, such as how the decisions were made as to who to terminate. She may think that the process was unfair and caused a number of her favorite colleagues to be let go. As for Jennifer, knowing that she is dominated by fear tells you that it is uncertainty about the future—perhaps her job might be cut next—that concerns her most. As their manager, having this more specific knowledge of Shelby's and Jennifer's emotions can guide your own actions. The following Take-Away Application (TAAP) builds on this scenario.

TAKE-AWAY APPLICATION—TAAP

Assume you are their manager and you know Shelby's dominant emotion related to the downsizing is anger and Jennifer's is fear:

1. What are two specific things you could do to alleviate Shelby's anger?
2. What are two specific things you could do to reduce Jennifer's fear?
3. What other things could you do to increase their positive emotions related to the changes?

How Can I Manage My Negative Emotions at Work?

Theoretically, you could simply translate your felt emotions into displayed emotions—unfiltered. Besides being unrealistic, this would be disastrous. Organizations have **emotion display norms,** or rules that dictate which types of emotions

are expected and appropriate for their members to show.[56] But what can you do when inevitably sometimes you feel negative emotions at work? See the following Example box that describes the costs and benefits of displaying anger at work.

EXAMPLE The Good and Bad of Anger at Work

Andrew Cornell, CEO of Cornell Iron Works, understands the days of the screaming boss are numbered. He deals with anger towards his employees by holding frequent and brief meetings, "rather than 'waiting until the end, throwing a nuclear bomb and leaving blood all over the wall.'"[57]

Screaming takes other forms too. At work you might receive a hostile e-mail berating you, copied to coworkers, in ALL CAPS. Science supports the many people who believe that "yelling" via e-mail or face-to-face is inappropriate and counterproductive. You may have been in a group meeting when someone was so angry he or she began to scream and bully another person. Bullying and yelling are unprofessional, are uncalled for, and damage the reputation of the perpetrator.

COSTS OF NEGATIVE EMOTIONS   Growing research evidence supports the undesirable outcomes from negative emotions that we all suspect. Negative emotions due to organizational change, for example, are linked to more sick time used and employee turnover.[58]

UNHAPPY CUSTOMERS MAY SUFFER TWICE   Customers' negative emotional displays (e.g., verbal aggression) have been shown to negatively affect employee job performance. Specifically, receivers of the aggression made more mistakes recalling and processing the customers' complaints![59] You may want to think twice before venting on a customer service representative.

WHAT ABOUT THE BENEFITS OF ANGER?   Expressing your anger sometimes can actually solve the problem. Your message is communicated, albeit forcefully, which can lead to better understanding. Displays of anger also are more likely to be beneficial if they are directed at organizational issues and problems instead of individuals. Being angry at the problem rather than the person is likely to be perceived more constructively and less defensively.[60]

YOUR THOUGHTS?

1. What advice would you give to managers on how to handle their own anger and other negative emotions at work?
2. What advice would you give to managers on how to handle the anger and negative emotions felt (and expressed) by their direct reports?
3. What has been the most productive way for you to deal with your negative emotions?

When executives get angry, they can get rude. In 2001, unhappy with an investor in a conference call who noted Enron seemed unable to produce its balance sheet, CEO Jeff Skilling said, "Well, thank you very much, we appreciate that, A--hole." Enron later declared bankruptcy in one of the biggest financial scandals at the start of the century. Skilling was convicted on 19 counts of securities and wire fraud in 2006.

Carol Bartz, CEO of Yahoo! from 2009 to 2011, told staff that if anyone leaked company secrets, she would "drop-kick" them "to f---ing Mars." Like Skilling's comment, Bartz's statement was widely reported. Bartz was most likely fired by Yahoo! for business reasons and not for tough talk.

Of course anger isn't the only negative emotion. Table 3.7 provides guidance on a variety of negative emotions and how to deal with them. As you study the table, think of your own experiences and reactions and how the recommendations in Table 3.7 could have helped.

TABLE 3.7 COMMON NEGATIVE EMOTIONS AND HOW TO HANDLE THEM

IF YOU'RE FEELING . . .	THEN YOU MIGHT WANT TO . . .
Fearful	Step back and try to see the situation objectively. Ask yourself: "Is my business or career truly at risk?" If not, then you may just be feeling nervous and excited rather than fearful.
Rejected	Do you actually respect the opinion of the person rejecting you? If the comment came from an idiot, someone you don't respect, the comment may actually be a backhanded compliment. If you do respect the person, then you may want to clarify by asking: "The other day you said _____ and I felt hurt. Can you clarify what happened?"
Angry	Get some distance from the situation to avoid blowing your top in the heat of the moment. Once you calm down, then precisely pinpoint the reason you are angry. In most every instance it's because somebody violated a rule or standard that is deeply important to you. Then find a way to communicate the importance of the rule or standard to the person so it doesn't happen again.
Frustrated	This happens at work when results don't meet your expectations, given the amount of time and energy you've applied. The goal often is achievable, but progress is slow. First, reassess your plan and behavior. Do they need modification? If no, then perhaps you simply need to be patient.
Inadequate	Even those with the highest self-esteem feel they don't measure up at times. Our discussion of self-efficacy and how to build it in Table 3.5 can guide your solution to this emotion.
Stressed	Time constraints are a major source of stress. Too many commitments, too little time. You therefore need to prioritize! Do what is important rather than what is urgent. For example, most e-mail is urgent but not important.

SOURCE: Adapted from G. James, "Feeling Negative? How to Overcome It," *Inc. Magazine*, November 26, 2012.

3.7 PRACTICE, LUCK, AND SUCCESS

MAJOR QUESTION

How can I be "deliberate" about success?

THE BIGGER PICTURE

You already know that luck can and does play a role in people's success. What isn't always as apparent is how some people work at being lucky. We define and explain how deliberate practice and preparing yourself for luck contribute to success.

In this chapter we've moved from fixed individual differences, such as intelligence and CSEs, to relatively flexible emotional intelligence and emotions. If given the choice, of course you'd rather have high intelligence than low. And if you're a manager or own your own business you'd rather hire intelligent people who also have high levels of conscientiousness and emotional intelligence. However, all of these individual differences are *relatively fixed* when compared to your behaviors. This means that you have far *more control over the things you do than over who you are*. We therefore conclude this chapter by describing deliberate practice and luck and their roles in your success.

Success = 10,000 Hours

While we cannot define *success* for you—it depends on your own history, expectations, goals and dreams, opportunities, and some of the IDs discussed in this chapter—we can provide some guidance on how to achieve success as *you* define it. To make the point, think of something you want to become really, *really* good at—world-class good. Perhaps you want to be truly excellent in a sport, playing an instrument, software design, or writing. Then take the advice from an old New York City joke: *Tourist:* "How do I get to Carnegie Hall?" *New Yorker:* "Practice, practice, practice."[61]

Okay, so how much practice? Try the 10,000-hour rule. After studying relevant research evidence, Malcolm Gladwell came to this conclusion in his best-selling book *Outliers: The Story of Success*:

> [T]he closer psychologists look at the careers of the gifted, the smaller the role innate talent seems to play and the bigger the role preparation seems to play. . . . [T]he people at the very top don't work just harder or even much harder than everyone else. They work much, *much* harder. . . . *Ten thousand hours is the magic number of greatness.*[62]

Generally, that works out to about 10 years of **deliberate practice, which is a demanding, repetitive, and assisted program to improve one's performance.**[63] Table 3.8 describes the hallmarks of deliberate practice.

TABLE 3.8 THE FIVE PROPERTIES OF DELIBERATE PRACTICE

CHARACTERISTIC	COMMENT
1. Designed to improve performance.	You start the process of skill development by identifying specific aspects of performance that need improvement. For example, if you want to become a better writer, you could study other writers and their books, and show your writing to other professional writers for feedback.
2. Can be repeated a lot.	It's all about repetition. The activity you are trying to improve must be something that can be repeated many, many times.
3. Provides feedback on a regular basis.	To evaluate how well you are doing something, you need objective valuation. And when you don't have feedback, it removes motivation to improve. Some tasks provide more of a challenge for feedback, as with music, public speaking, and auditioning for an acting role. That's why coaches or mentors matter.
4. Is highly demanding mentally.	Focusing on one or two targeted aspects of performance takes effort and concentration. This puts strains on our mental abilities. The best violinists, for instance, practice about three and a half hours a day, but not in one session. They find it helps to take a break in order to maintain their concentration. Chess champions also indicate that they spend a maximum of four or five hours practicing per day.
5. Isn't much fun.	Deliberate practice requires us to focus on things we are not good at doing. It would be more fun to repeat behaviors or activities at which we excel. Colvin, in his book "Talent Is Overrated," concluded that "if the activities that lead to greatness were easy and fun, then everyone would do them and they would not distinguish the best from the rest. The reality that deliberate practice is hard can even be seen as good news. It means that most people won't do it. So your willingness to do it will distinguish you all the more."[64]

SOURCE: G. Colvin, *Talent Is Overrated: What Really Separates World-Class Performers from Everybody Else* (New York: Penguin, 2008).

Tiger Woods. top rated golfer. Tiger Woods has the second most professional tours wins and is second in major tournament wins. Talented? Of course. But don't forget how much practice!

Talent Is Overrated—Practice Is the Key

Fortune magazine's Geoff Colvin, in his interesting book *Talent Is Overrated: What Really Separates World-Class Performers from Everybody Else*, says this about deliberate practice:

> It is activity designed specifically to improve performance, often with a teacher's help; it can be repeated a lot; feedback on results is continuously available; it's highly demanding mentally, whether the activity is purely intellectual, such as chess or business-related activities, or heavily physical, such as sports; *and it isn't much fun.*[65]

Tiger Woods, for example, relentlessly polished every aspect of his golf game since he was a toddler—first under his father's tutelage and later with the best coaches—to become the world's top golfer. Besides the troubles in his personal life, he also suffered injuries that further eroded his performance and cost him his top ranking. To his credit, however, he devoted himself to retooling his swing, engaged in immense deliberate practice over the period of years, and once again claimed the number one world ranking in early 2013.

Beyond sports, scientific research has given great attention to the benefits of deliberate practice in the training and performance of physicians. Simulation-based mastery is becoming a core principle in training doctors. Herein the elements of expert performance in a given practice area (e.g., gall bladder surgery) are identified, and then training, often including simulations, is built around practicing these elements.[66]

TAKE-AWAY APPLICATION—TAAP

1. Select two goals or endeavors at which you'd like to excel.

2. Create a deliberate practice plan for each that includes what you will do, how you will do it, when, and why (for what purpose).

3. Using Table 3.8, check or evaluate your plan in terms of (a) if it can be repeated a lot, (b) what you can do to combat the mental demands or fatigue, and (c) what you can do to help "add fun" into your practice plan.

Most Practice Is NOT Deliberate

Now you've learned that there is more to success than practice and talent. And while you and others may indeed spend considerable time practicing, it is important to point out that what most of us think of as practice is not *deliberate* practice. We want to call your attention to two particular qualities of deliberate practice that most people overlook—feedback and difficulty.

As a general rule, feedback is a necessary element of any type of development program. You need to know if you're making progress. During deliberate practice, feedback often comes from another person (e.g., a coach), not just yourself or the task (you'll learn much more about feedback in Chapter 6). Beyond this, deliberate practice is difficult. Instead of simply repeating a task over and over, like you've always done it, you need to get out of your comfort zone and stretch yourself. This means that many people with years of experience may not actually perform at a high level. We're not saying experience doesn't matter—of course it does. However, you can use deliberate practice to help you compete more effectively against somebody who has simply gone through the motions, operated in his or her comfort zone, for years and years.

Would I Rather Be Lucky or Good?

Actually, you don't have to decide. There's a third choice—both! Nevertheless, if you want to know about luck, then talk to lucky and unlucky people to see how they differ. It turns out that luck involves much more than simple random chance or coincidence. Lucky people, through how they think and behave, make their own good fortune. To help you improve your luck, we provide the following recommendations:

1. *Be active and involved.* Be open to new experiences and network with others to encounter more lucky chance opportunities.

2. *Listen to your hunches about luck.* Learn when to listen to your intuition or gut feelings. Meditation and mind-clearing activities can help.

3. *Expect to be lucky no matter how bad the situation.* Remain optimistic and work to make your expectations a self-fulfilling prophecy.

4. *Turn your bad luck into good fortune.* Take control of bad situations by remaining calm, positive, and focused on a better future.[67]

Many successful people made their own luck by making the best of life's hard knocks. We suggest you do the same. Turn lemons into lemonade. We expand on this positive perspective in Chapter 7.

what did i learn?

You learned that who you are affects performance because individual differences (IDs) play an important and often fundamental role in how you perform at school, at work, and in other contexts. Many practical applications of this learning will allow you to improve your own performance and work more effectively in any organizational setting, including one where you manage others. Reinforce your learning with the Key Points below. Consolidate your learning using the Integrative Framework. Then Challenge your mastery of the material by answering the Major Questions in your own words.

Key Points for Understanding Chapter 3
You learned the following key points.

3.1 THE DIFFERENCES MATTER

- Individual differences (IDs) is a broad category used to collectively describe the vast number of attributes (e.g., traits and behaviors) that describe you as a person.
- It is helpful to think of IDs in terms of their relative stability. Intelligence is relatively fixed whereas attitudes and emotions are more flexible and under your control.

3.2 INTELLIGENCES: THERE IS MORE TO THE STORY THAN IQ

- Intelligence represents an individual's capacity for constructive thinking, reasoning, and problem solving. It is more than IQ.
- Howard Gardner, in his theory of multiple intelligences, describes eight different intelligences—linguistic, logical, musical, kinesthetic, spatial, interpersonal, intrapersonal, and naturalist.
- Practical intelligence is the ability to solve everyday problems by utilizing knowledge gained from experience in order to purposefully adapt to, shape, and select environments.
- Knowledge of various forms of intelligence is useful for identifying intelligences relevant to particular jobs, which can then be used to select, place, and develop individuals accordingly.

3.3 PERSONALITY, OB, AND MY EFFECTIVENESS

- Personality is defined as the combination of stable physical, behavioral, and mental characteristics that give individuals their unique identities.

- A useful way to describe personality is using the Big Five personality dimensions. These are five basic dimensions that simplify more complex models of personality: extraversion, agreeableness, conscientiousness, emotional stability, and openness to experience.
- People with proactive personalities are relatively unconstrained by situational forces and often affect environmental change. Proactive people identify opportunities and act on them, show initiative, take action, and persevere until meaningful change occurs.
- Personality tests are commonly used by employers to select and place employees. However, it is important to know there is no ideal personality and personality testing often has flaws.

3.4 CORE SELF-EVALUATIONS: HOW MY SELF-EFFICACY, SELF-ESTEEM, LOCUS OF CONTROL, AND EMOTIONAL STABILITY AFFECT MY PERFORMANCE

- Core self-evaluations (CSEs) represent a broad personality trait comprising four narrower and positive individual traits: (1) self-efficacy, (2) self-esteem, (3) locus of control, and (4) emotional stability.
- Self-efficacy is a person's belief about his or her chances of successfully accomplishing a specific task.
- Self-efficacy beliefs can be improved via experience, behavior models, persuasion from others, and one's emotional state.
- The practical value of CSEs can be realized in selecting employees and training them to enhance elements of their CSEs.

3.5 THE VALUE OF BEING EMOTIONALLY INTELLIGENT

- Emotional intelligence (EI) is the ability to monitor one's own and others' feelings and emotions, to discriminate among them, and to use this information to guide one's thinking and actions.
- EI is associated with higher sales and improved retention, as well as leadership emergence, behavior, and effectiveness.
- You can develop your EI by building your personal competence (self-awareness and self-management) and social competence (social awareness and relationship management).

3.6 UNDERSTAND EMOTIONS TO INFLUENCE PERFORMANCE

- Emotions are complex, relatively brief responses aimed at a particular target, such as a person, information, experience, event, or nonevent.

- Most experiences at work and otherwise are a mixture of positive and negative emotions, rather than purely one or the other.

- Besides positive and negative emotions, it can be practically useful to understand and distinguish emotions in terms of their future orientation (e.g., anxiety) or past orientation (e.g., anger).

- Organizations have emotion display norms or rules that dictate which types of emotions are expected and appropriate for their members to show. It therefore is important to learn how to manage your emotions.

3.7 PRACTICE, LUCK, AND SUCCESS

- Deliberate practice can significantly affect your success in many areas of life; you can make your own luck.

- Some experts argue that practice is more important than raw talent.

- Deliberate practice is a well-proven path to success in many endeavors. It requires a program that is designed to improve actual performance, can be repeated, provides regular feedback, is highly demanding mentally, and isn't much fun.

- You can improve your chances of being lucky.

The Integrative Framework for Chapter 3

As shown in Figure 3.4, you learned how individual differences can present themselves, through the process of emotions (both felt and expressed) at the individual level, affecting many workplace outcomes at both the individual and group/team levels.

Challenge: Major Questions for Chapter 3

At the start of the chapter, we told you that after reading the chapter you should be able to answer the following questions. Unless you can, have you really processed and internalized the lessons in the chapter? Refer to the Key Points, Figure 3.4, the chapter itself, and your notes to revisit and answer the following major questions:

1. How does understanding the relative stability of individual differences benefit me?
2. How do multiple intelligences affect my performance?
3. How does my personality affect my performance?
4. How do self-evaluations affect my performance at work?
5. What is emotional intelligence and how does it help me?
6. How can understanding emotions make me more effective at work?
7. How can I be "deliberate" about success?

FIGURE 3.4   INTEGRATIVE FRAMEWORK FOR UNDERSTANDING AND APPLYING OB

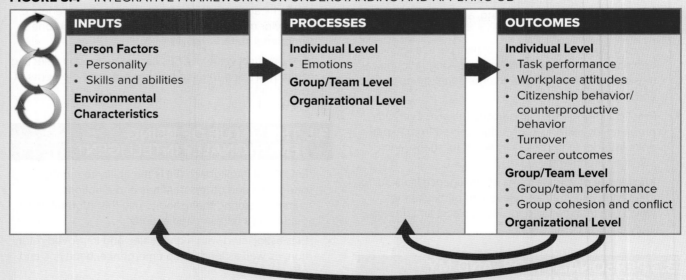

© 2014 Angelo Kinicki and Mel Fugate. All rights reserved. Reproduction prohibited without permission of the authors.

PROBLEM-SOLVING APPLICATION CASE (PSAC)

Why Are Employees Leaving Google? Facebook? Who's Next?

Use the knowledge of OB presented in this chapter to *apply the Integrative Framework of OB* and the problem-solving approach to the following case. Applying all of this knowledge should enable you to recommend realistic and effective solutions.

Many organizations recite a common mantra: "Our employees are our most valuable asset." How many companies then back this up and walk the talk is another matter. However, employees are indeed the most valuable asset of many knowledge-based companies, whose value resides in the experience, skills, and abilities of their employees. Google, one of the hottest companies to work for and repeatedly one of the most admired employers on the planet (no. 1 again in 2013),[68] is acutely aware of this fact. Google's talent (i.e., employees) is largely responsible for the company's tremendous success to date and will largely determine the company's future success. It is no wonder then that many other companies continually and intensely compete for Google's talent to drive their own growth and success. Notable examples are Sheryl Sandberg (Facebook), Marissa Mayer (Yahoo!), Lars Rasmussen (Facebook), and Richard Alfonsi (Twitter). (Some reports as far back as 2010 allege that over 140 Facebook employees are from Google.) Even Craig Silverstein, Google's third employee—after Sergey and Larry—left to work at Khan Academy.[69]

Despite Google's perennial status as one of the best places to work, it "competes for potential workers with Apple, Facebook, Amazon, Microsoft, and scores of start-ups, so every employee's departure triggers a costly, time-consuming recruiting process."[70] The pay and the perks don't seem to be enough either. In 2010, then CEO Eric Schmidt gave every employee a 10 percent pay raise. Google also was reported to offer enormous counteroffers—15 percent raise, 4x the stock benefits, and $500,000 cash bonus. Yet even this hasn't been enough to persuade some![71] As Robert Greene, a recruiter of engineers for tech start-ups, put it, "Google isn't the hot place to work" and has "become the safe place to work."[72]

Possible Reasons

Articles, blogs, and many other sources speculate and report a variety of potential reasons. For instance, one obvious one is because the company is no longer a start-up. It now qualifies as a behemoth with 30,000 employees. And because of the size it has many employees filling each and every role. However, rumor has it that if you are not an engineer, you are a second-class citizen. Similarly, if you don't office in Mountain View (the headquarters), then you have no connection or impact. Other employees simply report that it is now a large bureaucracy that is slow and inefficient.[73] These complaints occur despite the fact that employees get the famous "20% time" to work on projects of their choosing. To some employees this makes matters worse, as one devotes so much time to developing ideas, yet now there is little chance they get implemented.[74]

Is Facebook Next? What about the Next Hot Company?

If Google is victim to tech employees' lust for the latest, most exciting, and not yet public start-up, then is Facebook next? Is your company next? Should every successful start-up that matures into a full-fledged viable business expect the same fate for its essential, life-giving talent? For instance, Facebook's IPO in 2012 was enormous. And even though the stock fell sharply afterwards, many millionaires were created. And its average compensation seems to be similar to that offered at Google. Some reports, however, suggest that the luster is wearing off. Employee ratings of company satisfaction, compensation, and work–life balance have been declining since 2009. (The same survey reports Google's employee ratings of the same characteristics to be stable over this period.)[75] More recent data reveal that employee satisfaction at Google has once again surpassed that of Facebook employees.[76]

Apply the 3-Stop Problem-Solving Approach to OB

Stop 1: What is the problem?

- Use the Integrative Framework in Figure 3.4 to help identify the outcomes that are important in this case.
- Which of these outcomes are not being achieved in the case?
- Based on considering the above two questions, what is the most important problem in this case?

Stop 2: Use the Integrative Framework in Figure 3.4 to help identify the OB concepts or theories that help you to understand the problem in this case.

- What person factors are most relevant?
- What environmental characteristics are most important to consider?
- Do you need to consider any processes? Which ones?
- What concepts or theories discussed in this chapter are most relevant for solving the key problem in this case?

Stop 3: What are your recommendations for solving the problem?

- Review the material in the chapter that most pertains to your proposed solution and look for practical recommendations.
- Use any past OB knowledge or experience to generate recommendations.
- Outline your plan for solving the problem in this case.

Companies Shift Smoking Bans to *Smoker* Ban[77]

An increasing number of companies are using smoking as a reason to turn away job applicants. Employers argue that such policies increase worker productivity, reduce health care costs, and encourage healthier lifestyles. These policies up the ante on previous, less-effective efforts, such as no-smoking work environments, cessation programs, and higher health care premiums for smokers.

"Tobacco-free hiring" often requires applicants to submit to a urine test for nicotine, and, if hired, violations are cause for termination. The shift from "smoke-free" to "smoker-free" workplaces has prompted sharp debate about employers intruding into employees' private lives and regulating legal behaviors.

Some state courts have upheld the legality of refusing to employ smokers. For example, hospitals in Florida, Georgia, Massachusetts, Missouri, Ohio, Pennsylvania, Tennessee, and Texas, among others, stopped hiring smokers in the past year. Some justified the new policies as ways to reduce health care costs and to advance their institutional missions of promoting personal well-being.

Supporters of these policies note that smoking continues to be the leading cause of preventable death. About 20 percent of Americans still smoke, and smokers cost approximately $3,391 per year in lost productivity and additional health care expenses. Opponents argue that such policies are a slippery slope. Successful nonsmoker policies may lead to limits on other legal employee behaviors, like drinking alcohol, eating fast food, and participating in dangerous sports.

Many companies add their own wrinkle to the smoking ban and even forbid nicotine patches. And while most companies apply the rules only to new employees, a few have eventually mandated that existing employees must quit smoking or lose their jobs.

Questions: Managing Emotions While Managing a Smoking Problem

1. "Today's discrimination against smokers is equivalent to now illegal racial and gender discrimination years ago." Do you agree or disagree? Explain.
2. Assume you are the employee representative on the executive board at your company. You know the VP of HR plans to propose a smoker ban to begin June 1 for all new hires and the following January for all existing employees. However, you've been asked to keep the plans quiet. What would you do and why?
3. Now, assume you have permission to share the information. You know employees' responses are likely to be emotional (some positive and some negative). How would you present the information to them?
4. More generally, under what circumstances do companies have the right to consider and ban legal employee behaviors during the hiring process? Explain.
5. What is your position regarding policy changes (e.g., smoker ban) and applying them to existing employees who were hired under different guidelines? Explain your position.

GROUP EXERCISE

Anger Control Role Play

Objectives

1. To demonstrate that emotions can be managed.
2. To develop your interpersonal skills for managing both your own and someone else's anger.

Introduction

Personal experience and research tell us that anger begets anger. People do not make their best decisions when angry. Angry outbursts often inflict unintentional interpersonal damage by triggering other emotions (e.g., disgust in observers and subsequent guilt and shame in the angry person). Effective managers know how to break the cycle of negative emotions by defusing anger in themselves and others. This is a role-playing exercise for groups of four. You will have a chance to play two different roles. All the roles are generic, so they can be played as either a woman or a man.

Instructions

Your instructor will divide the class into groups of four. Everyone should read all five roles described. Members of each foursome will decide among themselves who will play which roles. All told, you will participate in two rounds of role playing (each round lasting no longer than eight minutes). In round one, one person will play Role 1 and another will play Role 3; the remaining two group members will play Role 5. In round two, those who played Role 5 in the first round will play Roles 2 and 4. The other two will switch to Role 5.

Role 1: The Angry (Out-of-Control) Shift Supervisor

You work for a leading electronics company that makes computer chips and other computer-related equipment. Your factory is responsible for assembling and testing the company's most profitable line of computer microprocessors. Business has been good, so your factory is working three shifts. The day shift, which you are now on, is the most desirable one. The night shift, from 11 pm to 7:30 am is the least desirable and least productive. In fact, the night shift is such a mess that your boss, the factory manager, wants you to move to the night shift next week. Your boss just broke this bad news as the two of you are having lunch in the company cafeteria. You are shocked and angered because you are one of the most senior and highly rated shift supervisors in the factory. Thanks to your leadership, your shift has broken all production records during the past year. As the divorced single parent of a 10-year-old child, the radical schedule change would be a major lifestyle burden. Questions swirl through your head. "Why me?" "What kind of reliable child care will be available when I sleep during the day and work at night?" "Why should I be 'punished' for being a top supervisor?" "Why don't they hire someone for the position?" Your boss asks what you think.

When playing this role, be as realistic as possible without getting so loud that you disrupt the other groups. Also, if anyone in your group would be offended by foul language, please refrain from cursing during your angry outburst.

Role 2: The Angry (Under-Control) Shift Supervisor

Same situation as in Role 1. But this role will require you to read and act according to the tips below (Guides for Action and Pitfalls to Avoid). You have plenty of reason to be frustrated and angry, but you realize the importance of maintaining a good working relationship with the factory manager.

Guides for Action

- Appreciate the potentially valuable lessons from anger.
- Use mistakes and slights to learn.
- Recognize that you and others can do well enough without being perfect.
- Trust that most people want to be caring, helpful family members and colleagues.
- Forgive others and yourself.
- Confront unrealistic, blame-oriented assumptions.
- Adopt constructive, learning-oriented assumptions.

Pitfalls to Avoid

- Assume every slight is a painful wound.
- Equate not getting what you want with catastrophe.
- See every mistake and slip as a transgression that must be corrected immediately.
- Attack someone for your getting angry.
- Attack yourself for getting angry.
- Try to be and have things perfect.
- Suspect people's motives unless you have incontestable evidence that people can be trusted.
- Assume any attempt to change yourself is an admission of failure.
- Never forgive.

Role 3: The (Hard-Driving) Factory Manager

You have a reputation for having a "short fuse." When someone gets angry with you, you attack. When playing this role, be as realistic as possible. Remember, you are responsible for the entire factory with its 1,200 employees and hundreds of millions of dollars of electronics products. A hiring freeze is in place, so you have to move one of your current supervisors. You have chosen your best supervisor because the night shift is your biggest threat to profitable operations. The night-shift supervisor gets a 10 percent pay premium. Ideally, the move will only be for six months.

Role 4: The (Mellow) Factory Manager

Same general situation as in Role 3. However, this role will require you to read and act according to the tips that follow (Guides for Action and Pitfalls to Avoid). You have a reputation for being results-oriented but reasonable. You are good at taking a broad, strategic view of problems and are a good negotiator.

Guides for Action

- Expect angry people to exaggerate.
- Recognize the other's frustrations and pressures.
- Use the provocation to develop your abilities.
- Allow the other to let off steam.
- Begin to problem-solve when the anger is at moderate levels.
- Congratulate yourself on turning an outburst into an opportunity to find solutions.
- Share successes with partners.

Pitfalls to Avoid

- Take every word literally.
- Denounce the most extreme statements and ignore more moderate ones.
- Doubt yourself because the other does.
- Attack because you have been attacked.
- Forget the experience without learning from it.

Role 5: Silent Observer

Follow the exchange between the shift supervisor and the factory manager without talking or getting actively involved. Jot down some notes (for later class discussion) as you observe whether the factory manager did a good job of managing the supervisor's anger.

Questions for Discussion

1. Why is uncontrolled anger a sure road to failure?
2. Is it possible to express anger without insulting others? Explain.
3. Which is more difficult, controlling anger in yourself or defusing someone else's anger? Why?
4. What useful lessons did you learn from this role-playing exercise?

Source: From D. Tjosvold, *Learning to Manage Conflict: Getting People to Work Together Productively,* 127–29. Copyright © 1993 Dean Tjosvold. Reprinted with permission of Lexington Books, Lanham, MD.

4 SOCIAL PERCEPTION AND MANAGING DIVERSITY

Why Are These Topics Essential for Success?

inputs

PERSON FACTORS
Demographics

ENVIRONMENTAL CHARACTERISTICS

processes

INDIVIDUAL LEVEL
Perceptions

GROUP/TEAM LEVEL
Group/team dynamics

ORGANIZATIONAL LEVEL

outcomes

INDIVIDUAL LEVEL
Well-being/flourishing

GROUP/TEAM LEVEL

ORGANIZATIONAL LEVEL
Employer of choice
Reputation

© 2014 Angelo Kinicki and Mel Fugate. All rights reserved.
Reproduction prohibited without permission of the authors.

MAJOR TOPICS I'LL LEARN AND QUESTIONS I SHOULD BE ABLE TO ANSWER

Winning at Work

For You: *What's ahead in this Chapter*

4.1 A SOCIAL INFORMATION PROCESSING MODEL OF PERCEPTION
MAJOR QUESTION: *How does the perception process affect the quality of my decisions and interpersonal relationships?*

4.2 STEREOTYPES
MAJOR QUESTION: *How can I use knowledge of stereotypes to make better decisions and manage more effectively?*

4.3 CAUSAL ATTRIBUTIONS
MAJOR QUESTION: *How do I tend to interpret employee performance?*

4.4 DEFINING AND MANAGING DIVERSITY
MAJOR QUESTION: *How does awareness about the layers of diversity help organizations effectively manage diversity?*

4.5 BUILDING THE BUSINESS CASE FOR MANAGING DIVERSITY
MAJOR QUESTION: *What is the business rationale for managing diversity?*

4.6 BARRIERS AND CHALLENGES TO MANAGING DIVERSITY
MAJOR QUESTION: *What are the most common barriers to implementing successful diversity programs?*

4.7 ORGANIZATIONAL PRACTICES USED TO EFFECTIVELY MANAGE DIVERSITY
MAJOR QUESTION: *What are organizations doing to effectively manage diversity, and what works best?*

INTEGRATIVE FRAMEWORK FOR UNDERSTANDING AND APPLYING OB

Demographics are a key input that affects important OB processes, most particularly perceptions, which in turn affect the individual-level outcome of well-being/ flourishing and the organizational outcomes of being an employer of choice and corporate reputation.

winning at work

PERCEPTION PLAYS A KEY ROLE IN GETTING A JOB

A recent survey of 400 human-resource professionals uncovered results that are important to college graduates looking for a job. The overwhelming conclusion? That "entry-level workers are an entitled, unprofessional bunch." About 45 percent of the HR professionals believed that the work ethic of new college graduates had slipped in the past five years.[1] Let's consider how you can avoid being perceived so negatively.

IMPRESSIONS FROM SOCIAL MEDIA

The Internet is a gold mine of information for recruiters, and some of it creates a bad impression. Photos of drunken behavior, or rants with foul language or that "bash" your employer, won't improve a recruiter's perception. You need to be careful about your online presence because approximately 20 percent of all organizations browse sites like LinkedIn, Facebook, MySpace, and Twitter to help screen employees.

Consider the experience of Pete Maulik, chief strategy officer at Fahrenheit 212. Maulik was ready to make an offer to an applicant, but first decided to check out the man's LinkedIn profile—and decided that the applicant was not a team player. "He took credit for everything short of splitting the atom," Mr. Maulik said. "Everything was 'I did this.' He seemed like a lone wolf. He did everything himself."

Maulik recalls another good applicant who used his Twitter account "to disparage just about every new innovation in the marketplace." Maulik concluded that the applicant "was much more comfortable as the critic than the collaborative creator."[2] This candidate was not hired either.

IMPRESSIONS FROM YOUR RÉSUMÉ

Typos, gaps in employment, and too much work history can leave negative impressions. Career coach Cheryl Palmer notes that using your employer's e-mail sends the message to potential employers "that the job seekers will not hesitate to use their equipment for personal use."[3]

RECOMMENDED TIPS

The following suggestions can help you manage the impression you are sending when applying for a job.

Do's

- Adjust your Facebook privacy settings so potential employers can't see your party photos.
- Use Twitter and LinkedIn to play up your professional interests (like posting relevant news articles).
- Cross-check your résumé and LinkedIn profile to make sure there aren't discrepancies.

Don'ts

- Don't badmouth a current or former employer, colleague, or company.
- Avoid using foul language and making negative remarks.
- Don't post anything that might be perceived as racist, biased, or illegal.[4]

Note: We cover impression management in more depth in Chapter 12.

FOR YOU   WHAT'S AHEAD IN THIS CHAPTER

We want to help you enhance your understanding of the perceptual process so you won't fall victim to common perceptual errors. We especially want to show you how perception influences the manner in which managers manage diversity. We discuss two of the outcomes of this perceptual process: stereotypes and causal attributions. Diversity should matter to you because how a business deals with diversity affects how you are perceived as an individual. Diversity should matter to the organization because it means taking advantage of the fullest range of human skill and talent. And we discuss barriers and challenges to managing diversity, and the practices organizations use to do so.

A SOCIAL INFORMATION PROCESSING MODEL OF PERCEPTION

major question

MAJOR QUESTION

How does the perception process affect the quality of my decisions and interpersonal relationships?

THE BIGGER PICTURE

Understanding the mechanics of how you process information will help you see how perception can impact a variety of important processes and outcomes in OB, as indicated in the Integrative Framework.

You're driving on a winding mountain road at dusk and suddenly you see something in the road. Is the object an animal, a rock, or a person? Should you stop, or just maneuver around it? Or you're in a team meeting and one of your teammates makes a negative statement about your work. Is the person being political or just having a bad day? Your mind is quickly trying to answer these questions before you make a response.

Perception is key to resolving the above situations. **Perception** *is a cognitive* **process that enables us to interpret and understand our surroundings.** Recognition of objects is one of this process's major functions. For example, both people and animals recognize familiar objects in their environments. You would recognize that the object in the road was a deer; dogs and cats can recognize their food dishes. People must recognize objects to meaningfully interact with their environment. But since organizational behavior's (OB's) principal focus is on people, the following discussion emphasizes *social* perception rather than object perception. (See the Example box on the perception of apologies in business.)

EXAMPLE How Perception of Apologies Differs in the United States and Japan

The frequency and meaning of apologies like "I'm sorry" vary around the world, particularly between Americans and Japanese. A recent study revealed that US students apologized 4.51 times a week while Japanese students used some type of apology 11.05 times a week. The findings highlight the importance of social perception.

WHAT DOES AN APOLOGY MEAN? "Americans see an apology as an admission of wrongdoing, whereas Japanese see it as an expression of eagerness to repair a damaged relationship, with no culpability necessarily implied." American students thus are less likely to apologize because they view it as an admission of guilt. This is consistent with the "psychological tendency among Westerners to attribute events to individuals' actions."[5] In contrast, Japanese students apologized even when they were not responsible. This is partly due to the fact that Asian countries possess more collective or group-oriented values that focus on doing things for the greater good over self-interests.

NEVER APOLOGIZE AND NEVER EXPLAIN An old John Ford film, *She Wore a Yellow Ribbon*, followed a cavalry brigade in the 1800s posted in the Indian Territory; it popularized a strand of American individualism in a phrase you may still hear today. John Wayne's character says, "Never apologize and never explain. It's a sign of weakness." But apologies do have a role in American business.

THE BUSINESS IMPACT OF APOLOGIES Apologizing can right legitimate wrongs, and it can save money for organizations. A study of medical malpractice suits revealed that 16 percent would not have sued had the hospital offered an apology. The University of Michigan Medical Center put these results to practice and "adopted a policy of 'full disclosure for medical errors,' including an apology; its rate of lawsuits has since dropped 65 percent."[6]

"Apologizing by admitting a mistake—to co-workers, employees, customers, clients, the public at large—tends to gain credibility and generate confidence in one's leadership," says Linda Stamato, of the Center for Negotiation and Conflict Resolution. She cites the apology by David Neeleman, chairman of Jet Blue, attempting to restore consumer trust, in his letter of apology to those ill-served by the air carrier during the havoc of winter storms in 2006. Although business leaders feel ambivalent about apologizing, Stamato says, "Taking responsibility for an error earns the privilege of being forgiven, and thus granted a second chance. Employees may well be relieved—after all, who has not made a mistake?—and more willing to help make the corrective action work better."[7]

YOUR THOUGHTS?

1. Do you think it pays to apologize even if you did not do something wrong? Explain.
2. What is your opinion about hospitals apologizing for medical errors?
3. What are some right ways and wrong ways to apologize in business settings?

Perception is an important process in the Integrative Framework for Understanding and Applying OB because it affects our actions and decisions. For example, *The Wall Street Journal* reported on a recent study that suggested "men with shaved heads are perceived to be more masculine, dominant and, in some cases, to have greater leadership potential than those with longer locks or with thinning hair."[8] Clearly, it is foolish to make hiring decisions based on the amount of hair on someone's head. But if you know the perceptual error, you can avoid it!

You can learn to avoid perceptual errors by understanding the process that guides perception. Figure 4.1 illustrates four stages of perception. Three of the stages—selective attention/comprehension, encoding and simplification, and storage and retention—describe how specific social information is observed and stored in memory. The fourth and final stage, retrieval and response, involves turning mental representations into real-world judgments and decisions.

We'll look at the four stages of social perception by following a simple everyday example. Suppose you were thinking of taking a course in, say, personal finance. Three professors teach the same course, using different types of instruction and testing procedures. Through personal experience, you now prefer good professors who rely on the case method of instruction and essay tests. According to social perception theory, you would likely arrive at a decision regarding which course to take based on the instructor, following the steps outlined in the following sections.

Stage 1: Selective Attention/Comprehension

People are constantly bombarded by physical and social stimuli in the environment. To avoid being overwhelmed, they selectively perceive subsets of environmental stimuli. This

FIGURE 4.1 SOCIAL PERCEPTION: A SOCIAL INFORMATION PROCESSING MODEL

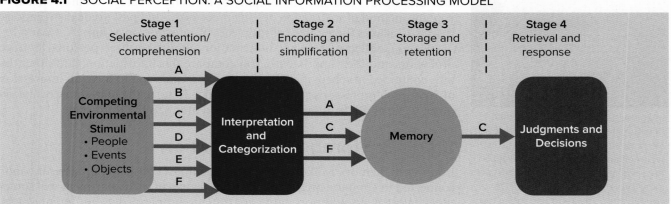

SOURCE: From R. Kreitner and A. Kinicki, *Organizational Behavior*, 10th ed., McGraw-Hill, 2013, p. 181. Reprinted with permission of McGraw-Hill Education.

is where attention plays a role. ***Attention* is the process of becoming consciously aware of something or someone.** The object of attention can come from the environment or from memory. Research has shown that people tend to pay attention to salient stimuli.

Salient Stimuli Something is *salient* when it stands out from its context. A 250-pound man would certainly be salient in a women's aerobics class but not at a meeting of the National Football League Players' Association. One's needs and goals often dictate which stimuli are salient. For a driver whose gas gauge shows empty, an Exxon or Shell sign is more salient than a McDonald's or Burger King sign. Moreover, research shows that people tend to find negative information more salient than positive information. This leads to a negativity bias.[9] This bias helps explain the gawking factor that slows traffic to a crawl following a car accident, and it can affect employee behavior at work.

Our Example You begin your search for the "right" personal finance professor by asking friends who have taken classes from the three available professors. You also may interview the various professors who teach the class to gather still more relevant information. In Figure 4.1, all the information you obtain shows as competing environmental stimuli labeled A through F. You interpret and categorize your notes.

Stage 2: Encoding and Simplification

Memory does not store observed information in its original form; encoding is required. Our brains interpret or translate raw information into mental representations. To accomplish this, perceivers assign pieces of information to **cognitive categories. "By category we mean a number of objects that are considered equivalent.** Categories are generally designated by names, e.g., *dog, animal.*"[10]

In social information processing theory, a particular category builds on a *schema*. A ***schema* represents a person's mental picture or summary of a particular event or type of stimulus.** For example, picture a sports car. Does the picture show a smaller vehicle with two doors? Is it red? If you answered yes, you would tend to classify all small, two-door, fire-engine-red vehicles as sports cars because this type of car possesses characteristics that are consistent with your sports car schema. We interpret and evaluate people, events, and objects by comparing their characteristics with information contained in schemata (the plural of schema).

Encoding We use encoding to interpret and evaluate our environment, using schemata and cognitive categories. We also use encoding and schemata to help us organize and remember information.

Simplification Relying on encoding helps us to simplify what might be a bewildering range of inputs. Encoding and schemata make the world more manageable.

Our Example Let's say you simplify by focusing on categories most salient to you: the method of instruction, testing procedures, and past grade distributions. Figure 4.1 shows these three salient pieces of information as lines A, C, and F.

Having collected relevant information about the three personal finance professors and their approaches, you compare this information with other details contained in schemata. This comparison leads you to form an impression of what each professor's course might be like. In turn, the relevant information (lines A, C, and F in Figure 4.1) are passed along to the third stage.

Stage 3: Storage and Retention

Long-term memory is like an apartment complex consisting of separate units connected to common areas. The different people in each apartment will sometimes interact. In addition, large apartment complexes have different wings, separately identifiable but connected. Long-term memory similarly consists of

Imagine the memory this individual has for parachuting off a mountain. He probably remembers the day, the weather, and the thrill of it all. Details from highly salient events like this are more likely to be remembered. Do you have any desire to engage in this activity? We don't!

separate but related categories. Specifically, long-term memory comprises three compartments (or wings), one each for events, semantic materials, and people.[11]

Event Memory   This compartment includes categories with information about both specific events (relying on unique details) and general events (relying on schemata). These memories describe appropriate sequences of events in well-known situations, such as going to a restaurant, going on a job interview, going to a food store, or going to a movie.

Semantic Memory   Semantic memory refers to general knowledge about the world, as a kind of mental dictionary of concepts. Each concept includes a definition (e.g., a good leader) and associated traits (outgoing), emotional states (happy), physical characteristics (tall), and behaviors (works hard). Concepts in semantic memory are stored as schemata; such schemata are often subject to cultural differences.

Person Memory   Categories within this compartment supply information about a single individual (your professor) or groups of people (professors). You are more likely to remember information about a person, an event, or an advertisement if it contains characteristics that are similar to something stored in the compartments of memory.

Our Example   As the time draws near for you to decide which personal finance professor to choose, your schemata of them are stored in the three categories of long-term memory. These schemata are available for immediate retrieval and comparison.

Stage 4: Retrieval and Response

People retrieve information from memory when they make judgments and decisions.

How Judgments Come   Ultimately judgments and decisions come about in one of two ways. Either we draw on, interpret, and integrate categorical information stored in long-term memory or we retrieve a summary judgment that was already made.

Our Example   On registration day you have to choose which professor to take for personal finance. After retrieving your schemata-based impressions from memory, you select a good professor who uses the case method and gives essay tests (line C in Figure 4.1). In contrast, you may choose your preferred professor by simply recalling the decision you made two weeks ago.

Managerial Implications

Social cognition is the window through which we all observe, interpret, and prepare our responses to people and events. A wide variety of managerial activities, organizational processes, and quality-of-life issues are thus affected by perception. We'll touch on hiring, performance appraisal, and leadership.

Hiring   Interviewers make hiring decisions based on their impression of how an applicant fits the perceived requirements of a job. Unfortunately, many of these decisions are made on the basis of implicit cognition. **Implicit cognition represents any thoughts or beliefs that are automatically activated from memory without our conscious awareness.** The existence of implicit cognition leads people to make biased decisions without an understanding that it is occurring.[12]

A recent study in the Netherlands demonstrated that the odds of being rejected for job openings were four times larger for Arabs than for Dutch applicants: The applicants were equally qualified.[13] Experts recommend two solutions for reducing the biasing effect of implicit cognition. First, managers can be trained to understand and reduce this type of hidden bias. Second, bias can be reduced by using structured as opposed to unstructured interviews, and by relying on evaluations from multiple interviewers rather than

Do you think that this woman may have any implicit cognitions that are affecting her dinner selection? Because she is drinking white wine, maybe this choice already activated a preference for fish or chicken. Do implicit cognitions affect your choices when dining out?

just one or two people. More and more companies are using virtual interviews as a tool for reducing problems associated with implicit cognition (see the Example box below).

EXAMPLE Virtual Interviews Can Improve the Accuracy of Job Interviews and Reduce Costs

A survey of managers from 500 companies revealed that 42 percent were using web-based video interviews as one component of the hiring process. Ocean Spray, a juice company in Massachusetts, is a good example. The company sends applicants an e-mail link that contains preset interview questions. The answers are recorded via webcam.

BENEFITS OF VIRTUAL INTERVIEWS   Standardization drives several benefits of virtual interviews.

Consistency. Video-enabled interviews standardize the process, which in turn leads to more reliable evaluations. For example, Walmart uses video interviews to help select pharmacists. Walmart recruiters believe that these interviews provide them with a better idea of how people will interact with customers. T.G.I. Friday's restaurant similarly uses video interviews to select restaurant managers for the same reason.

Collaboration. Experts suggest that "recruiters use recorded or live video interviews to foster collaboration around hiring decisions. With more stakeholders participating—by logging on to live interviews from multiple locations or leaving comments for colleagues to read on recorded interviews—more input leads to better candidate selection."

Saving Time and Money. Ocean Spray was experiencing an average cost of $1,000 per candidate for an in-person interview. Martin Mitchell, the company's manager of talent and diversity, said that "video interviews eliminated these costs" and they allowed the company to interview people more quickly while not forcing applicants to take time off work to travel for an interview.[14]

YOUR THOUGHTS?

1. The discussion you just read focuses on the positive aspects of this approach; what are the negative aspects of using video interviews?

2. How might you prepare for a video interview?

3. If you were relying on the videos to select candidates for a job, what would you look for?

Performance Appraisal   Faulty schemata about good versus poor performance can lead to inaccurate performance appraisals, which erode morale. A study of 166 production employees indicated that they trusted management more when they perceived that their performance appraisals were accurate.[15] Therefore, managers must accurately identify and communicate the behavioral characteristics and results they look for in good performance *at the beginning of a review cycle*.

Furthermore, because memory for specific instances of employee performance deteriorates over time, managers need a mechanism for accurately recalling employee behavior. Research shows that individuals can be trained to more accurately rate performance.[16] (See Chapter 6 for techniques to overcome common perception errors in the performance appraisal.)

Leadership   Research demonstrates that employees' evaluations of leader effectiveness are influenced strongly by their schemata of good and poor leaders. For example, a team of researchers found that in the employees' schema, good leaders would exhibit these behaviors:

1. Assigning specific tasks to group members.
2. Telling others that they had done well.
3. Setting specific goals for the group.
4. Letting other group members make decisions.
5. Trying to get the group to work as a team.
6. Maintaining definite standards of performance.[17]

4.2 STEREOTYPES

MAJOR QUESTION

How can I use knowledge of stereotypes to make better decisions and manage more effectively?

THE BIGGER PICTURE

Don't say you don't stereotype; that's how we humans think. Stereotypes help us process information faster. If you didn't rely on stereotypes, the world would seem chaotic. But stereotypes can also lead to bad decisions and undermine personal relationships. Understanding stereotypes can save you from such pitfalls.

Stereotypes represent a key component of the perception process because they are used during encoding. "A *stereotype* is an individual's set of beliefs about the characteristics or attributes of a group."[18] Stereotypes are not always negative. For example, the belief that engineers are good at math is certainly part of a stereotype. Stereotypes may or may not be accurate. Engineers may in fact be better at math than the general population.

Unfortunately, stereotypes can lead to poor decisions. Specifically they can create barriers for women, older individuals, people of color, and people with disabilities, all while undermining loyalty and job satisfaction. Examples follow.

Gender. A summary of research revealed that:

- People often prefer male bosses.
- Women have a harder time being perceived as an effective leader. (The exception: Women were seen as more effective than men only when the organization faced a crisis and needed a turnaround.)
- Women of color are more negatively affected by sex-role stereotypes than white women or men in general.[19]

Race. Studies of race-based stereotypes also demonstrated that people of color experienced more perceived discrimination, more racism-related stress, and less psychological support than whites.[20]

Age. Another example of an inaccurate stereotype is the belief that older workers are less motivated, more resistant to change, less trusting, less healthy, and more likely to have problems with work–life balance. A recent study refuted all of these negative beliefs about age.[21]

Stereotype Formation and Maintenance

Stereotyping is based on the following four-step process:

1. **Categorization.** We categorize people into groups according to criteria (such as gender, age, race, and occupation).
2. **Inferences.** Next, we infer that all people within a particular category possess the same traits or characteristics: women are nurturing, older people have more job-related accidents, African Americans are good athletes, and professors are absentminded.

3. **Expectations.** We form expectations of others and interpret their behavior according to our stereotypes.

4. **Maintenance.** We maintain stereotypes by:
    *   Overestimating the frequency of stereotypic behaviors exhibited by others.
    *   Incorrectly explaining expected and unexpected behaviors.
    *   Differentiating minority individuals from ourselves.

Research shows that it takes accurate information and motivation to reduce the use of stereotypes.[22]

Managerial Challenges and Recommendations

The key managerial challenge is to reduce the extent to which stereotypes influence decision making and interpersonal processes throughout the organization. We suggest three ways that this can be achieved.

1. **Managers should educate people about stereotypes and how they can influence our behavior and decision making.** We suspect that many people do not understand how stereotypes unconsciously affect the perception process.

2. **Managers should create opportunities for diverse employees to meet and work together in cooperative groups of equal status.** Social scientists believe that "quality" interpersonal contact among mixed groups is the best way to reduce stereotypes because it provides people with more accurate data about the characteristics of other groups of people.

3. **Managers should encourage all employees to strive to increase their awareness regarding stereotypes.** Awareness helps reduce the application of stereotypes when making decisions and when interacting with others.

What stands out in this photo? Did you notice the man working from a wheelchair? Do you think some people have negative stereotypes about people with disabilities? Research shows that there is a tendency to have such stereotypes.

CAUSAL ATTRIBUTIONS

MAJOR QUESTION

How do I tend to interpret employee performance?

THE BIGGER PICTURE

Consciously or unconsciously, you use *causal attributions* when you seek to explain the causes of behavior. So do most managers. You can avoid the *fundamental attribution bias* and *self-serving bias* if you learn how they distort our interpretation of observed behavior.

Attribution theory is based on a simple premise: People infer causes for observed behavior. Rightly or wrongly, we constantly formulate cause-and-effect explanations for how we and others behave. Formally defined, **causal attributions are suspected or inferred causes of behavior.** Managers need to understand how people formulate these attributions because the attributions profoundly affect organizational behavior. Consider the table below, in which how the manager understands the observed behavior drives him to take very different actions.

OBSERVED BEHAVIOR	MANAGER'S ATTRIBUTION	MANAGERIAL ACTION
Fails to meet minimum standards	Lack of effort	Reprimand
Fails to meet minimum standards	Lack of ability	Training

Kelley's Model of Attribution

Current models of attribution build on the pioneering work of the late Fritz Heider. Heider, the founder of attribution theory, who proposed that **behavior can be attributed either to *internal factors* within a person (such as ability) or to *external factors* within the environment (such as a difficult task).** Following Heider's work, Harold Kelley attempted to pinpoint specific antecedents of internal and external attributions. Kelley hypothesized that people make causal attributions by observing three dimensions of behavior: *consensus*, *distinctiveness*, and *consistency*.[23] These dimensions vary independently, forming various combinations and leading to differing attributions.

- *Consensus* compares an individual's behavior with that of his or her peers. There is high consensus when one acts like the rest of the group and low consensus when one acts differently.

- *Distinctiveness* compares a person's behavior on one task with his or her behavior on other tasks. High distinctiveness means the individual has performed the task in question in a significantly different manner than he or she has performed other tasks.

- *Consistency* judges if the individual's performance on a given task is consistent over time. Low consistency is undesirable for obvious reasons, and implies

FIGURE 4.2   SAMPLE CHARTS OF CONSENSUS, DISTINCTIVENESS, AND CONSISTENCY IN PERFORMANCE

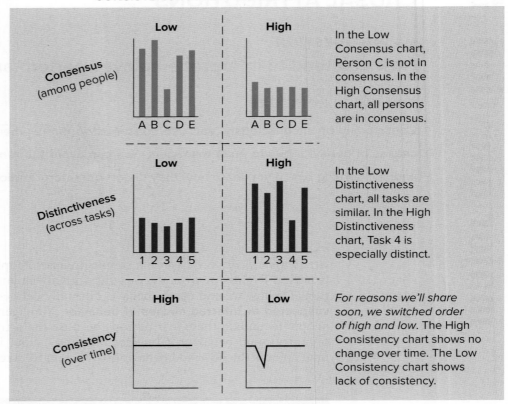

SOURCE: From K. A. Brown, "Explaining Group Poor Performance: An Attributional Analysis," *Academy of Management Review,* January 1984, p. 56. Copyright © 2001 by Academy of Management. Reprinted with permission of Academy of Management, via Copyright Clearance Center.

that a person is unable to perform a certain task at some standard level. High consistency implies that a person performs a certain task the same way, with little or no variation over time.

Figure 4.2 provides sample charts of these dimensions in both low and high incidence.

So how do these three dimensions of behavior lead to specific attributions? Kelley theorized that people attribute behavior to either *internal* causes (personal factors) or *external* causes (environmental factors) depending on the ranking of consensus, distinctiveness, and consistency as shown:

ATTRIBUTION	CONSENSUS (PEOPLE)	DISTINCTIVENESS (TASKS)	CONSISTENCY (TIME)
Internal	Low	Low	High
External	High	High	Low

While other combinations are possible, the two options shown above have been most frequently studied. **Note:** For another view of Kelley's theory, return to Figure 4.2. In the figure, we provided charts that, taken together, indicate Internal Attributions on the left-hand side and External Attributions on the right-hand side.

TAKE-AWAY APPLICATION—TAAP

1. Think of someone who recently disappointed you. It could be work-related (e.g., a peer did not complete part of a group assignment) or personal (e.g., a friend failed to remember your birthday).

2. Use Kelley's model to identify whether the unexpected behavior was due to internal or external causes.

3. Based on this attribution, what should you say or do to ensure that this type of behavior does not happen again?

Attributional Tendencies

Researchers have uncovered two attributional tendencies that distort one's interpretation of observed behavior—*fundamental attribution bias* and *self-serving bias.*

Fundamental Attribution Bias The ***fundamental attribution bias*** **reflects one's tendency to attribute another person's behavior to his or her personal characteristics, as opposed to situational factors.** This bias causes perceivers to ignore important environmental factors (again refer to the Integrative Framework) that often significantly affect behavior. This leads to inaccurate assessments of performance, which in turn foster inappropriate responses to poor performance.

Self-Serving Bias The ***self-serving bias*** **represents one's tendency to take more personal responsibility for success than for failure.** The self-serving bias suggests employees will attribute their success to internal factors (high ability or hard work) and their failures to uncontrollable external factors (tough job, bad luck, unproductive coworkers, or an unsympathetic boss). This tendency plays out in all aspects of life.

Managerial Application and Implications

Attribution models can explain how managers handle poorly performing employees. One study revealed that managers gave employees more immediate, frequent, and negative feedback when they attributed their performance to low effort. Another study indicates that managers tended to transfer employees whose poor performance was attributed to a lack of ability. These same managers also decided to take no immediate action when poor performance was attributed to external factors beyond an individual's control.[24]

The preceding observations offer useful lessons for all of us:

- **We tend to disproportionately attribute behavior to *internal* causes.** This can result in inaccurate evaluations of performance, leading to reduced employee motivation. The Integrative Framework for Understanding and Applying OB offers a simple solution for overcoming this tendency. You must remind yourself that behavior and performance are functions of both person factors and environmental characteristics.

- **Other attributional biases may lead managers to take inappropriate actions.** Such actions could include promotions, transfers, layoffs, and so forth. This can dampen motivation and performance.

- **An employee's attributions for his or her own performance have dramatic effects on subsequent motivation, performance, and personal attitudes such as self-esteem.** For instance, people tend to give up, develop lower expectations for future success, and experience decreased self-esteem when they attribute failure to a lack of ability. Employees are more likely to display high performance and job satisfaction when they attribute success to internal factors such as ability and effort.[25]

MAJOR QUESTION

How does awareness about the layers of diversity help organizations effectively manage diversity?

THE BIGGER PICTURE

Like seashells on a beach, people come in a variety of shapes, sizes, and colors. The global nature of your life requires you to interact with various and diverse people. It is important to be aware of the different layers of diversity and to know the difference between affirmative action and managing diversity.

Do you have any preconceived notions regarding diversity that are worth considering? Let's take a reality check:

- **Assumption: Gender diversity on boards of directors does not impact firm performance.** Wrong, says a study by the Credit Suisse Research Institute. Results from a study of 2,400 companies from 2005 to 2012 showed that "companies with at least one woman on the board would have outperformed stocks with no women on the board by 26 percent over the course of the last 6 years."[26]
- **Assumption: Organizations are having a hard time finding qualified employees during the recessionary period 2012–2013.** Yes, according to a study of 3,400 HR professionals. Two-thirds of the respondents said they had a hard time filling specific job openings; the most difficult jobs to fill included scientists, engineers, technicians and programmers, nurses, doctors, and executives; the biggest skill gaps involved critical thinking, problem solving, written communications, work ethic, and leadership.[27]
- **Assumption: Whites will constitute the majority among US racial groups through 2050.** No, according to the Census Bureau. Today, whites represent 63 percent of the population and this will drop below 50 percent in 2043.[28]

The United States is becoming more diverse in its gender, racial, educational, and age makeup—more working parents, more nonwhite, older, and so on—and the consequences are not always what you might expect. **Demographics are the statistical measurements of populations and their qualities (such as age, race, gender, or income) over time.** The study of demographics helps us to better appreciate diversity and helps managers to develop human resource policies and practices that attract, retain, and develop qualified employees. In the remainder of this chapter we hope to further your understanding of diversity and its managerial challenges.

Layers of Diversity

Diversity represents the multitude of individual differences and similarities that exist among people, making it an input in the Integrative Framework for Understanding and Applying OB. As you will learn, however, managing diversity impacts a variety of processes and outcomes within the Integrative Framework. This is why the topic is so important to managers.

Moreover, diversity pertains to everybody. It is not an issue of age, race, or gender; of being heterosexual, gay, or lesbian; or of being Catholic, Jewish, Protestant,

FIGURE 4.3 THE FOUR LAYERS OF DIVERSITY

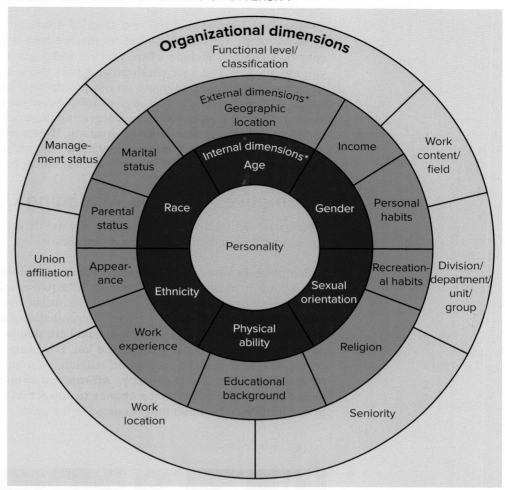

*Internal dimensions and external dimensions are adapted from M. Locken and J. B. Rosener, *Workforce America!* (Homewood, IL: Business One Irwin, 1991).

SOURCE: Reprinted from *Diverse Teams at Work: Capitalizing on the Power of Diversity* by L. Gardenswartz and A. Rowe, with permission of the Society for Human Resource Management (SHRM). © 2003 SHRM. All rights reserved.

or Muslim. Diversity pertains to the host of individual differences that make all of us unique and different from others.

Lee Gardenswartz and Anita Rowe, a team of diversity experts, identified four layers of diversity to help distinguish the important ways in which people differ (see Figure 4.3). Taken together, these layers define your personal identity and influence how each of us sees the world.

Figure 4.3 shows that *personality* is at the center of the diversity wheel because it represents a stable set of characteristics responsible for a person's identity. These are the dimensions of personality we discussed in Chapter 3. The next layer of diversity includes *internal dimensions* that are referred to as surface-level dimensions of diversity. **"Surface-level characteristics are those that are quickly apparent to interactants, such as race, gender, and age."**[29] Because these characteristics are viewed as unchangeable, they strongly influence our attitudes, expectations, and assumptions about others, which, in turn, influence our behavior. Take the encounter experienced by an African-American woman in middle management while vacationing at a resort. While she was sitting by the pool, "a large 50-ish white male approached me and demanded that I get him extra towels. I said, 'Excuse me?' He then said, 'Oh, you don't work here,' with no shred of embarrassment or apology in his voice."[30] Stereotypes regarding one or more of the primary dimensions of diversity most likely influenced this man's behavior toward the woman.

Figure 4.3 shows that the next layer of diversity comprises *external influences*. They represent individual differences that we have a greater ability to influence or control. Examples include where you live today, your religious affiliation, whether you are married and have children, and your work experiences. These dimensions also exert a significant influence on our perceptions, behavior, and attitudes. The final layer of diversity includes *organizational dimensions* such as seniority, job title and function, and work location. Integrating these last two layers results in what is called deep-level characteristics of diversity. **"*Deep-level characteristics* are those that take time to emerge in interactions, such as attitudes, opinions, and values."**[31] These characteristics are definitely under our control.

Affirmative Action vs. Managing Diversity

Affirmative action and managing diversity are driven by very different values and goals. This section highlights these differences.

Affirmative Action   It's important to understand that affirmative action is not a law in and of itself. It is an outgrowth of equal employment opportunity (EEO) legislation. The goal of this legislation is to outlaw discrimination and to encourage organizations to proactively prevent discrimination. ***Discrimination* occurs when employment decisions about an individual are due to reasons not associated with performance or are not related to the job.** For example, organizations cannot discriminate on the basis of race, color, religion, national origin, sex, age, physical and mental disabilities, and pregnancy. ***Affirmative action* is an artificial intervention aimed at giving management a chance to correct an imbalance, injustice, mistake, or outright discrimination that occurred in the past.**

Do the number of white males stand out in this picture? Congress is sometimes criticized for its lack of diversity. Congress is composed of 87 percent whites and 90 percent males.

Affirmative action:

- Can refer to both voluntary and mandatory programs.
- Does not legitimize quotas. Quotas are illegal. They can only be imposed by judges who conclude that a company has engaged in discriminatory practices.
- Does not require companies to hire unqualified people.
- Has created tremendous opportunities for women and minorities.
- Does not foster the type of thinking that is needed to manage diversity effectively.

Is the last point surprising? Research on affirmative action uncovered the following divisive trends. Affirmative action plans are:

1. Perceived more negatively by white males than women and minorities because white males see the plans as working against their own self-interests.
2. Viewed more positively by people who are liberals and Democrats than conservatives and Republicans.
3. Not supported by people who possess racist or sexist attitudes.[32]
4. Found to negatively affect the women and minorities expected to benefit from them. Research demonstrates that women and minorities, supposedly hired on the basis of affirmative action, feel negatively stigmatized as unqualified or incompetent.[33]

Helena Morrissey, CEO of Newton Investment, is a good example on that last point. When asked by a reporter to comment on women being selected to the company board in order to fill a quota, she said, "I find quotas condescending. I wouldn't want to be part of a board because I'm filling a quota."[34]

Managing Diversity   ***Managing diversity*** **enables people to perform up to their maximum potential.** It focuses on changing an organization's culture and infrastructure such that people provide the highest productivity possible. Ann Morrison, a diversity expert, attempted to identify the type of initiatives that companies use to manage diversity. She thus conducted a study of 16 organizations that successfully managed diversity. Her results uncovered three key strategies for success: education, enforcement, and exposure. She describes them as follows:

- **The educational component.** This "strategy has two thrusts: one is to prepare nontraditional managers for increasingly responsible posts, and the other is to help traditional managers overcome their prejudice in thinking about and interacting with people who are of a different sex or ethnicity."[35]
- **The enforcement component.** This strategy "puts teeth in diversity goals and encourages behavior change."[36]
- **The exposure component.** This strategy exposes people to others with different backgrounds and characteristics, which "adds a more personal approach to diversity by helping managers get to know and respect others who are different."[37]

In summary, both consultants and academics believe that organizations should strive to *manage* diversity rather than being forced to use affirmative action.

BUILDING THE BUSINESS CASE FOR MANAGING DIVERSITY

MAJOR QUESTION

What is the business rationale for managing diversity?

THE BIGGER PICTURE

After reviewing the business case for managing diversity, we also look at the demographic changes occurring in the US workforce that make the need to manage diversity all the more urgent. These demographic changes have major implications for OB.

The growing diversity in the United States is not a business initiative; it is a reality. Businesses can consciously choose to manage diversity or get caught short by the demographic changes facing the country.

Business Rationale

The rationale for managing diversity is more than its legal, social, or moral dimension. Quite simply, it's good business. Managing diversity gives the organization the ability to grow and maintain a business in an increasingly competitive marketplace. Here's what William Weldon, former chairman and CEO of Johnson & Johnson, said:

> Diversity and inclusion are part of the fabric of our businesses and are vital to our future success worldwide. The principles of diversity and inclusion are rooted in Our Credo [the company's values] and enhance our ability to deliver products and services to advance the health and well-being of people throughout the world. We cannot afford to reduce our focus on these critical areas in any business climate.[38]

Companies like Johnson & Johnson and Sodexo understand and endorse this proposition. Research also supports the logic of the strategy. For example, a recent study of 739 retail stores found support for the *access-and-legitimacy* perspective, defined in the following manner:

> An *access-and-legitimacy perspective* on diversity is based in recognition that the organization's markets and constituencies are culturally diverse. It therefore behooves the organization to match the diversity in parts of its own workforce as a way of gaining access to and legitimacy with those markets and constituent groups.[39]

This particular study discovered that customer satisfaction and employee productivity were higher when the racio-ethnic composition of customers matched that of store employees.[40]

These favorable results were taken one step further by another team of researchers. They wanted to know if customers would spend more money in stores when they perceived themselves as similar to the sales representatives. Results from 212 stores supported the idea that customer-employee similarity leads to more spending.[41] We hope you get the point. It pays to manage diversity, but organizations cannot use diversity as a strategic advantage if employees fail to contribute their full talents, abilities, motivation, and commitment. It is thus essential for an organization to create an environment or culture that allows all employees to reach their full potential. Managing diversity is a critical component of creating such an environment.

To help you in this endeavor, we review demographic characteristics of the US workforce and then discuss the managerial implications of demographic diversity.

Trends in Workforce Diversity

How is the US workforce changing? Let's examine five categories—gender, race, education, sexual orientation, and age.

Companies increasingly are trying to match the race of their workforce with that of their customers. Here we see African-American customers being helped by an employee of similar race. Why would customers prefer to be helped by someone of a similar race?

Women Break the Glass Ceiling—but Navigate a Labyrinth

Coined in 1986, **the term *glass ceiling* is used to represent an invisible but absolute barrier or solid roadblock that prevents women from advancing to higher-level positions.** Various statistics support the existence of a glass ceiling. The pay gap between men and women is one example. In 2012, the median weekly income in full-time management, professional, and related occupations was $1,328 for men in contrast to $951 for women. This gap continued for MBA graduates. Female graduates from top MBA programs earned 93 cents for every dollar earned by a male graduate, and the pay gap tends to increase over time.[42] Also, a recent WSJ/NBC national poll revealed that 40 percent of the women reported experiencing gender discrimination.[43]

Alice Eagly and her colleague Linda Carli conducted a thorough investigation into the organizational life of women and in 2007 published their conclusions that women had finally broken through the glass ceiling.[44] We updated data originally reported in Eagly and Carli's book and that led to their conclusion. There were many more female CEOs in 2014 (24 and 50 female CEOs within Fortune 500 and Fortune 1000 firms, respectively) and more women in managerial, professional, and related occupations than there were in the 1980s and 1990s.[45] Statistics further showed that women had made strides along several measures:

1. **Educational attainment** (women earned the majority of bachelor's and master's degrees from 2006 through 2012).
2. **Seats on boards of directors of Fortune 500 firms** (9.6% in 1995 and 16.6% in 2013).
3. **Leadership positions in educational institutions** (in 2010, women represented 18.7% of college presidents and 29.9% of board members).
4. **Federal court appointments** (in 2013, 32% and 30% of federal courts of appeals and US district court judges, respectively, were women).[46]

You can interpret the above statistics in one of two ways.

- **No Change.** On the one hand, you might see proof that women remain underpaid and underrepresented in leadership positions, victims of discriminatory organizational practices.
- **Positive Change.** Alternatively, you can agree with Eagly and Carli's conclusion that "men still have more authority and higher wages, but *women have been catching up*. Because some women have moved into the most elite leadership roles, *absolute barriers are a thing of the past*."[47]

Eagly and Carli propose that a woman's career follows a pattern more characteristic of traveling through a labyrinth. They use the labyrinth metaphor because they believe that a woman's path to success is not direct or simple, but rather contains twists, turns, and obstructions, particularly for married women with children.

Racial Groups Face Their Own Glass Ceiling and Perceived Discrimination

The US workforce is becoming increasingly diverse. Between 2012 and 2060, the Census Bureau predicts the following changes in ethnic representation:

- Growth: The Asian population (from 5.1% to 8.2%).
- Growth: The Hispanic population (from 17% to 31%).
- Mild growth: The African-American population (from 13.1% to 14.7%).
- Decline: Non-Hispanic whites (from 63% to 43%).[48]

A female's career is thought to resemble a labyrinth like this. Note the twists and turns that are needed to get through this maze. Have you experienced twists and turns in your career?

All told, the so-called minority groups will constitute approximately 57 percent of the workforce in 2060, according to the Census Bureau.[49] And yet, three additional trends suggest that current-day minority groups are stalled at their own glass ceiling.

Smaller percentage in the professional class. Hispanics, or Latinas/os, and African Americans have a smaller relative hold on managerial and professional jobs within their racial groupings. Women generally do better than men. The percentages shown below are the percentages of professionals *within* each category. When the listing shows Asian men with a 48 percent ranking in managerial/professional jobs, it does not mean that Asian men have 48 percent of all such jobs, but that among all working Asian males, almost one in two is a manager or a professional.[50]

MANAGERIAL/PROFESSIONAL JOBS *WITHIN* RACIAL CATEGORIES				
	ASIAN	WHITE	HISP./LATINA/O	BLACK
Men	**48%**	35%	15%	23%
Women	46%	**41%**	**24%**	**34%**

More discrimination cases. The number of race-based charges of discrimination that were deemed to show reasonable cause by the US Equal Employment Opportunity Commission increased from 294 in 1995 to 957 in 2013. Companies paid a total of $112 million to resolve these claims outside of litigation in 2013.[51]

Lower earnings. Minorities also tend to earn less personal income than whites. Median weekly earnings in 2010 were $1,103, $884, $1,275, and $895 for whites, blacks, Asians, and Hispanics, respectively. Interestingly, Asians had the highest median income.[52]

Mismatch between Education and Occupation Approximately 37 percent of the labor force has a college degree, and college graduates typically earn substantially more than workers with less education.[53] At the same time, however, three trends suggest a mismatch between educational attainment and the knowledge and skills needed by employers.

First, recent studies show that college graduates, while technically and functionally competent, are lacking in terms of teamwork skills, critical thinking, and analytic reasoning. Second, there is a shortage of college graduates in technical fields related to science, math, and engineering. Third, organizations are finding that high-school graduates working in entry-level positions do not possess the basic skills needed to perform effectively. This latter trend is partly due to a national high-school-graduation rate of only 75 percent and the existence of about 32 million adults in the United States who are functionally illiterate.[54]

Literacy is defined as "an individual's ability to read, write, and speak English, compute and solve problems at levels of proficiency necessary to function on the job and in society, to achieve one's goals, and develop one's knowledge and potential."[55] Many studies on illiteracy refer to illiteracy costing America around $60 billion a year in lost productivity. Such costs are worrisome to both government officials and business leaders (see the Example box).

Generational Differences in an Aging Workforce America's population and workforce are getting older, and the workforce includes greater generational differences than ever before. We already see four generations of employees working together, soon to be joined by a fifth (see Table 4.1). Managers need to deal effectively with these generational differences in values, attitudes, and behaviors. Many companies (including IBM, Lockheed Martin, Ernst & Young LLP, and Aetna) address this issue by providing training workshops on generational diversity.

EXAMPLE Why Is a Skills Gap Important to the United States?

The answer is all about the relationship between human capital and economic growth. Results from a global study presented in *The Wall Street Journal* showed that "countries with higher math and science skills have grown faster than those with lower-skilled populations."[56]

WHERE DOES THE UNITED STATES STAND AGAINST OTHER COUNTRIES? The United States, once the envy of the world, in 1990 had the largest percentage of 25- to 34-year-olds with at least a college degree. Now the United States lags behind 14 other developed countries according to the Organization for Economic Cooperation and Development (OECD).[57] More specifically, in 2009 the United States ranked 31st in math—similar to Portugal and Italy—on the OECD's Programme for International Student Assessment. If you consider "advanced" performance on math, "16 countries produced twice as many high achievers per capita than the U.S. did."

WHY IS THE UNITED STATES FALLING BEHIND? There are several reasons. Too many high school dropouts is one. Another has to deal with the degrees students are pursuing. "Not all bachelor's degrees are the same," Georgetown University's Center on Education and the Workforce said in an extensive analysis issue last year. "While going to college is undoubtedly a wise decision, what you take while you're there matters a lot, too."[58] Many students simply are majoring in subjects that are not in demand.

HOW IS THE UNITED STATES TRYING TO OVERCOME THE SKILLS GAP? Referencing this gap, President Obama declared that "by 2020 America will once again have the highest proportion of college graduates in the world."[59] While such rhetoric won't get the job done, it does point the country in the right direction. The president is also pushing for more student aid. Calls for federal and state governments, educators, associations, work councils, and organizations to cooperatively work together to solve this problem may yield results. One renewed idea is an increase in the use of apprenticeships. Apprenticeships let an organization train employees on the skills needed by the business. There were more than 375,000 people registered for apprenticeship programs in 2013.[60]

Educators are retooling the content of what they teach. Ellen Van Velso, a senior fellow at the Center for Creative Leadership, noted that "while undergraduate business administration and MBA programs provide students with a variety of technical skills, leadership and other soft skills are virtually absent in many programs."[61]

Educators are also changing how they teach, for example, with *personalized learning*. Personalized learning entails combining "a new generation of sophisticated adaptive courseware" with the "best of teacher- and computer-delivered instruction." In this vein, some schools in New York City are experimenting with a "comprehensive math program called School of One, in which each student receives a unique daily schedule, called a playlist, based on his or her academic strengths and needs. Students in the same classroom receive substantially different instruction every day, often from several teachers, both in person and online."[62]

YOUR THOUGHTS?

1. Are you hopeful that the United States can regain its dominance in human capital?

2. How valuable do you see each of the specific efforts to reduce the skills gap identified above?

3. What else would you recommend as a solution to cure the skills gap?

Based on the labels used in Table 4.1, how many different generations do you see? Do you think it's harder for a boomer to supervise a Millennial or vice versa?

Table 4.1 summarizes generational differences using common labels: Traditionalists, baby boomers, Gen Xers, Millennials/Gen Ys, and the incoming Gen 2020s. We use such labels (and resulting generalizations) for sake of discussion. There are always exceptions to the characterizations shown in Table 4.1.[63]

Millennials account for the largest block of employees in the workforce, followed by baby boomers. This is important because many Millennials are being managed by boomers who possess very different values and personal traits. Traits, discussed in Chapter 3, represent stable physical and mental characteristics that form an individual's identity. Conflicting values and traits are likely to create friction between people. For example, the workaholic and competitive nature of boomers is likely to conflict with the entitled and work–life balance perspective of Millennials. Managers and employees alike will need to be sensitive to the generational differences highlighted in Table 4.1.

TABLE 4.1 GENERATIONAL DIFFERENCES

	TRADITIONALISTS	BABY BOOMERS	GEN XERS	MILLENNIALS (GEN YS)	GEN 2020
Birth Time Span	1925–1945	1946–1964	1965–1979	1980–2001	2002–
Current Population	38.6 million	78.3 million	62 million	92 million	23 million
Key Historical Events	Great Depression, World War II, Korean War, Cold War era, rise of suburbs	Vietnam War, Watergate, assassinations of John and Robert Kennedy and Martin Luther King, women's rights, Kent State killings, first man on the moon	MTV, AIDS epidemic, Gulf War, fall of Berlin Wall, Oklahoma City bombing, 1987 stock market crash, Bill Clinton–Monica Lewinsky scandal	September 11th terrorist attack, Google, Columbine High School shootings, Enron and other corporate scandals, wars in Iraq and Afghanistan, Hurricane Katrina, financial crisis of 2008 and high unemployment	Social media, election of Barack Obama, financial crisis of 2008 and high unemployment
Broad Traits	Patriotic, loyalty, discipline, conformist, high work ethic, respect for authority	Workaholic, idealistic, work ethic, competitive, materialistic, seeks personal fulfillment	Self-reliance, work–life balance, adaptable, cynical, distrust authority, independent, technologically savvy	Entitled, civic minded, close parental involvement, cyberliteracy, appreciate diversity, multitasking, work–life balance, technologically savvy	Multitasking, online life, cyberliteracy, communicate fast and online
Defining Invention	Fax machine	Personal computer	Mobile phone	Google and Facebook	Social media and iPhone apps

SOURCE: Adapted from J. C. Meister and K. Willyerd, *The 2020 Workplace* (New York: Harper Collins, 2010), 54–55; and R. Alsop, *The Trophy Kids Grow Up* (San Francisco: Jossey-Bass, 2008), 5.

Have age-related differences at school or work caused any conflicts for you? The following Self-Assessment was created to assess your attitudes toward older employees. Because the term "older" is relative, we encourage you to define "older employees" in your own terms when completing the assessment.

Mc Graw Hill Education connect

SELF-ASSESSMENT 4.1 **Attitudes about Working with Older Employees**

Go to connect.mheducation.com and take Self-Assessment 4.1. Then consider the following questions:

1. What is your attitude about working with older employees? Are you surprised by the results?

2. What is your level of satisfaction working with older employees?

3. Based on your results, what can you do to improve your satisfaction associated with working with older employees?

4.6 BARRIERS AND CHALLENGES TO MANAGING DIVERSITY

MAJOR QUESTION

What are the most common barriers to implementing successful diversity programs?

THE BIGGER PICTURE

Wouldn't you rather know what obstacles lay ahead, instead of discovering them too late? We share 11 common challenges in effectively managing diversity.

Diversity is a sensitive, potentially volatile, and sometimes uncomfortable issue for people. For example, some think that diversity programs serve to create reverse discrimination against whites, and others believe that it is immoral to be anything other than heterosexual. It is therefore not surprising that organizations encounter significant barriers when trying to move forward with diversity initiatives. The following is a list of the most common barriers to implementing successful diversity programs:[64]

1. **Inaccurate stereotypes and prejudice.** This barrier manifests itself in the belief that differences are viewed as weaknesses. In turn, this promotes the view that diversity hiring will mean sacrificing competence and quality. A good example can be seen by considering a particular stereotype that significantly disadvantages women during salary negotiations. "Women are generally seen as low in competence but high in warmth, and men are seen as high in competence but low in warmth."[65] Research shows that women experience backlash when they engage in gender-incongruent behaviors like being an aggressive negotiator. The end result is that recruiters or hiring managers lose interest in hiring or working with women who violate the high-warmth, low-competence stereotype.[66]

2. **Ethnocentrism.** The ethnocentrism barrier represents the feeling that one's cultural rules and norms are superior or more appropriate than the rules and norms of another culture.

3. **Poor career planning.** This barrier is associated with the lack of opportunities for diverse employees to get the type of work assignments that qualify them for senior management positions.

4. **A negative diversity climate.** We define organizational climate in Chapter 7 as employee perceptions about an organization's formal and informal policies, practices, and procedures. **Diversity climate is a subcomponent of an organization's overall climate and is defined as the employees' aggregate "perceptions about the organization's diversity-related formal structure characteristics and informal values."**[67] Diversity climate is positive when employees view the organization as being fair to all types of employees; the concept of organizational fairness is raised again in Chapter 5. Recent research revealed that a positive diversity climate enhanced employees' psychological safety. **Psychological safety reflects the extent to which people feel safe to express their ideas and beliefs without fear of negative consequences.** As you might expect, psychological safety is positively associated with outcomes in the Integrative Framework.[68]

5. **An unsupportive and hostile working environment for diverse employees.** Sexual, racial, and age harassment are common examples of hostile work environments.

Whether perpetrated against women, men, older individuals, or LGBT people, hostile environments are demeaning, unethical, and appropriately called "work environment pollution." You certainly won't get employees' best work if they believe that the work environment is hostile toward them. Remember, a hostile work environment is perceptual. This means that people have different perceptions of what entails "hostility." It also is important to note that harassment can take place via e-mail, texting, and other forms of social media.

6. **Lack of political savvy on the part of diverse employees.** Diverse employees may not get promoted because they do not know how to "play the game" of getting along and getting ahead in an organization. Research reveals that women and people of color are excluded from organizational networks.[69] Some organizations attempt to overcome this barrier by creating employee-resource groups. These groups encourage individuals with similar backgrounds to share common experiences and success strategies. American Express has 16 network groups and Cisco has 11.[70]

7. **Difficulty in balancing career and family issues.** Women still assume the majority of the responsibilities associated with raising children. This makes it harder for women to work evenings and weekends or to frequently travel once they have children. Even without children in the picture, household chores take more of a woman's time than a man's time.

8. **Fears of reverse discrimination.** Some employees believe that managing diversity is a smoke screen for reverse discrimination. This belief leads to very strong resistance because people feel that one person's gain is another's loss.

9. **Diversity is not seen as an organizational priority.** This leads to subtle resistance that shows up in the form of complaints and negative attitudes. Employees may complain about the time, energy, and resources devoted to diversity that could have been spent doing "real work."

10. **The need to revamp the organization's performance appraisal and reward system.** Performance appraisals and reward systems must reinforce the need to effectively manage diversity. This means that success will be based on a new set of criteria. For example, General Electric evaluates the extent to which its managers are inclusive of employees with different backgrounds. These evaluations are used in salary and promotion decisions.[71]

11. **Resistance to change.** Effectively managing diversity entails significant organizational and personal change. As discussed in Chapter 16, people resist change for many different reasons.

Now that you know about the importance of the diversity climate, are you curious about the diversity climate in a current or former employer? If yes, take the Self-Assessment below. It measures the components of an organization's diversity climate and will enable you to determine if your employer has or had a favorable or unfavorable climate.

connect

SELF-ASSESSMENT 4.2   Assessing an Organization's Diversity Climate

Go to connect.mheducation.com and take Self-Assessment 4.2. Then consider the following questions:

1. What were the three highest- and lowest-rated survey items? What does this tell you about your employer?

2. Based on these scores, what advice would you give to the person in charge of human resources at the company you evaluated?

In summary, managing diversity is a critical component of organizational success. It is not an easy task, but it is important if you want to create an environment that engages and motivates employees to do their best.

ORGANIZATIONAL PRACTICES USED TO EFFECTIVELY MANAGE DIVERSITY

MAJOR QUESTION

What are organizations doing to effectively manage diversity, and what works best?

THE BIGGER PICTURE

Whether you manage a diverse work group or find yourself managed within a diverse work group, you'll do better by understanding the various ways in which organizations attempt to manage diversity. You'll be able to review eight options in the following. *Hint:* We recommend mutual adaptation.

What are organizations doing to effectively manage diversity? We can answer this question by first providing a framework for categorizing organizational initiatives.

Framework of Options

One especially relevant framework was developed by R. Roosevelt Thomas Jr., a diversity expert. He identified eight generic action options that can be used to address any type of diversity issue. After describing each action option, we discuss relationships among them.[72]

Option 1: Include/Exclude   This choice is an outgrowth of affirmative-action programs. Its primary goal is to either increase or decrease the number of diverse people at all levels of the organization. Shoney's restaurant chain represents a good example of a company that attempted to include diverse employees after settling a discrimination lawsuit. The company subsequently hired African Americans into positions of dining-room supervisors and vice presidents, added more franchises owned by African Americans, and purchased more goods and services from minority-owned companies.[73]

Option 2: Deny   People using this option deny that differences exist. Denial may manifest itself in proclamations that all decisions are color, gender, and age blind and that success is solely determined by merit and performance. Consider Novartis Pharmaceuticals, for example. The company lost a gender discrimination lawsuit to a class of 5,600 female representatives, costing the company $152 million. Holly Waters, one of the plaintiffs, charged that "she was not only paid less than her male equivalents at Novartis, but was fired when she was seven months pregnant after taking a few weeks off on advice of her doctors." Holly Waters was the highest performer in her district.[74] Novartis denied that gender discrimination was a companywide issue despite the fact that 5,600 women will receive compensation.[75]

Option 3: Assimilate   The basic premise behind this alternative is that all diverse people will learn to fit in or become like the dominant group. It only takes time and reinforcement for people to see the light. Organizations initially assimilate employees through their recruitment practices and the use of company-orientation programs. New hires generally are put through orientation programs that aim to provide employees with the organization's preferred values and a set of standard operating procedures. Employees then are encouraged to refer to the policies and procedures manual when they are confused about what to do in a specific situation. These practices create homogeneity among employees.

Option 4: Suppress   Differences are squelched or discouraged when using this approach. This can be done by telling or reinforcing others to quit whining and complaining about issues. The old "you've got to pay your dues" line is another frequently used way to promote the status quo.

Option 5: Isolate   This option maintains the current way of doing things by setting the diverse person off to the side. In this way the individual is unable to influence organizational change. Managers can isolate people by putting them on special projects. Entire work groups or departments are isolated by creating functionally independent entities, frequently referred to as "silos." Shoney Inc.'s employees commented to a *Wall Street Journal* reporter about isolation practices formerly used by the company:

> White managers told of how Mr. Danner [previous chairman of the company] told them to fire blacks if they became too numerous in restaurants in white neighborhoods; if they refused, they would lose their jobs, too. Some also said that when Mr. Danner was expected to visit their restaurant, they scheduled black employees off that day or, in one case, hid them in the bathroom. Others said blacks' applications were coded and discarded.[76]

Option 6: Tolerate   Toleration entails acknowledging differences but not valuing or accepting them. It represents a live-and-let-live approach that superficially allows organizations to give lip service to the issue of managing diversity. Toleration is different from isolation in that it allows for the inclusion of diverse people. However, differences are not really valued or accepted when an organization uses this option.

Option 7: Build Relationships   This approach is based on the premise that good relationships can overcome differences. It addresses diversity by fostering quality relationships—characterized by acceptance and understanding—among diverse groups. Marriott, for example, has paired younger and older employees into teams so that they can more effectively capitalize on their strengths and weaknesses.[77]

Marriott hotels is upgrading the look in its hotel rooms to appeal to a wider base of customers. Here we see J.W. Marriott Jr. (right) with his three sons, John (left), Steve (second left), and David pulling on a ceremonial gold rope to unveil a model of the new room design.

Option 8: Foster Mutual Adaptation   In this option, people are willing to adapt or change their views for the sake of creating positive relationships with others. This implies that employees and management alike must be willing to accept differences and, most important, agree that everyone and everything is open for change. Diversity training is one way to kick-start mutual adaptation. Research shows that such training can positively enhance people's attitudes and feelings about working with diverse employees.[78]

Conclusions about Action Options   Although the action options can be used alone or in combination, some are clearly better than others. Exclusion, denial, assimilation, suppression, isolation, and toleration are among the least preferred options. Inclusion, building relationships, and mutual adaptation are the preferred strategies. That said, Thomas reminds us that mutual adaptation is the only approach that unquestionably endorses the philosophy behind managing diversity. In closing this discussion, it is important to note that choosing how to best manage diversity is a dynamic process that is determined by the context at hand. For instance, some organizations are not ready for mutual adaptation. The best one might hope for in this case is the inclusion of diverse people.

How Companies Are Responding to the Challenges of Diversity

We close the chapter by sharing some examples and models that demonstrate how companies are responding to emerging challenges of managing diversity. If you compare the following actions against Thomas's framework, you'll find the greatest activity around Options 7 and 8, of building relationships or fostering mutual adaptation.

Response: Paying Attention to Sexual Orientation   A research project conducted by the Williams Institute at UCLA revealed that about 3.5 percent of adults identify as lesbian, gay, bisexual, and transgender (LGBT). This amounts to 9 million Americans.[79] But there are challenges. It is currently legal in 29 states to fire employees whose sexual orientation is something other than heterosexual, and it is legal in 34 states to fire transgender individuals.[80] This situation is likely to create negative job attitudes and feelings of marginalization for LGBT people. Corporate law firm Bingham McCutchen and Adobe Systems have tried to overcome this problem by instituting programs such as additional benefits for transgender employees and same-sex-partner benefits.[81]

Response: Responding to Changing Customer Demographics   A Citizens Union Bank branch in Louisville, Kentucky, designed and staffed the branch with the goal of attracting more Latina/o customers. The interior contains "bright, colorful walls of yellows and blues, large-scale photos of Latin American countries, comfortable couches, sit-down desks, a children's play area, a television tuned to Hispanic programming and even a vending area stocked with popular Latin American–brand soft drinks and snacks." The branch also took on a new name: Nuestro Banco, Spanish for "Our Bank." Branch deposits are setting records, and the CEO is planning to use this same model in other locations.[82]

The point to remember is that companies need to adopt policies and procedures that meet the needs of all employees. As such, programs such as day care and elder care, flexible work schedules, and benefits such as paternal leaves, less-rigid relocation policies, concierge services, and mentoring programs are likely to become more popular.

Response: Helping Women Navigate the Career Labyrinth   Organizations can make navigation easier by providing the developmental assignments that prepare women for promotional opportunities and providing flexible work schedules. For example, Boston Consulting Group "focuses heavily on recruiting and retaining women, offering part-time options, mentoring and professional-development programs." Companies like McKinsey & Co. and Goldman Sachs Groups are using "on-ramping" programs to attract former female employees to return to work. ***On-ramping* represents the process companies use to encourage people to reenter the workforce after a temporary career break.** Goldman, for example, instituted "returnship" programs that offer short-term job assignments to former employees.[83]

Response: Helping Hispanics Succeed   Miami Children's Hospital and Shaw Industries Inc. in Dalton, Georgia, attempted to improve employee productivity, satisfaction, and motivation by developing customized training programs to improve the communication skills of their Spanish-speaking employees.[84] Research further reveals that the retention and career progression of minorities can be significantly enhanced through effective mentoring.

Response: Providing both Community and Corporate Training to Reduce the Mismatch between Education and Job Requirements   To combat this issue on a more global level, companies like JPMorgan Chase & Co. are partnering with local communities. JPMorgan started The Fellowship Initiative (TFI) in New York in 2010 and expanded it to Chicago and Los Angeles in 2014. The goal of the program is to provide intensive academic and leadership training to young men of color. Jamie Dimon, chairman and CEO of JPMorgan, is committed to the program. He concluded that "these young men need access to high quality education and positive role models in and outside the classroom." New York City Mayor Michael Bloomberg applauded JPMorgan's effort by concluding that "we need more civic-minded companies and organizations to step up and join this work, and I congratulate JPMorgan Chase for being a leader in this effort and for making a real difference in the lives of young men of color in our city."[85]

At the individual corporate level, companies like Wheeler Machinery Co. in Salt Lake City have instituted specialized training programs that enable less-qualified people to perform more technically oriented jobs. Lockheed Martin and Agilent Technologies also offer some type of paid apprenticeship or internship to attract high-school students interested in the sciences.[86]

Response: Retaining and Valuing Skills and Expertise in an Aging Workforce
Here are seven initiatives that can help organizations to motivate and retain an aging workforce:

1. Provide challenging work assignments that make a difference to the firm.
2. Give the employee considerable autonomy and latitude in completing a task.
3. Provide equal access to training and learning opportunities when it comes to new technology.
4. Provide frequent recognition for skills, experience, and wisdom gained over the years.
5. Provide mentoring opportunities whereby older workers can pass on accumulated knowledge to younger employees.
6. Ensure that older workers receive sensitive, high-quality supervision.
7. Design a work environment that is both stimulating and fun.[87]

You'll see a number of these tactics at work in the employers who made AARP's 2013 list of best employers for older workers, as, for example, the training and learning opportunities provided by every employer who made the list. Employers making the list typically offer flextime, compressed work schedules, job sharing, and telecommuting. Representative winners: Scripps Health, National Rural Electric Cooperative Association, and S&T Bank.[88]

Response: Resolving Generational Differences   Traditional and boomer managers are encouraged to consider their approach toward managing the technologically savvy Gen Xers and Gen Ys. Gen Xers and Ys, for instance, are more likely to visit social networking sites during the work day, often perceiving this activity as a "virtual coffee break." In contrast, Traditional and boomer managers are more likely to view this as wasted time, thereby leading to policies that attempt to shut down such activity. Experts suggest that restricting access to social media will not work in the long run if an employer wants to motivate younger employees.

Would you like to improve your working relationships with diverse people? If yes, then the Self-Assessment shown on the following page can help. It asks you to compare yourself with a group of other people you interact with and then to examine the quality of the relationships between yourself and these individuals. This enables you to gain a better understanding of how similarities and differences among people influence your attitudes and behavior.

SELF-ASSESSMENT 4.3   How Does My Diversity Profile Affect My Relationships with Other People?

Go to connect.mheducation.com and take Self-Assessment 4.3. Then consider the following questions:

1. Which diversity dimensions have the greatest influence with respect to the quality of your interpersonal relationships?
2. Consider the person with whom you have the most difficulty working. Which dimensions of diversity may contribute to this bad relationship? What can you do to improve the relationship?

Response: Keep Working at It   Managing diversity takes commitment. Sodexo is a good example (see the box below). The company went from being highly regarded in managing diversity, to encountering diversity-related problems. The company is working to overcome these issues.

solving application

problem

Sodexo Encounters Diversity-Related Problems

Sodexo, one of the world's largest providers of food services and management, with nearly 420,000 employees in 80 countries, is a good example of a company that has attempted to effectively manage diversity. Sodexo has a deserved if well-groomed reputation for its diversity efforts, but the company's record is not perfect. Although the company was rated by DiversityInc in 2013 as the very best company for diversity based on its annual survey of 893 firms, Sodexo still is encountering diversity-related problems.[89]

Problems at Sodexo. Sodexo began its diversity program in 2002 in response to an anti-discrimination class-action lawsuit, brought by African-American employees who claimed they were not being promoted at the same rate as their white colleagues. The suit was eventually settled for $80 million in 2005. In 2010 NPR reported that "about a quarter of the company's managers are minorities, but only about 12 percent are black, which is not much of a change from five years ago, when the lawsuit was settled."[90]

Sodexo continues to have issues with labor and the law. Since the 2005 settlement, allegations of discrimination have continued, although often local in scope. The company has had other labor problems, with workers complaining about low wages. Also in 2010 Sodexo was called out by the Human Rights Watch in a 2010 report detailing the company's violations of workers' rights to unionize at several US

Executives from Sodexo speaking to employees.

locations. On the legal front Sodexo has fought isolated health code violations and charges of pocketing rebates from vendors to the detriment of several state clients.[91] In 2013 Sodexo agreed to pay $20 million in one such rebate fraud lawsuit brought by New York.[92]

YOUR CALL   *Apply the 3-Stop Problem-Solving Approach.*

Stop 1: What is the problem in this case?

Stop 2: Identify the OB concepts or theories to use to solve the problem.

Stop 3: What would you do to correct this situation?

what did i learn?

You learned that social perception and managing diversity are essential for success. Why? *Social perception*, so that you can better understand the perception process, improve how you are perceived, and adjust your own perception to avoid common perceptual errors; *managing diversity* (represented by demographics in our Integrative Framework), so that you can better optimize diversity's effect on individual and group/team outcomes. Reinforce your learning with the Key Points below. Then, consolidate your learning using the Integrative Framework. Finally, Challenge your mastery of the material by answering the Major Questions in your own words.

Key Points for Understanding Chapter 4

You learned the following key points.

4.1 A SOCIAL INFORMATION PROCESSING MODEL OF PERCEPTION

- Perception is a mental and cognitive process that enables us to interpret and understand our surroundings.
- Social perception is a four-stage process. The four stages are selective attention/comprehension, encoding and simplification, storage and retention, and retrieval and response (see Figure 4.1).
- Social perception affects a wide variety of organizational activities including hiring decisions, performance appraisals, leadership, and designing web pages.

4.2 STEREOTYPES

- Stereotypes are used during encoding and represent overgeneralized beliefs about the characteristics of a group.
- Stereotypes are not always negative, and they are not always inaccurate.
- Common stereotypes involve gender, race, and age.
- Stereotyping is a four-step process that includes categorization, inference, expectation formation, and maintenance.
- Stereotypes are maintained by (a) overestimating the frequency of stereotypic behaviors exhibited by others, (b) incorrectly explaining expected and unexpected behaviors, and (c) differentiating minority individuals from oneself.

4.3 CAUSAL ATTRIBUTIONS

- Causal attributions represent suspected or inferred causes of behavior.

- According to Kelley's model of causal attribution, external attributions tend to be made when consensus and distinctiveness are high and consistency is low. Internal (personal responsibility) attributions tend to be made when consensus and distinctiveness are low and consistency is high.
- The fundamental attribution bias involves emphasizing personal factors more than situational factors while formulating attributions. The self-serving bias involves personalizing the causes of one's success and externalizing the causes of one's failures.

4.4 DEFINING AND MANAGING DIVERSITY

- Diversity represents the individual differences that make people different from and similar to each other.
- Diversity varies along "surface-level" characteristics like race, gender, and age. It also varies along "deep-level" characteristics such as attitudes, opinions, and values.
- Affirmative action is an outgrowth of equal employment opportunity legislation and is an artificial intervention aimed at giving management a chance to correct past discrimination.
- Managing diversity entails creating a host of organizational changes that enable all people to perform up to their maximum potential.

4.5 BUILDING THE BUSINESS CASE FOR MANAGING DIVERSITY

- Managing diversity is predicted to be good business because it aims to engage employees and satisfy customers' unique needs.
- There are four key demographic trends: (a) women navigating a labyrinth after breaking the glass ceiling, (b) racial groups encountering a glass ceiling and perceived discrimination, (c) a mismatch existing between workers' educational attainment and occupational requirements, and (d) generational differences in an aging workforce.

4.6 BARRIERS AND CHALLENGES TO MANAGING DIVERSITY

- There are 11 barriers to successfully implementing diversity initiatives: (a) inaccurate stereotypes and prejudice, (b) ethnocentrism, (c) poor career planning, (d) a negative diversity climate, (e) an unsupportive and hostile working environment for diverse employees, (f) lack of political savvy on the part of diverse employees, (g) difficulty in balancing career and family issues, (h) fears of reverse discrimination, (i) diversity not seen as an organizational priority, (j) the need to revamp the organization's performance appraisal and reward system, and (k) resistance to change.

4.7 ORGANIZATIONAL PRACTICES USED TO EFFECTIVELY MANAGE DIVERSITY

• Organizations have eight options that they can use to address diversity issues: (a) include/exclude the number of diverse people at all levels of the organization, (b) deny that differences exist, (c) assimilate diverse people into the dominant group, (d) suppress differences, (e) isolate diverse members from the larger group, (f) tolerate differences among employees, (g) build relationships among diverse employees, and (h) foster mutual adaptation to create positive relationships.

The Integrative Framework for Chapter 4

As shown in Figure 4.4, you learned that demographics representing diversity serve as a key input and perceptions and group/team dynamics are crucial processes. These result in a variety of important outcomes, chief among them well-being/flourishing at the individual level and being the employer of choice and reputation at the organizational level. These outcomes appear in boldface. Other outcomes listed were touched upon in the chapter.

Challenge: Major Questions for Chapter 4

At the start of the chapter, we told you that after reading the chapter you should be able to answer the following major questions. Unless you can, have you really processed and internalized the lessons in the chapter? Refer to the Key Points, Figure 4.4, the chapter itself, and your notes to revisit and answer the following major questions:

1. How does the perception process affect the quality of my decisions and interpersonal relationships?

2. How can I use knowledge of stereotypes to make better decisions and manage more effectively?

3. How do I tend to interpret employee performance?

4. How does awareness about the layers of diversity help organizations effectively manage diversity?

5. What is the business rationale for managing diversity?

6. What are the most common barriers to implementing successful diversity programs?

7. What are organizations doing to effectively manage diversity, and what works best?

FIGURE 4.4 INTEGRATIVE FRAMEWORK FOR UNDERSTANDING AND APPLYING OB

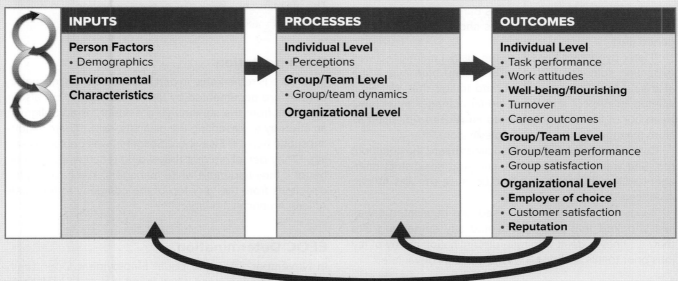

© 2014 Angelo Kinicki and Mel Fugate. All rights reserved. Reproduction prohibited without permission of the authors.

Seal of Disapproval

Wet Seal Inc. sells women's clothes and accessories under two brands in malls and shopping centers across the country (and Puerto Rico). Under the Wet Seal banner, nearly 470 stores target younger female customers aged 13 to 23 years old. Its Arden B brand, through some 80 stores, targets women aged 21 to 39.

These age ranges come from the company itself (at wetsealinc.com), which identifies Wet Seal as a "trend-right fashion retailer" and its target as "girls," with its core customer at 16 years of age, who loves fashion and shops frequently, both in the mall and online. The company identifies Arden B as a "contemporary fashion destination" with its target as "women," and its core customer at 28 years of age, who maintains a full social calendar and is always "dressed."

So far so good. But why would the company want to trigger a furor over outrageously callous and nearly unthinkable racist hiring practices? The issue went public in 2012 but has earlier roots.

Wrong by Race

For Nicole Cogdell the trouble started in 2009 when she and her associates at the Wet Seal store in King of Prussia, Pennsylvania, were preparing to welcome visiting Senior Vice President of Store Operations Barbara Bachman. After the meet and greet, Cogdell was shocked by what happened next.

"I later overheard her say to the district manager, 'I was expecting someone with blond hair and blue eyes.' She also said that I was not the brand image that Wet Seal wanted to project and the regional manager must have been out of her mind to promote an African American as store manager for the King of Prussia store."[93]

Cogdell said that her two associates heard the comment too. She was later terminated, and said her district manager told her she was being fired because she was African American.

"I was completely embarrassed and humiliated. I was just shocked that someone would say something like that. . . . I never dealt with race discrimination at any of my jobs prior to this situation. I was just overall devastated."

Consolation Job

The company offered her a new position. "That job consisted of a demotion from my previous position," she said, with "less pay and going back to the Springfield store. I declined the offer because the company refused to address their policies. I have always been a professional in the workplace, and I believe you should be judged by your performance and not the color of your skin."

Management Edicts

Cogdell's contention that racial bias was a matter of company policy has surprising collaboration. In a March 2009 e-mail to the Vice President of Store Operations and a district manager, under the heading "Global Issues," Bachman wrote, "Store Teams need diversity—African Americans dominate—huge issue." After observing a number of African-American employees working at a store, another senior executive ordered a district manager to "clean the entire store out."[94]

Lawsuit

In 2012 the Legal Defense Fund (LDF) of the National Association of Colored People (NAACP) filed *Cogdell v. Wet Seal*. The class action lawsuit alleged that "top executives at Wet Seal directed senior managers to get rid of African American store management employees for the sake of its 'brand image,' and to hire more white employees."[95]

Joining Cogdell as plaintiffs were two other former Wet Seal employees: Myriam Saint-Hilaire, also from the King of Prussia store, and Kai Hawkins, who had worked at Wet Seal locations in California, New Jersey, and Pennsylvania. The plaintiffs seek back pay, general damages, and punitive damages.

Documentation

"This case is remarkable in part because the discriminatory policies are documented by former managers, but also in an e-mail from the senior vice president," Brad Seligman, an attorney representing the plaintiffs, said. "There is nothing subtle here."[96] Elsewhere Seligman was quoted as saying, "They perceived that they would reach white markets better if they had more white managers. You have explicit directions from the very top of the company to terminate African American managers."[97]

EEOC Determination

In November 2012, the Equal Employment Opportunity Commission announced it had found that Wet Seal illegally discriminated against Cogdell. In its statement, citing unusually blatant evidence of racial discrimination, the director of the commission's Philadelphia office noted that Wet Seal's "corporate managers have openly stated they wanted employees who had the 'Armani look, were white, had blue eyes, thin and blond' to be profitable."[98] *Note:* By this time the EEOC had received over 20 complaints against Wet Seal.[99]

Resigned vs. Being Forced Out

In the suit, Wet Seal claimed that Cogdell had resigned her position for unknown reasons and therefore the company was not guilty of an adverse employment action. In contrast, the EEOC determination was that the hostile environment forced her to resign and that resignation was her only recourse.

Selective Diversity

In defending her e-mail in an August 2012 deposition, Bachman said she wrote her comments to stress the importance of having diversity in all stores. The EEOC determination noted that "witness interviews revealed that Bachman never expressed diversity concerns in stores with a predominantly white sales force but encouraged it because the sales force mirrored the community."[100] Bachman, by the way, left Wet Seal in 2011 and is now a retail consultant.

Race, Retail, Body Image

As of a recent visit to the Wet Seal site (wetseal.com), five photographs showed eight young women in all, with some models appearing more than once. All women were young, thin, and attractive; all but one model were clearly white. The one non-Caucasian model, who may be African American or of mixed race, appeared twice, once alone and once standing with another model. The site also has numerous links at the bottom of the page to stress the company's commitment to diversity.

Online Demographics

While Wet Seal does not publish the demographics of its customers beyond targeting specific age groups, a web analytics company purports to do just that. Quantcast Corporation routinely provides free analytics of web traffic to major vendors to induce the vendors to purchase its premium data services. Basically Quantcast extrapolates specific demographic data from known profiles developed from unique computer or ISP identifiers. With caveats that its statistics on wetseal.com are partial and include estimates, the stats are most useful as relative measures compared to the demographics associated with all web users.

A recent tally by Quantcast showed wetseal.com traffic in **gender** to be 64% female (vs. 51% for the net overall). In **age**, the under 18-component at 36% was highest, followed by the 18–24 group at 28% (vs. 18% and 12% for the net overall). In **race**, visitors were 49% Caucasian and 26% African American, followed by Hispanic and Asian segments (vs. 75% Caucasian and 9% African American, again followed by Hispanic and Asian). The figures relate only to visits and not sales.

Employee View

Meanwhile, current employee reviews of Wet Seal as an employer on the employer ranking site *glassdoor.com* do not mention racial discrimination, but some reviews complain of favoritism, especially on the basis of appearance.

Apply the 3-Stop Problem-Solving Approach to OB

Use the Integrative Framework in Figure 4.4 along the journey through all three stops to help identify inputs, processes, and outcomes relative to this case.

Stop 1. Define the problem.

Stop 2. Identify the OB concepts or theories to use to solve the problem.

Stop 3. Make recommendations and (if appropriate) take action.

And then . . .

- Justify your solution.
- Tell how you will evaluate the effectiveness of your solution.

LEGAL/ETHICAL CHALLENGE

Swastikas and Neonatal Care

This case involved an incident that occurred at Hurley Medical Center in Michigan. It resulted in a lawsuit.

Tonya Battle, a veteran black nurse in Hurley's neonatal intensive care unit, was taking care of a baby when a man walked into the unit. The man, who had a swastika tattoo, reached for the baby and was stopped by Tonya. She asked to see the wristband that identified him as the baby's parent. This was apparently hospital policy. "He abruptly told her he wanted to see her supervisor, who then advised Battle she should no longer care for the child."[101]

The man requested that no African-American nurses should take care of his child.

A note was subsequently put on the assignment clipboard saying, "No African American nurse to take care of baby." Tonya was "shocked, offended, and in disbelief that she was so egregiously discriminated against based on her race and re-assigned, according to the lawsuit, which asks for punitive damages for emotional stress, mental anguish, humiliation and damages to her reputation.[102] Battle could not understand why the hospital would accommodate the man's request. Although the note was later removed, black nurses were not allowed to care for the child for about a month.

It is important to note that the "American Medical Association's ethics code bars doctors from refusing to treat people based on race, gender, and other criteria, but there are no specific policies for handling race-based requests from patients." Further, a survey of "emergency physicians found patients often make such requests, and they are routinely accommodated. A third of doctors who responded said they felt patients perceive better care from providers of shared demographics, with racial matches considered more important than gender or religion."[103]

Your Views

What would you have done if you were a medical administrator at the time the request was made?

1. I would not have honored the man's request. I would have explained why Tonya Battle and other African-American nurses are best suited to take care of his child.

2. I would have done exactly what the hospital did. The man has a right to have his child taken care of by someone with a race or gender of his choosing.

What would you do about the lawsuit?

1. Fight it. It's ridiculous that someone would feel emotional stress and humiliation from simply being reassigned.

2. Settle the lawsuit and create a policy that prohibits honoring future requests like this.

3. Settle the lawsuit but not create a policy prohibiting accommodating such requests. Rather, hold a hospitalwide meeting explaining the rationale for why the hospital needs to accommodate such requests.

GROUP EXERCISE

Managing Diversity-Related Interactions

Objectives

1. To improve your ability to manage diversity-related interactions more effectively.

2. To explore different approaches for handling diversity interactions.

Introduction

The interpersonal component of managing diversity can be awkward and uncomfortable. This is partly due to the fact that resolving diversity interactions requires us to deal with situations we may never have encountered before. The purpose of this exercise is to help you manage diversity-related interactions more effectively. To do so, you will be asked to read three scenarios and then decide how you will handle each situation.

Instructions

Presented here are three scenarios depicting diversity-related interactions. Please read the first scenario, and then answer the three questions that follow it. Follow the same procedure for the next two scenarios. Next, divide into groups of three. One at a time, each person should present his or her responses to the three questions for the first scenario. The groups should then discuss the various approaches that were proposed to resolve the diversity interaction and try to arrive at a consensus recommendation. Follow the same procedure for the next two scenarios.

SCENARIO 1

Dave, who is one of your direct reports, comes to you and says that he and Scott are having a special commitment ceremony to celebrate the beginning of their lives together. He has invited you to the ceremony. Normally the department has a party and cake for special occasions. Mary, who is one of Dave's peers, has just walked into your office and asks you whether you intend to have a party for Dave.

A. How would you respond?

_____

_____

_____

B. What is the potential impact of your response?

_____

_____

_____

C. If you choose not to respond, what is the potential impact of your behavior?

_____

_____

_____

SCENARIO 2

You have an open position for a supervisor, and your top two candidates are an African-American female and a white female. Both candidates are equally qualified. The position is responsible for five white team leaders. You hire the white female because the work group likes her. The team leaders said that they felt more comfortable with the white female. The vice president of human resources has just called you on the phone and asks you to explain why you hired the white female.

A. How would you respond?

_____

_____

_____

B. What is the potential impact of not hiring the African American?

_____

_____

_____

C. What is the potential impact of hiring the African American?

_____

_____

_____

SCENARIO 3

While attending an off-site business meeting, you are waiting in line with a group of team leaders to get your lunch at a buffet. Without any forewarning, one of your peers in the line loudly says, "Thank goodness Terry is at the end of the line. With his size and appetite there wouldn't be any food left for the rest of us." You believe Terry may have heard this comment, and you feel the comment was more of a "weight-related" slur than a joke.

A. How would you respond?

_____

_____

_____

B. What is the potential impact of your response?

_____

_____

_____

C. If you choose not to respond, what is the potential impact of your behavior?

_____

_____

_____

Questions for Discussion

1. What was the recommended response for each scenario?

2. Which scenario generated the most emotion and disagreement? Explain why this occurred.

3. What is the potential impact of a manager's lack of response to Scenarios 1 and 3? Explain.

5 FOUNDATIONS OF EMPLOYEE MOTIVATION

How Can I Apply Motivation Theories?

inputs

PERSON FACTORS

ENVIRONMENTAL CHARACTERISTICS

processes

INDIVIDUAL LEVEL
Motivation

GROUP/TEAM LEVEL

ORGANIZATIONAL LEVEL

outcomes

INDIVIDUAL LEVEL

GROUP/TEAM LEVEL

ORGANIZATIONAL LEVEL

© 2014 Angelo Kinicki and Mel Fugate. All rights reserved. Reproduction prohibited without permission of the authors.

MAJOR TOPICS I'LL LEARN AND QUESTIONS I SHOULD BE ABLE TO ANSWER

5.1 THE WHAT AND WHY OF MOTIVATION
MAJOR QUESTION: *What is motivation and how does it affect my behavior?*

5.2 CONTENT THEORIES OF MOTIVATION
MAJOR QUESTION: *How would I compare and contrast the content theories of motivation?*

5.3 PROCESS THEORIES OF MOTIVATION
MAJOR QUESTION: *How would I compare and contrast the process theories of motivation?*

5.4 MOTIVATING EMPLOYEES THROUGH JOB DESIGN
MAJOR QUESTION: *What are the similarities and differences among top-down approaches, bottom-up approaches, and "idiosyncratic deals" in job design?*

INTEGRATIVE FRAMEWORK FOR UNDERSTANDING AND APPLYING OB

This chapter focuses on one key individual-level process—motivation—that has positive relationships with a number of important outcomes. As you read the chapter, note what outcomes are influenced by employee motivation.

winning at work

DISCUSSING PAY AT WORK

Ever wonder how your pay compares to that of someone else at the same company? Brian Bader did. He had just been hired for a technology-support job at Apple for $12 per hour and was told not to discuss salary with other employees. This requirement just made him curious. He decided to ask coworkers about their salary and found that most people were being paid between $10 and $12 per hour.

PAY INEQUITY

Brian was not upset about his relative pay at first, but it later became the cause of his decision to quit his job. He learned from performance data that were shared with work teams that he was twice as productive as the lowest performer on the team yet earned only 20 percent more. "It irked me. If I'm doing double the work, why am I not seeing double the pay?" he said when interviewed for *The Wall Street Journal*.[1] In OB we see his situation as an example of pay inequity.

HOW DO COMPANIES HANDLE DECISIONS ABOUT PAY?

Many companies tell employees not to discuss pay with coworkers. Others threaten to fire people who discuss pay at work. Why? Quite simply, when such disparities become public, they "can engender resentment, envy and dissatisfaction among workers." Keeping salaries private also helps companies "to retain the upper hand on salary negotiation and hope to keep flawed or even discriminatory compensation systems under wraps."[2]

Pay secrecy policies do not sit well with younger employees like Millennials, who are more willing to talk about pay and even discuss such things on social media. Other companies, like SumAll, are less secretive. This small data-analytics company in Manhattan believes that openness and transparency are more

likely to motivate Millennials. SumAll allows employees to see "investor agreements, company financials, performance appraisals, hiring decisions and employees' pay, along with each worker's equity and bonuses" on a shared drive.[3] Would you like to work at SumAll?

SHOULD YOU DISCUSS PAY WHILE AT WORK?

The answer depends on your role and position. Experts contend that the National Labor Relations Act prohibits companies from stopping the rank-and-file employees (i.e., people paid by the hour) from discussing salary and benefits packages outside of work time. This applies to social media as well. The rules are different, however, for managers and supervisors. They can legally be prevented from discussing pay.[4]

If you decide to discuss pay at work, keep the following recommendations in mind: (1) restrict your conversations to people you trust, (2) don't brag about your pay, and (3) understand your company's policy on the matter.

FOR YOU WHAT'S AHEAD IN THIS CHAPTER

We have all observed, or even worked in, dysfunctional organizations where managers don't seem to have a clue about how to motivate workers. OB supplies proven methods of how to motivate employees. These aren't just abstract theories. All spring from observation and study of the workplace, and they are validated in real-life testing. Business professionals treasure them as tools for making work better and more productive. We'll show you how they work and give practical tips and suggestions for implementation.

major question

What is motivation and how does it affect my behavior?

THE BIGGER PICTURE

You may feel we're about to get too personal. Intellectually you can identify motivation as a key process within the Integrative Framework to Understand and Apply OB, or study the psychological processes that drive it. But emotionally what you're about to read may remind you of a time when you worked in a group or organization and something made you stop and ask yourself why you even bothered. Or on the contrary, maybe you've been surprised by how consumed you have been by a particular job or volunteer effort.

For example, have you ever persisted at a difficult task when you seemed to be making no progress? Would you be willing to work extra hours for no pay? How about working extra hours for the *chance* of receiving more pay? Consider the deal offered by Hilcorp Energy, the third largest, privately held energy exploration and production company in the United States. The company "promised staff in 2010 that if the company doubles its production rate and reserves by 2015, every employee will get a check for $100,000."[5] Motivation theories help us understand our own behaviors in organizational settings and provide us tools for motivating others.

Motivation: What Is It, and Why Is It Important?

Motivation explains why we do the things we do. It explains why you are dressed the way you are right now and it can account for what you plan to do this evening. This chapter will guide how you can use principles of motivation to help achieve personal, team, and organizational goals.

How Does It Work?   The term *motivation* derives from the Latin word *movere*, meaning "to move." In the present context, **motivation refers to the psychological processes "that underlie the direction, intensity, and persistence of behavior or thought."**[6] "Direction pertains to *what* an individual is attending to at a given time, intensity represents the *amount* of effort being invested in the activity, and persistence represents *for how long* that activity is the focus of one's attention."[7] It can be tricky to understand motivation because you can't actually see it or know it in someone else. Motivation is inferred from one's behavior or from the results associated with behavior. Nonetheless, it is important to understand the principles of motivation if you want to direct your behavior toward achieving personal goals or to manage others in the pursuit of organizational goals.

You could start with the Integrative Framework to Understand and Apply OB (see beginning of chapter). Motivation is fueled by inputs that come from person and environmental factors. For example, our personality, values, and needs motivate us to behave in ways that satisfy our needs and goals. Just the same, many environmental characteristics impact motivation, including job design, discussed later in this chapter, rewards systems (discussed in Chapter 6), leadership (reviewed in Chapter 13), and organizational climate (introduced in Chapter 4).

Performers in many arenas—not just competitive dancing—are motivated to excel by extrinsic factors, such as prize money, praise, recognition from others, and titles. However, often times the key motivators are also, or instead, intrinsic, like a feeling of challenge and accomplishment.

There are two types of motivation: extrinsic motivation and intrinsic motivation.

- **Extrinsic motivation** results from the potential or actual receipt of extrinsic rewards. Extrinsic rewards like recognition, money, or a promotion represent a "payoff" received from others for performing a particular task. For example, Hilcorp Energy gave 400 employees a bonus of $50,000 toward the purchase of a new car when they achieved a specific performance goal. Would $50,000 motivate you to work harder in the future? The company believed so.

- **Intrinsic motivation** occurs when an individual is "turned on to one's work because of the positive internal feelings that are generated by doing well, rather than being dependent on external factors (such as incentive pay or compliments from the boss) for the motivation to work effectively."[8] As you can see we create our own intrinsic motivation by giving ourselves intrinsic rewards such as positive emotions, satisfaction, and self-praise. Consider the intrinsic motivation being displayed by the 2014 winners of *Dancing with the Stars*—Meryl Davis and Maksim Chmerkovskiy. The joy on their faces demonstrates the engagement and fun they are having while dancing.

Why Is Motivation Important?   Quite simply, motivation is the fuel that drives results and performance. That said, however, there are five generic reasons why managers care about motivation. They are:

1. **Join the organization.** Managers want to motivate high-quality job applicants to come to work for them.

2. **Stay with the organization.** Research shows that higher performers are more likely to leave an organization than average employees. Managers clearly want to motivate talented employees to remain with the company in good times and bad.[9]

3. **Be engaged at work.** We discussed in Chapter 2 that only 60 percent of the global workforce is engaged while at work.[10] Competitiveness suggests that it is crucial for managers to motivate employees in ways that lead to engagement.

4. **Perform organizational citizenship behaviors (OCBs).** OCBs were discussed in Chapter 2. They represent behaviors that go beyond the official duties or requirements of one's job, and they are positively related to other important OB outcomes.

5. **Help others.** Collaboration and cooperation are key in today's workplace. Managers want to motivate employees to help others in the pursuit of organizational goals.

The Two Fundamental Perspectives on Motivation: An Overview

Researchers have proposed two general categories of motivation theories: content theories and process theories. Content theories of motivation focus on identifying internal factors such as needs and satisfaction that energize employee motivation. Process theories of motivation focus on explaining the process by which internal factors and environmental characteristics influence employee motivation.[11] Process theories are more dynamic than content theories.

5.2 CONTENT THEORIES OF MOTIVATION

MAJOR QUESTION

How would I compare and contrast the content theories of motivation?

THE BIGGER PICTURE

You'll find that many theories deal with the content of what motivates individuals. Much of this will hit close to home as you think about what really motivates you in school or at work. Many of these theories come from other disciplines. So in other courses you may have already encountered Maslow's hierarchy of needs and related content theories like McGregor's Theory X and Theory Y, acquired needs theory, self-determination theory, and Herzberg's motivator-hygiene theory.

major question

Most **content theories of motivation** revolve around the notion that an employee's **needs influence motivation.** Content theorists ask, "What are the different needs that activate motivation's direction, intensity, and persistence." **Needs** are defined as **physiological or psychological deficiencies that arouse behavior.** They can be strong or weak and are influenced by environmental factors. Thus, human needs vary over time and place.

Content theories include:

- McGregor's Theory X and Theory Y
- Maslow's need hierarchy theory
- Acquired needs theory
- Self-determination theory
- Herzberg's motivator-hygiene theory

McGregor's Theory X and Theory Y

Douglas McGregor wrote a book entitled *The Human Side of Enterprise* in which he outlined his theory.[12] Drawing on his experience as a management consultant, McGregor formulated two sharply contrasting sets of assumptions about human nature. **Theory X** is a pessimistic view of employees: that they dislike work, must be monitored, and can only be motivated with rewards and punishment ("carrots and sticks"). McGregor felt this was the typical perspective of managers. To help managers break with this negative tradition, McGregor formulated his own Theory Y. **Theory Y** is a **modern and positive set of assumptions about people at work: that they are self-engaged, committed, responsible, and creative.** For example, a study of leaders in six top IT firms showed that Theory Y behaviors positively influenced virtual team members' trust, cooperation, and technology adaptation.[13]

Maslow's Need Hierarchy Theory: Five Levels of Needs

In 1943, psychologist Abraham Maslow published his now-famous need hierarchy theory of motivation. Although the theory was based on his clinical observation of

FIGURE 5.1 MASLOW'S NEED HIERARCHY

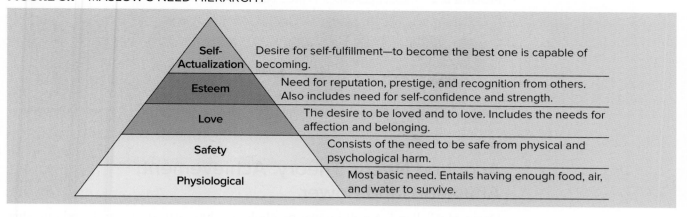

a few neurotic individuals, it has subsequently been used to explain the entire spectrum of human behavior. **The *need hierarchy theory* states that motivation is a function of five basic needs: physiological, safety, love, esteem, and self-actualization.** See Figure 5.1.

The Five Levels Maslow proposed that the five needs are met sequentially and relate to each other in a prepotent hierarchy (see Figure 5.1). "Prepotent" means that the current most-pressing need would be met first before the next need becomes the most powerful or potent. In other words, he believed human needs generally emerge in a predictable stair-step fashion. Thus when physiological needs are met, safety needs emerge, and so on up the need hierarchy, one step at a time. Once a need is satisfied, it activates the next higher need in the hierarchy. This process continues until the need for self-actualization is activated.[14]

Although research does not clearly support this theory of motivation, it remains popular among managers. For example, Chip Conley, founder and former CEO of Joie de Vivre, a boutique hotel chain with 28 locations, wrote a book (*Peak: How Great Companies Get Their Mojo from Maslow*) explaining how he used Maslow's theory to save the firm from going bankrupt. Conley believes that Maslow's theory helped him build employee, customer, and investor loyalty.[15]

Using Maslow's Theory to Motivate Employees For managers, Maslow's theory reminds us that employees have needs beyond earning a paycheck. For example, JM Family Enterprises, a Toyota distributor with 3,800 employees, is focused on helping employees cope with the cost of health care, a physiological need. The company offers primary health care, wellness exams, physicals, vaccines, and lab tests for employees at little or no cost.[16]

It also is important for managers to focus on satisfying employee needs related to self-concepts—self-esteem and self-actualization—because their satisfaction is significantly associated with a host of important OB outcomes. A final lesson revolves around the conclusion that satisfied needs lose their motivational potential. Therefore, managers are advised to motivate employees by devising programs or practices aimed at satisfying emerging or unmet needs. For example, a recent study by Adecco Group revealed that needs varied across generational groups. Younger workers wanted more flexibility than older employees and they expected to be promoted every two years. Managers should be careful when estimating employees' needs because research has showed that they have inaccurate beliefs about what motivates employees. Managers mistakenly estimated the importance of external rewards like pay and promotions while underestimating the motivation potential of intrinsic rewards.[17]

FIGURE 5.2 MCCLELLAND'S THREE NEEDS

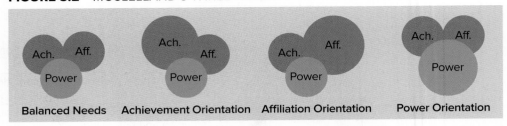

Balanced Needs   Achievement Orientation   Affiliation Orientation   Power Orientation

Acquired Needs Theory: Achievement, Affiliation, and Power

David McClelland, a well-known psychologist, has been studying the relationship between needs and behavior since the late 1940s. He proposed the ***acquired needs theory,*** **which states that three needs—achievement, affiliation, and power—are the key drivers of employee behavior.**[18] He used the term "acquired needs" because he believes that we are not born with our needs; rather we learn or acquire needs as we go about living our lives.

The Three Acquired Needs   McClelland's theory directs managers to drive employee motivation by appealing to three basic needs:

- ***Need for achievement,*** **the desire to excel, overcome obstacles, solve problems, and rival and surpass others.**
- ***Need for affiliation,*** **the desire to maintain social relationships, to be liked, and to join groups.**
- ***Need for power,*** **the desire to influence, coach, teach, or encourage others to achieve.**

Importantly, people vary in the extent to which they possess these needs, and often one need dominates the other two (see Figure 5.2).

McClelland identified a positive and negative form of the power need. The positive side is called *institutional power.* It manifests in the desire to organize people in the pursuit of organizational goals and help people obtain the feeling of competence. The negative face of power is called the need for *personal power.* People with this need want to control others, and they often manipulate people for their own gratification.

Are you curious about the status of your acquired needs? Can you guess which of the three needs is most dominant? Would you like to consider which of these needs is helping or hindering the achievement of your personal goals? Check your perceptions by taking the acquired needs Self-Assessment.

---

connect

SELF-ASSESSMENT 5.1   **What Is the Status of My Acquired Needs?**

Discover the status of your three acquired needs. Go to connect.mheducation.com and take Self-Assessment 5.1. Then consider the following questions:

1. Which of the three needs is dominant? Are you surprised by this result?
2. Which of the three needs is/are helping you to achieve your goals?
3. Are any of the needs affecting your level of flourishing (flourishing is discussed in Chapter 7)? Should you make any changes in your need states?

Sir James Dyson, founder of Dyson and inventor of the Dual Cyclone bagless vacuum cleaner, believes that the death of his father at an early age contributed to his achievement motivation. Do you think this is possible? Why?

Using Acquired Needs Theory to Motivate Employees

Applying the theory entails appealing to the preferences associated with each need when you (1) set goals, (2) provide feedback, (3) administer rewards, (4) assign tasks, and (5) design the job. Some suggestions are offered below.[19]

- **Need for achievement.** People motivated by this need, like James Dyson, inventor and manufacturer of the Dual Cyclone bagless vacuum cleaner, prefer working on challenging, but not impossible, tasks or projects. They like situations in which performance is due to effort and ability rather than luck, and like to be rewarded for their efforts. Factset Research Systems, a multinational financial data software company headquartered in Connecticut, used these recommendations to motivate employees. The company encouraged employees to pass the rigorous financial analyst certification exam, and they rewarded success with bonuses up to $17,500.[20] High achievers also like to receive a fair and balanced amount of positive and negative feedback. This enables them to improve their performance. Finally, high achievers prefer to work with other high achievers or by themselves. They get frustrated with slackers. Entrepreneurs were found to possess a high need for achievement.[21]

- **Need for affiliation.** People motivated by this need like to work in teams and in organizational climates characterized as cooperative and collegial. They also don't make the best managers because they tend to avoid conflict, have a hard time making difficult decisions without worrying about being disliked, and avoid giving others negative feedback.[22] Think twice before asking these people to lead groups or projects. It's also important to give balanced feedback to these people, but make it more personal. People high in affiliation may not like to stand out, so consider giving praise in private. Entrepreneurs were found to have lower needs for affiliation.[23]

- **Need for power.** People with a high need for power like to be in charge. They enjoy being in control of people and events and appreciate being recognized for this responsibility. You can delegate authority and responsibility to these people. The power need drives people to prefer goal-oriented tasks or projects, and they prefer direct feedback.

Self-Determination Theory: Competence, Autonomy, and Relatedness

Self-determination theory was developed by Edward Deci and Richard Ryan. In contrast to McClelland's belief that needs are learned over time, this theory identifies *innate* needs that must be satisfied for us to flourish—see discussion in Chapter 7. **Self-determination theory** assumes that three innate needs influence our behavior and well-being—competence, autonomy, and relatedness.[24]

Self-Determination Theory Focuses on Intrinsic Motivation This theory focuses on the needs that drive intrinsic motivation. It emphasizes intrinsic motivation because research shows that intrinsic motivation is longer lasting and has a more positive impact on task performance than extrinsic motivation.[25] The three needs of competence, autonomy, and relatedness are proposed to produce intrinsic motivation, which in turn is expected to enhance task performance according to self-determination theory. Research supports this proposition.[26]

The Three Innate Needs An innate need is something that we are born with. This suggests that everyone has a desire to satisfy all three of these needs in order to flourish. Managers thus are encouraged to recognize the importance of these three needs in themselves and others in order to foster work environments that fuel intrinsic motivation. The three innate needs are as follows:

1. **Competence Needs—"I need to feel efficacious."** This is the desire to feel qualified, knowledgeable, and capable to complete an act, task, or goal.

2. **Autonomy Needs—"I need to feel independent to influence my environment."** This is the desire to have freedom and discretion in determining what you want to do and how you want to do it.

3. **Relatedness Needs—"I want to be connected with others."** This is the desire to feel part of a group, to belong, and to be connected with others.

Although the above needs are proposed to be innate, their relative value can change over our lives and can vary across national cultures according to Deci and Ryan.

Using Self-Determination Theory to Motivate Employees Managers can apply this theory by trying to create work environments that support and encourage the opportunity to experience competence, autonomy, and relatedness. Here are some specific suggestions:

- **Competence.** Managers can provide tangible resources, time, contacts, and coaching to improve employee competence. (Coaching techniques are discussed in Chapter 6.) Managers can make sure that employees have the knowledge and information they need to perform their jobs. NetApp, a data storage company that was ranked as the 33rd best place to work in America in 2014 by *Fortune,* is noted for trying to enhance employees' competence. Managers regularly notify the vice chairman, Tom Mendoza, when they "catch someone doing something right." Mendoza then calls between 10 and 20 of these special employees every day to thank them.[27]

- **Autonomy.** Managers can empower employees and delegate meaningful assignments and tasks to enhance feelings of autonomy. Managers need to develop trust with their employees so they feel that their boss will back them up when they make decisions. Unilever is a great example of a company that helps to satisfy the need for autonomy. The company implemented what is called the Agile Working program. It allows "100,000 employees—everyone except factory production workers—to work anytime, anywhere, as long as they meet business needs. To support the effort, the company is investing in laptops, videoconferencing, soft-phones and smartphones, remote networks, webcams, and other technologies that help curtail travel."[28]

- **Relatedness.** Many companies use fun and camaraderie to foster relatedness. Nugget Market, an upscale supermarket chain in Sacramento, builds relatedness by creating a family-type work environment. One employee described the climate in this way: "The company doesn't see this as a workplace; they see it as a family. This is our home, where customers are treated as guests."[29] A positive and inspiring corporate vision also can be used to create a feeling of commitment to a common purpose. NetApp, just mentioned above, followed this suggestion by establishing a vision "to deliver the best possible results for the communities we serve by embracing and living a set of shared core values: Trust and Integrity, Leadership, Simplicity, Adaptability, Teamwork and Synergy, Go Beyond, Get Things Done."[30]

solving application

Life Is Good Co. Builds an Onsite Tavern to Foster Relatedness

Bert Jacobs, co-founder of the Life is Good Co., decided to open a tavern at corporate headquarters in Boston. The company, which designs, manufacturers, and sells clothing and accessories for men and women, has 4,500 retail store outlets in all 50 states. Jacobs told a reporter from *The Wall Street Journal* that he expects the tavern to build trust and enhance employees' well-being.

Why Build a Tavern? The idea is to blur the line between work and play, Jacobs said in an interview with *The Wall Street Journal* when announcing his plans. Jacobs wants the lounge, which will have lounge seating, a fireplace, and a stage, to become a place where

employees come after work to just hang out. His motivation is to provide an environment that is "homey and a place where people can put their feet up and relax. It can be both a place of work and fun. Every day, every employee will have a choice of where they want to work in the office. They might want to work in the tavern for an hour or two." The tavern will include booths where employees can meet with teammates for a meeting. He truly believes that the tavern will become a place for employees to bond, to feel a sense of belonging.

It's Not about Promoting Alcohol Jacobs was emphatic

about stating "that we're not promoting people to get drunk and go out and drive their cars. . . . If someone takes it too far and abuses it, they're probably not going to work out here. But if someone likes a cold beer every now and then, then I'm not going to freak out about it."

Jacobs' Goal Jacobs wants to create the tavern to increase trust among all employees and to enhance employee well-being. He simply wants a space where people can meet for fun or work in a relaxed environment. In the end, Jacobs believes that the tavern will enhance friendships and company performance.[31]

YOUR CALL

Stop 1: What problem is Bert Jacobs trying to address?

Stop 2: What OB concepts or theories support or refute what Jacobs is doing?

Herzberg's Motivator-Hygiene Theory: Two Ways to Improve Satisfaction

Frederick Herzberg's theory is based on a landmark study in which he interviewed 203 accountants and engineers.[32] These interviews sought to determine the factors responsible for job satisfaction and dissatisfaction. The results uncovered separate and distinct clusters of factors associated with job satisfaction and dissatisfaction. This pattern led to the **motivator-hygiene theory, which proposes that job satisfaction and dissatisfaction arise from two different sets of factors—satisfaction comes from *motivating factors* and dissatisfaction from *hygiene factors*.** In this view, managers can embrace two means of improving motivation: by improving motivators that drive satisfaction and improving hygiene factors that otherwise reduce job satisfaction.

- **Hygiene factors—"What makes employees dissatisfied?"** Job dissatisfaction was associated primarily with factors in the work *context* or environment. Herzberg labeled these as hygiene factors because each was associated with dissatisfaction. He hypothesized that such *hygiene factors*—including **company policy and administration, technical supervision, salary, interpersonal relations with one's supervisor, and working conditions—cause a person to move from a state of no dissatisfaction to dissatisfaction.** He did not consider their removal

FIGURE 5.3 ROLE OF JOB CONTENT AND JOB CONTEXT IN JOB SATISFACTION AND DISSATISFACTION

Job Content		**Job Context**	
Motivators		**Hygiene Factors**	
No Satisfaction → Satisfaction		No Dissatisfaction → Dissatisfaction	
Jobs that do not offer achievement, recognition, stimulating work, responsibility, and advancement.	Jobs offering achievement, recognition, stimulating work, responsibility, and advancement.	Jobs with good company policies and administration, technical supervision, salary, interpersonal relationships with supervisors, and working conditions.	Jobs with poor company policies and administration, technical supervision, salary, interpersonal relationships with supervisors, and working conditions.

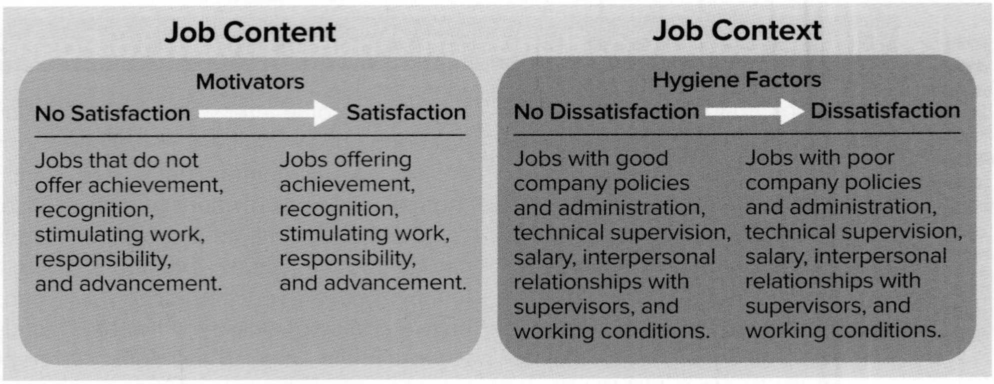

SOURCE: Adapted from D. A. Whitsett and E. K. Winslow, "An Analysis of Studies Critical of the Motivator-Hygiene Theory," *Personnel Psychology,* Winter 1997, 391–415.

as providing an immediate impact on satisfaction or increasing motivation (for that, see motivating factors following). At best, Herzberg proposed that individuals will experience the *absence* of job dissatisfaction when they have no grievances about hygiene factors.

- **Motivating factors—"What makes employees satisfied?"** Job satisfaction was more frequently associated with factors in the work *content* of the task being performed. Herzberg labeled these as *motivating factors* or *motivators* because each was associated with strong effort and good performance. He hypothesized that such **motivating factors, or motivators—including achievement, recognition, characteristics of the work, responsibility, and advancement—cause a person to move from a state of no satisfaction to satisfaction.** Therefore, Herzberg's theory predicts managers can motivate individuals by incorporating motivators into an individual's job.

For Herzberg, the groups of hygiene and motivating factors did not interact. "The opposite of job satisfaction is not job dissatisfaction, but rather no job satisfaction; and similarly, the opposite of job dissatisfaction is not job satisfaction, but no dissatisfaction."[33] Herzberg conceptualizes dissatisfaction and satisfaction as two parallel continuums. The starting point represents a null state at which *both* dissatisfaction and satisfaction are absent. Theoretically an organization member could have good supervision, pay, and working conditions (no dissatisfaction) but a tedious and unchallenging task with little chance of advancement (no satisfaction). See Figure 5.3.

Theory vs. Practice   Figure 5.3 shows how Herzberg looked at what created job satisfaction (as to job content) and what caused job dissatisfaction (as to job context). That is, he worked on two continuums, one for satisfaction and one for dissatisfaction, starting at a shared null point devoid of either. In practice, most managers work from the concept that removing dissatisfaction is just the first step in *improving* job satisfaction.

Managerial View of Job Satisfaction and Dissatisfaction   In practice managers learn from Herzberg but may apply his lessons differently from theory. Managers may even conceptualize a single continuum from dissatisfaction to satisfaction. Insights from Herzberg's theory allow managers to consider the dimensions of both job content and job context so they can manage for greater job satisfaction overall.

Employees at DreamWorks Animation and the Container Store might disagree that managing hygiene factors can only remove negative and not create positive job satisfaction. DreamWorks sends fresh-juice trucks to the campus every day and gives employees money to personalize their workstations. They also had a Banana Splats

FIGURE 5.4 A COMPARISON OF NEED AND SATISFACTION THEORIES

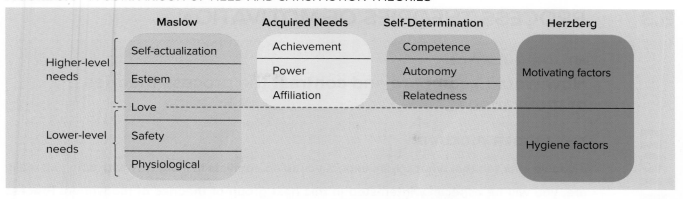

party after completing work on *Madagascar 3*. The Container Store has a strategy of paying hourly salespeople roughly *double* the industry average, approximately $46,925 a year in 2013.[34] We suspect that this approach creates plenty of employee motivation.

Using Herzberg's Theory to Motivate Employees   Research does not support the two-factor aspect of his theory nor the proposition that hygiene factors are unrelated to job satisfaction. However, there are three practical applications of the theory that help explain why it remains an important theory of OB.

1. **Hygiene First.** There are practical reasons to eliminate dissatisfaction before trying to use motivators to increase motivation and performance. You will have a harder time motivating someone who is experiencing pay dissatisfaction or otherwise struggling with Herzberg's hygiene factors.
2. **Motivation Next.** Once you remove dissatisfaction, you can hardly go wrong by building motivators into someone's job. This suggestion represents the core idea behind the technique of job design that is discussed in the final section of this chapter.
3. **A Few Well-Chosen Words.** Finally, don't underestimate the power of verbal recognition to reinforce good performance. Savvy managers supplement Herzberg's motivators with communication. Positive recognition can fuel intrinsic motivation, particularly for people who are engaged in their work. Chapter 6 will provide guidelines on the best ways to provide this type of positive feedback.

Figure 5.4 illustrates the overlap among the need and satisfaction theories discussed in this section. As you can see, the acquired needs and self-determination theories do not include lower-level needs. Remember, higher-level need satisfaction is more likely to foster well-being and flourishing.

TAKE-AWAY APPLICATION—TAAP

Considering all of the needs discussed within the content theories of motivation, and the list of motivators and hygiene factors:

1. Which ones have your highest levels of need satisfaction?
2. Which ones are most important for your success in school? How about in terms of your current/last/most-desired job?
3. Given that flourishing is related to satisfying higher-order needs, what can you do to increase your level of satisfaction for higher-level needs?

PROCESS THEORIES OF MOTIVATION

MAJOR QUESTION

How would I compare and contrast the process theories of motivation?

THE BIGGER PICTURE

If you've ever felt that what others expect you to do conflicts in a big way with who you really are, you will be especially interested in this next group of theories of motivation. Process theories examine how internal factors and environmental characteristics influence employee motivation. You'll be considering the three major process theories: equity/justice theory, expectancy theory, and goal-setting theory. Each theory offers unique ideas for motivating employees, or ways to help you understand how you feel about organizational expectations.

major question

Process theories of motivation attempt to describe *how* various person factors and environmental factors in the Integrative Framework affect motivation. They go beyond content theories by helping you understand *why* people with different needs and levels of satisfaction behave the way they do at work. (In contrast, content theories look at *what* motivates workers.)

In this section we discuss three process theories of motivation:

- Equity/justice theory
- Expectancy theory
- Goal-setting theory

Equity/Justice Theory: Am I Being Treated Fairly?

Defined generally, **equity theory** is a model of motivation that explains how people strive for *fairness* and *justice* in social exchanges or give-and-take relationships. Equity theory is based on cognitive dissonance theory, discussed in Chapter 2. According to this theory, people are motivated to maintain consistency between their beliefs and their behavior. Perceived inconsistencies create cognitive dissonance (or psychological discomfort), which, in turn, motivates corrective action. Accordingly, when victimized by unfair social exchanges, our resulting cognitive dissonance prompts us to correct the situation. Our response may range from a slight change in attitude or behavior to extremes (in rare cases) like sabotage or workplace violence. For example, supporters of WikiLeaks conducted cyberattacks against MasterCard and Visa because they thought that these companies were unfairly trying to

Julian Assange, Austalian publisher, journalist, and hacker, is best known as the editor-in-chief of WikiLeaks, which he cofounded in 2006. Assange became a person of interest to the United States when WikiLeaks published US military and diplomatic documents leaked by Chelsea Manning. He currently is facing sexual offense charges in Sweden and has obtained political asylum from Ecuador. He lives in the Embassy of Ecuador in London.

stifle WikiLeaks' dissemination of secret US diplomatic communications. Both MasterCard and Visa systems were temporarily down as a result of these attacks.[35]

Psychologist J. Stacy Adams pioneered the use of equity theory in the workplace. Let us begin by discussing his ideas and their current application. We then discuss the extension of equity theory into what is called *justice theory*. We conclude by discussing how to motivate employees with both equity and justice theory.

The Elements of Equity Theory: Comparing My Outputs and Inputs with Those of Others   The key elements of equity theory include outputs, inputs, and a comparison of the ratio of outputs to inputs; see Figure 5.5.

- **Outputs—"What do I perceive that I'm getting out of my job?"** Organizations provide a variety of outcomes for our work, including such things as pay/bonuses, medical benefits, challenging assignments, job security, promotions, status symbols, recognition, and participating in important decisions. Outcomes vary widely, depending on one's organization and rank. For example, very few companies use sabbaticals as an outcome due to their cost. In contrast, accounting and consulting firm Deloitte's "sabbatical program lets select employees spend three to six months at a nonprofit while earning full benefits and 40% of pay."[36]

FIGURE 5.5   ELEMENTS OF EQUITY THEORY

Equity theory compares how well you are doing to how well others are doing in similar jobs. Instead of focusing just on what you get out of the job (outputs) or what you put into the job (inputs), equity theory looks at the ratio between your ratio (of outputs to inputs) to the ratio of others.

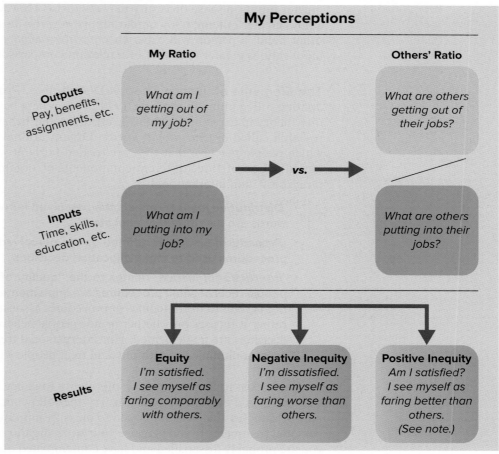

Note: Does positive inequity result in satisfaction? Some of us may feel so. But J. Stacy Adams recognized that employees often feel guilty about positive inequity, just as they might become angry about negative inequity. Your positive inequity is others' negative inequity. If your coworkers saw you as being favored unfairly in a major way, wouldn't they be outraged? How effective could you be in your job then?

- **Inputs—"What do I perceive that I'm putting into my job?"** An employee's inputs, for which he or she expects a just return, include education/training, skills, creativity, seniority, age, personality traits, effort expended, experience, and personal appearance.

- **Comparison—"How does my ratio of outputs to inputs compare with relevant others?"** Your feelings of inequity revolve around your evaluation of whether you are receiving adequate rewards to compensate for your collective inputs. In practice people perform these evaluations by comparing the perceived fairness of their output to input ratio to that of relevant others (see Figure 5.5). By dividing outputs by inputs, the larger the ratio, the greater the benefit. This comparative process was found to generalize across personalities and countries.[37] People tend to compare themselves to other individuals with whom they have close interpersonal ties such as friends, and to whom they are similar, such as people performing the same job or individuals of the same gender or educational level, rather than to dissimilar others. For example, the authors of your textbook work for universities. We do not compare our salaries to that of the head football coach at our respective schools. But we do consider our pay relative to other college business professors.

The Outcomes of an Equity Comparison Figure 5.5 shows the three different equity relationships resulting from an equity comparison: equity, negative inequity, and positive inequity. Because equity is based on comparing *ratios* of outcomes to inputs, inequity will not necessarily be perceived just because someone else receives greater rewards. If the other person's additional outcomes are due to his or her greater inputs, a sense of equity may still exist. However, if the comparison person enjoys greater outcomes for similar inputs, *negative inequity* will be perceived. On the other hand, a person will experience *positive inequity* when his or her outcome to input ratio is greater than that of a relevant comparison person.

The Elements of Justice Theory: Distributive, Procedural, and Interactional Justice Beginning in the later 1970s, researchers began to expand the role of equity theory in explaining employee attitudes and behavior. This led to a domain of research called *organizational justice*. Organizational justice reflects the extent to which people perceive that they are treated fairly at work. This, in turn, led to the identification of three different components of organizational justice: distributive, procedural, and interactional.[38]

- *Distributive justice* reflects the perceived fairness of how resources and rewards are distributed or allocated.

- *Procedural justice* is defined as the perceived fairness of the process and procedures used to make allocation decisions.

- *Interactional justice* relates to the "quality of the interpersonal treatment people receive when procedures are implemented."[39] This form of justice does not pertain to the outcomes or procedures associated with decision making, but rather it focuses on whether or not people believe they are treated fairly when decisions are implemented. Fair interpersonal treatment necessitates that managers communicate truthfully and treat people with courtesy and respect.

Tools exist to help us improve our ability to gauge the level of fairness or justice that exists in a current or past job. Try the following Self-Assessment. It contains part of a survey that was developed to measure employees' perceptions of fair interpersonal treatment. If you perceive your work organization as interpersonally unfair, you are probably dissatisfied and have contemplated quitting. In contrast, your organizational loyalty and attachment are likely greater if you believe you are treated fairly at work.

Mc Graw Hill connect

SELF-ASSESSMENT 5.2 Measuring Perceived Interpersonal Treatment

This Self-Assessment provides a measure of the extent to which a current or past employer is treating you fairly. If you want to know where you stand, go to connect .mheducation.com and take Self-Assessment 5.2. Then consider the following questions:

1. Does the level of fairness correlate to your work attitudes such as job satisfaction and organizational commitment?

2. What is causing your lowest level of perceived fairness? Can you do anything to change these feelings?

3. What do these results suggest about the type of company you would like to work for after graduation?

The Outcomes Associated with Justice   Doesn't it make sense that your perceptions of justice are related to outcomes in the Integrative Framework? Of course! This is why the study of organizational justice has flourished over the last 25 years. We created Figure 5.6 to summarize these research findings. The figure shows the strength of relationships between nine individual-level outcomes and the three components of organizational justice. By and large, distributive and procedural justice have consistently stronger relationships with outcomes. This suggests that managers would be better served paying attention to these two forms of justice. In contrast, interactional justice is not a leading indicator in any instance.

You can also see that certain outcomes, such as job satisfaction and organizational commitment, have stronger relationships with justice. All told, however, the majority of relationships are weak between justice and important OB outcomes. This reinforces the conclusion that motivating people via justice works for some outcomes but not for others.

Using Equity and Justice Theories to Motivate Employees   First, it is helpful to understand how strongly employees may feel about a perceived inequitable or unjust work situation. Frequently the primary source of their frustration is likely to be pay. A nationwide Gallup poll revealed that 51 percent of Americans felt underpaid.[40] You can motivate other employees by clearly understanding and communicating their opportunities to improve their situations. You can communicate reasonable expectations and make sure objective measures for rewards are well understood. Your knowledge of equity and justice theories will also allow you to hear out employees and better understand their concerns.

We share five practical lessons that can be drawn from equity and justice theories as follows:

1. **Employee Perceptions Are What Count.** No matter how fair management thinks the organization's policies, procedures, and reward system are, each employee's *perception* of the equity of those factors is what counts. Consider the situation of several thousand employees at Morgan Stanley. The company decided to pay 2012 bonuses in four equal installments starting in May 2013 through January 2016. "Employees who quit or are laid off before the payments stand to lose their deferred compensation unless they negotiate a separate deal with the company."[41] Executives at the company think that this is a good way to reduce risky behavior while employees think it is unfair. What do you think?

2. **Employees Want a Voice in Decisions That Affect Them.** Managers benefit by allowing employees to participate in making decisions about important work outcomes. In general, employees' perceptions of procedural justice are enhanced when they have a voice in the decision-making process. **Voice** is defined as

FIGURE 5.6 OUTCOMES ASSOCIATED WITH JUSTICE COMPONENTS

The three components of organizational justice have varying effects on workplace outcomes, listed here in rough order of strongest to weakest. Note that job satisfaction and organizational commitment lead the list of outcomes and most strongly align with justice components.

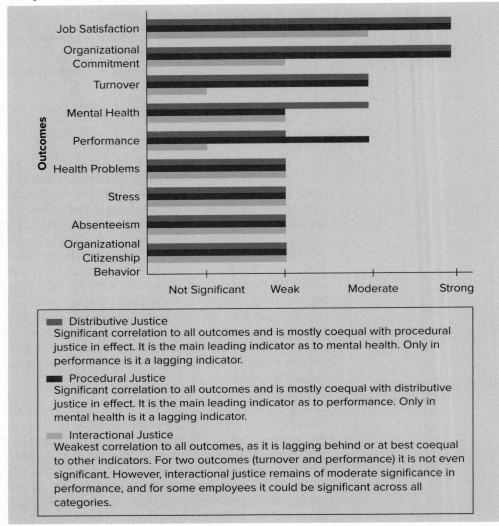

SOURCES: J. M. Robbins, M. T. Ford, and L. E. Tetrick, "Perceived Unfairness and Employee Health: A Meta-Analytic Integration," *Journal of Applied Psychology,* March 2012, 235–272; N. E. Fassina, D. A. Jones, and K. L. Uggerslev, "Meta-Analytic Tests of Relationships between Organizational Justice and Citizenship Behavior: Testing Agent-System and Shared-Variance Models," *Journal of Organizational Behavior,* August 2008, 805–828; Y. Chen-Charash and P. E. Spector, "The Role of Justice in Organizations: A Meta-Analysis," *Organizational Behavior and Human Decision Processes,* November 2001, 278–321; and J. A. Colquitt, D. E. Conlon, M. J. Wesson, C. O. L. H. Porter, and K. Y. Ng, "Justice at the Millenium: A Meta-Analytic Review of 25 Years of Organizational Justice Research," *Journal of Applied Psychology,* June 2001, 426.

"employees' upward expression of challenging but constructive opinions, concerns, or ideas on work-related issues to their managers."[42] Managers are encouraged to seek employee input on organizational changes that are likely to impact the workforce. Sadly, a recent study suggests that many managers are reluctant to follow this recommendation. Results demonstrated that employees were evaluated more negatively when they engaged in challenging forms of voice. Managers also were less likely to use these employees' ideas.[43] Be careful when you challenge your boss's decisions.

3. **Employees Should Be Given an Appeals Process.** Employees should be given the opportunity to appeal decisions that affect their welfare. Being able to appeal a decision fosters perceptions of distributive and procedural justice.

4. **Leader Behavior Matters.** Employees' perceptions of justice are strongly influenced by the leadership behavior exhibited by their managers (leadership is discussed in Chapter 13). Thus, it is important for managers to consider the justice-related implications of their decisions, actions, and public communications. For example, employees at Honeywell felt better about being asked to take furloughs—in which people get unpaid leave but remain employed—when they learned that David Cote, the company's chairman and CEO, did not take his $4 million bonus during the time employees were furloughed.[44]

5. **A Climate for Justice Makes a Difference.** Managers need to pay attention to the organization's climate for justice. For example, an aggregation of 38 research studies demonstrated that an organization's climate for justice was significantly related to team performance, an important outcome in the Integrative Framework for Understanding and Applying OB.[45] Researchers also believe a climate of justice can significantly influence the type of customer service provided by employees. In turn, this level of service is likely to influence customers' perceptions of "fair service" and their subsequent loyalty and satisfaction.

And as for yourself? You can work to improve equity ratios through your behavior or your perceptions. For example, you could work to resolve negative inequity by asking for a raise or a promotion (raising your outputs) or by working fewer hours or exerting less effort (reducing inputs). You could also resolve the inequity cognitively, by adjusting your perceptions as to the value of your salary or other benefits (outcomes) or the value of the actual work done by you or your co-workers (inputs).

Gabby Douglas began her gymnastics training at the age of seven, and battled back from a wrist fracture while a teenager, to become the first woman of color and the first African-American gymnast in Olympic history to become the individual all-around champion. She was also the first American gymnast to win gold in both the individual all-around and team competitions at the same Olympics. Gabby certainly had high expectations for success based on her training and experience.

Expectancy Theory: Does My Effort Lead to Desired Outcomes?

Expectancy theory **holds that people are motivated to behave in ways that produce desired combinations of expected outcomes.** Generally, expectancy theory can be used to predict behavior in any situation in which a choice between two or more alternatives must be made. For instance, it can be used to predict whether to quit or stay at a job; whether to exert substantial or minimal effort at a task; and whether to major in management, computer science, accounting, marketing, psychology, or communication.

The most widely used version of expectancy theory was proposed by Yale professor Victor Vroom. We now consider the theory's key elements and recommendations for its application.

The Elements of Vroom's Expectancy Theory: Expectancy, Instrumentality, and Valence
Motivation, according to Vroom, boils down to the decision of how much effort to exert in a specific task situation. This choice is based on a two-stage sequence of expectations (moving from effort to performance and from performance to outcome). First, motivation is affected by an individual's expectation that a certain level of effort will produce the intended performance goal. For example, if you do not believe increasing the amount of time you spend studying will significantly raise your grade on an exam, you probably will not study any harder than usual. Motivation also is influenced by the employee's perceived chances of getting various outcomes as a result of accomplishing his or her performance goal. Finally, individuals are motivated to the extent that they value the outcomes received (see Figure 5.7).

FIGURE 5.7 MAJOR ELEMENTS OF EXPECTANCY THEORY

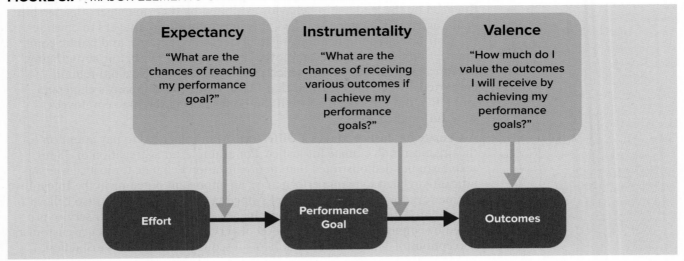

Let us consider the three key elements of Vroom's theory.

1. **Expectancy—"Can I achieve my desired level of performance?" An** *expectancy* **represents an individual's belief that a particular degree of effort will be followed by a particular level of performance.** In other words, it is an effort → performance expectation. Expectancies take the form of subjective probabilities. As you may recall from a course in statistics, probabilities range from zero to one. An expectancy of zero indicates effort has no anticipated impact on performance.

   > **EXAMPLE** Suppose you do not know how to use Excel. No matter how much effort you exert, your perceived probability of creating complex spreadsheets that compute correlations would be zero. An expectancy of one suggests that performance is totally dependent on effort. If you decided to take an Excel training course and practice using the program a couple of hours a day for a few weeks (high effort), you should be able to create spreadsheets that compute correlations.

   Research reveals that employees' expectancies are affected by a host of factors. Some of the more important ones include self-efficacy, time pressures, task difficulty, ability and knowledge, resources, and support from peers and one's boss.[46]

2. **Instrumentality—"What intrinsic and extrinsic rewards will I receive if I achieve my desired level of performance?" An** *instrumentality* **is how an individual perceives the movement from performance to outcome.** It represents a person's belief that a particular outcome is contingent on accomplishing a specific level of performance. Performance is instrumental when it leads to something else. Passing exams, for instance, is instrumental to graduating from college. The Problem-Solving Application illustrates how various boards of directors are reducing the instrumentality between CEO pay and corporate performance.

3. **Valence—"How much do I value the rewards I receive?** *Valence* **refers to the positive or negative value people place on outcomes.** Valence mirrors our personal preferences. For example, most employees have a positive valence for receiving additional money or recognition. In contrast, being laid off or being ridiculed for making a suggestion would likely be negatively valent for most individuals. In Vroom's expectancy model, *outcomes* refer to different consequences that are contingent on performance, such as pay, promotions, recognition, or celebratory events. For example, Aflac hosted a six-day appreciation week that included theme park visits, showing motion pictures, and daily gifts.[47] Would you value these rewards? Your answer would depend on your individual needs.

solving application

Corporate Boards Decide to Lower the Instrumentalities between CEO Performance and Pay

Alpha Natural Resources, a coal producer, gave its CEO, Kevin Crutchfield, a $528,000 bonus when the company had its largest financial loss in the company's history. The board said it wanted to reward him for his "tremendous efforts" in improving worker safety. This "safety bonus" was not tied to any corporate goals, and the company had never paid a specific bonus just for safety.

The board at generic drug maker Mylan made a similar decision. CEO Robert Coury received a $900,000 bonus despite poor financial results. The board felt that poor results were due to factors like the European sovereign-debt crisis and natural disasters in Japan. Not to be outdone, the board at Nationwide Mutual Insurance doubled the CEO's bonus, "declaring that claims from U.S. tornados shouldn't count against his performance metrics."

Is It Good to Relax Instrumentalities between Performance and Pay? Companies relax instrumentalities between performance and pay because they want to protect executives from being accountable for things outside their control, like a tornado or rising costs in natural resources. While this may make sense, it begs the question of what to do when good luck occurs. Companies do not typically constrain CEO pay when financial results are due to good luck. Blair Jones, an expert on executive compensation, noted that changing instrumentalities after the fact "only works if a board is willing to use it on the upside and the downside. . . . If it's only used for the downside, it calls into question the process."[48]

YOUR CALL

Stop 1: How would you describe the problem facing Alpha Natural Resources, Mylan, and Nationwide?

Stop 2: Did Alpha Natural Resources, Mylan, and Nationwide Mutual Insurance make decisions about CEO pay that were consistent with expectancy theory?

Stop 3: What does OB theory suggest that these companies should have done to compensate their CEOs?

According to expectancy theory, your motivation will be high when all three elements in the model are high. If any element is near zero, your motivation will be low. Whether you apply this theory on yourself, or managers apply it on their employees, it is critical to simultaneously consider the status of all three elements.

TAKE-AWAY APPLICATION—TAAP

This activity focuses on a past work- or school-related project that was unsuccessful. It would be best if it involved something that you would consider a failure.

1. Considering this project, what would you estimate was your expectancy for successfully completing the project? Use a 1–5 scale from (1) Very Low to (5) Very High.

2. What were the chances that you would receive outcomes/rewards that you valued had you successfully completed the project? Use a 1–5 scale from (1) Very Low to (5) Very High.

3. Considering the above two answers, what was your level of motivation? Was it high enough to achieve your performance goals?

4. What does expectancy theory suggest that you could have done to improve your chances of successfully completing the project? Provide specific suggestions.

5. How might you use the above steps to motivate yourself in the future?

Using Expectancy Theory to Motivate Employees There is widespread agreement that attitudes and behavior are influenced when organizations link rewards to targeted behaviors. For example, a recent study of college students working on group projects showed that group members put more effort into their projects when instructors "clearly and forcefully" explained how high levels of effort lead to higher performance—an expectancy—and that higher performance results in positive outcomes like higher grades and better camaraderie—instrumentalities and valent outcomes.[49]

Expectancy theory has important practical implications for individual managers and organizations as a whole (see Table 5.1). The following three practical lessons are essential for applying expectancy theory:

- **Enhance effort → performance expectancies.** This can be done by using tools and techniques associated with performance management, a topic discussed in Chapter 6. This leadership includes behaviors associated with goal setting, communication, feedback, coaching, providing consequences, and establishing/ monitoring performance expectations.

- **Determine desired levels of performance and set SMART goals.** Goals need to be **S**pecific, **M**easurable, **A**ttainable, **R**esults oriented, and **T**ime bound. Guidelines for establishing SMART goals are discussed in Chapter 6.

- **Link rewards to desired outcomes.** This means that you need to get to know your employees so that you can reward them with outcomes they value.

The following Problem-Solving Application illustrates expectancy theory in action at Westwood High School in Mesa, Arizona.

solving application

problem

A High School Principal Uses Principles of Expectancy Theory to Motivate Students

Tim Richard, principal at Westwood High School, decided to use a motivational program he called "celebration" to improve the grades of 1,200 students who were failing one or more courses. The school has a total of 3,000 students.

How Does the Program Work?
"Students are allowed to go outside and have fun with their friends for 28 minutes on four mornings a week," the principal explained to the local newspaper. "But those who have even one F must stay inside for 'remediation'—28 minutes of extra study, help from peer tutors or meetings with teachers." Richard,

who successfully implemented the program at a smaller high school, believes that the key to motivating students is to link a highly valued reward—socializing with friends outside—with grades. Socializing includes playing organized games, dancing and listening to music, eating snacks, and just plain hanging out. Results suggest that the program is working.

Positive results were found within two to three months of starting the motivation program. Students with failing grades dropped to 900. The principal's SMART goal is to achieve zero failing grades by the end of the year.

What Is the Student Reaction?
Students like the program. Ivana Baltazar, a 17-year-old senior, said, "you really appreciate celebration after you have been in remediation." She raised an F in economics to a B after receiving help in remediation. Good academic students like Joseph Leung also like the program. He is a tutor to students with failing grades. He believes that "the tricky part is getting people out of the mindset that they can't succeed. . . . A lot of times they just haven't done their homework. I try to help them understand that the difference between a person passing and failing is their work ethic."[50]

YOUR CALL

Stop 1: What problem is Tim Richard trying to address?

Stop 2: What OB concepts or theories are consistent with Mr. Richard's motivational program?

Stop 3: Do you agree with Mr. Richard's approach to improving student performance?

TABLE 5.1 MANAGERIAL AND ORGANIZATIONAL IMPLICATIONS OF EXPECTANCY THEORY

FOR MANAGERS	FOR ORGANIZATIONS
• Determine the outcomes that employees value.	• Reward people for desired performance, and do not keep pay decisions secret.
• Identify good performance so appropriate behaviors can be rewarded.	• Design challenging jobs.
• Make sure employees can achieve targeted performance levels.	• Tie some rewards to group accomplishments to build teamwork and encourage cooperation.
• Link desired outcomes to targeted levels of performance.	• Reward managers for creating, monitoring, and maintaining expectancies, instrumentalities, and outcomes that lead to high effort and goal attainment.
• Make sure changes in outcomes are large enough to motivate high effort.	• Monitor employee motivation through interviews or anonymous questionnaires.
• Monitor the reward system for inequities.	• Accommodate individual differences by building flexibility into the motivation program.

Goal-Setting Theory: How Can I Harness the Power of Goal Setting?

Regardless of the nature of their specific achievements, successful people tend to have one thing in common: Their lives are goal oriented. This is as true for politicians seeking votes as it is for world-class athletes. Research also supports this anecdotal conclusion. The results of more than 1,000 studies from a wide range of countries clearly show that goal setting helps individuals, teams, and organizations as a whole to achieve success.[51]

We want to help you harness the power of goal setting in your life. This necessitates that we review a theory of goal setting within a work context, and then explain the mechanisms that make goal setting so effective. We don't discuss the practical application of goal setting because it is presented in Chapter 6.

Edwin Locke and Gary Latham's Theory of Goal Setting After studying four decades of research on goal setting, two OB experts, Edwin Locke and Gary Latham, proposed a straightforward theory of goal setting. Here is how it works.[52]

- **Goals that are specific and difficult lead to higher performance than general goals like "do your best" or "improve performance."** This is why it is essential to set specific, difficult goals. **Goal specificity refers to the quantifiability of a goal.** For example, a goal of increasing the score on your next OB test by 10 percent is more specific than the goal of trying to improve your grade on the next test.

- **Certain conditions are necessary for goal setting to work.** People must have the ability and resources needed to achieve the goal, and they need to be committed to the goal. If these conditions are not met, goal setting does not lead to higher performance. Be sure that these conditions are in place as you pursue your goals.

- **Performance feedback and participation in deciding how to achieve goals are necessary but not sufficient for goal setting to work.** Feedback and participation enhance performance only when they lead employees to set and commit to a specific, difficult goal. Take Jim's Formal Wear, a tuxedo wholesaler in Illinois,

This informal group of NASA scientists and researchers has undertaken repeated climbs up Mt. Everest for research to help future space travelers. Do you think that these people are committed to the challenging goal of climbing Everest? If yes, what needs might motivate such commitment?

for example. "Once a week, employees meet with their teams to discuss their efforts and what changes should be made the next week. Employees frequently suggest ways to improve efficiency or save money, such as reusing shipping boxes and hangers."[53] The learning point is that goals lead to higher performance when you use feedback and participation to stay focused and committed to a specific goal.

- **Goal achievement leads to job satisfaction, which in turn reinforces employees to set and commit to even higher levels of performance.** Goal setting sets in motion a positive cycle of upward performance.

In sum, it takes more than setting specific, difficult goals to motivate yourself or others via goal setting. It is critical that the supporting conditions are put into place in order to gain the maximum value of goal setting.

What Are the Mechanisms Behind the Power of Goal Setting? Edwin Locke and Gary Latham, the same OB scholars who developed the motivational theory of goal setting just discussed, also identified the underlying mechanisms that explain how goals affect performance. There are four motivational mechanisms that fuel the power of goal setting.

1. **Goals Direct Attention.** Goals direct one's attention and effort toward goal-relevant activities and away from goal-irrelevant activities. If, for example, you have a term project due in a few days, your thoughts and actions tend to revolve

around completing that project. In reality, however, we often work on multiple goals at once. This highlights the importance of prioritizing your goals so that you effectively allocate your efforts over time.[54] For example, Nustar Energy, one of the largest asphalt refiners and operators of petroleum product terminals and petroleum liquids pipelines in the United States, has decided to give safety greater priority in its goals than profits. This prioritization paid off as the company celebrated three years of zero time off due to injuries in 2012, and corporate profits are doing just fine.[55]

2. **Goals Regulate Effort.** Goals have an energizing function in that they motivate us to act. As you might expect, harder goals foster greater effort than easy goals. Time deadlines also factor into the motivational equation. We expend greater effort on projects and tasks when deadlines are approaching. For example, an instructor's deadline for turning in your term project would prompt you to complete it, as opposed to going out with friends, watching television, or studying for another course.

3. **Goals Increase Persistence.** Within the context of goal setting, persistence represents the effort expended on a task over an extended period of time: It takes effort to run 100 meters; it takes persistence to run a 26-mile marathon. Persistent people tend to see obstacles as challenges to be overcome rather than as reasons to fail. A difficult goal that is important to an individual is a constant reminder to keep exerting effort in the appropriate direction. Peter Löscher, CEO of Siemens, wanted to build on the power of persistence by setting goals associated with "green consciousness" and increased wind-energy sales. To do this he hired Peter Solmssen from GE because "the one thing GE does better than anybody is execution," said Solmssen. "They set a target, and they achieve it. That's it." With Solmssen's help, Löscher's new goal-driven approach led to increased wind-energy sales and a 48 percent increase in stock price.[56]

4. **Goals Foster the Development and Application of Task Strategies and Action Plans.** Goals prompt us to figure out how they can be accomplished. This is a cognitive process of creatively developing a plan that outlines the steps, tasks, or activities that must take place to accomplish a goal. For example, teams of employees at Tornier, a medical device manufacturer in Amsterdam, meet every 45, 60, or 90 days to create action plans for completing their goals. Implementation of the plans can take between six and 18 months depending on the complexity of the goal.[57] A series of studies conducted in South Africa, Zimbabwe, and Namibia found that small businesses were more likely to grow and succeed if their owners engaged in "elaborate and proactive planning."[58]

TAKE-AWAY APPLICATION—TAAP

1. Set a goal for performance on the next exam in this class by filling in the following statement. "I want to increase the score on my next exam by ____% over the score on my previous exam." If you have not had an exam yet, pick a percentage grade you would like to achieve on your first exam.

2. Create a short action plan by listing four or five tasks or activities that are needed to help you achieve your goal. Identify actions that go beyond just reading.

3. Identify how you will assess your progress in completing the tasks or activities in your action plan.

4. Now work the plan, and get ready for success.

MAJOR QUESTION

What are the similarities and differences among top-down approaches, bottom-up approaches, and "idiosyncratic deals" in job design?

THE BIGGER PICTURE

Sometimes how happy you are in your job depends on who designs it. From an OB perspective, job design focuses on motivating employees by considering the environmental factors within the Integrative Framework for Understanding and Applying OB. Objectively, the goal of job design is to structure jobs and the tasks needed to complete them in a way that creates intrinsic motivation. We'll look at how potential motivation varies depending on who designs the job: management, you, or you in negotiation with management.

Completing tasks is the core of any job, and job design focuses on increasing employee-intrinsic motivation by changing the type of tasks we complete in the course of doing our jobs. **Job design,** also referred to as *job redesign* or *work design,* **"refers to any set of activities that involve the alteration of specific jobs or interdependent systems of jobs with the intent of improving the quality of employee job experience and their on-the-job productivity."**[59] As you can see from this definition, job design focuses on motivating employees by considering the environmental factors within the Integrative Framework.

In the last decade, more approaches to job design are now available.

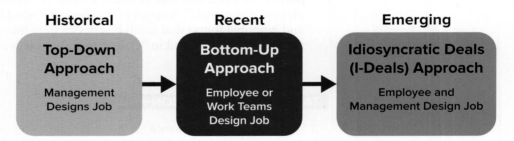

Historical	Recent	Emerging
Top-Down Approach	**Bottom-Up Approach**	**Idiosyncratic Deals (I-Deals) Approach**
Management Designs Job	Employee or Work Teams Design Job	Employee and Management Design Job

- **Top-Down.** Managers changed employees' tasks with the intent of increasing motivation and productivity. In other words, job design was management led.
- **Bottom-Up.** In the last 10 years, this perspective gave way to what have been called bottom-up processes, based on the idea that employees can proactively change or redesign their own jobs, thereby boosting their own motivation and engagement. Job design is driven by employees rather than managers according to bottom-up processes.
- **I-Deals.** The latest approach to job design attempts to merge these two historical perspectives and is referred to as *idiosyncratic deals.* This view envisions job design as a process in which employees and individual managers jointly negotiate the types of tasks employees complete at work. In other words, the process of job design is jointly owned by employees and managers.

This section provides an overview of these three conceptually different approaches to job design.[60] More coverage is given to top-down techniques and models because they have been used for longer periods of time and more research is available to evaluate their effectiveness.

Top-Down Approaches— "Management Designs Your Job"

In top-down approaches management creates efficient and meaningful combinations of work tasks for employees. If done correctly, in theory employees will display higher performance, job satisfaction, and employee engagement, and lower absenteeism and turnover. All of these are relevant outcomes in the Integrative Framework. But there are different approaches at work in top-down job creation. The five principal approaches are scientific management, job enlargement, job rotation, job enrichment, and the job characteristics model.

Scientific Management   Scientific management draws from research in industrial engineering and is most heavily influenced by the work of Frederick Taylor. Taylor, a mechanical engineer, developed the principles of scientific management based on research and experimentation to determine the most efficient way to perform jobs. ***Scientific management*** **is "that kind of management which conducts a business or affairs by** *standards* **established by facts or truths gained through** *systematic* **observation, experiment, or reasoning."**[61]

Designing jobs according to the principles of scientific management has both positive and negative consequences. Positively, employee efficiency and productivity are increased. On the other hand, research reveals that simplified, repetitive jobs also lead to job dissatisfaction, poor mental health, higher levels of stress, and low sense of accomplishment and personal growth.[62] Recognition of these negative consequences paved the way for the next four top-down approaches.

This automotive assembly line, which is using robotics, is a great example of scientific management. The principles of scientific management have aided auto manufacturers to produce cars more efficiently and with higher quality.

Job Enlargement   Companies first used this technique in the late 1940s in response to complaints about tedious and overspecialized jobs created from the principles of scientific management.   ***Job enlargement*** **involves putting more variety into a worker's job by combining specialized tasks of comparable difficulty.** Some call this *horizontally loading* the job. Researchers recommend using job enlargement as part of a broader approach that uses multiple motivational methods because, by itself, job enlargement does not have a significant and lasting positive effect on job performance.[63]

Job Rotation   As with job enlargement, companies use job rotation to give employees greater variety in their work.   ***Job rotation*** **calls for moving employees from one specialized job to another.** Rather than performing only one job, workers are trained and given the opportunity to perform two or more separate jobs on a rotating basis. Proposed benefits of job rotation include the following:[64]

- Increased engagement and motivation by providing employees with a broader perspective of the organization.
- Increased worker flexibility and easier scheduling because employees are cross-trained to perform different jobs.
- A vehicle to increase employees' knowledge and abilities, thus improving an employee's promotability and building a pipeline of internal talent.

You will find that more and more companies are hiring new college graduates into what are called "rotational programs." Many of our students have accepted such positions after graduation. Finally, the technique of job rotation has morphed into what is called *job swapping,* which tends to be used more frequently with senior-level managers. (See the Example box.)

EXAMPLE Job Swapping Is the Latest Application of Job Rotation

Nadim Hossain, vice president of marketing at San Francisco–based PowerReviews, went to a recent meeting in which he met with a marketing team and provided input on a proposed ad. Interestingly, he did not do this for his employer. *Fortune* magazine reported on what he was up to. "He traded roles for the day with Jon Miller, VP of marketing and co-founder of San Mateo, Calif., software firm Marketo, hoping to gain some insight into his own role by experiencing someone else's." This experiment is an example of an external job swap. Both individuals felt like they benefited from the experience. Mr. Hossain said that he got many ideas about how to motivate his sales team, and Mr. Miller left with a better idea of the challenges faced by chief marketing officers.

Job Swapping Can Be Done Internally Some companies are reluctant to do external "job swaps" because of confidentiality but take advantage of internal opportunities. For example, Jay Miletsky, CEO of online video start-up MyPod Studios, decided to change roles with an internal developer for a day. Sunil Verma, from mobile-ad company Velti, swaps jobs with executive-level peers every quarter in order to increase teamwork and improve communication. Steve Cody, CEO of Peppercom, a PR firm in New York, uses the practice to gain an understanding of the work experiences of entry-level employees. "He traded places with junior-level employees, including his receptionist, a junior account manager, and an account supervisor. He cleaned conference rooms, hung up coats, answered phones, and wrote press releases." Mr. Cody believes that he gained appreciation for employees' need for work–life balance based on the experience. "If you're open to a swap, you'll come out of it a much better leader," he said.[65]

YOUR THOUGHTS?

1. What are the pros and cons of job swaps?
2. What would be your ideal job swap?
3. If you managed a business, how would you feel about this option for your employees?

Job Enrichment Job enrichment is the practical application of Frederick Herzberg's motivator-hygiene theory of job satisfaction discussed earlier in this chapter. Specifically, **job enrichment entails modifying a job such that an employee has the opportunity to experience achievement, recognition, stimulating work, responsibility, and advancement.** These characteristics are incorporated into a job through vertical loading. Rather than giving employees additional tasks of similar difficulty (horizontal loading), *vertical loading* consists of giving workers more autonomy and responsibility. Intuit, for example, attempts to do this by encouraging employees "to spend 10% of their time pursuing projects they're passionate about."[66]

The Job Characteristics Model Two OB researchers, J. Richard Hackman and Greg Oldham, played a central role in developing the job characteristics approach. These researchers tried to determine how work can be structured so that employees experience intrinsic motivation. Hackman and Oldham proposed that intrinsic motivation is determined by three psychological states. In turn, these psychological states are fostered by the presence of five core job characteristics. The model is illustrated in Figure 5.8. In summary, the goal of **the *job characteristic model* is to promote high intrinsic motivation by designing jobs that possess the five core job characteristics.** Let us examine the core job characteristics.

The five core job characteristics are as follows:

- **Skill variety.** The extent to which the job requires an individual to perform a variety of tasks that require him or her to use different skills and abilities.

FIGURE 5.8   THE JOB CHARACTERISTICS MODEL

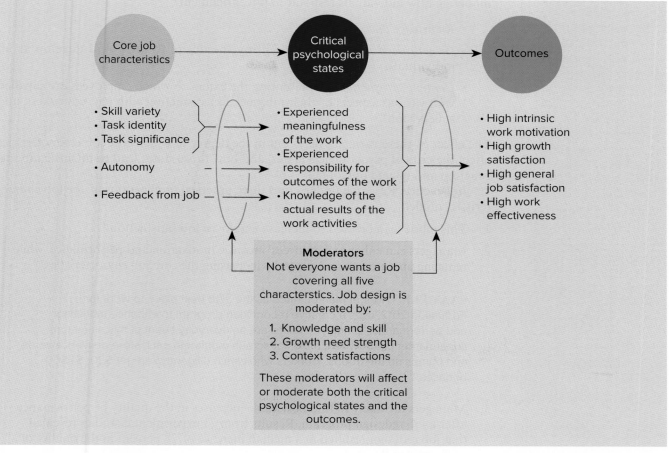

SOURCE: From J Richard Hackman and Greg R Oldham, *Work Redesign* (Prentice Hall Organizational Development Series), 1st ed © 1980, p 90. Reproduced by permission of Pearson Education, Upper Saddle River, NJ.

- **Task identity.** The extent to which the job requires an individual to perform a whole or completely identifiable piece of work. In other words, task identity is high when a person works on a product or project from beginning to end and sees a tangible result.

- **Task significance.** The extent to which the job affects the lives of other people within or outside the organization.

- **Autonomy.** The extent to which the job enables an individual to experience freedom, independence, and discretion in both scheduling and determining the procedures used in completing the job.

- **Feedback.** The extent to which an individual receives direct and clear information about how effectively he or she is performing the job.[67]

Moderators. See the box "Moderators" in Figure 5.8. Hackman and Oldham recognized that everyone does not want a job containing high amounts of the five core job characteristics. They incorporated this recognition into their model by identifying three person factors (inputs in our Integrative Framework) that affect or moderate how individuals respond to job enrichment:

- *Knowledge and skill.*
- *Growth need strength* (representing the desire to grow and develop as an individual).
- *Context satisfactions* (representing the extent to which employees are satisfied with various aspects of their job, such as satisfaction with pay, coworkers, and supervision).

The effect of these variables plays out in the degree to which core job characteristics affect the critical psychological states, and how those states lead to intrinsic job satisfaction and related outcomes.

In Practice. Research underscores three practical implications of the job characteristics model.

1. This model can be used to increase employee job satisfaction.[68]

2. Managers can enhance employees' intrinsic motivation and performance, while reducing absenteeism and stress, by increasing the core job characteristics.[69]

   EXAMPLE Nugget Market, rated as the 37th best place to work for by *Fortune* in 2012, uses a creative recognition program to enhance motivation and performance. "Employee rallies are an everyday event at this nine-store supermarket chain, where a big flat-screen monitor in each store delivers awards and pumps up the troops. Workers who watch diligently can get $20–$1,500 bonuses."[70]

3. Managers are likely to find noticeable increases in the quality of performance after a job redesign program. Results from 21 experimental studies revealed that job redesign resulted in a median increase of 28 percent in the quality of performance.[71]

Bottom-Up Approaches— "You Design Your Own Job"

As the term *bottom-up* suggests, this approach to job design is driven by employees rather than managers and is referred to as job crafting. **Job crafting is defined as "the physical and cognitive changes individuals make in the task or relational boundaries of their work."**[72] Employees are viewed as "job crafters" according to this model because they are expected to define and create their own job boundaries. As such, this approach to job design represents pro-active and adaptive employee behavior aimed at changing tasks, relationships, and cognitions associated with one's job.

Forms of Job Crafting Table 5.2 illustrates three forms of job crafting. The first involves changing one's *task boundaries*. You can do this by altering the scope or nature of tasks you complete at work or you can take on fewer or more tasks. The second entails changing the *relational nature* of one's job. Specifically, you can alter the quantity or quality of interactions you have with others at work, or you can establish new relationships. The third is *cognitive crafting*. It encompasses a change in how you perceive or think about the existing tasks and relationships associated with your job.

TABLE 5.2 FORMS OF JOB CRAFTING

CHANGES IN APPROACH	EXAMPLE	CHANGES IN RESULTS
Task boundaries: Number, scope, and type of job tasks.	Design engineers engage in relational tasks that move a project to completion.	Engineers are now guardians or movers of projects; they complete work in a more timely fashion.
Relational nature: Quality and/or amount of interaction with others encountered in a job.	Hospital cleaners actively care for patients and families and integrate themselves into the workflow of their floor units.	Cleaners are now helpers of the sick; they see the work of the floor unit as a vital part of an integrated whole.
Cognitive crafting: Perception of or thinking about tasks and relationships in your job.	Nurses take responsibility for all information and "insignificant" tasks so they can care more appropriately for a patient.	Nurses are now patient advocates; they provide high-quality, technical care.

SOURCE: Adapted from A. Wrzesniewski and J. E. Dutton, "Crafting a Job: Revisioning Employees as Active Crafters of Their Work," *Academy of Management Review*, April 2001, 185.

More and more people are crafting jobs that entail doing work from home. What are the challenges of managing people who work from home?

Outcomes of Job Crafting The right-hand column in Table 5.2 outlines the potential impact of job crafting on employee motivation and performance. You can see that job crafting is expected to change how employees perceive their jobs. Job crafting is expected to result in more positive attitudes about one's job, which in turn is expected to increase employee motivation, engagement, and performance. Preliminary research supports this proposition.[73]

Given that job crafting can lead to higher levels of engagement and satisfaction, you may be interested in understanding how you can apply the technique to a former, current, or future job. The following Self-Assessment explores the extent to which you may have applied job crafting to reduce job demands, seek resources, or seek challenges.

---

connect

SELF-ASSESSMENT 5.3 **To What Extent Have I Used Job Crafting?**

This survey measures the extent to which you are currently using job crafting. It assesses your efforts on three dimensions of job crafting: reducing work demands, seeking resources to do the job, and seeking challenges. Go to connect.mheducation .com and complete Self-Assessment 5.3. Then consider the following questions:

1. What are your strengths and weaknesses in terms of job crafting?
2. Were you happy in the job under consideration?
3. Do you think the average employee can affect all of the suggestions measured in the survey? Explain.

TAKE-AWAY APPLICATION—TAAP

Use the Results from Self-Assessment 5.3 to answer the following:

1. Use results from your assessment to identify three job crafting ideas you might use to increase your intrinsic motivation.
2. Using Table 5.2, identify two additional job crafting ideas.
3. What are the roadblocks to implementing the ideas identified in the above two steps?

Idiosyncratic Deals (I-Deals)— "You Negotiate the Design of Your Job"

This last approach to job design represents a middle ground between top-down and bottom-up methods and attempts to overcome their limitations. For example, top-down approaches are constrained by the fact that managers cannot always create changes in task characteristics that are optimum for everyone. Similarly, job crafting is limited by the amount of latitude people have in changing their own jobs. **Idiosyncratic deals (i-deals)** represent "employment terms individuals negotiate for themselves, taking myriad forms from flexible schedules to career development."[74] Although "star performers" have long negotiated special employment contracts or deals, demographic trends and the changing nature of work have created increased opportunities for more employees to negotiate i-deals.

I-deals tend to involve task and work responsibilities, schedule flexibility, location flexibility, and compensation.[75] The goal of such deals is to increase employee intrinsic motivation and productivity by allowing employees the flexibility to negotiate employment relationships that meet their needs and values. RSM McGladrey is a great example. The company promotes and encourages the creation of i-deals among its 8,000 employees. The focus of RSM McGladrey's program is to create innovative and flexible ways of working.[76]

Although this approach to job design is too new to have generated much research, preliminary evidence is positive. A recent study showed that i-deals were significantly correlated with employees' job satisfaction and organizational commitment.[77] Future study is needed to determine the generalizability of these encouraging results.

Consider how you might one day create an i-deal for yourself. This Self-Assessment will help you think through the process.

connect

SELF-ASSESSMENT 5.4   Creating an I-Deal

This survey measures the extent to which you are engaging in behaviors associated with creating i-deals. Go to connect.mheducation.com and complete Self-Assessment 5.4. Then consider the following questions:

1. What are your strengths and weaknesses in terms of creating an i-deal?
2. Assume you are applying for a job after graduation and you want to create an i-deal. What do your results suggest that you should discuss with your potential employer?

what did i learn?

You learned that motivation, a key individual-level process, is influenced by inputs such as needs, perceptions of justice, expectancies and instrumentalities, goals, and job design. You learned how various theories and models of motivation can be applied by managers to improve multiple outcomes. Reinforce your learning with the Key Points below. Consolidate your learning using the Integrative Framework. Then, Challenge your mastery of the material by answering the Major Questions in your own words.

Key Points for Understanding Chapter 5

You learned the following key points.

5.1 THE WHAT AND WHY OF MOTIVATION

- There are two types of motivation: intrinsic and extrinsic motivation.
- Extrinsic motivation results from the potential or actual receipt of extrinsic rewards.
- Intrinsic motivation is driven by positive internal feelings generated by doing well.
- Motivating employees is important for five reasons: why people join organizations, why people stay in organizations, why people are engaged at work, why people perform organizational citizenship behavior, and why people help their colleagues.

5.2 CONTENT THEORIES OF MOTIVATION

- Content theories are based on the idea that an employee's needs influence motivation. There are five key content theories.
- Douglas McGregor proposed a theory of motivation based on two opposing views of employees. Theory X people believe that employees dislike work and are motivated by rewards and punishment. Theory Y people believe that employees are self-engaged, committed, and responsible.
- Abraham Maslow proposed that motivation is a function of five basic needs—physiological, safety, love, esteem, and self-actualization—arranged in a prepotent hierarchy.
- David McClelland's acquired needs theory is based on the idea that motivation is a function of three basic needs: achievement, affiliation, and power.

- Self-determination theory assumes that three innate needs influence motivation: competence, autonomy, and relatedness.
- Frederick Herzberg's motivator-hygiene theory is based on the premise that job satisfaction and dissatisfaction arise from two different sets of factors. Satisfaction comes from motivating factors and dissatisfaction from hygiene factors.

5.3 PROCESS THEORIES OF MOTIVATION

- Process theories attempt to describe how various person factors and environmental factors affect motivation.
- Equity theory is a model of motivation that explains how people strive for fairness and justice in social exchanges. Fairness or equity is determined by comparing outputs and inputs with those of others.
- Three key types of justice include distributive, procedural, and interactive.
- Expectancy theory assumes that motivation is determined by one's perceived chances of achieving valued outcomes. The three key elements of this theory include expectancies, instrumentalities, and valence of outcomes.
- Goal-setting theory proposes that goals affect performance because they (1) direct one's attention, (2) regulate effort, (3) increase persistence, and (4) encourage the development of action plans.

5.4 MOTIVATING EMPLOYEES THROUGH JOB DESIGN

- Job design theories are based on the idea that motivation primarily is influenced by the tasks people perform and the characteristics of the immediate work environment.
- There are three broad approaches to job design: top-down, bottom-up, and emerging.
- The premise of top-down approaches is that management is responsible for creating efficient and meaningful combinations of work tasks for employees. Top-down approaches include scientific management, job enlargement, job rotation, job enrichment, and a contingency approach called the job characteristics model.
- Bottom-up approaches, which are referred to as job crafting, are driven by employees rather than managers. Employees create their own job boundaries.

- Emerging approaches include idiosyncratic deals (i-deals). This approach views job design as a process in which employees and managers jointly negotiate the types of tasks employees complete at work.

The Integrative Framework for Chapter 5

In this chapter we have seen how managers can apply various theories to the individual-level process of motivation, affecting outcomes at all three levels of the enterprise. See Figure 5.9.

Challenge: Major Questions for Chapter 5

At the start of the chapter, we told you that after reading the chapter you should be able to answer the following questions. Unless you can, have you really processed and internalized the lessons in the chapter? Review relevant portions of the text and your notes to answer the following major questions. With Figure 5.9 as your guide, look for inputs, processes, and outputs specific to each:

1. What is motivation and how does it affect my behavior?

2. How would I compare and contrast the content theories of motivation?

3. How would I compare and contrast the process theories of motivation?

4. What are the similarities and differences among top-down approaches, bottom-up approaches, and "idiosyncratic deals" in job design?

FIGURE 5.9 INTEGRATIVE FRAMEWORK FOR UNDERSTANDING AND APPLYING OB

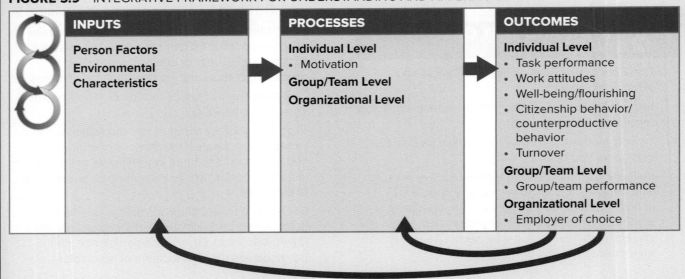

© 2014 Angelo Kinicki and Mel Fugate. All rights reserved. Reproduction prohibited without permission of the authors.

A Fickle Cat

Long-time employees complain that Caterpillar has changed.

John Arnold, a 35-year-old parts auditor at Caterpillar's distribution facility in Morton, Illinois, says some of his coworkers are on food stamps. Arnold has worked for Caterpillar since 1999. More than 10 years later, he's making $15.66 an hour.[78]

To succeed today, does an employer have to worry about motivation? In recent years, Caterpillar, a Wall Street darling and mainstay of American manufacturing, has rolled back traditional extrinsic motivators.

Item: Caterpillar laid off 30,000 workers in 2009.

Item: By the second quarter of 2012, Cat's profit had jumped 67 percent from the previous year. (Net profits in 2011 2Q of $1.01 billion, or $1.52 per share, rose to net profits of $1.69 billion or $2.54 per share in 2012 2Q.)

Item: About the same time, Cat was freezing wages and reducing benefits. New contracts created a two-tier system so that new hires were brought in on an even lower wage scale.[79]

Item: Further layoffs followed the newer, concessionary contracts.[80]

Disparities

In May 2013 a feature in *Bloomberg Businessweek* noted that while workers were losing jobs, pay, and benefits, CEO Oberhelman prospered. In 2011 his pay rose 60 percent to over $16 million, and in 2012 to more than $22 million.

So what serves as employee motivation in this environment? Maybe survival. The article quoted Emily Young, a welder at Caterpillar's Decatur plant: "You're basically expendable. For every one person who doesn't work, there's five waiting in line." The same article quoted CEO Oberhelman affirming, "We can never make enough profit."[81]

Weakened Unions. As *Businessweek* reported, Caterpillar toughed out a strike at its Illinois plant in 2012 for over three months. Eventually union workers agreed to virtually the same offer that caused the strike. Existing workers accepted a six-year wage freeze and reduced benefits. New workers would be brought in at a lower wage scale.

In Wisconsin in 2013, union workers didn't even try to strike. When their contract expired, workers simply stayed on the job. After a few months of on-again, off-again talks, the workers agreed to conditions similar to the Illinois contract.[82]

Worsening Results. Recently Cat's march to higher peaks of profit have stalled. With greater use of natural gas and dropping coal prices, sales of big mining trucks (used in surface coal mining) also declined. This forced the company to scale back production and lay off even more workers. This on top of an overall drop in spending in the Asian mining sector contributed to Cat's decline in earnings.[83]

A Money Problem

Some industry watchers see Caterpillar's worries as a money problem. As in too much of it. *Fortune* senior editor Matt Vella, in a *Fortune* Brainstorm podcast with magazine staff, sees it this way: "The criticism from labor is the company is doing better than ever; why aren't we seeing some of the rewards of that? The company will say, 'Well, we can't afford to give too much away because we don't know what's going to come down the road.'"[84]

The *Businessweek* article brought such questions to a head:

Caterpillar has become a symbol of the growing divergence in corporate America between profits and wages. As a percentage of gross domestic product, corporate earnings recently hit their highest level in more than 60 years, and wages fell to new lows, according to Moody's Analytics.

"What's interesting," says *Fortune* writer Nin-Hai Tseng, " . . . is that Caterpillar makes itself out to be this poster child of everything that went right with manufacturing in America. With that reputation carries a lot of responsibility. . . . [P]eople can ask . . . does it have a responsibility to pay its workers more?"

What Employees Say

While *Glassdoor.com* doesn't provide objective analysis, this job research site provides ready access to employee voices. The site includes posts by current and former company employees so people looking for work can research a potential employer. Most reviews include a simple yes or no on whether the reviewer would recommend the company as an employer. While there's no guarantee that all posts are legitimate, *Glassdoor.com* remains one of the best places to get a quick read on the way current and former employees likely feel.

Reviews for Caterpillar vary. Some workers say good things about their future with Caterpillar and the corporate culture. But more critique the company. Critics of the company's policies include both current and former employees. Tellingly, many current employees who would recommend the company as an employer have misgivings. Major themes include:

- Lack of chances to advance, stand out, prove one's worth, or improve one's compensation.
- Rueful acceptance of problems in the workplace because of the need to have a job.
- Over-management in face of shrinking pay.
- Overemphasis on cost-cutting programs by middle managers who frequently lack product or process knowledge.
- Lack of progressive vision for future growth, with single focus on reducing costs.

You get a sense of the tone of many comments in this post from a former employee, let go after eight years: "They will preach values, morality, safety, people, and quality, but in the end they only care about profit. Never been so disappointed in what a company has become as this one."[85]

The Executive View

When *Businessweek* asked Oberhelman about increasing wages, he sounded wistful. He can raise wages "when we start to see economic growth through GDP," he says. "Part of the reason we're seeing no inflation is because there's no growth. Inflation was driven by higher labor costs, not higher goods costs. Frankly, I'd love to see a little bit of that. Because I'd love to pay people more. I'd love to see rising wages for everybody."[86]

Real GDP has grown slightly during the period in which Oberhelman has reduced and frozen wages, from a negative 3.1% in 2009 up 2.4% in 2010, 1.8% in 2011, and 2.2% in 2012, according to the US Dept. of Commerce.[87]

In the meantime, Oberhelman justifies the growing disparity by invoking competitiveness. For Cat to be competitive, his executive salary needs to increase dramatically. For Cat to be competitive, workers' wages need to be reduced or frozen.

Then and Now

In contrast to its current frosty relations with labor, once Caterpillar was seen as an exemplar of an enlightened management that could justify spending to increase employee engagement by its return on investment.

As recently as 2006, a human resources guide on employee engagement cited Caterpillar as a success story. The guide noted Caterpillar's gains as follows:

- Annual savings of $8.8 million from decreased attrition, absenteeism, and overtime (Europe).
- Increase in output by 70% in less than 4 months (Asia Pacific).
- Decrease in break-even point by almost 50% in units/day, and of grievances by 80% (unionized plant).
- Increase of $2 million in profit and 34% in highly satisfied customers (start-up plant).[88]

Now Caterpillar has decided to increase profitability almost solely by going leaner. The staff at *Fortune* doubt that today's Caterpillar will ever restore the kinds of manufacturing jobs of the past—jobs that brought US workers into the middle class. Instead, Cat hews to a global view of managing labor costs.

The company continues to increase its overseas operations in places like Korea, Russia, and Brazil. Over half of its labor force and its profits are overseas. Domestically Caterpillar continues to reduce and reshape labor, moving to lower pay scales and benefits, and with a greater reliance on guest workers. (Oberhelman has lobbied to make it easier for corporations to bring in lower-cost, highly trained foreign PhDs.) As modern manufacturing continues to do more for less, organic demand for labor will continue to decrease.[89]

Time will tell if the company can remain competitive with a primary focus on managing costs only, or if it will find reason to elevate employee engagement as a company priority.

Apply the 3-Stop Problem-Solving Approach to OB

Stop 1: What is the problem?

- Use the Integrative Framework for Understanding and Applying OB (Figure 5.9) to help identify the outcomes that are important in this case.
- Which of these outcomes are not being achieved in the case?
- Based on considering the above two questions, what is the most important problem in this case?

Stop 2: Use the Integrative Framework to identify the OB concepts or theories that help you to understand the problem in this case.

- What person factors are most relevant?
- What environmental characteristics are most important to consider?
- Do you need to consider any processes? Which ones?
- What concepts or theories discussed in this chapter are most relevant for solving the key problem in this case?

Stop 3: What are your recommendations for solving the problem?

- Review the material in the chapter that most pertains to your proposed solution and look for practical recommendations.
- Use any past OB knowledge or experience to generate recommendations.
- Outline your plan for solving the problem in this case.

LEGAL/ETHICAL CHALLENGE

Should Senior Executives Receive Bonuses for Navigating a Company through Bankruptcy?

Consider this reportage from *The Wall Street Journal*: "On the way to bankruptcy court, Lear Corporation, a car-parts supplier, closed 28 factories, cut more than 20,000 jobs, and wiped out shareholders. Still, Lear sought $20.6 million in bonuses for key executives and other employees, including an eventual payout of more than $5.4 million for then-chief executive Robert Rossiter."

The US Justice Department objected to these bonuses, arguing that they violated a federal law established in 2005. The goal of the law was to restrict companies from paying bonuses to executives before and during a bankruptcy process. However, a judge ruled that the bonuses were legal because they were tied to the individuals meeting specific earning milestones. A company spokesperson further commented that the bonuses were "customary" and "fully market competitive." Lear has subsequently rebounded, adding 23,000 jobs since completing the bankruptcy process.

The practice of giving bonuses to senior executives who navigate a company through bankruptcy is quite common. A study of 12 of the 100 biggest corporate bankruptcies by *The Wall Street Journal* revealed that CEOs from these firms were paid more than $350 million in various forms of compensation.

"Over the past few years, fights have erupted during a handful of Chapter 11 bankruptcy cases," the newspaper reported. "The central argument has been over whether companies are adhering to federal laws when giving their executives the extra pay." While judicial decisions regarding this issue have been mixed, we want you to consider the ethics of paying executives large bonuses when "gutting" a company by laying off workers, closing plants, and eliminating health care and retirement benefits to retirees.[90]

Finding Answers to Solve the Challenge

Is it ethical to pay these bonuses? Respond to each of the following options.

1. Yes. Navigating a company through bankruptcy is hard work and involves making hard decisions. Executives at Lear, for example, earned those bonuses by staying with the company to shepherd it through tough times, helping to turn it around.

2. Yes, if all employees receive some sort of bonus for staying through a bankruptcy process. In other words, executives should be paid the same as other surviving employees. If everyone took a 10% pay cut or gets a 10% bonus, so should executives. What's fair for one is fair for all.

3. Absolutely not. It just is not right to close plants, displace employees, and eliminate retirement benefits while simultaneously giving executives hefty bonuses.

4. What is your ideal resolution to the challenge?

GROUP EXERCISE

Applying the Expectancy Theory

Objective

To practice applying expectancy theory.

Introduction

To increase someone's motivation via expectancy theory, you would make changes to the three components of expectancies, instrumentalities, and valence of rewards. In this exercise you will be asked to consider how you might do this by using a current or past job as a frame of reference.

Instructions

Your instructor will divide the class into groups of four to six. Each group member will work through Part 1 alone and then the group will convene to complete Part 2. If you are currently employed, use this job in answering the questions for Part 1. If you are not employed, then use your last job or a job you desire. Next, assume that you are responsible for managing the people doing that job. In other words, pretend you are managing yourself. Now you are ready to complete the steps in Part 1. Once you complete Part 1, follow the instructions for Part 2.

PART 1 (do this alone)

Step 1: Focusing on the valence component of expectancy theory, describe two ways you can determine the outcomes that employees doing this job would find valuable. What would you say or do?

Step 2: Focusing on instrumentality, explain two ways you can boost the instrumentality or link between performance and valent outcomes for an employee doing the focal job.

Step 3: Describe two ways you could increase expectancy, the likelihood that an employee's efforts will generate greater performance.

PART 2 (do this as a group)

Share your answers for each step in Part 1 with your group members. Don't just passively listen, but instead think of how you could apply their recommendations to the job you enriched in Part 1. Your goal is to gather four reasonable suggested actions for each of the steps in Part 1. This means that when you are finished you should have four different but feasible ways for determining valent outcomes, four ways of increasing instrumentality, and four ways for increasing expectancy.

Questions for Discussion

1. To what extent did your group members arrive at different ideas for steps 1–3 in Part 1. Did you find it valuable to share ideas in the group?

2. Do you think that the final set of ideas you summarized in Part 2 could reasonably be implemented? Explain why or why not.

3. What are the most difficult aspects of trying to apply expectancy theory? Explain.

6 PERFORMANCE MANAGEMENT

How Can You Use Goals, Feedback, Rewards, and Positive Reinforcement to Boost Effectiveness?

inputs

PERSON FACTORS
ENVIRONMENTAL CHARACTERISTICS

processes

INDIVIDUAL LEVEL
Performance management practices
GROUP/TEAM LEVEL
ORGANIZATIONAL LEVEL

outcomes

INDIVIDUAL LEVEL
GROUP/TEAM LEVEL
ORGANIZATIONAL LEVEL

© 2014 Angelo Kinicki and Mel Fugate. All rights reserved.
Reproduction prohibited without permission of the authors.

MAJOR TOPICS I'LL LEARN AND QUESTIONS I SHOULD BE ABLE TO ANSWER

6.1 PERFORMANCE MANAGEMENT PROCESSES
MAJOR QUESTION: *What are the elements of effective performance management, and how can this knowledge benefit me?*

6.2 STEP 1: DEFINE PERFORMANCE—EXPECTATIONS AND SETTING GOALS
MAJOR QUESTION: *How can improving my goal setting give me an advantage?*

6.3 STEP 2: PERFORMANCE MONITORING AND EVALUATION
MAJOR QUESTION: *How can performance monitoring and evaluation improve my performance and my ability to manage the performance of others?*

6.4 STEP 3: REVIEWING PERFORMANCE AND THE IMPORTANCE OF FEEDBACK AND COACHING
MAJOR QUESTION: *How can I use feedback and coaching to review and improve performance?*

6.5 STEP 4: PROVIDE CONSEQUENCES—ADMINISTER REWARDS AND PUNISHMENT
MAJOR QUESTION: *How can I use consequences to generate desired outcomes?*

6.6 REINFORCEMENT AND ADDITIONAL CONSIDERATIONS FOR PROVIDING APPROPRIATE CONSEQUENCES
MAJOR QUESTION: *How can you use various forms of reinforcement and consequences to improve performance?*

INTEGRATIVE FRAMEWORK FOR UNDERSTANDING AND APPLYING OB

Performance management is one of the most important individual-level processes in OB. It influences, for better and for worse, many outcomes for individuals, teams/departments, and organizations. We therefore encourage you to pay close attention to the numerous outcomes affected by performance management practices as you work through this chapter.

winning at work

EFFECTIVE RESPONSES DURING A PERFORMANCE REVIEW[1]

Performance reviews include a reviewer and a reviewee. Both roles are important. However, if you're the reviewee you typically have little control over the content of the message or how it is delivered. But you can control how you respond, and how you respond makes a world of difference in both the short and long run. Consider these tips.

1. *Don't get defensive.* Resist the urge! Keep an open mind and listen to the points that are highlighted in the review. It also is helpful to note the positives instead of fixating only on the negatives. This is difficult because the brain looks for and remembers negative information (recall our discussion in Chapter 3).

2. *Don't discuss the review with coworkers.* Don't vent to your coworkers. The news of a bad performance review often travels like wildfire through the organization. And as you may have seen for yourself, the message can and often does morph as it travels. Accurate, negative information can be painful enough, and nobody needs the additional pain of inaccurate or distorted negative information.

3. *Develop an action plan.* Instead of wallowing in misery, make a plan of how to respond and improve. You may also want to set a follow-up appointment with your boss and enlist his or her help in formulating your plan. Then, follow up to be sure you are on track and making progress.

4. *Make sure you understand the review.* Be sure to clarify, especially if the bad news is a surprise. Misunderstandings and miscommunication are common. It thus is important to remedy these disconnects so that both parties are clear.

5. *Don't take it personally.* Much easier said than done! Regardless of how the feedback is delivered, you can reframe it in terms of your performance rather than you as a person. After all, your action plan will focus on behaviors, not your personality or other fixed traits.

FOR YOU	WHAT'S AHEAD IN THIS CHAPTER

Performance management encompasses many of the topics and tools you've learned thus far. Therefore, in many ways this chapter serves as a sort of summary. And in other ways it serves as a rationale for your taking the course. If you want to know why OB is important, and why its theories, models, and tools matter, it comes down to improving performance at all three levels of OB—individual, team, and organizational. Our discussion focuses on several of the critical components of effective performance management: goal setting, feedback, rewards, and reinforcement. To effectively manage performance, managers and organizations need to determine and communicate clear expectations or goals, monitor and provide feedback regarding progress towards these goals, and then link and deliver appropriate consequences (such as rewards or punishment) for goal achievement. We also highlight how performance management is a powerful tool for motivating, developing, and retaining talent. We hope you will appreciate why an effective performance management system makes sure so many things go right at work.

MAJOR QUESTION

What are the elements of effective performance management, and how can this knowledge benefit me?

THE BIGGER PICTURE

Performance management occurs in many arenas of your life, notably school and work. And because it is a process that generates grades at school, and promotions and pay at work, it is important to understand how it works. Performance management is one of the most critical and far-reaching processes in the Integrative Model for Understanding and Applying OB. You'll see why opinions about the usefulness and effectiveness of performance management practices are often very negative. However, you'll also learn how performance management practices can indeed be beneficial, such as how they help reinforce and signal desired behaviors and outcomes across levels of OB.

major question

Our focus is on improving individual job performance, notably yours, as well as your ability to improve the performance of others. To do this, you need to draw on and apply many of the concepts and tools you've learned thus far, such as motivation, perceptions, individual differences, and human and social capital. The integration and application of this knowledge for the purposes of improved outcomes we refer to as *performance management*.

Performance management (PM) is a set of processes and managerial behaviors that involve defining, monitoring, measuring, evaluating, and providing consequences for performance expectations.[2] Defined in this way, PM is far more than the simple and common performance appraisal. Appraisals typically refer only to the actual performance review, an event. In contrast, effective PM is a continual process that includes much more. Let's see how.

Effective Performance Management

As illustrated in Figure 6.1, PM has multiple steps or components:

Step 1: Defining performance

Step 2: Monitoring and evaluating performance

Step 3: Reviewing performance

Step 4: Providing consequences

Successfully managing performance is a powerful means for improving individual, group, and organizational effectiveness.[3] Effective performance management generally influences important outcomes such as greater employee engagement and better organizational performance.[4] Managers who practice effective performance management generate exceptional results compared to those who don't:

- 50% less turnover
- 10–30% higher customer satisfaction ratings
- 40% higher employee commitment
- Double the net profits[5]

FIGURE 6.1 EFFECTIVE PERFORMANCE MANAGEMENT SYSTEM

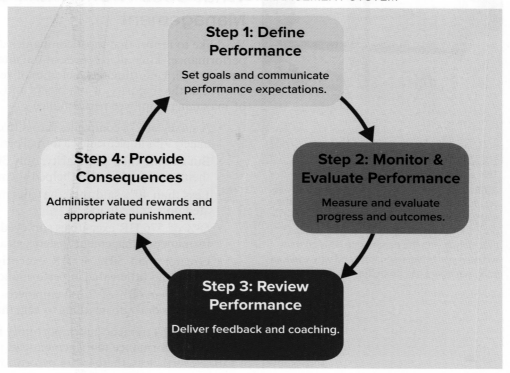

SOURCE: Adapted from A. J. Kinicki, K. J. L. Jacobson, S. J. Peterson, and G. E. Prussia, "Development and Validation of the Performance Management Behavior Questionnaire," *Personnel Psychology,* 2013, 1–45.

Performance management is an ever-present environmental factor, often exerted through the organization's managers and human resources policies and practices. In this chapter we consider its primary function as *process.* Before we are done we will see how PM links to a greater or lesser extent to outcomes across all levels in the Integrative Framework.

- Individual—Job satisfaction, OCBs, and turnover
- Team—Cohesiveness and performance
- Organization—Reputation and employer of choice

Common Uses of Performance Management

Most performance management processes have three primary functions.

1. *Make employee-related decisions.* For instance, your performance can be used to justify a pay raise, a promotion, and new assignments. PM can also generate documentation that could help justify termination and reduce the chances of a wrongful dismissal lawsuit.

2. *Guide employee development,* by assisting in identifying your strengths and weaknesses and highlighting your training and development needs. In fact, a performance management expert said that PM "is one of the most powerful talent management practices we have as HR professionals."[6]

3. *Send strong signals to employees* about what they are supposed to do and how to advance their careers within a given organization.

This final purpose also applies in school. Think about it: the components of your grade in this course signal what is important, what your professor expects you to do, and thus what is rewarded.

What Goes Wrong with Performance Management

This photo is typical of many performance reviews: a manager and a subordinate on opposite sides of a table; just once a year; the manager doing all/most of the talking; both uncomfortable; and both walking away less than happy with the experience. This chapter will help you understand how and why you and your managers can do better.

We'd like to report that most companies do a good job with managing performance. After all, it represents an internal variable over which they have control. Unfortunately, volumes of research and employee surveys show that the majority of managers and organizations do a poor job of managing employee performance.

- A survey of 278 companies across 15 countries showed that approximately 91% implemented a formal performance management system.
- But despite their popularity, only 30% of workers reported that their company's system helped them improve their performance.
- Less than 40% said their systems provided clear goals or generated honest feedback.[7]
- 58% of 576 HR executives surveyed graded their company's performance management systems as a C or worse.[8]
- Greater than 50% of HR executives and line managers said "they find little value in performance reviews."
- More than 60% of 2,200 employees surveyed by *Salary.com* said "reviews don't do anything to help their future performance."[9]

Such dismal statistics reveal a tremendous opportunity for individuals and organizations, as more effective performance management can improve numerous outcomes across levels of OB. Nevertheless, these awful perceptions beg the question: Why do companies often do so poorly with performance management?

First, often PM practices are *impractical*. They don't fit the situation and don't motivate the appropriate behaviors and outcomes. Such PM practices therefore are reduced to "chores" that involve little more than checking boxes. To illustrate, it is likely that you either have or will have a job in which your responsibilities shift and change as the demands of the market and your customers change. However, your employer's performance management practices may not adapt accordingly. This can result in a disconnect between the elements in your review and what you actually do day-to-day in your job.

Second, many experts also argue that the pitfalls of performance management frequently are due to *focusing on only one part of the process,* such as rating tools themselves (filling out the annual review form is the most common example) and only using measures that are available rather than measuring what is appropriate. For example, the amount of time spent with each customer is easy to measure but means less than the measure of customer satisfaction, or the number of new ideas generated versus the number of viable products taken to market. These shortcomings can result in employees and managers perceiving the whole process as simply administrative and one that doesn't accurately measure actual performance.

We therefore encourage you to study, learn, and apply all elements of performance management discussed in this chapter. Doing so will help you overcome these negative perceptions and show you that performance management is an important, practical process that connects many inputs and outcomes in the Integrative Framework of OB.

Importance of Good Management and Leadership

Research consistently shows that "over half of the most important drivers of employee engagement and performance are precisely the behaviors that define effective performance management: setting clear expectations, helping employees accomplish work, providing regular feedback, and finding new opportunities for employees to succeed and develop."[10] An excellent comprehensive application is provided in the following Example box. Learn how Tom Monaghan, the founder of Domino's Pizza, is now applying his extremely successful performance management techniques to home delivery hamburgers! While his burger venture is not thriving at the time we wrote this book, we present this Example here to introduce many of the PM topics and practices discussed throughout the chapter.

EXAMPLE Effective Performance Management: More Pizza and More Burgers

Tom Monaghan, the founder of Domino's Pizza, attributes much of his success to performance management. After starting Domino's Pizza in 1960, he grew the company to be the country's number one pizza delivery chain. He sold the company to Bain Capital for $1 billion in 1998.

He is now applying some of those same practices to a new business—Gyrene Burger. Like the 30-minute free-delivery promise at Domino's, Gyrene promises a hot, quality burger delivered free to your home in 10 minutes or less. To do this, the company delivers burgers and fries to customers within a 1½-mile radius of the store on bicycles and mopeds. Monaghan says, "If I know anything, it's how to deliver fast food." Gyrene is the nickname for a US Marine, which Monaghan served as for several years in the 1950s. The marines also inspired the camouflage themes of Gyrene's employee uniforms. He says the delivery burger business can be even bigger than that of Domino's Pizza, which at one point had 6,200 stores and was opening three more every day. To do this, Monaghan follows many of the elements of effective performance management shown in Figure 6.1.

CLEAR PERFORMANCE EXPECTATIONS   As is abundantly clear in Monaghan's autobiography, *Pizza Tiger,* the time element always matters. The 30-minute delivery guarantee was necessary. What would be the point of delivering a high-quality pizza, Monoghan asks, if it was cold? The emphasis on time extends to other parts of the business. Gary McCausland, Gyrene's COO and former head of International Operations at Domino's, still remembers when once he was late to an executive team meeting. Monaghan told him, "You're 12 minutes late; get up and get out of here and set your watch 10 minutes fast and you won't be late." Now for burgers at Gyrene, Monaghan is still a stickler for making the most of time. He personally shows employees how to run out the door. He also insists that all employees be able to run a 10-minute mile.

MONITORING, EVALUATING, AND REVIEWING PERFORMANCE   At Domino's Monaghan used a job planning and review (JP&R) system. At least once every three months, employees are required to fill out a form before sitting down with their manager. On the form employees are asked to describe their job functions or tasks. The purpose is to be sure that employees understand what is expected of them. The employees then describe what the manager is supposed to do to support their efforts in meeting these expectations. Then employees need to list goals for the month and action plans to achieve them. Monaghan explains that this helps employees build self-esteem via goal achievement, while at the same time helping managers hold people accountable. Finally, the manager completes a form that is shared with employees, who are given space and an opportunity to respond.

EXECUTIVES SET THE TONE   Executives were not exempt from the same standards; even more was expected of them. They were required to complete the above process once a month. Executives who reported directly to Monaghan had to give him a report every day describing the three or four things that they had done. Paul Roney, the former corporate treasurer at Domino's, described it this way: "When I first heard this I thought this is crazy." But he learned to appreciate such reports. "It's a communication mechanism, and it's a way to get constant feedback."[11]

REWARDING PERFORMANCE AND RETAINING TALENT   "I'm big on incentives," says Monaghan. At Domino's store managers earned 30 percent of profits in addition to their salaries. He also shares financial information (e.g., profit and loss statements) with all employees. Monaghan says, "Most businesses are embarrassed to show profits because of how low they are." Incentives also were used to retain talent. Domino's was losing key talent in the form of successful, proven managers. To help combat this, a system was put in place that rewarded franchisees for developing managers into store owners themselves. The franchisees then earned a percentage of the royalties from the new owner's stores.

YOUR THOUGHTS?

1. Do you think the practices that were so successful at Domino's Pizza will work at Gyrene Burgers? Why or why not?

2. What do you think are the pros and cons of Monaghan's performance management practices?

3. How effective do you think they would be where you work or have worked? Or if so far your job has been being a student, how effective would Monaghan's performance management practices be for you as a student? Explain.

As we delve deeper into the four steps of performance management, keep Gyrene Burgers and Monaghan's practices in mind. You'll find that Monaghan has used most every concept and tool covered in this chapter.

6.2 STEP 1: DEFINE PERFORMANCE—EXPECTATIONS AND SETTING GOALS

MAJOR QUESTION

How can improving my goal setting give me an advantage?

THE BIGGER PICTURE

Not all goals are created equal. You're about to learn the difference between performance goals and learning goals. More importantly, you'll pick up tips on how to manage the goal-setting process. You'll also benefit from practical guidance on what types of goals to use when.

Fisk Johnson, CEO of S. C. Johnson, strongly believes in setting goals. S. C. Johnson is the world's largest maker of household products, including Shout, Windex, Drano, and Scrubbing Bubbles. Here is what Johnson had to say when he accepted the Climate Leadership Award for Aggressive Goal Setting to reduce greenhouse gas emissions.[12]

> As a family company, we're committed to doing what's right for people and the planet, and we believe that to make an impact, you have to set measurable goals. In addition to the 27% reduction we've achieved versus our 2005 U.S. baseline, we will continue to raise the bar and hold ourselves accountable. By 2016, we plan to further reduce our greenhouse gas emissions by an additional 7% absolute reduction, and we're honored to be recognized for setting this goal.[13]

It makes sense that an important way to improve your performance and your ability to manage the performance of others is to create better goals. "When people have goals to guide them, they are happier and achieve more than they would without having them," according to a 2010 article in *Psychology Today*.[14] According to a Franklin Covey survey of workers in the United States, 56 percent don't "clearly understand their organization's most important goals" and an astounding 81 percent "don't have clearly defined goals."[15] It thus seems that an important way to improve your performance and your ability to manage the performance of others is to create better goals! "It simply is a fact: when people have goals to guide them, they are happier and achieve more than they would without having them. It's a brain thing. Achieving a goal you've set produces dopamine, a neurotransmitter responsible for feelings of pleasure. Reciprocally, dopamine activates neural circuitry that makes it easier to pursue new challenges. . . . Goals provide focus . . . enhance productivity and bolster self-esteem. And most of all, goals increase commitment, so you're more likely to achieve whatever you set out to conquer."[16]

Keep in mind that a challenge and prime responsibility for managers is to set and align goals across levels of OB—individual, department, and organizational. While this is true, our primary focus here is on the goals set at the individual level.

Two Types of Goals

The potentially vast number of goals you might set can generally be categorized into two types—performance goals and learning goals. **A *performance goal* targets a specific end result, and a *learning goal* involves enhancing your knowledge or skill.** Managers typically overemphasize the former and ignore the latter as they try to "motivate" greater effort and achieve final results. But if you lack necessary skills, experience, or direction from your supervisor, then performance goals can be more frustrating than motivating. When skills are lacking, it often is helpful to set learning goals first and then performance goals once you've developed some level of proficiency. Let's illustrate using a golf analogy, wherein a performance goal often distracts attention from the discovery of task-relevant strategies. For example, focusing on a golf score of 95 by novices may prevent them from concentrating on the fundamental elements of a sound golf swing and club selection. Both are essential for attaining that score. In short, the novice golfer must learn how to play the game before becoming concerned with a challenging performance outcome (e.g., score of 95).[17]

This also applies in college (and later in life). Given that about 25 percent of students who enroll in four-year colleges never finish, goal-setting skills need more attention. A study involving students who were struggling academically demonstrated the power of teaching students how to skillfully set and integrate both learning and performance goals. They participated in an intensive online tutorial on how to write and achieve personal goals, which led to significant improvement in academic achievement four months later.[18] The lesson? Learn about and apply goal setting to improve your grades now, if not also your performance at work.

Managing the Goal-Setting Process

There are four general steps to follow when implementing a goal-setting program (for yourself or others). Deficiencies in one step cannot be made up for with strength in the others. You need to diligently execute all four steps. We label these Step A, Step B, and so on to avoid confusion with the numbered steps of the Effective Performance Management System (compare Figure 6.1).

Step A: Set goals

Step B: Promote goal commitment

Step C: Provide support and feedback

Step D: Create action plans

Step A: Set Goals   Whether goals are imposed or set participatively, via a free exchange with your manager, they should be "SMART." ***SMART* applied to goals is an acronym for *specific, measurable, attainable, results* oriented, and *time* bound.** Table 6.1 lists practical guidelines for writing SMART goals.

TAKE-AWAY APPLICATION—TAAP

1. Select an important goal at school.

2. Make it "SMART" by being sure that it is: specific, measureable, attainable, results oriented, and time bound.

3. Refine it further still by assuring that it begins with "to _____," and pay particular attention to how it will be measured.

4. Do the same for a goal outside of school.

TABLE 6.1 GUIDELINES FOR WRITING SMART GOALS

Specific	Goals should be stated in precise rather than vague terms. For example, a goal that provides for 20 hours of technical training for each employee is more specific than stating that a manager should send as many people as possible to training classes. Goals should be quantified when possible.
Measurable	A measurement device is needed to assess the extent to which a goal is accomplished. Goals thus need to be measurable. It also is critical to consider the quality aspect of the goal when establishing measurement criteria. For example, if the goal is to complete a managerial study of methods to increase productivity, one must consider how to measure the quality of this effort. Goals should not be set without considering the interplay between quantity and quality of output.
Attainable	Goals should be realistic, challenging, and attainable. Impossible goals reduce motivation because people do not like to fail. Remember, people have different levels of ability and skill.
Results oriented	Corporate goals should focus on desired end results that support the organization's vision. In turn, an individual's goals should directly support the accomplishment of corporate goals. Activities that support the achievement of goals are outlined in action plans. To focus goals on desired end results, goals should start with the word *to*, followed by verbs such as *complete, acquire, produce, increase,* and *decrease.* Verbs such as *develop, conduct, implement,* or *monitor* imply activities and should not be used in a goal statement.
Time bound	Goals specify target dates for completion. (Recall the example of S. C. Johnson.)

SOURCE: From A. J. Kinicki, *Performance Management Systems* (Superstition Mt., AZ: Kinicki & Associates, 2011), 2–9. Reprinted with permission; all rights reserved.

Step B: Promote Goal Commitment   Goal commitment is important because employees are more motivated to pursue goals they view as personally relevant, obtainable, and fair. Table 6.2 provides practical advice to increase your goal commitment, while at the same time improving the quality of your goals and boosting your effectiveness.

TAKE-AWAY APPLICATION—TAAP

Build commitment to your goals.

1. Using a SMART goal you created from the previous TAAP box, apply the recommendations from Table 6.2 to increase your commitment to that goal.

2. Set a grade goal for the next exam in one of your courses. Apply the Table 6.2 recommendations to enhance your commitment and increase your chances of success.

Step C: Provide Support and Feedback   This step is about helping employees achieve their goals. Practical guidelines include the following:

- Make sure each employee has the necessary skills and information to reach his or her goals. Provide training if necessary, as it can boost one's expectancy (Chapter 5).

- Pay attention to employees' expectations about the movement from effort to performance, their perceived self-efficacy, and their reward preferences, and adjust accordingly.

- Be supportive and helpful. Empower employees as they grow.

- Give employees timely and task-specific feedback (knowledge of results) about what they are doing right and wrong.

- Provide monetary and nonmonetary incentives and reward meaningful progress too, and not just goal accomplishment.[19]

TABLE 6.2 TIPS FOR INCREASING GOAL COMMITMENT AND SUCCESS

Write Your Goals Down	You've heard it before, but writing your goals down makes a real difference. It helps guard against daydreaming or wishful thinking, in addition to making them SMART, and provides a record that you can go back and revise as you make progress or fine-tune your approach. Writing your goals down also clears room in your head—you don't have to remember them.
Identify Key Obstacles and Sources of Support	Be proactive and try to identify what or who might get in your way. Conversely, think of who or what might be able to help you reach your goal.
What's in It for YOU?	List the benefits of achieving the goal. Keeping your eyes on the prize will help you stay motivated over time.
Break It Down	Often your goals are large and/or take considerable time to achieve. It therefore is helpful to break them down into smaller, sub- or intermediate goals. Visualize. If you haven't tried this, do it; it works! Imagine not only how you will benefit by achieving your goal, but also how you feel. Adding the positive emotional component, as we discussed in Chapter 5, can be incredibly motivating.
Organize	Preparation is key. It gives you clarity, makes you more efficient, and helps you avoid wasting energy and time
Reward Yourself	We encourage you to reward yourself both for progress while pursuing your goal, as well as attaining the ultimate outcome. It is important to reinforce your efforts. Building in "small wins" and rewards along the way can help motivate you and keep you on track.[20]

Step D: Create Action Plans   What good is a goal without a plan for realizing it? For instance, planning the amount of time you intend to devote to training, rather than simply attending a session or doing it when you can, greatly improves the effectiveness of your learning. The same applies to studying—plan your study time, what you will study during that time, and research says you are more likely to stick with it and increase your learning.[21] The previous three steps all help tremendously in formulating your actions plans. Table 6.2 also offers useful tips. Besides these, we encourage you to look to your experience—what's worked in the past when pursuing a similar goal? If you can't rely on your own experience, then learn what others have done and follow their plan. No need to reinvent the wheel.

Next, visualize what achieving the goal looks like and work backwards. This is another instance where the characteristics of SMART goals are extremely valuable. Specific, results oriented, and time bound are fundamental characteristics of solid action plans. Finally, if you run into difficulties, then we've already provided you with an excellent tool—the problem-solving approach that we introduced you to in Chapter 1. This can help you identify and remedy roadblocks in your goal setting and action plans.

Applying the contingency approach we discussed in Chapter 1 to your goal setting is another way to be more effective and boost performance. Let's explore this next.

Contingency Approach to Defining Performance

Recall our discussion in Chapter 1 where we described how effective employees and managers (you!) should use a *contingency approach*. You learned there that it is important to do what the situation requires, rather than applying a one-size-fits-all approach and simply doing what has always been done, or only following your personal

TABLE 6.3 CONTINGENCY APPROACH TO DEFINING PERFORMANCE

BEHAVIORAL GOALS	OBJECTIVE GOALS	TASK OR PROJECT GOALS
• Can be used in most jobs.	• Best for jobs with clear and readily measured outcomes.	• Best for jobs that are dynamic, but in which nearer-term activities and milestones can be defined.
• Most relevant for knowledge work.	• Measure what matters, not just what can be measured.	• Similar to SMART goals.
• Example: Treat others with professionalism and respect; communicate clearly.	• Examples: sales quotas, production rates, error rates.	• Example: Complete your portion of the team project by Tuesday.

SOURCE: From E. D. Pulakos, R. A. Mueller-Hanson, R. S. O'Leary, and M. M. Meyrowitz, "Building a High-Performance Culture: A Fresh Look at Performance Management," *SHRM Foundations Effective Practice Guidelines Series,* July 24, 2012, 9. © 2012 Society for Human Resource Management, Alexandria, VA. Used with permission. All rights reserved.

preferences. Fit the behavior, policy, or practice to the situation. You are well served to remember and apply this same wisdom to goal setting.

To be clear, learning and performance goals have their place, and setting SMART goals can give you a significant advantage over your competitors. However, you can be more effective still if you define performance goals in ways *that match the situation*—not all performance can or should be measured in dollars and cents. Table 6.3 illustrates how some situations are best suited for behavioral goals, while others are best suited for objective goals, and others still, for task or project goals.

Goals and their associated consequences can powerfully affect performance, both positively and negatively. The following Example box shows both the advantages and disadvantages of goal setting in US hospitals.

EXAMPLE Green, Yellow, and Red Doctors[22]

Many for-profit hospital companies in the United States now utilize rigorous performance management systems for both doctors and administrators that include all of the steps in Figure 6.1. These organizations put a great emphasis on objective goals, and sometimes these same practices get them in trouble. For instance, physicians at Health Management Associates (HMA) were expected to admit at least 50 percent of all patients over the age of 65 that entered the emergency department. The intent of these goals was to align physician behaviors with the hospital's goals of increasing tests and admissions, which in turn would boost profits. Physician performance was posted on scorecards. Those who achieved the goal were noted in green; those who were close, in yellow; and those not meeting expectations, in red. A number of lawsuits have ensued alleging that unnecessary care was provided and bills artificially (fraudulently) inflated.

STEP 2: PERFORMANCE MONITORING AND EVALUATION

MAJOR QUESTION

How can performance monitoring and evaluation improve my performance and my ability to manage the performance of others?

THE BIGGER PICTURE

You're about to learn how monitoring and evaluating are the important next steps after defining and communicating performance expectations. To assure success, it is necessary to accurately measure and evaluate both your progress and ultimate completion of the goals you set in Step 1. You'll learn numerous practical tips to help with both monitoring and evaluating performance. Specifically, you'll learn how your perceptual errors can influence your evaluation of performance and how 360-degree feedback is a tool commonly used to help overcome shortcomings in the measurement and evaluation of performance.

Once performance expectations (goals) are defined and communicated it is necessary to monitor and evaluate your and others' progress and ultimate performance. We emphasize the importance of monitoring and evaluating *both* progress toward the final goal and the ultimate level of goal achievement, as doing so improves final outcomes. To make the point clearer, don't you prefer to know how you're doing in your classes sometime before your final grade report? Of course you do. Yet, in our consulting and own work experience we find that managers and organizations often only monitor and evaluate final outcomes, such as did you meet your sales quota or are your customers satisfied. Having no grades during the semester means you have to wait until you receive your final grade report to determine your performance, which is too late to take corrective action and may not capture all of the relevant aspects of your performance during the course. Therefore, accurately and appropriately monitoring and evaluating both progress and outcomes are critical components of effective performance management and your personal effectiveness.

Monitoring Performance—Measure Goals Appropriately and Accurately

Monitoring performance involves measuring, tracking, or otherwise verifying progress and ultimate performance. You use the information gathered through monitoring to identify problems (and successes) and opportunities to enhance performance during the pursuit of a goal, and your final outcomes. To do this effectively, you need to use or even create accurate and appropriate measures. So how do you do this? While there is no one right answer, and we could devote an entire book to the subject, the material on goal setting is quite helpful. Table 6.3 shows that many goals can be categorized as behavioral, objective, or task-oriented. How you measure these goals should match. Besides these, your measurement of performance, and thus your monitoring, can be improved further still by also considering and using four other types of measures, some of which overlap with those shown in Table 6.3:

Timeliness. Was the work completed on time? Many customer service roles require representatives to answer calls within a certain number of rings, or to respond to customer requests in a certain number of hours or days.

Quality. How well was the work done? A behavioral goal that could fit here is greeting customers warmly, personally, and with a smile by observing and/or reporting that these actually occurred.

Quantity. How much? Sales goals are common examples here, such as dollars sold or number of units.

Financial metrics. What were the profits, returns, or other relevant accounting-financial outcomes? For instance, some law firms measure the performance of attorneys and the larger firm by calculating profits in dollars per partner.[23]

After you've defined your performance goals and monitored them using accurate and appropriate measures, it is time to evaluate the level or quality of performance.

Evaluating Performance

It is important that your measures of performance are both relevant and accurate. There is nothing worse than being measured on something that does not matter, or having what is important not be measured. **Evaluating performance is the process of comparing performance at some point in time to a previously established expectation or goal.** Like the example above, every time you receive a grade for a midterm exam, you take that information and compare it with your goal for your final and overall grade for the course. The midterm grade is the means for both monitoring and evaluating your performance. That said, having this information isn't the end of the story. You then evaluate it—did you perform as you expected? Yes? No? Why? The answers to these questions are important and often influenced by your perceptual processes.

Perceptual Errors in Evaluating Performance As you learned in Chapter 4, your attributions and perceptions can greatly influence how you evaluate the information gathered via monitoring. Table 6.4 lists common perceptual errors and recommended solutions around the need to accurately monitor employee performance.

The best-laid goals from Step 1 can be completely undermined if performance toward those goals is not measured appropriately, or if performance is evaluated with bias. Many organizations and their managers have tried to overcome such problems using 360-degree feedback.

Vineet Nayar is the former CEO of HCL Technologies. He implemented an extensive and highly transparent 360-feedback system.

Overcoming Bias and Other Errors with 360-Degree Feedback In *360-degree feedback* individuals compare perceptions of their own performance with behaviorally specific (and usually anonymous) performance information from their manager, subordinates, and peers. Even outsiders, such as customers or suppliers, may be involved. For example, HCL Technologies, one of India's three largest IT services companies, implements a 360-degree feedback program for the CEO and 3,800 managers. The CEO's reviews are transparent, posted on the company's internal web for all 50,000 employees to see. The managers' results are posted too. Vineet Nayar, the former CEO who created the system, described the system as "reverse accountability," wherein managers are accountable to employees, opposite of the business norm.[24]

TABLE 6.4   COMMONLY FOUND PERCEPTUAL ERRORS RELATED TO PERFORMANCE EVALUATION

PERCEPTUAL ERROR	TENDENCY	EXAMPLE	RECOMMENDED SOLUTION: KEEP PERFORMANCE NOTES
Halo	To form an overall impression about a person or object and then use that impression to bias ratings about same.	Rating an employee positively across all dimensions of performance because the employee is so likable.	To record examples of positive and negative employee performance throughout the year. Remember that an employee's behavior tends to vary across different dimensions of performance.
Leniency	To consistently evaluate other people or objects in an extremely positive fashion.	Rating an employee high on all dimensions of performance regardless of actual performance.	To provide specific examples of both good and bad so you can help the employee improve. Remember that it does not help employees when they are given positive, inaccurate feedback. Be fair and realistic in evaluations.
Central tendency	To avoid all extreme judgments and rate people and objects as average or neutral.	Rating an employee as average on all dimensions of performance regardless of actual performance.	To define an accurate profile, with high and low points, so you can help the employee improve. Remember that it is normal to provide feedback that contains both positive and negative information.
Recency effects	To rely on most recent information. If the recent information is negative, the person or object is evaluated negatively.	Rating an employee based on the last portion of the review period.	To accumulate examples of performance over the entire rating period. Remember to look for trends but accept some variance as normal.
Contrast effects	To evaluate people or objects by comparing them with characteristics of recently observed people or objects.	Rating an employee as average, from a comparison of the employee's performance with the notable performance of a few top performers.	To evaluate employees against a standard rather than the performance of some of your most memorable employees. Remember that each employee deserves objectivity in evaluation that a standard can provide.

Collecting performance information from multiple sources helps a person being evaluated to get a broad view of his/her performance. The comparison of ratings across different raters also enables one to see if any potential biases and perceptual errors are occurring. Finally, it also makes it much more difficult for managers to unfairly favor or punish particular employees (recall our discussion of equity and fairness in Chapter 5).

PRACTICAL TIP   Research on upward and 360-degree feedback, combined with our consulting experience, leads us to *favor* anonymity and also to *discourage* use of 360-degree feedback for pay and promotion decisions. When it is used for pay and promotions, managers often resist and/or try to manipulate the process. However, this multisource feedback can be extremely helpful for manager training and development purposes.

Now that you have a sense of the importance of monitoring and evaluating performance, as well as some practical tips for doing this accurately, let's move on to the next step and review performance.

STEP 3: REVIEWING PERFORMANCE AND THE IMPORTANCE OF FEEDBACK AND COACHING

MAJOR QUESTION

How can I use feedback and coaching to review and improve performance?

THE BIGGER PICTURE

You're about to learn how different forms of feedback influence performance and how to deliver feedback more effectively. You'll also see how combining feedback with coaching is a powerful means for managing and improving your performance and that of others.

Most people agree that feedback—both giving and receiving—has the potential to boost performance. However, most people also admit that they neither receive nor provide feedback as often and as well as they would like. We therefore seek to help you understand some reasons why this happens and what you can do about it. It is safe to say, your feedback skills are some of the most valuable tools you can develop and use throughout your career. Now let's convince you that this bold statement is true.

The Importance of Feedback

Mike Duke, former president and CEO of Walmart, is a strong proponent of linking goal setting and feedback.

> Leadership is about . . . listening and getting feedback from a broad array of constituents. . . . It's about setting aggressive goals and not being afraid to go after very aggressive goals and targets. I think it's even better for a leader to set an aggressive goal and come up a little short than it would be to set a soft goal and to exceed it. . . . Hard feedback is in some environments viewed in a very threatening way, and people don't want to hear feedback. In our environment, I think there is a desire to hear candid feedback. When we leave a meeting, before we'll even drive away, I'll ask, "Well, give me feedback." I think a leader asking for feedback sets a good tone.[25]

Despite the clear and important role Mike Duke describes for feedback, it is dramatically underutilized in most every area of our lives. A Watson Wyatt Worldwide survey, for instance, revealed that 43 percent of employees said they "feel they don't get enough guidance to improve their performance." This is reinforced by a survey of 3,611 employees from 291 companies across the United States and Canada. Furthermore, 67 percent of employees felt they received too little positive feedback in general, and 51 percent too little constructive criticism from their bosses. Worse still, those who said they did not receive enough feedback were 43 percent less likely to recommend their employer to others![26] Clearly, feedback can affect outcomes across levels of the Integrative Framework.

What Effective Feedback Is . . . and Is Not

Students and employees alike appreciate feedback (at least those that are top performers). Both want to know how they're doing and how their performance compares to that of their peers. Feedback is an important, but not always present, cousin of goal setting. Feedback enables you to learn how your performance compares to the goal, which you can then use to modify your behaviors and efforts. We therefore define **feedback** **as information about (individual or collective) performance shared with those in a position to improve the situation.** It thus is no surprise that managers in well-run organizations follow up goal setting with a feedback program to facilitate adjustment and improvement, as described in the quote above from Mike Duke at Walmart.

Effective feedback is only information—it is not an evaluation. Subjective assessments such as, "You're lazy" or "You have a bad attitude," do not qualify as effective feedback. But hard data such as units sold, days absent, dollars saved, projects completed, customers satisfied, and quality rejects are all candidates for effective feedback programs. Christopher Lee, author of *Performance Conversations: An Alternative to Appraisals,* clarifies the concept of feedback by contrasting it with performance appraisals:

> Feedback is the exchange of information about the status and quality of work products. It provides a road map to success. It is used to motivate, support, direct, correct and regulate work efforts and outcomes. Feedback ensures that the manager and employees are in sync and agree on the standards and expectations of the work to be performed. Traditional appraisals, on the other hand, *discourage* two-way communication and treat employee involvement as a bad thing. Employees are discouraged from participating in a performance review, and when they do, their responses are often considered "rebuttals."[27]

Two Functions of Feedback

Experts say feedback serves two functions for those who receive it: one is *instructional* and the other *motivational*. Feedback instructs when it clarifies roles or teaches new behavior. For example, an assistant accountant might be advised to handle a certain entry as a capital item rather than as an expense item. Feedback motivates when it serves as a reward or promises a reward (remember our discussion in Chapter 5). Hearing the boss say, "You've completed the project ahead of schedule; take the rest of the day off," is a pleasant reward for hard work, but many employees also appreciate the attention and interest expressed by the very act of providing feedback, regardless of content.

Important Sources of Feedback— Including Those Often Overlooked

There are three common sources of feedback:

1. Others
2. Task
3. Self

It almost goes without saying that you receive feedback from *others* (e.g., peers, supervisors, lower-level employees, and outsiders). Perhaps less obvious is the fact that the *task* itself is a ready source of objective feedback. For instance, many tasks—computer programming, landing a jet airplane, or driving a golf ball—provide a steady stream of feedback about how well or poorly you are doing. A third source of feedback is *you,* but self-serving bias and other perceptual problems can contaminate this source (recall Chapter 4). Those high in self-confidence tend to rely on personal feedback more than those with low self-confidence. And this challenge increases as one moves up the organizational hierarchy because it is more difficult to get useful feedback from others. These challenges aside, feedback can be made even more useful when it is supported by senior managers, or is collected from departing employees and from customers. Each of these is discussed next.

The Role of Senior Managers and Leaders Nobody likes to give the boss negative feedback. And frankly, many bosses never ask because they don't want it. For example, one of the authors has worked at multiple universities and multiple companies in various industries, and none of his bosses have solicited feedback—not deans, not department chairs, not managers—none. This problem is compounded by the fact that task feedback is less feasible for senior managers because their day-to-day activities are more abstract than those of frontline employees (e.g., formulating strategy versus closing a sale). This predicament is consequential, as noted by Jim Boomer, a CPA and professional service firm consultant:

> [I]f you don't have a system for holding individuals accountable for their goals, all the work, time and effort that goes into developing these plans is diminished and you've your wasted effort. . . . Leadership tends to hold junior employees accountable but shies away from a formalized system to measure performance at the [senior manager/leader] level. . . . If [senior managers/leaders] are not willing to hold themselves accountable, employees will simply go through the motions and won't buy into a firm-wide performance system.[28]

So what can an executive or (high-level) manager do?

1. They can seek feedback from others by creating an environment in which employees feel they can be honest and open.

2. Separating feedback from the performance review process also helps, especially for executives who typically are not reviewed formally if at all.

3. They can create a mechanism to collect feedback anonymously. This is useful if the source of the feedback is not particularly important. For example, a CEO based at headquarters in Phoenix is curious how she is perceived by the design team in Shanghai. In this instance she doesn't need to know the views of any specific employee, just the views of employees from that location.[29]

The following Example box describes the unique approach to employee feedback at Zappos.

EXAMPLE How Do You Spell Feedback and Self-Improvement—Z-A-P-P-O-S!

Zappos is a perennial member of the *Fortune* 100 Best Companies to Work for List (no. 31 in 2012).[30] One of the key elements that enables Zappos to have rock star status with its customers and more than 1,200 employees is the company's approach to performance management. The company puts an extremely high premium on feedback, which it sees as fundamental to continuous improvement.[31]

FORM OF FEEDBACK Managers are explicitly instructed to provide only instructional feedback (e.g., amount of time spent on calls with customers)—not evaluative. Feedback is no longer quantified on 1–5 (unsatisfactory–satisfactory) scales. It instead is presented as number of times the manager witnessed a particular desirable behavior. The managers must give specific examples of the behavior.

LINKED TO VALUES These behaviors, and thus the feedback, are directly linked to the company's 10 core values—deliver WOW through service, embrace and drive change, create fun and a little weirdness, be creative and open-minded, pursue growth and learning, build open and honest relationships with communication, build a positive team and family spirit, do more with less, be passionate and determined, be humble. Their PM and associated feedback are all driven by and based on these values.

USE AND FREQUENCY OF FEEDBACK The company no longer does once-a-year reviews, but instead managers are expected to provide feedback and recognize employees continually, as they exhibit particular behaviors. This means managers decide how frequently. Moreover, "these assessments are not used for promotion, pay, or disciplinary purposes. Rather, their purpose is simply to provide feedback on how employees are perceived by others."[32]

NOT MEETING EXPECTATIONS? If this happens, and of course it does, then the company provides a number of free, on-site courses aimed at skill-building and improvement.

YOUR THOUGHTS?

1. What are the advantages to Zappos's approach to feedback?
2. What disadvantages are possible?
3. Explain why you would or would not want to be an employee with such a PM system.
4. Assume you are a manager at Zappos; what would be the pros and cons given this system for you?

Exit Interviews Employees quit jobs for many reasons, such as better opportunities, family issues, money, lack of fairness, bullying, and the most common—a horrible boss. Whatever the reason, exit interviews can provide the feedback that uncovers the true reasons. To illustrate, rather than assume that an employee left for family reasons (e.g., to be closer to family in order to help with young kids), we advise employees and employers to conduct exit interviews. The information gathered can help confirm or refute your assumptions. It also gives you guidance on what the organization needs to improve and what it does well. Perhaps the person actually left because of unethical conduct by boss or peers. Sometimes such feedback can uncover very serious misconduct that needs to be addressed urgently. For example, the cause of the fungal meningitis outbreak stemming from contaminated steroids distributed by New England Compounding Center (NECC) was uncovered, in part, by interviews with ex-employees of another company that was owned by the same people. These former employees revealed many shortcuts that compromised the quality and safety of NECC's products.[33]

Your Perceptions Matter

One reason people don't give or get more feedback is because they don't want it. If you don't want it, then how receptive will you be if you are given feedback? How likely will you be to give it if you think it's not wanted? As you learned in Chapter 2, your attitudes affect your intentions, which affect your behavior and also affect your perceptions. What are your attitudes toward feedback? Do you seek it out? Do you only want to hear it if it is positive? To answer these questions and better understand your desire for feedback, go to connect.mheducation.com and complete Self-Assessment 6.1.

connect

SELF-ASSESSMENT 6.1   What Is My Desire for Performance Feedback?

Go to connect.mheducation.com and take Self-Assessment 6.1 to learn your desire for feedback.

1. Think of a recent instance where you were given feedback by somebody.
2. How does your score help explain your reaction to that feedback?
3. Describe a specific way your desire for feedback (i.e., your score) helps (or hurts) you in college? At work?
4. Given your score, think of how you can improve your receptiveness for feedback.

Excerpted and adapted from D. M. Herold, C. K. Parsons, and R. B. Rensvold, "Individual Differences in the Generation and Processing of Performance Feedback," *Educational and Psychological Measurement*, February 1996, Table 1, p. 9, Copyright © 1996. Reproduced with permission of Sage Publications, Inc. via Copyright Clearance Center.

Many other factors potentially affect your perceptions of feedback. For instance, whether the feedback is negative, the source is credible, the feedback system is fair, and so on, all can influence your perceptions. And of course, your own mindfulness matters (recall Chapter 5).

Negative Feedback   Remember, feedback itself is simply information, neither positive nor negative. It only becomes positive or negative when you compare it to a goal or expectation. Such comparisons are the basis for improvement. (Note: Negative feedback is *not* negative reinforcement. You'll learn the important difference later in this chapter.) Generally, people tend to perceive and recall positive feedback more accurately than they do negative feedback. But negative feedback (e.g., being told your performance is below average) can have a *positive* motivational effect. In fact, in one study those who were told they were below average on a creativity test subsequently outperformed those who were led to believe their results were above average.

The subjects apparently took the negative feedback as a challenge and set and pursued higher goals. Those receiving positive feedback apparently were less motivated to do better.[34] Nonetheless, feedback with a negative message or threatening content needs to be administered carefully to avoid creating insecurity and defensiveness. Put another way, perception matters. Both negative and positive feedback need to provide clear guidance to improve performance. Feedback is most likely to be perceived accurately, and thus more likely to be acted on, when it is seen as instrumental (remember expectancy theory in Chapter 5) to an important or valued outcome.[35]

Self-efficacy also can be damaged by negative feedback, as discovered in a pair of experiments with business students. The researchers concluded, "To facilitate the development of strong efficacy beliefs, managers should be careful about the provision of negative feedback. Destructive criticism by managers which attributes the cause of poor performance to internal factors reduces both the beliefs of self-efficacy and the self-set goals of recipients."[36] One therefore needs to be careful when delivering feedback, due to the effect of feedback on goals.

Factors That Affect Your Perceptions of Feedback   Many factors influence how you, and people in general, perceive feedback. For instance, much of what you learned about attributions in Chapter 4 also applies here. All managers and employees are susceptible to the fundamental attribution bias (e.g., your manager attributes your poor performance entirely to you and things you control) and self-serving bias (e.g., you are likely to take credit for positive performance outcomes and attribute poor performance to other, extrinsic factors). Beyond attributions, the following also can influence your perceptions of feedback:

1. *Accuracy.* A common criticism of PM systems is that they either measure the wrong things or measure the right things wrong. Either way, the feedback received is inaccurate.

2. *Credibility of the sources.* If one of the members of your project team (for school or work) points out shortcomings in your work, you are likely to put more weight on his feedback if he is an "A" student or top performer than if not. Trust also is critical here. If you don't trust the person delivering the feedback, then you will likely be suspicious of his/her intentions and thereby discount its value.

3. *Fairness of the system.* If you perceive the process or outcomes—recall equity theory from Chapter 5—are unfair, then you are likely not only to discount the feedback but also to be outraged, withdraw, commit counterproductive work behaviors, and/or quit. Performance appraisals are one of the most common and critical aspects of organizational life that produce issues of fairness.

4. *Performance-reward expectancies.* Effective performance management, particularly ongoing and open feedback between you and your supervisors, is an important means for managing such expectancies.

5. *Reasonableness of the goals or standards.* Think goals—challenging is good, unattainable bad. An excellent example: if your manager says, "It is possible for you to earn a bonus up to 50 percent of your salary," then we encourage you to ask/consider if anybody has actually ever earned that much. If not, you may be the first, but it is more likely that the goal/standard is unreasonable.

Any feedback that fails to clear one or more of these cognitive hurdles will be rejected or discounted. Personal experience largely dictates how you weigh these factors. For

TABLE 6.5 FEEDBACK DO'S AND DON'TS

DON'T[37]	DO[38]
Use feedback to punish, embarrass, or put somebody down.	Keep feedback relevant by relating it to existing goals.
Provide feedback that is irrelevant to the person's work.	Deliver feedback as soon as possible to the time the behavior was performed.
Provide feedback that is too late to do any good.	Provide specific and descriptive feedback.
Provide feedback about something that is beyond the individual's control	Focus the feedback on things employees can control.
Provide feedback that is overly complex or difficult to understand.	Be honest, developmental, and constructive.

example, a review of research on disciplinary practices found that people have different perceptions of a disciplinary act based on the sex of the person delivering the discipline, the cultural characteristics of the people involved, and the supervisor's use of apologies and explanations.[39] Given these differences in perception, we recommend that supervisors utilize two-way communication, follow up with the employee to make sure the discipline was understood, use empathy (or apologies if appropriate) to lessen the employee's negative reactions (e.g., anger), and focus on helping the employee in the long run.

Feedback Do's and Don'ts

According to Anne Stevens and Greg Gostanian, managing partners at ClearRock, an outplacement and executive coaching firm, "Giving feedback to employees—and receiving feedback yourself—is one of the most misunderstood and poorly executed human resource processes."[40] Table 6.5 lists some important and fundamental do's and don'ts for giving feedback.

Coaching—Turning Feedback into Change

Coaching is a customized process between two or more people with the intent of enhancing learning and motivating change. Once goals and expectations are determined and communicated, performance is monitored, and feedback is collected, one potential next step is coaching. Coaching can either follow or encompass these other steps of performance management. One way to look at coaching is that it is an individualized and customized form of performance management. It is different from training, which typically involves only skill building with the same content delivered to a group of people. It also differs from mentoring, which most often has a career focus, more so than performance, and is exclusively from more senior or experienced employees to more junior. All of these differ from counseling that usually aims to overcome a problem, conflict, or dysfunctional behavior.[41]

Effective coaching is developmental, has specific performance goals, and typically involves considerable self-reflection, self-assessment, and feedback. In fact, "research from Gallup, McKinsey, and Harvard recommends that giving feedback should be the most used tool in a coach's toolbox."[42] The Self-Assessments throughout this book can serve as important elements for your own coaching.[43] When approached in this way, coaching is not only an important aspect of effective performance management, but also consistent with positive organizational behavior (POB) discussed in Chapter 7. Consider this: If coaching is done in the way described, then who wouldn't appreciate or benefit from coaching?

Anne Hawley Stevens, founder of ClearRock, is recognized as one of Boston's top executive coaches.

STEP 4: PROVIDE CONSEQUENCES—ADMINISTER REWARDS AND PUNISHMENT

MAJOR QUESTION

How can I use consequences to generate desired outcomes?

THE BIGGER PICTURE

Of course you like being rewarded, but in OB some rewards are more effective than others. You'll learn common types of rewards and the potential outcomes of specific reward systems. You'll see how organizations use various criteria (e.g., results and behaviors) to distribute rewards, as well as why rewards can fail to motivate as intended.

As illustrated in Figure 6.1, rewards are a critical component of a performance management system. And just as any particular motivational approach affects people differently (as you learned in Chapter 5), so do rewards. Some employees see their job as the source of a paycheck and little else. Others derive great pleasure from their job and association with coworkers. Even volunteers who donate their time to charitable organizations, such as the Red Cross, walk away with rewards in the form of social recognition and the pride of having given unselfishly of their time. It also is likely that in most instances people see such work as highly meaningful (recall our Chapter 3 discussion). Hence, the subject of organizational rewards includes, but goes far beyond, monetary compensation. This section examines key components of organizational reward systems.

Despite the fact that reward systems vary widely, it is possible to identify some common components. The model in Figure 6.2 focuses on three important components:

1. Types of rewards
2. Distribution criteria
3. Desired outcomes

Let us examine these components and then discuss pay for performance.

Types of Rewards

Financial, material, and social rewards qualify as *extrinsic rewards* because they come from the environment. Psychic rewards, however, are *intrinsic rewards* because they are self-granted. If you work primarily to obtain rewards such as money or praise, you would be considered extrinsically motivated. When you derive pleasure from the task itself (Chapter 5), feel your work is meaningful (Chapter 5), or have a sense of responsibility, you will likely become *engaged* with your work. Employee engagement, a very important outcome and first discussed in Chapter 2, is fueled by intrinsic motivation.

The relative importance of extrinsic and intrinsic rewards is a matter of culture and personal preferences.[44] To this end, it is critically important to know what types of rewards you or others value most. This knowledge can make the difference in managing others. It can also assist you in identifying employers with whom you fit.

For example, if you're hard-charging, a high income is very important to you, and you like to be rewarded based on your own efforts, then it would be advisable to look for companies with similar reward systems. You also can use your knowledge to "manage up." One of the authors of this book routinely told his managers, shortly after

FIGURE 6.2 KEY FACTORS IN ORGANIZATIONAL REWARD SYSTEMS

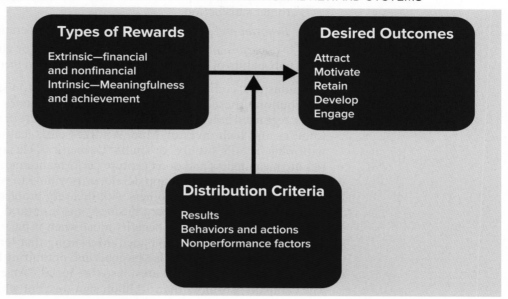

being hired, which of the rewards available for that particular job he valued most. This helped his managers choose and provide rewards that would have the most positive impact. It also is helpful to compare the rewards you value to a survey of employees and the rewards they value. To realize similar benefits, go to connect.mheducation.com and complete Self-Assessment 6.2 to find which rewards you value most. Then use the same results to complete the Take-Away Application (TAAP) that follows.

connect

SELF-ASSESSMENT 6.2   What Rewards Do I Value Most?

Go to connect.mheducation.com and complete Self-Assessment 6.2 to learn the value you place on a variety of rewards offered at work. Then do the following.

1. Were your perceptions accurate? Why or why not?

2. What would Vroom's expectancy theory suggest you should do?

3. Would you generalize the actual survey results to all nonmanagerial employees? Why or why not?

TAKE-AWAY-APPLICATION—TAAP

Using the results of Self-Assessment 6.2, answer the following:

1. Which rewards in the list are extrinsic? Intrinsic?

2. Do your personal top five most-valued items contain more intrinsic or extrinsic rewards?

3. What are your three most valued from the list?

4. Assume you are job hunting. How can you determine whether a given company provides the three rewards you value most?

Distribution Criteria

Three general criteria are used for distributing rewards:

- *Results.* Tangible outcomes such as individual, group, or organizational performance; quantity; and quality. These are commonly some type of accounting measure—sales, profit, or error rate. Increasingly these may also include customer satisfaction.

- *Behavior and actions.* Such as teamwork, cooperation, risk taking, and creativity.
- *Nonperformance considerations.* Customary or contractual, where the type of job, nature of the work, equity, tenure, level in hierarchy, etc., are rewarded.[45]

Industries, companies, and jobs differ and so too should their performance and distribution criteria. Many Internet-based companies, for example, boast of page views, registered users, and app downloads. These may or may not be relevant. LinkedIn founder and tech investor Marc Andreessen is leading a charge for doing away with what he calls "vanity" or "bull#$!% metrics." He argues that many common metrics are meaningless and don't capture performance meaningfully. "Download counts can easily be inflated if an app developer is willing to pay." Analytics company Mixpanel is attempting to help others with this very problem. Suhail Doshi, one of Mixpanel's founders, said: "Every business has a natural goal that correlates with its success. For instance, Yelp benefits most when it has more reviews, and Instagram when it has more photos uploaded. Measuring that 'one key metric' can lead to insights that are particular to that business and optimizing for it can give the company an edge versus competitors that are not so fine-tuned." An excellent example is Facebook. The company has more than 1 billion sign-ups, but what is more meaningful is how many have been active in the past 30 days. This is what the company tracks and promotes. It is an excellent metric for customer engagement, which is what many companies, not just those that live on the Web, want. In sum, measures, rewards, and distribution criteria need to be aligned to have effective PM.[46]

Desired Outcomes of the Reward System

As listed in Figure 6.2, a good reward system should attract and motivate talented people. A good reward system also should foster personal growth and development and keep talented people from leaving. A prime example is Tulsa-based QuikTrip: "Employees are treated so well at this 24-hour convenience chain—wages, benefits, and training—that they stay around for the long haul. More than 200 employees have been here more than 20 years."[47]

Be Sure You Get the Outcomes You Desire

In most instances, rewards are exchanges—you are given this for doing that. Professors sometimes give extra credit for doing, well, something extra (e.g., a special assignment or participating in research). At work, you may be paid a cash bonus or your commission rate may increase for performing above and beyond expectations (e.g., sales quota). And as we'll explore, rewards come in many forms—financial and nonfinancial. But whatever the case, it is important that whoever provides the reward gets what is desired or intended in exchange. There are three general outcomes from rewards:

1. *Desired outcome.* More of what you intended and for which you are rewarded.
2. *Nothing.* The reward can have no effect.
3. *Undesired side-effects.* Rewards reinforce or motivate the wrong behaviors.

To illustrate, in the current American health care system, providers (doctors and hospitals) are compensated for the services provided. This means that providers collect more revenues—make more money—when patients get sicker. Complications after surgical procedures are a case in point. Infections and procedure-related strokes are on average twice as profitable as the same procedures that go smoothly. A study by Harvard Medical School, Bain Consulting Group, and Texas Health Systems "found that private-insurance and Medicare payments soared when surgeries went awry, outpacing extra treatment costs. In one example, a complication during an intestinal surgery . . . could lead to an intensive care stay, boosting payments fivefold. . . . On average, procedures with complications netted $15,700 versus $7,600 for procedures that went well."[48] We're not judging or saying this is right or wrong—people should get paid for their expertise and work. But instead we make the point that performance management is both part of the cause and the solution to this enormous challenge. This also illustrates how performance management (e.g., rewards) can be both an input and a process in the Integrative Framework. The take-away: Be sure that your performance management system produces the *desired* outcomes and be mindful of undesirable side-effects.

Extrinsic, Total, and Alternative Rewards

Including the usual paycheck, the variety and magnitude of organizational rewards have evolved into a mind-boggling array—from child adoption and partner benefits, to college tuition reimbursement, and, of course, stock grants and options.[49] In fact, today it is common for your nonwage benefits to be 50 percent or more of your total compensation. A report by the Society for Human Resource Management describes the current and broader perspective that is "total rewards." **Total rewards encompass not only compensation and benefits, but also personal and professional growth opportunities and a motivating work environment that includes recognition, job design (Chapter 5), and work–life balance.** A total rewards perspective therefore includes:

- Compensation—base pay, merit pay, incentives, promotions, and pay increases.
- Benefits—health and wellness, paid time off, and retirement.
- Personal growth—training, career development, and performance management.[50]

This broader view of rewards is due in part to stiffer competition and challenging economic conditions, which have made it difficult for cost-conscious organizations to offer higher wages and more benefits each year. Employers have had to find alternative forms of rewards that cost less but still motivate employees to excel.

Alternatives to Money and Promotions The Great Recession often dramatically affected (extrinsic) rewards: salary freezes, reduced or eliminated bonuses, suspended 401(k) contributions, and even salary and benefit cuts. Many feared that such cuts would have negative effects on employee motivation and engagement. This predicament forced managers and companies to get more creative and consider the concept of "total rewards." However, it doesn't require a global financial cataclysm to cause companies to cut rewards. Many industries are inherently cyclical (e.g., oil and gas, automotive, housing), which means that financial resources expand and contract with some regularity.

Whatever the case, many business experts have proclaimed that the "new normal" is a situation in which rewards are permanently altered (constrained). Regardless of what your personal experience might be, research provides some encouraging insights pertaining to the link between extrinsic rewards and some of the outcomes in the Integrative Framework. For instance, results of a McKinsey survey of over 1000 executives revealed that "three noncash motivators—praise from immediate managers, leadership attention (for example, one-on-one conversations with leaders), and a chance to lead projects or task forces—[are] no less or even more effective motivators than the three highest-rated financial incentives: cash bonuses, increased pay, and . . . stock options."[51] These findings are consistent with a continuing trend in which companies are increasing their use of noncash rewards, such as implementing work–life programs, providing recognition, detailing formalized career paths, and providing special project opportunities.

Employee Values, Expectancies, and Voice One thing that can improve the effectiveness of most any reward system is employee involvement. Recall our discussion of motivation and procedural justice in Chapter 5. Involving employees in the design, selection, and assessment of rewards programs increases the chance that the rewards provided will be perceived as fair and valuable. (Valuable rewards are valent outcomes in expectancy theory from Chapter 5.) Involvement also fosters employee engagement—discussed in Chapter 2—as it makes them feel valued. Despite these benefits, only 11 percent of respondents in one study said their companies involved employees in the design of reward programs,[52] which means that 89 percent of companies do not involve employees. This may present you and your current or future employers with an opportunity: Involving employees is one way to get ahead of the competition. To increase your understanding and proficiency with rewards, the following Problem-Solving Application highlights some of the common reasons why rewards often fail to motivate. One way to use this is as a checklist. Examine rewards you receive at school, at work, and in other arenas of life using the eight elements in the box. Determine if any suffer such shortcomings. Applying your knowledge in this way can help assure that managers and employers get a bigger bang for their reward bucks!

solving application

Why Rewards Often Fail to Motivate

problem

Despite huge investments of time and money for organizational reward systems, the desired motivational effect often is not achieved. A management consultant and writer recently offered these eight reasons:

1. Too much emphasis on monetary rewards.
2. Absence of an "appreciation effect."
3. Sense in recipient that extensive benefits are entitlements.
4. Rewards encourage counterproductive behavior (as

discussed in Chapter 2). *Example:* In one case, city officials in Albuquerque, New Mexico, decided to pay trash truck crews for eight hours of work, no matter how long it actually took them to finish their routes. They wanted this move to encourage workers to finish the job quickly and thus lower the city's overtime expenses. Instead, the crews began to cut corners. They missed pickups, resulting in numerous complaints from customers. Some drove too

fast and caused accidents. Others incurred fines for driving to the dump with overloaded trucks.[53]

5. Too long of a delay between performance and rewards.
6. Too many one-size-fits-all rewards.
7. Use of one-shot rewards with a short-lived motivational impact.
8. Continued use of demotivating practices such as layoffs, across-the-board raises and cuts, and excessive executive compensation.[54]

YOUR CALL

Identify two rewards you receive in different arenas of your life (e.g., school, work, sports, etc.).

Stop 1: Which of the eight common flaws apply to each of the rewards you identified?

Stop 2: What new knowledge in OB could improve the effectiveness of these rewards (i.e., generate the desired outcomes)?

Stop 3: What are your recommendations to apply these learnings and make the incentives even more effective?

Pay for Performance

Pay for performance is the popular term for monetary incentives linking at least some portion of one's pay directly to results or accomplishments. It is compensation above and beyond basic wages and salary, and its use is consistent with recommendations derived from the expectancy theory of motivation discussed in the previous chapter. Many people refer to it simply as *incentive or variable pay.* The general idea behind pay-for-

Bernie Marcus, co-founder and former board member of Home Depot, was an early advocate of pay for performance and supported clawing back bonuses from executives who didn't meet performance expectations. In fact, during his time as a leader at the company he often refused bonuses.

performance schemes—including but not limited to merit pay, bonuses, and profit sharing—is to give employees an incentive for working harder and/or smarter. Proponents of incentive compensation say something extra is needed because hourly wages and fixed salaries do little more than motivate people to show up at work and put in the required hours. The most basic form of pay for performance is the traditional piece-rate plan. Here, the employee is paid a specified amount of money for each unit of work. Sales commissions, whereby a salesperson receives a specified amount of money for each unit sold, are another long-standing example of pay for performance.

Nutrisystem, the weight-loss program, provides a skillful and creative example of how to meet multiple organizational objectives via pay for performance. The company's plan aims to increase sales, staff particular working hours, and expand the customer base. Its call-center sales associates are paid the greater of either an hourly rate ($10 an hour for the first 40 hours per week, $15 an hour for any additional hours) or a flat-rate payment based on sales. Unlike conventional commissions, the flat rate is not tied to the sales price of the product. Instead, the payments vary depending on the shift during which the sale occurs and whether the sale resulted from an incoming or outgoing call. Higher payments are made for outgoing calls and for sales during off-peak times. This system incentivizes employees to work less-desirable hours and to make outgoing calls. It also allows the company to avoid overtime payments while at the same time rewarding the desired employee behaviors.[55] This example underscores the evolution and increasingly common practice of using performance versus nonperformance criteria in reward systems.

Making Pay for Performance Work

As with all other OB topics, we can use research and practice as a guide. Monetary rewards can work if they help people meet their basic needs (e.g., food and shelter), cause them to be respected by others (e.g., status), or enable them to provide for their families (e.g., nice house, good schools, and college for their children). Monetary rewards, however, do not increase knowledge, skills, and abilities, nor do they enrich jobs and enhance intrinsic motivation (Chapter 5).[56] Research results show mixed outcomes for pay for performance—some show increased performance and others decreased performance. A comprehensive review of the literature found only a modest positive relationship between financial incentives and performance *quantity* and no impact on performance *quality*.[57] The results are especially *unimpressive* for executives. Only a weak link was found between large executive bonuses paid out in good years and improvement in corporate profitability in subsequent years.[58] However, companies with the best pay-for-performance results:

- Paid top performers substantially higher than the other employees
- Reduced "gaming" of the system by increasing transparency
- Utilized multiple measures of performance
- Calibrated performance measures to assure accuracy and consistency

It also is important that a company's culture supports such practices, and leadership support is considered the most important contributor to such a culture (you'll learn about these topics in Chapters 13 and 14). Even with limited compensation dollars "the best pay for performance organizations often carve out funds for extra rewards to high performers and tend to see fewer employees whose performance is rated as high," noted a PM consultant.[59]

REINFORCEMENT AND ADDITIONAL CONSIDERATIONS FOR PROVIDING APPROPRIATE CONSEQUENCES

MAJOR QUESTION

How can you use various forms of reinforcement and consequences to improve performance?

THE BIGGER PICTURE

Whether at school, at work, or even in your social life, your behavior is influenced in many ways. In this section, you'll learn about three especially effective and practical means for influencing your behavior and that of others: the law of effect and how it relates to respondent and operant conditioning; common types of reinforcement; and how managers can increase the effectiveness of reinforcement using a variety of reinforcement schedules.

As noted earlier, providing consequences (both rewards and punishments) is the last stage of the performance management process. Unfortunately, many managers can't seem to get it right. Consider these scenarios:

- You stop making suggestions on how to improve your department because your boss never acts on your ideas.

- Your colleague, the ultimate political animal in your office, gets a great promotion while her more skilled coworkers (like you) scratch their heads and gossip about the injustice.

In the first instance, a productive behavior faded away for lack of encouragement. In the second, unproductive behavior was unwittingly rewarded. How rewards, and consequences more generally, are administered can make or break performance management efforts. Fortunately, OB tools and skills can help you and your employers be more effective. This is particularly important given that rewards are often important career outcomes in the Integrative Framework (e.g., pay raises, bonuses, and promotions). And such outcomes can often influence subsequent perceptions (fairness), intentions (thoughts of quitting your job), processes (emotions), and behaviors (actual turnover). Thanks to the pioneering work of Edward L. Thorndike, B. F. Skinner, and many others, behavior modification and *reinforcement* techniques help managers, and you, achieve the desired effect when providing feedback and granting rewards.

The Law of Effect—Linking Consequences and Behaviors

During the early 1900s, psychologist Edward L. Thorndike observed in his lab that a cat would behave randomly and wildly when placed in a small box with a secret trip lever that opened a door. However, once the cat accidentally tripped the lever and escaped, the animal would go straight to the lever when placed back in the box. Hence, Thorndike formulated his famous ***law of effect,*** **which says behavior with favorable consequences tends to be repeated, while behavior with unfavorable consequences tends to disappear.**[60] This was a dramatic departure from previous notions that behavior was the product of inborn instincts.

Using Reinforcement to Condition Behavior

B. F. Skinner refined Thorndike's conclusion that behavior is controlled by its consequences. Skinner's work became known as *behaviorism* because he dealt strictly with observable behavior. As a behaviorist, Skinner believed it was pointless to explain behavior in terms of unobservable inner states such as needs, drives, attitudes, or thought processes.[61] To this end, Skinner drew an important distinction between two types of behavior: respondent and operant behavior.[62] **He labeled unlearned reflexes or stimulus–response (S–R) connections *respondent behavior.*** This category of behavior was said to describe a very small proportion of adult human behavior, such as shedding tears while peeling onions and reflexively withdrawing one's hand from a hot stove.[63] **Skinner attached the label *operant behavior* to behavior that is learned when one "operates on" the environment to produce desired consequences. Some call this the response–stimulus (R–S) model.** Years of controlled experiments with pigeons in "Skinner boxes" helped Skinner develop a sophisticated technology of behavior control, or *operant conditioning.* For example, he taught pigeons how to pace figure eights and how to bowl by reinforcing the underweight (and thus hungry) birds with food whenever they more closely approximated target behaviors. Skinner's work has significant implications for OB because the vast majority of organizational behavior falls into the operant category.[64]

Contingent Consequences

Contingent consequences, according to Skinner's operant theory, control behavior by responding to a target behavior in one of four ways: positive reinforcement, negative reinforcement, punishment, and extinction. The term *contingent* means there is a purposeful if-then linkage between the target behavior and the consequence. This represents an instrumentality according to expectancy theory.

It therefore is helpful for you *first* to think of the target behavior, whether you want to increase or decrease it, and then choose the consequence you will provide (see Figure 6.3).

Increase Desired Behaviors   ***Positive reinforcement* is the process of strengthening a behavior by contingently presenting something pleasing.** (Importantly, a behavior is strengthened when it increases in frequency and weakened when it decreases in frequency.) For instance, in the wake of the BP oil spill in 2010, newly appointed CEO Bob Dudley made 100 percent of variable pay (bonuses) based on safety for the fourth quarter of 2010.[65]

***Negative reinforcement* also strengthens a desired behavior by contingently withdrawing something displeasing.** For example, many probationary periods for new hires are applications of negative reinforcement. During probation periods (often your first 30, 60, or 90 days on a new job) you need to have weekly meetings with your boss

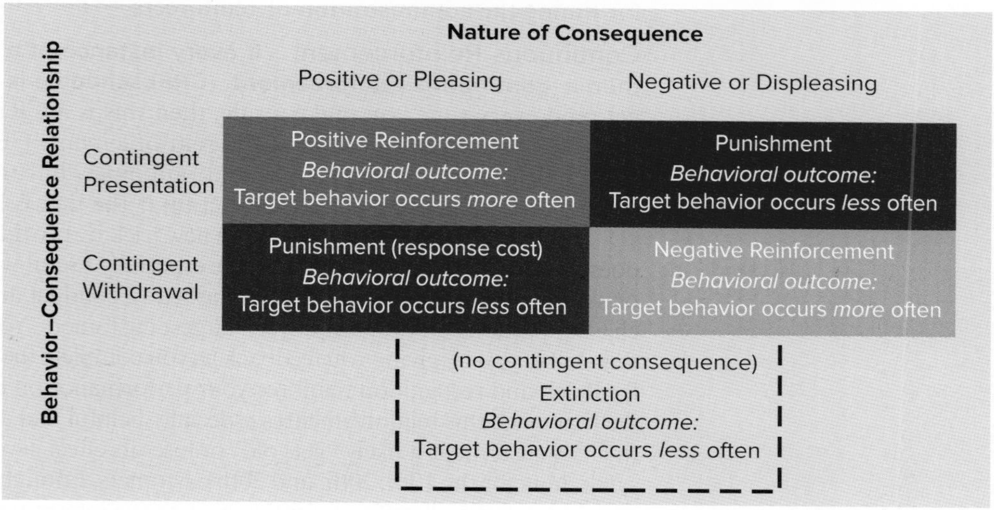

FIGURE 6.3   CONTINGENT CONSEQUENCES IN OPERANT CONDITIONING

or have somebody sign off on your work. Once you've demonstrated your skill, these requirements are removed. Unfortunately, the vast majority of people *confuse negative reinforcement with negative feedback,* which is a form of punishment. They are indeed different and have opposite effects on behavior. Negative reinforcement, as the word *reinforcement* indicates, strengthens a behavior because it provides relief from something undesirable (e.g., paperwork, meetings, and yelling).

Decrease Undesired Behaviors **Punishment** **is the process of weakening behavior through either the contingent presentation of something displeasing or the contingent withdrawal of something positive.** For example, the US Department of Transportation now fines airlines up to $27,500 per passenger for planes left on the tarmac for more than three hours. This reduced the reported cases to 12 from 535 from one year to the next.[66] Carnival Cruise Lines, which has had multiple mishaps and disasters in the past few years (e.g., Costa *Concordia,* which capsized off the coast of Italy), cut the compensation of two of its top executives. Then CEO Micky Arison's incentive pay was reduced 27 percent and the head of the Costa division had his cut 37 percent.[67] And while an increasing number of companies incentivize employees to engage in healthy behaviors, some companies are now punishing employees for unhealthy behaviors. CVS Caremark, for instance, now requires its 12,000 employees to participate in health screenings or pay an extra $600 for their health care premiums.[68]

Weakening a behavior by ignoring it or making sure it is not reinforced is referred to as **extinction.** Getting rid of a former boyfriend or girlfriend by refusing to return his/her phone calls or texts, or unfriending him/her on Facebook, is an extinction strategy. These action will reduce not only communications with this person but also the heartache. A good analogy for extinction is to imagine what would happen to your houseplants if you stopped watering them. Like a plant without water, a behavior without occasional reinforcement eventually dies. Although very different processes, both punishment and extinction have the same weakening effect on behavior.

The bottom line: Knowing the difference between these various forms of contingent consequences provides you with a number of powerful tools with which to manage yourself and others. Put another way, you just learned four tools for influencing behavior. Most people think of and use only two—positive reinforcement and punishment. Apply your knowledge and get ahead!

You can supercharge or at least enhance the effectiveness of your positive reinforcement efforts (e.g., rewards) by managing the timing or schedule of reinforcement delivery.

Positive Reinforcement Schedules

It's not just the reinforcement that influences behavior, but also *when* it is administered. Continuous and intermittent reinforcement schedules are two common means for timing the administration of reinforcers.

Continuous Reinforcement **If every instance of a target behavior is reinforced then a** **continuous reinforcement** **(CRF) schedule is in effect.** For instance, if you get paid every time you make a sale, then this is a CRF schedule. The sale is the desired behavior, and payment is the reinforcement. CRF is useful for making early links between desired behaviors and outcomes, but they are susceptible to perceptions of entitlement and rapid extinction if the link is broken.

Just like you train your dog to do a new trick by providing a reward each time he or she does it successfully, CRF schedules are especially useful when employees learn a new task or skill. For example, assume you are asked to conduct an analysis of the individual purchasing patterns of your employer's largest customers. Your manager could help develop this skill in you by giving you feedback as you complete the analysis for each customer. This feedback and recognition reinforce your performance on this new task. However, you can see that while this reinforcement is especially helpful and appreciated with analyses for the first few customers, it likely "gets old" or loses its effect if your manager continues to do the same thing for the 10th, 20th, and 30th customers. Enough already! One way to help guard against the fading benefit of reinforcers is to use intermittent schedules.

TABLE 6.6 REINFORCEMENT SCHEDULES, EXAMPLES, ADVANTAGES, AND DISADVANTAGES

REINFORCEMENT SCHEDULE	EXAMPLES	ADVANTAGES	DISADVANTAGES
Fixed ratio	Piece-rate pay; bonuses tied to the sale of a fixed number of units	Clear and predictable link between the behavior and the reinforcer	Costly to monitor performance and administer reinforcers (e.g., money); reinforcers lose effect over time
Variable ratio	Slot machines that pay after a variable number of pulls; lotteries that pay after a variable number of tickets sold	Strong motivation to continue until reinforcer is received; less costly than fixed ratio	Some desired behaviors will not be rewarded; potentially long periods between reinforcers (e.g., payouts)
Fixed interval	Paychecks (every two weeks or once a month); annual bonuses; and probationary periods	Clear and predictable link between the behavior and reinforcer; less costly than fixed ratio	Inconsistent effort and performance over the interval (majority of effort/performance occurs near reinforcer)
Variable interval	Random supervisor "pats on the back"; spot rewards; random audits (e.g., financial); random drug tests of athletes and employees; pop quizzes	Consistent and strong motivation to perform over time; least costly schedule due to relatively little monitoring and administration	Some desired behaviors will not be reinforced; potentially long periods between reinforcers (e.g., payouts)

Intermittent Reinforcement Unlike CRF schedules, *intermittent reinforcement involves reinforcement of some but not all instances of a target behavior.* There are four subcategories of intermittent schedules. Table 6.6 shows these along with examples.

Work Organizations Typically Rely on the Weakest Schedule

Generally, variable ratio and variable interval schedules of reinforcement produce the strongest behavior that is most resistant to extinction. As gamblers will attest, variable schedules hold the promise of reinforcement after the next deal of cards, roll of the dice, or spin of the wheel (target response). In contrast, continuous and fixed schedules are the least likely to have the desired effects over time. Such time-based pay schemes such as hourly wages and yearly salaries are still the rule in today's workplaces, despite the trend toward pay for performance. The majority of work organizations rely on fixed intervals of reinforcement.

Reinforcement Schedules and Performance Figure 6.4 illustrates the relative effect of the schedules on performance over time. To elaborate, consider three professors who teach different sections of the same undergraduate OB course. Also assume the students are essentially equal across the three sections. Given this scenario, Professor Blue bases student grades solely on short quizzes given at the beginning of every class (continuous reinforcement). Professor Black bases grades on a midterm and final of equal weight (fixed interval). Professor Red uses a number of unannounced or pop quizzes (variable interval).

We expect the level of preparation for each class and their overall performance (preparation and learning) to follow the patterns in Figure 6.4. Professor Blue's students would start fast and prepare diligently for each class. However, they then would "settle into a routine" and a common level of preparation. Over time it is likely that they will figure out what is required and do less. Ultimately some students may even quit preparing once they have a clear sense of what their overall grade will be. The pattern for Professor Black's students is all too common. The students start slow knowing there is plenty of time before the midterm. When that time grows near, the intensity of

FIGURE 6.4 REINFORCEMENT SCHEDULES AND PERFORMANCE

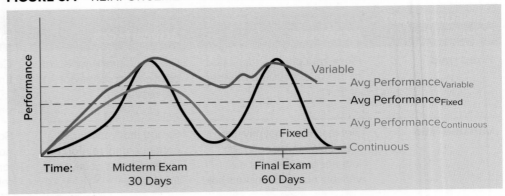

SOURCE: © 2014 Mel Fugate. All rights reserved. Reproduction prohibited without permission of the author.

their preparation (cramming for some) grows until exam time. Then, once the midterm passes they disconnect for a while until they ramp up again for the final. In contrast, Professor Red's students will likely maintain a level of preparation that is on average higher throughout the course, as there is a chance they will have a pop quiz and be graded each and every session throughout the course.

The bottom line: Students generally don't like unannounced or pop quizzes. However, if the professor's goal is student preparation and learning, then variable interval grading is one means for generating a higher average level of performance. These same patterns and results apply in business settings too. For instance, many sales and professional service (accounting and law) jobs have monthly numbers, either sales or billable hours. This often results in far more work getting done in the last few days of the month than in the beginning (see Figure 6.4—30 days, 60 days, etc.).

Practical Implications for Using the Strongest Schedule

You are unlikely to change your employer's pay and bonus schedules from once a month and once a year. It also is unlikely that you'll change your professor's grading format. However, there are many ways you can put your knowledge of positive reinforcement schedules to use within the confines of existing practices.

Spot Rewards. At work, spot rewards are incredibly effective. For instance, if your coworker has worked her butt off to make your project a success, then you might take the time to recognize her efforts via e-mail to the entire team including your manager. Your manager, in turn, may decide to give Friday off to those who complete their work in a quality fashion and ahead of schedule.

Variable Rewards/Bonuses. Entrepreneurs can especially benefit from applying knowledge of reinforcement schedules. Assume that you started your own business, and like many new businesses you are short on cash. And while you would like to provide regular bonuses and pay raises, you simply can't afford to. Instead you can pay bonuses only when, and to celebrate, your company secures a new customer or a big order. The variable nature of these rewards not only recognizes employees' efforts and success, but also motivates them to work hard in the future because they know that such efforts are recognized/reinforced.

"Celebrations." As for school, we advocate celebrating (reinforcing) "victories," such as completion of a paper, a good score on an exam, and the end of the semester in which you worked hard and performed well. Scattering these reinforcers throughout the semester can help to motivate and reenergize you to work hard in the future, especially if you make these rewards contingent on good behavior.

All three of these examples apply variable schedules. Think of your own examples and consider their effectiveness. Better still, take this knowledge and apply it for your own benefit. Reinforcement schedules, like the larger process of performance management, are often limited only by your creativity and willingness to apply your knowledge. We therefore encourage you to use the knowledge of PM gained in this chapter to both better understand existing practices and improve those you control.

what did i learn?

In our coverage of performance management, you learned how you can use goals, feedback, rewards, and reinforcement to boost effectiveness. Reinforce your learning with the Key Points below, and then consolidate it using the Integrative Framework. Challenge your mastery of the material by answering the Major Questions in your own words.

Key Points for Understanding Chapter 6

You learned the following key points.

6.1 PERFORMANCE MANAGEMENT PROCESSES

- Effective performance management (PM) is a process of defining, monitoring, reviewing, and providing consequences.

- PM is often used for employee-related decisions and development. It also is a powerful means for signaling what is wanted or not.

- Employee perceptions of the value and effectiveness of PM are often very low.

- Managers and leaders are critical to the perceived and actual success of PM.

6.2 STEP 1: DEFINE PERFORMANCE—EXPECTATIONS AND SETTING GOALS

- Goal setting is critical to effective PM.
- Both learning and performance goals can be used.
- SMART goals are more likely to be achieved.
- Goal commitment, support and feedback, as well as action plans foster goal achievement.
- PM can be improved using behavioral, objective, and task/project goals.

6.3 STEP 2: PERFORMANCE MONITORING AND EVALUATION

- Monitoring performance requires effective measurement, such as the timeliness, quality, quantity, or financial nature of performance goals.

- Evaluation involves comparing performance measures to expectations or goals.

- Performance evaluation is often hampered by perceptual errors.

- Multi-rater or 360-degree feedback is commonly used to help improve the accuracy of performance evaluation.

6.4 STEP 3: REVIEWING PERFORMANCE AND THE IMPORTANCE OF FEEDBACK AND COACHING

- Two basic functions of feedback are to instruct and motivate.

- Sources of feedback include others, the task, and yourself.

- Leaders and managers often don't receive useful feedback, yet both are critical in assuring that others do.

- The effectiveness of (positive and negative) feedback is greatly influenced by the receiver's perceptions.

- Coaching helps translate feedback into desired change.

6.5 STEP 4: PROVIDE CONSEQUENCES—ADMINISTER REWARDS AND PUNISHMENT

- Rewards can be categorized as extrinsic or intrinsic.

- Results, behavior, and nonperformance considerations are common criteria by which rewards are distributed.

- Rewards are tools to help achieve desired outcomes, such as to attract, motivate, retain, develop, and engage employees.

- Several alternative rewards practices are increasingly used today—total rewards, noncash, and pay for performance.

6.6 REINFORCEMENT AND ADDITIONAL CONSIDERATIONS FOR PROVIDING APPROPRIATE CONSEQUENCES

- According to the law of effect, behaviors are either repeated or diminished depending on the desirability of the consequences to which they are linked.

- Contingently providing consequences is fundamental to effective reinforcement.

- Both positive and negative reinforcement increase desired behaviors.

- Punishment and extinction both decrease undesirable behaviors.

- The schedule of when and how reinforcers are administered can increase their effectiveness.

The Integrative Framework for Chapter 6

As shown in Figure 6.5, you learned that performance management practices are associated with nearly every outcome across the three levels of OB. At the individual level these are task performance, work attitudes (e.g., job satisfaction), well-being/flourishing, citizenship and counterproductive behaviors, turnover, career outcomes, and creativity. Group and team-level performance, along with group satisfaction, cohesion, and conflict, are similarly related. As for the organizational level, performance management practices link to accounting/financial performance, customer satisfaction, reputation, and even an organization's overall survival.

Challenge: Major Questions for Chapter 6

At the start of the chapter, we told you that after reading the chapter you should be able to answer the following major questions. Unless you can, have you really processed and internalized the lessons in the chapter? Refer to the Key Points, Figure 6.5, the chapter itself, and your notes to revisit and answer the following major questions:

1. What are the elements of effective performance management, and how can this knowledge benefit me?

2. How can improving my goal setting give me an advantage?

3. How can performance monitoring and evaluation improve my performance and my ability to manage the performance of others?

4. How can I use feedback and coaching to review and improve performance?

5. How can I use consequences to generate desired outcomes?

6. How can I use various forms of reinforcement and consequences to improve performance?

FIGURE 6.5 INTEGRATIVE FRAMEWORK FOR UNDERSTANDING AND APPLYING OB

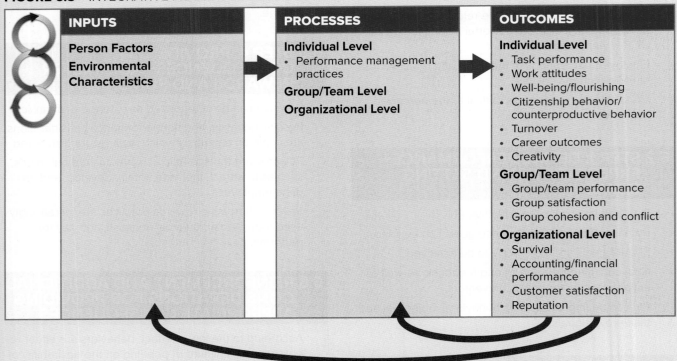

© 2014 Angelo Kinicki and Mel Fugate. All rights reserved. Reproduction prohibited without permission of the authors.

PROBLEM-SOLVING APPLICATION CASE (PSAC)

Improving Customer Satisfaction at McDonald's

McDonald's performed well throughout most of the economic downturn by sticking to its strategy of rolling out a steady stream of new menu items at a range of prices—from inexpensive snack wraps to more costly fruit smoothies—intended to appeal to more consumers. It also remodeled and tidied up many of its 14,000 US restaurants. However, satisfying customers with speedy and friendly service was a persistent challenge.

The bad news about customer satisfaction became a companywide focus in March 2013 during a webcast with franchise owners. (Approximately 90% of McDonald's restaurants are owned by franchisees.) McDonald's executives noted that 1 in 5 customer complaints was related to friendliness issues and that the problem was "increasing."

A slide from Steve Levigne, vice president of business research for McDonald's USA, stated ominously: "Service is broken." The top complaint was "rude or unprofessional employees"; complaints and speed of service had "increased significantly over the past six months"; and some customers even found the service "chaotic." The news was soon picked up in the business press.

McDonald's First Response. In the webcast, McDonald's asked franchisees to hire more employees and provide better training to deal with complaints. McDonald's, for its part, began to roll out a new system for taking orders, new software to better manage the workload and number of employees on the line, and a structure that provides managers more direct responsibility for specific areas of operation (e.g., the kitchen or customer service).[69]

Admitting Its Mistakes. McDonald's has acknowledged its role in creating service challenges due to its aggressive expansion of the menu. "Jeff Stratton, president of McDonald's USA, said the chain introduced several new products and limited-time offers this year to give customers more variety," reported *The Wall Street Journal.* It quoted Stratton as admitting, "The pace of product introduction in my opinion: too fast."[70]

The PR Battle. McDonald's made its effort to deal with such problems part of its PR strategy. "The company's response could serve as a case study in using customer criticism as a basis for a brand-building PR campaign," writes Richard Brownwell, a content manager for the *PRNews* website.[71] Brownwell praises the company for listening to its customers, then further improving communications with a new feedback system, and being open and candid about its troubles.

That openness was evident during the webcast wherein the company shared many steps it was willing to take to address customer satisfaction. For example, the company changed its 2014 business plan to invest in better food prep tables and improve training.

Work in Process. McDonald's has further to go. Late in 2013 *QSR Magazine,* which routinely reports on the average speed of service of various fast-food chains, found McDonald's average service time not only lagged its competitors, but it was the slowest reported over the 18 years that QSR has kept track.[72]

Moreover, early in 2014 the company apologized further when the CEO, Don Thompson, admitted, "We've lost some of our customer relevance." Thompson announced other likely adjustments to the menu, including customized burgers and a stronger emphasis on breakfast.[73]

Employee Wages. Although McDonald's has been open on most topics, it has not talked much about one factor that may be affecting service—employee compensation. Articles and critics in the business press connect poor service to the high rate of turnover, which they connect to low pay. McDonald's does not publicly report its turnover rates, but fast-food restaurants typically run an average annual turnover rate of 60%.[74] Taken together, this suggests that when unhappy customers are added to low pay, McDonald's may be experiencing even higher rates.

Apply the 3-Stop Problem-Solving Approach to OB

Use the Integrative Framework in Figure 6.5 along the journey through all 3-Stop to help identify inputs, processes, and outcomes relative to this case.

Stop 1: What is the problem?

- Use the Integrative Framework for Understanding and Applying OB (see Figure 6.5) to help identify the outcomes that are important in this case.
- Which of these outcomes are not being achieved in the case?
- Based on considering the above two questions, what is the most important problem in this case?

Stop 2: Use the Integrative Framework to identify the OB concepts or theories that help you to understand the problem in this case.

- What person factors are most relevant?
- What environmental characteristics are most important to consider?
- Do you need to consider any processes? Which ones?
- What concepts or theories discussed in this chapter are most relevant for solving the key problem in this case?

Stop 3: What are your recommendations for solving the problem?

- Review the material in the chapter that most pertains to your proposed solution and look for practical recommendations.

- Use any past OB knowledge or experience to generate recommendations.

- Outline your plan for solving the problem in this case.

LEGAL/ETHICAL CHALLENGE

Timing of Stock Vesting to Reduce Taxes

Goldman Sachs granted 10 directors and executives more than $65 million worth of stock just before new tax laws went into effect January 1, 2013. The stock in question was awarded for the previous year. And while it is not uncommon for companies to advance the vesting time, which is the point at which the stock options or grants can be sold or cashed in, Goldman and many other companies routinely do this in January when they make the rest of their compensation decisions and pay out bonuses for the previous year.

A company spokesperson said that the bonuses were not limited just to top executives. However, the company refused to elaborate on who else was given early awards or the motives for doing so. "Goldman's decision is the latest illustration of the lengths large U.S. companies have gone to shield their stakeholders from higher taxes that loomed throughout the so-called fiscal cliff standoff at the end of 2012. . . . Goldman's move could shield its executives from increased tax rates, which will rise as high as 39.6% in 2013 from 35% last year."

Goldman's actions were criticized in part due to CEO Lloyd Blankfein's op-ed in *The Wall Street Journal* in which he said tax increases are a necessary part of US fiscal reform.

To be fair, Goldman is not the only culprit. Four hundred eighty-three companies announced special dividends in December of 2012, compared to 142 the year before. The December 2012 number was more than for any year since 1955![75]

What Would You Do?

What would you do if you were the CEO of Goldman Sachs, and you were in charge of such compensation decisions?

1. Move the vesting time up just as the company did. It is appropriate for companies to help shareholders, including executives, reduce their tax burdens. Explain your argument for this position.

2. Not change the vesting time and do it in January, just as your company typically does. Explain your argument for this position.

3. Think of another alternative/argument and explain.

GROUP EXERCISE

Rewards, Rewards, Rewards

Objectives

1. To tap the class's collective knowledge of organizational rewards.
2. To appreciate the vast array of potential rewards.
3. To contrast individual and group perceptions of rewards.
4. To practice your group creativity skills.

Introduction

Rewards are a centerpiece of organizational life. Both extrinsic and intrinsic rewards motivate us to join and continue contributing to organized effort. But not all rewards have the same impact on work motivation. Individuals have their own personal preferences for rewards. The best way to discover people's reward preferences is to ask them, both individually and collectively. This group brainstorming and class discussion exercise requires about 20 to 30 minutes.

Instructions

Your instructor will divide your class randomly into teams of five to eight people. Each team will go through the following four-step process:

1. Each team will have a six-minute brainstorming session, with one person acting as recorder. The objective of this brainstorming session is to list as many different organizational rewards as the group can think of. Your team might find it helpful to think of rewards by category (such as rewards from the work itself, rewards you can spend, rewards you can eat and drink, rewards you can feel, rewards you can wear, rewards you can share, rewards you cannot see, etc.). Remember, good brainstorming calls for withholding judgments about whether ideas are good or not. Quantity is wanted. Building upon other people's ideas also is encouraged.

2. Next, each individual will take four minutes to write down, in decreasing order of importance, 10 rewards he or she wants from the job. *Note:* These are your *personal* preferences, your "top 10" rewards that will motivate you to do your best.

3. Each team will then take five minutes to generate a list of "today's 10 most powerful rewards." List them in decreasing order of their power to motivate job performance. Voting may be necessary.

4. A general class discussion of the questions listed below will conclude the exercise.

Questions for Discussion

1. How did your personal top 10 list compare with your group's top 10 list? If there is a serious mismatch, how would it affect your motivation? (To promote discussion, the instructor may have several volunteers read their personal top 10 lists to the class.)

2. Which team had the most productive brainstorming session? (The instructor may request each team to read its brainstormed list of potential rewards and top 10 list to the class.)

3. Were you surprised to hear certain rewards getting so much attention? Why?

4. How can managers improve the incentive effect of the rewards most frequently mentioned in class?

5. What is the likely future of organizational reward plans? Which of today's compensation trends will probably thrive, and which are probably passing fads?

7 POSITIVE ORGANIZATIONAL BEHAVIOR

How Can I Flourish at School, Work, and Home?

inputs

PERSON FACTORS
Emotions
Mindfulness
Psychological capital

ENVIRONMENTAL
CHARACTERISTICS
Organizational climate

processes

INDIVIDUAL LEVEL

GROUP/TEAM LEVEL

ORGANIZATIONAL LEVEL

outcomes

INDIVIDUAL LEVEL
Well-being/flourishing

GROUP/TEAM LEVEL

ORGANIZATIONAL LEVEL

© 2014 Angelo Kinicki and Mel Fugate. All rights reserved. Reproduction prohibited without permission of the authors.

MAJOR TOPICS I'LL LEARN AND QUESTIONS I SHOULD BE ABLE TO ANSWER

7.1 THE IMPORTANCE OF POSITIVE OB
MAJOR QUESTION: *How does understanding Positive OB benefit me?*

7.2 THE POWER OF POSITIVE EMOTIONS
MAJOR QUESTION: *What is the role of positive emotions in POB, and how can they make me more effective at school, at work, and in other arenas of life?*

7.3 FOSTERING MINDFULNESS
MAJOR QUESTION: *How can mindfulness contribute to my effectiveness?*

7.4 POSITIVE PSYCHOLOGICAL CAPITAL: CAPITAL THAT I OWN AND CONTROL
MAJOR QUESTION: *How can my inner HERO benefit me at work and in my career?*

7.5 CREATING A CLIMATE THAT FOSTERS POSITIVE OB
MAJOR QUESTION: *How can managers create an organizational climate that fosters Positive OB?*

7.6 FLOURISHING: THE DESTINATION OF POSITIVE OB
MAJOR QUESTION: *What can I do to enhance my level of flourishing?*

INTEGRATIVE FRAMEWORK FOR UNDERSTANDING AND APPLYING OB

This chapter focuses on four inputs—positive emotions, mindfulness, psychological capital, and organizational climate—that influence individuals' well-being and level of flourishing. As you read the chapter, take note of the other outcomes that are influenced by the inputs and processes associated with Positive OB.

winning at work

WHAT YOU DO IS WHAT YOU GET

If emotions are products of our thoughts, behaviors, and experiences, then it makes sense that managing our thoughts and behaviors can allow us to experience more positive emotions. Here are some specific things you can do.

- **Manage Expectations.** Some people say, "You get what you expect." If this is true, then start your day with a positive expectation. Think of something positive that you will do or that you know will happen that day.

- **Take Time to Plan and Organize.** The most common source of stress is the perception that you have too much work to do. Rather than obsess about it, pick one thing that if done today will move you closer to your most important goal, then do that first.

- **Give a Gift to Other People.** Not a conventional, neatly wrapped present, but instead a positive or kind gesture. It can be as simple as a smile, compliment, or words of encouragement. Volumes of research show that helping others is one of the most fulfilling things that people do. The more you give, the more you'll get.

- **Deflect Partisan Conversations.** Some topics breed conflict, such as religion and politics. You can politely bow out by saying, "Talking about that stuff makes my head hurt."

- **Assume People Have Good Intentions.** You can't read minds and don't really know the "why" behind what people do. Assuming that others have evil motives can only bring you down. Try to assume the best or at least non-negative intentions.

- **Focus on the Job in Front of You.** One of the prime enemies of your positivity is worry. We often worry about things that we can't control, including things from the past (it's done—you can't go back). You're better off looking ahead than looking back. Don't worry about the past or what you can't control.

- **End the Day with Gratitude.** Just before you go to bed, write down at least one wonderful thing that happened that day, or something that you are particularly grateful for. It might be something small, making your mom laugh when you talked to her on the phone, or something big like acing a final exam or closing a big deal at work. Whatever it is, be grateful for that day because it will never come again.[1]

FOR YOU   WHAT'S AHEAD IN THIS CHAPTER

We're concluding Part One and our discussion of the individual level by introducing you to one of the most exciting and fastest growing areas of OB, *positive organizational behavior (POB)*. The exciting news is that research suggests that you can enhance your life and job satisfaction by following some of the ideas presented in this chapter. Many inputs in the Integrative Framework contribute to POB, and it in turn affects important outcomes across all levels. We explore the importance of POB and then expand on several of the elements that help foster your own personal positivity and—as shown in the growing reports and research in the *Harvard Business Review* and the major journals in OB—the benefits of positive workplaces. Positive emotions are one such element (individual level process), as are mindfulness (person input), positive psychological capital (person input), and organizational climate (environmental characteristic input). Combined, these elements create a positive workplace environment and enable people, teams, and organizations to flourish. Flourishing is the ultimate individual-level outcome of POB and comprises positive emotions, engagement, constructive relationships, meaningfulness, and achievement.

MAJOR QUESTION

How does understanding Positive OB benefit me?

THE BIGGER PICTURE

You can benefit at school or work by understanding Positive OB (POB), a purposefully positive approach to managing the behavior of individuals, groups, and organizations. You'll see some of these potential benefits when you explore three ways in which Positive OB affects a broader set of outcomes. You'll then see the benefits of POB illustrated in detail.

Two Modes of Viewing Organizations

Let's set the stage by establishing two scenarios as set out in an early presentation of POB.

First Scenario   The first scenario begins, "Imagine a world in which almost all organizations are typified by greed, selfishness, manipulation, secrecy, and a single-minded focus on winning."[2] Wealth is the ultimate measure of success. Feelings of distrust, anxiety, self-absorption, fear, burnout, and abuse are common. Members often experience conflict, treat each other disrespectfully, and break agreements to each other. Managers, researchers, and teachers in this context focus on problem solving, managing uncertainty, overcoming resistance, achieving profitability, and figuring out how to best the competition.

Second Scenario   Now imagine a world in which appreciation, collaboration, virtuousness, vitality, and meaningfulness are the rule. Well-being and thriving for individuals, groups, and organizations are the markers of success. Trustworthiness, resilience, wisdom, humility, and positive energy are common features. Relationships and interactions are described as compassionate, loyal, honest, respectful, and forgiving. Managers, researchers, and teachers emphasize theories of excellence, positive deviance, extraordinary performance, and positive spirals of flourishing.

Emphasis, Not Rejection, of Business Realities   Many professionals who first encounter POB ideas assume it simply rejects the hard business realities in the first scenario: the need to solve problems, to manage uncertainty, to overcome resistance, to achieve profitability, and to compete successfully. But something else is happening in POB.

Positive organizational behavior "does not reject the value and significance of the phenomena in the first worldview. Rather, it emphasizes the phenomena represented in the second."[3] A more recent review of POB described it like this:

> **Positive OB (POB)** involves the study and application of positively oriented human resource strengths and psychological capacities that can be measured, developed, and effectively managed for performance improvement in today's workplace.[4]

Most research, writing, and teaching have until recently focused largely on the first view described above. We choose to complement this traditional view with a more contemporary and clearly more positive and constructive approach in this chapter. We want to show you how identifying and applying the many positive attributes of individuals, groups, and organizations is yet another and especially powerful way of increasing your effectiveness *especially* in the business environment.

FIGURE 7.1 A MODEL OF POSITIVE ORGANIZATIONAL BEHAVIOR

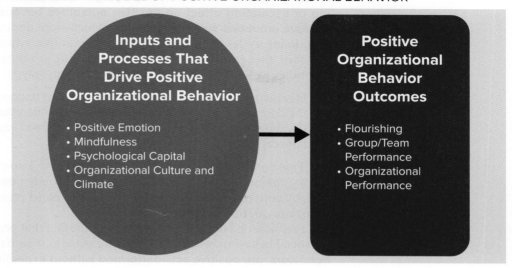

Inputs and Processes That Drive Positive Organizational Behavior

- Positive Emotion
- Mindfulness
- Psychological Capital
- Organizational Culture and Climate

Positive Organizational Behavior Outcomes

- Flourishing
- Group/Team Performance
- Organizational Performance

Figure 7.1 previews how this chapter organizes the topic. Certain inputs and a specific process from the Integrative Framework drive Positive OB. In turn, Positive OB is expected to elevate positive outcomes across the individual, group/team, and organizational levels.

How Positivity Works

Research on POB is relatively new and undeveloped, but it is growing quickly. Already we have enough evidence to support the conclusion that positive organizational practices drive outcomes across all three levels of the Integrative Framework.[5] This conclusion in turn has generated interest in understanding how positive practices affect OB-related outcomes. Figure 7.2 illustrates this process.

FIGURE 7.2 THE FLOW OF POSITIVE INFLUENCE

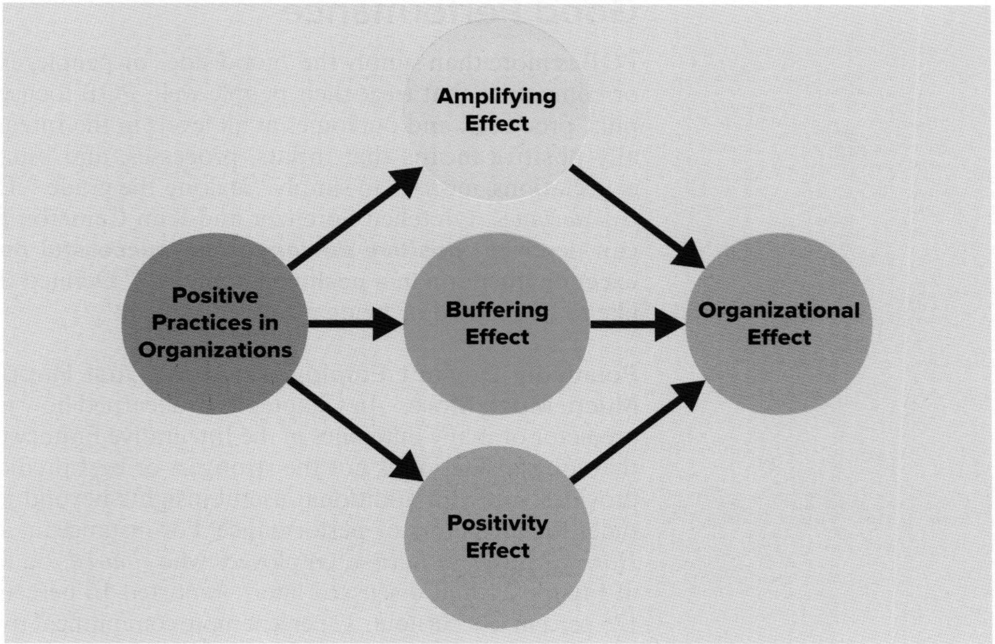

Amplifying Effect

Positive Practices in Organizations

Buffering Effect

Organizational Effect

Positivity Effect

SOURCE: Adapted from K. Cameron, C. Mora, T. Leutscher, and M. Calarco, "Effects of Positive Practices on Organizational Effectiveness," *The Journal of Applied Behavioral Science,* September 2011, 287. Reprinted with permission of Sage Publications, Inc.

Amplifying Effect In the *amplifying effect,* positive practices have an amplifying or escalating effect on positive outcomes because of their association with positive emotions and social capital, which were discussed in Chapter 1. Mutually reinforcing cycles of positivity occur, for example, when we observe kindness, compassion, and gratitude. Barbara Fredrickson, a renowned researcher on positive emotions, explained the amplifying effect in this way:

> Elevation increases the likelihood that a witness to good deeds will soon become the doer of good deeds, then elevation sets up the possibility for some sort of upward spiral . . . and organizations are transformed into more compassionate and harmonious places.[6]

This conception of positive emotions is also known as the broaden-and-build theory, maintaining that positive emotions broaden one's attention and cognition, and, by consequence, allow the individual to build greater emotional well-being, as though on an upward spiral.

Fredrickson's description underscores the fact that people are more likely to exhibit prosocial behaviors when POB is taking place in their work environments. *Prosocial behaviors* are positive acts performed without expecting anything in return.[7]

Buffering Effect To buffer means to reduce or counteract the effects of something that is happening in our lives. In the *buffering effect,* positive practices buffer or reduce the impact of negative events and stressors. They do this by enhancing what is called psychological capital. As you will learn later in this chapter, *psychological capital* represents a set of personal characteristics that help us to flourish and be resilient in the face of adversity or challenging obstacles.

Positivity Effect The *positivity effect* "is the attraction of all living systems toward positive energy and away from negative energy, or toward that which is life giving and away from that which is life depleting."[8] Organizations that use positive practices are more likely to create an atmosphere of positive energy, which in turn fuels increased performance.[9]

The Benefits of POB Extend beyond Good Performance

POB is more than simply the "good side" of people, examples of good performance, or companies that treat their people well. POB focuses on *exceptionally positive* inputs, processes, and outcomes at all levels in the Integrative Framework. Exceptionally positive means that inputs, processes, and outcomes are above and beyond expectations, more than simply "making the grade." This is often referred to as *positive deviance.* Gretchen Spreitzer and Kim Cameron from the University of Michigan describe *positive deviance* as "successful performance that dramatically exceeds the norm in a positive direction."[10] Defined this way, we suspect you would like to be accused of being positively deviant!

Positively Deviant Employees Aren't Just Happy and Satisfied—They Are Much, Much More In Chapter 2, you learned how job satisfaction is an important predictor of many outcomes in the Integrative Framework. However, you also learned that job satisfaction is not the strongest or best predictor of job performance. POB provides you with additional useful insights beyond job satisfaction and other attitudes for predictors of performance. For instance, in a recent study published in the *Harvard Business Review*, employees who *flourish*—a key component of POB shown in Figure 7.1 and discussed later—reported 16 percent higher overall performance, 125 percent less burnout, 32 percent more commitment to their employers, and 46 percent more job satisfaction, and they missed less work.[11] These outcomes are compelling often make *Fortune*'s 100 Best Companies to Work For list because they consistently value employees more than their competitors. They also tend to hold environmental and community responsibilities in a higher regard than most, and they walk the talk in terms of being stewards of people, planet, and profits. What would be your personal benefits of working for such a company? You might want to pursue a job at a CC company based on our discussion.

solving application

problem

Conscious Capitalism at Whole Foods

The company, based in Austin, Texas, is a perennial favorite on *Fortune*'s 100 Best Companies to Work For list.[19] One reason why is its transparency. Employees vote on every new hire and are able to see everyone's pay. Another reason is its CEO, John Mackey, and his approach to business, which he describes in a book, *Conscious Capitalism*. Fundamental to this notion is a higher purpose.

A Higher Purpose Is the Destination *and* the Vehicle. While you'll learn about visions and leadership in Chapter 13, a higher purpose is a very particular type of vision in conscious capitalism. It requires a focus on something other than profitability, shareholders, and economic gain. And it guides all other business activities.

Choose Talent Carefully. A clear and compelling purpose helps identify, attract, and hire the most appropriate new employees. But to assure they actually walk the

John Mackey, CEO of Whole Foods, wrote the book on conscious capitalism.

talk, new hires begin with a 30–90-day probationary period, at the end of which two-thirds of their team members must vote to keep them. Such conscious practices have resulted in a turnover rate of

less than 10 percent, which makes it easier to justify investments in employee development.[20]

Teamwork Unlocks Creativity and Improves Decisions. "It's deeply fulfilling for people to be part of a team, where their contributions are valued and the team encourages them to be creative and make contributions."[21] You'll learn more about teamwork in Chapter 8, but teams can generate more than the sum of their parts. At Whole Foods teams create their own identities and names (e.g., Green Produce Monsters). They also make all of their own hiring, product, and compensation decisions.

Conscious Capitalism Is Self-Reinforcing. Purpose feeds talent, it guides and coheres teams, and both in turn help fulfill the purpose. Such continual reinforcement creates *positive spirals,* which we'll discuss more later in the chapter.

YOUR CALL *Apply the 3-Stop Problem-Solving Approach.*

Stop 1: How did Mackey define the problem?

Stop 2: Which inputs and processes from the Integrative Framework are evident?

Stop 3: Would you want to work for a company that practices CC? Why or why not? Assume you were to start your own business. What would be three benefits of modeling after CC principles?

MAJOR QUESTION

What is the role of positive emotions in POB, and how can they make me more effective at school, at work, and in other arenas of life?

THE BIGGER PICTURE

At school, at work, or in your personal life, you've already seen how powerfully and sometimes unexpectedly emotions can arise. OB recognizes emotions as an important and ever-present individual-level process. In the section ahead you can see if your positive emotional experience matches our list and definitions of the 10 most common positive emotions. Then, you'll see how positivity is more than happiness and painting a smile on your face. You'll also find tips on how to foster your own positive emotions and how to apply them at school, work, and home.

Recall that in Chapter 3 we introduced emotions as relatively brief psychological and physiological reactions that have a particular target, such as a person (e.g., unethical and bullying boss), situation (e.g., a night out with your closest friends), event (e.g., scoring well on an exam), or nonevent (e.g., your forgot to brush your teeth). Our discussion then focused largely on the various types of negative emotions and how to manage their expression. We now turn our attention to positive emotions. Like their negative cousins, positive emotions are relatively flexible individual differences and are important processes in the Integrative Framework. And while it is true that you, like most people, simply think of emotions in terms of positive-negative, "I'm happy, I'm sad," you'll learn there is much more to the story.

Beyond Good vs. Bad

Positive and negative emotions are not polar opposites. The emotional world is not simply good versus bad. Negative emotions spur you to act in quite narrow or specific ways. Fear may motivate you to flee and anger may motivate you to fight. Positive emotions in contrast tend to broaden your mindset, open you to consider new, different, if not better alternatives when trying to solve a problem. If you think of emotions in this way, then you can see that negative emotions are limiting and positive emotions are resources that fuel individual, group, and organizational flourishing. (*Flourishing* is discussed in detail in the last section of this chapter.) Barbara Fredrickson explains positive emotions this way:

> To get a feel for the ways positive emotions can build life resources, envision for a moment something that made you feel joyful, playful, or intensely alive—when you wanted to smile, cheer, or jump up and dance around. Maybe it was . . . sharing a meal with lots of laughter with a friend you haven't seen in ages . . . maybe it was dancing with the group of friends as your favorite band played. Whatever comes to mind for you, take a moment to relive the experience in your mind, letting joy rekindle. Consider how you felt and what you felt like doing. What we've learned about joyful experiences like these is that the playful urges they carry build resources, and in times of trouble, these gains in resources can help you in important ways—strengthen relationships, boost performance at school and work, and improve your health.[22]

The bottom line: Positive emotions help you build social (e.g., relationships), psychological (e.g., well-being), and physical (e.g., lower stress and a healthy heart) resources that support your efforts and effectiveness in all arenas of your life—school, work, and family. Positive emotions also help combat negative emotions. Therefore, positive emotions are processes that influence many of the outcomes in the Integrative Framework. More than that, the benefits of positive emotions have been shown to endure over long periods of time.

Table 7.2 lists the 10 most common positive emotions from the most to the least frequently experienced. Love is a special case, however. Despite being at the bottom

TABLE 7.2 DESCRIPTION OF THE 10 MOST FREQUENT POSITIVE EMOTIONS

POSITIVE EMOTION	DESCRIPTION
Joy	Visualize this: your surroundings are safe and familiar. Things are going your way, even better than you expected at the moment. Choice requires little effort on your part. Colors are more vivid. There's a spring in your step. And your face lights up in a smile and with an inner glow.
Gratitude	Imagine you've realized that someone has gone out of his or her way to do something different. Your mentor gently steers your career in the right direction. Your physician goes out of her way to meet you at the office on the weekend. Gratitude opens your heart and generates an urge for you to give back, to do something good in return, either for the person who helped you work or for someone else.
Serenity	Like joy, serenity includes safe surroundings. Serene situations are familiar and require little effort on your part. But unlike joy, serenity is much more low key. It's when you went on a long, relaxing ride or walk, engaged in fulfilling conversation, or got wrapped up in a good book at the pool or beach while on vacation.
Interest	Something novel or different draws your attention, filling you with a sense of possibility or mystery. Unlike joy and serenity, the circumstances call for effort on your part. You're pulled to immerse yourself in what you're discovering.
Hope	Hope is different from most other positive emotions, which you experience when you're safe and/or satisfied. You are hopeful when something isn't going your way, but you believe that it can.
Pride	You know pride's evil cousins—shame and guilt—and the painful feelings that overcome you when you are to blame for something. Pride is the opposite; you're "to blame" for something good, something for which you can take credit or when you recognize that you made a positive difference to someone else. (However, unchecked pride is hubris.)
Amusement	Sometimes something unexpected happens that simply makes you laugh. Amusement is social; it most often happens in the company of and as a result of others. Heartfelt laughter often accompanies amusement.
Inspiration	Every so often, you come across true human excellence—people doing exceptional things. Feeling inspired rivets your attention, warms your heart, and draws you in. Inspiration doesn't simply feel good; it makes you want to act, to improve, or even to be the best that you can be.
Awe	Closely related to inspiration, awe happens on a grand scale. You literally feel overwhelmed. You feel small and humble. Awe makes you stop in your tracks. Sometimes people are awed by nature, such as the Grand Canyon or Niagara Falls.
Love	Love is not a single positive emotion. It incorporates many of the others. When these good feelings stir our hearts within a safe, often close relationship, we call it love. Early stages of such relationships involve intense interest in everything and anything the person says. You share amusements and laughter together. As your relationship builds great joy, you begin to share your hopes and dreams for the future together. When the relationship becomes more solid, you experience serenity and can be proud of your partner's achievements, as if they are your own.

SOURCE: Adapted from B. L. Fredrickson, *Positivity* (New York: Three Rivers Press, 2009).

of the list, love actually is the most frequently experienced positive emotion. After reading and learning about each of the other positive emotions, you'll understand why it was inserted last in the table.

TAKE-AWAY APPLICATION—TAAP

Complete the following to apply your new knowledge regarding positive emotions.

1. Choose three emotions, other than love, from Table 7.2.
2. Now think of a time when you experienced each. What were the circumstances?
3. What were the benefits to you?
4. Did anybody else benefit? If so, how?
5. Think of ways you can create and experience each of these at either school, work, or home.

Positive Emotions Lead to Success at School, at Work, and in Life

People have often wondered and long debated whether happiness leads to success or vice versa. The answer is: both! Interestingly, however, recent research provides compelling evidence that positive emotions lead to or foster many desirable behaviors and outcomes:

- **Stronger social relationships.** Positive emotions energize others, make you more attractive, and are contagious.
- **Prosocial behaviors.** Positive emotions foster helping others, altruism, and openness.
- **Liking of yourself and others.** Positive emotions are linked to improved self-esteem and self-efficacy.
- **Stronger bodies and immune systems.** Positive emotions help lower stress hormones and blood pressure, pain, and the frequency of colds.[23]
- **Original thinking.** Positive emotions enhance creativity, openness to more alternatives, and collaboration.[24]

Many experiments and other forms of research reveal a compelling amount of evidence for the benefits of positivity and positive emotions. And while many are impressive, one in particular is worthy of specific note: That is that positivity begets positivity. It has been shown time and again that if you help somebody in a meaningful, or even small, way, he or she is more likely to help others. As Barbara Fredrickson says, "Beyond the dance of positivity between you and the person you helped, those who witness your good deed may well feel inspired, their hearts uplifted and elevated."[25] This means that not only do you reap the benefits of helping somebody else, but that person also benefits, and so does the person he or she helps, and so on, and so on. This self-reinforcing and perpetuating aspect of positive emotions, and positivity more generally, is what leads to **upward spirals of positivity, where your positive behaviors, feelings, and attitudes feed your own and those of others in a continual, reinforcing process.**

How Much Positivity Is Enough?

We again want to underscore the valuable role of negative emotions—life is not all sunshine and roses. And forcing (or deluding) yourself to feel or act that everything is great all the time is absurd, if not pathological. Eternally rose-colored glasses certainly would undermine your effectiveness, health, and overall well-being. Even the most positive person feels the intense emotional pain associated with experiences of loss and betrayal. Positive people get angry when they or others are treated unfairly. So this begs the question: How much positivity is enough?

Multiple Positives for Every Negative   Thankfully, recent research gives you some guidance. While some researchers have argued for specific ratios of positive to negative, and others have disputed specific numbers, they all agree that positive and negative experiences are not equivalent.[26] This means that you can't simply remedy a negative experience with a positive one. Instead, to flourish and experience the benefits of POB discussed in this chapter you must have three, five, or more positive experiences for every negative. It also is helpful to know that you don't need to focus on which positive emotions you feel at a particular time; just be sure that you have multiple positives for every one negative

Fundamental to this idea of multiple positive emotions for every negative is the well-established fact that our brains respond differently to positive and negative experiences.

- **Negative experiences** activate a survival orientation, which leads us to be more responsive to negative information. Interestingly, our brains actually look more for negative information and stimuli over positive ones during daily activities.[27] This is probably one explanation for why managers tend to give more negative than positive feedback to employees.

- **Positive experiences** activate a supportive orientation, which leads us to be more responsive to positive information. This is part of the reason why managers, and people more generally, seem receptive to new ideas when they are in a "good mood."

This discussion underscores how important it is for managers to focus on the good things employees are doing, and for all of us to focus on the positive qualities of coworkers, classmates, partners, friends, and spouses. Practical advice on how to build your positive emotions follows in the next section.

Strategies to Increase Your Positivity   The following activities can help you increase your positive experiences and decrease your negative ones.[28]

Create high-quality connections. Any social interaction, whether with family, coworkers, classmates, or the person ahead of you in line, is a chance to create a high-quality connection. Such connections are energizing and enhance your positivity. To transform ordinary interactions into high-quality connections, try the following tips:

Sports like golf are one way to "goof off" and have fun. To make this work, however, you need to enjoy the activity for the activity's sake. Too many people ruin the fun of playing golf by taking their scores too seriously.

1. **The only person in the room.** Engage the other person by being present, attentive, and affirming. Act as if he/she is the only person in the room.

2. **Support.** Do what you can to encourage the person and help him/her achieve a goal or attain success.

3. **Give trust.** Believe you can depend on this person to meet your expectations, and let it show.

4. **Goof off.** Play! Have no goals or intentions other than to goof off.

Cultivate kindness. Give yourself the goal of performing five new acts of kindness in a single day. Aim for actions that really make a difference and come at no cost to you. Assess what those around you might need most and make a plan, but execute your plan so that your acts of kindness all occur on the same day.

Develop distractions. One of the best ways to break from negativity is to distract yourself. The more attention a distraction requires the better. To do this, make two lists: healthy distractions and unhealthy distractions. Brainstorm and think of ways—old and new—to distract yourself from negative thoughts. Be sure to try to think of things you can do at school, at home, or at work. Negativity can creep in anywhere and at any time; you therefore need your lists of distractions handy and practical. Healthy distractions could be going for a run, for a bike ride, or to the driving range. Unhealthy distractions might be drinking, food, TV, or video games. Be careful of these, and for each unhealthy one, challenge yourself to add another healthy distraction.

Dispute negative self-talk and thoughts. Get a stack of 3 × 5 cards and write your common negative thoughts or emotions about yourself, about a relationship, or about a situation at school, work, or home. Then, in a private place where nobody can hear you, read the cards one at a time. After reading each one aloud, then quickly, without thought, dispute or counter that negative thought. Beat it down and disprove it with something positive about yourself, the situation, or facts. Be sure to do this with enthusiasm, as it will build your conviction. Practice this. Your goal is to dispute negative thoughts as quickly as they enter your mind.

Platitudes = Fake = Bad Outcomes

It is important for you to remember, however, that simply uttering positive words or forcing a smile isn't enough. Humans are excellent detectors of insincerity.[29] If your positivity is not heartfelt and genuine, then you will not reap any of the benefits discussed (e.g., improved performance, relationships, and health). Worse still, insincere attempts at positivity may even do harm, as others are likely to see your lack of authenticity, which can erode their trust in you and your influence and credibility with them. (Many of these topics are discussed in later chapters—influencing others in Chapter 12 and leadership in Chapter 13.) To apply this knowledge, and learn which positive emotions you experience, take Self-Assessment 7.1.

Mc Graw Hill Education connect

SELF-ASSESSMENT 7.1   What Is My Positivity Ratio?

Go to connect.mheducation.com and take Self-Assessment 7.1 to learn the ratio of your positive to negative emotions. Then do the following:

1. What is your reaction to the results?
2. Considering the individual differences (IDs) we discussed in Chapter 3, which ones do you think are contributing to your ratio?
3. Do others see you as more or less positive than your ratio suggests? Why?
4. If you do this for two different dimensions of your life (e.g., school and work), then to what do you attribute these differences?
5. Describe three things you can do to improve your positivity ratio for school.

From *Positivity: Groundbreaking Research Reveals How to Embrace the Hidden Strength of Positive Emotions, Overcome Negativity, and Thrive,* by Barbara Fredrickson, Copyright © 2009 by Barbara Fredrickson, Ph.D. Used by permission of Crown Books, an imprint of the Crown Publishing Group, a division of Random House LLC. All rights reserved.

My Level of Positivity

To make this discussion come to life for you, it is helpful to know the relative frequency of your positive to negative emotions. This knowledge can help you understand many things about yourself, such as how likely you are to reap the benefits of positive emotions and POB. Remember that emotions are short-lived and that any measure of your emotions captures only your feelings about a specific event, person, or dimension of your life at a particular point in time. We therefore encourage you to take the Self-Assessment for the past day of your life, which is intended to capture your positivity for life more generally. Then, do it focusing on school as your target. If you're working, calculate your ratio of positive to negative emotions for work and compare it to your ratio for life more generally. This will give you knowledge of your positivity in various arenas of your life and help you better understand this important personal resource.

FOSTERING MINDFULNESS

MAJOR QUESTION

How can mindfulness contribute to my effectiveness?

THE BIGGER PICTURE

You may be more aware of mindfulness by its absence, that is, in the aftermath of when you realize you've done something foolish or thoughtless. You will be encouraged to learn that you can improve your focus and attention through practice. You're about to learn what inhibits mindfulness and two of the most effective techniques you can use to increase it.

The concept of mindfulness has been studied for over 30 years. It has historical roots in Buddhism in that it represents a state of consciousness that is cultivated through meditative practice. But mindfulness, just like meditation itself, is not tied to any religion. Psychologists are keenly interested in fostering mindfulness because it is positively associated with many indicators of physical and mental health. The field of OB, however, has only recently started to examine the concept.[30] We are discussing mindfulness in this chapter due to its potential to positively impact many of the outcomes in the Integrative Framework. For example, mindfulness will enhance your ability to use managerial skills associated with performance management like giving feedback, coaching, and recognizing others.

In this section, we discuss the difference between mindfulness and mindlessness, the inhibitors of mindfulness, the benefits of mindfulness, and techniques you can use to practice mindfulness.

Mindlessness vs. Mindfulness

Imagine that you are sitting in your seat during an airplane flight that is beginning its descent to your destination. Across the aisle, you notice that a two-year-old baby starts to cry due to altitude changes and the mother begins to soothe him. Suddenly, a man sitting in the same row as the crying baby tells the mom to "shut that (N-word) baby up." Despite her attempts to quiet the baby boy, he continues to cry. Unexpectedly, the man reaches around and slaps the child in the face with an open hand, which results in louder screams from the baby, along with a scratch below the eye.

This alleged event occurred on a Delta Air Lines flight, according to the boy's mother and corroborated by another witness. The offensive man, Joe Rickey Hundley, pleaded guilty to a simple assault charge and was sentenced to 8 months in federal prison. He subsequently was discharged by his employer—AGC Aerospace & Defense.[31]

This is an example of *mindless* behavior, at the least. **Mindlessness "is a state of reduced attention. It is expressed in behavior that is rigid,"** or thoughtless.[32] Mr. Hundley certainly wasn't thinking about the repercussions of his behavior, and he clearly failed to control his emotions, which is a key component of *mindfulness*. Mindlessness requires minimal information processing and we often do it rather automatically. In this case a man's emotional state apparently took complete control of him. A more common example would be driving to and from work. We get in the car, take off, and then all of a sudden we remember arriving at our destination wondering how we got there. Mindlessness can also be purposive when we refuse to "acknowledge or attend to a thought, emotion, motive, or object of perception."[33]

An example is forgetting someone's name 30 seconds after being introduced for the first time. A lack of attention simply sends the name into our pile of forgotten information. Not surprisingly, mindlessness is associated with poor mental and physical health, less satisfying relationships, and lower task performance.[34] Mindfulness is completely different.

Mindfulness **is defined as "the awareness that emerges through paying attention on purpose, in the present moment, and nonjudgmentally to the unfolding of experience moment by moment."**[35] In essence, mindfulness represents the extent to which we are *aware and attentive* to what is happening around us at a given moment. This awareness and attention pertain to both our inner (How am feeling at this moment? What am I thinking?) and outer (What are others feeling and doing? What is that noise? Who has the most power in this group?) worlds. Mindfulness requires effort because our brains work in ways that detract from staying focused. For example, we all have a "thinking mind" that likes to judge everything we see and hear. This leads to the "mental chatter" that detracts from the inner quiet needed to stay focused and aware of what is going on around us. Further, our minds have an automatic pilot of unawareness. It's simply easier to let the mind aimlessly wander around than it is to concentrate on the present moment. Left unchecked, the mind will drive us toward mindlessness.[36]

Mindfulness improves our interpersonal communications because it keeps us focused on other persons we're involved with and the details of what they are saying. Herb Kelleher, former CEO of Southwest Airlines, was noted as a very mindful person. Here is what Doug Parker, CEO of US Airways, had to say about a typical interaction with Herb: "He is completely engaged and never looks over your shoulder to see who else is in the room. It's not out of principle; it's just who he is." Mr. Parker told a *Fortune* reporter that he changed his approach to communicating with employees based on observing Mr. Kelleher. He has shunned large group meetings for smaller ones containing 30 or 40 people. He said that this enables him to be more attentive to employee needs and to "really" listen to their concerns.[37] Doug Parker's actions represent mindfulness in action.

Mindfulness requires attentional balance, which reflects your ability to maintain sustained, nonemotional attention in a specific situation. Does wearing headphones at work help or hinder attentional balance? The Example box below discusses some interesting conclusions about the use of headphones at work.

EXAMPLE   Does the Use of Headphones Help Achieve Mindfulness?

More and more companies are allowing employees to use earbuds and noise-canceling headphones at work. Some people listen to music while others just want to reduce the general level of noise. The feeling among many employees is that it helps block distractions like loud coworkers, ringing phones, and machine-related noises. Not all companies agree with this conclusion, however, and some employers have banned their use.

LISTENING TO MUSIC WHILE STUDYING AND WORKING.   Research on students provided little support for listening to music while studying. A study of Taiwanese students revealed that concentration levels went down when participants studied while listening to music with lyrics. Adult reading-test scores also were lower when people listened to hip-hop music while reading.

Neuroscientists believe that "listening to music with lyrics while trying to read or write can distract employees by overtaxing verbal-processing regions of the brain." Dr. Robert Desimone, director of Brain Research at MIT, concluded that "the prefrontal cortex, the brain's control center, must work harder to force itself not to process any strong verbal stimuli, such as catchy lyrics, that compete with the work you're attempting."[38]

INDIVIDUAL DIFFERENCES EXIST.   Research shows that people pay more or less attention to music they like or dislike, respectively. In other words, we are more distracted by music we like. Familiar music that does not contain lyrics also was found to serve as a sound-blocker. Other individuals also benefit from noise-canceling headphones because they reduce the amount of high-frequency sound and general activity occurring in an office environment.

At the same time, the use of earbuds and headphones can cause conflict and resentment at work. It becomes hard for colleagues to get each other's attention when one or more people are listening to music or wearing noise-reducing headphones. This can lead people to throw things to get someone else's attention. Further, some people believe that the use of such equipment at work violates norms of etiquette.

DO HEADPHONES HELP? We would not recommend them when you are reading or studying. Otherwise, it seems that individual differences and office norms should rule.[39]

YOUR THOUGHTS?

1. If you are going to listen to music while working, what artists or types of music would be most suitable for you?
2. What's your opinion about students who want to listen to music while studying?
3. Assume you're on a team project with other students; would it bother you if other team members wore headphones and listened to music? Explain.
4. What's your opinion about workers who want to listen to music at work?
5. Assume at work you're promoted to supervise a group of employees; would it bother you if some workers in the group wore headphones and listened to music? Explain.

Let's consider the inhibitors to attentional balance.

Inhibitors of Mindfulness

There are two key inhibitors of mindfulness: attentional deficit and attentional hyperactivity.[40] It is important to understand these inhibitors so that you can avoid them.

Attentional Deficit An *attentional deficit* reflects the inability to focus vividly on an object. This can easily occur in a classroom when students feel bored, listless, or uninterested in what is being discussed. Surfing the Internet during class certainly will contribute to this inhibitor. Attentional deficit also stems from a lack of sleep, a cold, conflicting priorities, or counterfactual thinking. Counterfactual thinking represents the tendency to think about "what could have been" or "what might be" as opposed to what is actually taking place or being said. The recommendation here is to stay focused on the moment and don't let your attention sway toward the past or the future.

Sometimes we become distracted instead of paying attention to the present moment. What might this boy miss by letting his attention sway from the ball game? A home run? A ball hit his way? It takes effort to stay focused on what is happening around us.

Attentional Hyperactivity *Attentional hyperactivity* **happens when our minds are racing or wandering, resulting in compulsive daydreaming or fantasizing.** This is also called "rumination." For example, fantasizing about your lunch or evening plans during class prohibits you from paying attention to what your professor is saying. Research reveals that all of us do a lot of mind wandering on a daily basis.[41] Bestselling author and psychology professor Daniel Gilbert estimates that people mind wander about 50 percent of the workday. Can you imagine the cost in terms of lost productivity? Gilbert's research reveals that most mind wandering is centered on personal rather than business concerns.[42] Mind wandering is likely to increase when we are highly aroused, such as drinking three Red Bull drinks before 10:00 am, or when we have a lot of commitments. The recommendation here is be aware when your mind wanders. When it happens, don't be overly attentive to it and don't be mad at yourself for doing it. Just give soft recognition to the fact that your mind is wandering and then return your focus to the present moment.

Benefits of Mindfulness

There are four broad benefits of mindfulness.[43]

1. **Increased physical, mental, and interpersonal effectiveness.** This occurs because people are more aware of physical sensations, personal feelings, personal emotions, and the feelings and emotions of others.

2. **More effective communications.** Mindfulness fosters more effective listening, greater use of empathy, and more attention to nonverbal cues during conversations.

3. **More balanced emotions.** Paying attention to internal emotions and the emotions of others leads us to be more balanced and less reactive. This in turn helps reduce conflict with others.

4. **Personal effectiveness.** Mindfulness enhances your ability to contribute during class sessions or meetings at work, to provide social support to others, to ask for help when needed, and to develop and sustain loving relationships.

Recent OB research revealed that mindfulness was significantly related to several outcomes in the Integrative Framework. Specifically, mindfulness was positively associated with task performance, job satisfaction, and decreased emotional exhaustion. Given the newness of this concept within the field of OB, future research may uncover additional benefits of mindfulness.[44]

Would you like to improve your overall well-being? How about the effectiveness of your social interactions and relationships? If yes, then you will gain valuable insight about enhancing your level of mindfulness in pursuit of these positive outcomes by taking the following Self-Assessment. It measures your level of mindfulness. You can use your scores to develop an improvement plan.

---

connect

SELF-ASSESSMENT 7.2 **What Is My Level of Mindfulness?**

Go to connect.mheducation.com and take Self-Assessment 7.2. Then answer the following questions.

1. What questions reflect your greatest inhibitors? (Select the three items with the lowest scores.)

2. What is the cause of these inhibitors?

3. Examine the techniques listed in the next section and determine which one might be best suited for your needs. Start using the technique on a daily basis.

Copyright © 2003 by the American Psychological Association. Adapted with permission from K. W. Brown and R. M. Ryan, "The Benefits of Being Present: Mindfulness and Its Role in Psychological Well-Being," *Journal of Personality and Social Psychology, 84*(4), 826.

Practicing Mindfulness

The goal of practicing mindfulness is to help you become more calm and collected in all circumstances. The 2009 book *The Leader's Way* explains: "When the mind is disturbed by anger, jealousy, hate, impatience, fear, lack of self-confidence, or negative emotions about things that happened in the past, it is wasting valuable time that instead should be used for constructive thinking."[45] Practicing mindfulness helps you focus your mind on productive activities while constraining counterproductive thinking and mind wandering.

The good news is that mindfulness can be learned by using a variety of simple meditative techniques on a regular basis. Although there are many good books you can consult for details regarding these techniques,[46] we review two approaches that are easily learned: a breathing meditation and a walking meditation. Research shows that practicing short meditative techniques like these reduces stress and negative emotions, and increases emotional regulation, task performance, and memory.[47]

The Wall Street Journal, covering the growing influence of meditation, interviewed Dr. Muali Doraiswamy, a psychiatry professor at Duke University Medical Center. He discussed the physiological process underlying the positive outcomes of mediation, which the *Journal* summarized as follows: "Some forms of meditation have been found to activate the parasympathetic nervous system, which stimulates the body's relaxation response, improves blood supply, slows down heart rate and breathing and increases digestive activity, he said. It also slows down the release of stress hormones, such as cortisol."[48] You will find both physiological and cognitive benefits from practicing mindfulness. Give it a try!

Breathing Meditation   Breathing meditations are easy and can be done almost anywhere. Focusing on breath reminds us of the "here and now" because it brings us back to a fundamental and vital function of life. This technique requires nothing more than just tuning into the feelings associated with breathing in and out. Two experts recommend the following simple approach for getting started:

- Place your hand on your stomach a couple of inches beneath the upside-down V at the center of your rib cage. Look down, breathe normally, and watch your hand. You'll probably see it move only a little bit, and sort of up and down.
- Leaving your hand in place, now breathe in such a way that your hand moves out and back, perpendicular to your chest. Try to breathe into your hand with real oomph, so that it travels back and forth half an inch or more with each breadth.[49]

Start out by trying these two steps for about 10–20 breaths. Once you are comfortable with this form of diaphragm breathing, you can take your practice to the next level with these additional instructions:

- Sit comfortably in a chair, feet firmly on the ground and your back relatively erect. Feel like you are a "proud mountain" of stability. Close your eyes and take a deep inhale that fills your belly and lungs. Now exhale, noticing how your belly contracts. Do this twice.
- Add counting to your breathing. Count to four or five as you both inhale and exhale. This will ensure that you take deep breaths. Try doing this for five minutes twice a day. You can extend the length of time you practice breathing meditations as you become more comfortable with the technique.

Your mind is likely to wander while using the above techniques. You also will notice sounds around you. Not to worry, it's normal. When this happens, just acknowledge the thoughts and sounds and return your focus to your breath. Don't try to chase the thoughts away or give them much attention. Just recognize the thoughts and sounds and let them pass. The thoughts will move away like a white cloud being moved by the wind in a blue sky.

Walking Meditation   This is one of your authors' favorite forms of meditation because it can be done anytime you are walking, and no one will know that you are doing it. It's important to start this technique by forming an intention. An *intention* **represents an end point or desired goal you want to achieve.** In this context, the intention sends a signal to the mind that guides its attentiveness and awareness during the meditative practice.[50] A sample intention would be "I will focus on the act of walking while ignoring other sounds and thoughts." Begin walking keeping your intention in mind. Concentrate on the placement of one footstep after another. Feel the rhythmic nature of your steps. Focus on how it feels to lift and place your feet on the surface. Train your mind to be aware of your footsteps. Notice the speed at which you walk and the pressure being felt by your feet. Consider changing the length of your stride and notice how it feels. If your mind starts to wander or you begin thinking about something you have to do, just recognize the thought and then drop it. Return your attention and awareness to your intention, which is the act of walking. You will be amazed at what you can observe.[51] Try this for five minutes.

Another variant of this technique involves taking a walk with a different intention. Examples are "I will focus on all sounds during my walk" or "I will focus on all smells during my walk." If you use an intention aimed at sound, begin walking and concentrate on what you hear. Listen for all types of sounds like footsteps, birds, mechanical objects operating, wind, tree branches rustling, voices, clanging of objects, airplanes, etc. The key is to allow your mind to focus on anything that can be heard. Again, recognize stray or wandering thoughts, and then let them passively go away by returning to your intention. Try this for five to ten minutes.

Practice Makes Perfect   Mindfulness can be learned via practice, and the benefits are substantial. Google, General Mills, and McKinsey & Company recognize this conclusion by investing in company-sponsored training programs.[52] Yes, it takes time, practice, and, most importantly, commitment. The above techniques can get you started, and you can consult additional resources noted above if you want to expand your practice. We would like to close with a thought by Jon Kabat-Zinn, the founder and director of the Stress Reduction Clinic at the University of Massachusetts Medical Center and professor of Medicine. Here is what Professor Kabat-Zinn had to say about meditation:

> It is not some weird cryptic activity, as our popular culture might have it. It does not involve becoming some kind of Zombie, vegetable, self-absorbed narcissist, navel gazer, "space cadet," cultist, devotee, mystic, or Eastern philosopher. Meditation is simply about being yourself and knowing something about who that is. . . . Meditation is the process by which we go about deepening our attention and awareness, refining them, and putting them to greater practical use in our lives.[53]

In summary, increasing your level of mindfulness is likely to positively impact the processes shown in the Integrative Framework, which in turn should foster positive outcomes across the individual, group/team, and organizational levels. We strongly encourage you to give it a try.

TAKE-AWAY APPLICATION—TAAP

- Begin by thinking of a time when you were not paying attention in class.

  1. What do you think was the cause of your lack of mindfulness? Was it due to attentional deficit or attentional hyperactivity?

  2. What can you do in class to stay focused on what is being discussed?

- Think of a time when you were talking with someone and you completely missed part of what the person said because your mind was wandering.

  3. How can you remain mindful in one-on-one conversations?

POSITIVE PSYCHOLOGICAL CAPITAL: CAPITAL THAT I OWN AND CONTROL

MAJOR QUESTION

How can my inner HERO benefit me at work and in my career?

THE BIGGER PICTURE

Positive psychological capital is a relatively new concept in OB and is part of the POB movement. It is a key person input in the Integrative Framework. Often you'll find the concept explained in terms of its components: hope, efficacy, resiliency, and optimism (HERO). So you're about to learn how to develop and benefit from your inner HERO or psychological capital.

Fred Luthans, a renowned professor at the University of Nebraska and POB expert, says that **those with high levels of *positive psychological capital (PsyCap)* have high levels of hope, efficacy, resilience, and optimism (HERO).** They are characterized by the following:

H	**Hope.** Persevering toward goals and, when necessary, redirecting paths to goals (hope) in order to succeed.
E	**Efficacy.** Having confidence (efficacy) to take on and put in the necessary effort to succeed at challenging tasks.
R	**Resilience.** When beset by problems and adversity, sustaining and bouncing back and even beyond (resilience) to attain success.
O	**Optimism.** Making a positive attribution (optimism) about succeeding now and in the future.[54]

Moreover, you can develop your PsyCap!

As we discussed in Chapter 3, individual differences that are relatively flexible (e.g., emotional intelligence) versus those that are fixed (e.g., intelligence) present opportunities for you and managers to harness, develop, and utilize them. It is important to understand the components of your PsyCap because it is flexible and it has been shown to predict many of the outcomes in the Integrative Framework in desirable ways, such as increased job satisfaction, organizational commitment, and well-being, and decreased intentions to quit, job stress, anxiety, and counterproductive work behaviors.[55] This section provides the information you need to develop your PsyCap and that of others.

Hope = Willpower + "Waypower"

You're probably thinking, "Of course I know what hope is; what else is there to know?" You also likely see yourself as more hopeful than the average person. If this is your view, then you might be surprised to learn that hope actually has two components. Knowledge about these components can help you understand why hope works, when it doesn't, and how to build it.

The two components of hope are *willpower* and *waypower*. This means **to have *hope* you need to have a goal and the determination to achieve it (willpower), and you need to see one or more alternative paths to achieve your goal, even when faced with adversity (waypower).**[56] The Example box on the next page highlights the role of willpower when entrepreneurs start and grow a business. Hope therefore requires both a goal and means for achieving that goal.

EXAMPLE   It Takes Hope to Build a Business

Ben Horowitz, the renowned venture capitalist, puts a high premium on the willpower of entrepreneurs. Willpower, along with genius, are in his mind the two most crucial characteristics of successful entrepreneurs. "Building a company is hard and lonely. It demands relentless focus. And no matter how well you do, you must be ready to be pummeled again and again."[57] It takes willpower to persist. Horowitz himself demonstrated enormous willpower when Loudcloud, a previous venture he did with Marc Andreesen, nearly failed a half dozen times before ultimately being revived, strengthened, and sold to HP for $1.6 billion. "Horowitz used 'force of personality and willpower to make a business out of it,' says Herb Allen III, the CEO of Allen & Co."[58]

Brothers John (on the left) and Bert Jacobs started Life Is Good T-shirts with very little resources. Through a combination of hope and the belief that optimism is powerful they built a $100 million apparel business.

Brothers Bert and John Jacobs relied on willpower to start and grow their Life Is Good T-shirts company. The brothers started the company in 1989 by driving a used van up and down the East Coast selling T-shirts printed with their artwork. They survived on peanut butter and jelly and lived in the van. Showers were a rarity. After five years, they had $78 in the bank, but that didn't cause them to give up.

Success started to come when the brothers concluded that "people seemed worn down by the media's constant focus on the negative side of information. That led to a keg party at our apartment where we put drawings up on a wall. We had done a lot of music-inspired, cool, funky designs. But when we asked friends to write notes next to the drawings, we got a lot of comments about one drawing [a stick figure that smiled]. We decided to pair the figure with the words LIFE IS GOOD and printed up 48 T-shirts with it. We went to a street fair and sold all of them in the first hour. It confirmed that people were craving something positive that focused on the good, instead of what's wrong with the world." The rest is history.

In 2012 the company started a partnership with Hallmark to develop and market greeting cards and stationery using the brothers' saying and artwork. The company also has partnerships with Smucker's and Plant Dog. Today the company has over $100 million in annual revenue and 4,500 retail shops sell their wares.[59]

YOUR THOUGHTS?

1. Why is hope so important in starting and growing a business?
2. Did the Jacobs brothers display hope? How so?
3. Why do you think the Jacobs brothers did not give up after only having $78 in the bank after five years of running their business?
4. Do you have the type of willpower needed to start and grow a business? Explain.

What you learned in Chapter 6 about effective goal setting can also assist you in building hope in yourself and others. The problem-solving approach we introduced you to starting in Chapter 1 is another helpful tool for building hope, as it can assist you in identifying both potential obstacles and support, as well as alternative feasible paths by which to reach your goal

TAKE-AWAY APPLICATION—TAAP

Complete the following to apply your new knowledge regarding hope.

1. Think of a situation at school, work, or home that you'd like to positively influence.
2. Now describe a specific goal you'd like to achieve.
3. Formulate a plan of action to achieve this goal.
4. To increase the level of hope for achieving your goal, think of a plan B or alternative to your first plan. These steps should make you more hopeful of having a positive influence.

Efficacy

We discussed efficacy in Chapter 3 and won't provide much detail here. But remember efficacy also is a component of your core self-evaluations (CSEs) and represents confidence in your ability to do something. As such, your self-efficacy influences how you perceive the world around you and your ability to deal with the inherent challenges and opportunities. Also remember from Chapter 3 (see Figure 3.3) that you can do many things to improve your self-efficacy. We'll explore how efficacy is related to your stress in detail in Chapter 16, but for now, just recall the example we provided in Chapter 3 of how your efficacy with public speaking affects your attitudes, performance, and stress related to this activity. Applying your knowledge of self-efficacy will help you realize its important role in your positive psychological capital—greater efficacy makes you both more confident and more positive.

Resilience

If you're *resilient* then you have the capacity to consistently bounce back from adversity and to sustain yourself in the face of the demands of positive events. This means that resiliency helps you when things go your way and when they don't—it is your built-in shield and recovery characteristic. Luthans and his colleagues stated that resiliency "is arguably the most important positive resource to navigating a turbulent and stressful workplace."[60] What gives resilience its power? Resilient people are open to new experiences, flexible to changing demands, and emotionally stable when confronted with adversity.[61] Given these characteristics, resilience is a clear component of psychological capital and POB.

Optimism

Optimists are both realistic and flexible. Think about it. If you aren't realistic, then you are setting yourself up to fail. And if you fail too often, then even the most optimistic people lose their motivation and inspiration. Similarly, true optimists are flexible. This means that they are willing to revise their views as situations change. (Recall the contingency approach to management discussed in Chapter 1?) To clarify, optimists don't see everything as positive. If they did they would be Pollyanna-ish or delusional. Recall also from Chapter 4 that particular ways of making attributions (i.e., the ways in which people perceive causes of events) characterize optimists, such that **optimists often view successes as due to their "personal, permanent, and pervasive causes, and negative events to external, temporary, and situation-specific ones."**[62]

That said, did you ever wonder why people are optimistic in the first place? What function does it serve? One school of thought claims that optimism is self-inspiration—it is our mind's way of motivating us to move forward even if the future is uncertain. The rationale is that if humans didn't think that the future would be bright—an improvement over today—then they might be crippled with fear and uncertainty, never take risks, never better themselves or their situation. After all, humans have the unique ability to think ahead, and everybody knows they will die someday. And if the mind didn't have some way of combatting this, then many people would be stuck in or preoccupied with gloom (similar to those that suffer from severe depression), wouldn't save money or invest in children. Therefore, a belief that things can or will be better in the future not only helps keep our minds at ease, but also reduces stress (discussed in Chapter 16) and helps us paint our decisions in a positive, appealing light. It keeps us moving forward. For example, optimism helps motivate us to continue to achieve and progress at work because

Reed Hastings, CEO of Netflix, is an entrepreneurial optimist. He left the military to work for the Peace Corp. He then started his first company, Pure Software, and left it to co-found Netflix in 1997. Netflix has experienced tremendous growth under Hastings' leadership.

some people become CEOs and fabulously wealthy (like Reed Hastings and Mark Zuckerberg). Many people pursue such aspirations even though the probability of becoming a billionaire is infinitesimally small. In contrast, optimism also motivates most people to get married, despite the fact that in America 50 percent of marriages end in divorce. Scientists argue that optimism is part of what alters our views of the likely outcomes (probabilities) in our lives and motivates us to act.[63]

How I Can Develop My PsyCap

Like human and social capital in Chapter 1, PsyCap is a form of capital that is valuable to develop. It can help you flourish in your personal life and work life. The good news is that the PsyCap components are mutually reinforcing—developing one often helps develop the others. Try putting the following recommendations into practice in order to develop your PsyCap.

- **Hope development.** Generate a work-related goal that is important to you, attainable yet challenging; create multiple plans for achieving this goal. Share these with others—coworkers or classmates—to get their feedback and recommendations.
- **Efficacy development.** Besides recommendations from Chapter 3, break your larger goal into smaller subgoals as discussed in Chapter 6. Create plans for achieving the subgoals and share them with others to get feedback and recommendations.
- **Resilience development.** Make a list of your personal talents, skills, and social networks (recall our discussion of social capital in Chapter 1); specify how these can be used to help you achieve your goal; identify potential obstacles and determine how to avoid or reduce their impact.[64]
- **Optimism development.** Hope development bolsters your optimism, but it also is helpful to identify obstacles and negative expectations. On your own, check to see if those that you identify are valid, and then have others challenge your assumptions.

We conclude this section with a Self-Assessment of PsyCap. Learning your personal PsyCap score can help you understand and improve your ability to find a job (job search efficacy), increase your creativity and innovativeness, and reduce the stress in your life.[65] Your score will also serve as the basis for developing hope, efficacy, resiliency, and optimism, as described above.

connect

SELF-ASSESSMENT 7.3 What Is My Level of PsyCap?

Go to connect.mheducation.com and complete Self-Assessment 7.3. The four scores obtained after completing Self-Assessment 7.3 represent your hope, efficacy, resiliency, and optimism, respectively. Then answer the following questions:

1. Which is the highest? Lowest? Complete the PsyCap development protocol described above and be sure to utilize your highest/strongest component and pay extra attention to the development of the lowest/weakest.

2. In the Integrative Framework identify a process at all three levels—individual, group, and organizational—that PsyCap is likely to influence.

3. Describe one thing you can do to further develop each component of your PsyCap.

Adapted from F. Luthans, C. M. Youseff, and B. J. Avolio, *Psychological Capital: Developing the Human Competitive Edge,* Oxford, UK: Oxford University Press, 2006.

major question

MAJOR QUESTION

How can managers create an organizational climate that fosters Positive OB?

THE BIGGER PICTURE

OB has a term for how you and your cohorts might view the school you attend or the workplace you share: *organizational climate*. As you see in the Integrative Framework, displayed at the beginning of this chapter and in Figure 7.1, this input operates along with other environmental characteristics. But what factors contribute to the organizational climate? You're about to find out.

Just as a car needs gasoline or electric power to run, Positive OB needs the right environment in order to flourish. OB scholars discuss the "right environment" in terms of what is called organizational culture and organizational climate. We focus on organizational climate in this section because organizational culture is thoroughly discussed in Chapter 14.

Organizational climate is defined as employees' perceptions "of formal and informal organizational policies, practices, procedures, and routines."[66] In plain language, organizational climate represents employees' beliefs about what they "see" going on at work and beliefs about "what" is happening to them. These perceptions can range from positive and uplifting to negative and debilitating. Obviously, positive climates are more likely to create the type of environment needed for Positive OB to take root in an organization.

Figure 7.3 presents a model outlining the key contributors to an organizational climate that fosters Positive OB: organizational values, organizational practices, and virtuous leadership. Let us consider each of these contributors.

Organizational Values

We defined *values* in Chapter 2 as abstract ideals that guide one's thinking and behavior across all situations. In the current context, organizational values represent the ideals that are endorsed, shared, and supported by the organization as a whole. A team of researchers identified three global values that are essential for promoting Positive OB (see Figure 7.3). Each one is defined below.[67]

1. **Restorative justice** reflects "a shared belief in the importance of resolving conflict multilaterally through the inclusion of victims, offenders, and all other stakeholders."[68] Organizations that subscribe to this value tend to resolve conflict by giving all parties a chance to express their thoughts and feelings. This in turn leads to healing when there has been hurt or offense, thereby producing solutions that focus on the greater good.

2. **Compassion is a shared value that drives people to help others who are suffering.** It is associated with behaviors related to sympathy, kindness, tenderness, warmth, and love.[69]

3. **Temperance is a shared belief in showing restraint and control when faced with temptation and provocation. It promotes self-control, humility, and prudence.** All told, temperance helps people to avoid egocentric and heated emotional responses in favor of patience and restraint.

Organizational Practices

Organizational practices **refer to a host of procedures, policies, practices, routines, and rules that organizations use to get things done.** Figure 7.3 shows that training programs, support programs, and human resource practices and policies represent three key sets of practices that impact organizational climate.[70] For example, safety training not only reduces accidents, but demonstrates to employees that the organization cares about their well-being. Companies like General Motors, Hyatt, Charles Schwab, American Airlines, MGM Resorts International, and AIG offer progressive human resource practices to support "inclusion and diversity for lesbian, gay, bisexual, and transgender (LGBT) employees. These progressive corporations, and hundreds like them, have not only adopted policies that prohibit discrimination based on sexual orientation and gender identity, they are also offering equivalent medical benefits for same-sex partners and, in many cases, insurance coverage for gender reassignment surgery."[71]

The point to remember is that employees have greater commitment, satisfaction, citizenship behavior, and performance, and lower absenteeism and intentions to quit, when they believe that organizational practices support them professionally or personally.[72] Consider the practices used by Boston Consulting Group and Kimpton Hotels & Restaurants in San Francisco. Boston Consulting Group relies on a "red zone report" to identify when people "are working too many long weeks." New employees also "can delay their start date by six months and receive $10,000 to volunteer at a nonprofit." Management at Kimpton Hotels "sends flowers and gift baskets" to employees' loved ones when they have to work excessive hours. "It also hosts fireside chats with top executives and has rewarded great work with spa days, extra paid time off, and flat-screen TVs."[73]

Virtuous Leadership

Virtuousness **represents "what individuals and organizations aspire to be when they are at their very best."**[74] The focus of virtuous leadership is to help individuals, groups, and organizations to elevate, enrich, and flourish. Although Chapter 12 provides a broad discussion of leadership, we consider it here due to its significant relationship with organizational climate.[75]

It is important to note that virtuous leadership will not positively affect organizational climate unless it is voluntarily done as an end in itself. In other words, something is virtuous only when it is done for the purpose of creating positive deviance. For example, if kindness is displayed for the sole reason of getting someone to help you, then your actions become manipulation rather than kindness.[76] Let us examine the key components of virtuous leadership and its consequences.

Components of Virtuous Leadership   OB scholars have proposed a variety of traits and individual differences that underlie virtuous leadership. The four shown in Figure 7.3 were selected because they are most frequently discussed in OB research. Virtuous leaders are more focused on the *greater good* than self-interest. They tend to do things that benefit the largest number of people possible. For example, Antony Jenkins, CEO of Barclays PLC, decided to dismantle "a self-serving and aggressive culture by abolishing commissions on financial-product sales, among other things." He felt that the incentive system was fostering individualistic rather than collective behavior, which ultimately led to misconduct among employees.[77]

Virtuous leaders tend to promote *trust* by making sure that their words match their actions. They walk the talk. Trust also is enhanced by treating people with respect and dignity. *Integrity,* which reflects living a life guided by morals and honesty, is surely going to foster Positive OB. Consider the case of Suzanne Garvin.

> Suzanne Garvin, a personal banker in Los Angeles, tells of an instance in which she mistakenly drew a large check from the wrong account. Her supervisor, a kindly looking older lady, had blown by Garvin's desk and initialed the check without looking at the account number. When the error was discovered, the supervisor obscured her signoff and tried to blame Garvin. (She'd kept a photocopy of the check and quietly presented it during the inquisition that followed.) "Our bosses were disturbed and assured me they would look into it," recalls Garvin. Yet the punishment was slight; just a brief talking to, no more.[78]

This episode reduced the trust between Garvin and her boss and with senior management. This example shows how a lack of virtuous leadership undermines attempts at creating Positive OB.

The final component of virtuous leadership, **forgiveness, is defined as "the capacity to foster collective abandonment of justified resentment, bitterness, and blame, and, instead, it is the adoption of positive, forward-looking approaches in response to harm or damage."**[79] In addition to promoting Positive OB, forgiveness can affect your health. Research shows that *unforgiveness* is associated with adverse health conditions like poor immune system functioning, cardiovascular disease, and premature death.[80]

Mike Rice, former coach of Rutgers, was fired because of his behavior toward basketball players. Would you like to be coached by someone who threw basketballs at players during practice? Can people learn to be more virtuous?

Effects of Virtuous Leadership   Historically, there is little research on this important topic. More recently, however, several studies done at the organizational level of analysis demonstrated that virtuous leadership was related to outcomes like financial performance, customer satisfaction, positive organizational climate, and subjective measures of organizational effectiveness over periods of one to two years later.[81] In contrast, a lack of virtuous leadership negatively affects individuals and organizations alike. Consider what happened at Rutgers University. Head basketball coach Mike Rice was fired after a video surfaced showing him "kicking players and throwing basketballs at them while using gay slurs." The athletic director subsequently resigned and the university is experiencing backlash from the investment community. Investors of state and local bonds have demanded "extra yield to own university securities since the video of Rice made headlines."[82] Remember, both positive and negative emotions spread, but negative emotions and information spread faster.

major question

THE BIGGER PICTURE

Asked what you want out of life, you might reply that you want to be happy. One early leader in the positive psychology movement eventually went beyond that goal and proposed another goal: *Flourishing.* You may find this broadened goal to include even more of your true aspirations. Flourishing, a key individual-level outcome in the Integrative Framework, includes five elements. They are positive emotions, engagement, relationships, meaning, and achievement (PERMA).

Martin Seligman, a renowned psychologist from the University of Pennsylvania, has been studying happiness and well-being for over 30 years. He is credited as being the driver of today's positive psychology movement, which is the forerunner of research on Positive OB.[83] Seligman originally believed that happiness was the most important outcome in our lives. He changed his mind over the years. He now feels that people equate happiness with being cheerful, and you don't have to be cheerful to be physically or psychologically healthy. He also was discouraged by methods used to assess happiness because they were strongly determined by the rater's immediate mood. Quite simply, the concept of happiness turned out to be too narrow for evaluating a person's overall well-being and it was very difficult to accurately measure. We know as OB researchers that you can't study and change something if you can't measure it.

These observations led Seligman to change his view of well-being. He equates well-being to the weather. There is not one unique component that defines our weather. Rather, it combines several *measurable* factors such as temperature, level of humidity, and wind speed. The same is true of our well-being. **Well-being is the combined impact of five elements—positive emotions, engagement, relationships, meaning, and achievement (PERMA).** There is one essential consideration to remember about these elements. We must pursue them for their own sake, not as a means to obtain another outcome. In other words, well-being comes about by freely pursuing one or more of the five elements in PERMA.[84]

Flourishing **represents the extent to which our lives contain PERMA.** When we flourish, our lives result in "goodness . . . growth, and resilience."[85] We should all strive to flourish because of its association with other positive health outcomes like lower cardiovascular risk, lower inflammation, longer life, greater REM sleep, and positive mental health.[86] PERMA elements also are positively related to other important outcomes in the Integrative Framework—task performance, career satisfaction, organizational commitment, and turnover. Managers also should care about employees' level of flourishing because it is positively related to outcomes at both the group/team level—team performance—and the organizational level—overall productivity and financial performance.[87] Interestingly, Jerome Dodson, fund manager for the Parnassus Workplace Fund, is using the extent to which a company has a flourishing environment as one criterion for selecting investment opportunities (see the Problem-Solving Application).

solving application

Ethical Investing

The Parnassus Workplace Fund was started in 2005 by Jerome Dodson. In 2013 the fund had $312 million invested in 35 holdings. Dodson's initial investment philosophy for this fund was grounded in the belief that ethical companies with positive working environments are good investments. Dodson said that "it made a lot of intuitive sense to me that companies that treat their employees well should in return get good efforts from their employees and they should be more successful as a business."[88] Dodson admits that he makes investment decisions by integrating old-fashioned financial research with information obtained from interviewing managers and employees from companies under consideration. He also assesses the "positivity" of work environments by examining annual rankings contained in independent sources such as *Fortune* and *Working Mother.*

Let's consider whether Dodson's philosophy holds up by comparing returns achieved by the Workplace Fund versus the S&P 500. Dodson's fund realized 19.8%, 13%, and 12.5% gains for one-, three-, and five-year periods. In contrast, the S&P 500 obtained returns of 7.7%, 1.7%, and 6.9% during these same time periods.[89]

YOUR CALL   *Apply the 3-Stop Problem-Solving Approach.*

Stop 1:   What is the problem Mr. Dodson faced?

Stop 2:   Use the Integrative Framework to explain why flourishing environments lead to financial performance.

Stop 3:   Do you think Dodson's philosophy will stand the test of time? Explain.

We now consider the elements contained in PERMA. As you read, keep in mind that research suggests that less than 20 percent of U.S. adults flourish.[90] Sadly, this statistic suggests that many American adults are languishing. We hope that this section provides insights into enhancing your level of flourishing.

Positive Emotions

Although we thoroughly discussed positive emotions in the last section, there is one aspect of Barbara Fredrickson's "broaden and build" theory that we want to repeat because it enhances your ability to experience the other components of PERMA. Positive emotions *broaden* your perspective about how to overcome challenges in your life, such as the emotion of joy is more likely to lead you to envision creative ideas during a brainstorming session. Positive emotions also *build* on themselves, resulting in a spreading of positive emotions within yourself and with others around you. For instance, thinking lovingly about someone in your life is likely to activate other positive emotions like gratitude and interest. These emotions in turn foster the desire to play, explore, and savor time with loved ones.[91]

Our students report two interesting comments when we talk about positive emotions. First, they view positive emotions as something that "happens to them" rather than something they "create." Secondly, they sometimes find it hard to be positive given all their commitments and activities. Although both of these comments are partly accurate, they can be overcome by following Martin Seligman's suggestions for *proactively* increasing positivity in your life. Try this one after reading about it. Close your eyes and envision the face of someone still alive who helped you in the past. It should be someone who made a major impact on your life, and someone that you never properly thanked. Now imagine meeting that person next week face-to-face. Are you feeling gratitude?

The emotion of gratitude makes us happy and satisfied. We also strengthen relationships with others—the "R" component in PERMA—when we express gratitude to others. The problem with showing gratitude is that we frequently do it quickly with a passing "thank you." This approach can appear meaningless. Instead, Seligman recommends using a "Gratitude Visit." Here is how it works.

Write a letter of gratitude to someone and deliver it in person. The letter should be about 300 words: be specific about what the person did and how his/her actions affected you. Punch up the level of appreciation. Next, call the person and tell him/her that you would like to meet, but don't indicate why. When you meet, read the letter word for word. If the person interrupts, ask him/her to please wait until you finish reading. Once you are done reading, discuss the content of the letter and your feelings for each other. Seligman's research shows that people feel happier and less sadness over time after using this technique.[92]

Engagement

We thoroughly discussed the topic of employee engagement in Chapter 2. You may recall that engagement reflects the extent to which you are physically, cognitively, and emotionally involved with an activity, task, or project. Being engaged in something has been referred to as being in the "zone" or in a state of "flow." **Flow "is defined as the state of being completely involved in an activity for its own sake."**[93] Flow is a positive state because well-being is positively impacted by deep attention and engagement with an activity. A recent study of flow over a four-day period, for instance, revealed that people were more energized in the evenings if they experienced flow during the workday.[94]

Engagement and positive emotions are not one and the same. For example, when we are *in flow,* we are not necessarily thinking about anything; we are just doing! Our concentration is so high during flow that we use all of our cognitive and emotional resources needed for thought and feelings. This conclusion underscores the point that you can create positive emotions much easier than flow.

How can you create engagement or flow for yourself? Seligman and others suggest that this is a two-part sequence that involves (1) identifying your signature strengths and (2) learning to use them in daily personal and work activities. For us, working on this book, teaching, and playing golf put us into flow. Once you identify your strengths, you also can work with your manager to determine how these strengths can be incorporated into your job. If you are interested in identifying your strengths, we encourage you to take the strengths Self-Assessment created by Martin Seligman and his colleagues.

■ connect

SELF-ASSESSMENT 7.4 **What Are My Signature Strengths?**

Would you like to be more engaged with your school, work, and leisure activities? If yes, then this assessment will help you because it identifies your signature strengths that must be present for you to experience flow. You can use your scores to assess how you might build your strengths into your daily activities.

Go to www.authentichappiness.org and take the free self-assessment. Then consider the following questions:

1. What are your highest strengths?
2. What are your weaknesses (i.e., the components with the lowest scores)?
3. Which of your strengths are you using on a daily basis?
4. What can you do to incorporate your strengths into your school, work, and leisure activities?

Relationships

Think of the last time you boisterously laughed, the last time you felt joyous, or the last time you felt inspired or experienced awe. Were you with someone else in each case? We suspect so because positive emotions often are associated with activities involving others.

Biologists have concluded that we are creatures of the hive. After studying insects such as wasps, termites, and ants, researchers concluded that "the group" is a natural unit of selection. In other words, insects and people both like to be in groups and to collaboratively work with others in getting things done. For insects, it's the building of a fortress or hive, and for us its activities like completing tasks and projects, socializing, sharing memories, and traveling.

While others sometimes get on our nerves, positive relationships are a strong contributor to our well-being. They buffer us from stressors and provide resources that enable us to more effectively get things done. Positive relationships fuel the giving and receiving of social support. **Social support** **is the amount of perceived helpfulness derived from social relationships.** We receive four types of social support from others.

- *Esteem support.* Providing information that a person is accepted and respected despite any problems or inadequacies.
- *Informational support.* Providing help in defining, understanding, and coping with problems.
- *Social companionship.* Spending time with others in leisure and recreational activities.
- *Instrumental support.* Providing financial aid, material resources, or needed services.[95]

The above discussion suggests that your level of flourishing is enhanced by seeking social support. You also will flourish by providing support to others, particularly in the form of kindness. Research reveals that the exhibition of kindness produces significant increases in well-being. We therefore want to encourage you to conduct a kindness exercise. Simply do a completely unexpected thing for someone else. It can

What types of support do you see in this photo of the aftermath of the Boston marathon bombing? What other aspects of PERMA would be activated by helping others in a tragedy like this?

be as simple as holding a door open for another to pass through or helping someone with directions. Then notice how you feel. You should experience one or more positive emotions.

Meaningfulness

Viktor Frankl, an Austrian neurologist and psychiatrist who survived the Holocaust, was a strong proponent of using meaningfulness to promote well-being. His best-selling book *Man's Search for Meaning* chronicled his experiences in concentration camps and summarized what he learned from these events. His conclusion was that "striving to find a meaning in one's life is the primary motivational force" for people.[96] In other words, it is the drive to find meaning in our lives that instills us with a sense of purpose and motivation to pursue goals.

Meaningfulness is defined as "belonging to and serving something that you believe is bigger than the self."[97] In our case, for instance, we derive meaning from writing this book because we believe that it can positively enrich your life and help you to manage others more effectively. The concept of meaningfulness is both subjective and objective. For example, we had a past colleague who hated teaching undergraduate students. In contrast, we love teaching undergraduates. For our colleague, teaching undergraduates was not meaningful, but it was and is for us! Objectively, we also derive meaning when we read student feedback and teaching evaluations. There is nothing more satisfying than hearing that we impacted a student's life.

We have three suggestions for building meaning into your life.

1. **Identify activities you love doing—you have a passion for them.** Then try to do more of these activities or find ways to build them into your work role. This will create a sense of purpose for you. Some jobs are so vital that they inherently foster a strong sense of meaningfulness. Consider the case of Michelle Catts at America's largest nuclear power plant in Arizona.

   > By 6 am, Michelle Catts is making her way to the office past guards armed with automatic weapons, ultrasensitive X-ray machines, electronic gates and sensors that sniff out explosives. . . . Catts is one of our Nuclear Regulatory Commission inspectors at the plant serving as government watchdogs to make sure Arizona Public Service Co. finds problems before they affect safety. . . . "My job every day is to make sure this plant is operating safely," Catts said. "That's a pretty important job. It's a good feeling at the end of the day to know I found important things to ask about."[98]

2. **Find a way to build your natural strengths into your personal and work life.** Your signature strengths were assessed earlier in Self-Assessment 7.4.

3. **Go out and help someone.** Research shows that people derive a sense of meaningfulness by helping others. We also should note that people with high meaningfulness in their lives are more likely to help others.[99] All told, helping others creates the upward spiral of positivity discussed earlier in this chapter.

Achievement

This component of PERMA pertains to the extent to which you have a self-directed "achieving life." In other words, we flourish when we pursue achievement for its own sake. Doing so fosters feelings of mastery, which in turn enhances our self-esteem and self-efficacy. Qualcomm, ranked as the 32nd best company to work for by *Fortune* in 2014, attempts to encourage achievement among its technology employees. The company encourages employees to submit innovative ideas in research papers. In 2012, engineers submitted nearly 200 papers, and winners of best paper submissions were asked to present at a forum and other speaking engagements.[100] McDonald's is another company that has been trying to help employees achieve, but they are taking a different approach than Qualcomm (see Example box).

EXAMPLE   McDonald's Helps Employees to Flourish

In the United Kingdom, McDonald's spends around $55 million a year to help employees acquire nationally recognized academic qualifications in things like math and English. The company has awarded about 35,000 such certifications since the start of the program in 2006. McDonald's is one of the largest apprenticeship providers in the country.

McDonald's also invests heavily in both executive level training and management training to "restaurant general managers, department managers, and shift managers who, as the day-to-day leaders on the front lines, are taught the communications and coaching skills they need to motivate crews and to hit their shift's sales targets. The return on the company's investment is measured not in terms of increased revenue or profitability but in lower turnover of hourly managers and their crews. Turnover has declined steadily since the programs were initiated." McDonald's consistently has been ranked as one of the top 50 best workplaces by the Great Place to Work Institute.[101]

YOUR THOUGHTS?

1. If you worked on the Problem-Solving Application Case at the end of Chapter 6, you saw McDonald's in a less favorable light, at least for customer service in the United States. How could a company have a problem with customer service and still be a great place to work?

2. How does investing in academic certifications and management development contribute to flourishing among McDonald's employees?

3. What are notable examples you've seen at school or work to help people flourish?

McDonald's invests heavily in training, which is evidenced by McDonald's Hamburger Universities, one in Chicago, Illinois, and another in Shanghai. The rationale is that improving employees' knowledge and skills will boost their achievement, and thus their flourishing and its benefits at work.

what did i learn?

In our coverage of positive organizational behavior in this chapter, you learned that Positive OB focuses on creating work environments in which people flourish and that there are a number of techniques you can use to increase positivity even at an individual level at school and home. Reinforce your learning with the Key Points below. Then consolidate your learning using the Integrative Framework. Challenge your mastery of the material by answering the Major Questions in your own words.

Key Points for Understanding Chapter 7

You learned the following key points.

7.1 THE IMPORTANCE OF POSITIVE OB

- Positive OB emphasizes positive emotion, mindfulness, psychological capital, and organizational culture and climate to foster flourishing and performance across all three levels of OB.

- POB operates via three principle effects: *amplifying, buffering,* and *positivity*. These combined generate positive outcomes.

- Conscious capitalism is a business philosophy and approach to POB that involves a higher purpose, stakeholder interdependence, conscious leadership, and conscious culture.

7.2 THE POWER OF POSITIVE EMOTIONS

- Negative emotions cause you to narrow your focus while positive emotions cause you to broaden your thinking.

- Positive emotions are associated with stronger social relationships, prosocial behaviors, stronger bodies and immune systems, and original thinking.

- Research shows that you need multiple positive experiences to overcome or compensate for each negative.

7.3 FOSTERING MINDFULNESS

- Mindlessness is a state of reduced attention while *mindfulness* is fostered by paying attention to the present moment in a nonjudgmental way.

- Two key inhibitors of mindfulness are attentional deficits and attentional hyperactivity.

- Mindfulness can be learned by using a variety of simple "meditative" techniques on a regular basis.

7.4 POSITIVE PSYCHOLOGICAL CAPITAL: CAPITAL THAT I OWN AND CONTROL

- Positive psychological capital is comprised of hope, efficacy, resilience, and optimism.

- Hope includes not only a goal and determination to achieve it, but also one or more clear paths for achieving your goal.

- Resilience is your ability to bounce back after adversity and sustain yourself.

- Optimism attributes positive events to personal, permanent, and pervasive factors.

7.5 CREATING A CLIMATE THAT FOSTERS POSITIVE OB

- Organizational climate represents employees' perceptions of an organization's policies, practices, procedures, and routines.

- Positive organizational climates are a function of organizational values, organizational practices, and virtuous leadership.

- Positive climates are driven by values pertaining to (1) restorative justice, (2) compassion, and (3) temperance.

- The key components of virtuous leadership include a focus on the greater good, trust, integrity, and forgiveness.

7.6 FLOURISHING: THE DESTINATION OF POSITIVE OB

- Flourishing reflects the extent to which our lives contain five elements indicated by the acronym PERMA: positive emotions, engagement, relationships, meaning, and achievement. It is a key outcome in the Integrative ramework.

- Engagement and positive emotions are not one and the same. Engagement can be increased by using your signature strengths in everyday activities.

- Four key types of social support include esteem support, informational support, social companionship, and instrumental support.

The Integrative Framework for Chapter 7

As shown in Figure 7.4, you learned that positive emotions, mindfulness, psychological capital, and organizational climate are all inputs that fuel Positive OB. These inputs are associated with outcomes across the three levels of OB. At the individual level, related outcomes include task performance, work attitudes, well-being/flourishing, citizenship behavior/ counterproductive behavior, turnover, career outcomes, and creativity. At the group/team level, outcomes include group/team performance and group cohesion and conflict. Finally, at the organizational level, outcomes include financial performance, overall organizational performance, customer satisfaction, and reputation.

Challenge: Major Questions for Chapter 7

At the start of the chapter, we told you that after reading the chapter you should be able to answer the following major questions. Unless you can, have you really processed and internalized the lessons in the chapter?

Refer to the Key Points, Figure 7.4, the chapter itself, and your notes to revisit and answer the following major questions:

1. How does understanding Positive OB benefit me?
2. What is the role of positive emotions in POB, and how can they make me more effective at school, at work, and in other arenas of life?
3. How can mindfulness contribute to my effectiveness?
4. How can my inner HERO benefit me at work and in my career?
5. How can managers create an organizational climate that fosters Positive OB?
6. What can I do to enhance my level of flourishing?

FIGURE 7.4   INTEGRATIVE FRAMEWORK FOR UNDERSTANDING AND APPLYING OB

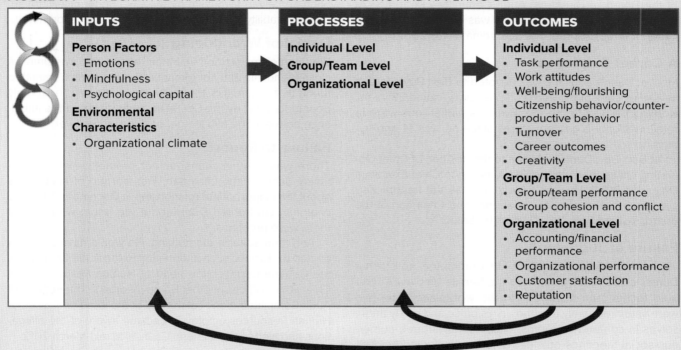

© 2014 Angelo Kinicki and Mel Fugate. All rights reserved. Reproduction prohibited without permission of the authors.

Best Buy: Trouble at the Top

You could say that Best Buy had enough problems. Competition is stiff in consumer electronics, even without online merchants, and margins are thin. At its height in April 2006, Best Buy was selling for over $56 a share. But its stock shifted wildly with the changing market, dipping under $18 in 2008, rising to over $47 in 2010, and settling for $30 and change by the end of March 2012.

Then improprieties came to light that led to the resignation of its CEO and the demotion of its founder. At issue was "an allegedly inappropriate relationship" between then CEO Brian Dunn and a female subordinate, in the language of the Board of Directors' Audit Committee Report.[102] At the time of the 2012 report, Dunn was married, 51, and the father of three children. The subordinate was 29.

A Career Employee

Most of Dunn's adult life was devoted to Best Buy. Starting as a sales clerk at the age of 24, he stayed some 28 years, working his way to the top. Even his earlier jobs were in retail, working in grocery stores since he was 14 and bypassing college.[103]

At Best Buy, Dunn had risen to the position of Chief Operating Officer and was again promoted to Chief Executive Officer in 2009. He was widely seen as the handpicked successor to the company's founder and Chairman of the Board, Richard Schulze, 20 years his senior.[104]

Failure of Judgment

The report of the Board's Audit Committee noted that Dunn's close relationship with the female employee "created friction and disruption in the workplace." The two were seen frequently together in his office and off by themselves in conference rooms. They acknowledged numerous social meetings outside the office, including lunches and drinks, sometimes during the week and sometimes on the weekend. The female employee spoke openly about the favors she received from the CEO, which included tickets to concerts and sporting events.

The committee noted that in two trips abroad, totaling nine days in 2011, Dunn contacted the female employee by cell phone at least 224 times, including 33 phone calls, 149 text messages, and 42 picture or video messages, "for which there was no identifiable business purpose." The CEO's cell phone contained photos with messages expressing affection, one of which included the female employee's initials.

Work Environment

The Audit Committee report concludes that Dunn acted unprofessionally and damaged the work environment, demonstrating "a lack of the judgment expected of the most senior executive officer of the Company."

In 45 interviews, the Audit Committee spoke with 34 current or former employees. The report states that the relationship, as it became better known, "damaged employee morale and created unnecessary distraction in the workplace." Some employees complained that "they felt that the rules appeared to apply to every employee except the CEO." Some of the employees questioned senior management's commitment to Best Buy's stated policies and ethical guidelines.

Matters were not helped by the female employee's frequent mentions of the attention and perks she was receiving. Such perceived favoritism by the CEO undermined the supervisor's ability to manage the employee, the report noted.

Denial of Wrongdoing

Both parties maintained that their relationship was simply a close friendship and not romantic. But the Audit Committee found that regardless, the relationship showed "extremely poor judgment" by the CEO. The auditors noted the imbalance between the two in age, position, and power.

Failure to Report

There was another management problem: extended silence. Schulze, the chairman, first learned of allegations about the inappropriate relationship in December 2011. The chairman confronted Dunn about the issue, who denied there were problems.

And then Schulze did nothing. He would have been expected to disclose such information to the Audit Committee, the General Counsel, the head of Human Resources, the Chief Ethics Officer, or other Board members. The Board and Audit Committee didn't catch wind of the issue until a senior Human Resources employee became aware of the allegations and alerted the General Counsel in mid-March 2012.

Conclusions

The Audit Report found that as CEO, Dunn had violated company policy as to inappropriate conduct, conflicts of interest, and vendor gifts (he had solicited a free concert ticket for the employee). It concluded that Chairman Schulze failed to appropriately report the allegations, a lapse that risked employee retaliation or other liability.

Departure

In the month before the report came out in May 2012, Dunn walked. He and the Audit Committee agreed on a separation package of $6.6 million, comprising bonuses and stock grants already awarded, compensation for unused vacation, and severance pay.[105]

Schulze complied with the request to step down as acting chairman, although he remains on the board in the created role of Chairman Emeritus.

Employee Uncertainty

The local public radio news uncovered an objective measure of how the fallout from the scandal and the board's reaction unsettled staff employees. During the three months of the spring of 2011, nearly 1,800 Best Buy employees joined LinkedIn, the employment-oriented social networking website, Minnesota Public Radio reported. "That's more new LinkedIn members just from Best Buy than from Cargill, 3M, General Mills, Medtronic and St. Jude Medical combined," all major employers in the state.[106] This surge implies a large number of employees losing confidence in the long-term status of their jobs and feeling the need to extend their professional networking.

Aftermath

Many business analysts responded favorably to the shakeup, expressing hope that the change would allow management to take a fresh look at the company's growing challenges (including competition from online retailers).[107] But the market punished the stock further, taking it to a low in the $11 range by the end of 2012. In 2013, a year after the Audit Report, the stock had climbed back to the $25 range and higher, with analysts split as to whether Best Buy was at best a buy, sell, or hold.

Apply the 3-Stop Problem-Solving Approach to OB

Referring to Figure 7.4 and your notes, apply the knowledge of OB presented in this chapter to the above case.

Applying this knowledge should enable you to recommend realistic and effective solutions.

Stop 1: What is the problem?

- Identify the outcomes that are important in this case.
- Which of these outcomes are not being achieved in the case?
- Based on considering the above two questions, what is the most important problem in this case?

Stop 2: Use the material in this chapter to help you understand the problem in this case.

- What person factors are most relevant?
- What environmental characteristics are most important to consider?
- Do you need to consider any processes? Which ones?
- What concepts or tools discussed in this chapter are most relevant for solving the key problem in this case?

Stop 3: What are your recommendations for solving the problem?

- Review the material in the chapter that most pertains to your proposed solution and look for practical recommendations.
- Use any past OB knowledge or experience to generate recommendations.
- Outline your plan for solving the problem in this case.

LEGAL/ETHICAL CHALLENGE

Tracking Sensors Invade the Workplace: Devices on Workers and Furniture Offer Clues for Boosting Productivity[108]

Does face time matter? What about in call centers? Bank of America (BoA) wanted to answer these questions. To do so, it asked about 90 workers to wear badges with sensors to measure their movements and conversations. They found that the most productive employees were members of close-knit teams and spoke frequently with their colleagues.

What did they do? For one, BoA scheduled group rather than individual breaks. This boosted productivity by at least 10 percent.

Many companies are now using similar technology to collect real-time data. Sensors are fastened to furniture or worn on lanyards to measure how often employees get up, where they congregate, and with whom they communicate. These data are then used to structure the environment and modify policies to facilitate work, interactions, and communication. Some see this as a new tool to foster collaboration and productivity.

Cubist Pharmaceuticals, like BoA, found positive correlations between employees' productivity and face-to-face

interactions. In particular, it found that social activity dropped off significantly during lunch time, as many employees retreated to their desks to check e-mails, rather than chatting with one another. The company then decided to make its once-dingy cafeteria more inviting, improving the lighting and offering better food, to encourage workers to lunch together, instead of at their desks. Kimberly Clark Corp. also used this technology to learn that its employees commonly met in groups of 3 or 4, but did so in conference rooms designed for much larger groups. It reconfigured its meeting spaces.

Putting badges on workers is just the beginning of a broader trend, researchers say. As companies rethink their offices, many are looking into "smart buildings," wired with technologies that show workers' location in real time and suggest meetings with colleagues nearby.

But there's a fine line between Big Data and Big Brother, at least in the eyes of some employees, who might shudder at the idea of the boss tracking their every move. Sensor proponents, however, argue that smartphones and corporate ID badges already can transmit their owner's location. As a result, many such studies allow employees to opt out. They instead wear "mock" sensors so others don't know whether they are participants or not.

Legally, current sensing technologies don't seem to violate employment laws. "It's not illegal to track your own employees inside your own building," says Dr. Ben Waber, CEO of Sociometric Solutions, a company that provides sensors and measurement. But others argue that such monitoring is a slippery slope. Providers of such services are likely to be pressured to provide individual employee data; while not illegal, some are concerned that this would be too invasive.

What Are Your Views?

1. Assume you're the owner of a company and you choose to use this technology. Justify your decision and describe how you will explain it to your employees.

2. Consider you are the employee representative on the executive board of the same company in the first question. You learn that management plans to use this technology, but employees are against it. Make your case to the board. On what grounds do you object?

3. Despite your compelling argument in question 2, management decides to go ahead and use the technology. However, it is willing to negotiate the boundaries. Describe the boundaries you and other employees are comfortable with.

GROUP EXERCISE

Disputing Negative Beliefs

Objectives
1. To learn how to combat negative thinking and emotions.
2. To practice cognitive reframing.

Introduction
Negative thinking and negative emotions serve to undermine your performance, attitudes, and moods. The bad news is that the brain is wired to pay attention to negative information. This is why negative emotions and beliefs tend to roll out of our minds automatically. The overall goal of this exercise is to provide you with a way to combat the snowballing of negative thinking and emotions. This should in turn foster the creation of positive emotions. The technique is called "cognitive reframing," and Martin Seligman developed a five-step process you can use. He labeled it the "ABCDEs."

Instructions
1. Take out a piece of paper and write down a response to the following items.[109]

   A. *Identify something that is causing you distress or negative emotions.* It could be a problem you are currently facing or something that might happen in the future. (For example: My roommate is moving out and I can't afford the rent by myself.)

   B. *List the negative beliefs you have about the event or problem.* (For example: I don't have any prospects for a new roommate and may have to move. I might have to move back home and quit school. I could ask my parents for money, but they really can't afford to pay my rent. I could move to a lower-priced single apartment in a bad area of town.)

   C. *Identify the consequences of your beliefs.* (For example: I am going to move back home for spring semester and return to campus in the fall.)

   D. *Formulate a disputation of your beliefs.* It is important to remember that pessimistic thoughts are generally overreactions, so the first step is to correct inaccurate or distorted thoughts. (For example: I have not studied my finances closely and may be able to afford the apartment. Even if I can't afford the apartment right now, I could get a part-time job that would cover the additional expenses. I don't have to accept a bad roommate, but worst case scenario is that I have to carry the added expenses for one semester.)

   E. *Describe how energized and empowered you feel at the moment.* (For example: I'm motivated to find a new roommate and get a part-time job. I have taken care of myself throughout college and there is no reason I can't continue to resolve this short-term problem.)

2. Pair up with someone else in the class and share your responses for the ABCDEs.

3. Each of you should provide feedback about Steps D—disputing negative beliefs—and E—describe positive feelings. In doing this, feel free to offer additional ideas for Step D.

Questions for Class Discussion
1. What are your reactions to this exercise?

2. Did the exercise help you to reframe negative beliefs into positive ones? Provide examples.

3. How might you use this technique in a more immediate way. In other words, which of the ABCDEs would be most important to use when negative thinking starts to dominate your thinking? Explain.

Groups

8 GROUPS AND TEAMS

How Can Working with Others Increase Everybody's Performance?

inputs

PERSON FACTORS

ENVIRONMENTAL CHARACTERISTICS

processes

INDIVIDUAL LEVEL

GROUP/TEAM LEVEL
Group & Team Dynamics

ORGANIZATIONAL LEVEL

outcomes

INDIVIDUAL LEVEL

GROUP/TEAM LEVEL

ORGANIZATIONAL LEVEL

© 2014 Angelo Kinicki and Mel Fugate. All rights reserved. Reproduction prohibited without permission of the authors.

MAJOR TOPICS I'LL LEARN AND QUESTIONS I SHOULD BE ABLE TO ANSWER

8.1 GROUP CHARACTERISTICS

MAJOR QUESTION: *How can knowledge of groups and their key characteristics make me more successful?*

8.2 THE GROUP DEVELOPMENT PROCESS

MAJOR QUESTION: *How can understanding the group development process make me more effective at school and work?*

8.3 TEAMS AND THE POWER OF COMMON PURPOSE

MAJOR QUESTION: *What are the characteristics of effective team players and team building, and how does this knowledge improve my performance in various types of teams?*

8.4 TRUST BUILDING AND REPAIR— ESSENTIAL TOOLS FOR SUCCESS

MAJOR QUESTION: *How can I build and repair trust in ways that make me more effective at school, work, and home?*

8.5 KEYS TO TEAM EFFECTIVENESS

MAJOR QUESTION: *What are the keys to effective teams, and how can I apply this knowledge to give me an advantage?*

INTEGRATIVE FRAMEWORK FOR UNDERSTANDING AND APPLYING OB

This chapter focuses on group and team dynamics. You will learn that these group-level processes relate to important outcomes at not only the group, but also the individual and organizational levels in the Integrative Framework. As such, group and team dynamics are critically important processes in the study and practice of OB.

winning at work

USING TEAM CHARTERS TO BOOST EFFECTIVENESS

When working in teams, most students, and employees, often hurry into the task at hand. While this works sometimes, social scientists and OB professionals have identified a better approach. They recommend that individuals in the team should first examine member strengths, share personal expectations, set common goals, ascertain levels of commitment, agree on processes for communication and decision making, and decide how to measure and control contributions from members.

Without this preparation, many teams fail to realize the synergies of the collective input of team members and get bogged down in unproductive conflict. Team charters can help avoid or overcome many of these challenges. Charters outline why a team exists, what its goals are, and how members are expected to behave to achieve said goals. Charters also establish norms that govern individual behavior, provide criteria for measuring team outcomes, and develop guidelines for assessing member behavior. Effective *team charters* have the following components:

1. *Mission statement:* The team's purpose; why the team exists; what the team needs to accomplish.

2. *Team vision:* A clear and concise statement of the ideal end state the team desires to achieve in terms of all of the entities that will be affected by the team's outcomes.

3. *Team identity:* Includes a team name and logo that represent member composition and goals; a team roster with each member's name, phone number, e-mail address; and an assessment of each member's strengths and improvement goals.

4. *Boundaries:* Clarifies policies, procedures, and values the team subscribes to that cannot be violated; limitations on the team's performance; the decisions the team can make on its own versus needing permission from others; the activities that are legitimate for the team to engage in; the stakeholders affected by the team's activities.

5. *Operating guidelines:* Describes the team structure and processes including how leaders will function, how decisions will be made, how work will be allocated, communication procedures, how conflict will be managed, and how member growth and development will be facilitated.

6. *Performance norms and consequences:* Describes norms needed to facilitate goal attainment in member satisfaction, including the standards of performance; how team and member performance will be evaluated; how members will treat each other; how dysfunctional behaviors will be managed; how team members will be disciplined for not adhering to team norms; the due process for terminating a member from the team; expectations for team meetings; expectations for team project contributions; consequences for work that is late or is of poor quality; how grades for team projects will be allocated to individual team members.

7. *Charter endorsement:* All team members sign the team charter agreement to verify their endorsement and commitment to uphold the team charter. Those not agreeing to all terms should leave the team for reassignment.

SOURCE: From "Increasing Student-Learning Team Effectiveness with Team Charters," by Phillip Hunsaker, Cynthia Pavett, and Johanna Hunsaker, *Journal of Education for Business 86,* 2011, 127–138. (Figure 2, p. 130). Reprinted by permission of the publisher, Taylor & Frances Ltd., http://www.tandf.co.uk/journals.

FOR YOU   WHAT'S AHEAD IN THIS CHAPTER

We begin Part Two of this book with a discussion of groups and teams. Your success at work or school improves when you understand the differences between formal and informal groups, as the two have different functions, roles, norms, and dynamics. Next we describe the group and team development process for the same reason. We then differentiate groups from teams and explore important team characteristics, such as team competencies, teamwork and team building, and finally two important types of teams—self-managed and virtual. The importance of trust is covered next as it is a critical element to group and team functioning. We close by exploring facilitators for team effectiveness such as common purpose, composition, cooperation, and team size.

major question

MAJOR QUESTION
How can knowledge of groups and their key characteristics make me more successful?

THE BIGGER PICTURE

Groups are often labeled formal or informal and serve multiple functions. As a member of such groups, you can play many different roles. Group roles and norms are the means by which expectations are communicated to groups and their members. Roles and norms therefore are powerful forms of social control that influence group and member behavior. They also impact a number of important outcomes across levels in the Integrative Framework.

Drawing from the field of sociology, we define a *group* as (1) two or more freely interacting individuals who (2) share norms and (3) goals and have a (4) common identity.[1] People form groups for many reasons. Most fundamental among these reasons is that groups usually accomplish more than individuals. Furthermore, research consistently shows that groups routinely outperform the average of their individual members, particularly with quantitative tasks. Examples include financial forecasts, sales estimates, and climate change predictions.

It seems that simply interacting with others improves both individual and team accuracy in such tasks. Building on what you learned in Chapter 6, these performance benefits increase further still if the team receives feedback that describes which member's approach is most effective. The rationale is that the team becomes more efficient, focuses on the best approach, and then applies the knowledge and efforts to improving on the best approach, which raises performance even more.[2]

It is useful to distinguish the group from a crowd or organization. Here is how organizational psychologist E. H. Schein helps make the distinctions clear:

> The size of a *group* is . . . limited by the possibilities of mutual interaction and mutual awareness. Mere aggregates of people do not fit this definition because they do not interact and do not perceive themselves to be a group even if they are aware of each other as, for instance, a *crowd* on a street corner watching some event. A total department, a union, or a whole *organization* would not be a group in spite of thinking of themselves as "we," because they generally do not all interact and are not all aware of each other. However, work teams, committees, subparts of departments, cliques, and various other informal associations among organizational members would fit this definition of a group.[3]

The size of a group is thus limited by the potential for mutual interaction and mutual awareness.[4] Think of the various groups to which you belong. Does each group satisfy the four criteria in our definition? Have a look at Figure 8.1, which illustrates the four criteria. To increase your understanding of groups, we next address their functions, roles, norms, and dynamics.

Formal and Informal Groups

Individuals join or are assigned to groups for various purposes. **A *formal group* is assigned by organizations or their managers to accomplish specific goals.** Such groups often have labels: work group, team, committee, or task force. **An *informal group* exists when the members' overriding purpose of getting together is friendship**

FIGURE 8.1 FOUR CRITERIA OF A GROUP

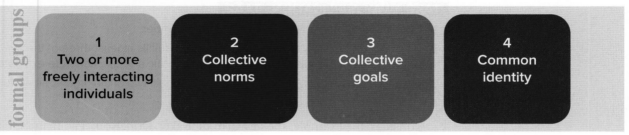

formal groups

| 1 Two or more freely interacting individuals | 2 Collective norms | 3 Collective goals | 4 Common identity |

Whole Foods has effectively applied the concept of formal groups to their stores. For instance, employees clearly identify with their particular store and compete against other stores.

or a common interest.[5] Formal and informal groups often overlap, such as when a team of corporate auditors heads for the tennis courts after work. Friendships forged on the job can be so strong as to outlive the job itself in an era of job hopping, reorganizations, and mass layoffs.

For example, membership in organized corporate "alumni" groups is increasingly popular. There are now alumni groups for hundreds of companies, including Hewlett-Packard, Ernst & Young, and Texas Instruments. Some groups are started by former employees, while others are formally sanctioned by employers as a way to stay in touch, creating a potential pool of boomerang workers that employers can draw from when hiring picks up.[6] A quick Google search revealed more than 8,500 ex-employee groups, many of which are facilitated by Facebook.

The desirability of overlapping formal and informal groups is debatable.[7] Some managers firmly believe personal friendship fosters productive teamwork on the job, while others view such relationships as a serious threat to productivity. Both situations are common, and it is the manager's job to strike a workable balance based on the maturity and goals of the people involved. A survey of 1,000 US adults revealed that 61 percent consider their bosses to be friends. However, approximately a third of those who are connected with their boss on a social networking site wish they weren't![8] This is food for thought.

Functions of Formal Groups

Researchers point out that formal groups fulfill two basic functions: *organizational* and *individual* (see Table 8.1).[9] Complex combinations of these functions can be found in formal groups at any given time.

TABLE 8.1 FORMAL GROUPS FULFILL ORGANIZATIONAL AND INDIVIDUAL FUNCTIONS

ORGANIZATIONAL FUNCTIONS	INDIVIDUAL FUNCTIONS
1. Accomplish complex, interdependent tasks that are beyond the capabilities of individuals.	1. Satisfy the individual's need for affiliation.
2. Generate new or creative ideas and solutions.	2. Develop, enhance, and confirm the individual's self-esteem and sense of identity.
3. Coordinate interdepartmental efforts.	3. Give individuals an opportunity to test and share their perceptions of social reality.
4. Provide a problem-solving mechanism for complex problems requiring varied information and assessments.	4. Reduce the individual's anxieties and feelings of insecurity and powerlessness.
5. Implement complex decisions.	5. Provide a problem-solving mechanism for personal and interpersonal problems.
6. Socialize and train newcomers.	

formal groups

SOURCE: Adapted from E. H. Schein, *Organizational Psychology*, 3rd ed. (Englewood Cliffs, NJ: Prentice-Hall, 1980), 149–151.

TAKE-AWAY APPLICATION—TAAP

1. Think of a formal group in which you're a member.
2. Describe how being a member of that group fulfills at least three of the five individual functions listed in Table 8.1. Be specific and use concrete examples.
3. Now describe in detail how the team fulfills at least two of the organizational functions.

Consider, for example, the law firm of Baker Donelson. The firm highly values community service and has doubled its number of pro bono hours each year since 2008. To formalize their commitment to such work, they appointed Lisa Borden as pro bono shareholder and created a pro bono committee.[10] Not only does this show the alignment of cultural values and norms you'll learn about in Chapter 14, but it also illustrates both the organizational and individual functions of formal groups. Specifically, the committee helps coordinate pro bono work across the many offices and practice areas of the firm (organizational function). And free services support Baker Donelson's organizational values and goals of being a good citizen in their communities and increasing attorney satisfaction (organizational functions). In addition, providing pro bono work most likely fulfills individual functions, such as confirming an attorney's sense of identity (as a kind, caring individual), building strong work relationships, and living according to one's values.

Roles and Norms—Social Building Blocks for Group and Organizational Behavior

Work groups transform individuals into functioning organizational members through subtle yet powerful social forces. These social forces, in effect, turn "I" into "we" and "me" into "us." Group influence weaves individuals into the organization's social fabric by communicating and enforcing both role expectations and norms. Group members positively reinforce those who adhere to current roles and norms with friendship and acceptance. On the other hand, nonconformists experience criticism and even ostracism or rejection by group members. Anyone who has experienced the "silent treatment" from a group of friends knows what a potent social weapon ostracism can be. The usefulness of roles and norms is enhanced by understanding how they develop and why they are enforced.

Roles A *role* is a set of expected behaviors for a particular position, and a *group role* is a set of expected behaviors for members of the group as a whole.[11] Therefore each role you play is defined in part by the expectations of that role. As a student, you are expected to be motivated to learn, conscientious, participative, and attentive. Professors are expected to be knowledgeable, prepared, and genuinely interested in student learning. Sociologists view roles and their associated expectations as a fundamental basis of human interaction and experience.

In the many arenas of life (e.g., work, family, and school), people often play multiple roles. At work, for example, employees frequently play roles that go beyond duties in a job description, such as helping coworkers and suggesting improvements.[12] Employees often serve in multiple groups and may play one or more roles within each. Two types of roles are particularly important—*task* and *maintenance*. Effective groups ensure that both roles are fulfilled (see Table 8.2).[13] But before continuing with your learning about group roles, it will be helpful to learn about your own group role preferences by completing Self-Assessment 8.1. Knowing which types of roles you prefer can help you understand why you might have been more or less satisfied with a particular group or team of which you've been a member. Playing roles that don't match your preferences is likely to be less satisfying. Moreover, if you understand your own preferences, you can set yourself up to win (be happy and productive) in future groups, as you can volunteer or position yourself to play the roles you prefer.

TABLE 8.2 TASK AND MAINTENANCE ROLES

TASK ROLES	DESCRIPTION
Initiator	Suggests new goals or ideas
Information seeker/giver	Clarifies key issues
Opinion seeker/giver	Clarifies pertinent values
Elaborator	Promotes greater understanding through examples or exploration of implications
Coordinator	Pulls together ideas and suggestions
Orienter	Keeps group headed toward its stated goal(s)
Evaluator	Tests group's accomplishments with various criteria such as logic and practicality
Energizer	Prods group to move along or to accomplish more
Procedural technician	Performs routine duties (e.g., handing out materials or rearranging seats)
Recorder	Performs a "group memory" function by documenting discussion and outcomes
MAINTENANCE ROLES	**DESCRIPTION**
Encourager	Fosters group solidarity by accepting and praising various points of view
Harmonizer	Mediates conflict through reconciliation or humor
Compromiser	Helps resolve conflict by meeting others "halfway"
Gatekeeper	Encourages all group members to participate
Standard setter	Evaluates the quality of group processes
Commentator	Records and comments on group processes/dynamics
Follower	Serves as a passive audience

SOURCE: Adapted from discussion in K. D. Benne and P. Sheats, "Functional Roles of Group Members," *Journal of Social Issues,* Spring 1948, 41–49.

connect

SELF-ASSESSMENT 8.1 **Group and Team Role Preference Scale**

Go to connect.mheducation.com and take Self-Assessment 8.1 to learn which roles you prefer to play in group and team settings.

1. Does your preferred role match your perceptions? Justify your answer using examples of your behavior.

2. Given your preferred role (the one with the highest score), describe how you could be most effective in group assignments? What challenges might your preferred role cause for you? For your group?

3. Given your least preferred role (the one with the lowest score), describe how this has been problematic for you and one of your teams. Explain two ways you could improve your performance and that of your team by working on this deficiency.

Task roles enable the work group to define, clarify, and pursue a common purpose, and **maintenance roles** foster supportive and constructive interpersonal relationships. In short, task roles keep the group on *track* while maintenance roles keep the group *together*. A project team member is performing a task function when he or she says at an update meeting, "What is the real issue here? We don't seem to be getting anywhere." Another individual who says, "Let's hear from those who oppose this plan," is performing a maintenance function. Importantly, each of the various task and maintenance roles may be played in varying combinations and sequences by either the group's leader or any of its members.[14]

TAKE-AWAY APPLICATION—TAAP

1. Think of a (formal or informal) group of which you're a member.

2. Describe how at least three task roles are fulfilled. Explain how the roles are fulfilled using examples of specific people and behaviors.

3. Do the same for at least three maintenance roles.

(Note: If necessary use more than one group, but be sure to describe at least three task and three maintenance roles.)

Sallie Krawcheck, from interview on her purchase of the networking company 85 Broads.

The task and maintenance roles listed in Table 8.2 can serve as a handy checklist for managers and group leaders who wish to ensure proper group effectiveness and development (discussed in the next section of this chapter). Roles that are not always performed when needed, such as those of coordinator, evaluator, and gatekeeper, can be performed in a timely manner by the formal leader or assigned to other members. Leaders can further ensure that roles are fulfilled by clarifying specifically what is expected of employees in the group.

Sallie Krawcheck, one of the most powerful women on Wall Street and former executive at Citibank and Bank of America (B of A), provides an excellent example. When she took over as president of the Global Wealth and Investment Management (GWIM) group at B of A, she was quick to fulfill both task and maintenance roles. At the embattled bank she quickly tended to task roles and appointed eight executives to oversee various operations within the group, such as heads of the US brokerage force and private wealth management. New goals were set; she also worked diligently to integrate and harmonize the dual cultures (maintenance roles) of both B of A and Merrill Lynch, which it acquired at the height of the financial crisis.[15]

The task roles of initiator, orienter, and energizer are especially important because they are *goal-directed* roles. Research studies on group goal setting confirm the motivational power of challenging goals. As with individual goal setting (Chapters 5 and 6), difficult but achievable goals are associated with better group results.[16] Also in line with individual goal-setting theory and research, group goals are more effective if group members clearly understand them and are both individually and collectively committed to achieving them. Initiators, orienters, and energizers can be very helpful in this regard. Moreover, international managers need to be sensitive to cultural differences regarding the relative importance of task and maintenance roles. For example, Asian cultures often value maintenance roles more than groups from the West.

Many important maintenance roles are often fulfilled by people referred to as "office moms." They may or may not have children of their own, but they are the colleagues who are most likely to remember birthdays, circulate cards, and bring cupcakes to celebrate. Office moms may play important mentoring-type roles—listening to employees and giving helpful advice regarding work and life more generally. Sometimes they even offer a shoulder to cry on. They are known to tell you what you need to hear, such as "she knows your significant other is all wrong for you—and will say so." In short, office moms offer all kinds of support and advice, informally, for work and life matters that fall outside of more formal task roles and company infrastructure (e.g., human resources).[17]

Norms   "A *norm* is an attitude, opinion, feeling, or action—shared by two or more people—that guides behavior."[18] Norms help create order and allow groups to function more efficiently, as they prevent groups from having to progress through the development process each and every time they meet. Can you imagine having to establish guidelines over and over again? Norms are more encompassing than roles, which tend to be at the individual level in the Integrative Framework and pertain to a specific job or situation. Norms, in contrast, are shared phenomena and apply to the group, team, or organization level.

Although norms are typically unwritten and seldom discussed openly, they have a powerful influence on group and organizational behavior. As you'll learn in Chapter 14 (organizational culture), individual and group behavior are guided in part via the shared nature of expectations and norms. For example, the 3M Company has a norm wherein employees devote 15 percent of their time to think big, pursue new ideas, or further develop something spawned from their other work. The "15 percent time" program, as it is called, was started in 1948 and supports the culture of innovation 3M is known for. Google, as well as other tech companies, implements a similar program and allows employees to allocate 20 percent of their time to ideas and projects beyond their own jobs. It is alleged, but not confirmed, that projects developed during this time were Gmail and Google Earth.[19]

Norms serve many purposes and are thus reinforced. Some of these reasons are listed in Table 8.3.

TABLE 8.3   WHY NORMS ARE REINFORCED

NORM	REASON	EXAMPLE
"Make our department look good in top management's eyes."	Group/organization survival	After vigorously defending the vital role played by the Human Resources Management Department at a divisional meeting, a staff specialist is complimented by her boss.
"Success comes to those who work hard and don't make waves."	Clarification of behavioral expectations	A senior manager takes a young associate aside and cautions him to be a bit more patient with coworkers who see things differently.
"Be a team player, not a star."	Avoidance of embarrassment	A project team member is ridiculed by her peers for dominating the discussion during a progress report to top management.
"Customer service is our top priority."	Clarification of central values/unique identity	Two sales representatives are given a surprise Friday afternoon party for having received prestigious best-in-the-industry customer service awards from an industry association.

Norms emerge either on their own, over time, or as a more conscious effort. For instance, think of the group of friends you hung out with on Friday night. What are some of the common behaviors and unspoken norms of behavior? Were these norms the result of discussion or did they just kind of happen? In contrast, norms can also be purposefully created, which is what we advocate. (Why leave things to chance at work when you can directly influence them for the better?) The World Health Organization (WHO) provides an excellent example. The mission of the organization is to improve health for people around the world. The WHO took on the challenge of improving surgical outcomes. To do this, its member group World Alliance for Public Safety created the Safe Surgery Checklist that identifies three stages of surgery and the important tasks associated with each. They recommend that a surgery coordinator (a specific task role) be assigned to assure that each task is complete before moving to the next stage.

> *Stage 1—(Sign In) Before Administering Anesthesia:* Confirm patient identity, site, procedure, and consent; mark the site of the surgery; anesthesia safety check; pulse oximeter on.

> *Stage 2—(Time Out) Before Incision:* Confirm all team members have introduced themselves by name and role; surgeon, anesthesiologist, and nurse confirm patient, procedure, and site; surgeon reviews critical steps and potential challenges; anesthesiologist checks for potential problems; nursing team reviews that all equipment and personnel are in place; confirm appropriate medications have been administered.

> *Stage 3—(Sign Out) Before Patient Leaves Operating Room:* Nurse verbally confirms with the team—name of procedure recorded; instrument, sponge, and needle counts are correct; specimen is labeled and includes patient's name; surgeon, anesthesiologist, and nurse review post-op concerns, medications, and pain management.

"By following a few critical steps," the World Alliance for Public Safety notes, "health care professionals can minimize the most common and avoidable risks endangering the lives and well-being of surgical patients."[20]

solving application

problem

No Cash Bonuses at Wooga?! But Everybody Else Gets Them!

Wooga, a German social gaming company, doesn't pay performance bonuses. This is hard to believe given the common practice among its competitors to provide generous bonuses.

For instance, rival Zynga pays top performers with lavish gifts, which can include $100,000 in stock. Its hard-driving culture promotes competition within, tracks individual performance, and demotes or fires those who don't keep pace. These practices seem to work. Zynga has produced such online hits as Mafia Wars, Farmville, and Zynga Poker.

Wooga's games are almost as well known, including Diamond Dash, Bubble Island, Pearl's Peril, Monster World, and Jelly Splash.

So Why Doesn't Wooga Pay Bonuses? If bonuses work for Zynga, why not for Wooga? Jens Begemann, founder and CEO, says: "I don't believe in them. . . . If people are not motivated, you may need bonuses to make sure they work. But I don't think that's the right incentive." Bonuses work against Wooga's culture of openness and collaboration. The company creates games for social platforms (e.g., Facebook) with teams of developers. Sharing all knowledge is essential—within and between teams as well as between management and employees. Begemann doesn't want teams comparing and competing with each other for ideas, talent, or *users* (a critical performance measurement in gaming). He reasons that if a team competes for users, it may be unlikely to allow a user to be directed to a Wooga game from a competing team. Performance bonuses could get in the way of Wooga's overall success.

Besides, Begemann notes, in Germany cash bonuses are taxed at nearly 50 percent. "Sometimes, people don't even realize they received a bonus." Part of this no-bonus practice can be attributed to the European approach to start-ups. In contrast to the winner-take-all approach in US companies, European companies tend not to single out individuals and differentiate their compensation so dramatically. Note, however, that Wooga does use a financial incentive—ownership. Wooga provides employees with initial shares in the company to give workers a stake in the company's overall success.

It Seems to Work and Venture Capital Agrees In 2011 alone, users grew by 185 percent to 40 million monthly users, up from 14 million a year earlier. The practice also has attracted private investors (the company is not yet public). One investor raved, "I fell in love with this philosophy. [Begemann] basically does not believe that running competitive teams is the best way to build the company." In contrast to just having people work harder, the investor said, "It's very important people work smarter."

Market Share Update Ranking changes fast in this market. Based on daily active users, Wooga—which by the end of 2012 was Zynga's closest rival—had slipped to third place as King, the makers of Candy Crush Saga and Pet Rescue Saga, soared to number one. In the first half of 2013 Zynga claimed 52 million users and King 66 million.[21]

SOURCE: Adapted from P. Glader, "Wooga, A Case Study in No-Cash Bonus Culture," *Fast Company*, February 21, 2012, http://www.fastcompany.com/1816541/wooga-case-study-no-cash-bonus-culture, accessed April 28, 2013.

YOUR CALL

Stop 1: What potential problems do you see with Wooga's no-bonus policy?

Stop 2: How can your knowledge of group norms help you explain why Wooga's no-bonus practices foster effective groups?

Stop 3: Describe what you would recommend, above and beyond what they already do, to help overcome the challenges associated with Wooga's no-bonus policy.

Another way to think about roles and norms is peer pressure. Peer pressure is about expectations, and we all know what peer pressure is and how effective or problematic it can be. But at its root, peer pressure is simply the influence of the group on the individual, and the expectations of associated roles and norms are the means of this influence. (You'll learn much more about influencing others in Chapter 12.)

Now that you've learned what groups are and the importance of roles and norms, let's move on and explore how to develop effective groups. Combining this knowledge enables you to influence key outcomes at the individual, group, and organizational levels in the Integrative Framework.

MAJOR QUESTION

How can understanding the group development process make me more effective at school and work?

THE BIGGER PICTURE

You'll find working in groups and teams much easier when you recognize and understand they often follow a five-stage development process. We put each stage in context to help you understand the problems and benefits common to groups and teams as they evolve. Your understanding and application of this knowledge will enable you to more effectively manage individual- and group-level outcomes in the Integrative Framework and perform more successfully in work and school groups.

At work and school, groups and teams go through a maturation process. Their development is much like the life-cycle processes found in many disciplines—products in marketing and human development in biology. All of these processes are described in terms of stages that differ in terms of number, sequence, length, and nature.[22] Bruce Tuckman formulated perhaps the most popular group development process. His process originally had four stages but was later expanded to five—forming, storming, norming, performing, and adjourning (see Figure 8.2).[23]

A word of caution: Similar to Maslow's theory of needs discussed in Chapter 5, Tuckman's theory has not withstood rigorous empirical testing. However, many researchers and practitioners like Tuckman's five-stage model of group development because it is easy to remember and has commonsense appeal. Let's learn a little bit about this process and its individual stages.

Notice in Figure 8.2 how individuals give up a measure of their independence when they join and participate in a group. Also, the various stages are not necessarily of the same duration or intensity. For instance, the storming stage may be practically nonexistent or painfully long, depending on the goal clarity and the commitment and maturity of the members. You can make this process come to life by relating the various stages to your own experiences with work groups, committees, athletic teams, fraternities/sororities, religious groups, or class project teams. Some group experiences that surprised you when they occurred may now make sense or strike you as inevitable when seen as part of a natural development process.

Stage 1: Forming

During this "ice-breaking" stage, group members tend to be uncertain and anxious about such things as their roles, the people in charge, and the group's goals. Mutual trust is low, and there is a good deal of holding back to see who takes charge and how.

Interestingly, research has shown that this is just the time in a group's development where some conflict among group members is beneficial. A study of 71 technology project teams revealed that conflict in the early stages of the group development process *increased* creativity.[24] However, the results can be quite different in other situations. For example, in life-and-death situations sometimes faced by surgical teams and airline cockpit crews, the uncertainty inherent in the early stages of development (e.g., forming and storming) can be dangerous.

FIGURE 8.2 TUCKMAN'S FIVE-STAGE MODEL OF GROUP DEVELOPMENT

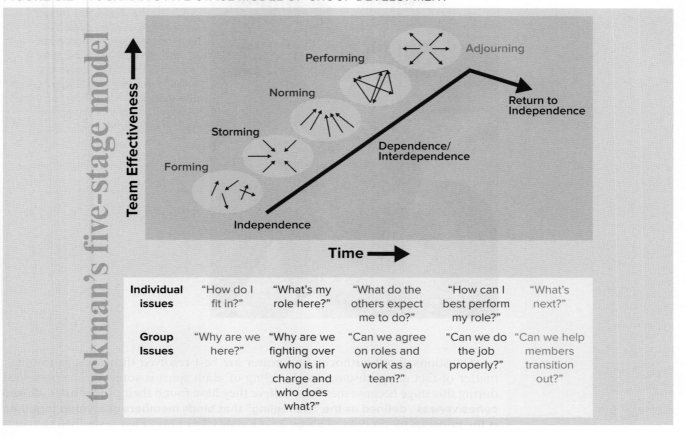

Individual issues	"How do I fit in?"	"What's my role here?"	"What do the others expect me to do?"	"How can I best perform my role?"	"What's next?"
Group Issues	"Why are we here?"	"Why are we fighting over who is in charge and who does what?"	"Can we agree on roles and work as a team?"	"Can we do the job properly?"	"Can we help members transition out?"

According to the National Transportation Safety Board, "73% of commercial airline pilots' serious mistakes happen on crews' first day together."[25] If the formal leader (e.g., a supervisor) does not assert his or her authority, an emergent leader will often step in to fulfill the group's need for leadership and direction (the details of leadership are discussed in Chapter 13).

Stage 2: Storming

This is a time of testing. Individuals test the leader's policies and assumptions as they try to determine how they fit into the power structure. Subgroups take shape, and subtle forms of rebellion, such as procrastination, occur.

In fact, some management experts say the reason many new CEOs don't survive is because they never get beyond the storming stage. Ron Johnson at JCPenney, for example, never really got employees and other top managers on board with his radical rebranding of the retailer. He fired thousands of employees, and much of the old guard, but many of those who remained resisted his plan. The situation was made worse still by a lack of support from the Board of Directors.[26] Many groups stall in Stage 2 because of how power and politics (topics we'll cover in Chapter 12) can erupt into open rebellion.

Stage 3: Norming

Groups that make it through Stage 2 generally do so because a respected member, other than the leader, challenges the group to resolve its power struggles so something can be accomplished.

Professional race car drivers, including Danica Patrick, shown here, rely on their teams to develop strategies and implement them effectively to win races. To do this, it is essential that such teams to both reach and maintain the performing stage of group development. Describe how you think the stages of group development unfold in race car teams?

Questions about authority and power are best resolved through unemotional, matter-of-fact group discussion. A feeling of team spirit is sometimes experienced during this stage because members believe they have found their proper roles. **Group cohesiveness**, defined as the "we feeling" that binds members of a group together, is the principal by-product of Stage 3.[27] Google CEO Larry Page reshuffled the company's top management team in early 2013, as reported in *The Wall Street Journal*, to "weed out perceived inefficiencies and a lack of cohesion among some of the Internet company's core product groups." He restructured jobs and responsibilities and reassigned people.[28] Current research supports these actions and shows that increasing team member interactions and the interdependence of their work tasks can help overcome the conflicts and boost team cohesion and performance.[29]

Stage 4: Performing

Activity during this vital stage is focused on solving task problems, as contributors get their work done without hampering others.

This stage is often characterized by a climate of open communication, strong cooperation, and lots of helping behavior. Conflicts and job boundary disputes are handled constructively and efficiently. Cohesiveness and personal commitment to group goals help the group achieve more than could any one individual acting alone.

Stage 5: Adjourning

The work is done; it is time to move on to other things. The return to independence can be eased by rituals celebrating "the end" and "new beginnings."

Parties, award ceremonies, and graduations can punctuate the end. Leaders need to emphasize valuable lessons learned during the adjourning stage.

major question

What are the characteristics of effective team players and team building, and how does this knowledge improve my performance in various types of teams?

THE BIGGER PICTURE

When you better understand the difference between groups and teams, you'll be well equipped to perform better in both. You'll find practical tips in our discussion of critical competencies of effective team players along with guidance on teamwork and team building. This section concludes with a discussion of two particularly important and contemporary types of teams—*self-managed* and *virtual*.

A **team** is "a small number of people with complementary skills who are committed to a common purpose, performance goals, and approach for which they hold themselves mutually accountable." Besides being a central component of the Integrative Framework, teams are a cornerstone of work life. General Electric's CEO Jeffrey Immelt offers this blunt overview: "You lead today by building teams and placing others first. It's not about you."[30] This means practically all employees need to develop their skills related to being good team players and building effective teams.

While Immelt's position is accepted by many CEOs across industries, some also are quick to emphasize the important roles of individual team members. For instance, JP Morgan's CEO Jamie Dimon stated, "While teamwork is important and often code for getting along, equally important is an individual's ability to have the courage to stand alone and do the right thing."[31] Dimon's view was put to the test during the Great Recession and financial scandals in the recent past (e.g., the London Whale). Research supports these views. Executives from 300 companies indicated that teamwork was the single most desirable soft skill (64 percent of executives). Interpersonal, social, and managerial skills were also noted.[32]

In today's team-focused work environment, organizations need leaders who are adept at teamwork themselves and can cultivate the level of trust necessary to foster constructive teamwork. Employees reported that the three traits of their most admired bosses were trust in employees, honesty/authenticity, and great team-building skills.[33] To help you be more effective in the team context, let's begin by differentiating groups and teams.

A Team Is More Than Just a Group

Management consultants at McKinsey & Company say it is a mistake to use the terms *group* and *team* interchangeably. After studying many different kinds of teams—from athletic to corporate to military—they concluded that successful teams tend to take on a life of their own. A group becomes a team when the following criteria are met:

1. *Leadership* becomes a shared activity.
2. *Accountability* shifts from strictly individual to both individual and collective.
3. The group develops its own *purpose* or mission.
4. *Problem solving* becomes a way of life, not a part-time activity.
5. *Effectiveness* is measured by the group's collective outcomes and products.[34]

Bob Lane, the former CEO of Deere & Company, emphasizes the purpose and effectiveness of teams when he talks about his company being a team, not a family. A reporter summarized his words this way: "While family members who don't pull their weight may not be welcome at the Thanksgiving dinner table, they remain members of the family. But if you're not pulling your weight here, I'm sorry, you're not part of the team."[35] Mr. Lane clearly has strong views on the difference.

Let's make this more personal for you. As you know, well-functioning groups or teams can be incredibly effective in achieving goals and quite fulfilling for members. However, you also know that they can be a tremendous waste of time. It therefore would be beneficial for you to be able to differentiate the former from the latter. Some experts describe this difference in terms of "maturity." Mature groups are more effective. Completing Self-Assessment 8.2 will help you better understand the maturity level of a current or past team of which you're a member. The individual items provide excellent insights into the causes of the team's success, or lack thereof, and can guide improvements.

connect

SELF-ASSESSMENT 8.2 **Is This a Mature Work Group or a Team?**

Go to connect.mheducation.com and take Self-Assessment 8.2 to determine the maturity (effectiveness characteristics) of one of your current or past groups/teams.

1. Does your evaluation help explain why the group or team was successful or not? Explain.
2. Was (or is) there anything you could have done (or can do) to increase the maturity of this group? Explain.
3. How will this evaluation instrument help you be a more effective group member or leader in the future?

Teams in Terms of Group Development Stage Compared to our discussion of groups and group development in the previous sections, teams are task groups that have matured to the *performing* stage. Because of conflicts due to power, authority, and unstable interpersonal relations, many work groups never qualify as a real team. The distinction was clarified this way: "The essence of a team is common commitment. Without it, groups perform as individuals. With it, they become a powerful unit of collective performance."[36] This underscores two other important distinctions between teams and groups: Teams assemble to accomplish a common task and require collaboration.[37]

The following Example box describes how important building an effective team is to Kevin Ryan, the former president of DoubleClick (one of the original Internet banner ad companies eventually purchased by Google) and founder and current CEO of Gilt Groupe (a specialty apparel, accessories, and home décor club). He clearly acknowledges that teams take time to develop. But he also is clear that he expects managers to control the process. We then discuss teamwork competencies and being a team player.

EXAMPLE ## Team Building Is an Important Part of Talent Management[38]

Kevin Ryan knows a bit about building successful teams. He's done it at a number of companies (e.g., DoubleClick and Gilt Groupe) and is regarded as one of the country's leading Internet entrepreneurs. His leadership style emphasizes talent management (Chapter 1), which he sees as the number one responsibility of CEOs, and rigorous performance management (Chapter 6). Both of these converge in his expectations for managers' ability to build effective teams. These views are illustrated in his description of a conversation with a new manager.

CLEAR EXPECTATIONS "Five months from now, you need to have a great team. Earlier would be better, but five months is the goal. To do that, you'll need to spend the next month evaluating the people you have right now. I hope they're good. But if they're not, we'll make changes to replace them. If you need to promote people internally, we'll do that. If you need to go outside, we'll do that. You also need to make sure you retain your best people. I'm going to be really disturbed if I see that people we wanted to keep have started leaving your area."

CONSEQUENCES Sadly, the manager didn't build a strong team. At four months two key positions were still open and two key individuals had left. Mr. Ryan then asked: "Tell us what we can do to help. . . . If you need us to double your recruiting resources, we'll do that." At six months the situation had not improved. Mr. Ryan then said, "We're done."

YOUR THOUGHTS?

1. What are the benefits to Kevin Ryan's approach to team building?
2. What are the potential shortcomings?
3. Explain why you would or would not want to be a manager for Kevin Ryan.

Developing Your Teamwork Competencies and Being a Team Player Instead of a "Free-Rider"

Forming teams and urging employees to be team players are good starting points on the road to creating effective teams. But they are not enough. Teamwork competencies need to be role modeled and taught. These include group problem solving, mentoring, conflict management skills (Chapter 10), and emotional intelligence (Chapter 3). Put another way, many of the inputs and processes across various levels in the Integrative Framework also are important elements of effective teams and team building. Research suggests that teams collaborate most effectively when companies develop and encourage teamwork competencies. This means that teamwork competencies should be measured and rewarded, too (recall our discussion of performance management in Chapter 6). If teamwork is important, then how can you measure it? Thankfully, this is well researched but not necessarily commonly practiced. Researchers have distilled five common teamwork competencies. These are outlined in Table 8.4.

TABLE 8.4 COMMON TEAMWORK COMPETENCIES

COMPETENCY	EXAMPLES OF MEMBER BEHAVIORS
1. Contributes to the Team's Work	• Completed work in a timely manner • Came to meetings prepared • Did complete and accurate work
2. Constructively Interacts with Team Members	• Communicated effectively • Listened to teammates • Accepted feedback
3. Keeps Team on Track	• Helped team plan and organize work • Stayed aware of team members' progress • Provided constructive feedback
4. Expects Quality Work	• Expected team to succeed • Cared that the team produced quality work
5. Possesses Relevant Knowledge, Skills, and Abilities (KSAs) for Team's Responsibilities	• Possessed necessary KSAs to contribute meaningfully to the team • Applied knowledge and skill to fill in as needed for other members' roles

Notice that all of these competencies are action oriented. This means that being a team player is more than a state of mind: it is about action!

Evaluating Teamwork Competencies There are at least two ways to use Table 8.4 and knowledge of teamwork competencies. The first is as a tool to enhance your self-awareness. The second is to use these competencies as a way to measure your performance and the performance of other members of your team. Self-Assessment located at connect.mheducation.com can be useful for both. Many of your business courses require team assignments and some require peer evaluations. Complete Self-Assessment to learn about your own teamwork competencies and/or the performance of the members of one of your teams at school (e.g. sport, club, or fraternity/sorority). For example, knowledge of your team competencies can help you determine which competencies are your strongest are opportunities for improvement. You can then choose to play and/or develop your deficiencies.

SELF-ASSESSMENT 8.3 Evaluate Team Member F

After completing the Self-Assessment, do the following

1. Which competencies are your strongest (i.e., hav

2. Do these scores match your own impressions

3. Which is your lowest? Describe two things display this competency.

4. Which competency do you feel is mos in the teams on which you're a mem

5. Describe the pros and cons of usi assignments in school.

Adapted from M. W. Ohland, M. L. Loughr
H. R. Pomeranz, and D. G. Schmucker, "
Development of a Behaviorally Anchored
Learning & Education, 2012, 609–30. Repr

clearly acknowledges that teams take time to develop. But he also is clear that he expects managers to control the process. We then discuss teamwork competencies and being a team player.

EXAMPLE   Team Building Is an Important Part of Talent Management[38]

Kevin Ryan knows a bit about building successful teams. He's done it at a number of companies (e.g., DoubleClick and Gilt Groupe) and is regarded as one of the country's leading Internet entrepreneurs. His leadership style emphasizes talent management (Chapter 1), which he sees as the number one responsibility of CEOs, and rigorous performance management (Chapter 6). Both of these converge in his expectations for managers' ability to build effective teams. These views are illustrated in his description of a conversation with a new manager.

CLEAR EXPECTATIONS   "Five months from now, you need to have a great team. Earlier would be better, but five months is the goal. To do that, you'll need to spend the next month evaluating the people you have right now. I hope they're good. But if they're not, we'll make changes to replace them. If you need to promote people internally, we'll do that. If you need to go outside, we'll do that. You also need to make sure you retain your best people. I'm going to be really disturbed if I see that people we wanted to keep have started leaving your area."

CONSEQUENCES   Sadly, the manager didn't build a strong team. At four months two key positions were still open and two key individuals had left. Mr. Ryan then asked: "Tell us what we can do to help. . . . If you need us to double your recruiting resources, we'll do that." At six months the situation had not improved. Mr. Ryan then said, "We're done."

YOUR THOUGHTS?

1. What are the benefits to Kevin Ryan's approach to team building?

2. What are the potential shortcomings?

3. Explain why you would or would not want to be a manager for Kevin Ryan.

Developing Your Teamwork Competencies and Being a Team Player Instead of a "Free-Rider"

Forming teams and urging employees to be team players are good starting points on the road to creating effective teams. But they are not enough. Teamwork competencies need to be role modeled and taught. These include group problem solving, mentoring, conflict management skills (Chapter 10), and emotional intelligence (Chapter 3). Put another way, many of the inputs and processes across various levels in the Integrative Framework also are important elements of effective teams and team building. Research suggests that teams collaborate most effectively when companies develop and encourage teamwork competencies. This means that teamwork competencies should be measured and rewarded, too (recall our discussion of performance management in Chapter 6). If teamwork is important, then how can you measure it? Thankfully, this is well researched but not necessarily commonly practiced. Researchers have distilled five common teamwork competencies. These are outlined in Table 8.4.

TABLE 8.4 COMMON TEAMWORK COMPETENCIES

COMPETENCY	EXAMPLES OF MEMBER BEHAVIORS
1. Contributes to the Team's Work	• Completed work in a timely manner • Came to meetings prepared • Did complete and accurate work
2. Constructively Interacts with Team Members	• Communicated effectively • Listened to teammates • Accepted feedback
3. Keeps Team on Track	• Helped team plan and organize work • Stayed aware of team members' progress • Provided constructive feedback
4. Expects Quality Work	• Expected team to succeed • Cared that the team produced quality work
5. Possesses Relevant Knowledge, Skills, and Abilities (KSAs) for Team's Responsibilities	• Possessed necessary KSAs to contribute meaningfully to the team • Applied knowledge and skill to fill in as needed for other members' roles

Notice that all of these competencies are action oriented. This means that being a team player is more than a state of mind: it is about action!

Evaluating Teamwork Competencies   There are at least two ways to use Table 8.4 and knowledge of teamwork competencies. The first is as a tool to enhance your self-awareness. The second is to use these competencies as a way to measure your performance and the performance of other members of your team. Self-Assessment 8.3 located at connect.mheducation.com can be useful for both. Many of your business courses require team assignments and some require peer evaluations. Complete this Self-Assessment to learn about your own teamwork competencies and/or to evaluate the performance of the members of one of your teams at school (e.g., for a class, sport, club, or fraternity/sorority). For example, knowledge of your teamwork competencies can help you determine which competencies are your strongest and those that are opportunities for improvement. You can then choose to play to your strengths and/or develop your deficiencies.

connect

SELF-ASSESSMENT 8.3 **Evaluate Team Member Effectiveness**

After completing the Self-Assessment, do the following:

1. Which competencies are your strongest (i.e., have the highest average scores)?

2. Do these scores match your own impressions of your teamwork competencies?

3. Which is your lowest? Describe two things you can do to further develop and display this competency.

4. Which competency do you feel is most often the one lacking by low performers in the teams on which you're a member?

5. Describe the pros and cons of using this tool to do peer evaluations for team assignments in school.

Adapted from M. W. Ohland, M. L. Loughry, D. J. Woehr, L. G. Bullard, R. M. Felder, C. J. Finelli, R. A. Layton, H. R. Pomeranz, and D. G. Schmucker, "The Comprehensive Assessment of Team Member Effectiveness: Development of a Behaviorally Anchored Rating Scale for Self- and Peer Evaluation," *Academy of Management Learning & Education,* 2012, 609–30. Reprinted with permission of Academy of Management.

Being a Team Player   So, what does it mean to be a team player? Understanding and exhibiting the competencies noted above is an excellent start. And while everybody has her or his own ideas of what is most important, it is likely that most people's views include the 3 Cs of team players:

Committed
Collaborative
Competent[39]

Put another way, the 3 Cs are the "cover charge" or the bare minimum to be considered a team player. Think of a team on which you either are or were a member. It would be difficult to consider any individual member a team player if he or she didn't possess and exhibit all three. Effective team players therefore don't just *feel* the 3 Cs—they *display* them. To make the point, think of somebody on one of your teams who clearly displays the 3 Cs and somebody who does not. How do the differences affect you? The team? While there are many potential reasons that people are not team players, a particularly common and problematic one is *social loafing* (i.e., "anti-team player").

Social Loafing   ***Social loafing* is the tendency for individual effort to decline as group size increases.** To illustrate the point, consider a group or team of which you're a member and ask yourself: "Is group performance less than, equal to, or greater than the sum of its parts?" Can three people working together, for example, accomplish less than, the same as, or more than they would working separately? An interesting study conducted more than a half-century ago found the answer to be "less than." In a rope-pulling exercise ("tug-of-war"), three people pulling together achieved only two-and-a-half times the average individual rate. Eight pullers achieved less than four times the individual rate.[40] Social loafing is problematic because it typically involves more than simply "slacking off." Free riders (i.e., "loafers") produce not only low-quality work, which causes others to work harder to compensate, but they often also distract or disrupt the work of other team members. Research involving business students revealed two common reasons why individuals loaf—apathy and social disconnectedness. Apathy means they are uninterested in the task, don't care about their grade, and/or are unconcerned about the effect of their poor work on others. A loafer's social disconnection may be due to simply not liking or getting along with one or more members of the team, or they may feel like outsiders or not part of the clique.[41] You undoubtedly have many of your own examples. Let's briefly analyze this threat to group effectiveness with an eye toward avoiding it.

Guarding Against Loafing   Consistent with the definition above, social loafing generally increases as group size increases and work is more widely dispersed. What makes this worse is that loafers "expect others to pick up the slack even as they receive the same rewards."[42] To combat such problems:

1. Limit group size.

2. Assure equity of effort to mitigate the possibility that a member can say, "Everyone else is goofing off, so why shouldn't I?" Your knowledge of equity and justice from Chapter 5 can offer you some ideas on how to avoid or fix this.

3. Hold people accountable—don't allow members to feel that they are lost in the crowd and think "who cares?" Motivation (Chapter 5) and performance management (Chapter 6) practices also can be helpful.

Recent research with four-member teams showed that ***hybrid rewards*—those that include team and individual components**—reduced social loafing and improved information sharing. Hybrid rewards hold members accountable both as individuals and as a team.[43] A particularly interesting finding was that self-reliant "individualists" were more prone to social loafing than were group-oriented "collectivists." Why do you think this is?

1. Think of a group or team situation in which one of the members was "loafing."

2. Given what you just learned, what do you think was the cause of her/him to free-ride or loaf?

3. Describe, in detail, two things you could have done to prevent this from happening.

4. Describe what you can do in a future group assignment in school to avoid or reduce social loafing. Be specific.

Now let's discuss how to build teams. Team building is another key element to your near- and long-term career success and a critical means for influencing many of the outcomes at different levels in the Integrative Framework (e.g., your individual job performance, team cohesiveness, and organizational profitability).

Team Building

Team building is a catchall term for a host of techniques aimed at improving the internal functioning of work groups. Whether conducted by company trainers, hired consultants, or you, team-building workshops strive for greater cooperation, better communication, and less dysfunctional conflict (different forms of conflict and how to manage them are discussed in Chapter 10). Rote memorization and lectures are discouraged by team builders who prefer *active* versus passive learning. Greater emphasis is placed on *how* work groups get the job done than on the task itself. Experiential learning techniques such as interpersonal trust exercises, conflict role-play sessions, and competitive games are common if not expected. While there are many alternatives, we need to ask: Does team building work? Is it worth the investment of time, people, and money?

Does Team Building Work?   It's hard to say. While many businesspeople are confident that development efforts yield results (e.g., Kip Tindell, CEO of the Container Store), cost-conscious executives increasingly insist on determining the return on investment (ROI) for team building and other talent-development investments. One

Full-time employees of the Container Store receive 263 hours of training their first year. Communication and transparency also are highly valued. CEO Kip Tindell believes that all information and data (except salaries) should be shared with employees. Such practices foster trust, teamwork, and organizational effectiveness at the company. Besides trust, what are the benefits of transparency and investments in training?

estimate is that fewer than 20 percent of companies that invest in development actually calculate the ROI.[44] Part of the problem is that many if not most organizations do not set clear objectives for team building (or training more generally). Three fundamental elements are recommended for those interested in establishing the ROI for team building:

- *Clear objectives.* This is the starting point for ROI estimates. Many outcomes are possible, but it is important to identify which are most relevant for a particular team, such as increased sales, increased customer satisfaction, timeliness, or quality. To illustrate, if the objective is simply to get team members to know each other and have fun, then an engaging exercise or a happy hour is enough. If instead the objective is to translate the training into action, such as on-the-job collaboration, then it is recommended to follow up, use reminders, and somehow measure that it is happening.[45]

- *Validation.* Not to be confused with the objectives, validation involves confirming that team-building efforts actually link to the desired changes in behavior and attitudes. For example, a positive attitude toward customers likely affects the quality of work produced by the team. You can validate (verify) this link using your knowledge of goal setting and performance management from the previous two chapters.

- *Performance information.* What data are needed to track the previous two elements and how will they be obtained?[46] Attitudes toward customers can be measured with employee surveys, quality can be gauged by the number of reworked products, and customer satisfaction can be determined with surveys or interviews.

How to Build Effective Teams—Quickly Like goal setting, creating and communicating performance expectations for teams is extremely important. However, the reality is that today teams are often put together in a hurry; they are assemblies of people who do not routinely work together but must get results—quickly. It therefore is necessary for effective teams to be built and start performing in real time. Knowing how to do this can give you a real advantage when looking for a job, and then (quickly) distinguishing yourself as a top performer after you get a job. Today's dynamic workplace often requires different people to come together across boundaries (e.g., departments, experience levels, knowledge, age, and even employers if you partner with vendors and suppliers). Businesses sometimes need to build effective teams fast. Here are some practical tips to do just that. These six actions can help accelerate the development of your team and get it performing sooner rather than later.

1. **Break the ice.** Have each member share relevant details about his or her experience. Doing so helps everybody learn what types of skills and abilities the team possesses, and it also facilitates cooperation because team members can use each other's experiences as a shared history, which substitutes for the history that they don't actually have together. Sample questions: "Please tell us about the types of teams in which you've participated." "What are some of the biggest challenges and how were they dealt with?"

2. **Don't reinvent the wheel.** Ask team members what has worked in the past. This can help signal respect for their competence and judgment and lead to greater engagement and commitment (recall our discussions from Chapter 2).

3. **Communicate a purpose and a plan.** Clearly explain the team's purpose and how they will work together. Do more than simply hand out assignments, but instead explain why the team was created, the problem to be solved, and the benefits of success. Describe milestones, or key dates, and the main deliverables.

4. **Play to strengths.** Set individuals and the larger team up to win. This means match individual members' skills to responsibilities and goals of the team. Fit is likely to lead to higher performance and show that you were listening to individuals and care about their success.

5. **Clarify decision making.** Think about and explain how you approach decision making in dealing with conflicts (you'll learn more about this in Chapter 11). Decisions that will affect the team's final product, for example, are often handled by the team leader (or boss). Beware, however, not to interfere in decisions that should be made within the team.

6. **Information is essential—make it flow.** Establish clear processes and expectations for sharing information within the team—e-mails, face-to-face meetings, voicemail, Dropbox, SharePoint, Skype, etc. Explicitly include your expectations for giving and receiving feedback.[47]

All sorts of interesting approaches to teams and teamwork can be found in the workplace today. Technology and global competitiveness motivate organizations to be more flexible and responsive. The next section profiles two different approaches to teams—*self-managed* and *virtual*. We selected these particular types of teams because of their pervasive use, supporting research evidence, and their varying degrees of empowerment (discussed more in Chapter 12).

Self-Managed Teams

Self-managed teams are defined as groups of workers who are given administrative oversight for their task domains. Administrative oversight involves delegated activities such as planning, scheduling, monitoring, and staffing. These are "chores" normally performed by managers. In short, employees in these unique work groups act as their own supervisor. Leadership responsibilities often are shared and shift as the demands on the team change and members step up.[48] This contrasts with hierarchical or centralized types of management typically found in teams. Accountability is maintained *indirectly* by outside managers and leaders. More than 75 percent of the top 1,000 US companies currently use some form of self-managed team.[49] For example, Google X is the now famous although low-profile special research lab for the company. Google is synonymous with research and innovation, and such activities occur throughout the company. But Google X includes teams with especially broad latitude and whose members flow in and out of projects over time. Members of these fluid and largely self-directed teams are charged with "moonshot" projects—those that can change the world *and* be commercially viable—such as driverless cars, Google Glass, and broadband transmitters on high-altitude balloons.[50]

Typically, self-managed teams schedule work and assign duties, with managers present to serve as trainers and facilitators. Self-managed teams—variously referred to as semiautonomous work groups, autonomous work groups, and superteams—come in every conceivable format today, some more autonomous than others. It is important to know, however, that *self-managed* does not mean simply turning workers loose to do their own thing. Indeed, an organization embracing self-managed teams should be prepared to undergo revolutionary changes in management philosophy, structure, staffing and training practices, and reward systems. The traditional notions of managerial authority (discussed in detail in Chapter 12) and control are turned on their heads. Not surprisingly, many managers strongly resist giving up the reins of power to people they view as subordinates. They see self-managed teams as a threat to their job security. Nevertheless, members of (self-managed) teams are increasingly from different functional areas of the organization (e.g., finance, operations, marketing, and R&D).

Cross-Functionalism **Cross-functionalism** occurs when specialists from different areas are put on the same team. New product development is a popular area in which organizations utilize cross-functional teams. An example was provided by Brian Walker, the CEO of furniture maker Herman Miller. Mr. Walker described how the company uses self-management and cross-functional teams to leverage the talents of employees in product development and boost company performance:

> We strive to realize the potential of all our employees and allow them to enjoy what they do. This often involves moving people beyond their current jobs and areas of expertise. If I can have 5,000 or 6,000 people who are passionate about what they do, using every bit of their capabilities in solving problems and finding solutions to our customers' problems, I'm going to be much better off than if I leave that to 10 percent of that population who tell the other people what to do. . . .
>
> [To do this] we're big believers in putting teams together . . . we're very willing to move folks around between departments. In our design process, for example, we deliberately create tension by putting together a cross-functional team that includes people from manufacturing, finance, research, ergonomics, marketing and sales. The manufacturing guys want something they know they can make easily and fits their processes. The salespeople want what their customers have been asking for. The tension comes from finding the right balance, being willing to follow those creative leaps to the new place, and convincing the organization it's worth the risk.[51]

Are Self-Managed Teams Effective? Research from the 1990s and 2000s showed mixed results. Self-managed teams have been shown to improve work–life quality, customer service, and productivity. However, other studies reported low or no improvement in these same outcomes.[52] A review of dozens of individual studies concluded that self-managed teams had a positive effect on productivity and on specific attitudes relating to self-management (e.g., responsibility and control). But self-managed teams had no significant effect on general attitudes (e.g., job satisfaction and organizational commitment) and no significant effect on absenteeism or turnover.[53] More recent research provides some guidance on the importance of different team member personality types (remember the Big Five from Chapter 3) for self-managed team performance. Specifically, teams with members who are very similar in terms of conscientiousness, but highly different in terms of extraversion, performed best.[54] This suggests that conscientious people prefer to work with or at least perform better when they work with other conscientious people, but a team full of extraverts is less than optimal. Think about this? How can your knowledge of OB help you explain these results?

Results for self-managed teams are generally encouraging but do not qualify as a sweeping endorsement. Nonetheless, experts say the trend toward self-managed work teams will continue upward in North America because of a strong cultural bias in favor of direct participation. What are your views? Would you prefer to work in a self-managed team or a more conventional format? Why? Regardless of how you answer these questions, it is insightful to learn what it is that some of the most effective organizations do to make their self-managed teams successful. Read the Example box to find out.

EXAMPLE The Art of the Self-Managing Team[55]

Many argue, and some convincingly, that great teams don't last. Many of them disassemble because their members move on to other if not better opportunities. One implication of this fact is that organizations and their leaders obsess too much over choosing the best members—chances are they will leave. Thankfully, however, companies like W.L. Gore, Worthington Industries, Semco, and Morning Star provide insights into how to overcome this common hurdle or assumption and continually create top-performing self-managed teams.

THE OPPOSITE OF CHAOS Some managers fear teams that are not under direct managerial control. But effective self-managed teams are not "loosey-goosey, unstructured or chaotic. They're just the opposite: focused, disciplined, and more effective over the long haul than typical teams." Founder Bill Gore says, "At Gore we don't manage people. . . . We expect people to manage themselves."[56]

Self-managed teams at these companies commonly share three characteristics:

1. Competence
2. Clear Goals and Expectations
3. Shared Values

Let's look at each in more detail.

1. **Competence Rules the Day.** Most employees and team members do not have job titles. However, a lack of job titles does not mean a lack of leadership. Everybody knows who the leaders are, and they typically are those who have "served their colleagues best, have offered the most useful ideas, and have worked the hardest and most effectively for the team's success. At W.L. Gore, they say you find out if you're a leader by calling a meeting and seeing if anyone comes." Even assigned or explicit leaders are "transparently competence-based." A strict hierarchy is followed by most emergency room teams—attending physicians, fellows, and finally residents.

2. **Clear Goals and Expectations.** Recall what you learned in Chapters 5 and 6 about goals and goal setting. Most organizations do this poorly and all can do better. That said, each employee at Morning Star, a tomato processor, creates a "letter of understanding" with colleagues who are most affected by his or her work. This letter explains in great detail what each can expect. This not only clarifies goals and expectations, but also boosts goal commitment (see Chapter 6 and the Integrative Framework).

3. **Shared Values.** Effective (self-managed) teams are clear about what they value. Surgical teams are keenly focused on patient safety and good medical outcomes. This focus is shared by every member of often large surgical teams and despite the fact that members routinely come and go.

YOUR THOUGHTS?

1. These organizations make self-managed teams look simple. If this is true, then why do you think more organizations don't use them?
2. Assume you're a founder and CEO of a company. Argue both for and against using self-managed teams.

Now we turn our attention to virtual teams, which are another important and increasingly popular form of work team.

Virtual Teams

Technology not only allows people to communicate where, when, and with whom they wish, but also allows many people (and organizations) to work without offices. For you personally, what would be/are the advantages and disadvantages of telecommuting and virtual work?

Virtual teams work together over time and distance via electronic media to combine effort and achieve common goals.[57] Virtual teams are a product of evolving information technologies that allow people to connect from anywhere most anytime (e.g., via e-mail, texting, WebEx, Skype, GoToMeeting, Google Hangout, and many others). Traditional team meetings, for example, are location-specific. You and other team members are either (physically) present or absent. Members of virtual teams report in from different locations, different organizations, often different time zones and countries. In other words, the workforce is *distributed*. Distributed workers often have no permanent office at their companies, preferring to work in home offices, at cafés, at airports, in client conference rooms, at the beach, or at other places. Advocates say virtual teams are very flexible and efficient because they are driven by information and skills, not by time and location.[58] People with needed information and/or skills can be team members, regardless of where or when they actually do their work.[59] Today it seems that most people are connected to work remotely at least some of the time. Recent research indicates that 46 percent of all organizations use virtual teams, and 66 percent of multinational organizations use such teams.[60]

Best Uses for Virtual Teams   Virtual teams and distributed workers present many potential benefits: reduced real estate costs (limited or no office space); ability to leverage diverse knowledge, skills, and experience across geography and time (e.g., one doesn't have to have an SAP expert in every office); ability to share knowledge of diverse markets; and reduced commuting and travel expenses. The flexibility often afforded by virtual teams also can reduce work–life conflicts for employees, which some employers contend makes it easier for them to attract and retain talent.[61] The vast majority of organizations (72%) that use virtual teams indicate that brainstorming ideas or solutions to problems is the most successful task for such teams. Goal setting for team initiatives was a close second (68%) and developing plans to realize these goals was next (63%).[62]

Obstacles for Virtual Teams   Virtual teams have challenges, too. Compared to traditional face-to-face teams, it is more difficult to establish team cohesion, work satisfaction, trust, cooperative behavior, and commitment to team goals.[63] You'll notice that many of these are important elements in the Integrative Framework. So, virtual teams should be used with caution. It is no surprise that it is more difficult building team relations when members are distributed. About one-half of companies reported this challenge, followed closely by time zone differences (48%). When virtual teams cross country borders, then culture differences, holidays, and local laws and customs also can cause problems. Interpersonally, members of virtual teams reported the inability to observe nonverbal cues and a lack of collegiality.[64] Different time zones and the inability to observe nonverbals are challenges that apply to virtual teams more generally, not only those that cross national borders, as does the ability to lead such teams.[65] As you'll learn in Chapter 13, shared leadership produces better performance in virtual teams than does more common, hierarchical, command-and-control leadership.[66]

Effective Virtual Team Participation and Management   Research and practice provide a number of useful recommendations to help team members and teams as a whole to overcome the above challenges. Many "how to" articles exist on managing remote workers and virtual teams. We put together a collection of best practices to help focus your efforts and accelerate your success:[67]

1. **Adapt communications.** Learn how the various remote workers function, including their preferences for e-mail, texts, and phone calls. It often is advisable to have regularly scheduled calls (Skype or cell). Be strategic and talk to the right people, at the right times, about the right topics. Don't just blanket everybody via e-mail—focus the message. Accommodate the different time zones in a fair and consistent manner.

2. **Share the love.** Use your company's intranet or other technology to keep distributed workers in the loop. Acknowledging birthdays and recognizing accomplishments are especially important for those who are not in the office (regularly). Newsletters also can help and serve as a touch point and vehicle for communicating best practices and success stories.

3. **Develop productive relationships with key people on the team.** This may require extra attention, communication, and travel, but do what it takes. Key people are the ones you can lean on and the ones that will make or break the team assignment.

4. **Partner.** It is common that members of virtual teams are not direct employees of your employer (e.g., contractors). Nevertheless, your success and that of your team depend on them. *Treat them like true partners and not hired help.* You need them and presumably they need you.

5. **Availability.** Managers and remote workers all need to know when people can be reached, where, and how. Let people know and make yourself available.

6. **Pace.** Because of different time zones, some projects can receive attention around the clock, as they are handed off from one zone to the next. Doing this effectively requires that both senders and receivers clearly specify what they have completed and what they need in each transfer.

7. **Updates.** Even if you are not the boss, or your boss doesn't ask for them, be sure to provide regular updates on your progress to the necessary team members.[68]

8. **Select the right people.** "The best virtual workers tend to be those who thrive in interdependent work relationships . . . [and] are self-reliant and self-motivated. . . . Virtual work requires independent thought and willingness to take initiative. Those who tend to struggle in virtual team situations are people who wait for instructions and want to be told what to do."[69]

9. **Communication skills are essential.** Because so much communication happens with the written word, virtual team members must have excellent communication skills. They must be able to write well in easy-to-understand and to-the-point language. For this reason, "lone-wolfs" typically do not do well, despite preferring to work on their own, due to poor communication skills.

Face Time   Researchers and consultants are consistent about one aspect of virtual teams—*there is no substitute for face-to-face contact*. Members need to put faces to names and work. Meeting in person is especially beneficial early in virtual team development, and team leaders are encouraged to meet even more frequently with key members.[70] Face-to-face interactions can be as simple as lunch, water-cooler conversations, social events, or periodic meetings. Whatever the case, such interactions enable people to get familiar with each other and build credibility, trust, and understanding. This reduces misunderstandings and makes subsequent virtual interactions more efficient and effective, and it also increases job performance and reduces conflict and intentions to quit.[71]

The bottom line:

1. People bond when they see each other.

2. Virtual means you pay less attention (your brain treats video images of your team members on your computer screen like images on the TV).

One of the primary, but not the only, purposes of open work spaces is to increase the ability to collaborate with others. The rationale is simple, if office doors and walls aren't in the way, then people are more likely to interact.

3. Casual conversations have lasting benefits (unplanned conversations often spur new ideas and boost collaboration).[72]

Steve Jobs, when in charge at Pixar, was a big believer in face-to-face interactions. As a result, he was intimately involved in and spent great sums of money designing and building the company's office space. Instead of three buildings, he insisted on one and put the cafeteria and bathrooms right in the center. Doing these things meant every employee inevitably ran into others sometime, or even multiple times, during each workday.[73]

Furthermore, virtual teams cannot succeed without some additional and old-fashioned factors, such as effective decision making, communication, training, a clear mission and specific objectives, effective leadership, schedules, and deadlines.[74] Underlying many of these is one of the truly essential elements to effective teams of all types—trust!

8.4 TRUST BUILDING AND REPAIR—ESSENTIAL TOOLS FOR SUCCESS

major question

MAJOR QUESTION

How can I build and repair trust in ways that make me more effective at school, work, and home?

THE BIGGER PICTURE

Trust sometimes seems like a rare commodity in today's turbulent workplace. But you're about to see why it's so important at all levels of the Integrative Framework. You'll learn how OB considers trust as a collection of hard operational components, and not just a soft and vague ideal. With this understanding you'll be empowered to apply your knowledge to build trust and to repair it when damaged or diminished.

Trust **is a reciprocal belief that another person will consider how his or her intentions and behaviors will affect you.** The reciprocal (give and take) nature of trust means that when we feel or observe that others trust us, we are more likely to trust them. The converse also is true. That said, the importance of trust in organizational life cannot be overstated. Trust is the interpersonal lubricant for relationships within and between all organizational levels—individual, group, and organizational—and drives many important team-level outcomes found in the Integrative Framework (e.g., cooperation, communication, performance, and innovation). Yet, these have not been good times for trust in the corporate world. Recall our discussion of ethics and the successive waves of scandals in Chapter 1. These, along with years of mergers, layoffs, bloated executive bonuses, and widespread incivility (face-to-face and online) have left many of us cynical about trusting our manager, coworkers, employers, and politicians.

Public opinion polls show that "less than one-fifth of the general public believes business leaders and government officials will tell the truth when confronted with a difficult issue." The situation is even worse if you look at the differences between "business" and "business leaders." People surveyed reported a 32-point greater trust of business than for its leaders. Yikes! This led one corporate governance writer to claim: "The real crisis is one of leadership. About one-half of the global population trusts business to tell the truth while only 18% trust business leaders to do so."[75] Americans are especially harsh—15 percent trust business leaders to be truthful and only 10 percent expect political leaders to be truthful.

This is an extremely grim commentary, and as you learned in Chapters 2 and 4, your trust-related perceptions and attitudes are important determinants of your behavior.[76] Because trust is so important, we will explore ways in which to build trust and repair it when it is damaged. But let's first learn about different forms of trust.

Three Forms of Trust

For our purposes in OB, we discuss three particular forms of trust:

1. *Contractual trust.* Trust of character. Do people do what they say they are going to do? Do managers and employees make clear what they expect of one another?

2. *Communication trust.* Trust of disclosure. How well do people share information and tell the truth?

3. *Competence trust.* Trust of capability. How effectively do people meet or perform their responsibilities and acknowledge other people's skills and abilities?[77]

Answering these questions provides both a good assessment of trustworthiness and a guide for building trust.

TAKE-AWAY APPLICATION—TAAP

1. Describe a person with whom you have a high level of contractual trust, then a person with whom you have a low level. What are the implications for your relationship?

2. Think of an instance where you demonstrated communication trust by telling somebody something that was difficult, maybe even costly to you, but you did so to preserve communication trust. Now think of a time when somebody violated this type of trust with you. What were your reactions?

3. Describe an instance when competence trust was violated, by you or somebody else. What was the result? (Hint: Group assignments in school often provide examples.)

Building Trust

According to our definition of trust, we tend to give what we get: Trust begets trust; distrust begets distrust. Therefore, the practical application of this knowledge is to act in ways that demonstrate each of the aforementioned forms of trust. Doing so builds trust. Beyond this, you can benefit by practicing the following behaviors for building and maintaining trust:

Communication. Keep team members and employees informed by explaining policies and decisions and providing accurate feedback. Be candid about one's own problems and limitations. Tell the truth.[78]

Support. Be available and approachable. Provide help, advice, coaching, and support for team members' ideas.

Respect. Delegation, in the form of real decision-making authority, is the most important expression of managerial respect. Delegating meaningful responsibilities to somebody shows trust in him or her. Actively listening to the ideas of others is a close second.

Fairness. Be quick to give credit and recognition to those who deserve it. Make sure all performance appraisals and evaluations are objective and impartial.

Predictability. Be consistent and predictable in your daily affairs. Keep both expressed and implied promises.

Competence. Enhance your credibility by demonstrating good business sense, technical ability, and professionalism.[79]

If trust is reciprocal (give and take), then it would be helpful to know how trusting you are of others. Self-Assessment 8.4 can help you learn about different aspects of your interpersonal trust. Besides improving your self-awareness, knowledge of your interpersonal trust can also provide guidance in how to more effectively build trust with others—friends, classmates, coworkers, and bosses.

connect

SELF-ASSESSMENT 8.4   How Trusting Am I?

Go to connect.mheducation.com and complete Self-Assessment 8.4 to learn about the value you place on a variety of rewards offered at work. Then consider the following questions.

1. Which particular items in this trust questionnaire are most central to your idea of trust? Why?

2. Does your score accurately depict the degree to which you trust (or distrust) the target person?

3. Why do you trust (or distrust) this individual?

4. If you trust this person to a high degree, how hard was it to build that trust? Explain.

5. Given your inclination (score on the assessment) to trust others, describe three implications for your work in group assignments and project teams at school.

Repairing Trust

Just as trust can be built, it can be eroded. Violating, or even the perception of violating, another's trust can diminish trust and lead to *distrust*. As you know from personal experience, trust is violated in many different ways—sometimes unknowingly and other times seemingly purposefully. In either case, it is important to repair trust when it is damaged. Regardless of who is responsible for eroding or damaging trust, both parties need to be involved in the repair of trust. Figure 8.3 describes a popular approach to trust repair. Dennis and Michelle Reina studied thousands of instances of broken trust in business and developed seven steps for regaining trust. We illustrate their recommendations as a staircase with the first step at the bottom to show how individuals must work their way back up from distrust, one step at a time, to finally regain the trust that had been damaged. The seven-step process shown in Figure 8.3 can help, whether you are the perpetrator or victim.

We then conclude the chapter with a discussion of keys to team effectiveness.

FIGURE 8.3   REINA SEVEN-STEP MODEL FOR REBUILDING TRUST

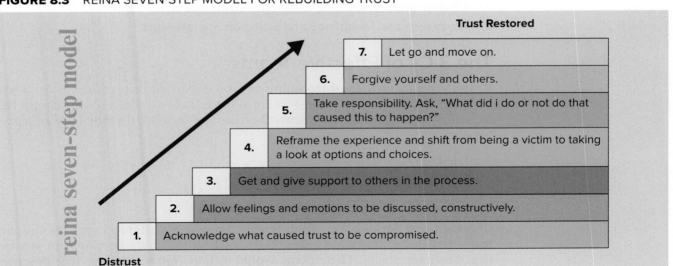

SOURCE: Adapted from D. Reina and M. Reina, *Rebuilding Trust in the Workplace: Seven Steps to Renew Confidence, Commitment, and Energy* (San Francisco, CA: Berrett-Koehler, 2010), 13. See also R. Hastings, "Broken Trust Is Bad for Business," *Society of Human Resource Management,* March 7, 2011.

major question

What are the keys to effective teams, and how can I apply this knowledge to give me an advantage?

THE BIGGER PICTURE

You will thrive in team settings when you better understand the characteristics of effective teams. You can use such characteristics as facilitators to function more successfully in group and team settings. You will also benefit from the practical suggestions, supported by research and practice, with which we conclude the chapter.

Characteristics of High-Performing Teams

A nationwide survey asked respondents, "What is a high-performance team?" Participants were also asked to describe their peak experiences in teams. The following eight attributes of high-performance teams emerged:

1. *Participative leadership.* Creating interdependency by empowering, freeing up, and serving others.
2. *Shared responsibility.* Establishing an environment in which all team members feel as responsible as the manager for the performance of the work unit.
3. *Aligned on purpose.* Having a sense of common purpose about why the team exists and the function it serves.
4. *High communication.* Creating a climate of trust and open, honest communication.
5. *Future focused.* Seeing change as an opportunity for growth.
6. *Focused on task.* Keeping meetings focused on results.
7. *Creative talents.* Applying individual talents and creativity.
8. *Rapid response.* Identifying and acting on opportunities.[80]

The 3 Cs of Effective Teams

Recent research provides three additional and important factors to consider when building effective teams. (These 3 Cs are at the team level, which contrasts with the 3 Cs of *effective team players* discussed earlier that focus on the individual or member level.)

Charters and strategies

Composition

Capacity

Charters and Strategies Both researchers and practitioners urge groups and teams to plan before tackling their tasks, early in the group development process (e.g., storming stage). These plans should include **team charters** that describe **how the team will operate, such as processes for sharing information and decision making (teamwork).** Team charters were discussed in the Winning at Work feature at the beginning of this chapter. Teams should also create and implement

major question

MAJOR QUESTION

How can I build and repair trust in ways that make me more effective at school, work, and home?

THE BIGGER PICTURE

Trust sometimes seems like a rare commodity in today's turbulent workplace. But you're about to see why it's so important at all levels of the Integrative Framework. You'll learn how OB considers trust as a collection of hard operational components, and not just a soft and vague ideal. With this understanding you'll be empowered to apply your knowledge to build trust and to repair it when damaged or diminished.

Trust is a reciprocal belief that another person will consider how his or her intentions and behaviors will affect you. The reciprocal (give and take) nature of trust means that when we feel or observe that others trust us, we are more likely to trust them. The converse also is true. That said, the importance of trust in organizational life cannot be overstated. Trust is the interpersonal lubricant for relationships within and between all organizational levels—individual, group, and organizational—and drives many important team-level outcomes found in the Integrative Framework (e.g., cooperation, communication, performance, and innovation). Yet, these have not been good times for trust in the corporate world. Recall our discussion of ethics and the successive waves of scandals in Chapter 1. These, along with years of mergers, layoffs, bloated executive bonuses, and widespread incivility (face-to-face and online) have left many of us cynical about trusting our manager, coworkers, employers, and politicians.

Public opinion polls show that "less than one-fifth of the general public believes business leaders and government officials will tell the truth when confronted with a difficult issue." The situation is even worse if you look at the differences between "business" and "business leaders." People surveyed reported a 32-point greater trust of business than for its leaders. Yikes! This led one corporate governance writer to claim: "The real crisis is one of leadership. About one-half of the global population trusts business to tell the truth while only 18% trust business leaders to do so."[75] Americans are especially harsh—15 percent trust business leaders to be truthful and only 10 percent expect political leaders to be truthful.

This is an extremely grim commentary, and as you learned in Chapters 2 and 4, your trust-related perceptions and attitudes are important determinants of your behavior.[76] Because trust is so important, we will explore ways in which to build trust and repair it when it is damaged. But let's first learn about different forms of trust.

Three Forms of Trust

For our purposes in OB, we discuss three particular forms of trust:

1. *Contractual trust.* Trust of character. Do people do what they say they are going to do? Do managers and employees make clear what they expect of one another?

2. *Communication trust.* Trust of disclosure. How well do people share information and tell the truth?

3. *Competence trust.* Trust of capability. How effectively do people meet or perform their responsibilities and acknowledge other people's skills and abilities?[77]

Answering these questions provides both a good assessment of trustworthiness and a guide for building trust.

TAKE-AWAY APPLICATION—TAAP

1. Describe a person with whom you have a high level of contractual trust, then a person with whom you have a low level. What are the implications for your relationship?

2. Think of an instance where you demonstrated communication trust by telling somebody something that was difficult, maybe even costly to you, but you did so to preserve communication trust. Now think of a time when somebody violated this type of trust with you. What were your reactions?

3. Describe an instance when competence trust was violated, by you or somebody else. What was the result? (Hint: Group assignments in school often provide examples.)

Building Trust

According to our definition of trust, we tend to give what we get: Trust begets trust; distrust begets distrust. Therefore, the practical application of this knowledge is to act in ways that demonstrate each of the aforementioned forms of trust. Doing so builds trust. Beyond this, you can benefit by practicing the following behaviors for building and maintaining trust:

Communication. Keep team members and employees informed by explaining policies and decisions and providing accurate feedback. Be candid about one's own problems and limitations. Tell the truth.[78]

Support. Be available and approachable. Provide help, advice, coaching, and support for team members' ideas.

Respect. Delegation, in the form of real decision-making authority, is the most important expression of managerial respect. Delegating meaningful responsibilities to somebody shows trust in him or her. Actively listening to the ideas of others is a close second.

Fairness. Be quick to give credit and recognition to those who deserve it. Make sure all performance appraisals and evaluations are objective and impartial.

Predictability. Be consistent and predictable in your daily affairs. Keep both expressed and implied promises.

Competence. Enhance your credibility by demonstrating good business sense, technical ability, and professionalism.[79]

If trust is reciprocal (give and take), then it would be helpful to know how trusting you are of others. Self-Assessment 8.4 can help you learn about different aspects of your interpersonal trust. Besides improving your self-awareness, knowledge of your interpersonal trust can also provide guidance in how to more effectively build trust with others—friends, classmates, coworkers, and bosses.

Design firm IDEO supports web entrepreneurs in launching and growing sustainable global businesses, and part of their job is to educate clients on the importance of building a diverse team. Here's a quick peak at their website, www.openideo.com.

team performance strategies, which are deliberate plans that outline what exactly the team is to do, such as goal setting and defining particular member roles, tasks, and responsibilities.[81]

Composition *Team composition* is a term that describes the collection of jobs, personalities, knowledge, skills, abilities, and experience of team members. Defined in this way it is no surprise that team composition can and does affect team performance. It is important that team member characteristics fit the responsibilities of the team for the team to be effective. *Fit* facilitates team effectiveness and *misfit* impedes it—you need the right people on your team. Recent research shows that in the early stages of team development (i.e., forming and storming) teams perform better when members have a high tolerance for uncertainty (a personality trait). This same finding applies to self-managed and virtual teams, due to the relative lack of direction and face-to-face communication.[82] Recall also our discussion of the Big Five personality characteristics in Chapter 3. Team research shows that teams with members who possess high levels of openness or emotional stability deal with task conflict better than those without these composition characteristics.[83] The bottom line: Create teams with the composition to match the desired objectives. Knowledge of OB and the Integrative Framework, in particular, can be very helpful in this regard.

Capacity Research shows that *team adaptive capacity* (i.e., adaptability) is important to meet changing demands and to effectively transition members in and out. It is fostered by individuals who are motivated both to achieve an accurate view of the world (versus an ethnocentric or self-centered view) and to work effectively with others to achieve outcomes.[84]

Rewards, Competition, and Collaboration

Of course rewards matter, and they are a common cause for suboptimal team performance. Microsoft, for instance, used to force rank individual employees as "top performers, good, average, below average, and poor regardless of the team's overall performance. . . . This stacked ranking created a culture in which employees competed with one another rather than against other companies."[85] Separating teams into A, B, and C players does just that—it divides and separates the team. In contrast, Whole Foods Market uses teams extensively throughout the organization. And consistent with this, most incentives are team versus individual based.[86] If a team's department or store reduces costs and/or boosts revenues, then the team earns a share of the benefits. Organizations that foster the greatest collaboration and most effective teams typically use hybrid rewards and recognize both individual and team performance. Doing this appropriately motivates at both the individual and team levels, and it also positively influences many important outcomes across levels in the Integrative Framework.

EXAMPLE Exemplary Teamwork at NASA

National Aeronautics and Space Administration (NASA) is an organization that epitomizes teamwork. The organization "has been at the forefront in structuring and facilitating multi-team teams to provide dynamic flight control since the first NASA flight." Notably, three different global sites have controlled the International Space Station (ISS) by rotating responsibilities 24 hours a day, 365 days a year, for 11 years! Effective coordination and collaboration occur almost seamlessly, even as team members come and go and responsibilities repeatedly cross international borders from one site to another. NASA overcomes common challenges faced by many teams today.

DYNAMIC COMPOSITION   The members of the various teams continually change. Astronauts (and cosmonauts), for example, routinely change as their time on board the ISS is limited. But imagine the amount of time and resources required to continually prepare new members of the ISS. Technical, physical, and cultural training requirements are immense. It then is essential that they effectively execute their respective responsibilities when onboard. More generally, the ISS was built and is maintained by five space agencies representing 23 countries!

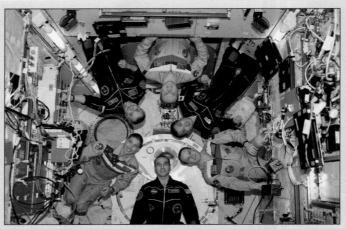

Here crew members of Expedition 30 pose for an in-flight crew portrait in the European Space Agency's Automated Transfer Vehicle *Edoardo Amaldi* (ATV-3), currently docked with the International Space Station.

TECHNOLOGY AND DISTANCE   Communication is critical and an ever-present challenge. Ground control not only needs to communicate with the ISS, but also must communicate with each other. It's not as simple as making a cell phone call or Skyping. Distance is an obvious obstacle. NASA must overcome the "us" versus "them" dynamic between the flight crew and mission control. Language differences, at both misson control and in the ISS, and isolation also are problematic. Astronauts often are aboard for months at a time, and the confined spaces and lack of communication with family and friends are incredibly stressful. Thankfully, new technology enables the flight crew to communicate more frequently and privately with others on the ground.

THE ULTIMATE TELECOMMUTERS   "Astronauts and cosmonauts can be viewed as the original [and the most extreme] telecommuters!" Most if not all of the challenges discussed in this chapter are experienced by those involved in the ISS—both on the ground and in space.[87]

YOUR THOUGHTS?

Imagine that you're a member and leader of the ISS flight crew.

1. What team challenges do you think would be most enjoyable for you?
2. What team challenges do you think would be most problematic for you?
3. What would you be inclined to do to assure the team works effectively (and safely)?

Effective Team Size

Researchers generally find that teams range between 2 and 25 team members. Effective teams, however, typically have fewer than 10 members. This conclusion was echoed in a survey of 400 workplace team members in the United States and Canada: "The [mean] average North American team consists of 10 members. Eight is the most common size [the mode]."[88]

These findings are consistent with more recent recommendations by a world-renowned expert on teams, who suggests limiting teams to nine or fewer people. Coordinating any more becomes too difficult, if not counterproductive.[89] In a practical sense, we all are well advised not to fixate on any particular team size. Team size instead should be determined by the requirements of the task at hand—recall our discussion of a contingency approach to management in Chapter 1. "As projects get larger in size, [they] may also . . . need to add personnel. Similarly, as the task is complex and uncertain, team members with diverse skill sets and knowledge bases must be included in the team to address task complexity, and the team must collaborate closely to integrate this knowledge."[90]

what did i learn?

You learned that working with others can increase everybody's performance because groups and teams can, and often do, accomplish more than individuals. You learned that roles and norms are the building blocks of team behavior. You learned about the group development process, the characteristics of effective team players, team building, and how different forms of teams are ways to realize the benefits of groups and teams. You learned you can boost your personal effectiveness further still by understanding trust and how to repair it. And you learned the value of particular means for building team effectiveness. Reinforce your learning with the Key Points below and consolidate it using the Integrative Framework. Challenge your mastery of the material by answering the Major Questions in your own words.

Key Points for Understanding Chapter 8

You learned the following key points:

8.1 GROUP CHARACTERISTICS

- Groups are two or more individuals who share norms, goals, and identity.
- Both formal and informal groups are important.
- Roles are expected behaviors for a particular job or position, and group roles set expectations for members of a group.
- Norms are shared attitudes, opinions, feelings, or actions that help govern the behaviors of groups and their members.

8.2 THE GROUP DEVELOPMENT PROCESS

- Groups often evolve or develop along five defined steps: forming, storming, norming, performing, and adjourning.
- Knowledge of these steps can help you understand group dynamics and be more effective in groups and teams.

8.3 TEAMS AND THE POWER OF COMMON PURPOSE

- Teams differ from groups in terms of leadership, accountability, purpose, problem solving, and effectiveness.
- Teams are groups in the performing stage.

- Team players are committed, collaborative, and competent.
- Common contemporary forms of teams are self-managed, cross-functional, and virtual.

8.4 TRUST BUILDING AND REPAIR—ESSENTIAL TOOLS FOR SUCCESS

- Trust is a reciprocal belief that another person will consider how their intentions and behaviors will affect you.
- Three common forms of trust are contractual, communication, and competence.
- Repairing trust can be accomplished using a seven-step process and is critical to your short- and long-term success.

8.5 KEYS TO TEAM EFFECTIVENESS

- High-performing teams have several characteristics, such as participative leadership, aligned purpose, future focused, and creativity.
- Charters and strategies, composition, and capacity are the 3 Cs of effective teams.
- Reward, competition, and collaboration are all means for fostering team effectiveness.

The Integrative Framework for Chapter 8

As shown in Figure 8.4, you learned how the process of group/team dynamics leads to a large number of outcomes at all three levels in the Integrative Framework.

Challenge: Major Questions for Chapter 8

At the start of the chapter, we told you that after reading the chapter you should be able to answer the following questions. Unless you can, have you really processed and internalized the lessons in the chapter? Refer to the Key Points, Figure 8.4, the chapter itself, and your notes to revisit and answer the following major questions:

1. How can knowledge of groups and teams and their key characteristics make me more successful?
2. How can understanding the group development process make me more effective at school and work?
3. What are the characteristics of effective team players and team building, and how does this knowledge improve my performance in various types of teams?
4. How can I build and repair trust in ways that make me more effective at school, work, and home?
5. What are the keys to effective teams, and how can I apply this knowledge to give me an advantage?

FIGURE 8.4 INTEGRATIVE FRAMEWORK FOR UNDERSTANDING AND APPLYING OB

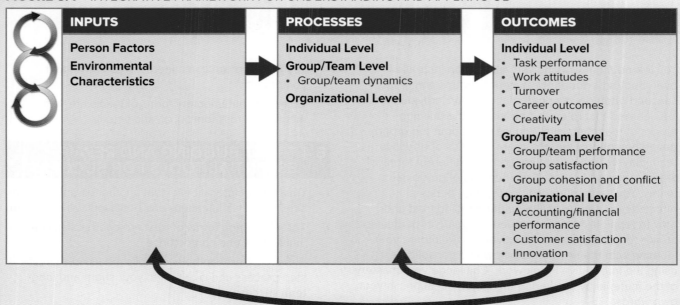

© 2014 Angelo Kinicki and Mel Fugate. All rights reserved. Reproduction prohibited without permission of the authors.

Group Forms to Amp Up Research

Major drug companies and nonprofit research groups would never put aside fierce competition and conflicting agendas just to crack some of the world's most challenging diseases, would they?

Except they did.

In early 2014, the National Institutes of Health (NIH) announced the creation of the Accelerating Medicines Partnership (AMP) to target some of the most challenging diseases. And to accelerate potential cures, they all agreed to share "scientists, tissue and blood samples, and data, in a five-year collaborative effort."[91]

Competition through Cooperation

This deal, put together by the NIH, creates wins for all participants. "By pooling their brightest minds and best lab discoveries," *The Wall Street Journal* reports, "they hope to put together a research system that can decipher the diseases in ways each hasn't been able to on its own."[92] The *Journal* notes that the costs to the participants are much lower than they would be when working on their own. In fact, the total budget for the partnership is $213 million, split roughly between the NIH at $118.9 million and industry at $110.6 million. These amounts are dramatically lower than the $350 million average cost for the discovery and development of a single drug. Beyond reducing the financial costs, this collaboration also spreads the risk, as 95% of experimental medicines fail to be both effective and safe.[93]

Not Just Cost Savings

The NIH identifies benefits beyond cutting research costs: shorter development time, improved prospects for success, and increased range of therapies. "Understanding the biological pathways underlying disease and the specific biological targets that can alter disease will lead to more rational drug design and better tailored therapies,"[94] the NIH says. The agency predicts that the projects will enable more robust clinical trials and reduce the number of failures in Phase II and Phase III clinical trials.

Early Stage and Open Source

One reason why the coalition works is because the competitors are collaborating on the earliest stage of the research. The NIH says that the project shouldn't face antitrust concerns because it consists of early research and will make all results freely available to the public.

Three Projects

Scientists from the NIH and its industry partners selected three focal diseases:

- Alzheimer's disease.
- Type 2 diabetes.
- The auto-immune diseases of rheumatoid arthritis and lupus.

Egos at the Door?

The project is unique. "We are getting together in a way that has not happened before," Dr. Francis S. Collins, director of the National Institutes of Health, told *The New York Times*. "We are bringing scientists from different perspectives into the same room. They will leave their egos at the door, leave their affiliations at the door."[95]

The *Times* reports that such a collaboration would have been impossible five years ago, quoting Dr. Mikael Dolsten, president of worldwide research and development at Pfizer. "It was a different time," Dr. Dolsten said. "Companies had the view that going alone would be sufficient."[96]

Who's Who

Industry participants include household names. The ten commercial partners are AbbVie, Biogen Idec, Bristol-Myers Squibb, GlaxoSmithKline, Johnson & Johnson, Lilly, Merck, Pfizer, Sanofi, and Takeda. Nonprofit partners are the Alzheimer's Association, the American Diabetes Association, the Arthritis Foundation, the Lupus Foundation of America, the Lupus Research Institute/Alliance for Lupus Research, the Foundation for the NIH, the Geoffrey Beene Foundation, PhRMA, the Rheumatology Research Foundation, and USAgainstAlzheimer's.[97]

Apply the 3-Stop Problem-Solving Approach to OB

Referring to Figure 8.4 and your notes, apply the knowledge of OB presented in this chapter to the above case. Applying this knowledge should enable you to recommend realistic and effective solutions.

Stop 1: What is the problem?

- Identify the outcomes that are important in this case.
- Which of these outcomes are not being achieved in the case?
- Based on considering the above two questions, what is the most important problem in this case?

Stop 2: Use the material in this chapter to help you understand the problem in this case.

- What person factors are most relevant?
- What environmental characteristics are most important to consider?
- Do you need to consider any processes? Which ones?
- What concepts or tools discussed in this chapter are most relevant for solving the key problem in this case?

Stop 3: What are your recommendations for solving the problem?

- Review the material in the chapter that most pertains to your proposed solution and look for practical recommendations.
- Use any past OB knowledge or experience to generate recommendations.
- Outline your plan for solving the problem in this case.

LEGAL/ETHICAL CHALLENGE

When an "A" Is Not an "A"—Who's Responsible?

It is well known that the Wall St. Meltdown and Great Recession were intimately tied to the mortgage market. At the heart of this was the pursuit of greater and greater returns. Financial institutions of all sorts (e.g., mortgage lenders, banks, investment banks, and insurance companies) got increasingly "creative" with their mortgage-related products and qualifications. This creativity enabled financial institutions to sell more homes, more mortgages, more mortgage-backed securities, and more insurance than they could otherwise. This also enabled millions of Americans to purchase homes that they otherwise could not qualify for or afford. Then the bubble popped! Home values dropped, credit dried up, returns fell, and so on. Millions of homeowners were forced to foreclose or were underwater (i.e., obligated to pay more than market value). Countless, mostly smaller, financial institutions went out of business while many of the largest were acquired or bailed out.

One important character in this story is missing, however: ratings agencies! S&P, Moody's, and Fitch are the three biggest in the United States. They assign grades much like school—As, Bs, and Cs—to the securities created by pooling many mortgages into packages (e.g., bonds and other mortgage-backed securities). These grades were (and still are) fundamentally important to the entire market, as they determined to whom and at what terms these securities were sold. For example, many institutions (e.g., pension funds) can only purchase A-graded securities. It also is important to note that the agencies were and are paid for their "grading services" by the firms whose products they grade. Citigroup, for instance, pooled many mortgages it bought into packages (e.g., bonds). They then took these bonds to S&P to be graded, grades for which they paid. (A-rated bonds have more buyers than Bs, which have more than Cs.) It is no surprise

then that those financial institutions shopped around for higher grades.

As it is now well known, the agencies' grades were often inaccurate. Like a professor assigning grades to papers without looking at them, they assigned As to many securities that weren't worthy. If this wasn't problem enough, under current law, the agencies are not legally responsible for their ratings or grades. (It's like randomly assigning As to everybody in the class with no consequences to the professor.) The agencies have long contended that their conclusions are simply "opinions" and are protected by the First Amendment.[98] While pending legislation intends to hold agencies accountable and liable, as it stands today they are not responsible for the grades they assign.

What Should Be Done about the Ratings Agencies?

1. Ratings agencies should be liable for their ratings. If financial institutions that create and sell fraudulent securities (e.g., those they expect to fail) can be prosecuted, then so too should the agencies that rated them as secure and sellable (e.g., an A rating).

2. Ratings agencies cannot be expected to fully understand the increasingly complex financial products presented to them. It is unreasonable for them to be held accountable.

3. Neither #1 nor #2 matters. The entire situation would take care of itself if the financial institutions were not the ones paying agencies for their ratings. An alternative payment arrangement would remedy the situation.

4. Invent another alternative and explain.

A Committee Decision—The Johnny Rocco Case

Objectives

1. To give you firsthand experience with work group dynamics through a role-playing exercise.
2. To develop your ability to evaluate group effectiveness.

Introduction

Please read the following case before going on:

Johnny has a grim personal background. He is the third child in a family of seven. He has not seen his father for several years, and his recollection is that his father used to come home drunk and beat up every member of the family. Everyone ran when his father came staggering home.

His mother, according to Johnny, wasn't much better. She was irritable and unhappy, and she always predicted that Johnny would come to no good end. Yet she worked when her health allowed her to do so in order to keep the family in food and clothing. She always decried the fact that she was not able to be the kind of mother she would like to be.

Johnny quit school in the seventh grade. He had great difficulty conforming to the school routine—he misbehaved often, was truant frequently, and fought with schoolmates. On several occasions he was picked up by the police and, along with members of his group, questioned during several investigations into cases of both petty and grand larceny. The police regarded him as "probably a bad one."

The juvenile officer of the court saw in Johnny some good qualities that no one else seemed to sense. Mr. O'Brien took it on himself to act as a "big brother" to Johnny. He had several long conversations with Johnny, during which he managed to penetrate to some degree Johnny's defensive shell. He represented to Johnny the first semblance of personal interest in his life. Through Mr. O'Brien's efforts, Johnny returned to school and obtained a high school diploma. Afterwards, Mr. O'Brien helped him obtain a job.

Now 20, Johnny is a stockroom clerk in one of the laboratories where you are employed. On the whole Johnny's performance has been acceptable, but there have been glaring exceptions. One involved a clear act of insubordination on a fairly unimportant matter. In another, Johnny was accused, on circumstantial grounds, of destroying some expensive equipment. Though the investigation is still open, it now appears the destruction was accidental.

Johnny's supervisor wants to keep him on for at least a trial period, but he wants "outside" advice as to the best way of helping Johnny grow into greater responsibility. Of course, much depends on how Johnny behaves in the next few months. Naturally, his supervisor must follow personnel policies that are accepted in the company as a whole. It is important to note that Johnny is not an attractive young man. He is rather weak, and sickly, and he shows unmistakable signs of long years of social deprivation.

A committee is formed to decide the fate of Johnny Rocco. The chairperson of the meeting is Johnny's supervisor and should begin by assigning roles to the group members. These roles [shop steward (representing the union), head of production, Johnny's coworker, director of personnel, and social worker who helped Johnny in the past] represent points of view the chairperson believes should be included in this meeting. (Johnny is not to be included.) Two observers should also be assigned. Thus, each group will have eight members.

Instructions

After roles have been assigned, each role player should complete the personal preference part of the worksheet, ranking from 1 to 11 the alternatives according to their appropriateness from the vantage point of his or her role.

Once the individual preferences have been determined, the chairperson should call the meeting to order. The following rules govern the meeting: (1) The group must reach a consensus ranking of the alternatives; (2) the group cannot use a statistical aggregation, or majority vote, decision-making process; (3) members should stay "in character" throughout the discussion. Treat this as a committee meeting consisting of members with different backgrounds, orientation, and interests who share a problem.

After the group has completed the assignment, the observers should conduct a discussion of the group process, using the Group Effectiveness Questions here as a guide. Group members should not look at these questions until after the group task has been completed.

Group Effectiveness Questions

A. Referring to Table 8.2 in this chapter, what task roles were performed? By whom?
B. What maintenance roles were performed? By whom?
C. Were any important task or maintenance roles ignored? Which?
D. Was there any evidence of social loafing? Explain.

Questions for Class Discussion

1. Did your committee do a good job? Explain.
2. What, if anything, should have been done differently?
3. How much similarity in rankings is there among the different groups in your class? What group dynamics apparently were responsible for any variations in rankings?

Worksheet

PERSONAL PREFERENCE	GROUP DISCUSSION	
_____	_____	Warn Johnny that at the next sign of trouble he will be fired.
_____	_____	Do nothing, as it is unclear if Johnny did anything wrong.
_____	_____	Create strict controls (dos and don'ts) for Johnny with immediate strong punishment for any misbehavior.
_____	_____	Give Johnny a great deal of warmth and personal attention and affection (overlooking his present behavior) so he can learn to depend on others.
_____	_____	Fire him. It's not worth the time and effort spent for such a low-level position.
_____	_____	Talk over the problem with Johnny in an understanding way so he can learn to ask others for help in solving his problems.
_____	_____	Give Johnny a well-structured schedule of daily activities with immediate and unpleasant consequences for not adhering to the schedule.
_____	_____	Do nothing now, but watch him carefully and provide immediate punishment for any future behavior.
_____	_____	Treat Johnny the same as everyone else, but provide an orderly routine so he can learn to stand on his own two feet.
_____	_____	Call Johnny in and logically discuss the problem with him and ask what you can do to help him.
_____	_____	Do nothing now, but watch him so you can reward him the next time he does something good.

9 COMMUNICATION IN THE DIGITAL AGE

How Can I Become a More Effective Communicator?

inputs

PERSON FACTORS

ENVIRONMENTAL CHARACTERISTICS

processes

INDIVIDUAL LEVEL
Communication

GROUP/TEAM LEVEL
Communication

ORGANIZATIONAL LEVEL
Communication

outcomes

INDIVIDUAL LEVEL

GROUP/TEAM LEVEL

ORGANIZATIONAL LEVEL

© 2014 Angelo Kinicki and Mel Fugate. All rights reserved. Reproduction prohibited without permission of the authors.

MAJOR TOPICS I'LL LEARN AND QUESTIONS I SHOULD BE ABLE TO ANSWER

9.1 BASIC DIMENSIONS OF THE COMMUNICATION PROCESS

MAJOR QUESTION: *How can knowledge about the basic communication process help me communicate more effectively?*

9.2 COMMUNICATION COMPETENCE

MAJOR QUESTION: *What are the key aspects of interpersonal communication that can help me improve my communication competence?*

9.3 GENDER, GENERATIONS, AND COMMUNICATION

MAJOR QUESTION: *Do I need to alter how I communicate based on the gender and age of my audience?*

9.4 SOCIAL MEDIA AND OB

MAJOR QUESTION: *How can social media increase my effectiveness at work and in my career?*

9.5 COMMUNICATION SKILLS TO BOOST YOUR EFFECTIVENESS

MAJOR QUESTION: *How can I increase my effectiveness using skills related to presenting, crucial conversations, and managing up?*

INTEGRATIVE FRAMEWORK FOR UNDERSTANDING AND APPLYING OB

Communication represents a key process variable that is important at the individual, group/team, and organizational levels. Because of its impact at all three levels, you will learn that communication affects a host of outcomes across the same three levels. Be attentive to the outcomes associated with communication processes as you read this chapter.

winning at work

COMMUNICATION COUNTS IN LANDING A JOB

As a job seeker, it is your responsibility to prove that you're the best candidate for the job. Effective communication skills enable you to sell yourself and to calm your nerves. Performing well during an interview depends on both what you say and how you say it!

WHAT YOU SAY

• *Direct the conversation.* Many people simply wait to be asked questions. Small talk can get things started, but whatever you choose be sure it is short and noncontroversial.

• *Pick your selling points.* Identify and focus on your top two or three selling points. If you have little experience, then perhaps focus on personal qualities. If you have experience, then highlight significant achievements.

• *Substantiate.* Provide evidence (such as stories and/or data) to illustrate your selling points.

• *What's in it for them?* Ask not what the job will do for you, but what you can do on the job. Explain why you're a good match and what you bring to the party.

• *Don't forget to do your homework.* Be sure to thoroughly research the company, using the Web and other resources. Look for information relevant to past, current, and future company events and initiatives. Use this knowledge when talking or asking questions about the company.

• *Anticipate challenging questions.* Know that you will be asked, "What are your weaknesses?" The key here is to identify a challenge briefly, then discuss how you solved the problem.

HOW YOU SAY IT

• *Show them that you'll "bring it."* Express your enthusiasm and willingness to do anything, not just the most interesting stuff.

• *Smile.* It's one of the easiest ways to win people over.

• *Take your time.* Nerves often make us rush through an answer—just to get it over with. Slow yourself down and speak in a normal conversational tone.

• *Eye contact.* Don't stare in the other person's eyes, but don't stare at the floor or out the window either.

• *Dress how they dress.* Regardless of your own style or wardrobe, your choices need to match what is common at the company. The rule: "anything that distracts, detracts."

• *Close with a handshake.* End the interview with a "thank you" and a firm handshake.

• *Follow-up.* At the end of the interview ask when the interviewer would like you to follow up. Then drop your interviewer a note of thanks.

FIGHTING NERVES

• Prepare
• Breathe
• Pause before answering
• Never say you're nervous
• Use positive self-talk and visualization[1]

FOR YOU   WHAT'S AHEAD IN THIS CHAPTER

We're about to give you practical guidance on how to communicate effectively. Communication is a critically important process at all levels of OB—individual, group, and organizational—and in most arenas of your life. We'll guide you through important elements at each level, beginning with how individuals process information. We'll also highlight the characteristics of competent communicators and show you how to more successfully communicate within and between generations and genders. We'll conclude with the most practical tips of all: the dos and don'ts of social media in your professional life, which effective presentation and conversational skills to develop, and how to manage up.

BASIC DIMENSIONS OF THE COMMUNICATION PROCESS

major question

MAJOR QUESTION

How can knowledge about the basic communication process help me communicate more effectively?

THE BIGGER PICTURE

You probably already understand the logic of how communication is a critical process at all three levels in OB as shown in the Integrative Framework. But you'll get more benefit out of your understanding from the model of the communication process that follows. You'll be able to analyze communication in a more detailed and practical fashion. One useful tool is a model of the communication process that includes a sender, message, and receiver; encoding and decoding; a medium; feedback; and dealing with "noise" or interference. You also will learn that it is important to match your choice of communication medium to the situation at hand.

Have you had misunderstandings with others that involve written or oral communication? Has a professor ever given you instructions or expectations that were unclear? Did this affect your performance? Or has it ever happened that someone e-mailed you and you responded with an over-the-top response? Was the outcome positive? Probably not.

These examples illustrate the challenges in effectively communicating in today's 24/7 digitally connected world. They also underscore how important it is to understand the underlying communication process and the dynamics of communicating as technology continues to evolve.

The study of communication is fundamentally important because every managerial function and activity involves some form of direct or indirect communication. This explains why communication is a critical "process" at all three levels in the Integrative Framework. Whether planning and organizing or directing and leading, managers find themselves communicating with and through others. This implies that everyone's communication skills affect both personal and organizational effectiveness.[2] For example, a study of medical errors by the Agency for Healthcare Research and Quality for the US Senate revealed that communications problems were the most common cause of death due to preventable errors.[3] The seriousness of this finding is accentuated by the fact that preventable medical errors are the *third* leading cause of death among Americans.[4]

Defining Communication

Communication **is defined as "the exchange of information between a sender and a receiver, and the inference (perception) of meaning between the individuals involved."**[5] This definition highlights that communication is a process that takes place between two or more people. It's a very important process for managers because they tend to spend the majority of their time sending, receiving, and interpreting messages.

The fact that managers spend a great deal of time communicating does not mean that they are necessarily good at it. A study of 2,115 executives by the American Management Association, for example, showed that "more than half (51.4%) . . .

said their employees were only average in effective communications skills (versus 38.1% who rated them above average)."[6]

This study emphasizes the importance of understanding the communication process.

How the Communication Process Works

As we all know, communicating is not that simple or clear-cut. Communication is fraught with miscommunication. Researchers recognize this and have begun to examine communication as a form of social information processing (recall the discussion in Chapter 4) in which receivers interpret messages by cognitively processing information. This view led to development of a perceptual model of communication that depicts communication as a process in which receivers create meaning in their own minds. Let us consider the parts of the process and then integrate them with an example.

Sender, Message, and Receiver The sender is the person wanting to communicate information—the message. The receiver is the person, group, or organization for whom the message is intended.

Encoding Communication begins when a sender encodes an idea or thought. Encoding entails translating thoughts into a code or language that can be understood by others. This forms the foundation of the message. For example, if a professor wants to communicate to you about an assignment, he or she must first think about what information he or she wants to communicate. Once the professor resolves this issue in his or her mind (encoding), he or she can select a medium with which to communicate.

Selecting a Medium Managers can communicate through a variety of media. Potential media include face-to-face conversations and meetings, telephone calls, charts and graphs, and the many digital forms (e.g., e-mail, texting, voice mail, videoconferencing, Twitter, Facebook, Blackboard, etc.). Choosing the appropriate media depends on many factors, including the nature of the message, its intended purpose, the type of audience, proximity to the audience, time horizon for disseminating the message, and personal preferences.

All media have advantages and disadvantages. Face-to-face conversations, for example, are useful for communicating about sensitive or important issues that require feedback and intensive interaction.[7] In contrast, telephones are convenient, fast, and private but lack nonverbal information. Although writing memos or letters

FIGURE 9.1 COMMUNICATION PROCESS IN ACTION

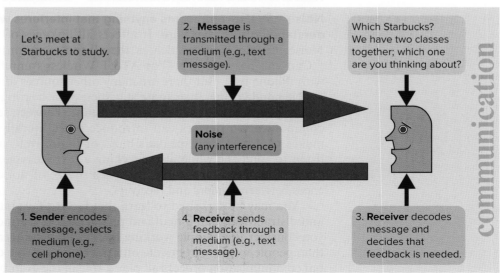

Trying to communicate via cell phone while sitting in a café is likely to be affected by noise and the quality of your connection. The person's cell phone conversation can also represent noise to someone at the next table.

is time consuming, it is a good medium when it is difficult to meet with the other person, when formality and a written record are important, and when face-to-face interaction is not necessary to enhance understanding. We have more to say in the next section about choosing media.

Decoding and Creating Meaning   Decoding occurs when receivers receive a message. It is the process of interpreting and making sense of a message. Returning to our example of a professor communicating about an assignment, decoding would occur among students when they receive the message from the professor.

The perceptual model of communication is based on the belief that a receiver creates the meaning of a message in his or her mind. This means that the same message can be interpreted differently by different people. Consider the following example that occurred to a reporter from *The Wall Street Journal* when he was on assignment in China.

I was riding the elevator a few weeks ago with a Chinese colleague here in the *Journal*'s Asian headquarters. I smiled and said, "Hi." She responded, "You've gained weight." I might have been appalled, but at least three other Chinese co-workers also have told me I'm fat. I probably should cut back on the pork dumplings. In China, such an intimate observation from a colleague isn't necessarily an insult. It's probably just friendliness.[8]

This example highlights that decoding and creating the meaning of a message are influenced by cultural norms and values. Cross-cultural communication is discussed later in this chapter.

Feedback   Have you ever been on your cell phone and thought that you lost your connection with the person you were talking to? If yes, something like the following probably occurred. "Hello, Donna are you there?" "Donna, can you hear me?" The other person may say back, "Yes, I can hear you, but your voice is cutting in and out." This is an example of feedback—the receiver expresses a reaction to the sender's message.

Noise   *Noise* **represents anything that interferes with the transmission and understanding of a message.** It affects all linkages of the communication process. Noise includes factors such as the all-too-common unreliable or slow networks ("Can you hear me now?" or AT&T Wireless's unreliable connections associated with iPhone use). But there are many other sources of noise: speech impairment, illegible handwriting, inaccurate statistics, poor hearing and eyesight, environmental noises, people talking, and physical distance between sender and receiver. Our many communication devices can introduce noise literally, as when your smartphone makes your desktop's speakers buzz, or figuratively, as when a person is trying to listen to someone while also checking a text message. Nonverbal communication, discussed later in this chapter, also is a source of noise, as are cross-cultural differences between senders and receivers.

You may be surprised to learn that face-to-face interruptions create more noise and distractions than e-mail and phone calls. This finding is more important when you consider that people working in cubicles get interrupted 29 percent more often than people working in private offices.[9] Noise and the other elements of the sequential communication process all play a role in the example in Figure 9.1

Selecting the Right Medium

You have all kinds of communication media to choose from when you want to communicate with others, ranging from face-to-face conversations to the use of mass media. That said, your communication effectiveness is partly based on using the medium that is most appropriate for the situation at hand. The same is true for managers. Consider how Fred Hassan, former chairman of the board and CEO of pharmaceutical company Schering-Plough, used multiple methods of communicating with his employees while he initiated a major change in the company's sales culture (see Problem-Solving Application box).

solving application

problem

Using Multiple Communication Media to Implement Organizational Change

When Fred Hassan joined Schering-Plough, the company's revenue was declining and it was burning through cash. The US sales organization was not meeting its sales targets and employees were frustrated. Some of the company's sales and marketing practices were also being investigated by US attorneys for possible violation.

What Did Mr. Hassan Do? He believed that the company needed a new sales culture. He proposed that "instead of focusing, as usual, on high-pressure tactics to maximize short-term results, our sales reps needed to become more professional, more focused on building deep, long-lasting customer relationships." Mr. Hassan wanted customers to view sales reps as trusted consultants rather than

salespeople. He concluded that "a wholesale change in the mind-set of our sales reps and their attitudes about their role" was needed.

The change effort required the support and buy-in of the 400 district sales managers who supervised Schering-Plough's 4,000 US sales reps. During his first two years on the job, Mr. Hassan decided to work closely in one-on-one meetings with the district managers. He did this because he wanted to discuss his new vision, get their support, and coach them on the new behaviors he wanted them to model for sales reps. He then held an annual meeting of the entire sales force explaining his vision, the new corporate values, and a new strategy based on "business integrity" and "putting customers first."

After the meeting, he made it a practice to regularly meet one-on-one with the district managers "to discuss the specific challenges each was facing with his or her reps and to ask how I might help." He then created a handbook used in a companywide frontline management training program. He also participated in small group meetings with employees to discuss the change initiatives.

What Happened over Time? Under Mr. Hassan's leadership, sales grew from $9 billion to $20 billion and the company "increased the number of late-stage drugs in the firm's portfolio from five to 12, and upped blockbusters from zero to five, making the company one of the top growth companies among its peers."[10]

YOUR CALL

Stop 1: What is the problem that Mr. Hassan faced upon joining the company?

Stop 2: What OB theories or concepts can explain Mr. Hassan's approach toward organizational change?

Stop 3: What is your evaluation of Mr. Hassan's approach to communication? Would you recommend anything?

Media Richness

Media richness involves the capacity of a given communication medium to convey information and promote understanding.[11] Alternative media can vary from rich to lean. The richer a medium, the better it is at conveying information.

Jeff Zucker, the current President of CNN Worldwide and the former CEO of NBC Universal, understands the power of a handwritten note.

Four Factors of Media Richness

1. **Feedback** (ranging from fast to very slow).
2. **Channel** (ranging from the combined visual and audio characteristics of a videoconference to the limited visual aspects of a computer report).
3. **Type** of communication (ranging from personal to impersonal).
4. **Language source** (ranging from the natural body language and speech involved in a face-to-face conversation to the numbers contained in a financial statement).

A two-way face-to-face conversation is the richest form of communication. It provides immediate feedback and allows for the observation of multiple cues such as body language and tone of voice. You might find it interesting to note that face-to-face meetings dominate a CEO's day "because such personal interactions are critical to learning the information necessary to run a company effectively."[12] In contrast, telephone conversations and videoconferencing are not as informative as face-to-face exchanges even though they are relatively high in richness. At the other end of the scale, newsletters, computer reports, and general e-mail blasts are lean media because feedback is very slow, the channels involve only limited visual information, and the information provided is generic or impersonal. E-mail and social media messages vary in media richness: leaner if they impersonally blanket a large audience and richer if they mix personal textual and video information that prompts quick conversational feedback.[13] Another case altogether is a handwritten note!

EXAMPLE   NBC Universal President Jeff Zucker put handwritten invitations in the rooms of the 1,600 attendees of the Association of National Advertisers annual meeting in 2010. Recipients of the invitations said that the handwritten nature of NBC's Zucker stood out from other events.[14]

Zucker could have easily used e-mail or Twitter to convey his message, but he went to the richer form of handwritten notes because he wanted to create a more personal impression with his audience.[15]

TAKE-AWAY APPLICATION—TAAP   Analyzing a Miscommunication

In your recent past, think of a situation in which you had a key miscommunication with an individual or group. Now answer the following questions:

1. Based on the process model of communication shown in Figure 9.1, what went wrong?
2. Based on what has been presented so far on various communication media, did you choose the most appropriate medium? Explain.
3. Based on your answers to the above two questions, what would you do differently?

9.2 COMMUNICATION COMPETENCE

major question

MAJOR QUESTION

What are the key aspects of interpersonal communication that can help me improve my communication competence?

THE BIGGER PICTURE

You probably have a good sense of how well you communicate, and you might even rate yourself on a 10-point scale. OB gives you a term for this: communication competence. It reflects your ability to effectively communicate with others. You'll be happy to learn you can improve this skill, which is crucial because it ties to career progression and the quality of your interpersonal relationships. So look in this section for how various communication styles or skills affect your communication competence.

Although there is no universally accepted definition of **communication competence,** it is a performance-based index of an individual's abilities to effectively use communication behaviors in a given context.[16]

Are you curious about your level of communication competence? Is it low, medium, or high? Find out by completing the following Self-Assessment. If your score is lower than you prefer, find ideas in the chapter for improving your interpersonal communication skills.

---

connect

SELF-ASSESSMENT 9.1   Assessing My Communication Competence

This scale measures your communication competence. Go to connect.mheducation.com and take Self-Assessment 9.1. Then answer the following questions.

1. Are you happy with the results?
2. What are your top three strengths and your three biggest weaknesses—use the items' scores to determine strengths and weaknesses.
3. How might you use your strengths more effectively in your role as a student?
4. How might you improve on your weaknesses?

Let's consider three communication skills that affect your communication competence in a big way:

- Nonverbal communication
- Active listening
- Nondefensive communication

Sources of Nonverbal Communication

Nonverbal communication is "[a]ny message sent or received independent of the written or spoken word. . . . [I]t includes such factors as use of time and space, distance between persons when conversing, use of color, dress, walking behavior, standing, positioning, seating arrangement, office locations and furnishings."[17]

Experts estimate that 65 to 95 percent of every conversation is interpreted through nonverbal communication.[18] It thus is important to ensure that your nonverbal signals are consistent with your intended verbal messages. Because of the prevalence of nonverbal communication and its significant effect on organizational behavior—including, but not limited to, perceptions of others, hiring decisions, work attitudes, turnover, and the acceptance of one's ideas in a presentation—it is important that managers become consciously aware of the sources of nonverbal communication. For instance, a recent study found that 81 percent of job-interview candidates lied, and experts believe that liars have nonverbal "tells."[19] Can you guess what they are?

Carol Kinsey Goman, author of the book *The Truth About Lies in the Workplace: How to Spot Liars and What to Do About Them,* suggested some possible clues. "Body language that might indicate deception includes touching an eyebrow or squeezing the bridge of the nose while closing the eyes. Or, a liar may show nervousness through increased foot movement." She also says that people display verbal cues about lying. They include "unnecessary elaboration to a story, changing a subject or offering qualifiers such as 'to the best of my knowledge.'"[20]

Let's consider four key sources of nonverbal messages:

- Body movements and gestures
- Touch
- Facial expressions
- Eye contact

Body Movements and Gestures   Body movements (e.g., leaning forward or backward) and gestures (e.g., pointing) provide additional nonverbal information that can either enhance or detract from the communication process. Open body positions, such as leaning backward or gesturing with palms facing up, communicate *immediacy,* a term used to represent openness, warmth, closeness, and availability for communication. *Defensiveness* is communicated by gestures such as folding arms, crossing hands, and crossing one's legs. It is important to recognize defensiveness in ourselves and others because we tend to stop listening when we become defensive.[21] Nondefensive communication is discussed later in this section.

Although it is both easy and fun to interpret body movements and gestures, it is important to remember that body-language analysis is subjective, easily misinterpreted, and highly dependent on the context and cross-cultural differences.[22] Thus, managers need to be careful when trying to interpret body movements. Inaccurate interpretations can create additional "noise" in the communication process.

Touch   Touching is another powerful nonverbal cue. People tend to touch those they like. A meta-analysis of gender differences in touching indicated that women do more touching during conversations than men.[23] Touching conveys an impression of warmth and caring and can be used to create a personal bond between people. Hugs, for example, have replaced the handshake according to some. Nearly 50 percent of respondents to a Greenlight Community survey said they routinely hug at work instead of shaking hands.[24] Be careful about touching people from diverse cultures, however, as norms for touching vary significantly around the world.

Facial Expressions   Facial expressions convey a wealth of information. Smiling, for instance, typically represents warmth, happiness, or friendship, whereas frowning conveys dissatisfaction or anger. Do you think these interpretations apply to different cultural groups? A summary of relevant research revealed that the association between facial expressions and emotions varies across cultures.[25] A smile, for example, does not convey the same emotion in different countries. One study showed that people from the United States and Japan were able to accurately associate facial

Bill Gates, first as the founder and CEO of Microsoft and now as an active philanthropist, has had to communicate and persuade many people in many places. He undoubtedly understands that his message and effectiveness depend on more than just his words.

TABLE 9.1 ADVICE TO IMPROVE NONVERBAL COMMUNICATION SKILLS

Positive nonverbal actions include the following:
- Maintaining eye contact.
- Nodding your head to convey that you are listening or that you agree.
- Smiling and showing interest.
- Leaning forward to show the speaker you are interested.
- Using a tone of voice that matches your message.

Negative nonverbal behaviors include the following:
- Avoiding eye contact and looking away from the speaker.
- Closing your eyes or tensing your facial muscles.
- Excessive yawning.
- Using body language that conveys indecisiveness or lack of confidence (e.g., slumped shoulders, head down, flat tones, inaudible voice).
- Speaking too fast or too slow.

nonverbal skills

expressions with personality traits for politicians from both countries. They also were able to predict electoral success of these same candidates, but only for those from their own cultures.[26] Therefore, managers need to be careful when interpreting facial expressions among diverse groups of employees.

Eye Contact Eye contact is a strong nonverbal cue that varies across cultures. Westerners are taught at an early age to look at their parents when spoken to. In contrast, Asians are taught to avoid eye contact with a parent or superior in order to show obedience and subservience.[27] Once again, managers should be sensitive to different orientations toward maintaining eye contact with diverse employees.

Practical Tips It is important to have good nonverbal communication skills in light of the fact that they are related to the development of positive interpersonal relationships. Table 9.1 offers insights into improving your nonverbal communication skills.

As children we all were instructed to listen. However, many adults, particularly managers and leaders, are never instructed to listen and seemingly don't. To communicate and perform better, we'd all benefit from listening more effectively.

Active Listening

Listening involves much more than hearing a message. Hearing is merely the physical component of listening. **Listening is the process of *actively* decoding and interpreting verbal messages.** Listening requires cognitive attention and information processing; hearing does not. There is general consensus that listening is a cornerstone skill of communication competence.

In support of this conclusion, listening effectiveness is positively associated with customer satisfaction and negatively associated with employee intentions to quit. Tom Folliard, CEO of CarMax, recognizes this conclusion and makes an effort to communicate with employees (see the Example box). In contrast, poor communication between employees and management was cited as a primary cause of employee discontent and turnover.[28] Moreover, John Beeson, an executive coach and succession planning consultant, noted that weak interpersonal communication skills, including listening, are major reasons managers are passed over for promotions to executive positions.[29]

EXAMPLE   The CEO of CarMax Proactively Listens to Employees

CarMax is the largest used-car retailer in the United States. The company has 110 locations and about 12,000 employees.[30] Current CEO Tom Folliard believes that he can improve profitability and customer satisfaction by listening to employees.

THE COMPANY LOWERS COSTS BY LISTENING TO AN EMPLOYEE   A few years ago an employee suggested that the company should siphon gas from wholesale cars it purchased. Mr. Folliard listened to the idea and CarMax now draws thousands of gallons of gas from wholesale cars and then transfers it to the tanks of its retail cars. This one idea has saved the company over a half a million dollars. The original idea came from a town hall meeting that Folliard was hosting with employees from one of the company's retail stores.

CEO FOLLIARD TRAVELS TO LISTEN TO EMPLOYEES   Folliard visited about 70 stores in 2012. He "hosted grand openings, town halls, and steak cookouts for offices that met monthly sales goals (he does the grilling). He and his team use the visits to connect with associates, answer questions, and solicit feedback from the field." Andy Garzia, a purchasing officer in Houston, said that management is trying "to get to know us on a personal level and to hear our perspective."[31]

YOUR THOUGHTS?

Why would employees be more motivated when their managers or senior executives listen to them?

Unfortunately, many of us think we are good listeners when evidence suggests just the opposite. For example, researchers estimate that typical listeners only retain 20 to 50 percent of what they hear.[32]

Why do you think we miss or lose so much of what we hear? One reason is that we have the cognitive capacity to process words at a much higher rate than people speak. This means that our cognitive processes are being underutilized, leading to daydreaming and distractions. Noise is another reason. A third reason, and one that you can control, relates to your motivation to listen and your listening style. It takes effort to actively listen. You won't be a better listener unless you are motivated to do so.

What's Your Listening Style—or Styles?   You can improve your communication competence by understanding your typical listening style. There are four styles:[33]

1. **Active—I'm fully invested.** Active listeners are "all in." That is, they are motivated to listen and give full attention when others are talking. They focus on what is being communicated and expend energy participating in the discussion. They also use body language such as leaning in or direct eye contact to convey interest.

2. **Involved—I'm partially invested.** Involved listeners devote some, but not all, of their attention and energy to listening. They reflect on what is being said and partially participate in the discussion. Their use of nonverbal cues also tends to be inconsistent or intermittent. Involved listeners can show nonverbal signs of interest and noninterest in the same conversation.

3. **Passive—It's not my responsibility to listen.** Passive listeners are not equal partners in a speaking-listening exchange. They assume that the speaker is responsible for the quality of the interaction and their role is to passively take in information. Passive listeners will display attentiveness, but it can be faked at times. Overall, they don't expend much motivation or energy into receiving and decoding messages.

4. **Detached—I'm uninterested.** Detached listeners tend to withdraw from the interaction. They appear inattentive, bored, distracted, and uninterested. They may start using mobile devices during the speaking-listening exchange. Body language will reflect lack of interest, such as slumping and avoiding direct eye contact.

Which of the four styles do you tend to use? Do you consistently use one or two styles, or does your style vary from one situation to the next. You can answer these questions by taking the following Self-Assessment.

Mc Graw Hill Education connect®

SELF-ASSESSMENT 9.2 Assessing My Listening Style

Go to connect.mheducation.com and complete Self-Assessment 9.2 to measure your listening style. Then answer the following questions:

1. Based on your results, how would you classify your style?
2. Are you surprised by the results?
3. Identify three things you can do to improve your listening skills.

Becoming a More Effective Listener   Effective listening is a learned skill that requires effort and motivation. It basically comes down to *paying attention to the content of the message.* The suggestions in Table 9.2 can be used to increase your listening skills. They can be practiced at school, home, and work.

TABLE 9.2   TIPS FOR EFFECTIVE LISTENING

TIP	EXPLANATION
Show respect.	Give everyone the opportunity to explain his/her ideas without interrupting. Actively try to help the sender convey his/her message.
Listen from the first sentence.	Turn off your internal thoughts and whatever you were thinking about prior to the interaction.
Be mindful.	Stay in the moment and focus on the sender. Don't try to figure out what the speaker is going to say.
Keep quiet.	You have two ears and one mouth; use them accordingly. Try to use the 80/20 rule. Your conversation partner should speak 80 percent of the time and you should speak 20 percent.
Ask questions.	Asking questions clarifies what is being said and demonstrates that you are listening.
Paraphrase and summarize.	Paraphrasing amounts to repeating back to someone what you just heard him/her say. Summarizing is used to integrate or consolidate an entire conversation. Both of these techniques enhance communication accuracy because they help to ensure the messages are being understood correctly.
Remember what was said.	Either take notes or make an effort to log critical information into your mental computer.
Involve your body.	Use nonverbal cues to demonstrate interest and involvement.

SOURCE: Based on J. Keyser, "Active Listening Leads to Business Success," *T+D,* July 2013, 26–28; and B. Brooks, "The Power of Active Listening," *The American Salesman,* December 2010, 28–30.

Nondefensive Communication

Have you ever been in an auto accident? If yes, then you likely have intimate knowledge of defensiveness. In situations like this, one party often tries to blame the other while both defend themselves. Which of the toward defensiveness styles in Table 9.3 are likely to occur in such situations?

Defensiveness occurs when people perceive that they are being attacked or threatened. This perception in turn leads to defensive listening and destructive behaviors such as shutting down or being passive-aggressive, standing behind rules or policies, creating a diversion, or counterattacking. In turn, defensiveness from one person results in a defensive chain that activates defensiveness in the other party. All told, defensiveness from either party in an exchange fosters inaccurate and inefficient communication.[34]

You may be surprised to learn that defensiveness often is started by the poor choice of words we use and/or the nonverbal posture used during interactions. In the language of behavior modification, the inappropriate choice of words and body language serve as *antecedents* of defensiveness. For example, using absolutes like "always" or "never" is very likely to create a defensive response. You should try to avoid using absolutes because they are rarely true. You can increase your communication competence by avoiding the defensive antecedents and employing the positive antecedents of nondefensive communication shown in Table 9.3.

TAKE-AWAY APPLICATION—TAAP

1. Think of an interaction you had with someone that resulted in defensiveness from either the sender or receiver.
2. Referring to Tables 9.2 and 9.3, where were the potential causes of the defensive communication pattern?
3. Again referring to Tables 9.2 and 9.3, identify three things you could have done differently to facilitate nondefensive communication.

TABLE 9.3 ANTECEDENTS OF DEFENSIVE AND NONDEFENSIVE COMMUNICATION

TOWARD DEFENSIVENESS		TOWARD NONDEFENSIVENESS	
STYLE	**EXAMPLE**	**STYLE**	**EXAMPLE**
Evaluative	"Your work is sloppy."	**Descriptive**	"Your work was two days late."
Controlling	"You need to . . ."	**Problem solving**	*Mutually trying to find solutions to problems.*
Strategizing	*Concealing your true intentions.*	**Straightforward**	*Don't hide your intentions or agenda.*
Neutral	*Acting detached or showing no interest.*	**Empathetic**	*Convey understanding of the person's feelings about the issue.*
Superior	*Conveying that you are smarter or more experienced.*	**Equal**	*Have two-way problem-solving discussions.*
Certain	*Conveying that you know all the answers.*	**Honest and open**	*Use I-messages:* "I am angry about the way you spoke to the customer because our department looked unresponsive."

SOURCE: Based on J. R. Gibb, "Defensive Communication," *Journal of Communication*, 1961, 141–148; and "Reach Out: Effective Communication," *Sunday Business Post*, April 14, 2013.

9.3 GENDER, GENERATIONS, AND COMMUNICATION

MAJOR QUESTION

Do I need to alter how I communicate based on the gender and age of my audience?

THE BIGGER PICTURE

Would you agree that women and men have communicated differently since the dawn of time? Some stereotypes about gender lead to coarse jokes but don't improve understanding. But social scientists have specific insights into gender differences in communication that go beyond stereotype. As you learned in Chapter 4, the same holds true for people from different generations, who also have different values and expectations about how best to communicate. You can improve your communication competence by understanding and accommodating communication differences among men and women and various generations.

Differences in communication between men, women, and generations are partly caused by the array of linguistic styles people use. Deborah Tannen, a communication expert, defines *linguistic style* as follows:

> **Linguistic style** refers to a person's characteristic speaking pattern. It includes such features as directness or indirectness, pacing and pausing, word choice, and the use of such elements as jokes, figures of speech, stories, questions, and apologies. In other words, linguistic style is a set of culturally learned signals by which we not only communicate what we mean but also interpret others' meaning and evaluate one another as people.[35]

Linguistic style not only helps explain communication differences between women and men and across generations, but also has been used to more efficiently deal with the customer complaints made via e-mail. Coding and adding linguistic style information to the text (words themselves) enabled companies to more effectively address customer concerns and achieve satisfaction via an automated complaint management system.[36] These results suggest that linguistic styles matter both in person and over the Internet. Therefore, increased awareness of linguistic styles can improve communication accuracy and communication competence.

This section strives to increase your understanding of interpersonal communication between women and men and across generations. To do this, we discuss alternative explanations for differences in linguistic styles, various communication differences between groups (e.g., genders and generational), and recommendations for improving communication between them.

Communication Differences between Women and Men

Although researchers do not completely agree on the cause of communication differences between women and men, there are two competing explanations that involve the well-worn debate between *nature* and *nurture*. Some researchers believe that interpersonal differences between women and men are due to inherited biological differences between the sexes. This perspective, which also is called the "evolutionary psychology" or "Darwinian perspective," attributes gender differences in communication to drives, needs, and conflicts associated with reproductive strategies used by women and men.

The Male Perspective   Males are expected to communicate more aggressively, interrupt others more than women, and hide their emotions because they have an inherent desire to possess features attractive to females. Men also see conversations as negotiations in which people try to achieve and maintain the upper hand. It thus is important for males to protect themselves from others' attempts to put them down or push them around. This perspective increases a male's need to maintain independence and avoid failure.[37] Although males are certainly not competing for mate selection during a business meeting, evolutionary psychologists propose that men cannot turn off the biologically based determinants of their behavior.[38]

The Female Perspective   According to "social role theory," females and males learn ways of speaking while growing up. Research shows that girls learn conversational skills and habits that focus on rapport and relationships, whereas boys learn skills and habits that focus on status and hierarchies. Accordingly, women come to view communication as a network of connections in which conversations are negotiations for closeness. This orientation leads women to seek and give confirmation and support more so than men.

What Does Research Reveal?   Research demonstrates that women and men communicate differently in a number of ways.[39] Women are more likely to share credit for success, to ask questions for clarification, to tactfully give feedback by mitigating criticism with praise, and to indirectly tell others what to do. A study found that management teams with a higher proportion of women monitored feedback and employee development more closely. The same teams also tended to promote more interpersonal communication and employee involvement in decision making.[40] In contrast, men are more likely to boast about themselves, to bluntly give feedback, and to withhold compliments, and are less likely to ask questions and to admit fault or weaknesses.

Generational Differences in Communication

As discussed in Chapter 4, today's workplace often involves people from four different generations—traditionalists, baby boomers, Gen Xers, and Millennials (Gen Ys). (Refer to Table 4.1 for additional details and characteristics.) Among the challenges in this scenario is the fact that Millennials are the largest cohort in the workforce, and they are most likely to be managed by boomers. A consultant on the issue described the scenario this way: "Gen Y workers might have excellent technology skills but many need to improve their business writing and interpersonal communication skills."[41] Whether or not you agree with this statement, or see it simply as another stereotype, it is true that Millennials "don't remember a world without computers, and in many cases they have honed their communication skills via e-mails, instant messages, and text messages rather than by talking on the phone or in person, or by writing letters, memos, and reports."[42] Many, but certainly not all, Gen Xers were introduced to communication technologies at work, and their careers have paralleled the evolution of communication technologies and practices. The opposite assumption can be made for traditionalists. Some people in this generation either resist technology altogether if their employers allow them to or do only what is necessary.[43]

Expectations and *norms* about communication represent the key issues when considering communication across generations. For example, traditionalists and boomers are more likely to regard texting and surfing during a meeting as inappropriate as compared to Millennials. Younger employees also are more likely to use the Internet and social media to accomplish their tasks. Patty Baxter, publisher at Metro Guide

Publishing in Halifax, Nova Scotia, has firsthand knowledge about this communication pattern.

Patty learned that advertising sales were down because her staff, all under the age of 35, were e-mailing sales pitches rather than calling potential clients on the phone. She noted, "e-mail won't cut it in professions like sales, where personal rapport matters. You're not selling if you're just asking a question and getting an answer back."[44] Patty wanted her employees to start calling prospective clients. Not everyone agrees, however, with Ms. Baxter. Stephanie Shih, 27, a marketing manager at Paperless Post in New York, concluded that phones are "outdated." Kevin Castle, 32-year-old chief technology officer at Technossus in Irvine, California, stated that "unplanned calls are such an annoyance that he usually unplugs his desk phone and stashes it in a cabinet. Calling someone without e-mailing first can make it seem as though you're prioritizing your needs over theirs."[45]

Improving Communications between the Sexes and Generations

It is important to remember not to generalize any trends, preferences, or perceptions to all men, women, or members of a particular generation. Some men, for instance, are less likely to boast about their achievements while some women are less likely to share the credit. Some traditionalists embrace technology and "younger" communication practices, while not all members of Gen Y are technological whizzes. The point is that there are always exceptions to the rule. Additional helpful suggestions were offered by trainer Dana Brownlee in an interview with *Forbes:*

- **Match degree of formality with the culture.** Old-school formality and new-school informality can cause culture clashes. Older generations often feel younger people cross the line, writing e-mails to clients and coworkers as if they are texting or not taking the time to check grammar and spelling. It is wise for all employees to be aware of the cultural norms and follow those—formal or otherwise—as that is what coworkers and clients have come to expect.

- **Use a variety of communication tools.** Regardless of your preferred mode of communication (e.g., face-to-face or texting), it is important that employees from all generations use a variety. This avoids alienating any particular generation.

- **Avoid stereotypes.** Don't assume based on somebody's age that he or she only likes one mode or dislikes another. Learn people's preferences and try to be accommodating. A good place to start is to share your own preferences with others.

- **Be aware of different values and motives.** Older workers often believe that younger workers are needy or high maintenance, while younger workers sometimes feel as if they are cut out of the loop or unappreciated. Both are part of the solution. Leaders need to realize how important that acknowledgment is, but the younger generations need to realize they're not going to get an IV drip of praise.

- **Be willing to learn and teach.** Every generation has something give to and take from the others.[46]

We conclude with the following advice for managers: Utilize the similarities between genders and between generations, before trying to understand or deal with differences. Doing so is not only practical, but it also is consistent with current trends in positive organizational behavior.

The final section of this chapter also offers some generic suggestions for increasing your communication effectiveness that can be used when communicating with men, women, and people from any generation.

MAJOR QUESTION

How can social media increase my effectiveness at work and in my career?

THE BIGGER PICTURE

You won't be surprised that employees use social media for personal purposes at work. They have from the start. Now employers are getting into the action, and are still getting it wrong. You're about to learn how to leverage the advantages and avoid the pitfalls of social media, at any level of the organization. You'll expand your understanding of how to use social media (especially e-mail) productively, how to handle privacy issues, and how to navigate or even improve social media policies.

As you know, *social media* uses web-based and mobile technologies to generate interactive dialogue with members of a network. Social media is now woven throughout the fabric of our lives, and because it affects so many subjects covered in this book, it highlights the importance of communication as an OB topic. And despite the stereotypes for the Millennial generation's love of technology and connectivity (Chapter 4), accurate or not, social media is used by a significant proportion of people across all age groups (see Figure 9.2). Consider the following utilization rates of social media across different age groups:[47]

Age	Percent Using Social Media
• 13–18	81
• 19–29	89
• 30–49	78
• 50–64	60
• 65+	43

These statistics suggest that employers and managers are wise to utilize social media tools with employees across all generations. A human resource expert put it this way:

> Used correctly, social media can benefit an organization. However, if not managed effectively, it can create many legal, financial and personnel risks. Given the potential risks and benefits of social media in the workplace, it is critical for managers to develop policies and procedures governing its appropriate use.[48]

The same applies to you and other employees. It is important to realize the benefits and avoid the pitfalls. To do this, let's begin our discussion with what experts and researchers say about the effects of social media on productivity.

Social Media and Increased Productivity

A fundamental driving force behind technology (of all forms) at work, including social media, is to boost productivity. The key for employees, managers, and employers is to harness the potential and enhance performance at the individual, group, and organizational levels. The following quote clearly articulates this argument:

> [W]ork is becoming a place to collaborate, exchange ideas, and communicate with colleagues and customers. Your value as an employee will be determined not only by how well you perform your job but also by how much you contribute your knowledge and ideas back to the organization. The ways in which companies develop this culture of collaboration will become a significant competitive factor in attracting and engaging top talent in the twenty-first century.[49]

Social media is clearly a tool that can help both you and your employers realize these productivity benefits.

Employee Productivity   Evidence is mounting that shows a host of benefits for employees, such as

- Increased job satisfaction and better work–life balance.[50]
- Performance and retention.[51]
- More creativity and collaboration.[52]

Interestingly, two studies involving thousands of employees even showed that those who used five or more social networking sites had higher sales numbers than those that used only one to four.[53] This implies that more is better for salespeople! While you should be careful about drawing conclusions from these findings, they are nonetheless interesting. Furthermore, if you think that employees' opinions matter, then you'll find it useful that a study by Microsoft revealed that 46 percent of employees across generations and industries felt that social media tools would make them more productive at work.

To make sense of this claim, consider that many workers "waste an average of 74 minutes per day trying to contact partners or customers and 67 minutes per day trying to find business information."[54] This scenario is worse still if you consider that other studies show that many high-skilled knowledge workers spend approximately 28 percent of their workweek on e-mail and 20 percent sifting through information to find what is needed or useful. "But, when companies use social media internally, messages become content; a searchable record of knowledge can reduce, by as much as 35 percent, the time employees spend searching for company information. . . . Just think what you could do with 35 percent more time in a week!"[55] It also is important to consider that many of the benefits for employees also translate into benefits for their employers.

Employer Productivity   It is clear that companies of all sizes and industries believe in the benefits of social media. Procter and Gamble, for instance, now devotes more than a third of its US marketing budget to digital media. "Company executives say digital media in many cases is proving to be a faster and cheaper way for P&G's brands to reach consumers, and feedback is also faster."[56] If deployed effectively, social media enables businesses to

- **Connect in real time and over distances with many key stakeholders.** Stakeholders include employees, customers (past, current, and future), communities, suppliers, prospective talent, former employees (sources of future talent), and many others.
- **Connect sources of knowledge across the organization, offices, and time zones.** Linking knowledge in these ways is a means to realizing the potential of employee diversity (covered in Chapter 4) and enhancing productivity. Social media is by definition a way of connecting people virtually, so its effective implementation will likely benefit virtual teamwork (Chapter 8).

- **Expand and open the traditional boundaries to involve outsiders in problem solving.** Social networks can become the "circulatory system" for organizational innovation and effectiveness (Chapter 15). The Example box describes how a couple of well-known companies now use social media to innovate and solve problems using crowdsourcing. ***Crowdsourcing* occurs when companies invite nonemployees to contribute to particular goals and manage the process via the Internet.**

EXAMPLE Expanding Organizational Boundaries with Crowdsourcing

A particularly interesting and important aspect of social media at work is its ability to redefine conventional organizational boundaries and structure.

- GE's Ecomagination Challenge, for instance, asked people outside of the company for ideas to create the next-generation smart power grid.
- Lego used crowdsourcing to design new products. Lego reviews proposed designs three times a year and people receive 1 percent of their toy's net revenue if their design is selected.[57]
- PepsiCo has a similar ongoing program that solicits advertising ideas from outside the company. The winner receives $1 million. One of these programs generated more than 5,600 entries for their 2013 Super Bowl spot.[58]

PepsiCo crowdsourced its 2013 Pepsi "countdown" ad with 400 images and photos, all user-supplied content.

Connections with people inside and outside the organization greatly expand a company's human and social capital (Chapter 1). A more subtle yet more common example of crowdsourcing is seeking recommendations for a restaurant, a new car, or a professor on sites such as Yelp, Facebook, Twitter, or RateMyProfessor.

YOUR THOUGHTS?

1. Describe at least two ways you crowdsource and the sites you use.
2. Now, think of a service that you use and that you also believe would benefit from crowdsourcing. To clarify, this does not simply mean soliciting your opinions or satisfaction. Crowdsourcing instead is the practice of involving stakeholders (e.g., customers or even competitors) in solving problems.

Costs of Social Media

Many managers believe that social media at work is a distraction and erodes productivity. Consider fantasy football:

- The U.S. Bureau of Labor Statistics estimates that employers should expect to lose approximately one hour of work per week for each employee who plays fantasy football.
- Roughly 23 million people had fantasy football teams for the 2013–2014 season.
- Use the average pay rate of $23.98 per hour for nonfarm workers.
- The loss equates to $551 million per week in the US economy.
- There are 15 weeks in the season, which means the total estimated cost of lost productivity is $8 billion![59]

This is just fantasy football. To make this more real for you, assume you own a business and know that many of your employees play in a fantasy leagues. Does this change your attitude about access to and use of social media at work? What would you do?

Another and often overlooked cost of social media, and mobile connectivity more generally, is *multitasking*. The Winning at Work feature at the beginning of Chapter 11 offers some extremely provocative and helpful findings about this topic. You may even want to skip ahead and give that a quick read now. That will be a perfect setup for the pros and cons of e-mail, discussed next, which is not only one of the most useful communication tools but also one of the main causes or temptations of multitasking.

Make E-mail Your Friend, Not Your Foe

We give particular attention to e-mail in this section because it is so important, and as the statistics above show, it can be a major consumer of your time and enemy of your productivity. In our many years of teaching and consulting with employees across organizational levels and industries, we continually hear that e-mail is an ever-present challenge and often an enormous time drain. To be clear, most acknowledge that e-mail is essential. But handling e-mail effectively can make it your friend instead of your foe. See Table 9.4 for the benefits, drawbacks, and some tips on managing e-mail.

TABLE 9.4   E-MAIL: BENEFITS, DRAWBACKS, AND SUGGESTIONS FOR MANAGING IT

Benefits

- **Reduced costs of distributing information.** E-mail allows information to be sent electronically, thereby reducing the costs of sending information to employees and customers.
- **Increased teamwork.** Users can send messages to colleagues anywhere in the world and receive immediate feedback.
- **Reduced paper costs.** An expert estimates these savings at $9,000 per employee.
- **Increased flexibility.** Employees can access e-mail from anywhere.

Drawbacks

- **Wasted time and effort.** E-mail can distract people from completing their work responsibilities.
- **Information overload.** The average corporate employee receives 171 messages a day, and 10–40% of these messages are unimportant.
- **Increased costs to organize, store, and monitor.** Systems are needed to protect privacy. The Federal Rules of Civil Procedure require organizations to keep tabs on e-mail and produce them in case of litigation.
- **Neglect of other media.** People unsuccessfully attempt to solve complex problems with e-mail. E-mail reduces the amount of face-to-face communication.

Managing E-Mail

- **Do not assume e-mail is confidential.** Employers are increasingly monitoring all e-mail. Assume your messages can be read by anyone.
- **Be professional and courteous.** Recommendations include delete trailing messages, don't send chain letters and jokes, don't type in all caps—it's equivalent to shouting, don't respond immediately to a nasty e-mail, refrain from using colored text and background, don't expose your contact list to strangers, and be patient about receiving replies.
- **Avoid sloppiness.** Use a spell checker or reread the message before sending.
- **Don't use e-mail for volatile or complex issues.** Use a medium that is appropriate for the situation at hand.
- **Keep messages brief and clear.** Use accurate subject headings and let the reader know what you want right up front.
- **Save people time.** Type "no reply necessary" in the subject line or at the top of your message if appropriate.
- **Be careful with attachments.** Large attachments can crash someone's system and use up valuable time downloading. Send only what is necessary, and get permission to send multiple attachments.

SOURCE: C. Graham, "In-Box Overload," *The Arizona Republic,* March 16, 2007, A14; M. Totty, "Rethinking the Inbox," *The Wall Street Journal,* March 26, 2007, R8; A. Smith, "Federal Rules Define Duty to Preserve Work E-Mails," *HR Magazine,* January 2007, 27, 36; M. Totty, "Letter of the Law," *The Wall Street Journal,* March 26, 2007, R10; and "The Top 10 E-Mail Courtesy Suggestions," *Coachville Coach Training,* March 22, 2000, http://topten.org.content/tt.BN122.htm.

Social Media Concerns and Remedies— What Companies Can Do

Related to productivity, it is true that *some* employees waste time at work. This has been and always will be true. But when it comes to social media, approximately 20 percent of employers block access to social media sites at work to help combat such waste and loss of productivity (see Figure 9.2).[60] However, the evidence is growing that restricting or completely blocking the use of social media by employees at the office can backfire.

Be Careful about Blocking Access Banning access can damage employee morale and loyalty—potentially leading to even greater losses in productivity.[61] Some experts argue, and most employees would agree, that small breaks during the workday help boost productivity. Such breaks can take the form of going outside to get a breath of fresh air, talking with a colleague over a cup of coffee, or checking personal e-mail or Facebook, or checking/sending Tweets.[62]

If these "re-energizing" benefits of social (media) breaks are not convincing enough for you or your employer, then consider other potential and undesirable implications of blocking policies:

- *Could alienate (younger) employees.* Young, old, or in between, many people are accustomed to being plugged into social sites throughout the day. Blocking their access therefore can be off-putting to employees. Moreover, organizations

FIGURE 9.2 PERCENTAGE OF US EMPLOYEES WHO HAVE VARIOUS SOCIAL MEDIA SITES BLOCKED

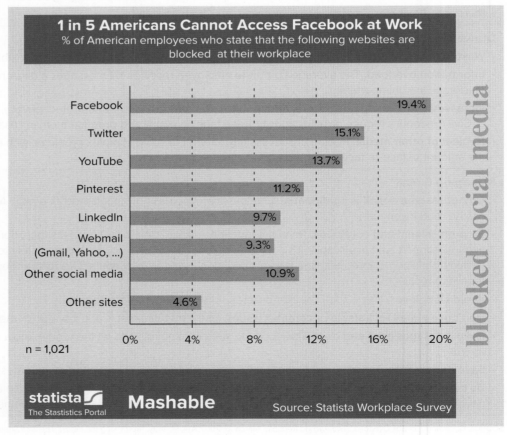

1 in 5 Americans Cannot Access Facebook at Work
% of American employees who state that the following websites are blocked at their workplace

Facebook	19.4%
Twitter	15.1%
YouTube	13.7%
Pinterest	11.2%
LinkedIn	9.7%
Webmail (Gmail, Yahoo, ...)	9.3%
Other social media	10.9%
Other sites	4.6%

n = 1,021

statista — The Statistics Portal   Mashable   Source: Statista Workplace Survey

SOURCE: Data for this graph from "Why Banning Facebook at Work Is a Stupid Move," *Business Insider,* October 2, 2013, http://www.businessinsider.com/why-banning-facebook-at-work-is-a-stupid-move-2013-10.

can block access on company devices, but so many people have smartphones, tablets, and other devices of their own. As a result, many employees continue their typical use of social media but simply do so on their own devices—still on company time.

- *Fairness—you can't have it one way.* If employers expect employees to be connected and responsive 24/7 to work-related e-mails (e.g., those from managers, coworkers, clients, or suppliers), then it only seems fair to allow them to tend to their "own business" during work hours. This is especially true if employees also do work outside of prescribed hours (e.g., at home in the evenings or on the weekend).
- *Suggests a lack of trust.* "Banning social media may send a message to your employees that you don't trust them. . . . This can cause a sharp divide in the team atmosphere you want to create."[63] As you learned in Chapter 8, it is difficult to manage and influence others without trust, and one of the basic ways of gaining trust from others is to trust them first.

You may also find it interesting that at least seven states forbid employers from demanding passwords and access to employees' social networking sites.[64] What is truly shocking to us is that any employer would ask and that any state would allow it! Whether you share this view or not, the likelihood of what any given organization will consider depends in part on leaders' social media attitudes.

Assess and Manage Leadership's Social Media Attitudes At this point in our discussion it is helpful to consider the social media readiness of an organization to which you belong. Self-Assessment 9.3 helps you assess leadership's attitude toward social media, such as how supportive management is of creating communities, how well the culture fosters collaboration and knowledge sharing, and how widely social media is used to collaborate. With this knowledge you can determine how well your own attitudes fit with those of the organization, and it may even provide you opportunities to improve the organization's readiness.

---

connect

SELF-ASSESSMENT 9.3 Assess Social Media Readiness

Go to connect.mheducation.com and take Self-Assessment 9.3. Then answer the following questions.

1. Which of the three dimensions has the highest score?
2. What are the implications for the employees/members?
3. What are the implications for the organization and how it interacts with stakeholders other than employees/members?
4. Which dimension is the lowest?
5. Describe two things that could be done to improve the organization's readiness in this area.

If the attitudes you find are not as positive as you would like, have no fear. Thankfully, and as you learned in Chapter 2, attitudes can be changed. Favorable leadership attitudes open the door to other productive applications of social media, such as developing and implementing a social media strategy.

Create and Implement a Social Media Strategy Despite the pervasive use of social media, less than 50 percent of companies have an actual social media policy.[65] If you believe that social media can be an effective tool at work, then you and your employer are well advised to create a formal strategy. Generally speaking, social media has three primary uses for organizations, and a strategy assists in determining for which and how social media is most useful:

1. **Recruiting talent.** The web, and services like LinkedIn, can help identify and engage both active and passive job candidates and introduce them to the organization's brand and job opportunities.

2. **Knowledge sharing.** Intranets and social media can facilitate the collection, dissemination, and use of knowledge, skills, abilities, and relationships both within and outside the organization.

3. **Reinforcing the brand.** Social media is a critical tool for introducing, reinforcing, and otherwise managing an organization's brand with all types of stakeholders (e.g., customers, suppliers, and employees).

Even organizations that have no official social media presence still in actuality likely have one because their employees and customers are interacting on the web and creating one. It therefore is wise to give genuine strategic attention to your organization's social media strategy. See "How to Be Strategic about Social Media" below for some excellent guiding questions to help you determine if and how social media can be used in your organization.

Use these questions as a starting point and guide.

How to Be Strategic about Social Media

- What are the organizational benefits and risks of using or not using social media?
- For what strategic goals or purposes could social media be used?
- In what ways could social media help support or implement the organization's business strategy?
- Who are the relevant stakeholders affected by social media?
- Who is ultimately responsible and accountable for the social media strategy?
- Are there sufficient resources to appropriately implement and maintain social media?
- What mechanisms are in place to respond to potential risks, should they occur?
- Ultimately, how will the organization as a whole and employees as individuals engage in social media?[66]

Privacy Any discussion of the effective use of social media for employees or their employers must include privacy issues. Employers and their employees have identities, and these identities are reflected in their reputations. Both are built over time and can be extremely consequential professionally. This is why you and your employers are well advised to pay close attention to privacy issues. This view is captured well in the following quote:

> The erosion of privacy provides troubling prospects, including the wearing down of the notion of "consent" as ineffective means are provided to opt-out of or to remove incorrect information in certain social media venues. Without privacy, individuals are denied physical and symbolic spaces for moral reflection as well as the resources needed to build and maintain their reputations.[67]

Reputations, both yours and your employer's, can be damaged in a variety of ways, such as loss of employment or business, social stigma, embarrassment and stress, lost job or business opportunities, and, of course, legal action. Many legal professionals now routinely include online profiles, e-mail, instant messaging, videos, photos, and other information retrieved from social media to make their cases for and against individuals and organizations.[68]

What Can You Do to Protect Yourself and Your Personal Brand (Reputation)?
Follow the aforementioned recommendations for starters. Assume no privacy, and keep your worlds separate. A clear and extreme example is provided by Stephanie Marchesi of the marketing firm Fleishman-Hillard in New York. She was well

Facebook is now an important communication and marketing tool for many organizations the world over. However, along with the benefits come challenges. Mark Zuckerberg, the company's founder and CEO, has had to address persistent issues related to privacy. What challenges does Facebook create for companies that use it? Describe other challenges that may confront companies that use Facebook.

known for maintaining four devices to segment her professional and personal worlds: an iPhone and iPad for family and social uses and a BlackBerry and laptop for work. She also has separate e-mail accounts and calendars, so that members of one world cannot "see" the other.[69] Establishing and maintaining multiple accounts, and using discretion about what you post, can be a challenge or even impossible. But think of the potential implications—your reputation or job!

Creating a social media policy can be tremendously useful in helping organizations outline which social media tools can be used, when, by whom, and how.

Create a Social Media Policy If the costs and concerns noted above aren't enough to motivate your employer to create a *social media policy* **that describes the who, how, when, for what purposes, and consequences for noncompliance of social media usage,** then one only needs to consider the impact of any one of a growing number of online nightmares for companies. For instance, do you recall the photos and videos of Taco Bell and Domino's Pizza employees in disgusting acts with food? "These viral moments do more than turn stomachs," writes business commentator Anthonia Akitunde. "[T]hey point to a troubling trend: employees abusing social media on the job to the detriment of the brand."[70] The elements of effective social media policies are outlined in Table 9.5.

The Example box below describes the Coca-Cola Company's social media policy.

EXAMPLE Coke's Online Social Media Principles

The company formulated its policies with the motive "to help empower our associates to participate in this new frontier of marketing and communications, represent our Company, and share the optimistic and positive spirits of our brands . . . we always remember who we are (a marketing company) and what our role is in the social media community (to build our brands)."

1. **Adhere to Coke's Code of Business Conduct and Other Policies.** All employees, from the chairman to interns, must abide by our codes governing information protection, privacy, insider information, and disclosure.

2. **You Are Responsible for Your Actions.** Anything you post that can potentially tarnish the Company's image will ultimately be your responsibility. We do encourage you to participate in the online social media space, but urge you to do so properly, exercising sound judgment and common sense.

3. **Be a "Scout" for Compliments and Criticism.** If you encounter comments online you feel are important, then please forward them to the designated online media office (e-mail address included).

4. **Let the Experts Respond to Negative Posts.** If you see negative or disparaging comments online, please do not engage but instead forward these to those trained to address such concerns (e-mail address included).

5. **Be Wise When Mixing Business and Personal Lives.** Our worlds intersect online. "The Company respects the free speech rights of all of its associates, but you must remember that customers, colleagues and supervisors often have access to the online content you post. Keep this in mind . . ." as information intended for family and friends can be forwarded. "NEVER disclose non-public information of the Company, and be aware that taking public positions online that are counter to the company's interests may cause a conflict."

YOUR THOUGHTS?

1. What are two benefits you see in Coke's policy?

2. What gaps do you notice, based on your experiences and what you've studied in this chapter?

SOURCE: Adapted from "Social Media Principles," *Coca Cola website*, http://www.coca-colacompany.com/stories/online-social-media-principles, accessed February 9, 2014.

TABLE 9.5 EIGHT ELEMENTS OF AN EFFECTIVE SOCIAL MEDIA POLICY

ELEMENT	DESCRIPTION
Create safe channels for employee concerns before going online.	The key words here are *safe* and *before*. Conflicts happen, as you will learn in Chapter 10, but what is important is that managers and organizations provide means by which employees' concerns are reported and handled without retaliation.
Clarify what is confidential.	Clearly explain what information employees can and cannot share online. Providing an approval process may help too.
Outline consequences for violations.	Make it known that employees can be held responsible for what they post and the consequences (e.g., videos of behavior on the job or in the company uniform).
Designate a spokesperson for online policies.	You don't want every and any employee fielding questions regarding company policies; identify a person(s) so interpretations and communications are consistent.
Discuss appropriate ways to engage others online.	Similar to the above, it typically is ill advised to have any and all employees responding to others' comments about the company online. Instruct them to be polite and nonconfrontational, and then to notify the designated person.
Explain what is considered illegal.	This refers to proprietary information, trademarks, and copyrights. It is the organization's responsibility to educate employees on these matters.
Align social media policy with the organization's culture.	Your company's social media policy is a great place to reaffirm what you want your company culture to be, while conveying your stance on this serious topic.
It educates employees.	It's not enough to have a social media policy; it is necessary to educate and train people about it and to embed it in social media practices. (One of the authors, for instance, could not locate a social media policy, or a person responsible for it, at his university.)

SOURCE: Adapted from A. Akitunde, "Employees Gone Wild: Eight Reasons You Need a Social Media Policy TODAY," *Open Forum*, August 15, 2013, https://www.openforum.com/articles/employee-social-media-policy/, accessed September 9, 2013.

COMMUNICATION SKILLS TO BOOST YOUR EFFECTIVENESS

MAJOR QUESTION

How can I increase my effectiveness using skills related to presenting, crucial conversations, and managing up?

THE BIGGER PICTURE

Master these three communication skills, and they will enhance your performance and career success throughout your life. The skills are

- **Presenting**
- **Crucial Conversations**
- **Managing Up**

These individual-level process skills make you more effective when working with others and influence a host of outcomes at both the individual and group levels in the Integrative Framework for Understanding and Applying OB.

Some jobs require you to present regularly and others never, but you can bet that you'll need to present formally or informally to some degree in your professional lives. How well you present can greatly affect others' perceptions of you and your professional opportunities. We therefore devote this section to some practical skills to help make you a more effective presenter. Improving your presentation skills is always valuable, given that relatively few people are truly at ease or actually enjoy speaking or presenting to a group.

In this section, you'll also explore how to effectively conduct *crucial conversations* and to *manage up!*

Presenting—Do You Give Reports or Do You Tell Stories?

You should probably start by answering the question in the above heading. Reports are packed with data and information and can be exhausting in their detail. Stories, in contrast, are short in all of these elements but are rich in emotion and help the presenter connect with the audience. As you learned earlier, different communication media are better than others for any given message. The challenge for you is to know what your audience wants and needs, and then to construct and deliver your presentation accordingly. It generally is best (more effective) if you can present your message more as a colorful story with emotion than as a detail-laden report. The people that organize the TED (Technology, Education, Design) talks have a five-step protocol that they use with many of their presenters to help them deliver presentations with impact.[71]

The TED Five-Step Protocol for Effective Presentations

1. Frame your story.
2. Plan your delivery.
3. Develop your stage presence.

Part of Elon Musk's—co-founder of PayPal, Tesla, SpaceX, and SolarCity—appeal is his ability to communicate his visions for innovative designs to investors, employees, and the general public. His TED Talk is one of the most frequently viewed.

4. Plan your multimedia.
5. Put it together.

Let's consider these steps in more detail.

Step 1—Frame Your Story   Think of your presentation as a journey and decide where you want to start and end. Consider what your audience already knows about your subject, start there, and quickly explain why it matters to you or why it should matter to them. Include only the most relevant details or points and try to bring them to life with examples. Don't try to do too much. Put another way, don't just skim over all of the potential points, but instead pick the best and dive deeper on each of those. Beware of jargon, boasting, or mind-numbing details. As for conclusions or where to end, try to plan your journey to end with a solution. Or you can even conclude with a question to spur audience engagement or give them something to think about afterwards. For example, we have presented as a journey the 3-Stop Problem-Solving Approach applied throughout this book. Perhaps your presentation might be structured similarly—what is the problem? what are potential causes or explanations? and what is your recommendation for action?

Step 2—Plan Your Delivery   There are three basic ways to deliver a talk:

1. Read it from a script.
2. Use bullet lists that outline what will be covered in each section and guide both the presenter and audience.
3. Memorize everything you wish to say and REHEARSE.

Generally, reading is ineffective. You will almost certainly lose your connection with the audience, if you ever connect in the first place. (TED forbids presenters to read.) Memorizing can work, if your audience is expected to simply sit and listen, but it takes a tremendous amount of time and practice. Unless you have it completely ingrained in your memory, then again, your audience can easily realize you are not as prepared as you hoped. If you use the bullet list approach, be sure you know not only the content for each point, but also how you want to transition from one to the next.

Step 3—Develop Your Stage Presence   "Getting the words, story and substance right is a much bigger determinant of success or failure than how you stand or whether you're visibly nervous." Beware of how much you move—not too much or too little. If you're really nervous, then pay particular attention to your lower body to prevent rocking or shifting from one leg to the other. Walking around is fine, if it is natural for you. Otherwise you may be well served to stand in particular spots for different lengths of time or points. The nonverbal communication pointers you learned earlier in this chapter are helpful too. Your body aside, the most important element of stage presence is eye contact! Find a handful of friendly faces around the room and deliver your talk while looking them in the eyes.

As for nervousness, there are many ways to help overcome this, and many of them you've learned in this book. For instance, what you learned about self-efficacy in Chapter 3 can be especially helpful, and preparation is a critical element of building your efficacy. But perhaps one of the most useful things you can do to overcome nervousness is to realize that people expect you to be nervous. Don't make too much of it.

Step 4—Plan Your Multimedia   Don't feel compelled to use the latest and greatest or any technology at all. But whatever you choose, keep it simple and don't let it distract the audience. If photos or images are appropriate, then use them. People of course respond differently to pictures and videos than they do to words. Images

TABLE 9.6 TEN TIPS FOR MORE EFFECTIVE POWERPOINT PRESENTATIONS

TIP	PUT IT IN ACTION
1. Write a script	Figure out what you want to say—beginning, middle, and end—before trying to put it on slides. Too many people start with slides and then fill in content.
2. One thing at a time	The only thing on the slide should be what you are talking about. If you put multiple points on the slide, then people will always read ahead and not focus on what you're saying.
3. No paragraphs	Don't put everything you want to say on a slide. No "big blocky chunks of text," otherwise you will "kill a room full of people—cause of death, terminal boredom poisoning."
4. Pay attention to design	Avoid the temptation to dress up your slides with cheesy effects and focus instead on simple design basics: use simple font styles, sizes, and colors; place dark text on light background; and avoid clutter.
5. Use images sparingly	Some people think images are stimulating and others think they are distracting. Split the difference.
6. Think outside the screen	"YOU are the focus when you're presenting, no matter how interesting your slides are."
7. Have a hook	Open with something surprising or intriguing to hook your audience. The best openers are often those that appeal to the audience's emotions—wow them, scare them, surprise them.
8. Ask questions	Questions engage the audience or pique their interest, so use them!
9. Modulate	Speak like you speak to your friends rather than reading off of index cards. Keeping a lively and personal tone of voice can go a long way.
10. Break the rules	Of course, like anything else, feel free to violate any of these rules if you think it's a good idea. Breaking rules because you have a good reason is different than not following them because you didn't know.

SOURCE: Adapted from D. Wax, "10 Tips for More Effective PowerPoint Presentations," *Lifehack*, November 24, 2012, http://www.lifehack.org/articles/technology/10-tips-for-more-effective-powerpoint-presentations.html, accessed October 7, 2013.

(videos and pictures) convey emotion better than words. However, if you use video clips, try to keep them to 60 seconds or less to prevent losing members of the audience. Since PowerPoint is so widely used, and "bad PowerPoint happens to good people and quite often the person giving the presentation is just as much a victim as the poor sods listening," the tips in Table 9.6 are very helpful.

Step 5—Put It Together   Be prepared far enough in advance—think weeks if possible, not days, hours, or minutes. If you practice in front of others, which is a good idea, be selective. Anybody in the practice audience role will feel compelled to give you feedback, but you need valuable feedback, not just any feedback. Preparation aside, remember to focus on the framing and substance of your journey and don't get too wrapped up in the other steps and details. If you don't think you have a compelling story, then go back to the drawing board and create one. Lastly, be yourself. Use the steps as a guide and don't try to copy somebody else—learn but don't copy.

Crucial Conversations

"Crucial conversations are discussions between two or more people where (1) the stakes are high, (2) opinions vary, and (3) emotions run strong."[72] Such conversations can and do occur in all arenas of your life—school, work, and socially. Examples include:

- Ending a relationship.
- Talking to a coworker or classmate who behaves offensively.
- Giving the boss or professor feedback.
- Critiquing a classmate or colleague's work.

Many of your important conversations with coworkers, friends, and classmates are full of emotions. Applying some of the communication skills and tools described in this chapter can help you improve the outcomes of crucial and other types of conversations.

- Asking a roommate to move out.
- Talking to a team member who isn't keeping commitments.
- Giving an unfavorable performance review.[73]

Please note that what you learned in Chapter 6 related to feedback also is very helpful with most crucial conversations.

Depending on how you handle such conversations the consequences can be enormous for your job, career, department, performance (school and work), social success and satisfaction, health, and many others. When confronted with such high stakes interactions, you basically have three choices—avoid them, face them and handle them poorly, or face them and handle them well. We'll focus on the last one. But before we do this, let's first explore why people often do so poorly in crucial situations, as it will serve as a bit of review of things you've learned already.

When It Matters Most, We Do Our Worst "When conversations turn from routine to crucial, we're often in trouble. That's because emotions don't exactly prepare us to converse effectively."[74] Our negative emotions (Chapter 3) kick in and the fight-or-flight response takes over. Moreover, crucial conversations often happen unexpectedly, which means you typically are unprepared. When this happens, again, your negative emotions can dominate and your self-efficacy decline (Chapter 3). The knowledge you gained in Chapter 7 on positive emotions and positive OB can help you in crucial situations. Specifically, a good way to prepare for crucial conversations is to foster your own positive state. Then, you can use the STATE technique described next to conduct your crucial conversations more effectively.

STATE to Be Effective When It's Crucial The acronym **STATE** will help you address even the most difficult conversations with a plan or path to follow.

- **Share your facts.** Start with the least controversial, most persuasive elements that support what you want for yourself and for the relationship.
- **Tell your story.** Enhance what you want by describing what has happened, how you've arrived where you are, how you'd like to see it change, and why. It may help to add in what you don't want personally or for the relationship.
- **Ask for others' facts and stories.** This is key to creating dialogue, which is essential if you're to have a productive crucial conversation. Don't *talk at* but instead *talk with* others. It is important that you approach crucial conversations as two-way exchanges. Don't be accusatory, but instead simply describe the situation, how you feel, and what you would like to see happen. Use "I" instead of "you." What you learned about effective feedback in Chapter 6 can also help here.
- **Talk tentatively.** Keep in mind that you're telling a story, not stating facts. The facts came first, then you add "color" or describe the impact on you via your story.
- **Encourage testing.** Make it safe for others to share their (opposing) views. It is critical to maintain mutual respect during crucial conversations. One way to do this is to explain and focus on mutual purpose—what you both stand to gain. You must also be sure that the other person respects you in order to avoid defensiveness (recall what you learned earlier in this chapter) and conflict. Apologize if it's appropriate to get back on track.[75]

TAKE-AWAY APPLICATION—TAAP

1. Think of somebody with whom you need or want to have a crucial conversation.
2. Use **STATE** to guide your planning.
3. Schedule and have the crucial conversation. Then review how it went using **STATE** to see how well you did and the benefits.

Managing Up

You learned in Chapter 6 about more contemporary forms of feedback (e.g., 360 degree), and that knowledge is helpful here. We are going to build on that and on crucial conversations to give you some guidance on how to manage your boss.

Gauge Receptiveness to Coaching Many organizations now claim that they believe in the merits of employee involvement and feedback, even upward. Note that translating these espoused values into enacted values requires skill. The place to begin is with your manager's receptiveness. Regardless of your organization's policy or comments from senior leadership, you're wise to put your efforts elsewhere if your manager is not receptive. You can't coach a boss that doesn't want to be coached. To gauge receptiveness, it is recommended that you:[76]

1. Learn your manager's view of coaching. What are his/her expectations? What are yours?

2. Explain what's in it for him or her.

3. Ask for permission to provide coaching or feedback. For instance, "Ms. Boss, would you mind if I share a different perspective, one that might help us solve the problem?"

4. Find how best to deliver criticism. Learn where, when, and how he or she wants to hear criticism—in the moment, in private, via e-mail, face-to-face, or another way.

5. Ask for agreement and commitment. After the first two, confirm that your boss is interested.

What to Do Next If your boss is receptive, be sure to read the following box, "Effective Upward Management," on how to coach your boss. If your boss is not receptive, read "Effective Upward Management" anyway, as it provides some helpful insight for managing others and helping others manage you.

Effective Upward Management[77]

Many efforts to manage your boss can be considered crucial conversations. It therefore is especially important to do so effectively. These steps and tips can help you prepare, deliver, and follow through.

Step 1—Prepare your message. Unlike crucial conversations that often happen in the moment, attempts to manage up or coach your boss are an agreed-upon arrangement that occurs over time. Therefore, use time to your advantage and prepare.

- Know what you want to accomplish.
- Support your points with examples, data, or other evidence.

Step 2—Plan your delivery and tactics. Plan how you will deliver your message—the tone and choice of words and influence tactics (Chapter 12) that will most likely achieve your desired result. Role playing is a very valuable tool—use it!

Step 3—Deliver. When conducting the coaching conversation, be sure you:

- *Are sensitive.* Your boss has feelings just like you, and just as you don't like to get hammered with how horrible and disappointing you are, neither does your boss.
- *Don't generalize behavior.* Speak to specific areas of his/her job, specific behaviors, and specific situations.
- *Provide ideas or suggestions.* Don't introduce your ideas as if they are the only ones that will work, or use language like "you must" or "you should."

Step 4—Follow up. Coaching and managing both involve more than simply providing feedback. You need to follow up to see or share how your boss has been doing in the areas discussed. Also ask what you can do to help him or her going forward.

YOUR THOUGHTS?

1. How well do you think this could work for you?
2. How could this approach be improved (are any steps or details missing)?
3. Can you think of somebody you could use this approach on? Describe.

what did i learn?

You learned that you can become a more effective communicator by understanding communication as a process that operates at all levels of the organization. At the individual level, you learned specific approaches to improve interpersonal communication. At the group/team level, and the organizational level, you learned how to manage your social media brand or impression and how to develop effective presentations in formal settings. At the organizational level, you learned how the proper approach to communication can allow you to manage up to higher levels in the organization. Across all three levels, you learned how to prepare for the kinds of crucial conversations that often find us at our worst, but potentially can be our best. Reinforce your learning with the Key Points below. Then consolidate your learning using the Integrative Framework. Challenge your mastery of the material by answering the Major Questions in your own words.

Key Points for Understanding Chapter 9

You learned the following key points.

9.1 BASIC DIMENSIONS OF THE COMMUNICATION PROCESS

- All communication involves a sender, message, and receiver.
- Noise has many sources and types and can interfere with communications.
- The medium is an important consideration for effective communication.
- Media richness helps convey information and promote understanding. It is influenced by feedback, channel, type, and language source.

9.2 COMMUNICATION COMPETENCE

- Communication competence refers to an individual's ability to effectively use communication behaviors in a given context.
- Nonverbal communication is extremely important to effective communication and includes many potential elements, such as body movements and gestures, touch, facial expressions, and eye contact.
- Listening is the process of actively decoding and interpreting verbal messages.
- Four common listening styles are active, involved, passive, and detached.

9.3 GENDER, GENERATIONS, AND COMMUNICATION

- Linguistic styles represent a person's characteristic speaking pattern.
- Women and men communicate differently. Women are more likely to share credit and ask clarifying questions, and men are more likely to give blunt feedback and withhold compliments.
- Generational differences are important to consider, as each generation has its own norms and preferences.
- Despite any differences or similarities, be careful not to generalize anything about communication to entire genders or generations.

9.4 SOCIAL MEDIA AND OB

- Social media can increase employee and employer productivity.
- The use of social media at work also has many costs, some potentially significant and consequential.
- E-mail can increase teamwork and flexibility and reduce costs of paper and distributing information. But it also has costs: wasted time, information overload, and increased costs of time and money organizing, storing, and monitoring.
- Social media policies help outline what is expected and what is forbidden. They also help guard employers against liability and undesirable events.
- It is important to monitor and manage privacy issues in the digital space. It is also important to monitor and manage your personal brand and your employer's brand.

9.5 COMMUNICATION SKILLS TO BOOST YOUR EFFECTIVENESS

- Effective presenters are more likely to tell stories than give reports. It is helpful to frame your story, plan the delivery, develop stage presence and multimedia, and put it all together.
- Crucial conversations are discussions between two or more people where the stakes are high, opinions vary, and emotions run strong.
- Managing up is more effective if you gauge your manager's receptiveness, ask for permission to provide feedback/input, prepare your message, plan your delivery and tactics, and follow up.

The Integrative Framework for Chapter 9

As shown in Figure 9.3, you learned that communication is a key individual, group/team, and organizational level process. While we touched on a host of inputs, both person factors (personality, experience, skills and abilities, and mindfulness) and environmental characteristics (job design, relationship quality, leadership, organizational climate and culture, and stressors), our primary focus was on processes and outputs. Communication links to outcomes across the three levels of OB. At the individual level, communication relates to task performance, work attitudes, well-being/flourishing, citizenship behavior/counterproductive behavior, turnover, career outcomes, and creativity. Communication also correlates with group/team performance, group satisfaction, and group cohesion and conflict. Finally, communication impacts organizational outcomes such as employer of choice, survival, accounting/financial performance, customer satisfaction, reputation, and innovation.

Challenge: Major Questions for Chapter 9

At the start of the chapter, we told you that after reading the chapter you should be able to answer the following questions. Unless you can, have you really processed and internalized the lessons in the chapter? Refer to the Key Points, Figure 9.3, the chapter itself, and your notes to revisit and answer the following major questions:

1. How can knowledge about the basic communication process help me communicate more effectively?

2. What are the key aspects of interpersonal communication that can help me improve my communication competence?

3. Do I need to alter how I communicate based on the gender and age of my audience?

4. How can social media increase my effectiveness at work and in my career?

5. How can I increase my effectiveness using skills related to presenting, crucial conversations, and managing up?

FIGURE 9.3   INTEGRATIVE FRAMEWORK FOR UNDERSTANDING AND APPLYING OB

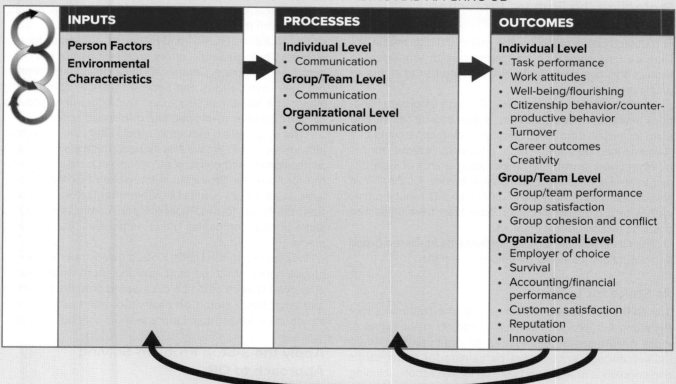

SOURCE: © 2014 Angelo Kinicki and Mel Fugate. All rights reserved. Reproduction prohibited without permission of the authors.

Costco Management Walks Tightrope with Social Media

Job seekers and employers have long known that risqué revelations on Facebook can jeopardize career prospects. But now companies are facing their own challenges for alleged blunders in dealing with social media.

Take Costco Wholesale Corporation. Analysts say that the company offers the best pay and benefits in retail.[78] In fact, Wall Street critics have even accused Costco of favoring employees *too* much and want to see lower compensation costs and higher returns.[79]

So how did Costco catch the attention of the National Labor Review Board (NLRB)? Costco was charged with perceived violations of labor rights, due to language in the company's employee handbook related to employees' use of the Internet and social media. The NLRB ruled that Costco's employee policies violated labor law (discussed below), and it required the company to rewrite its policies.[80]

Protecting the Firm vs. Protecting Workers' Rights

The Costco action highlights the way that digital media has increased the need for even greater care by employers to protect the company while still protecting the rights of employees.

Here's what started the trouble: Costco's employee handbook prohibited its employees, subject to discipline and even dismissal, from electronically posting statements that "damage the Company . . . or . . . any person's reputation."

What's wrong with that? From many points of view this language would seem reasonable and wise. Costco has a responsibility to protect the company and its reputation, as well as to protect the rights of individuals from unwanted postings by someone it employs.

The NLRB saw the Costco language as much too broad and potentially infringing on employees' rights.

At Stake for Labor

The NLRB oversees compliance with the National Labor Relations Act (NLRA). The NLRA protects basic rights of most private-sector employees to organize into trade unions, engage in collective bargaining for better terms and conditions at work, and take collective action including protests and strikes.

The NLRB puts a high priority on digital speech rights under the Act. It comes down to employees' rights to "concerted activity," under Section 7 of the statute, "when two or more employees take action for their mutual aid or protection regarding terms and conditions of employment." This means that employees are allowed to speak out and do so together. But there must be limits.

At Stake for Companies

The NLRA applies *whether or not* employees belong to a union, so most companies are affected. All companies must now walk a tightrope in making sure they fulfill their obligations to ownership (e.g., shareholders) and employees. If they err too far in one direction, they infringe the rights of employees. If they err too far in the other, they risk the reputation and value of the company.

Employers "desiring to implement a social media policy," writes one law firm specializing in the area, "must walk a very fine line between prohibiting unwanted conduct—such as revealing confidential information or making disparaging comments about the company—and avoiding undue restrictions on protected activities."[81]

A Moving Target

Companies trying to get the right balance face a moving target because regulatory institutions are still playing catchup with the implications of social media.

The NLRB has issued—and reissued—guidelines for employers. Their guidance offers suggestions but not "pre-approved" language. Companies must individually hammer out their own policies and hope they are in compliance. (Note: The NLRB has suggested that companies provide helpful examples of allowed and disallowed speech.)

"The core issue is that social media alters the way we as individuals share who we are, merging our roles as people, professionals, and consumers," writes Nick Hayes, an analyst for Forrester Research, in the wake of Costco's problems. In all, Hayes counts 12 different regulatory agencies, from the NLRB to the Federal Trade Commission, with a stake in how companies guide employees' use of social media.[82]

In response to the NLRB, Costco quietly rewrote its employee handbook to be more specific about what kinds of employee speech could be considered grounds for action and what kinds would be protected. No doubt the new handbook is longer than before and will continue to grow.

Apply the 3-Stop Problem-Solving Approach to OB

Stop 1: What is the problem?

- Use the Integrative Framework of OB to help identify the outcomes that are important in this case.

- Which of these outcomes are not being achieved in the case?

- Based on considering the above two questions, what is the most important problem in this case?

Stop 2: Use the Integrative Framework and the discussion in this chapter to help identify the OB concepts or theories that help you to understand the problem in this case.

- What person factors are most relevant?
- What environmental characteristics are most important to consider?
- Do you need to consider any processes? Which ones?
- What concepts or theories discussed in this chapter are most relevant for solving the key problem in this case?

Stop 3: What are your recommendations for solving the problem?

- Review the material in the chapter that most pertains to your proposed solution and look for practical recommendations.
- Use any past OB knowledge or experience to generate recommendations.
- Outline your plan for solving the problem in this case.

LEGAL/ETHICAL CHALLENGE

Should an Employee Be Fired Because She Complained about Customers via Facebook?

This case involves a waitress at a Famous Dave's BBQ restaurant in Bismarck, ND. Someone posted a picture on Facebook showing her holding a sign that implied that Native Americans were poor tippers. The picture was posted during the United Tribes International Powwow being held in Bismarck. Not only was the women in the photo fired, but so was the person who took the photo.

The owner of this Famous Dave's franchise posted the following statement: "When an employee decides to make an ass of his or herself they can now do it for all to see. Sadly, for reasons unknown to me, often times bitter employees also try to embarrass the employers and taint the businesses where they work. Clearly a recent post by a now former employee fits this description."

Many people agreed that linking the comment about tipping to the reference of the International Powwow implied that Native Americans "are as a class poor tippers." The

original post caused very negative reactions among the local community.[83]

If You Were an Executive from Corporate Headquarters, What Would You Do?

1. Commend the franchise owner for firing the woman. The waitress showed bad judgment and the negative publicity could adversely affect sales at the restaurant.
2. I think the waitress was making a joke, albeit in bad taste. She doesn't deserve to be fired. I would reinstate her if she were willing to make a public apology.
3. The employee should be fired, but we need to create a policy about communicating on social media about our restaurants. I would discourage franchise owners from writing posts like this one.
4. Invent other options.

GROUP EXERCISE

Practicing Different Styles of Communication

Objectives

1. To demonstrate the relative effectiveness of communicating assertively, aggressively, and nonassertively.
2. To give you hands-on experience with different styles of communication.

Introduction

Research shows that assertive communication is more effective than either an aggressive or nonassertive style. This *role-playing exercise* is designed to increase your

ability to communicate assertively. Your task is to use different communication styles while attempting to resolve the work-related problems of a poor performer.

While we identified various communication styles in the chapter, please refer to Table 9.7, which consolidates and further expands on such styles.

Instructions

Divide into groups of three and read the "Poor Performer" and "Store Manager" roles provided here. Then decide who will play the poor performer role, who will play the managerial role, and who will be the observer. The observer

TABLE 9.7 COMMUNICATION STYLES AND BEHAVIOR PATTERNS

STYLE	DESCRIPTION	NONVERBAL	VERBAL
Nonassertive	Inhibited, self-denying, encourages others to take advantage.	Poor eye contact Downward glance Slumped Constantly shifting weight Wringing hands Weak or whiny voice	Qualifiers ("maybe"; "kind of") Fillers ("uh," "you know," "well") Negaters ("It's not really that important," "I'm not sure")
Assertive	Expressive and self-enhancing without intruding on others; permits others to influence outcomes; pushing hard without attacking.	Good eye contact Comfortable but firm posture Strong, steady, audible voice Facial expressions match message Appropriately serious tone	Direct and unambiguous language No attributions or evaluations of others' behavior Use of "I" statements and cooperative "we" statements
Aggressive	Expressive and self-enhancing at others' expense; taking advantage of others.	Glaring eye contact Moving or leaning too close Threatening gestures (pointed finger, clenched fist) Loud voice	Swear words and abusive language Attributions and evaluations of others' behavior Sexist or racist terms Explicit threats or put-downs

communication styles & behavior

SOURCE: Adapted in part from J. Walters, "Managerial Assertiveness," *Business Horizons*, September–October 1982, 24–29.

will be asked to provide feedback to the manager after each role-play. When playing the managerial role, you should first attempt to resolve the problem by using an aggressive communication style. Attempt to achieve your objective by using the nonverbal and verbal behavior patterns associated with the aggressive style shown in Table 9.7. Take about four to six minutes to act out the instructions. The observer should give feedback to the manager after completing the role-play. The observer should comment on how the employee responded to the aggressive behaviors displayed by the manager.

After feedback is provided on the first role-play, the person playing the manager should then try to resolve the problem with a nonassertive style. Observers once again should provide feedback. Finally, the manager should confront the problem with an assertive style. Once again, rely on the relevant nonverbal and verbal behavior patterns presented in Table 9.7 and take four to six minutes to act out each scenario. Observers should try to provide detailed feedback on how effectively the manager exhibited nonverbal and verbal assertive behaviors. Be sure to provide positive and constructive feedback.

After completing these three role-plays, switch roles: manager becomes observer, observer becomes poor performer, and poor performer becomes the manager. When these role-plays are completed, switch roles once again.

Role: Poor Performer

You sell shoes full time for a national chain of shoe stores. During the last month you have been absent three times without giving your manager a reason. The quality of your work has been slipping. You have a lot of creative excuses when your boss tries to talk to you about your performance.

When playing this role, feel free to invent a personal problem that you may eventually want to share with your manager. However, make the manager dig for information about this problem. Otherwise, respond to your manager's comments as you normally would.

Role: Store Manager

You manage a store for a national chain of shoe stores. In the privacy of your office, you are talking to one of your salespeople who has had three unexcused absences from work during the last month. (This is excessive, according to company guidelines, and must be corrected.) The quality of his or her work has been slipping. Customers have complained that this person is rude, and coworkers have told you this individual isn't carrying his or her fair share of the work. You are fairly sure this person has some sort of personal problem. You want to identify that problem and get him or her back on the right track.

Questions for Class Discussion

1. What drawbacks of the aggressive and nonassertive styles did you observe?

2. What were major advantages of the assertive style?

3. What were the most difficult aspects of trying to use an assertive style?

4. How important was nonverbal communication during the various role-plays? Explain with examples.

10 MANAGING CONFLICT AND NEGOTIATIONS

How Can These Skills Give Me an Advantage?

inputs

PERSON FACTORS

ENVIRONMENTAL CHARACTERISTICS

processes

INDIVIDUAL LEVEL

GROUP/TEAM LEVEL
Conflict and Negotiation

ORGANIZATIONAL LEVEL

outcomes

INDIVIDUAL LEVEL

GROUP/TEAM LEVEL

ORGANIZATIONAL LEVEL

MAJOR TOPICS I'LL LEARN AND QUESTIONS I SHOULD BE ABLE TO ANSWER

10.1 A CONTEMPORARY VIEW OF CONFLICT
MAJOR QUESTION: *How can understanding a modern perspective of conflict make me more effective at school, work, and home?*

10.2 CONVENTIONAL FORMS OF CONFLICT
MAJOR QUESTION: *What are some types of conflict and how can I manage them to my benefit?*

10.3 FORMS OF CONFLICT INTENSIFIED BY TECHNOLOGY
MAJOR QUESTION: *What can I do to manage work–family conflict and incivility to make me more effective at school, work, and home?*

10.4 EFFECTIVELY MANAGING CONFLICT
MAJOR QUESTION: *What can I do to prevent, reduce, or even overcome conflicts?*

10.5 NEGOTIATION
MAJOR QUESTION: *What are some best practices for effective negotiation?*

INTEGRATIVE FRAMEWORK FOR UNDERSTANDING AND APPLYING OB

Conflict and negotiation are ever-present and consequential group/team level processes in OB. Both are related to most outcomes across levels of OB. We challenge you to identify these outcomes as you read this chapter and learn about conflict and negotiation.

© 2014 Angelo Kinicki and Mel Fugate. All rights reserved. Reproduction prohibited without permission of the authors.

NEGOTIATING YOUR SALARY FOR A NEW JOB

Experts offer this advice for getting the best compensation you can.

- **Know the market rate.** Research what companies are paying other employees with similar jobs in the same area.

- **Know your own value.** Can you justify making more than the market rate? Be ready to offer specific examples of your experience and accomplishments; tell how you benefited your past and present employers.

- **Be honest.** Don't exaggerate your pay or accomplishments.

- **Don't go first.** Try to wait for the other person to name a number. You might say you want to be paid the going rate for someone with your qualifications. If you have to give an answer, give a range, not a specific dollar figure.

- **Consider benefits, too.** Some of the most valuable parts of your compensation package may be insurance and retirement savings. Retirement may seem like eons away, but an employer match of 5 percent to your 401(k) plan is like an extra 5 percent of pay—without an immediate tax bite.

- **Look at the long term.** If you can't get a big pay package, consider whether you can ask for something else that will help your long-term career, for example, a chance to work on an important assignment.

NEGOTIATING A PAY RAISE

Preparation is critical. You therefore need information, and the following are some valuable sources and techniques for acquiring it.

- **Current colleagues.** They, of course, are the best but also the toughest source. The best strategy is to be honest and say: "I'm not sure my salary reflects market value, so I'm checking with colleagues to find out what the current salary range is in our field. Would you be willing to talk about compensation?" Assure them you'll keep it confidential, and then, if they're willing, start by giving them a range for where your salary falls and asking them how it compares with theirs.

- **Former colleagues.** Ask them what they think is an appropriate range for your job in a company of your

size and industry. It may also help to be explicit about asking their advice and keeping the discussion in the third person: "What do you think is a competitive or appropriate salary for a solid performer doing X in a company like mine (or a company like hers/his)?"

- **Give to get.** Another effective approach is to offer your salary and then ask: "Does that sound competitive with what you're making or what your company offers?"

- **Social capital and recruiters.** One of the very best sources is recruiters who place people in jobs and companies like yours. Salary is almost always part of their discussions. So, if you're going to build out your network, adding a recruiter or two who will share such info can be extremely valuable. But you need the relationship first. It's no use cold calling a recruiter and expecting him/her to share such info—that expertise is part of what recruiters get paid for!

SOURCES: For "Negotiating Your Salary at a New Job": adapted from B. Brophy, "Bargaining for Bigger Bucks: A Step-by-Step Guide to Negotiating Your Salary," *Business 2.0,* May 2004, 107, http://money.cnn.com/ S. Curran, "Compensation Advice for New Grads," *Bloomberg Businessweek,* April 30, 2007, http://www.businessweek.com/ and F. Di Meglio, "Job Searchers Face a New Reality," *Bloomberg Businessweek,* April 3, 2008, http://www.businessweek.com/. For "Negotiating a Pay Raise": E. Zimmerman, "How to Benchmark Your Salary," *CBS News,* April 23, 2009, http://www.cbsnews.com/accessed June 12, 2013.

> ### FOR YOU WHAT'S AHEAD IN THIS CHAPTER
>
> We continue our discussion of the group and team level in the Integrative Framework and address conflict and negotiation in this chapter. Conflict is an inevitable part of organizational life. We describe some of the common causes of conflict at work, people's frequent reactions, as well as the language or metaphors often used to describe conflict. Both common (e.g., personality) and contemporary (e.g., cyber bullying) forms of conflict are discussed. We then provide practical guidance on how to manage various forms of conflict, which is followed by an explanation of negotiation, including types of negotiations and ethical pitfalls.

A CONTEMPORARY VIEW OF CONFLICT

MAJOR QUESTION

How can understanding a modern perspective of conflict make me more effective at school, work, and home?

THE BIGGER PICTURE

Conflict is an ever-present part of your life and an important group-level process in the Integrative Framework for Applying and Understanding OB. To help you better understand and manage conflict, we explore several common causes of conflict at school and work today. Then, you'll learn about what it means to have too little, too much, or enough conflict (the conflict continuum). We expand this further and explain that not all conflict is bad or dysfunctional; some forms are functional or desirable. Next, we describe some of the desired outcomes of functional conflict.

Conflict is a pervasive part of the human experience. Some surveys report that employees spend two or more hours per week, or one day per month, dealing with some type of conflict at work. Not only is conflict time-consuming, but employees also report many other undesirable consequences, such as absences (25%), avoiding work-related events (24%), quitting (18%), terminations (16%), and project failures (9%).[1] Whether these statistics move you or not, you can safely assume that all forms of conflict at work are underreported. Due to these consequences, and the fact that conflicts can and do occur within and between levels in the Integrative Framework of OB, managing conflict effectively is essential for individual, departmental, and organizational effectiveness. It therefore is no surprise that "a considerable effort on the part of management is devoted to dealing with conflict and its aftermath."[2]

However, it is important to realize that conflict has *both* positive and negative consequences. We learned in Chapter 4, for example, that diversity within work groups can create conflict, but that training can be used to help diverse groups to achieve higher levels of performance. The goal of this chapter therefore is to help you understand how to avoid the negative side of conflict while also gaining from its positive outcomes. We begin by providing a foundation for understanding conflict and then discuss the major forms of conflict. We next review methods and tools for managing conflict and conclude by exploring the skill of negotiation.

A Modern View of Conflict and Escalation

Conflict occurs when one **"party perceives that its interests are being opposed or negatively affected by another party."**[3] The word *perceives* reminds us that sources of conflict and issues can be real or imagined, just like our discussion of fairness, equity, and justice in Chapter 5. If you perceive you were screwed, then you feel you were screwed. A lack of fairness, perceived or real, is a major source of conflict at work. For example, associates at a major New York law firm, Cravath, Swaine, & Moore, felt that their $34,000 bonus checks were "an insult" given that they had received as much as $95,000 before. This conflict was made worse by the fact that since the economy has recovered, partners in the firm have kept a larger share of the profits—almost at pre-recession levels.[4] Associates felt they shared the pains but not the gains.

This example illustrates another important and common characteristic of conflicts—they can escalate! Consider the example in the following Problem-Solving Application.

solving application

Seemingly Small Incidents Can Escalate

Since 9/11 heightened airline security has increased frustrations for both airline employees and passengers. Passengers have to abide by more and more rules that employees must enforce. For instance, on a flight from Europe to the United States a simple passenger request escalated quickly. "Bill Pollock asked a flight attendant about a sign telling passengers not to venture beyond the curtain separating economy class from the rest of the plane," the *New York Times* reported. "He wanted to stretch his legs and visit his wife seated on the opposite aisle, using the passageway behind the galley in the plane's midsection. But when he questioned a flight attendant on the policy and began recording their conversation using his cellphone, the situation quickly escalated: The flight attendant grabbed his phone and nearby federal air marshals intervened."

They held him against the wall with his hands behind his back. Pollock said, "I wasn't violent, I didn't use four-letter words. All I did

Heightened airline security since 9/11 has increased frustrations and conflicts in passengers and employees.

was ask this guy about the sign on the curtain and they flipped out." Afterwards Mr. Pollock wondered about his rights and the rules, such as being restricted to particular cabins and not just bathrooms, as well as the right to video/audio record flight crew. A spokesperson

for the Federal Aviation Administration responded and said that there is no rule limiting passenger movement on planes, but "no person may assault, threaten, intimidate or interfere with a crew member in the performance of the crew member's duties."[5] What is your reaction?

YOUR CALL *Apply the 3-Stop Problem-Solving Approach.*

Stop 1: What is the problem?

Stop 2: Which OB concepts can help you explain the cause of the problem?

Stop 3: What recommendations do you have to prevent and/or resolve this and similar problems?

Escalation of Conflict When conflict escalates, the intensity increases and often leads to "cycles of provocation and counter-provocation eventually resulting in the replacement of substantive debate with increasingly hateful and sometimes violent confrontations directed more at hurting opponents than at advancing interests."[6] The result is positions that are increasingly extreme and increasingly unjustifiable. Conflict escalation often exhibits these five characteristics:

1. **Change in tactics**—Parties often move from "light tactics" (e.g., persuasive arguments, promises, and efforts to please the other side) to "heavy tactics" (e.g., threats, power plays, and violence).

2. **Number of issues grows**—More and more issues that bother each party are raised and included in the conflict.

3. **Issues move from specific to general**—Small and specific concerns often become more vague or general and can evolve into a general disliking or intolerance of the other party.

4. **Number of parties grows**—More people and groups are drawn into the conflict.

5. **Goals change**—Parties change their focus from "doing well" or resolution to winning and even hurting the other party.[7]

Since conflicts by nature are between people, a good place to start our discussion is for you to learn about your own tendencies for conflicts with others. You likely believe that you have relatively few conflicts and are easy to get along with, which you might indeed be. However, this is likely just what the most problematic bosses of the coauthors of this book thought/think of themselves. It therefore is valuable to "test" your impressions of yourself by completing Self-Assessment 10.1.

connect

SELF-ASSESSMENT 10.1 Interpersonal Conflict Tendencies

Go to connect.mheducation.com and take Self-Assessment 10.1 to learn how well you get along with others at work and/or school.

1. Does your score match your perception of yourself?

2. The Assessment measures how well you get along with others and how they treat you; both are sources of conflict. If you were to improve the measure, what other things do you think should be included?

Because conflict, particularly when it escalates, can be so damaging, employees and managers both need to understand the dynamics of conflict and know how to handle it effectively. A good place to start is to consider some of the situations that commonly cause conflict.

Some Common Causes of Conflict   Certain situations produce more conflict than others. By knowing the antecedents or causes of conflict, you and managers are better able to anticipate conflict and take steps to resolve it if it becomes dysfunctional. Table 10.1 lists many of the situations that tend to produce either functional or dysfunctional conflict. Which of these situations have happened to you?

Proactive managers carefully read these early warnings and take appropriate action. For example, group conflict sometimes can be reduced by making decisions on the basis of majority approval rather than striving for a consensus.

TAKE-AWAY APPLICATION—TAAP

1. Identify an important conflict that you've experienced at school, at work, or in your personal life.

2. Determine which characteristics of conflict escalation were evident.

3. Now, using Table 10.1, think of *personal* examples for each of the situations that commonly produce conflict.

A Conflict Continuum   Ideas about managing conflict underwent an interesting evolution during the 20th century. Initially, management experts believed all conflict ultimately threatened management's authority and thus had to be avoided or quickly resolved. They later recognized the inevitability of conflict and advised managers to learn to live with it. Emphasis remained on resolving conflict whenever possible, however. Beginning in the 1970s, OB specialists realized conflict had both positive and negative outcomes. This

TABLE 10.1   SITUATIONS THAT COMMONLY PRODUCE CONFLICT

Incompatible personalities or value systems		Inadequate communication
Overlapping or unclear job boundaries		Interdepartment/intergroup competition
Competition for limited resources		Unreasonable deadlines or extreme time pressure
Unreasonable or unclear policies, standards, or rules	*situations that produce conflict*	Decision making by consensus (dissenters may feel coerced)
Organizational complexity (conflict tends to increase as the number of hierarchical layers and specialized tasks increases)		Collective decision making (the greater the number of people participating in a decision, the greater the potential for conflict)
Interdependent tasks (e.g., one person cannot complete his or her assignment until others have completed their work)		Unmet expectations (employees who have unrealistic expectations about job assignments, pay, or promotions are more prone to conflict)

SOURCES: Adapted in part from discussion in A. C. Filley, *Interpersonal Conflict Resolution* (Glenview, IL: Scott, Foresman, 1975), 9–12; and B. Fortado, "The Accumulation of Grievance Conflict," *Journal of Management Inquiry,* December 1992, 288–303. See also D. Tjosvold and M. Poon, "Dealing with Scarce Resources: Open-Minded Interaction for Resolving Budget Conflicts," *Group & Organization Management,* September 1998, 237–255.

perspective introduced the revolutionary idea that organizations could suffer from either *too little* or *too much* conflict. Neither scenario is good.

Appropriate types and levels of conflict energize people in constructive directions.[8] The relationship between conflict intensity and outcomes is illustrated in Figure 10.1. These differences lead to the distinction between functional and dysfunctional conflict.

Functional vs. Dysfunctional Conflict

The distinction between *functional conflict* and *dysfunctional conflict* pivots on whether the organization's interests are served. **Functional conflict is commonly referred to in management circles as constructive or cooperative conflict and is characterized by consultative interactions, a focus on the issues, mutual respect, and useful give and take.** In such situations people often feel comfortable disagreeing and presenting opposing views. Positive outcomes frequently result. Each of these elements is lacking or even opposite in cases of *dysfunctional conflict,* **which threatens an organization's interests.**[9] This highlights the important role of management, and your own actions, in determining whether conflict is more or less positive. Let's explain this in a bit more detail in the Example box.

FIGURE 10.1   RELATIONSHIP BETWEEN CONFLICT INTENSITY AND OUTCOMES[10]

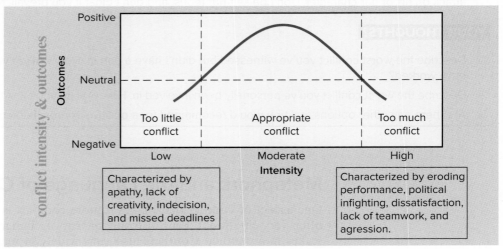

EXAMPLE How to Take a Positive Approach to Conflict

The importance of taking a positive approach to conflict is underscored by a recent, somewhat mysterious incident that led to criticism of a CEO and his public apology.

Jim Hagedorn, CEO of Scotts Miracle-Gro, has used "salty" (i.e., profane) language in the past, and in June 2013 the company publicly reprimanded him for an outburst, possibly during a board meeting. Three board members resigned and Hagedorn publicly apologized. The company issued a press release that it also filed with the SEC:

> The resignations were delivered to the Company following a unanimously supported reprimand of Hagedorn that stemmed from the use of inappropriate language. All three former board members confirmed that their departures were not related to any disagreement relating to the Company's operations, policies, practices or financial reporting.
>
> "While I have a tendency to use colorful language, I recognize my comments in this case were inappropriate and I apologize," Hagedorn said. "I, along with the rest of our board members, consider the matter resolved and I have made a personal commitment to prevent a future recurrence."[11]

Jim Hagedorn, CEO of Scotts Miracle-Gro, has used salty language in the past, and in June 2013 the company publicly reprimanded him for an outburst; Hagedorn publicly apologized.

While we can't say what happened in the boardroom with certainty, we can say that outbursts are often the result of a negative approach to conflict. Here are some *tips for a positive approach.*

1. **Personal Integrity.** When you process your conflicts with integrity, they lead to growth, increased awareness, and self-improvement. Uncontrolled anger, defensiveness, and shame defeat these possibilities. Everyone feels better when they overcome their problems and reach resolution, and worse when they succumb and fail to resolve them. It is a bitter truth that victories won in anger lead to long-term defeat. Those defeated turn away, feeling betrayed and lost, and carry this feeling with them into their next conflict.

2. **Opportunity to Learn and Problem Solve.** Conflict can be seen simply as a way of learning more about what is not working and discovering how to fix it. The usefulness of the solution depends on the depth of your understanding of the problem. This depends on your ability to listen to the issue as you would to a teacher, which depends on halting the cycle of escalation and searching for opportunities for improvement.[12]

3. **Empathy.** The key, oddly enough, is to empathize with the person you're confronting. Not only does it help you understand the other's position, but he/she is likely to be more receptive to you and your position in return.

4. **Focus on Facts and the Issue.** To this end, utilize useful facts rather than impressions, offer alternatives along with your objections, and limit comments to the deed, not the doer. Your opponent won't hear anything you say after an attack on his or her character. Don't be self-righteous, and don't gloat if you prevail. Nobody likes a poor winner.[13]

YOUR THOUGHTS?

1. Describe the worst conflict you've witnessed but didn't have a part in. How well do you think the above tips would have worked?

2. Describe the worst conflict you've personally been involved in. How well do you think these tips would have worked?

3. Are there any other options that you would recommend for a positive approach to conflict?

Metaphors and the Language of Conflict

One aspect of conflict that makes it more complex is the language people use. It's often very emotional. Fear of losing or fear of change quickly raises the emotional stakes in a conflict. Conflicts also vary widely in magnitude. Conflicts have both participants and observers. Some observers may be interested and active while others are disinterested and passive. Consequently, the term *conflict* can take on vastly different meanings depending on the circumstances and one's involvement. For example, consider these three metaphors and accompanying workplace expressions:

Conflict as war: "We shot down that idea."

Conflict as opportunity: "What will it take to resolve this disagreement?"

Conflict as journey: "Let's search for common ground and all learn something useful."[14]

Anyone viewing a conflict as war or a sports contest is likely to try to win at all costs and wipe out the enemy. For example, Donald Trump has said, "In life, you have fighters and nonfighters. You have winners and losers. I am both a fighter and a winner."[15] Alternatively, those seeing a conflict as an opportunity and a journey will tend to be more positive, open-minded, and constructive. In a hostile world, combative and destructive warlike thinking often prevails.

But typical daily workplace conflicts are *not* war. So when dealing with organizational conflicts, we are challenged to rely less on the metaphor and language of war and more on the metaphors and language of *opportunity* and *journey*. We want you to keep the following instructive observation in mind for the balance of this chapter:

> **EXAMPLE**   Conflict gives you an opportunity to deepen your capacity for empathy and intimacy with your opponent. Your anger transforms the "other" into a stereotyped demon or villain. Similarly, defensiveness will prevent you from communicating openly with your opponents, or listening carefully to what they are saying. On the other hand, once you engage in dialogue with that person, you will resurrect the human side of his/her personality—and express your own as well.[16]

Okay, so you can take a more positive and constructive approach to conflict—it isn't all bad. But if this is possible, then why do so many people avoid conflict?

Why People Avoid Conflict

Are you uncomfortable in conflict situations? Do you go out of your way to avoid conflict? If so, you're not alone. Many of us avoid conflict for a variety of both good and bad reasons. Some of the most common are combinations of fear of:

- Harm
- Rejection
- Damage to or loss of relationships
- Anger
- Being seen as selfish
- Saying the wrong thing
- Failing
- Hurting someone else
- Getting what you want[17]

This list is self-explanatory, except for the fear of "getting what you want." This refers to people who, for personal reasons, feel undeserving or fear the consequences of success and thus tend to sabotage themselves. Of course, avoiding conflict doesn't make it go away. The conflict situation is likely to continue or even escalate. What is the alternative? The Example below provides some useful suggestions. For our purposes, it is sufficient to become consciously aware of our fears and practice overcoming them. Reading, understanding, and acting on the material in this chapter, and OB more generally, are steps in a positive direction.

> **EXAMPLE**   Avoiding Conflict Makes It Grow!
> When you're tempted to avoid conflict, you may be well served to do the following instead.
>
> 1. **Stop ignoring a conflict.** Ignoring or working around a conflict won't make it go away and may cause further escalation. Instead, bring both sides together to address the issues.

2. **Act decisively to improve the outcome.** Delay only causes the problem, real or perceived, to fester. Addressing a conflict in short order can help unveil misunderstandings or simple oversights before they grow into something more or spread.

3. **Make the path to resolution open and honest**. Involve all relevant parties, collect information, and determine a desired outcome. Doing so helps resolve misunderstandings and focuses everybody on the end state instead of wallowing in the (alleged) offenses.

4. **Use descriptive language instead of evaluative.** Beware of accusations and judgmental language. Both put people on the defensive and impede progress. Instead, focus on the problem (behaviors, feelings, implications) and solution rather than the perpetrator.

5. **Make the process a team-building opportunity.** If the problem affects the team, then it may be beneficial to approach the conflict and its solution as a team. Such resolutions may improve relationships in such a way that the team functions even better than it did before the conflict.

6. **Keep the upside in mind.** Effective conflict resolution creates "success momentum." In other words, conflicts are signs along the road to the final and desired destination. Don't get bogged down and lose sight of the ultimate goal or bigger picture.[18]

TAKE-AWAY APPLICATION—TAAP

1. Think of a conflict, or a situation that is strained, one that you either haven't addressed or have purposefully avoided.

2. Then describe how you could apply suggestions 2–4 in the Example above.

3. If the situation involves a team or a group of people, then describe how you might use this as an opportunity for team-building (suggestion 5).

4. Identify and focus on the upside (suggestion 6), as it will help motivate you to follow the other suggestions and prevent you from getting discouraged.

At this point in our discussion it is useful to remind ourselves of what we get for our efforts. After all, embracing conflict or taking a more positive and constructive view can be difficult and counterintuitive. What are the desired outcomes of our efforts?

Desired Outcomes of Conflict Management

Conflict management is more than simply a quest for agreement. If progress is to be made and dysfunctional conflict minimized, a broader agenda is in order. An influential model of cooperative conflict outlines three desired outcomes:

1. *Agreement.* But at what cost? Equitable and fair agreements are best. An agreement that leaves one party feeling exploited or defeated will tend to breed resentment and subsequent conflict.

2. *Stronger relationships.* Good agreements enable conflicting parties to build bridges of goodwill and trust for future use. Moreover, conflicting parties who trust each other are more likely to keep their end of the bargain.

3. *Learning.* Functional conflict can promote greater self-awareness and creative problem solving. Like the practice of management itself, successful conflict handling is learned primarily by doing. Knowledge of the concepts and techniques in this chapter is a necessary first step, but there is no substitute for hands-on practice. There are plenty of opportunities to practice conflict management in today's world.[19]

major question

MAJOR QUESTION

What are some types of conflict and how can I manage them to my benefit?

THE BIGGER PICTURE

You can think of many types of conflicts from your own life, and likely have a good idea of what caused most of them. But in this section we focus on two of the most common and consequential types of conflict in organizations—*personality* and *intergroup*. The first occurs at the individual level and the other at the group level. Understanding both types will make you more effective at managing an extremely valuable group-level process in the Integrative Framework.

Opposition in and of itself is not usually a problem, as it can be a constructive way of challenging the status quo and improving behaviors, processes, and outcomes. New ideas by definition are in opposition to old ideas or ways of doing things. However, opposition becomes an issue if and when it turns into dysfunctional conflict and impedes progress and performance. *Personality conflict* and *intergroup conflict* can both impede progress and performance, and cause a number of other undesirable outcomes across levels of the Integrative Framework of OB.

Hopefully, none of your personality or other types of conflict will result in violence. But if conflicts are not taken seriously and addressed, they often escalate and the negative consequences grow. Think of personality conflicts you've had at work or school. What were the consequences to you? The other person? Members of your team, department, or class?

Personality Conflicts

As discussed in Chapter 3, your *personality* is the package of stable traits and characteristics that create your unique identity. Given the many possible combinations of personality traits, it is clear why personality conflicts are inevitable. We define a **personality conflict as interpersonal opposition based on personal dislike or disagreement.** This is an important topic, as evidenced by a survey of 173 managers in the United States. When the managers were asked what makes them most uncomfortable, an overwhelming 73 percent said, "Building relationships with people I dislike." "Asking for a raise" (25%) and "speaking to large audiences" (24%) were the distant second and third responses.[20]

How to Deal with Personality Conflicts

"I just don't like him. We don't get along." How often have you thought or said something like this about a classmate, coworker, or friend of a friend? One of the many reasons for these feelings and statements is personality conflicts. Such conflicts are common and often pose nightmares for managers and employees more generally. Remember that you learned in Chapter 3 that personality traits, by definition, are stable and resistant to change. Moreover, according to the American Psychiatric Association's *Diagnostic and Statistical Manual of Mental Disorders,* there are 410 psychological disorders that can and do show up in the workplace.[21] The existence of such disorders raises unique legal issues.

Employees in the United States suffering from psychological disorders such as depression and mood-altering diseases such as alcoholism are protected from discrimination by the Americans with Disabilities Act.[22]

(Other nations have similar laws.) Also, sexual harassment and other forms of discrimination can grow out of apparent personality conflicts. And personality conflicts that are ignored or avoided often escalate. For example, Mozilla, the maker of the Firefox web browser, suffered the consequences of personality conflict when it's former CEO, Brendan Eich, donated money to a referendum on legislation that banned same-sex marriage. While some of the coders in the Firefox community agreed with his views and actions, others vehemently disagreed. Mr. Eich refused to discuss or explain his views, which caused things to escalate, which led to conflicts with the board of directors and ultimately his resignation. All of this occurred just two weeks after he took the job.[23] It therefore is critically important to identify and remedy such conflicts.[24]

EXAMPLE   A CEO Who Planned a "Food Fight"

Kevin Reddy, the CEO of Noodles & Co. Restaurants, hired Dan Fogarty as chief marketing officer knowing that his personality clashed with that of the company's president, Keith Kinsey. (Fogarty and Kinsey previously worked together at Chipotle.)

Reddy knew that Kinsey was analytical and pragmatic, while Fogarty was unstructured and creative. The CEO counted on and took advantage of their different personalities and heated debates. Reddy believed that executives who challenge one another—rather than validating each others' ideas—produced the best thinking. He said, "I don't mind if it gets a little bloody as long as it's merely a flesh wound."[25]

Table 10.2 presents practical tips for both you and managers who are involved in or affected by personality conflicts. Best practices vary, depending on the party. Steps 2 through 4 in the table show how to escalate your concern if the conflict is not resolved.

Our later discussions of handling dysfunctional conflict and alternative dispute resolution techniques also apply.

TABLE 10.2   HOW TO RESPOND WHEN AN EMPLOYEE EXPERIENCES A PERSONALITY CONFLICT

FOR THE EMPLOYEE	FOR THIRD-PARTY OBSERVERS	FOR THE EMPLOYEE'S MANAGER
1. All employees need to be familiar with and *follow* company policies for diversity, antidiscrimination, and sexual harassment.		
2. Communicate directly with the other person to resolve the perceived conflict (emphasize problem solving and common objectives, not personalities).	Do not take sides in someone else's personality conflict.	Investigate and document the conflict; if appropriate, take corrective action (e.g., feedback or behavior modification).
3. Avoid dragging coworkers into the conflict.	Suggest the parties work things out for themselves in a constructive and positive way.	If necessary, attempt informal dispute resolution.
4. If dysfunctional conflict persists, seek help from direct supervisors or human resource specialists.	If dysfunctional conflict persists, refer the problem to the parties' direct supervisors.	Refer difficult conflicts to human resource specialists or hired counselors for formal resolution attempts and other interventions.

Intergroup Conflict

Conflict among work groups, teams, and departments is a common threat to individual and organizational effectiveness, as illustrated in the Integrative Framework. For example, the conflict between the National Football League (NFL) Owners Association and the League's referees had widely publicized and dramatic consequences. A number of botched calls by "substitute" referees were witnessed not only by the players and owners, but millions of fans on television. And at least one of these calls changed the outcome of a game.[26] The conflicts between these two parties caused tremendous problems at many levels for those affected, such as referees, players, teams, the NFL, and the owners.

Conflict States and Processes It is useful to distinguish between two forms of intergroup conflict:

- *Conflict states*—shared perceptions among members of the team about the intensity of disagreement over either tasks (i.e., goals, ideas, and performance strategies) or relationships (i.e., personality clashes and interpersonal styles).
- *Conflict processes*—members' interactions aimed at working through task and interpersonal disagreements.[27]

Recent research strongly supports what you likely suspect: *conflict processes,* or how teams manage differences, matter. Much like what you learned in Chapter 5 about distributive and procedural justice, *process always matters!*[28] So much so that a leading expert and her colleagues concluded, "The truth about team conflict: Conflict processes, that is, how teams interact regarding their differences, are at least as important as conflict states, that is, the source and intensity of their perceived incompatibilities."[29] This argument was highlighted in the merger between American Airlines and US Airways. Unions representing dispatchers and mechanics felt that the "American workers got moved ahead of them" in the negotiations. As a result they will be working side-by-side with people who will make nearly 30% more for the same job and work fewer hours.[30]

Conflict processes are often critically important in mergers, as was the case when US Airways merged with American Airlines. Tom Horton, former CEO of American Airlines (right), handed over control of the merged company to US Airways CEO, Doug Parker (left). Both played critical roles in solving conflicts and gaining the support of airline employees and unions.

In-Group Thinking—"Us vs. Them" As we discussed in Chapter 8, *cohesiveness*—a "we feeling" binding group members together—can be a good or bad thing. A certain amount of cohesiveness can turn a group of individuals into a smooth-running team. Too much cohesiveness, however, can breed groupthink because a desire to get along pushes aside critical thinking. The study of in-groups by small group researchers has revealed an array of challenges associated with increased group cohesiveness and in-group thinking. Specifically,

- Members of in-groups view themselves as a collection of unique individuals, while they stereotype members of other groups as being "all alike."
- In-group members see themselves positively and as morally correct, while they view members of other groups negatively and as immoral.
- In-groups view outsiders as a threat.
- In-group members exaggerate the differences between their group and other groups. This typically involves a distorted perception of reality.[31]

Managers cannot eliminate in-group thinking, but they certainly should not ignore it when handling intergroup conflicts. Let's explore some options for managers—and you.

How to Handle Intergroup Conflict

Drawing on your past experiences, how have you attempted to solve conflicts between a team of which you are a member and another team? While many techniques are successful in particular situations, research and practice support three specific approaches:

- Contact hypothesis
- Conflict reduction
- Creating psychologically safe climates

Making an effort to understand and appreciate differing company, industry, or cultural customs is an effective way to avoid conflicts and make all parties more comfortable.

Contact Hypothesis   The ***contact hypothesis*** **suggests that the more members of different groups interact, the less intergroup conflict they will experience.** Those interested in improving race, international, and union–management relations typically encourage cross-group interaction. The hope is that *any* type of interaction, short of actual conflict, will reduce stereotyping and combat in-group thinking.

But research has shown this approach to be naive and limited. For example, a study of ethnic majority (in-group) and ethnic minority (out-group) students from Germany, Belgium, and England revealed that contact did in fact reduce prejudice. Specifically, contact over time resulted in a lower desire for social distance and fewer negative emotions related to the out-group. The quality of contacts mattered too, especially regarding equal status, cooperation, and closeness. It wasn't enough simply to encounter members of the out-group (e.g., just an introduction). However, *prejudice also reduced contact.* Those in the out-group were more reluctant to engage or contact the in-group. Moreover, contact had no effect on reducing prejudice of the minority out-group on the majority in-group.[32] One interpretation of these results is that contact matters, quality contact matters more, but both matter most from the in-group's perspective.

Nevertheless, intergroup friendships are still desirable, as is documented in many studies.[33] But they are readily overpowered by negative intergroup interactions. Thus, the top priority for managers faced with intergroup conflict is to identify and root out specific negative linkages between or among groups.

Conflict Reduction   Considering these facts, managers are wise to note negative interactions between members and groups and consider options for reducing conflict. Several alternative actions are recommended:

- Work to eliminate specific negative interactions (obvious enough).
- Conduct team building to reduce intragroup conflict and prepare for cross-functional teamwork (discussed in Chapter 8).
- Encourage and facilitate friendships via social events (e.g., happy hours, sports leagues, and book clubs).
- Foster positive attitudes (e.g., empathy and compassion).

- Avoid or neutralize negative gossip.
- Practice the above—be a role model.[34]

TAKE-AWAY APPLICATION—TAAP

1. Think of an example of intergroup conflict in your own life. Your example should include a description of a group, team, or department of which you either are or were a member, as well as the nature (task or relationship) of the conflict.

2. Then describe how the conflict was handled. Was the conflict resolved?

3. Regardless of your answer to question 2, explain how one or more of the above recommendations could have been applied to reduce, eliminate, or even prevent the conflict described in question 1.

Creating a Psychologically Safe Climate   As we've discussed, conflict occurs at all levels in the Integrative Framework. This means that the causes and remedies can also occur at individual, group, and organizational levels. Recall our discussion of climate in Chapter 5. **Climate represents employees' shared perceptions of policies, practices, and procedures.** Specific to psychological safety, a **"*psychological safety climate* refers to a shared belief held by team members that the team is a safe place for interpersonal risk taking and captures a 'sense of confidence that the team will not embarrass, reject, or punish someone for speaking up.'"**[35] When employees feel psychologically safe they are more likely to speak up and present their ideas and less likely to take disagreements personally. This results in better functioning teams (e.g., less conflict) and higher individual and team performance.[36]

So, how can you and your employers create or foster a climate for psychological safety? Here are three fundamental and widely applicable practices:

1. Assure leaders are inclusive and accessible.

2. Hire and develop employees who are comfortable expressing their own ideas and receptive and constructive to those expressed by others.

3. Celebrate and even reinforce the value of differences between group members and their ideas.[37]

Find out the level of psychological safety in one of your groups, teams, or organizations by completing Self-Assessment 10.2. It's a quick, accurate, and valuable way to get a sense of this important environmental characteristic. Knowing the level of psychological safety can help you understand why some conflicts occur and how effectively they are likely to be handled.

connect

SELF-ASSESSMENT 10.2   Psychological Safety Climate

Go to connect.mheducation.com and take Self-Assessment 10.2 to evaluate how open groups of which you're a member are to addressing conflicts.

1. Identify a group at school or work of which you are a member. It helps if the one you choose has to deal with opposing views and make decisions. Complete Self-Assessment 10.2 focusing on this group.

2. Which items help you understand why the group deals with conflicts as it does?

3. Explain three things you and your group members can do to increase psychological safety and reduce conflict.

Excerpted from A. Edmondson, "Psychological Safety and Learning Behavior in Work Teams," *Administrative Science Quarterly 44,* 1999, 350–383. Copyright © 1999. Reproduced with permission of Sage Publications, Inc. via Copyright Clearance Center.

major question

MAJOR QUESTION

What can I do to manage work–family conflict and incivility to make me more effective at school, work, and home?

THE BIGGER PICTURE

We focus our discussion on two particular forms of conflict that are increasingly relevant in today's busy world of work and school—work–family conflict and incivility (e.g., bullying). You, for instance, have demands at school and other arenas of your life (e.g., work, your social life, and perhaps a family), and these demands can compete and cause conflicts. Such conflicts, along with uncivil behavior or mistreatment, can have dramatic and undesirable effects on individual-level (and other) outcomes noted in the Integrative Framework.

Students, employees, and people everywhere have always experienced conflicts between the various arenas of their lives, notably between work, school, and home. Bullying and other forms of mistreatment also are common parts of the human experience. But what makes both of these especially relevant today is the 24/7 connectivity we all experience. Technology enables us to be "plugged in" everywhere and all the time. This means that the boundaries between the various arenas of work, home, social, and school are blurred and the potential for conflicts is greater. This contrasts with the recent past when these activities and their demands were confined to the physical locations in which they occurred (e.g., work happened largely at the office). Not anymore. Technology also changes and extends bullying. The Internet and social media are new and devastating tools for bullies and other bad actors. These are reasons why we give special attention to these forms of conflict.

Work–Family Conflict

Work–family conflict occurs when the demands or pressures from work and family domains are mutually incompatible. Work–family conflict can take two distinct forms: work interference with family and family interference with work.[38] And in either case, these conflicts can be social (e.g., between the expectations of your boss and those of your professor), or they can be cognitive (e.g., your thoughts about school interfere with work or vice versa). For example, suppose two managers in the same department have daughters playing on the same soccer team. One manager misses the big soccer game to attend a last-minute department meeting; the other manager skips the meeting to attend the game. Both may experience work–family conflict. These conflicts matter because they can negatively affect many important outcomes in the Integrative Framework and your larger life domain (see Table 10.3).

What about you? What level of conflict do you think you experience between school and other domains of your life? Self-Assessment 10.3 will help you know. We strongly encourage you to complete this Assessment, as it will help you see such conflicts from the point of view of others, not just your own perceptions. Moreover, the Self-Assessment can help you identify which conflicts are the greatest and least, and this knowledge can assist you in determining what to do about it.

TABLE 10.3 NEGATIVE CONSEQUENCES OF CONFLICTS BETWEEN WORK, FAMILY, AND OTHER LIFE DOMAINS

WORK INTERFERES WITH FAMILY	FAMILY INTERFERES WITH WORK	POTENTIAL OUTCOMES
Job satisfaction	Marital satisfaction	Life satisfaction
Intentions to quit	Family satisfaction	Health problems
Absenteeism	Family-related strain	Depression
Performance	Family-related performance	Substance use/abuse

SOURCE: Adapted from F. T. Amstad, L. L. Meier, U. Fasel, A. Elfering, and N. K. Semmer, "A Meta-Analysis of Work-Family Conflict and Various Outcomes with a Special Emphasis on Cross-Domain versus Matching Domain Relations," *Journal of Occupational Health Psychology,* 2011, 151–169.

connect

SELF-ASSESSMENT 10.3 **School–Non-School Conflict**

Go to connect.mheducation.com and take Self-Assessment 10.3 to evaluate the level and sources of conflicts between school and other arenas of your life.

1. What is your reaction?
2. Do any of your responses and sources of conflict surprise you?
3. Which do you think is greater, the social dimension (questions 1–6) or the cognitive dimension (questions 7–9)?
4. What can you do to prevent or reduce the conflicts you identified?

Adapted from S. R. Ezzedeen and P. M. Swiercz, "Development and Initial Validation of a Cognitive-Based Work-Nonwork Conflict Scale," *Psychological Reports,* 2007, 979–99. Reprinted with permission of Ammons Scientific Ltd.

Because the consequences of such conflict can be numerous and very problematic, researchers and managers alike have devoted extensive attention and effort to understanding and reducing such conflicts. From a practical perspective, it is helpful to think of *balance.*

Balance Is the Key to Reducing Conflict Ideally, you will be able to avoid or remove conflicts completely. But more often than not you cannot eliminate such conflicts and instead have to manage or balance demands between the different domains of your life. Here are some ideas to consider.

Sheryl Sandberg, COO of Facebook. She used to stay late, along with the programmers. But she now goes home around 5:00 pm. This doesn't mean she doesn't do any work after 5:00, but she often does it from home.

- *Work–family balance begins at home.* Case studies of successful executives reveal that family and spousal support is critical for reaching senior-level positions.[39] This in turn suggests that both men and women need help with domestic responsibilities if there is any chance of achieving work–family balance. This same message was reinforced by Sheryl Sandberg of Facebook, who recently argued in her book, *Lean In,* that women who want it all can indeed have it, but they also need support at home—they can't do it alone.

- *An employer's family-supportive philosophy is more important than specific programs.* This means that the organizational culture must support the use of family-friendly programs for employees to use them. For instance, it's not enough to simply provide child care; employees must also feel supported and comfortable using it. The same goes for leaving early to attend a child's sporting event or recital.

- *The importance of work–family balance varies across generations.* A study of work values across 16,000 people from different generational groups suggests that organizations should consider implementing work policies that are targeted toward different generational groups.[40] (Recall our discussion in Chapter 4.) For example, flextime and compressed work programs can be used to attract and retain both Gen Ys and Gen Xers, while job enrichment discussed in Chapter 5 may be a more effective way to motivate baby boomers.

Flexspace vs. Flextime and Your Supervisor   Balance requires flexibility, which is a key aspect of many efforts to eliminate or reduce conflicts. That said, not all flexibility is the same. Understanding the differences can help you better balance your own demands between not only work and family, but school and the rest of your life too.

> *Flexspace*, such as telecommuting, is when policies enable employees to do their work from different locations besides the office (e.g., coffee shops, home, or the beach).

> *Flextime* is flexible scheduling, either when work is expected to be completed (e.g., deadlines) or during which particular hours of the day (e.g., 10–5, or anytime today).

While this all makes sense to you, it is critically important to emphasize the role of supervisors. The value of most any type of flexible work arrangement can be undermined if your immediate supervisor isn't supportive. Put another way, supportive policies matter, but what good is a policy if you aren't allowed to use it?[41]

Incivility—Treating Others Poorly Has Real Costs

Incivility is any form of socially harmful behavior, such as aggression, interpersonal deviance, social undermining, interactional injustice, harassment, abusive supervision, and bullying.[42] Incivility is common, so much so that recent research reports that 98 percent of employees stated they had experienced some form of incivility and 50 percent said they had been treated rudely at least once a week![43] Table 10.4 describes some of employees' common responses to incivility and their frequencies. Besides the obvious—that you don't like to be mistreated—experts on the matter describe the costs of incivility this way:

> The costs chip away at the bottom line. Nearly everybody who experiences workplace incivility responds in a negative way, in some cases overtly retaliating. Employees are less creative when they feel disrespected, and many get fed up and leave.[44]

One estimate is that 13 percent of executives' time at Fortune 1000 companies is spent dealing with incivility. This equates to seven weeks per year![45]

TABLE 10.4   EMPLOYEES' RESPONSES TO AND THE COSTS OF INCIVILITY AT WORK

48% intentionally decreased their work effort
47% intentionally decreased the time spent at work
38% intentionally decreased the quality of their work
63% lost work time avoiding the offender
66% said performance declined
25% admitted to taking frustration out on customers
12% said they left their job because of it

SOURCE: Reprinted by permission of *Harvard Business Review*. Exhibit from "The Price of Incivility—Lack of Respect Hurts Morale and the Bottom Line," by C. Porath and C. Pearson, January–February 2013. Copyright © 2013 by the Harvard Business School Publishing Corporation; all rights reserved.

FIGURE 10.2   CAUSES, FORMS, AND OUTCOMES OF INCIVILITY AT WORK

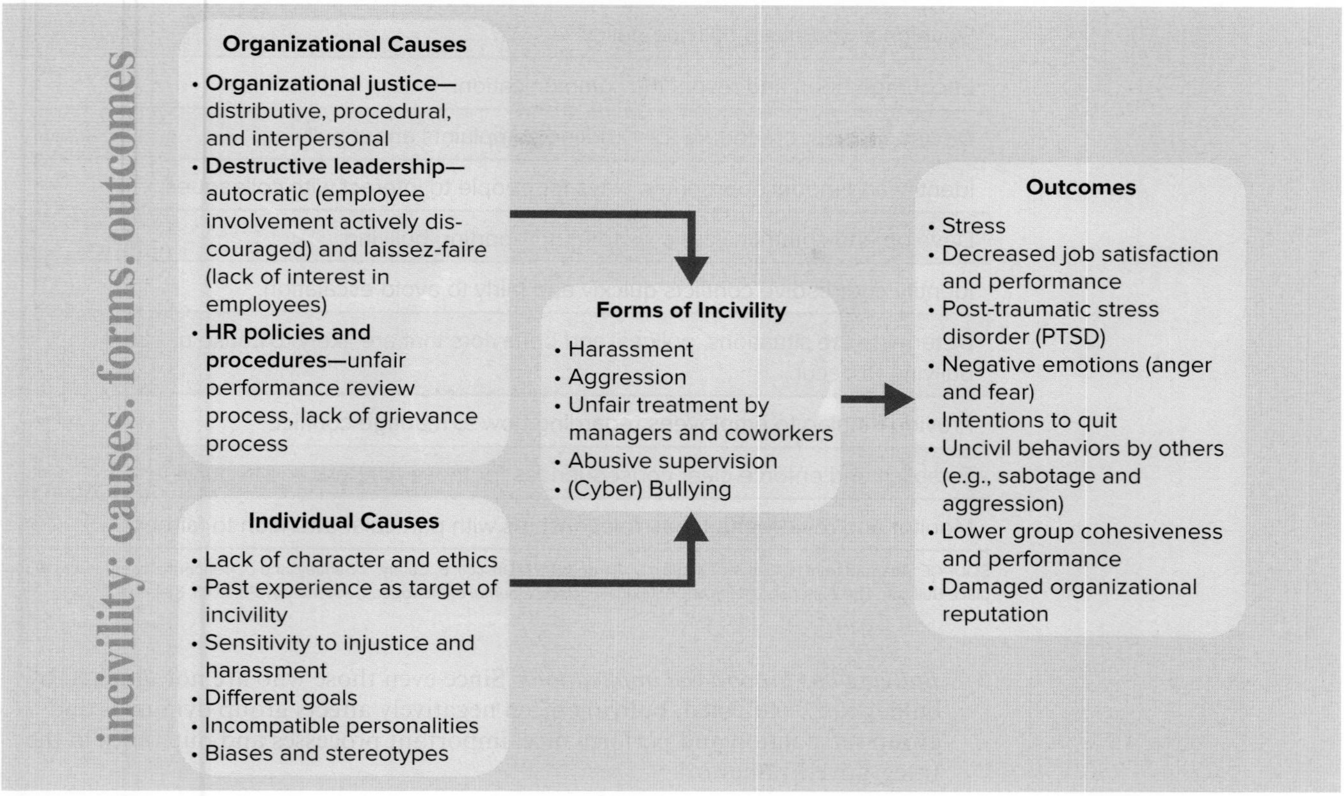

incivility: causes, forms, outcomes

Organizational Causes

- **Organizational justice**—distributive, procedural, and interpersonal
- **Destructive leadership**—autocratic (employee involvement actively discouraged) and laissez-faire (lack of interest in employees)
- **HR policies and procedures**—unfair performance review process, lack of grievance process

Individual Causes

- Lack of character and ethics
- Past experience as target of incivility
- Sensitivity to injustice and harassment
- Different goals
- Incompatible personalities
- Biases and stereotypes

Forms of Incivility

- Harassment
- Aggression
- Unfair treatment by managers and coworkers
- Abusive supervision
- (Cyber) Bullying

Outcomes

- Stress
- Decreased job satisfaction and performance
- Post-traumatic stress disorder (PTSD)
- Negative emotions (anger and fear)
- Intentions to quit
- Uncivil behaviors by others (e.g., sabotage and aggression)
- Lower group cohesiveness and performance
- Damaged organizational reputation

SOURCE: Inspired by and adapted from R. Singleton, L. A. Toombs, S. Taneja, C. Larkin, and M. G. Pryor, "Workplace Conflict: A Strategic Leadership Imperative," *International Journal of Business and Public Administration 8,* 2011, 149–156.

Causes of Incivility   It's no surprise that both individuals and their employers can be the root cause of mistreatment at work. Figure 10.2 illustrates some common causes of various forms of incivility (e.g., aggression, harassment, and bullying).

Note that the causes, just like the outcomes, can occur at all three levels in the Integrative Framework. This means that bad behavior is truly an organizational problem, even it if starts with a single individual.

Bullying   Recall our discussion of counterproductive work behaviors and bullying in Chapter 2. The chapter-opening Winning at Work and in-chapter Problem-Solving Application addressed bullying from the target's or individual's perspective. We are going to build on this here and explore the implications of bullying at the group and organization levels. To this end, it is useful to note that bullying is different from other forms of mistreatment or incivility in at least three ways.[46]

1. *Bullying is most often evident to others.* Bullies at work don't have to push you down or take your lunch money, like they do in elementary school. But even when they are less obvious and nonviolent, coworkers are commonly aware that someone is being bullied through either gossip or other forms of communication (e.g., meetings, e-mail, and social media).

2. *Bullying affects even those who are NOT bullied.* Recent research shows that employees who are simply aware of bullying of colleagues, but not themselves a target, are more likely to quit their jobs. This means that bullying has costs that extend well beyond the person being bullied.[47] This is similar to what you learned in Chapter 5 about a lack of justice. Simply witnessing or being aware that one of your colleagues is mistreated has negative effects on you.

TABLE 10.5 ANTI-BULLYING STRATEGIES FOR GROUPS AND ORGANIZATIONS

Develop a workplace bullying policy.
Encourage open and respectful communication.
Develop a clear procedure for handling complaints about bullying.
Identify and model appropriate ways for people to interact with colleagues.
Develop and communicate a system for reporting bullying.
Identify and resolve conflicts quickly and fairly to avoid escalation.
Determine the situations, polices, and behaviors that are likely to cause or allow bullying to occur.
Provide training to employees regarding how to manage conflict.
Establish and enforce clear consequences for those who engage in bullying.
Monitor and review employee relationships with particular attention to fairness.

SOURCE: Adapted from H. Cooper-Thomas, D. Gardner, M. O'Driscoll, B. Cately, T. Bentley, and L. Trenberth, "Neutralizing Workplace Bullying: The Buffering Effects of Contextual Factors," *Journal of Managerial Psychology 28,* 2013, 384–407.

3. *Bullying has group-level implications.* Since even those who are not targeted by bullies can be affected, bullying often negatively affects group dynamics and group satisfaction and performance, important processes and outcomes in the Integrative Framework.

Given the costs of bullying, what can you and employers do? Table 10.5 provides a collection of best practices from business and research.

Cyber Bullying and Harassment   As noted above, among the ways advances in technology have changed school and work is in the area of conflict.[48] The Web, our everywhere connectivity, and particularly social media create new avenues and weapons for bullies at school, at work, and in our social lives. Many researchers now report that virtual bullying is more common that face-to-face bullying, although the two often co-occur.[49] Worse still, both face-to-face and cyber bullying affect their victims in two ways. Not only do the uncivil acts directly harm the targeted person, but the *fear of future mistreatment amplifies this effect.* So, what can you and managers do to avoid bullying and other forms of incivility? The practices described in Table 10.5 above are a good start. But it is useful for you and your employers to take specific actions to prevent and address virtual incivility (harassment and bullying) in e-mails and social media.

Policies
- Create and enforce policies on acceptable computer technology usage
- Assure that company technology (e.g., computers and smartphones) cannot be used anonymously
- Communicate expectations for e-mail and social media communications outside of work that affect the organization and its members.

Practices
- Be wary of
  - Using BOLD lettering and underlining and punctuation
  - Messages that are mean-spirited
  - Demeaning phrases
  - Personal insults

- Avoid sending copies to people who don't need to receive the message—so as not to embarrass the recipient.
- Think before you hit the send button (good idea to wait until the next day).
- Take appropriate action when you become aware of "conflict-producing" e-mail.[50]

Victim, Witness, or Perpetrator?   You've learned about various forms of conflict, as well as potential causes and solutions. Let's conclude this section by having you assess not just your experience, but also your actions. Completing Self-Assessment 10.4 can help you improve your own effectiveness.

■ connect®

SELF-ASSESSMENT 10.4   Bullying Scale

This will highlight the forms of bullying you experience, witness, or commit.

1. Which three example items do you most commonly experience?
2. What do you think are the causes of these examples? Try to identify causes across individual, group, and organizational levels using your OB knowledge.
3. To what extent do your most commonly experienced match those you most commonly engage in?
4. Describe some things that could be done to prevent or reduce these acts of bullying.

From T. Glomb, "Predicting Workplace Aggression: Reciprocal Aggression, Organizational, and Individual Responses," *International Journal of Organization Theory and Behavior 13*, 2010, 249–291. Reprinted with permission.

Another way to be a more effective and helpful when witnessing bullying is to take the perspective of the target. Consciously think of what it is like to be him/her, walk in his/her shoes, and experience the effects of being bullied. Research has shown that you may realize both obvious and not so obvious benefits by doing so, such as:[53]

- They may like you more (obvious)
- Your interactions with that person are likely to improve (obvious)
- There may be reduced stereotyping of the target, or target group, and increased empathy (not so obvious)
- There may be an increased sense of shared or common goals and experiences (i.e., interpersonal overlap)

In a practical sense, perspective taking can serve as a low-cost and highly effective intervention to help mitigate many of the prejudices and bad behaviors often observed in work and school settings. It also can be used when mediating conflicts, as in the heat of the conflict most parties often are so focused on themselves that they never think to consider the other's view.

Remember that mistreatment has more victims than the immediate targets. We therefore urge you not to be a silent bystander but do your part to prevent and remedy various forms of incivility at school, work, and home.

MAJOR QUESTION

What can I do to prevent, reduce, or even overcome conflicts?

THE BIGGER PICTURE

So far in this chapter you've learned about many forms of conflict along with potential causes and solutions. We extend your knowledge in this section by introducing a number of practical means for dealing with a variety of conflicts. Specifically, we explore how to program or create functional conflict and how to implement alternative forms of dispute resolution (ADR). This makes sense given our knowledge that too little conflict is undesirable. You then will learn about various conflict-handling styles and have the opportunity to identify your own. The practical knowledge in this section will make you more effective by enabling you to better manage conflicts and important outcomes in the Integrative Framework.

We now turn our attention to the active management of both functional and dysfunctional conflict and discuss how to stimulate functional conflict, how to handle dysfunctional conflict, and how third parties can help.

Programming Functional Conflict

Have you ever been on a team at school or member of a committee that got so bogged down in details and procedures that nothing was accomplished? Of course you have. Such experiences are both a waste of time and frustrating. One way to break out of such unproductive ruts is to generate and monitor *functional conflict.* When done effectively, collaboration, creativity, and results can soar. As one expert put it: "Conflict is oxygen and brings issues into the open."[52] The challenge is to do it in a functional rather than dysfunctional manner. To do this, managers essentially have two options.

1. *Fan the fire and get more of the same.* Managers can urge coworkers to hunker down and slog through—simply persist. While this may work, this approach can be unreliable (conflict can escalate) and slow.

2. *Program conflict.* Alternatively, managers can resort to programmed conflict. Experts in the field define **programmed conflict** as "conflict that raises different opinions regardless of the personal feelings of the managers."[53] The challenge is to get contributors to either defend or criticize ideas based on relevant facts rather than on the basis of personal preference or political interests. This requires disciplined role-playing and effective leadership. Two programmed conflict techniques with proven track records are *devil's advocacy* and the *dialectic method.* Let's explore these two ways of stimulating functional conflict.

Devil's Advocacy   This technique gets its name from a traditional practice within the Roman Catholic Church. When someone's name comes before the College of Cardinals for elevation to sainthood, it is absolutely essential to ensure that he or she had a spotless record. Consequently, one individual is assigned the role of *devil's advocate* to uncover and air all possible objections to the person's canonization. In today's organizations **devil's advocacy** involves assigning someone the role of critic. Figure 10.3 shows the steps involved in this approach. Note how devil's advocacy alters the usual decision-making process in steps 2 and 3 on the left side of the figure.

FIGURE 10.3 TECHNIQUES FOR STIMULATING FUNCTIONAL CONFLICT: DEVIL'S ADVOCACY AND THE DIALECTIC METHOD

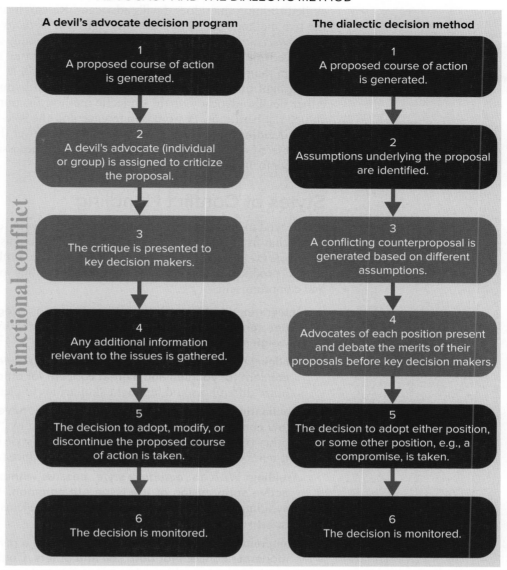

SOURCE: From R. A. Casler and R. C. Schwenk, "Agreement and Thinking Alike: Ingredients for Poor Decisions," *Academy of Management Executive*, February 1990, 72–73. Reproduced with permission of The Academy of Management, via Copyright Clearance Center.

The Dialectic Method Like devil's advocacy, the dialectic method is a time-honored practice. This particular approach to programmed conflict traces all the way back to ancient Greece. Plato and his followers attempted to synthesize truths by exploring opposite positions (called *thesis* and *antithesis*). Court systems in the United States and elsewhere rely on directly opposing points of view for determining guilt or innocence. Accordingly, today's **dialectic method calls for managers to foster a structured debate of opposing viewpoints prior to making a decision.**[54] Steps 3 and 4 in the right half of Figure 10.3 set the dialectic approach apart from common decision-making processes.

Pros, Cons, and Practical Advice on Programmed Conflict It is a good idea to rotate the job of devil's advocate so no one person or group develops a strictly negative reputation. Moreover, periodically playing the devil's advocacy role is good training for developing analytical and communication skills and emotional intelligence. As for the dialectic method, it is intended to generate critical thinking and reality testing. A major drawback of the dialectic method is that "winning the debate" may overshadow the issue at hand. Also, the dialectic method requires more skilled training than does devil's advocacy. Research on the relative effectiveness of the two methods ended in a tie, although *both methods were more effective than consensus decision making.*[55] However, a laboratory study showed that devil's advocacy produced more potential solutions and made better recommendations for a case problem than did groups using the dialectic method.[56]

In light of this mixed evidence, managers and you have some latitude in using either devil's advocacy or the dialectic method for pumping creative life back into stalled deliberations. Personal preference and the role-players' experience may well be the deciding factors in choosing one approach over the other. The important thing is to actively stimulate functional conflict when necessary, such as when the risk of blind conformity or groupthink is high.

Styles of Conflict Handling

People tend to handle (negative) conflict in similar ways, referred to as *styles.* Figure 10.4 shows that five of the most common styles are distinguished based on relative concern for others (*x*-axis) and concern for self (*y*-axis). The combinations of these two characteristics produce the conflict-handling styles integrating, obliging, dominating, avoiding, and compromising.[57]

Integrating (problem solving): When using an ***integrating style,*** **interested parties confront the issue and cooperatively identify the problem, generate and weigh alternatives, and select a solution.**

Obliging (smoothing): If you have an ***obliging style,*** **then you tend to show low concern for yourself and a great concern for others.** Such people tend to minimize differences and highlight similarities to please the other party.

Dominating: Those with a ***dominating style*** **have a high concern for self and low concern for others,** often characterized by "I win, you lose" tactics. The other party's needs are largely ignored. This style is often called *forcing* because it relies on formal authority to force compliance (discussed in Chapter 12).

Avoiding: With an ***avoiding style,*** **passive withdrawal from the problem and active suppression of the issue are common.** We addressed the pitfalls of avoiding conflict earlier, as well as the problems associated with suppressing negative emotions.

Compromising: The ***compromising*** **style is a give-and-take approach with a moderate concern for both self and others.** Compromise is appropriate when parties have opposite goals or possess equal power.

FIGURE 10.4 FIVE COMMON CONFLICT-HANDLING STYLES

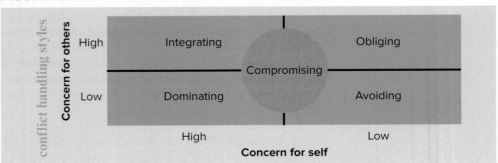

SOURCE: From M. A. Rahim, "A Strategy for Managing Conflict in Complex Organizations," *Human Relations*, 1985, Vol. 38. No. 1, 84. Reproduced with permission of Sage Publications Ltd. via Copyright Clearance Center.

Before you learn about the characteristics of these styles, and the best situations in which to use them, take Self-Assessment 10.5 to learn your own style. If you know your own style, you'll be able to see if what you learn matches your style. Better still, you'll know the situations in which your preferred style helps versus hurts you when handling conflict. For instance, wouldn't you like to know when an *avoiding* style (perhaps yours?) is most effective?

---

connect

SELF-ASSESSMENT 10.5 Preferred Conflict-Handling Style

Go to connect.mheducation.com and learn what your tendencies are for handling conflicts.

1. What is your style? On the surface, before reading below, does this make sense to you? Why or why not?

2. Describe a conflict you've experienced in which your conflict-handling style helped you.

3. Describe a conflict in which your style didn't serve you well. Explain why.

4. Explain which style you think would have been best for that particular conflict?

The complete instrument may be found in M. A. Rahim, "A Measure of Styles of Handling Interpersonal Conflict," *Academy of Management Journal,* June 1983, 368–376. Copyright © 1983. Reproduced with permission of Academy of management via Copyright Clearance Center.

When to Apply the Various Conflict-Handling Styles Consistent with the contingency approach described throughout this book, there is no "one style fits all" when it comes to handling conflict. Research and practice thankfully provide some guidance regarding which styles seem to work best in particular situations (see Table 10.6).

TAKE-AWAY APPLICATION—TAAP

1. Think of a conflict in your own life.

2. Then describe how the conflict was handled. Which style best describes how you handled the conflict? Was it the appropriate style?

3. Explain which style would have been most appropriate and why?

Why Styles Matter Because conflict is so pervasive it is no surprise that researchers and managers have both devoted considerable attention to the topic. Some key points:

1. **Culture.** Recent research shows that conflict-handling styles are not just an individual-level phenomenon. Departments and entire organizations can develop the same sort of styles (e.g., integrating, dominating, and avoiding). And leaders' own styles have the greatest influence in determining which style gets embedded. (Culture and how to embed it will be covered in detail in Chapter 14.)

2. **Results.** Cooperative styles (integrating and obliging) improved new product development (NPD) performance between buyers and suppliers across several industries in Hong Kong. In contrast, uncooperative styles (dominating and avoiding) increased numerous types of conflicts and hampered NPD performance. Compromising had no effect on performance in these same situations.[58] NPD relationships are increasingly important in the global economy; it therefore is wise to give careful consideration to the styles used when working with such partners.

3. **Reduced turnover.** Particularly noteworthy is the considerable attention given to conflict in the nursing occupation. For instance, nurses with high levels of emotional intelligence (covered in Chapter 3) were more inclined to use collaborative

TABLE 10.6 STYLES FOR HANDLING INTERPERSONAL CONFLICT AND THE SITUATIONS WHERE THEY ARE APPROPRIATE AND INAPPROPRIATE

STYLE	APPROPRIATE	INAPPROPRIATE
Integrating	1. Issues are complex. 2. Synthesis of ideas is needed to come up with better solutions. 3. Commitment is needed from other parties for successful implementation. 4. Time is available for problem solving. 5. One party alone cannot solve the problem. 6. Resources possessed by different parties are needed to solve their common problem.	1. Task or problem is simple. 2. Immediate decision is required. 3. Other parties are unconcerned about outcome. 4. Other parties do not have problem-solving skills.
Obliging	1. You believe that you may be wrong. 2. Issue is more important to the other party. 3. You are willing to give up something in exchange for something from the other party in the future. 4. You are dealing from a position of weakness. 5. Preserving relationship is important.	1. Issue is important to you. 2. You believe that you are right. 3. The other party is wrong or unethical.
Dominating	1. Issue is trivial. 2. Speedy decision is needed. 3. Unpopular course of action is implemented. 4. Necessary to overcome assertive subordinates. 5. Unfavorable decision by the other party may be costly to you. 6. Subordinates lack expertise to make technical decisions. 7. Issue is important to you.	1. Issue is complex. 2. Issue is not important to you. 3. Both parties are equally powerful. 4. Decision does not have to be made quickly. 5. Subordinates possess high degree of competence.
Avoiding	1. Issue is trivial. 2. Potential dysfunctional effect of confronting the other party outweighs benefits of resolution. 3. Cooling-off period is needed.	1. Issue is important to you. 2. It is your responsibility to make decision. 3. Parties are unwilling to defer. 4. Prompt attention is needed.
Compromising	1. Goals of parties are mutually exclusive. 2. Parties are equally powerful. 3. Consensus cannot be reached. 4. Integrating or dominating style is not successful. 5. Temporary solution to a complex problem is needed.	1. One party is more powerful. 2. Problem is complex enough to need problem-solving approach.

interpersonal conflict

SOURCE: From M. A. Rahim, "Toward a Theory of Managing Organizational Conflict," *The International Journal of Conflict Management 13*, 2002, 206–235. Copyright © Emerald Group Publishing Limited, all rights reserved.

styles and less likely to use accommodating conflict-handling styles in a sample of nurses.[59] Given the intense shortage of nurses in many parts of the world, turnover is a critical and top-of-the-mind issue for nursing managers and health care administrators alike. Therefore, reducing conflict (e.g., bullying) is an important and effective means for reducing turnover.

4. **Contingency approach.** No one style is best for every situation. Employees and managers are both well served to apply a contingency approach (see our Chapter 1 discussion) to conflict-handling styles.

Third-Party Interventions: Alternative Dispute Resolution

Disputes between employees, between employees and their managers/employers, and between companies too often end up in lengthy and costly court battles. US businesses spend hundreds of billions of dollars per year on *direct legal costs*. But this number is puny when compared to *indirect legal costs,* such as opportunities not pursued due to litigation concerns, disclaimers, and extra testing. All such costs are ultimately passed on to consumers in the form of higher prices.[60] It therefore is no wonder that a more constructive, less expensive approach called alternative dispute resolution has seen enthusiastic growth in recent years. The benefit of **alternative dispute resolution (ADR)** is that it **"uses faster, more user-friendly methods of dispute resolution, instead of traditional, adversarial approaches (e.g., unilateral decision making or litigation)."**[61]

The Many Forms and Progression of ADR You undoubtedly know of many forms of ADR but didn't realize it. The techniques listed below represent a progression of steps third parties can take to resolve organizational conflicts.[62] They are ranked from easiest and least expensive to most difficult and costly. A growing number of organizations have formal ADR policies involving an established sequence of various combinations of these techniques:

Facilitation	A third party, usually a manager, informally urges disputing parties to deal directly with each other in a positive and constructive manner.
Conciliation	A neutral third party informally acts as a communication conduit between disputing parties. This is appropriate when conflicting parties refuse to meet face to face. The immediate goal is to establish direct communication, with the broader aim of finding common ground and a constructive solution.
Peer review	A panel of trustworthy coworkers, selected for their ability to remain objective, hears both sides of a dispute in an informal and confidential meeting. Any decision by the review panel may or may not be binding, depending on the company's ADR policy. Membership on the peer review panel often is rotated among employees.[63]
Ombudsman	Someone who works for the organization, and is widely respected and trusted by his or her coworkers, hears grievances on a confidential basis and attempts to arrange a solution. This approach, more common in Europe than North America, permits someone to get help from above without relying on the formal hierarchy chain.
Mediation	"The mediator—a trained, third-party neutral—actively guides the disputing parties in exploring innovative solutions to the conflict. Although some companies have in-house mediators who have received ADR training, most also use external mediators who have no ties to the company."[64] Unlike an arbitrator, a mediator does *not* render a decision. It is up to the disputants to reach a mutually acceptable decision.
Arbitration	Disputing parties agree ahead of time to accept the decision of a neutral arbitrator in a formal courtlike setting, often complete with evidence and witnesses. Statements are confidential. Decisions are based on legal merits. Trained arbitrators, typically from outside agencies such as the American Arbitration Association, are versed in relevant laws and case precedents. In many instances,

employee arbitration is mandatory for resolving disputes. Heated debate has occurred, however, over the past several years regarding mandatory versus voluntary arbitration. On the one hand, many employers have not realized the time and cost savings promised by arbitration and now prefer to litigate. On the other, many employees feel that arbitration unfairly benefits employers who have skilled arbitrators whose job it is to handle such disputes (recall the issues of equity and justice covered in Chapter 5).[65]

ADR in Action Georgia Pacific, a paper, pulp, and packaging company, has embraced ADR with impressive results. The company's ADR program saved approximately $42 million in the first 10 years of the program. This is remarkable even for a company with annual revenues in the billions.[66] The Example box provides some excellent and practical guidance for implementing an ADR system similar to Georgia Pacific's.

EXAMPLE Implementing ADR at Your Company

The legal team at Georgia Pacific (GP) was the first Fortune 500 company to implement an effective alternative dispute resolution system. Aided by top management support, the company's ADR program is a deeply embedded dispute resolution tool. The leaders at GP recommend the following for companies that seek to realize similar benefits:

- *Get top management support.* Show economic benefits of early case resolution versus winning at all costs.
- *Start training.* While attorneys often are familiar with ADR, they need training on using it effectively.
- *Start small.* Don't attempt a wholesale change of processes and procedures. Choose cases that are best suited for ADR and try those first.
- *Incorporate ADR.* Build ADR into contracts and other agreements and practices.
- *Grant authority.* Devote a person or persons with authority to handle ADR.
- *Begin immediately.* Speed is an advantage of ADR; use it. To do this, set up a process for quickly screening cases and identifying those that qualify for ADR.
- *Build and collect ADR resources.* Like other forms of institutional knowledge, build "libraries" or repositories of ADR cases and information.
- *Don't be afraid to litigate.* Not all cases are appropriate for ADR.
- *Measure results.* Measuring actual and potential costs is both art and science. Get uncomfortable and devise a means to capture the appropriate outcomes (e.g., time, money, and relationships).
- *Be patient.* Effective ADR programs evolve over time.

SOURCE: Excerpted and adapted from P. M. Armstrong, P. J. Hall, and E. A. Infante, "Anatomy of a Successful Mediation," Association of Corporate Counsel, 2006. Retrieved March 24, 2011, from http://www.acc.com/vl/public/ProgramMaterial/loader.cfm.

YOUR THOUGHTS?

Assume you are the owner and primary decision maker of a company.

1. Describe at least three benefits of ADR that you see.
2. What disadvantages do you see?
3. Based on these pros and cons, would you or would you not use ADR?

Make Your Rivals Allies Sadly, rivals at school and work can negatively affect your success or at least make you miserable—a classmate or colleague threatened by your performance, a superior unwilling to acknowledge your good ideas, or a subordinate who undermines you. Ignoring or avoiding such rivals rarely works. We therefore recommend the following three-step process to convert enemies into friends. It involves 3 Rs: redirection, reciprocity, and rationality.

1. **Redirection.** Redirect your rival's negative emotions away from you. For example, the conflict or source of tension may actually be the result of somebody

else's actions. Your employer assigned you the responsibilities for the new customer. This was not your doing. Or your professor assigned your final project teams; you didn't select them yourself.

2. **Reciprocity.** Give before you ask! Cooling a conflict often begins with giving up something of value instead of asking for something first, or directly asking for a trade. Be strategic, however, and provide something that your rival perceives as valuable but can also reasonably reciprocate. For instance, allow him to participate in meetings with the new client in exchange for his support and ideas.

3. **Rationality.** Clearly and honestly explain your intentions for your actions and your desire to cooperate for mutual benefit. Don't leave your rival guessing the motives of your actions.[67]

Apply Your Conflict Management Knowledge

The Problem-Solving Application illustrates how a manager of a small business transformed dysfunctional conflict into functional conflict. It also gives you the opportunity to apply many of the tools you've learned thus far in the chapter.

solving application

problem

Transforming Dysfunctional into Functional Conflict

Trevor David is a manager of a small security company in the Midwestern United States. The Great Recession hit that part of the country especially hard and pushed many auto suppliers and dealerships to close, some of whom had been Trevor's largest customers. When big chunks of business are lost, management is forced to cut payroll to align with reduced income. Historically, David simply laid off employees who worked for the customer accounts they lost. On the one hand this approach was functional—he reduced the payroll to align with reduced revenues—but it also had dysfunctional side effects. He lost some of his best and most loyal employees simply because they

worked for customers who left. The same employees felt unappreciated and resentful, which made it difficult to rehire them when new accounts were added or past customers returned. The remaining employees commonly politicked to work on the accounts they perceived to be more stable to mitigate the likelihood of being laid off in the future (politics are discussed in detail in Chapter 12). Making matters worse, some employees quit when they heard that the account on which they worked was struggling or laying off its own employees.

These experiences caused David to do things differently when a customer recently closed its Michigan operations. This time he

involved employees in the decision-making process (recall the discussion of procedural justice in Chapter 5; participative decision making is covered in Chapter 11). He shared the number of hours that needed to be reduced and then asked employees to generate solutions for closing the gap. To his surprise and delight, employees willingly accepted fewer hours to avoid layoffs, accepted shifts they didn't normally work, and considered employee seniority and performance factors in their decisions. Although the business environment is still difficult for David's company, he has more committed employees and a stronger financial position because he transformed dysfunctional into functional conflict.[68]

YOUR CALL

Stop 1: What was/is Trevor David's problem?

Stop 2: Which concepts from this chapter help you understand and overcome this problem?

Stop 3: Apply your knowledge to generate other recommendations beyond what Mr. David already implemented.

major question

major question

MAJOR QUESTION

What are some best practices for effective negotiation?

THE BIGGER PICTURE

You are negotiating with someone about something throughout your life. It therefore is valuable to better understand negotiation and related strategies. We discuss negotiation in this section because negotiations are both the cause and remedy of many conflicts. Given this, it is no surprise that negotiations can influence outcomes across all three levels of the Integrative Framework. To help you excel at negotiation and be more effective, we explore different forms of negotiations and tactics.

Negotiation is a give-and-take decision-making process involving two or more parties with different preferences. Common examples include labor-management negotiations over wages, hours, and working conditions and negotiations between supply chain specialists and vendors involving price, delivery schedules, and credit terms. Self-managed work teams with overlapping task boundaries also need to rely on negotiated agreements. Negotiation is even more important today given that the workplace is increasingly complex and competitive.

Two Basic Types of Negotiation

Negotiation experts often distinguish between two fundamental types of negotiation—*distributive* and *integrative.* Understanding the difference has great practical implications.

Distributive vs. Integrative   A **distributive negotiation** usually involves a single issue—a "fixed pie"—in which one person gains at the expense of another. This "win–lose" approach is arguably the most common. For example, haggling over the price of a car is a distributive negotiation. However, in the conflicts discussed in this chapter, often more than one issue is at stake and each party values the issues differently. The outcomes available are no longer a fixed pie divided among all parties. Such scenarios describe **integrative negotiation, where an agreement can be found that is better for both parties than what they would have reached through distributive negotiation.**[69] Distributive negotiation involves traditional win–lose thinking. Integrative negotiation calls for a progressive win–win strategy.[70]

> **EXAMPLE:**   Fred Krupp, president of the Environmental Defense Fund, helps the nonprofit organization achieve more of its objectives by seeking win–win negotiations with businesses:
>
> - The Fund opened a Bentonville, Arkansas, office near Walmart's headquarters to help that company achieve goals for energy efficiency and packaging reduction.
> - When other environmental groups wanted to combat acid rain with strict limits on sulfur dioxide emissions, the Environmental Defense Fund partnered with utilities to push for a cap-and-trade system that offers business greater flexibility while still reducing emissions.[71]

Many people say we are negotiating all of the time and throughout our lives. Buying a car is one such instance. These transactions are excellent opportunities to apply your OB knowledge and improve your outcomes—more car for less money.

Factors to Consider When Choosing Which Approach to Take Finding areas of common ground can be difficult; successful negotiators are able to weigh multiple issues affecting a problem and gather information about which issues are most important to the other parties and why. Research and practice provide some helpful hints:

- **Know Who You Are.** Personality matters. Recent research shows that people with high levels of agreeableness (recall our discussion of the Big Five personality dimensions in Chapter 3) are best suited for integrative negotiations, whereas those low in this personality characteristic are better at distributive negotiations.[72] Why do you think this is?

- **Manage Outcome Expectations.** In most negotiations each party has an expected outcome, and this is compared to the actual outcome.[73] Skilled negotiators therefore manage expectations in advance of actual negotiations.

EXAMPLE If two people paid $35,000 for a car, then the one who expected to pay $33,000 was disappointed and the one who expected to pay $37,000 was delighted.

EXAMPLE Managers will often send out a message saying "it's been a tough year" in advance of annual reviews and salary discussions.

You can smile, laugh, or flinch in reaction to a first offer. This signals to your counterparty that they are outside of your **zone of possible agreement (ZOPA) — the range of possibilities you are willing to accept.**[74]

- **Consider the Other Person's Outcome.**[75] Of course you negotiate for your own benefit. But it often also matters how the other party makes out—are they satisfied?

EXAMPLE American Airlines negotiations with the pilots union in 2003 provides an example. The entire industry was in turmoil after 9/11. Many airlines went bankrupt (e.g., Delta) and the future of American was highly uncertain. The unions accepted huge concessions—$10 billion over six years (e.g., wage cuts of 15–23 percent). They perceived this as necessary and appropriate given the situation. However, this all changed when they learned that six top American executives arranged for bonuses equal to twice their salaries, and that 45 executives set up a pension fund in case the airline went bankrupt.

- **Adhere to Standards of Justice.**[76] Not only do the outcomes need to be perceived as fair (distributive justice), but so too do the processes by which they were attained. For instance, nobody likes to be taken advantage of, such as a negotiation expert challenging you or when you have incomplete information. Again, think of buying a new car. The dealer knows all of the numbers, and despite the best information the Web has to offer, you still never know the numbers as well as he/she does.

- **Remember Your Reputation.**[77] You may "win" today, only to foreclose opportunities in the future. Put another way, winning at all costs often has significant costs!

Added-Value Negotiation

One practical application of the integrative approach is **added-value negotiation (AVN). During AVN, the negotiating parties cooperatively develop multiple deal packages while building a productive long-term relationship.** AVN consists of these five steps:

1. *Clarify interests.* After each party identifies its tangible and intangible needs, the two parties meet to discuss their respective needs and find common ground for negotiation.

2. *Identify options.* A marketplace of value is created when the negotiating parties discuss desired elements of value (such as property, money, behavior, rights, and risk reduction).

3. *Design alternative deal packages.* While aiming for multiple deals, each party mixes and matches elements of value from both parties in workable combinations.

4. *Select a deal.* Each party analyzes deal packages proposed by the other party. Jointly, the parties discuss and select from feasible deal packages, with a spirit of creative agreement.

5. *Perfect the deal.* Together the parties discuss unresolved issues, develop a written agreement, and build relationships for future negotiations.[78]

Emotions and Negotiations

Many people believe that good negotiators show no emotion, like Roger Federer on the tennis court. But as you've learned in Chapters 3 and 7, emotions are indeed an integral part of the human experience and part of most everything we do. Negotiation experts and researchers acknowledge this and provide guidance on how to use emotions to your advantage. Remember that emotions are contagious. If you want the other party to be calm, creative, or energetic, then consider showing these emotions yourself. The specifics are outlined following.

Tips for Negotiating with Emotion   Preparation is critical to effective negotiations. Only the arrogant think otherwise. The following tips can help you prepare emotionally for an impending negotiation.

1. **Ideal emotions.** How do you want to feel going into the negotiation? Why? Many people answer this question quickly and say, "calm but assertive." When probed further they reveal other combinations, if not competing emotions. The challenge for you is to realize which will best suit your objectives and be mindful of them while negotiating.

2. **Managing emotions.** What can you do in advance to put yourself in the ideal emotional state? We provided several tools in the chapter on positive organizational behavior (Chapter 7) to help you project and promote positive emotions. Choose appropriately—meditation to calm you down or perhaps music by Godsmack (a favorite of one of the authors) to pump you up. If you are surprised or ambushed and put on the spot (e.g., with a phone call or somebody stopping by your office), then buy some time and say, "I just need to wrap up what I'm doing, and I'll call you back in 10 minutes." This will give you time to achieve the appropriate emotional state.

3. **Hot buttons.** What can throw you off balance? Some people seem eternally patient, while others frustrate easily. And some negotiators try to push your hot buttons as a tactic. Know your own tendencies and be sure to manage them appropriately.

4. **Keeping balance.** Everyone loses balance once in a while. How will you regain it if lost? Taking a break is a good idea. Stepping out, going to the restroom, or simply calling a "time out" can provide a break in the action and enable you to regroup. These same tactics can be used to redirect a negotiation that has gone/ is going in the wrong direction. You also may want to redirect the discussion to higher-level issues, especially if the discussion is getting bogged down in details.

5. **Emotions after.** How do you want to feel when you're finished? Many people say "relieved," which signifies the stress many of us feel while negotiating. Others say "satisfied," which speaks more to performance. Whatever the case, it is good to set goals for emotions just like other outcomes in negotiations (and other outcomes in the Integrative Framework).[79]

TAKE-AWAY APPLICATION—TAAP

Identify an upcoming negotiation, or an existing conflict that you need to address.

1. Make a plan using the questions above.
2. What do you anticipate the benefits will be for the situation you chose?
3. After implementing your plan, reflect on the outcome. Which of the above tips were most helpful?

Ethics and Negotiations

The success of negotiations is often influenced to a large extent by the *quality* of information exchanged. Telling lies, hiding key facts, and engaging in other potentially unethical tactics listed in Table 10.7 erodes trust and goodwill, both vital in win–win and other successful negotiations. An awareness of these dirty tricks can keep good-faith bargainers from being unfairly exploited. Unethical negotiating tactics need to be factored into organizational codes of ethics (recall our discussion in Chapter 1).

As we've noted, conflict and negotiations are affected by and in turn influence many elements in the Integrative Framework. More specifically, they can determine your personal satisfaction and performance throughout your professional life. We therefore encourage you once again to add the knowledge and tools in this chapter to your own skill set.

TABLE 10.7 QUESTIONABLE AND UNETHICAL TACTICS IN NEGOTIATIONS

TACTIC	DESCRIPTION/CLARIFICATION/RANGE
Lies	Subject matter for lies can include limits, alternatives, the negotiator's intent, authority to bargain, other commitments, acceptability of the opponent's offers, time pressures, and available resources.
Puffery	Among the items that can be puffed up are the value of one's payoffs to the opponent, the negotiator's own alternatives, the costs of what one is giving up or is prepared to yield, importance of issues, and attributes of the products or services.
Deception	Acts and statements may include promises or threats, excessive initial demands, careless misstatements of facts, or asking for concessions not wanted.
Weakening the opponent	The negotiator here may cut off or eliminate some of the opponent's alternatives, blame the opponent for his own actions, use personally abrasive statements to or about the opponent, or undermine the opponent's alliances.
Strengthening one's own position	This tactic includes building one's own resources, including expertise, finances, and alliances. It also includes presentations of persuasive rationales to the opponent or third parties (e.g., the public, the media) or getting mandates for one's position.
Nondisclosure	Includes partial disclosure of facts, failure to disclose a hidden fact, failure to correct the opponents' misperceptions or ignorance, and concealment of the negotiator's own position or circumstances.
Information exploitation	Information provided by the opponent can be used to exploit his weaknesses, close off his alternatives, generate demands against him, or weaken his alliances.
Maximization	Includes demanding the opponent make concessions that result in the negotiator's gain and the opponent's equal or greater loss. Also entails converting a win–win situation into win–lose.

SOURCE: From H. J. Reitz, J. A. Wall Jr., and M. S. Love, "Ethics in Negotiation: Oil and Water or Good Lubrication?", *Business Horizons,* May–June 1998. Reprinted with permission from Elsevier.

what did i learn?

In this chapter you learned that by managing conflict and applying sound principles in negotiation, you gain an advantage in working for better outcomes at work, school, and home, and across all levels of organizations. Reinforce what you learned with the Key Points below. Then consolidate your learning using the Integrative Framework. Finally, Challenge your mastery of this chapter by answering the Major Questions in your own words.

Key Points for Understanding Chapter 10
You learned the following key points.

10.1 A CONTEMPORARY VIEW OF CONFLICT

- Conflict occurs when one party perceives that its interests are opposed or negatively affected by another.
- Conflict can be both negative and positive along a continuum.
- The distinction between functional and dysfunctional conflict is important and useful.
- People avoid conflict for many reasons, but doing so can make it grow.
- Positive outcomes of conflict often fit into three categories: agreement, stronger relationships, and learning.

10.2 CONVENTIONAL FORMS OF CONFLICT

- Common or conventional forms of conflict are personality and intergroup.
- Personality conflicts can be avoided or overcome by communicating directly with the other party(ies), avoiding involving others, and, if needed, pursuing help from superiors or human resource specialists.
- Intergroup conflicts can be avoided or overcome by distinguishing between conflict states and processes, and applying the contact hypothesis.

10.3 FORMS OF CONFLICT INTENSIFIED BY TECHNOLOGY

- Work–family conflict occurs when the demands or pressures from work and family domains are mutually incompatible.
- Work–family conflict can be addressed in many ways, such as balancing demands between the different domains and implementing supportive employee

policies and managerial practices, such as flexspace and flextime.
- Incivility (e.g., bullying and harassment) has negative consequences for not only targeted employees but also coworkers who witness it.
- Cyber bullying is a particularly problematic form of incivility that must be monitored and addressed by organizational policies and practices.

10.4 EFFECTIVELY MANAGING CONFLICT

- Functional conflict can be fostered using several approaches, such as programmed conflict, devil's advocacy, and the dialectic method.
- People have a variety of conflict-handling tendencies or styles; five common styles are integrating, obliging, dominating, avoiding, and compromising.
- Many forms of alternative dispute resolution (ADR) are used—facilitation, conciliation, peer-review, ombudsman, mediation, and arbitration—to more quickly and cheaply reduce conflicts.

10.5 NEGOTIATION

- Negotiation is a give-and-take decision-making process involving two or more parties with different preferences.
- Distributive and integrative are two common forms of negotiation.
- Distributive negotiation usually involves a single issue—a "fixed pie"—in which one person gains at the expense of another.
- Integrative negotiation involves agreements that are better for both parties than what they would have reached through distributive negotiation.
- During added-value negotiations (AVN), negotiating parties cooperatively develop multiple deal packages while building a productive long-term relationship.
- It is important to consider implications of both emotions and ethics in any and all negotiations.

The Integrative Framework for Chapter 10
As shown in Figure 10.5, you learned that conflict is an inevitable part of organizational life and serves as an especially important group/team-level process in the Integrative Framework. How effectively you manage conflict can potentially impact outcomes across all levels of OB. You also learned how the process of negotiation is a valuable tool for both preventing and managing conflict.

Challenge: Major Questions for Chapter 10

At the start of the chapter, we told you that after reading the chapter you should be able to answer the following questions. Unless you can, have you really processed and internalized the lessons in the chapter? Refer to the Key Points, Figure 10.5, the chapter itself, and your notes to revisit and answer the following major questions:

1. How can understanding a modern perspective of conflict make me more effective at school, work, and home?

2. What are some types of conflict and how can I manage them to my benefit?

3. What can I do to manage work–family conflict and incivility to make me more effective at school, work, and home?

4. What can I do to prevent, reduce, or even overcome conflicts?

5. What are some best practices for effective negotiation?

FIGURE 10.5 INTEGRATIVE FRAMEWORK FOR UNDERSTANDING AND APPLYING OB

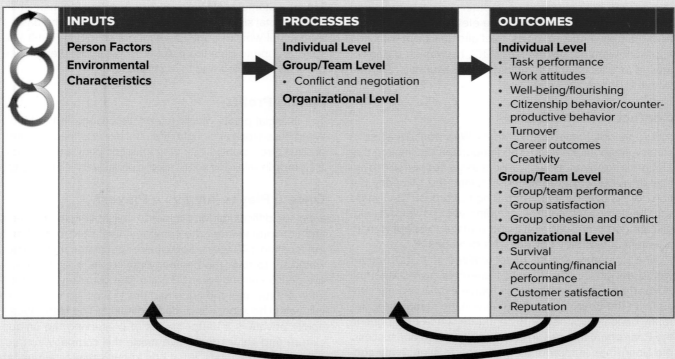

INPUTS	PROCESSES	OUTCOMES
Person Factors **Environmental Characteristics**	**Individual Level** **Group/Team Level** • Conflict and negotiation **Organizational Level**	**Individual Level** • Task performance • Work attitudes • Well-being/flourishing • Citizenship behavior/counter-productive behavior • Turnover • Career outcomes • Creativity **Group/Team Level** • Group/team performance • Group satisfaction • Group cohesion and conflict **Organizational Level** • Survival • Accounting/financial performance • Customer satisfaction • Reputation

SOURCE: © 2014 Angelo Kinicki and Mel Fugate. All rights reserved. Reproduction prohibited without permission of the authors.

Without George Zimmer, Does Men's Wearhouse Like the Way It Looks?

What happens when a company fires its own founder, and the founder "fires" back? Men's Wearhouse provides an excellent example.

Company founder and spokesperson George Zimmer became famous as the face and voice of its company's media ads. "You're going to like the way you look," he'd say. "I guarantee it."

In 2011 Zimmer had handed the leadership reins to Doug Ewert but continued on in other ways. He remained on the board of directors with the elevated title of Executive Chairman and kept on as chief pitchman. But with little apparent warning, on June 19, 2013, he was fired and removed as Executive Chairman. He subsequently resigned from the Board.[80]

Conflict with the Board

Although not immediately, Men's Wearhouse issued a statement about the firing. The announcement implied that Zimmer's termination was a necessary response "to an ego-driven power grab aimed at taking the company private for his own benefit," according to *Forbes*. "The board said he demanded control, including veto power over significant corporate decisions, and refused to support management unless they bowed to his demands."[81]

The company should have realized that its founder would not go quietly. Zimmer issued his own statement: "Over the past several months I have expressed my concerns to the Board about the direction the company is currently heading. Instead of fostering the kind of dialogue in the Boardroom that has, in part, contributed to our success, the Board has inappropriately chosen to silence my concerns by terminating me as an executive officer."

Conflict with the CEO?

Another point of likely contention was suggested by a subsequent event. A few weeks after Zimmer was out, Men's Wearhouse bought the designer Joseph Abboud and its US factory for $97.5 million in cash. In other words, the company bought out one of its suppliers and even acquired a means of production. This move was intended to broaden branded product offerings and increase profit margins, which contrasted with Zimmer's approach of only offering wholesale brands. "It's really a reshaping of the whole business model," CEO Ewert said, approvingly.[82]

Foundering Identity

Men's Wearhouse has been struggling to manage a new public identity without Zimmer in the picture. (The company has the legal right to use Zimmer's name and catchphrase for a year, but has chosen not to.) Its first major TV spot played up the role of Men's Wearhouse in making men look good through the decades. A young thin male model walked city streets through brief vignettes each representing its own decade with the clothing style changing to match—the seventies, the eighties, the nineties, the oughts, and the current day.

Laura Stampler of *Business Insider* called the male character "a total sleaze." She noted that "every time he passes a beautiful woman—one is wearing a schoolgirl outfit—he spins around to ogle them. A Men's Wearhouse employee gives an approving nod to each scene."[83]

Falling Profits

The financial press, which noted little change in the Men's Wearhouse stock price right after Zimmer was fired, was less positive three months later when the company announced a 2.3% drop in sales and a 28% drop in profit over the last quarter.

Once a Player, Always a Player?

It may be difficult for Mr. Zimmer to resist trying to intervene and continue to steer the company he started in 1973 and ran for almost 40 years. Some have speculated that Zimmer would try to take the company private as a hostile takeover.[84] He currently owns 3.6% of the company. Zimmer's letter shortly after the firing had this to say: "To be clear, at this point I have not concluded that taking The Men's Wearhouse private is a better means of preserving the unique culture and values that have made the company so successful over the years. What I do know is that as a founder and large shareholder, I am greatly concerned about the future of the company if this culture and these values are lost, and believe that the Board should be open to at least consider the full range of possibilities that could optimize the future value of the company for all stakeholders."

At the time of Zimmer's statement, financial analysts reported that management has "unanimous board support and is not in favor of a buyout."[85] More recently, other analysts note that if Zimmer did want to take the company private, it is already 10% cheaper than before.[86]

Apply the 3-Stop Problem-Solving Approach to OB

Stop 1: What is the problem?

- Use the Integrative Framework to help identify the outcomes that are important in this case.

- Which of these outcomes are not being achieved in the case?

- Based on considering the above two questions, what is the most important problem in this case?

Stop 2: Use the Integrative Framework to help identify the OB concepts or theories that help you to understand the problem in this case.

- What person factors are most relevant?

- What environmental characteristics are most important to consider?

- Do you need to consider any processes? Which ones?

- What concepts or theories discussed in this chapter are most relevant for solving the key problem in this case?

Stop 3: What are your recommendations for solving the problem?

- Review the material in the chapter that most pertains to your proposed solution and look for practical recommendations.

- Use any past OB knowledge or experience to generate recommendations.

- Outline your plan for solving the problem in this case.

LEGAL/ETHICAL CHALLENGE

It's Not My Problem . . . Or Is It?

You are the most junior financial analyst in your department of seven people. You've been in this job for three years, and you feel you have good relationships with all the members of your department and many others outside the department. Your department manager, along with the managers of five other departments, reports directly to the president, with whom you also have a very positive relationship. While the personalities of the members of your department are very different, most everybody has seemed to get along during your time at the company. This, however, changed when your department manager had a conflict with one of your more senior coworkers. He began to treat him unfairly, assigned him the most undesirable jobs, and talked about him disparagingly to other employees both inside and outside of your department. You feel that he is indeed being mistreated.

If this wasn't bad enough, the situation escalated when your poorly treated colleague confronted your manager about the mistreatment. Your manager then persuaded two of the department's most senior employees to join him in his personal attacks and attempts to damage your colleague's reputation both inside and outside the company. The situation got so bad that in one meeting the manager and other two senior members screamed at your colleague. Your colleague didn't scream back and nobody else in the department said anything.

The situation continues to escalate and is negatively affecting your department and your own satisfaction at work.

What Should You Do?

1. Let the conflict and mistreatment continue. While the situation is unfortunate, it's not your responsibility to intervene. Explain your reasoning.

2. Intervene and talk to your manager. Everybody has a responsibility to address unethical behavior and conflict. Explain your reasoning.

3. Make the president aware. You have a positive relationship with the president and feel that you could talk to her about the situation. Explain your reasoning.

4. Create and explain other alternatives.

GROUP EXERCISE

Bangkok Blowup—A Role-Playing Exercise

Objectives

1. To further your ability to diagnose the causes of an interpersonal conflict.

2. To give you a firsthand opportunity to try to resolve a relationship conflict.

Introduction

This is a role-playing exercise intended to develop your ability to diagnose and solve an interpersonal conflict. There is no single best way to resolve the conflict in this exercise. One style might work for one person, while another gets the job done for someone else.

Instructions

Read the following short case, "Can Larry Fit In?" Pair up with someone else and decide which of you will play the role of Larry and which will play the role of Melissa, the office manager. Pick up the action from where the case leaves off. Try to be realistic and true to the characters in the case. The manager is primarily responsible for resolving this conflict situation. Whoever plays Larry should resist any unreasonable requests or demands and cooperate with any personally workable solution. Note: To conserve time, try to resolve this situation in less than 15 minutes.

CAN LARRY FIT IN?

You're Melissa, Office Manager

You are the manager of an auditing team sent to Bangkok, Thailand, to represent a major international accounting firm headquartered in New York. You and Larry, one of your auditors, were sent to Bangkok to set up an auditing operation. Larry is about seven years older than you and has five more years' seniority in the firm. Your relationship has become very strained since you were recently designated as the office manager. You feel you were given the promotion because you have established an excellent working relationship with the Thai staff as well as a broad range of international clients. In contrast, Larry has told other members of the staff that your promotion simply reflects the firm's heavy emphasis on affirmative action. He has tried to isolate you from the all-male accounting staff by focusing discussions on sports, local night spots, and so forth.

You are sitting in your office reading some complicated new reporting procedures that have just arrived from the home office. Your concentration is suddenly interrupted by a loud knock on your door. Without waiting for an invitation to enter, Larry bursts into your office. He is obviously very upset, and it is not difficult for you to surmise why he is in such a nasty mood.

You recently posted the audit assignments for the coming month, and you scheduled Larry for a job you knew he wouldn't like. Larry is one of your senior auditors, and the company norm is that they get the choice assignments. This particular job will require him to spend two weeks away from Bangkok in a remote town, working with a company whose records are notoriously messy.

Unfortunately, you have had to assign several of these less-desirable audits to Larry recently because you are short of personnel. But that's not the only reason. You have received several complaints from the junior staff (all Thais) recently that Larry treats them in a condescending manner. They feel he is always looking for an opportunity to boss them around, as if he were their supervisor instead of an experienced, supportive mentor. As a result, your whole operation works more smoothly when you can send Larry out of town on a solo project for several days. It keeps him from coming into your office and telling you how to do your job, and the morale of the rest of the auditing staff is significantly higher.

Larry slams the door behind him and proceeds to express his anger over this assignment.

You're Larry, Senior Auditor

Why is Melissa deliberately trying to undermine your status in the office? She knows that the company norm is that senior auditors get the better jobs. It's unwritten policy! You've paid your dues, and now you expect to be treated with respect. And this isn't the first time this has happened. Since she was made the office manager, she has tried to keep you out of the office as much as possible. It's as if she doesn't want her rival for leadership of the office around. When you were asked to go to Bangkok, you assumed that you would be made the office manager because of your seniority in the firm. It's obvious that the reason management picked Melissa was political, another example of reverse discrimination against white males.

In staff meetings, Melissa has talked about the need to be sensitive to the feelings of the office staff as well as the clients in this multicultural setting. "Where does she come off preaching about sensitivity! What about *my* feelings, for heaven's sake?" you wonder. This is nothing more than a straightforward power play. She is probably feeling insecure about being the only female accountant in the office and being promoted over someone with more experience. "Sending me out of town," you decide, "is a clear case of 'out of sight, out of mind.'"

Well, it's not going to happen that easily. You are not going to roll over and let her treat you unfairly. It's time for a showdown. If she doesn't agree to change this assignment and apologize for the way she's been treating you, you're going to register a formal complaint with her boss in the New York office. You are prepared to submit your resignation if the situation doesn't improve.

Questions for Discussion

1. What are the causes of the conflict between Melissa and Larry?

2. What can be done to reduce the conflict?

3. Now that you have heard how others handled the conflict, what do you think is the optimum way to handle this situation?

Source: From D. A. Whetten and K. S. Cameron, *Developing Management Skills*, 6th ed. Copyright © 2005. Printed and Electronically reproduced by permission of Pearson Education, Inc., Upper Saddle River, New Jersey.

11 DECISION MAKING AND CREATIVITY

How Critical Is It to Master These Skills?

inputs

PERSON FACTORS

ENVIRONMENTAL CHARACTERISTICS

processes

INDIVIDUAL LEVEL
Decision Making

GROUP/TEAM LEVEL
Decision Making

ORGANIZATIONAL LEVEL

outcomes

INDIVIDUAL LEVEL
Creativity

GROUP/TEAM LEVEL

ORGANIZATIONAL LEVEL

MAJOR TOPICS I'LL LEARN AND QUESTIONS I SHOULD BE ABLE TO ANSWER

11.1 RATIONAL AND NONRATIONAL MODELS OF DECISION MAKING
MAJOR QUESTION: *How can people integrate rational and nonrational models of decision making?*

11.2 DECISION-MAKING BIASES: RULES OF THUMB OR "HEURISTICS"
MAJOR QUESTION: *It's hard to be rational. What are the biases that get in the way?*

11.3 EVIDENCE-BASED DECISION MAKING
MAJOR QUESTION: *How can I more effectively use evidence-based decision making?*

11.4 FOUR DECISION-MAKING STYLES
MAJOR QUESTION: *How do I decide to decide?*

11.5 A ROAD MAP TO ETHICAL DECISION MAKING
MAJOR QUESTION: *How can I assess the ethics of my decisions?*

11.6 GROUP DECISION MAKING
MAJOR QUESTION: *What are the pros and cons of group decision making and the various problem-solving tools?*

11.7 CREATIVITY
MAJOR QUESTION: *How can I increase my own creative behavior and that of my employees?*

INTEGRATIVE FRAMEWORK FOR UNDERSTANDING AND APPLYING OB

This chapter focuses on decision making, a key process variable at the individual and group/team level, and the individual level outcome of creativity. You will learn that decision making is associated with a host of other individual, group/team, and organizational level outcomes. Try to make note of the different outcomes related to decision making as you read this chapter.

© 2014 Angelo Kinicki and Mel Fugate. All rights reserved. Reproduction prohibited without permission of the authors.

DOES MULTITASKING IMPROVE MY EFFECTIVENESS?

All of our lives are filled with daily activities that lead us to try to do more than one thing at a time. Examples are driving a car and talking on the phone, studying and listening to music, or listening to a classroom lecture and texting a friend.

MULTITASKING AND STUDENT PERFORMANCE

A team of researchers studied the effects of multitasking in a university setting. Undergraduates agreed to allow the researchers to install spyware to record their laptop use during class. Two types of multitasking were measured. *Distractive multitasking* involved tasks or activities in which students directed cognitive resources to non–class activities. *Productive multitasking* entailed using laptops for tasks or activities that were related to the class. Results demonstrated that students spent 42 percent of classroom time on *distractive* multitasking. Further, higher ratios of distractive to productive multitasking were associated with lower grades.[1]

MULTITASKING AT WORK

Numerous studies with employees in their actual work environments have shown that multitasking is associated with lower efficiency. It seems that multitaskers end up switching tasks hundreds of times a day.[2] In contrast, we found one study that showed a positive relationship between multitasking and performance for call-center employees. However, this positive effect disappeared when the researchers accounted for intelligence. In other words, intelligence is more important for performance than your ability to multitask.[3]

Researchers' best estimate is that only 2.5 percent of people can effectively multitask, although many people think they can. Most of us aren't good at multitasking because "our brains are wired for 'selective attention' and can focus on only one thing at a time."[4]

TIPS FOR MULTITASKING

If you are going to multitask, start with a list of what you need to accomplish, prioritize the items, and then work the list. Try to eliminate distractions so that you can focus on one thing at a time. Finally, you need to control your use of social networking websites as they can distract you from doing key tasks. Also consider putting your cell phone on silent mode or switching it off when you want to focus on a task.[5]

FOR YOU	WHAT'S AHEAD IN THIS CHAPTER

We contrast rational and nonrational decision making and explain why it's important to understand both. We also show you eight decision-making biases and the benefits of evidence-based decision making. We also show how companies are leveraging big data for making decisions. Next, we discuss general decision-making styles and ethical decision making. We conclude by distinguishing the pros and cons of group decision making, group problem-solving techniques, and the process of creativity. All of this information will help you improve your ability to make decisions.

RATIONAL AND NONRATIONAL MODELS OF DECISION MAKING

MAJOR QUESTION

How can people integrate rational and nonrational models of decision making?

THE BIGGER PICTURE

Decision making is a key process within the Integrative Framework for Understanding and Applying OB. We have been encouraging you to use this framework throughout this book in order to enhance your ability to solve problems. Use of the framework helps you identify and choose alternative solutions that lead to a desired outcome. This process varies along a continuum of rational to nonrational. Four steps in making rational decisions are (1) identify the problem, (2) generate alternative solutions, (3) evaluate alternatives and select a solution, and (4) implement and evaluate the solution. Examples of nonrational models include (1) satisficing and (2) intuition.

Decision making matters deeply in your personal and work life. Let's consider the impact of decisions made by a few college graduates during the interview process. One job applicant took a nonemergency call on his smartphone 15 minutes into the interview. Do you think this decision made a positive impression? Another decided to bring his father into a 45-minute interview: The recruiter was shocked. Paula Welch, a Cigna HR representative, similarly noted how one recent grad asked his father to call and negotiate a higher salary after receiving a job offer. Here's a really good decision: A college senior brought her cat to the interview in a cage, and then proceeded to play with it during the interview. The end results of these decisions were bad in all cases.[6]

Decision making entails identifying and choosing alternative solutions that lead to a desired state of affairs. The above examples illustrate how one's decision making affects the chances of getting a job after graduation, but the importance of decision making is much broader. As a case in point, the annual Global Leadership Development study conducted by *Training* magazine uncovered that critical thinking/ problem solving was the second most important competency desired by organizations in 2012 and 2013.[7] You would be well served to improve your decision-making skills.

Let's look at two different methods managers can use to make decisions. They can follow a rational model or several nonrational models.

Rational Decision Making: Managers Make Logical and Optimal Decisions

The **rational model of decision making** explains how managers *should* make decisions. It assumes that managers are completely objective and possess complete information when making decisions. Decisions thus demonstrate excellent logic and optimize the organization's best interests.

FIGURE 11.1 THE FOUR STAGES IN RATIONAL DECISION MAKING

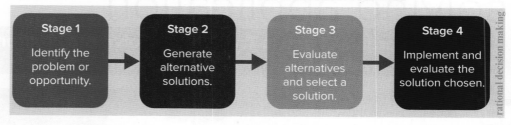

Stage 1	Stage 2	Stage 3	Stage 4
Identify the problem or opportunity.	Generate alternative solutions.	Evaluate alternatives and select a solution.	Implement and evaluate the solution chosen.

There are four generic stages associated with rational decision making (see Figure 11.1).

Stage 1: Identify the Problem or Opportunity—Determining the Actual versus the Desirable

We defined a *problem* in Chapter 1 as a difference or gap between an actual and desired situation. By now you know that problem identification is the first stop in solving any type of problem. We did not mention in our earlier discussion, however, that managers also have to make decisions regarding opportunities. **An *opportunity* represents a situation in which there are possibilities to do things that lead to results that exceed goals and expectations.** For example, US medical schools must prepare to produce 5,000 more graduates a year by 2019. Unfortunately, this wonderful opportunity will require some tough decisions because the number of funded residencies has been frozen since 1997. Residencies entail the three to seven years of additional on-the-job training that medical students need before they can practice medicine on their own. Without more residency positions, the Association of American Medical Colleges predicts a shortage of 62,900 doctors by 2015, and potentially as many as 140,000 by 2025.[8]

Whether you face a problem or an opportunity, the goal is always the same: to make improvements that change conditions from their current state to a more desirable one. This requires you to diagnose the causes of the problem (or the nature of the opportunity).

Stage 2: Generate Alternative Solutions—Both the Obvious and the Creative

For many people this is the exciting part of decision making, the step where you get to be creative, think outside the box, and share your ideas of how things should be done. *Brainstorming,* for instance, is a common technique used by both individuals and groups to generate potential solutions. Brainstorming is discussed later in this chapter. Unfortunately, a research study of 400 strategic decisions revealed that managers struggled during this stage because of three key decision-making blunders:

1. **Rushing to judgment.** Managers simply make decisions too quickly without considering all relevant information.

2. **Selecting readily available ideas or solutions.** Managers take the easy solution without rigorously considering alternatives. This can tend to happen when emotions are high about the problem at hand.

3. **Making poor allocation of resources to study alternative solutions.** Managers don't invest the resources to properly study the problem and alternative courses of action.

Decision makers thus are encouraged to slow down when making decisions, to evaluate a broader set of alternatives, and to invest in studying a greater number of potential solutions.[9] The Problem-Solving Application on the next page illustrates how these blunders may have impacted J.P. Morgan Chase's response to the "London whale" trading problem in 2012 and 2013.

solving application

J.P. Morgan Chase Is Trying to Resolve the London Whale Trading Fiasco

J. P. Morgan Chase is one of the largest banks in the world, and it ran afoul of regulators in 2012 and 2013 in what is dubbed the "London whale" fiasco. Since that time, US regulators have been rigorously investigating the situation.

What Happened? Three former London-based traders made large investment bets that led to a nearly $6 billion loss for the company. A French-born employee named Bruno Michel Iksil was called the "London whale" because his bets created the most losses. After the news originally broke, Chase CEO Jamie Dimon referred to the scandal as a "tempest in a teapot." He later described it as an isolated risk that the bank had taken care of. He wanted the problem to go away.

Regulators are investigating whether or not these three former employees, and the bank itself, "tried to hide some of the mounting losses during the first quarter of this year [2013]."[10] They think there was a cover-up.

The Company's Response Over time Dimon concluded that he underestimated the losses because he "relied on advice from

Jamie Dimon of J.P. Morgan Chase testifying to a governmental committee.

colleagues that losses wouldn't worsen." A US Senate panel did not agree with this interpretation. The committee concluded that Chase "brushed off internal warnings and misled regulators and investors about the score of the losses tied to the trades."

Dimon denies these charges, saying that no one at the company "thought we had a big problem" but rather "we knew we had a small problem." The company estimated the problem at $300 million, not $6 billion. In response to the comment that the company withheld

information from regulators, Dimon said, "We tried to tell them but we didn't know sometimes."

Dimon is now vigorously defending the company's integrity and decisions. He said, "I don't know what more I can say. Bad strategy, badly vetted, badly monitored, badly controlled. Embarrassing. Terrible. Sorry." He also told investors at a conference hosted by Morgan Stanley that "there was no hiding, there was no lying, there was no b—s—."[11] He further promised to fight any lawsuits that are filed against the company.

YOUR CALL

Stop 1: What is the problem in this case from CEO Dimon's perspective?

Stop 2: Which of the above stage 2 blunders were committed by Chase?

Stop 3: Rolling back time, what decisions do you think Chase should have made when it first discovered the losses?

Stage 3: Evaluate Alternatives and Select a Solution—Ethics, Feasibility, and Effectiveness In this stage, you need to evaluate alternatives in terms of several criteria. Not only are costs and quality important, but you should consider the following questions: (1) Is it ethical? (If not, don't consider it.) (2) Is it feasible? (If time is an issue, costs are high, resources are limited, technology is needed, or customers are resistant, for instance, then the alternative is not feasible.) (3) Will it remove the causes and solve the problem?

Stage 4: Implement and Evaluate the Solution Chosen   Once a solution is chosen, it needs implementation. And after implementation, stakeholders need to evaluate how effectively the solution solves the problem. To be effective, the solution should eliminate or significantly reduce the difference between the earlier, actual problem state and the desired outcome. If the gap is not closed, the implementation fails, and either the problem was incorrectly identified or the solution was inappropriately conceived or executed. If the solution fails, management can return to the first step, problem identification. If the problem was correctly identified, management should consider implementing one of the previously identified, but untried, solutions. This process can continue until all feasible solutions have been tried or the problem has changed.

What's Good and Bad about the Rational Model?   The rational model is prescriptive, outlining a logical process that managers *should* use when making decisions. As such, the rational model is based on the notion that managers *optimize* when making decisions. Optimizing involves solving problems by producing the best possible solution and is based on a set of highly desirable conditions—having complete information, leaving emotions out of the decision-making process, honestly and accurately evaluating all alternatives, having abundant and accessible time and resources, and having people willing to implement and support decisions. Practical experience, of course, tells us that these conditions are all rarely met, and assumptions to the contrary are unrealistic. Herbert Simon in 1978 earned the Nobel Prize for his work on decision making. He put it this way: "The assumptions of perfect rationality are contrary to fact. It is not a question of approximation; they do not even remotely describe the processes that human beings use for making decisions in complex situations."[12]

That said, there are three benefits of trying to follow a rational process as much as realistically possible:

- **Quality.** The quality of decisions may be enhanced, in the sense that they follow more logically from all available knowledge and expertise.
- **Transparency.** It makes the reasoning behind a decision transparent and available to scrutiny.
- **Responsibility.** If made public, it discourages the decider from acting on suspect considerations (such as personal advancement or avoiding bureaucratic embarrassment) and therefore encourages more responsible decisions.[13]

Nonrational Models of Decision Making: Decision Making Does Not Follow an Orderly Process

Nonrational models of decision making **explain how managers actually make decisions.** The models typically build on assumptions that decision making is uncertain, that decision makers do not possess complete information, and that managers struggle to make optimal decisions. Two nonrational models are Herbert Simon's *normative* model and the *intuition* model.

Simon's Normative Model: "Satisfactory Is Good Enough"   Herbert Simon proposed this model to describe the process that managers actually use when making decisions. The process is guided by a decision maker's bounded rationality. *Bounded rationality* **represents the notion that decision makers are "bounded" or restricted by a variety of constraints when making decisions.** These constraints include any personal characteristics or internal and external resources that reduce rational decision making. Personal characteristics include the limited capacity of the human mind, personality, and time constraints. Consider gender: Males tend to make more risky decisions than females.[14] Examples of internal resources are the organization's human and social capital, financial resources, technology, plant and equipment, and internal processes and systems. External resources include things the organization cannot directly control such as employment levels in the community, capital availability, and government policies.[15] Tom Albanese, former CEO of Rio Tinto, the second largest mining company in the world, experienced these constraints when he decided to acquire Riverside Mining Ltd. (see the Example box).

EXAMPLE   Bounded Rationality Dooms an Acquisition Decision

In 2013 Tom Albanese stepped down as Rio Tinto's CEO after a series of bad decisions. One involved the acquisition of Riverside Mining Ltd. for $3.7 billion. Albanese was interested in Riverside's coking-coal operations in Africa.

THE FATAL DECISION   There were few bidders for Riverside because of "concerns about getting the steel ingredient out of Mozambique's bush country." The price of coking was $290 a ton at the time of the acquisition decision in 2011. The price was $165 a ton in January 2013.

"Rio Tinto had planned to ship the coal along the Zambezi River, but that strategy proved unworkable when the company ran into trouble dredging the river and failed to secure government approval for shipments." The effects of this decision resulted in the company writing down $3 billion of lost costs, and the resignation of Albanese and the company's head of strategy, Doug Ritchie.[16]

Through its Diavik Diamond Mine subsidiary, Rio Tinto operates the Diavik mine in the subarctic tundra of Canada's Northwest Territories.

YOUR THOUGHTS?

1. How does bounded rationality explain what happened in this example?

2. What constraints of internal and external resources—directly identified or implied—acted as boundaries to the decisions made?

3. What could Albanese have done differently?

Ultimately, these limitations result in the tendency to acquire manageable rather than optimal amounts of information. In turn, this practice makes it difficult for managers to identify all possible alternative solutions. In the long run, the constraints of bounded rationality cause decision makers to fail to evaluate all potential alternatives, thereby causing them to *satisfice.*

Satisficing consists of choosing a solution that meets some minimum qualifications, one that is "good enough." Satisficing resolves problems by producing solutions that are satisfactory, as opposed to optimal. Finding a radio station to listen to in your car is a good example of satisficing. You cannot optimize because it is impossible to listen to all stations at the same time. You thus stop searching for a station when you find one playing a song you like or do not mind hearing.

The Intuition Model: "It Just Feels Right"   Many entrepreneurs start businesses on the basis of intuition. Consider the following:

EXAMPLE   Ignoring recommendations from advisers, Ray Kroc purchased the McDonald's brand from the McDonald brothers: "I'm not a gambler and I didn't have that kind of money, but my funny bone instinct kept urging me on." Ignoring the fact that 24 publishing houses had rejected the book and her own publishing house was opposed, Eleanor Friede gambled on a "little nothing book," called *Jonathan Livingston Seagull:* "I felt there were truths in this simple story that would make it an international classic."[17]

Intuition **represents judgments, insights, or decisions that "come to mind on their own, without explicit awareness of the evoking cues and of course without explicit evaluation of the validity of these cues."**[18] Unfortunately, the use of intuition does not always lead to blockbuster decisions such as those by Ray Kroc or Eleanor Friede. To enhance your understanding of the role of intuition in decision making, this section reviews a model of intuition and discusses the pros and cons of using intuition to make decisions.

A Model of Intuition Figure 11.2 presents a model of intuition. Note that the model shows two forms of intuition:

1. **A** **holistic hunch** **represents a judgment that is based on a subconscious integration of information stored in memory.** People using this form of intuition may not be able to explain why they want to make a certain decision, except that the choice "feels right."

2. **Automated experiences** **represent a choice that is based on a familiar situation and a partially subconscious application of previously learned information related to that situation.** For example, when you have years of experience driving a car, you react to a variety of situations without conscious analysis.

In Figure 11.2, you can see that intuition is represented by two distinct processes. One is automatic, involuntary, and mostly effortless. The second is quite the opposite in that it is controlled, voluntary, and effortful. For example, when trying to answer one of the Your Thoughts? questions at the end of the Example boxes, you may spontaneously have an answer pop into your mind based on your recollection of what you previously read (an automatic process). Upon further reflection (controlled process), however, you may decide your initial thought is wrong and that you need to

FIGURE 11.2 A MODEL OF INTUITION

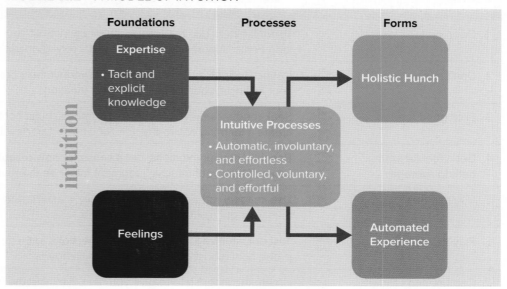

SOURCES: Based in part on D. Kahneman and G. Klein, "Conditions for Intuitive Expertise," *American Psychologist*, September 2009, 515–526; E. Sadler-Smith and E. Shefy, "The Intuitive Executive: Understanding and Applying 'Gut Feel' in Decision Making," *Academy of Management Executive*, November 2004, 76–91; and C. C. Miller and R. D. Ireland, "Intuition in Strategic Decision Making: Friend or Foe in the Fast-Paced 21st Century," *Academy of Management Executive*, February 2005, 19–30.

go back and reread some material to arrive at another answer. This in turn may cause novel ideas to come to mind, and the two processes continue. These intuitive processes are influenced by two sources: expertise and feelings (see Figure 11.2). Expertise represents an individual's combined **explicit knowledge** (i.e., information that can easily be put into words) and **tacit knowledge** (i.e., information gained through experience that is difficult to express and formalize) regarding an object, person, situation, or decision opportunity.

> **EXAMPLE**   Steve Jobs used a combination of explicit and tacit knowledge to create new products. The feelings component reflects the automatic, underlying effect one experiences in response to an object, person, situation, or decision opportunity. An intuitive response builds on the interaction between one's expertise and feelings in a given situation.

- **Pros and Cons of Using Intuition.** There are two benefits of using intuition to make decisions. (1) It can speed up the decision-making process, which is valuable when you are under time constraints.[19] (2) It is useful when resources are limited. On the downside, however, intuition is subject to the same types of biases associated with rational decision making, biases we discuss in the next section of this chapter. In addition, the decision maker may have difficulty convincing others that the intuitive decision makes sense, so a good idea may be ignored.

- **What Is the Bottom Line on Intuition?** We believe that intuition and rationality are complementary and that managers should attempt to use both when making decisions.[20] We thus encourage you to use intuition when making decisions. You can develop your intuitive awareness by using the recommendations in Table 11.1.

Improving Your Intuitive Awareness   Do you think being intuitive is a good thing? Would you like to become more intuitive? If yes, then you will find the Self-Assessment on the next page valuable.

TABLE 11.1   GUIDELINES FOR DEVELOPING INTUITIVE AWARENESS

RECOMMENDATION	DESCRIPTION
1. Open up the closet	To what extent do you experience intuition; trust your feelings; count on intuitive judgments; suppress hunches; covertly rely upon gut feel?
2. Don't mix up your I's	Instinct, insight, and intuition are not synonymous; practice distinguishing among your instincts, your insights, and your intuitions.
3. Elicit good feedback	Seek feedback on your intuitive judgments; build confidence in your gut feel; create a learning environment in which you can develop better intuitive awareness.
4. Get a feel for your batting average	Benchmark your intuitions; get a sense for how reliable your hunches are; ask yourself how your intuitive judgment might be improved.
5. Use imagery	Use imagery rather than words; literally visualize potential future scenarios that take your gut feelings into account.
6. Play devil's advocate	Test out intuitive judgments; raise objections to them; generate counterarguments; probe how robust gut feel is when challenged.
7. Capture and validate your intuitions	Create the inner state to give your intuitive mind the freedom to roam; capture your creative intuitions; log them before they are censored by rational analysis.

SOURCE: From E. Sadler-Smith and E. Shefy, "The Intuitive Executive: Understanding and Applying 'Gut Feel' in Decision Making," *Academy of Management Executive*, November 2004, 88. Reproduced with permission of The Academy of Management, via Copyright Clearance Center.

SELF-ASSESSMENT 11.1 Am I Intuitive?

Go to connect.mheducation.com and complete Self-Assessment 11.1 to assess your intuitiveness. Then answer the following questions:

1. What is your level of intuitiveness? Do you agree with this assessment?

2. What are the two highest items driving your intuition? When do you tend to use these characteristics?

3. What are your two lowest items that detract from your intuition? When do they get in the way of your making intuitive decisions?

TAKE-AWAY APPLICATION—TAAP

Use the results of Self-Assessment 11.1 and Table 11.1 to answer the following:

1. Examine the recommendations in Table 11.1 and evaluate each one as either a strength of yours—something you do—or a weakness—something you tend not to do.

2. For those recommendations in Table 11.1 that you think might be your weaknesses, consider whether results from the intuition Self-Assessment can help you to turn the weaknesses to strengths.

3. Develop a plan to further develop your self-assessment strengths on the basis of the recommendations in Table 11.1 for increasing your intuitive awareness.

Integrating Rational and Nonrational Models Applying the idea that decisions are shaped by characteristics of both problems and the contexts in which decision makers have to solve the problems, consultants David Snowden and Mary Boone have come up with their own approach that responds to the challenging environments facing today's organizations. They essentially integrate rational and nonrational models by identifying four kinds of decision environments and an effective method of decision making for each.[21]

1. **Simple.** A simple context is stable, with clear cause-and-effect relationships, so the best answer can be agreed upon.

    Effective: *The rational model.* Decision makers gather information, categorize it, and respond in an established way.

2. **Complicated.** There is a clear relationship between cause and effect, but some people may not see it, and more than one solution may be effective.

    Effective: *The rational model.* Decision makers investigate and analyze options.

3. **Complex.** There is one right answer, but many unknowns obscure cause-and-effect relationships.

    Effective: *Intuition.* Decision makers start by experimenting, testing options, and probing to see what might happen as they look for a creative solution.

4. **Dynamic/Chaotic.** Cause-and-effect relationships change so fast that no pattern emerges.

    Effective: Both *intuition* and *evidence-based decision making*, discussed in Section 11.3 of this chapter. Decision makers act first to establish order and then find areas where it is possible to identify patterns so that aspects of the problem can be managed.[22]

DECISION-MAKING BIASES: RULES OF THUMB OR "HEURISTICS"

major question

MAJOR QUESTION

It's hard to be rational. What are the biases that get in the way?

THE BIGGER PICTURE

You and everyone else use "heuristics" when making decisions. By better understanding the nature of these various rules of thumb, you can improve your ability to make more rational decisions. Heuristics fall into eight categories: availability bias, representativeness bias, confirmation bias, anchoring bias, overconfidence bias, hindsight bias, framing bias, and escalation of commitment bias.

Ever had a hard time explaining why you made a particular decision? It would be normal because all of us use shortcuts or "rules of thumb" when making decisions. Academics call them judgmental heuristics, pronounced "hyur-ris-tiks." ***Judgmental heuristics*** **represent cognitive shortcuts or biases that are used to simplify the process of making decisions.**[23]

There are both pros and cons to the use of heuristics. Because these shortcuts derive from knowledge gained from past experience, they can help managers make decisions. At the same time, however, they can lead to bad decisions, particularly for people facing severe time constraints, an unfortunately notorious example being primary health care doctors. For example, a recent study of medical malpractice claims showed that diagnostic errors, which are partly caused by misapplied judgmental heuristics, result in up to 160,000 deaths per year. Bad decisions are very costly in this context, in human suffering and in plain dollars. Between 1986 and 2010, diagnosis-related errors cost doctors and hospitals about $38.8 billion.[24]

Here are eight biases that commonly affect decision making:

1. Confirmation bias
2. Overconfidence bias
3. Availability bias
4. Representativeness bias
5. Anchoring bias
6. Hindsight bias
7. Framing bias
8. Escalation of commitment bias

Knowledge about these biases or heuristics can help you to avoid using them in the wrong situation or being blinded by not knowing you are in fact using them.

1. **Confirmation Bias.** The confirmation bias has two components. The decision maker (1) subconsciously decides something even before investigating why it is the right decision, for example, making a snap decision to purchase a particular smartphone; and (2) seeks information that supports purchasing this particular phone while discounting information that does not.[25]

2. **Overconfidence Bias.** Most of us tend to be overconfident about estimates or forecasts. For example, most of us regard ourselves as better than average drivers.[26] This bias grows in strength when people are asked moderate to extremely

difficult questions rather than easy ones. (See the Problem-Solving Application on the BP Oil Spill.) Entrepreneurs especially fall prey to this bias when deciding to start and sustain new ventures. Sadly, one entrepreneurial success frequently leads to investing in a poor opportunity later on. Experienced investment analysts also were found to be more prone to overconfidence.[27] Our advice: Don't assume that overconfident and assertive people have the best recommendations.

solving application

problem

Heuristics Partly to Blame for BP Oil Spill

CNN summed up the months of bad news this way: "The drill rig Deepwater Horizon exploded and sank in April 2010, killing 11 men aboard and unleashing an undersea gusher from a BP-owned well called Macondo a mile under water. It took three months to cap the well, and federal officials estimate nearly 5 million barrels of oil—more than 200 million gallons—poured into the Gulf in that time."[28]

What Happened? According to Bob Bea, an engineering professor at the University of California, Berkeley, "Technological disasters, like the BP oil spill, follow a well-worn 'trail of tears.'" Bea has investigated 630 different types of disasters and is an expert on offshore drilling.

The Associated Press interviewed Bea in the spill's aftermath. Bea thinks the BP spill falls into the category of disasters that result when an organization simply ignores warning signs through overconfidence and incompetence. He pointed to congressional testimony: BP ignored problems with a dead battery, leaky cement job, and loose hydraulic fittings.

"Disasters don't happen because of 'an evil empire,'" Bea said. "It's hubris, arrogance, and indolence."

Because cutting-edge technology often works flawlessly, Bea said,

people get lulled into complacency. "Corners get cut, problems ignored. Then boom."[29]

The Confirmation Bias at Work The finance industry saw the disaster as resulting from BP's failure to "debias" its investigation. "Transocean workers conducted two pressure tests, a positive pressure test and a negative pressure test," according to the *Quarterly Journal of Finance*. "The positive pressure test involves increasing the pressure inside the well by pumping fluid, to see whether fluids leak from the well. . . . The result was favorable.

"The negative pressure test involves decreasing pressure from the well, to see whether fluids leak. . . . The test results were unusual, and Transocean workers struggled to interpret the readings. Pressure built up unexpectedly with no clear reason as to why." This situation was deemed to be "non-problematic."

"However, other Transocean workers were not persuaded that the problems had been resolved. For example, Wyman Wheeler, who supervised the drilling crew for

The Deepwater Horizon oil rig disaster.

twelve hours per day, was not convinced that all was in order. Yet, when Wheeler's shift ended at 6 pm his replacement, Jason Anderson, assured both his Transocean coworkers (and for that matter, his BP colleagues) that the pressure readings were normal."[30]

The Final Outcome? BP settled charges with the US Department of Justice by pleading guilty to "11 counts of manslaughter, two misdemeanors, and a felony count of lying to Congress. BP also agreed to four years of government monitoring of its safety practices and ethics. . . . As of February 2013, criminal and civil settlements and payments to a trust had cost the company $42.2 billion."[31]

YOUR CALL

Stop 1: What was the problem in this example?

Stop 2: How did the confirmation bias and overconfidence bias contribute to this disaster?

Stop 3: What would you recommend that BP do differently in the future to avoid such disasters?

Some people are afraid of flying because they overestimate the chances of being in a plane crash. Plane crashes are "low probability" events. There was only one large airplane flying passengers that crashed in 2014, the Malaysian Boeing 777. If you consider all airplanes flying around the world, there were 138 and 155 crashes in 2013 and 2012, respectively.

3. **Availability Bias.** The availability heuristic represents a decision maker's tendency to base decisions on information that is readily available in memory. This leads us to overestimate the importance of information we recently received or thought about. The problem, of course, is that recent information is not necessarily the best or most accurate information.

   This bias can be fueled by news media, which likes to emphasize negative or unusual events, like plane crashes or high-school shootings. This heuristic is likely to cause people to overestimate the occurrence of these unlikely events.[32] This bias also is partially responsible for the recency effect noted in Table 4.1 in Chapter 4. For example, a manager is more likely to give an employee a positive performance evaluation if the employee exhibited excellent performance over the last few months.

4. **Representativeness Bias.** The representativeness heuristic is used when people estimate the probability of an event occurring. It reflects the tendency to assess the likelihood of an event occurring based on one's impressions about similar occurrences. A manager, for example, may hire a graduate from a particular university because the past three people hired from this university turned out to be good performers. In this case, the "school attended" criterion is used to facilitate complex information processing associated with employment interviews. Unfortunately, this shortcut can result in a biased decision. Similarly, an individual may believe that he or she can master a new software package in a short period of time because a different type of software was easy to learn. This estimate may or may not be accurate. For example, it may take the individual a much longer time to learn the new software because it involves learning a new programming language.

5. **Anchoring Bias.** How would you answer the following two questions? Is the population of Iraq greater than 40 million? What's your best guess about the population of Iraq? Was your answer to the second question influenced by the number *40 million* suggested by the first question? If yes, you were affected by the anchoring bias. The anchoring bias occurs when decision makers are influenced by the first information received about a decision, even if it is irrelevant. This bias happens because initial information, impressions, data,

Hostess Twinkies have been produced in a Chicago bakery since the 1930s. The company recently closed the plant as part of its reorganization strategy. Employees and the union were devasted as they thought the production of Twinkies was part of the company's future.

feedback, or stereotypes anchor our subsequent judgments and decisions.

6. **Hindsight Bias.** Imagine yourself in the following scenario: You are taking an OB course that meets Tuesday and Thursday, and your professor gives unannounced quizzes each week. It's the Monday before a class, and you are deciding whether to study for a potential quiz or to watch Monday night football. Two of your classmates have decided to watch the game rather than study because they don't think there will be a quiz the next day. The next morning you walk into class and the professor says, "Take out a sheet of paper for the quiz." You turn to your friends and say, "I knew we were going to have a quiz; why did I listen to you?" The hindsight bias occurs when knowledge of an outcome influences our belief about the probability that we could have predicted the outcome earlier. The danger of this bias is that, in retrospect, we get overconfident about our foresight, which leads to bad decisions.[33] For example, investors prone to this bias will confidently think they are predicting good investment opportunities, on the basis of such experiences, only to find out that they invested in dogs.[34]

7. **Framing Bias.** This bias relates to the manner in which a question is posed or framed. For example, customers have been found to prefer meat that is framed as "85% lean meat" instead of "15% fat," although, of course, they are the same thing. Framing is important because it shows that our decisions are influenced by the manner in which a problem or question is framed.[35] You are encouraged to frame decision questions in alternative ways in order to avoid this bias.

8. **Escalation of Commitment Bias.** The *escalation of commitment bias* refers to the tendency to stick to an ineffective course of action when it is unlikely that the bad situation can be reversed. Personal examples might include investing more money into an old or broken car and putting more effort into improving a personal relationship that is filled with conflict. A business example would be Hostess asking investors to reinvest in the company during its second bankruptcy. One of the company's lenders described it this way: "If you look in the dictionary at the definition of throwing good money after bad, there should be a picture of Hostess beside it."[36]

   Researchers recommend the following actions to reduce the escalation of commitment:

   • Set minimum targets for performance, and have decision makers compare their performance against these targets.
   • Regularly rotate managers in key positions throughout a project.
   • Encourage decision makers to become less ego-involved with a project.
   • Make decision makers aware of the costs of persistence.[37]

TAKE-AWAY APPLICATION—TAAP

Using the list of decision-making biases, answer the following questions:

1. Think of a bad decision you made in the last 6 to 12 months.
2. Now consider which of the eight decision-making biases may have influenced your decision.
3. Based on your answer, and your knowledge of judgmental heuristics, what could you have done differently to avoid the bad decision?

EVIDENCE-BASED DECISION MAKING

major question

MAJOR QUESTION

How can I more effectively use evidence-based decision making?

THE BIGGER PICTURE

You can improve the quality of your decisions by looking for the best evidence and the best available data to make, inform, or support the decision. This section of the chapter will help you understand the role of evidence in decision making and the move toward "big data."

Interest in the concept of evidence-based decision making stems from two sources. The first is the desire to avoid the decision-making biases discussed previously, and the second is research done on evidence-based medicine.[38] In health care, the goal is to increase the quality of care while reducing costs. Proponents believe that ***evidence-based decision making*** **(EBDM), which is defined as a process of conscientiously using the best available data and evidence when making managerial decisions,** can help make this happen. Results from its application in other industries suggests that this is possible.

Consider the applications to dairy farming and professional sports.

EXAMPLE "A Canadian company, Dairy Quality, unveiled a new product called Milk Guardian, a small black box that slides onto the back of an iPhone. A farmer inserts a plastic slide containing a milk sample from one of his cows, and the device counts the number of somatic cells. (A high somatic cell count can be an indicator of mastitis, an infection of the udder tissue.) Counting somatic cells used to require sending milk to an offsite lab and waiting a week or more for results; using a microscope and an app, Milk Guardian can analyze a sample on location in six seconds or less. The accessory and app cost $1,800."[39]

(Left) Milk Guardian provides hardware and an app to modify an iPhone so it can count somatic cells from a sample to identify udder infection; *(right)* the Lely Astronaut a4 robot milks cows so farmers can sleep through pre-dawn milking.

EXAMPLE More than 50 percent of NBA basketball teams use EBDM to improve their team's performance.

- **Wearable monitors.** During practice, for example, players wear a silver dollar–sized chip to monitor their physiological indicators, movements, and posture. Coaches leverage the data to customize a training regiment for each player, all to improve each player's conditioning and range of motion.

- **Camera analysis.** During games, cameras track players' movements, and software converts the images to data points like "contested rebounds (with an opponent within 3½ feet), catch-and-shoot success rates, live-ball turnovers and the speed and distance players travel. . . . The cameras detect the percentage players walk, jog, run and sprint, and use those motions to determine the 'mechanical load' on players' legs." Teams use the data to customize how players train on off days and how they can prevent injuries.[40]

A Model of Evidence-Based Decision Making (EBDM)

Figure 11.3 illustrates a model of EBDM. You can see that evidence is used in three different ways: to make a decision, to inform a decision, and to support a decision.

"Evidence is used to *make* a decision whenever the decision follows directly from the evidence." For example, if you wanted to purchase a particular used car (e.g., Toyota Prius) based on price and color (e.g., red), you would obtain data from the Internet and classified ads and then choose the seller offering the lowest-priced red Prius. "Evidence is used to *inform* a decision whenever the decision process combines hard, objective facts with qualitative inputs, such as intuition or bargaining with stakeholders." For instance, in hiring new college graduates, objective data about applicants' past experience, education, and participation in student organizations

FIGURE 11.3   THE USE OF EVIDENCE IN DECISION MAKING

In each of the three scenarios following, the role of evidence is increasingly diminished, until in the final scenario evidence becomes an *output* of the decision process. Note also that the risks increase with each succeeding scenario.

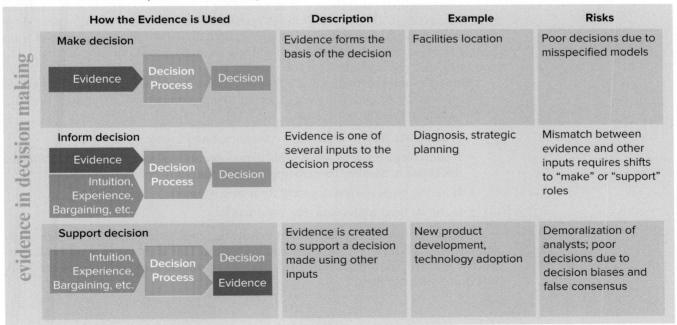

How the Evidence is Used	Description	Example	Risks
Make decision	Evidence forms the basis of the decision	Facilities location	Poor decisions due to misspecified models
Inform decision	Evidence is one of several inputs to the decision process	Diagnosis, strategic planning	Mismatch between evidence and other inputs requires shifts to "make" or "support" roles
Support decision	Evidence is created to support a decision made using other inputs	New product development, technology adoption	Demoralization of analysts; poor decisions due to decision biases and false consensus

SOURCE: From P. M. Tingling and M. J. Brydon, "Is Decision-Based Evidence Making Necessarily Bad?," *MIT Sloan Management Review,* Summer 2010, 73. Copyright © 2010 from MIT Sloan Management Review/Massachusetts Institute of Technology. All rights reserved. Distributed by Tribune Content Agency, LLC.

would be relevant input to making a hiring decision. Nonetheless, subjective impressions garnered from interviews and references would typically be combined with the objective data to make a final decision. These two uses of evidence are clearly positive and should be encouraged. The same cannot be said about using evidence to support a decision.

"Evidence is used to *support* a decision whenever the evidence is gathered or modified for the sole purpose of lending legitimacy to a decision that has already been made."[41] This application of evidence has both positive and negative effects. On the positive side, manufactured evidence can be used to convince an external audience that the organization is following a sound course of action in response to a complex and ambiguous decision context. This can lead to confidence and goodwill about how a company is responding to environmental events. On the negative side, this practice can stifle employee involvement and input because people will come to believe that management is going to ignore evidence and just do what it wants. You know how discouraging this can be if it ever happened to you. There are two takeaways about using evidence to support a decision. First, this practice should not always be avoided. Second, because this practice has both pros and cons, management needs to carefully consider when it "might" be appropriate to ignore disconfirming evidence and push its own agenda or decisions.

Big Data: The Next Frontier in EBDM

A recent study says that the digital universe will reach 40 zettabytes (ZB) by 2020. This reflects a 50 percent growth in information from 2010. To put this in perspective, there are 700,500,000,000,000,000,000 grains of sand on the beaches around the world. Forty ZB is equal to 57 times the number of grains of sand.[42] The term **big data** **reflects the vast quantity of data available for decision making.** It also encompasses "the collection, sorting, and analysis of that information, and the techniques to do so."[43] The analysis of big data is expected to revolutionize all aspects of our lives, and many companies are not prepared for this change. For example, a survey of 800 people by the American Management Association revealed that only 1 in 4 organizations has the ability to handle big data.[44]

Experts estimate that there will be a need for 1.5 million experts in data analytics over the next 5–10 years. Guess who is responding to this need? Universities. More and more universities are offering majors in data analytics. These degrees will train people to use quantitative and statistical tools to analyze and interpret big data. Do you think that you are suited for this career?

Managers and companies that effectively utilize big data, such as Kroger (see the Problem-Solving Application), are expected to gain competitive advantage. Big data creates value in the following ways:

- It can make information more transparent and usable.
- It allows organizations, like Kroger, to measure and collect all types of performance information, enabling them to implement initiatives to enhance productivity.
- It allows more narrow segmentation of customers.
- It can be used to develop new products.[45]

One problem with big data is that private or sensitive information is more easily obtained, which means it can be leaked to others. This is precisely what NSA contractor Edward Snowden did in 2013. He leaked information about what the NSA was doing with big data.[46]

solving application

Kroger Uses Big Data to Improve Customer Service and Profits

Behind the scenes at this Kroger supermarket, computers, using infra-red cameras, count shoppers in line to alert managers when to open new lanes and even to predict future traffic.

Kroger is using big data from infra-red cameras to reduce the wait time in checkout lines. Kroger's system, which is referred to as QueVision, is operating in roughly 95 percent of its stores. Sales have increased since the system was installed, reports *The Wall Street Journal*.

How Does the System Work?
The cameras detect body heat and they are placed "at the entrances and above cash registers at most of Kroger's roughly 2,400 stores. Paired with in-house software that determines the number of lanes that need to be open, the technology has reduced the customer's average wait time to 26 seconds. That compares with an average of four minutes before Kroger began installing the cameras in 2010."

The data also uncovered some additional trends that led to increased sales. "The system showed that there were more customers than Kroger realized buying a small number of items in the morning and during lunchtime, and that the express lanes were backing up. So Kroger added 2,000 new express lanes to its stores nationwide, which it credits with growing the number of those small orders over the last two years."[47]

YOUR CALL

Stop 1: What problem was Kroger trying to solve by installing QueVision? Based on Figure 11.3, how is Kroger using the data it is capturing?

Stop 2: What are the causes of different spending patterns and customer service responses?

Stop 3: What is your evaluation of Kroger's use of QueVision? Briefly summarize ethical and privacy issues around their customer service effort.

11.4 FOUR DECISION-MAKING STYLES

major question

MAJOR QUESTION

How do I decide to decide?

THE BIGGER PICTURE

Your decision-making style reflects the manner in which you perceive and comprehend information. You will find it as an input in the Integrative Framework. Knowing the four general styles of decision making will help you understand how your managers and coworkers are making their decisions; and it will help you know yourself that much better, too. The four decision-making styles are directive, analytical, conceptual, and behavioral.

We make countless decisions on a daily basis—from what to wear, to what to eat, to what route to take driving to school, to whether or not to confront a negative colleague. These decisions are guided by our decision-making style. **A *decision-making style* is how an individual perceives and comprehends stimuli and the general manner in which he or she chooses to respond to such information.**[48] A team of researchers developed a model of decision-making styles that is based on the idea that styles vary along two different dimensions: value orientation and tolerance for ambiguity.[49]

Value Orientation and Tolerance for Ambiguity

Value orientation reflects the extent to which an individual focuses on either task and technical concerns or people and social concerns when making decisions. Some people, for instance, are very task focused at work and do not pay much attention to people issues, whereas others are just the opposite. The second dimension pertains to a person's *tolerance for ambiguity.*

This individual difference indicates the extent to which a person has a high need for structure or control in his or her life. Some people desire a lot of structure in their lives (a low tolerance for ambiguity) and find ambiguous situations stressful and psychologically uncomfortable. In contrast, others do not have a high need for structure and can thrive in uncertain situations (a high tolerance for ambiguity). Imagine the ambiguity faced by brain surgeons when doing surgery. Ambiguous situations can energize people with a high tolerance for ambiguity.

When the dimensions of value orientation and tolerance for ambiguity are combined, they form four styles of decision making: directive, analytical, conceptual, and behavioral (see Figure 11.4).

The Directive Style: Action-Oriented Decision Makers Who Focus on Facts

People with a *directive* style have a low tolerance for ambiguity and are oriented toward task and technical concerns when making decisions. They are efficient, logical, practical, and systematic in their approach to solving problems. People with this style are action oriented and decisive and like to focus on facts. In their pursuit of speed and results, however, these individuals tend to be autocratic, exercise power and control, and focus on the short run.

FIGURE 11.4 DECISION-MAKING STYLES

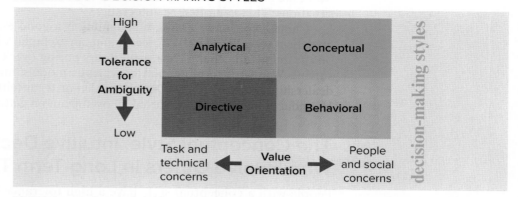

SOURCE: Based on discussion in A. J. Rowe and R. O. Mason, *Managing with Style: A Guide to Understanding, Assessing, and Improving Decision Making* (San Francisco: Jossey-Bass, 1987), 1–17.

Interestingly, a directive style seems well suited for an air-traffic controller. Here is what Paul Rinaldi, president of the National Air Traffic Controllers Association, had to say about his decision-making style to a reporter from *Fortune*:

> It's not so much analytical as it is making a decision quickly and sticking with it. . . . You can't back out. You've constantly got to be taking into account the speed of the airplane, its characteristics, the climb rate, and how fast it's going to react to your instructions. You're taking all that in and processing it in a split second, hoping that it'll all work together. . . . We can't make mistakes.[50]

The Analytical Style: Careful and Slow Decision Makers Who Like Lots of Information

People with this style have a much higher tolerance for ambiguity and tend to overanalyze a situation. They like to consider more information and alternatives than do those with a directive style. Analytical individuals are careful decision makers

Elon Musk, on the right, is CEO of SpaceX, CEO of Tesla Motors, and chair of SolarCity. Musk believes that SpaceX will commercialize space travel. He is known to have both an analytical and conceptual style of decision making.

who take longer to make decisions but who also respond well to new or uncertain situations. They can often be autocratic.

Chinese consumer Zhang Guangming is a good example of someone with an analytical style. *BusinessWeek* sees in him an exemplar of other potential car buyers on the mainland. Zhang "has spent hours poring over Chinese car buff magazines, surfing Web sites to mine data on various models, and trekking out to a dozen dealerships across Beijing." Once he settled on a car (either a Volkswagen Bora or a Hyundai Sonata sedan) he started all over again on getting the best deal.[51]

The Conceptual Style: Intuitive Decision Makers Who Involve Others in Long-Term Thinking

People with a conceptual style have a high tolerance for ambiguity and tend to focus on the people or social aspects of a work situation. They take a broad perspective to problem solving and like to consider many options and future possibilities. Conceptual types adopt a long-term perspective and rely on intuition and discussions with others to acquire information. They also are willing to take risks and are good at finding creative solutions to problems. On the downside, however, a conceptual style can foster an idealistic and indecisive approach to decision making.

The Behavioral Style: Highly People-Oriented Decision Makers

This style is the most people oriented of the four styles. People with this style work well with others and enjoy social interactions in which opinions are openly exchanged. Behavioral types are supportive, are receptive to suggestions, show warmth, and prefer verbal to written information. Although they like to hold meetings, people with this style have a tendency to avoid conflict and to be too concerned about others. This can lead behavioral types to adopt a wishy-washy approach to decision making and to have a hard time saying no to others and to have difficulty making difficult decisions.

Which Style Are You?

Research reveals that very few people have only one dominant decision-making style. Rather, most managers have characteristics that fall into two or three styles. Studies also show that decision-making styles vary by age, occupations, personality types, gender, and countries.[52] The following self-assessment will enhance your understanding about your decision making style.

connect

SELF-ASSESSMENT 11.2 What Is My Decision-Making Style?

Go to connect.mheducation.com and complete Self-Assessment 11.2 to measure your decision-making style. Then answer the following questions:

1. Do you agree with your results? Explain.

2. Which of these styles is most important in your role as a student and in your current job?

3. Based on your answer to question 2, what might you do to modify your decision-making style?

© Dr. Alan J. Rowe, Distinguished Emeritus Professor. Revised December 18, 1998. Reprinted with permission.

A ROAD MAP TO ETHICAL DECISION MAKING

MAJOR QUESTION

How can I assess the ethics of my decisions?

THE BIGGER PICTURE

Sometimes you may find yourself confused about the ethics of a situation. One way to gain some certainty is to graph the situation with a decision tree. A decision tree provides a framework for ethical decision making.

In Chapter 1 we discussed the importance of ethics and the growing concern about the lack of ethical behavior among business leaders and students. Unfortunately, research shows that many types of unethical behavior go unreported, and unethical behavior is negatively related to employee engagement.[53] While this state of affairs partially explains the passage of laws to regulate ethical behavior in corporate America, we believe we can turn to another place to look for improvement—the decision-making process people engage in. Ethical acts ultimately involve individual or group decisions. It thus is important to consider the issue of ethical decision making. Harvard Business School Professor Constance Bagley suggests that a *decision tree* can help managers to make more ethical decisions.[54]

A **decision tree** **is a graphical representation of the process underlying decisions,** and it shows the consequences of making various choices. Decision trees are used to aid in decision making. You can follow Bagley's decision tree, shown in Figure 11.5, by asking the following questions:

1. **Is the proposed action legal?** This may seem like common sense, but you would be surprised how some managers and companies overlook this question. For example, Synthes, a medical device maker, decided to market Norian XR, a cement that potentially turns into bone when injected into humans, for spine surgeries despite being told not to by the Food and Drug Administration. At least five people died on the operating table after being injected with Norian.[55]

2. **If "yes," does the proposed action maximize shareholder value?** A decision maximizes shareholder value when it results in a more favorable financial position (e.g., increased profits) for an organization. Whether or not an action maximizes shareholder value, the decision tree shows that managers still need to consider the ethical implications of the decision or action.

3. **If "yes," is the proposed action ethical?** The answer to this question is based on considering the positive effect of the action on an organization's other key constituents (customers, employees, the community, the environment, suppliers) against the benefit to the shareholders. For example, Bangladesh factory owners bullied employees to work in a building despite warnings from engineers

The 2013 building collapse in Rana Plaza in Bangladesh is the largest garment factory accident in history. Sadly, 1,129 people died in this tragedy. This tragedy could have been prevented by better management.

FIGURE 11.5 AN ETHICAL DECISION TREE

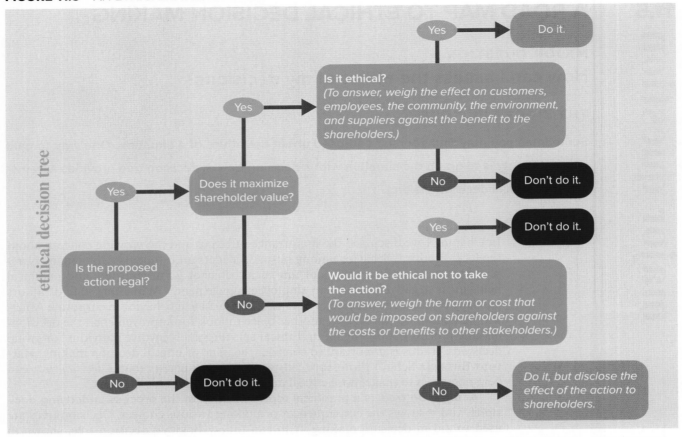

SOURCE: Reprinted by permission of *Harvard Business Review*. Exhibit from "The Ethical Leader's Decision Tree" by C. E. Bagley, February 2003. Copyright © 2003 by the Harvard Business School Publishing Corporation; all rights reserved.

that an exterior crack made it unsafe. They did this out of fear of losing business, a negative impact on shareholder value.

As you may know, the building collapsed, killing 1,129 people. In this case, the decision to force workers to enter the building may have benefited the shareholders, but it was very bad for employees and the country.[56] Ethically, then, managers should not have encouraged workers to enter the building, obviously.

4. **If "no," would it be ethical not to take the proposed action?** If an action would not directly benefit shareholders, you need to consider whether it would be ethical not to take the proposed action.

Returning to the example of factory owners bullying workers to enter a damaged building in Bangladesh, this decision was harmful to other stakeholders—employees and the country. Thus, the ethical conclusion might be to ask employees to enter the building after fixing the structural problems and to ask customers for some leeway in filling orders.

It is important to keep in mind that the decision tree cannot provide a quick formula that managers and organizations can use to evaluate every ethical question. Ethical decision making is not always clear-cut and is affected by cross-cultural differences. Organizations are encouraged to conduct ethics training and to increase awareness about cross-cultural issues when the work involves people with mixed cultural backgrounds.[57] That said, the decision tree does provide a framework for considering the trade-offs between managerial and corporate actions and managerial and corporate ethics. Try using this decision tree the next time you are faced with a significant ethical question or problem.

major question

MAJOR QUESTION

What are the pros and cons of group decision making and the various problem-solving tools?

THE BIGGER PICTURE

You've probably seen both good and bad come out of a group decision. OB confirms that group decisions can lead to mixed results. It identifies five potential advantages and four disadvantages. Knowing them arms you with information to help you maximize the advantages and minimize the disadvantages. In this section you will find contingency recommendations for involving groups in decision making and three helpful group problem-solving techniques: brainstorming, the nominal group technique, and computer-aided decision making.

The popular press and movies celebrate individual heroes like Robert Downey Jr. (aka Tony Stark) in *Iron Man*. Stark made his own decisions in saving the planet from ruin. Most managers, however, work with others and make decisions by involving others. Although groups don't generally make as effective decisions as the *best* individual acting alone, research reveals that groups make better decisions than *most* individuals acting alone.[58] It thus is valuable for you to learn about decision making in groups.

Advantages and Disadvantages of Group Decision Making

We often have to decide whether to make a decision alone or to consult with others. The following list of advantages and disadvantages can help you decide what to do.

Advantages   The following five advantages are most likely to be found when the group has experience with the issue at hand and when it is diverse in terms of characteristics like personalities, gender, attitudes, and experience.[59]

- **Greater pool of knowledge.** A group possesses more information and knowledge than one individual acting alone.
- **Different approaches to a problem.** Individuals with different backgrounds and experiences bring varied perspectives to diagnosing and solving problems.
- **Greater commitment to a decision.** Participation and a voice in decision making are more likely to result in commitment to a decision. This in turn leads group members to accept and feel responsible for implementing a proposed solution.
- **Better understanding of decision rationale.** Participating in a decision increases group members' understanding about why a decision is being made and what must occur to implement it. This in turn reduces miscommunication among people.
- **More visible role modeling.** Less experienced group members learn about group dynamics and how to solve problems.[60]

Disadvantages   The disadvantages of group-aided decision making involve group dynamics and interpersonal interactions.[61]

- **Social pressure.** The desire to remain in good standing within the group leads to conformity and stifles creativity.
- **A few people dominate.** The quality of a group's decision can be influenced by a few vocal people who dominate the discussion. This is particularly problematic when the vocal person is perceived as a powerful individual.
- **Goal displacement.** When evaluating alternatives, secondary considerations such as winning an argument, getting back at a rival, or trying to impress the boss can override the primary goal of solving a problem. **Goal displacement occurs when the primary goal is overridden by a secondary goal.**
- **Groupthink.** **Groupthink is "a mode of thinking that people engage in when they are deeply involved in a cohesive in-group, when members' strivings for unanimity override their motivation to realistically appraise alternative courses of action."**[62] Groupthink is thoroughly discussed in the next section.

Groupthink

Swissair (Schweizerische Luftverkehr) was the national airline for Switzerland and thrived for decades, but poor decisions sealed its doom in the economic downturn of 2001. Swissair went bankrupt, and most of its planes, routes, and personnel were taken over by Swiss International Air Lines. Which of the groupthink symptoms may have contributed to the company's demise?

The term *groupthink,* defined above, originated from an analysis of the decision-making processes underlying the war in Vietnam and other US foreign policy fiascoes. Modern managers can all too easily become victims of groupthink (e.g., space shuttle *Challenger* disaster, Enron debacle, and Iraq war after 9/11) if they passively ignore the danger. Groupthink happens when members fail to exercise sufficient reality testing and moral judgment due to pressures from the group. Groupthink is more likely when there are high levels of **cohesiveness or a sense of "we-ness" that overrides individual differences and motives.** Members of groups tend to be cohesive for two fundamental reasons: (1) simply because they like and enjoy each other's company and (2) because they need each other to achieve a common goal. When described this way, you can easily see how cohesiveness is a double-edged sword and how it affects group-level outcomes in the Integrative Framework. It can help you and your team reduce conflict, but it can also reduce performance if it limits questioning and critical thinking and results in groupthink.[63] It therefore is important to be aware of groupthink.

Symptoms of Groupthink   There are eight common symptoms of groupthink. The greater the number of symptoms, the higher the probability of groupthink:

1. *Invulnerability.* An illusion that breeds excessive optimism and risk taking.
2. *Inherent morality.* An assumption groups are prey to that encourages the group to ignore ethical implications.
3. *Rationalization.* Protects personal or "pet" ideas and assumptions.
4. *Stereotyped views of opposition.* Cause group to underestimate opponents.
5. *Self-censorship.* Stifles critical debate.
6. *Illusion of unanimity.* Silence of members interpreted to mean consent.
7. *Peer pressure.* Loyalty of dissenters is questioned.
8. *Mindguards.* Self-appointed protectors against adverse information.[64]

Prevention Is Better than Treatment   Prevention is better than treatment or cure when dealing with groupthink. Table 11.2 provides some excellent recommendations. Using the techniques shown in Table 11.2 should remove barriers to minority dissent. **Minority dissent reflects the extent to which group members feel comfortable**

TABLE 11.2 TECHNIQUES FOR PREVENTING GROUPTHINK

1. Each member of the group should be assigned the role of critical evaluator. This role involves actively voicing objections and doubts.
2. Top-level executives should not use policy committees to rubber-stamp decisions that have already been made.
3. Different groups with different leaders should explore the same policy questions.
4. Managers should encourage subgroup debates and bring in outside experts to introduce fresh perspectives.
5. Someone should be given the role of devil's advocate when discussing major alternatives. This person tries to uncover every conceivable negative factor.
6. Once a consensus has been reached, everyone should be encouraged to rethink his/her position to check for flaws.

SOURCE: Adapted from discussion in I. L. Janis, *Groupthink,* 2nd ed. (Boston: Houghton Mifflin, 1982), ch. 12.

disagreeing with other group members. Research reveals that minority dissent is positively related to participation in decision making and job satisfaction.[65]

Are you working on any project teams at school or work? If yes, you may be interested in assessing the level of minority dissent and participation in decision making. Results from the following Self-Assessment can help you to improve your effectiveness within these teams.

connect

SELF-ASSESSMENT 11.3 **What Is the Level of Minority Dissent and Participation in Group Decision Making in One of My Work Groups?**

Go to connect.mheducation.com and complete Self-Assessment 11.3. Then answer the following questions:

1. What is your level of minority dissent and participation in decision making?
2. Are you happy with these results?
3. How might you increase the level of minority dissent and participation in this group? Consider the ideas in Table 11.2.

The items in the survey were developed from C. K. W. De Dreu and M. A. West, "Minority Dissent and Team Innovation: The Importance of Participation in Decision Making," *Journal of Applied Psychology 86*(6), December 2001, 1191–1201.

Practical Contingency Recommendations about Group Decision Making

Routine and Frequent If the decision occurs frequently and is of a routine nature—such as deciding on promotions or who qualifies for a loan—use groups because they tend to produce more consistent decisions than do individuals.

Time Constraints Given time constraints, let the most competent individual, rather than a group, make the decision.

Information and Communication In the face of environmental threats such as time pressure and potential serious effects of a decision, groups use less information and fewer communication channels. This increases the probability of a bad decision.

Recommendation With complex tasks, managers should devise mechanisms to enhance communication effectiveness. (The quality of communication strongly affects a group's productivity.)

Reaching Consensus: The Goal of Group Problem-Solving Techniques

Using groups to make decisions generally requires that they reach a consensus. According to a decision-making expert, a **consensus** "is reached when all members can say they either agree with the decision or have had their 'day in court' and were unable to convince the others of their viewpoint. In the final analysis, everyone agrees to support the outcome."[66] This definition indicates that consensus does not require unanimous agreement because group members may still disagree with the final decision but are willing to work toward its success. It is important that group members honestly and accurately communicate with each other when trying to reach a consensus.

Practical Problem-Solving Techniques

Decision-making experts have developed a host of problem-solving techniques to aid in problem solving. Three we discuss here are (1) brainstorming, (2) the Delphi technique, and (3) decision support systems.

Brainstorming: A Tool for Generating Ideas **Brainstorming is used to help groups generate multiple ideas and alternatives for solving problems.** Developed by advertising executive A. F. Osborn, the technique is used in a variety of contexts.[67] Applications include solving problems, developing creative ideas for new products or removing performance roadblocks, and developing action plans to achieve goals. Brainstorming sessions begin by asking participants to silently generate ideas or solutions, which then are collected either in public or anonymously and summarized in some fashion (e.g., on a white board or a flip chart).

> **TIP** It's good to collect the ideas/solutions anonymously if the issue is emotional, political, or highly salient/sensitive to some group members.[68]

A second session is generally used to critique and evaluate the alternatives. Today, many brainstorming sessions are conducted electronically. **Electronic brainstorming, sometimes called *brainwriting*, allows participants to submit their ideas and alternatives over a computer network.** Webinars are a good tool to use for this purpose.[69]

Managers are advised to follow the seven rules for brainstorming used by IDEO, a product design company (see Table 11.3).

Brainstorming is an effective technique for generating new ideas/alternatives, and research reveals that people can be trained to improve their brainstorming skills.

The Delphi Technique This problem-solving method was originally developed by the RAND Corporation for technological forecasting.[70] It now is used as a multipurpose planning tool. **The *Delphi technique* is a group process that anonymously generates ideas or judgments from physically dispersed experts.**

This technique is useful when face-to-face discussions are impractical, when disagreements and conflict are likely to impair communication, when certain individuals might severely dominate group discussion, and when groupthink is a probable outcome of the group process.[71]

Decision Support Systems The increased globalization of organizations, the existence of big data, and the advancement of information technology have led to the development of decision support systems. **Decision support systems (DSS) are "computer-based interactive systems that help decision makers to use data and models to solve unstructured**

Imagine the amount of brainstorming and decision support systems being used in large data centers like this one.

TABLE 11.3 SEVEN RULES FOR BRAINSTORMING

RULE	DETAILS
1. Defer judgment.	Don't criticize during the initial stage of generating ideas. Avoid phrases such as "We've never done it that way," "It won't work," "It's too expensive," and "Our manager will never agree."
2. Build on the ideas of others.	Encourage participants to extend others' ideas by avoiding "buts" and using "ands."
3. Encourage wild ideas.	Encourage out-of-the-box thinking. The wilder and more outrageous the ideas, the better.
4. Go for quantity over quality.	Guide participants to generate and write down as many new ideas as possible. Focusing on quantity encourages people to think beyond their favorite ideas.
5. Be visual.	Use different colored pens (e.g., red, purple, blue) to write on big sheets of flip chart paper, white boards, or poster board that is put on the wall.
6. Stay focused on the topic.	Appoint a facilitator to keep the discussion on target.
7. One conversation at a time.	Set ground rules that no one interrupts another person, dismisses someone's ideas, shows disrespect, or otherwise behaves rudely.

SOURCE: B. Nussbaum, "The Power of Design," *BusinessWeek,* May 17, 2004, 86–94.

problems."[72] Today, these systems are used to solve any type of problem, structured or unstructured. For example, Best Buy, Google, GE, Intel, and Microsoft all use internal intranets to obtain input from employees. Both Best Buy and Google found that these systems were helpful in estimating the demand for new products and services.[73] These systems also were found to improve information processing and decision making within virtual teams.[74]

solving application

problem

Rosemont Center Addresses Employee-Related Issues

Rosemont Center, a social services agency in Columbus, Ohio, provides services to youth and low-income families. The center is funded by federal, state, and local agencies, along with insurers and private donors.

The center's rate of employee turnover grew from 41 percent to 72 percent over three years. This compares to national turnover rates between 50 and 60 percent for community health facilities. Rosemont also found that employee motivation and engagement declined during this period, as did the quality of service provided.

Sonya Latta, the HR director for the center, was tasked with examining turnover. She put together a team to examine the causes of turnover. The team examined results from previous job satisfaction surveys and exit interviews: Exit interviews consist of asking departing employees about the reasons why they are quitting. The following themes were identified from this analysis: People quit because of "demanding work, work/life balance issues relating to night and weekend work, low salaries, on-call responsibilities without additional compensation for certain programs," poor career development opportunities, and lack of support for managers.

Sonya did not know how to eliminate these potential causes of turnover. She thus decided to ask the task force to interview managers from other social service agencies in Ohio to determine how they were handling similar organizational issues.[75]

YOUR CALL

Let's apply the 3-Stop Approach to problem solving.

Stop 1: What is the problem in this case?

Stop 2: What concepts or theories of OB help to explain the reasons why people are quitting?

Stop 3: What would you do to resolve the problem?

major question

MAJOR QUESTION

How can I increase my own creative behavior and that of my employees?

THE BIGGER PICTURE

Could you become more creative if you needed to? As a manager could you improve the creativity of your group? When you consider creativity from an OB perspective, you will see it as both a process and an outcome (see the Integrative Framework). The process aspect of creativity includes four key behaviors: problem formulation/definition, preparation/information gathering, idea generation, and idea evaluation/validation. And the good news is that research and the insights of creators show that you can manage these behaviors for employees and for yourself. That is, you can increase creativity by following certain practical recommendations.

Creativity is defined here as the process of producing **"new and useful ideas concerning products, services, processes, and procedures."**[76] It can be as simple as locating a new place to hang your car keys or as complex as developing a pocket-size microcomputer. One can create something new (creation), one can combine or synthesize things (synthesis), or one can improve or change things (modification).

You probably already recognize that creativity expands the options available to the decision maker. So we now consider a model of creativity for insight into how you can increase your own creativity and, as a manager, do the same for your employees.

A Model of Creativity

Figure 11.6 illustrates a model of creativity. You can see that it flows nicely from the General Model of OB in that a combination of person factors and environmental characteristics influences creative performance behaviors, which in turn influences creative outcome effectiveness. Let's explore this model, starting with a discussion of the difference between creative performance behaviors and creative outcome effectiveness.

FIGURE 11.6 A MODEL OF CREATIVITY

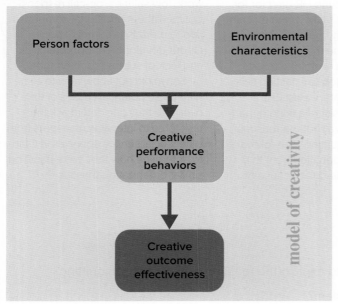

model of creativity

Creative Performance Behaviors Produce Creative Outcome Effectiveness *Creative performance behaviors* represent four key behaviors that drive the production of creative outcomes. *Creative outcome effectiveness* is defined "as the joint novelty and usefulness (quality) of a product or service" as judged by others.[77]

Researchers believe that the four behaviors constituting *creative performance behaviors* unfold according to the following sequence.[78]

- **Problem formulation/definition.** You will recognize this as the by-now-familiar Stop 1 in our 3-Stop Approach to problem solving. We have asked you to make this stop on the problem-solving journey numerous times while reading this book. The practice of accurately defining the problem will enhance your creativity.

- **Preparation/information gathering.** The preparation stage reflects the notion that creativity starts from a base of knowledge. Experts suggest that creativity involves a convergence between tacit and explicit knowledge. Renowned choreographer Twyla Tharp emphasizes the significance of preparation in the creative process: "I think everyone can be creative, but you have to prepare for it with routine." Tharp's creativity-feeding habits include reading literature, keeping physically active (which stimulates the brain as well as the rest of the body), and choosing new projects that are very different from whatever she has just completed.[79] These behaviors facilitate the development of "remote associations." This is one reason why daydreaming has been found to foster creativity.[80] Preparation/information gathering also includes intentional behaviors associated with actively searching for new information related to a problem.

- **Idea generation.** This takes making new mental connections regarding the creative task or problem at hand. This behavior is emphasized in brainstorming.

- **Idea evaluation/validation.** This involves selecting the most creative and promising idea from multiple options.

Drivers of Creative Performance Behaviors   Figure 11.6 shows that person factors and environmental characteristics go into producing the four creative performance behaviors: Note that these person factors and environmental characteristics are inputs in the Integrative Framework of OB. Here is a summary of person factors and environmental characteristics identified through research that drive creative performance behaviors:

- **Person Factors.** First, creativity requires motivation and domain-relevant knowledge. In other words, people need to be motivated to apply their knowledge and capabilities to create new ideas, new products, and solutions to all sorts of problems. The Big Five personality dimensions, an innovative cognitive style, self-efficacy, willingness to tolerate ambiguity, and proactive personality, all are positively associated with creative performance behaviors.[81]

- **Environmental Characteristics.** Meaningful work, positive relationships with supervisors and coworkers, informational feedback, and spatial configuration of work settings all have a positive impact on creative performance behaviors.[82] For example, many organizations, such as Google, Zappos, Salesforce.com, and Yahoo!, are designing the work environment to encourage casual conversations among employees who don't generally work together. They are doing this by "squeezing workers into smaller spaces so they are more likely to bump into each other." They also are "installing playful prompts, like trivia games, to get workers talking in traditional conversational dead zones, such as elevators."[83]

Organizational climate, which was discussed in Chapters 4 and 7, and organizational culture, which is discussed in Chapter 15, also contribute to the exhibition of creative behaviors.[84] Managerial behavior and organizational policies and procedures are key ways to influence organizational climate and culture. The following Self-Assessment measures *creativity climate*. If you are curious whether or not a current or former employer has a "climate for creativity," we encourage you to complete this Assessment.

The Virgin Group, which was the brainchild of Sir Richard Branson (shown in foreground), consists of 400 companies. The companies operate multiple airlines around the world under the Virgin name.

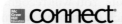

SELF-ASSESSMENT 11.4 Assessing Climate for Creativity

Go to connect.mheducation.com and complete Self-Assessment 11.4. Then answer the following questions.

1. What items most and least contributed to the company's creative climate?

2. Based on your results and Table 11.4, what would you do to increase the level of creativity in this organization?

Practical Recommendations for Increasing Creativity

While some consultants recommend hypnotism as a good way to increase employees' creativity, we prefer suggestions derived from research and especially from three executives leading creative or innovative companies: Jeffrey Katzenberg, CEO of Dreamworks Animation; Ed Catmull, cofounder of Pixar; and David Kelley, founder of IDEO. Both research and their practical experience underscore the conclusion that creativity can be enhanced by effectively managing the four creative performance behaviors. Research also has uncovered some practical tips that all of us can use to increase our creativity (see Table 11.4).

All three executives further recommend that management should create a "safe" work environment that encourages risk taking, autonomy, collaboration, and trusting relationships among employees.[85] These executives suggest that it is important to develop a "peer environment" in which people are more concerned about working for the greater good than for their own personal success. This norm can be nurtured through the use of transformational leadership, which is discussed in Chapter 13.[86] The willingness to give and accept ongoing feedback in a nondefensive manner is another critical component of a culture dedicated to creativity. For example, Pixar uses daily reviews or "dailies" as a process of giving and receiving constant feedback. This will be most effective if organizations train managers in the process of providing effective feedback. Ed Catmull and David Kelly also emphasize the importance of hiring great people who possess some of the person factors discussed earlier. This can be done by asking job applicants "for a story, example or insight that reveals thinking, judgment and problem-solving skills." For example, you might ask an individual to describe a situation in which he or she improvised or how he or she handled a complex problem in a previous job.[87] Finally, these executives also suggest that management should stay connected with innovations taking place in the academic community. For example, Dreamworks invites academics to deliver lectures, and Pixar encourages technical artists to publish and attend academic conferences.

TABLE 11.4 TIPS FOR SPARKING CREATIVITY

1. Put effort into it. Creativity requires motivation.
2. Let the subconscious mind do its work. Trying to force your mind to come up with ideas can stifle creativity. Take a walk, relax, or just plain focus on something else.
3. Daydream. Build time for daydreaming into your daily activities.
4. Seek out the unusual. Watching, visiting, or listening to novel or weird stuff can spark fresh ideas.
5. Surround yourself by the color **blue.** The color blue promotes relaxation and associative thinking.
6. Think like a child. Imagine yourself at a young age and think how you would have solved the problem at that age.
7. Find time to laugh. Watch a short video or comedic presentation as it spurs more insights.
8. Try to solve problems when you are groggy. Grogginess fosters creativity.

SOURCE: These suggestions were derived from S. Shellenbarger, "Even People Who Lack Ideas Can Set the Scene for Inspiration; Just Walk Away," *The Wall Street Journal,* April 3, 2013, D1–2; "How to Come Up with a Great Idea," *The Wall Street Journal,* April 29, 2013, R1–2; and J. Lehrer, "How to Be Creative," *The Wall Street Journal,* March 10–11, 2012, C1–2.

what did i learn?

You learned that it is critical to master the skills of both decision making and creativity and that you have tools and techniques available to you to do just that. Reinforce your learning with the Key Points below. Consolidate your learning using the Integrative Framework. Then Challenge your mastery of the material by answering the Major Questions in your own words.

Key Points for Understanding Chapter 11

You learned the following key points.

11.1 RATIONAL AND NONRATIONAL MODELS OF DECISION MAKING

- The rational model explains how managers *should* make decisions.
- The four stages of rational decision making are (1) identify the problem or opportunity, (2) generate alternative solutions, (3) evaluate alternatives and select a solution, and (4) implement and evaluate the solution chosen.
- Nonrational models explain how managers actually make decisions. Two nonrational models are the normative model and the intuitive model.
- According to the normative model, decision makers are guided by bounded rationality, which represents the fact that decision makers are "bounded" or restricted by different constraints. This leads to satisficing.
- There are two types of intuition: holistic hunches and automated experiences. Intuition is represented by two distinct processes: one is automatic and the second is controlled; and there are two sources of intuition: expertise and feelings.

11.2 DECISION-MAKING BIASES: RULES OF THUMB OR "HEURISTICS"

- Decision-making bias occurs as the result of using judgmental heuristics. The eight biases are (a) confirmation, (b) overconfidence, (c) availability, (d) representativeness, (e) anchoring, (f) hindsight, (g) framing, and (h) escalation of commitment.

11.3 EVIDENCE-BASED DECISION MAKING

- The goal of evidence-based decision making (EBDM) is to conscientiously use the best data when making decisions.

- EBDM is used for three purposes: to make decisions, to inform decisions, and to support decisions.
- Big data denotes the vast quantity of data available for decision making. The benefits of using big data include the following: makes information more transparent and usable, allows organizations to measure and collect many types of performance data, allows the segmentation of customers, and can be used to develop new products.

11.4 FOUR DECISION-MAKING STYLES

- The model of decision-making styles is based on the idea that styles vary along two dimensions: value orientation and tolerance for ambiguity.
- There are four styles of decision making: analytical, conceptual, behavioral, and directive.

11.5 A ROAD MAP TO ETHICAL DECISION MAKING

- A decision tree is a graphical representation of the process underlying decisions.
- The ethical decision tree represents a structured approach for making ethical decisions.
- You work through the tree by answering a series of questions and the process leads to a recommended decision.

11.6 GROUP DECISION MAKING

- Although groups typically make better decisions than the average individual, there are both pros and cons to involving groups in the decision-making process.
- The advantages to using groups include (1) greater pool of knowledge, (2) different approach to a problem, (3) greater commitment to decisions, and (4) more visible role modeling.
- The disadvantages to using groups include (1) social pressure to make particular decisions, (2) a few people dominate, (3) goal displacement, and (4) groupthink.
- Groupthink reduces the quality of decisions and is caused by high levels of cohesiveness among group members. This cohesiveness overrides individual differences.
- There are seven symptoms of groupthink that can be used to diagnose its occurrence.
- You should use a contingency approach in deciding whether or not to include groups in the decision-making process.

- Three commonly used problem-solving tools include brainstorming, the Delphi technique, and decision support systems.

11.7 CREATIVITY

- Creativity is defined as the process of using imagination and skill to develop a new or unique product, object, process, or thought.

- There are four creative performance behaviors you can use to increase your creativity: problem formulation/definition, preparation/information gathering, idea generation, and idea evaluation/validation.

- Creative behaviors are influenced by a host of person factors and environmental characteristics.

- Table 11.4 presents a list of tips for increasing your creativity.

The Integrative Framework for Chapter 11

You learned that decision making is a key process at both the individual and group/team levels, and it is affected by person factors like personality, skills and abilities, values, and needs. Decision making also is influenced by environmental characteristics associated with job design, leadership, and organizational climate. As shown in Figure 11.7, you further learned that decision making is associated with the individual outcomes of task performance, career outcomes, and creativity. At the group level, decision making impacts group/team performance and group cohesion and conflict. Finally, decision making impacts an organization's overall financial performance.

Challenge: Major Questions for Chapter 11

At the start of the chapter, we told you that after reading the chapter you should be able to answer the following questions. Unless you can, have you really processed and internalized the lessons in the chapter? Refer to the Key Points, Figure 11.7, the chapter discussion, and your notes to revisit and answer the following major questions:

1. How can people integrate rational and nonrational models of decision making?

2. It's hard to be rational. What are the biases that get in the way?

3. How can I more effectively use evidence-based decision making?

4. How do I decide to decide?

5. How can I assess the ethics of my decisions?

6. What are the pros and cons of group decision making and the various problem-solving tools?

7. How can I increase my own creative behavior and that of my employees?

FIGURE 11.7 INTEGRATIVE FRAMEWORK FOR UNDERSTANDING AND APPLYING OB

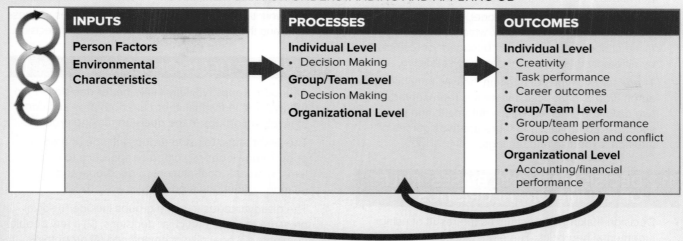

© 2014 Angelo Kinicki and Mel Fugate. All rights reserved. Reproduction prohibited without permission of the authors.

Redeeming Groupon

The meteoric if bumpy rise of Groupon highlights the issues of decision making and creativity. For this case we will look at Groupon's earliest days, into and including its successful IPO, under leadership of its first CEO and cofounder, Andrew Mason.

No one doubts Mason was creative, or that he was a fearless decision maker. Let's start with the main idea: reinventing coupon marketing by leveraging social media. The potential of the idea was huge.

"There was always a sense that Groupon had a lot of good ideas but no real focus," Benchmark Capital analyst Daniel Kurnos said of this period.[88] Mason is "the type of guy who comes up with wild ideas that often have no beginning or end, and then lets them rip," wrote *Vanity Fair* in a 2011 profile. "Finding out where—or if—they land is part of the fun."[89]

Examples of Business Issues and Lack of Focus

The same brashness that let Groupon cut deals in ways that were out of the ordinary may have blinded the company to the need for mundane business diligence. Ben Edelman, associate professor of business administration at Harvard Business School, said that management had "very little patience. . . . Groupon was not hesitant to jump into these businesses before they had figured out the important details that may have deterred others from jumping in," Edelman said.[90]

During Groupon's rise, many business critics were worried that it was growing too fast, working in areas where it lacked expertise, overspending on marketing and staff levels, and always running losses.

IPO as Turning Point

Such issues came to the fore before and after Groupon's IPO, its successful November IPO, thanks to higher levels of transparency and heightened scrutiny.

Before getting to the IPO stage, the seas were choppy. Problems included:

- Multiple disagreements about the offering price.
- Major issues with financial statements requiring multiple filings and corrections.[91]
- Ongoing complaints from merchants about the value they received from the service given its cost.

Following the IPO, more chop followed the initial euphoria. Over the next year, Groupon saw valuation pop as high as over $27 and then drop as low as $2.60 a share. Among its problems:

- **Accounting.** In March of 2012, the company blamed an "internal weakness" in its controls and had to report an even larger net loss. (The drop in revenue resulted from the company having to pay higher refunds to merchants than had been stated.)[92]
- **Slower growth.** Although in 2012, its first full year as a public company, Groupon's revenue increased 45 percent, this is nowhere the explosive growth that initially made it a Wall Street darling. (Revenues had increased five-fold in 2011 and 22-fold in 2010.)

While Groupon was riding high, Mason's shortcomings were overlooked. But as valuation plummeted, business writers became more critical. Here's Adam Hartung in *Forbes*:

> CEO Andrew Mason deserves a lot of credit for building the sales machine that outperformed everyone else—including Google and Amazon. But the other side of his performance was complete inexperience in how to manage finances, operations or any other part of a large publicly traded corporation. Unprofessional analyst presentations, executive turnover, disrespectful comments to investors and chronic unprofitableness all were acceptable if—and only if—he kept up that torrid growth pace.[93]

You may already know that Mason lost his position in February 2013. But for the sake of developing your problem-solving skills, we will be asking you to analyze Groupon's situation up to that point and to consider other steps than a change in leadership.

Apply the 3-Stop Problem-Solving Approach to OB

Stop 1: What is the problem?

- Use the Integrative Framework for Understanding and Applying OB to help identify the outcomes that are important in this case.
- Which of these outcomes are not being achieved in the case?
- Based on considering the above two questions, what is the most important problem in this case?

Stop 2: Use the Integrative Framework to help identify the OB concepts or theories that help you to understand the problem in this case.

- What person factors are most relevant?
- What environmental characteristics are most important to consider?
- Do you need to consider any processes? Which ones?
- What concepts or theories discussed in this chapter are most relevant for solving the key problem in this case?

Stop 3: What are your recommendations for solving the problem?

- Review the material in the chapter that most pertains to your proposed solution and look for practical recommendations.

- Use any past OB knowledge or experience to generate recommendations.

- Outline your plan for solving the problem in this case.

LEGAL/ETHICAL CHALLENGE

Hospitals Are Using Big Data to Evaluate Doctors at Work: Is It a Good Idea?

"MemorialCare is part of a movement by hospitals around the U.S. to change how doctors practice by monitoring their progress toward goals, such as giving recommended mammograms." Although many doctors do not like this approach, Barry Arbuckle, MemorialCare's CEO, believes that tracking doctors' performance is "absolutely key" to the hospital's future.

"Cardiologist Venkat Warren said he worried that 'some bean-counter will decide what performance is.' He wondered whether doctors would be pushed to avoid older and sicker patients who might drag down their numbers. 'If it isn't cost-cutting, what is it?' Dr. Warren asked." CEO Arbuckle counters that he wants to create an "integrated health system that operates efficiently and hits quality goals."

"Technology is making it easier to monitor doctors' work as patients' details are compiled electronically instead of on paper charts." A host of software companies are starting to market programs that hospitals can use to track physicians' decisions and performance. Given the push to reduce the cost of health care in the United States, it is likely that more hospitals will consider using big data to make decisions.

MemorialCare is using big data and it does not have plans to stop. It currently keeps data on a variety of per-formance measures and uses them to determine a doctor's level of pay. Some doctors don't like this approach because they feel it is hard to quantity good patient care and that big data can put too much pressure on doctors. One doctor commented that "physicians are going to feel that you're whipping them to do more, and they're going to burn out."[94]

Do You Like the Practice of Using Big Data to Evaluate Physician Performance?

1. Yes. Tracking physician performance and patient outcomes is good for everyone. Big data can be published so that patients can use it to select doctors, and hospitals can use it to reward doctors.

2. No. Trying to quantify something as complex as the quality of patient care is likely to demotivate the very physicians we need to improve the health care system.

3. I think it would be useful for certain specialties but not others. I agree with Dr. Warren that the use of such data might lead doctors to avoid "sicker" patients.

4. Identify another option.

GROUP EXERCISE

Ethical Decision Making

Objectives

1. To apply the rational model of decision making.
2. To examine the ethical implications of a managerial decision.

Introduction

In this chapter we learned there are four steps in the rational model of decision making. The third step involves evaluating alternatives and selecting a solution. Part of this evaluation entails deciding whether or not a solution is ethical. The purpose of this exercise is to examine the steps in decision making and to consider the issue of ethical decision making. You may want to reexamine the material on ethics in Chapter 1.

Instructions

Break into groups of five or six people and read the following case. As a group, discuss the decision made by the company and answer the questions for discussion at the end of the case. Before answering questions 4 and 5, however, brainstorm alternative decisions the managers at TELECOMPROS could have made. Finally, the entire class can reconvene and discuss the alternative solutions that were generated.

The Case of TELECOMPROS

For large cellular service providers, maintaining their own customer service call center can be very expensive. Many have found they can save money by outsourcing their customer service calls to outside companies.

TELECOMPROS is one such company. It specializes in cellular phone customer service. TELECOMPROS saves large cellular companies money by eliminating overhead costs associated with building a call center, installing additional telephone lines, and so forth. Once TELECOMPROS is hired by large cellular service providers, TELECOMPROS employees are trained on the cellular service providers' systems, policies, and procedures. TELECOMPROS' income is derived from charging a per hour fee for each employee.

Six months ago, TELECOMPROS acquired a contract with Cell2u, a large cellular service provider serving the western United States. In the beginning of the contract, Cell2U was very pleased. As a call center, TELECOMPROS has a computer system in place that monitors the number of calls the center receives and how quickly the calls are answered. When Cell2U received its first report, the system showed that TELECOMPROS was a very productive call center and it handled the call volume very well. A month later, however, Cell2U launched a nationwide marketing campaign. Suddenly, the call volume increased and TELECOMPROS's customer service reps were unable to keep up. The phone monitoring system showed that some customers were on hold for 45 minutes or longer, and at any given time throughout the day there were as many as 50 customers on hold. It was clear to Cell2U that the original number of customer service reps it had contracted for was not enough. It renegotiated with upper management at TELECOMPROS and hired additional customer service reps. TELECOMPROS was pleased because it was now receiving more money from Cell2U for the extra employees, and Cell2U was happy because the call center volume was no longer overwhelming and its customers were happy with the attentive customer service.

Three months later, though, TELECOMPROS's customer service supervisors noticed a decrease in the number of customer service calls. It seemed that the reps had done such a good job that Cell2U customers had fewer problems. There were too many people and not enough calls. With little to do, some reps were playing computer games or surfing the Internet while waiting for calls to come in.

Knowing that if Cell2U analyzed its customer service needs, it would want to decrease the reps to save money, TELECOMPROS's upper management made a decision. Rather than decrease its staff and lose the hourly pay from Cell2U, the upper management told customer service supervisors to call the customer service line. Supervisors called in and spent enough time on the phone with reps to ensure that the computer registered the call and the time it took to "resolve" the call. Then they would hang up and call the call center again. TELECOMPROS did not have to decrease its customer service reps, and Cell2U continued to pay for the allotted reps until the end of the contract.

Questions for Discussion

1. Was the decision made by TELECOMPROS an ethical one? Why or why not?

2. If you were a manager at TELECOMPROS, what would you have done when your manager asked you to call the customer service line? What are the ramifications of your decision? Discuss.

3. Where did the decision-making process at TELECOMPROS break down? Explain.

4. What alternative solutions to the problem at hand can you identify? What is your recommended solution? Explain why you selected this alternative.

5. How would you implement your preferred solution? Describe in detail.

12 POWER, INFLUENCE, AND POLITICS

How Can I Apply These to Increase My Effectiveness?

inputs

PERSON FACTORS

ENVIRONMENTAL CHARACTERISTICS

processes

INDIVIDUAL LEVEL

GROUP/TEAM LEVEL
Power, Influence, and Politics

ORGANIZATIONAL LEVEL

outcomes

INDIVIDUAL LEVEL

GROUP/TEAM LEVEL

ORGANIZATIONAL LEVEL

© 2014 Angelo Kinicki and Mel Fugate. All rights reserved. Reproduction prohibited without permission of the authors.

MAJOR TOPICS I'LL LEARN AND QUESTIONS I SHOULD BE ABLE TO ANSWER

12.1 POWER AND ITS BASIC FORMS
MAJOR QUESTION: *What are the basic forms of power and how can they help me achieve my desired outcomes?*

12.2 POWER SHARING AND EMPOWERMENT
MAJOR QUESTION: *How can sharing power increase my power?*

12.3 EFFECTIVELY INFLUENCING OTHERS
MAJOR QUESTION: *How do my influence tactics affect my personal effectiveness?*

12.4 POLITICAL TACTICS AND HOW TO USE THEM
MAJOR QUESTION: *What are the many forms of politics, and how can understanding them make me more effective at school, at work, and socially?*

12.5 IMPRESSION MANAGEMENT
MAJOR QUESTION: *Do I seek only to impress, or to make a good impression?*

INTEGRATIVE FRAMEWORK FOR UNDERSTANDING AND APPLYING OB

Power, influence, and politics are some of the most common means by which you affect the behavior of others and they affect yours. Learning these tools will increase your effectiveness in managing individual, group, and organizational level outcomes.

winning at work

"If you had to identify, in one word, the reason why the human race has not achieved, and never will achieve, its full potential, that word would be 'meetings.'"[1] This cynical and funny quote resonates with employees everywhere. You've probably never heard, nor ever will hear, somebody pleading for more meetings. One estimate is that the average worker spends four hours a week in meetings and feels that at least half that time is wasted.[2] Even worse, a sample of CEOs revealed that they spend on average 18 hours per week in meetings.[3] Yet despite the pain, we know that people need to meet, and when managed effectively, groups and teams of people can accomplish great things. We therefore give you some practical tools to get the most out of your meetings, colleagues, and your time. And in the process everybody will appreciate you even more.

LET'S START WITH COMMON COMPLAINTS

Three of the most common complaints are that meetings:

1. Are unnecessary.
2. Don't accomplish much.
3. Are too long. Smartphones only make this worse, as people are commonly distracted (busy texting) until they are asked to speak.

WHAT TO DO

1. *Make and distribute an agenda.* Do more than simply state purpose, day, time, and location. Also tell participants specifically what they need to do to prepare.

2. *Set and communicate a goal for the meeting.* Tell participants in advance, and when you convene, what the end will look like. Explain what you want to accomplish by the time you conclude the meeting, such as a decision or plan of action.

3. *Assign responsibilities.* Assign roles and responsibilities for the meeting itself, and then verbally assign expectations for who is to do what as follow-up or next steps.

4. *Set a time limit.* Some experts suggest that meetings be limited to no more than 45 minutes. There are at least two benefits to this practice: (1) people typically schedule calendar items on the hour, and a 45-minute limit gives them time to get to and prepare for their next appointment; and (2) tasks expand to fill the time you give them (45 minutes will help keep you disciplined and on task).[4]

5. *Experiment.* For instance, if you typically do two meetings a week, or four per month, then try cutting that number in half. Doing more, or even the same, in fewer meetings is a benefit for everybody. Try it.

6. *Be concise.* Tell everybody that you expect concise comments that are on topic, and reinforce this by modeling the same behavior.

7. *Marry complaints with solutions.* Establish the expectation that if somebody raises an issue or complaint that they must also provide a potential solution.

8. *Stick to a schedule.* Start on time and end on time.

FOR YOU | WHAT'S AHEAD IN THIS CHAPTER

The purpose of this chapter is to give you a survival kit for the rough-and-tumble side of organizational life. We do so by exploring the interrelated topics of power, empowerment, influence and persuasion, organizational politics, and impression management. These topics are in the group and team section of the book because they are about influencing others—individuals *and* groups. They also are important group-level processes in the Integrative Framework for Applying and Understanding OB. We will help you understand that how you influence others impacts their response and your effectiveness. The appropriate, skilled, and ethical use of the knowledge in this chapter will not only help set you apart from your peers, but also close the gap between you and those with more experience and bigger titles.

major question

What are the basic forms of power and how can they help me achieve my desired outcomes?

THE BIGGER PICTURE

You try to influence people all day, every day of your life, sometimes with great effort and other times without even being aware. And others are doing the same to you. To influence people, you draw on various types of power. Depending on the situation, you might simply tell the person to do what you want (such as if you're his or her manager), or you might inspire the person with your charismatic personality and persuasive prowess (such as if you're his or her coworker). How you choose to influence others, what types of power you use, can have important implications for how they respond. We will help you understand what the different types of power are and how they generate different responses in others. Such knowledge can make you more effective at managing outcomes across the levels of the Integrative Framework for Understanding and Applying OB.

Power is defined as the ability to marshal human, informational, and other resources to get something done. Defined this way, power is all about influencing others. The more influence you have, the more powerful you are, and vice versa. The term *power* commonly evokes mixed and often passionate reactions. To skeptics, Lord Acton's time-honored declaration that "power corrupts and absolute power corrupts absolutely" is truer than ever. However, like it or not, power is a fact of life in modern organizations. According to one management writer,

> Power must be used because managers must influence those they depend on. Power also is crucial in the development of managers' self-confidence and willingness to support subordinates. From this perspective, power should be accepted as a natural part of any organization. Managers should recognize and develop their own power to coordinate and support the work of subordinates; it is powerlessness, not power, that undermines organizational effectiveness.[5]

To make our discussion of power more practical, we distinguish between five common forms or bases of power.

Five Bases of Power

A popular and useful distinction is made between five bases of power: legitimate, reward, coercive, expert, and referent. (See Figure 12.1.) Each involves a different approach to influencing others and has advantages and drawbacks. Let's learn more.

Legitimate Power   This base of power is what most people think of as authority and is anchored to one's formal position. Thus, **managers who obtain compliance**

FIGURE 12.1 THE FIVE BASES OF POWER

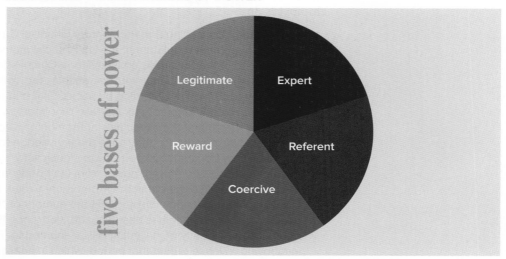

primarily because of their formal authority to make decisions have *legitimate power.* Legitimate power may be expressed either positively or negatively.

- *Positive legitimate* power focuses constructively on job performance.

    EXAMPLE The HP board utilized this form of power when it ousted CEO Mark Hurd for inappropriately using company funds and sexually harassing a contractor with whom he had an affair.[6]

- *Negative legitimate power,* in contrast, tends to be threatening and demeaning to those being influenced, if not simply an exercise in building the power holder's ego.

    EXAMPLE Many US politicians have used their legislative position power to name various "monuments" after themselves, from the Charles Rangel Center for Public Service (New York) to the Ted Stevens Airport (Alaska). The late Robert Byrd from West Virginia had more than 30 monuments named after him.[7]

Yet other instances of legitimate power or authority mix positive and negative aspects. Can you think of an example?

Reward Power Individuals or organizations have *reward power* **if they can obtain compliance by promising or granting rewards.** Pay-for-performance plans and positive reinforcement practices attempt to exploit reward power.

EXAMPLE When Exide Batteries provided quality products and services that were attractive to Walmart, it was rewarded with more than $100 million of annual business. But when Walmart withdrew its business and went to a competitor, Exide was forced into bankruptcy.[8]

Coercive Power The ability to **make threats of punishment and deliver actual punishment gives an individual** *coercive power.*

EXAMPLE The Federal Trade Commission filed and won a lawsuit against Roll International, the owner of popular beverages Fiji Water and Pom Wonderful. The FTC charged that the company made false health claims about the pomegranates in its Pom Wonderful juice. The company must now stop making such claims about its products.[9]

Expert Power **Valued knowledge or information gives an individual** *expert power* over those who need such knowledge or information. The power of supervisors is enhanced because they know about work assignments and schedules before their employees do.

> **EXAMPLE** Consulting firm Promontory Financial Group is composed mainly of former government regulators of the US financial industry, such as Mary Shapiro, former head of the Securities and Exchange Commission. The firm helps banks challenge rules and influence reforms, such as the Volker Rule that, among other things, puts curbs on risky trading by banks. One bank executive said that "they sometimes hired Promontory to appease regulators, who think highly of the firm's expertise." Given that the executives at Promontory are themselves former regulators, it is no surprise they have the knowledge to influence today's regulators. However, they boost their expert power significantly by also drawing heavily on their relationships or referent power from their previous positions in government.[10] This issue is much bigger than the Promontory Group, as a recent report by the Sunlight Foundation indicated that the number of "lobbyists with former government experience has nearly quadrupled since 1998. . . . Those revolving door lobbyists, mostly from Captial Hill, accounted for nearly all of the huge growth in lobbying revenue during that period, which increased to $1.32 billion [in 2012] from $703 million in 1998."[11]

Referent Power ***Referent power*** **comes into play when one's personal characteristics and social relationships become the reason for compliance.** Charisma is commonly associated with referent power, but one does not need to be the life of the party to possess referent power. In Asian cultures, for instance, characteristics such as age, gender, or family name are sources of social status and referent power. One often-overlooked and underestimated source of referent power is your network of relationships.

> **EXAMPLE** Say a coworker calls and asks if you can help her with a project. You tell her that you don't have the knowledge or skill yourself, but that Susan, a member of another department who you happen to know, can provide the help your coworker requires. You make the introduction. Because you introduced your coworker to somebody who helped her, you have referent power by virtue of your relationships.

Referent power drives the success of a number of marketing schemes, as with companies like Tupperware and MaryKay, which use independent contractors to throw home parties to display and sell goods to friends and families. More recently, the solar power industry is using referent power (including companies like SunWize, SmartPower, and SolarCity) to expand its business. Like Tupperware, they assume that "the best sales people are often enthusiastic customers willing to share their experiences with friends and neighbors—and perhaps earn a referral fee on any sales that result."[12] The solar companies have found that this approach is both an easier and more effective means for finding new customers. This shows that people are more trusting of and therefore more easily influenced by people they know.

One's reputation is another example of referent power. Many companies hire new CEOs, in part, to reap the benefits of the executive's reputation. Ford Motor Company, for example, hired Alan Mulally as CEO because of his stellar reputation and success at Boeing.

Now that you've learned about the five bases of power, complete Self-Assessment 12.1 to identify which bases of power you commonly use. Answering the associated questions will help you understand how the various forms of power can both help and hurt you when trying to influence others.

Some residential solar companies are using the referent power of customers' relationships (e.g., their families and friends), to market and sell their products via home parties, like Tupperware and MaryKay have done successfully for years.

![connect logo] **SELF-ASSESSMENT 12.1** **How Much Power Do I Have?**

Go to connect.mheducation.com and take Self-Assessment 12.1 to learn which bases of power you use.

1. Which of the five bases of power do you use the most?

2. Describe how this form of power helps you at school, at work, and socially.

3. Which of the five bases do you have the least of? What are the implications for you at school, at work, and socially?

4. What two specific things can you do to increase your expert power? Two things to increase your referent power?

Copyright © 1989 by the American Psychological Association. Adapted with permission from T. R. Hinkin and C. A. Schriesheim, "Development and Application of New Scales to Measure the French and Raven (1959) Bases of Social Power," *Journal of Applied Psychology,* 74(4), 1989, 567.

Position v. Personal Power

The first three (legitimate, reward, and coercive) are often referred to as ***position power*** **because the source of influence is associated with a particular job or position within an organization.** Managers, for instance, have legitimate, reward, and coercive power because they control your pay, your work assignments, and your evaluations. In contrast, expert and referent are forms of ***personal power,*** **as they are sources of influence that you possess independent of your position or job.** (See Figure 12.2.) These two general sources of power frequently collide when you are promoted and then must manage the people who just yesterday were your peers. Such transitions are especially important and difficult for you to manage. The following Example box offers good advice.

FIGURE 12.2 BASES OF POWER: POSITION AND PERSONAL

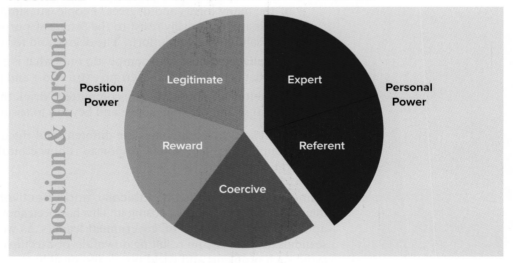

EXAMPLE From Teammate to Manager: Taking Charge

If you've been promoted to lead your group, you suddenly have more legitimate power. But to be an effective leader, you need to exercise that power carefully in a way that doesn't alienate but motivates your former coworkers. This applies at all levels of organizations, including the executive suite. For instance, Satya Nadella confronted such challenges when he became CEO at Microsoft. Mr. Nadella's position power increased when he assumed the CEO role, which makes him every employee's boss, including other executives who were until then his peers.[13] This was not easy, as some of these executives left Microsoft, while others were promoted. Mr. Nadella, and most anybody who is promoted to a management position, would benefit from the following advice on how to influence their former peers who are now subordinates:

1. *Don't show off.* It might be tempting to strengthen your leadership role with an aggressive, dominating style, overseeing every detail. But that approach stirs resentment.

2. *Do accept responsibility.* Trying to stay buddies with group members will undermine your ability to get the job done and will erode respect for you and your ability to handle the position. Collaborate when it's the best way to accomplish goals, not to save a friendship.

3. *Do your homework.* Work with your new supervisor to define goals for yourself and your team. Strengthen your network of mentors to improve your management skills. Meet with your staff to go over your vision and expectations. Setting a direction for the team enhances your credibility (expert power).

4. *Pay attention to team members' concerns.* Show them how meeting the group's goals will put them on track toward meeting their own needs.

YOUR THOUGHTS?

1. What do you think would be the greatest challenge to being promoted and having to manage your peers?

2. Consider, for example, if you suddenly were responsible for grading classmates. Explain how you would apply the four recommendations given above.

Power, but for What Purpose?

Asserting or using power is a necessary and sometimes even subconscious part of our lives. However, what we often overlook or don't consider directly are the potential outcomes of our efforts to influence others. People tend to have three primary reactions to our attempts to manage and otherwise influence them—resistance, compliance, and commitment.

- **Resistance.** Of course, you know what resistance is. But have you ever thought of the many forms and degrees? People can simply be indifferent, be passive-aggressive, or actively resist to the extent of purposefully undermining you or even sabotaging your efforts. The degree and form of resistance thus matter.

- **Compliance.** Those who comply do only what is expected, nothing more. They do what is required and exert no extra effort and provide no extra input.

- **Commitment.** Those who are committed "drink the Kool-Aid." They believe in the cause and often go above and beyond to assure its success.[14]

As you can see, these outcomes are different and the differences matter! One thing that certainly can affect others' responses is how ethically or responsibly you utilize any form of power.

Using Power Responsibly, Ethically, and Effectively   Leaders who do not use their power responsibly risk losing it. This has been shown time and again in political uprisings and the ouster of government leaders, as well as the persistent waves of scandals in business and resulting downfalls of executives. For managers who want to avoid such problems and wield power responsibly, a step in the right direction is understanding the difference between commitment and mere compliance. Responsible managers strive for using power for the good of others, rather than simply using it for personal gain. Former NATO commander General Wesley Clark put it this way:

> Sometimes threatening works, but it usually brings with it adverse consequences—like resentment and a desire to get even in some way. People don't like to be reminded that they are inferior in power or status. And so, in business, it is important to motivate through the power of shared goals, shared objectives, and shared standards.[15]

FIGURE 12.3 BASES OF POWER: COMMITMENT V. COMPLIANCE

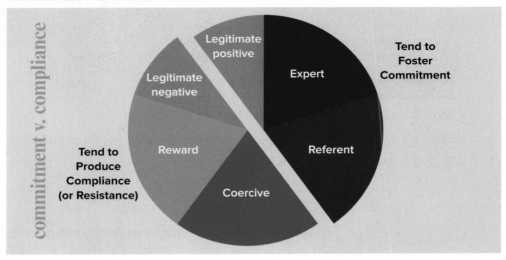

As General Clark describes, sometimes you only need somebody to comply (simply do as you need, ask, or say), but other times you need his or her genuine commitment. You therefore should choose the types of power you use accordingly.

How Does this Relate to the Five Bases of Power? Research, practice, and perhaps your own experiences show that:

- Reward, coercive, and *negative* legitimate power tend to produce *compliance* (and sometimes, resistance).
- *Positive* legitimate power, expert power, and referent power tend to foster *commitment*.

See Figure 12.3. Once again, commitment is superior to compliance because it is driven by internal or intrinsic motivation (Chapter 5). Committed employees tend to be self-starters who do not require close supervision. These are important success factors in today's flatter, team-oriented organizations. In contrast, employees who merely comply require frequent "jolts" of power from the boss to keep them going. The following Problem-Solving Application illustrates the point.

solving application

problem

A Heavy Hand at J&J

One day a batch of more than 1 million bottles of St. Joseph aspirin failed a quality test because a sample didn't dissolve properly, according to two employees involved in the testing process. Following company procedures, the employees blocked the batch from being shipped. As reported in *Fortune*, their manager then called the two into his office. "He said, 'You like working here?'" one of the workers recalls. "'This should pass. There's no reason this should fail.'"

Ultimately the two quality workers were ordered to retest the drugs and then average the new scores to arrive at a passing grade so that the pills could ship.

Says one of them: "You get to the point where, like me, you end up doing what you're told." The manager they accused denies knowledge of the incident. Tellingly, though, he acknowledges that there were ethical issues in the department and in turn blames another supervisor.[16]

YOUR CALL

Stop 1: What is/are the problem(s) in the J&J scenario?

Stop 2: Which OB concepts help explain the problem(s) identified in Stop 1?

Stop 3: What do you recommend?

Bases of Power and Outcomes in the Integrative Framework Research gives us some insights into how different bases of power affect important outcomes in the Integrative Framework, such as job performance, job satisfaction, and turnover.

- Expert and referent power had a generally positive effect.
- Reward and legitimate power had a slightly positive effect.
- Coercive power had a slightly negative effect.[17]

These relationships are summarized in Figure 12.4.

Now that you have a clearer sense of what power is and how it operates, let's learn about how sharing power can actually increase your own power.

FIGURE 12.4 BASES OF POWER AND EFFECTIVENESS OF OUTCOMES

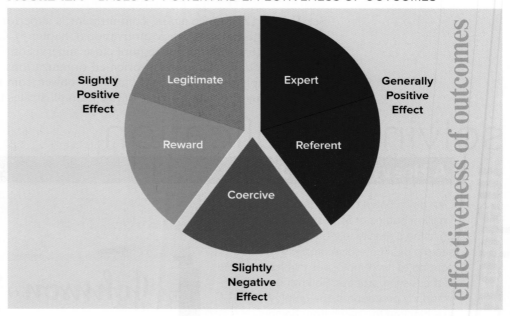

12.2 POWER SHARING AND EMPOWERMENT

major question

MAJOR QUESTION

How can sharing power increase my power?

THE BIGGER PICTURE

How much do you like being told what to do? Chances are you didn't like it as a kid and like it even less as an adult at work. Thankfully, many managers and organizations are looking to employees to solve problems and make decisions, instead of always telling them what to do and how to do it. This increased participation and sharing of authority is referred to as empowerment. Empowerment is a process that influences many important outcomes in the Integrative Framework for Understanding and Applying OB. We therefore explain different forms of empowerment (structural and psychological), various degrees of empowerment, and how to foster it in individuals, teams, and organizations.

A trend continues in today's workplace wherein employees are given greater influence, instead of the more traditional top-down, command-and-control, centralized management practices. This trend is often referred to as **empowerment, which is defined as efforts to "enhance employee performance, well-being, and positive attitudes."**[18] Like our discussion of positive organizational behavior in Chapter 7, empowerment has been shown to favorably influence many outcomes in the Integrative Framework, such as job satisfaction, organizational commitment, performance, turnover, and employee stress.[19] The research and practice related to empowerment have focused on two general forms—*structural* and *psychological*.

Structural Empowerment

Structural empowerment is based on transferring authority and responsibilities from management to employees. Some of the common ways to do this are via the job design and job characteristics forms of motivation that you learned about in Chapter 5. Therefore, managers and their employers can boost employee empowerment by changing policies, procedures, job responsibilities, and team designs. Any of these that increase the effectiveness of employee decision making (Chapter 11) are likely also to increase their performance, well-being, and job-related attitudes. To better understand and apply this knowledge about empowerment, it is necessary to think about the issue correctly.

Thinking the Right Way about Empowerment   Effective empowerment does *not* include giving decision-making authority to just any employee in any and every situation. That would be both foolish and irresponsible—not empowerment! Instead, decision-making authority and other broader responsibilities should only be shared with those who are competent to do what is necessary. It therefore is necessary to avoid two pitfalls to more effectively understand and apply empowerment:

1. Empowerment is *not a zero-sum game* where one person's gain is another's loss. *Sharing power, via empowerment, is a means for increasing your own power.* As Frances Hesselbein, the woman credited with modernizing the Girl Scouts of

FIGURE 12.5 THE EVOLUTION OF POWER FROM DOMINATION TO DELEGATION

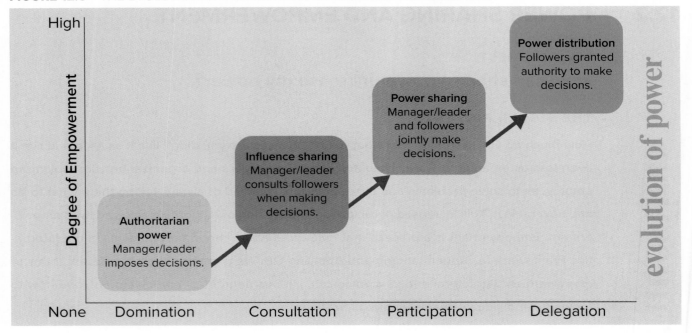

the USA, put it: "The more power you give away, the more you have."[20] Authoritarian managers who view employee empowerment as a threat to their own power are missing the point because of their win–lose thinking.

2. Empowerment is **a matter of degree,** not an either–or proposition. Figure 12.5 illustrates how power can be shifted to the hands of nonmanagers step by step. The overriding goal is to increase productivity and competitiveness in organizations. Each step in this evolution increases the power of organizational contributors who traditionally were told what, when, and how to do things.

Sharing Power to Increase Your Power and Performance A common element of empowerment involves pushing decision-making authority down to lower levels. For example, Homewood Suites offers a 100 percent money-back guarantee if a guest isn't satisfied. Any employee—from housekeeper to manager—can make good on that guarantee; they don't have to seek approval. And the guest doesn't have to go through a chain of command to have a complaint resolved. "The return we get on every dollar refunded is 20 to 1," executive Frank Saitta says, based on repeat business and referrals from those refunded guests. The return on engaged employees "is much higher."[21]

Now that you have an understanding of structural empowerment, let's move on and learn about psychological empowerment.

Psychological Empowerment

Psychological empowerment occurs when employees feel a sense of:

Meaning—Belief that your work values and goals align with those of your manager, team, or employer.

Competence—Personal evaluation of your ability to do your job.

Self-determination—Sense that you have control over your work and its outcomes.

Impact at work—Feeling that your efforts make a difference and affect the organization.[22]

Simply giving employees more responsibilities or tasks does not mean they will feel empowered. Would you feel empowered if your manager allowed you to clean toilets because you've done such an excellent job of cleaning sinks?!

While structural empowerment draws on job design and characteristics, psychological empowerment is related to self-efficacy (Chapter 3) and intrinsic motivation (Chapter 5). "It is less concerned with the actual transition of authority and responsibility but instead focuses on employees' perceptions or cognitive states regarding empowerment."[23] Put simply, if you feel that your work has meaning, that you are competent, and that you have some control (self-determination), then you are very likely to feel highly efficacious and perform at a high level. It therefore is necessary to do more than simply delegate more responsibilities if you wish to psychologically empower others. Let's illustrate with an example.

EXAMPLE   Assume you're a janitor and you clean sinks, and you do it very well. Would you feel empowered if your manager said, "Because you clean the sinks so well, now I'd like you to clean the toilets too." Empowered? No. Where is the sense of meaning or impact? This is simply delegating more work to you (similar to job enlargement discussed in Chapter 5).

Put plainly, don't feel too confident that you're empowering others if they don't feel empowered!

Psychological Empowerment at the Team and Organizational Levels   Recent research and practice have shown that the same four elements that foster psychological empowerment for individuals apply to teams and organizations.[24] Team empowerment grew from the knowledge that teams affect individuals' emotions, attitudes, and performance (recall Chapter 8). This led both managers and experts to explore whether teams (and entire organizations) could be empowered. The conclusion: yes! Moreover, the benefits to individuals also apply to teams and organizations—higher team performance and satisfaction[25] and more positive emotions within the team.[26]

EXAMPLE   Toyota has successfully empowered teams for decades. Teams in Toyota manufacturing facilities, for example, are expected to identify and solve problems as they occur and not simply pass them along to management to fix. Employees are also encouraged to make efficiency and quality improvement suggestions to management. These are typically reviewed by management, but the problems are often assigned to employee teams charged with identifying and implementing solutions. Toyota's practices have been so effective that they have been adopted by not only other auto companies, but manufacturers in many other industries the world over.

Since we've explored different forms of empowerment and its various degrees and levels, let's conclude this section with a discussion of how to increase or develop empowerment in individuals, teams, and organizations.

How to Empower Individuals, Teams, and Organizations

Empowering others is not simple, but what makes it easier is that the same levers can be used to influence empowerment across levels of an organization. Figure 12.6 illustrates some of the key inputs to empower others and the resulting outcomes. Notice how many of these also are elements in the Integrative Framework.

Empowerment Inputs   Structural empowerment is an input to psychological empowerment. This makes sense, as job characteristics, policies, and practices can either facilitate or impede the feelings of empowerment for individuals and teams. This has in fact been shown in recent research with nurses in hospitals. Policies and practices

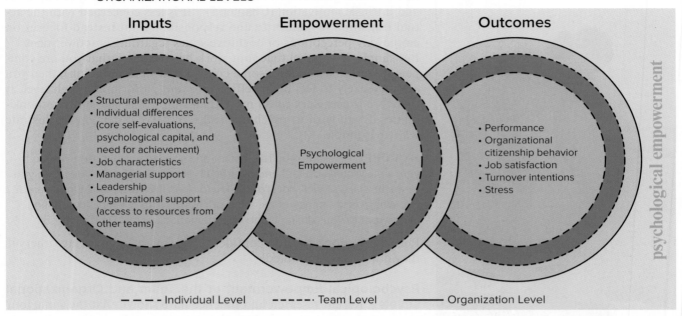

SOURCE: Adapted from M. T. Maynard, L. L. Gilson, and J. E. Mathieu, "Empowerment—Fad or Fab? A Multilevel Review of the Past Two Decades of Research," *Journal of Management 20,* 2012, 1–51.

were changed (structural empowerment) that helped nurse leaders to feel greater meaningfulness in their jobs and provide more participative decision making and less bureaucracy. This in turn increased their feelings of psychological empowerment and their actual empowering behaviors.[27]

Similarly, the extent to which employees have positive self-evaluations, such as core self-evaluations (Chapter 3) and positive psychological capital (Chapter 7), likely enhances their sense of empowerment. What you learned about motivation in Chapter 5 is also helpful to understanding and fostering empowerment across levels of the Integrative Framework. Specifically, job characteristics that generate intrinsic motivational states (sense of meaningfulness and responsibility) clearly can help, as can leadership, which you'll learn about in the next chapter. Finally, if teams have access to the resources such as the people and their ideas in other teams, then they too are more likely to be empowered.

Empowerment Outputs   As with many of the topics covered in this book, empowerment is important because it positively influences performance for individuals, teams, and organizations. Past and current research consistently show this. But the benefits extend beyond performance and also include citizenship behaviors, job satisfaction, and turnover intentions (Chapter 2). Empowerment also reduces stress for individuals and teams.[28]

While empowerment can be a challenge to implement, we are confident that with the knowledge and tools you are learning in this chapter you'll be able to find jobs that are empowering to you, and that you in turn will more effectively empower others. To help your empowerment efforts, we turn our attention in the next section to particular tools for influencing others.

EFFECTIVELY INFLUENCING OTHERS

MAJOR QUESTION

How do my influence tactics affect my personal effectiveness?

THE BIGGER PICTURE

How do you get others to do as you wish? Do you attempt to dazzle them with your knowledge and logical arguments? Or do you prefer a less direct approach, such as promising to return the favor? Whatever approach you use, the crux of the issue is social influence. A large measure of interpersonal interaction involves attempts to influence others, including parents, bosses, coworkers, professors, friends, spouses, and children. Let's start sharpening your influence skills by exploring influence tactics and their effective and ethical application.

In a perfect world, individual and collective interests would be closely aligned and everyone would move forward as one. But the world isn't perfect. We instead often find a rather messy situation in which self-interests often override the collective mission of the department or organization. Personal and hidden agendas are pursued, political coalitions are formed, false impressions are made, and people end up working against rather than with each other. Managers, and you, need to be able to guide diverse individuals with their own interests to pursue common objectives. At stake in this tug-of-war between individual and collective interests is effectiveness, at the personal, group, and organizational levels. And your tools for managing such challenges are *influence tactics*.

Common Influence Tactics

Influence tactics **are conscious efforts to affect and change a specific behavior in others.** Researchers identified nine of the most common ways that people try to get their bosses, coworkers, and subordinates to do what they want. The following tactics are listed in rank order, beginning with most frequently used.

1. *Rational persuasion.* Trying to convince someone with reason, logic, or facts.
2. *Inspirational appeals.* Trying to build enthusiasm by appealing to others' emotions, ideals, or values.
3. *Consultation.* Getting others to participate in planning, making decisions, and changes.
4. *Ingratiation.* Getting someone in a good mood prior to making a request; being friendly and helpful and using praise, flattery, or humor. A particular form of ingratiation is "brown nosing."
5. *Personal appeals.* Referring to friendship and loyalty when making a request.
6. *Exchange.* Making explicit or implied promises and trading favors.
7. *Coalition tactics.* Getting others to support your efforts to persuade someone.
8. *Pressure.* Demanding compliance or using intimidation or threats.
9. *Legitimating tactics.* Basing a request on one's authority or right, organizational rules or policies, or explicit/implied support from superiors.

Hedge fund manager Bill Ackman, of Pershing Square Capital LP, used coalition, rational appeals, pressure, and legitimating tactics to leverage a partial stake in JC Penney to gain control of the company, which under his watch eventually failed and resulted in his departure—and an estimated loss of $700 million for Pershing.[29]

These are considered *generic* influence tactics because they characterize social influence in all directions. And research has shown this ranking to be fairly consistent regardless of whether the direction of influence is downward, upward, or lateral.[30]

Hard v. Soft Tactics   Some refer to the first five influence tactics—rational persuasion, inspirational appeals, consultation, ingratiation, and personal appeals—as *"soft" tactics* because they are friendlier than, and not as coercive as, the last four tactics—exchange, coalition, pressure, and legitimating tactics, which are *"hard" tactics* because they involve more overt pressure.

Which Do I Use Most? Least?   It's likely when you read the list of tactics that each meant something to you. But let's put this to the test, so to speak, and have you learn which of these tactics you most commonly use. Knowing which tactics you tend to use most and least can help you better choose the appropriate tactic for any given situation. The contingency approach that we've utilized throughout this book also applies to influence tactics. Just as with bases of power, it is important to use the tactic that is most appropriate for the situation and your desired outcome. Applying this knowledge can increase your effectiveness. The next step to realizing these benefits is to complete Self-Assessment 12.2.

connect

SELF-ASSESSMENT 12.2   **Which Influence Tactics Do I Use?**

Go to connect.mheducation.com and take Self-Assessment 12.2 to learn which of the nine influence tactics you use and in what order of frequency.

1. Is your rational persuasion score the highest? Regardless, give some specific examples of how you use this tactic.

2. Which tactic is your least preferred (lowest score)? Provide examples of situations of when and how you may use this tactic.

Match Tactics to Influence Outcomes

Research and practice provide us some useful lessons about the relative effectiveness of influence tactics along with other instructive insights. Some insights are intuitive and may match your personal experiences, while others may not.

- **Strong at the core.** *Core influence tactics*—rational persuasion, consultation, collaboration, and inspirational appeals—are most effective at building commitment. Do not rely on pressure and coalition tactics. Interestingly, in one study, managers were not very effective at downward influence. They relied most heavily on inspiration (an effective tactic), ingratiation (a moderately effective tactic), and pressure (an ineffective tactic).

- **Important, enjoyable, friendly.** Commitment is more likely when the influence attempt involves something important and enjoyable and is based on a friendly relationship.

- **Believable and trustworthy.** Credible people tend to be the most persuasive.

- **Consultative trumps legitimating.** Some employees are more apt to accept change when managers rely on a consultative strategy and are more likely to resist change when managers use a legitimating tactic.
- **Schmoozing benefits are short-lived.** Ingratiation improved short-term but reduced long-term sales goal achievement in a study of salespeople. Schmoozing can help today's sales but not tomorrow's.
- **Subtlety wins long term.** Subtle flattery and agreeing with the other person's opinion (both are forms of ingratiation) were shown to increase the likelihood of executives being recommended to sit on boards of directors.
- **We can learn to influence.** Research with corporate managers of a supermarket chain showed that influence tactics can be taught and learned. Managers who received 360-degree feedback on two occasions regarding their influence tactics showed an increased use of core influence tactics.

So what's the bottom line? The influence tactics listed above can be learned and improved to move resisters to compliance, and those who are compliant to commitment.

TAKE-AWAY APPLICATION—TAAP   Using Influence Tactics to Achieve My Goals

1. Think of a goal at school, work, or socially. Be sure this goal also requires somebody else's help for you to achieve.

2. Determine if you need this person's compliance or commitment.

3. Then, using whichever tactic in Self-Assessment 12.2 is your highest, describe specifically how you can use this tactic to achieve your chosen goal. Does this tactic match the desired outcome (compliance or commitment)?

4. Identify a second tactic that can help you achieve this goal, then describe specifically how you can apply it. Be sure the tactic you choose matches your desired outcome (compliance or commitment).

How Can I Increase My Own Influence?

The appropriate choice and application of the power and influence tactics described already provide a good place to start. But there are many other tools that can help you enhance your ability to influence others.[31]

Know what you want and believe you can get it. State your (influence) goals in a positive way. For example, say, "I would like to be part of the decision-making process," instead of, "I don't think anybody will take me seriously." Put another way, tell people what you want instead of what you don't want.

Credibility. People are more likely to listen to those with credibility. Highlight yours by emphasizing your expertise, reputation, and/or track record.

Trustworthiness. It is difficult to influence others if they don't trust you. To build and maintain trust, be authentic, deliver on what you promise, consider the interests of others, and don't do anything to diminish your trustworthiness.

Empathy. It often is best to assume somebody else's position before your own. People are more easily influenced when they feel others understand their situation.

Strong communication capability. All other personal characteristics aside, the ability to effectively communicate your ideas and listen to others bolsters your influence.

Be inspirational. Enthusiasm is contagious. If you're excited, others are more likely to be excited and to follow.

Open-mindedness. Truly influential people are not afraid of being influenced themselves.

Your ability to persuade others can be enhanced further still by understanding and applying the six principles of persuasion. Let's explore these now.

Six Principles of Persuasion

Experiments by Robert Cialdini and others have identified six principles for influencing people.[32] These principles are based on the idea that people have fundamental responses, and if your efforts align with these responses, your influence increases. Learn the following and see what you think.

1. *Liking.* People tend to like those who like them. Learning about another person's likes and dislikes through informal conversations builds friendship bonds. So do sincere and timely praise, empathy, and recognition.

2. *Reciprocity.* The belief that both good and bad deeds should be repaid in kind is virtually universal. Managers who act unethically and treat employees with contempt can expect the same in return. Worse still, those same employees are likely to treat each other and their customers unethically and with contempt. Managers need to be positive and constructive role models and fair-minded to benefit from the principle of reciprocity.

3. *Social proof.* People tend to follow the lead of those most like themselves. Role models and peer pressure are powerful cultural forces in social settings. Managers are advised to build support for workplace changes by first gaining the enthusiastic support of informal leaders who will influence their peers.

4. *Consistency.* People tend to do what they are personally committed to do. A manager who can elicit a verbal commitment from an employee has taken an important step toward influence and persuasion.

5. *Authority.* People tend to defer to and respect credible experts. Too many managers and professionals take their expertise for granted, as in the case of a hospital where the physical therapy staff was frustrated by the lack of follow-through by patients. No matter how much they emphasized the importance of continuing therapy, many patients stopped once they returned home. An investigation of the causes revealed that patients were unaware of the professional/clinical qualifications of their therapists. Once they were informed, and their many diplomas and certifications were hung on the walls in the clinic, patient compliance was remarkable. Compliance increased 34 percent![33]

Robert Cialdini is one of the world's foremost authorities on influence. His principles are based in research and proven in practice. You too can benefit from the application of these principles in every arena of your life—school, work, and socially.

- **Consultative trumps legitimating.** Some employees are more apt to accept change when managers rely on a consultative strategy and are more likely to resist change when managers use a legitimating tactic.
- **Schmoozing benefits are short-lived.** Ingratiation improved short-term but reduced long-term sales goal achievement in a study of salespeople. Schmoozing can help today's sales but not tomorrow's.
- **Subtlety wins long term.** Subtle flattery and agreeing with the other person's opinion (both are forms of ingratiation) were shown to increase the likelihood of executives being recommended to sit on boards of directors.
- **We can learn to influence.** Research with corporate managers of a supermarket chain showed that influence tactics can be taught and learned. Managers who received 360-degree feedback on two occasions regarding their influence tactics showed an increased use of core influence tactics.

So what's the bottom line? The influence tactics listed above can be learned and improved to move resisters to compliance, and those who are compliant to commitment.

TAKE-AWAY APPLICATION—TAAP Using Influence Tactics to Achieve My Goals

1. Think of a goal at school, work, or socially. Be sure this goal also requires somebody else's help for you to achieve.
2. Determine if you need this person's compliance or commitment.
3. Then, using whichever tactic in Self-Assessment 12.2 is your highest, describe specifically how you can use this tactic to achieve your chosen goal. Does this tactic match the desired outcome (compliance or commitment)?
4. Identify a second tactic that can help you achieve this goal, then describe specifically how you can apply it. Be sure the tactic you choose matches your desired outcome (compliance or commitment).

How Can I Increase My Own Influence?

The appropriate choice and application of the power and influence tactics described already provide a good place to start. But there are many other tools that can help you enhance your ability to influence others.[31]

Know what you want and believe you can get it. State your (influence) goals in a positive way. For example, say, "I would like to be part of the decision-making process," instead of, "I don't think anybody will take me seriously." Put another way, tell people what you want instead of what you don't want.

Credibility. People are more likely to listen to those with credibility. Highlight yours by emphasizing your expertise, reputation, and/or track record.

Trustworthiness. It is difficult to influence others if they don't trust you. To build and maintain trust, be authentic, deliver on what you promise, consider the interests of others, and don't do anything to diminish your trustworthiness.

Empathy. It often is best to assume somebody else's position before your own. People are more easily influenced when they feel others understand their situation.

Strong communication capability. All other personal characteristics aside, the ability to effectively communicate your ideas and listen to others bolsters your influence.

6. *Scarcity.* People want items, information, and opportunities that have limited availability. Special opportunities and privileged information are influence-builders for managers.

Importantly, Cialdini recommends using these six principles in combination, rather than separately, for maximum impact. Because of potential ethical implications, one's goals need to be worthy and actions need to be sincere and genuine when using these six principles.

Apply Your Knowledge

We conclude this section by giving you an opportunity to apply your knowledge in a scenario that is both common and important to many students. It is valuable to realize that effective influence starts with a plan. Follow these steps to create your own influence plan.

> **Step 1:** Set a goal and get a clear idea of what it is you want to achieve.
>
> **Step 2:** Identify the person or persons who can help you achieve that goal.
>
> **Step 3:** Determine what type of influence outcome—compliance or commitment— you want or need from the person(s) identified in step 2.
>
> **Step 4:** Decide which bases of power and tactics are most appropriate for the influence outcome you desire. (Be realistic as to which of these bases and tactics are available to you.)
>
> **Step 5:** Explicitly describe how you apply the bases of power and tactics you chose.

Now, apply this approach to the following scenario. Assume that you want to get a job at Interstate Batteries in their Talent Group. This is your goal. To do this, it is helpful to learn more about the organization and who the decision makers are. Thankfully, Interstate hired Jennifer, who went to your school, two years ago. (You learned this through the career services center.) You attained her info and plan to contact her, with the hopes that she will share her experiences and put you in touch with the hiring manager in the Talent Group. You do not need Jennifer's enthusiastic commitment to your employment efforts, as she doesn't even know you. But what you would like is her "compliance" with your desire for more information and an introduction to the Talent Group manager. She likely is willing to do this, if for no other reason than she is an alumna of your school, and you were very charming in your e-mail and phone communications. Now, you need to decide which of the bases of power and influence tactics you have available with Jennifer, and which of these are most appropriate for gaining her compliance.

TAKE-AWAY APPLICATION—TAAP

1. Using the scenario above, which bases of power are most appropriate to gain Jennifer's compliance?

2. Describe, specifically, how you would apply the base or bases of power identified in question 1.

3. Which of the nine influence tactics are most appropriate to influence Jennifer?

4. Describe how you would use each one to achieve your desired outcome.

We hope the practical tools you've gained in this section whetted your appetite for learning more about how you can influence others, affect many processes and outcomes in the Integrative Framework, and thus increase your personal effectiveness. Let's continue to build your knowledge and skills and focus on political tactics next.

MAJOR QUESTION

What are the many forms of politics, and how can understanding them make me more effective at school, at work, and socially?

THE BIGGER PICTURE

When you hear the word "politics," what comes to mind? The president, deadlocked congress, or your conniving, self-serving, untrustworthy boss or coworker? Whatever the case, it is unlikely that a smile comes to your face or that your heart is warmed. But it is important to realize that politics are not all bad. To make this point, and increase your effectiveness at school, at work, and socially, we explore this important and interesting topic by defining the term *organizational politics,* exploring some fundamental causes of politics, discussing nine common political tactics, identifying three levels of political action, and finally providing recommendations on how to manage politics in your favor. All this will help you better understand and manage this ever-present aspect of organizational life and key group-level process in the Integrative Framework.

major question

As just described, organizational politics are typically viewed as negative or counter-productive behaviors (e.g., manipulation, controlling information, undermining). This is a narrow and inaccurate view of organizational politics because they also entail positive behaviors, such as persuading others to accept one's point of view and aligning people to efficiently execute strategic objectives.[34] It therefore is important for you to understand organizational politics to realize the upside and avoid or manage the downside.

Organizational Politics—The Good and the Bad

Organizational politics are intentional acts of influence to enhance or protect the self-interest of individuals or groups that are not endorsed by or aligned with those of the organization. The critical aspect is the emphasis on *self-interest,* as this distinguishes politics from other forms of influence. Managers are endlessly challenged to achieve a workable balance between employees' self-interests and organizational interests. When a proper balance or alignment exists, the pursuit of self-interest may also serve the organization's interests. In contrast, when political activities are out of balance and/or conflict with the organization's interests, they are considered negative and not endorsed by the organization. This means that they are not an integral part of an employee's job role and not approved.

Causes of Political Behavior   Political behavior has causes at all three levels of the Integrative Framework. Specifically, research shows that organizational justice (Chapter 5) is the strongest organizational influence on politics. Trust in coworkers (Chapter 8) and negative affect (negative emotions—Chapter 3) are the strongest work environment and individual difference predictors, respectively.[35] Underlying most of these causes is a more fundamental or root cause—uncertainty.

Arthur Levitt, former SEC chairman, supports putting term limits on auditor–client relationships, requiring them to rotate every few years. The motive is to reduce conflicts of interest that undoubtedly occur and to increase objectivity and independence. Congress passed a bill that blocked such regulations and thus allows companies and their auditors to do business as usual. On average such relationships last nearly 25 years for S&P 500 companies.[36]

Uncertainty Triggers Political Actions   A lack of justice, such as unfair performance appraisal procedures and outcomes (procedural and distributive justice, Chapter 5), generates uncertainty in your performance ratings and pay. A lack of trust in a boss or coworker almost certainly boosts the uncertainty as to whether he or she will undermine you and steal credit. While each of these scenarios creates uncertainty for you, research shows that political maneuvering is triggered by five common sources of uncertainty within organizations:

1.   Unclear objectives
2.   Vague performance measures
3.   Ill-defined decision processes
4.   Strong individual or group competition[37]
5.   Any type of change

Performance, Change, and Politics   Closely related to the second item of the above list—vague performance measures—is the problem of *unclear performance-reward linkages* (recall our discussion of expectancy motivation theory in Chapter 5). This is a significant problem. Over 10,000 employees were asked to respond to the statement: "Employees who do a better job get paid more." While 48 percent of the responding managers agreed, only 31 percent of the nonmanagers agreed.[38] Besides being a sad commentary on performance management and motivation, these results matter because employees tend to resort to "politicking" when they are unsure about what it takes to get ahead.

   Related to the fifth factor—any type of change—an organization development specialist noted: "Whatever we attempt to change, the political subsystem becomes active. Vested interests are almost always at stake and the distribution of power is challenged."[39] Tools for combating resistance to change are discussed in Chapter 16. Before we move on and learn more about organizational politics, it is useful for you to get a sense of how political you are. This is another one of those attributes, similar to trust, about which people often think more highly of themselves than others do.

Complete Self-Assessment 12.3 and learn about your own level of politics. There is an added benefit, as this particular Assessment also taps into ethics and manipulation. It could be telling to have some friends complete this same short Assessment in terms of how they see you!

connect

SELF-ASSESSMENT 12.3   How Political Am I?

Go to connect.mheducation.com and take Self-Assessment 12.3 to learn about your own political tendencies.

1. Does your score accurately capture your tendencies toward organizational politics? Why or why not?

2. Do you think a true organizational politician would complete the Assessment honestly? Explain.

3. Given knowledge of your political tendencies, describe how they could both help or hurt you at school, at work, and in your career.

Frequently Used Political Tactics

Anyone who has worked in an organization has firsthand knowledge of blatant politicking. Although there are many different ways to describe and categorize political tactics, Table 12.1 shows some of the most commonly used political tactics and a description of each.

TABLE 12.1   MOST COMMONLY USED POLITICAL TACTICS

TACTIC	DESCRIPTION
1. Building a network of useful contacts	Cultivating a support network both inside and outside the organization
2. Using "key players" to support initiatives	Getting prior support for a decision or issue. Building others' commitment via participation
3. Making friends with power brokers	Teaming up with powerful people who can get results
4. Bending the rules to fit the situation	Interpreting or (not) enforcing rules to serve your own interests
5. Self-promotion	Blowing your own horn, but not doing the same for others' accomplishments
6. Creating a favorable image (also known as *impression management.*)	Dressing for success. Adhering to organizational norms and drawing attention to one's successes and influence. Taking credit for others' accomplishments
7. Praising others (ingratiation)	Making influential people feel good ("brown nosing")
8. Attacking or blaming others	Used to avoid or minimize association with failure. Reactive when scapegoating is involved. Proactive when goal is to reduce competition for limited resources
9. Using information as a political tool	Involves the purposeful withholding or distortion of information. Obscuring an unfavorable situation by overwhelming superiors with information

SOURCE: Adapted from R. W. Allen, D. L. Madison, L. W. Porter, P. A. Renwick, and B. T. Mayes, "Organizational Politics: Tactics and Characteristics of Its Actors," *California Management Review,* Fall 1979, 77–83.

It is likely that you view some of the tactics in the table very favorably, such as building a network of useful contacts. And of course doing this is a means of serving your own interests. In fact, many management experts and career counselors agree that it is wise for businesspeople to build, maintain, and use networks both internal and external to one's employer. This is a positive use of politics and consistent with what you learned about social capital in Chapter 1. However, let's explore another common and not-so-positive political tactic—blaming others.

Failure, Blame, and Politics

You may have noticed in our discussion up to this point that politicking often occurs when things don't work out, that is, in situations of underperformance. How one responds to underperformance (failure) is very important. Research involving several hundred thousand managers from a large variety of industries in the United States showed that 70 percent of the population tends to assign blame for failures in one of the following three ways:

1. Blame others
2. Blame oneself
3. Deny blame[40]

These tendencies are stable, just like personality and many of the other individual differences discussed in Chapter 3. And like other individual differences, one's "blaming style" likely fits some situations well and is problematic in others. It is helpful to assess your own tendencies, as well as those of your coworkers and people you must influence at work. It also is helpful to realize that politicking can and does occur at three different levels, which we discuss next.

Three Levels of Political Action

Although much political maneuvering occurs at the individual level, it also can involve group or collective action. Figure 12.7 illustrates three different levels of political action: the individual level, the coalition level, and the network level.[41] Each level has its distinguishing characteristics. At the individual level, self-interests are pursued by the individual. The political aspects of coalitions and networks are not so obvious, however, and thus require a bit of explanation.

Coalition-Level Politics   A *coalition* is an informal group bound together by the *active* pursuit of a *single* issue. Coalitions may or may not coincide with formal

FIGURE 12.7   LEVELS OF POLITICAL ACTION IN ORGANIZATIONS

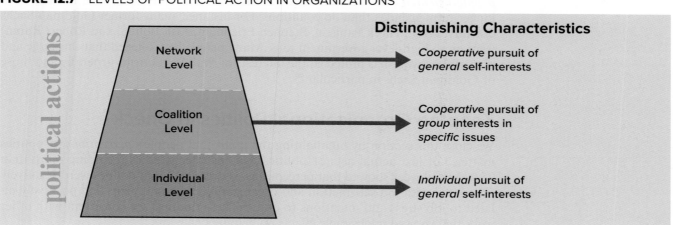

The "ice bucket challenge" was a sensation in the late summer of 2014. Besides boosting financial donations to research for ALS disease nearly fourfold, it also was an excellent example of political tactics and levels of political action. For instance, many celebrities were challenged to participate, which brought attention to the cause and demonstrated the power of influential others (political tactic #2 in Table 12.1). And because so many people joined together to support a common cause (ALS), it also illustrated coalition-level political action.

group membership. When the target issue is resolved (a sexually harassing supervisor is fired, for example), the coalition disbands. Experts note that political coalitions have "fuzzy boundaries," meaning they are fluid in membership, flexible in structure, and temporary in duration.[42] Coalitions are a potent political force in organizations. For instance, a coalition representing farmers and airlines persuaded the Commodity Futures Trading Commission (CFTC) to exempt these industries from new legislation that requires companies that trade futures contracts, in commodities such as grain and jet fuel, to put up greater amounts of collateral.[43]

Network-Level Politics   A third level of political action involves networks. Unlike coalitions, which pivot on specific issues, networks are loose associations of individuals seeking social support for their general self-interests. Politically, *networks are people-oriented, while coalitions are issue-oriented.* Networks have broader and longer-term agendas than do coalitions. For instance, many former Goldman Sachs executives (e.g., Hank Paulson, Stephen Friedman, Josh Bolten, and Robert Rubin) went on to high-level government jobs. Many people have alleged that this large and powerful network has protected the interests of Wall Street firms generally and those of Goldman Sachs in particular.[44]

Keeping Organizational Politics in Check

We close this section by highlighting the point that people's *perceptions* of politics matter, not just actual acts of politics. For instance, studies including more than 25,000 employees showed that perceptions of organizational politics were negatively associated with job satisfaction and organizational commitment, and positively related to job stress and intentions to quit.[45] These findings are consistent with other work that showed undesirable effects on helping behaviors.[46]

Do these results suggest that managers should attempt to stop people from being political? Good luck. Organizational politics cannot be eliminated. A manager would be naïve to believe this is possible. But political maneuvering can and should be managed to keep it constructive and within reasonable bounds. One expert put it this way: "People can focus their attention on only so many things. The more it lands on politics, the less energy—emotional and intellectual—is available to attend to the problems that fall under the heading of real work."[47]

Not Too Much and Not Too Little   An individual's degree of politicalness is a matter of personal values, ethics, and temperament. People who are either strictly nonpolitical or highly political generally pay a price for their behavior. The former may experience slow promotions and feel left out, while the latter may run the risk of being called self-serving and lose their credibility. People at both ends of the political spectrum may be considered poor team players. A moderate amount of prudent political behavior generally is considered a survival tool in complex organizations. Experts remind us that "political behavior has earned a bad name only because of its association with politicians. On its own, the use of power and other resources to obtain your objectives is not inherently unethical. It all depends on what the preferred objectives are."[48] What are your thoughts?

How to Build Support for My Ideas   Taken together, our discussion of politics probably leaves you wondering, "What should I do?" How do I avoid the bad and take advantage of the good? Thankfully, both research and practice provide some useful and specific advice on how to build support for your ideas. Here are eight recommendations:

1. Create a simple slogan that captures your idea.
2. Get your idea on the agenda. Describe how it addresses an important need or objective and look for ways to make it a priority.
3. Score small wins early and broadcast them widely. Results build momentum and make it easier for other people to commit.
4. Form alliances with people who have the power to decide, fund, and implement.
5. Persist and continue to build support. It is a process, not an event.
6. Respond and adjust. Be flexible and accepting of other people's input; the more names on it, the more likely you are to succeed.
7. Lock it in. Anchor the idea into the organization through budgets, job descriptions, incentives, and other operating procedures.
8. Secure and allocate credit. You don't want your idea to be hijacked, nor do you want to blow your own horn. You need others to sing your praises to assure you get the credit you deserve.[49]

TAKE-AWAY APPLICATION—TAAP

1. Make politics work for you and select an idea—something you would like to change, a new program, a new policy or practice—for an organization to which you belong.
2. Work through and apply as many of the eight recommendations in the list above as are relevant. (Don't be too quick to skip any particular recommendation; give each some real thought.)
3. Execute your plan. Regardless of the level of success, compare what you actually did with what you planned to do (how many of the eight recommendations did you actually use?).
4. If you're happy with the outcome, then hopefully this showed you the positive power of politics. If you were less than pleased with the results, revise your plan and be sure to follow it.

THE BIGGER PICTURE

We all want to look good in the eyes of others, and to do this we often engage in impression management. Like the other topics discussed in this chapter, impression management involves techniques we engage in to influence others in all arenas of life. To help you manage your own impressions, we define the term *impression management* and discuss what it means to make good and bad impressions, as well as how to remedy bad impressions and make effective apologies. You will see how practical knowledge in this area helps boost your effectiveness across levels of outcomes in the Integrative Framework.

We pursue the basic human desire to impress others not only because it makes us feel good about ourselves, but also because others often can provide things we desire, such as a job, a good grade, or a date! Many of our attempts to influence others in such ways are "impression management." We conclude this chapter with a discussion of this particular form of influence.

What Is Impression Management?

Impression management is defined as any attempt to control or manipulate the images related to a person, organization, or idea.[50] This encompasses things such as speech, behavior, and appearance. Most impression management attempts are directed at making a good impression on important others, although there are exceptions, as we will see. It is important to remember that anyone can be the intended target of impression management—parents, teachers, peers, employees, and customers are all fair game. For instance, by positioning themselves as socially responsible (CSR), companies can create positive impressions with many stakeholders, such as potential customers, and in turn boost sales.[51] Let's dive into good and bad impressions in more detail.

Good Impressions

Research conducted in the context of job interviews shows that impressions are formed very quickly and often subtly. Interviewers gather information on job candidates based on their handshake, smile, and manner of dress. All of this information is communicated before any questions are asked! More importantly, it was shown that these same factors were related to ultimate job offers.[52]

How to Make a Killer First Impression   You've undoubtedly heard the saying: "You have only one chance to make a first impression." Some argue that people judge you within one second of meeting you. Researchers tested this belief and found that after viewing only a microsecond of a video of a political candidate, subjects predicted with 70 percent accuracy who would win an election! To help you overcome the

Craig's List founder Craig Newmark and CEO Jim Buckmaster seemingly pay little attention to impression management. Their office is in a small storefront; Buckmaster takes public transportation to work while Newmark drives himself in a modest car. Buckmaster says that neither of them is interested in being wildly wealthy and dealing with the associated challenges. Stopping short and avoiding the hassles is just fine for them. Also interesting is the fact that Newmark, despite being the wealthy founder, currently works in a customer service role with no managerial responsibilities at CraigsList.[53]

pressure, and assure that people's snap judgments of you are favorable, we make the following five recommendations:

1. **Set an intention.** Once again goal setting from Chapters 5 and 6 comes into play. When you're preparing for an event (a meeting, social event, conference), think of whom you'd like to meet and what you'd like to achieve from that introduction. Then, plan your energy, intro, and comments accordingly.

2. **Consider your ornaments.** We're not talking about Christmas trees or party favors, but instead your jewelry, makeup, and clothes. This advice is for both men and women. Men, don't overlook your watch, for instance. Many people will draw conclusions from the type of watch you wear and how it aligns with your clothes (e.g., sporty, gaudy, trendy). Women, of course, should not forget that their makeup and jewelry are judged similarly. Be sure they match your personality and your intended message.

3. **Remember that your body speaks.** We've all heard that body language makes a difference, but people very rarely actually do anything about it. Pay attention to the nonverbals you learned about in Chapter 9. And if you're serious about managing your body language, then find a way to video yourself in a social setting. Use this to help you manage your tendencies in the future.

4. **Bust bad moods and bad days.** If you can't shake a bad mood or prevent your bad day from spilling over into your event, then stay home. This requires you to manage your emotions and mood. The knowledge and tools you acquired in Chapter 7 on Positive OB can help here. If you're in a bad mood before an important event, then find a way to snap out of it—play some of your favorite music, work out, go shopping—or reschedule. People will pick up on your mood, and you don't want your body language to convey: "Hello, my name is Bad Mood Bob."

5. **Be interested to be interesting.** The best way to appear interesting is *to appear interested*. People tend to like people who like them; at least this is a good place to start. Rather than blather on about yourself, an excellent way to show interest is to ask questions about the other person. Depending on the situation, you may be able to do some research about the person or persons you'll meet, and then make it part of your intention or goal to ask them about interesting things you learned about them.[54]

TAKE-AWAY APPLICATION—TAAP

1. Which of the five rules for making a first impression do you most often overlook? Which one do you think you could gain the most from?

2. Think of somebody you'd like to positively impress, and assume you'll be able to meet this person next week at a networking event.

3. Describe your intention or goal for the introduction.

4. Describe how you can appear interested. What questions might you ask?

5. Now, assume that the day of the networking event arrives and you're in a bad mood. Explain two things you could do to break out of this mood and prepare yourself for the event.

Reciprocity and Impression Management   Recall our discussion of reciprocity earlier in this chapter ("Six Principles of Persuasion")—the benefits of giving in order to receive. An interesting stream of research shows that when a CEO makes positive comments about another, and the other's company, Wall Street analysts give more favorable reports for both the CEO and the company when they miss earnings.[55] Put another way, if I say something positive about you to the media, then they are likely to be more forgiving if or when your performance is low. This is obviously a powerful form of influence—one that really pays!

Ethics and Impression Management   Impression management often strays into questionable, if not unethical, territory. And, like the last example, CEOs often engage in impression management with Wall Street analysts. This is to be expected, and in and of itself is not a problem. However, a study of more than 600 CEOs of companies with more than $100 million in revenues showed that unfavorable analyst comments prompted CEOs to verbally communicate that their companies do indeed have policies and practices that are in shareholders' best interests. Related research showed that CEOs also routinely communicated that their own compensation plan was aligned with shareholder interests, although, in both instances, it was found that CEOs regularly misrepresented these issues.[56] For example, their companies often made job and R&D cuts that undermined the long-term health of the company (counter to shareholder interests), and their personal compensation often was increased even when the share price of their company plummeted.

How about this story of impression management from a large bank:

> After 7 pm, people would open the door to their office, drape a spare jacket on the back of their chair, lay a set of glasses down on some reading material on their desk—and then go home for the night. The point of this elaborate gesture was to create the illusion that they were just out grabbing dinner and would be returning to burn the midnight oil.[57]

While these examples highlight some ethically questionable impression management practices, entire industries have transformed themselves using impression management. The venture capital (VC) industry, for instance, historically shunned any publicity. The norm in the industry was for the owners to stay out of the limelight, keep low profiles, and keep their mouths shut. Now, however, VC firms are aggressively engaged in impression management and hire PR firms, blog, and tweet. The following Example box provides some interesting details and insights.

EXAMPLE Impression Management Venture Capital Style[58]

Self-promotion by venture capitalists was frowned upon until about 2009. Until that point those that did "take the stage" were criticized and called "parade jumpers." But since 2009 VC firms old (e.g., Bessemer Venture Partners) and new (e.g., Founders Fund) actively engage in impression management with investors, the media, and other VC firms. Today some of the founders and lead rainmakers in VC firms are celebrities with publicity, status, and influence to match their often immense wealth. Below are some of the reasons why VC firms across the industry now pursue impression management with enthusiasm and perhaps the most successful one today.

Marc Andreessen and Ben Horowitz entered the venture capital industry with a bang, or more like a flash. They embraced (self-)promotion and other impression management techniques and achieved greater growth than any other VC. Their tactics and performance also garnered them incredible status and influence. They are now seen as the most desirable source of financing for entrepreneurs in San Francisco and New York.

- *Poor returns.* Venture capital firms averaged 4.6 percent returns in the last 10 years. This means that investors are putting their money in other places; therefore, VCs have to compete more aggressively.

- *Knock on doors.* This increased competition has motivated VCs to reach out to and differentiate themselves with investors and entrepreneurs, which contrasts with the recent past where investors and entrepreneurs needed some sort of inside connection to get a meeting with VCs.

- *Andreessen & Horowitz.* This VC firm, started by the founder of Netscape (one of the first Web companies) and one of its executives, entered the market in 2009 with a completely different approach—they courted entrepreneurs, used social media (blogs and Twitter), and marketed themselves aggressively. Their "public" approach was motivated by the belief that "each year 15 deals account for 97 percent of all venture capital profits. To be successful, they would have to pursue those 15 companies. And they would do it by aggressively marketing their expertise to the reporters and bloggers who follow start-ups." To execute this strategy they didn't just hire a PR firm, but they made the PR firm's founder (Margit Wennmacher) a partner in Andreesen & Horowitz.

- *Success.* Andreessen & Horowitz quickly became the fastest-growing VC firm in the industry.

YOUR THOUGHTS?

1. What are your thoughts about aggressively managing the impressions of investors and customers, like Andreessen & Horowitz and other VC firms have done?
2. Think of the job you have now, or one you've had in the past. With whom and how could they use impression management to improve or grow their business?
3. What ethical standards would you apply to impression management?

Favorable Upward Impression Management Tactics On a positive note, both research and practice have revealed three categories of favorable upward impression management techniques:[59]

1. *Job-focused*—presenting information about one's job performance in a favorable light.
2. *Supervisor-focused*—praising and doing favors for one's supervisor.
3. *Self-focused*—presenting oneself as a polite and nice person.

Before going further, let's have you learn about your own tendencies for favorable impression management. More specifically, Self-Assessment 12.4 will help you understand the types of impression management—job-, supervisor-, and self-focused—you tend to use in work settings.

connect

SELF-ASSESSMENT 12.4   **Your Impression Management—How and Who**

Go to connect.mheducation.com and take Self-Assessment 12.4 to learn both how you manage your impressions and with whom.

1. Are you better suited for "Hollywood," or are you better described as safe or a free agent?

2. What are the benefits of your impression management tendencies?

3. What are the drawbacks?

4. Look at all of the items in the Assessment, select the two that could be most useful to you, and describe specifically how you could use them.

Let's be clear: a moderate amount of upward impression management is a necessity for the average employee today. For example, ingratiation can slightly improve your performance appraisal results and make your boss like you significantly more.[60] Engage in too little impression management and busy managers are liable to overlook some of your valuable contributions when they make job assignment, pay, and promotion decisions. Too much, and you run the risk of being branded a "schmoozer," a "phony," and other unflattering things by your coworkers.[61] Consider, for instance, that noticeable flattery and ingratiation can backfire by embarrassing the target person and damaging your credibility.[62]

Bad Impressions—The Common if Not Subtle Kind

Remarkably, some people actually try to make a bad impression. But because these people are relatively rare, we instead focus on common, if not subtle, ways people make bad impressions at work. In addition to the many obvious faux pas—don't cheat, don't lie, don't steal—many employees often make bad impressions without knowing it. Some common ways this happens and how to overcome them are:

- *Doing only the minimum.* Many employees aren't aware that not making the often simple extra effort to fulfill a coworker's request can be costly. Going the extra mile to check the status of a report, for instance, can go a long way toward conveying a positive impression.

- *Having a negative mindset.* Most people consider themselves positive, but sometimes others have a different view. When presented with a new initiative, do you immediately think of and point out the potential pitfalls or complain? If so, then it is possible that others see you as negative. And managers prefer people who are supportive, not necessarily "yes men and women," but those who are constructive versus eternal naysayers.

- *Overcommitting.* Initiative is often good, but biting off more than you can chew means you might choke! The inability to deliver on-time or quality work is a sure way to make a bad impression. Prioritize and deliver, which requires saying no sometimes.

- *Taking no initiative.* The opposite of overcommitting—failing to take action when something needs to get done—can also make you look bad. If coworkers (including your boss) frequently come to you with the same questions or challenges, then step up and try to proactively solve the issue.
- *Waiting until the last minute to deliver bad news.* Of course you shouldn't report to or consult with your boss on every little hiccup in your work. But worse still is to inform her or him just before a deadline that you are having difficulties. This puts your boss in a bad spot too. Be smart; put yourself in the other person's shoes and consider if and when you would want to know the information you have.[63]

Spinning Bad into Good, or Good into Better

One final point is that much of impression management involves "spinning" a bad situation into something better. Public relations (PR), for instance, is impression management at the organizational level and often involves "managing the message," such as reducing the damage of bad press associated with a scandal. The massive BP oil spill is a prime example. The company downplayed the estimates of how much oil was leaking—first 1,000 barrels per day, then 5,000, and then nearly 50,000! It was later learned that the company knowingly underestimated the extent of the leak. Doing so dramatically undermined the credibility of a company that billed itself as: "BP—Beyond Petroleum—a paragon of environmental sustainability."[64]

As CEO of BP during the massive Deepwater Horizon oil spill in 2010, Tony Hayward was criticized for being evasive and blaming others. By not handling the incident effectively, he damaged the reputation of the company and lost his job. How would you have handled the situation if you were CEO of BP?

The company also attempted to deflect blame for the spill onto contractors and downplayed the environmental impact. This made the company appear insensitive and led people to believe they were simply trying to avoid legal liabilities. Months after the spill began, the company unleashed a barrage of television spots featuring BP employees from the Gulf, highlighting its commitment to the cleanup. According to one PR expert:

It was one of the worst PR approaches that I've seen in my 56 years in the business. . . . They tried to be opaque. They had every excuse in the book. Right away they should have accepted responsibility and recognized what a disaster they faced. They basically thought they could spin their way out of catastrophe. It doesn't work that way.[65]

A communications professor summed it up this way: "BP could apologize every day . . . [but] until the oil stopped, there was nothing that could be done to make it better, but there was plenty that could be said to make it worse."[66]

How to Prepare for and Deal with Bad Events So how can organizations best handle crises? A PR executive who represents the New York Yankees and News Corp. suggests that all organizations should create a crisis plan that includes:

1. How information is to be gathered.
2. How to formulate a response.
3. Who will deliver the message, and via which media channels.
4. Don't minimize a given problem. No matter how small it is in the company's eyes, it is a big deal to somebody else.
5. Be understanding and empathetic.

After these, get on with doing business—whatever the organization does well (e.g., finding and creating petroleum products, as in the case of BP).[67] Of course, let's not forget that apologies often are necessary and have a place in impression management.

Apologies   One way to remedy or at least reduce the impact of bad impressions, negative uses of power, or poor performance is with an apology. Apologies are a form of trust repair (discussed in Chapter 8) where one acknowledges an offense and frequently offers to make amends. It is a widely held norm in the United States and other cultures (e.g., Japan) to apologize when one's actions (or lack of action) cause harm to another, whether intentional or not. And much like our discussion of equity in Chapter 5, harm can be perceived or actual, but in either case it is real to the offended. Apologies are important and are considered effective to the extent they restore trust and positively affect your ability to influence the offended party in the future.[68]

We know from life that not all people apologize, and when they do, the effects differ. But in business perhaps the better questions are when to apologize and how. Table 12.2 describes the primary reasons leaders should apologize along with their associated motives.

Table 12.2 can be helpful for nonleaders too, and you may consider apologizing in any of the following situations:

- Doing so will serve an important purpose (see Table 12.2).
- The offense is of serious consequence.
- It's appropriate to assume responsibility for the offense.
- No one else can get the job done.
- The cost of saying something is likely to be lower than the cost of staying silent.

Whether the apology is from a leader or not, all effective apologies have the following four characteristics:

1.   Acknowledgment of wrongdoing
2.   Acceptance of responsibility
3.   Expression of regret
4.   Promise that the offense will not be repeated[69]

It also is helpful to consider that a failure to apologize, or to do so in a timely manner, can turn a bad situation worse.[70]

TABLE 12.2   PURPOSES FOR LEADER APOLOGIES AND THEIR DESIRED OUTCOMES

PURPOSE	MOTIVE OR DESIRED OUTCOME
Individual—Leader offended other.	Encourage followers to forgive and forget.
Institution—Follower offended another organizational member.	Restore functioning within the group or organization when one member offends another member(s).
Intergroup—Follower offended external party.	Repair relations with an external group that perceived harm by a member of the leader's group.
Moral—Genuine regret for wrongdoing.	Request for forgiveness and redemption for regrettable (in)action.

SOURCE: Based on B. Kellerman, "When Should a Leader Apologize—and When Not?", *Harvard Business Review*, April 1, 2006.

You are now far better equipped to influence people in many arenas of life. We close this chapter with a reminder: you don't need to have a big, fancy title or corner office to have power. You typically have more power than you think. We encourage you to be more purposeful and accurate in your application of power, empowerment, influence, politics, and impression management. Doing so will dramatically increase your effectiveness across levels of the Integrative Framework. Besides, you'll get your way more often!

what did i learn?

You learned that you can increase your effectiveness by applying power, influence, and politics. You learned the bases of power, common influence tactics, the causes of politics, and which forms are most effective in different situations. You also learned that sharing power and empowering others are important means for building your own influence and improving your performance. Reinforce what you learned with the Key Points below. Then consolidate your learning using the Integrative Framework. Finally, Challenge your mastery of this chapter by answering the Major Questions in your own words.

Key Points for Understanding Chapter 12

You learned the following key points.

12.1 POWER AND ITS BASIC FORMS

- Power is defined as the ability to marshal human, informational, and other resources to get something done.

- The five main bases of power are legitimate, reward, coercive, expert, and referent.

- The first three bases are considered forms of position power and the last two, forms of personal power.

12.2 POWER SHARING AND EMPOWERMENT

- Empowerment is defined as efforts to enhance employee performance, well-being, and positive attitudes.

- Structural empowerment is based on transferring authority and responsibilities from management to employees.

- Power sharing can be described on a continuum from domination to consultation, participation, and finally delegation.

- Psychological empowerment occurs when employees feel a sense of meaning, competence, self-determination, and impact at work.

12.3 EFFECTIVELY INFLUENCING OTHERS

- Influence tactics are conscious efforts to affect and change a specific behavior in others. The tactics you use often determine how people respond to your influence attempts.

- We studied nine common influence tactics: rational persuasion, inspirational appeals, consultation, ingratiation, personal appeals, exchange, coalition tactics, pressure, and legitimating tactics.

- You can expand your effectiveness further still by using six principles of persuasion: liking, reciprocity, social proof, consistency, authority, and scarcity.

12.4 POLITICAL TACTICS AND HOW TO USE THEM

- Organizational politics are intentional acts of influence to enhance or protect the self-interest of individuals or groups that are not endorsed by or aligned with those of the organization.

- Competition along with uncertainty regarding objectives, performance measures, decision processes, and change are major drivers or causes of political actions.

- Political action occurs at three levels—individual, coalition, and network.

12.5 IMPRESSION MANAGEMENT

- Impression management is defined as any attempt to control or manipulate the images related to a person, organization, or idea.

- Because impressions have been shown to relate to subsequent job offers, it is important to make good first impressions by being interested, focusing on body language, setting goals or intentions, and displaying a positive mood and emotions.

- Common ways to make bad impressions are doing only the minimum, having a negative mindset, over-committing, taking no initiative, and waiting until the last minute to deliver bad news.

- Organizations need a recovery plan in case of disaster; an apology for a transgression can be effective.

The Integrative Framework for Chapter 12

As shown in Figure 12.8, you learned practical tools to help you influence others—power, empowerment, influence, politics, and impression management. Collectively, these tools represent important group-level processes. And how you use these tools often determines whether people resist, comply with, or actually commit to your wishes. You learned how using these tools relates to individual-level outcomes, such as performance, attitudes, well-being, (counter)productive citizenship behaviors, turnover, and career outcomes. Power and influence are also associated with satisfaction,

FIGURE 12.8 THE INTEGRATIVE FRAMEWORK FOR UNDERSTANDING AND APPLYING OB

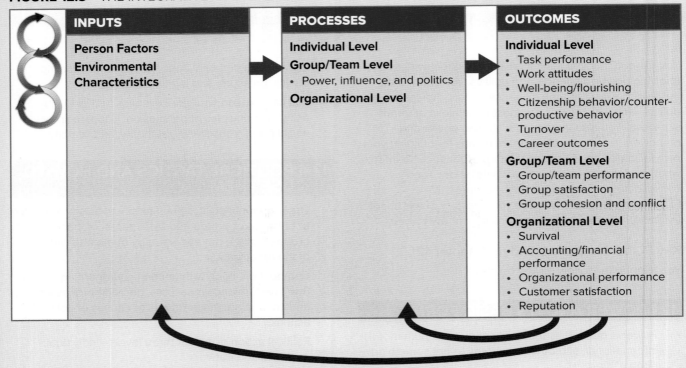

© 2014 Angelo Kinicki and Mel Fugate. All rights reserved. Reproduction prohibited without permission of the authors.

cohesion, and conflict at the group/team level, and with survival, financial performance, customer satisfaction, and reputation at the organizational level. Beyond this, you explored the notion of empowerment and how sharing power with others can increase your own power and influence.

Challenge: Major Questions for Chapter 12

At the start of the chapter, we told you that after reading the chapter you should be able to answer the following questions. Unless you can, have you really processed and internalized the lessons in the chapter? Refer to the Key Points, Figure 12.8, the chapter itself, and your notes to revisit and answer the following major questions:

1. What are the basic forms of power and how can they help me achieve my desired outcomes?

2. How can sharing power increase my power?

3. How do my influence tactics affect my personal effectiveness?

4. What are the many forms of politics, and how can understanding them make me more effective at school, at work, and socially?

5. Do I seek only to impress, or to make a good impression?

Writing the Book (Review) on Conflict of Interest

If you're not getting glowing online reviews for your product, maybe you could buy them. One entrepreneur tried that business model in the realm of self-publishing, and for a while, it worked out fine.

Pay for Play in Online Book Reviews

An article in the *New York Times* featured someone who had been selling online book reviews to the authors who wanted them. Besides confirming the worst suspicions of many, the story raises issues of ethics and trust in online reviews.

GettingBookReviews.com. Todd Rutherford was doing press releases for hire for self-published authors. Authors wanted the press releases to increase the likelihood that their books would get more attention, whether in published or consumer reviews. In 2010 Rutherford realized he could help his clients more directly by simply writing the reviews himself under assumed names. And so he advertised that very service.

He launched GettingBookReviews.com (the site is no longer active), blatantly setting out his terms. A single five-star review would be written and posted for only $99. And soon he offered bulk discounts—20 reviews for only $499, 50 reviews for $999.

In some ways it's a wonder he lasted as long as he did. His house of cards tumbled with increased notoriety driven by one unhappy customer—but not before he had published some 4,500 online reviews. By the time the 2012 article in the *New York Times* came out, Rutherford had folded his tent and moved on. Last heard, he was selling RVs in Oklahoma.[71]

Puffery Is Legal

Advertising in general, and the book business in particular, has always relied on puffery, of inflating the positive aspects of their products. A good example is the book jacket blurbs a publisher will often solicit from authors it publishes to support books from other authors on its roster.

Moreover, it is not uncommon for the friends or associates of an author to help, often by posting positive reviews. These actions are not illegal. The reviews are clearly sourced, and the individuals who write them are entitled to their opinions. (While it may be more ethical for the reviewers to note their relationship to the author, it is not a legal requirement.)

Opinion Spamming Is Not

Bing Liu is a professor of computer science at the University of Illinois at Chicago who studies data mining and more specifically the abuse of online reviews. He defines opinion spamming as the illegal effort behind everything from fake reviews to bogus blogs and websites.

"Positive opinions can result in significant financial gains and/or [renown] for businesses, organizations and individuals," Liu writes on his faculty website. "This, unfortunately, gives strong incentives for opinion spamming."[72]

As to online book reviews, it is illegal for a reviewer to receive compensation for a positive review and then post it on most sites, including Amazon.com.

Comparatively new slang terms for authors who post reviews pretending to be someone else are "sock puppets" or "sock monkeys." That these terms exist suggests such behavior is common.

The successful and award-winning British author R. J. Ellory wouldn't seem to need such help, but in 2012 he was called out by fellow author Jeremy Duns for multiple reviews (posted under fictional names, of course) on Amazon.com. ABC News broke the story, after the website Gawker published Duns' complaints on his Twitter feed. The scandal was then written up in *The Huffington Post.*

"Ellory writes 5-star reviews of his own work on Amazon. Long, purple tributes to his own magnificent genius," Duns tweeted. "RJ Ellory also writes shoddy, sh----y sniping reviews of other authors' work on Amazon, under an assumed identity."[73]

The Importance of Trust

Can trust be restored in online reviews? Maybe, but not soon. Liu estimates that about a third of all online reviews are false. He notes that the need to be able to identify bogus reviews will only increase. One of his research areas is the creation of algorithms to help identify false reviews. He's skeptical that without computer help one could tell the difference. In the current environment, consumers should train themselves to be skeptical, and where possible balance online reviews with trusted third-party resources. This is easier in the electronic product area than in the world of e-books but not impossible.

One can also envisage a future where it is clear that the results of opinion spamming create their own deterrent. "Once someone finds out you paid a book reviewer, your reputation is toast," writes Angelo Hoy, owner/operator of the *Writers Weekly* website.[74] Her site offers its own e-book for authors on e-marketing their books by legal means.

Apply the 3-Stop Problem-Solving Approach to OB

Stop 1: What is the problem?

- Use the Integrative Framework to help identify the outcomes that are important in this case.
- Which of these outcomes are not being achieved in the case?
- Based on considering the above two questions, what is the most important problem in this case?

Stop 2: Use the Integrative Framework shown at the start of this chapter to help identify the OB concepts or theories that help you to understand the problem in this case.

- What person factors are most relevant?
- What environmental characteristics are most important to consider?

- Do you need to consider any processes? Which ones?
- What concepts or theories discussed in this chapter are most relevant for solving the key problem in this case?

Stop 3: What are your recommendations for solving the problem?

- Review the material in the chapter that most pertains to your proposed solution and look for practical recommendations.
- Use any past OB knowledge or experience to generate recommendations.
- Outline your plan for solving the problem in this case.

LEGAL/ETHICAL CHALLENGE

Secret Banking Elite Rules Trading in Derivatives

Until recently, nine people had a standing meeting in Manhattan one Wednesday each month. This was a highly secretive group of powerful people across Wall Street, known by critics as the "derivatives dealers club." The membership and discussions were strictly confidential. The focus: Protect the interests of the largest firms on Wall Street that serve as dealers in the highly lucrative derivatives market. Derivatives (swaps and options) are financial products used like insurance to hedge financial risk. Because derivatives do not trade on formal exchanges, like stocks on the New York Stock Exchange (NYSE), and are largely unregulated by agencies such as the Securities and Exchange Commission (SEC), their creation and trading are largely self-managed by the firms themselves. This secretive group helped oversee and control this multitrillion-dollar market.

The dealers' club attempted to block the efforts of other banks to enter the market and compete with select few member firms. It also blocked many efforts by regulators and others to get full and free disclosure of dealer prices and fees. The situation is similar to a real estate agent selling a house and the buyer only knowing what he or she paid, the seller only knowing what he or she received, and the agent pocketing the rest in fees. These fees would not be known to either the buyer or the seller.

This lack of disclosure has implications far beyond the biggest banks. Pension funds, states, cities, airlines, food companies, and some small businesses use derivatives to offset and manage risk. These parties argue that without transparency they cannot determine if they receive a fair price. What is known, however, is that Wall Street's largest firms collect billions of dollars in undisclosed fees each year from trading these derivatives—fees that certainly would be smaller if there was more transparency and competition. These concerns have spurred investigation of anticompetitive practices by the Department of Justice and threats by some legislators. The firms, however, have powerful allies—the many politicians in Washington to whom they've made substantial campaign contributions.

Derivatives dealers' defense is that derivative prices are complex. Unlike shares of Netflix stock, which are all equivalent—one share has the same price as all the rest—terms of oil derivatives can vary greatly. The complexity therefore requires customization, and greater transparency is impractical if not impossible.

What Is Your Position on Derivatives Trading?

1. Regulators should assert influence over the derivatives market, like they do with stocks, and require derivatives to be traded on an open exchange where buyers and sellers disclose prices and fees.

2. Nothing should be done to change how derivatives are bought and sold. If buyers and sellers don't like the lack of dealer transparency, then they can choose not to trade derivatives.

3. The derivatives market should be modified only slightly to allow other players (e.g., banks) to provide derivatives. If they then choose to disclose prices and fees, that is their choice, just as it is the choice of others to buy derivatives.

4. Invent other alternatives and explain.

You Make Me Feel So Good!

Objectives

1. To introduce a different type of impression management and sharpen your awareness of impression management.

2. To promote self-awareness and diversity awareness by comparing your perceptions and ethics with those of others.

Introduction

This is a group discussion exercise designed to enhance your understanding of impression management. Personal interpretations are involved, so there are no strictly right or wrong answers.

Researchers recently have explored *beneficial* impression management, the practice of helping friends and significant others look good. This new line of inquiry combines the established OB topics of social support (discussed relative to stress in Chapter 16) and impression management (discussed in this chapter). In this exercise, we explore the practical and ethical implications of "strategically managing information to make your friends look good." We also consider impression management in general.

Instructions

This is a two-stage exercise: a private note-taking part, followed by a group discussion.

Stage 1 (5 to 7 minutes): Read the two scenarios below and then rate each one according to the following three scales:

How strongly do you approve of this tactic? (Mark an "X" for scenario 1 and an "O" for scenario 2.)

Disapprove   Approve

1 _____ 2 _____ 3 _____ 4 _____ 5 _____ 6 _____ 7

How effective is this tactic likely to be in the longer run?

Very ineffective   Highly effective

1 _____ 2 _____ 3 _____ 4 _____ 5 _____ 6 _____ 7

How ethical is this tactic?

Unethical   Ethical

1 _____ 2 _____ 3 _____ 4 _____ 5 _____ 6 _____ 7

Scenarios[75]

1. A high school ballplayer buoys the spirits of a teammate who struck out at a key moment by emphasizing the latter's game-winning hit last week and noting that even the greatest big-league hitters fall about 7 times out of 10. He may privately suspect his teammate has only mediocre baseball talent, but by putting the best side to his comments and not sharing his doubts, he makes the teammate feel better, builds his confidence so he can face tomorrow's game in a more optimistic frame of mind, and boosts the teammate's image in front of the other players who can hear his reassuring words.

2. At a party, a college student describes her roommate to a potential date she knows her friend finds extremely attractive. She stresses her friend's intelligence, attractiveness, and common interests but fails to mention that her friend can also be quite arrogant.

Stage 2 (10 to 15 minutes): Join two or three others in a discussion group and compare scores for both scenarios.

Are there big differences of opinion, or is there a general consensus? Next, briefly discuss these questions: How do *you* create a good first impression in *specific* situations? What goes through your mind when you see someone trying to make a good impression for him- or herself or for someone else? *Note:* Your instructor may ask you to pick a spokesperson to briefly report the results of your discussion to the class. If so, be sure to keep notes during the discussion.

Questions for Discussion

1. Is the whole practice of impression management a dishonest waste of time, or does it have a proper place in society? Why?

2. In what situations can impression management attempts backfire?

3. How do you know when someone has taken impression management too far?

4. How would you respond to a person who made this statement? "I never engage in impression management."

13 LEADERSHIP EFFECTIVENESS
What Does It Take to Be Effective?

inputs

PERSON FACTORS

ENVIRONMENTAL CHARACTERISTICS
Leadership

processes

INDIVIDUAL LEVEL

GROUP/TEAM LEVEL
Leadership

ORGANIZATIONAL LEVEL

outcomes

INDIVIDUAL LEVEL

GROUP/TEAM LEVEL

ORGANIZATIONAL LEVEL

© 2014 Angelo Kinicki and Mel Fugate. All rights reserved. Reproduction prohibited without permission of the authors.

MAJOR TOPICS I'LL LEARN AND QUESTIONS I SHOULD BE ABLE TO ANSWER

13.1 MAKING SENSE OF LEADERSHIP THEORIES

MAJOR QUESTION: *How does an integrated model of leadership help me become an effective leader?*

13.2 TRAIT THEORIES: DO LEADERS POSSESS UNIQUE TRAITS AND PERSONAL CHARACTERISTICS?

MAJOR QUESTION: *How can I use the takeaways from trait theories to improve my ability to lead?*

13.3 BEHAVIORAL STYLE THEORIES: WHICH LEADER BEHAVIORS DRIVE EFFECTIVENESS?

MAJOR QUESTION: *Do effective leaders behave in similar ways?*

13.4 SITUATIONAL THEORIES: DOES EFFECTIVE LEADERSHIP DEPEND ON THE SITUATION?

MAJOR QUESTION: *How do I know when to use a specific leader behavior?*

13.5 TRANSFORMATIONAL LEADERSHIP: HOW DO LEADERS TRANSFORM EMPLOYEES' MOTIVES?

MAJOR QUESTION: *How can I use transformational leadership when working with others?*

13.6 ADDITIONAL PERSPECTIVES ON LEADERSHIP

MAJOR QUESTION: *How can I improve the relationship with my boss?*

INTEGRATIVE FRAMEWORK FOR UNDERSTANDING AND APPLYING OB

This chapter focuses on leadership, a critical input and process variable within the Integrative Framework. As you might expect, you will learn that leadership affects a large number of outcomes across all three levels of OB. Try to keep track of the outcomes associated with leadership as you read this chapter.

winning at work

LEARNING TO LEAD

You will learn later in this chapter that leadership effectiveness is more a function of your behavior than a set of traits you are born with. This implies that leadership skills can be learned, a conclusion supported by research.[1]

learning because they focus on what can be learned from both success and failure, and they encourage us to seek input, guidance, and coaching from effective leaders. We encourage you to set learning goals associated with leadership development such as "learn how to run better meetings," "learn to improve my influence skills," or "learn to provide more effective feedback."

STEP 1: HOW CAN I BEGIN THE LEARNING PROCESS?

The learning process starts with self-awareness. You may recall that we discussed the importance of self-awareness in Chapter 1. This is why we have encouraged you to complete a host of Self-Assessments while reading this book. If you want to learn how to lead, the first step is to identify the type of leader behaviors you tend to use.[2] You will be given this opportunity in this chapter. You can use this knowledge to experiment with trying different styles of leadership in different situations. As one management consultant noted, "Finding one's style of leadership is a growing experience and one of introspection and personal development. Leadership is a trial-and-error encounter, and potential leaders must remember they will fail many times and make mistakes."[3]

STEP 2: CLAIM A LEADER IDENTITY

How we think of ourselves, which is referred to as our *identity*, affects our willingness to take on leadership roles. This means that it is important to see yourself as a leader. You can do this in two ways. The first is a direct approach in which you refer to yourself as a leader of some group, project, or task or you engage in stereotypical leadership acts. For example, if you are meeting with a student group to complete an assignment, you can walk into the meeting with an agenda and then start running the meeting. The second way consists of indirect claims of leadership such as sitting at the head of table for a meeting, mentioning your relationship with recognized leaders, or "dressing the part."[4]

STEP 3: DEVELOP A LEARNING GOAL ORIENTATION

In Chapter 6 we discussed the difference between learning and performance goals. Learning goals promote

STEP 4: EXPERIMENT AND SEEK FEEDBACK

Situational theories of leadership tell us that the effectiveness of specific leadership behaviors depends on the situation at hand. Try experimenting with the different leader behaviors discussed later in this chapter in different situations. Next, assess the impact of your experimental approach to leadership. This is feedback. We encourage you to seek feedback from those you trust and to reflect on what "could" be learned from your many educational and work experiences. A recent experimental study with students, for example, showed that leadership effectiveness increased over time for those students who consistently spent time reflecting on what "could" be learned from their experiences.[5]

FOR YOU   WHAT'S AHEAD IN THIS CHAPTER

Regardless of your role at work or in life, how well you understand leadership will let you be more effective. To a significant degree, leadership is available to all. Genetics and privilege neither guarantee leadership abilities, nor are they required. We all know individuals with all the "right" advantages who are ineffective leaders. We are about to help you navigate the many theories of leadership, appreciate how leadership traits and behaviors can be learned and developed, identify and apply styles of leadership, and finally understand how what you learn about leadership helps you to be a better follower and more effective at any level in an organization.

major question

MAJOR QUESTION

How does an integrated model of leadership help me become an effective leader?

THE BIGGER PICTURE

You're about to learn why leadership is both an input and process in the Integrative Framework for Understanding and Applying OB. Organizations can't really start up without leadership, nor can they sustain operations. You'll acquire an overall model of leadership that integrates the many leadership theories that have been proposed. Then you'll hone your understanding of effective leadership and parse the difference between leading and managing.

Leadership is defined as "a process whereby an individual influences a group of individuals to achieve a common goal."[6] Note that you do not need to have a formal position of authority to be a leader. Anyone who exerts influence over others in the pursuit of organizationally relevant matters is a leader.

This definition underscores the broad impact that leaders have on organizations. Consider the following statistics. Gallup research has shown that employee disengagement

Do singers exert leadership when they perform? Would a group of well-known singers like this exert more influence than one singer performing alone? Why or why not?

in the United States costs $450 to $550 billion per year, and ineffective leadership is a key driver of disengagement.[7] Researchers also have estimated that approximately 50 percent of all managers around the world are incompetent or ineffective. The cost of this incompetence is greater the higher up you go in an organization. For example, one study estimated that the cost of a failed senior leader is $2.7 million.[8]

From a scientific perspective, the topic of leadership has generated more OB-related research than any other topic except motivation. This is why OB scholars have developed a great number of theories to help guide managers to improve their leadership effectiveness.

We recognize that there are far too many leadership theories to cover in this one chapter. So we have created a model that integrates the major leadership theories and we use it to structure the content covered in this chapter. We follow that by focusing on theories that have received some level of research support.

An Integrated Model of Leadership

Figure 13.1 presents an integrated model of leadership. Starting at the far right of the model, you see that leadership effectiveness is the outcome we are trying to explain in this chapter. Note that effective leadership is influenced by four types of leadership behavior: task-oriented, relationship-oriented, passive, and transformational. Effective leadership also is affected by a combination of task-oriented traits and interpersonal attributes. Recall from Chapter 3 that individual differences significantly impact performance, and they vary from relatively fixed (intelligence) to somewhat flexible (self-efficacy).

Moreover, Figure 13.1 represents how demographic characteristics such as gender and age, task-oriented traits, and interpersonal attributes influence an individual's use of leader behaviors. The final component (situational factors) influencing leadership effectiveness involves our earlier discussions of contingency theory. That is, effective leadership requires using the "right" behavior at the "right" time.

What Is Effective Leadership?

The answer to this question is more complicated than you might think because leadership effectiveness is more than simply gaining commitment with our influence attempts. Assessing leadership effectiveness entails consideration of three issues.[9]

FIGURE 13.1   AN INTEGRATED MODEL OF LEADERSHIP

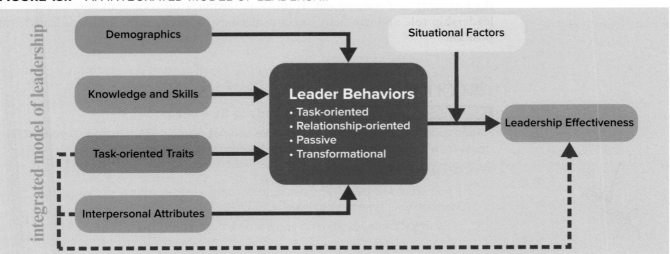

Issue 1. The Content of the Evaluation: "What Criteria Are Being Used to Assess Effectiveness?" Effectiveness depends on what the evaluator wants. For example, the content of effectiveness can entail criteria such as task performance, quality, customer satisfaction, sales, employee job satisfaction, turnover, or an overall evaluation of leadership effectiveness.

Issue 2. The Level of the Evaluation: "At What Level Are the Criteria Being Measured?" As you know from the Integrative Framework, effectiveness can be measured at the individual, group, or organizational levels. Evaluations at different levels also can produce difference conclusions. For example, sales performance may be a good measure of performance for one store location, but not across a geographic region.

Issue 3. The Rater's Perspective: "Who Is Doing the Evaluation?" Assessments of effective leadership can be made by different people or groups, and their view of effective leadership may vary.[10] For example, a manager may be perceived as effective by a direct report, but not by the entire work unit or the boss.

What Is the Difference between Leading and Managing?

Bernard Bass, a leadership expert, concluded that "leaders manage and managers lead, but the two activities are not synonymous."[11] Broadly speaking, managers typically perform functions associated with planning, investigating, organizing, and control, and leaders deal with the interpersonal aspects of a manager's job. Leaders inspire others, provide emotional support, and try to get employees to rally around a common goal. Leaders also play a key role in creating a vision and strategic plan for an organization. Managers, in turn, are charged with implementing the vision and strategic plan. There are several conclusions to be drawn from this discussion.

First, good leaders are not necessarily good managers, and good managers are not necessarily good leaders. Second, effective leadership requires effective managerial skills at some level. For example, JetBlue ex-CEO David Neeleman was let go after an ice storm revealed managerial deficiencies in how he handled the situation.[12] In contrast, both Tim Cook, CEO of Apple, and Alan Mulally, CEO of Ford Motor Company, are recognized for the use of managerial skills when implementing corporate strategies.[13]

Do you want to lead others, or understand what makes a leader tick? Then take the following Self-Assessment. It provides feedback on your readiness to assume a leadership role and can help you consider how to prepare for a formal leadership position.

connect

SELF-ASSESSMENT 13.1 Am I Ready to Be a Leader?

Go to connect.mheducation.com and take Self-Assessment 13.1. It measures your readiness for a leadership role. Then answer the following questions:

1. Do you agree with your results?

2. If you scored below 60 and desire to become a leader, what might you do to increase your readiness to lead?

3. How might these results help you become a more effective leader?

TRAIT THEORIES: DO LEADERS POSSESS UNIQUE TRAITS AND PERSONAL CHARACTERISTICS?

major question

MAJOR QUESTION

How can I use the takeaways from trait theories to improve my ability to lead?

THE BIGGER PICTURE

You'll see in the Integrative Framework that just as skills and abilities (as person factors) were an input in Chapter 3, leadership traits are an input (as environmental characteristics). Trait theories attempt to identify personal characteristics that differentiate effective leaders from followers. After identifying key traits established by research, we discuss the importance of gender and perceptions in determining what it takes to be an effective leader.

Trait theory is the successor to what was called the "great man" theory of leadership. This approach was based on the assumption that leaders such as Abraham Lincoln, Martin Luther King Jr., or Mark Zuckerberg were born with some inborn ability to lead. In contrast, trait theorists believed that leadership traits were not innate, but could be developed through experience and learning. **The *trait approach* attempts to identify personality characteristics or interpersonal attributes that can be used to differentiate leaders from followers.**

What Are the Core Traits Possessed by Leaders?

Early research demonstrated that five traits tended to differentiate leaders from average followers:

1. Intelligence.
2. Dominance.
3. Self-confidence.
4. Level of energy and activity.
5. Task-relevant knowledge.[14]

Over the years, researchers and consultants began to consider more and more traits, making it very difficult to determine the traits that truly differentiate leaders from followers. This led to crazy claims like effective leaders are taller, bald, and wear glasses. While some leaders may possess these characteristics, these are not generalized characteristics that managers should consider when hiring or promoting people to leadership positions.

If you believe in making conclusions based on science, then OB researchers have come up with an answer to the question at hand by using a statistical technique called meta-analysis. A meta-analysis is a statistical procedure that effectively computes an average relationship between two variables. Table 13.1 is a summary of what we know from this research. Instead of the five basic traits from early research (see above), note the emphasis on task-orientation and the expansion into interpersonal attributes.[15]

TABLE 13.1 KEY TASK-ORIENTED TRAITS AND INTERPERSONAL ATTRIBUTES

POSITIVE TASK-ORIENTED TRAITS	POSITIVE/NEGATIVE INTERPERSONAL ATTRIBUTES
• Intelligence	• Extraversion (+)
• Conscientiousness	• Agreeableness (+)
• Open to Experience	• Communication Skills (+)
• Emotional Stability	• Emotional Intelligence (+)
	• Narcissism (−)
	• Machiavellianism (−)
	• Psychopathy (−)

All of the traits and interpersonal attributes listed in Table 13.1 have been defined elsewhere in this book except for the "dark side" traits of narcissism, Machiavellianism, and psychopathy.[16] Let's consider them now.

- **Narcissism** **is defined as having "a self-centered perspective, feelings of superiority, and a drive for personal power and glory."**[17] Individuals with this trait have inflated views of themselves, have fantasies of being in control of everything, and like to attract the admiration of others. Although narcissistic leaders have an upside of being more charismatic and passionate, they also were found to promote counterproductive work behaviors from others[18]—recall our discussion in Chapter 2.

- **Machiavellianism** **entails the use of manipulation, a cynical view of human nature (e.g., all people lie to get what they want), and a moral code that puts results over principles (e.g., you have to cheat to get ahead).** It's not surprising that this characteristic is associated with counterproductive behavior.

- **Psychopathy** **is characterized as a lack of concern for others, impulsive behavior, and a lack of remorse or guilt when one's actions harm others.** It's no surprise that this type of person is toxic at work.

There are two more conclusions to note about Table 13.1. First, personality is more important than intelligence when selecting leaders.[19] Second, displaying the "dark side" traits tends to result in career derailment—being demoted or fired.[20] You definitely want to avoid these traits.

Margaret Thatcher, prime minister of the United Kingdom from 1979 to 1990, served three terms. She was the longest-serving prime minister of the previous century. Which of the positive traits were likely possessed by Margaret Thatcher?

Pol Pot (on the left) was the communist dictator of Cambodia from 1975 to 1979, whose programs and policies led to the deaths of between 2 and 3 million people, roughly a quarter of the Cambodian population. Do you think Pol Pot possessed any of the "dark side" traits?

What Is the Role of Emotional Intelligence in Leadership Effectiveness?

We discussed emotional intelligence in Chapter 3. Recall that *emotional intelligence* is the ability to manage oneself and one's relationships in mature and constructive ways: The components of emotional intelligence are shown in Table 3.6. Given that leadership is an influence process between leaders and followers, it should come as no surprise that emotional intelligence is predicted to be associated with leadership effectiveness. While Daniel Goleman, the psychologist who popularized the concept, and other consultants contend that they have evidence to support this conclusion,[21] it has not been published in scientific journals. That said, scientific evidence supports two conclusions:[22]

1. **Emotional intelligence is an input to transformational leadership.** In other words, emotional intelligence helps managers to effectively enact the behaviors associated with transformational leadership, which is discussed later in this chapter.

2. **Emotional intelligence has a small, positive, and significant association with leadership effectiveness.** This suggests that emotional intelligence will help you to lead more effectively, but it is not the secret elixir of leadership effectiveness as suggested by Daniel Goleman.

Do Women and Men Display the Same Leadership Traits?

The increase of women in the workforce has generated much interest in understanding the similarities and differences in female and male leaders. Research reveals the following four conclusions:

1. Men and women were seen as displaying more task and social leadership, respectively.[23]

2. Women used a more democratic or participative style than men, and men used a more autocratic and directive style than women.[24]

3. Men and women were equally assertive.[25]

4. Women executives, when rated by their peers, managers, and direct reports, scored higher than their male counterparts on a variety of effectiveness criteria.[26]

Lynn Tilton, CEO of Patriarch Partners, possesses many of the positive leadership traits identified by researchers. Her holding company manages 75 companies with over $8 billion in revenues.

TABLE 13.2 FOUR BASIC SKILLS FOR LEADERS

WHAT LEADERS NEED		AND WHY
Cognitive abilities to identify problems and causes for rapidly changing situations.		Leaders must sometimes derive effective solutions in short time spans with limited information.
Interpersonal skills to influence and persuade others.	skills for leaders	Leaders need to work well with diverse people.
Business skills to maximize the use of organizational assets.		Leaders increasingly need such skills as they advance up through an organization.
Strategic skills to craft an organization's mission, vision, strategies, and implementation plans.		Obviously, this latter skill-set matters most for individuals at the top ranks in an organization.

SOURCE: Adapted from T. V. Mumford, M. A. Campion, and F. P. Morgeson, "Leadership Skills Strataplex: Leadership Skill Requirements across Organizational Levels," *Leadership Quarterly*, 2007, 154–166.

How Important Are Knowledge and Skills?

Extremely! A team of researchers identified four basic skills needed by leaders. See Table 13.2.

Do Perceptions Matter?

The answer is yes according to what is called implicit leadership theory. **Implicit leadership theory is based on the idea that people have beliefs about how leaders should behave and what they should do for their followers.** These beliefs are summarized in what is called a *leadership prototype.*[27] **A leadership prototype is a mental representation of the traits and behaviors that people believe are possessed by leaders.** It is important to understand the content of leadership prototypes because we tend to perceive that someone is a leader when he or she exhibits traits or behaviors that are consistent with our prototypes. Although past research demonstrated that people were perceived as leaders when they exhibited masculine-oriented traits and behaviors associated with masculinity, and dominance,[28] more recent studies showed an emphasis on more feminine traits and styles that emphasize empowerment, fairness, compassion, and supportiveness.[29] This change in prototypes bodes well for reducing bias and discrimination against women in leadership roles.

What Are the Takeaways from Trait Theory?

There are four.

1. **We can no longer afford to ignore the implications of leadership traits.** Traits play a central role in how we perceive leaders, and they ultimately impact leadership effectiveness. For example, the Cardiac Rhythm Disease Management Group within Medtronic Inc. identified nine types of traits and skills (e.g., giving clear performance feedback and being courageous) that were necessary for leaders. The company then designed a leadership development program to help its employees learn and apply these traits.[30]

    More and more companies are using management development programs to build a pipeline of leadership talent. This is a particularly important recommendation in light of results from corporate surveys showing that the majority of companies do not possess adequate leadership talent to fill future needs.

2. **The list of positive traits and "dark side" traits shown in Table 13.1 provides guidance regarding the leadership traits you should attempt to cultivate and avoid if you want to assume a leadership role in the future.** Personality tests, which were

What Is the Role of Emotional Intelligence in Leadership Effectiveness?

We discussed emotional intelligence in Chapter 3. Recall that *emotional intelligence* is the ability to manage oneself and one's relationships in mature and constructive ways: The components of emotional intelligence are shown in Table 3.6. Given that leadership is an influence process between leaders and followers, it should come as no surprise that emotional intelligence is predicted to be associated with leadership effectiveness. While Daniel Goleman, the psychologist who popularized the concept, and other consultants contend that they have evidence to support this conclusion,[21] it has not been published in scientific journals. That said, scientific evidence supports two conclusions:[22]

1. **Emotional intelligence is an input to transformational leadership.** In other words, emotional intelligence helps managers to effectively enact the behaviors associated with transformational leadership, which is discussed later in this chapter.

2. **Emotional intelligence has a small, positive, and significant association with leadership effectiveness.** This suggests that emotional intelligence will help you to lead more effectively, but it is not the secret elixir of leadership effectiveness as suggested by Daniel Goleman.

Do Women and Men Display the Same Leadership Traits?

The increase of women in the workforce has generated much interest in understanding the similarities and differences in female and male leaders. Research reveals the following four conclusions:

1. Men and women were seen as displaying more task and social leadership, respectively.[23]

2. Women used a more democratic or participative style than men, and men used a more autocratic and directive style than women.[24]

3. Men and women were equally assertive.[25]

4. Women executives, when rated by their peers, managers, and direct reports, scored higher than their male counterparts on a variety of effectiveness criteria.[26]

Lynn Tilton, CEO of Patriarch Partners, possesses many of the positive leadership traits identified by researchers. Her holding company manages 75 companies with over $8 billion in revenues.

TABLE 13.2 FOUR BASIC SKILLS FOR LEADERS

WHAT LEADERS NEED		AND WHY
Cognitive abilities to identify problems and causes for rapidly changing situations.		Leaders must sometimes derive effective solutions in short time spans with limited information.
Interpersonal skills to influence and persuade others.	skills for leaders	Leaders need to work well with diverse people.
Business skills to maximize the use of organizational assets.		Leaders increasingly need such skills as they advance up through an organization.
Strategic skills to craft an organization's mission, vision, strategies, and implementation plans.		Obviously, this latter skill-set matters most for individuals at the top ranks in an organization.

SOURCE: Adapted from T. V. Mumford, M. A. Campion, and F. P. Morgeson, "Leadership Skills Strataplex: Leadership Skill Requirements across Organizational Levels," *Leadership Quarterly,* 2007, 154–166.

How Important Are Knowledge and Skills?

Extremely! A team of researchers identified four basic skills needed by leaders. See Table 13.2.

Do Perceptions Matter?

The answer is yes according to what is called implicit leadership theory. **Implicit leadership theory is based on the idea that people have beliefs about how leaders should behave and what they should do for their followers.** These beliefs are summarized in what is called a *leadership prototype.*[27] **A *leadership prototype* is a mental representation of the traits and behaviors that people believe are possessed by leaders.** It is important to understand the content of leadership prototypes because we tend to perceive that someone is a leader when he or she exhibits traits or behaviors that are consistent with our prototypes. Although past research demonstrated that people were perceived as leaders when they exhibited masculine-oriented traits and behaviors associated with masculinity, and dominance,[28] more recent studies showed an emphasis on more feminine traits and styles that emphasize empowerment, fairness, compassion, and supportiveness.[29] This change in prototypes bodes well for reducing bias and discrimination against women in leadership roles.

What Are the Takeaways from Trait Theory?

There are four.

1. **We can no longer afford to ignore the implications of leadership traits.** Traits play a central role in how we perceive leaders, and they ultimately impact leadership effectiveness. For example, the Cardiac Rhythm Disease Management Group within Medtronic Inc. identified nine types of traits and skills (e.g., giving clear performance feedback and being courageous) that were necessary for leaders. The company then designed a leadership development program to help its employees learn and apply these traits.[30]

   More and more companies are using management development programs to build a pipeline of leadership talent. This is a particularly important recommendation in light of results from corporate surveys showing that the majority of companies do not possess adequate leadership talent to fill future needs.

2. **The list of positive traits and "dark side" traits shown in Table 13.1 provides guidance regarding the leadership traits you should attempt to cultivate and avoid if you want to assume a leadership role in the future.** Personality tests, which were

What Is the Role of Emotional Intelligence in Leadership Effectiveness?

We discussed emotional intelligence in Chapter 3. Recall that *emotional intelligence* is the ability to manage oneself and one's relationships in mature and constructive ways: The components of emotional intelligence are shown in Table 3.6. Given that leadership is an influence process between leaders and followers, it should come as no surprise that emotional intelligence is predicted to be associated with leadership effectiveness. While Daniel Goleman, the psychologist who popularized the concept, and other consultants contend that they have evidence to support this conclusion,[21] it has not been published in scientific journals. That said, scientific evidence supports two conclusions:[22]

1. **Emotional intelligence is an input to transformational leadership.** In other words, emotional intelligence helps managers to effectively enact the behaviors associated with transformational leadership, which is discussed later in this chapter.

2. **Emotional intelligence has a small, positive, and significant association with leadership effectiveness.** This suggests that emotional intelligence will help you to lead more effectively, but it is not the secret elixir of leadership effectiveness as suggested by Daniel Goleman.

Do Women and Men Display the Same Leadership Traits?

The increase of women in the workforce has generated much interest in understanding the similarities and differences in female and male leaders. Research reveals the following four conclusions:

1. Men and women were seen as displaying more task and social leadership, respectively.[23]

2. Women used a more democratic or participative style than men, and men used a more autocratic and directive style than women.[24]

3. Men and women were equally assertive.[25]

4. Women executives, when rated by their peers, managers, and direct reports, scored higher than their male counterparts on a variety of effectiveness criteria.[26]

Lynn Tilton, CEO of Patriarch Partners, possesses many of the positive leadership traits identified by researchers. Her holding company manages 75 companies with over $8 billion in revenues.

TABLE 13.2 FOUR BASIC SKILLS FOR LEADERS

WHAT LEADERS NEED		AND WHY
Cognitive abilities to identify problems and causes for rapidly changing situations.		Leaders must sometimes derive effective solutions in short time spans with limited information.
Interpersonal skills to influence and persuade others.	skills for leaders	Leaders need to work well with diverse people.
Business skills to maximize the use of organizational assets.		Leaders increasingly need such skills as they advance up through an organization.
Strategic skills to craft an organization's mission, vision, strategies, and implementation plans.		Obviously, this latter skill-set matters most for individuals at the top ranks in an organization.

SOURCE: Adapted from T. V. Mumford, M. A. Campion, and F. P. Morgeson, "Leadership Skills Strataplex: Leadership Skill Requirements across Organizational Levels," *Leadership Quarterly,* 2007, 154–166.

How Important Are Knowledge and Skills?

Extremely! A team of researchers identified four basic skills needed by leaders. See Table 13.2.

Do Perceptions Matter?

The answer is yes according to what is called implicit leadership theory. **Implicit leadership theory is based on the idea that people have beliefs about how leaders should behave and what they should do for their followers.** These beliefs are summarized in what is called a *leadership prototype.*[27] **A leadership prototype is a mental representation of the traits and behaviors that people believe are possessed by leaders.** It is important to understand the content of leadership prototypes because we tend to perceive that someone is a leader when he or she exhibits traits or behaviors that are consistent with our prototypes. Although past research demonstrated that people were perceived as leaders when they exhibited masculine-oriented traits and behaviors associated with masculinity, and dominance,[28] more recent studies showed an emphasis on more feminine traits and styles that emphasize empowerment, fairness, compassion, and supportiveness.[29] This change in prototypes bodes well for reducing bias and discrimination against women in leadership roles.

What Are the Takeaways from Trait Theory?

There are four.

1. **We can no longer afford to ignore the implications of leadership traits.** Traits play a central role in how we perceive leaders, and they ultimately impact leadership effectiveness. For example, the Cardiac Rhythm Disease Management Group within Medtronic Inc. identified nine types of traits and skills (e.g., giving clear performance feedback and being courageous) that were necessary for leaders. The company then designed a leadership development program to help its employees learn and apply these traits.[30]

   More and more companies are using management development programs to build a pipeline of leadership talent. This is a particularly important recommendation in light of results from corporate surveys showing that the majority of companies do not possess adequate leadership talent to fill future needs.

2. **The list of positive traits and "dark side" traits shown in Table 13.1 provides guidance regarding the leadership traits you should attempt to cultivate and avoid if you want to assume a leadership role in the future.** Personality tests, which were

Do these results suggest that managers should attempt to stop people from being political? Good luck. Organizational politics cannot be eliminated. A manager would be naïve to believe this is possible. But political maneuvering can and should be managed to keep it constructive and within reasonable bounds. One expert put it this way: "People can focus their attention on only so many things. The more it lands on politics, the less energy—emotional and intellectual—is available to attend to the problems that fall under the heading of real work."[47]

Not Too Much and Not Too Little   An individual's degree of politicalness is a matter of personal values, ethics, and temperament. People who are either strictly nonpolitical or highly political generally pay a price for their behavior. The former may experience slow promotions and feel left out, while the latter may run the risk of being called self-serving and lose their credibility. People at both ends of the political spectrum may be considered poor team players. A moderate amount of prudent political behavior generally is considered a survival tool in complex organizations. Experts remind us that "political behavior has earned a bad name only because of its association with politicians. On its own, the use of power and other resources to obtain your objectives is not inherently unethical. It all depends on what the preferred objectives are."[48] What are your thoughts?

How to Build Support for My Ideas   Taken together, our discussion of politics probably leaves you wondering, "What should I do?" How do I avoid the bad and take advantage of the good? Thankfully, both research and practice provide some useful and specific advice on how to build support for your ideas. Here are eight recommendations:

1. Create a simple slogan that captures your idea.
2. Get your idea on the agenda. Describe how it addresses an important need or objective and look for ways to make it a priority.
3. Score small wins early and broadcast them widely. Results build momentum and make it easier for other people to commit.
4. Form alliances with people who have the power to decide, fund, and implement.
5. Persist and continue to build support. It is a process, not an event.
6. Respond and adjust. Be flexible and accepting of other people's input; the more names on it, the more likely you are to succeed.
7. Lock it in. Anchor the idea into the organization through budgets, job descriptions, incentives, and other operating procedures.
8. Secure and allocate credit. You don't want your idea to be hijacked, nor do you want to blow your own horn. You need others to sing your praises to assure you get the credit you deserve.[49]

TAKE-AWAY APPLICATION—TAAP

1. Make politics work for you and select an idea—something you would like to change, a new program, a new policy or practice—for an organization to which you belong.

2. Work through and apply as many of the eight recommendations in the list above as are relevant. (Don't be too quick to skip any particular recommendation; give each some real thought.)

3. Execute your plan. Regardless of the level of success, compare what you actually did with what you planned to do (how many of the eight recommendations did you actually use?).

4. If you're happy with the outcome, then hopefully this showed you the positive power of politics. If you were less than pleased with the results, revise your plan and be sure to follow it.

MAJOR QUESTION

Do I seek only to impress, or to make a good impression?

THE BIGGER PICTURE

We all want to look good in the eyes of others, and to do this we often engage in impression management. Like the other topics discussed in this chapter, impression management involves techniques we engage in to influence others in all arenas of life. To help you manage your own impressions, we define the term *impression management* and discuss what it means to make good and bad impressions, as well as how to remedy bad impressions and make effective apologies. You will see how practical knowledge in this area helps boost your effectiveness across levels of outcomes in the Integrative Framework.

We pursue the basic human desire to impress others not only because it makes us feel good about ourselves, but also because others often can provide things we desire, such as a job, a good grade, or a date! Many of our attempts to influence others in such ways are "impression management." We conclude this chapter with a discussion of this particular form of influence.

What Is Impression Management?

Impression management is defined as any attempt to control or manipulate the images related to a person, organization, or idea.[50] This encompasses things such as speech, behavior, and appearance. Most impression management attempts are directed at making a good impression on important others, although there are exceptions, as we will see. It is important to remember that anyone can be the intended target of impression management—parents, teachers, peers, employees, and customers are all fair game. For instance, by positioning themselves as socially responsible (CSR), companies can create positive impressions with many stakeholders, such as potential customers, and in turn boost sales.[51] Let's dive into good and bad impressions in more detail.

Good Impressions

Research conducted in the context of job interviews shows that impressions are formed very quickly and often subtly. Interviewers gather information on job candidates based on their handshake, smile, and manner of dress. All of this information is communicated before any questions are asked! More importantly, it was shown that these same factors were related to ultimate job offers.[52]

How to Make a Killer First Impression   You've undoubtedly heard the saying: "You have only one chance to make a first impression." Some argue that people judge you within one second of meeting you. Researchers tested this belief and found that after viewing only a microsecond of a video of a political candidate, subjects predicted with 70 percent accuracy who would win an election! To help you overcome the

Do these results suggest that managers should attempt to stop people from being political? Good luck. Organizational politics cannot be eliminated. A manager would be naïve to believe this is possible. But political maneuvering can and should be managed to keep it constructive and within reasonable bounds. One expert put it this way: "People can focus their attention on only so many things. The more it lands on politics, the less energy—emotional and intellectual—is available to attend to the problems that fall under the heading of real work."[47]

Not Too Much and Not Too Little   An individual's degree of politicalness is a matter of personal values, ethics, and temperament. People who are either strictly nonpolitical or highly political generally pay a price for their behavior. The former may experience slow promotions and feel left out, while the latter may run the risk of being called self-serving and lose their credibility. People at both ends of the political spectrum may be considered poor team players. A moderate amount of prudent political behavior generally is considered a survival tool in complex organizations. Experts remind us that "political behavior has earned a bad name only because of its association with politicians. On its own, the use of power and other resources to obtain your objectives is not inherently unethical. It all depends on what the preferred objectives are."[48] What are your thoughts?

How to Build Support for My Ideas   Taken together, our discussion of politics probably leaves you wondering, "What should I do?" How do I avoid the bad and take advantage of the good? Thankfully, both research and practice provide some useful and specific advice on how to build support for your ideas. Here are eight recommendations:

1. Create a simple slogan that captures your idea.
2. Get your idea on the agenda. Describe how it addresses an important need or objective and look for ways to make it a priority.
3. Score small wins early and broadcast them widely. Results build momentum and make it easier for other people to commit.
4. Form alliances with people who have the power to decide, fund, and implement.
5. Persist and continue to build support. It is a process, not an event.
6. Respond and adjust. Be flexible and accepting of other people's input; the more names on it, the more likely you are to succeed.
7. Lock it in. Anchor the idea into the organization through budgets, job descriptions, incentives, and other operating procedures.
8. Secure and allocate credit. You don't want your idea to be hijacked, nor do you want to blow your own horn. You need others to sing your praises to assure you get the credit you deserve.[49]

TAKE-AWAY APPLICATION—TAAP

1. Make politics work for you and select an idea—something you would like to change, a new program, a new policy or practice—for an organization to which you belong.
2. Work through and apply as many of the eight recommendations in the list above as are relevant. (Don't be too quick to skip any particular recommendation; give each some real thought.)
3. Execute your plan. Regardless of the level of success, compare what you actually did with what you planned to do (how many of the eight recommendations did you actually use?).
4. If you're happy with the outcome, then hopefully this showed you the positive power of politics. If you were less than pleased with the results, revise your plan and be sure to follow it.

IMPRESSION MANAGEMENT

MAJOR QUESTION

Do I seek only to impress, or to make a good impression?

THE BIGGER PICTURE

We all want to look good in the eyes of others, and to do this we often engage in impression management. Like the other topics discussed in this chapter, impression management involves techniques we engage in to influence others in all arenas of life. To help you manage your own impressions, we define the term *impression management* and discuss what it means to make good and bad impressions, as well as how to remedy bad impressions and make effective apologies. You will see how practical knowledge in this area helps boost your effectiveness across levels of outcomes in the Integrative Framework.

We pursue the basic human desire to impress others not only because it makes us feel good about ourselves, but also because others often can provide things we desire, such as a job, a good grade, or a date! Many of our attempts to influence others in such ways are "impression management." We conclude this chapter with a discussion of this particular form of influence.

What Is Impression Management?

Impression management is defined as any attempt to control or manipulate the images related to a person, organization, or idea.[50] This encompasses things such as speech, behavior, and appearance. Most impression management attempts are directed at making a good impression on important others, although there are exceptions, as we will see. It is important to remember that anyone can be the intended target of impression management—parents, teachers, peers, employees, and customers are all fair game. For instance, by positioning themselves as socially responsible (CSR), companies can create positive impressions with many stakeholders, such as potential customers, and in turn boost sales.[51] Let's dive into good and bad impressions in more detail.

Good Impressions

Research conducted in the context of job interviews shows that impressions are formed very quickly and often subtly. Interviewers gather information on job candidates based on their handshake, smile, and manner of dress. All of this information is communicated before any questions are asked! More importantly, it was shown that these same factors were related to ultimate job offers.[52]

How to Make a Killer First Impression   You've undoubtedly heard the saying: "You have only one chance to make a first impression." Some argue that people judge you within one second of meeting you. Researchers tested this belief and found that after viewing only a microsecond of a video of a political candidate, subjects predicted with 70 percent accuracy who would win an election! To help you overcome the

Craig's List founder Craig Newmark and CEO Jim Buckmaster seemingly pay little attention to impression management. Their office is in a small storefront; Buckmaster takes public transportation to work while Newmark drives himself in a modest car. Buckmaster says that neither of them is interested in being wildly wealthy and dealing with the associated challenges. Stopping short and avoiding the hassles is just fine for them. Also interesting is the fact that Newmark, despite being the wealthy founder, currently works in a customer service role with no managerial responsibilities at CraigsList.[53]

pressure, and assure that people's snap judgments of you are favorable, we make the following five recommendations:

1. **Set an intention.** Once again goal setting from Chapters 5 and 6 comes into play. When you're preparing for an event (a meeting, social event, conference), think of whom you'd like to meet and what you'd like to achieve from that introduction. Then, plan your energy, intro, and comments accordingly.

2. **Consider your ornaments.** We're not talking about Christmas trees or party favors, but instead your jewelry, makeup, and clothes. This advice is for both men and women. Men, don't overlook your watch, for instance. Many people will draw conclusions from the type of watch you wear and how it aligns with your clothes (e.g., sporty, gaudy, trendy). Women, of course, should not forget that their makeup and jewelry are judged similarly. Be sure they match your personality and your intended message.

3. **Remember that your body speaks.** We've all heard that body language makes a difference, but people very rarely actually do anything about it. Pay attention to the nonverbals you learned about in Chapter 9. And if you're serious about managing your body language, then find a way to video yourself in a social setting. Use this to help you manage your tendencies in the future.

4. **Bust bad moods and bad days.** If you can't shake a bad mood or prevent your bad day from spilling over into your event, then stay home. This requires you to manage your emotions and mood. The knowledge and tools you acquired in Chapter 7 on Positive OB can help here. If you're in a bad mood before an important event, then find a way to snap out of it—play some of your favorite music, work out, go shopping—or reschedule. People will pick up on your mood, and you don't want your body language to convey: "Hello, my name is Bad Mood Bob."

5. **Be interested to be interesting.** The best way to appear interesting is *to appear interested*. People tend to like people who like them; at least this is a good place to start. Rather than blather on about yourself, an excellent way to show interest is to ask questions about the other person. Depending on the situation, you may be able to do some research about the person or persons you'll meet, and then make it part of your intention or goal to ask them about interesting things you learned about them.[54]

TAKE-AWAY APPLICATION—TAAP

1. Which of the five rules for making a first impression do you most often overlook? Which one do you think you could gain the most from?
2. Think of somebody you'd like to positively impress, and assume you'll be able to meet this person next week at a networking event.
3. Describe your intention or goal for the introduction.
4. Describe how you can appear interested. What questions might you ask?
5. Now, assume that the day of the networking event arrives and you're in a bad mood. Explain two things you could do to break out of this mood and prepare yourself for the event.

Reciprocity and Impression Management   Recall our discussion of reciprocity earlier in this chapter ("Six Principles of Persuasion")—the benefits of giving in order to receive. An interesting stream of research shows that when a CEO makes positive comments about another, and the other's company, Wall Street analysts give more favorable reports for both the CEO and the company when they miss earnings.[55] Put another way, if I say something positive about you to the media, then they are likely to be more forgiving if or when your performance is low. This is obviously a powerful form of influence—one that really pays!

Ethics and Impression Management   Impression management often strays into questionable, if not unethical, territory. And, like the last example, CEOs often engage in impression management with Wall Street analysts. This is to be expected, and in and of itself is not a problem. However, a study of more than 600 CEOs of companies with more than $100 million in revenues showed that unfavorable analyst comments prompted CEOs to verbally communicate that their companies do indeed have policies and practices that are in shareholders' best interests. Related research showed that CEOs also routinely communicated that their own compensation plan was aligned with shareholder interests, although, in both instances, it was found that CEOs regularly misrepresented these issues.[56] For example, their companies often made job and R&D cuts that undermined the long-term health of the company (counter to shareholder interests), and their personal compensation often was increased even when the share price of their company plummeted.

How about this story of impression management from a large bank:

> After 7 pm, people would open the door to their office, drape a spare jacket on the back of their chair, lay a set of glasses down on some reading material on their desk—and then go home for the night. The point of this elaborate gesture was to create the illusion that they were just out grabbing dinner and would be returning to burn the midnight oil.[57]

While these examples highlight some ethically questionable impression management practices, entire industries have transformed themselves using impression management. The venture capital (VC) industry, for instance, historically shunned any publicity. The norm in the industry was for the owners to stay out of the limelight, keep low profiles, and keep their mouths shut. Now, however, VC firms are aggressively engaged in impression management and hire PR firms, blog, and tweet. The following Example box provides some interesting details and insights.

EXAMPLE Impression Management Venture Capital Style[58]

Self-promotion by venture capitalists was frowned upon until about 2009. Until that point those that did "take the stage" were criticized and called "parade jumpers." But since 2009 VC firms old (e.g., Bessemer Venture Partners) and new (e.g., Founders Fund) actively engage in impression management with investors, the media, and other VC firms. Today some of the founders and lead rainmakers in VC firms are celebrities with publicity, status, and influence to match their often immense wealth. Below are some of the reasons why VC firms across the industry now pursue impression management with enthusiasm and perhaps the most successful one today.

Marc Andreessen and Ben Horowitz entered the venture capital industry with a bang, or more like a flash. They embraced (self-)promotion and other impression management techniques and achieved greater growth than any other VC. Their tactics and performance also garnered them incredible status and influence. They are now seen as the most desirable source of financing for entrepreneurs in San Francisco and New York.

- *Poor returns.* Venture capital firms averaged 4.6 percent returns in the last 10 years. This means that investors are putting their money in other places; therefore, VCs have to compete more aggressively.

- *Knock on doors.* This increased competition has motivated VCs to reach out to and differentiate themselves with investors and entrepreneurs, which contrasts with the recent past where investors and entrepreneurs needed some sort of inside connection to get a meeting with VCs.

- *Andreessen & Horowitz.* This VC firm, started by the founder of Netscape (one of the first Web companies) and one of its executives, entered the market in 2009 with a completely different approach—they courted entrepreneurs, used social media (blogs and Twitter), and marketed themselves aggressively. Their "public" approach was motivated by the belief that "each year 15 deals account for 97 percent of all venture capital profits. To be successful, they would have to pursue those 15 companies. And they would do it by aggressively marketing their expertise to the reporters and bloggers who follow start-ups." To execute this strategy they didn't just hire a PR firm, but they made the PR firm's founder (Margit Wennmacher) a partner in Andreesen & Horowitz.

- *Success.* Andreessen & Horowitz quickly became the fastest-growing VC firm in the industry.

YOUR THOUGHTS?

1. What are your thoughts about aggressively managing the impressions of investors and customers, like Andreessen & Horowitz and other VC firms have done?
2. Think of the job you have now, or one you've had in the past. With whom and how could they use impression management to improve or grow their business?
3. What ethical standards would you apply to impression management?

Favorable Upward Impression Management Tactics   On a positive note, both research and practice have revealed three categories of favorable upward impression management techniques:[59]

1. *Job-focused*—presenting information about one's job performance in a favorable light.
2. *Supervisor-focused*—praising and doing favors for one's supervisor.
3. *Self-focused*—presenting oneself as a polite and nice person.

Before going further, let's have you learn about your own tendencies for favorable impression management. More specifically, Self-Assessment 12.4 will help you understand the types of impression management—job-, supervisor-, and self-focused—you tend to use in work settings.

SELF-ASSESSMENT 12.4 **Your Impression Management—How and Who**

Go to connect.mheducation.com and take Self-Assessment 12.4 to learn both how you manage your impressions and with whom.

1. Are you better suited for "Hollywood," or are you better described as safe or a free agent?
2. What are the benefits of your impression management tendencies?
3. What are the drawbacks?
4. Look at all of the items in the Assessment, select the two that could be most useful to you, and describe specifically how you could use them.

Let's be clear: a moderate amount of upward impression management is a necessity for the average employee today. For example, ingratiation can slightly improve your performance appraisal results and make your boss like you significantly more.[60] Engage in too little impression management and busy managers are liable to overlook some of your valuable contributions when they make job assignment, pay, and promotion decisions. Too much, and you run the risk of being branded a "schmoozer," a "phony," and other unflattering things by your coworkers.[61] Consider, for instance, that noticeable flattery and ingratiation can backfire by embarrassing the target person and damaging your credibility.[62]

Bad Impressions—The Common if Not Subtle Kind

Remarkably, some people actually try to make a bad impression. But because these people are relatively rare, we instead focus on common, if not subtle, ways people make bad impressions at work. In addition to the many obvious faux pas—don't cheat, don't lie, don't steal—many employees often make bad impressions without knowing it. Some common ways this happens and how to overcome them are:

- *Doing only the minimum.* Many employees aren't aware that not making the often simple extra effort to fulfill a coworker's request can be costly. Going the extra mile to check the status of a report, for instance, can go a long way toward conveying a positive impression.

- *Having a negative mindset.* Most people consider themselves positive, but sometimes others have a different view. When presented with a new initiative, do you immediately think of and point out the potential pitfalls or complain? If so, then it is possible that others see you as negative. And managers prefer people who are supportive, not necessarily "yes men and women," but those who are constructive versus eternal naysayers.

- *Overcommitting.* Initiative is often good, but biting off more than you can chew means you might choke! The inability to deliver on-time or quality work is a sure way to make a bad impression. Prioritize and deliver, which requires saying no sometimes.

- *Taking no initiative.* The opposite of overcommitting—failing to take action when something needs to get done—can also make you look bad. If coworkers (including your boss) frequently come to you with the same questions or challenges, then step up and try to proactively solve the issue.
- *Waiting until the last minute to deliver bad news.* Of course you shouldn't report to or consult with your boss on every little hiccup in your work. But worse still is to inform her or him just before a deadline that you are having difficulties. This puts your boss in a bad spot too. Be smart; put yourself in the other person's shoes and consider if and when you would want to know the information you have.[63]

Spinning Bad into Good, or Good into Better

One final point is that much of impression management involves "spinning" a bad situation into something better. Public relations (PR), for instance, is impression management at the organizational level and often involves "managing the message," such as reducing the damage of bad press associated with a scandal. The massive BP oil spill is a prime example. The company downplayed the estimates of how much oil was leaking—first 1,000 barrels per day, then 5,000, and then nearly 50,000! It was later learned that the company knowingly underestimated the extent of the leak. Doing so dramatically undermined the credibility of a company that billed itself as: "BP—Beyond Petroleum—a paragon of environmental sustainability."[64]

As CEO of BP during the massive Deepwater Horizon oil spill in 2010, Tony Hayward was criticized for being evasive and blaming others. By not handling the incident effectively, he damaged the reputation of the company and lost his job. How would you have handled the situation if you were CEO of BP?

The company also attempted to deflect blame for the spill onto contractors and downplayed the environmental impact. This made the company appear insensitive and led people to believe they were simply trying to avoid legal liabilities. Months after the spill began, the company unleashed a barrage of television spots featuring BP employees from the Gulf, highlighting its commitment to the cleanup. According to one PR expert:

> It was one of the worst PR approaches that I've seen in my 56 years in the business. . . . They tried to be opaque. They had every excuse in the book. Right away they should have accepted responsibility and recognized what a disaster they faced. They basically thought they could spin their way out of catastrophe. It doesn't work that way.[65]

A communications professor summed it up this way: "BP could apologize every day . . . [but] until the oil stopped, there was nothing that could be done to make it better, but there was plenty that could be said to make it worse."[66]

How to Prepare for and Deal with Bad Events   So how can organizations best handle crises? A PR executive who represents the New York Yankees and News Corp. suggests that all organizations should create a crisis plan that includes:

1. How information is to be gathered.
2. How to formulate a response.
3. Who will deliver the message, and via which media channels.
4. Don't minimize a given problem. No matter how small it is in the company's eyes, it is a big deal to somebody else.
5. Be understanding and empathetic.

After these, get on with doing business—whatever the organization does well (e.g., finding and creating petroleum products, as in the case of BP).[67] Of course, let's not forget that apologies often are necessary and have a place in impression management.

Apologies   One way to remedy or at least reduce the impact of bad impressions, negative uses of power, or poor performance is with an apology. Apologies are a form of trust repair (discussed in Chapter 8) where one acknowledges an offense and frequently offers to make amends. It is a widely held norm in the United States and other cultures (e.g., Japan) to apologize when one's actions (or lack of action) cause harm to another, whether intentional or not. And much like our discussion of equity in Chapter 5, harm can be perceived or actual, but in either case it is real to the offended. Apologies are important and are considered effective to the extent they restore trust and positively affect your ability to influence the offended party in the future.[68]

We know from life that not all people apologize, and when they do, the effects differ. But in business perhaps the better questions are when to apologize and how. Table 12.2 describes the primary reasons leaders should apologize along with their associated motives.

Table 12.2 can be helpful for nonleaders too, and you may consider apologizing in any of the following situations:

- Doing so will serve an important purpose (see Table 12.2).
- The offense is of serious consequence.
- It's appropriate to assume responsibility for the offense.
- No one else can get the job done.
- The cost of saying something is likely to be lower than the cost of staying silent.

Whether the apology is from a leader or not, all effective apologies have the following four characteristics:

1. Acknowledgment of wrongdoing
2. Acceptance of responsibility
3. Expression of regret
4. Promise that the offense will not be repeated[69]

It also is helpful to consider that a failure to apologize, or to do so in a timely manner, can turn a bad situation worse.[70]

TABLE 12.2   PURPOSES FOR LEADER APOLOGIES AND THEIR DESIRED OUTCOMES

PURPOSE	MOTIVE OR DESIRED OUTCOME
Individual—Leader offended other.	Encourage followers to forgive and forget.
Institution—Follower offended another organizational member.	Restore functioning within the group or organization when one member offends another member(s).
Intergroup—Follower offended external party.	Repair relations with an external group that perceived harm by a member of the leader's group.
Moral—Genuine regret for wrongdoing.	Request for forgiveness and redemption for regrettable (in)action.

SOURCE: Based on B. Kellerman, "When Should a Leader Apologize—and When Not?", *Harvard Business Review*, April 1, 2006.

You are now far better equipped to influence people in many arenas of life. We close this chapter with a reminder: you don't need to have a big, fancy title or corner office to have power. You typically have more power than you think. We encourage you to be more purposeful and accurate in your application of power, empowerment, influence, politics, and impression management. Doing so will dramatically increase your effectiveness across levels of the Integrative Framework. Besides, you'll get your way more often!

what did i learn?

You learned that you can increase your effectiveness by applying power, influence, and politics. You learned the bases of power, common influence tactics, the causes of politics, and which forms are most effective in different situations. You also learned that sharing power and empowering others are important means for building your own influence and improving your performance. Reinforce what you learned with the Key Points below. Then consolidate your learning using the Integrative Framework. Finally, Challenge your mastery of this chapter by answering the Major Questions in your own words.

Key Points for Understanding Chapter 12

You learned the following key points.

12.1 POWER AND ITS BASIC FORMS

- Power is defined as the ability to marshal human, informational, and other resources to get something done.
- The five main bases of power are legitimate, reward, coercive, expert, and referent.
- The first three bases are considered forms of position power and the last two, forms of personal power.

12.2 POWER SHARING AND EMPOWERMENT

- Empowerment is defined as efforts to enhance employee performance, well-being, and positive attitudes.
- Structural empowerment is based on transferring authority and responsibilities from management to employees.
- Power sharing can be described on a continuum from domination to consultation, participation, and finally delegation.
- Psychological empowerment occurs when employees feel a sense of meaning, competence, self-determination, and impact at work.

12.3 EFFECTIVELY INFLUENCING OTHERS

- Influence tactics are conscious efforts to affect and change a specific behavior in others. The tactics you use often determine how people respond to your influence attempts.
- We studied nine common influence tactics: rational persuasion, inspirational appeals, consultation, ingratiation, personal appeals, exchange, coalition tactics, pressure, and legitimating tactics.
- You can expand your effectiveness further still by using six principles of persuasion: liking, reciprocity, social proof, consistency, authority, and scarcity.

12.4 POLITICAL TACTICS AND HOW TO USE THEM

- Organizational politics are intentional acts of influence to enhance or protect the self-interest of individuals or groups that are not endorsed by or aligned with those of the organization.
- Competition along with uncertainty regarding objectives, performance measures, decision processes, and change are major drivers or causes of political actions.
- Political action occurs at three levels—individual, coalition, and network.

12.5 IMPRESSION MANAGEMENT

- Impression management is defined as any attempt to control or manipulate the images related to a person, organization, or idea.
- Because impressions have been shown to relate to subsequent job offers, it is important to make good first impressions by being interested, focusing on body language, setting goals or intentions, and displaying a positive mood and emotions.
- Common ways to make bad impressions are doing only the minimum, having a negative mindset, overcommitting, taking no initiative, and waiting until the last minute to deliver bad news.
- Organizations need a recovery plan in case of disaster; an apology for a transgression can be effective.

The Integrative Framework for Chapter 12

As shown in Figure 12.8, you learned practical tools to help you influence others—power, empowerment, influence, politics, and impression management. Collectively, these tools represent important group-level processes. And how you use these tools often determines whether people resist, comply with, or actually commit to your wishes. You learned how using these tools relates to individual-level outcomes, such as performance, attitudes, well-being, (counter)productive citizenship behaviors, turnover, and career outcomes. Power and influence are also associated with satisfaction,

FIGURE 12.8 THE INTEGRATIVE FRAMEWORK FOR UNDERSTANDING AND APPLYING OB

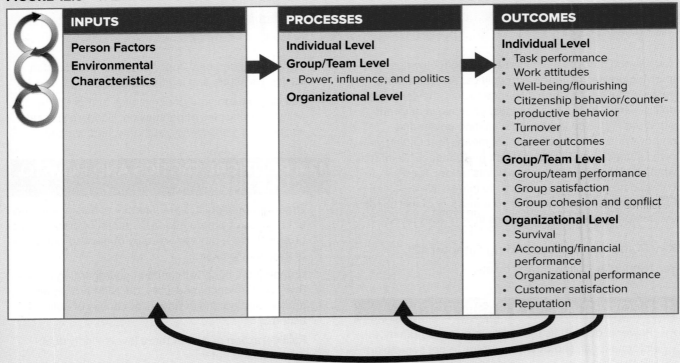

© 2014 Angelo Kinicki and Mel Fugate. All rights reserved. Reproduction prohibited without permission of the authors.

cohesion, and conflict at the group/team level, and with survival, financial performance, customer satisfaction, and reputation at the organizational level. Beyond this, you explored the notion of empowerment and how sharing power with others can increase your own power and influence.

Challenge: Major Questions for Chapter 12

At the start of the chapter, we told you that after reading the chapter you should be able to answer the following questions. Unless you can, have you really processed and internalized the lessons in the chapter? Refer to the Key Points, Figure 12.8, the chapter itself, and your notes to revisit and answer the following major questions:

1. What are the basic forms of power and how can they help me achieve my desired outcomes?

2. How can sharing power increase my power?

3. How do my influence tactics affect my personal effectiveness?

4. What are the many forms of politics, and how can understanding them make me more effective at school, at work, and socially?

5. Do I seek only to impress, or to make a good impression?

Writing the Book (Review) on Conflict of Interest

If you're not getting glowing online reviews for your product, maybe you could buy them. One entrepreneur tried that business model in the realm of self-publishing, and for a while, it worked out fine.

Pay for Play in Online Book Reviews

An article in the *New York Times* featured someone who had been selling online book reviews to the authors who wanted them. Besides confirming the worst suspicions of many, the story raises issues of ethics and trust in online reviews.

GettingBookReviews.com. Todd Rutherford was doing press releases for hire for self-published authors. Authors wanted the press releases to increase the likelihood that their books would get more attention, whether in published or consumer reviews. In 2010 Rutherford realized he could help his clients more directly by simply writing the reviews himself under assumed names. And so he advertised that very service.

He launched GettingBookReviews.com (the site is no longer active), blatantly setting out his terms. A single five-star review would be written and posted for only $99. And soon he offered bulk discounts—20 reviews for only $499, 50 reviews for $999.

In some ways it's a wonder he lasted as long as he did. His house of cards tumbled with increased notoriety driven by one unhappy customer—but not before he had published some 4,500 online reviews. By the time the 2012 article in the *New York Times* came out, Rutherford had folded his tent and moved on. Last heard, he was selling RVs in Oklahoma.[71]

Puffery Is Legal

Advertising in general, and the book business in particular, has always relied on puffery, of inflating the positive aspects of their products. A good example is the book jacket blurbs a publisher will often solicit from authors it publishes to support books from other authors on its roster.

Moreover, it is not uncommon for the friends or associates of an author to help, often by posting positive reviews. These actions are not illegal. The reviews are clearly sourced, and the individuals who write them are entitled to their opinions. (While it may be more ethical for the reviewers to note their relationship to the author, it is not a legal requirement.)

Opinion Spamming Is Not

Bing Liu is a professor of computer science at the University of Illinois at Chicago who studies data mining and more specifically the abuse of online reviews. He defines opinion spamming as the illegal effort behind everything from fake reviews to bogus blogs and websites.

"Positive opinions can result in significant financial gains and/or [renown] for businesses, organizations and individuals," Liu writes on his faculty website. "This, unfortunately, gives strong incentives for opinion spamming."[72]

As to online book reviews, it is illegal for a reviewer to receive compensation for a positive review and then post it on most sites, including Amazon.com.

Comparatively new slang terms for authors who post reviews pretending to be someone else are "sock puppets" or "sock monkeys." That these terms exist suggests such behavior is common.

The successful and award-winning British author R. J. Ellory wouldn't seem to need such help, but in 2012 he was called out by fellow author Jeremy Duns for multiple reviews (posted under fictional names, of course) on Amazon.com. ABC News broke the story, after the website Gawker published Duns' complaints on his Twitter feed. The scandal was then written up in *The Huffington Post.*

"Ellory writes 5-star reviews of his own work on Amazon. Long, purple tributes to his own magnificent genius," Duns tweeted. "RJ Ellory also writes shoddy, sh----y sniping reviews of other authors' work on Amazon, under an assumed identity."[73]

The Importance of Trust

Can trust be restored in online reviews? Maybe, but not soon. Liu estimates that about a third of all online reviews are false. He notes that the need to be able to identify bogus reviews will only increase. One of his research areas is the creation of algorithms to help identify false reviews. He's skeptical that without computer help one could tell the difference. In the current environment, consumers should train themselves to be skeptical, and where possible balance online reviews with trusted third-party resources. This is easier in the electronic product area than in the world of e-books but not impossible.

One can also envisage a future where it is clear that the results of opinion spamming create their own deterrent. "Once someone finds out you paid a book reviewer, your reputation is toast," writes Angelo Hoy, owner/operator of the *Writers Weekly* website.[74] Her site offers its own e-book for authors on e-marketing their books by legal means.

Apply the 3-Stop Problem-Solving Approach to OB

Stop 1: What is the problem?

- Use the Integrative Framework to help identify the outcomes that are important in this case.

- Which of these outcomes are not being achieved in the case?

- Based on considering the above two questions, what is the most important problem in this case?

Stop 2: Use the Integrative Framework shown at the start of this chapter to help identify the OB concepts or theories that help you to understand the problem in this case.

- What person factors are most relevant?

- What environmental characteristics are most important to consider?

- Do you need to consider any processes? Which ones?

- What concepts or theories discussed in this chapter are most relevant for solving the key problem in this case?

Stop 3: What are your recommendations for solving the problem?

- Review the material in the chapter that most pertains to your proposed solution and look for practical recommendations.

- Use any past OB knowledge or experience to generate recommendations.

- Outline your plan for solving the problem in this case.

LEGAL/ETHICAL CHALLENGE

Secret Banking Elite Rules Trading in Derivatives

Until recently, nine people had a standing meeting in Manhattan one Wednesday each month. This was a highly secretive group of powerful people across Wall Street, known by critics as the "derivatives dealers club." The membership and discussions were strictly confidential. The focus: Protect the interests of the largest firms on Wall Street that serve as dealers in the highly lucrative derivatives market. Derivatives (swaps and options) are financial products used like insurance to hedge financial risk. Because derivatives do not trade on formal exchanges, like stocks on the New York Stock Exchange (NYSE), and are largely unregulated by agencies such as the Securities and Exchange Commission (SEC), their creation and trading are largely self-managed by the firms themselves. This secretive group helped oversee and control this multitrillion-dollar market.

The dealers' club attempted to block the efforts of other banks to enter the market and compete with select few member firms. It also blocked many efforts by regulators and others to get full and free disclosure of dealer prices and fees. The situation is similar to a real estate agent selling a house and the buyer only knowing what he or she paid, the seller only knowing what he or she received, and the agent pocketing the rest in fees. These fees would not be known to either the buyer or the seller.

This lack of disclosure has implications far beyond the biggest banks. Pension funds, states, cities, airlines, food companies, and some small businesses use derivatives to offset and manage risk. These parties argue that without transparency they cannot determine if they receive a fair price. What is known, however, is that Wall Street's largest firms collect billions of dollars in undisclosed fees each year from trading these derivatives—fees that certainly would be smaller if there was more transparency and competition. These concerns have spurred investigation of anticompetitive practices by the Department of Justice and threats by some legislators. The firms, however, have powerful allies—the many politicians in Washington to whom they've made substantial campaign contributions.

Derivatives dealers' defense is that derivative prices are complex. Unlike shares of Netflix stock, which are all equivalent—one share has the same price as all the rest—terms of oil derivatives can vary greatly. The complexity therefore requires customization, and greater transparency is impractical if not impossible.

What Is Your Position on Derivatives Trading?

1. Regulators should assert influence over the derivatives market, like they do with stocks, and require derivatives to be traded on an open exchange where buyers and sellers disclose prices and fees.

2. Nothing should be done to change how derivatives are bought and sold. If buyers and sellers don't like the lack of dealer transparency, then they can choose not to trade derivatives.

3. The derivatives market should be modified only slightly to allow other players (e.g., banks) to provide derivatives. If they then choose to disclose prices and fees, that is their choice, just as it is the choice of others to buy derivatives.

4. Invent other alternatives and explain.

You Make Me Feel So Good!

Objectives

1. To introduce a different type of impression management and sharpen your awareness of impression management.

2. To promote self-awareness and diversity awareness by comparing your perceptions and ethics with those of others.

Introduction

This is a group discussion exercise designed to enhance your understanding of impression management. Personal interpretations are involved, so there are no strictly right or wrong answers.

Researchers recently have explored *beneficial* impression management, the practice of helping friends and significant others look good. This new line of inquiry combines the established OB topics of social support (discussed relative to stress in Chapter 16) and impression management (discussed in this chapter). In this exercise, we explore the practical and ethical implications of "strategically managing information to make your friends look good." We also consider impression management in general.

Instructions

This is a two-stage exercise: a private note-taking part, followed by a group discussion.

Stage 1 (5 to 7 minutes): Read the two scenarios below and then rate each one according to the following three scales:

How strongly do you approve of this tactic? (Mark an "X" for scenario 1 and an "O" for scenario 2.)
Disapprove   Approve
1 _____ 2 _____ 3 _____ 4 _____ 5 _____ 6 _____ 7

How effective is this tactic likely to be in the longer run?
Very ineffective   Highly effective
1 _____ 2 _____ 3 _____ 4 _____ 5 _____ 6 _____ 7

How ethical is this tactic?
Unethical   Ethical
1 _____ 2 _____ 3 _____ 4 _____ 5 _____ 6 _____ 7

Scenarios[75]

1. A high school ballplayer buoys the spirits of a teammate who struck out at a key moment by emphasizing the latter's game-winning hit last week and noting that even the greatest big-league hitters fall about 7 times out of 10. He may privately suspect his teammate has only mediocre baseball talent, but by putting the best side to his comments and not sharing his doubts, he makes the teammate feel better, builds his confidence so he can face tomorrow's game in a more optimistic frame of mind, and boosts the teammate's image in front of the other players who can hear his reassuring words.

2. At a party, a college student describes her roommate to a potential date she knows her friend finds extremely attractive. She stresses her friend's intelligence, attractiveness, and common interests but fails to mention that her friend can also be quite arrogant.

Stage 2 (10 to 15 minutes): Join two or three others in a discussion group and compare scores for both scenarios.

Are there big differences of opinion, or is there a general consensus? Next, briefly discuss these questions: How do *you* create a good first impression in *specific* situations? What goes through your mind when you see someone trying to make a good impression for him- or herself or for someone else? *Note:* Your instructor may ask you to pick a spokesperson to briefly report the results of your discussion to the class. If so, be sure to keep notes during the discussion.

Questions for Discussion

1. Is the whole practice of impression management a dishonest waste of time, or does it have a proper place in society? Why?

2. In what situations can impression management attempts backfire?

3. How do you know when someone has taken impression management too far?

4. How would you respond to a person who made this statement? "I never engage in impression management."

13 LEADERSHIP EFFECTIVENESS

What Does It Take to Be Effective?

inputs

PERSON FACTORS

ENVIRONMENTAL CHARACTERISTICS
Leadership

processes

INDIVIDUAL LEVEL

GROUP/TEAM LEVEL
Leadership

ORGANIZATIONAL LEVEL

outcomes

INDIVIDUAL LEVEL

GROUP/TEAM LEVEL

ORGANIZATIONAL LEVEL

MAJOR TOPICS I'LL LEARN AND QUESTIONS I SHOULD BE ABLE TO ANSWER

13.1 MAKING SENSE OF LEADERSHIP THEORIES

MAJOR QUESTION: *How does an integrated model of leadership help me become an effective leader?*

13.2 TRAIT THEORIES: DO LEADERS POSSESS UNIQUE TRAITS AND PERSONAL CHARACTERISTICS?

MAJOR QUESTION: *How can I use the takeaways from trait theories to improve my ability to lead?*

13.3 BEHAVIORAL STYLE THEORIES: WHICH LEADER BEHAVIORS DRIVE EFFECTIVENESS?

MAJOR QUESTION: *Do effective leaders behave in similar ways?*

13.4 SITUATIONAL THEORIES: DOES EFFECTIVE LEADERSHIP DEPEND ON THE SITUATION?

MAJOR QUESTION: *How do I know when to use a specific leader behavior?*

13.5 TRANSFORMATIONAL LEADERSHIP: HOW DO LEADERS TRANSFORM EMPLOYEES' MOTIVES?

MAJOR QUESTION: *How can I use transformational leadership when working with others?*

13.6 ADDITIONAL PERSPECTIVES ON LEADERSHIP

MAJOR QUESTION: *How can I improve the relationship with my boss?*

INTEGRATIVE FRAMEWORK FOR UNDERSTANDING AND APPLYING OB

This chapter focuses on leadership, a critical input and process variable within the Integrative Framework. As you might expect, you will learn that leadership affects a large number of outcomes across all three levels of OB. Try to keep track of the outcomes associated with leadership as you read this chapter.

© 2014 Angelo Kinicki and Mel Fugate. All rights reserved. Reproduction prohibited without permission of the authors.

winning at work

LEARNING TO LEAD

You will learn later in this chapter that leadership effectiveness is more a function of your behavior than a set of traits you are born with. This implies that leadership skills can be learned, a conclusion supported by research.[1]

learning because they focus on what can be learned from both success and failure, and they encourage us to seek input, guidance, and coaching from effective leaders. We encourage you to set learning goals associated with leadership development such as "learn how to run better meetings," "learn to improve my influence skills," or "learn to provide more effective feedback."

STEP 1: HOW CAN I BEGIN THE LEARNING PROCESS?

The learning process starts with self-awareness. You may recall that we discussed the importance of self-awareness in Chapter 1. This is why we have encouraged you to complete a host of Self-Assessments while reading this book. If you want to learn how to lead, the first step is to identify the type of leader behaviors you tend to use.[2] You will be given this opportunity in this chapter. You can use this knowledge to experiment with trying different styles of leadership in different situations. As one management consultant noted, "Finding one's style of leadership is a growing experience and one of introspection and personal development. Leadership is a trial-and-error encounter, and potential leaders must remember they will fail many times and make mistakes."[3]

STEP 2: CLAIM A LEADER IDENTITY

How we think of ourselves, which is referred to as our *identity,* affects our willingness to take on leadership roles. This means that it is important to see yourself as a leader. You can do this in two ways. The first is a direct approach in which you refer to yourself as a leader of some group, project, or task or you engage in stereotypical leadership acts. For example, if you are meeting with a student group to complete an assignment, you can walk into the meeting with an agenda and then start running the meeting. The second way consists of indirect claims of leadership such as sitting at the head of table for a meeting, mentioning your relationship with recognized leaders, or "dressing the part."[4]

STEP 3: DEVELOP A LEARNING GOAL ORIENTATION

In Chapter 6 we discussed the difference between learning and performance goals. Learning goals promote

STEP 4: EXPERIMENT AND SEEK FEEDBACK

Situational theories of leadership tell us that the effectiveness of specific leadership behaviors depends on the situation at hand. Try experimenting with the different leader behaviors discussed later in this chapter in different situations. Next, assess the impact of your experimental approach to leadership. This is feedback. We encourage you to seek feedback from those you trust and to reflect on what "could" be learned from your many educational and work experiences. A recent experimental study with students, for example, showed that leadership effectiveness increased over time for those students who consistently spent time reflecting on what "could" be learned from their experiences.[5]

FOR YOU   WHAT'S AHEAD IN THIS CHAPTER

Regardless of your role at work or in life, how well you understand leadership will let you be more effective. To a significant degree, leadership is available to all. Genetics and privilege neither guarantee leadership abilities, nor are they required. We all know individuals with all the "right" advantages who are ineffective leaders. We are about to help you navigate the many theories of leadership, appreciate how leadership traits and behaviors can be learned and developed, identify and apply styles of leadership, and finally understand how what you learn about leadership helps you to be a better follower and more effective at any level in an organization.

major question

MAJOR QUESTION

How does an integrated model of leadership help me become an effective leader?

THE BIGGER PICTURE

You're about to learn why leadership is both an input and process in the Integrative Framework for Understanding and Applying OB. Organizations can't really start up without leadership, nor can they sustain operations. You'll acquire an overall model of leadership that integrates the many leadership theories that have been proposed. Then you'll hone your understanding of effective leadership and parse the difference between leading and managing.

Leadership is defined as "a process whereby an individual influences a group of individuals to achieve a common goal."[6] Note that you do not need to have a formal position of authority to be a leader. Anyone who exerts influence over others in the pursuit of organizationally relevant matters is a leader.

This definition underscores the broad impact that leaders have on organizations. Consider the following statistics. Gallup research has shown that employee disengagement

Do singers exert leadership when they perform? Would a group of well-known singers like this exert more influence than one singer performing alone? Why or why not?

in the United States costs $450 to $550 billion per year, and ineffective leadership is a key driver of disengagement.[7] Researchers also have estimated that approximately 50 percent of all managers around the world are incompetent or ineffective. The cost of this incompetence is greater the higher up you go in an organization. For example, one study estimated that the cost of a failed senior leader is $2.7 million.[8]

From a scientific perspective, the topic of leadership has generated more OB-related research than any other topic except motivation. This is why OB scholars have developed a great number of theories to help guide managers to improve their leadership effectiveness.

We recognize that there are far too many leadership theories to cover in this one chapter. So we have created a model that integrates the major leadership theories and we use it to structure the content covered in this chapter. We follow that by focusing on theories that have received some level of research support.

An Integrated Model of Leadership

Figure 13.1 presents an integrated model of leadership. Starting at the far right of the model, you see that leadership effectiveness is the outcome we are trying to explain in this chapter. Note that effective leadership is influenced by four types of leadership behavior: task-oriented, relationship-oriented, passive, and transformational. Effective leadership also is affected by a combination of task-oriented traits and interpersonal attributes. Recall from Chapter 3 that individual differences significantly impact performance, and they vary from relatively fixed (intelligence) to somewhat flexible (self-efficacy).

Moreover, Figure 13.1 represents how demographic characteristics such as gender and age, task-oriented traits, and interpersonal attributes influence an individual's use of leader behaviors. The final component (situational factors) influencing leadership effectiveness involves our earlier discussions of contingency theory. That is, effective leadership requires using the "right" behavior at the "right" time.

What Is Effective Leadership?

The answer to this question is more complicated than you might think because leadership effectiveness is more than simply gaining commitment with our influence attempts. Assessing leadership effectiveness entails consideration of three issues.[9]

FIGURE 13.1   AN INTEGRATED MODEL OF LEADERSHIP

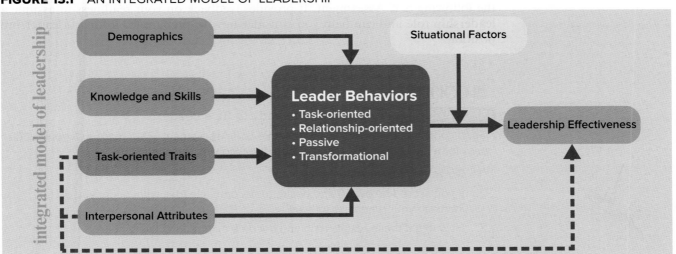

Issue 1. The Content of the Evaluation: "What Criteria Are Being Used to Assess Effectiveness?" Effectiveness depends on what the evaluator wants. For example, the content of effectiveness can entail criteria such as task performance, quality, customer satisfaction, sales, employee job satisfaction, turnover, or an overall evaluation of leadership effectiveness.

Issue 2. The Level of the Evaluation: "At What Level Are the Criteria Being Measured?" As you know from the Integrative Framework, effectiveness can be measured at the individual, group, or organizational levels. Evaluations at different levels also can produce difference conclusions. For example, sales performance may be a good measure of performance for one store location, but not across a geographic region.

Issue 3. The Rater's Perspective: "Who Is Doing the Evaluation?" Assessments of effective leadership can be made by different people or groups, and their view of effective leadership may vary.[10] For example, a manager may be perceived as effective by a direct report, but not by the entire work unit or the boss.

What Is the Difference between Leading and Managing?

Bernard Bass, a leadership expert, concluded that "leaders manage and managers lead, but the two activities are not synonymous."[11] Broadly speaking, managers typically perform functions associated with planning, investigating, organizing, and control, and leaders deal with the interpersonal aspects of a manager's job. Leaders inspire others, provide emotional support, and try to get employees to rally around a common goal. Leaders also play a key role in creating a vision and strategic plan for an organization. Managers, in turn, are charged with implementing the vision and strategic plan. There are several conclusions to be drawn from this discussion.

First, good leaders are not necessarily good managers, and good managers are not necessarily good leaders. Second, effective leadership requires effective managerial skills at some level. For example, JetBlue ex-CEO David Neeleman was let go after an ice storm revealed managerial deficiencies in how he handled the situation.[12] In contrast, both Tim Cook, CEO of Apple, and Alan Mulally, CEO of Ford Motor Company, are recognized for the use of managerial skills when implementing corporate strategies.[13]

Do you want to lead others, or understand what makes a leader tick? Then take the following Self-Assessment. It provides feedback on your readiness to assume a leadership role and can help you consider how to prepare for a formal leadership position.

---

connect

SELF-ASSESSMENT 13.1 Am I Ready to Be a Leader?

Go to connect.mheducation.com and take Self-Assessment 13.1. It measures your readiness for a leadership role. Then answer the following questions:

1. Do you agree with your results?
2. If you scored below 60 and desire to become a leader, what might you do to increase your readiness to lead?
3. How might these results help you become a more effective leader?

in the United States costs \$450 to \$550 billion per year, and ineffective leadership is a key driver of disengagement.[7] Researchers also have estimated that approximately 50 percent of all managers around the world are incompetent or ineffective. The cost of this incompetence is greater the higher up you go in an organization. For example, one study estimated that the cost of a failed senior leader is \$2.7 million.[8]

From a scientific perspective, the topic of leadership has generated more OB-related research than any other topic except motivation. This is why OB scholars have developed a great number of theories to help guide managers to improve their leadership effectiveness.

We recognize that there are far too many leadership theories to cover in this one chapter. So we have created a model that integrates the major leadership theories and we use it to structure the content covered in this chapter. We follow that by focusing on theories that have received some level of research support.

An Integrated Model of Leadership

Figure 13.1 presents an integrated model of leadership. Starting at the far right of the model, you see that leadership effectiveness is the outcome we are trying to explain in this chapter. Note that effective leadership is influenced by four types of leadership behavior: task-oriented, relationship-oriented, passive, and transformational. Effective leadership also is affected by a combination of task-oriented traits and interpersonal attributes. Recall from Chapter 3 that individual differences significantly impact performance, and they vary from relatively fixed (intelligence) to somewhat flexible (self-efficacy).

Moreover, Figure 13.1 represents how demographic characteristics such as gender and age, task-oriented traits, and interpersonal attributes influence an individual's use of leader behaviors. The final component (situational factors) influencing leadership effectiveness involves our earlier discussions of contingency theory. That is, effective leadership requires using the "right" behavior at the "right" time.

What Is Effective Leadership?

The answer to this question is more complicated than you might think because leadership effectiveness is more than simply gaining commitment with our influence attempts. Assessing leadership effectiveness entails consideration of three issues.[9]

FIGURE 13.1 AN INTEGRATED MODEL OF LEADERSHIP

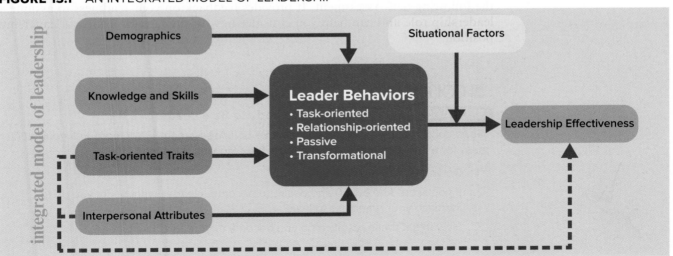

Issue 1. The Content of the Evaluation: "What Criteria Are Being Used to Assess Effectiveness?" Effectiveness depends on what the evaluator wants. For example, the content of effectiveness can entail criteria such as task performance, quality, customer satisfaction, sales, employee job satisfaction, turnover, or an overall evaluation of leadership effectiveness.

Issue 2. The Level of the Evaluation: "At What Level Are the Criteria Being Measured?" As you know from the Integrative Framework, effectiveness can be measured at the individual, group, or organizational levels. Evaluations at different levels also can produce difference conclusions. For example, sales performance may be a good measure of performance for one store location, but not across a geographic region.

Issue 3. The Rater's Perspective: "Who Is Doing the Evaluation?" Assessments of effective leadership can be made by different people or groups, and their view of effective leadership may vary.[10] For example, a manager may be perceived as effective by a direct report, but not by the entire work unit or the boss.

What Is the Difference between Leading and Managing?

Bernard Bass, a leadership expert, concluded that "leaders manage and managers lead, but the two activities are not synonymous."[11] Broadly speaking, managers typically perform functions associated with planning, investigating, organizing, and control, and leaders deal with the interpersonal aspects of a manager's job. Leaders inspire others, provide emotional support, and try to get employees to rally around a common goal. Leaders also play a key role in creating a vision and strategic plan for an organization. Managers, in turn, are charged with implementing the vision and strategic plan. There are several conclusions to be drawn from this discussion.

First, good leaders are not necessarily good managers, and good managers are not necessarily good leaders. Second, effective leadership requires effective managerial skills at some level. For example, JetBlue ex-CEO David Neeleman was let go after an ice storm revealed managerial deficiencies in how he handled the situation.[12] In contrast, both Tim Cook, CEO of Apple, and Alan Mulally, CEO of Ford Motor Company, are recognized for the use of managerial skills when implementing corporate strategies.[13]

Do you want to lead others, or understand what makes a leader tick? Then take the following Self-Assessment. It provides feedback on your readiness to assume a leadership role and can help you consider how to prepare for a formal leadership position.

connect

SELF-ASSESSMENT 13.1 Am I Ready to Be a Leader?

Go to connect.mheducation.com and take Self-Assessment 13.1. It measures your readiness for a leadership role. Then answer the following questions:

1. Do you agree with your results?
2. If you scored below 60 and desire to become a leader, what might you do to increase your readiness to lead?
3. How might these results help you become a more effective leader?

MAJOR QUESTION

How can I use the takeaways from trait theories to improve my ability to lead?

THE BIGGER PICTURE

You'll see in the Integrative Framework that just as skills and abilities (as person factors) were an input in Chapter 3, leadership traits are an input (as environmental characteristics). Trait theories attempt to identify personal characteristics that differentiate effective leaders from followers. After identifying key traits established by research, we discuss the importance of gender and perceptions in determining what it takes to be an effective leader.

Trait theory is the successor to what was called the "great man" theory of leadership. This approach was based on the assumption that leaders such as Abraham Lincoln, Martin Luther King Jr., or Mark Zuckerberg were born with some inborn ability to lead. In contrast, trait theorists believed that leadership traits were not innate, but could be developed through experience and learning. **The *trait approach* attempts to identify personality characteristics or interpersonal attributes that can be used to differentiate leaders from followers.**

What Are the Core Traits Possessed by Leaders?

Early research demonstrated that five traits tended to differentiate leaders from average followers:

1. Intelligence.
2. Dominance.
3. Self-confidence.
4. Level of energy and activity.
5. Task-relevant knowledge.[14]

Over the years, researchers and consultants began to consider more and more traits, making it very difficult to determine the traits that truly differentiate leaders from followers. This led to crazy claims like effective leaders are taller, bald, and wear glasses. While some leaders may possess these characteristics, these are not generalized characteristics that managers should consider when hiring or promoting people to leadership positions.

If you believe in making conclusions based on science, then OB researchers have come up with an answer to the question at hand by using a statistical technique called meta-analysis. A meta-analysis is a statistical procedure that effectively computes an average relationship between two variables. Table 13.1 is a summary of what we know from this research. Instead of the five basic traits from early research (see above), note the emphasis on task-orientation and the expansion into interpersonal attributes.[15]

TABLE 13.1 KEY TASK-ORIENTED TRAITS AND INTERPERSONAL ATTRIBUTES

POSITIVE TASK-ORIENTED TRAITS	POSITIVE/NEGATIVE INTERPERSONAL ATTRIBUTES
• Intelligence	• Extraversion (+)
• Conscientiousness	• Agreeableness (+)
• Open to Experience	• Communication Skills (+)
• Emotional Stability	• Emotional Intelligence (+)
	• Narcissism (−)
	• Machiavellianism (−)
	• Psychopathy (−)

All of the traits and interpersonal attributes listed in Table 13.1 have been defined elsewhere in this book except for the "dark side" traits of narcissism, Machiavellianism, and psychopathy.[16] Let's consider them now.

- ***Narcissism*** **is defined as having "a self-centered perspective, feelings of superiority, and a drive for personal power and glory."**[17] Individuals with this trait have inflated views of themselves, have fantasies of being in control of everything, and like to attract the admiration of others. Although narcissistic leaders have an upside of being more charismatic and passionate, they also were found to promote counterproductive work behaviors from others[18]—recall our discussion in Chapter 2.

- ***Machiavellianism*** **entails the use of manipulation, a cynical view of human nature (e.g., all people lie to get what they want), and a moral code that puts results over principles (e.g., you have to cheat to get ahead).** It's not surprising that this characteristic is associated with counterproductive behavior.

- ***Psychopathy*** **is characterized as a lack of concern for others, impulsive behavior, and a lack of remorse or guilt when one's actions harm others.** It's no surprise that this type of person is toxic at work.

There are two more conclusions to note about Table 13.1. First, personality is more important than intelligence when selecting leaders.[19] Second, displaying the "dark side" traits tends to result in career derailment—being demoted or fired.[20] You definitely want to avoid these traits.

Margaret Thatcher, prime minister of the United Kingdom from 1979 to 1990, served three terms. She was the longest-serving prime minister of the previous century. Which of the positive traits were likely possessed by Margaret Thatcher?

Pol Pot (on the left) was the communist dictator of Cambodia from 1975 to 1979, whose programs and policies led to the deaths of between 2 and 3 million people, roughly a quarter of the Cambodian population. Do you think Pol Pot possessed any of the "dark side" traits?

What Is the Role of Emotional Intelligence in Leadership Effectiveness?

We discussed emotional intelligence in Chapter 3. Recall that *emotional intelligence* is the ability to manage oneself and one's relationships in mature and constructive ways: The components of emotional intelligence are shown in Table 3.6. Given that leadership is an influence process between leaders and followers, it should come as no surprise that emotional intelligence is predicted to be associated with leadership effectiveness. While Daniel Goleman, the psychologist who popularized the concept, and other consultants contend that they have evidence to support this conclusion,[21] it has not been published in scientific journals. That said, scientific evidence supports two conclusions:[22]

1. **Emotional intelligence is an input to transformational leadership.** In other words, emotional intelligence helps managers to effectively enact the behaviors associated with transformational leadership, which is discussed later in this chapter.

2. **Emotional intelligence has a small, positive, and significant association with leadership effectiveness.** This suggests that emotional intelligence will help you to lead more effectively, but it is not the secret elixir of leadership effectiveness as suggested by Daniel Goleman.

Do Women and Men Display the Same Leadership Traits?

The increase of women in the workforce has generated much interest in understanding the similarities and differences in female and male leaders. Research reveals the following four conclusions:

1. Men and women were seen as displaying more task and social leadership, respectively.[23]

2. Women used a more democratic or participative style than men, and men used a more autocratic and directive style than women.[24]

3. Men and women were equally assertive.[25]

4. Women executives, when rated by their peers, managers, and direct reports, scored higher than their male counterparts on a variety of effectiveness criteria.[26]

Lynn Tilton, CEO of Patriarch Partners, possesses many of the positive leadership traits identified by researchers. Her holding company manages 75 companies with over $8 billion in revenues.

TABLE 13.2 FOUR BASIC SKILLS FOR LEADERS

WHAT LEADERS NEED		AND WHY
Cognitive abilities to identify problems and causes for rapidly changing situations.		Leaders must sometimes derive effective solutions in short time spans with limited information.
Interpersonal skills to influence and persuade others.	skills for leaders	Leaders need to work well with diverse people.
Business skills to maximize the use of organizational assets.		Leaders increasingly need such skills as they advance up through an organization.
Strategic skills to craft an organization's mission, vision, strategies, and implementation plans.		Obviously, this latter skill-set matters most for individuals at the top ranks in an organization.

SOURCE: Adapted from T. V. Mumford, M. A. Campion, and F. P. Morgeson, "Leadership Skills Strataplex: Leadership Skill Requirements across Organizational Levels," *Leadership Quarterly*, 2007, 154–166.

How Important Are Knowledge and Skills?

Extremely! A team of researchers identified four basic skills needed by leaders. See Table 13.2.

Do Perceptions Matter?

The answer is yes according to what is called implicit leadership theory. **Implicit leadership theory is based on the idea that people have beliefs about how leaders should behave and what they should do for their followers.** These beliefs are summarized in what is called a *leadership prototype*.[27] **A *leadership prototype* is a mental representation of the traits and behaviors that people believe are possessed by leaders.** It is important to understand the content of leadership prototypes because we tend to perceive that someone is a leader when he or she exhibits traits or behaviors that are consistent with our prototypes. Although past research demonstrated that people were perceived as leaders when they exhibited masculine-oriented traits and behaviors associated with masculinity, and dominance,[28] more recent studies showed an emphasis on more feminine traits and styles that emphasize empowerment, fairness, compassion, and supportiveness.[29] This change in prototypes bodes well for reducing bias and discrimination against women in leadership roles.

What Are the Takeaways from Trait Theory?

There are four.

1. **We can no longer afford to ignore the implications of leadership traits.** Traits play a central role in how we perceive leaders, and they ultimately impact leadership effectiveness. For example, the Cardiac Rhythm Disease Management Group within Medtronic Inc. identified nine types of traits and skills (e.g., giving clear performance feedback and being courageous) that were necessary for leaders. The company then designed a leadership development program to help its employees learn and apply these traits.[30]

   More and more companies are using management development programs to build a pipeline of leadership talent. This is a particularly important recommendation in light of results from corporate surveys showing that the majority of companies do not possess adequate leadership talent to fill future needs.

2. **The list of positive traits and "dark side" traits shown in Table 13.1 provides guidance regarding the leadership traits you should attempt to cultivate and avoid if you want to assume a leadership role in the future.** Personality tests, which were

transactional leadership is based on using rewards and punishment to drive motivation and performance.

> **EXAMPLE**   Consider how Stephen Greer, founder of Hartwell Pacific, a scrap metal recycling business in Asia, used transactional leadership to combat several million dollars in fraud and theft from his employees in Mexico and his operations in Asia.
>
> For Hartwell Pacific, the biggest strain was a lack of control systems. Greer was so focused on new markets that he glossed over niceties like accounting procedures, inventory audits, and reference checks for new hires. . . .
>
> When he finally realized the extent of the fraud in his nascent empire, Greer pulled back, eventually liquidating the operation in Mexico. He also instituted a system of close oversight. He appointed local finance managers who reported directly to headquarters, creating checks and balances on local general managers. He started requiring three signatories for all company checks. He installed metal detectors to prevent theft. Once a month, the local managers flew to headquarters, where they compared revenues, costs, and overall performance. If one plant seemed to be overpaying for supplies, or if revenues seemed out of line with inventory, Greer began asking hard questions—ones he should have been asking all along.[37]

Greer's use of transactional leadership helped to correct the fraud and theft problems and the company ultimately experienced profitable growth. Research supports a positive association between transactional leadership and leader effectiveness and group performance.[38]

Nick Saban, head football coach at the University of Alabama, also uses task-oriented leadership with his players (see Example box). The success of his approach is confirmed by winning a national championship at Louisiana State University and two with the University of Alabama.

EXAMPLE   Nick Saban Uses Task-Oriented Leadership to Achieve National Championships in Football

Nick Saban has lots of energy and he puts in long hours as a head coach. He spent so much time traveling to evaluate high school players that the NCAA came up with the "Saban rule." It prevents college coaches from traveling to high schools in the spring to watch players. More importantly, Saban is known for what people in Tuscaloosa, Alabama, call "the process." It is very regimented and detailed.

HOW DOES "THE PROCESS" WORK?   He "defines expectations for his players athletically, academically, and personally." He also "sets expectations so that everyone understands what he wants, and then he can pull back." For example, he wants to know players' workout routines for each day, including the amount of weight they can bench press. "If a lineman is above his target body-fat percentage, Saban wants to know what the staff is doing to fix it."

Alabama head coach Nick Saban holds the Coaches Trophy after the 2013 BCS National Championship college football game against Notre Dame in Miami.

Saban also is very supportive to his staff. Once they make a game plan, Saban leaves its execution to the coaching staff. He also takes ownership for mistakes or losses. Defensive coordinator Kirby Smart said that Saban "has always taken the blame and never pointed at a coach or a person or a kid. And I think that helps the whole organization. It gives you confidence before the game that 'Hey, we've got a plan. We've outworked everybody at this point. Let's go execute it and do it.'"

Saban has hired trainers to coach him and the staff. He believes that you only get better by focusing on the small things that make a difference on game day. For example, he brought in a martial arts expert to teach the players martial arts because he thought it would help players gain leverage when blocking. He also added Pilates to the team's workout after he experienced it himself.[39]

YOUR THOUGHTS?

1. Do you think Saban's "process" goes too far in terms of its demands on college football players?
2. What aspects of Saban's approach do you see as most applicable in a business organization?
3. What aspects would you rather see modified or abandoned in a business organization?

Relationship-Oriented Leader Behavior

The purpose of relationship-oriented leadership is to enhance employees' skills and to create positive work relationships among coworkers and between the leader and his/her employees. Examples include behaviors that are supporting (e.g., helping people deal with stressful events), developmental (e.g., providing career advice or assigning people to assignments that allow them to learn), appreciative (e.g., providing positive praise or an award), and empowering (e.g., allowing employees to make decisions).[40]

OB researchers have primarily investigated the impact of three relationship-oriented behaviors:

- Consideration
- Empowerment
- Servant-leadership

Consideration   As with initiating structure, this type of leader behavior was identified by researchers at The Ohio State University. **Consideration involves leader behavior associated with creating mutual respect or trust and focuses on a concern for group members' needs and desires.** This is an important type of behavior to use in addition to task leadership because it promotes social interactions and identification with the team and leader. In fact, researchers at Ohio State initially proposed that a high–initiating structure, high-consideration style would be the one best style of leadership. Overall, research results did not support this prediction. On its own, however, considerate leader behavior has a moderately strong positive relationship with measures of leadership effectiveness.[41]

What do you think is your relative style of using initiating structure and consideration when interacting with student peers or with work colleagues? Which of these two types of leader behavior is a strength, opportunity, or weakness for you? You can answer these questions by taking the following Self-Assessment.

connect

SELF-ASSESSMENT 13.2   **My Task- and Relationship-Oriented Leadership Style**

This Assessment measures the extent to which you use initiating structure and consideration when working with others at school or work. Go to connect.mheducation.com and take Self-Assessment 13.2 and then answer the following questions.

1. Are you better at using initiating structure or consideration?
2. Based on identifying your two lowest scores for each type of leader behavior, suggest ways to improve your leader behavior.

Empowering Leadership   We need to define two terms in order to explain the positive effects of empowering leadership. **Empowering leadership represents the extent to which a leader creates perceptions of psychological empowerment in others. Psychological empowerment, which reflects employees' belief that they have control over their work,** is expected to drive intrinsic motivation.[42] Let's consider how leaders can create psychological empowerment.

Leaders increase psychological empowerment by engaging in behaviors that enhance perceptions of meaning, self-determination or choice, competence, and impact.

- **Leading for meaningfulness.** Managers lead for meaningfulness by *inspiring* their employees and *modeling* desired behaviors. One way to do this is by helping employees to identify their passions at work and creating an exciting organizational vision employees feel connected to. For example, employees at Millennium are highly motivated by the drug maker's vision—to cure cancer.[43]

- **Leading for self-determination or choice.** Managers lead for choice by *delegating* meaningful assignments and tasks. This is how Gail Evans, an executive vice president at Atlanta-based CNN, feels about leading for choice. Evans said that "delegating is essential. If you refuse to let your staff handle their own projects, you're jeopardizing their advancement—because they aren't learning new skills and adding successes to their resume—and you're wasting your precious hours doing someone else's work."[44]

- **Leading for competence.** This involves *supporting* and *coaching* employees. Managers first need to make sure employees have the knowledge needed to successfully perform their jobs. Deficiencies can be handled through training and mentoring. Providing positive feedback and sincere recognition can also be coupled with the assignment of a challenging task to fuel employees' intrinsic motivation.

- **Leading for progress.** Managers lead for progress by *monitoring* and *rewarding* others. We thoroughly discussed how best to do this in Chapter 6.

Research supports the use of empowering leadership. Empowering leadership fosters psychological empowerment, which in turn impacts outcomes like intrinsic motivation, creativity, and performance.[45]

Servant-Leadership   The term *servant-leadership* was coined by Robert Greenleaf in 1970. Greenleaf believed that great leaders act as servants, making the needs of others, including employees, customers, and community, their first priority. **Servant-leadership focuses on increased service to others rather than to oneself.**[46] Because the focus of servant-leadership is serving others over self-interest, servant-leaders are less likely to engage in self-serving behaviors that hurt others. Embedding servant-leadership into an organization's culture requires actions as well as words.

> **EXAMPLE**   Afni, Inc., a global customer contact services provider, launched a leadership development program aimed at enhancing both servant and empowering leadership. Heather Cushing, Senior Manager of Leadership Development, said the goal of the program is to help managers "exhibit an attitude of servant-hood, caring for the coaching and development of each level reporting up through them." Afni wants managers to empower "others to reach their full potential, while also inspiring teamwork and loyalty and improving employee engagement."[47]

Servant-leadership is expected to promote leadership effectiveness because it focuses on providing support and growth opportunities to employees. As you may recall from our discussion of perceived organizational support (POS) in Chapter 2, people generally reciprocate with increased effort aimed at collective performance when they feel supported. Servant-leaders have the characteristics listed in Table 13.3.

TABLE 13.3 CHARACTERISTICS OF THE SERVANT-LEADER

SERVANT-LEADERSHIP CHARACTERISTICS	DESCRIPTION
1. Listening	Servant-leaders focus on listening to identify and clarify the needs and desires of a group.
2. Empathy	Servant-leaders try to empathize with others' feelings and emotions. An individual's good intentions are assumed even when he or she performs poorly.
3. Healing	Servant-leaders strive to make themselves and others whole in the face of failure or suffering.
4. Awareness	Servant-leaders are very self-aware of their strengths and limitations.
5. Persuasion	Servant-leaders rely more on persuasion than positional authority when making decisions and trying to influence others.
6. Conceptualization	Servant-leaders take the time and effort to develop broader-based conceptual thinking. Servant-leaders seek an appropriate balance between a short-term, day-to-day focus and a long-term, conceptual orientation.
7. Foresight	Servant-leaders have the ability to foresee future outcomes associated with a current course of action or situation.
8. Stewardship	Servant-leaders assume that they are stewards of the people and resources they manage.
9. Commitment to the growth of people	Servant-leaders commit to people beyond their immediate work role. They foster an environment that encourages personal, professional, and spiritual growth.
10. Building community	Servant-leaders strive to create a sense of community both within and outside the work organization.

SOURCE: Adapted from L. C. Spears, "Introduction: Servant-Leadership and the Greenleaf Legacy," in *Reflections on Leadership: How Robert K. Greenleaf's Theory of Servant-Leadership Influenced Today's Top Management Thinkers*, ed. L. C. Spears (New York: Wiley, 1995), 1–14.

Does your current manager display the traits shown in Table 13.3? If yes, then you are more likely to be happier, more productive, more creative, and more willing to go above and beyond your role. This is precisely what researchers have uncovered.[48] The following Self-Assessment measures the extent to which a current or former manager uses servant-leadership behaviors. Results from the Assessment will enhance your understanding of what it takes to really be a servant-leader.

connect

SELF-ASSESSMENT 13.3 Is My Boss a Servant-Leader?

Go to connect.mheducation.com and complete Self-Assessment 13.3 to evaluate your manager's status as being a servant-leader. Then do the following:

1. If you were able to give your boss feedback based on these results, what would you recommend?

2. To what extent do you think you engage in servant-leader behaviors?

3. How might you demonstrate more servant-leadership in your teams at work or school? Be specific.

Sam Palmisano, former chairman and CEO of IBM, is a good example of a servant-leader. Here is what he had to say about his approach to leadership:

> Over the course of my IBM career I've observed many CEOs, heads of state, and others in positions of great authority. I've noticed that some of the most effective leaders don't make themselves the center of attention. They are respectful. They listen. This is an appealing personal quality, but it's also an effective leadership attribute. Their selflessness makes the people around them comfortable. People open up, speak up, contribute. They give those leaders their very best.[49]

Research on servant-leadership is relatively new. We expect that future results will continue to confirm the value of using this leader behavior to promote individual, group, and organizational flourishing. In the meantime, we encourage you to practice this style of leadership.

TAKE-AWAY APPLICATION—TAAP

Using Relationship-Oriented Leadership

1. Think about the group projects you currently are working on. Now describe how you might attempt to use both empowering leadership and servant-leadership in team meetings.

2. How would you evaluate whether or not these leader behaviors are effective?

Passive Leadership

Passive leadership is best illustrated by what OB scholars call *laissez-faire* leadership. **Laissez-faire leadership represents a general failure to take responsibility for leading.** Examples of laissez-faire leadership include avoiding conflict, failing to provide coaching on difficult assignments, failing to assist employees in setting performance goals, failing to give performance feedback, failing to address issues associated with bullying, or being so hands-off that employees have little idea about what they should be doing. Given these examples, you should not be surprised to learn that laissez-faire leadership had a greater negative impact on employees' perceptions of leadership effectiveness than did the unique positive contributions from positive leadership traits, initiating structure, transactional leadership, consideration, and transformational leadership.[50]

What does this suggest? Laissez-faire leadership can be demoralizing and it makes employees feel unsupported. We thus suggest that organizations should use employee feedback to identify managers who lead with this style. Once identified, people can be trained to use behaviors associated with other forms of task and relational leadership. All told, however, if a person in a leadership role is not willing to perform the role and responsibilities of being a leader, then he or she should be removed from the position.

What gender do you think engages in more laissez-faire leadership? A meta-analysis revealed that men displayed more of this type of leadership than women.[51]

What Are the Takeaways from Behavioral Styles Theory?

There are three.

1. **Leader behavior is more important than leader traits when it comes to effectiveness.**[52] Our mantra for leaders is "every behavior matters."

2. **Leader behaviors can be systematically improved and developed.**[53] Organizations are encouraged to continue to invest in leadership development programs.

3. **There is no one best style of leadership.** The effectiveness of a particular leadership style depends on the situation at hand.

MAJOR QUESTION

How Do I Know When to Use a Specific Leader Behavior?

THE BIGGER PICTURE

If you're inclined to think about which leadership approach a particular situation suggests, you are already sympathetic to situational leadership. Proponents believe that effective leadership depends on the situation. Situational leadership attempts to help managers determine when they should use particular types of leader behavior. While many such theories have been proposed, only two have received extensive research examination: Fred Fiedler's *contingency model* and Robert House's *path-goal theory*. We conclude by discussing the application of situational theories.

Situational leadership theories grew out of the realization that there is not a single "best" style of leadership. **Situational theories propose that the effectiveness of a particular style of leader behavior depends on the situation.** As situations change, different styles become appropriate. The concept makes a lot of common sense. As you will learn, however, the application of situational theories is more complicated than it appears.

Let's examine two alternative situational theories: Fiedler's contingency model and House's path-goal theory.

Fiedler's Contingency Model

The oldest situational theory was developed by Fred Fiedler. He labeled the model **contingency theory because it is based on the premise that a leader's effectiveness is contingent on the extent to which a leader's style fits or matches characteristics of the situation at hand.** To understand how this matching process works, we need to consider the key leadership styles identified by Fiedler and the situational variables that constitute what Fiedler labels *situational control*.[54]

Two Leadership Styles: Task Orientation versus Relationship Orientation
Fiedler believed that leaders have one dominant or natural leadership style that is resistant to change. A leader's style is described as either task-motivated or relationship-motivated. You are familiar with these two orientations from our previous discussion in this chapter. Task-motivated leaders focus on accomplishing goals, whereas relationship-motivated leaders are more interested in developing positive relationships with followers. To determine an individual's leadership style, Fiedler developed the least preferred coworker (LPC) scale. The scale asks you to evaluate a coworker you least enjoy working with on 16 pairs of opposite characteristics (such as friendly/unfriendly or tense/relaxed). High scores on the survey (high LPC) indicate that an individual is relationship-motivated, and low scores (low LPC) suggest a task-motivated style.

Three Dimensions of Situational Control Situational control refers to the amount of control and influence the leader has in her or his immediate work environment. There are three dimensions of situational control: *leader–member relations, task structure,* and *position power.*

- **Leader–member relations** reflect the extent to which the leader has the support, loyalty, and trust of the work group. This dimension is the most important component of situational control. Good leader–member relations suggest that the leader can depend on the group, thus ensuring that the work group will try to meet the leader's goals and objectives.

- **Task structure** is concerned with the amount of structure contained within tasks performed by the work group. For example, a managerial job contains less structure than that of a bank teller. Because structured tasks have guidelines for how the job should be completed, the leader has more control and influence over employees performing such tasks. This dimension is the second most important component of situational control.

- **Position power** refers to the degree to which the leader has formal power to reward, punish, or otherwise obtain compliance from employees.

The dimensions of situational control vary independently, forming eight combinations of situational control that vary from high to low (see Figure 13.2). High control implies that the leader's decisions will produce predictable results because the leader has the ability to influence work outcomes. Low control implies that the leader's decisions may not influence work outcomes because the leader has very little influence.

When Is Each Style Most Effective? Neither leadership style is effective in all situations. Figure 13.2 illustrates when task- and relationship-motivated leadership are expected to be most effective.

- **When task-oriented leadership is best.** Task-oriented leadership should be most effective in either *high-control* (situations I–III in Figure 13.2) or *low-control* situations (situation VIII).

FIGURE 13.2 REPRESENTATION OF FIEDLER'S CONTINGENCY MODEL

Fiedler's contingency model	Situational Control	High-Control Situations			Moderate-Control Situations				Low-Control Situations
	Leader–Member Relations	Good	Good	Good	Good	Poor	Poor	Poor	Poor
	Task Structure	High	High	Low	Low	High	High	Low	Low
	Position Power	Strong	Weak	Strong	Weak	Strong	Weak	Strong	Weak
	Situation	I	II	III	IV	V	VI	VII	VIII
	Optimal Leadership Style	Task-Motivated Leadership			Relationsip-Motivated Leadership				Task-Motivated Leadership

SOURCE: Adapted from F. E. Fiedler, "Situational Control and a Dynamic Theory of Leadership," in *Managerial Control and Organizational Democracy,* ed. B. King, S. Streufert, and F. E. Fiedler (New York: Wiley, 1978), 114.

HIGH-CONTROL EXAMPLE Suppose you are taking the lead in preparing a 10-page report for a class project that requires extensive use of Excel. In this situation, you have strong influence across a majority of the dimensions, as shown:

Leader–member relations: Good. Your teammates like you and they realize that you have the most experience with using Excel.

Task structure: High. You know the professor's expectations and you have the skills needed to crunch numbers with Excel.

Position power: Weak. You do not have the authority to evaluate your teammates and dole out rewards or punishment.

As shown in Figure 13.2, this high-control situation calls for a task-oriented style of leadership.

LOW-CONTROL EXAMPLE Suppose as before that you are working on the same class project preparing a 10-page report for a class project requiring extensive use of Excel. This time, however, you have less control:

Leader–member relations: Poor. Your teammates perceive that you use "dark side" leadership traits,

Task structure: Low. The professor did not clearly explain the performance expectations for the project.

Position power: Weak. You do not have the authority to evaluate your teammates and dole our rewards or punishment.

As shown in Figure 13.2, this low-control situation also calls for task-oriented leadership.

- **When relationship-oriented leadership is best.** Relationship-oriented leadership should be most effective in situations of *moderate control* (situations IV–VII in Figure 13.2).

MODERATE-CONTROL EXAMPLE Again, suppose you are working on the same class project preparing a 10-page report for a class project that requires extensive use of Excel. This time, you have a moderate amount of control:

Leader–member relations: Good. Your teammates like you and they realize that you have the most experience with using Excel.

Task structure: Low. The professor did not clearly explain the performance expectations for the project.

Position power: Weak. You do not have the authority to evaluate your teammates and dole our rewards or punishment.

As shown in Figure 13.2, this moderate-control situation calls for a relationship-oriented leadership style.

What should you do if your dominant leadership style—task or relationship—does not match the situation? Then, Fiedler suggests, it is better to move the leader to a more suitable situation than to try to change the leader's leadership style. This response is contrary to the behavioral styles approach, which assumes that we can learn different leader behaviors. Fiedler believes that people cannot change their leadership style. Do you agree with this proposition?

Takeaways from Fiedler's Model Although research provides only partial support for this model and the LPC scale,[55] there are three key takeaways from Fiedler's model.

1. *Leadership effectiveness goes beyond traits and behaviors.* The fit between a leader's style and the situational demands is important. As a case in point, a team of researchers examined the effectiveness of 20 senior-level managers from GE who left the company for other positions. The researchers concluded that "not

all managers are equally suited to all business situations. The strategic skills required to control costs in the face of fierce competition are not the same as those required to improve the top line in a rapidly growing business or balance investment against cash flow to survive in a highly cyclical business. . . . We weren't surprised to find that relevant industry experience had a positive impact on performance in a new job, but that these skills didn't transfer to a new industry."[56]

2. ***Organizations should attempt to hire or promote people whose leadership styles fit or match situational demands.*** For example, Bill Marriott, Marriott's executive chairman, decided to select the first nonfamily CEO because he felt that his son John was not suited for the position despite spending his entire life working his way up through the company (see Problem-Solving Application). If a manager is failing in a certain context, management should consider moving the individual to another situation. Don't give up on a high-potential person simply because he or she was a poor leader in one context.

3. ***Leaders need to modify their style to fit a situation.*** For example, a recent study found that too much task-oriented leader behavior was viewed negatively by employees whereas excessive relationship leadership was not. Leaders need to experiment with finding the "right" amount of leadership to exhibit in different situations.[57]

solving application

problem

Bill Marriott Selects Arne Sorenson to Be CEO over His Son

Bill Marriot became CEO of the company at the age of 32. He was selected by his father after working in the company since he was 14. Under his leadership, the company grew from $85 million in 1964 to $11.8 billion in 2012.

Bill's Dilemma After suffering a heart attack at the age of 57, Bill Marriott began to consider a succession plan. He wanted one of his four children to take over because the 85-year-old company had always been run by a family member.

John Marriott was the most capable to take over. John started as a cook in the kitchen and went on to work in every aspect of the business. Bill said that John "spent most of his adult life preparing to succeed me as CEO. He devoted

his heart and soul to learning the business. . . . But as time went on, I realized that it wasn't the right fit—not for John and not for Marriott."

Bill's Response Bill Marriott saw that the company needed a CEO with strong people skills. He noted that "our culture is focused on people, because treating one another well is essential to creating an atmosphere in which everyone treats guests well, and that's the most fundamental element of our business."

The company had hired lawyer Arne Sorenson to help represent the company in 1993. Bill thought Sorenson had great financial skills so he hired him at a later time to head up mergers and acquisitions. Sorenson became chief financial officer in 1998. Over time, Bill Marriott

observed that his CFO developed very keen people skills.

As Sorenson's task and relationship skills grew, John Marriott became unhappy working at headquarters. He simply did not like managing the bureaucracy of such a large company. Bill concluded that his son was a "natural born entrepreneur" who did not have the personality to run a company like Marriott.

The Outcome Father and son agreed that John would be happier working in another role. In 2005, John became vice chairman of the board, and he started a medical testing company. He also is CEO of JWM Family Enterprises, a family trust company. Bill turned over the CEO reigns to Arne in March 2012. Arne is flourishing in his new role.[58]

YOUR CALL

Stop 1: What is the problem in this case?

Stop 2: What leadership concepts or theories helped Bill Marriott to make a decision about his successor?

Stop 3: Do you agree with Bill Marriott's decision? Explain.

The mountaineering guide in yellow is a great example of a path-goal leader. His job is to reduce roadblocks during an ascent and to provide coaching and support during the journey. Of the two climbers, who do you think has the most fun? Who has the greatest sense of accomplishment?

House's Path-Goal Theory

A second popular situational theory, proposed by Robert House in the 1970s and revised in 1996, is the ***path-goal theory, which holds that leader behaviors are effective when employees view them as a source of satisfaction or as paving the way to future satisfaction.*** Leaders are expected to do this by (1) reducing roadblocks that interfere with goal accomplishment, (2) providing the guidance and support needed by employees, and (3) linking meaningful rewards to goal accomplishment.

House's revised model is presented in Figure 13.3. You can see that leadership effectiveness is influenced by the interaction between eight leadership behaviors and a variety of contingency factors.

What Determines Leadership Effectiveness? The Match Between Leadership Behavior and Contingency Factors   Figure 13.3 shows that two contingency factors—employee characteristics and environmental factors—are expected to cause different leadership behaviors to be more effective than others.

- **Employee characteristics.** Five important employee characteristics are locus of control, task ability, need for achievement, experience, and need for clarity.
- **Environmental factors.** Two relevant environmental factors are task structure (independent versus interdependent tasks) and work group dynamics.
- **Leader behaviors.** Figure 13.3 reveals that House has expanded the number of task- and relationship-oriented leader behaviors beyond those previously discussed. A description of these leader behaviors is presented in Table 13.4.

FIGURE 13.3   A REPRESENTATION OF HOUSE'S REVISED PATH-GOAL THEORY

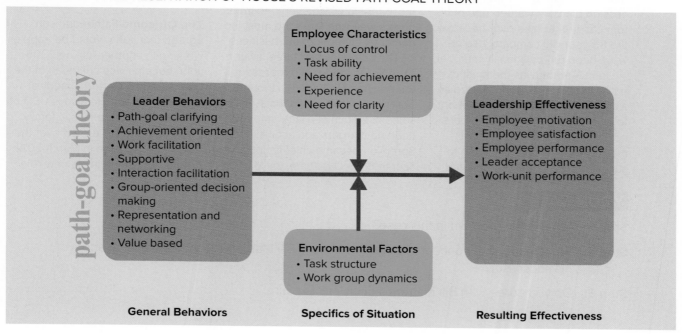

TABLE 13.4 CATEGORIES OF LEADER BEHAVIOR WITH THE REVISED PATH-GOAL THEORY

LEADER BEHAVIORS	WHAT IT MEANS
Path-goal–clarifying behaviors	Clarifying employees' performance goals; providing guidance on how employees can complete tasks; clarifying performance standards and expectations; use of positive and negative rewards contingent on performance.
Achievement-oriented behaviors	Setting challenging goals; emphasizing excellence; demonstrating confidence in employees' abilities.
Work-facilitation behaviors	Planning, scheduling, organizing, and coordinating work; providing mentoring, coaching, counseling, and feedback to assist employees in developing their skills; eliminating roadblocks; providing resources; empowering employees to take actions and make decisions.
Supportive behaviors	Showing concern for the well-being and needs of employees; being friendly and approachable; treating employees as equals.
Interaction-facilitation behaviors	Resolving disputes; facilitating communication; encouraging the sharing of minority opinions; emphasizing collaboration and teamwork; encouraging close relationships among employees.
Group-oriented decision-making behaviors	Posing problems rather than solutions to the work group; encouraging group members to participate in decision making; providing necessary information to the group for analysis; involving knowledgeable employees in decision making.
Representation and networking behaviors	Presenting the work group in a positive light to others; maintaining positive relationships with influential others; participating in organizational social functions and ceremonies; doing unconditional favors for others.
Value-based behaviors	Establishing a vision, displaying passion for it, and supporting its accomplishment; demonstrating self-confidence; communicating high-performance expectations and confidence in others' abilities to meet their goals; giving frequent positive feedback.

SOURCE: Adapted from R. J. House, "Path-Goal Theory of Leadership: Lessons, Legacy, and a Reformulated Theory," *Leadership Quarterly*, 1996, 323–352.

Putting the Theory into Action   To better understand how these contingency factors influence leadership effectiveness, we consider locus of control (see Chapter 3), an employee characteristic, and task structure, an environmental factor.

EXAMPLE   **Locus of Control.** Can be internal or external.

Internal. Employees with an internal locus of control are

- More likely to prefer participative or achievement-oriented leadership because they believe they have control over the work environment.
- Unlikely to be satisfied with directive leader behaviors that exert additional control over their activities.

External. Employees with an external locus

- Tend to view the environment as uncontrollable, thereby preferring the structure provided by supportive or directive leadership.

EXAMPLE   **Task Structure.** Task structure can be low or high.

Low. Low task structure occurs when

- Employees are not clear about their roles or performance expectations—high role ambiguity.

Directive and supportive leadership should help employees experiencing role ambiguity.

High. High task structure occurs when

- Employees work on routine and simple tasks.

Directive leadership is likely to frustrate such employees. Supportive leadership is most useful in this context.

Does the Revised Path-Goal Theory Work?   There are not enough direct tests of House's revised path-goal theory to draw overall conclusions. Nonetheless, there are three important takeaways from this theory.

1. *Use more than one style of leadership.* Effective leaders use multiple types of leader behavior. Thus, you are encouraged to familiarize yourself with the eight types of leader behavior outlined in path-goal theory and to try new behaviors when the situation calls for them.

   EXAMPLE   Consider the leader behaviors exhibited by Bob Iger, CEO of Walt Disney Company. Iger prefers to work behind the scenes and does not host any Disney TV productions. He is known to say hello to everyone he encounters on the Disney campus and participates in a Disney team that competes in the Malibu, California, triathlon to raise money for charity. Since taking over the helm at Disney, Iger patched up the rocky relationship between Pixar and Disney and ultimately purchased Pixar for $7 billion. He also resolved several contentious issues with former director Roy Disney and Comcast. Iger empowers his employees and allows them plenty of freedom to make decisions. At the same time, he holds people accountable for their work.[59]

   This example illustrates that Iger uses path-goal–clarifying behaviors, achievement-oriented behaviors, work-facilitation behaviors, supportive behaviors, interaction-facilitation behaviors, and representation and networking behaviors. See Table 13.4.

2. *Help employees achieve their goals.* Leaders are encouraged to clarify the paths to goal accomplishment and to remove any obstacles that may impair an employee's ability to achieve his or her goals. In so doing, managers need to guide and coach employees during the pursuit of their goals.

3. *Modify your leadership style to fit various employee and environmental characteristics.* A small set of employee characteristics (i.e., ability, experience, and need for independence) and environmental factors (task characteristics of autonomy, variety, and significance) are relevant contingency factors.[60]

Applying Situational Theories

Although researchers and practitioners support the logic of situational leadership, the practical application of such theories has not been clearly developed. A team of researchers thus attempted to resolve this problem by proposing a general strategy that managers can use across a variety of situations. The general strategy contains five steps.[61] We explain how to implement the steps by using the examples of a head coach of a sports team and a sales manager.

Step 1: Identify important outcomes. Managers must first determine the goals they want to achieve. For example, the head coach may have games to win or wish to avoid injury to key players whereas a sales manager's goals might be to increase sales by 10 percent or decrease customers' complaints.

Step 2: Identify relevant leadership behaviors. Next managers need to identify the specific types of behaviors that may be appropriate for the situation at hand. The list of behaviors shown in Table 13.4 is a good starting point. A head coach in a championship game, for instance, might focus on achievement-oriented and work-facilitation behaviors. In contrast, a sales manager might find path-goal–clarifying, work-facilitation, and supportive behaviors more relevant for the sales team. Don't try to use all available leadership behaviors. Rather, select the one or two that appear most helpful.

Step 3: Identify situational conditions. Fiedler and House both identify a set of potential contingency factors to consider, but there may be other practical considerations. For example, a star quarterback on a football team may be injured, which might require the team to adopt a different strategy toward winning the game. Similarly, managing a virtual sales team from around the world will affect the types of leadership that are most effective in this context.

Step 4: Match leadership to the conditions at hand. There simply are too many possible situational conditions for us to provide specific advice. This means that you should use your knowledge about organizational behavior to determine the best match between leadership styles/behaviors and the situation at hand. The coach whose star quarterback is injured might use supportive and values-based behaviors to instill confidence that the team can win with a different quarterback. Our virtual sales manager also might find it useful to use the empowering leadership associated with work-facilitation behaviors and to avoid directive leadership.

Step 5: Determine how to make the match. Managers can either use guidelines from contingency theory or path-goal theory. Either you can change the person in the leadership role or the leader can change his or her style or behavior. Returning to our examples, it is not possible to change the head coach in a championship game. This means that the head coach needs to change his or her style or behavior to meet the specific challenge. In contrast, the organization employing the sales manager might move him or her to another position because the individual is too directive and does not like to empower others. Alternatively, the sales manager could change his or her behavior, if possible.

Caveat When Applying Situational Theories

Can you think of any downside to applying situational theories? Consider this scenario. A manager has three employees reporting to her and one of them is exceeding her goals by 30 percent. The other two have satisfactory levels of performance. Because of the superior performance by one employee, the manager decides to reward this person by assigning her to a new, hot project. Part of this assignment entails attending a week-long training session in Phoenix, Arizona, in January. The employee is ecstatic!

The other two employees hear about this assignment and they are mad. Rather than seeing this situational leadership as positive, they feel inequity and are claiming favoritism. This will likely result in lower engagement and performance. Are you surprised by this outcome? Do you have any idea why this happened?

A team of OB researchers investigated the possibility that there are unintended negative consequences when managers use a situational approach with members from a team. Study findings revealed that treating group members differently resulted in some employees feeling that they were not among the leader's "in-group" (i.e., a partnership characterized by mutual trust, respect, and liking). The concept of in-groups and out-groups is discussed later in the chapter. These negative feelings in turn had a counterproductive effect on employees' self-efficacy and subsequent group performance. The point to remember is that leaders of teams need to be careful when treating individual team members differently. There are potential pros and cons to the application of situational theories in a team context.[62]

TRANSFORMATIONAL LEADERSHIP: HOW DO LEADERS TRANSFORM EMPLOYEES' MOTIVES?

MAJOR QUESTION

How can I use transformational leadership when working with others?

THE BIGGER PICTURE

Transformational leaders use a combination of charisma, interpersonal skills, and leader behaviors to transform followers' goals, motives, and behavior. Four key behaviors used by transformational leaders are inspirational motivation, idealized influence, individualized consideration, and intellectual stimulation. We discuss a process by which these behaviors help produce positive outcomes.

Transformational leadership represents a broad type of leader behavior that goes beyond task and relational leadership. Its origins date back to the 1940s when German sociologist Max Weber discussed the pros and cons of charismatic leadership.[63] **_Charisma_ is a form of interpersonal attraction that inspires acceptance, devotion, and enthusiasm.** Weber's initial ideas were examined and then incorporated into different models of transformational leadership during the 1970s and 80s. The dominant model of transformational leadership was proposed by a renowned OB scholar named Bernard Bass.[64] Bass believed that transformational leaders used key leader behaviors to influence others.

A Model of Transformational Leadership

Transformational leaders transform followers to pursue organizational goals over self-interests. They do this by using leader behaviors that appeal to followers' self-concepts—namely their values, motives, and personal identity. There are *four key behaviors of transformational leaders*. Figure 13.4 provides a sketch of how transformational leaders rely on these four key leader behaviors (second column from left): inspirational motivation, idealized influence, individualized consideration, and intellectual stimulation. Let's look at each in more detail.

Inspirational Motivation "Let me share a vision that transcends us to a greater good." **_Inspirational motivation,_ which includes the use of charisma, involves establishing an attractive vision of the future, the use of emotional arguments, and exhibition of optimism and enthusiasm.** A vision is "a realistic, credible, attractive future for your organization."[65] According to Burt Nanus, a leadership expert, the "right" vision unleashes human potential because it serves as a beacon of hope and common purpose. It does this by attracting commitment, energizing workers, creating meaning in employees' lives, establishing a standard of excellence, promoting high ideals, and bridging the gap between an organization's present problems and its future goals and aspirations.

> **EXAMPLE** Biotechnology firm Genentech "inspires employees with tear-jerking presentations by patients whose lives have been helped by Genentech products." One employee commented that "there is a sense of purpose when you share clients' stories. We are all working toward the same goal: life."[66]

FIGURE 13.4 A TRANSFORMATIONAL MODEL OF LEADERSHIP

transformational model of leadership	Individual and organizational characteristics	Leader behavior	Effects on followers and work groups	Outcomes
	• Traits	• Inspirational motivation	• Increased self-efficacy and collective self-efficacy	• Increased individual, group, and organizational performance
	• Life experiences	• Idealized influence	• Increased identification with the leader and work group members	• Positive work attitudes
	• Organizational culture	• Individualized consideration	• Increased perceptions of psychological empowerment and perceived organizational support	• Increased individual and group creativity/innovation
		• Intellectual stimulation	• Increased positive affect • Increased perceptions of task meaningfulness • Increased perceptions of organizational justice • Increased trust and liking with the leader • Increased perceptions of positive climates and work group processes	• Reduced stress and turnover • Increased organizational citizenship behavior • Increased customer service • Positive perceptions of leader effectiveness

SOURCE: Adapted from D. A. Waldman and F. J. Yammarino, "CEO Charismatic Leadership: Levels-of-Management and Levels-of-Analysis Effects," *Academy of Management Review,* April 1999, 266–285; and D. V. Knippenberg and S. B. Sitkin, "A Critical Assessment of Charismatic-Transformational Leadership Research: Back to the Drawing Board," *The Academy of Management Annals,* 2013, 1–60.

EXAMPLE Civil rights leader Martin Luther King Jr. had a vision or "dream" of racial equality. He both inspired a movement of people and helped the country envision a brighter future.

EXAMPLE Lloyd Dean, CEO of Dignity Health, has a vision of human kindness.[67] He believes that humanity is the core of health care.

Yvon Chouinard (on the left) at a cocktail party mingling with several of his employees and celebrity guests.

Idealized Influence "Let me demonstrate how to work hard and do the 'right' thing." The focus of ***idealized influence* is to instill pride, respect, and trust within employees.** Managers do this by sacrificing for the good of the group, being a role model, and displaying high ethical standards.

EXAMPLE Yvon Chouinard, founder of the outdoor clothing brand Patagonia, is a role model of running a business with goals that go far beyond profits. He wants the company to be a great place to work and has instituted policies to support employees. For example, an on-site cafeteria serves healthful food and the company provides on-site child care. Chouinard is dedicated to environmental issues. He committed "the company to 'tithing' for environmental activism, committing 1 percent of sales or 10 percent of profits, whichever is greater. The commitment include[s] paying employees working on local environmental projects so they could commit their efforts full-time." He also committed the company to using all pesticide-free cotton because the standard process for producing cotton was bad for the environment. The company's flex-time policies allow employees to come and go as they want as long as goals and deadlines are being met.[68]

Individualized Consideration "Let me provide tangible support to help you reach your goals." This component of transformational leadership is relationship-oriented. Specifically, **_individualized consideration_ entails behaviors associated with providing support, encouragement, empowerment, and coaching to employees.** These behaviors necessitate that leaders pay special attention to the needs of their followers and search for ways to help people develop and grow. You can do this by spending time talking with people about their interests and by identifying new learning opportunities for them.

> **EXAMPLE** Jeff Immelt, CEO of General Electric, invites one of the company's officers to his home every other Friday for a casual evening of drinks, some laughs, dinner, and conversation about world events. On Saturday, they get back together to talk about the individual's career. This "high touch" approach is a great way for Immelt to get to know his employees and to serve as a mentor.[69]

Intellectual Stimulation "Let's establish challenging and meaningful goals." This component of transformational leadership is more task-oriented. **_Intellectual stimulation_ involves behaviors that encourage employees to question the status quo and to seek innovative and creative solutions to organizational problems.** This behavior aims to encourage employee creativity, innovation, and problem solving. If used effectively, employees are more likely to view organizational problems as "my problems" and to proactively attempt to overcome performance roadblocks.

> **EXAMPLE** At San Diego's WD-40, makers of lubricants and cleaners, managers are held accountable for employee engagement. Managers set improvement goals based on employee surveys, and then they meet with upper management every 90 days to discuss progress against goals. Speaking of goals, CEO Garry Ridge said, "Our goals are tied not only to financial performance but to the cultural performance of our company, which includes the level of engagement scores."[70]

How Does Transformational Leadership Work?

Figure 13.4 shows on the left-hand side that transformational leader behavior is first influenced by both individual and organizational characteristics. For example, on the individual side, research reveals that transformational leaders tend to have personalities that are more extraverted, agreeable, and proactive and less neurotic than non-transformational leaders. They also have higher emotional intelligence.[71] Female leaders also were found to use transformational leadership more than male leaders.[72] It is important to note, however, that transformational leadership is less trait-like and more susceptible to managerial influence. This conclusion reinforces the notion that an individual's life experiences play a role in developing transformational leadership and that transformational leadership can be learned. Finally, Figure 13.4 shows that organizational culture influences the extent to which leaders are transformational. Cultures that are adaptive and flexible rather than rigid and bureaucratic are more likely to create environments that foster the opportunity for transformational leadership to be exhibited.

Figure 13.4, in the third column from the left, further shows that the use of transformational leadership creates positive effects on followers and work groups. In turn, these positive effects are expected to lead to positive outcomes (in the right-hand column) like individual, group, and organizational performance;

organizational commitment; organizational citizenship behaviors (OCBs); and safety behaviors.[73] By and large, research supports these proposed linkages.[74]

Have you worked for a transformational leader? The following Self-Assessment measures the extent to which a current or former manager used transformational leadership. Taking the Assessment provides a good idea about the specific behaviors you need to exhibit if you want to lead in a transformational manner.

connect

SELF-ASSESSMENT 13.4 Is My Manager Transformational?

Go to connect.mheducation.com and complete Self-Assessment 13.4. Then answer the following questions.

1. What could your manager have done to be more transformational?
2. Use the survey questions to identify three behaviors you can exhibit to increase your application of transformational leadership.

Implications for Managers Support for transformational leadership underscores five important managerial implications.

- **The establishment of a positive vision of the future—inspirational motivation—should be considered a first step at applying transformational leadership.** Why? Because the vision represents a long-term goal, and it is important for leaders to begin their influence attempts by gaining agreement and consensus about where the team or organization is headed. It also is critical to widely communicate the vision among the team or entire organization.[75] People can't get excited about something they don't know about or don't understand.

- **The best leaders are not just transformational.** Effective leaders also rely on other task-oriented and relationship-oriented behaviors, and they avoid a laissez-faire or "wait-and-see" style.[76] We encourage you to use all types of leader behavior discussed in this chapter, when appropriate.

Just like Optimus Prime and other Transformers can change their form, managers need to morph their styles to fit the situation at hand. Why do you think some people struggle with changing their leadership style across situations?

- **Transformational leadership affects outcomes at the individual, group, and organizational levels.**[77] Managers can thus use the four types of transformational leadership shown in Figure 13.4 (second column from left) as a vehicle to improve a host of important outcomes. The key point to remember is that transformational leadership transforms individuals as well as teams and work groups, ultimately creating widespread positive influence.

- **Transformational leadership works virtually.** If you lead geographically dispersed people, then it is important to focus on how you can display the four transformational leader behaviors in your e-mails, tweets, webinars, and conference calls.[78]

- **Transformational leaders can be ethical or unethical.** Whereas ethical transformational leaders enable employees to enhance their self-concepts, unethical ones select or produce obedient, dependent, and compliant followers.

MAJOR QUESTION

How can I improve the relationship with my boss?

THE BIGGER PICTURE

You are about to discover the most recent addition to OB's understanding of leadership: *leader-member exchange theory.* You will also discover that OB has meaningful insights into the role of the follower.

Two additional perspectives on leadership deserve attention:

- Leader-member exchange (LMX) theory.
- A follower perspective.

The Leader-Member Exchange (LMX) Model of Leadership

Over the last two decades, LMX has been the second-most-researched theory of leadership. This theory differs considerably from those previously discussed, as it focuses on the *quality of relationships* between managers and subordinates as opposed to the *behaviors or traits* of either leaders or followers. It also differs in that it does not assume that leader behavior is characterized by a stable or average leadership style as do the previously discussed models. In other words, most models of leadership assume a leader treats all employees in about the same way.

In contrast, the **leader-member exchange (LMX) theory is based on the assumption that leaders develop unique one-to-one relationships with each of the people reporting to them.** Behavioral scientists call this sort of relationship a *vertical dyad.* The forming of vertical dyads is said to be a naturally occurring process, resulting from the leader's attempt to delegate and assign work roles. In turn, the quality of these relationships is expected to affect a host of outcomes in the Integrative Framework of OB such as performance, work attitudes, and turnover. Two distinct types of LMX relationships are expected to evolve.[79]

In-Group versus Out-Group Exchanges LMX relationships are based on the leader's attempt to delegate and assign work roles. This process results in two types of leader-member dyads.

- **In-group exchange: Creating trust and mutual obligation.** High LMX relationships are characterized by a partnership of reciprocal influence, mutual trust, respect and liking, and a sense of common fates. These relationships become more social over time.
- **Out-group exchange: Creating more formality in expectations and rewards.** Low LMX relationships tend to focus on the economic exchange between leaders and followers. In other words, the relationship tends to be more formal and revolves around specifically negotiating the relationship between performance and pay. This relationship does not create a sense of mutual trust, respect, or common fate.[80]

Does the Quality of an LMX Matter? Yes! LMXs have widespread influence on many important outcomes. For example, a positive LMX is associated with individual-level behavioral outcomes like performance, turnover, and organizational citizenship behavior, and attitudinal outcomes such as organizational commitment, job satisfaction, and justice.[81] Differential treatment of team members can also be problematic. A team of researchers found that differential treatment among members of soccer, hockey, and basketball teams led to negative team atmospheres, which in turn promoted poor perceptions of team performance.[82] Low-quality leader-member exchanges are not good for individuals or groups.

You might not be surprised to learn that the quality of leader-member exchanges varies in importance across Western and Asian countries. While outcomes in Asian cultures are influenced by the quality of an LMX, employees in Asian countries also are influenced by collective interests and role-based obligations more so than Western-based employees.[83]

How Are LMX Relationships Formed? The quality of an LMX is influenced by three categories of variables: follower characteristics, leader characteristics, and interpersonal relationship variables.[84]

1. **Follower characteristics.** As we learned in Chapter 4, initial perceptions of others are based on individual characteristics. Leaders tend to create more positive LMXs with employees perceived as possessing competence, positive personalities, agreeableness, conscientiousness, and extraversion.

2. **Leader characteristics.** Leaders that use transactional and transformational leadership tend to have more positive LMXs. Not surprisingly, extraverted and agreeable leaders also tend to have more positive LMXs.

When this photo was taken in September 2013, just prior to the G20 Summit, Barack Obama and Vladimir Putin had numerous reasons to distrust each other and veer from a more solid one-to-one relationship. Differences over an appropriate response to civil war in Syria and Russia's embrace and protection of NSA turncoat Edward Snowden were only two of many irksome issues creating friction between their countries. Certainly their relationship would not be characterized as an in-group exchange. Do you think it is important for world leaders to have in-group exchanges? If yes, how might their relationship be improved?

3. **Interpersonal relationship variables.** There are far too many interpersonal factors that affect an LMX, so we note three that have the greatest impact on a leader-member relationship. High LMXs tend to occur when the parties:

- Trust each other.
- Perceive themselves as similar in terms of interests (both like sports or action movies), values (both value honesty), and attitudes (both want work–life balance).
- Like each other.

Managerial and Personal Implications of LMX Theory   There are three important implications.

- **Expectations.** Leaders are encouraged to establish high-performance expectations for all of their direct reports because favoritism and differential treatment within teams lead to negative outcomes.
- **Diversity.** Because personality and demographic similarity between leaders and followers are associated with higher LMXs, managers need to be careful that they don't create a homogenous work environment in the spirit of having positive relationships with their direct reports.
- **Initiative.** It is important to take positive actions at improving a poor LMX. We encourage you to take the lead as opposed to waiting for your boss to change the relationship. The following Self-Assessment was designed with this application in mind. Taking this Assessment will help you diagnose the quality of your relationship with a boss and determine how you can improve it.

Mc Graw Hill **connect**

SELF-ASSESSMENT 13.5   **Assessing My Leader-Member Exchange**

Go to connect.mheducation.com and complete Self-Assessment 13.5. It measures the quality of a current or former leader-member exchange. Then answer these questions.

1. Are you surprised by the results? Explain.
2. Based on your results, what do you think are the key causes of the LMX with your boss? Be specific.

SOURCE: Survey items were taken from R. C. Liden and J. M. Maslyn, "Multidimensionality of Leader-Member Exchange: An Empirical Assessment through Scale Development," *Journal of Management,* 1998, 56. Reproduced with permission of Sage Publications Ltd. via Copyright Clearance Center.

A management consultant offers the following tips for improving the quality of leader-member exchanges.[85]

- *Stay focused on your department's goals and remain positive about your ability to accomplish your goals.* An unsupportive boss is just another obstacle to be overcome.
- *Focus on changing things you can control.* Take control in changing the relationship and empower yourself to get things done. Stop dwelling on circumstances you cannot control.

   EXAMPLE   Laura Stein, general counsel at Clorox Co., found herself reporting to a new CEO brought from the outside, and she did not know much about him, so she studied up on his values and preferred communications style. And she was proactive: "[S]he volunteered to informally advise colleagues about revamping [company] strategy in China, where she previously had worked." The new CEO, Donald Knauss, was impressed. He concluded that Laura would "help anyone who asks for help," and he subsequently broadened her duties "to cover additional areas such as crisis management."[86]

- *Work on improving your relationship with your manager.* Begin by examining the level of trust between the two of you and then try to improve it by frequently and effectively communicating. You can also increase trust by following through on your commitments and achieving your goals.
- *Use an authentic, respectful, and assertive approach to resolve differences with your manager.* It also is useful to use a problem-solving approach when disagreements arise.

TAKE-AWAY APPLICATION—TAAP

Using results from your Self-Assessment and the recommendations above:

1. What aspects of your relationship are most in need of improvement?
2. What do you think are the main causes of your LMX?
3. Describe three things you can do to improve your LMX.

The Role of Followers in the Leadership Process

All of the previous theories discussed in this chapter have been leader-centric. That is, they focused on understanding leadership effectiveness from the leader's point of view. We conclude this chapter by discussing the role of followers in the leadership process.

To start, note how both leaders and followers are closely linked. You cannot lead without having followers, and you cannot follow without having leaders. Each needs the other, and the quality of the relationship determines how we behave as followers. This is why it is important for both leaders and followers to focus on developing a mutually rewarding and beneficial relationship.

Let's consider "types" of followers and steps you can take to be a better follower.

What Do Leaders Want from Followers?   Followers vary in terms of the extent to which they commit to, comply with, and resist a leader's influence attempts. For example, one researcher identified three types of followers: helpers, independents, and rebels.

- *Helpers* show deference to and comply with the leadership.
- *Independents* distance themselves from the leadership and show less compliance.
- *Rebels* show divergence from the leader and are least compliant.

The same researcher notes other types of followers, moderate in compliance: *diplomats, partisans*, and *counselors*.[87] Leaders obviously want followers who are

1. Productive
2. Reliable
3. Honest
4. Cooperative
5. Proactive
6. Flexible

Leaders do not benefit from followers who hide the truth, withhold information, fail to generate ideas, are unwilling to collaborate, provide inaccurate feedback, or are unwilling to take the lead on projects and initiatives.[88]

What Do Followers Want from Leaders?   Followers seek, admire, and respect leaders who foster three emotional responses in others:

- Significance
- Community
- Excitement

That is, followers want organizational leaders to create feelings of *significance* (what one does at work is important and meaningful), *community* (a sense of unity encourages people to treat others with respect and dignity and to work together in pursuit of organizational goals), and *excitement* (people are engaged and feel energy at work).[89]

How Can I Become a Better Follower?   A pair of OB experts developed a four-step process for followers to use in managing the leader–follower relationship.[90]

1. **It is critical to understand your boss.** You should attempt to gain an appreciation for your manager's leadership style, interpersonal style, goals, expectations, pressures, and strengths and weaknesses. One way of doing this is to ask your manager to answer the following seven questions:[91]

   a. How would you describe your leadership style? Does your style change when you are under pressure?

   b. When would you like me to approach you with questions or information? Are there any situations that are off limits (e.g., a social event)?

   c. How do you want me to communicate with you?

   d. How do you like to work?

   e. Are there behaviors or attitudes that you will not tolerate? What are they?

   f. What is your approach toward giving feedback?

   g. How can I help you?

2. **You need to understand your own style, needs, goals, expectations, and strengths and weaknesses.**

3. **Conduct a gap analysis between the understanding you have about your boss and the understanding you have about yourself.** With this information in mind, you are ready to proceed to the final step of developing and maintaining a relationship that fits both parties' needs and styles.

4. **Build on mutual strengths and adjust or accommodate the leader's divergent style, goals, expectations, and weaknesses.**[92] For example, you might adjust your style of communication in response to your boss's preferred method for receiving information. Other adjustments might be made in terms of decision making. If the boss prefers a participative approach, then you should attempt to involve your manager in all decisions regardless of your decision-making style—recall our discussion of decision-making styles in Chapter 11. Good use of time and resources is another issue for you to consider. Most managers are pushed for time, energy, and resources and are more likely to appreciate followers who save rather than cost them time and energy. You should not use up your manager's time discussing trivial matters.

We'll leave you with two final thoughts on being a successful follower or employee in the organization:

Recognize Conflict. The fact is, sometimes you may not be able to accommodate a leader's style, expectations, or perhaps weaknesses, and may have to seek a transfer or quit to reconcile the discrepancy. We recognize that there are personal and ethical trade-offs that one may not be willing to make when managing the leader–follower relationship.

Enhance Success. Finally, recognize the importance of working at being a good follower, when that is your role. We can all enhance our boss's leadership effectiveness and our employer's success by becoming better followers, and thus create our own success. Remember, it is in your best interest to be a good follower because leaders need and want competent employees.[93]

what did i learn?

You learned that to be an effective leader requires appropriate leadership behavior that can be learned and developed. The chapter provided an integrated model of leadership to allow you to understand the many contributing factors to leadership effectiveness. You also learned the importance of being a good follower. Reinforce your learning with the Key Points below. Consolidate your learning using the Integrative Framework. Then Challenge your mastery of the material by answering the Major Questions in your own words.

Key Points for Understanding Chapter 13
You learned the following key points.

13.1 MAKING SENSE OF LEADERSHIP THEORIES

- You do not need to have a formal position of authority to lead.
- Figure 13.1 shows an integrated model of leadership. The extent to which people effectively use the four key leader behaviors—task-oriented, relationship-oriented, passive, and transformational—is a function of demographic characteristics, knowledge and skills, task-oriented traits, and interpersonal attributes.
- Effective leadership requires effective managerial skills at some level.

13.2 TRAIT THEORIES: DO LEADERS POSSESS UNIQUE TRAITS AND PERSONAL CHARACTERISTICS?

- Table 13.1 summarizes the positive task-oriented traits and positive/negative interpersonal attributes possessed by leaders.
- Emotional intelligence impacts the use of transformational leadership and is positively associated with leadership effectiveness.
- There are both similarities and differences between leadership traits possessed by men and women.
- Leaders need four key skills: cognitive abilities, interpersonal skills, business skills, and strategic skills.
- People possess prototypes of effective and ineffective leaders.

13.3 BEHAVIORAL STYLE THEORIES: WHICH LEADER BEHAVIORS DRIVE EFFECTIVENESS?

- There are four categories of leader behavior: task-oriented, relationship-oriented, passive, and transformational.
- Task-oriented leadership includes the use of initiating structure and transactional leadership.
- Relationship-oriented leadership includes the use of consideration, empowerment, and servant leadership.
- Psychological empowerment is experienced when leaders create perceptions of meaningfulness, self-determination or choice, competence, and impact.
- Servant-leadership focuses on increased service to others rather than to oneself. Servant-leaders display the characteristics in Table 13.3.
- Passive leadership, also known as laissez-faire leadership, is demoralizing and makes employees feel unsupported. Avoid it!

13.4 SITUATIONAL THEORIES: DOES EFFECTIVE LEADERSHIP DEPEND ON THE SITUATION?

- Situational theories are based on the idea that effective leadership depends on the situation at hand.
- Fiedler believes leadership effectiveness depends on an appropriate match between leadership style and situational control. Leaders are either task or relationship oriented and the situation is composed of leader-member relations, task structure, and position power.
- House's path-goal theory holds that leader behaviors are effective when employees view them as a source of satisfaction or as paving the way to future satisfaction. In this respect, leaders exhibit eight styles or categories of leader behavior. In turn, the effectiveness of these styles depends on various employee characteristics and environmental factors.
- Researchers suggest a five-step approach for applying situational theories.

13.5 TRANSFORMATIONAL LEADERSHIP: HOW DO LEADERS TRANSFORM EMPLOYEES' MOTIVES?

- Transformational leaders motivate employees to pursue organizational goals above their own self-interests.
- Transformational leaders rely on four unique types of leader behavior: inspirational motivation, idealized

influence, individualized consideration, and intellectual stimulation.

- Individual characteristics and organizational culture influence the extent to which people use transformational leadership.

- The use of transformational leadership has positive effects on followers and work groups. In turn, these positive effects foster positive individual, group, and organizational performance.

13.6 ADDITIONAL PERSPECTIVES ON LEADERSHIP

- The LMX model revolves around the development of dyadic relationships between managers and their direct reports. These leader-member exchanges result in either in-group or out-group relationships.

- It is hard for leaders to be effective if they have bad followers. Leaders want followers who are productive, reliable, honest, cooperative, proactive, and flexible. People are more likely to be positive followers when the leader creates feelings of significance, community, and excitement.

- Followers can use a four-step process for improving the relationship with their boss. First, it is critical to understand your boss. Second, followers need to understand their own style, needs, goals, expectations, and strengths and weaknesses. Third, conduct a gap analysis between the understanding followers have about their boss and themselves. Finally, build on mutual strengths and adjust to or accommodate the leader's different style, goals, expectations, and weaknesses.

The Integrative Framework for Chapter 13

As shown in Figure 13.5, you learned that leadership is a critical input and process associated with the person factors of personality, emotions, demographics, and skills and abilities, and the environmental characteristic of relationship quality. You also learned that leadership is associated with many OB outcomes. At the individual level, leadership is related to task performance, work attitudes, well-being/flourishing, citizenship behavior, turnover, and creativity. Leadership further impacts the group-level outcomes of team performance, satisfaction, and cohesion and conflict. Finally, effective leadership is correlated with five organizational-level outcomes.

Challenge: Major Questions for Chapter 13

At the start of the chapter, we told you that after reading the chapter you should be able to answer the following questions. Unless you can, have you really processed and internalized the lessons in the chapter? Refer to the Key Points, Figure 13.5, the chapter itself, and your notes to revisit and answer the following major questions:

1. How does an integrated model of leadership help me become an effective leader?
2. How can I use the takeaways from trait theories to improve my ability to lead?
3. Do effective leaders behave in similar ways?
4. How do I know when to use a specific leader behavior?
5. How can I use transformational leadership when working with others?
6. How can I improve the relationship with my boss?

FIGURE 13.5   THE INTEGRATIVE FRAMEWORK FOR UNDERSTANDING AND APPLYING OB

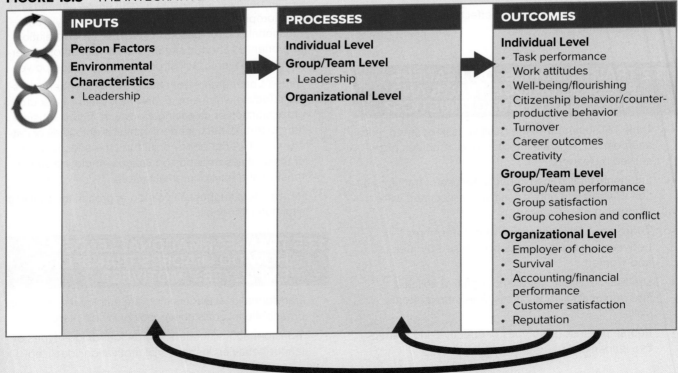

INPUTS	PROCESSES	OUTCOMES
Person Factors **Environmental Characteristics** • Leadership	**Individual Level** **Group/Team Level** • Leadership **Organizational Level**	**Individual Level** • Task performance • Work attitudes • Well-being/flourishing • Citizenship behavior/counter-productive behavior • Turnover • Career outcomes • Creativity **Group/Team Level** • Group/team performance • Group satisfaction • Group cohesion and conflict **Organizational Level** • Employer of choice • Survival • Accounting/financial performance • Customer satisfaction • Reputation

© 2014 Angelo Kinicki and Mel Fugate. All rights reserved. Reproduction prohibited without permission of the authors.

Leadership Style and Substance at Dignity Health

Catholic Healthcare West (now Dignity Health) may have hired Lloyd Dean as much for his leadership style as his résumé. Yes, in 2000 the résumé showed eight years' experience in health care at Evangelical Health Systems and more before that in pharmaceuticals. But something else gave him the edge.

Dean stands out "as an unconventional leader in a staid, grave industry," a 2013 profile in *Fortune* declared, based on such recent glimpses into Dean's leadership style as follows:

- **Energetic and Positive.** Coworkers know Dean's early arrival every morning at work by his bellowing laugh as he exits the elevators.

- **Eyes and Ears.** Dean will sometimes show up in sweats and sunglasses to hang in the lobbies of his hospitals so he can check on customer service and hear their complaints.

- **Customer Focus and Communication.** When Dean uncovers a problem, he'll write a memo for staff called "Just Thinking." Staff members realize they should read "Just Thinking" as "Just Fix It."

- **Outreach and Engagement.** Once, the late Senator Ted Kennedy was running late. He was supposed to introduce Dean at a Washington Hilton to executives, policy makers, and congressional staff. By the time Kennedy arrived, Dean had already made the rounds of the room and done Kennedy's job for him.

- **Authentic and Sincere.** Kathleen Sebelius, the former U.S. Secretary of Health and Human Services under President Obama, noted that unlike most health care CEOs with whom she consulted, Dean never failed to ask her how she was doing and to offer his help. "There's a personal side that isn't phony or fake," she said.

- **Personal Brand and Reputation.** Dean's personal brand of fairness and integrity precedes him and affords him more credibility with elected officials "than [with] almost any other corporate executive," says Willie Brown, former mayor of San Francisco.

- **Balance and Tact.** *Fortune* praised Dean for his poise and diplomacy in balancing religiosity and secularity, quite a feat considering he's not even Catholic."[94]

Teachers and CEOs Have Much in Common

In a recent interview, Dean ties success as a CEO to what he learned as a public school teacher.

> Successful educators tend to have three key attributes. One, you have to be able to listen. Two, be able to take complex principles and ideas and put them in a language that people will understand. Three, motivate and create the desire in individuals to learn—to get them to focus together on a common project. It's the same in business. It's what a CEO does.[95]

Personal Values

Dean's engagement with his current job runs deep, he explains.

> I'd always asked myself, how can I use the opportunity I have, the gifts I've been given, to have an impact on the kinds of communities that I came from? And I began to realize that in health care, faith-based organizations were really focused on the poor and most vulnerable. As someone who grew up in a religious family, and also wanted to help those communities, that really resonated with me. . . . I love health care. What greater opportunity do you have to impact large numbers of people? To help people really sustain life, or change the path that they're on in a positive way?[96]

A Historic Challenge

Leadership style and substance came to the forefront in 2000, when Catholic Healthcare West (CHW) recruited Dean to save their system. CHW was in crisis and was close to insolvent.

Back then, CHW was a collection of dozens of religious and community hospitals and care facilities. It had all started in 1986, when two congregations of the Sisters of Mercy joined their 10 hospitals together. The goal was to use aggregated size to better serve the community. Soon other hospitals were added, Catholic, Lutheran, Methodist, nondenominational, and governmental in nature.

CHW had hoped to improve operating efficiencies through amalgamated size for more clout in dealing with vendors to control costs. It grew in two ways: vertically by acquiring physician networks and horizontally by acquiring hospitals.

Specific Challenges at CHW: A Weak Empire

James C. Robinson and Sandra Dratler studied CHW's transition in detail. They argue that Dean arrived to find a business that enjoyed few of the benefits and many disadvantages of its size. The situation was dire. CHW had been losing a million dollars a day *for the last three years*.[97]

The specifics aren't pretty. CHW had:

- Suffered severe losses from conglomerate overexpansion.

- Placed its most prominent and often multiple facilities in Los Angeles, Sacramento, and San Francisco, where competition and utilization were at national lows.

- Bet on centralized billing, purchasing, and information technology (IT) at the corporate level with poor results.
- Tracked financial performance at the regional level, allowing management to overlook operational shortfalls when covered by investment earnings.
- Developed little understanding of the incremental revenues and costs attributable to each site and service.
- Acquired hospitals with independent community boards and medical staffs, hampering economies of scale.
- Failed to resolve conflicts between centralized corporate authority and local facilities that retained autonomous control over spending.
- Never achieved the potential benefit of consolidating its financial assets (because of local autonomy) to use surpluses in established markets to invest in communities with more potential growth.

Robinson and Dratler called CHW of that time "a weak empire of strong principalities, a holding company whose distinct businesses hoarded any profit and clamored for subsidies to cover any loss."[98]

For the purposes of this case, we're asking you to apply your problem-solving skills to CHW as it existed when Dean took the helm. Drive your recommendations from the specifics above. Use what you learned about Dean from the case and leadership styles in the chapter to inform your recommendations.

Apply the 3-Stop Problem Solving Approach to OB

Stop 1: What is the problem?

- Use the Integrative Framework for Understanding and Applying OB to help identify the outcomes that are important in this case.
- Which of these outcomes are not being achieved in the case?
- Based on considering the above two questions, what is the most important problem in this case?

Stop 2: Use the Integrative Framework to help identify the OB concepts or theories that help you to understand the problem in this case.

- What person factors are most relevant?
- What environmental characteristics are most important to consider?
- Do you need to consider any processes? Which ones?
- What concepts or theories discussed in this chapter are most relevant for solving the key problem in this case?

Stop 3: What are your recommendations for solving the problem?

- Review the material in the chapter that most pertains to your proposed solution and look for practical recommendations.
- Use any past OB knowledge or experience to generate recommendations.
- Outline your plan for solving the problem in this case.

LEGAL/ETHICAL CHALLENGE

Is GlaxoSmithKline Effectively Responding to Allegations about Inappropriately Rewarding Doctors?

This case involves allegations that U.K. drug maker GlaxoSmithKline PLC's salespeople are rewarding doctors in China for prescribing Botox.

"Internal Glaxo documents and e-mails reviewed by *The Wall Street Journal* show Glaxo's China sales staff was apparently instructed by local managers to use their personal e-mail addresses to discuss marketing strategies related to Botox. In the personal e-mails, sales staff discuss rewarding doctors for prescribing Botox with cash payments, credits that could be used to meet medical-education requirements, and other rewards."

An anonymous person reported the issue to Glaxo and indicated that its "China sales staff provided doctors with speaking fees, cash payments, dinners and all-expenses-paid trips" for prescribing company products between 2004 and 2010. Glaxo did an investigation and concluded that there was no evidence of wrongdoing.

The tipster sent a follow-up note in May 2013 revealing that the practices had continued during the past year. Glaxo again denied the charges and said they came from the same source who complained in the past.

The *Journal* did a follow-up examination of internal documents and e-mails and discovered that the company had a marketing strategy that targeted 48 doctors in China. A PowerPoint presentation uncovered by the *Journal* revealed that targeted doctors and hospitals were given sales goals and told, "if the hospital did not make it [the sales goal], the doctor cannot get bonus even if he made it to the sales target." There is no direct evidence that any money was paid to physicians. Internal e-mails further showed that about

16 salespeople discussed this marketing program on their personal e-mails.

E-mails from April 2013 revealed that Glaxo managers were reminding Botox salespeople about the above marketing plan and required them to submit sales data.[99]

What Would You Do If You Were a Member of Glaxo's Senior Leadership Team?

1. Nothing. The company has already concluded there was no wrongdoing and the recent charges come from the same individual.

2. Continue to do business, but launch a more thorough investigation with the help of Chinese officials. They are more likely to help the company get to the truth.

3. Fire or suspend all the managers whose names are associated with the internal e-mails that show interest in this alleged marketing scheme. I also would contact every Botox salesperson in China and tell them to discontinue any support for this marketing program. I would warn them that they will be terminated for failing to abide by this directive.

4. Invent other options.

GROUP EXERCISE

Exhibiting Leadership within the Context of Running a Meeting

Objectives

1. To consider the types of problems that can occur when running a meeting.

2. To identify the leadership behaviors that can be used to handle problems that occur in meetings.

Introduction

Managers often find themselves playing the role of formal or informal leader when participating in a planned meeting (e.g., committees, work groups, task forces). As a leader, individuals often must handle a number of interpersonal situations that have the potential of reducing the group's productivity. For example, if an individual has important information that is not shared with the group, the meeting will be less productive. Similarly, two or more individuals who engage in conversational asides could disrupt the normal functioning of the group. Finally, the group's productivity will also be threatened by two or more individuals who argue or engage in personal attacks on one another during a meeting. This exercise is designed to help you practice some of the behaviors necessary to overcome these problems and at the same time share in the responsibility of leading a productive group.

Instructions

Your instructor will divide the class into groups of four to six. Once the group is assembled, briefly summarize the types of problems that can occur when running a meeting—start with the material presented in the preceding introduction. Write your final list on a piece of paper. Next, for each problem on the group's list, the group should brainstorm a list of appropriate leader behaviors that can be used to handle the problem. Use the guidelines for brainstorming discussed in Chapter 11. Try to arrive at a consensus list of leadership behaviors that can be used to handle the various problems encountered in meetings.

Questions for Discussion

1. What types of problems that occur during meetings are most difficult to handle? Explain.

2. Are there any particular leader behaviors that can be used to solve multiple problems during meetings? Discuss your rationale.

3. Was there a lot of agreement about which leader behaviors were useful for dealing with specific problems encountered in meetings? Explain.

Organizational Processes

14 ORGANIZATIONAL CULTURE, SOCIALIZATION, AND MENTORING

How Can I Use These Concepts for Competitive Advantage?

inputs

PERSON FACTORS

ENVIRONMENTAL CHARACTERISTICS
Culture (national and organizational)

processes

INDIVIDUAL LEVEL

GROUP/TEAM LEVEL

ORGANIZATIONAL LEVEL
Culture, socialization, and mentoring

outcomes

INDIVIDUAL LEVEL

GROUP/TEAM LEVEL

ORGANIZATIONAL LEVEL

MAJOR TOPICS I'LL LEARN AND QUESTIONS I SHOULD BE ABLE TO ANSWER

14.1 THE FOUNDATION OF ORGANIZATIONAL CULTURE: UNDERSTANDING ITS DRIVERS AND FUNCTIONS

MAJOR QUESTION: *What is culture and why is it important to understand its layers and functions?*

14.2 THE IMPACT OF ORGANIZATIONAL CULTURE TYPES ON OUTCOMES

MAJOR QUESTION: *To what extent are the different types of organizational culture related to important outcomes?*

14.3 THE PROCESS OF CULTURE CHANGE

MAJOR QUESTION: *What are the mechanisms I can use to implement culture change?*

14.4 THE ORGANIZATIONAL SOCIALIZATION PROCESS

MAJOR QUESTION: *How can the practical lessons of socialization research be integrated within the three phases of socialization?*

14.5 EMBEDDING ORGANIZATIONAL CULTURE THROUGH MENTORING

MAJOR QUESTION: *What are the four developmental networks and how can I use them to advance my career?*

INTEGRATIVE FRAMEWORK FOR UNDERSTANDING AND APPLYING OB

This chapter focuses on organizational culture and the socialization and mentoring that allow new members to become part of the culture of the organization. The Integrative Framework shows how culture functions as both an environmental input and an organizational process.

© 2014 Angelo Kinicki and Mel Fugate. All rights reserved. Reproduction prohibited without permission of the authors.

winning at work

HOW WOULD I ASSESS PERSON–ENVIRONMENT FIT (PE) WHEN APPLYING FOR JOBS?

"Employment site Glassdoor provides information on salaries, organizational cultures, and interview questions by using anonymous posts from employees and people seeking employment. In 2012 the company obtained 285,000 questions used by hiring managers. Here are the four most frequently asked interview questions: *What's your favorite movie? What's your favorite website? What's the last book you read for fun? What makes you uncomfortable?*[1]

"WHY ARE COMPANIES ASKING THESE QUESTIONS?

"Although these questions have nothing to do with performance, recruiters ask them because they are trying to assess whether or not an applicant will "fit in" with the company's culture. A recent study of people hiring undergraduate and graduate students revealed that more than 50 percent of the evaluators considered "fit" to be the most important criterion during the interview process.[2]

"WHAT DOES IT MEAN TO "FIT"?

Person–environment fit (PE) reflects "the compatibility between an individual and a work environment that occurs when their characteristics are well matched."[3] Although there are many types of fit, we are interested in what is called **person–organization fit (PO),** which reflects the extent to which your personality and values match the climate and culture in an organization. PO fit is important because it is associated with more positive work attitudes and task performance and lower intentions to quit and stress.[4]

"HOW CAN YOU ASSESS "FIT"?

"It will take some effort on your part. First conduct an evaluation of your strengths, weaknesses, and values.

Next, do the same for the company or department at hand by doing research about the company on the Internet or talking with current employees. This information will now enable you to prepare a set of diagnostic questions to ask during the interview process. These questions need to focus on determining your level of fit. For example, if you value recognition for hard work, then ask a recruiter how the company rewards performance. If the answer does not support a strong link between performance and rewards, you probably will have a low PE fit and will not be happy working at this company.

We have created a Take-Away Application later in this chapter to help you practice the process of assessing person–organization fit.

FOR YOU | WHAT'S AHEAD IN THIS CHAPTER

This chapter begins your exploration of what is called "macro" organizational behavior. Macro OB is concerned with studying OB from the perspective of the organization as a whole. We use the graphical image of the Integrative Framework of OB on the previous page to illustrate how organizational culture is a key input that influences a host of processes and outcomes. We begin by exploring the foundation of organizational culture so that you can understand its drivers and functions. Next we review the four key types of organizational culture and consider their relationships with various outcomes. This is followed by a discussion of how managers can change organizational culture. Finally, we discuss how socialization and mentoring are used to embed organizational culture, and focus on how you can use knowledge of these processes to enhance your career success and happiness.

major question

MAJOR QUESTION

What is culture and why is it important to understand its layers and functions?

THE BIGGER PICTURE

Although you may have a small impact on your employer's organizational culture, you undoubtedly are affected by it. Culture affects outcomes at the individual, group, and organizational level. You are going to learn what creates organizational culture and how culture in turn affects other organizational processes. You also will understand the three levels that constitute culture and the functions it serves for organizations.

The quote "culture eats strategy for breakfast" was attributed to management expert Peter Drucker. But it really caught everyone's attention when Mark Fields, CEO at Ford Motor Company, used it in 2006. The slogan currently hangs in the company's "war room." Ford's former CEO Alan Mulally created the war room, which contains charts, graphs, and lists of products, as a meetingplace for executives to discuss the execution of Ford's corporate strategies. The culture slogan serves as a reminder of the importance of organizational culture to Ford's success.[5]

What is the point of this slogan? It's quite simple. A company can have the best vision and strategy in the world, but it won't be able to execute them unless the culture is aligned with the strategy. This is a lesson that successful companies like Lincoln Electric, Southwest Airlines, and SAS Institute have applied for years. Lincoln Electric has the largest share of the global welding market, Southwest is the largest airline in the United States, and SAS is the world's largest privately held software firm.[6] All of these firms exert significant effort at creating and reinforcing the type of culture that helps them achieve their strategic goals.

One of our primary goals in this chapter is to help you understand how managers can use organizational culture as a competitive advantage. Let us start by considering the foundation of organizational culture.

Defining Culture and Exploring Its Impact

Organizational culture is defined as "the set of shared, taken-for-granted implicit assumptions that a group holds and that determines how it perceives, thinks about, and reacts to its various environments."[7] This definition highlights four important characteristics of organizational culture:

- **Shared concept.** Organizational culture consists of beliefs and values that are shared among a group of people.
- **Learned over time.** It is passed on to new employees through the process of socialization and mentoring, topics discussed later in this chapter.
- **Influences our behavior at work.** This is why "culture eats strategy for breakfast."
- **Impacts outcomes at multiple levels.** Culture affects outcomes at the individual, group/team, and organizational levels.

FIGURE 14.1 DRIVERS AND FLOW OF ORGANIZATIONAL CULTURE

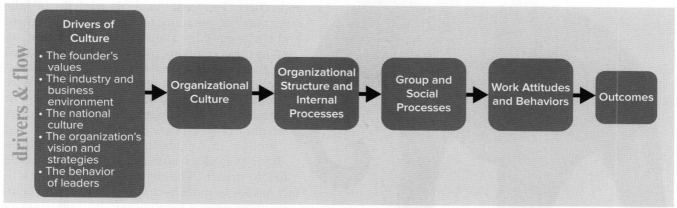

SOURCE: Adapted from C. Ostroff, A. J. Kinicki, and R. S. Muhammad, "Organizational Culture and Climate," in I. B. Weiner, N. W. Schmitt, and S. Highhouse, eds., *Handbook of Psychology*, vol. 12, 2nd ed. (Hoboken, NJ: Wiley, 2012), 643–676. Reprinted with permission of John Wiley & Sons, Inc.

Figure 14.1 provides a conceptual framework for understanding the drivers and effects of organizational culture. Five elements drive organizational culture:

- The founder's values
- The industry and business environment
- The national culture
- The organization's vision and strategies
- The behavior of leaders

In turn, *organizational culture* influences the type of *organizational structure* adopted by a company and a host of *internal processes* (including human resource practices, policies, and procedures) implemented in pursuit of organizational goals. These organizational characteristics then affect a variety of *group and social processes*.[8] This sequence ultimately affects employees' *work attitudes and behaviors* and a variety of organizational *outcomes*. All told, Figure 14.1 tells us that organizational culture has a wide span of influence, ultimately impacting a host of individual, group, and organizational outcomes.[9] Once again, this is why culture eats strategy for breakfast.

The Three Levels of Organizational Culture

Organizational culture operates on three levels:

1. Observable artifacts
2. Espoused values
3. Basic underlying assumptions

Each level varies in terms of outward visibility and resistance to change, and each level influences another level.

Level 1: Observable Artifacts At the more visible level, culture represents observable artifacts. ***Artifacts* consist of the physical manifestation of an organization's culture.** Organizational examples include:

- Acronyms
- Manner of dress
- Awards
- Myths and stories told about the organization
- Published lists of values
- Observable rituals and ceremonies
- Special parking spaces
- Decorations

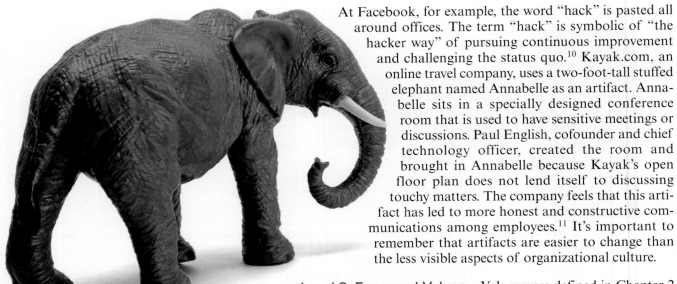

At Facebook, for example, the word "hack" is pasted all around offices. The term "hack" is symbolic of "the hacker way" of pursuing continuous improvement and challenging the status quo.[10] Kayak.com, an online travel company, uses a two-foot-tall stuffed elephant named Annabelle as an artifact. Annabelle sits in a specially designed conference room that is used to have sensitive meetings or discussions. Paul English, cofounder and chief technology officer, created the room and brought in Annabelle because Kayak's open floor plan does not lend itself to discussing touchy matters. The company feels that this artifact has led to more honest and constructive communications among employees.[11] It's important to remember that artifacts are easier to change than the less visible aspects of organizational culture.

Annabelle the Elephant is an artifact of the corporate culture at Kayak.com, provided as a catalyst to make sure employees do not ignore an important but difficult topic, the so-called elephant in the room. Can you think of other artifacts that might prime people to give honest feedback?

Level 2: Espoused Values   Values were defined in Chapter 2 as abstract ideals that guide one's thinking and behavior across all situations. In the context of organizational culture, it is important to distinguish between values that are espoused versus those that are enacted.

- *Espoused values* **represent the explicitly stated values and norms that are preferred by an organization.** They are generally established by the founder of a new or small company and by the top management team in a larger organization. Most companies have a short of list of espoused values. For example, Procter and Gamble's list of values includes integrity, leadership, ownership, passion for winning, and trust.[12] In contrast, Google and Zappos have 10 espoused values.

Because espoused values represent aspirations that are explicitly communicated to employees, managers hope that those values will directly influence employee behavior. Unfortunately, aspirations do not automatically produce the desired behaviors because people do not always "walk the talk."

EXAMPLE   Energy company BP, for instance, has long claimed that it values safety, yet the company had a refinery fire in Texas City, Texas, that killed 15 people in 2005. In 2006, a pipeline leak in Alaska lost over 200,000 gallons of crude, and the 2010 Deepwater Horizon spill in the Gulf lost more than 200 million gallons according to the US government.[13]

- *Enacted values* **represent the values and norms that actually are exhibited or converted into employee behavior.** They represent the values that employees ascribe to an organization based on their observations of what occurs on a daily basis. It is important for managers to reduce gaps between espoused and enacted values because they can significantly influence employee attitudes and organizational performance.

Consider that a survey from the Ethics Resource Center showed that employees were more likely to behave ethically when management behavior set a good ethical example and kept its promises and commitments.[14] This finding was underscored by another study of 129 mergers. Employees were more productive and post-merger performance was higher when employees believed that the post-merger behavior within the newly formed firm was consistent with the espoused values.[15] It pays to walk the talk when it comes to integrating companies after a merger.

EXAMPLE   Juniper Networks spent considerable effort to align its espoused values of trust, delivering excellence, pursuing bold aspirations, and making a meaningful difference with employee behavior. The company started by selecting 200 employees from around the world to come up with a list of behaviors that exemplified each of the values. These behaviors were then infused into the human resource practices of hiring, training, evaluating, and promoting people. The company completely revamped its process of performance appraisal.

- **Old.** Employees felt the old system violated the company's values. Previously the company evaluated all employees and then forced a distribution curve across the entire population.

- **New.** The new system builds on a "conversation day." On such days, "employees and managers discuss areas for improvement and areas for growth, set stretch goals, and align the goals with employees' career aspirations. There is no rating given or a specific measure of improvement." An employee survey revealed that 66 percent of Juniper's employees felt that the new system was helpful or extremely helpful.[16]

Level 3: Basic Underlying Assumptions **Basic underlying assumptions con-stitute organizational values that have become so taken for granted over time that they become assumptions that guide organizational behavior.** They represent deep-seated beliefs that employees have about their company and thus constitute the core of organizational culture. As you might expect, basic underlying assumptions are highly resistant to change. Consider how Unilever CEO Paul Polman reinforces a core belief in sustainability (see Example box).

Sustainability **represents "a company's ability to make a profit without sacri-ficing the resources of its people, the community, and the planet."**[17] Sustainability also is referred to as "being green," and Pulitzer Prize–winning political commenta-tor Thomas Friedman believes that "outgreening" other nations can renew America and even defeat al-Qaeda.[18]

EXAMPLE   Unilever Strives to Promote a Sustainability Culture

When Paul Polman took over as CEO of Unilever in 2009, he told Wall Street analysts that the company would no longer pro-vide earnings guidance and quarterly profit statements. This is unheard of! Analysts revolted and the stock price immediately dropped.

WHAT WAS POLMAN TRYING TO ACCOMPLISH?

Polman wanted to instill a deep-seated belief regarding sustain-ability within all employees at Unilever. He started this effort by creating a "Sustainable Liv-ing Plan." The plan contained goals to "double its sales even

Paul Polman, CEO at Unilever.

as it cuts its environmental footprint in half and sources all its agricultural products in ways that don't degrade the earth by 2020." The company also set a goal to improve the well-being of 1 billion people by influencing them to wash their hands and brush their teeth and by selling foods with less salt and fat.

Polman told investors that "if you don't buy into this, I respect you as a human being, but don't put your money in our company." He believes that shareholder return should not override nobler goals. He also said, "Our purpose is to have a sustainable business model that is put at the service of the greater good. It's as simple as that."

WHAT ARE THE RESULTS OF UNILEVER'S PUSH FOR A SUSTAINABILITY CULTURE? Polman believes that employees are more engaged and the company is a more desirable place to work. As evidence, Unilever "is one of the five most-searched-for employers, behind Google, Apple, Microsoft, and Facebook." In 2012, sales grew in every region Unilever operates in around the globe, and the company cut costs through its Sustainable Living plan.

Employees at Unilever "say that doing good is in the company's DNA." This is what we call a basic underlying assumption![19]

YOUR THOUGHTS?

1. What do you think was the driving force behind Polman's desire to create a culture of sustainability?

2. Do you agree with Polman about the tangible business benefits of Unilever's cultural values?

3. Whether you agree with Polman or not, was he wise to tell investors not to put money in the Unilever if they did not also buy into the Sustainable Living plan?

The Four Functions of Organizational Culture

An organization's culture fulfills four important functions (see Figure 14.2):

1. Organizational identity
2. Collective commitment
3. Social system stability
4. Sense-making device

To help bring these four functions to life, let's consider how each of them has taken shape at Southwest Airlines. Southwest is a particularly instructive example

FIGURE 14.2 FOUR FUNCTIONS OF ORGANIZATIONAL CULTURE

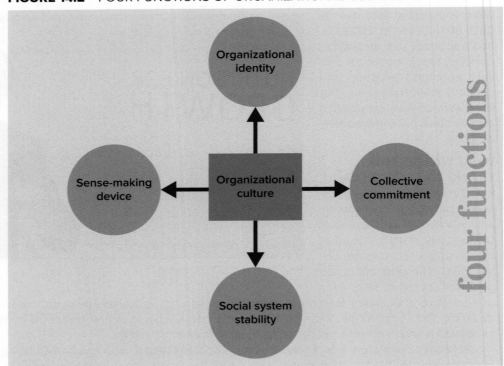

SOURCE: Adapted from discussion in L. Smircich, "Concepts of Culture and Organizational Analysis," *Administrative Science Quarterly*, September 1983, 339–358. Copyright © 1983. Reprinted with permission of Sage Publications, Inc.

because it has grown to become the largest carrier in the United States serving more customers domestically than any other airline and has achieved 40 consecutive years of profitability. *Fortune* named Southwest the seventh Most Admired Company in the World, and it was recognized in 2012 by *Chief Executive Magazine* as one of the 40 Best Companies for Leaders based on outstanding company culture and internal professional development.[20]

Function 1: Culture Provides Employees with an Organizational Identity

Southwest Airlines is known as a fun place to work that values employee satisfaction and customer loyalty over corporate profits. Gary Kelly, Southwest's CEO, highlighted this theme by noting that "our people are our single greatest strength and our most enduring long-term competitive advantage."[21]

The company has a catastrophe fund based on voluntary contributions for distribution to employees who are experiencing serious personal difficulties. Southwest's people-focused identity is reinforced by the fact that it is an employer of choice. Southwest contributed $228 million into its employee-based profit-sharing program in 2013. The company also was rated as providing outstanding opportunities for women and Hispanics by *Professional Women* magazine and *Hispanic* magazine, respectively, and *National Conference on Citizenship* ranked Southwest as one of The Civic 50 for use of time, talent, and resources in civic engagement.

Function 2: Culture Facilitates Collective Commitment

The mission of Southwest Airlines "is dedicated to the highest quality of Customer Service delivered with a sense of warmth, friendliness, individual pride, and Company Spirit."[22] Southwest's

This photo demonstrates Southwest's culture. You see employees having fun in an airport terminal, which can be a frustrating experience for passengers. Do you think these employees can lighten the spirit of the travelers in the background?

nearly 46,000 employees are committed to this mission. As evidence, Southwest was rated number one in Customer Service by the 2013 Airline Quality Ratings and JD Power named them 2012 Customer Service Champion for performance in People, Presentation, Price, Process, and Product.

Function 3: Culture Promotes Social System Stability

Social system stability reflects the extent to which the work environment is perceived as positive and reinforcing, and the extent to which conflict and change are effectively managed. Southwest is noted for its philosophy of having fun, having parties, and celebrating. For example, each city in which the firm operates is given a budget for parties. Southwest also uses a variety of performance-based awards and service awards to reinforce employees. The company's positive and enriching environment is supported by the lowest turnover rates in the airline industry and the employment of 1,355 married couples. In 2013 Southwest was recognized with the Employee Choice Awards Best Place to Work, by *Glassdoor.com*.

Function 4: Culture Shapes Behaviors by Helping Members Make Sense of Their Surroundings

This function of culture helps employees understand why the organization does what it does and how it intends to accomplish its long-term goals. Keeping in mind that Southwest's leadership originally viewed ground transportation as their main competitor in 1971, employees come to understand why the airline's primary vision is to be the best primarily short-haul, low-fare, high-frequency, point-to-point carrier in the United States. Employees understand they must achieve exceptional performance, such as turning a plane around in 20 minutes, because they must keep costs down in order to compete against Greyhound and the use of automobiles. In turn, the company reinforces the importance of outstanding customer service and high-performance expectations by using performance-based awards and profit sharing. Employees own about 13 percent of the company stock.[23]

TAKE-AWAY APPLICATION—TAAP **Assessing the Levels of Culture at My Current Employer**

Answer the following questions by considering your current or a past employer. (If you do not have experience yet as an employee, substitute your current school/university or a company you are researching as an employer of choice.)

1. What artifacts can you see at work? What do these artifacts tell you about your employer?

2. What are the company's espoused values? Do you think management's enacted behaviors are consistent with the espoused values?

3. Identify three key beliefs you have about your employer: You may want to ask a colleague the same question. Are these beliefs consistent with the meaning of the artifacts you described in question 1?

4. How does your employer's culture compare to that of Southwest?

MAJOR QUESTION

To what extent are the different types of organizational culture related to important outcomes?

THE BIGGER PICTURE

Do you think that companies rated on *Fortune*'s List of 100 Best Places to Work have unique cultures? How do we know what type of culture exists at these companies or your current employer? You will learn about the four types of culture that are defined by the competing values framework. You also will discover the extent to which these four culture types are related to important outcomes.

To address the above Major Question, we need to provide a taxonomy of culture types. You can imagine that it is hard to get agreement on a common set of organizational culture types given culture's complexity. While consultants tend to invent their own proprietary assessments, academics have proposed and scientifically tested three different frameworks. This section discusses the *competing values framework* because it is the most widely used approach for classifying organizational culture. It also was named as one of the 40 most important frameworks in the study of organizations and has been shown to be a valid approach for classifying organizational culture.[24] We then discuss relationships among culture types and outcomes.

Identifying Culture Types with the Competing Values Framework

The **competing values framework (CVF) provides a practical way for managers to understand, measure, and change organizational culture.** It identifies four fundamental types of organizational culture as shown in Figure 14.3.[25]

The CVF was originally developed by a team of researchers who were trying to classify different ways to assess organizational effectiveness. This research showed that measures of organizational effectiveness varied along two fundamental dimensions or axes. One axis pertained to whether an organization focuses its attention and efforts on internal dynamics and employees or outward toward its external environment and its customers and shareholders. The second was concerned with an organization's preference for flexibility and discretion or control and stability. Combining these two axes creates four types of organizational culture that are based on different core values and different sets of criteria for assessing organizational effectiveness.

Figure 14.3 shows the strategic thrust associated with each cultural type along with the means used to accomplish this thrust and the resulting ends or goals pursued by each cultural type. Before beginning our exploration of the CVF, it is important to note that organizations can possess characteristics associated with each culture type. That said, however, organizations tend to have one type of culture that is more dominant than the others. Let us begin our discussion of culture types by starting in the upper-left-hand quadrant of the CVF.

FIGURE 14.3 THE COMPETING VALUES FRAMEWORK

Culture varies along two continua of competing values: flexibility and discretion vs. stability and control, and internal focus and integration vs. external focus and differentiation. This leads to four categories of organizations, each with its own unique thrust.

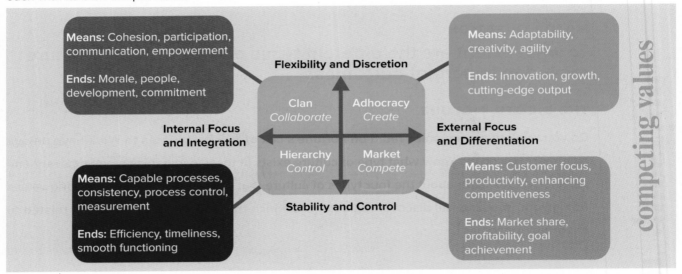

SOURCE: Adapted from K. S. Cameron, R. E. Quinn, J. Degraff, and A. V. Thakor, *Competing Values Leadership* (Northampton, MA: Edward Elgar, 2006), 32.

Clan Culture Companies with a *clan culture* have **an internal focus and value flexibility rather than stability and control.** These resemble a family-type organization in which effectiveness is achieved by encouraging collaboration, trust, and support among employees. This type of culture is very "employee-focused" and strives to instill cohesion through consensus and job satisfaction and commitment through employee involvement. Clan organizations devote considerable resources to hiring and developing their employees, and they view customers as partners. Collaborating is the strategic thrust of this culture.

> **EXAMPLE** Google is the number 1 company to work for in 2014.[26] Larry Page, Google's co-founder and CEO, describes the culture as a "family" environment. He said, "my job in the company is to make sure everybody in the company has great opportunities, and that they feel they're having a meaningful impact and are contributing to the good of society. . . . It's important that the company be a family, that people feel that they're part of the company, and that the company is like a family to them. When you treat people that way, you get better productivity."[27] Google also holds weekly all-hands ("TGIF") meetings so that employees can ask Larry, Sergey Brin—a Google co-founder—and other executives questions about anything involving the company. This practice enhances employee communication and morale, two aspects of a clan culture.

> **EXAMPLE** Edward Jones, the privately held financial services firm, was ranked as the 4th best company to work for in 2014. Edward Jones has over 11,000 small offices and 7 million clients worldwide. The company maintains a close-knit culture by using a variety of celebratory events. Its 8% turnover rate is one of the lowest in the industry and more than 33% of its financial advisors are more than 50 years old.[28]

Adhocracy Culture Companies with an *adhocracy culture* have **an external focus and value flexibility.** Creation of new products and services is the strategic thrust of this culture, which is accomplished by being adaptable, creative, and fast to respond to changes in the marketplace. Adhocracy cultures do not rely on the type

Edward Jones launched a program that provides tablet PCs to its financial advisors. As shown, advisors take tablets on the road as they make personal visits to existing and potential clients. The goal is to reduce the amount of time advisors spend on administrative tasks, leaving them more time to build strong relationships with clients.

of centralized power and authority relationships that are part of market and hierarchical cultures. They empower and encourage employees to take risks, think outside the box, and experiment with new ways of getting things done.

A recent article in *The Wall Street Journal* noted that adhocracy-type cultures are decreasing in the United States as many companies are becoming risk averse. The downside of this trend is that "reasonable" risk taking is needed to create new businesses, products, and ultimately jobs. On the positive side, however, pockets of risk taking are taking place in different industries such as technology and energy and different regions like the coastal cities of San Francisco and Boston and college towns like Boulder, Colorado, and Austin, Texas.[29]

EXAMPLE   Biopharmaceutical firm AstraZeneca "is experimenting with new ways to organize research to improve productivity. Scientists now are responsible for candidate drugs until they begin the final human trials, ending a culture of handing off early-stage products to other researchers as if on an assembly line."[30]

EXAMPLE   The Tata group, a multinational conglomerate headquartered in Mumbai, India, has 100 operating companies in more than 80 countries. Tata takes innovation so seriously that it developed an "Innometer." The conglomerate measures creative goals and accomplishments vs. domestic or global benchmarks while instilling a sense of urgency among employees.[31]

Market Culture   Companies with a ***market culture*** have a strong external focus and value stability and control. Competition is the strategic thrust of these organizations. They have a strong desire to deliver results and accomplish goals. Because this type of culture is focused on the external environment, customers and profits take precedence over employee development and satisfaction. The major goal of managers is to drive toward productivity, profits, and customer satisfaction.

EXAMPLE   Grupo Bimbo is the world's largest bakery company. Bimbo managers operate in a low-margin business and thus focus heavily on execution. "Profits

Imagine having to deliver over 10,000 products across 22 countries. Do you think this takes a lot of planning and detailed execution? Bimbo's market-based culture contributes to this effort.

depend heavily on getting the right amount of highly perishable products to stores at the right moment and at a reasonable cost. . . . For instance, it uses tricycle delivery bikes in urban areas of China where streets are too narrow for trucks, a practice it first implemented in Latin America."[32] The company operates 171 plants and delivers over 10,000 products across 22 countries.

EXAMPLE Canada's Bombardier is the largest train manufacturer in the world. Bombardier's culture focuses on the importance of setting and achieving goals. CEO Pierre Beaudoin said, "Connecting goals to each person's day-to-day work is important. . . . What I like most, though, is that we now have an organization that wants to get better. And that's the key. We always talk about why we're not there yet; we're on a journey—how close are we to those world-class metrics. We used to make excuses for why our performance was good enough. Today we say, 'what will it take to get to world class?'" Can you see the cultural focus on productivity, goal achievement, and competitiveness?[33]

Hierarchy Culture   Control is the strategic thrust within a hierarchy culture. The **hierarchy culture has an internal focus, which produces a more formalized and structured work environment, and values stability and control over flexibility.** This orientation leads to the development of reliable internal processes, extensive measurement, and the implementation of a variety of control mechanisms. Effectiveness in a company with this type of culture is likely to be assessed with measures of efficiency, timeliness, quality, safety, and reliability of producing and delivering products and services.[34] Hierarchical cultures have been found to have both negative and positive effects.

EXAMPLE   Consider the positive example of Mumbai's *dabbawalas*, individuals who deliver prepared meals to customers' homes or offices and then return empty *dabbas*—metal lunch boxes—later in the day. To do their jobs effectively, dabbawalas rely on a hierarchical culture (see the Problem-Solving Application).

EXAMPLE   Consider the negative impact at General Motors. Mary Barra, GM's former product officer and current CEO, has been "attacking GM's bureaucracy, slashing the number of required HR reports by 90 percent and shrinking the company's employee policy manual by 80 percent. But loosening the dress code drew a flood of calls and e-mails from employees asking if they could, in fact, wear jeans." The answer was yes. "Barra saw the dress code, along with other changes, as an opportunity to have a conversation about responsibility. 'There was a culture in the past where the rule was the rule and when you weren't empowered to make the decision you could all just complain about the rule. Well, now we were really empowering virtually every single person,' Barra says." One of her major goals is to reduce the complexity associated with producing cars.[35] This means that she wants more flexibility, which is a component of either a clan or adhocracy culture. Bara was promoted to the CEO position at GM in January 2014.

solving application

The Dabbawalas Rely on a Hierarchical Culture to Effectively Deliver Food

Over 5,000 dabbawalas in Mumbai deliver more than 130,000 lunchboxes every day. The need for this service grew from the strong cultural reliance by the working population on a hot meal for lunch. The dabbawalas pick up the prepared lunchboxes in late morning and return the empty containers after lunch. Vendors also use the delivery service for getting their commercial hot lunches to customers. Workers are willing to pay for the service and the illiterate dabbawalas are so skilled in execution that the service remains affordable for many workers.

Each dabbawala belongs to a group, and the groups manage themselves "with respect to hiring, logistics, customer acquisition and retention, and conflict resolution." Within each group individuals have a very clear hierarchical role to play. Despite a high degree of self-management, the independent groups must collaborate and coordinate to deliver lunch within the fourth-largest city in the world. Mistakes are rare even though these employees complete over 260,000 transactions during a day, and they do it six days a week, 52 weeks a year.

How Does a Hierarchical Culture Help? First off, the dabbawalas don't use any IT system or cell phones. These workers have integrated organization, management, process, and culture to achieve their goals. It all begins with using the Mumbai Suburban Railway. A workday starts with a worker picking up a dabba from a customer—customers prepare their own lunch and dabbawalas pick them up and transport them. The dabba is then taken to "the nearest train station, where it is sorted and put onto a wooden crate according to its destination. It is then taken by train to the station closest to its destination. There it is sorted again and assigned to another worker, who delivers it to the right office before lunchtime." The process reverses in the afternoon when the dabbas are picked up and returned to the customer's home.

The railway system's schedule effectively sets the timing of what needs to be done. For example, "workers have 40 seconds to load the crates of dabbas onto a train at major stations and just 20 seconds at interim stops." This requires the workers to determine the most efficient way to get these key tasks completed.

Workers also build some slack into the system. Each group has 2 or 3 extra workers who help out wherever they are needed. This works because employees are cross-trained in the major tasks of collecting, sorting, transporting, and customer relations.

How Do the Independent Workers Communicate? The dabbawalas use a very basic system of symbols to communicate. Three key markings are included on the lid of a dabba. The first indicates where the dabba must be delivered. The second is a series of characters: a number is used to indicate which employee is making the delivery, "an alphabetical code (two or three letters) for the office building, and a number indicating the floor. The third—a combination of color and shape, and in some instances, a motif—indicates the station of origin." Customers also provide their own unique small bags for carrying dabbas, which helps workers remember who gets which dabba.

Does It Work? Yes. Not only does this work system result in the reliable distribution of lunches, but the dabbawalas tend to stay in the same work group their entire working lives. Employees genuinely care about each other.[36]

YOUR CALL

Stop 1: What is the major problem dabbawalas want to avoid?

Stop 2: What OB concepts help explain why the dabbawalas are effective?

Stop 3: Would you recommend a similar system for a comparable firm in the United States? Explain.

Cultural Types Represent Competing Values It is important to note that certain cultural types reflect opposing core values. These contradicting cultures are found along the two diagonals in Figure 14.3. For example, the clan culture—upper-left quadrant—is represented by values that emphasize an internal focus and flexibility, whereas the market culture—bottom-right quadrant—has an external focus and concern for stability and control. You can see the same conflict between an adhocracy culture that values flexibility and an external focus and a hierarchy culture that endorses stability and control along with an internal focus. Why are these contradictions important?

They are important because an organization's success may depend on its ability to possess core values that are associated with competing cultural types. While this is difficult to pull off, it can be done. 3M is a good example.

EXAMPLE 3M is a global innovation company that is structured around five business groups. 3M tried to merge competing cultural characteristics from an adhocracy with those from a hierarchy. Reflecting an adhocracy culture, 3M released 1,000 new products in 2009, and it awards annual Genesis Grants, "worth as much as $100,000, to company scientists for research. The money is allocated by their peers and is spent on projects for which 'no sensible, conventional person in the company would give money,'" says Chris Holmes, a 3M division vice president. The company has a goal to generate 30 percent of its revenue from products developed in the last five years. In contrast, 3M pursued a hierarchical culture by implementing quality management techniques to reduce waste and defects and increase efficiency. Although 3M achieved better efficiency and earnings in the short run, new product revenue decreased and scientists complained that the quality initiatives were choking off innovation. One engineer quipped that "it's really tough to schedule invention." 3M's CEO, George Buckley, was made aware of these cultural conflicts and decided to reduce the conflict within company labs by decreasing hierarchical policies/procedures while simultaneously increasing those related to adhocracy. The company continues to emphasize quality and reliability in its factories. To date, results indicate a successful transition as the company achieved both its efficiency and new product revenue goals in 2010.[37]

Are you curious about the type of culture that exists in a current or past employer? Do you wonder if you possess person–organization fit? The following Self-Assessment allows you to consider these questions.

connect

SELF-ASSESSMENT 14.1 **What Is the Organizational Culture at My Current Employer?**

Go to connect.mheducation.com and complete Self-Assessment 14.1. Then answer the following questions.

1. How would you describe the organizational culture?

2. Do you think that this type of culture is best suited to help the company achieve its strategic goals? Explain.

Outcomes Associated with Organizational Culture

Both managers and academic researchers believe that organizational culture can drive employee attitudes, performance, and organizational effectiveness, thereby leading to competitive advantage. To test this possibility, various measures of organizational culture have been correlated with a variety of individual and organizational outcomes. So what have we learned? A meta-analysis involving over 1,100 companies uncovered the results shown in Figure 14.4.[38]

Figure 14.4 illustrates the strength of relationships among eight different organizational outcomes and the culture types of clan, adhocracy, and market: Hierarchy

FIGURE 14.4 CORRELATES OF ORGANIZATIONAL CULTURE

Note: The category of organizational commitment was associated with only clan and market structures, and not adhocracy, and therefore shows only two bars.

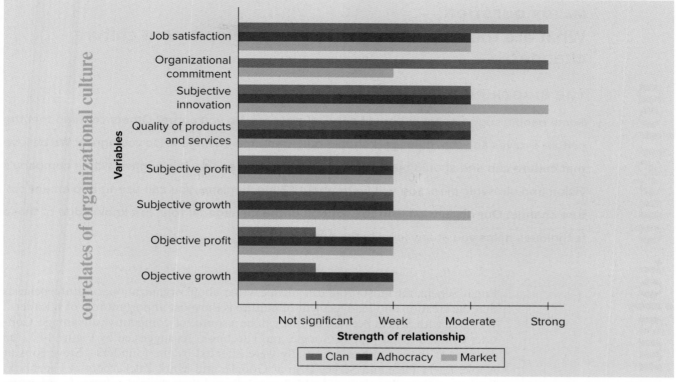

SOURCE: Data supplied from C. A. Hartnell, A. Y. Ou, and A. J. Kinicki, "Organzational Culture and Organizational Effectiveness: A Meta-Analytic Investigation of the Competing Values Framework's Theoretical Suppositions," *Journal of Applied Psychology*, July 2011, 677–694.

was not included due to a lack of research on this type. Results reveal that the eight types of organizational outcomes had significant and positive relationships with clan, adhocracy, and market cultures. The majority of these relationships were of moderate strength, indicating that they are important to today's managers. Closer examination of Figure 14.4 leads to the following five conclusions:

Five Lessons

1. **Organizational culture is related to measures of organizational effectiveness.** This means that an organization's culture can be a source of competitive advantage.

2. **Employees are more satisfied and committed to organizations with clan cultures.** These results suggest that employees prefer to work in organizations that value flexibility over stability and control and those that are more concerned with satisfying employees' needs than customer or shareholder desires.

3. **Innovation and quality can be increased by building characteristics associated with clan, adhocracy, and market cultures into the organization.** Managers may want to use a combination of all three types of culture to produce these outcomes.

4. **An organization's financial performance (growth in profit and growth in revenue) is not strongly related to organizational culture.** Managers should not expect to increase financial performance immediately by trying to change their organization's culture. (This is not an argument against all cultural change. Some changes in culture can improve competitive advantage, which then results in financial benefits, as we will see.)

5. **Companies with market cultures tend to have more positive organizational outcomes.** Managers are encouraged to consider how they might make their cultures more market oriented.

major question

What are the mechanisms I can use to implement culture change?

THE BIGGER PICTURE

Some people suggest that culture change takes years. Do you agree? Others contend that the culture evolves and that managers should not attempt to manage it. Do you agree? We believe that culture can and should be nurtured and developed so that it is aligned with a company's vision and strategic plan. You will learn about 12 mechanisms you can use to implement culture change. Our discussion is in the context of the managerial role, but knowledge of these techniques helps you at any level in the organization.

Edgar Schein, the most prolific academic writer about organizational culture, believes that the creation and management of culture is the most important role of a leader.[39] We agree with Schein because culture can be a source of competitive advantage. Consider companies like Apple, Google, and Facebook. As suggested by Figure 14.1, the cultures at these companies initially were affected by the founders—Steve Jobs at Apple, Larry Page and Sergey Brin at Google, and Mark Zuckerberg at Facebook. Over time, these founders embedded or reinforced their desired cultures by adopting specific types of organizational structure and implementing a host of human resource practices, policies, and procedures. Although it is not an easy task to change an organization's culture, this section provides an overview of how to create cultural change.

Before describing the specific ways in which managers can change organizational culture, let's review four truths about culture change.

1. **Leaders are the architects and developers of organizational culture.** This suggests that culture is not determined by fate. It is formed and shaped by the ongoing behavior of everyone who works at a company. Herb Kelleher, former CEO of Southwest Airlines, noted that culture change is not formulaic. "It's not a job that you do for six months and then you just say, 'Well that's behind us.' It's something you do every day."[40]

2. **Changing culture starts with targeting one of the three levels of organizational culture—observable artifacts, espoused values, and basic underlying assumptions.**

Sergey Brin (on the left) and Larry Page started Google in 1998. They met as Ph.D. students at Stanford. Today, Sergey directs special projects and Larry is the CEO. The company runs more than 1 million servers and processes over 1 billion searches per day.

The fastest way to start a culture change project is through the use of observable artifacts. For example, if you wanted to foster a market culture, you could post graphs of performance metrics around the office. These charts would reinforce the importance of high performance. That said, culture will not change in a significant way unless managers are able to change basic underlying assumptions.[41] It takes time to change this deep-seated aspect of culture.

3. **Consider how closely the current culture aligns with the organization's vision and strategic plan.** Remember the quote "culture eats strategy for breakfast" whenever you pursue culture change. It is essential that an organization's culture is consistent with its vision and strategic goals. **A *vision* represents a long-term goal that describes "what" an organization wants to become. A *strategic plan* outlines an organization's long-term goals and the actions necessary to achieve those goals.**

    EXAMPLE   Walt Disney's original *vision* for Disneyland included the following components: Disneyland will be something of a fair, an exhibition, a playground, a community center, a museum of living facts, and a showplace of beauty and magic. It will be filled with the accomplishments, the joys and hopes of the world we live in. And it will remind and show us how to make those wonders part of our lives.[42]

    Failing to align vision, strategic goals, and organizational goals will likely result in "culture eating strategy for breakfast."

4. **Use a structured approach when implementing culture change.** Chapter 16 can help you in this regard as it presents several models that provide specific steps to follow when implementing any type of organizational change. Our experience as consultants tells us that culture change is frequently met with resistance. This happens because people become accustomed to the culture and they prefer to leave things as they are. Chapter 16 outlines several techniques you can use to overcome such resistance.

Let's now consider the specific methods or techniques that managers can use to change an organization's culture.

Twelve Mechanisms for Creating Culture Change

Schein notes that changing organizational culture involves a teaching process. That is, organizational members teach each other about the organization's preferred values, beliefs, norms, expectations, and behaviors. He further articulates specific mechanisms for changing organizational culture, and from his writing we identify 12 of the most potent, summarized in Table 14.1.[43]

1. Formal Statements   This method for embedding culture relies on using formal statements of organizational philosophy, mission, vision, values, and materials used for recruiting, selection, and socialization: They represent observable artifacts.

    EXAMPLE   Sam Walton, the founder of Walmart, established three basic beliefs or values that represent the core of the organization's culture. They are (a) respect for the individual, (b) service to our customer, and (c) striving for excellence.

    EXAMPLE   Nucor Corporation attempts to emphasize the value it places on its people by including every employee's name on the cover of the annual report. This practice also reinforces the clan type of culture the company wants to encourage.[44]

2. The Design of Physical Space, Work Environments, and Buildings   Physical spacing among people and buildings and the location of office furniture are different ways to send messages about culture. For example, an open office environment is more appropriate for an organization that wants to foster collaboration.

TABLE 14.1 TWELVE MECHANISMS FOR CHANGING ORGANIZATIONAL CULTURE

MECHANISM	LEVEL		
	OBSERVABLE ARTIFACT	ESPOUSED VALUE	BASIC ASSUMPTION
1. Formal statements	X	X	
2. Design of physical space, work environments, and buildings	X		X
3. Slogans, language, acronyms, and sayings	X	X	
4. Deliberate role modeling, training programs, teaching, and coaching by others	X	X	X
5. Explicit rewards, status symbols, and promotion criteria	X	X	X
6. Stories, legends, or myths about key people and events	X	X	X
7. Organizational activities, processes, or outcomes		X	X
8. Leader reactions to critical incidents and organizational crises			X
9. Rites and rituals	X	X	X
10. The workflow and organizational structure	X		X
11. Organizational systems and procedures	X	X	X
12. Organizational goals and criteria throughout employee cycle (hire to retire)	X	X	X

EXAMPLE Novartis AG in Basel, Switzerland, did it by using "common workspaces, sofas, soft lighting and cappuccino machines to encourage people to talk, share ideas and build relationships." They also invested in laptops for employees so that they would not be tied down to cubicles.[45]

3. Slogans, Language, Acronyms, and Sayings These elements of corporate culture often have a profound effect on the organization over time because they are easy to remember and repeat.

EXAMPLE Aetna was losing money and customers in the 2000s, and culture was partly the cause. The company had a dysfunctional reverence for its 150-year history. "Once openly known among workers as 'Mother Aetna,' the culture encouraged employees to be steadfast to the point that they'd become risk-averse, tolerant of mediocrity, and suspicious of outsiders. The prevailing executive mind-set was 'We take care of our people for life, as long as they show up every day and don't cause trouble.'"[46] Obviously, the "Mother Aetna" tag was not good for the company.

4. Deliberate Role Modeling, Training Programs, Teaching, and Coaching by Others Many companies structure training to provide an in-depth introduction about their organizational values' basic underlying assumptions.

EXAMPLE EMC Corporation, a global information technology company with over 60,000 employees, devotes much effort and resources to embed cultural characteristics associated with clan, market, and hierarchy cultures. All new employees begin by completing an online program called "FastStart" that informs them about the company's history, vision, values, and expectations. In turn, specific hiring departments use job-specific orientations. For example, "sales education conducts a five-day, intensive case study–driven program culminating in sales presentations, and our Global Services organization delivers a two-week orientation to introduce organizational goals, measurements, contributions, and roles."[47]

5. Explicit Rewards, Status Symbols, and Promotion Criteria   This mechanism has a strong impact on employees due to its highly visible and meaningful nature. Reward systems are one of the strongest ways to embed organizational culture. It is important to remember what you learned about motivation in Chapter 5 when attempting to change culture via rewards. It is essential to consider the various forms of justice.

> **EXAMPLE**   At Triage Consulting Group, employees at the same level of their career earn the same pay, but employees are eligible for merit bonuses, reinforcing a culture of achievement—market culture. The merit bonuses are partly based on coworkers' votes for who contributed most to the company's success—clan culture. The employees who receive the most votes are recognized each year at the company's "State of Triage" meeting—market culture.[48]

6. Stories, Legends, or Myths About Key People and Events   Storytelling is a powerful way to send messages to others about the values and behaviors that are desired by the organization.

> **EXAMPLE**   Jeff Bezos, Amazon's CEO, told an interviewer from the *Harvard Business Review* that "there are stories we tell ourselves internally about persistence and patience, long-term thinking, staying focused on the customer."[49] This would reinforce a market culture.

Stories of heroism frequently follow plane crashes. While these individuals are not pulling people from a burning plane, they are heroes in the sense of determining the cause of the crash. Such information helps airlines and the aviation industry to design safer planes, which benefits all of us.

EXAMPLE   At the Olive Garden, "leaders share with staff members letters from customers describing how they chose to celebrate meaningful events at the company's restaurants." The company believes that sharing these stories "is a powerful reminder of the value of continued quality improvements and innovation," which promotes beliefs and behaviors associated with hierarchy and adhocracy cultures.[50]

EXAMPLE   Allianz Life Insurance encourages employees to share stories about their work experiences with coworkers. "Favorite" stories are then considered for a reward of up to $500.[51] Such stories might be used to support any of the four cultural types.

7. Organizational Activities, Processes, or Outcomes   Leaders pay special attention to those activities, processes, and outcomes that they can measure and control. This in turn sends strong messages to employees about acceptable norms and behavior.

EXAMPLE   When Ron Sargent took over as chief executive of Staples, he wanted to increase the focus on customer service. He started by investigating what values the office supply retailer's employees already held, and they told him they cared about helping others. Sargent used that value as the basis for developing their skill in serving customers. Staples began teaching employees more about the products they sell and now offers bonuses for team performance. Sargent also pays frequent visits to stores so he can talk directly to employees about what customers like and dislike.[52] Sargent's actions would clearly promote an adhocracy and market-based culture.

8. Leader Reactions to Critical Incidents and Organizational Crises   Neuroscience research shows that people learn and pay attention to the emotions exhibited by leaders. Positive emotions spread, but negative emotions travel faster and farther.[53]

EXAMPLE   BP's new CEO after the Gulf oil spill—Bob Dudley—responded quickly to criticism that the company valued profit and efficiency more than safety—a focus on a market rather than hierarchy culture. In order to foster more of a hierarchical culture, he sent a memo to all employees indicating "that safety would be the sole criterion for rewarding employee performance in its operating business for the fourth quarter."[54] These types of rewards will need to be offered long term if the company truly wants to change employees' basic underlying assumptions regarding safety.

9. Rites and Rituals   The power of this dimension of organizational culture is seen again and again. ***Rites and rituals* represent the planned and unplanned activities and ceremonies that are used to celebrate important events or achievements.**

EXAMPLE   Employees at Boston advertising agency Arnold Worldwide like to meet at a beer vending machine in the office, nicknamed Arnie, after completing the day's meetings with clients. "As they sip bottles of home-brewed beer, employees exchange ideas and chitchat, often sticking around the office instead of heading to a nearby bar." While this ritual can surely facilitate clan, adhocracy, and market cultures, organizations need to be careful about encouraging drinking at work. Employment lawyers caution that drinking at work "can lead to driving intoxicated, assault, sexual harassment or rape. Plus, it may make some employees uncomfortable while excluding others, such as those who don't drink for health or religious reasons."[55]

Financial and human resources staffing firm Salo LLC, located in Minneapolis, uses a "safer" set of rites and rituals to reinforce a clan and market-based culture (see Example box).

EXAMPLE Salo LLC Uses Rites and Rituals to Embed a Clan and Market Culture

When customer requests come in to a particular office, "they are posted on a wall-sized whiteboard, and can only be recorded, altered or erased by the salesperson who landed the client."

A WHITEBOARD AND GONG ARE USED AS KEY ARTIFACTS The whiteboards are visible to everyone and they have become "a center hub of activity," according to Adam Sprecher, a managing director at the firm. When a new client name goes up on the board, Sprecher says, "there's a little anxiety of 'OK, here we go! Now it's time to perform.' It's an adrenaline rush."

Colored pens are used to indicate the status of a project. Initial clients are listed in black, and then updated in "blue or orange as candidates are added or eliminated. A red check mark means it is time to start thinking about new ideas."

Another artifact, a big brass gong, is used to reinforce a market orientation. When a deal is completed, the salesperson rings the gong. "People get up and cheer and clap." Other teams in the company replace the gong with chest bumps or victory dances.

RITUALS ALSO USED TO AVOID JINXING A DEAL Salo employees have developed rituals aimed at increasing sales. Managing director Gwen Martin said, "When we are about to lock a deal down, it's bad luck to high-five each other, because you might jinx it." But some acknowledgment seemed appropriate. "So you do a 'pinkie-five' instead."[56]

YOUR THOUGHTS?

1. How are clan and market cultures being reinforced by Salo?

2. How comfortable would you be working at a company like Salo that so overtly organizes culture around rites, rituals, and even the need to avoid jinxes?

3. Which industries are the best fit for Salo's cultural approach, and why?

10. The Workflow and Organizational Structure Hierarchical structures are more likely to embed an orientation toward control and authority than a flatter organization. This partly explains why leaders from many organizations are increasingly reducing the number of organizational layers in an attempt to empower employees and increase employee involvement.

> **EXAMPLE** Novartis AG changed its organizational structure to foster the creativity and productivity associated with adhocracy and market cultures. "Leaders are seeing results from cross-functional product development teams. Job rotation and cross-training are also successful. Creating informal networking opportunities sounds trivial, but the evidence is strong that relationships heavily impact productivity and creativity."[57]

In contrast, both pharmaceutical maker Pfizer Inc. and water technology system provider Xylem Inc. added organizational layers—more hierarchy—in order to comply with the Foreign Corrupt Practices Act and to keep accurate records. The law prohibits US-based companies from bribing foreign officials in exchange for business.[58]

> **EXAMPLE** Pfizer consolidated its compliance systems by combining "separate departments around the world into one office, based in New York, which reports to the company's chief executive."

> **EXAMPLE** Xylem created a global anticorruption program. "It placed 'oversight committees' in each of the company's three divisions to help implement the program. The groups report to a broader oversight committee at the company's headquarters in White Plains, N.Y."[59]

11. Organizational Systems and Procedures Companies are increasingly using electronic networks as a tool to promote different types of cultures. Disney, for example, has invested over \$1 billion in big data technology in order to determine the best way to provide customer service, a characteristic of market cultures.[60]

EXAMPLE   Employees of Canada-based International Fitness Holdings, a health club group, use a Facebook-like application to "recognize peers by posting messages to a public 'team wall' as well as through private e-mails. . . . Each employee receives an annual bank of 300 Kudos points to award to coworkers. Once awarded, these points may be traded for prizes such as paid time off, gas cards or restaurant gift certificates." Employees can allocate points in 5-to-50-point increments depending on the importance of the behavior.[61] What type of culture would this system promote?

EXAMPLE   In San Francisco, Hearsay Social Inc., a social-media software company, uses online technology to collect peer performance feedback, which can promote any of the four culture types in the CVF. The feedback in turn is used to determine employees' performance evaluation. Managers feel that the performance evaluations are more accurate because they are based on input from multiple people.[62]

EXAMPLE   LifeSize Communications, a video conferencing company in Austin, Texas, uses an internal online network to promote collaboration (clan) and increased sales (market). A salesperson recently used the system to close a deal. The person wanted "advice about how to sell a product against a competitor." To get ideas, the salesperson logged onto the network "to access content posted by a LifeSize partner in South Africa. It describes an approach he used to win business against that competitor."[63]

12. Organizational Goals and Criteria throughout the Employee Cycle   How a company handles basic HR duties—for recruitment, selection, development, promotion, layoffs, and retirement of people—defines and perpetuates a company culture. Zappos, ranked as the 38th best place to work by *Fortune* in 2014, spends a great deal of time trying to hire people who fit into its clan-based culture (see Example box).

EXAMPLE   Zappos Works Hard to Recruit and Select People Who Fit Its Culture

Here is what Rebecca Ratner, Zappos's HR director, had to say about the company's approach to recruitment and selection. "We spend seven to 10 hours over four occasions at happy hours, team building events, or other things outside the office. We can see them, and they can us." The process seems to be good for retention. "In 2009, we had a 20 percent turnover rate," says Ratner. That is impressive for call centers. What keeps people at Zappos? "We pay 100 percent of employee benefits," . . . and then there's the wow factor.

"We can't ask people to wow a customer if they haven't been wowed by us," says Ratner. Zappos is so eager to wow employees and make sure who they hire is committed that they offer people \$3,000 after they've been trained to walk away if they feel they and Zappos aren't a good fit. Almost no one takes the \$3,000 walk-away money. But many trainees return for more Zappos training to become managers.[64]

YOUR THOUGHTS?

1. Why would Zappos's approach to recruiting result in greater person–organization fit?

2. As a potential employee, what would your concerns be attending a happy hour as part of your employer's selection process?

3. Identify one of the unique things that Zappos does in its recruitment, and explain how that one thing adds to culture.

Don't Forget about Person–Organization Fit Now that we have described the four key types of organizational culture and the mechanisms managers can use to change culture, it's time to reflect on your person–organization (PO) fit. Recall that PO fit reflects the extent to which your personality and values match the climate and culture in an organization. Your PO fit matters because it links to positive work attitudes and performance.[65]

We have two activities for you to complete to determine your level of fit and what you can do about it. The first is to take Self-Assessment 14.2. It measures your preference for the four types of culture in the CVF. The second is a Take-Away Application that asks you to compute the gap between your organization's current culture and your preferred culture. These gaps will then be used to make a plan of action for improving your PO fit.

---

connect

SELF-ASSESSMENT 14.2 **What Type of Organizational Culture Do I Prefer?**

Go to connect.mheducation.com and complete Self-Assessment 14.2. It measures your preferred type of organizational culture. After answering the following questions, results from this assessment will be used in the associated Take-Away Application.

1. What is the rank order of your preferred culture types?
2. To what extent does your preferred culture type affect your job satisfaction?

TAKE-AWAY APPLICATION—TAAP **What Is My Level of Person–Organization Fit?**

Use results from Self-Assessments 14.1 and 14.2 to answer the following questions.

1. First, compute the gap between your preferred and actual culture types for clan, adhocracy, market, and hierarchy. Do this by subtracting the actual culture type score (Self-Assessment 14.1) from the preferred type score (Self-Assessment 14.2). Where are your largest gaps?

2. Make a plan to improve your person–organization fit. Focusing on your two largest culture type gaps, determine what is causing the gaps. You will find it helpful to look at the survey items that measure these types to determine the cause of the gaps.

3. Now use the 12 embedding mechanisms just discussed and suggest at least two things you can do and two things your manager might do to improve your level of fit.

4. How would you assess whether or not the changes you identified in question 3 are working? Be specific.

MAJOR QUESTION

How can the practical lessons of socialization research be integrated within the three phases of socialization?

THE BIGGER PICTURE

Take a moment and think back to the last time you started a new job. Were you nervous and confused about what to do? Did someone help guide you through the transition? If not, you probably had an uncomfortable few days. If someone did help, then you experienced a form of proactive socialization. All of us have been socialized at one time or another. It's a natural aspect of starting a new job at any company. It's important to understand the socialization process because it ultimately affects your work attitudes and performance. You will learn about a three-phase model of organizational socialization and practical lessons based on socialization research.

Organizational socialization is defined as "the process by which a person learns the values, norms, and required behaviors which permit him to participate as a member of the organization."[66] This definition highlights that organizational socialization is a key mechanism used by organizations to embed their organizational cultures, particularly for new employees. In short, organizational socialization turns outsiders into fully functioning insiders by promoting and reinforcing the organization's core values and beliefs. This section introduces a three-phase model of organizational socialization and examines the practical application of socialization research.

A Three-Phase Model of Organizational Socialization

One's first year in a complex organization can be confusing. There is a constant swirl of new faces, strange jargon, conflicting expectations, and apparently unrelated events. Some organizations treat new members in a rather haphazard, sink-or-swim manner. More typically, though, the socialization process is characterized by a sequence of identifiable steps.

Organizational behavior researcher Daniel Feldman has proposed a three-phase model of organizational socialization that promotes deeper understanding of this important process. As illustrated in Figure 14.5, the three phases are:

1. Anticipatory socialization
2. Encounter
3. Change and acquisition

Each phase has its associated perceptual and social processes. Feldman's model also specifies behavioral and affective outcomes that can be used to judge how well an individual has been socialized. The entire three-phase sequence may take from a few weeks to a year to complete, depending on individual differences and the complexity of the situation.

Imagine the feelings that this new employee might have about starting a job. What emotions might he be experiencing? Excitement? Worry? Challenge? How can companies help new employees to "fit in" during the first few weeks of employment?

FIGURE 14.5 A MODEL OF ORGANIZATIONAL SOCIALIZATION

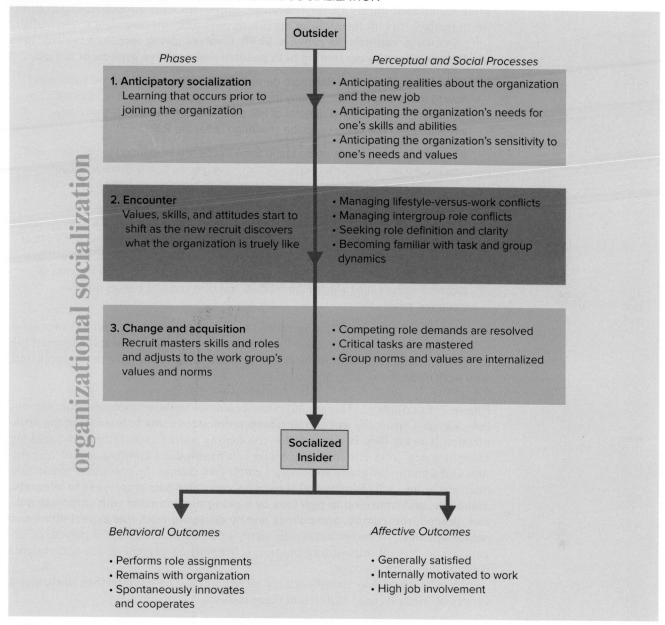

SOURCE: Adapted from D. C. Feldman, "The Multiple Socialization of Organization Members," *Academy of Management Review*, April 1981, 309–381. Copyright © 1981 by Academy of Management. Reprinted with permission of Academy of Management, via Copyright Clearance Center.

Phase 1: Anticipatory Socialization   The ***anticipatory socialization phase*** **occurs before an individual actually joins an organization.** It is represented by the information people have learned about different careers, occupations, professions, and organizations. Anticipatory socialization information comes from many sources. An organization's current employees are a powerful source of anticipatory socialization. So are the Internet and social media. For example, a recent survey of PricewaterhouseCoopers (PwC), the largest professional services firm in the world, uses several web-based sources to attract potential employees. "PwC's early identification strategy is supported by the pwc.tv website, *Feed Your Future* magazine (downloadable through pwc.tv; it showcases the lives/careers of PwC professionals), and Leadership Adventure (face-to-face learning programs that emphasize the PwC Behaviors).[67]

Unrealistic expectations about the nature of the work, pay, and promotions are often formulated during Phase 1. Because employees with unrealistic expectations are more likely to quit their jobs in the future, organizations may want to use realistic job previews. A *realistic job preview (RJP)* **involves giving recruits a realistic idea of what lies ahead by presenting both positive and negative aspects of the job.**

EXAMPLE   The Hilton Baltimore demonstrates to housekeeping job applicants how to make a bed. The company then asks the applicant to do it him/herself. Tishuana Hodge, regional director of HR, said, "We can see who is genuinely interested and physically up to the challenge" after the RJP.[68]

EXAMPLE   "Applicants of the Idaho State Police are introduced to the sights and sounds of a law enforcement environment, bringing them into immediate contact with future colleagues—and unsavory characters that create a need for police."[69]

EXAMPLE   AT&T, which has used RJPs for over 20 years, uses face-to-face meetings and videos to provide applicants RJPs. "One of its newer live realistic job previews gives insight to potential technicians responsible for installing AT&T's fiber optic technology and computer networking. Technicians also teach customers how to use the merchandise." AT&T does this because it needs "someone who has the technical knowledge to install the product and who can also deliver premier customer service."[70]

Research revealed that RJPs were related to higher performance and to lower attrition from the recruitment process. Results also demonstrated that RJPs lowered job applicants' initial expectations and led to lower turnover among those applicants who were hired.[71]

Phase 2: Encounter   This second phase begins when the employment contract has been signed. During the *encounter phase* **employees come to learn what the organization is really like.** It is a time for reconciling unmet expectations and making sense of a new work environment. Many companies use a combination of orientation and training programs to socialize employees during the encounter phase. Onboarding is one such technique. *Onboarding* **programs help employees to integrate, assimilate, and transition to new jobs by making them familiar with corporate policies, procedures, culture, and politics and by clarifying work-role expectations and responsibilities.**[72] A recent corporate survey revealed that roughly 73 percent of organizations rely on onboarding programs, but only 51 percent of the respondents believed they were effective.[73]

There is no set way to onboard a new employee. The Example box illustrates a variety of methods used at different organizations.

EXAMPLE   Companies Use Different Approaches to Onboard Employees

The first day on the job can be filled with completing boring paperwork regarding benefits and dull presentations about the company's history, mission, and values. While these activities are important, other companies try to find more creative ways for employees to spend their first few days and weeks at work.

FACEBOOK USES A BOOTCAMP   Facebook asks new hires to complete all necessary paperwork prior to starting work. This enables the company to send new employees right into its "Bootcamp" program. This six-week program is used for new engineering recruits. Bootcampers are first given a computer and desk and then are asked to open their laptops. They generally find six e-mails. "One welcomes them to the company; the other five describe tasks they're supposed to perform, including fixing bugs on the Facebook site." The program has multiple goals. One is to establish the belief that employees "have the power to push changes directly onto the Facebook site. . . . Another is to foster independence and creativity. At Facebook there isn't one way to solve problems; there are many—and everyone is encouraged to come up with his own approach." Bootcampers also are paired up with mentors who coach employees on how to best get through the first few weeks.[74]

ROVER.COM, RACKSPACE INC., AND BAZAARVOICE USE NOVEL METHODS

Dog-boarding site *Rover.com* asks new developers to create live updates on the company's website on their first day at work. Web-hosting firm Rackspace uses a four-day orientation complete with "games, skits, costumes, thumping music, and a limbo bar" to onboard its new employees. Bazaarvoice, a company that markets social commerce solutions to business problems, "sends incoming employees on a weeklong scavenger hunt designed to bring them up to speed on company culture and lingo."[75]

APPLE FOCUSES ON SECRECY

Apple's onboarding is a combination of a standard orientation, challenges, secrecy threats, and peer coaching. "Many employees are hired into so-called dummy positions, roles that aren't explained in detail until after they join the company." New employees are given very limited information outside of the half-day orientation that includes a welcome package containing all the paperwork to be completed. For example, employees are not taught how to connect their newly issued computers to the network. It is assumed that this complicated endeavor is no big deal for tech-savvy

These individuals are playing a game at an onboarding session. How can playing games help someone adjust during the encounter phase?

individuals. Employees also are given a "secrecy briefing," which is referred to as Scared Silent. Employees are warned about the importance of secrecy and security and are told that swift termination comes to anyone who talks about Apple's secrets outside of work. Apple does help new employees in one important way. They are assigned an "iBuddy," a peer outside the primary work team "who can serve as a sounding board, someone for the bewildered new employee to ask questions."[76]

AMERICAN INFRASTRUCTURE LIKES THE BUDDY SYSTEM

This civil construction, mining, and manufacturing company assigns new employees an onboarding "buddy." The buddy is supposed to help the recruit learn about the corporate culture "and to provide them with the opportunity to ask questions, gain clarification, and share best practices from their previous organizations." All new employees also are required "to wear a 'green' hard hat on all of their job locations for the first 90 days in order to signal to their fellow employees that they are new to the organization." This enables new employees to be treated with special care and concern at active jobsites.[77]

YOUR THOUGHTS?

1. Which of these onboarding methods is most appealing to you? Why?
2. Which of these onboarding methods is least appealing to you? Why?
3. What are the drawbacks of Apple's approach of hiring employees into dummy positions (for reasons of secrecy)? What are the trade-offs?

Phase 3: Change and Acquisition The ***change and acquisition phase*** requires **employees to master important tasks and roles and to adjust to their work group's values and norms.** This will occur only when employees have a clear understanding about their roles and they are effectively integrated within the work unit. Being successful in Phase 3 also necessitates that employees have a clear understanding regarding the use of social media. It is easy for you to create problems for yourself by not being aware of expectations regarding surfing, texting during meetings, and sending personal messages on company equipment. Experts suggest setting ground rules on the first day of employment, coaching employees on norms, and discussing how guidelines have changed over time.[78] Finally, success during this phase is enhanced when companies take a long-term approach toward socialization. Miami Children's Hospital (MCH) is a great example in that it uses goal setting, continued support, employee feedback, incentives, and a graduation ceremony to help employees through this final phase of socialization.

> **EXAMPLE**   Socialization at Miami Children's Hospital (MCH) is driven by the need to reduce turnover among new employees. The goal is to reduce new employee turnover by 50 percent. Support is provided in two ways. First, all new employees are assigned an MCH "buddy" who is trained in communication, coaching, and mentoring skills. New recruits shadow their buddy for the first 40 hours at work and then meet weekly to discuss any issues that come up. New employees also are supported by their direct supervision through this phase. This is facilitated by mandatory lunch meetings at 30- and 60-day milestones to discuss the onboarding experience. For feedback on the newcomer's transition, the hospital uses an online survey that employees complete at 30, 60, and 90 days. Results are reviewed monthly by management and further actions are taken whenever the socialization process appears to be failing. These results also are used to motivate the buddies, who are rewarded when the new hire rates the onboarding experience as effective. Finally, "new employees reunite at 90 days for a two-day culture-shaping retreat where they get to engage with their peers and experience the 'MCH Way.' This includes a graduation celebration that is attended by senior leaders and managers."[79]

Table 14.2 presents a list of socialization processes or tactics used by organizations to help employees through this adjustment process. Turning to Table 14.2, can you identify the socialization tactics used by MCH?

To what extent have you been adequately socialized? If it is high, then all is well. If your socialization is medium to low, you may need to find a mentor: Mentoring is discussed in the next section. Take a moment to complete Self-Assessment 14.3. It measures the extent to which you have been socialized into your current work organization.

Mc Graw Hill Education connect

SELF-ASSESSMENT 14.3   Have You Been Adequately Socialized?

Go to connect.mheducation.com and complete Self-Assessment 14.3. Then answer the following questions:

1. What is your level of socialization? Are you surprised by the results?
2. Based on your results and what you have learned about socialization, what advice would you provide to your organization to improve its socialization process?

Practical Application of Socialization Research

Past research suggests five practical guidelines for managing organizational socialization.

1. Effective onboarding programs result in increased retention, productivity, and rates of task completion for new hires.[80] This reinforces the conclusion that managers should avoid a haphazard, sink-or-swim approach to organizational socialization because formalized and proactive socialization tactics positively affect new hires.[81]

2. More and more organizations use socialization tactics to reinforce a culture that promotes ethical behavior. Managers are encouraged to consider how they might best set expectations regarding ethical behavior during all three phases of the socialization process.[82]

3. Managers need to help new hires integrate within the organizational culture and overcome the stress associated with working in a new environment. The

TABLE 14.2 SOCIALIZATION TACTICS

Examples in each row illustrate one or the other of the alternatives. Which one?

ALTERNATIVE TACTICS AND DESCRIPTION			WHICH IS THIS AN EXAMPLE OF?
COLLECTIVE	**VS.**	**INDIVIDUAL**	**EXAMPLE**
Grouping newcomers and exposing them to a common set of experiences.		Treating each newcomer individually and exposing him or her to more or less unique experiences.	All new hires attend an orientation session on the same day.
SEQUENTIAL	**VS.**	**RANDOM**	**EXAMPLE**
Segregating a newcomer from regular organization members during a defined socialization period.		No effort to clearly distinguish a newcomer from more experienced members.	Army recruits must attend boot camp before they are allowed to work alongside established soldiers.
FIXED	**VS.**	**VARIABLE**	**EXAMPLE**
Management setting a timetable for the assumption of the role.		Management setting no timetable and relying on contingencies for assumption of role.	American university students typically spend one year apiece as freshmen, sophomores, juniors, and seniors.
SERIAL	**VS.**	**DISJUNCTIVE**	**EXAMPLE**
The newcomer socialized over time with help of an experienced member.		The newcomer not provided a role model.	A buddy system of orientation.
INVESTITURE	**VS.**	**DIVESTITURE**	**EXAMPLE**
The affirmation of a newcomer's incoming global and specific role identities and attributes.		The denial and stripping away of the newcomer's existing sense of self and the reconstruction of self in the organization's image.	During police training, cadets are required to wear uniforms and maintain an immaculate appearance; they are addressed as "officer" and told they are no longer ordinary citizens but representatives of the police force.

SOURCE: Descriptions adapted from B. E. Ashforth, *Role Transitions in Organizational Life: An Identity-Based Perspective* (Mahwah, NJ: Lawrence Erlbaum Associates, 2001), 149–183.

type of orientation program used to socialize employees affects their expectations and behavior. A study of 72 new Asian international graduate students revealed that they had more accurate expectations, felt less stress, reported better adjustment, and had higher retention rates when the orientation program focused on coping with new-entry stress.[83] Consider the approach used by John Chambers, CEO of Cisco Systems: "He meets with groups of new hires to welcome them soon after they start, and at monthly breakfast meetings workers are encouraged to ask him tough questions."[84]

4. Support for stage models is mixed. Although there are different stages of socialization, they are not identical in order, length, or content for all people or jobs.[85] Managers are advised to use a contingency approach toward organizational socialization. In other words, different techniques are appropriate for different people at different times.

5. Managers should pay attention to the socialization of *diverse* employees. Research has demonstrated that diverse employees, particularly those with disabilities, experienced different socialization activities than other newcomers. In turn, these different experiences affected their long-term success and job satisfaction.[86]

MAJOR QUESTION

What are the four developmental networks and how can I use them to advance my career?

THE BIGGER PICTURE

Everyone can benefit from mentoring. We have! This section can help you to improve your development networks underlying mentoring, which ultimately should help you obtain career satisfaction and promotions.

The modern word *mentor* derives from Mentor, the name of a wise and trusted counselor in Greek mythology. Terms typically used in connection with mentoring are *teacher, coach, sponsor,* and *peer*. **Mentoring** is defined as the process of forming and maintaining intensive and lasting developmental relationships between a variety of developers (i.e., people who provide career and psychosocial support) and a junior person (the protégé, if male; or protégée, if female).[87] Mentoring can serve to embed an organization's culture when developers and the protégé/protégée work in the same organization for two reasons. First, mentoring contributes to creating a sense of oneness by promoting the acceptance of the organization's core values throughout the organization. Second, the socialization aspect of mentoring also promotes a sense of membership.

Not only is mentoring important as a tactic for embedding organizational culture, but research suggests it can significantly influence the protégé/protégée's future career.[88] This section reviews the functions of mentoring, the developmental networks underlying mentoring, and the personal and organizational implications of mentoring.

Functions of Mentoring

Kathy Kram, a Boston University researcher, conducted in-depth interviews with both members of 18 pairs of senior and junior managers. As a by-product of this study, Kram identified two general functions—career and psychosocial—of the mentoring process.

Five *career functions* that enhanced career development were:

1. Sponsorship
2. Exposure and visibility
3. Coaching
4. Protection
5. Challenging assignments

Big Brothers Big Sisters is the largest volunteer mentoring network in the United States. The organization has paired adults with children for over 100 years. A survey of former children in the progam revealed that 83 percent obtained values and principles that influenced them throughout their lives.

Four *psychosocial functions* were:

1. Role modeling
2. Acceptance and confirmation
3. Counseling
4. Friendship

The psychosocial functions clarified the participants' identities and enhanced their feelings of competence.[89]

Developmental Networks Underlying Mentoring

Mentoring is currently viewed as a process in which protégés and protégées seek developmental guidance from a network of people, who are referred to as *developers*. McKinsey & Company tells its associates, "Build your own McKinsey." This slogan means the consulting firm expects its people to identify partners, colleagues, and subordinates who have related goals and interests so that they can help one another develop their expertise. Each McKinsey associate is thus responsible for his or her own career development—and for mentoring others. As McKinsey's approach recognizes, the diversity and strength of a person's network of relationships are instrumental in obtaining the type of career assistance needed to manage his or her career.[90]

Figure 14.6 presents a developmental network typology based on integrating the diversity and strength of developmental relationships.[91]

Diversity of Developmental Relationships *Diversity of developmental relationships* **reflects the variety of people within the network an individual uses for developmental assistance.** There are two subcomponents associated with network diversity: (1) the number of different people the person is networked with and (2) the various social systems from which the networked relationships stem (e.g., employer, school, family, community, professional associations, and religious affiliations). As shown in Figure 14.6, developmental relationship diversity ranges from low (few people or social systems) to high (multiple people or social systems).

FIGURE 14.6 DEVELOPMENTAL NETWORKS ASSOCIATED WITH MENTORING

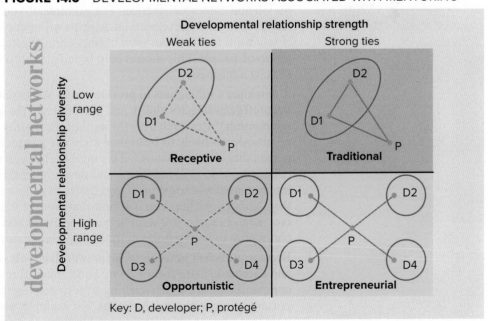

Key: D, developer; P, protégé

SOURCE: From M. Higgins and K. Kram, "Reconceptualizing Mentoring at Work: A Developmental Network Perspective," *Academy of Management Review*, April 2001, 270. Copyright © 2001 by Academy of Management. Reprinted with permission of Academy of Management, via Copyright Clearance Center.

Developmental Relationship Strength **Developmental relationship strength** represents the quality of relationships among the individual and those involved in his or her developmental network. For example, strong ties are reflective of relationships based on frequent interactions, reciprocity, and positive affect. Weak ties, in contrast, are based more on superficial relationships. Together, the diversity and strength of developmental relationships result in four types of developmental networks (see Figure 14.6): receptive, traditional, entrepreneurial, and opportunistic. It is important that you do not ignore weak ties because they very frequently lead to job opportunities.[92]

A *receptive* developmental network is composed of a few weak ties from one social system such as an employer or a professional association. The single oval around D1 and D2 in Figure 14.6 indicates two developers who come from one social system. In contrast, a *traditional* network contains a few strong ties between an employee and developers that all come from one social system. An example would be your creating a strong developmental relationship with your boss and one colleague at work. An entrepreneurial network, which is the strongest type of developmental network, is made up of strong ties among several developers (D1–D4) who come from four different social systems. In this case, you would develop strong ties with your boss and one internal colleague, but you also would develop a good network with people from other organizations. Finally, an opportunistic network is associated with having weak ties with multiple developers from different social systems.

Personal and Organizational Implications

There are six key implications to consider:

1. **You should foster a broad developmental network because the number and quality of your contacts will influence your career success.** In doing this, keep in mind the comments of two networking experts: "Relationships are living, breathing things. Feed, nurture, and care about them; they grow. Neglect them; they die.[93] It's very important to invest time in your developmental relationships.

2. **Look to the consistency or congruence between your career goals and the type of developmental network at your disposal.** This alignment has a big influence on job and career satisfaction. For example, if you are interested in a job in finance, then try to develop relationships with people with a finance background. If you want to start your own business one day, try to network with a diverse group of people. This should help broaden your understanding of what it takes to start a business.

3. **A developer's willingness to provide career and psychosocial assistance depends on the protégé/protégée's ability and potential and the quality of the interpersonal relationship.**[94] Research also shows that the quality of the mentoring relationship is likely to be higher when the parties have common values and personality characteristics.[95] This implies that you must take ownership for enhancing your skills, abilities, and developmental networks as well as your interpersonal relationships if you desire to experience career advancement throughout your life. You will find that you get what you give. Don't just contact mentors when you want something. Build and maintain relationships by continuing to have regular contact with people in your developmental network.

4. **Become proficient at using social networking tools such as Twitter, LinkedIn, and Facebook.** Data from Jobvite and LinkedIn reveal that the majority of US companies use social networking sites to help recruit employees.[96] It's also important to stay active on these sites. For example, when you learn from a LinkedIn note that someone is celebrating a birthday or work anniversary, send them a note. People like to feel appreciated for who they are rather than for what they can do for you.

5. **Develop a mentoring plan.** Experts suggest that this plan should include the following components:[97]
   - Identify and prioritize your mentoring goals. These goals should be based on a determination of what you want to learn.
   - Identify people who are skilled or experienced in areas you want to improve. Don't overlook your peers as they are a good source of functional, technical, and organizational knowledge.
   - Determine how best to build a relationship with these "targeted" individuals.
   - Determine how you can provide value to your mentor. Because mentoring is a two-way street, others are more likely to help you if they see some value in assisting you in the pursuit of your career goals.
   - Determine when it is time to move on. Mentors are not forever. If you believe that your mentor is ineffective, or worse yet, causing more harm than benefit, find a new mentor. It's easy to become stuck with one mentor. Expanding your horizons will not only benefit you, but it can help the mentor to develop his or her mentoring skills as well.

6. **Incorporate mentoring into the organization's leadership development programs.** Disney, Walsh Construction, and LMA Consulting all obtained long-lasting positive benefits by formally including mentoring into employees' personal development plans.[98]

Are you being adequately mentored? If not, you are more likely to experience adverse work attitudes, performance, and career outcomes. Self-Assessment 14.4 was created so that you can take stock of your level of mentoring.

connect

SELF-ASSESSMENT 14.4 Assessing My Level of Mentoring

Go to connect.mheducation.com and complete Self-Assessment 14.4. Then answer the following questions:

1. What is your level of mentoring?
2. After identifying your three lowest scoring items in the survey, propose things you can do to improve your level of mentoring?
3. How would you evaluate the success of these ideas?

In conclusion, mentoring can help you and the organizations in which you may work. For example, mentoring enhances the effectiveness of organizational communication. Specifically, mentoring increases the amount of vertical communication both up and down an organization. It also provides a mechanism for modifying or reinforcing organizational culture. Benefits such as these are leading more and more companies to set up formal mentoring programs.

what did i learn?

You learned that organizational culture helps managers to create competitive advantage. You examined the function and types of culture and considered how managers can change culture. Finally, you now know that socialization and mentoring are two processes that organizations use to embed organizational culture. As an employee this same knowledge helps you understand your employer's culture and how to best to fit in. Reinforce what you learned with the Key Points below. Then consolidate your learning using the Integrative Framework. Finally, Challenge your mastery of this chapter by answering the Major Questions in your own words.

Key Points for Understanding Chapter 14

You learned the following key points.

14.1 THE FOUNDATION OF ORGANIZATIONAL CULTURE: UNDERSTANDING ITS DRIVERS AND FUNCTIONS

- Culture is a shared concept that is learned over time. It also influences our behavior at work and outcomes at multiple levels.

- The three levels of organizational culture are observable artifacts, espoused values, and basic underlying assumptions.

- Espoused values represent the explicitly stated values and norms that are preferred by an organization. Enacted values, in contrast, reflect the values and norms that actually are exhibited or converted into employee behavior.

- Four functions of organizational culture are organizational identity, collective commitment, social system stability, and a device for sense-making.

14.2 THE IMPACT OF ORGANIZATIONAL CULTURE TYPES ON OUTCOMES

- The competing values framework identifies four different types of organizational culture. A clan culture has an employee focus. Adhocracy and market cultures have external foci that emphasize innovation/growth and market share/profitability, respectively. Hierarchical cultures are internally focused on efficiency and smooth functioning.

- There are five conclusions about outcomes associated with organizational culture: (1) culture is related to measures of organizational effectiveness; (2) employees are more satisfied and committed to compa-

nies with clan cultures; (3) innovation and quality can be increased by building characteristics associated with clan, adhocracy, and market cultures; (4) an organization's financial performance is not strongly related to culture; and (5) companies with market cultures tend to have more positive organizational outcomes.

14.3 THE PROCESS OF CULTURE CHANGE

- There are four caveats about culture change. First, leaders are the architects and developers of organizational culture. Second, the process of culture change begins with targeting the three layers of culture. Third, culture needs to be aligned with a company's vision and strategic plan. Finally, it is important to use a structured approach when implementing culture change.

- There are 12 key ways that managers can change organizational culture.

- Person–organization fit is important because it is associated with positive work attitudes and performance.

14.4 THE ORGANIZATIONAL SOCIALIZATION PROCESS

- Organization socialization is a key mechanism used by organizations to embed their organizational cultures. It turns outsiders into fully functioning insiders.

- Daniel Feldman proposed a three-phase model of socialization. The three phases are anticipatory socialization, encounter, and change and acquisition.

- There are six socialization tactics. They are collective versus individual, formal versus informal, sequential versus random, fixed versus variable, serial versus disjunctive, and investiture versus divestiture.

- Research supports a number of practical applications of socialization tactics.

14.5 EMBEDDING ORGANIZATIONAL CULTURE THROUGH MENTORING

- Mentoring serves to embed organizational culture for two reasons. First, mentoring contributes to creating a sense of oneness by promoting the acceptance of the organization's values. Second, the socialization aspect of mentoring promotes a sense of membership.

- Mentoring has two general functions: career and psychosocial.

- Current models of mentoring view it as a developmental network of relationships that help people to learn and develop.

- There are four key developmental networks underlying effective mentoring. A receptive network is composed of a few weak ties from one social system. Having a few strong ties with developers from one social system is referred to as a traditional network. An entrepreneurial network is made up of strong ties among several developers. An opportunistic network is associated with having weak ties from different social systems.

- There are six important personal and organizational implications of effective mentoring.

The Integrative Framework for Chapter 14

As shown in Figure 14.7, you learned that the input of national and corporate culture as an environmental characteristic drives organizational-level processes of culture, socialization, and mentoring. These processes affect five outcomes across the individual, group/team, and organizational levels.

Challenge: Major Questions for Chapter 14

At the start of the chapter, we told you that after reading the chapter you should be able to answer the following questions. Unless you can, have you really processed and internalized the lessons in the chapter? Refer to the Key Points, Figure 14.7, the chapter itself, and your notes to revisit and answer the following major questions:

1. What is culture and why is it important to understand its layers and functions?

2. To what extent are the different types of organizational culture related to important outcomes?

3. What are the mechanisms I can use to implement culture change?

4. How can the practical lessons of socialization research be integrated within the three phases of socialization?

5. What are the four developmental networks and how can I use them to advance my career?

FIGURE 14.7 INTEGRATIVE FRAMEWORK FOR UNDERSTANDING AND APPLYING OB

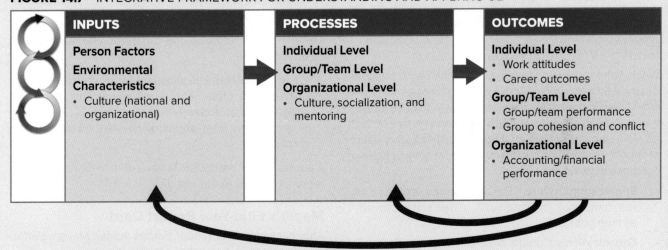

© 2014 Angelo Kinicki and Mel Fugate. All rights reserved. Reproduction prohibited without permission of the authors.

Changing the Culture at Yahoo! Inc.

You might call Yahoo! the original Internet company. Starting in the mid-1990s by almost accidentally discovering the need for good search engines, Yahoo! became a wildly popular web portal whose valuation shot high during the creation of the dot-com bubble.

But over the years Yahoo! lost its way—trying to be too many things to too many people. After a string of CEOs and failed attempts to halt a steady loss in value, Yahoo! tapped Marissa Mayer, somewhat famous as one of Google's early hires, in July 2012. Her task? To lead the charge and help Yahoo! regain and fulfill its promise as a major player in Internet and mobile.

For this case we will focus on Mayer's challenges in transforming Yahoo! culture and business performance.

Wall Street: Happy

Response on the street has continued to be positive. As of this writing, Yahoo! has seen its stock price rise by over 100 percent. Investors applaud Mayer and her plans—and they drove the stock even higher after revenue reports for the third quarter of 2013 exceeded expectation.[99]

Industry Watchers: Hopeful

When Yahoo! announced Mayer's appointment, many industry watchers immediately had high hopes that she would help Yahoo! gain some Google mojo to drive netizen traffic. Rafe Needleman at CNET is representative of such opinion, when he set out what he saw as the top five issues at Yahoo!. Google and culture make his list several times in comparison to Yahoo!:

- **Engineering Culture.** "The best Google services are fast, functional, and continually tested and improved as time goes on."

- **Organizational Culture.** Needleman quotes Salim Ismael, one critic of Yahoo!'s organizational structure: "On the Internet you need speed and you need to take risks. Yahoo! accidentally adopted a matrix organization structure that's antithetical to both." (Authors' note: We discuss matrix organizational design in Chapter 15.)

- **Killing Projects.** Google "maintains an optimism about its direction even as it chops down its underperformers."

- **Long-Term Visions.** Needleman suggests that Google can weather setbacks (as with Google's attempts in social media) because it commits to a long-term vision.

- **Culture of Experimentation.** Google tries many things, from self-driving cars to eyeglasses that

augment reality. Such pure research can pay off in unexpected ways. However, he notes Yahoo! doesn't have Google's fat wallet to fund such R&D.[100]

Yahoo!'s Long Problems with Focus

From one point of view, all of Yahoo!'s challenges can be linked to a well-discussed lack of focus. In 2006 *The New York Times* published an article critical of Yahoo!,[101] and in response Brad Garlinghouse, then a Yahoo! senior vice president, wrote an internal memo published by *The Wall Street Journal*.

> We lack a focused, cohesive vision for our company. We want to do everything and be everything—to everyone. We've known this for years, talk about it incessantly, but do nothing to fundamentally address it. . . . I've heard our strategy described as spreading peanut butter across the myriad opportunities that continue to evolve in the online world. The result: a thin layer of investment spread across everything we do and thus we focus on nothing in particular.

Garlinghouse also notes the organizational result of this cultural dilemma:

> We are separated into silos that far too frequently don't talk to each other. And when we do talk, it isn't to collaborate on a clearly focused strategy, but rather to argue and fight about ownership, strategies and tactics.[102]

A succession of Yahoo! CEOs have tried to fix Yahoo! in this regard. How has Mayer fared?

Mayer's First-Year Report Card

After her first year at Yahoo!, *Forbes* graded Mayer's performance across its own set of categories:

- **Advertising [Revenue]: D.** Yahoo! was still struggling with reversing declines in ad revenue while its competitors were increasing revenue.

- **Earnings: C.** Revenues were flat in 2012 and declined in the first part of 2013. (This was prior to a bump in the third quarter of 2013.)

- **Products: B–.** *Forbes* liked the increase in decisions to kill old products (like Altavista) and bring new products to market.

- **Acquisitions: B.** *Forbes* called out the acquisition of Tumblr, among others.

- **Morale: B+.** *Forbes* noted that former employees were returning and job applications were way up.

An OB View of Mayer's Performance

From an OB perspective, looking at Mayer's first 16 months, we can note the following achievements. Mayer has:

- Opened up communications and transparency including frequent internal and public announcements, bolstered internally with a Friday FYI "ask anything" session with employees.[103]

- Used PR to leverage her (perhaps enhanced) legend of achievement at Google to inspire investors and the troops at Yahoo!.

- Removed some business-only executives and replaced them with tech- and product-savvy employees.

- Restored Yahoo! as an employer of choice.[104]

- Energized Yahoo! engineers into optimism about the future.[105]

- Made the tough change in telecommuting policy to help make Yahoo! more productive. (See discussion below.)

- Addressed Yahoo!'s lack of a social community (and outflanked Google) by purchasing Tumblr.[106]

About That Telecommuting Decision, Other Bumps in the Road

You have already read about Mayer's decision to ban telecommuting for most employees in Chapter 2's Problem-Solving Application on Yahoo! (see page 77). We can now reconsider this controversial decision in the context of the need to change Yahoo!'s comfortable and staid culture. Here's *Forbes* magazine on the topic:

> Whether you agree with Mayer's decision or not, she needed to do something. She is facing what some would say are significant challenges at Yahoo!, which is considered stodgy and lethargic in comparison to its competitors. To combat that perception, she is searching for innovative ways to make magic happen—always a tough spot for leaders under siege.[107]

Mayer's decisions will continue to generate controversy, from a fashion shoot in *Vogue* magazine to the teleconferencing decision to reengineering the e-mail structure.[108]

Early in 2014 Mayer fired her hand-picked COO based on lackluster sales.[109] While bumps in the road are to be expected, the true test will be how well Yahoo! stays on course and makes corrections. As an example, following the decision on telecommuting, Mayer reclaimed some lost support among employees when she significantly expanded parental leave benefits.[110] The decision was announced in May 2013, the month before the telecommuting policy took effect.

Apply the 3-Stop Problem-Solving Approach to OB

Stop 1: What is the problem?

- Use the Integrative Framework of OB (see Figure 14.7) to help identify the outcomes that are important in this case.

- Which of these outcomes are not being achieved in the case?

- Based on considering the above two questions, what is the most important problem in this case?

Stop 2: Use the Integrative Model of OB shown at the start of this chapter to help identify the OB concepts or theories that help you to understand the problem in this case.

- What person factors are most relevant?

- What environmental characteristics are most important to consider?

- Do you need to consider any processes? Which ones?

- What concepts or theories discussed in this chapter are most relevant for solving the key problem in this case?

Stop 3: What are your recommendations for solving the problem?

- Review the material in the chapter that most pertains to your proposed solution and look for practical recommendations.

- Use any past OB knowledge or experience to generate recommendations.

- Outline your plan for solving the problem in this case.

LEGAL/ETHICAL CHALLENGE

Is an Apology Enough?

The dilemma in this case pertains to a scandal at the University of North Carolina (UNC). Organizational culture is at the core of the case because the events that occurred indirectly involve the values and beliefs about the role of athletics within a university.

The scandal revolved around whether or not the school's Department of African and Afro-American Studies offered courses that never met and sponsored hundreds of independent study classes of limited value to student athletes. The university did an internal review and, as reported in *Bloomberg Businessweek*, determined the department "offered more than 200 lecture courses that never met. The department also sponsored hundreds of independent study classes of dubious value. Internal reviews have identified forged faculty signatures and more than 500 grades changed without authorization. The students affected were disproportionately football and basketball players."[111]

College athletics is a $16 billion industry, and schools enjoy the related revenues in light of their nonprofit, tax-exempt status as organizations dedicated to education and research. This means that it is important for the "stars" to keep playing and win games.

Management at UNC took action and eight employees either resigned or were fired, including the chancellor. The new chancellor, Carol Foyt, initially resisted calls for further investigation, but changed her mind in January 2014. An investigation is currently taking place.

The scandal was exposed by Mary Willingham, a campus reading specialist. Mary told reporters that she and other academic advisers "knowingly steered some of their charges into the fake classes to keep the sports stars eligible." She said that "18 out of about 180 athletes whose records she assessed could be considered to read at a grammar school level."[112] Willingham's comments resulted in her being demoted and stripped of her supervisory title and public condemnation by some school officials. For example, James Dean Jr., the executive vice chancellor and

provost, said that "Mary Willingham has done our students a great disservice." He initially declared that Willingham was a liar, but later apologized stating that he had misspoken. Head basketball coach Roy Williams said that "Willingham had impugned the moral character of his players." He claimed that "every one of the kids that we've recruited in 10 years you'd take home and let guard your grandchildren." Sadly, Willingham has in turn received e-mails containing death threats, and recent reports in *Businessweek* reveal that Dean continues to attack Willingham in internal meetings.[113]

Solving the Dilemma

Assume that you are the chancellor; what would you do at this point in the case?

1. Acknowledge wrongdoing, reinstate Mary Willingham to her former position, and continue the internal investigation.

2. Acknowledge wrongdoing, but Mary stays where she is. She should not have blown the whistle to local reporters without first going to upper management at the university.

3. Reprimand both James Dean and the basketball coach for their comments, and continue the internal investigation.

4. Invent other options.

GROUP EXERCISE

Assessing the Organizational Culture at Your School

Objectives

1. To provide you with a framework for assessing organizational culture.

2. To conduct an evaluation of the organizational culture at your school.

3. To consider the relationship between organizational culture and organizational effectiveness.

Introduction

Academics and consultants do not agree about the best way to measure an organization's culture. Some people measure culture with surveys, while others use direct observation or information obtained in interviews/workshops with employees. This exercise uses an informal group-based approach to assess the three levels of organizational culture discussed in this chapter. This approach has successfully been used to measure organizational culture at a variety of organizations.

Instructions

Your instructor will divide the class into groups of four to six people. Each group member should then complete the Cultural Assessment Worksheet by him- or herself. It asks you to identify the artifacts, espoused values, and basic assumptions that are present at your current school. You may find it useful to reread the material on layers of organizational culture discussed earlier. When everyone is done, meet as a group and share the information contained on your individual worksheets. Create a summary worksheet based on a consensus of the cultural characteristics present at each level of culture. Next, compare the information contained on the summary worksheet with the cultural descriptions shown in Figure 14.3 and discuss what type of culture your school possesses. Again, strive to obtain a consensus opinion. Finally, the group should answer the discussion questions that follow the Cultural Assessment Worksheet.

Cultural Assessment Worksheet

Artifacts (physical or visible manifestations of culture; they include jargon, heroes, stories, language, ritual, dress, material objects, mascots, physical arrangements, symbols, traditions, and so forth)	Espoused Values (the stated values and norms preferred by the organization)	Basic Assumptions (taken-for-granted beliefs about the organization that exist on an unconscious level)

Questions for Discussion

1. What are the group's consensus artifacts, espoused values, and basic assumptions? Are you surprised by anything on this list? Explain.

2. What type of culture does your school possess? Do you like this organizational culture? Discuss why or why not.

3. Do you think the organizational culture identified in question 2 is best suited for maximizing your learning? Explain your rationale.

4. Is your school in need of any cultural change? If yes, discuss why and recommend how the school's leaders might create this change. The material on embedding organizational culture would help answer this question.

15 ORGANIZATIONAL DESIGN, EFFECTIVENESS, AND INNOVATION

How Can Understanding These Key Processes and Outcomes Help Me Succeed?

inputs

PERSON FACTORS

ENVIRONMENTAL CHARACTERISTICS
Organizational Structure

processes

INDIVIDUAL LEVEL

GROUP/TEAM LEVEL

ORGANIZATIONAL LEVEL
Organizational Design and Effectiveness

outcomes

INDIVIDUAL LEVEL

GROUP/TEAM LEVEL

ORGANIZATIONAL LEVEL
Accounting/Financial Performance
Innovation

MAJOR TOPICS I'LL LEARN AND QUESTIONS I SHOULD BE ABLE TO ANSWER

15.1 THE FOUNDATION OF AN ORGANIZATION
MAJOR QUESTION: *How can knowledge about an organization's foundation help me in my career?*

15.2 ORGANIZATION DESIGN
MAJOR QUESTION: *What are the seven basic ways in which organizations are structured, and how do these structures relate to the organization's purpose?*

15.3 THE CONTINGENCY APPROACH TO DESIGNING ORGANIZATIONS
MAJOR QUESTION: *How can I use knowledge about contingency organization design to find an employer that fits my needs and preferences?*

15.4 STRIVING FOR ORGANIZATIONAL EFFECTIVENESS
MAJOR QUESTION: *What does an organization's choice of how it measures its effectiveness tell me about the organization?*

15.5 ORGANIZATIONAL INNOVATION
MAJOR QUESTION: *How can I better understand how companies innovate so I can support my company in innovation?*

INTEGRATIVE FRAMEWORK FOR UNDERSTANDING AND APPLYING OB

Organizational structure is a key environmental input that impacts organizational level processes and outcomes.

© 2014 Angelo Kinicki and Mel Fugate. All rights reserved. Reproduction prohibited without permission of the authors.

winning at work

WORKING VIRTUALLY TAKES SPECIAL PREPARATIONS

Advances in social networking, video conferencing, cloud storage, and mobile technology have enabled more and more employees to work virtually. Whether you work for a company like Kalypso LP, a consulting firm with 150 employees and no corporate offices, or a company that prefers that employees show up at the office, it is likely that you will perform some of your work away from the office. For example, today about 2.5 percent of the US workforce works exclusively from home whereas roughly 20 percent of workers around the world telecommute and conduct some of their work from home.[1]

WHY IS IT HARD TO WORK VIRTUALLY?

Although you can work virtually from almost anywhere, most virtual work takes place from your home. There are three primary issues that make it hard for most people to work from home. The first involves the need for personal contact and social interaction. Many of us enjoy the social contact and camaraderie that comes with working in an office. Second, many people have difficulty creating boundaries between their work and home life. Finally, it takes discipline to work from home. There are no managers or colleagues around to motivate or prompt you to get things done.

TIPS FOR WORKING VIRTUALLY

1. **Create an effective work area.** You need dedicated space to work, free of clutter and distractions (like the TV). It should feel like an office—include pictures and such, be well-lit, and allow for privacy. Some people like to include green plants because it helps them concentrate.

2. **Set your work hours.** Too much flexibility can lead to wasting time and distractions. Commit to specific hours just like you would if you were going to an office.

3. **Set expectations with family and friends.** Talk to family and friends about the need to minimize distractions while working from home. You need to be left alone. It must be clear that working from home doesn't mean that you are available to answer personal questions any more than if you worked at an office. Interruptions should be allowed for important issues.

4. **Establish goals and to-do lists.** A list of things you need to get done will help to focus on the work and avoid distractions or the tendency to procrastinate.

5. **Communicate with people in your professional network.** Out of sight, out of mind. Be sure to maintain contact with people in your professional network. This obviously includes your boss and coworkers, but also might involve customers, vendors, or personal contacts.

6. **Get the desired level of human interaction.** Schedule time to meet face-to-face with coworkers and friends. You will have to make a special effort as you are the one away from the office.[2]

FOR YOU   WHAT'S AHEAD IN THIS CHAPTER

This second chapter on macro OB highlights how organizational structure and design affect organizational-level outcomes. We begin by exploring the basic foundation of an organization and then review seven basic ways organizations are structured. Next we review the contingency approach to organizational design and then discuss four generic effectiveness criteria used by organizations. We conclude by exploring innovation and how it can be fostered.

MAJOR QUESTION

How can knowledge about an organization's foundation help me in my career?

THE BIGGER PICTURE

We interact with people in organizations on a daily basis. Whether they are for-profit, non-profit, or mutual benefit, organizations possess some common characteristics. The better you understand these foundations, the better prepared you will be to perform at any level of the organization. You'll explore these commonalities and more: the difference between a closed and open system; and how organizations can become learning organizations. As a necessary springboard for this chapter, we formally define the term *organization,* clarify the meaning of organization charts, and explore two open-system perspectives of organizations.

What Is an Organization?

From a design perspective, an **organization** is "a system of consciously coordinated activities or forces of two or more persons."[3] Earlier in this book, the common understanding of organization was adequate for our discussions. But now this formal definition is especially helpful because the phrase "consciously coordinated" underscores the importance of organizational design.

Embodied in the *conscious coordination* aspect of this definition are four common denominators of all organizations: coordination of effort, aligned goals, division of labor, and a hierarchy of authority.[4]

- **Coordination of effort** is achieved through formulation and enforcement of policies, rules, and regulations.
- **Aligned goals** start from the development of a companywide strategic plan. These strategic goals are then cascaded down through the organization so the employees are aligned in their pursuit of common goals.
- **Division of labor** occurs when the common goal is pursued by individuals performing separate but related tasks.
- **Hierarchy of authority,** also called the chain of command, is a control mechanism dedicated to making sure the right people do the right things at the right time. Historically, managers have maintained the integrity of the hierarchy of authority by adhering to the unity of command principle. The **unity of command principle** specifies that each employee should report to only one manager. Otherwise, the argument goes, inefficiency would prevail because of conflicting orders and lack of personal accountability. (Indeed, these are problems in today's more fluid and flexible organizations based on innovations such as cross-functional, self-managed, and virtual teams.) Managers in the hierarchy of authority also administer rewards and punishments.

When operating in concert, the four foundational factors—coordination of effort, a common goal, division of labor, and a hierarchy of authority—enable an organization to come to life and function.

Organization Charts

An organization chart is a graphic representation of formal authority and division of labor relationships. To the casual observer, the term *organization chart* means the family tree–like pattern of boxes and lines posted on workplace walls. Within each box one usually finds the names and titles of current position holders. To organization theorists, however, organization charts reveal much more. The partial organization chart in Figure 15.1 reveals four basic dimensions of organizational structure: (1) hierarchy of authority (who reports to whom), (2) division of labor, (3) spans of control, and (4) line and staff positions.

Hierarchy of Authority   As Figure 15.1 illustrates, there is an unmistakable structure or chain of command. Working from bottom to top, the 10 directors report to the two executive directors who report to the president who reports to the chief executive officer. Ultimately, the chief executive officer answers to the hospital's board of directors. The chart in Figure 15.1 shows strict unity of command up and down the line. A formal hierarchy of authority also delineates the official communication network and speaks volumes about compensation. Research shows that there is an increasing wage gap between layers over time. That is, the difference in pay between successive layers tends to increase over time.[5]

Division of Labor   In addition to showing the chain of command, the sample organization chart indicates extensive division of labor. Immediately below the hospital's president, one executive director is responsible for general administration while another is responsible for medical affairs. Each of these two specialties is

FIGURE 15.1   SAMPLE ORGANIZATION CHART FOR A HOSPITAL (EXECUTIVE AND DIRECTOR LEVELS ONLY)

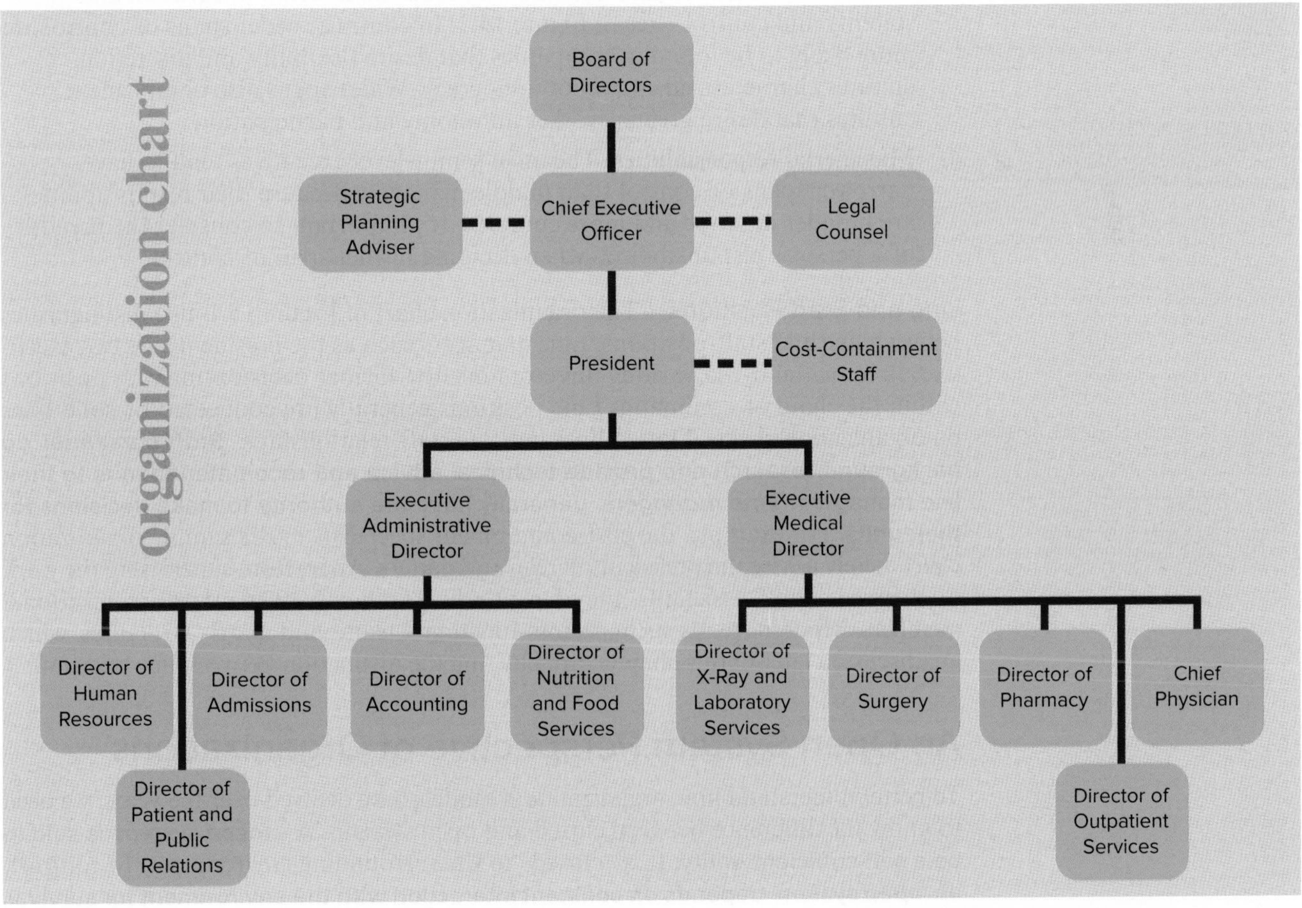

further subdivided as indicated by the next layer of positions. At each successively lower level in the organization, jobs become more specialized.

Spans of Control   **Span of control refers to the number of people reporting directly to a given manager.** Spans of control can range from narrow to wide. For example, the president in Figure 15.1 has a narrow span of control of two. (Staff assistants usually are not included in a manager's span of control.) Narrow spans of control tend to create "taller" organizations or those that are more hierarchical. In contrast, a wide span of control leads to a "flat" organization. The executive administrative director in Figure 15.1 has a wider span of control of five. Historically, spans of 7 to 10 people were considered best. More recently, however, corporate restructuring and improved communication technologies have increased the typical span of control.[6]

Although there is no consensus regarding the optimal span of control, managers should consider four factors when determining spans of control: organizational size, skill level, organizational culture, and managerial responsibilities. Let's consider each of these factors.[7]

1. **Organizational size.** Larger organizations tend to have narrower spans of control and more organizational layers, whereas smaller ones have a wider span of control. Costs tend to be higher in organizations with narrow spans due to the increased expense of having more managers. Communication also tends to be slower in narrow spans because it must travel throughout multiple organizational layers.

2. **Skill level.** Complex tasks require more managerial input, thereby suggesting a narrow span of control. Conversely, routine tasks do not require much supervision, leading to the use of a wider span of control.

3. **Organizational culture.** Narrow spans of control are more likely in companies with a hierarchical culture because they focus on internal integration and stability and control—recall Figure 14.3. In contrast, wider spans of control are more likely to be found in companies that desire flexibility and discretion, cultures characterized as clan or adhocracy. Wider spans also complement cultures that desire greater worker autonomy and participation.

4. **Managerial responsibilities.** The most senior-level executives tend to have narrower spans of control than middle managers because their responsibilities are broader in scope and more complex. It's important to consider the breadth of a person's responsibilities when deciding his/her span of control.

Line and Staff Positions   The organization chart in Figure 15.1 also distinguishes between line and staff positions. Line managers such as the president, the two executive directors, and the various directors occupy formal decision-making positions within the chain of command. Line positions generally are connected by solid lines on organization charts. Dotted lines indicate staff relationships. **Staff personnel do background research and provide technical advice and recommendations to their line managers. Line managers generally have the authority to make decisions for their units.** For example, the cost-containment specialists in the sample organization chart merely advise the president on relevant matters. Apart from supervising the work of their own staff assistants, they have no line authority over other organizational members. Modern trends such as cross-functional teams and matrix structures, which are discussed later in this chapter, are blurring the distinction between line and staff.

An Open-System Perspective of Organizations

To better understand how organizational models have evolved over the years, we need to know the difference between closed and open systems. **A closed system is said to be a self-sufficient entity.** It is "closed" to the surrounding environment. In contrast, **an open system depends on constant interaction with the environment for survival.** The distinction between closed and open systems is a matter of degree. Because every worldly system is partly closed and partly open, the key question is: How great a role does the environment play in the functioning of the system? For instance, a battery-powered clock is a relatively closed system. Once the battery is inserted, the clock performs its time-keeping function hour after hour until the battery goes dead. The human body, on the other hand, is a highly open system because it requires a constant supply of life-sustaining oxygen from the environment. Nutrients also are imported from the environment. Open systems are capable of self-correction, adaptation, and growth, thanks to feedback from the environment.

The fact that college tuitions always seem to be on the rise is a good example of an open system. While we might hope that tuition is rationally set in a closed system where knowledgeable administrators work from clear inputs on costs and expenses, in reality tuition is set in a much more open system. Consider that public universities mostly see the amount of public subsidy reduced as politicians respond to political pressure. Given that most people do not want to pay more taxes to finance education, universities thus are pushed to either raise tuition or cut costs and services. Private universities similarly see a decrease in private donations due to limited funds and an abundance of caution due to uncertainty with the U.S. economy. University presidents also may be trying to manage demands from directors or chancellors to improve academic ratings (if not the football team). So you see, universities do not have the ability to function as closed systems in most cases, especially as to tuition. Over time, at least generally, a systems approach suggests that demands for increased performance go up and subsidizing resources go down.

Historically, management theorists downplayed the environment as they used closed-system thinking to characterize organizations as either well-oiled machines or highly disciplined military units. They believed rigorous planning and control would eliminate environmental uncertainty. But that approach proved unrealistic. Drawing on the field of general systems theory that emerged during the 1950s, organization theorists suggested a more dynamic model for organizations.[8] The resulting open-system model likened organizations to the human body. Accordingly, the model in Figure 15.2 reveals the organization to be a living organism that transforms inputs into various outputs. The outer boundary of the organization is permeable. People, information, capital, and goods and services move back and forth across this boundary.

Moreover, each of the five organizational subsystems—goals and values, technical, psychosocial, structural, and managerial—is dependent on the others. Feedback

FIGURE 15.2 THE ORGANIZATION AS AN OPEN SYSTEM

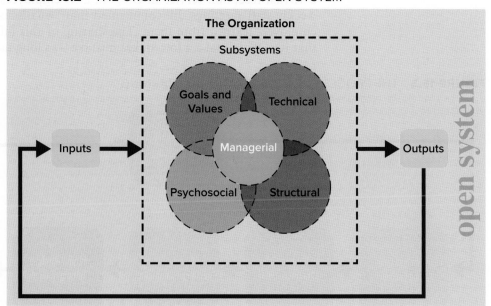

SOURCE: This model is synthesized from Figures 5-2 and 5-3 in F. E. Kast and J. E. Rosenzweig, *Organization and Management: A System and Contingency Aproach,* 4th ed. (New York: McGraw-Hill, 1986), 112, 114.

about such things as sales and customer satisfaction or dissatisfaction enables the organization to self-adjust and survive despite uncertainty and change. In effect, the organization is alive.

Learning Organizations

In recent years, organizational theorists have extended the open-system model by adding a "brain" to the "living body." Organizations are said to have humanlike cognitive functions, such as the abilities to perceive and interpret, solve problems, store information, and learn from experience. This has led to a stream of research that examines the process by which organizations learn. Peter Senge, a professor at the Massachusetts Institute of Technology, popularized the term *learning organization* in his best-selling book *The Fifth Discipline.* He described a learning organization as "a group of people working together to collectively enhance their capacities to create results that they truly care about."[9] A practical interpretation of these ideas results in the following definition. **A *learning organization* is one that proactively creates, acquires, and transfers knowledge and that changes its behavior on the basis of new knowledge and insights.**[10]

It is important to understand how organizations learn because learning is essential to an organization's continuous improvement and renewal over time. As such, it is no surprise that organizational learning is positively associated with organizational performance and innovation, a topic discussed later in this chapter.[11] Researchers have shown that organizations learn by using five independent subprocesses (see Figure 15.3): information acquisition, information distribution, information interpretation, knowledge integration, and organizational memory. Let us consider how these processes work.

Step 1: Information Acquisition *Information acquisition,* also known as *scanning,* "refers to the process through which an organization obtains information from internal and external sources."[12] Because this is the first step of learning, it is advantageous for organizations to include breadth in their acquisition of information. For example, discussions about past success and failure, a process called "post-mortems," represent critical sources of information.

Step 2: Information Distribution *Information distribution* pertains to the processes or systems that people, groups, or organizational units use to share information among themselves. For example, Jill Nelson, the founder of Ruby Receptionists, a virtual reception service in Oregon, asks employees to discuss their mistakes at weekly staff meetings. Jill commented that "we discuss the mistakes and what the employees learned from them. The sharing of this information sends the message that it's OK to make a low-stakes mistake—as long as you learn from it and share

FIGURE 15.3 THE PROCESS OF ORGANIZATIONAL LEARNING

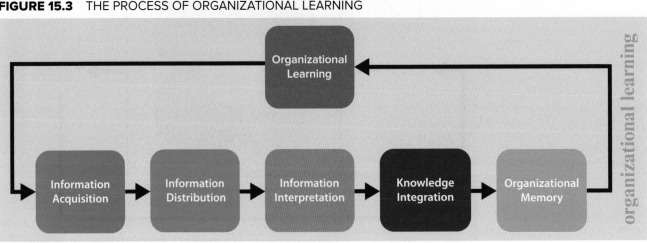

This unit of firefighters has to rely on organizational learning to effectively fight fires. The unit has to work as a team while adjusting to things like weather, temperature, and breadth of the fire. Fire units also are known for having post-mortems after a fire to discuss lessons learned.

your lesson with others."[13] We encourage all organizations to follow Jill's lead.

Step 3: Information Interpretation   This step is all about making sense of the information that organizations have acquired and distributed. It is important to remember that this step is affected by the perceptual biases discussed in Chapter 4 and the decision-making biases reviewed in Chapter 11.

Step 4: Knowledge Integration   *Knowledge integration* occurs when information is integrated across different sources. Integration leads to shared understanding among individuals and groups. This step can be accomplished by having post-mortems in which different people or groups present their ideas about an opportunity or problem. The point is to seek consensus about the meaning of information being considered.

Step 5: Organizational Memory   Learning will not last unless the organization finds a method to save it. Knowledge needs to be put into some type of repository or organizational memory if it is to be used in the future. Organizational memory is not an object. Rather, it represents the combined process of "encoding, storing, and retrieving the lessons learned from an organization's history, despite the turnover of personnel."[14]

What Can Be Done to Improve Organizational Learning?   We have two recommendations. The first is to improve on the five steps just discussed. This might begin by using a survey to assess the extent to which an organization is following these steps. The Self-Assessment below was created so that you could make this assessment on a current or former employer. Results from such an assessment then can be used to target organizational changes aimed at improving learning.

connect

SELF-ASSESSMENT 15.1   Am I Working for a Learning Organization?

Go to connect.mheducation.com and complete Self-Assessment 15.1. Then answer the following questions:

1. To what extent is the company a learning organization? Are you surprised by the results?
2. Identify the three items receiving the lowest ratings. Now, propose solutions for how the organization might improve on these three areas.

Second, realize that leader behavior and organizational culture drive organizational learning. If leaders do not support a vision and culture that promote the value of learning, it won't happen.

EXAMPLE   Consider A. G. Lafley, CEO of Procter & Gamble from 2000 to 2009. Lafley told a reporter from *Harvard Business Review* that he made plenty of mistakes and that he had "my fair share of failure. But you have to get past the disappointment and the blame and really understand what happened and why it happened. And then, more important, decide what you have learned and what you are going to do differently next time."[15] Lafley's views on learning certainly contributed to P&G's success under his leadership: "sales doubled, profits quadrupled, and P&G's market value increased by more than $100 billion."[16] P&G's poor performance after his departure led to his return as CEO in 2013. The company is hoping that Lafley can use what he has learned about leadership and strategic management to help turn the company around.[17]

The rationale of open systems led Jack Welch, former CEO of GE, to coin the term *boundaryless organization.* **A *boundaryless organization* is one "where management has largely succeeded in breaking down barriers between internal levels, job functions and departments, as well as reducing external barriers between the association [organization] and those with whom it does business."**[22] Members of boundaryless organizations communicate primarily with e-mail, phone, and other virtual methods. This type of structure is fluid and flexible and relies on telecommuting between geographically dispersed people.[23] This suggests that this structure is most appropriate for businesses in fast-changing industries or environments.

While the introduction and apparent ascendancy of each of these categorical forms of organization ties to a specific point in history, all of these forms are in use today, often to the maximum potential. All structures are valid if matched with an organization's vision and strategies. For example, Zappos recently adopted a horizontal structure called a "holocracy" in order to give employees more voice in getting things done. The design attempts to eliminate the role of traditional managers and get rid of job titles.[24]

Seven Types of Organizational Structures

The following seven types of organizational structure cover almost all organizations. We provide historical background, with examples and schematic diagrams for each.

FUNCTIONAL STRUCTURE

Work is organized into separate vertical functions, such as finance, sales, production, and human resources.

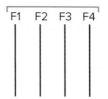

Functional Structure   **A *functional structure* groups people according to the business functions they perform, for example, manufacturing, marketing, and finance.** A manager is responsible for the performance of each of these functions, and employees tend to identify strongly with their particular function, such as sales or engineering.

> EXAMPLE   The organization chart in Figure 15.1 illustrates a functional structure. Responsibility at this hospital is first divided into administrative and medical functions, and within each category, directors are responsible for each of the functions. This arrangement puts together people who are experts in the same or similar activities. Thus, as a small company grows and hires more production workers, salespeople, and accounting staff, it typically groups them together with a supervisor who understands their function.

Some organizations have concluded that using a functional structure divides people too much, ultimately creating silos within the organization. This in turn detracts from the extent to which employees collaborate and share best practices across functions.

DIVISIONAL STRUCTURE

Work is organized into separate vertical divisions, which may focus on products or services, or customers or clients, or even geography.

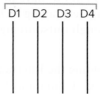

Divisional Structure   In a ***divisional structure,* employees are segregated into organization groups based on similar products or services, customers or clients, or geographic regions.** The divisional structure is sometimes called a product structure or profit center approach.

> EXAMPLE   General Electric has four businesses (major product divisions): GE Capital, GE Energy, GE Technology Infrastructure, and GE Home & Business Solutions. These major business areas are subdivided further into either product or geographic divisions.[25] Typically, within each division it maintains its own internal functional structure.

As with functional structures, some organizations have concluded that using a divisional structure can also create silos within the organization.

Matrix Structure   Organizations use matrix structures when they need stronger horizontal alignment or cooperation in order to meet their goals. **A *matrix structure* combines a vertical structure with an equally strong horizontal overlay.** This generally combines functional and divisional chains of command to form a grid with two command structures, one shown vertically by function and the other shown horizontally, by product line, brand, customer group, or geographic region.

MATRIX STRUCTURE

The matrix can be used with a variety of vertical and horizontal elements. Shown here are four different functions interlinked to four product lines.

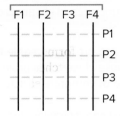

HORIZONTAL STRUCTURE

Several flexible teams—T1–T4—organize around the horizontal workflow or processes. Some vertical functions remain, but they are minimized.

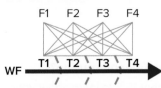

EXAMPLE Pharmaceutical maker Bristol-Myers Squibb is highly committed to this structure. Jane Luciano, vice president of global learning and organization development, said, "We have the matrix every way it can be organized, including geographically, functionally, and on a product basis." The company is very pleased with its matrix structure. Ms. Luciano noted that "the matrix has enabled us to upgrade and promote excellence around core capabilities, so we can be very purposeful in developing functional expertise in specific disciplines, such as marketing, medical, HR, or finance excellence."[26]

Such a structure can provide a reasonable counterbalance among important stakeholders.

Application of a matrix structure is not easy. Matrix organizations have a bad reputation for being too complex and confusing. The reality is that it takes much more collaboration and integration to effectively implement this structure. Jay Galbraith, an expert on matrix structures, noted that matrix structures frequently fail because management fails to create complementary and reinforcing changes to the organization's IT systems, human resource procedures (e.g., performance appraisals, rewards, selection criteria), planning and budgeting processes, organizational culture, internal processes, and so on. He concluded that "organization structures do not fail; managements fail at implementation."[27] This type of structure increasingly is being used by companies expanding into international markets.

Horizontal Structure In a ***horizontal structure,*** **teams or workgroups, either temporary or permanent, are created to improve collaboration and work on common projects.**

This horizontal approach to organizational design tends to focus on work processes. A process consists of every task and responsibility needed to meet a customer need, such as developing a new product or filling a customer order. Completing a process requires input from people in different functions, typically organized into a cross-functional team (described in Chapter 8).

EXAMPLE W.L. Gore & Associates is a good example of a company that has successfully implemented this structure (see Example box).

Teamwork is a common feature of organizations designed horizontally.

EXAMPLE W.L. Gore & Associates Operates with a Horizontal Design

W.L. Gore is a technologically driven company that focuses on product innovation. It develops and manufactures products that provide highly reliable performance in varied environments, ranging from the surface of Mars, to inside the heart. In 2012, the company received its 15th consecutive recognition from *Fortune* as one of the 100 Best Places to Work. It was ranked as the 22nd best in 2014. Employees are called associates.

Founder Bill Gore said, "The objective of the Enterprise is to make money and have fun doing so."[28] The company has followed this premise for over 50 years. The culture is built on the following beliefs:[29]

- **Belief in the individual**—employees are encouraged to trust and believe in each other.
- **Power of small teams**—a team-based structure with minimum hierarchy is used.

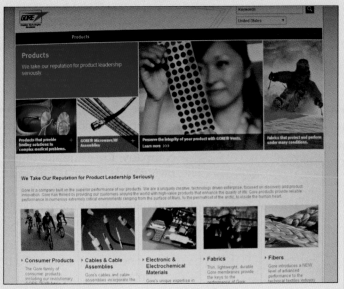

Gore links strategy, culture, and structure.

- **All in the same boat**—employees are part owners through a stock plan.
- **Long-term view**—investments are based on long-term payoffs.

Gore avoids hierarchy and is less formal than most companies. Interactions among associates are informal, and people are encouraged to treat each other "respectfully and fairly. This type of environment naturally promotes social interaction."[30]

Gore's structure is consistent with its strategy and culture. It has a "team-based flat lattice organization that fosters personal initiative. There are no traditional organizational charts, no chains of command, nor predetermined channels of communication."

HOW DOES THE STRUCTURE WORK?   Associates "communicate directly with each other and are accountable to fellow members of our multi-disciplined teams. We encourage hands-on innovation, involving those closest to a project in decision making. Teams organize around opportunities and leaders emerge. This unique kind of corporate structure has proved to be a significant contributor to associate satisfaction and retention."

Associates "are hired for general work areas. With the guidance of their sponsors (not bosses) and a growing understanding of opportunities and team objectives, associates commit to projects that match their skills. All of this takes place in an environment that combines freedom with cooperation and autonomy with synergy."[31]

YOUR THOUGHTS?

1. What are the pros of Gore's structure?
2. What are the drawbacks?
3. Do you think this type of structure would work in most organizations? Explain.

The final three types of structures are all examples of open organizations. Before learning about them in more detail, find out how well suited you are for telecommuting. Telecommuting is a common practice in companies that use open designs.

connect

SELF-ASSESSMENT 15.2   **What Is My Preference for Telecommuting?**

Go to connect.mheducation.com and complete Self-Assessment 15.2 to learn about your preferences for working in a traditional environment versus telecommuting. Then answer the following questions:

1. Do you prefer telecommuting or a traditional work environment?
2. What bothers you most about telecommuting?
3. How might managers assess an employee's preference for telecommuting in a job interview?

HOLLOW STRUCTURE

Within the organization, a number of functions are outsourced.

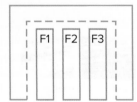

Hollow Structure   A **_hollow structure_**, also known as a **_network structure_**, is designed around a central core of key functions and outsources other functions to other companies or individuals who can do them cheaper or faster. An athletic shoe company, for example, might decide that it can excel at developing new designs, owing to its design talent and knowledge of the market. Then it might find outsourcing partners to handle other activities such as manufacturing, order taking, shipping, and managing employee benefits. The more processes that are outsourced, the more the resulting organization is "hollow"—and focused on what it does best.

EXAMPLE   Herman Miller, the furniture company, goes outside the organization for design expertise. CEO Brian Walker explained the advantages. "This external network ensures that we are always taking a fresh look at problems faced by our customers without subjecting [them] to our own filters. If you have only an internal design staff, even an enormously talented one, you are inherently limited by their existing world view and experiences. Our ability to tap into a broader outside network lets us . . . get a fresh perspective on existing or emerging problems." The company also uses other organizations for manufacturing; Walker says the company is "more . . . an integrator than a manufacturer," which makes it less resistant to new product ideas because it doesn't have to change manufacturing processes itself.[32]

A hollow structure is useful when an organization is faced with strong price competition and there are enough companies to perform the required outsourced processes.

The growing number of hollow structures has increased demand for freelance workers. This in turn has created an online industry that helps companies hire people for micro-tasks or short-term assignments (see the Problem-Solving Application).

solving application

Freelancers Use the Internet to Obtain Work

TaskRabbit, located in San Francisco, operates like an eBay for odd jobs. The online service helps link people looking for short-term work with organizations or people that need someone to complete specific tasks.

How Does It Work? Assume that an individual has an errand he or she wants done and doesn't have time to do it, or a company wants a unique task completed and it doesn't have a skilled person to do it. The person or organization looking for help goes to TaskRabbit .com and posts the task and the amount to be paid for the work. Members of TaskRabbit, called

TaskRabbits, then place bids to get the work. "Generally, the lowest bidder wins. TaskRabbit gets a cut of the transaction."

TaskRabbit "makes people undergo a rigorous process to become a TaskRabbit, including a video interview, federal background check, Social Security number trace and, lastly, a test to see if applicants have what it takes."[33]

Is the Concept Spreading? Yes, according to Dane Stangler, director of research and policy at the Ewing Marion Kauffman Foundation. Dane estimates that 10 percent of US workers are freelancers. Consider the experience of Elance Inc., an

online job networking site. Elance, which "lets freelancers bid for jobs like programming or designing that they can complete over the Internet, has attracted more than 500,000 businesses and 2 million freelancers, about a third of whom are based in the United States." The company estimates that it will pay workers about $300 million in 2013.

Is There a Downside? Sara Horowitz, founder and executive director of the Freelancers Union, thinks so. She thinks that sites like TaskRabbit or Elance will lead people to accept jobs with no benefits and poor work conditions.[34]

YOUR CALL

Stop 1: What is the problem that led to the creation of companies like TaskRabbit and Elance?

Stop 2: What OB theories or concepts underscore the value of the service being offered by TaskRabbit and Elance?

Stop 3: Would you use online services like this to find a job? Would you recommend them to friends?

Modular Structure A modular organization, like a hollow organization, uses outsourcing. But instead of outsourcing processes, it outsources parts of a product, such as components of a jet or subroutines of a software program. **In a _modular structure,_ the company assembles product parts, components, or modules provided by external contractors.** The modular organization also is responsible for ensuring that the parts meet quality requirements, that the parts arrive in a timely fashion, and that the organization is capable of efficiently combining the parts into

MODULAR STRUCTURE

The main part of the organization (M) is structured and managed to make it easy to plug in vendors for well-defined functions (F1 through F3) as parts of the business process.

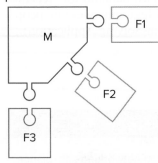

VIRTUAL STRUCTURE

One or more companies (here we show companies A and B) create or manage a wide network of virtually connected employees, represented by the dots, for a specific business process that otherwise appears as a traditional company.

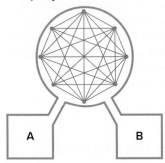

the final whole. This design is useful when a company can identify product modules and create design interfaces that allow it to assemble parts into a working order.

> **EXAMPLE** A good example is Boeing, in its production of the 787 Dreamliner. Modular structures are used in other industries such as automobile manufacturing, bicycle production, home appliances, consumer electronics, and software development.

Virtual Structure The concept of virtual organizations originated in the 1990s. It was an outgrowth of the benefits associated with information technology. **A *virtual structure* is one whose members are geographically apart, usually working with e-mail and other forms of information technology, yet which generally appears to customers as a single, unified organization with a real physical location.**

> **EXAMPLE** Automattic, Inc., a web designer, has 291 employees working in 26 countries, 94 cities, and 28 states in the United States. The company, which hosts servers for the blogging platform WordPress.com, allows workers to work from anywhere. Virtual meetings are commonplace. "The company has a San Francisco office for occasional use, but project management, brainstorming and water-cooler chatter take place on internal blogs. If necessary, team members fly around the world to meet each other face to face. And if people have sensitive questions, they pick up the phone."[35]

The primary benefits of virtual structures like that of Automattic are the ability for organizations to tap into a wider talent pool, to increase the speed in getting things done, and to reduce costs because there is less need for physical facilities and travel budgets.

The nature of virtual organizations has expanded since their inception. Today, virtual structures are classified into two different types: internal and networked.[36]

Toni Schneider was CEO of Automattic from 2006–January 2014. The use of a virtual structure helped the company to grow from its inception in 2005 to over $1 billion in revenue. Toni currently serves in a role associated with product building.[37]
SOURCE: Automattic, Inc., at http://automattic.com/map/.

TABLE 15.2 SEVEN STRUCTURES OF ORGANIZATIONAL DESIGN

STRUCTURE	BEST FOR	PROS	CONS
Functional F1 F2 F3 F4	Small companies, some large government organizations and divisions of large companies (see following).	Clear roles and responsibilities.	Coordination and communication across functional silos can be an issue; most companies use dotted line or other informal means to combat this potential limitation.
Divisional D1 D2 D3 D4	Large companies with separate divisions built on different technologies, geographies, or different bases of customers.	Clear roles and responsibilities. Workers in each division can have more product focus, accountability, and flexibility than in a functional structure.	Coordination and communication across divisional silos can be an issue (as with functional structures, most companies use dotted line or other informal means to combat this potential limitation).
Matrix F1 F2 F3 F4 P1 P2 P3 P4	Organizations looking to more formally escape problems associated with silos by using a formal level of horizontal integration. Increasingly used by international organizations.	Lines of formal authority along two dimensions, such as functional/product or product/region, can allow organization to work more cohesively.	Management can sometimes fail to provide adequate processes to ensure its success. Because some employees report to two bosses simultaneously, there is the potential for conflict if the managers fail to coordinate.
Horizontal F1 F2 F3 F4 WF T1 T2 T3 T4	Companies needing to create better value by improving internal coordination for greater efficiency or flexibility in rapid response to customer needs.	Rapid communication and reduction in cycle time of work done; greater flexibility; faster organizational learning; improved responsiveness to customers.	Potential conflicts between processes and nonprocess functions; nonprocess parts of the organization could suffer neglect; fewer opportunities for functional specialization.
Hollow F1 F2 F3	When there is heavy price competition with pressure to cut costs and markets outside the organization can perform required processes.	Lower cost of entry and overhead; access to best sources of specialization and technology; market discipline that leads to supplier competition and innovation; potential for further cost reduction and quality improvement.	Loss or decrease of in-house skills, internal capacity to innovate, control over supply; costs of transitioning to hollow state; higher monitoring to align incentives; competitive threat of being supplanted by suppliers.
Modular M F1 F2 F3	When it is possible to specify the nature of product modules and to design interfaces that allow multiple vendors to join up and function.	Potential for cost savings, faster responsiveness, competence beyond one's boundary; ability to switch vendors for best fit and product improvement.	Not all products may be amenable to chunking into modules; poorly specified interfaces can hinder modules and hamper assembly; laggards can hold up innovation that occurs concurrently across a chain of collaborators.
Virtual A B	When it is possible to explore a new market opportunity by partnering with other organizations or rapidly deploying a new potential business model.	Ability to respond nimbly to market opportunity, to provide product extension or one-stop-shop service to leverage organizational assets distributed across partners forming the virtual firm; low exit costs if initial opportunity vanishes.	Requires high level of communication to avoid redundancy; wide distribution of employees can undermine trust and coordination; likely fails to promote strong employee loyalty or organizational identification.

seven structures of organizational design

SOURCE: Adapted from N. Anand and R. L. Daft, "What Is the Right Organizational Design?," *Organizational Dynamics,* June 2007, Vol. 36, No. 4, 329–344. Reprinted with permission of Elsevier.

1. **Internal virtual structures.** Internal virtual structures pertain to work arrangements that are used to coordinate the work of geographically dispersed employees working for one organization, such as those at Automattic, Inc., or e-mailing marketing firm Emma. Emma has 100 employees working across the United States. This structure primarily relies on the use of information technology, but also requires managers to consider three key issues:

   • **Do I have the right people?** Not everyone is suited to work virtually, as you may have learned from taking Self-Assessment 15.2. This implies that it is essential for managers to consider the personal characteristics, needs, and values of people who might work virtually. For example, a recent study of upper-division business students revealed that the Big Five personality trait of agreeableness was positively associated with attitudes toward telecommuting.[38] Clint Smith, CEO of Emma, likes to hire employees who are self-confident and skilled in proactively communicating. He believes that these skills are needed to ensure that employees take initiative to be kept in the loop on what is going on.

   • **How often should people get together?** There is no clear answer to this question. At Emma, for instance, employees are patched into 45-minute video meetings every two weeks. The CEO also encourages all employees to return to headquarters in Nashville for big events or holiday parties. Our recommendation is to use a contingency approach. More frequent contact is needed at the start of a project, and we suggest that regular milestone meetings should be held online.

   • **What type of technology should be used to coordinate activities?** Of course remote workers can stay connected with a host of technology. The choice depends on the skills and resources at hand. That said, we concur with Clint Smith's conclusion about not underestimating "the power of the voice, the power of the face and the power of the face to face." Emma has purchased a variety of group-chat tools and collaboration tools to foster productive communication among its dispersed employees.[39]

2. **Networked virtual structures.** This structure is used to establish a collaborative inter-organizational network of independent firms or individuals in order to create a virtual entity. The networked individuals or companies join forces because each possesses core competencies needed for a project or product. This structure is used in the movie/entertainment industry. For example, writers, producers, actors, and studios join forces, not as one legal entity, but rather as a collaborative network to make a movie. Once again, a variety of information technology is used to coordinate the efforts of the different members within the network.

   Now that we have reviewed all 7 designs, consider Table 15.2. It shows the pros and cons for each design and suggests situations when a design may be most effective.

TAKE-AWAY APPLICATION—TAAP **What Is My Preferred Type of Organizational Structure?**

Use the seven fundamental types of organizational structure to answer these questions:

1. Which of the seven types is most consistent with how you like to work and your preferred working environment? Explain.

2. Have you ever worked in a company that had a structure that did not fit your needs and style? How did you feel working there?

3. How would you assess whether or not a future employer had your preferred organizational structure?

THE CONTINGENCY APPROACH TO DESIGNING ORGANIZATIONS

MAJOR QUESTION

How can I use knowledge about contingency organization design to find an employer that fits my needs and preferences?

THE BIGGER PICTURE

You know that every job has its pros and cons. The same is true about an organization's design. You will learn that there is no singular structure that is appropriate to all organizations. This awareness led to the contingency approach to designing organizations. After reviewing a landmark study about the difference between mechanistic and organic organizations, we discuss when each of the seven organizational designs previously discussed is most likely to be effective.

According to the **contingency approach to organization design,** organizations tend to be more effective when they are structured to fit the demands of the situation. One of the first design considerations is whether the organization would flourish with centralized or decentralized decision making. This distinction underscores the difference between mechanistic and organic organizations.

Mechanistic versus Organic Organizations

A landmark contingency design study was reported by a pair of British behavioral scientists, Tom Burns and G. M. Stalker. In the course of their research, they drew a very instructive distinction between what they called *mechanistic* and *organic* organizations.

Mechanistic organizations are rigid bureaucracies with strict rules, narrowly defined tasks, and top-down communication. A mechanistic organization generally would have one of the traditional organizational designs described earlier in this chapter and a hierarchical culture—recall the discussion of culture types in Chapter 14. The "orderliness" of this structure is expected to produce reliability and consistency in internal processes, thereby resulting in higher efficiency, quality, and timeliness. You can imagine how valuable this type of structure might be for a company in the nuclear power industry, where mistakes and errors can be catastrophic. It is important to note that being mechanistic does not mean that an organization should not be responsive to employee and customer feedback. Toyota, a company noted for being more mechanistic, fell into this trap and ended up with recalls involving faulty accelerator pedals and rusted spare-tire carriers.[40]

Organic organizations are flexible networks of multitalented individuals who perform a variety of tasks. Organic organizations are more likely to use horizontal designs or those that open boundaries between organizations. Whole Foods Market is a prime example (see the Example box).

EXAMPLE Whole Foods Market Uses an Organic Structure

Whole Foods Market has grown by merger, acquisition, and expansion to over 370 stores, over 58,000 employees, and revenues in the range of $9–12 billion.[41] It operates in the United States, Canada, and the United Kingdom. Founder and co-CEO John Mackey stated that "Whole Foods is a social system. . . . It's not a hierarchy."[42] The company does not pass down lots of rules from corporate headquarters in Austin, Texas. Rather, it relies on a team-based structure that promotes commitment to productivity, innovation, and decentralized decision making across 12 geographic regions.

THE STRUCTURE IS BASED ON FOUR CORE PRINCIPLES

1. **Self-directed teams.** Each store is an autonomous profit center that is structured around an average of 10 self-managed teams. Each team has a designated leader and a set of performance goals. Teams meet regularly to discuss operations, solve problems, and recognize each other. They also have the power to make hiring decisions, and everyone's pay is publicly shown on the company's intranet. It's clear that important decisions are made at the store level, and teams provide key input to these decisions.

2. **"No-secrets" management.** The company measures a host of productivity indices and then shares the data with all employees. For example, stores regularly post sales broken down by team, year-to-date, and sales against the same day last year. Each month, the stores get detailed data on profitability. Productivity measures such as "sales per labor hour" also are tied to team member bonuses.

3. **Accountability and competition are essential.** Teams are expected to establish and achieve stretch performance targets. Teams are encouraged to compete against other teams in pursuit of key goals like sales per labor hour. Teams compete against teams in their own store as well as teams in different stores and regions. Peer reviews and responses to its ongoing store tours (provided and promoted at all individual locations) are used to evaluate performance within a store.

4. **Shared fate.** The company does not believe in entitlements. Rather, it promotes a shared fate by using a "salary cap that limits the compensation (wages plus profit incentive bonuses) of any team member to nineteen times the average total compensation of all full-time team members in the company."[43]

YOUR THOUGHTS?

1. What are some of the key ways Whole Foods avoids excess hierarchy?

2. Based on your knowledge of OB, why would employees like to work in this type of work environment?

3. Whole Foods has the luxury of selling many of its products at a premium to a more affluent section of the market. To what degree would its horizontal and organic approach work in other demographics? Ordinarily profit margins in the retail food industry are thin.

Different Approaches to Decision Making   Decision making tends to be centralized in mechanistic organizations and decentralized in organic organizations. **Centralized decision making** occurs when key decisions are made by top management. **Decentralized decision making** occurs when important decisions are made by middle- and lower-level managers. Generally, centralized organizations are more tightly controlled while decentralized organizations are more adaptive to changing situations.

Experts on the subject warn against extremes of centralization or decentralization. For example, Ron Johnson, former CEO of JC Penney, created problems for the company when he unilaterally pushed his "no-discounts" strategy without heeding advice of internal managers and industry norms. Johnson, a former executive at Apple, implemented ideas that were contrary to Penney's brand and customers' preferences. He also was unwilling to test his ideas on a subset of stores before rolling them out across all stores.[44] The challenge is to achieve a workable balance between the two extremes. A management consultant put it this way:

> The modern organization in transition will recognize the pull of two polarities: a need for greater centralization to create low-cost shared resources; and a need to improve market responsiveness with greater decentralization. Today's winning organizations are the ones that can handle the paradox and tensions of both pulls. These are the firms that analyze the optimum organizational solution in each particular circumstance, without prejudice for one type of organization over another. The result is, almost invariably, a messy mixture of decentralized units sharing cost-effective centralized resources.[45]

Practical Research Insights   When they classified a sample of actual companies as either mechanistic or organic, Burns and Stalker discovered one type was not superior to the other. Each type had its appropriate place, depending on the environment. When the environment was relatively stable and certain, the successful organizations tended to be *mechanistic*. The successful ones tended to be *organic* organizations when the environment was unstable and uncertain.[46] Research on this topic reveals two key conclusions.

1. **Bureaucracy begets greater bureaucracy.** This conclusion comes from a study of 42 voluntary church organizations. As the organizations became more mechanistic (more bureaucratic), the intrinsic motivation of their members decreased. Mechanistic organizations apparently undermined the volunteers' sense of freedom and self-determination. Additionally, the researchers believe their findings help explain why bureaucracy tends to feed on itself: "A mechanistic organizational structure may breed the need for a more extremely mechanistic system because of the reduction in intrinsically motivated behavior."[47] Thus, bureaucracy begets greater bureaucracy.

2. **Communication patterns follow structure.** Field research in two factories, one mechanistic and the other organic, found expected communication patterns. Command-and-control (downward) communication characterized the mechanistic factory. Consultative or participative (two-way) communication prevailed in the organic factory.[48]

Getting the Right Fit

All of the organization structures described in this chapter are used today because each structure has advantages and disadvantages that make it appropriate in some cases. For example, the clear roles and strict hierarchy of an extremely mechanistic organization are beneficial when careful routines and a set of checks and balances are important, as at a nuclear power facility. In a fast-changing environment with a great deal of uncertainty, an organization would benefit from a more organic structure that lowers boundaries between functions and organizations.

Experts suggest that managers should consider four key issues when making decisions about how best to design an organization: strategy and goals, technology, size, and human resources.[49]

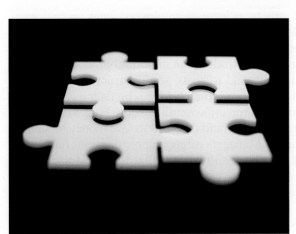

Determining the best organizational design is akin to putting together a puzzle. The pieces of strategy, technology, size, and human resources must fit together like this puzzle.

1. **Strategy and goals.** An organization's strategy is the cornerstone of determining the most appropriate design. Because corporate strategy requires an organization to decide how it will compete given both internal and external considerations, it is essential that organizational design be developed in tandem with establishing strategy.

2. **Technology.** Technology represents the information technology, equipment, tools, and processes needed to transform inputs to outputs. Technology enables products and serviced to be created and distributed. This implies that the technology being used by a company is a key consideration in deciding the best way to organize in pursuit of strategic goals.

3. **Size.** Size is indicated by things such as the number of employees, volume of sales, amount of assets, and geographical locations. Greater size generally requires more complex organizational designs.

4. **Human resources.** Human resources refers to the level of employees' human capital. Highly skilled employees typically prefer designs that allow freedom, autonomy, and empowerment. Flexible structures that allow for decentralized

Which of these environments appears to be mechanistic and organic? What cues did you use to make this determination? When would a company want to be more or less mechanistic and organic?

decision making are more likely to be a good design choice for organizations employing a large segment of highly skilled and professional employees.

Let us now consider how these four issues pertain to contingency design for the seven basic organization designs.

Functional Structures A functional structure can save money by grouping together people who need similar materials and equipment. Quality standards can be maintained because supervisors understand what department members do and because people in the same function develop pride in their specialty. Workers can devote more of their time to what they do best. These benefits are easiest to realize in a stable environment, where the organization doesn't depend on employees to coordinate their efforts to solve varied problems. Today fewer organizations see their environment as stable, so more are moving away from strictly functional structures.

Divisional Structures Divisional structures increase employees' focus on customers and products. Managers have the flexibility to make decisions that affect several functions in order to serve customer needs. This enables the organization to move faster if a new customer need arises or if a competitor introduces an important product. However, duplicating functions in each division can add to costs, so this structure may be too expensive for some organizations. Also, divisions sometimes focus on their own customer groups or products to the exclusion of the company's overall mission. Ford Motor Company has struggled to unify its geographic and brand divisions to save money by sharing design, engineering, and manufacturing. Managers of geographic divisions have introduced new car models on different time lines and insisted that their customers want different features.[50] In contrast, geographic divisions have helped McDonald's grow by freeing managers to introduce menu items and décor that locals appreciate.[51]

Matrix Structures A matrix structure tries to combine the advantages of functional and divisional structures. This advantage is also the structure's main drawback: it violates the unity of command principle, described previously in the chapter. Employees have to balance the demands of a functional manager and a product or project manager. When they struggle with this balance, decision making can slow to a crawl, and political behavior can overpower progress. The success of a matrix organization therefore requires superior managers who communicate extensively, foster commitment and collaboration, manage conflict, and negotiate effectively to establish goals and priorities consistent with the organization's strategy. One organization that has made matrix structures work for decades is Procter & Gamble. To manage over 129,000 employees in more than 180 countries, the company has a matrix structure in which global business units are responsible for a brand's development and production, while market development organizations focus on the customer needs for particular regions and the way the brands can meet those needs. Employees have to meet objectives both for the brand and for the market, with different managers responsible for each.[52]

Horizontal Structures   Horizontal designs generally improve coordination and communication in organizations.[53] Cross-functional teams can arrive at creative solutions to problems that arise in a fast-changing environment. Teams can develop new products faster and more efficiently than can functions working independently in a traditional structure. Horizontal designs also encourage knowledge sharing. However, because lines of authority are less clear, managers must be able to share responsibility for the organization's overall performance, build commitment to a shared vision, and influence others even when they lack direct authority. This type of structure is a good fit when specialization is less important than the ability to respond to varied or changing customer needs. It requires employees who can rise to the challenges of empowerment. Best Buy decided that a horizontal design would be a good way for it to increase sales.

> **EXAMPLE**   Best Buy decided that it would follow a strategy of excellent customer service in order to create competitive advantage. It had to be something that consumers could not get at another store or online. The design effort began by spending millions to train employees in all products sold so that they would be "an undisputed point of reference." The company then redesigned the stores, placing "Solution Central" in the middle of the store: "Best Buy's version of Apple's Genius Bar, where Geek Squad members help customers figure out how to get their iPads to work with their laptops, iPhones, and TVs, so they leave the store with working gear instead of a 'box of problems,' says Best Buy Vice President Josh Will."[54]

Open Boundary Structures (Hollow, Modular, Virtual)   Organizations that open their boundaries to become hollow, modular, or virtual can generate superior returns by focusing on what they do best.[55] Like functional organizations, they tap people in particular specialties, who may be more expert than the generalists of a divisional or horizontal organization. The downside of these structures is that organizations give up expertise and control in the functions or operations that are outsourced. Still, like divisional and horizontal organizations, they can focus on customers or products, leaving their partners to focus on their own specialty area.

The success of organizations that work across boundaries depends on managers' ability to get results from people over whom they do not have direct formal authority by virtue of their position in the organization. Boeing, for example, has been embarrassed by its setbacks in manufacturing the Dreamliner from components provided by a network of suppliers, which did not always meet their commitments to Boeing. Also, individuals in these organizations may not have the same degree of commitment as employees of a traditional organization, so motivation and leadership may be more difficult. Therefore, these designs are the best fit when organizations have suitable partners they trust; efficiency is very important; the organization can identify functions, processes, or product components to outsource profitably; and in the case of a virtual organization, when the need to be met is temporary.[56]

major question

What does an organization's choice of how it measures its effectiveness tell me about the organization?

THE BIGGER PICTURE

Do you pay more attention in class if you know the material will show up on a test? If yes, then you understand the power of measurement and accountability. Organizations similarly tend to hold employees accountable for important outcomes. The purpose of this section is to discuss the effectiveness criteria used by organizations.

Assessing organizational effectiveness is an important topic for an array of people, including managers, stockholders, government agencies, and OB specialists. We consider a generic model of organizational effectiveness and explore its practical application.

Generic Effectiveness Criteria

A good way to better understand this complex subject is to consider four generic approaches to assessing an organization's effectiveness (see Figure 15.4.) They are:

- Goal accomplishment
- Internal processes
- Strategic constituencies satisfaction
- Resource acquisition

These effectiveness criteria apply equally well to large or small and profit or not-for-profit organizations. Moreover, as denoted by the overlapping circles in Figure 15.4, the four effectiveness criteria can be used in various combinations. The key thing to remember is "no single approach to the evaluation of effectiveness is appropriate in all circumstances or for all organization types."[57] Let's consider the four dimensions of organizational effectiveness.

Goal Accomplishment Goal accomplishment is the oldest and most widely used effectiveness criterion for organizations.[58] Key organizational results or outputs are compared with previously stated goals or objectives. Deviations, either plus or minus, require corrective action. This is simply an organizational variation of the personal goal-setting process discussed in Chapter 5. Effectiveness, relative to the criterion of goal accomplishment, is gauged by how well the organization meets or exceeds its goals.

Productivity metrics like revenue per employee or total output produced divided by number of employees are common organization-level goals. Goals also may be set for organizational efforts such as minority recruiting, sustainability, customer satisfaction, employee satisfaction, quality improvement, and output.[59]

> **EXAMPLE** McDonald's Corp.'s key goal is to improve customer service. The company believes that accomplishing this goal will lead to increased revenue and profits. McDonald's wants its franchises to improve the friendliness of their staff. National data reveal that one in five customer complaints is related to "friendliness issues." The company also is trying to improve its speed of service. This is needed because data show that competitors have faster response times. The average

FIGURE 15.4   FOUR DIMENSIONS OF ORGANIZATIONAL EFFECTIVENESS

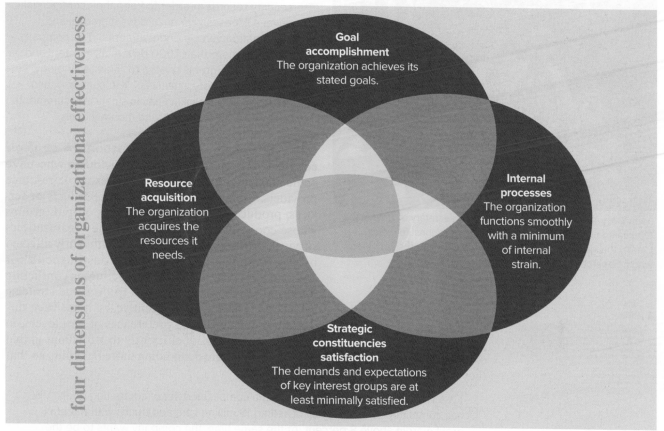

four dimensions of organizational effectiveness

Goal accomplishment
The organization achieves its stated goals.

Resource acquisition
The organization acquires the resources it needs.

Internal processes
The organization functions smoothly with a minimum of internal strain.

Strategic constituencies satisfaction
The demands and expectations of key interest groups are at least minimally satisfied.

SOURCE: Adapted from discussion in K. Cameron, "Critical Questions in Assessing Organizational Effectiveness," *Organizational Dynamics,* Autumn 1980, 66–80; and K. S. Cameron, "Effectiveness as Paradox: Consensus and Conflict in Conceptions of Organizational Effectiveness," *Management Science,* May 1986, 539–553.

service time for drive-through service was 188.83 seconds for McDonald's and 129.75 for Wendy's. To achieve its customer service goal, McDonald's is changing its model for staffing restaurants and is implementing a new system for taking orders.[60]

Internal Processes   This dimension of effectiveness focuses on "what the organization must excel at" to effectively meet its financial objectives and customers' expectations. A team of researchers has identified four critical high-level internal processes that managers are encouraged to measure and manage. These processes influence productivity, efficiency, quality, safety, and a host of other internal metrics. The processes include organizational activities associated with:

1.   Innovation.
2.   Customer service and satisfaction.
3.   Operational excellence.
4.   Being a good corporate citizen.[61]

Companies tend to adopt continuous improvement programs in pursuit of improving their internal processes. Consider how Con-way Freight attempts to meet its goals for safety and quality.

> **EXAMPLE**   Con-way Freight dispatches over 9,600 trucks from 365 service centers on a daily basis. The company picks up deliveries, consolidates them, and then delivers them to customers. "Thirty-six percent are delivered the next day and another 43 percent within two days. . . . Drivers are held to high standards and charged with safely operating trucks that back into dozens of customers' docks.

John Kerry—with the microphone—is the secretary of state in the Obama administration. Who are his strategic constituencies? Clearly this group of people, young and old, are constituents to whom Senator Kerry must pay attention.

They are required to maintain excellent safety and security records in order to keep their commercial driver's licenses with hazardous materials and combination-vehicle endorsements." The company also uses more than 1,000 drivers as mentors and trainers of programs related to "new technology rollouts and safety initiatives." The company also rewards safety by linking pay to safety measurements taken on a daily, weekly, and monthly basis.[62]

Strategic Constituencies Satisfaction A ***strategic constituency*** **is any group of individuals who have some stake in the organization**—for example, resource providers, users of the organization's products or services, producers of the organization's output, groups whose cooperation is essential for the organization's survival, or those whose lives are significantly affected by the organization.[63] Strategic constituencies (or *stakeholders*) generally have competing or conflicting interests. This forces executives to do some strategic juggling to achieve workable balances. For example, in recent years, it has been difficult for many organizations to satisfy the needs and preferences of employees, in part because of investors' pressure to operate more efficiently to withstand global competition at the same time many employees are demanding more flexibility so that they can fulfill competing roles.

> **EXAMPLE** Volkswagen is pursuing a complicated set of competing goals. VW has committed to a 2018 goal of selling 10 million cars and trucks with a pretax profit margin above 8 percent. At the same time, the company wants to be the "world's most fascinating and sustainable" company. VW's ability to meet these goals is fostered by the competitive advantage it gets from "platform sharing." This procedure enables the company "to build different models with the same components—without the customer noticing. Done poorly, parts sharing can destroy equity in a brand, as GM discovered in the 1980s when it produced the Chevrolet-based Cadillac Cimarron and the 'lookalike' cars. Done right . . . it becomes a money machine."[64]

It is difficult to satisfy the needs or demands of different constituencies. As the Volkswagen example illustrates, it takes careful planning and detailed execution to meet the needs of varying groups.

Resource Acquisition The final criterion, resource acquisition, relates to inputs rather than outputs. An organization is deemed effective in this regard if it acquires necessary factors of production such as raw materials, labor, capital, and managerial and technical expertise. Charitable organizations such as the Salvation Army and United Way judge their effectiveness in terms of how much money they raise from private and corporate donations.

Our consulting experience reveals that this dimension of effectiveness is an issue for many companies. The issue is this: Companies often have visions and goals that they cannot afford to execute. For example, a recent client wanted to grow its revenue in international markets, but it did not have the money to start an international sales organization. The company ultimately abandoned its plans due to a lack of resources.

Mixing Effectiveness Criteria: Practical Guidelines

Experts on the subject recommend a multidimensional approach to assessing the effectiveness of modern organizations. This means no single criterion is appropriate

Southwest Airlines is the envy of the beleaguered commercial airline industry because it is consistently effective at turning a profit by satisfying its customers and employees with a low-cost, on-time strategy and a no-layoff policy. Southwest's response to the accident with this plane is an example of its responsiveness to customer and safety issues. Southwest uses many of the theories and recommendations discussed in this book to pave the way to its continued success.

for all stages of the organization's life cycle. Nor will a single criterion satisfy competing stakeholders. Well-managed organizations mix and match effectiveness criteria to fit the unique requirements of the situation.

EXAMPLE Irdeto Holdings, which provides content protection for pay TV and video recordings, decided on a structural change after determining that sales were growing fastest in Asia, which already accounted for almost 40 percent of the company's revenues. To meet business goals for serving this important geographic market, Irdeto's executives decided to convert the company's Beijing office into a second headquarters (the first headquarters is located near Amsterdam). This change serves an important constituency—Asian customers—but has raised concerns with Amsterdam employees. Responding to that second constituency, Irdeto's CEO, Graham Kill, announced plans to build a new Amsterdam office building and explained that employees can enjoy an exciting career path if they are willing to rotate between the two headquarters' cities. Management also has had to address internal processes, especially in developing Chinese managers to take initiative in decision making and to think about issues affecting the entire corporation, not just its Asian markets.[65]

Managers need to identify and seek input from strategic constituencies. This information, when merged with the organization's stated mission and philosophy, enables management to derive an appropriate *combination* of effectiveness criteria. The following guidelines are helpful in this regard:

- **The goal accomplishment approach** is appropriate when "goals are clear, consensual, time-bounded, measurable."[66]
- **The internal processes approach** is appropriate when organizational performance is strongly influenced by specific processes (e.g., cross-functional teamwork).
- **The strategic constituencies approach** is appropriate when powerful stakeholders can significantly benefit or harm the organization.
- **The resource acquisition approach** is appropriate when inputs have a traceable effect on results or output. For example, the amount of money the American Red Cross receives through donations dictates the level of services provided.

Unforeseen events or accidents represent another set of factors that should be considered when evaluating organizational effectiveness.

EXAMPLE Southwest Airlines focused its attention on airplane safety after the fuselage ruptured on one of its Boeing 737 models, causing a 5-foot-long tear in the plane's ceiling. Southwest canceled 300 flights as it voluntarily conducted inspections on 79 of its older planes.[67]

This example illustrates how a company can quickly change its focus on specific goals in response to an accident.

major question

MAJOR QUESTION

How can I better understand how companies innovate so I can support my company in innovation?

THE BIGGER PICTURE

Managers agree that the ability to innovate affects long-term success, and you will undoubtedly be asked to help your employer do so. This section provides insights into how organizations approach the goal of innovation. After discussing the types of innovation pursued by companies, we review the myths about innovation, the seeds of innovation, why it is important to learn from failure, and the supporting forces needed to fuel innovation.

Accenture, a worldwide consulting, technology services, and outsourcing company, recently conducted a worldwide survey of executives on the topic of innovation. Results revealed that 90 percent of the respondents believed that their company's success depended on its ability to innovate.[68] **Innovation** "is the creation of something new that makes money; it finds a pathway to the consumer."[69] Innovation is more likely to occur when organizations have the proper supporting forces. We now take a closer look at innovation and how it is fostered in organizations.

Innovation is different from *invention,* which entails the creation of something new, and *creativity,* which was defined in Chapter 11 as a process of developing something new or unique. CEO of Procter & Gamble A. G. Lafley discussed this distinction in an interview with *BusinessWeek:* "You need creativity and invention, but until you can connect that creativity to the customer in the form of a product or service that meaningfully changes their lives, I would argue you don't have innovation."[70] Innovation also is different from *integration,* which involves actions associated with getting multiple people, units, departments, functions, or sites to work together in pursuit of a goal, idea, or project.[71] As you will learn in this section, successful innovation relies on invention, creativity, and integration.

Types of Innovation: Product or Process, Core or Transformational

Innovations can take place along various dimensions.

Product versus Process Innovations   Managers often need to improve a product or service they offer in response to competition or customer feedback. This often amounts to a technological innovation. Alternatively, managers may need to improve the process by which a product is made or a service is offered. This typically amounts to a process improvement.

More specifically, a **product innovation** is a change in the appearance or the performance of a product or a service or the creation of a new one. A **process innovation** is a change in the way a product or a service is conceived, manufactured, or distributed.

Core versus Transformational Innovations   This continuum of innovation pertains to distinctions of *where* and *how* a company intends to innovate. **Core innovations** are

targeted at existing customers and rely on optimizing existing products/services for existing customers. These types of innovations are more incremental and are less likely to generate significant amounts of new revenue.

> EXAMPLE   With new packaging, Nabisco's launched a 100-calorie packet of Oreos for people on the go.[72]

> EXAMPLE   With a slight product reformulation, Procter & Gamble launched one of its dishwashing detergents as a powder in a concentrated pouch instead of a liquid.

In contrast, **_transformational innovations_ are targeted at creating new markets and customers and rely on developing breakthroughs and inventing things that don't currently exist.**

> EXAMPLE   Keurig created a new category of coffee and tea preparation by creating a product that offered a cup-at-a-time pod-style brewing. In 2012, sales of Keurig products exceeded $3.8 billion. Research on _Fortune_'s list of the 100 fastest-growing companies revealed that transformational innovations produced much faster growth and more positive valuations from investors than companies engaging in core innovations.[73]

Myths about Innovation

There are two myths about innovation that need to be dispelled.

Myth #1: Innovation Involves an Epiphany or Eureka Moment   Many people think that innovation is a spur-of-the-moment thing in which an idea is hatched, such as Isaac Newton discovering gravity after being hit on the head by an apple while sitting under a tree. This is a nice story, but it does not represent reality. Others conceive innovation as something that occurs when a person is in the right place at the right time. Nothing could be further from the truth. Innovation does not occur like a thunderbolt. In the words of Jack and Suzy Welch, "it emerges incrementally, in bits and chugs, forged by a mixed bag of co-workers from up, down, and across an organization, sitting and wrangling it out in the trenches."[74]

Myth #2: Innovation Can Be Systematized   Apple's former CEO Steve Jobs once was asked, "How do you systematize innovation?" He answered, "You don't."[75] If innovation could be codified and standardized, everyone would do it. There simply are too many challenges associated with innovation that make its success unpredictable. That said, we will shortly discuss several supporting forces that help organizations to innovate.

The Seeds of Innovation: The Starting Point of Innovation

The process of growing a tree is a useful metaphor for understanding how organizations can become more innovative. Seeds are the starting point for growing trees. Over time, seeds evolve into trees with strong trunks if they receive the proper water, oxygen, nutrients, and sunlight—supporting forces. A healthy trunk enables a tree to survive and produce a canopy for all to enjoy. Innovation follows a similar process. **_Seeds of innovation_ represent the starting points for organizational innovation.** After studying hundreds of innovations, an expert identified six seeds of innovation.[76]

1. Hard Work in a Specific Direction   Most innovations come from dedicated people diligently working to solve a well-defined problem. This hard work can span many years.

2. Hard Work with Direction Change   Innovations frequently occur when people change their approach toward solving a problem. In other words, hard work closes some doors and opens others.

3. Curiosity and Experimentation Innovations can begin when people are curious about something of interest, and experimentation is used to test for the viability of curious ideas.[77] This seed of innovation requires an organizational culture that supports experimentation. Jim Donald, CEO of Extended Stay America, encountered a problem with this seed when he joined the company.[78] The Problem-Solving Application illustrates what the company did to grow this seed.

solving application

problem

Extended Stay America Tries to Increase Innovation

Jim Donald took the helm at the national hotel chain after it had gone through bankruptcy. Employees were suffering from job insecurity and they avoided decisions that might cost the company money. "They were waiting to be told what to do," said Donald.

What Did the Company Do to Increase Innovation? Employees were told that the company needed them to generate daring ideas and take calculated risks in order to improve customer service and profitability. To make this happen, Mr. Donald decided that he needed to provide a safety net to employees in order to get them to avoid the fear of failure. He thus created the "Get Out of Jail, Free" cards and distributed them to the company's 9,000 employees.

Mr. Donald also emphasized that employees could turn in the card "when they took a big risk on behalf of the company—no questions asked." The card became a way of giving employees permission to

make mistakes in behalf of trying to do something innovative.

What Was the Result of the Program? The cards have been trickling in since the program started. For example, "one California hotel manager recently called to redeem her card . . . confessing that she nabbed 20 business

cards from a fishbowl in the lobby of nearby rival La Quinta in an attempt to find prospective customers. Another manager in New Jersey cold-called a movie-production company when she heard it would be filming in the area. The film crew ended up booking $250,000 in accommodations at the hotel."[79]

YOUR CALL

1. What problem was Mr. Donald trying to resolve?
2. What OB theories or concepts help explain the causes of the problem?
3. What do you think about Mr. Donald's solution? Explain.

4. Wealth and Money Innovations frequently occur because an organization or an individual simply wants to make money.

> **EXAMPLE** Unilever's stagnant sales drove the company to look for innovative ways to cut costs and increase the introduction of new products. This is why the company cut excess layers of management and began to focus on releasing a smaller number of new, innovative products. These efforts significantly improved Unilever's market share and profitability.[80]

5. Necessity   Many innovations grow from the desire to achieve something or to complete a task that is needed to accomplish a broader goal. Here are two examples where the goal was to expand market opportunities.

> **EXAMPLE**   "Xerox hired two researchers the company calls 'innovation managers.'" Their job is to hunt for inventions and products from Indian start-ups that Xerox might adapt for North America.[81]

> **EXAMPLE**   Similarly, Hewlett-Packard has repurposed resources in its research lab in India to look for web-interface applications for mobile phones in Asia and Africa that it could migrate to developed markets.[82]

6. Combination of Seeds   Many innovations occur as a result of multiple factors.

Learning from Failure

Failure **occurs when an activity fails to deliver its expected results or outcomes.**[83] Unfortunately, failure or mistakes are generally feared and penalized, which creates an environment of risk aversion. This in turn reduces innovation. Bill Gates, founder and former CEO at Microsoft, concluded that "it's fine to celebrate success, but it's more important to heed the lessons of failure. How a company deals with mistakes suggests how well it will bring out the best ideas and talents of its people, and how effectively it will respond to change."[84]

> **EXAMPLE**   Jill Nelson, founder of Ruby Receptionist, a virtual reception service in Portland, Oregon, put Gates's comments into action. "In my firm, I have employees talk about their small mistakes at weekly staff meetings. We discuss the mistakes and what the employees learned from them. The sharing of this information sends the message that it's OK to make a low-stakes mistake—as long as you learn from it and share your lesson with others."[85]

We conclude by noting results from a recent study on organizational learning. The researchers wanted to know if organizations learn more from success or failure. What do you think? Results indicated that organizations learned from both success and failure, but learning was stronger and longer lasting when it was based on failure.[86]

The Supporting Forces for Innovation

Innovation won't happen as a matter of course. It needs to be nurtured and supported. Organizations can support innovation by providing the appropriate resources:

1. The necessary human capital.
2. The right organizational culture and climate.
3. The appropriate resources.
4. The required structure and processes.

To gauge a company's likely success in innovation, we can ask about these resources.

Does the Company Have the Necessary Human Capital?   We defined human capital in Chapter 1 as the productive potential of an individual's knowledge and actions: a person factor in the Integrative Framework of OB. Research has identified several employee characteristics that can help organizations innovate. For example, innovation was positively associated with the individual characteristics associated with creativity, the level of skills and abilities possessed by people, employees' self-efficacy for innovation, and the quality of the relationship between managers and employees.

> **EXAMPLE**   GE is aware of the importance of human capital for innovation. In Louisville, for example, the company has hired "more than 300 industrial designers, engineers, and other salaried team members with new skills and expertise in areas such as wireless technology and advanced manufacturing."[87]

StubHub was founded in 2000 by two Stanford Business School students. Today, the company is owned by eBay and is the largest ticket marketplace in the world. StubHub clearly hired the "right" people to help it grow.

EXAMPLE Jeff Flour, co-founder of StubHub, also recognizes the importance of hiring the right people as he begins to hire for his latest endeavor—Spreecast .com, a social video platform. He said, "The mistakes I made in hiring at StubHub have helped inform my decisions this time around. I'll be treading more carefully in bringing in senior people and look for different qualities. I'll focus on experience and skill set and be more interested in personality, raw intelligence, and drive to make the person a better fit with the existing team."[88]

Does the Company Have the Right Organizational Culture and Climate? Organizational culture, composed of core values and beliefs held by employees, and organizational climate, which consists of employees' perceptions of formal and informal organizational policies, practices, procedures, and routines, impact innovation. For example, a recent meta-analysis revealed that innovation was positively associated with market, adhocracy, and clan cultures—recall our discussion in Chapter 14.[89]

EXAMPLE GE already has put this research finding into use in a training program called "Leadership, Innovation, and Growth." Teams attending the training complete an internal assessment regarding the extent to which the culture is supportive of creativity. Participants then use the results to discuss how they might make the work environment more innovation friendly.[90]

Moreover, employees also were more innovative when the human resources policies and procedures encouraged employees to innovate and when the company linked rewards to innovative behavior.[91] Have you worked for a company that has an innovative climate? Are you wondering what it takes to create an innovative climate? If yes, then we encourage you to take the innovation climate Self-Assessment.

connect

SELF-ASSESSMENT 15.3 Assessing the Innovation Climate of My Organization

Go to connect.mheducation.com and complete Self-Assessment 15.3 to determine the extent to which one of your past employers has an innovative climate. Then answer the following:

1. What is the level of innovation? Are you surprised by the results? Explain.

2. Select the three lowest survey item scores. Use the content of these items to provide recommendations for what the company could do to become more innovative.

Does the Company Devote Enough Resources to Innovation? Organizations need to put their money where their mouths are. If managers want innovation, they must dedicate resources to its development. Resources come in multiple forms. They can include dollars, time, energy, and focus.

EXAMPLE Heineken spent $2 million on training employees on beer basics to help them innovate.[92]

Does the Company Have the Required Structure and Processes? Organizational structure is a prime contributor to innovation.

> **EXAMPLE** Larry Page, Google's CEO, decided to revamp the company's old structure, comprised of large engineering and product-management groups. The new structure is based on seven product-focused units "dedicated to areas like search, ad products, Android, and commerce. The executives heading each of the units now have full responsibility—and accountability—for their fates. Getting a new product started no longer requires convincing executives from across the company to get on board."[93]

In Chapter 1, we defined organizational processes as an organization's capabilities in management, internal processes, and technology that are used to turn inputs into outcomes. Processes play a critical role in innovation. IDEO, for example, employs a unique process when it helps companies to innovate (see Example box). *Crowdsourcing*, defined as "the practice of obtaining needed services, ideas, or content by soliciting contributions from a large group of people" typically via the ***Internet***, is being used by more companies to help innovate.[94] Although crowdsourcing has pros and cons, and limited research has examined its effectiveness, we agree with the conclusion of two experts: "In the end, though, crowds expand the capabilities of companies; they should be viewed as another tool for organizational problem solving."[95]

EXAMPLE Design Thinking Your Way to Innovative Solutions

IDEO (pronounced "eye-di-oh") is a unique, award-winning, highly respected and influential global design firm. They are responsible for innovative products, such as the first mouse for Apple, heart defibrillators that walk a user through the steps, and TIVO's "thumbs up–thumbs down" button. An intense focus on end-user behavior is the foundation of all they do and is embedded in the three steps of their *design thinking*. Their approach will be of interest to anyone interested in encouraging innovation.

- **Inspiration.** As defined by David Kelley, IDEO's legendary founder, inspiration is the problem or opportunity that motivates the search for solutions.
- **Ideation.** This is the process of generating, developing, and testing ideas.
- **Implementation.** The final step is what links the problem solving to people's lives.

Observing user behavior and working with prototypes are important aspects of each step. They help IDEO's diverse problem-solving teams both define client problems and gauge the effectiveness of their solutions.

Thinking like a Designer. The company's consulting approach to products, services, processes, and strategy brings together what is desirable from a human point of view with what is technologically feasible and economically viable. It also allows people who are trained as designers to use creative tools to address a vast range of challenges. The goal: to tap into abilities we all have but get overlooked by more conventional problem-solving practices. It relies on your ability "to be intuitive, to recognize patterns, [and] to construct ideas that are emotionally meaningful as well as functional."

Beyond Product Design. IDEO's design thinking has been so successful that many nonbusiness and nonproduct organizations are now engaging the company. For instance, the company is now working with health care and education, as well as sustainable processes for clean drinking water. It also is working with the National Football League to improve how to help players more successfully transition to life after football.[96]

As an Organization. IDEO has over 550 employees in a dozen offices, both in major US cities and overseas in London, Shanghai, Singapore, and Tokyo.[97] The result of organic design, the firm is the result of merging four different design firms. Its current structure builds on project teams and a flat hierarchy, in support of individual autonomy and creativity, and relying on socialization of recruits and engineer buy-in.[98]

YOUR THOUGHTS?

1. What is appealing to you about IDEO?
2. Describe how you could apply their process to solve one of your own challenges.
3. Earlier in this chapter, you read that innovation cannot be systematized. To what degree does IDEO's "design thinking" vary from an attempt to systematize innovation? Explain your answer.

---

what did i learn?

You learned that at any level of the organization your knowledge of organizational design, effectiveness, and innovation gives you the ability to help both you and an organization to achieve desired goals. Reinforce your learning with the Key Points below. Then consolidate your learning with the Integrative Framework. Finally, Challenge your mastery of the material by answering the Major Questions in your own words.

Key Points for Understanding Chapter 15

You learned the following key points.

15.1 THE FOUNDATION OF AN ORGANIZATION

- Coordination of effort, aligned goals, division of labor, and hierarchy of authority are four common denominators of all organizations.

- There is no consensus about the optimal span of control. In deciding span of control, managers should consider the organization's size, the skill level needed to complete tasks, the organization's culture, and managerial responsibilities.

- Closed systems, such as a battery-powered clock, are relatively self-sufficient. Open systems, such as the cost of college tuition, are highly dependent on the environment for survival. Organizations are said to be open systems.

- A learning organization is one that proactively creates, acquires, and transfers knowledge and changes its behavior on the basis of new knowledge and insights.

- Figure 15.3 illustrates the five-step process underlying organizational learning.

15.2 ORGANIZATIONAL DESIGN

- There are three broad types of organizational design: traditional, horizontal, and open. Each is based on a different focus and is associated with specific types of structure.

- There are seven basic ways organizations are structured. Traditional designs include (a) functional structures, in which work is divided according to function; (b) divisional structures, in which work is divided according to product or customer type or location; and (c) matrix structures, with dual-reporting structures based on product and function. Organizations also may be designed (d) horizontally, with cross-functional teams responsible for entire processes. Organization design also may reduce barriers between organizations, becoming (e) hollow

organizations, which outsource functions; (f) modular organizations, which outsource the production of a product's components; or (g) virtual organizations, which temporarily combine the efforts of members of different companies in order to complete a project.

- Table 15.2 summarizes the pros and cons of each of the seven types of organizational design.

15.3 THE CONTINGENCY APPROACH TO DESIGNING ORGANIZATIONS

- Mechanistic (bureaucratic, centralized) organizations tend to be effective in stable situations. In unstable situations, organic (flexible, decentralized) organizations are more effective. These findings underscore the need for a contingency approach to organization design.

- Managers should consider four key issues when making decisions about how best to design an organization: strategy and goals, technology, size, and human resources.

- Mechanistic organizations and functional structures may be necessary when tight control is important and the environment is stable. Organic organizations allow for innovation in a rapidly changing environment. Divisional structures are a good fit when the organization needs deep knowledge of varied customer groups and the ability to respond to customer demands quickly. A matrix organization can deliver the advantages of functional and divisional structures if the company has superior managers who communicate extensively, foster commitment and collaboration, and negotiate effectively to establish goals and priorities consistent with the organization's strategy.

- A horizontal design is a good fit when specialization is less important than the ability to respond to varied or changing customer needs. Hollow, modular, and virtual designs are best when organizations have suitable partners they trust; efficiency is very important; the organization can identify functions, processes, or product components to outsource; and in the case of a virtual organization, when the need to be met is temporary.

15.4 STRIVING FOR ORGANIZATIONAL EFFECTIVENESS

- There are four generic organizational effectiveness criteria. They are goal accomplishment (satisfying stated objectives), resource acquisition (gathering the necessary productive inputs), internal processes (building and maintaining healthy organizational systems), and strategic constituencies satisfaction (achieving at least minimal satisfaction for all key stakeholders).

- There is not one measure of effectiveness that fits all organizations. Well-managed organizations mix and match effectiveness criteria to fit the unique requirements of the situation.

15.5 ORGANIZATIONAL INNOVATION

- Innovation is creating something new, something which is commercialized. In contrast, invention is simply the creation of something new and creativity is the process of developing something new or unique. Integration involves actions associated with getting multiple people, units, departments, functions, or sites to work together in pursuit of a goal, idea, or project. Innovation relies on invention, creativity, and integration.

- Innovations can take two fundamental forms. They can entail product or process innovations. They also can be core, which are targeted at existing customers, or transformational, which are focused on creating new markets and customers.

- There are two key myths about innovation. The first is the myth that innovation involves an epiphany or eureka moment. The second is that innovation can be systematized.

- Seeds of innovation are the starting point for organizational innovation. They include (1) hard work in a specific direction, (2) hard work with direction change, (3) curiosity and experimentation, (4) wealth and money, (5) necessity, and (6) combination of seeds.

- Innovation is enhanced when people spend time learning from failure.

- Innovation must be nurtured and supported. Four ways to do this are by providing the necessary human capital, the right organizational culture and climate, the appropriate resources, and the required structure and processes.

The Integrative Framework for Chapter 15

As shown in Figure 15.5, you learned that multiple environmental factors support the primary input of organizational structure, and that decision making at the individual and group/team levels is an important process to support organizational design and effectiveness. Supporting organizational processes include HR policies and culture, socialization, and mentoring. The organizational outputs include both innovation and accounting/financial performance.

Challenge: Major Questions for Chapter 15

At the start of the chapter, we told you that after reading the chapter you should be able to answer the following questions. Unless you can, have you really processed and internalized the lessons in the chapter? Refer to the Key Points, Figure 15.5, the chapter itself, and your notes to revisit and answer the following major questions:

1. How can knowledge about an organization's foundation help me in my career?

2. What are the seven basic ways in which organizations are structured, and how do these structures relate to the organization's purpose?

3. How can I use knowledge about contingency organization design to find an employer that fits my needs and preferences?

4. What does an organization's choice of how it measures its effectiveness tell me about the organization?

5. How can I better understand how companies innovate so I can support my company in innovation?

FIGURE 15.5 INTEGRATIVE FRAMEWORK FOR UNDERSTANDING AND APPLYING OB

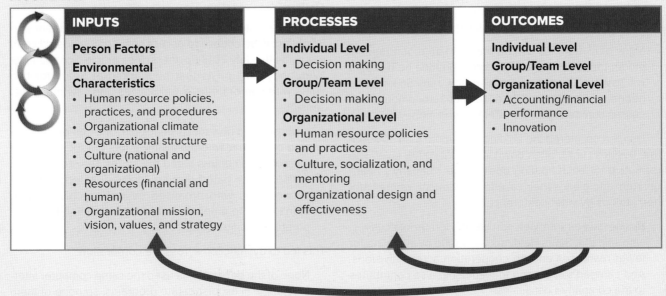

© 2014 Angelo Kinicki and Mel Fugate. All rights reserved. Reproduction prohibited without permission of the authors.

Sears Holding and Organizational Structure

Most business leaders have their critics. But Edward S. Lampert of Sears Holding Corporation has more critics than most.[99]

Lampert, a hedge fund billionaire, acquired control of Kmart—emerging from bankruptcy—in 2003 through his hedge fund ESL Investments. In 2005 Lampert used Kmart as a platform to acquire the financially troubled Sears, creating the Sears Holding Corporation. Lampert's ESL Investments controls some 56 percent of the holding company.

Thanks to aggressive cost-cutting, Sears Holdings thrived at first, and its stock price soared. But by 2007, profits had declined 45 percent. The stock, at an all-time high of $182, began a long descent (to a low of $36 two years later). The stock has had some mild increases since then but returned to the $30–$40 range in 2012 and 2013.

Throughout, finding a good CEO was problematic; not many stayed on. Interim CEOs often stood in while search committees looked. In January 2013, Lampert took over directly from CEO Lou D'Ambriosio, who left to deal with a family medical matter, according to published reports.[100] Under Lampert's direction, Sears Holding has gone up and down but not retained any of its mild increases in valuation.

Lampert's problems relate in part to organization.

Structure

On acquisition, Sears was organized like a classic retailer. Department heads ran their own product lines, but under the same merchandising and marketing leaders and toward the same financial goals. For several years, Lambert kept the structure intact: until 2008.

Bloomberg Businessweek questions the impact of Lampert's reorganization on Sears Holding:

> Many of its troubles can be traced to an organizational model the chairman implemented, an idea he has said will save the company. Lampert now runs Sears like a hedge fund portfolio, with dozens of autonomous businesses competing for his attention and money.[101]

Lampert splintered the holdings into more than 30 separate business units, often down to a profit center level. The executive for each holding goes to the company's headquarters and pleads their case for investment, where Lampert attends by videoconference.

> *Businessweek* interviewed over 40 former executives, who said that Sears Holdings is ravaged by infighting for fewer resources and no cooperation across divisions. And Lampert's approach to leadership also contributes to the company's difficulties.

While technically the company may be seen as employing a divisional structure, Lampert's approach seems to remove coordination and unity of vision at the top. Rather than existing as silos, each division is treated as an orphan with no claims to family loyalty. You might say this is an *atomized* structure.

Style

A fan of Ayn Rand's Objectivist philosophy that selfishness begets effective and rational business decisions, Lampert likes the idea of forcing divisions to compete *within* the organization the same way they compete *outside* in the open market.

At the annual teleconferences with business division heads, Lampert often appears to be ignoring the executive entirely, checking on e-mail and not asking questions, until he hears something that triggers his attention. Once aroused, he may pepper the executive with comments and questions, or he may lecture the executives on fine points of retail. One trigger is the use of standard retail jargon like *vendors* or *consumers*. Some executives privately refer to Lampert as the Wizard of Oz for such performances.

Part of Lampert's style may have been forged by his earlier successes with ESL, when he would hold a portfolio of real estate holdings, stripping them of assets strategically to achieve maximum return. But in 2008, *The Wall Street Journal* judged that Lampert was failing because his strategies did not fit the times. "The best time for acquisitions or creating value by stripping out and selling embedded assets such as real estate is, for now, past."[102]

Culture

Corporate culture under Lampert is fraught with fear and infighting, if we choose to accept some of the posted comments on the July 2013 *Businessweek* article. For example, "VideoboyMatt" posts that he worked at Sears for two years with corporate-level employees and saw much dissension:

> I was amazed how much smack talk one center, or office said of another who did a similar job, but for a different division. Call centers hated the stores, the stores hated online, online hated delivery, delivery hated customer service reps who promised everything, blue ribbon didn't listen to employees (blue ribbon being their corporate escalation dept.) . . .

This led to dysfunction across the corporation:

> None of the departments used the same computer interface, they all used separate programs, so none of them

could look up the same info. So if you ordered an appliance online in NY, it would be sent to a warehouse in Georgia, and then the warehouse, or customer service rep who took the customer's phone call could not look up any info on it, or track it down.[103]

Incentives

Bob Sutton is an organizational psychologist and author who used his own blog to expand on the *Businessweek* article. He points out how Lampert's structure incentivizes dysfunction.

> Lampert defends this structure as "decentralized," but that confuses a structure where individual units have autonomy to act largely as they please with one where there is no incentive (or worse, a disincentive) to support the company's overall performance. Google, for example, is quite decentralized, but there have always been both cultural and financial pressures to do what is best for the company as a whole.[104]

Integrated Retail

In May of 2013, Lampert decried his company's "unacceptable" losses, and as reported in *Businessweek,* repeatedly invoked a strategy of "integrated retail," of combining digital interaction with bricks-and-mortar retail. Lampert explained:

> I think that the broad-based, everybody-gets-the-same-deal marketing that Sears and Kmart and many others have engaged in for a long time will be changing. I'm not predicting that the retail industry will become like the airline industry where 10 people . . . across a row on a plane all pay different prices for their seat or five people on the floor of a hotel room all pay different prices for their hotel room.[105]

Wall Street responded favorably with a mild bump in stock price, but the price soon drifted down again. Later in the year, a bigger rise came when Lampert announced plans to spin off more assets from the holding company,

but again the stock returned to the mid-$30 range. Some critics describe the company's progress as a death spiral; some have identified Lampert as one of the worst CEOs in the country for not wanting to understand retail or improve investment in the company instead of wringing profits from it.[106]

Apply the 3-Stop Problem-Solving Approach to OB

Stop 1: What is the problem?

- Use the Integrative Framework for Understanding and Applying OB (Figure 15.5) to help identify the inputs, processes, and outcomes that are important in this case.
- Which of the outcomes are not being achieved in the case?
- Based on considering the above two questions, what is the most important problem in this case?

Stop 2: Use the Integrative Framework to identify the OB concepts or theories that help you to understand the problem in this case.

- What person factors are most relevant?
- What environmental characteristics are most important to consider?
- Do you need to consider any processes? Which ones?
- What concepts or theories discussed in this chapter are most relevant for solving the key problem in this case?

Stop 3: What are your recommendations for solving the problem?

- Review the material in the chapter that most pertains to your proposed solution and look for practical recommendations.
- Use any past OB knowledge or experience to generate recommendations.
- Outline your plan for solving the problem in this case.

LEGAL/ETHICAL CHALLENGE

One of the Fastest-Growing Businesses Involves Spying on Consumers: Is This Ethical?[107]

Many companies believe that the use of sophisticated software that tracks our Internet behavior is an innovative way to get information that can be used to increase their revenue.

"Hidden inside Ashley Hayes-Beaty's computer, a tiny file helps gather personal details about her, all to be put up

for sale for a tenth of a penny. The file consists of a single code . . . that secretly identifies her as a 26-year-old female in Nashville, Tennessee."

The code knows that her favorite movies include *The Princess Bride, 50 First Dates,* and *10 Things I Hate About You.* It knows she enjoys the *Sex and the City* series. "It knows she browses entertainment news and likes to take quizzes."

Upon learning about the file, Ashley concluded it was "eerily correct." Ms. Hayes's behavior is being monitored without her knowledge or permission by Lotame Solutions. The company uses special software called a "beacon" to track what people type on websites. "Lotame packages that data into profiles about individuals, without determining a person's name, and sells the profiles to companies seeking customers." That said, Eric Porres, Lotame's chief marketing officer, indicated that the profile can be segmented "all the way down to one person." Lotame also claimed that you can remove yourself from their system, assuming you even know that you are being tracked by the system.

"The information that companies gather is anonymous, in the sense that Internet users are identified by a number assigned to their computer, not by a specific person's name."

Many companies are unaware that their websites were tagged with beacons and that intrusive files were being attached to anyone who visited their website. The courts have not ruled on the legality of these complex tracking procedures.

How Do You Feel about the Practice of Someone Tracking Your Internet Behavior without Your Approval or Awareness?

1. Give me a break; this is the Internet age. Tracking is fair game and provides useful information to companies so they can target products that meet our needs. Besides, you can get off Lotame's system if you don't want to be tracked. Further, tracking can be used to catch pedophiles and other types of criminal behavior.

2. I can accept the idea of tracking, but companies like Lotame should get our approval before they start collecting data.

3. This is an invasion of my privacy and it should be disallowed by the courts.

4. I am against any attempts to police what goes on when we use the Internet.

GROUP EXERCISE

Strategic Constituent Analysis

Objectives

1. To continue developing your group interaction and teamwork skills.

2. To engage in open-system thinking.

3. To conduct a strategic constituencies audit and thus more fully appreciate the competing demands placed on today's managers.

4. To establish priorities and consider trade-offs for modern managers.

Introduction

According to open-system models of organizations, environmental factors—social, political, legal, technological, and economic—greatly affect what managers can and cannot do. This exercise gives you an opportunity to engage in open-system thinking within a team setting. It requires a team meeting of about 20 to 25 minutes followed by a 10- to 15-minute general class discussion. Total time required for this exercise is about 30 to 40 minutes.

Instructions

Your instructor will randomly assign you to teams with five to eight members each. Choose one team member to act as recorder/spokesperson. Either at your instructor's prompting or as a team, choose one of these two options:

1. Identify an organization that is familiar to everyone on your team (it can be a local business, your college or university, or a well-known organization such as McDonald's, Walmart, or Southwest Airlines).

2. Select an organization from any of the Problem-Solving Application Cases following each chapter in this book.

Next, do a *strategic constituency audit* for the organization in question. Begin by brainstorming the key strategic constituents for your chosen organization. Your team will need to make reasonable assumptions about the circumstances surrounding your target organization.

Finally, your team should select the three (or more) *high-priority* strategic constituents on your team's list. Rank them number one, number two, and so on. (*Tip:* A top-priority constituent is one with the greatest short-term impact on the success or failure of your target organization.) Be prepared to explain to the entire class your rationale for selecting each high-priority strategic constituent.

Questions for Discussion

1. How does this exercise foster open-system thinking? Give examples.

2. Did this exercise broaden your awareness of the complexity of modern organizational environments? Explain.

3. Why do managers need clear priorities when it comes to dealing with strategic constituents?

4. How many *trade-offs* (meaning one party's gains at another's expense) can you detect in your team's list of strategic constituents? Specify them.

5. How difficult was it for your team to complete this assignment? Explain.

16 MANAGING CHANGE AND STRESS

How Can You Apply OB and Show What You've Learned?

inputs

PERSON FACTORS

ENVIRONMENTAL CHARACTERISTICS

processes

INDIVIDUAL LEVEL

GROUP/TEAM LEVEL

ORGANIZATIONAL LEVEL
Leading Change and Managing Stress

outcomes

INDIVIDUAL LEVEL

GROUP/TEAM LEVEL

ORGANIZATIONAL LEVEL

MAJOR TOPICS I'LL LEARN AND QUESTIONS I SHOULD BE ABLE TO ANSWER

16.1 FORCES FOR CHANGE

MAJOR QUESTION: *What are the common forces or drivers of change at work, and how can this knowledge improve my personal effectiveness?*

16.2 TYPES AND MODELS OF CHANGE

MAJOR QUESTION: *How can different approaches to change make me and my organization more effective managers of change?*

16.3 UNDERSTANDING RESISTANCE TO CHANGE

MAJOR QUESTION: *Why do people resist change and what can I do about it?*

16.4 THE GOOD AND BAD OF STRESS

MAJOR QUESTION: *How can stress affect my effectiveness—positively and negatively?*

16.5 EFFECTIVE CHANGE AND STRESS MANAGEMENT

MAJOR QUESTION: *How can OB knowledge and tools help me effectively manage change and stress?*

INTEGRATIVE FRAMEWORK FOR UNDERSTANDING AND APPLYING OB

Leading change and managing stress are ultimate tests of your understanding and ability to apply OB knowledge and tools. As you'll learn, effectively leading change processes requires you to consider both person and environmental inputs and outcomes across organizational levels. Because of the complexity and broad impact of organizational change, it also is a major source of stress at work. We therefore encourage you to use this final chapter as a test of the knowledge you've accumulated thoughout this book and course.

© 2014 Angelo Kinicki and Mel Fugate. All rights reserved. Reproduction prohibited without permission of the authors.

winning at work

HOW TO W.I.N. AT STRESS AND CHANGE

We chose this fitting acronym for the final Winning at Work in this book. Everybody has stress and everybody is confronted with change. And as you'll learn in this chapter, change is often stressful. We therefore offer some simple and practical recommendations you can apply to school, work, and other arenas of your life.

DETERMINE WHAT YOU CAN AND CANNOT CONTROL

Many people, including a large number of researchers, find that the more control you have over your environment the less stress you'll experience. This also applies to dealing with change. For example, changes at work are typically much less stressful if you are involved in the planning and have some say (control) over the processes and outcomes of the changes. Therefore, a good place to start when managing stress and change in the many arenas of your life is with determining what you can control and what you can't. Once you've done this, then you'll be well on your way to applying what Sharon Melnick, a noted stress researcher, calls *W-I-N at Change*.[1] First, identify a change in some arena of your life—school, work, a relationship. Then follow the three steps below and see if you don't reduce your stress and increase your success at managing change.

Written Inventory. Make a three-column chart. Write the implications of the change for you personally in column one. In the second column, describe your reactions to these implications. Pay particular attention to your emotions (Chapter 3) and how they affect your reactions.

Individual Responsibility. Describe in the third and final column what specific things you can do to address the implications and your reactions. Do you need to manage your emotions? Would it be helpful to seek some support from a classmate, colleague, or friend? It might be helpful to consider your attributions (Chapter 4), potential biases

(Chapter 6), or the possibility of miscommunication (Chapter 9). Be sure to focus on the aspects that you can control, and don't get distracted or bogged down in what you can't.

New Learning Plan. Situations that cause stress and/or require change are often excellent opportunities for learning. You can learn what triggered your stress and how to avoid or prevent it in the future. But we also encourage you to be purposeful and identify what specific skills you need to effectively *manage* the change. Then, describe what you need and can do to learn these skills. Consider finding a mentor or coach, as this can also help build your social capital (Chapter 1). Set goals, make a plan, and work the plan (Chapters 5 and 6).

| FOR YOU | WHAT'S AHEAD IN THIS CHAPTER |

We know you've heard the statement: "The only constant in life is change." But we want you now to think about what this might mean for your job and career. We created this chapter not only to help you answer this question, but also to give you practical knowledge and tools to help you manage change at different levels in the Integrative Framework of OB. To do this, we'll explore common forces or drivers for change, as well as learn about some popular models for understanding and managing change. It also is common for people to resist change. It therefore is useful to learn about some of the causes of resistance and what you can do about it. Because change is a major cause of stress at work, and in your life as a whole, we then help you understand both the positive and negative aspects of stress. The chapter concludes with suggestions on how to manage resistance, stress, and change more generally.

FORCES FOR CHANGE

MAJOR QUESTION

What are the common forces or drivers of change at work, and how can this knowledge improve my personal effectiveness?

THE BIGGER PICTURE

There are a great many potential causes or forces for organizational change. Therefore, to understand and manage them more effectively, we've organized them into two broad categories— internal and external forces. Making this distinction will enable you to better manage this important organizational-level process to achieve a variety of outcomes across levels in the Integrative Framework of OB.

Before we dive into a general discussion of the forces for change, we think a good place to start is to assess your own general attitudes toward change. Remember from Chapter 2 that attitudes are tendencies to respond either favorably or unfavorably to a given object or situation. Complete Self-Assessment 16.1 to learn about your own predisposition toward change. Then use all of what you learn in this chapter to help you strengthen an already positive attitude, or improve one that is not.

connect

SELF-ASSESSMENT 16.1   What Are My General Attitudes Toward Change?

Go to connect.mheducation.com and take Self-Assessment 16.1 to learn about your general attitudes toward changes at school or work.

1. What is your overall attitude? Are you surprised?
2. Think of three examples from your school or work life that are consistent with your score.
3. Now think of a personal example where you think you possessed a clearly negative attitude toward a particular change. What made this different from/similar to your general attitudes toward change?
4. Drawing on what you learned in Chapter 2 about attitudes, describe two specific ways you can improve your attitudes toward change.

SOURCE: Adapted from Miller, V. D., Johnson, J. R., & Grau, J. "Antecedents and willingness to participate in a planned organizational change," *Journal of Applied Communication Research,* 1994, 22: 59–80.

Now that you have a sense of your own attitudes toward change, consider this question about organizations: How do they know when they should change? What cues should an organization look for? Although there are no clear-cut answers to these questions, one way we can find cues signaling the need for change is to monitor the forces for change. These forces often differ greatly, and to help make sense of the variety we categorize them into external and internal forces (see Figure 16.1).

External Forces

External forces for change **originate outside the organization.** Such forces often apply to your organization and its competitors or even entire industries. External

FIGURE 16.1 EXTERNAL AND INTERNAL FORCES FOR CHANGE

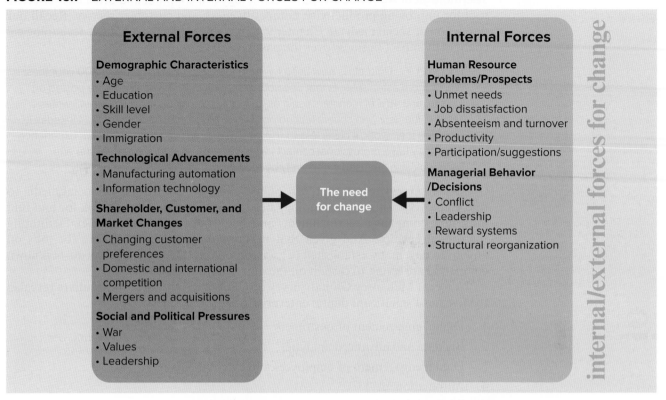

External Forces

Demographic Characteristics
- Age
- Education
- Skill level
- Gender
- Immigration

Technological Advancements
- Manufacturing automation
- Information technology

Shareholder, Customer, and Market Changes
- Changing customer preferences
- Domestic and international competition
- Mergers and acquisitions

Social and Political Pressures
- War
- Values
- Leadership

The need for change

Internal Forces

Human Resource Problems/Prospects
- Unmet needs
- Job dissatisfaction
- Absenteeism and turnover
- Productivity
- Participation/suggestions

Managerial Behavior /Decisions
- Conflict
- Leadership
- Reward systems
- Structural reorganization

internal/external forces for change

forces therefore can dramatically affect why an organization exists, as well as which markets it participates in and how. For instance, external changes can either present new opportunities for organizations to realize and grow (e.g., smartphones for consumers and Apple's iPhone), or they can cause the ultimate demise or failure of a business (e.g., smartphones for consumers and Blackberry). Let us now consider the four key external forces for change: demographic characteristics, technological advancements, market changes, and social and political pressures.

Lehman Brothers was the fourth largest investment bank to collapse in the wake of the Wall Street meltdown of 2008. The meltdown destroyed people's lives and life savings, and its effects are still seen today. Lehman's bankruptcy is considered the largest in U.S. history.

Demographic Characteristics Chapter 2 provided a detailed discussion of demographic changes occurring in the US workforce. You learned that organizations are changing benefits and aspects of the work environment in order to attract, motivate, and retain diverse employees. Organizations also are changing the way in which they design and market their products and services and design their store layouts based on generational differences. For example, Ken Romanzi, North American chief operating officer for Ocean Spray Cranberries Inc., told a *Wall Street Journal* reporter that "we don't do anything to remind boomers that they are getting older."[2]

Persistently high unemployment levels among young people around the world are creating a strong force for change by governments and organizations alike. Experts believe that much of the current unrest in the Middle East is being fueled by a younger population that cannot find meaningful employment opportunities.[3]

Technological Advancements   Technology is a common and often cost-effective tool for improving productivity, competitiveness, and customer service. Recall our discussion of social media in Chapter 9, as it is one of the most notable technological changes to impact business over the past several years.

> **EXAMPLE**   LinkedIn is now used by more than 225 million people in 200 countries. What's more astonishing is that one source reports that 77% of all jobs are posted on the site, and 48% of recruiters use it as their only recruiting tool! "Simply put," writes Jamie Cifuentes, who covers technology for *PC Magazine,* "recruiters love LinkedIn. It simplifies their work, it costs less to use, and users can't lie about their work experience when they have professional contacts who can view what they post." Twitter and Facebook also are used extensively by recruiters, 54% and 66%, respectively.[4]

Other surveys report that 98% of recruiters use some form of social media to find employees. This one technology has changed how employees look for and find jobs, how companies recruit talent, and how companies make money facilitating these relationships. And given that millions of people are looking for jobs on any given day, many established (e.g., Facebook and Google) and yet-to-be-known companies are trying to cash in on the opportunities.[5]

A recent McKinsey Global Survey of CEOs and other senior executives revealed the five most significant digital enterprise trends in business:[6]

1. Digital engagement of customers
2. Big data and advanced analytics
3. Digital engagement of employees and external partners
4. Automation
5. Digital innovation

Each of these may present job and career opportunities for you. To be sure, OB will play a central role in the level of success individuals and organizations have with each. Put another way, it is people who design and use such technological tools, interpret the data, and then ultimately formulate and apply them effectively. "[D]espite the host of technical challenges in implementing digital [approaches]," McKinsey notes, ". . . success (or failure) of these programs ultimately relies on organization and leadership, rather than technology considerations."[7]

Shareholder, Customer, and Market Changes   Shareholders have become more involved with pressing for organizational change in response to ethical lapses from senior management and anger over executives' compensation packages. For instance, since 2011 public companies are required to allow shareholders to vote on executive compensation. These are referred to as "say on pay" provisions and are part of the Dodd-Frank Act. Although the votes are nonbinding, which means the company is not obligated to comply with the vote, the policy has indeed resulted in changes. In 2012 approximately 50 out of 3,000 companies received no votes, such as Citigroup, McKesson, and Abercrombie & Fitch. Nabors Industries, an oil services company, failed all three years such votes have been required. Many companies are now hiring firms (well-known examples include Institutional Shareholder Services and Glass, Lewis, & Co.) to advise them on changes to their compensation practices, all in efforts to win future approval and support from shareholders.[8]

To the right of President Obama, US Senators Chris Dodd and Barney Frank watch the signing of the Wall Street Reform and Consumer Protection Act in 2010.

Customers also are increasingly sophisticated and demand the companies with whom they do business to deliver higher value products and services. If they don't get what they want, then they will shop elsewhere. This has led more and more companies to seek customer feedback about a wide range of issues in order to attract and retain customers because "turning a potential negative situation into visible positive sentiment is social media's biggest potential advantage," writes Lauren McCrea of the Ignite Social Media Agency.[9]

> **EXAMPLE** Walmart collects feedback from millions of customers to help improve service and merchandising.

> **EXAMPLE** UPS takes customer service to another level. It not only includes the names and pictures of its customer service representatives on its Facebook page—so you can "see" who you're dealing with—but it also provides direct e-mail and phone contact info! Yes, you can contact a person directly![10]

Social and Political Pressures These forces are created by social and political events. For example, widespread concern about the impact of climate change and rising energy costs have been important forces for change in almost every industry around the world. Companies have gone "green," looking for ways to use less energy themselves and to sell products that consume less energy and are safer to use. For example, Esquel, one of the world's largest producers of premium cotton shirts, received pressure from retail customers such as Nike and Marks & Spencer to improve its environmental and social performance. These retailers pressed Esquel to produce more cotton organically.

This is very difficult to do because most of Esquel's cotton comes from Xinjiang, "an arid province in northwestern China that depends mainly on underground sources of water," according to Stanford's Hua L. Lee. "The traditional method of irrigation there was to periodically flood the fields—an inefficient approach that created a perfect breeding ground for insects and diseases. Heavy pesticide use was a necessity." This pressure ultimately caused Esquel to closely work with farms to implement sustainable farming techniques. "For example, it assisted them in adopting drip irrigation to decrease their water use and in establishing natural pest- and disease-control programs such as breeding disease-resistant strains of cotton, to reduce reliance on pesticides. (The new variety of cotton plants also produced stronger fiber, resulting in less scrap during fabric manufacturing than conventional cotton did.)"[11]

Political events, such as the wars and unrest in the Middle East, also can create substantial change. Many defense contractors and infrastructure companies find opportunities due to such events. Events aside, governments can apply political pressures that can force or block changes. French pharmaceutical company Sanofi has been restructuring its research and development facilities around the world. Part of these changes included closing a lab in Toulouse that was not producing enough new drug discoveries to continue operating. However, the French government intervened and blocked the closing in French courts. The labor laws in the country make it easier for the government to prevent profitable companies from cutting jobs, particularly in high-tech industries that French politicians want to foster. This is challenging for Sanofi, which wants to consolidate specific operations to particular cities around the globe, like early drug research in Boston and infectious diseases in Lyon (another French city).[12]

Internal Forces

***Internal forces for change* come from inside the organization.** These forces may be subtle, such as low job satisfaction, or can manifest in outward signs, such as low productivity, conflict, or strikes. Internal forces for change come from both human resource problems and managerial behavior and decisions.

Human Resource Problems or Prospects These problems stem from employee perceptions about how they are treated at work and the match between individual and organization needs and desires. Chapter 2 highlighted the relationship between an employee's unmet needs and job dissatisfaction. Dissatisfaction is a symptom of an underlying employee problem that should be addressed.

EXAMPLE Employees at Foxconn, one of Apple's major Chinese suppliers, went on strike after managers required harsh production demands for the iPhone 5. Workers slowed production to a halt and even had violent clashes with management and inspectors. Tensions with the incredibly stringent quality standards were intensified when the company disallowed vacation time during the holidays to meet production goals. Apple has since taken a more active role in assuring higher wages and better working conditions at Foxconn and other suppliers.[13]

It also is common for new executives to "clean house." When new CEOs take charge they often bring in their own people. About a quarter of CFOs, for example, are gone within one year of a new chief executive taking the reins. CFOs that have survived such changes in leadership offer three pieces of advice that executives and others can benefit from:

1. *Communicate.* "It's better to err on the side of over communication . . . there's so much [the incoming CEO] needs to learn." Share both job-critical details and information about the culture, people, and customers.

2. *Identify the CEO's strengths and compensate for the weaknesses.* It can be helpful to learn the knowledge and skill gaps and do what you can to cover them. This will prevent the new executive from being blindsided. Complement his or her skills and knowledge.

3. *Don't be an obstacle or resister.* Embrace the change. "If you don't believe in the direction the boss is going, and you don't say why, and you sit there and simmer with resentment, that's not a good place to be."[14]

Unusual or high levels of absenteeism and turnover also represent forces for change. Organizations might respond to these problems by using the various approaches to job design discussed in Chapter 5, and by removing the different stressors discussed later in this chapter. To help combat these challenges, leaders and managers of change are well served to encourage employee participation and suggestions.

Managerial Behaviors and Decisions Excessive interpersonal conflict between managers and their subordinates or the board of directors is a sign that change is needed.

EXAMPLE Andrew Mason, founder and former CEO of Groupon, was fired due to his strategy and underperformance. He decided to take the firm aggressively into selling goods and not just coupons for discounts with local merchants. These actions, combined with underperforming international expansion, led the board to conclude that his decisions and direction were not right for the company. (See the Problem-Solving Application Case at the end of Chapter 11.)

"After four and a half intense and wonderful years as CEO of Groupon, I've decided that I'd like to spend more time with my family. Just kidding—I was fired today." Farewell memo to Groupon employees from Andrew Mason, its founder and former CEO.[15]

BP not only changed is senior leadership but also its practices related to safety, motivated by the disastrous spill in the Gulf of Mexico in 2010 and previous explosion in a Texas facility in 2005. Current CEO Bob Dudley knows all aspects of the oil business and has spent $14 billion on cleanup efforts and another $11 billion for settlements. Dudley is determined "not to let unethical and potentially criminal behavior worm its way into the final settlements." His attitude—and the company's approach—is "instead of stressing the safety for the sake of complying with regulatory guidelines or passing an audit, BP's goal is to build a behavior-based safety culture, one in which everyone on the job is committed to performing their work safely, even when no one is looking over their shoulder." He brought in retired admiral Frank Bowman, of the U.S. Navy's nuclear fleet, to oversee the safety program. And to be sure he has adequate influence, Mr. Bowman is also on the BP board of directors.[16]

MAJOR QUESTION

How can different approaches to change make me and my organization more effective managers of change?

THE BIGGER PICTURE

Researchers and managers alike have tried to identify effective ways to manage the change process, given its importance for organizational survival. This section provides insights into general types of organizational changes, as well as reviews of Lewin's change model, a systems model of change, Kotter's eight steps for leading organizational change, and the organizational development approach. Each serves as an organizational-level tool that affects many outcomes across the levels of our Integrative Framework of OB.

Given the incredible variety of changes that occur, how are you supposed to manage them effectively? Do you just "wing it" and do whatever you feel in the moment? Or do you develop a particular approach and manage any and all changes the same way? The contingency approach in Chapter 1 suggests that you'd be wise to have a variety of approaches or change management tools and use the one best suited for a particular change. We provide such knowledge and tools in this section. Let's start our discussion by looking at general types of changes.

Three General Types of Change

A useful way to organize and think about change is displayed in Figure 16.2. You'll notice that this is similar to the common types of innovation you learned in Chapter 15—product, process, core, or transformational. These similarities make sense, as innovation requires change. Therefore, the common types of change differ in degree of change much like the types or degrees of innovation. With this in mind, many if not most organizational changes can be put into one of these three categories.

1. *Adaptive change* is the least complex, costly, and uncertain. It involves reimplementation of a change in the same organizational unit at a later time or

FIGURE 16.2 A GENERIC TYPOLOGY OF ORGANIZATIONAL CHANGE

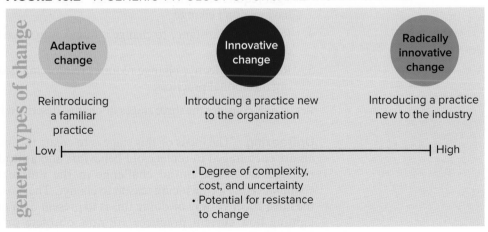

general types of change

Adaptive change — Reintroducing a familiar practice

Innovative change — Introducing a practice new to the organization

Radically innovative change — Introducing a practice new to the industry

Low |————————————————————————————| High

- Degree of complexity, cost, and uncertainty
- Potential for resistance to change

imitation of a similar change by a different unit. For example, an adaptive change for a department store would be to rely on 12-hour days during the annual inventory week. The store's accounting department could imitate the same change in work hours during tax preparation time. Adaptive changes are not particularly threatening to employees because they are familiar.

2. *Innovative change* **falls midway on the continuum of complexity, cost, and uncertainty.** Many companies now utilize flextime and flexspace work arrangements (recall our discussion from Chapter 10). If other companies in their industry already utilize such practices, then this would qualify as an innovative change. Intel, for example, is embarking on innovative changes as they try to compete in the smartphone and tablet markets. While these are quite different from the PC markets where Intel made its name, many of its competitors (e.g., ARM Holdings) are doing the same.[17] Innovative changes are therefore more complex, as organizations need to learn new behaviors, as well as create, implement, and enforce new policies and practices. These situations both have more uncertainty and cause more fear than adaptive changes.

3. *Radically innovative change* **is at the high end of the continuum of complexity, cost, and uncertainty.** Changes of this sort are the most difficult to implement and tend to be the most threatening to managerial confidence and employee job security. At the same time, however, radically innovative changes potentially realize the greatest benefits. Radical changes must also be supported by an organization's culture. Organizational change is more likely to fail if it is inconsistent with any of the three levels of organizational culture: observable artifacts, espoused values, and basic assumptions (see the discussion in Chapter 14).

Now that you've learned how to categorize types of change, let's turn our attention to specific models of how to manage change.

Lewin's Change Model

Most models of organizational change originated from the landmark work of social psychologist Kurt Lewin. Lewin developed a three-stage model of planned change that explained how to initiate, manage, and stabilize the change process.[18] The three stages are *unfreezing*, *changing*, and *refreezing*. Before reviewing each stage, it is important to highlight some key assumptions underlying this model and many of the others:[19]

1. **Learn and unlearn.** The change process involves learning something new, as well as discontinuing or unlearning current attitudes, behaviors, or organizational practices.

2. **Motivation.** Change will not occur unless there is motivation to change. This is often the most difficult part of the change process.

3. **People make or break.** People are the key to all organizational changes. Any change, whether in terms of structure, group process, reward systems, or job design, requires individuals to change. Organizations don't change if employee behaviors don't change.

4. **Resistance.** Resistance to change is found even when the goals of change are highly desirable.

5. **Reinforce.** Effective change requires reinforcing new behaviors, attitudes, and organizational practices.

Let us now consider the three stages of change described by Lewin. Refer to Figure 16.3.

Unfreezing The focus of this stage is to create the motivation to change. Individuals are encouraged to replace old behaviors and attitudes with new ones (desired by management). The initial challenge in the unfreezing process is creating and communicating a convincing reason to change. The most common, but not necessarily the most effective, way of doing this is to present data or compelling arguments highlighting how current practices are now obsolete or less than ideal, such as low

FIGURE 16.3 LEWIN MODEL OF CHANGE

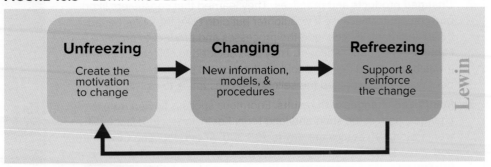

employee or customer satisfaction data, or market share gains made by competitors. This approach is exactly the same as the rational persuasion influence tactic you learned about in Chapter 12, and it helps employees understand the need for change.

> **EXAMPLE** Facebook had less than two dozen engineers working on mobile applications in 2012. The fact that it now has hundreds is a strong signal that mobile is at the center of the company's new strategy. This change was motivated in part by the company being public and needing to please shareholders, as well as the desire to monetize or make revenue from its immense user base.[20] The company thus needed to reallocate many of the resources (human and financial) from building its business around desktop computers to smartphones and tablets.

To unfreeze the organization, CEO Mark Zuckerberg and others shared growing criticisms that Facebook's app on iPhones didn't function well—it was slow and frequently crashed. The situation was made worse by other companies gaining enormous popularity in the mobile space. This led Mike Shaver, Facebook's director of mobile engineering, to say, "If we are going to be a mobile company at scale, we needed to do something qualitatively different . . . we needed a nuclear option."[21] After attempting to compete with Instagram's photo-sharing service, Facebook decided instead to buy the company for $1 billion in 2012.

Changing This is where the rubber meets the road and change occurs. Because change involves learning and doing things differently, this stage entails providing employees with new information, new behavioral models, new processes or procedures, new equipment, new technology, or new ways of getting the job done. How does management know what to change? There is no simple answer to this question. Organizational change can be aimed at improvement or growth, or it can focus on solving a problem such as poor customer service or low productivity. The Example box provides an excellent illustration of how Jin Zhiguo, former chairman of Tsingtao Beer, responded to serious production difficulties at a newly acquired brewery.

EXAMPLE Jump-Starting a Sluggish Company[22]

Tsingtao (ching-dow) is the #1 selling Chinese beer in America. In the mid-1990s the company acquired another brewery, and Jin Zhiguo, who at the time was an assistant managing director, learned that the new facility was producing 1,000 per day—bottles not cases! This was undesirable to say the least, as the company had about 1,000 employees (1 bottle per day per employee). What did he do?

1. **Gathered data.** He gathered not only production, cost, and profit data, but also customer insights. In the mid-1990s Chinese companies still were not all that concerned with such metrics, particularly customer insights. Jin himself, along with his salespeople, went out into the communities and learned why people drank which beers and with which types of food.

---

2. **Changed products and practices.** They learned that consumers liked one competitor because it was lighter but didn't like the other because it had sediment. Jin changed the processes and product to produce a lighter beer without sediment. They also decided to chill their beer after it was brewed and deliver it cold. At the time, all producers delivered beer warm and expected the sellers and consumers to chill it.

3. **Reinforced changes with results.** Enormous success flowed from these changes, both in the short and long term. For instance, that first facility went from 1,000 bottles per day to 790,000. After becoming CEO in 2001 and spreading these changes across the entire company, Tsingtao is now the fifth largest beer producer in the world and has double-digit profit growth annually.

Zhiguo Jin spent his entire career at Tsingtao and retired as a director in 2012.

YOUR THOUGHTS?

1. What are your impressions of Mr. Jin's approach?
2. What do you think were his biggest challenges?
3. Which of the three actions do you think was the most important?

Change also can be targeted at different levels in an organization. Sending managers to leadership training programs can improve many individuals' job satisfaction and productivity.

> **EXAMPLE** Safelite Autoglass designed and implemented a training program for 1,000 of its managers to equip them to implement a wholesale culture change at the company. The dramatic changes were intended to focus every employee on customer satisfaction and double the business in four years.[23]

In contrast, installing new information technology can be the change required to increase work group productivity and overall corporate profits. The point to keep in mind is that change should be targeted at some type of desired end result. The systems model of change, which is the next model to be discussed, provides managers with a framework to diagnose the target of change.

Refreezing The goal of this stage is to support and reinforce the change. Change is supported by helping employees integrate the changed behavior or attitude into their normal way of doing things. This is accomplished by first giving employees the chance to exhibit the new behaviors or attitudes. Once this happens, positive reinforcement is used to encourage the desired change. More specifically, early in the change process it is especially helpful to use continuous reinforcement with extrinsic rewards (e.g., recognition, feedback, bonuses), as we discussed in Chapter 6. This helps establish clear links between the desired new behaviors and the reinforcing reward or recognition. And don't forget role modeling. Walking the talk of change is arguably the most powerful way to get others to follow.

A Systems Model of Change

A systems approach to change is based on the notion that any change, no matter how large or small, has a cascading effect throughout an organization. For example, promoting an individual to a new work group affects the group dynamics in both the old and new groups. Similarly, creating project or work teams may necessitate the need to revamp compensation practices. These examples illustrate that change creates additional change.

A systems model of change is similar to the systems framework used in the Integrative Framework of OB. However, it is a bit more complex, as shown in Figure 16.4. This model includes inputs, strategic plans, target elements of change, and outputs.

FIGURE 16.4 A SYSTEMS MODEL OF CHANGE

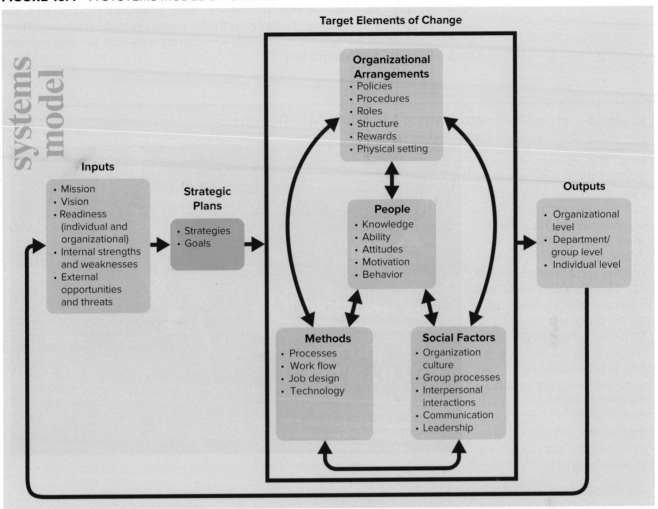

SOURCE: Adapted from D. R. Fuqua and D. J. Kurpius, "Conceptual Models in Organizational Consultation," *Journal of Counseling and Development*, July–August 1993, 602–618; and D. A. Nadler and M. L. Tushman, "Organizational Frame Bending: Principles for Managing Reorientation," *Academy of Management Executive*, August 1989, 194–203.

It is a very practical approach and can be used to diagnose *what* to change and to determine *how* to evaluate the success of a change effort. Let's explore the individual components.

Inputs The starting point for organizational change should be asking and answering the question: "Why change?" Leaders need to get clear on the overarching motive or reason for change. It then is essential to assure that the intended changes align with the organization's mission, vision, and resulting strategic plan.[24]

Mission statements represent the "reason" organizations exist. Some examples of clear and effective missions:

- Instagram, the photo-sharing service, has a simple mission—"To capture and share the world's moments."[25]
- Southwest Airline's is legendary—"To give people the freedom to fly."
- Charles Schwab—"A relentless ally for the individual investor."
- Interface—"To be the first company that, by its deeds, shows the entire industrial world what sustainability is in all its dimensions: People, process, product, place and profits—by 2020—and in doing so we will become restorative through the power of influence."

While each of these is interesting, you and most people in business wonder—how does an organization create an effective mission? Sally Jewell, the CEO of REI, the outdoor clothing and equipment retailer, provides an excellent description of how she and her team of 150 leaders went about formulating a mission for the company. The details are in the Example box.

EXAMPLE How to Formulate a Meaningful Mission

Missions are big-picture, long term, and existential. These qualities mean they are often quite general. But it is important that they are not too general, which would make them abstract and meaningless. Sally Jewell, the CEO of outdoor clothing and adventure retailer REI, followed a very useful and repeatable process when refining the company's mission. She began by assembling a representative team of leaders. It's best to be inclusive rather than exclusive. Involving people in the process will help assure that their interests are reflected in the mission and that they will be more likely to "live it." Then ask the members:

Sally Jewell, CEO of REI, the retailer of outdoor gear and clothing.

1. Why does our organization exist? Ask this question three to five times to get a deeper, richer view.
2. What would happen if our organization went away?
3. Why do I devote my creative energies to this organization?
4. Compile and consolidate the answers to these questions.[26]

This process resulted in REI's mission: "To inspire, educate and outfit for a lifetime of outdoor adventure and stewardship."

YOUR THOUGHTS?

1. This approach was successful for REI, but how successful do you think it would be for an organization to which you belong?
2. What are the benefits of this approach?
3. What are the shortcomings or ways to improve it?

As you learned in Chapter 14, a **vision** is a compelling future state for an organization, and it also is another important input in the systems model of change. Consider how the difference between mission and vision affects organizational change. Missions typically imply little or nothing about change, but instead simply define the organization's overall purpose, like those of Instagram, Southwest, and Charles Schwab noted above. In contrast, effective *visions* describe a highly desirable future and outline how the organization will get there; which markets, services, products, and people will be involved; and how all of these elements align with the organization's values. Interface

Inc., a world leader in sustainability and commercial interiors, captures all of these and more in its vision:

> Interface® will become the first name in commercial and institutional interiors worldwide through its commitment to **people, process, product, place and profits.** We will strive to create an organization wherein all people are accorded unconditional respect and dignity; one that allows each person to continuously learn and develop. We will focus on product (which includes service) through constant emphasis on process quality and engineering, which we will combine with careful attention to our customers' needs so as always to deliver superior value to our customers, thereby maximizing all stakeholders' satisfaction. We will honor the places where we do business by endeavoring to become the first name in industrial ecology, a corporation that cherishes nature and restores the environment. Interface will lead by example and validate by results, including profits, leaving the world a better place than when we began, and we will be restorative through the power of our influence in the world.[27]

Readiness for change **is defined as beliefs, attitudes, and intentions regarding the extent to which changes are needed and the capacity available to successfully implement those changes.** Defined in this way, you can see how readiness can be both an individual- and/or an organizational-level input.[28] Put another way, effective change at work requires both the employees and the employer to be willing and able to change (i.e., have high readiness). Readiness has four components:

1. Necessity for change
2. Top management support for change efforts
3. Personal ability to cope with changes
4. Perceived personal consequences of change

Self-Assessment 16.2 will help you determine your own readiness for change. It also can be used to determine the readiness of an organization to which you belong.

---

connect

SELF-ASSESSMENT 16.2   **What Is Your Readiness for Change?**

Think of a change at school, work, or another arena of your life. Then go to connect .mheducation.com and take Self-Assessment 16.2 to learn the extent of your readiness for change, or that of the organization in which the change needs to occur.

1. Of the four components which is the lowest?
2. How do you think this will affect the success of the particular change? Be specific.
3. Who seems to be "most ready," you (components 1 and 2) or the organization (components 3 and 4)?
4. Given what the readiness measure tells you, what do you recommend to improve the readiness for both you and the organization?

Strategic Plans   A strategic plan outlines an organization's long-term direction and the actions necessary to achieve planned results. Among other things, strategic plans are based on results from a SWOT—strengths, weaknesses, opportunities, and threats—analysis. This analysis aids in developing an organizational strategy to attain desired goals, such as profits, customer satisfaction, quality, adequate return on investment, and acceptable levels of turnover and employee satisfaction.

Target Elements of Change   Target elements of change are the components of an organization that may be changed. They essentially represent change levers that managers can push and pull to influence various aspects of an organization. The choice of which lever to use, however, is based on a diagnosis of a problem, or problems, or the actions needed to accomplish a goal. A problem exists when managers are not obtaining the results they desire—when a gap exists, as explained in Chapter 1 and used in the 3-Stop Problem-Solving Approach. The target elements of change are used to diagnose problems and to identify change-related solutions. As shown in Figure 16.4, there are four targeted elements of change:

1. Organizational arrangements
2. Social factors
3. Methods
4. People

Each target element of change contains a subset of more detailed organizational features. For instance, the "social factors" component includes consideration of an organization's culture, group processes, interpersonal interactions, communication, and leadership. (All of these are OB topics discussed in this book and included in the Integrative Framework of OB.)

There are two final issues to keep in mind about the target elements. First, the double-headed arrows in the figure connecting each target element of change convey the message that change ripples across an organization. For example, changing a reward system to reinforce team rather than individual performance (an organizational arrangement) is likely to impact organizational culture (a social factor). Second, the "people" component is placed in the center of the target elements of change box because all organizational change ultimately impacts employees and vice versa. Organizational change is more likely to succeed when managers proactively consider the impact of change on employees.

Outputs   Outputs represent the desired end results or goals of a change. Once again, these end results should be consistent with an organization's strategic plan. Figure 16.4 indicates that change may be directed at the individual, group, or organizational level. Change efforts are more complicated and difficult to manage when they are targeted at the organizational level. This occurs because organizational-level changes are more likely to affect multiple target elements of change shown in the model.

Now that you've learned the details of the systems approach to change, we shift our focus to one of the most popular approaches to organizational change since the 1990s—Kotter's Eight Steps.

Kotter's Eight Steps for Leading Organizational Change

John Kotter, an expert in leadership and change management, believes that organizational change most often fails not because of inadequate planning but because of ineffective implementation. To help overcome this, he proposed an eight-step process for leading change (see Table 16.1). This approach differs from the systems model in that it does not help in diagnosing the need for or targets of change. It is, however, somewhat like Lewin's model in that it guides managers through the process of effective organizational change. For instance, you could map the first four steps onto Lewin's "unfreezing" stage; steps 5, 6, and 7 to "moving" or "changing"; and step 8 to the "refreezing" stage.

The value of Kotter's steps is that they provide specific recommendations about behaviors and activities needed to successfully lead organizational change. Notice that vision and strategy are central components to Kotter's approach, as they are in the systems model. But it also is helpful to know that Kotter insists that the steps need to be followed in sequence and none skipped. It therefore requires a tremendous

TABLE 16.1 EIGHT STEPS TO LEADING ORGANIZATIONAL CHANGE

STEP	DESCRIPTION
1. Establish a sense of urgency.	Unfreeze the organization by creating a compelling reason for why change is needed.
2. Create the guiding coalition.	Create a cross-functional, cross-level group of people with enough power to lead change.
3. Develop a vision and strategy.	Create a vision and strategic plan to guide the change process.
4. Communicate the change vision.	Create and implement a communication strategy that consistently communicates the new vision and strategic plan.
5. Empower the broad-based action.	Eliminate barriers to change and use target elements of change to transform the organization. Encourage risk and creative problem solving.
6. Generate short-term wins.	Plan for and create short-term "wins" or improvements. Recognize and reward people who contribute to the wins.
7. Consolidate gains and produce more change.	The guiding coalition uses credibility from short-term wins to create more change. Additional people are brought into the change process as change cascades throughout the organization. Attempts are made to reinvigorate the change process.
8. Anchor new approaches in the culture.	Reinforce the changes by highlighting connections between new behaviors and processes and organizational success. Develop methods to ensure leadership development and succession.

SOURCE: Reprinted by permission of Harvard Business School Press. From *Leading Change* by J. P. Kotter, Boston, MA, 1996. Copyright © 1996 by the Harvard Business School Publishing Corporation; all rights reserved.

commitment of resources (time, money, and people) to implement Kotter's eight steps. The result is that this approach is very difficult for organizations, and even more so for individuals, to utilize. These challenges are in part overcome by our final approach to change—organizational development (OD).

Creating Change through Organization Development

Organization development (OD) differs from the previously discussed models of change. And while its origins are in Lewin's approach,[29] it does not entail a structured sequence as proposed by Lewin and Kotter. OD does, however, possess the same diagnostic focus associated with the systems model of change. That said, OD is much broader in orientation than any of the previously discussed models. Academics Bernard Burnes and Bill Cooke reviewed the long history of organizational development and identify its appeal this way:

> OD processes could really transform people, make them psychologically healthier. . . . Then, through the use of these improved interpersonal skills, people in the organization would develop more powerful ways to solve problems, increase their participation, share power and decision making.[30]

If you think this sounds much like empowerment discussed in Chapter 12, then you are correct. Many OD experts and practitioners argue that employee empowerment is central to this approach to change. Now let's learn a bit about the history of OD and how it works.

The History and Philosophy of OD Throughout its history OD has combined academic rigor with practical application, which has led some experts to say it is the most common approach to organizational change today. Three fundamental aspects have helped it earn this distinction:

1. OD is about planned change aimed at increasing "an organization's ability to improve itself as a humane and effective system."

2. OD takes theories and results from the laboratory and applies them to the real-life work settings. In this way, OD is very similar to the applied problem-solving approach taken in this book. We've presented theories, research, and practical tools in ways that make their application clear and effective.

3. OD takes a distinctly democratic and participative approach to solving conflict and problems. This means that an organizational development approach to organizational change is not simply a top-down approach where senior leaders prescribe changes or directives to be followed by employees. Instead, OD advocates the involvement of all players in identifying needed changes, planning how to make such changes, and then the ultimate implementation and evaluation of change efforts.

How OD Works One way to think of OD is to follow a medical metaphor and approach the organization as if it were a "sick" patient: "diagnose" its ills, prescribe and implement an "intervention," and "evaluate" progress. If the evaluation reveals that positive change has not occurred, this information provides feedback that is used to refine the diagnosis and/or consider the extent to which the intervention was effectively implemented (see Figure 16.5).

Let's improve your understanding by exploring each of these components in a bit more detail.

1. **Diagnosis:** *What is the problem and its causes?* Many means can be used to answer this question: interviews, surveys, meetings, written materials, and direct observation. We recommend the 3-Stop Problem-Solving Approach and the Integrative Framework of OB to help. The target elements in the systems model of change can also be useful. For example, you might ask, "To what extent does the structure or reward system contribute to the problem?"

2. **Intervention:** *What can be done to solve the problem?* The treatment or intervention represents the changes being made to solve the problem. Treatments are selected based on the causes of the problem. For example, if the cause of low

FIGURE 16.5 THE OD PROCESSES

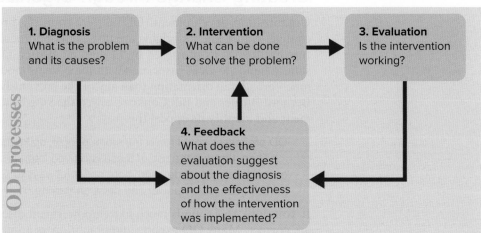

SOURCE: Adapted from W. L. French and C. H. Bell Jr., *Organization Development: Behavioral Interventions for Organizational Improvement* (Englewood Cliffs, NJ: Prentice Hall, 1978).

quality is poor teamwork, then team building (see Chapter 8) might be used as the intervention. In contrast, training may be appropriate if poor leadership is the cause of low quality (see Chapter 13). The key thing to remember is that there is not one "set" of intervention techniques that applies to all situations. Rather, you can use any number of interventions based on the knowledge and tools you learned in this book and course. Remember the contingency approach from Chapter 1 and used throughout this book, which suggests that the "best" solution or intervention depends on the particular situation.

3. *Evaluation: Is the intervention working?* Evaluation requires measurement of effectiveness—draw on what you learned about performance management in Chapter 6 and organizational effectiveness in Chapter 15. The measures must match the problem. For instance, if the problem is job performance, then part of the problem may be the way performance is measured. It is highly unlikely that teamwork or quality of service can be evaluated if you only measure sales volume. It also is helpful if the final evaluation is based on comparing measures of effectiveness obtained before and after the intervention.

4. *Feedback: What does the evaluation suggest about the diagnosis and the effectiveness of how the intervention was implemented?* If the evaluation reveals that the intervention worked, then the OD process is complete and you can consider how best to "refreeze" the changes. However, a negative evaluation means one of two things: either (1) the initial diagnosis was wrong or (2) the intervention was not effectively implemented. Negative evaluations generally require you to collect more information about steps 1 and 2 in the OD process shown in Figure 16.5.

OD and the Integrative Framework of OB OD has been shown to positively influence a number of outcomes in the Integrative Framework of OB.

- Employee satisfaction with change was higher when top management was highly committed to the change effort.[31]
- Varying one target element of change created changes in other target elements. Also, there was a positive relationship between individual behavior change and organizational-level change.[32]
- Interventions using more than one OD technique were more effective in changing job attitudes and work attitudes than interventions that relied on only one human process or structural approach.[33]
- US and European firms used OD interventions more frequently than firms from China and Japan, and some OD interventions are "culture free" (i.e., are more or less effective depending on the national culture) and some are not.[34]

EXAMPLE OD and the Big Shift

International consulting firm, Deloitte, created a Shift Index to help organizations determine how they measure up to 20,000 U.S. firms in terms of three fundamental drivers of change and performance: (1) developments in technology and politics; (2) market changes, such as flows of capital, information, and talent; and (3) impacts of change on competition, volatility, and performance. Comparisons in these areas, using the Shift Index, can serve as a tool for applying the OD process—diagnosis, intervention, evaluation, and feedback.[35]

---

major question

Why do people resist change and what can I do about it?

THE BIGGER PICTURE

You can't think about change without also thinking about resistance. Change and resistance are intimately related. Therefore, if you are going to effectively manage change you need to understand and manage resistance. Your ability to do this is fundamental to your effectiveness at managing this important process and its many related outcomes in the Integrative Framework of OB. Quite simply, resistance can either make or break the best change efforts and your personal success.

We begin our discussion by defining ***resistance to change*** **as any thought, emotion, or behavior that does not align with real or potential changes to existing routines.** This means that people resist both actual and imagined events. With this in mind, it is helpful to think about resistance by recalling our discussion of influence in Chapter 12. Viewing change in this way is helpful because managing resistance and change are fundamentally attempts to influence employees to think, feel, or behave differently. This perspective underscores that resistance is one of the three possible influence outcomes—the other two being compliance and commitment. This perspective has led many people to conclude that resistance to change represents a failed influence attempt. And while resistance can indeed spell failure, we are going to challenge this assumption and approach resistance in a different and more useful way, and help you gain more compliance and commitment to change.

A Dynamic View of Resistance

Historically, and still, many managers of change see resistance as employees pursuing their own interests and attempting to undermine the interests of the manager or larger organization. This view suggests that there is a victim, either the manager of change who must "fight" or overcome the lack of compliance or commitment by employees, or employees who are victims of uncaring or inconsiderate managers and employers who serve their interests at the expense of employees. These two perspectives are why resistance is commonly viewed as a negative and individual-level outcome in the change process (and in the Integrative Framework of OB).

While both of these views are possible, and at times are very real, there is much more to the resistance story. Specifically, it is equally likely that resistance is caused by two other key factors:

1. Change agent's characteristics, actions, inactions, and perceptions. **A *change agent* is someone who is a catalyst in helping organizations to deal with old problems in new ways.** Change agents can be external consultants or internal employees.

2. Quality of the relationship between change agents and change recipients.

When viewed in this way, resistance is a dynamic form of feedback (see Figure 16.6). You learned at several points in this book (e.g., Chapter 6) about the many practical

FIGURE 16.6   A DYNAMIC MODEL OF RESISTANCE TO CHANGE

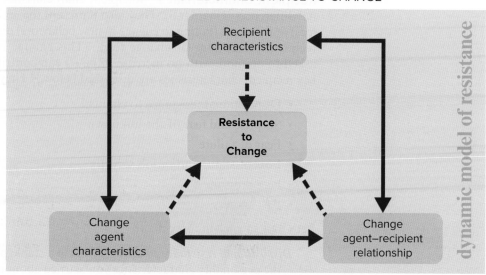

and powerful uses of feedback. Let's explore some fundamental causes of resistance to change to help you better understand and manage a dynamic approach to resistance more effectively.

Causes of Resistance to Change

Resistance can be subtle or overt. Figure 16.6 presents a model of resistance that illustrates the relationships among the three key causes of resistance. Resistance is a dynamic interaction among the three sources, rather than being caused solely by irrational and stubborn recipients of change. For example, recipients resist partly based on their perceptions of change, which are very much influenced by the attitudes and behaviors exhibited by change agents and the level of trust between change agents and recipients. Similarly, change agents' actions and perceptions are affected by the recipients' actions and inactions and the quality of relationships with recipients. Let's consider each source of resistance.

To better understand the nature of resistance to change, it will be helpful for you to learn about the level of your own dispositional resistance to change by completing Self-Assessment 16.3. Knowing this about yourself will help you manage your own tendencies and better recognize them in others. Both will make you more successful with organizational change throughout your career.

McGraw Hill Education connect

SELF-ASSESSMENT 16.3   How Resistant Are You to Change?

Go to connect.mheducation.com and take Self-Assessment 16.3 to learn the extent of your dispositional resistance to change.

1. Which of the four components is highest?

2. Given your answer to question 1, what are the potential implications if your manager changes?

3. Describe two things you can do to help reduce the negative impact of your attribute with the lowest score.

4. Describe two things you can do to help reduce the negative impact of your attribute with the second lowest score.

Copyright © 2003 by the American Psychological Association. Adapted with permission from S. Oreg, "Resistance to Change: Developing an Individual Differences Measure," *Journal of Applied Psychology, 88*(4), 682.

Recipient Characteristics   Recipient characteristics include a variety of individual differences (Chapter 3). They also represent the actions (engaging in new behaviors) or inactions (failing to engage in new behaviors) displayed by recipients. Finally, recipient perceptions of change (e.g., "This change is unfair because I am being asked to do more with no increase in pay") can contribute to resistance. Six of the key recipient characteristics are discussed below.[36] They are:

- Dispositional resistance to change
- Surprise and fear of the unknown
- Fear of failure
- Loss of status and/or job security
- Peer pressure
- Past success

Let's look at each in more depth.

Dispositional resistance to change. This is a stable personality trait, like many of the personality characteristics you learned about in Chapter 3. Individuals with a high **dispositional resistance to change** are "less likely to voluntarily initiate changes and more likely to form negative attitudes toward the changes [they] encounter."[37] Dispositional resistance comprises four attributes:

1. *Routine seeking*—extent to which you enjoy and seek out stable environments.
2. *Emotional reaction*—degree to which you feel stressed and uncomfortable when change is imposed.
3. *Short-term focus*—extent you are preoccupied with inconveniences in the near term due to the changes instead of long-term benefits.
4. *Cognitive rigidity*—stubbornness or lack of willingness to consider alternative ways of doing things.

Surprise and fear of the unknown. When innovative or radically different changes are introduced without warning, affected employees become fearful of the implications. The same is true when managers announce new goals without explaining the specific plans for how the goals will be achieved. Imagine how you would feel if your boss stated that your department was going to increase sales by 25 percent without hiring any new employees. Failing to set expectations around a change effort or the setting of new goals is a key contributor to resistance.[38]

Fear of failure. Intimidating changes on the job can cause employees to doubt their capabilities. Self-doubt erodes self-confidence and cripples personal growth and development. Recall our discussion about self-efficacy in Chapter 3.

Loss of status and/or job security. Administrative and technological changes that threaten to alter power bases or eliminate jobs generally trigger strong resistance. For example, most corporate restructuring involves the elimination of managerial jobs. One should not be surprised when middle managers resist restructuring and other programs (e.g., empowerment) that reduce their authority and status.

Peer pressure. Someone who is not directly affected by a change may actively resist it to protect the interests of his or her friends and coworkers.

Past success. Success can breed complacency. It also can foster a stubbornness to change because people come to believe that what worked in the past will work in the future. Decades ago the Green Revolution alleviated hunger in Asia and Latin America by equipping farmers with more productive strains of wheat and rice. But in the words of Usha Tuteja, who heads the Agricultural Economics Research Center at Delhi University, "People got complacent." Governments,

Potential Stressors   The model begins with four potential types of *stressors*, **which are factors that produce stress.** The four types are:

1. **Individual level.** Job demands are the most common, but work overload, unclear or conflicting expectations, everyday hassles, perceived control over events occurring in the work environment, and job characteristics can also be problematic.[47] One of the very worst is job loss, which negatively affects most every aspect of people's lives (e.g., financial, professional, health, and interpersonal relationships). Let's not overlook the stress associated with a nightmare manager or an otherwise miserable job. If you lack opportunities for advancement, have a fear of being laid off, or work at a job that is not in your desired career path, then you too are likely to be stressed. Hopefully you not one of the 40 million Americans who report sleep problems, many of which are linked to work stress.[48]

2. **Group level.** Recall our discussion in Chapter 8 about the challenges of working in groups and it will be obvious how many of these can cause stress. For instance, managers create stress for employees by (1) exhibiting inconsistent behaviors, (2) failing to provide support, (3) showing lack of concern, (4) providing inadequate direction, (5) creating a high-productivity environment, and (6) focusing on negatives while ignoring good performance. Sexual harassment experiences and bullying (Chapter 10) represent other group-level stressors. And, of course, let's not forget annoying coworkers, as they are one of the most common if not problematic sources of group-level stress.[49]

3. **Organizational level**. Organizational culture, which was discussed in Chapter 14, is a potential stressor in itself. For instance, a high-pressure environment that fuels employee fear about performing up to standard can increase the stress response. The increased use of information technology is another source of organizational stress, as continual connectivity causes employees to be "on call" anytime.[50] One study revealed that 59 percent of the respondents are overloaded and stressed by the amount of information they process at work. Unfortunately, a majority of these individuals report coping with this stressor by either deleting or ignoring work information.[51] We don't recommend this coping strategy.

4. **Extra-organizational.** Extra-organizational stressors are those caused by factors outside the organization. For instance, in Chapter 10 we discussed how conflicts associated with balancing school with one's career or family life are stressful. Socioeconomic status is another extra-organizational stressor. Stress is higher for people with lower socioeconomic status, which represents a combination of income, education, and occupation.[52]

Fighting Fatigue   As noted above, sleep disorders affect millions of Americans. Recent reports are that 30 percent of workers routinely do not get enough sleep (7–9 hours per night). This results in lost productivity of about 11.3 days per employee per year, or $2,280 per year on average. It also is linked to increases in absenteeism and *presenteeism,* **which is when employees show up but are sick or otherwise in no condition to work productively.** The most extreme and tragic effects are the number of injuries and accidents that occur. For instance, every year a number of bus accidents occur and people are killed, and some proportion of these are ultimately attributed to driver error in which the drivers were tremendously sleep deprived. Thankfully, you and your employer can do a number of things to fight fatigue and its negative effects.

1. **Staffing.** Maintain adequate staffing to cover the workload. This is especially important for companies that have downsized, as they are likely to simply spread the same amount of work across a smaller number of employees.

Employee productivity obviously is zero when they are unconscious at work. How does being tired affect your performance at school and/or work? Provide at least three specific examples.

2. **Scheduling.** Consider overtime and time spent commuting when scheduling workers to help assure they have enough time between shifts to sleep the needed amount. Rotate shifts forwards, and not back, to avoid messing up people's circadian rhythms.

3. **Environment.** Light, sound, temperature, and other workplace elements can have subtle but important effects on worker fatigue.

4. **Education.** Educate workers to better manage their sleep and factors that can affect it. Covering sleep-disorder screening also can help, as many people have underlying clinical/health problems that negatively affect their sleep.[53]

Cognitive Appraisals You've undoubtedly heard the expression: "It's not what happens to you but how you respond that matters." This essentially describes cognitive appraisal, which is the process by which people evaluate the meaning of events and demands (e.g., stressors) for their own well-being. Put another way, what makes stressors actually stressful is how they are cognitively appraised. There are two types of appraisals that determine whether a particular stressor is actually experienced as stress, and to what degree it is stressful.

1. *Primary appraisals* are perceptions of whether a stressor is irrelevant, positive, or negative. Stress appraisals are obviously the most important in terms of our current discussion because they imply that a situation or stressor is perceived as harmful, threatening, or challenging.

2. *Secondary appraisals* are perceptions of how able you are to deal or cope with a given demand. During this evaluation a person considers which coping strategies are available and which ones are most likely to help resolve the situation at hand.

Combined, these appraisals influence the choice of your coping strategies and in turn the subsequent outcomes.

Coping Strategies Coping strategies are characterized by the specific behaviors and cognitions used to cope with a situation. People use a combination of three approaches to cope with stressors and stress (see Figure 16.7). The first, called a *control strategy,* consists of using behaviors and cognitions to directly anticipate or solve problems. A control strategy has a take-charge tone. Examples include talking to your professor or boss about workload if you feel overwhelmed with your responsibilities and confronting someone who is spreading negative rumors. Research consistently, but not always, shows health and other benefits for control coping.[54] People are more apt to use control coping when they possess high self-esteem, self-efficacy, and problem-solving skills.[55]

Escape strategies are those in which you avoid or ignore stressors. These strategies can be beneficial if you have no control over the stressors or their causes. Like people with an internal locus of control, if you have no control over the situation (e.g., the president of your company is an unpredictable and unlikeable individual, but thankfully is not your direct supervisor), then it is best not to attempt to utilize control coping and instead avoid or escape stressful encounters with him/her.

Symptom management strategies, which focus on reducing the symptoms of stress, are the third type of strategy commonly used, such as relaxation, meditation, medication, or exercise to manage the symptoms of occupational stress. A vacation, for example, can be a good way to reduce the symptoms of stress. Other people may drink or take drugs to reduce stress. In contrast, one of this book's authors plays with his sweet and savage Jack Russell terrier to relieve stress.

Stress Outcomes   Stress has psychological/attitudinal, behavioral, cognitive, and physical health consequences or outcomes. Besides your own personal experiences, a large body of research supports the negative effects of perceived stress on many aspects of our lives.[56] Workplace stress is associated with many undesirable effects on many outcomes in the Integrative Framework of OB:

- Decreases in job satisfaction, organizational commitment, organizational citizenship behavior, positive emotions, and performance.
- Increases in emotional exhaustion, burnout, absenteeism, and turnover.[57]

The undesirable effects extend beyond these, however. Stress is linked to many counterproductive behaviors, like yelling, verbal abuse, and violence toward others. It also is associated with the frequency of drinking and taking illicit drugs.[58] These stress outcomes are very costly to individuals and organizations alike. Finally, ample evidence supports the conclusion that stress negatively affects our physical and psychological health. Stress contributes to the following physical and mental health problems:

- Lessened ability to ward off illness and infection
- High blood pressure
- Coronary artery disease
- Tension headaches
- Back pain
- Gastrointestinal problems
- Psychological well-being[59]

We think that it is stressful just to think about all of these problems! That said, let's close the chapter with some suggestions on how to manage stress and change effectively.

EXAMPLE   Barrie D'Rozario DiLorenzo (BD'D) Takes Advertising, Marketing, and Employee Stress *Very Seriously*!

The Minnesota-based agency boasts an intensely people-centered culture. Not only is the work environment open and stimulating to foster interaction, but the firm's leadership took it much, much further. It offered each of its 18 employees 500 hours of paid time off to pursue their passions! The firm was entering the summer slow season, and instead of paying employees simply to show up or to do less than a full-day's work, Stuart D'Rozario, the agency's president and chief creative director, told employees to take 500 hours to do something they haven't done because of a lack of time. (Think of it as four years' worth of vacation in one summer!) He clarified, doing nothing was not an option. Employees were required to identify something specific, make a plan, and execute.

There's more to the story. BD'D had built up considerable cash reserves and decided to complete the 500-hour project before soliciting and taking on new business. Of course, existing clients would be served, but employees would be paid from existing reserves.

Some employees traveled, at least one made music, another painted, and one even designed a hands-free dog leash! Employees' choices often were, but were never required, to be consistent with the spirit of the firm, which is creativity, enthusiasm, and passion.

To keep the firm running during this time, employees were expected to split their time—25 percent BD'D business and 75 percent for their passion project.

"D'Rozario believes the 500 hours will make the agency better, but that was never the explicit purpose. 'Honestly, my big hope for this is now that they're back, people realize the things you wanted to do, you could always be doing and find a place for it in your lives,' he says. Year after year we let the sun go down on our dreams because we can't take time. Maybe it's time to start giving it."[60]

YOUR THOUGHTS?

1. If you are currently working, then what effect do you think a 500-hour project would have on you?
2. What effect do you think it had on employee stress? Employee engagement?

major question

MAJOR QUESTION

How can OB knowledge and tools help me effectively manage change and stress?

THE BIGGER PICTURE

Your are about to receive practical suggestions on how to manage change and stress. Since organizational change often has implications for nearly every element of the Integrative Framework of OB, it is an excellent opportunity to apply your knowledge and conclude the book. OB provides many practical tools to make you a more effective manager of change. Specifically, we'll describe how to apply the systems model you learned about earlier for strategic planning and diagnosis. We then provide advice on how to overcome resistance to change and manage stress, which is followed by some practical tips for successful change management.

Applying the Systems Model of Change—Strategic Planning and Diagnosis

There are two different ways to apply the systems model of change. The first is as an aid during the strategic planning process. Once a group of managers have determined their vision and strategic goals, the target elements of change can be considered when developing action plans to support the accomplishment of goals (see Figure 16.4).

> **EXAMPLE** Following the merger of Adolph Coors Company and Molson, the management team of Molson Coors Brewing established goals of cutting costs by $180 million, making Coors Light a global brand, and developing new high-end brands of beer. Target elements of change included strengthening shared values of the predecessor companies (social factors), keeping production and distribution employees focused on their existing functions (motivation, a people factor), creating a general-management development program (another people factor), and establishing a subsidiary to specialize in new products (organizational arrangements).[61]

The following Problem-Solving Application illustrates how to apply the systems model of change to diagnose problems and determine the need for change.

solving application

Systems Model of Change

A CEO of a software company was intensely frustrated when he realized his company had lost a bid for business with a new customer. The reason: Two of the three division presidents at the software company submitted a proposal for the same project to the potential customer. The customer was appalled by having received two proposals from the same company. To get to the root of the issue, employees were interviewed using questions that pertained to each of the target elements of change. The interviews revealed that the lack of collaboration among the division presidents was due to the reward system (an organizational arrangement), a competitive culture and poor communications (social factors), and poor work flow (a methods factor).

problem

Stop 1: What is the problem?

Stop 2: How can you apply the systems model of change to diagnose the problem? What might you find?

Stop 3: What recommendations do you have?

How to Overcome Resistance to Change

We previously noted that resistance is a form of feedback and managers need to understand why it is occurring before trying to overcome it. This can be done by considering the extent to which the three sources of resistance shown in Figure 16.6 are contributing to the problem.

Employee and Change Recipient Characteristics and Reactions Employees are more likely to resist when they perceive that the personal costs of change outweigh the benefits. If this is the case, then managers are advised to:

1. Provide as much information as possible to employees about the change.
2. Inform employees about the reasons/rationale for the change.
3. Conduct meetings to address employees' questions regarding the change.
4. Provide employees the opportunity to discuss how the proposed change might affect them.

Change Agent–Employee Relationships The four recommendations just described also will improve the agent–recipient relationship by enhancing the level of trust between the parties.

> **EXAMPLE**   When Sergio Marchionne took over as CEO of Chrysler Motors, the company was in dire straits. The US government had bailed it out by taking a large ownership position. Mr. Marchionne knew that he had to take drastic action—shore up finances, revamp product lines, reduce costs, and increase revenues. However, he also knew that to be successful he needed the commitment of the company's 60,000 employees. He was the change agent who desperately needed productive relationships with the change recipients. To this end, he spent much of the $6 billion from the bailout to upgrade automotive design and production technology, as well as to integrate many of Chrysler's operations and products with those of Fiat, for whom Marchionne is also the CEO. He also eliminated the chairman's role, giving the CEO more power and control, and changed the organization's structure so that the key 26 managers now report directly to him.[62]

Organizational Processes and Practices Here again the Integrative Framework of OB can be very useful. The lesson of Figure 16.6 is that managers should not assume that people are consciously resisting change. Resistance has a cause that generally involves some obstacle in the work environment, such as job design (Chapter 5), performance management practices (Chapter 6), and organizational change (current chapter).[63] Obstacles in the organization's structure or in a "performance appraisal system [that] makes people choose between the new vision and their own self-interests" impedes change more than an individual's direct resistance.[64]

Sergio Marchionne, CEO of both Fiat and Chrysler, was instrumental in saving Chrysler during the Great Recession. He is widely regarded as a masterful change agent in the industry.

This perspective implies that it is important for management to obtain employee feedback about any obstacles that may be affecting their ability or willingness to accept change. In the end, change agents should not be afraid to modify the targeted elements of change or their approach toward change based on employee resistance. If people are resisting for valid reasons, then a new change initiative is needed.

A Contingency Approach to Overcoming Resistance As you learned in Chapter 1, effective managers apply the knowledge and tools to match the requirements of the situation (one size does not fit all). A similar contingency approach is recommended for avoiding or overcoming resistance to change. Table 16.2 describes six managerial strategies, the appropriate situations in which to take such actions, along with their respective advantages and drawbacks.

TABLE 16.2 SIX STRATEGIES FOR OVERCOMING RESISTANCE TO CHANGE

APPROACH	COMMONLY USED WHERE	ADVANTAGES	DRAWBACKS
Education & Communication	There is a lack of information or inaccurate information and analysis.	Once persuaded, people will often help with the implementation of the change.	Time-consuming if lots of people are involved.
Participation & Involvement	The initiators do not have all the information they need to design the change and others have considerable power to resist.	People who participate will be committed to implementing change, and any relevant information they have will be integrated into the change plan.	Time-consuming if participators design an inappropriate change.
Facilitation & Support	People are resisting because of adjustment problems.	No other approach works as well with adjustment problems.	Can be time-consuming and expensive and still fail.
Negotiation & Agreement	Someone or some group will clearly lose out in a change and that group has considerable power to resist.	Sometimes it is relatively easy to avoid major resistance.	Too expensive if it alerts others to negotiate for compliance.
Manipulation & Co-optation	Other tactics will not work or are too expensive.	It can be a relatively quick and inexpensive solution to resistance problems.	Leads to future problems if people feel manipulated.
Explicit & Implicit Coercion	Speed is essential and the initiators of change possess considerable power.	It is speedy and can overcome any kind of resistance.	Risky if it leaves people mad at the initiators.

overcoming resistance to change

SOURCE: Reprinted by permission of *Harvard Business Review.* Exhibit from "Choosing Strategies for Change," by J. P. Kotter and L. A. Schlesinger, March/April 1979 Copyright © 1979 by the Harvard Business School Publishing Corporation; all rights reserved.

How to Manage Stress

Stress is costly to individuals, groups, and organizations as a whole. The American Institute of Stress, for instance, estimates that work stress costs US industries about $300 billion a year. It thus is not surprising that organizations are increasingly implementing a variety of stress-reduction programs to help employees cope with modern-day stress.[65] Let's explore some that may benefit you, other employees, and your employers.

Stress-Reduction Techniques   The four most frequently used stress reduction techniques are muscle relaxation, biofeedback, meditation, and cognitive restructuring. Each method involves somewhat different ways of coping with stress (see Table 16.3).

Beyond the benefits of all these techniques, research shows that leisure activities (e.g., playing or watching sports, shopping, reading) also can help you combat stress. And the effectiveness of these activities is boosted further still if you are intrinsically motivated to do them (recall our discussion in Chapter 5 regarding intrinsic versus extrinsic motivation).[66] However, it also shows that cognitive restructuring is the most effective.[67]

The ABCDEs of Cognitive Restructuring   Recall our discussion of positive organizational behavior in Chapter 7. Many of the techniques described there can also help you in avoiding and reducing stress, such as fostering positive emotions, mindfulness, flourishing, and a positive organizational climate. In addition to these, the following five-step process of cognitive restructuring can help you stop thinking

TABLE 16.3   STRESS-REDUCTION TECHNIQUES

TECHNIQUE	HOW IT WORKS	ASSESSMENT
Muscle relaxation	Uses slow, deep breathing and systematic muscle tension relaxation.	Inexpensive and easy to use; may require a trained professional to implement.
Biofeedback	Electronic monitors train people to detect muscular tension; muscle relaxation is then used to alleviate this symptom of stress.	At one time expensive due to costs of equipment; however, equipment continues to be more affordable and can be used to evaluate effectiveness of other stress-reduction programs.
Meditation	Practitioners relax by redirecting their thoughts away from themselves, often following a structured procedure to significantly reduce mental stress.	Least expensive, simple to implement, and can be practiced almost anywhere.
Cognitive restructuring	Irrational or maladaptive thoughts are identified and replaced with those that are rational or logical.	Expensive because it requires a trained psychologist or counselor.
Holistic wellness	A broad, interdisciplinary approach that goes beyond stress reduction by advocating that people strive for personal wellness in all aspects of their lives.	Involves inexpensive but often behaviorally difficult lifestyle changes.

stress reduction

pessimistically about an event or problem. It's called the ABCDEs, as illustrated below.[68]

A—Name the event or problem. For example:

My roommate is going to move out, and I can't afford to pay the rent by myself.

B—List your beliefs about the event or problem.

I don't have any prospects for a new roommate, and I may have to move. I might have to move back home and quit school. I could ask my parents for money, but they really can't afford to pay my rent. I could move to a lower-priced single apartment in a bad part of town.

C—Identify the consequences of your beliefs.

I'm going to move back home for spring semester and will return in the fall.

D—Formulate a counterargument to your initial thoughts and beliefs. It is important to remember that pessimistic thoughts are generally overreactions, so the first step is to correct inaccurate or distorted thoughts.

I have not studied my expenses closely, and I may be able to afford the apartment. Even if I can't afford the apartment right now, I could get a part-time job that would cover the additional expenses. I could advertise on Craigslist or the school newspaper for a new roommate. I don't have to accept a bad roommate, but the worst-case scenario is that I have to carry the added expenses for one semester.

E—Describe how energized and empowered you feel at the moment.

I'm motivated to find a new roommate and get a part-time job. I have taken care of myself throughout college and there is no reason I can't continue to resolve this short-term problem.

TAKE-AWAY APPLICATION—TAAP

1. Think of a stressor in your life, preferably at school or work.
2. Then describe how you can use the ABCDEs of cognitive restructuring.
3. Do you feel more confident in your ability to overcome or reduce this stressor?
4. Does simply making this plan make you feel better, less stressed?

Research and practice show that this technique works well over time. The key is to stay with your ABCDEs and not to expect "instantaneous" results.

Pulling It All Together—Change Management Tips for Managers

We conclude the chapter and book by asking you to return to the Integrative Framework of OB. Hopefully, you realize that both person and environmental inputs can have a major impact on what needs to change, how it needs to change, and the ultimate success of any change initiatives. And as you learned in Chapter 5 on equity approaches to motivation—process always matters. Effective managers of change therefore carefully consider the relevant inputs and processes for any given change effort, as these are critical determinants of outcomes in the Integrative Framework of OB, which likely overlap with the goals of a given change. You therefore may choose to start with the end in mind, as suggested in the following Example box that details five keys to change management success.

┌───┐

EXAMPLE   Your Future: Five Tips for Successful Managers of Change[69]

Every other Example box in your textbook has focused on what has happened at a real company. This is an exception. Here we are asking you to consider an example of your own future.

We can safely predict that your future is going to involve change and related stress. While change is neither simple nor easy, here are our best tips to help "stack the deck" in your favor and improve your chances for success. While some tips specifically address the manager's role, all will help you at any level of the organization.

1. **Set Realistic Change Goals.** Leaders of change often think big and bold. This is fine so long as the objectives are realistic and attainable for the situation and organization. Just like you learned in Chapter 5, SMART goals are challenging but attainable.

2. **Assure Senior Leader Involvement and Commitment.** CEOs and other senior leaders must get their "hands dirty" and be *visibly* involved in change initiatives. They must not simply sit in the ivy tower and dictate change. They need to be planners, cheerleaders, and doers. Such involvement will help shape employee perceptions (Chapter 4) and beliefs that leaders are serious about the changes and that they care about employees.

3. **Walk the Talk.** Change can be difficult, even scary, for many employees. It thus is beneficial if senior leaders and managers "jump first." If employees are asked to make sacrifices (e.g., pay concessions, work overtime, take on additional responsibilities), then leaders and managers should make them first and in-kind. Leaders and managers of change need to make their actions visible and make them count. This is similar to role modeling you learned about in Chapter 13.

4. **Be Clear on "Why."** Everybody (beyond the top management team) wants to know "why" the changes are happening. What are the motives, what will be the personal impact, and what role will they play in shaping the outcomes? Your organization must not suffer from "the lower you go, the less you know" phenomenon. Everybody responsible for and affected by the change must clearly understand why it is happening. Understanding why is fundamental to building commitment to change and reducing resistance. To do this effectively requires communicating and training.

5. **Align Performance Management Practices.** It is very difficult, if not foolish, to expect your salespeople to give full attention to selling your company's new product if the bulk of their compensation is still focused on the old product. It therefore is not only necessary to align goals, but also important that recognition and other rewards are aligned with the change-related goals. As you learned in Chapter 7, different types and schedules of reinforcement can dramatically modify behavior and affect your change management effectiveness.

YOUR THOUGHTS?

1. Which of the five tips above do you think is most often missing when change efforts fail? Explain why.

2. What other tips would you offer managers of change, based either on knowledge and tools from this particular chapter or on other things you learned in this book?

3. What immediate challenges do you see on the horizon that will let you apply these five tips?

└───┘

Whether you work for somebody else or run your own business, effectively managing change is something that will benefit you throughout your career. It is neither simple nor easy. However, the rewards are enormous if you can do it well. The knowledge and tools we've provided here can give you a real competitive edge on other employees and managers.

And don't forget that managing change is about *doing*. Perhaps Charlie Strong, the recently hired football coach for the University of Texas, put it best when outlining his expectations for players, particularly the team's leaders: "They can lead the new culture or be run over by it. . . . 'I don't want to talk about things. I'd rather do things. We just talked. Now it's time to do."[70]

what did i learn?

You learned that change and stress will be two companions throughout your professional life. You learned how you can apply OB to help you recognize and respond appropriately to drivers of change and to manage both the positive and negative sides of stress for greater effectiveness. Reinforce what you learned with the Key Points below. Then consolidate your learning using the Integrative Framework. Finally, Challenge your mastery of this chapter by answering the Major Questions in your own words.

Key Points for Understanding Chapter 16

You learned the following key points.

16.1 FORCES FOR CHANGE

- The potentially many forces for change can be categorized as external and internal.
- External forces are demographic, technological, shareholder and market, and social and political.
- Internal forces often pertain to human resources and managerial behavior and decisions.

16.2 TYPES AND MODELS OF CHANGE

- The many kinds of change are often described in terms of three general types—adaptive, innovative, and radically innovative—based on their relative complexity, cost, and uncertainty.
- Lewin's change model is a popular and often-applied model and involves three stages: unfreezing, changing, and refreezing.
- A systems model of change is similar to the Integrative Framework of OB in that it includes inputs, strategic plans, target elements of change, and outputs.
- An organizational development (OD) approach to change involves diagnosing, intervening, evaluating, and feeding this information back to assess change effectiveness.

16.3 UNDERSTANDING RESISTANCE TO CHANGE

- Resistance to change is any thought (cognitive), emotion, or behavior that does not align with real or potential changes to existing routines.

- Dynamic perspectives of resistance describe the causes as an interplay of change recipient characteristics, change agent characteristics, and the relationship between the two.

16.4 THE GOOD AND BAD OF STRESS

- Stress is an adaptive response to environmental demands that can be physical, emotional, and/ or behavioral.
- The occupational stress process has four basic elements: stressors, cognitive appraisal, coping strategies, and outcomes.
- Stressors can occur at multiple levels—individual, group, organizational, and extra-organizational.
- Primary and secondary are the two common forms of cognitive appraisal.
- Common coping strategies are control, escape, and symptom management.

16.5 EFFECTIVE CHANGE AND STRESS MANAGEMENT

- The systems model of change provides multiple targets for effective change management, such as change recipient characteristics, change agent characteristics, and their relationship.
- Education and communication, involvement, negotiation, and coercion are among the many means for overcoming resistance to change.
- Many stress reduction techniques are supported by research: muscle relaxation, biofeedback, meditation, cognitive restructuring, and holistic wellness.

The Integrative Framework for Chapter 16

As shown in Figure 16.8, you learned that the process of leading and managing change and stress at the organizational level often involves a range of inputs, processes, and outcomes across all levels of the organization.

Challenge: Major Questions for Chapter 16

At the start of the chapter, we told you that after reading the chapter you should be able to answer the following questions. Unless you can, have you really processed and internalized the lessons in the chapter? Refer to the Key

Points, Figure 16.8, the chapter itself, and your notes to revisit and answer the following major questions:

1. What are the common forces or drivers of change at work, and how can this knowledge improve my personal effectiveness?

2. How can different approaches to change make me and my organization more effective managers of change?

3. Why do people resist change and what can I do about it?

4. How can stress affect my effectiveness—positively and negatively?

5. How can OB knowledge and tools help me effectively manage change and stress?

FIGURE 16.8 INTEGRATIVE FRAMEWORK FOR UNDERSTANDING AND APPLYING OB

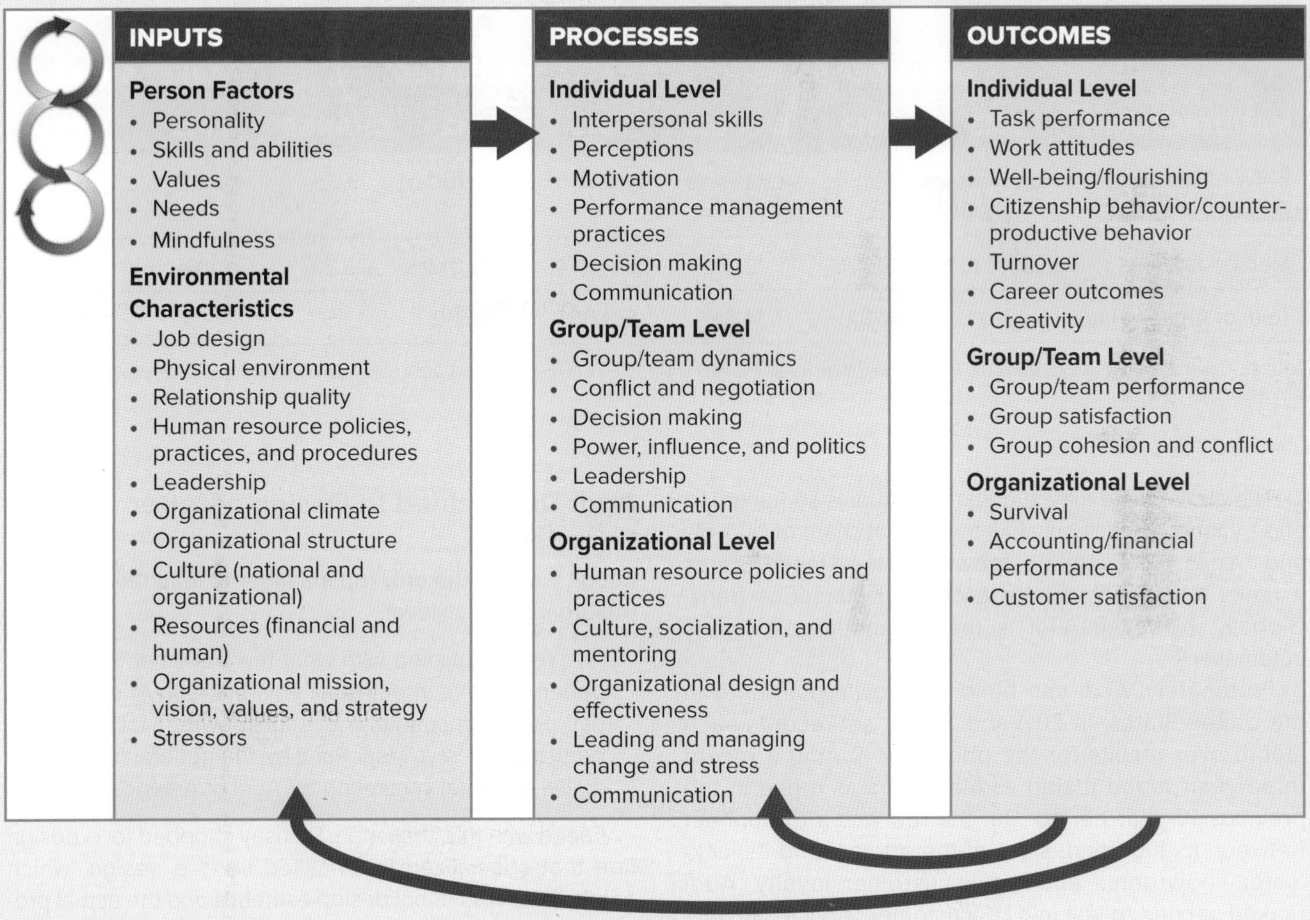

INPUTS	PROCESSES	OUTCOMES
Person Factors • Personality • Skills and abilities • Values • Needs • Mindfulness **Environmental Characteristics** • Job design • Physical environment • Relationship quality • Human resource policies, practices, and procedures • Leadership • Organizational climate • Organizational structure • Culture (national and organizational) • Resources (financial and human) • Organizational mission, vision, values, and strategy • Stressors	**Individual Level** • Interpersonal skills • Perceptions • Motivation • Performance management practices • Decision making • Communication **Group/Team Level** • Group/team dynamics • Conflict and negotiation • Decision making • Power, influence, and politics • Leadership • Communication **Organizational Level** • Human resource policies and practices • Culture, socialization, and mentoring • Organizational design and effectiveness • Leading and managing change and stress • Communication	**Individual Level** • Task performance • Work attitudes • Well-being/flourishing • Citizenship behavior/counter-productive behavior • Turnover • Career outcomes • Creativity **Group/Team Level** • Group/team performance • Group satisfaction • Group cohesion and conflict **Organizational Level** • Survival • Accounting/financial performance • Customer satisfaction

© 2014 Angelo Kinicki and Mel Fugate. All rights reserved. Reproduction prohibited without permission of the authors.

PROBLEM-SOLVING APPLICATION CASE (PSAC)

Audi Is Driving Change

Over half of your customers never come back. Do you have a problem?

Audi thinks so. Audi sees 46 percent repeat business among its North American customers, while other German imports average 55 percent.[71] Here is how Audi compares to its closest competitors:

Ranking German Luxury Car Manufacturers in the United States by Sales

MANUFACTURER	DECEMBER SALES			YTD SALES			CHANGE IN MARKET SHARE	
	2013	2012	CHANGE	2013	2012	CHANGE	2013	2012
BMW of North America Inc.	37,389	37,399	. . .	309,280	281,460	9.9%	2.0%	1.9%
Mercedes-Benz	35,835	30,376	18.0%	334,344	295,013	13.3%	2.1%	2.0%
Audi of America Inc.	17,013	14,841	14.6%	158,061	139,310	13.5%	1.0%	1.0%

SOURCE: "Sales and Share of Total Market by Manufacturer," Auto Sales, *The Wall Street Journal Online,* January 3, 2014, http://online.wsj.com/mdc/public/page/2_3022-autosales.html.

The above table may suggest why Audi is so hungry to make changes. It has only half the market share of its rivals and needs to accelerate growth. In the United States it ranks third, behind both BMW and Mercedes Benz. Globally, however, Audi is the second-largest luxury automaker.[72]

Fortunately, Audi can build on growing strength in the United States. In 2011 and 2012 it set records each month over results for the prior year. During a recent three-year period it sold as many cars as it had in the previous 10-year period. But the rub was a disconnect between its high-end, state-of-the-art cars and its lackluster showrooms and weak customer loyalty. Audi ranked second to last in a US customer service satisfaction poll of car buyers.

The Economic Value of Customer Service

This gap is expensive. A 2012 study from Maritz Research estimated that the average car dealership could sell upwards of *217 additional cars per year by improving customer service.*

So in September 2012, Audi of America President Scott Keogh began visiting dealers around the country. *Businessweek* reported that he told them "he attributed the low numbers partly to the dealership experience, and that he wanted to focus on customer service."

Audi Determined to Design a Better Experience

Keogh was not the only top manager to lead the charge at the organizational level.

"We're not satisfied with what the customer service experience is like in our retail environment. At dealers today, people encounter a lot of unknowns, a lot of waiting, bottlenecks," says Mark Ramsey, the general manager of digital and retail marketing for Audi of America.

Faced with this challenge, Ramsey shopped for a design firm that specialized in so-called *service design*, which emphasizes traditional design esthetics *and* the actual process of buying a product. They chose US-based Continuum.

More Functional and Modern Showrooms

In late 2013 Audi began sharing more information about Continuum's approach to changing the Audi showrooms. Keogh was even more encouraged, given the high level of dealer cooperation he received from his many visits to individual dealerships. Now customers will find smaller open consulting areas with ready information available by iPad and giant tablet screens. And behind the sleek and fashion-forward showrooms are improved systems and software to improve the experience.

Other news coming out of Audi seems to indicate more of the experience is being modified than just the showroom and sales experience. For instance, the iPads that will be part of the sales experience in the showroom also will be extended to the parts and service departments. Audi drives this implementation by providing discounted iPads to dealers that don't use them already and free software to those that do. Audi says 80 percent of its US dealers have already placed orders for the subsidized iPads.[73]

Apply the 3-Stop Problem-Solving Approach to OB

Stop 1: What is the problem?

- Use the Integrative Model of OB in Figure 16.8 to help identify the outcomes that are important in this case.

- Which of these outcomes are not being achieved in the case?

- Based on considering the above two questions, what is the most important problem in this case?

Stop 2: Use the Integrative Framework of OB shown at the start of this chapter to help identify the OB concepts or theories that help you to understand the problem in this case.

- What person factors are most relevant?

- What environmental characteristics are most important to consider?

- Do you need to consider any processes? Which ones?

- What concepts or theories discussed in this chapter are most relevant for solving the key problem in this case?

Stop 3: What are your recommendations for solving the problem?

- Review the material in the chapter that most pertains to your proposed solution and look for practical recommendations.

- Use any past OB knowledge or experience to generate recommendations.

- Outline your plan for solving the problem in this case.

LEGAL/ETHICAL CHALLENGE

Job Cuts and Legal Settlements . . . Two Ways to Profit

The major US banks have rebounded since the Great Recession. Many posted record profits in 2013 and 2014. For instance, the industry reported over $40 billion in profits in just one quarter in 2013![74] Looking only at profits might lead you to believe that times are good for big banks and all their employees. Certainly the big bank CEOs have done well. Jamie Dimon, CEO of JP Morgan Chase (JPM), was awarded $20 million, and Brian Moynihan of Bank of America (BofA) received $14 million, but both trailed industry CEO compensation leader Lloyd Blankfein of Goldman Sachs (GS), whose board agreed to $23 million in compensation for 2013.[75]

In response to the financial crisis, changing markets, and new regulations, the big banks changed their strategies and significantly restructured their companies. Many of these changes focused on reducing their involvement in the mortgage business that was at the center of the crisis.

On the one hand, some argue that the rich rewards are just and appropriate given the enormous changes overseen and led by these CEOs. However, another point of view argues that these profits are in large part the result of massive layoffs, cuts that continue even in the face of record profits and generous CEO compensation. JPM cut more than 15,000 employees, BofA 30,000, and Citigroup nearly 25 percent of its workforce. Eliminating such large numbers of employees reduces expenses and helps boost profits even when revenues are not growing.[76]

Moreover, many of these same CEOs were at the helm when their companies plunged into the crisis. Their associated misconduct has resulted in billions of dollars of legal expenses (fees and settlements). For instance, JPM's Dimon was prominent in negotiating nearly $20 billion in 2013 alone to cover legal expenses related to settlements involving the "London Whale" scandal and misconduct related to Bernie Madoff and mortgage investments. BofA, for its part, has paid out nearly $50 billion since the crisis to cover its own legal obligations related to the mortgage meltdown.[77]

What is your position on rewarding CEOs (and other executives) for profits in the wake of employee job cuts and legal expenses?

What Is Your Position?

1. CEOs should continue to be rewarded for profits, even if they occur as the result of massive job cuts and despite legal expenses for misconduct during their time on the job. Explain this position.

2. From an organizational change perspective, what are the advantages and disadvantages of this position?

3. CEOs are the ultimate leaders of their organizations and the buck should stop with them. Their compensation should not increase if large numbers of jobs are cut and/or significant legal liabilities are incurred.

4. From an organizational change perspective, what are the advantages and disadvantages of this position?

5. If you were a member of the board of directors at a big bank, what would you recommend for compensating the CEO in light of job cuts and legal settlements? Explain.

Creating Personal Change through Force-Field Analysis

Objectives

1. To apply force-field analysis to a behavior or situation you would like to change.

2. To receive feedback on your strategies for bringing about change.

Introduction

The theory of force-field analysis is based on the premise that people resist change because of counteracting positive and negative forces. Positive forces for change are called *thrusters*. They propel people to accept change and modify their behavior. In contrast, *counterthrusters* or *resistors* are negative forces that motivate an individual to maintain the status quo. People frequently fail to change because they experience equal amounts of positive and negative forces to change.

Force-field analysis is a technique used to facilitate change by first identifying the thrusters and resistors that exist in a specific situation. To minimize resistance to change, it is generally recommended to first reduce or remove the negative forces to change. Removing counterthrusters should create increased pressure for an individual to change in the desired direction. Managers can also further increase motivation to change by following up the reduction of resistors with an increase in the number of positive thrusters of change.

Instructions

Your instructor will pair you up with another student. The two of you will serve as a team that evaluates the completeness of each other's force-field analysis and recommendations. Once the team is assembled, each individual should independently complete the Force-Field Analysis Form presented after these instructions. Once both of you complete this activity, one team member should present results from steps 2 through 5 from the five-step Force-Field Analysis Form. The partner should then evaluate the results by considering the following questions with his or her team member:

1. Are there any additional thrusters and counterthrusters that should be listed? Add them to the list.

2. Do you agree with the strength evaluations of thrusters and counterthrusters in step 4? Ask your partner to share his or her rationale for the ratings. Modify the ratings as needed.

3. Examine the specific recommendations for change listed in step 5, and evaluate whether you think they will produce the desired changes. Be sure to consider whether the focal person has the ability to eliminate, reduce, or increase each thruster and counterthruster that is the basis for a specific recommendation. Are there any alternative strategies you can think of?

4. What is your overall evaluation of your partner's intervention strategy?

Force-Field Analysis Form

STEP 1

In the space provided, please identify a number of personal problems you would like to solve or aspects of your life you would like to change. Be as imaginative as possible. You are not limited to school situations. For example, you may want to consider your work environment if you are currently employed, family situation, Interpersonal relationships, club situations, and so forth. It is important that you select some aspects of your life that you would like to change but up to now have made no effort to do so.

_____

_____

_____

_____

_____

_____

STEP 2

Review in your mind the problems or aspects listed in step 1. Now select one that you would really like to change and that you believe lends itself easily to force-field analysis. Select one that you will feel comfortable talking about to other people.

STEP 3

On the form following step 4, indicate existing forces that are pushing you in the direction of change. Thrusters may be forces internal to the self (pride, regret, fear) or they may be external to the self (friends, the boss, a professor). Also list existing forces that are preventing you from changing. Again, the counterthruster may be internal to the self (uncertainty, fear) or external to the self (poor instruction, limited resources, lack of support mechanisms).

STEP 4

In the space to the right of your list of thrusters and counterthrusters indicate the relative strength. For consistency, use a scale of 1 to 10, with 1 indicating a weak force and 10 indicating a high force.

THRUSTERS   STRENGTH

_____ _____
_____ _____
_____ _____
_____ _____
_____ _____

COUNTERTHRUSTERS   STRENGTH

_____ _____
_____ _____
_____ _____
_____ _____
_____ _____

STEP 5

Analyze your thrusters and counterthrusters, and develop a strategy for bringing about the desired change. Remember that it is possible to produce the desired results by strengthening existing thrusters, introducing new thrusters, weakening or removing counterthrusters, or some combination of these. Consider the impact of your change strategy on the system's internal stress (i.e., on yourself and others), the likelihood of success, the availability of resources, and the long-term consequences of planned changes. Be prepared to discuss your recommendations with the partner in your group.

_____
_____
_____
_____
_____

Questions for Discussion

1. What was your reaction to doing a force-field analysis? Was it insightful and helpful?

2. Was it valuable to receive feedback about your force-field analysis from a partner? Explain.

3. How would you assess the probability of effectively implementing your recommendations?

EPILOGUE   A REVIEW AND FINAL APPLICATION OF WHAT YOU'VE LEARNED

major question

MAJOR QUESTION

How can I use my knowledge about OB to help me achieve personal and professional effectiveness?

THE BIGGER PICTURE

This final section provides a high level of summary of what you have learned and offers suggestions for applying your OB knowledge and tools at work.

We wrote this epilogue to serve two primary functions: (1) this material can serve as a review for a final exam at the end of your course and/or (2) it can be used as a "sneak peek" at the beginning of the course to foreshadow what you will learn.

Let's begin by considering our reasons for writing this book. We'll then briefly review our approach to problem solving and the components of the Integrative Framework of OB. To reinforce your knowledge, we provide one more problem solving application of OB as a reminder for how you can apply what you have learned to help you achieve personal and professional effectiveness.

Why Did We Write This Book?

The answer is simple. We passionately believe that knowledge about OB can help you flourish both personally and professionally. Writing this book thus represents our small way of assisting you along the path of personal and professional development.

Books generally provide knowledge about a particular subject (e.g., accounting, finance, economics, and marketing), but they often fall short in helping people apply this knowledge. We tried to overcome this limitation in two ways. First, we focused intensely on application. To do this we used a problem-solving approach that focuses on using OB knowledge to understand and solve problems at work, school, and your larger life space. Second, we incorporated this problem-solving perspective within the Integrative Framework of OB. We did this because the Integrative Framework provides a structure to help you classify, organize, and apply the many OB concepts and theories that exist. Without some type of organizing structure, we find that students experience information overload and fail to see how concepts are related, which in turn reduces their ability to apply what they are learning.

The 3-Stop Problem-Solving Approach

Our efforts to improve your problem-solving effectiveness began by showing you that common sense often is not common practice. We instead taught you to think critically and add rigor and structure to your problem solving by thinking of it as a 3-Stop Journey:

Stop 1: Define the Problem. To be an effective problem solver, you must define the problem accurately.

Stop 2: Identify Potential Causes Using OB Concepts and Theories. The many OB theories and concepts you learned are extremely useful in helping to determine the underlying causes of the problem you defined in Stop 1.

Stop 3: Make Recommendations and (if Appropriate) Take Action. Once your problem is defined and its cause(s) identified, it is time for you to plan and implement recommendations. Again, your vast OB knowledge and tools can be applied to the underlying causes from Stop 2 to remedy the defined problem.

We believe that you can become a more effective problem solver in all arenas of your life (school, work, and home) by applying your OB knowledge within this 3-Stop approach. In turn, your improved problem-solving abilities will lead to better performance for you, your team, and your organization. This is important because problem solving is one of the most sought-after skills by employers across industries and job levels. This is the reason you were provided numerous opportunities in every chapter to apply your OB knowledge using Problem-Solving Applications, Self-Assessments, Take-Away Applications, and end-of-chapter Problem-Solving Application Cases.

The Integrative Framework of OB

The Integrative Framework uses a systems approach and was created to help you organize the many concepts and theories that define the field of OB. The structure of the framework, which includes inputs, processes, and outcomes, can help you execute the 3-Stop Approach to problem solving. Let's consider each of these components.

Inputs: The Person-Environment Distinction   As explained in Chapter 1, a general way to categorize OB inputs is in terms of those that reside within you (person factors), such as values and work attitudes (Chapter 2), individual differences and emotions (Chapter 3), perceptions and diversity (Chapter 4), and those outside or external to you (environmental characteristics), like performance management (Chapter 6), leader behavior (Chapter 13), organizational culture (Chapter 14), and design (Chapter 15). This categorization helps you organize or classify what you learn about OB into these two easily understood categories or buckets. This will assist you when trying to identify what OB concepts or theories are relevant for a particular problem because every new concept or theory represents a possible cause of a problem.

Processes at Individual, Group/Team, and Organizational Levels   Another key aspect and benefit of the Integrative Framework is the distinction between levels of OB analysis. The book was divided into three parts to highlight the importance of thinking about and applying OB knowledge in terms of levels—individual, group/ team, and organizational. You learned not only that many OB concepts exist at particular levels, such as personality at the individual level, but also that some concepts like performance management and conflict can affect outcomes across all levels.

Outcomes at Individual, Group/Team, and Organizational Levels   OB is an applied field and there are many different outcomes that can be improved by using knowledge of OB. These outcomes occur at one or more of the individual level (e.g., task performance and turnover), the group/team level (e.g., group/team performance and group cohesion and conflict), and the organizational level (e.g., financial performance and innovation).

The Complete Integrative Framework of OB   Figure E.1 illustrates the complete Integrative Framework. It provides a summary of the many concepts and theories you learned by reading this book. The framework further illustrates how the various concepts and theories are related to each other: Inputs affect processes, which in turn influence outcomes. If you want to test your retention of the many theories and concepts you learned while reading this book, try to match each topic in Figure E.1 to its corresponding chapter.

FIGURE E.1 COMPLETE INTEGRATIVE FRAMEWORK OF OB

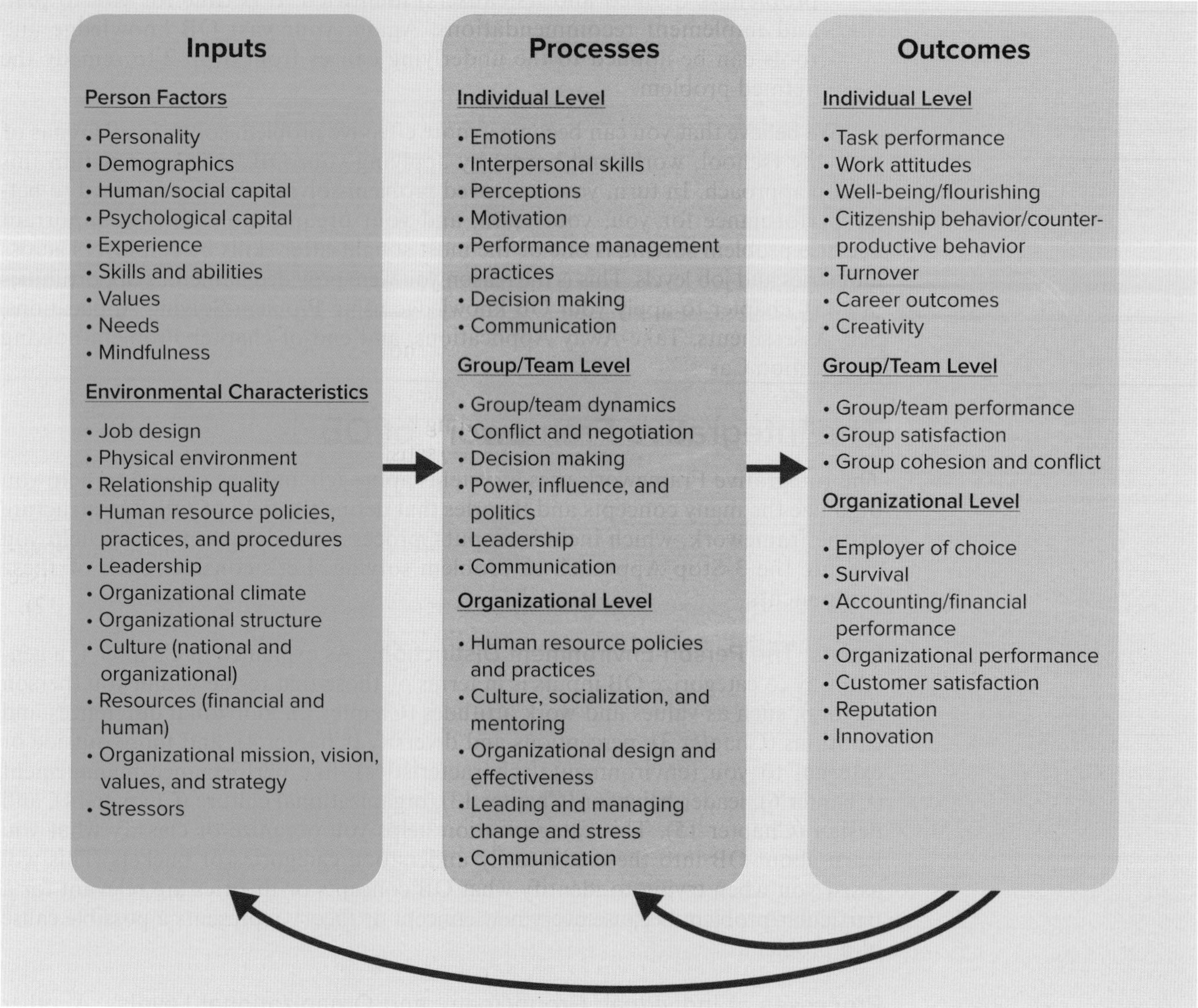

Inputs	Processes	Outcomes
Person Factors	**Individual Level**	**Individual Level**
• Personality	• Emotions	• Task performance
• Demographics	• Interpersonal skills	• Work attitudes
• Human/social capital	• Perceptions	• Well-being/flourishing
• Psychological capital	• Motivation	• Citizenship behavior/counter-productive behavior
• Experience	• Performance management practices	• Turnover
• Skills and abilities	• Decision making	• Career outcomes
• Values	• Communication	• Creativity
• Needs		
• Mindfulness	**Group/Team Level**	**Group/Team Level**
	• Group/team dynamics	• Group/team performance
Environmental Characteristics	• Conflict and negotiation	• Group satisfaction
	• Decision making	• Group cohesion and conflict
• Job design	• Power, influence, and politics	
• Physical environment	• Leadership	**Organizational Level**
• Relationship quality	• Communication	
• Human resource policies, practices, and procedures		• Employer of choice
• Leadership	**Organizational Level**	• Survival
• Organizational climate		• Accounting/financial performance
• Organizational structure	• Human resource policies and practices	• Organizational performance
• Culture (national and organizational)	• Culture, socialization, and mentoring	• Customer satisfaction
• Resources (financial and human)	• Organizational design and effectiveness	• Reputation
• Organizational mission, vision, values, and strategy	• Leading and managing change and stress	• Innovation
• Stressors	• Communication	

© 2014 Angelo Kinicki and Mel Fugate. All rights reserved. Reproduction prohibited without permission of the authors.

Hypothetical Problem-Solving Scenario

Let's reinforce your problem-solving skills one more time using the Integrative Framework and the 3-Stop Approach. We'll use a scenario first introduced in Chapter 1. It involved the problem of employee turnover, an individual-level outcome. For this application assume that *you* are a valued junior employee who is thinking of quitting. While one person quitting may not be a problem, your thoughts about quitting coincide with the fact that many other talented junior employees quit your department in the past couple of years.

Stop 1: Define the Problem Recall that a problem is a gap between a current situation and a desired situation or outcome. In this hypothetical scenario, your organization desires to have the appropriate number of talented people in its most crucial jobs. Due to excessive turnover of its best junior talent, however, there is a shortage or gap of qualified employees—the problem. Note that defining the problem this way is different than simply saying more people quit your company this year than did last year, or that your employer has higher turnover than its competitors. If your worst performers quit instead of your best, then you could argue that your organization is better off due to a reduction in "dead wood" rather than having a problem. To elaborate, it isn't necessarily a problem to lose people, especially those with obsolete skills or who underperform, but if your organization's most valuable and high-performing people quit, then a problem likely exists. This sort of reasoning highlights the importance of defining the problem accurately.

Now that we've confidently completed the first stop and defined the problem accurately—an insufficient number of talented, high-performing, junior employees due to excessive turnover—let's continue our journey and identify the potential causes of this turnover problem.

Stop 2: Use OB to Highlight the Causes   The Integrative Framework is particularly helpful at this Stop. While people quit for a variety of reasons, a good place to start is to consider both person and environmental inputs and then various processes as potential causes of your organization's turnover problem (see Figure E-1).

- **Potential Cause 1**—Person factors often represent key causes of turnover. Possibly the junior employees are quitting because their jobs don't fulfill their personal values (see Chapter 2). Low job satisfaction (Chapter 2) and demotivating job characteristics (see Chapter 5) also might be causing turnover.

- **Potential Cause 2**—Environmental factors frequently constitute causes for turnover. For example, people may be quitting because they have poor relationships with their boss (see Chapter 13) or they are working in a culture (see Chapter 14) characterized with too much political behavior (see Chapter 12).

- **Potential Cause 3**—Individual, group/team, and organizational processes can also cause turnover. Conflict, a team-level process (see Chapter 10) may constitute a cause of turnover. Possibly your turnover problem results from a faulty performance management system (an organizational-level process—Chapter 6) that unfairly distributes raises, bonuses, and recognition. As you learned in Chapter 5, a lack of justice (distributive, procedural, or relational) is often a powerful driver of employee turnover.

Notice that the potential causes are located in different components (i.e., inputs and processes) and levels within the Integrative Framework. Using the Integrative Framework to identify potential causes increases the likelihood that you'll identify the appropriate cause(s) of your organization's turnover problem, which is essential to creating and implementing the best solution in Stop 3.

Stop 3: Generate Effective Recommendations Using OB   Now it's time for you to review the potential causes and determine which ones are the most likely causes of the problem. Returning to our scenario, we describe brief recommendations for each of the potential causes outlined above. We'll address all three to highlight how much you've learned and the practical value of that knowledge.

- **Response to Cause 1: Recommendations for Improving Personal Factors.** OB provides a host of ideas for solving this problem: These ideas come from Chapters 2 and 5. The values of your most valuable employees could potentially be better met by allowing them to work on projects that satisfy their values of self-direction or achievement. Job satisfaction might be increased by providing rewards that equitably meet employees' needs. Finally, motivation can be enhanced by allowing people to assume more responsibility for projects (job enrichment) and by determining how and when to do their work (autonomy).

- **Response to Cause 2: Recommendations for Improving Environmental Characteristics.** Manager-employee relationships can suffer for many reasons, but let's assume that in this hypothetical scenario some key and more junior employees in your department feel they are in the "out group," instead of the "in group," which is largely older and more senior employees who have known and worked with your manager for many years. This cause sounds like poor leader-member exchange (LMX in

Chapter 13), which may be remedied by training managers to be more inclusive and implementing formal mentoring and development programs. The political behavior driving a negative culture might be improved by acknowledging the issue and discontinuing the practice of rewarding people who are too political. Finally, team-building (see Chapter 8) can be used to reduce the conflict among employees.

- **Cause 3: Recommendations for Improving Processes.** Chapter 6, along with your knowledge related to justice and goal setting in Chapter 5, provides a host of ideas for improving performance management practices. A good place to start is to use Figure 6-1 and clearly define and communicate performance goals and expectations. If these goals are SMART, then they are more likely to be achieved. It also is necessary to monitor progress towards these goals and provide feedback. Finally, it is important to provide consequences (e.g., rewards) for goal achievement. The effectiveness of rewards can be increased by explicitly making clear links between particular levels of performance and rewards (instrumentality). While these steps can avoid or remedy many performance management issues, it is necessary to also determine whether this process and the resulting consequences are fair (procedural and distributive justice). To do this it may also be helpful to implement 360 feedback to provide more diverse performance data, thereby improving the accuracy of performance evaluations.

Are you surprised by the many causes and potential solutions for this problem? As we just illustrated, the 3-Stop Approach, combined with the Integrative Framework, can help you to more effectively solve problems. This in turn will contribute to your personal and professional effectiveness and opportunities.

Our Parting Wishes for You

We hope you enjoyed your OB journey! Remember, OB is more than common sense or simply possessing certain knowledge. *Those who outperform others over time are those who apply their knowledge.* We therefore encourage you to apply your new knowledge of OB to achieve a more successful and fulfilling career. This was our ultimate wish for you and our goal for writing this book.

We wish you happiness, health, and success! Enjoy the journey!

CHAPTER 1

Page 3: © porocrex/Getty Images/RF; p. 8: © Ariel Skelley/Getty Images; p. 10: © epa european pressphoto agency b.v./Alamy; p. 11: © Ingram Publishing; p. 14: © Press Association via AP Images; p. 16: © Scott J. Ferrell/Congressional Quarterly/Alamy; p. 19: © Associated Press; p. 20: © Pete Souza/The White House; p. 21: © McGraw-Hill Education/Gary He, photographer; p. 24: © David Jones/Getty Images/RF; p. 28: © Johnny Green/PA Wire URN:5896390. Press Association via AP Images; p. 29: © Scott Carson/ZUMA Press, Inc./Alamy.

CHAPTER 2

Page 39: © Christine Glade/Getty Images/RF; p. 42: © DC Stock/Alamy; p. 45: © Paul Bradbury/age footstock; p. 46: © AP Photo/New School for Social Research; p. 47: © Blend Images/Ariel Skelley/Getty Images; p. 49: © Fuse/Getty Images; p. 52: © Adam Gault/age footstock; p. 54: © Stuart C. Wilson/Getty Images for Red Bull; p. 56: © ZUMA Press, Inc./Alamy; p. 59: © AP Photo/The Daily Progress/Damien Dawson; p. 62: © Radius Images/Alamy.

CHAPTER 3

Page 73: © winhorse/Getty Images/RF; p. 77 (top): © Jason Bye/Alamy; p. 77 (bottom): © London Entertainment/Alamy; p. 81 (top): © ZUMA Press, Inc./Alamy; p. 81 (bottom): © ZUMA Press, Inc./Alamy; p. 84: © AP Photo/Rafiq Maqbool; p. 86: © epa european pressphoto agency b.v./Alamy; p. 87: © ZUMA Press, Inc./Alamy; p. 91: © Pixtal/AGE Fotostock; p. 93: © AP Photo/Tony Gutierrez; p. 96: © Rex Features via AP Images; p. 100 (left): © AP Photo/Jessica Kourkounis; p. 100 (right): © AP Photo/Manu Fernandez; p. 103: © AP Photo/Phelan M. Ebenhack.

CHAPTER 4

Page 111: © Tom Nulens/Getty Images/RF; p. 114: © Brand X Pictures/Superstock; p. 115: © Dave Mason/Blend Images LLC p. 118: © Pixtal/AGE Fotostock; p. 124: © AP Photo/Susan Walsh; p. 127: © Blend Images/Alamy/RF; p. 128: © baur/Alamy/RF; p. 129: © Profimedia.CZ a.s./Alamy; p. 134: © AP Photo/Richard Drew; p. 137: © Sipa via AP Images.

CHAPTER 5

Page 145: © James Brey/Getty Images/RF; p. 147: © Andy Kropa/Invision/AP; p. 151: © Bruno Vincent/Getty Images; p. 156: © AP Photo/Anthony Devlin; p. 161: © ZUMA Press, Inc/Alamy; p. 166: © Glenn Coombridge/Getty Images/RF; p. 169: © Glow Images; p. 173: © Colin Anderson/Blend Images LLC.

CHAPTER 6

Page 181: © mattjeacock/Getty Images/RF; p. 184: © Chris Ryan/age footstock; p. 185: © AP Photo/J. Pat Carter; p. 186: © Jeffrey Phelps/AP Images for SC Johnson; 192: © Graham Crouch/Bloomberg via Getty Images; p. 196: © Ronda Churchill/Bloomberg via Getty Images; p. 199: © ClearRock, Inc.; p. 205: © AP Photo/Ric Feld.

CHAPTER 7

Page 217: © iconeer/Getty Images/RF; p. 221: © AP Photo/Gerald Herbert; p. 223: © Dustin Finkelstein/Getty Images for SXSW; p. 227: © Ingram Publishing; p. 231: © Patrick Herrera/Getty Images; p. 236: © Michael Dwyer/AP Images; p. 237: © AP Photo/The Canadian Press/Adrien Veczan; p. 241: © AP Photo/Frank Franklin II; p. 245: © AP Photo/MetroWest Daily News, Ken McGagh; p. 247: © Associated Press.

CHAPTER 8

Page 255: © Image Source, all rights reserved; p. 257: © Jim West/Alamy; p. 260: © Peter Foley/Bloomberg via Getty Images; p. 262: © Carsten Koal/Getty Images; p. 266: © McClatchy-Tribune Information Services/Alamy; p. 269: © Bloomberg via Getty Images; p. 272: © Denver Post via Getty Images; p. 276: © Image Source/Getty Images; p. 278: © AP Photo/Keystone, Walter Bieri; p. 283: © Troels Graugaard/Getty Images; p. 284: © Rex Features via AP Images.

CHAPTER 9

Page 293: © Tuomas Kujansuu/Getty Images/RF; p. 296: © Juice Images/Cultura/Getty Images/RF; p. 298: © ZUMA Press, Inc./Alamy; p. 300: © Richard Ellis/Alamy; p. 301: © McGraw-Hill Education/Eclipse Studios; p. 304: © Chris Ryan/age footstock; p. 310: © Mark Davis/Getty Images for Pepsi; p. 315: © Justin Sullivan/Getty Images; p. 318: © Bloomberg via Getty Images; p. 320: © Design Pics/Don Hammond.

CHAPTER 10

Page 329: © Michael Goldman/Getty Images; p. 331: © Jim West/Alamy; p. 334: © Bloomberg via Getty Images; p. 337: © Ryan Lane/Getty Images/RF; p. 339: © AP Photo/LM Otero; p. 340: © Blend Images/Alamy/RF; p. 343: © Spencer Platt/Getty Images; p. 357: © OJO Images Ltd./Alamy/RF.

CHAPTER 11

Page 367: © jamtoons/Getty Images/RF; p. 370: © Kristoffer Tripplaar/Alamy; p. 372: Photo Courtesy of The Diavik Diamond Mine; p. 377: © Everett Collection/Alamy; p. 378: © AF Archive/Alamy; p. 379: © AP Photo/Mark Lennihan; p. 380 (left): © Roberts Publishing Services. All rights reserved; p. 380 (right): © Danita Delimont/Alamy; p. 383: © Bloomberg via Getty Images; p. 385: © NASA Photo/Alamy; p. 387: © ZUMA Press, Inc./Alamy; p. 390: © Alistair Scott/Alamy; p. 392: © Rex Features via AP Images; p. 395: © Don Arnold/Getty Images.

CHAPTER 12

Page 403: © Influx Productions/Stockbyte/Getty Images/RF; p. 406: © SasPartout/age footstock; p. 409: © Bloomberg via Getty Images; p. 413: © Blend Images/Alamy/RF; p. 416: © epa european pressphoto agency b.v./Alamy; p. 418: Photo released into public domain by Dr. Robert Cialedini; p. 421: © AP Photo/Manuel Balce Ceneta; p. 424: © Andy Kropa/Invision/AP; p. 427: © AP Photo/Jeff Chiu; p. 429: © AP Photo/Paul Sakuma; p. 431: © Daily Mail/Rex/Alamy.

CHAPTER 13

Page 439: © Anthia Cumming/Getty Images/RF; p. 440: © Kevin Winter/WireImage/Getty Images; p. 444 (left): © Brian Harris/Alamy; p. 444 (right): © AFP/Getty Images; p. 445: © PRNewsFoto/Patriarch Partners, Courtney Grant Winston; p. 449: © AP Photo/Gerald Herbert; p. 458: © Image Source/Javier Perini CM; p. 463: © Brad Barket/Getty Images; p. 465: © Gustavo Caballero/Getty Images; p. 467: © epa european pressphoto agency b.v./Alamy.

CHAPTER 14

Page 479: © Tarik Kizilkaya/E+/Getty Images/RF; p. 482: © photonic 2/Alamy/RF; p. 483: © epa european pressphoto agency b.v./Alamy; p. 485: © Denver Post via Getty Images; p. 489: © PRNewsFoto/Edward Jones; p. 490: © Scott Olson/Getty Images;

photo credits

CR-1

photo credits

p. 494: © Bloomberg via Getty Images; p. 497: © NTSB/Alamy; p. 502: © Oli Kellett/Getty Images; p. 505: © Wire Images/Getty Images; p. 508: © AP Photo/Connecticut Post, Ned Gerard.

CHAPTER 15

Page 519: © Piet Mall/Stock 48/Getty Images; p. 525: © AP Photo/The Huntsville Times, Eric Schultz; p. 529: © Roberts Publishing Services. All rights reserved; p. 532: © Bloomberg via Getty Images; p. 537: © Adam Gault/age footstock; p. 538 (left): © skynesher/Getty Images; p. 538: (right): © Monty Rakusen/Getty Images; p. 542: © Kerry-Edwards 2004, Inc./Sharon Farmer, photographer; p. 543: © AP Photo/Ross D. Franklin; p. 546: © jeremy sutton-hibbert/Alamy; p. 548: © NetPhotos/Alamy.

CHAPTER 16

Page 557: © JGI/Jamie Grill/Getty Images; p. 559: © AP Photo/Kirsty Wigglesworth; p. 560: © AP Photo/Charles Dharapak; p. 562: © Christoph Soeder/dapd/AP Images; p. 566: © Imaginechina via AP Images; p. 568: © Matt Peyton/AP Images for REI; p. 578: © epa european pressphoto agency b.v./Alamy; p. 582: © Design Pics/Darren Greenwood; p. 586: © Bill Pugliano/Getty Images.

CHAPTER NOTES

Chapter 1

1. J. Pfeiffer and R. I. Sutton, *The Knowing-Doing Gap: How Smart Companies Turn Knowledge into Action* (Boston: Harvard Business School, 2000).
2. A. Fisher, "Executives to New Grads: Shape Up!" *Fortune,* February 1, 2012.
3. Ibid.
4. As quoted in P. LaBarre, "The Industrialized Revolution," *Fast Company,* November 2003, 116, 118.
5. F. Manjoo, "How Google Became Such a Great Place to Work," *Slate.com,* January 21, 2013.
6. M. Moskowitz, R. Levering, O. Akhtar, E. Fry, C. Leahey, and A. Vandermey, "The 100 Best Companies to Work For," *Fortune,* February 4, 2013, 87.
7. N. Smith, "How Common Sense and Hindsight Blind Us to the Future," *BusinessNewsDaily,* March 28, 2011, http://www.businessnewsdaily.com/804-common-sense-fails-scientific-method.html.
8. M. S. Rao, "Myths and Truths about Skills," *T&D,* May 7, 2012.
9. R. Alsop, "MBA Recruiter Survey: Something Old, Something New," *The Wall Street Journal,* September 20, 2006.
10. M. Casserly, "The 10 Skills That Will Get You Hired in 2013," *Forbes,* December 12, 2012, http://www.forbes.com/sites/meghancasserly/2012/12/10/the-10-skills-that-will-get-you-a-job-in-2013/.
11. M. Robles, "Executive Perception of the Top 10 Skills Needed in Today's Workplace," *Business Communication Quarterly,* 2012, 453–465.
12. Ibid.
13. R. Hori, "Why Soft Skills Matter," *Bloomberg Businessweek,* December 5, 2012, http://www.businessweek.com/printer/articles/84916-why-soft-skills-matter, accessed June 14, 2013.
14. Bureau of Labor Statistics, February 24, 2013, http://www.BLS.gov/nls/nlsfaqs.htm#anch41.
15. R. E. Ployhart, J. A. Weekley, and J. Ramsey, "The Consequences of Human Resource Stocks and Flows: A Longitudinal Examination of Unit Service Orientation and Unit Effectiveness," *Academy of Management Journal,* 2009, 996–1015.
16. See B. Groysberg, L. Eling Lee, and R. Abrahams, "What It Takes to Make Star Hires Pay Off," *Sloan Management Review,* January 1, 2010; and A. Pomeroy, "C-Suite Worries over Succession Planning," *HR Magazine,* December 2007, 22.
17. K. Jiang, D. P. Lepak, J. Hu, and J. C. Baer, "How Does Human Resource Management Influence Organizational Outcomes? A Meta-Analytic Investigation of Mediating Mechanisms," *Academy of Management Journal,* 2012, 1264–1294.
18. J. Tyrangiel, "Tim Cook's Freshman Year," *Fortune,* December 16, 2012, 62–76; and A. Lashinshky, "How Tim Cook Is Changing Apple," *Fortune Tech,* May 24, 2012.
19. R. E. Ployhart and T. P. Moliterno, "Emergence of the Human Capital Resource: A Multilevel Model," *Academy of Management Review,* 2011, 127–150.
20. R. R. Hastings, "Build Social Capital with Relationships," *SHRM,* June 26, 2012.
21. R. Kortes and S. Lin, "Getting on Board: Organizational Socialization and the Contribution of Social Capital," *Human Relations,* March 2013, 407–428.
22. N. D. Schwartz, "In Hiring, a Friend in Need Is a Prospect, Indeed," *New York Times,* January 27, 2013.
23. L. Bossidy and R. Charan, *Execution* (London, England: Random House, 2011), 81.
24. S. Williams, M. Tanner, and J. Beard, "How to Cure the Cheating Pandemic," *BizEd,* July/August 2012, 58–59.
25. S. Jayson, "Teens Face Up to Ethics Choices—If You Can Believe Them," *USA Today,* December 6, 2006, 6D.
26. Josephson Institute Center for Youth Ethics, "2012 Report Card on the Ethics of American Youth," November 20, 2012, and "2010 Report Card on the Ethics of American Youth," February 10, 2011, http://charactercounts.org/programs/reportcard/2012/index.html and http://charactercounts.org/programs/reportcard/2010/index.html.
27. M. H. Bazerman and A. E. Tenbrunsel, "Ethical Breakdowns: Good People Often Let Bad Things Happen, Why?," *Harvard Business Review,* April 2011.
28. D. Barboza and C. Duhigg, "Pressure, Chinese and Foreign, Drives Changes at FoxConn," *The New York Times,* February 20, 2012, B1.
29. D. Koenig and S. Mayerowitz, "American Airlines Stumbles on Path to Recovery," *USAToday,* October 11, 2012.
30. J. Eaglesham, "Missing: Stats on Crisis Convictions," *The Wall Street Journal,* May 13, 2012.
31. J. Strasburg and J. Chung, "Investors Exit Fund Dogged by Probe," *The Wall Street Journal,* February 15, 2013.
32. S. Harrington, "Successful Companies Are Led by CEOs Who Take a People-Centered Approach," *Human Resources,* July–August 2010, 4.
33. L. Berlin, "JPMorgan Chase Whistleblower: 'Essentially Suicide' to Stand Up to Bank," *Huffington Post,* February 21, 2013.
34. A. Farnham, "7 Purchase Snitches: Time to Rat Out Your Boss?," *ABCNews.com,* September 17, 2012.
35. Berlin, "J. P. Morgan Chase Whistleblower."
36. Bazerman and Tenbrunsel, "Ethical Breakdowns."
37. D. L. McCabe, K. D. Butterfield, and L. K. Trevino, "Academic Dishonesty in Graduate Business Programs: Prevalence, Causes, and Proposed Action," *Academy of Management Learning & Education,* 2006, 294–305.
38. P. Babcock, "Spotting Lies," *HR Magazine,* October 2003, 47. Also see D. Macsai, ". . . And I Invented Velcro," *BusinessWeek,* August 4, 2008, 15.
39. B. Tepper, "When Managers Pressure Employees to Behave Badly: Toward a Comprehensive Response," *Business Horizons* 53, 2010, 591–598.
40. Based on M. C. Gentile, "Keeping Your Colleagues Honest," *Harvard Business Review,* March 2010.
41. M. A. Rutherford, L. Parks, D. E. Cavazos, and C. D. White, "Business Ethics as a Required Course: Investigating the Factors Impacting the Decision to Require Ethics in the Undergraduate Business Core Curriculum," *Academy of Management Learning & Education,* 2012, 174–186.
42. Ibid.
43. L. Gary, "Want Better Results? Boost Your Problem Solving Power," *Harvard Business Review,* October 2004.
44. L. Petrecca, "Always Working," *USA Today,* March 7, 2013, 1A–2A.
45. S. Ovide, "Meet the New Mobile Workers," *The Wall Street Journal,* March 12, 2013, B4.
46. Ibid.
47. J. R. Terborg, "Interactional Psychology in Research on Human Behavior in Organizations," *Academy of Management Review,* 1981, 569–576.
48. S. Sonnentag, E. J. Mojza, E. Demerouti, and A. B. Bakker, "Reciprocal Relations between Recovery and Work Engagement: The Moderating Role of Job Stressors," *Journal of Applied Psychology,* July 2012, 842–853.
49. M. Moskowitz, R. Levering, O. Akhtar, E. Fry, C. Leahey, and A. Vandermey, "The 100 Best Companies to Work For," *Fortune,* February 4, 2013, 73–82.
50. R. L. Ackoff, "On the Use of Models in Corporate Planning," *Strategic Management Journal,* 1981, 353–359. See also R. Kreitner, *Management,* 9th ed. (New York: Houghton-Mifflin, 2002), 271.

51. N. Morgan, "Are You Getting the Best Solutions for Your Problems?," *Harvard Business Review,* January 1, 2002, http://cb.hbsp.harvard.edu/cb/web/he/product_view.seam?R=C0201D-PDF-ENG&T=EC&C=SEARCH&CS=05149d1977477612e265fff9eb8043c2, accessed March 5, 2013.

Chapter 2

1. A. Casey, "Five Cases of Workplace Bullying That Led to Tragedy," *Highest Five,* September 17, 2012, http://www.highestfive.com/money/5-cases-of-workplace-bullying-that-led-to-tragedy/.

2. C. R. Cook, K. R. Williams, N. G. Guerra, T. E. Kim, and S. Sadek, "Predictors of Bullying and Victimization in Childhood and Adolescence: A Meta-Analytic Investigation," *School Psychology Quarterly,* June 2010, 65–83.

3. "Results of the 2007 WBI U.S. Workplace Bullying Survey," http://www.workplacebullying.org/wbiresearch/wbi-2007/, accessed February 21, 2013.

4. "Etc. Competition," *Bloomberg Businessweek,* November 26–December 2, 2012, 94–95.

5. See M. Weinstein, "Intimidation Elimination," *Training,* May/June 2014, 46–48; and R. Sherwood, "Solutions for Bullying in the Workplace," http://voices.yahoo.com/solutions-bullying-workplace-11361976.html, May 17, 2012.

6. A. Bardi and S. H. Schwartz, "Values and Behavior: Strength and Structure of Relations," *Personality and Social Psychology Bulletin,* October 2003, 1208.

7. Ibid., 1207–1220; and M. L. Arthaud-Day, J. C. Rode, and W. H. Turnley, "Direct and Contextual Effects of Individual Values on Organizational Citizenship Behavior in Teams," *Journal of Applied Psychology,* July 2012, 792–807.

8. S. H. Schwartz, "An Overview of the Schwartz Theory of Basic Values," *Online Readings in Psychology and Culture* 2(1), December 1, 2012, 8, http://dx.doi.org/10.9707/2307-0919.1116.

9. M. Moskowitz and R. Levering, "The 100 Best Companies to Work For," *Fortune,* February 4, 2013, 88.

10. L. Winerman, "A Healthy Mind, a Longer Life," *Monitor on Psychology,* November 2006, 42–44.

11. D. A. Harrison, D. A. Newman, and P. L. Roth, "How Important Are Job Attitudes? Meta-Analytic Comparisons of Integrative Behavioral Outcomes and Time Sequences," *Academy of Management Journal,* April 2006, 305–325; and M. Riketta, "The Causal Relation between Job Attitudes and Performance: A Meta-Analysis of Panel Studies," *Journal of Applied Psychology,* March 2008, 472–481.

12. L. Festinger, *A Theory of Cognitive Dissonance* (Stanford, CA: Stanford University Press, 1957).

13. I. Ajzen, "The Theory of Planned Behavior," *Organizational Behavior and Human Decision Processes,* 1991, 188.

14. Excerpted from S. Reddy, "'I Don't Smoke, Doc,' and Other Patient Lies," *The Wall Street Journal,* February 19, 2013, D3.

15. R. P. Steel and N. K. Ovalle II, "A Review and Meta-Analysis of Research on the Relationship between Behavioral Intentions and Employee Turnover," *Journal of Applied Psychology,* November 1984, 673–686.

16. J. D. Westaby, "Behavioral Reasoning Theory: Identifying New Linkages Underlying Intentions and Behavior," *Organizational Behavior and Human Decision Processes,* 2005, 97–120, and J. D. Westaby, T. M. Probst, and B. C. Lee, "Leadership Decision-Making: A Behavioral Reasoning Theory Analysis," *The Leadership Quarterly,* June 2010, 481–495.

17. "Smart Ways to Perk Up Your Staff," *Fortune,* February 6, 2012, 113–115.

18. M. S. Christian, A. S. Garza, and J. E. Slaughter, "Work Engagement: A Quantitative Review and Test of Its Relations with Task and Contextual Performance," *Personnel Psychology,* 2011, 89–136; and A. Kinicki, F. McKee-Ryan, C. Schriesheim, and K. Carson, "Assessing the Construct Validity of the Job Descriptive Index (JDI): A Review and Meta-Analysis," *Journal of Applied Psychology,* February 2002, 14–32.

19. J. P. Meyer and L. Herscovitch, "Commitment in the Workplace: Toward a General Model," *Human Resource Management Review,* Autumn 2001, 301.

20. See T. W. H. Ng, D. C. Feldman, and S. S. K. Lam, "Psychological Contract Breaches, Organizational Commitment, and Innovation-Related Behaviors: A Latent Growth Modeling Approach," *Journal of Applied Psychology,* July 2010, 744–751.

21. Moskowitz and Levering, "The 100 Best Companies to Work For."

22. M. Moskowitz, R. Levering, and N. Tseng, "10 Top-Paying Companies 2013," *Fortune* on *CNN/Money,* updated June 11, 2013.

23. M. Moskowitz , R. Levering, and L. Stangel, "Google's 10 Best Perks: Cars, Sleep Pods—You Name It," *Silicon Valley Business Journal,* April 15, 2013.

24. W. A. Kahn, "Psychological Conditions of Personal Engagement and Disengagement at Work," *Academy of Management Journal,* December 1990, 695.

25. W. A. Macy, B. Schneider, K. M. Barbera, and S. A. Young, *Employee Engagement: Tools for Analysis, Practice, and Competitive Advantage* (West Sussex, UK: Wiley-Blackwell, 2009), 20.

26. Aon Hewitt, "2012 Engagement Distribution," *2013 Trends in Global Employee Engagement,* 8.

27. See M. S. Christian, A. S. Garza, and J. E. Slaughter, "Work Engagement: A Quantitative Review and Test of Its Relations with Task and Contextual Performance," *Personnel Psychology,* 2011, 89–136; and P. Petrou, E. Demerouti, M. C. W. Peeters, W. B. Schaufeli, and J. Hetland, "Crafting a Job on a Daily Basis: Contextual Correlates and the Link to Work Engagement," *Journal of Organizational Behavior,* November 2012, 1120–1141.

28. S. Sonnentag, E. J. Mojza, E. Demerouti, and A. B. Bakker, "Reciprocal Relations between Recovery and Work Engagement: The Moderating Role of Job Stressors," *Journal of Applied Psychology,* July 2012, 842–853.

29. Aon Hewitt, "Key Drivers of Employee Engagement," *2013 Trends in Global Employee Engagement,* 17.

30. See J. Robison, "Building Engagement in This Economic Crisis," *Gallup Management Journal,* February 19, 2009, http://gmj.gallup.com/content/115213/Building-Engagement-Economic-Crisis.aspx.

31. See Christian, Garza, and Slaughter, "Work Engagement: A Quantitative Review and Test of Its Relations with Task and Contextual Performance"; M. S. Cole, F. Walter, A. G. Bedeian, and E. H. O'Boyle, "Job Burnout and Employee Engagement: A Meta-Analytic Examination of Construct Proliferation," *Journal of Management,* September 2012, 1550–1581; and K. M. Barbera, "Driving Customer Satisfaction and Financial Success through Employee Engagement," *People & Strategy,* 2009, 22–27.

32. J. Robison, "How the Ritz-Carlton Manages the Mystique," *Gallup Management Journal,* December 11, 2008, http://gmj.gallup.com/content/112906.

33. See R. Tartell, "Employee Engagement—Why Care?," *Training,* July/August 2012, 10–11; and C. Suddath, "Sweating in Secret," *Bloomberg Businessweek,* April 2–April 8, 2002, 82–83.

34. A. Braithwaite, "Eight-Hour Energy," *Bloomberg Businessweek,* August 27–September 2, 2012, 72–73.

35. L. Freifeld, "I Want to Work There!" *Training,* July/August 2012, 16–24.

36. B. Groysberg and M. Slind, "Leadership Is a Conversation," *Harvard Business Review,* June 2012, 76–84.

37. Moskowitz and Levering, "The 100 Best Companies to Work For."

38. L. Rhodes and R. Eisenberger, "Perceived Organizational Support: A Review of the Literature," *Journal of Applied Psychology,* August 2002, 698–714.

39. Ibid.; and M. K. Shoss, R. Eisenberger, S. L. D. Restubog, and T. J. Zagenczyk, "Blaming the Organization for Abusive Supervision: The Roles of Perceived Organizational Support and Supervisor's Organizational Embodiment," *Journal of Applied Psychology,* January 2013, 158–168.

40. D. A. Kaplan, "Salesforce's Happy Workforce," *Fortune,* February 6, 2012, 106.

41. M. G. Danaher, "Back Pay for Retaliation May Be Based on Loss of Job Opportunity," *HR Magazine,* June 2012, 113.

42. P. C. Smith, L. M. Kendall, and C. L. Hulin, *The Measurement of Satisfaction in Work and Retirement* (Skokie, IL: Rand-McNally, 1969).

43. E. Mendes, "U.S. Job Satisfaction Struggles to Recover to 2008 Levels," *Gallup,* May 31, 2011, http://www.gallup.com/poll/147833/Job-Satisfaction-Struggles-Recover-2008-Levels.aspx.

44. "2012 Employee Job Satisfaction and Engagement," *Society for Human Resources Management,* October 2012, http://www.shrm.org/Research/SurveyFindings/Articles/Documents/SHRM-Employee-Job-Satisfaction-Engagement.pdf.

45. E. F. Stone, "A Critical Analysis of Social Information Processing Models of Job Perceptions and Job Attitudes," in *Job Satisfaction: How People Feel about Their Jobs and How It Affects Their Performance,* ed. C. J. Cranny, P. Cain Smith, and E. F. Stone (New York: Lexington Books, 1992), 21–52.

46. J. P. Wanous, T. D. Poland, S. L. Premack, and K. S. Davis, "The Effects of Met Expectations on Newcomer Attitudes and Behaviors: A Review and Meta-Analysis," *Journal of Applied Psychology,* June 1992, 288–297.

47. Results can be found in J. Cohen-Charash and P. E. Spector, "The Role of Justice in Organizations: A Meta-Analysis," *Organizational Behavior and Human Decision Processes,* November 2001, 278–321.

48. N. A. Bowling, E. A. Hendricks, and S. H. Wagner, "Positive and Negative Affectivity and Facet Satisfaction: A Meta-Analysis," *Journal of Business Strategy,* December 2008, 115–125.

49. See R. D. Arvey, T. J. Bouchard Jr., N. L. Segal, and L. M. Abraham, "Job Satisfaction: Environmental and Genetic Components," *Journal of Applied Psychology,* April 1989, 187–192.

50. See C. Dormann and D. Zapf, "Job Satisfaction: A Meta-Analysis of Stabilities," *Journal of Organizational Behavior,* August 2001, 483–504.

51. P. Wakeman, "The Good Life and How to Get It," *Inc.,* February 2001, 50.

52. M. C. Noonan and J. L. Glass, "The Hard Truth about Telecommuting," *Monthly Labor Review,* June 2012, 38–45; and C. Suddath, "Work-from-Home Truths, Half-Truths, and Myths," *Bloomberg Businessweek,* March 4–March 10, 2013, 75.

53. P. Cohan, "4 Reasons Marissa Mayer's No-At-Home-Work Policy Is an Epic Fail," *Forbes,* February 26, 2013, http://www.forbes.com/sites/petercohan/2013/02/26/4-reasons-marissa-mayers-no-at-home-work-policy-is-an-epic-fail/; and N. L. Pesce, "Marissa Mayer Bans Telecommuting at Yahoo! and Becomes the Mother of Dissension," *New York Daily News,* March 4, 2013, http://www.nydailynews.com/life-style/n-y-moms-react-yahoo-ban-telecommuting-article-1.1277492.

54. S. P. Brown, "A Meta-Analysis and Review of Organizational Research on Job Involvement," *Psychological Bulletin,* September 1996, 235–255.

55. P. W. Hom and A. J. Kinicki, "Toward a Greater Understanding of How Dissatisfaction Drives Employee Turnover," *Academy of Management Journal,* October 2001, 975–987.

56. I. Robertson and C. Cooper, *Well-Being: Productivity and Happiness at Work* (London, UK: Palgrave Macmillan, 2011).

57. Based on Casey, "Five Cases of Workplace Bullying That Led to Tragedy"; and H. Westerman, "In Harm's Way," *The Age,* March 10, 2010, http://www.theage.com.au/small-business/in-harms-way-20100309-pvxm.html.

58. T. A. Judge, C. J. Thoresen, J. E. Bono, and G. K. Patton, "The Job Satisfaction–Job Performance Relationship: A Qualitative and Quantitative Review," *Psychological Bulletin,* May 2001, 376–407.

59. Ibid.

60. D. S. Whitman, D. L. Van Rooy, and C. Viswesvaran, "Satisfaction, Citizenship Behaviors, and Performance in Work Units: A Meta-Analysis of Collective Relations," *Personnel Psychology,* Spring 2010, 41–81.

61. D. W. Organ, *Organizational Citizenship Behavior: The Good Soldier Syndrome* (Lexington, MA: Lexington Books, 1988), 4.

62. D. W. Organ, "The Motivational Basis of Organizational Citizenship Behavior," in *Research in Organizational Behavior,* ed. B. M. Staw and L. L. Cummings (Greenwich, CT: JAI Press, 1990), 46.

63. Results can be found in B. J. Hoffman, C. A. Blair, J. P. Meriac, and D. J. Woehr, "Expanding the Criterion Domain? A Quantitative Review of the OCB Literature," *Journal of Applied Psychology,* March 2007, 555–566.

64. See N. P. Podsakoff, S. W. Whiting, P. M. Podsakoff, and B. D. Blume, "Individual- and Organizational-Level Consequences of Organizational Citizenship Behaviors: A Meta-Analysis," *Journal of Applied Psychology,* January 2009, 122–141; and Whitman, Van Rooy, and Viswesvaran, "Satisfaction, Citizenship Behaviors, and Performance in Work Units."

65. S. J. Motowidlo and H. J. Kell, "Job Performance," in *Handbook of Psychology* (Vol. 12), ed. N. W. Schmitt and S. Highhouse (Hoboken, NJ: John Wiley & Sons, Inc., 2012).

66. M. Conlin, "To Catch a Corporate Thief," *BusinessWeek,* February 16, 2009, 52.

67. J. R. Detert, L. K. Treviño, E. R. Burris, and M. Andiappan, "Managerial Modes of Influence and Counterproductivity in Organizations: A Longitudinal Business-Unit-Level Investigation," *Journal of Applied Psychology,* July 2007, 993–1005.

68. H. Boushey and S. J. Glynn, "There Are Significant Business Costs to Replacing Employees," *Center for American Progress,* November 16, 2012, http://www.americanprogress.org/issues/labor/report/2012/11/16/44464/there-are-significant-business-costs-to-replacing-employees.

69. A. Nyberg, "Retaining Your High Performers: Moderators of the Performance–Job Satisfaction–Voluntary Turnover Relationship," *Journal of Applied Psychology,* May 2010, 440–453.

70. J. McGregor, "Giving Back to Your Stars," *Fortune,* November 1, 2010, 53–54; and J. Martin and C. Schmidt, "How to Keep Your Top Talent," *Harvard Business Review,* May 2010, 54–61.

71. See M. VanHook, "All Aboard! ALEX(R) Survey Finds Many Companies Miss the Onboarding Boat," June 4, 2014, http://www.reuters.com/article/2014/06/04/idUSnMKWjQ9P1a+1d4+MKW20140604.

72. "A Signature New-Hire Experience," http://mycareer.deloitte.com/us/en/life-at-deloitte/leadership/learning-and-development/a-signature-new-hire-experience accessed June 24, 2014.

73. M. C. Sturman, L. Shao, and J. H. Katz, "The Effect of Culture on the Curvilinear Relationship between Performance and Turnover," *Journal of Applied Psychology,* January 2012, 46–62.

74. A. Quirk, "The Business Case for Flex," *HR Magazine,* April 2012, 44–46.

75. Based on C. Hannan, "Management Secrets from the Meanest Company in America," *Bloomberg Businessweek,* January 7–13, 2013, 46–51; "The Complete Company Rankings," *MSN Money,* July 9, 2012, http://money.msn.com/investing/the-complete-company-rankings-2012.aspx; DISH Network, "A Whole New Animal in Whole-Home Entertainment: DISH Network Annual Report Year Ending December 31, 2011"; SEC Annual Report, http://www.sec.gov/Archives/edgar/vprr/0000/1202/12026847.pdf; "Drink the Kool-Aid," *Glassdoor.com,* http://www.glassdoor.com/Reviews/Employee-Review-DISH-RVW1241473.htm, accessed March 11, 2013; D. A. McIntyre, A. C. Allen, and M. B. Sauter, "America's Worst Companies to Work For," *Fox Business News,* August 10, 2012, http://www.foxbusiness.com/personal-finance/2012/08/10/americas-worst-companies-to-work-for/; D. A. McIntyre, M. B. Sauter, A. E. M. Hess, and S. Weigley, "America's Worst Companies to Work For," *Fox Business News,* July 24, 2013, http://www.foxbusiness.com/industries/2013/07/24/americas-worst-companies-to-work-for/; and Liz Ryan, "Dish Network the Country's Worst Employer? CEO: 'That's Ridiculous!'" *Huffington*

Post, August 29, 2012, http://www.huffingtonpost.com/liz-ryan/dish-network-the-countrys_b_1790994.html.

76. M. Lorenz, "Two in Five Employers Use Social Media to Screen Candidates," Careerbuilder, July 1, 2013, http://thehiringsite.careerbuilder.com/2013/07/01/two-in-five-employers-use-social-media-to-screen-candidates/.

77. Based on S. McFarland, "Job Seekers Getting Asked for Facebook Passwords," *USA Today,* March 22, 2013, http://usatoday30.usatoday.com/tech/news/story/2012-03-20/job-applicants-facebook/53665606/1.

78. This exercise was based on S. Dunphy and K. Aupperle, "Flight Plan: Motivation," *Training & Development,* October 2001, 18–19.

Chapter 3

1. N. M. Davis, "Google's Top Recruiter," *HR Magazine,* July 2012, 40–41.

2. J. King, "6 Things New Hires Should Do in the First 30 Days," *T+D Magazine,* July 20, 2012, http://blog.softwareadvice.com/articles/hr/new-hire-checklist-1071312/, accessed March 27, 2013.

3. Society of Human Resource Management (SHRM), "Onboarding Practices Survey Findings," April 13, 2011, http://www.shrm.org/Research/SurveyFindings/Articles/Pages/OnboardingPractices.aspx, accessed March 27, 2013.

4. S. N. Kaplan, "Persistence Is Best Predictor of CEO Success," *Bloomberg.com,* October 26, 2011, http://www.bloomberg.com/news/2011-10-26/persistence-is-best-predictor-of-ceo-success-steven-n-kaplan.html, accessed March 27, 2013.

5. Z. Zhang, M. Wang, and J. Shi, "Leader-Follower Congruence in Proactive Personality and Work Outcomes: The Mediating Role of Leader-Member Exchange," *Academy of Management Journal* 55(1), February 2012, 111–130.

6. D. A. Briley and E. M. Tucker-Drob, "Genetic and Environmental Continuity in Personality Development: A Meta-Analysis," *Psychological Bulletin,* June 23, 2014, 1–29.

7. T. A. Judge, L. S. Simon, C. Hurst, and K. Kelley, "What I Experienced Yesterday Is Who I Am Today: Relationship of Work Motivations and Behaviors to Within-Individual Variation in the Five-Factor Model of Personality," *Journal of Applied Psychology,* 99, 2014, 199–221.

8. J. W. B. Lang, M. Kersting, U. R. Hulsheger, and J. Lang, "General Mental Ability, Narrower Cognitive Abilities, and Job Performance: The Perspective of the Nested-Factor Model of Cognitive Abilities," *Personnel Psychology* 63, 2010, 595–640.

9. S. Kanazawa, "Evolutionary Psychology and Intelligence Research," *American Psychologist,* May–June 2010, 279–289.

10. See R. A. Weinberg, "Intelligence and IQ," *American Psychologist,* 1989, 98–104; and W. A. Walker and C. Humphries, "Starting the Good Life in the Womb," *Newsweek,* September 17, 2007, 56, 58.

11. B. Azar, "People Are Becoming Smarter—Why?," *APA Monitor,* June 1996, 20. See also K. Baker, "Why Do IQ Scores Vary by Nation?," *Newsweek,* August 2, 2010, 14; S. Begley, "Can You Build a Better Brain?," *Newsweek,* January 10–17, 2011, 40–45; and S. Begley, "Get Smarter: A Group of Thinkers Explains How," *Newsweek,* January 24, 2011, 42. For interesting reading on intelligence, see J. R. Flynn, "Searching for Justice: The Discovery of IQ Gains over Time," *American Psychologist,* January 1999, 5–20; and E. Benson, "Intelligent Intelligence Testing," *Monitor on Psychology,* February 2003, 48–54.

12. H. Gardner, *Frames of Mind: The Theory of Multiple Intelligences,* 10th ed. (New York: Basic Books, 1993). See also H. Gardner, *Intelligence Reframed: Multiple Intelligences for the 21st Century* (New York: Basic Books, 2000); and B. Fryer, "The Ethical Mind: A Conversation with Psychologist Howard Gardner," *Harvard Business Review,* March 2007, 51–56.

13. R. J. Sternberg, "WICS: A Model of Leadership in Organizations," *Academy of Management Learning and Education,* December 2003, 388. Emphasis added.

14. D. Hambrick, "I.Q. Points for Sale, Cheap," *The New York Times,* May 6, 2012.

15. G. Kolata, "Power in Numbers," *The New York Times,* January 2, 2012.

16. M. Grinblatt, M. Keloharju, and J. T. Linnainmaa, "IQ, Trading Behavior, and Performance," *Journal of Financial Economics,* 2012, 339–362.

17. J. Bell, "Watch Out Wonderlic, There's a New Combine Test in Town," *USA Today,* February, 17, 2013.

18. Judge, Simon, Hurst, and Kelley, "What I Experienced Yesterday"; Briley and Drob, "Genetic and Environmental Continuity"; and C. J. Ferguson, "A Meta-Analysis of Normal and Disordered Personality across the Life Span," *Journal of Personality and Social Psychology,* 2010, 659–667. See also C. J. Hopwood, M. B. Donnellan, D. M. Blonigen, R. F. Krueger, M. McGue, W. G. Iacono, and S. A. Burt, "Genetic and Environmental Influences on Personality Trait Stability and Growth During the Transition to Adulthood: A Three-Wave Longitudinal Study," *Journal of Personality and Social Psychology,* January 17, 2011, 1–12.

19. The landmark report is J. M. Digman, "Personality Structure: Emergence of the Five-Factor Model," *Annual Review of Psychology* 41, 1990, 417–440. Also see P. Warr, D. Bartram, and A. Brown, "Big Five Validity: Aggregation Method Matters," *Journal of Occupational and Organizational Psychology,* September 2005, 377–386.

20. Data from S. V. Paunonen et al., "The Structure of Personality in Six Cultures," *Journal of Cross-Cultural Psychology,* May 1996, 339–353.

21. For supporting evidence see D. P. Schmitt, J. Allik, R. R. McCrae, and V. Benet-Martinez, "The Geographic Distribution of Big Five Personality Traits," *Journal of Cross-Cultural Psychology,* March 2007, 173–212.

22. T. S. Bateman and M. J. Crant, "The Proactive Component of Organizational Behavior: A Measure and Correlates," *Journal of Organizational Behavior* 14(2), March 1993, 103–118. See also J. P. Thomas, D. S. Whitman, and V. Chockalingam, "Employee Proactivity in Organizations: A Comparative Meta-Analysis of Emergent Proactive Constructs," *Journal of Occupational & Organizational Psychology,* June 2010, 275–300.

23. Bateman and Crant, "The Proactive Component of Organizational Behavior."

24. Z. Zhang, M. Wang, and J. Shi, "Leader-Follower Congruence in Proactive Personality and Work Outcomes: The Mediating Role of Leader-Member Exchange," *Academy of Management Journal,* 2012, 111–130.

25. T. Snyder, "The 2007 Inc. 5000: How I Did It: Rachel Coleman, CEO, Two Little Hands Productions," *Inc.,* http://www.inc.com/inc5000/, accessed March 26, 2008.

26. Khan Academy website: http://www.khanacademy.org/.

27. M. R. Barrick and M. K. Mount, "The Big Five Personality Dimensions and Job Performance: A Meta-Analysis," *Personnel Psychology,* Spring 1991, 21. See also I. S. Oh, G. Wang, and M. K. Mount, "Validity of Observer Ratings of the Five-Factor Model of Personality Traits: A Meta-Analysis," *Journal of Applied Psychology,* December 13, 2010, 1–12.

28. Barrick and Mount, "The Big Five Personality Dimensions and Job Performance," 21.

29. J. Dikkers, P. G. Jansen, A. de Lange, C. Vinkenburg, and D. Kooij, "Proactivity, Job Characteristics, and Engagement: A Longitudinal Study," *Career Development International,* 2010, 59–77; T. Kim, A. H. Hon, and J. M. Crant, "Proactive Personality, Employee Creativity, and Newcomer Outcomes: A Longitudinal Study," *Journal of Business Psychology,* 2009, 93–103; and J. M. Crant, "The Proactive Personality Scale as a Predictor of Entrepreneurial Intentions," *Journal of Small Business Management,* 1996, 42–50.

30. D. Zielinski, "Effective Assessments," *HR Magazine,* January 2011, 61–64.

31. Oh, Wang, and Mount, "Validity of Observer Ratings of the Five-Factor Model of Personality Traits," 1–12. For details on test bias see H. Aguinis, S. A. Carpenter, and C. A. Pierce, "Revival of Test Bias Research in Pre-Employment Testing," *Journal of Applied Psychology 94*(10), 2010, 648–680. For a discussion and advice on using pre-employment tests see T. Minton-Eversole, "Avoiding Bias in Pre-Employment Testing," *HR Magazine*, December 2010, 77–80.

32. Based in part on T. A. Judge, "Core Self-Evaluations and Work Success," *Current Directions in Psychological Science,* 2009, 58–62.

33. Oh, Wang, and Mount, "Validity of Observer Ratings of the Five-Factor Model of Personality Traits."

34. Z. Simsek, C. Heavey, and J. F. Veiga, "The Impact of CEO Core Self-Evaluation on the Firm's Entrepreneurial Orientation," *Strategic Management Journal*, 2010, 110–119.

35. F. Giblin and B. Lakey, "Integrating Mentoring and Social Support Research within the Context of Stressful Medical Training," *Journal of Social and Clinical Psychology*, 2010, 771–796.

36. A. Lang and B. Thomas, "Crossing the Canyon," *T+D Magazine*, March 2013, 36–39.

37. Taken from D. L. Ferris, H. Lian, D. J. Brown, F. X. J. Pang, and L. M. Keeping, "Self-Esteem and Job Performance: The Moderating Role of Self-Esteem Contingencies," *Personnel Psychology*, 2010, 561–593.

38. See P. C. Earley and T. R. Lituchy, "Delineating Goal and Efficacy Effects: A Test of Three Models," *Journal of Applied Psychology,* February 1991, 81–98.

39. See P. Tierney and S. M. Farmer, "Creative Self-Efficacy: Its Potential Antecedents and Relationship to Creative Performance," *Academy of Management Journal,* December 2002, 1137–1148.

40. See W. S. Silver, T. R. Mitchell, and M. E. Gist, "Response to Successful and Unsuccessful Performance: The Moderating Effect of Self-Efficacy on the Relationship between Performance and Attributions," *Organizational Behavior and Human Decision Processes*, June 1995, 286–299.

41. E. Diener and M. Diener, "Cross-Cultural Correlates of Life Satisfaction and Self-Esteem," *Journal of Personality and Social Psychology*, April 1995, 662.

42. Giblin and Lakey, "Integrating Mentoring and Social Support Research."

43. W. J. McGuire and C. V. McGuire, "Enhancing Self-Esteem by Directed-Thinking Tasks: Cognitive and Affective Positivity Asymmetries," *Journal of Personality and Social Psychology*, June 1996, 1124.

44. For an instructive update, see J. B. Rotter, "Internal versus External Control of Reinforcement: A Case History of a Variable," *American Psychologist*, April 1990, 489–493.

45. B. K. Fuller, M. C. Spears, and D. F. Parker, "Entrepreneurial Tendencies: Evidence from China and India," *International Journal of Management and Marketing Research*, 2010, 39–52.

46. For an overall review of research on locus of control, see P. E. Spector, "Behavior in Organizations as a Function of Employee's Locus of Control," *Psychological Bulletin,* May 1982, 482–497.

47. Adapted from S. Craig, "DealBook: A Female Wall Street Financial Chief Avoids Pitfalls That Stymied Others," *The New York Times,* November 9, 2010.

48. See the box titled "Get Happy Carefully" in D. Goleman, R. Boyatzis, and A. McKee, "Primal Leadership: The Hidden Driver of Great Performance," *Harvard Business Review,* Special Issue: Breakthrough Leadership, December 2001, 49.

49. N. Easton. "Christine Lagarde: How to Get What You Want Without Being Aggressive," *Fortune* Interview, March 24, 2014. Found at: https://www.youtube.com/watch?v=1NetrLREQlg. Downloaded June 26, 2014.

50. B. Kidwell, D. M. Hardesty, B. R. Murtha, and S. Sheng, "Emotional Intelligence in Marketing Exchanges," *Journal of Marketing,* January 2011, 78–95.

51. J. D. Mayer, R. D. Roberts, and S. G. Barsade, "Human Abilities: Emotional Intelligence," *Annual Review of Psychology*, 2008, 507–36.

52. F. Walter, M. S. Cole, and R. H. Humphrey, "Emotional Intelligence: Sine Qua Non of Leadership or Folderol?," *Academy of Management Perspectives,* February 2011, 45–59.

53. M. Fugate, A. J. Kinicki, and G. E. Prussia, "Employee Coping with Organizational Change: An Examination of Alternative Theoretical Perspectives and Models," *Personnel Psychology,* 2008, 1–36.

54. S. D. Pugh, M. Groth, and T. Hennig-Thurau, "Willing and Able to Fake Emotions: A Closer Examination of the Link between Emotional Dissonance and Employee Well-Being," *Journal of Applied Psychology*, 2011, 377–90.

55. R. S. Lazarus, *Emotion and Adaptation* (New York: Oxford University Press, 1991), chs. 6, 7.

56. K. L. Wang and M. Groth, "Buffering the Negative Effects of Employee Surface Acting: The Moderating Role of Employee-Customer Relationship Strength and Personalized Services," *Journal of Applied Psychology, 99,* 2014, 341–350.

57. S. Shellenbarger, "When the Boss Is a Screamer," *The Wall Street Journal,* August 15, 2012.

58. Fugate, Kinicki, and Prussia, "Employee Coping with Organizational Change."

59. A. Rafaeli, A. Erez, S. Ravid, R. Derfler-Rozin, D. Treister, and R. Scheyer, "When Customers Exhibit Verbal Aggression, Employees Pay Cognitive Costs," *Journal of Applied Psychology,* 2012, 931–950.

60. D. Geddes and R. R. Callister, "Crossing the Line(s): A Dual Threshold Model of Anger in Organizations," *Academy of Management Review,* 2007, 721–746.

61. As quoted in H. Mackay, "Always Follow the Advice of D. Lou," *The Arizona Republic*, January 18, 2009, D2.

62. M. Gladwell, *Outliers: The Story of Success* (New York: Little, Brown, 2008), 38–41.

63. E. K. Coughlan, A. M. Williams, A. P. McRogbert, and P. R. Ford, "How Experts Practice: A Novel Test of Deliberate Practice Theory," *Journal of Experimental Psychology, Learning, Memory, & Cognition, 40,* March 2014, 449–458.

64. G. Colvin, *Talent Is Overrated: What Really Separates World-Class Performers from Everybody Else* (New York: Penguin, 2008), 66.

65. Ibid.

66. W. C. McGaghie, "The Science of Learning Medical Education," *British Journal of Medical Education, 48,* February 2014, 106–108.

67. For more, see R. Wiseman, *The Luck Factor: The Four Essential Principles* (New York: Miramax, 2004); and D. H. Pink, "How to Make Your Own Luck," *Fast Company,* July 2003, 78–82.

68. M. Moskowitz, R. Levering, O. Akhtar, E. Fry, C. Leahey, and A. Vandermey, "The 100 Best Companies to Work For," *Fortune,* February 4, 2013, 87.

69. P. Cohan, "Google's Talent Drain: Why Its Best Brains Are Bolting," *Daily Finance,* November 29, 2010; and K. Swisher, "End of an Era: Google's Very First Employee, Craig Silverstein—Technically No. 3—Leaving," *All Things D,* February 9, 2012.

70. F. Manjoo, "How Google Became Such a Great Place to Work," *Slate.com,* January 21, 2013.

71. M. Arrington, "Google Making Extraordinary Counteroffers to Stop Flow of Employees to Facebook," *TechCrunch,* September 1, 2010.

72. Excerpted from A. Efrati and P. W. Tam, "Google Battles to Keep Talent," *The Wall Street Journal,* November 11, 2010.

73. M. Lynley, "The Main Reasons Googlers Leave the Best Place in the World to Work," *Business Insider,* February 22, 2012.

74. Cohan, "Google's Talent Drain."

75. T. Kelly, "Google Trumps Facebook Employee Satisfaction, Glassdoor Survey Finds," *The Huffington Post,* March 23, 2012.

76. E. Protalinski, "Google Overtakes Facebook in Employee Satisfaction," *ZDNET,* March 22, 2012.

77. A. G. Sulzberger, "Hospitals Shift Smoking Bans to Smoker Ban," *The New York Times,* February 10, 2011.

Chapter 4

1. R. E. Silverman, "At Work: Recent College Grads Lack Professionalism," *The Wall Street Journal,* March 20, 2013, B8.

2. L. Kwoh, "Beware: Potential Employers See the Dumb Things You Do Online," *The Wall Street Journal,* October 29, 2012, B8.

3. "12 Top Job-Search Errors," *The Arizona Republic,* December 30, 2012, D6.

4. Kwoh, "Beware: Potential Employers See the Dumb Things You Do Online."

5. Excerpted from W. W. Maddux, P. H. Kim, T. Okumura, and J. M. Brett, "Why 'I'm Sorry' Doesn't Always Translate," *Harvard Business Review,* June 2012, 26.

6. J. Paskin, "Don't Apologize," *Bloomberg Businessweek,* April 22–28, 2013, 88.

7. L. Stamato, "Should Business Leaders Apologize?," *Ivey Business Journal,* July/August 2008, http://iveybusinessjournal.com/topics/leadership/should-business-leaders-apologize-why-when-and-how-an-apology-matters.

8. R. E. Silverman, "Bald Is Powerful," *The Wall Street Journal,* October 3, 2012, B1, B6.

9. The negative bias was examined by A. Weinberg and G. Hajcak, "Beyond Good and Evil: The Time-Course of Neural Activity Elicited by Specific Picture Content," *Emotion,* December 2010, 767–782.

10. E. Rosch, C. B. Mervis, W. D. Gray, D. M. Johnson, and P. Boyes-Braem, "Basic Objects in Natural Categories," *Cognitive Psychology,* July 1976, 383. Emphasis added.

11. D. M. Amodio and K. G. Ratner, "A Memory Systems Model of Implicit Social Cognition," *Current Directions in Psychological Science,* June 2011, 143–148.

12. C. D. Cameron, J. L. Brown-Iannuzzi, and B. K. Payne, "Sequential Priming Measures of Implicit Social Cognition: A Meta-Analysis of Associations with Behavior and Explicit Attitudes," *Personality and Social Psychology Review,* November 2012, 330–350.

13. E. Dervous, A. M. Ryan, and H. D. Nguyen, "Multiple Categorization in Resume Screening: Examining Effects on Hiring Discrimination Against Arab Applicants in Field and Lab Settings," *Journal of Organizational Behavior,* May 2012, 544–570.

14. Excerpted and drawn from D. Zielinski, "The Virtual Interview," *HR Magazine,* July 2012, 55–58.

15. See R. C. Mayer and J. H. Davis, "The Effect of the Performance Appraisal System on Trust for Management: A Field Quasi-Experiment," *Journal of Applied Psychology,* February 1999, 123–136.

16. The effectiveness of rater training was supported by D. V. Day and L. M. Sulsky, "Effects of Frame-of-Reference Training and Information Configuration on Memory Organization and Rating Accuracy," *Journal of Applied Psychology,* February 1995, 158–167.

17. Leadership categorization is studied by J. S. Phillips and R. G. Lord, "Schematic Information Processing and Perceptions of Leadership in Problem-Solving Groups," *Journal of Applied Psychology,* August 1982, 486–492; and S. Melwani, J. S. Mueller, and J. R. Overbeck, "Looking Down: The Influence of Contempt and Compassion on Emergent Leadership Categorizations," *Journal of Applied Psychology,* November 2012, 1171–1185.

18. C. M. Judd and B. Park, "Definition and Assessment of Accuracy in Social Stereotypes," *Psychological Review,* January 1993, 110. Emphasis added.

19. See J. V. Sanchez-Hucles and D. D. Davis, "Women and Women of Color in Leadership," *American Psychologist,* April 2010, 171–181; and S. Bruckmüller and N. R. Branscombe, "How Women End Up on the 'Glass Cliff,'" *Harvard Business Review,* January–February 2011, 26.

20. See T. DeAngelis, "Unmasking 'Racial Micro Aggressions,'" *Harvard Business Review,* February 2009, 42–46.

21. T. W. H. Ng and D. C. Feldman, "Evaluating Six Common Stereotypes about Older Workers with Meta-Analytical Data," *Personnel Psychology,* 2012, 821–858.

22. See E. L. Paluck and D. P. Green, "Prejudice Reduction: What Works? A Review and Assessment of Research and Practice," *Annual Review of Psychology,* 2009, 339–367.

23. Kelley's model is discussed in detail in H. H. Kelley, "The Processes of Causal Attribution," *American Psychologist,* February 1973, 107–128.

24. See S. E. Moss and M. J. Martinko, "The Effects of Performance Attributions and Outcome Dependence on Leader Feedback Behavior Following Poor Subordinate Performance," *Journal of Organizational Behavior,* May 1998, 259–274.

25. See J. Silvester, F. Patterson, and E. Ferguson, "Comparing Two Attributional Models of Job Performance in Retail Sales: A Field Study," *Journal of Occupational and Organizational Psychology,* March 2003, 115–132.

26. "Does Gender Diversity Improve Performance?," http://sponsorship.credit-suisse.com/app/article/indexcfm?fuseaction=OpenArticle&aoid=360157&coid=72934&lang=EN, July 31, 2012, accessed May 13, 2013.

27. T. Minton-Eversole, "Skills Gaps Often Very Basic: English, Critical Thinking, Solving Problems," *HR Magazine,* May 2013, 20.

28. "U.S. Census Bureau Projections Show a Slower Growing, Older, More Diverse Nation a Half Century from Now," http://www.census.gov/newsroom/releases/archives/population/cb12-243.html. See also L. Meckler, "Hispanic Future in the Cards," *The Wall Street Journal Online,* http://online.wsj.com/article/SB20001424127887323981504578175284228844590.html, December 13, 2012.

29. M. R. Hebl and D. R. Avery, "Diversity in Organizations," in N. W. Schmitt and S. Highhouse, eds., *Handbook of Psychology* (Vol. 12) (Hoboken, NJ: John Wiley, 2013), 678. Emphasis added.

30. H. Collingwood, "Who Handles a Diverse Work Force Best?," *Working Women,* February 1996, 25.

31. Hebl and Avery, "Diversity in Organizations," 678. Emphasis added.

32. Results can be found in D. A. Harrison, D. A. Kravitz, D. M. Mayer, L. M. Leslie, and D. Lev-Arey, "Understanding Attitudes Toward Affirmative Action Programs in Employment: Summary and Meta-Analysis of 35 Years of Research," *Journal of Applied Psychology,* September 2006, 1013–1036.

33. For a thorough review of relevant research, see M. E. Heilman, "Affirmative Action: Some Unintended Consequences for Working Women," in B. M. Staw and L. L. Cummings, eds., *Research in Organizational Behavior* (Vol. 16) (Greenwich, CT: JAI Press, 1994), 125–169.

34. D. Brady, "Etc. Hard Choices: Helena Morrissey on Founding the 30% Club," *Bloomberg Businessweek,* October 1–7, 2012, 88.

35. A. M. Morrison, *The New Leaders: Guidelines on Leadership Diversity in America* (San Francisco: Jossey-Bass, 1992), 78.

36. Ibid.

37. Ibid.

38. Excerpted from "No. 1 Johnson & Johnson," http://www.diversityinc.com/article/5449/Mo-1-Johnson—Johnson/, accessed December 27, 2010.

39. R. J. Ely and D. A. Thomas, "Cultural Diversity at Work: The Effects of Diversity Perspectives on Work Group Processes and Outcomes," *Administrative Science Quarterly,* 2001, 243. Emphasis added.

40. D. R. Avery, P. F. McKay, S. Tonidandel, S. D. Volpone, and M. A. Morris, "Is There Method to the Madness? Examining How Racio-ethnic Matching Influences Retail Store Productivity," *Personnel Psychology,* 2012, 167–199.

41. R. G. Netemeyer, C. M. Heilman, and J. G. Maxham III, "Identification with the Retail Organization and Customer-Perceived Employee Similarity: Effects on Customer Spending," *Journal of Applied Psychology,* September 2012, 1049–1058.

42. See "Catalyst Quick Take: Women's Earnings and Income," *Catalyst,* New York, 2013, http://www.catalyst.org/knowledge/womens-earnings-and-income; A. Damast, "She Works Hard for Less Money," *Bloomberg Businessweek,* December 24, 2012–January 6, 2013, 31–32; and S. Datta, A. Guha, and M. Iskandar-Datta, "Ending the Wage Gap," *Harvard Business Review,* May 2013, 30.

43. C. McCain Nelson, "Poll: Most Women See Bias in the Workplace," *The Wall Street Journal,* April 12, 2013, A4.

44. See A. H. Eagly and L. L. Carli, *Through the Labyrinth* (Boston: Harvard Business School Press, 2007).

45. See "Number of Fortune 500 Women CEOs Reaches Historic High," June 3, 2014, http://fortune.com/2014/06/03/number-of-fortune-500-women-ceos-reaches-hostoric-high/; and "Women EOs of the Fortune 1000," June 10, 2014, http://www.catalyst.org/knowledge/women-ceos-fortune-1000.

46. See "Educational Attainment," http://www.census.gov/hhes/socdemo/education/data/cps/2012/tables.html, last revised January 2013; "Women in the Board Room and in the President's Office: What Differences Does It Make?," http://www.agb.org/events/annual-meeting/2011/2011-agb-national-conference-trustreeship/sessions/women-board-room-and-pr, accessed December 29, 2010; and "Women in the Federal Judiciary: Still a Long Way to Go," http://www.nwlc.org/resource/women-federal-judiciary-still-long-way-to-1, April 26, 2013.

47. Eagly and Carli, *Through the Labyrinth,* 26–27. Emphasis added.

48. "U.S. Census Bureau Projections Show a Slower Growing, Older, More Diverse Nation a Half Century from Now," U.S. Census Bureau Press Release, December 12, 2012, https://www.census.gov/newsroom/releases/archives/population/cb12-243.html.

49. Meckler, "Hispanic Future in the Cards."

50. Bureau of Labor Statistics, U.S. Department of Labor, *The Editor's Desk,* "Earnings and Employment by Occupation, Race, Ethnicity, and Sex, 2010," http://www.bls.gov/opub/ted/2011/ted_20110914.htm, accessed May 17, 2013.

51. See U.S. Equal Employment Opportunity Commission, "Race-Based Charges FY 1997–FY 2013," http://www.eeoc.gov/eeoc/statistics/enforcement/race.cfm, accessed June 25, 2014.

52. Bureau of Labor Statistics, "Earnings and Employment by Occupation, Race, Ethnicity, and Sex, 2010."

53. U.S. Bureau of Labor Statistics, "Table A-4. Employment Status of the Civilian Population 25 Years and over by Educational Attainment," http://www.bls.gov/news.release/empsit.t04.htm, last modified November 8, 2013; and "Earnings and Unemployment Rates by Educational Attainment," Current Population Survey, http://www.bls.gov/emp/ep_table_001.htm, last modified May 22, 2013. Includes persons with bachelor's, master's, professional, and doctoral degrees.

54. See L. Freifeld, "Bridging the Skills Gap," *Training,* March/April 2013, 16–21; and "Illiteracy Statistics," U.S. Department of Education, National Institute of Literacy, http://www.statisticbrain.com/number-of-american-adults-who-cant-read/, April 28, 2013.

55. "Facts on Literacy," *National Literacy Facts,* August 27, 1998, http://www.svs.net/wpci/Litfacts.htm (this posting on http://www.svs.net/wpci/Litfacts.htm is no longer extant); "Workplace Literacy Facts," http://wplrc.losrios.edu/pagem111300.html.

56. G. P. Shultz and E. A. Hanushek, "Education Is the Key to a Healthy Economy," *The Wall Street Journal,* May 11, 2012, A15.

57. See S. Childress, "Rethinking School," *Harvard Business Review,* March 2012, 77–79; and D. Wessel and S. Banchero, "Education Slowdown Threatens U.S.," *The Wall Street Journal,* April 26, 2012, A1, A12.

58. Wessel and Banchero, "Education Slowdown Threatens U.S."

59. "Remarks of President Barack Obama—As Prepared for Delivery, Address to Joint Session of Congress Tuesday, February 24, 2009," http://www.whitehouse.gov/the_press_office/Remarks-of-President-Barack-Obama-Address-to-Joint-Session-of-Congress.

60. See "Registered Apprenticeship National Results Fiscal Year 2013," U.S. Department of Labor, http://www.doleta.gov/oa/data_statistics/cfm, accessed June 25, 2014.

61. Freifeld, "Bridging the Skills Gap."

62. Childress, "Rethinking School."

63. For a review of generational research, see S. Lyons and L. Kuron, "Generational Differences in the Workplace: A Review of the Evidence and Directions for Future Research," *Journal of Organizational Behavior,* February 2014, 139–57.

64. These barriers were taken from discussions in M. Loden, *Implementing Diversity* (New York: McGraw-Hill, 1995); E. E. Spragins, "Benchmark: The Diverse Work Force," *Inc.,* January 1993, 33; and Morrison, *The New Leaders.*

65. C. T. Kuli and M. Olekalns, "Negotiating the Gender Divide: Lessons from the Negotiation and Organizational Behavior Literatures," *Journal of Management,* July 2012, 1387–1415.

66. Ibid.

67. J. A. Gonzalez and A. DeNisi, "Cross-Level Effects of Demography and Diversity Climate on Organizational Attachment and Firm Effectiveness," *Journal of Organizational Behavior,* January 2009, 24.

68. See B. Singh, D. E. Winkel, and T. T. Selvarajan, "Managing Diversity at Work: Does Psychological Safety Hold the Key to Racial Differences in Employee Performance?" *Journal of Occupational and Organizational Psychology,* June 2013, 242–263; A. Groggins and A. M. Ryan, "Embracing Uniqueness: The Underpinnings of a Positive Climate for Diversity," *Journal of Occupational and Organizational Psychology,* June 2013, 264–282; and E. H. Buttner, K. B. Lowe, and L. Billings-Harris, "An Empirical Test of Diversity Climate Dimensionality and Relative Effects on Employee of Color Outcomes," *Journal of Business Ethics,* 2012, 247–258.

69. Hebl and Avery, "Diversity in Organizations."

70. See J. S. Lublin, "To Climb the Ladder, Try Joining a Group," *The Wall Street Journal,* December 26, 2012, B6; and M. Moskowitz and R. Levering, "The 100 Best Companies to Work For," *Fortune,* February 4, 2013.

71. G. Colvin, "Lafley and Immelt: In Search of Billions," *Fortune,* December 11, 2006, 70–72.

72. This discussion is based on R. R. Thomas Jr., *Redefining Diversity* (New York: AMACOM, 1996).

73. D. J. Gaiter, "Eating Crow: How Shoney's, Belted by a Lawsuit, Found the Path to Diversity," *The Wall Street Journal,* April 16, 1996, A1, A11.

74. E. Friedman, "Jury Finds Novartis Liable for Female Employee Discrimination Complaints," *ABC News,* May 18, 2010, http://abcnews.go.com/Business/novartis-pharmaceuticals-corp-found-guilty-gender-discrimination/story?id=10678178.

75. T. Roth, "$152.5 Million Settlement in Novartis Gender Discrimination Suit," *Findlaw.com,* July 15, 2010, http://blogs.findlaw.com/decided/2010/07/1525-million-settlement-in-novartis-gender-discrimination-suit.html.

76. Gaiter, "Eating Crow."

77. K. Gurchiek, "Options for Older Workers," *HR Magazine,* June 2012, 18.

78. See Z. T. Kalinoski, D. Steele-Johnson, E. J. Peyton, K. A. Leas, J. Steinke, and N. A. Bowling, "A Meta-Analytic Evaluation of Diversity Training Outcomes," *Journal of Organizational Behavior,* November 2013, 1076–1104.

79. G. J. Gates, "How Many People Are Lesbian, Gay, Bisexual, and Transgender?" http://:williamsinstitute.law.ucla.edu/wp-content/uploads/Gates-How-Many-People-LGBT-Apr-2011.pdf, April 2011.

80. E. Margolin, "The Fight for ENDA: Think You Can't Be Fired for Being Gay? Think Again," *MSNBC,* April 25, 2013, http://www.msnbc.com/thomas-roberts/the-fight-enda-think-you-cant-be-fired. See also N. Wing, "It's 2013, and It's Still Perfectly Legal to

Fire Somebody for Being Gay," *Huffington Post,* August 16, 2013, http://www.huffingtonpost.com/2013/08/16/enda-gay-discrimination_n_3767043.html.

81. These examples can be found in M. Moskowitz, R. Levering, and C. Tkaczyk, "100 Best Companies to Work For," *Fortune,* February 8, 2010, 75–88.

82. S. J. Wells, "Say Hola! to the Majority Minority," *HR Magazine,* September 2008, 38.

83. See L. Kwoh, "McKinsey Tries to Recruit Mothers Who Left the Field," *The Wall Street Journal,* February 20, 2013, B1, B8; and J. Schramm, "On-Ramps Lead Back to Work," *HR Magazine,* September 2012, 120.

84. S. Boehle, "Voices of Opportunity," *Training,* January 2009, 39.

85. JPMorgan Chase & Co., "JPMorgan Chase & Co. Announces Expansion of Intensive Academic Program for Young Men of Color in New York, Chicago, and Los Angeles," June 25, 2014, http://finance.yahoo.com/news/jpmorgan-chase-co-announces-expansion-130000315.html.

86. See S. Harris, "Drilling Down into the Skills Gap," *Training,* March/April 2013, 22–23; and B. Mirza, "Build Employee Skills, Help Nonprofits," *HR Magazine,* October 2008, 30.

87. G. M. McEvoy and M. J. Blahana, "Engagement or Disengagement? Older Workers and the Looming Labor Shortage," *Business Horizons,* September–October 2001, 50.

88. "Best Employers for Workers over 50 Winners," *AARP,* June 2013, http://www.aarp.org/work/on-the-job/info-06-2013/aarp-best-employers-winners-2013.html.

89. "Sodexo: No. 1 in the DiversityInc Top 50," http://www.diversityinc.com/sodexo/, accessed May 16, 2013.

90. "Introspection after Allegations of Discrimination," *NPR.org,* January 12, 2010, http://www.npr.org/templates/story/story.php?storyId=122456071.

91. "Sodexo," *Sourcewatch,* The Center for Media and Democracy, accessed December 7, 2013, http://www.sourcewatch.org/index.php/Sodexo#Consistent_Pattern_of_Denying_Worker_Rights.

92. E. Bruske, "Sodexo to Pay New York $20 Million for School-Meal Rebate Fraud," *Grist.org,* July 22, 2010, http://grist.org/article/food-sodexo-to-pay-new-york-20-million-for-fraud/.

93. Chanel Hill, "Wet Seal Employee Files Bias Suit," *Philadelphia Tribune,* July 16, 2012. Unless otherwise noted, quotations in this Problem-Solving Application Case are from the Hill article.

94. "Cogdell v. Wet Seal," *LDF News,* July 12, 2012, http://www.naacpldf.org/case-issue/cogdell-v-wet-seal.

95. Ibid.

96. Hill, "Wet Seal Employee Files Bias Suit."

97. A. Veiga, "Wet Seal Workers Sue Retailer for Racial Discrimination," *Huffington Post,* July 12, 2012.

98. S. H. Lewis, "Determination of the U.S. Equal Employment Opportunity Commission," Charge Number 530-2009-01834, November 26, 2011. Lewis is director of the Philadelphia District Office of the EEOC.

99. "Cogdell v. Wet Seal."

100. Lewis, "Determination of the U.S. Equal Employment Opportunity Commission."

101. R. Erb, "Hospital Settles Nurse's Discrimination Suit," *USA Today,* February 22, 2013, http://www.usatoday.com/story/news/nation/2013/02/22/hospital-settles-discrimination-suit/1940575/.

102. R. Erb, "Nurse Sues Hospital over Racial Request," *The Arizona Republic,* February 19, 2013, A2.

103. J. Karoub, "Hospitals Often Appease Bigotry," *The Arizona Republic,* February 24, 2013, D1, D3.

Chapter 5

1. L. Weber and R. E. Silverman, "Workers Share Their Salary Secrets," *The Wall Street Journal,* April 17, 2013, B1, B8.

2. Ibid.

3. R. E. Silverman, "Psst . . . This Is What Your Co-Worker Is Paid," *The Wall Street Journal,* January 30, 2013, B6.

4. See W. Schnotz, "Federal Laws for Employees' Right to Share Salary Information," *Houston Chronicle,* http://smallbusiness.chron.com/federal-laws-employees-right-share-salary-information-other-employees-12899.html, accessed May 21, 2013; and Weber and Silverman, "Workers Share Their Salary Secrets."

5. M. Moskowitz and R. Levering, "The 100 Best Companies to Work For," *Fortune,* February 4, 2013, 87.

6. A. M. Schmidt, J. W. Beck, and J. Z. Gillespie, "Motivation," in N. W. Schmitt and S. Highhouse, eds., *Handbook of Psychology* (vol. 12) (Hoboken, NJ: John Wiley & Sons, 2013), 311.

7. Ibid.

8. J. R. Hackman, G. R. Oldham, R. Janson, and K. Purdy, "A New Strategy for Job Enrichment," *California Management Review,* Summer 1975, 58.

9. A. Nyberg, "Retaining Your High Performers: Moderators of the Performance–Job Satisfaction–Voluntary Turnover Relationship," *Journal of Applied Psychology,* May 2010, 440–453.

10. "2012 Trends in Global Employee Engagement," Aon Hewitt (London, England: 2012), 23, http://www.aon.com/attachments/human-capital-consulting/2012_TrendsInGlobalEngagement_Final_v11.pdf.

11. A review of content and process theories of motivation is provided by "Motivation in Today's Workplace: The Link to Performance," *Research Quarterly* (Society for Human Resource Management), Second Quarter 2010, 1–9.

12. See D. McGregor, *The Human Side of Enterprise* (New York: McGraw-Hill, 1960).

13. See D. Thomas and R. Bostrom, "Building Trust and Cooperation through Technology Adaptation in Virtual Teams: Empirical Field Evidence," *Information Systems Management,* 2010, 45–56. For evidence related to measuring and using theory X and theory Y, see R. Kopelman, D. Prottas, and A. L. Davis, "Douglas McGregor's Theory X and Y: Toward a Construct-Valid Measure," *Journal of Managerial Issues,* Summer 2008, 255–271.

14. For a complete description of Maslow's theory, see A. H. Maslow, "A Theory of Human Motivation," *Psychological Review,* July 1943, 370–396.

15. C. Conley, *How Great Companies Get Their Mojo from Maslow* (San Francisco: Jossey-Bass, 2007).

16. Moskowitz and Levering, "The 100 Best Companies to Work For," 90.

17. See A. Hood, "Grow the Young Workforce," *The Arizona Republic,* May 5, 2013, CL1; and D. Facer, "Motivation Misunderstanding," *Training,* July/August 2012, 26–28.

18. D. C. McClelland, *Human Motivation* (New York: Guilford Press, 1985).

19. Some of these recommendations are based on "McClelland's Human Motivation Theory," *Mind Tools,* http://www.mindtools.com/pages/article/human-motivation-theory.htm, accessed May 22, 2013.

20. Moskowitz and Levering, "The 100 Best Companies to Work For," 92.

21. J. Fahed-Sreih and S. Morin-Delerm, "A Perspective on Leadership in Small Businesses: Is the Need for Achievement a Motive in Predicting Success," *International Journal of Entrepreneurship,* 2012, 1–23.

22. S. W. Spreier, M. H. Fontaine, and R. L. Malloy, "Leadership Run Amok," *Harvard Business Review,* June 2006, 72–82.

23. W. H. Decker, T. J. Calo, and C. H. Weer, "Affiliation Motivation and Interests in Entrepreneurial Careers," *Journal of Managerial Psychology,* 2012, 302–320.

24. R. M. Ryan and E. L. Deci, "Self-Determination Theory and the Facilitation of Intrinsic Motivation, Social Development, and Well-Being," *American Psychologist,* January 2000, 68–78.

25. E. L. Deci, R. Koestner, and R. M. Ryan, "A Meta-Analytic Review of Experiments Examining the Effects of Extrinsic Rewards on Intrinsic Motivation," *Psychological Bulletin,* November 1999, 627–668.

26. R. A. Kusurkar, T. J. Ten Cate, C. M. P. Vos, P. Westers, and G. Croisset, "How Motivation Affects Academic Performance: A Structural Equation Modelling Analysis," *Advances in Health Science Education,* March 2013, 57–69; and C. M. Moran, J. M. Diefendorff, T.-Y. Kim, and Z.-Q. Liu, "A Profile Approach to Self-Determination Theory Motivations at Work," *Journal of Vocational Behavior,* December 2012, 354–363.

27. Moskowitz and Levering, "The 100 Best Companies to Work For," 87.

28. R. J. Grossma, "Phasing Out Face Time," *HRMagazine,* April 2013, 33–34.

29. Moskowitz and Levering, "The 100 Best Companies to Work For," 90.

30. "Go Further, Faster with NetApp—Our Story," *NetApp.com,* http://www.netapp.com/us/company/our-story/, accessed May 22, 2013.

31. Abstracted from interview with CEO Bert Jacobs by L. Kwoh, "How a Tavern Makes a Healthy, Happy Office," *The Wall Street Journal,* May 14, 2013, D4.

32. F. Herzberg, B. Mausner, and B. B. Snyderman, *The Motivation to Work* (New York: John Wiley & Sons, 1959).

33. F. Herzberg, "One More Time: How Do You Motivate Employees?" *Harvard Business Review,* January–February 1968, 56.

34. Moskowitz and Levering, "The 100 Best Companies to Work For," 88.

35. R. G. Satter and J. Lawless, "WikiLeaks Supporters Protest via Cyberattacks," *The Arizona Republic,* December 10, 2010, A15.

36. Moskowitz and Levering, "The 100 Best Companies to Work For," 92.

37. P. Bamberger and E. Belogolovsky, "The Impact of Pay Secrecy on Individual Task Performance," *Personnel Psychology,* Winter 2010, 965–996; and M. C. Bolino and W. H. Turnley, "Old Faces, New Places: Equity Theory in Cross-Cultural Contexts," *Journal of Organizational Behavior,* January 2008, 29–50.

38. For a thorough review of organizational justice theory and research, see R. Cropanzano, D. E. Rupp, C. J. Mohler, and M. Schminke, "Three Roads to Organizational Justice," in G. R. Ferris, ed., *Research in Personnel and Human Resources Management* (vol. 20) (New York: JAI Press, 2001), 269–329.

39. J. A. Colquitt, D. E. Conlon, M. J. Wesson, C. O. L. H. Porter, and K. Y. Ng, "Justice at the Millennium: A Meta-Analytic Review of 25 Years of Organizational Justice Research," *Journal of Applied Psychology,* June 2001, 426.

40. D. Jacobe, "Half of Americans Say They Are Underpaid," Gallup Organization, August 18, 2008, http://www.gallup.com/poll/109618/Half-Americans-Say-They-Underpaid.aspx.

41. A. Lucchetti and B. Philbin, "Bankers Get IOUs Instead of Bonus Cash," *The Wall Street Journal,* January 16, 2013, A1.

42. S. Tangirala and R. Ramanujam, "Ask and You Shall Hear (but Not Always): Examining the Relationship Between Manager Consultation and Employee Voice," *Personnel Psychology,* 2012, 251–252.

43. E. R. Burris, "The Risks and Rewards of Speaking Up: Managerial Responses to Employee Voice," *Academy of Management Journal,* August 2012, 851–875.

44. D. Cote, "Honeywell's CEO on How He Avoided Layoffs," *Harvard Business Review,* June 2013, 43–46.

45. D. S. Whitman, S. Caleo, N. C. Carpenter, M. T. Horner, and J. B. Bernerth, "Fairness at the Collective Level: A Meta-Analytic Examination of the Consequences and Boundary Conditions of Organizational Justice Climate," *Journal of Applied Psychology,* July 2012, 776–791.

46. Schmidt, Beck, and Gillespie, "Motivation."

47. Moskowitz and Levering, "The 100 Best Companies to Work For," 96.

48. Z. R. Mider and J. Green, "Heads or Tails, Some CEOs Win the Pay Game," *Bloomberg Businessweek,* October 8–14, 2012, 23–24.

49. P. K. Tyagi, "Expectancy Theory and Social Loafing in Marketing Research Group Projects," *The Business Review,* Summer 2010, 22–27.

50. C. Creno, "Program Helps Students Succeed," *The Arizona Republic,* November 27, 2012, B2.

51. G. H. Seijts and G. P. Latham, "Knowing When to Set Learning versus Performance Goals," *Organizational Dynamics,* 2012, 1–6.

52. Ibid.; and E. A. Locke and G. P. Latham, "Building a Practically Useful Theory of Goal Setting and Task Motivation," *American Psychologist,* September 2002, 705–717.

53. D. Meinert, "An Open Book," *HRMagazine,* April 2013, 46.

54. The case of multiple goals is discussed by J. B. Vancouver, J. M. Weinhardt, and A. M. Schmidt, "A Formal, Computational Theory of Multiple-Goal Pursuit: Integrating Goal-Choice and Goal-Striving Processes," *Journal of Applied Psychology,* November 2010, 985–1008.

55. Moskowitz and Levering, "The 100 Best Companies to Work For," 90.

56. R. Weiss and B. Kammel, "How Siemens Got Its Geist Back," *Bloomberg Businessweek,* January 31–February 6, 2011, 18–20.

57. A. Fox, "Put Plans into Action," *HRMagazine,* April 2013, 27–31.

58. M. Frese, S. I. Krauss, N. Keith, S. Escher, R. Grabarkiewicz, S. T. Luneng, C. Heers, J. Unger, and C. Friedrich, "Business Owners' Action Planning and Its Relationship to Business Success in Three African Countries," *Journal of Applied Psychology,* November 2007, 1481–1498.

59. J. L. Bowditch and A. F. Buono, *A Primer on Organizational Behavior* (New York: John Wiley & Sons, 1985), 210.

60. A review of these approaches is provided by S. Hornung, D. M. Rousseau, J. Glaser, P. Angerer, and M. Weigl, "Beyond Top-Down and Bottom-Up Work Redesign: Customizing Job Content through Idiosyncratic Deals," *Journal of Organizational Behavior,* February 2010, 187–215; and G. R. Oldham and J. R. Hackman, "Not What It Was and Not What It Will Be: The Future of Job Design," *Journal of Organizational Behavior,* February 2010, 463–479.

61. G. D. Babcock and R. Trautschold, *The Taylor System in Franklin Management,* 2nd ed. (New York: Engineering Magazine Company, 1917), 31.

62. See the related discussion in S. Wagner-Tsukamoto, "An Institutional Economic Reconstruction of Scientific Management: On the Lost Theoretical Logic of Taylorism," *Academy of Management Review,* January 2007, 105–117; and P. R. Lawrence, "The Key Job Design Problem Is Still Taylorism," *Journal of Organizational Behavior,* February 2010, 412–421.

63. This type of program was developed and tested by M. A. Campion and C. L. McClelland, "Follow-Up and Extension of the Interdisciplinary Costs and Benefits of Enlarged Jobs," *Journal of Applied Psychology,* June 1993, 339–351.

64. J. Brunold and S. Durst, "Intellectual Capital Risks and Job Rotation," *Journal of Intellectual Capital,* 2012, 178–195.

65. J. Alsever, "Job Swaps: Are They for You?" *Fortune,* October 29, 2012, 47–48.

66. Moskowitz and Levering, "The 100 Best Companies to Work For," 88.

67. Definitions of the job characteristics were adapted from J. R. Hackman and G. R. Oldham, "Motivation through the Design of Work: Test of a Theory," *Organizational Behavior and Human Performance,* August 1976, 250–279.

68. S. E. Humphrey, J. D. Nahrgang, and F. P. Morgeson, "Integrating Motivational, Social, and Contextual Work Design Features: A Meta-Analytic Summary and Theoretical Extension of the Work Design Literature," *Journal of Applied Psychology,* September 2007, 1332–1356.

69. Ibid.

70. M. Moskowitz, R. Levering, and C. Tkaczyk, "1000 Best Companies to Work For," *Fortune,* February 7, 2011, 93.

71. Productivity studies are reviewed in R. E. Kopelman, *Managing Productivity in Organizations* (New York: McGraw-Hill, 1986).

72. A. Wrzesniewski and J. E. Dutton, "Crafting a Job: Revisioning Employees as Active Crafters of Their Work," *Academy of Management Review,* April 2001, 179.

73. P. Petrou, E. Demerouti, M. C. W. Peeters, W. B. Schaufeli, and J. Hetland, "Crafting a Job on a Daily Basis: Contextual Correlates and the Link to Work Engagement," *Journal of Organizational Behavior,* November 2012, 1120–1141.

74. Hornung, Rousseau, Glaser, Angerer, and Weigl, "Beyond Top-Down and Bottom-Up Work Redesign," 188.

75. C. C. Rosen, D. J. Slater, C.-H. Chang, and R. E. Johnson, "Let's Make a Deal: Development and Validation of the Ex Post I-Deals Scale," *Journal of Management,* March 2013, 709–742.

76. T. Hopke, "Go Ahead, Take a Few Months Off," *HRMagazine,* September 2010, 71–74.

77. Rosen, Slater, Chang, and Johnson, "Let's Make a Deal."

78. M. Kimes, "Caterpillar's Doug Oberhelman: Manufacturing's Mouthpiece," *Bloomberg Businessweek,* May 16, 2013, http://www.businessweek.com/articles/2013-05-16/caterpillars-doug-oberhelman-manufacturings-mouthpiece#rshare=email_article.

79. Ibid.

80. R. Kirchen, "'Just Crazy' . . . Former Bucyrus CEO Slams Caterpillar for Layoffs," *Milwaukee Business Journal,* June 18, 2013. See also B. Tita, "Wisconsin Caterpillar Workers Approve Contract with Company," *The Wall Street Journal,* June 12, 2013, B9, http://online.wsj.com/article/SB10001424127887323949904578539341459718214.html.

81. Kimes, "Caterpillar's Doug Oberhelman: Manufacturing's Mouthpiece."

82. Tita, "Wisconsin Caterpillar Workers Approve Contract with Company."

83. B. Tita, "Caterpillar Expected to Cut 2013 Forecasts," *The Wall Street Journal,* April 21, 2013, http://online.wsj.com/article/SB10001424127887323551004578436740377768474.html.

84. *Fortune* Brainstorm Podcast, "Caterpillar CEO Doug Oberhelman," May 24, 2013, hosted by S. DuBois, *Fortune* reporter, with senior editor M. Vella and writer N.-H. Tseng, http://money.cnn.com/2013/05/24/leadership/fortune-brainstorm-podcast-caterpillar-ceo.fortune/index.html.

85. *Glassdoor.com.* Comments were harvested from six months' worth of reviews covering the new contracts discussed in the article.

86. Kimes, "Caterpillar's Doug Oberhelman: Manufacturing's Mouthpiece."

87. U.S. Department of Commerce, Bureau of Economic Analysis, Table 1.1.1, Percent Change from "Preceding Period in Real Gross Domestic Product [Annual View]," last revised June 26, 2013, http://www.bea.gov/iTable/iTable.cfm?ReqID=9&step=1#reqid=9&step=3&isuri=1&910=X&911=0&903=1&904=2008&905=2013&906=A.

88. R. J. Vance, *Effective Practice Guidelines: Employee Engagement and Commitment* (Alexandria, Va.: SHRM Foundation, 2006).

89. *Fortune* Brainstorm Podcast, "Caterpillar CEO Doug Oberhelman."

90. This case was drawn from M. Spector and T. McGinty, "The CEO Bankruptcy Bonus," *The Wall Street Journal,* January 27, 2012, A1, A12.

Chapter 6

1. Adapted from J. A. Johnson, "Bad Performance Review? Don't Lose Your Cool," *The Arizona Republic,* August 22, 2010.

2. Adapted from A. J. Kinicki, K. J. L. Jacobson, S. J. Peterson, and G. E. Prussia, "Development and Validation of the Performance Management Behavior Questionnaire," *Personnel Psychology,* 2013, 1–45.

3. H. Aguinis, H. Joo, and R. K. Gottfredson, "What Monetary Rewards Can and Cannot Do: How to Show Employees the Money," *Business Horizons,* 2013, 241–249.

4. E. D. Pulakos, R. A. Mueller-Hanson, R. S. O'Leary, and M. M. Meyrowitz, "Building a High-Performance Culture: A Fresh Look at Performance Management," *SHRM Foundations Effective Practice Guidelines Series,* July 24, 2012.

5. *The High Cost of Doing Nothing: Quantifying the Impact of Leadership on the Bottom Line* (Escondido, CA: Ken Blanchard Companies, 2009).

6. K. Gurchiek, "We're Looking at Performance Management in the Wrong Way," *SHRM online,* http://www.shrm.org/hrdisciplines/employeerelations/articles/pages/performance-management-wrong.aspx, accessed April 18, 2013.

7. W. F. Cascio, "Global Performance Management Systems," in I. Bjorkman and G. Stahl, eds., *Handbook of Research in International Human Resources Management* (London, UK: Edward Elgar Ltd., 2006), 176–196. See also E. D. Pulakos, *Performance Management: A New Approach for Driving Business Results* (West Sussex, UK: Wiley-Blackwell, 2009).

8. J. Light, "Human Resource Executives Say Reviews Are Off Mark," *The Wall Street Journal,* November 7, 2010.

9. A. Fox, "Curing What Ails Performance Reviews," *SHRM Special Report,* http://www.shrm.org/Publications/hrmagazine/EditorialContent/Pages/0109fox.aspx, accessed April 18, 2013.

10. Pulakos, *Performance Management,* 4.

11. J. Gruss, "Burger Hustle," *Business Observer,* November 2, 2012. See also T. Monaghan and R. Anderson, *Pizza Tiger* (New York: Random House, 1996).

12. S. C. Johnson, press release, February, 28, 2013, https://www.scjohnson.com/en/press-room/press-releases/02-28-2013/SC-Johnson-Awarded-Goal-Setting-Certificate-by-EPA%E2%80%99s-Climate-Leadership-Program.aspx, accessed April 19, 2013.

13. Ibid.

14. H. E. Marano, "The Goals That Guide Us," *Psychology Today,* November 11, 2010.

15. Adapted and quoted from "ThermoSTAT," *Training,* July–August 2003, 16.

16. Marano, "The Goals That Guide Us."

17. G. H. Seijts and G. P. Latham, "Knowing When to Set Learning Versus Performance Goals," *Organizational Dynamics 40*(1), January–March 2012, 1–6.

18. D. Morisano, J. B. Hirsh, J. B. Peterson, R. O. Pihl, and B. M. Shore, "Setting, Elaborating, and Reflecting on Personal Goals Improves Academic Performance," *Journal of Applied Psychology,* March 2010, 255.

19. See E. A. Locke, "Linking Goals to Monetary Incentives," *Academy of Management Executive,* November 2004, 130–133.

20. Adapted from Marano, "The Goals That Guide Us."

21. T. Sitzmann and S. K. Johnson, "The Best Laid Plans: Examining the Condition under Which a Planning Intervention Improves Learning and Reduces Attrition," *Journal of Applied Psychology,* September 2012, 967–981.

22. J. Cresswell and R. Abelson. "Hospital Chain Said to Scheme to Inflate Bills," *The New York Times,* January 23, 2014.

23. E. D. Pulakos, *Performance Management: A New Approach for Driving Business Results* (Malden, MA: Wiley-Blackwell, 2009).

24. A. Bryant, "He's Not Bill Gates, or Fred Astaire," *The New York Times,* February 14, 2010.

25. As quoted in A. D. Innocenzio and R. Beck, "AP Interview: Wal-Mart CEO Talks Leadership, Life," *Associated Press,* February 6, 2011.

26. K. Tyler, "One Bad Apple," *HR Magazine,* December 2004, 85. Data taken from "Managers Are Ignoring Their Employees," *LeadershipIQ,* December 2, 2009.

27. C. D. Lee, "Feedback, Not Appraisal," *HR Magazine,* November 2006, 111.

28. J. Boomer, "Accountability—The Key to Firm Success," *CPAPracticeAdvisor.com,* January 2013, http://www.cpapracticeadvisor.com/article/10831608/accountability-the-key-to-firm-success, accessed April 20, 2013.

29. D. Debow, "When You're the Boss, Who Gives You Reviews?," *Fortune,* December 22, 2010.

30. M. Moskowitz and R. Levering, "The 100 Best Companies to Work For," *Fortune,* February 4, 2013, 87.

31. Pulakos, *Performance Management,* 15.

32. Ibid.

33. R. Maurer, "Using Exit Interviews to Prevent Disaster," *SHRM online,* April 5, 2013, http://www.shrm.org/hrdisciplines/safetysecurity/articles/Pages/Exit-Interviews-Prevent-Disaster.aspx, accessed April 24, 2013.

34. For complete details, see P. M. Podsakoff and J.-L. Farh, "Effects of Feedback Sign and Credibility on Goal Setting and Task Performance," *Organizational Behavior and Human Decision Processes,* August 1989, 45–67.

35. A. J. Kinicki, G. E. Prussia, B. Wu, and F. M. McKee-Ryan, "A Covariance Structure Analysis of Employees' Response to Performance Feedback," *Journal of Applied Psychology,* 2004, 1057–1069.

36. W. S. Silver, T. R. Mitchell, and M. E. Gist, "Responses to Successful and Unsuccessful Performance: The Moderating Effect of Self-Efficacy on the Relationship between Performance and Attributions," *Organizational Behavior and Human Decision Processes,* June 1995, 297.

37. Adapted from C. Bell and R. Zemke, "On-Target Feedback," *Training,* June 1992, 36–44. A model feedback program is discussed by M. Weinstein, "Leadership Leader," *Training,* February 2008, 41–46.

38. For a comprehensive collection of articles and research related to feedback, see "Guide to Giving Effective Feedback," *Harvard Business Review,* February 9, 2011.

39. L. E. Atwater, J. F. Brett, and A. C. Charles, "The Delivery of Workplace Discipline: Lessons Learned," *Organizational Dynamics,* 2007, 392–403.

40. "Friendly Feedback," *Training,* May 2007, 11.

41. "What Is Coaching?," *ASTD Publications,* December 4, 2009, http://www.astd.org/Publications/Newsletters/ASTD-Links/ASTD-Links-Articles/2009/12/What-Is-Coaching, accessed April 15, 2013.

42. M. Wayland, "Providing Positive Feedback to Your Sales Stars," *ASTD Publications,* August 17, 2012, http://www.astd.org/Publications/Blogs/Sales-Enablement-Blog/2012/08/Providing-Positive-Feedback-to-Your-Sales-Stars, accessed April 22, 2013.

43. "Coaching in a Business Environment," *SHRM Templates,* March 21, 2013.

44. See D. Brady, "Hard Choices: Joe Torre," *Bloomberg Businessweek,* June 21–27, 2010, 96; J. Shambora, "From Leverage to Corkage," *Fortune,* December 6, 2010, 80; and K. Nicholas, "Where the Wild Things Are," *Bloomberg Businessweek,* January 17–23, 2011, 74.

45. Adapted from M. Von Glinow, "Reward Strategies for Attracting, Evaluating, and Retaining Professionals," *Human Resource Management,* Summer 1985, 193.

46. L. Gannes, "Andreessen and Mixpanel Call for an End to 'Bullshit Metrics,'" *All Things D,* December 17, 2012, http://allthingsd.com/20121217/andreessen-and-mixpanel-call-for-an-end-to-bullshit-metrics/, accessed April 12, 2013.

47. R. Levering and M. Moskowitz, "100 Best Companies to Work For: And the Winners Are . . . ," *Fortune,* February 2, 2009, 67–78.

48. C. Weaver, "Treatment Woes Can Bolster Hospital's Profit," *The Wall Street Journal,* April 16, 2013.

49. For example, see B. Nelson, *1001 Ways to Reward Employees,* 2nd ed. (New York: Workman Publishing, 2005).

50. Excerpted and adapted from R. L. Heneman and E. E. Coyne, "Implementing Total Rewards Strategies," *Society for Human Resource Management,* October 21, 2010, http://www.shrm.org/about/foundation/products/Pages/ImplementingTotalRewards.aspx.

51. M. Dewhurst, M. Guthridge, and E. Mohr, "Motivating People: Getting Beyond Money," *McKinsey Quarterly,* November 2009, 2.

52. Ibid.

53. Excerpted from "How Effective Is Incentive Pay?," *HR Magazine,* January 2008, 12.

54. S. Miller, "Satisfaction with Pay, Benefits Falling," *HR Magazine,* January 2007, 38–39; and C. Palmeri, "Workers Say: 'We Want an Upgrade,'" *BusinessWeek,* April 16, 2007, 11.

55. J. M. Minami and M. M. May, "3rd Circuit: Employees Who Received Flat-Rate Payments Tied to Sales Are Exempt," *Society of Human Resource Management,* September 24, 2010, http://www.shrm.org/LegalIssues/FederalResources/Pages/3rdFlatRatePayments.aspx.

56. Aguinis, Joo, and Gottfredson, "What Monetary Rewards Can and Cannot Do," 242.

57. For details, see G. D. Jenkins Jr., N. Gupta, A. Mitra, and J. D. Shaw, "Are Financial Incentives Related to Performance? A Meta-Analytic Review of Empirical Research," *Journal of Applied Psychology,* October 1998, 777–787.

58. L. A. Bebchuk and J. M. Fried, "Pay without Performance: Overview of the Issues," *Academy of Management Perspectives,* February 2006, 5–24.

59. Excerpted and adapted from S. Miller, "Study: Keys to Effective Performance Pay," *Society for Human Resource Management,* December 15, 2010.

60. See E. L. Thorndike, *Educational Psychology: The Psychology of Learning,* vol. II (New York: Columbia University Teachers College, 1913).

61. For more recent discussion, see J. W. Donahoe, "The Unconventional Wisdom of B. F. Skinner: The Analysis-Interpretation Distinction," *Journal of the Experimental Analysis of Behavior,* September 1993, 453–456.

62. See B. F. Skinner, *The Behavior of Organisms* (New York: Appleton-Century-Crofts, 1938).

63. For modern approaches to respondent behavior, see B. Azar, "Classical Conditioning Could Link Disorders and Brain Dysfunction, Researchers Suggest," *APA Monitor,* March 1999, 17.

64. For interesting discussions of Skinner and one of his students, see M. B. Gilbert and T. F. Gilbert, "What Skinner Gave Us," *Training,* September 1991, 42–48.

65. G. C. Hazan and D. Mattioli, "BP Links Pay to Safety in Fourth Quarter," *The Wall Street Journal,* October 19, 2010.

66. W. Neuman, "Flights at JFK Sit on Tarmac for Hours," *The New York Times,* December 29, 2010.

67. G. Strauss, "Carnival CEO's Compensation Drops," *USA Today,* March 8, 2013, 6B.

68. "Workers' Health Habits Have Growing Effect on Premiums," *Dallas Morning News,* April 18, 2013.

69. Adapted from J. Jargon, "McDonald's Says 'Service Is Broken,' Tries a Fix," *The Wall Street Journal,* April 11, 2013, B1, and at http://online.wsj.com/article/SB10001424127887324010704578414901710175648.html.

70. Ibid.

71. R. Brownell, "McDonald's Makes Point of Repairing Its Service Issues in Public," *PRNews,* November 15, 2013, http://www.prnewsonline.com/water-cooler/2013/11/15/mcdonalds-a-mini-case-study-in-effective-communications/.

72. S. Oches, "Special Report: The Drive-Thru Performance Study," *QSR Magazine,* October 2013, http://www.qsrmagazine.com/reports/drive-thru-performance-study.

73. J. Jargon, "McDonald's Acknowledges Service Has Suffered," *The Wall Street Journal,* November 14, 2013, http://online.wsj.com/

news/articles/SB1000142405270230378960457919843249969 9844. See also S. Berfeld, "McDonald's Admits It Has a 'Customer Relevance' Problem," *Bloomberg Businessweek,* January 23, 2014, http://www.businessweek.com/articles/2014-01-23/mcdonalds-admits-it-has-a-customer-relevance-problem.

74. Jargon, "McDonald's Says. . . ." See also A. Lutz, "McDonald's Customer Service Has Never Been Worse," *Business Insider,* October 2, 2013, http://www.businessinsider.com/mcdonalds-needs-better-customer-service-2013-10; and A. Hartung, "Will the Living Wage Trend Kill or Make McDonald's and Walmart?," *Forbes,* August 1, 2013, http://www.forbes.com/sites/adamhartung/2013/08/01/will-the-living-wage-trend-kill-or-make-mcdonalds-and-walmart/.

75. L. Moyer, S. Russolillo, and P. McGee, "Goldman Awards Stock Ahead of Tax Rise," *The Wall Street Journal,* January 2, 2013.

Chapter 7

1. G. James, "9 Daily Habits That Will Make You Happier," *Inc. Magazine,* November 5, 2012.

2. K. S. Cameron, J. E. Dutton, and R. E. Quinn, *Positive Organizational Scholarship: Foundations of a New Discipline* (San Francisco, CA: Berrett-Koehler, 2003), 3–4.

3. Ibid., 4.

4. F. Luthans and B. J. Avolio, "The 'Point' of Positive Organizational Behavior," *Journal of Organizational Behavior,* 2009, 291–307.

5. See K. Cameron, C. Mora, T. Leutscher, and M. Calarco, "Effects of Positive Practices on Organizational Effectiveness," *The Journal of Applied Behavioral Science,* September 2011, 266–308; and R. Takeuchi, G. Chen, and D. Lepak, "Through the Looking Glass of a Social System: Cross-Level Effects of High-Performance Work Systems on Employees' Attitudes," *Personnel Psychology,* Spring 2009, 1–29.

6. B. L. Fredrickson, "Positive Emotions and Upward Spirals in Organizations," in Cameron, Dutton, and Quinn, *Positive Organizational Scholarship,* 163–175.

7. K. S. Cameron, D. Bright, and A. Caza, "Exploring the Relationships Between Organizational Virtuousness and Performance," *The American Behavioral Scientist,* February 2004, 766–790.

8. Cameron, Mora, Leutscher, and Calarco, "Effects of Positive Practices on Organizational Effectiveness," 288.

9. Ibid., as basis of discussion of the three effects.

10. G. Spreitzer and K. Cameron, "Applying the POS Lens to Bring out the Best in Organizations," *Organizational Dynamics,* 2012, 85–88.

11. G. Spreitzer and C. Porath, "Creating Sustained Performance," *Harvard Business Review,* January-February 2012, 3–9.

12. A. Bryant, "Three Good Hires? He'll Pay More for One Who's Great," *The New York Times,* March 13, 2010, http://www.nytimes.com/2010/03/14/business/14corners.html?pagewanted=all&_r=0, accessed April 1, 2013.

13. *NBC Nightly News,* "Food for Thought: An Actor's New Role in the Grocery Store," http://dailynightly.nbcnews.com/_news/2013/04/02/17571711-food-for-thought-an-actors-new-role-in-the-grocery-store.

14. J. Black, "In New Orleans, an Actor Turns Grocer," *The New York Times,* March 6, 2012, http://www.nytimes.com/2012/03/07/dining/wendell-pierce-to-open-a-grocery-store-in-new-orleans.html?pagewanted = all, accessed April 3, 2013.

15. *NBC Nightly News,* "Food for Thought."

16. S. S. Pillay and R. S. Sisodia, "A Case for Conscious Capitalism: Conscious Leadership through the Lens of the Brain," *Ivey Business Online,* September–October 2011, http://www.iveybusinessjournal.com/topics/leadership/a-case-for-conscious-capitalism-conscious-leadership-through-the-lens-of-brain-science#.UV7qUaMo670, accessed April 2, 2013.

17. Ibid.

18. J. Fox, "What Is It That Only I Can Do?" *Harvard Business Review,* January–February 2011, 3–7.

19. M. Moskowitz and R. Levering, "The 100 Best Companies to Work For," *Fortune,* February 4, 2013, 87.

20. J. Mackey and R. Sisodia, "Want to Hire Great People? Hire Consciously," *CNNMoney,* January 17, 2013, http://management.fortune.cnn.com/2013/01/17/best-companies-whole-foods-mackey/, accessed April 3, 2013.

21. Ibid.

22. B. L. Fredrickson, *Positivity* (New York: Three Rivers Press, 2009), 22.

23. Ibid.

24. S. Lyubomirsky, L. King, and E. Diener, "The Benefits of Frequent Positive Affect: Does Happiness Lead Success?" *Psychological Bulletin,* 2005, 803–855.

25. Fredrickson, *Positivity,* 70.

26. B. L. Fredrickson, "Updated Thinking on Positivity Ratios," *American Psychologist,* 2013, 814–822.

27. See D. Goleman, *Focus: The Hidden Driver of Excellence* (New York: Harper Collins, 2013).

28. Advice in this section comes from Fredrickson, *Positivity.*

29. Ibid.

30. For reviews, see O. Marianetti and J. Passmore, "Mindfulness at Work: Paying Attention to Enhance Well-Being and Performance," in P. A. Linley, S. Harrington, and N. Garcea, eds., *Oxford Handbook of Positive Psychology and Work* (New York: Oxford University Press, 2010), 189–200; and E. Dane, "Paying Attention to Mindfulness and Its Effects on Task Performance in the Workplace," *Journal of Management,* July 2011, 997–1018.

31. R. Ward and M. Martinez, "Man Accused of Slapping Crying Boy on Delta Flight Is Out of a Job," http://cpf.cleanprint.net/cpf/cpf?action=print&type=filePrint&key=cnn&url=http%3A%2F, February 18, 2013; "Man Accused of Slapping Baby on Flight Pleads Not Guilty," http://www.myfoxaltnata.com/story/21749757/man-accused-of-slapping-baby-on-flight-pl, March 27, 2013.

32. E. J. Langer, "Minding Matters: The Consequences of Mindlessness-Mindfulness," *Advances in Experimental Social Psychology,* 1989, 138.

33. K. W. Brown and R. M. Ryan, "The Benefits of Being Present: Mindfulness and Its Role in Psychological Well-Being," *Journal of Personality and Social Psychology,* 2003, 823.

34. E. J. Langer, "Minding Matters: The Consequences of Mindlessness-Mindfulness," *Advances in Experimental Social Psychology,* 1989, 137–173.

35. J. Kabat-Zinn, "Mindfulness-Based Interventions in Context: Past, Present, and Future," *Clinical Psychology: Science and Practice,* Summer 2003, 145.

36. J. Kabat-Zinn, *Wherever You Go There You Are* (New York: Hyperion, 1994).

37. D. Parker, "The Best Advice I Ever Got," *Fortune,* October 25, 2012, 120.

38. Abstracted from S. Shellenbarger, "At Work, Do Headphones Really Help?" *The Wall Street Journal,* May 29, 2012, D1, D4.

39. Ibid.

40. These inhibitors are discussed by B. A. Wallace and S. L. Shapiro, "Mental Balance and Well-Being," *American Psychologist,* October 2006, 690–701.

41. Dane, "Paying Attention to Mindfulness."

42. D. Gilbert, "The Science Behind the Smile," *Harvard Business Review,* January–February 2012, 85–90.

43. See Dane, "Paying Attention to Mindfulness"; see also Brown and Ryan, "The Benefits of Being Present."

44. U. R. Hülsheger, H. J. E. M. Alberts, A. Feinholdt, and J. W. B. Lang, "Benefits of Mindfulness at Work: The Role of Mindfulness in Emotion Regulation, Emotional Exhaustion, and Job Satisfaction," *Journal of Applied Psychology,* March 2013, 310–325.

45. His Holiness the Dalai Lama and L. V. D. Muyzenberg, *The Leader's Way* (New York: Broadway Books, 2009), 49–50.

46. Kabat-Zinn, *Wherever You Go;* R. Hanson and R. Mendius, *Buddha's Brain: The Practical Neuroscience of Happiness, Love, and Wisdom* (Oakland, CA: New Harbinger Publications, 2009); and Dalai Lama and Muyzenberg, *The Leader's Way.*

47. J. J. Arch and M. G. Craske, "Mechanisms of Mindfulness: Emotion Regulation Following a Focused Breathing Induction," *Behavior Research and Therapy,* 2006, 1849–1858; and D. M. Levy, J. O. Wobbrock, A. W. Kaszniak, and M. Ostergren, "The Effects of Mindfulness Meditation Training on Multitasking in a High-Stress Information Environment," *Graphics Interface,* May 2012, 45–52.

48. S. Reddy, "Doctor's Orders: 20 Minutes of Meditation Twice a Day," *The Wall Street Journal,* April 16, 2013, D1, D2.

49. Hanson and Mendius, *Buddha's Brain,* 81.

50. S. L. Shapiro, L. E. Carlson, J. A. Astin, and B. Freedman, "Mechanisms of Mindfulness," *Journal of Clinical Psychology,* March 2006, 373–386.

51. Based on Dalai Lama and Muyzenberg, *The Leader's Way.*

52. See J. Barsh and J. Lavoie, *Centered Leadership* (New York: Crown Business, 2014); and J. Marturano, *Finding the Space to Lead: A Practical Guide to Mindful Leadership* (New York: Bloomsbury Press, 2014).

53. Kabat-Zinn, *Wherever You Go.*

54. Luthans and Avolio, "The 'Point' of Positive Organizational Behavior."

55. A. Newman, D. Ucbasaran, F. Zhu, and G. Hirst. "Psychological Capital: A Review and Synthesis," *Journal of Organizational Behavior,* 2014, 120–138.

56. J. B. Avey, F. Luthans, and S. M. Jensen, "Psychological Capital: A Positive Resource for Combating Employee Stress and Turnover," *Human Resource Management,* September–October 2009, 677–693.

57. M. Helft, "Silicon Valley's Stealth Power," *Fortune,* February 27, 2014, http://money.cnn.com/2014/02/27/technology/ben-horowitz.pr.fortune/.

58. Ibid.

59. D. Eng, "Life Is Good in the T-shirt Business," *Fortune,* May 19, 2014, 39–42.

60. Avey, Luthans, and Jensen, "Psychological Capital," 682.

61. Ibid.

62. Ibid., 681.

63. T. Sharot, "The Optimism Bias," *Time Magazine,* June 6, 2011, 40–46.

64. F. Luthans, J. B. Avey, B. J. Avolio, and S. J. Peterson, "The Development and Resulting Performance Impact of Positive Psychological Capital," *Human Resource Development Quarterly,* Spring 2010, 41–66.

65. J. B. Avey, R. J. Reichard, F. Luthans, and K. H. Mhatre, "Meta-Analysis of the Impact of Positive Psychological Capital on Employee Attitudes, Behaviors, and Performance," *Human Resource Development Quarterly,* 2011, 127–152. See also M. H. Jafri, "Psychological Capital and Innovative Behavior: An Empirical Study on Apparel Fashion Industry," *The Journal Contemporary Management Research,* 2012, 42–52.

66. C. Ostroff, A. J. Kinicki, and R. S. Muhammad, "Organizational Culture and Climate," in I. B. Weiner, N. W. Schmitt, and S. Highhouse, eds., *Handbook of Psychology,* vol. 12 (Hoboken, NJ: John Wiley & Sons, 2013), 651.

67. Definitions based on R. Fehr and M. J. Gelfand, "The Forgiving Organization: A Multilevel Model of Forgiveness at Work," *Academy of Management Review,* October 2012, 664–688.

68. Ibid., 669.

69. A. S. Tsui, "On Compassion in Scholarship: Why Should We Care?," *Academy of Management Review,* April 2013, 167–180.

70. See R. R. Kehoe and P. M. Wright, "The Impact of High-Performance Human Resource Practices on Employees' Attitudes and Behaviors," *Journal of Management,* February 2013, 366–391.

71. S. Caminiti, "Taking the Lead," *Fortune,* February 4, 2013, S2–3.

72. R. Eisenberger and F. Stinglhamber, *Perceived Organizational Support: Fostering Enthusiastic and Productive Employees* (Washington, DC: APA, 2011); and J. D. Nahrgang, F. P. Morgeson, and D. A. Hofmann, "Safety at Work: A Meta-Analytic Investigation of the Link between Job Demands, Job Resources, Burnout, Engagement, and Safety Outcomes," *Journal of Applied Psychology,* January 2011, 71–94.

73. Moskowitz and Levering, "The 100 Best Companies to Work For," 87, 89.

74. K. Cameron, D. Bright, and A. Caza, "Exploring the Relationships Between Organizational Virtuousness and Performance," *American Behavioral Scientist,* February 2004, 767.

75. Ostroff, Kinicki, and Muhammad, "Organizational Culture and Climate."

76. K. Cameron, "Responsible Leadership as Virtuous Leadership," *Journal of Business Ethics,* January 2011, 25–35; and R. D. Hackett and G. Wang, "Virtues and Leadership: An Integrating Conceptual Framework Founded in Aristotelian and Confucian Perspectives and Virtues," *Management Decision,* 2012, 868–899.

77. J. S. Lublin, "This CEO Used to Have an Office," *The Wall Street Journal,* March 13, 2013, B1.

78. C. Bonanos, "The Lies We Tell at Work," *Bloomberg Businessweek,* February 4–10, 2013, 72.

79. K. Cameron and A. Caza, "Organizational and Leadership Virtues and the Role of Forgiveness," *Journal of Leadership and Organizational Studies,* 2002, 39.

80. Ibid.

81. Cameron, "Responsible Leadership"; and Cameron, Mora, Leutscher, and Calarco, "Effects of Positive Practices on Organizational Effectiveness."

82. Bloomberg News, "Rutgers Basketball Coach Abuse Scandal Puts Chris Christie on the Defensive," *Newsday,* April 9, 2013, http://long-island.newsday.com/search/rutgers-basketball-coach-abuse-scandal-puts-chris-christie-on-the-defensive-1.5037001, accessed April 17, 2013.

83. F. Luthans, "The Need for Meaning of Positive Organizational Behavior," *Journal of Organizational Behavior,* September 2002, 695–706.

84. M. P. Seligman, *Flourish* (New York: Free Press, 2011).

85. B. L. Fredrickson and M. F. Losada, "Positive Affect in the Complex Dynamics of Human Flourishing," *American Psychologist,* 2005, 678–86.

86. C. D. Ryff, B. H. Singer, and G. D. Love, "Positive Health: Connecting Well-Being with Biology," *Philosophical Transactions of the Royal Society of London, Biological Sciences,* 2004, 1383–1394; C. L. M. Keyes and E. J. Simoes, "To Flourish or Not: Positive Mental Health and All-Cause Mortality," *American Journal of Public Health,* November 2012, 2164–2172; Seligman, *Flourish.*

87. Cameron, Mora, Leutscher, and Calarco, "Effects of Positive Practices on Organizational Effectiveness," 266–308; and M. Losada and E. Heaphy, "The Role of Positivity and Connectivity in the Performance of Business Teams," *American Behavioral Scientist,* February 2004, 740–765.

88. "Parnassus Workplace Fund," *U.S. News and World Report,* Money & Investing section, http://money.usnews.com/funds/mutual-funds/large-growth/parnassus-workplace-fund/parwx, accessed April 4, 2013.

89. P. Ortiz, "Why Happy Workers Lead to Bigger Profits," *Ignites, A Service of the Financial Times,* http://www.ignites.com/c/486491/54461/happy_workers_lead_bigger_profits, accessed March 11, 2013.

90. Fredrickson and Losada, "Positive Affect in the Complex Dynamics of Human Flourishing."

91. B. Fredrickson, "The Role of Positive Emotions in Positive Psychology," *American Psychologist,* March 2001, 218–226.

92. Both gratitude exercises were based on Seligman, *Flourish,* 30–31. See also S. Achor, "Positive Intelligence," *Harvard Business Review,* January–February 2012, 100–102.

93. B. A. Wallace, "Mental Balance and Well-Being: Building Bridges between Buddhism and Western Psychology," *American Psychologist,* October 2006, 696.

94. E. Demerouti, A. B. Bakker, S. Sonnentag, and C. J. Fullagar, "Work-Related Flow and Energy at Work and at Home: A Study on the Role of Daily Recovery," *Journal of Organizational Behavior*, February 2012, 276–295.

95. S. Cohen and T. A. Wills, "Stress, Social Support, and the Buffering Hypothesis," *Psychological Bulletin*, September 1985, 310–357.

96. V. E. Frankl, *Man's Search for Meaning* (New York: Pocket Books, 1959).

97. Seligman, *Flourish*, 17.

98. R. Randazzo, "Nuclear Watchdog," *The Arizona Republic*, November 2, 2008, D1.

99. E. E. Smith, "There's More to Life Than Being Happy," *The Atlantic*, January 9, 2013, http://www.theatlantic.com/health/archive/2013/01/theres-more-to-life-than-being-happy/266805/; and M. F. Steger and T. B. Kashdan, "The Unbearable Lightness of Meaning: Well-Being and Unstable Meaning in Life," *The Journal of Positive Psychology*, March 2013, 103–115.

100. Moskowitz and Levering, "The 100 Best Companies to Work For," 88.

101. R. Goffee and G. Jones, "Creating the Best Workplace on Earth," *Harvard Business Review*, May 2013, 103.

102. "Report of the Audit Committee of the Board of Directors of Best Buy to the Board of Directors of Best Buy Regarding Investigation of Alleged Misconduct by Former Chief Executive Officer," May 12, 2012. The report was filed as an exhibit to the Best Buy Form 8-K of event date. Publicly traded U.S corporations must file a Form 8-K with the Securities and Exchange Commission for disclosure within four business days of a significant event affecting the company, in this case the departure of the CEO.

103. N. Parmer, "Interview with Best Buy CEO Brian Dunn," *SmartMoney*, June 28, 2010.

104. M. Bustillo, "Best Buy Chairman to Resign after Probe," *The Wall Street Journal*, May 15, 2012.

105. E. Carlyle, "Best Buy CEO Brian Dunn Gets $6.6 Million Severance Package after 'Friendship' with 29-Year-Old Employee," *Forbes*, May 14, 2012.

106. A. Baxter and M. Moylan, "Best Buy Workers Weigh Company's Ruin or Revival," *Minnesota Public Radio*, June 21, 2012.

107. Associated Press, Reuters, and L. Cox, "Best Buy Founder Forced to Quit after Failing to Tell Board about CEO's Affair with Employee," *Daily Mail Online*, May 14, 2012.

108. R. E. Silverman, "Tracking Sensors Invade the Workplace: Devices on Workers, Furniture Offer Clues for Boosting Productivity," *The Wall Street Journal*, March 7, 2013.

109. Adapted from R. Kreitner and A. Kinicki, *Organizational Behavior*, 10th ed. (Burr Ridge, IL: McGraw-Hill, 2013) 559–560.

Chapter 8

1. This definition is based in part on one found in D. H. Smith, "A Parsimonious Definition of 'Group': Toward Conceptual Clarity and Scientific Utility," *Sociological Inquiry*, Spring 1967, 141–167.

2. S. Schultze, A. Mojzisch, and S. Schulz-Hardt, "Why Groups Perform Better Than Individuals at Quantitative Judgment Tasks: Group-to-Individual Transfer as an Alternative to Differential Weighting," *Organizational Behavior and Human Decision Processes*, 2012, 24–26.

3. E. H. Schein, *Organizational Psychology*, 3rd ed. (Englewood Cliffs, NJ: Prentice Hall, 1980), 145. Emphasis added. For more, see L. R. Weingart, "How Did They Do That? The Ways and Means of Studying Group Process," in L. L. Cummings and B. M. Staw, eds., *Research in Organizational Behavior*, vol. 19 (Greenwich, CT: JAI Press, 1997), 189–239.

4. Schein, *Organizational Psychology*, 145.

5. See R. Cross, N. Nohria, and A. Parker, "Six Myths about Informal Networks—and How to Overcome Them," *MIT Sloan Management Review*, Spring 2002, 67–75; and C. Shirky, "Watching the Patterns Emerge," *Harvard Business Review*, February 2004, 34–35.

6. Excerpted from S. Armour, "Company 'Alumni' Groups Keep Word Out after Workers Go," *USA Today*, August 30, 2005, 4B.

7. See J. Janove, "FOB: Friend of Boss," *HR Magazine*, June 2005, 153–156.

8. Taken from K. Gurchiek, "Gap Exists between What Workers Need and Get from the Boss," *Society for Human Resource Management*, November 22, 2010, http://www.shrm.org/Publications/HRNews/Pages/NeedGetFromBoss.aspx.

9. Schein, *Organizational Psychology*, 149–153.

10. M. Moskowitz, R. Levering, and C. Tkaczyk, "Fortune's 100 Best Companies to Work For, 2010," *Fortune*, February 7, 2011, 96.

11. S. E. Humphrey, F. P. Morgeson, and M. J. Mannor, "Developing a Theory of the Strategic Core of Teams: A Role Composition Model of Team Performance," *Journal of Applied Psychology*, 2009, 48–61.

12. G. Graen, "Role-Making Processes within Complex Organizations," in *Handbook of Industrial and Organizational Psychology*, ed. M. D. Dunnette (Chicago: Rand McNally, 1976), 1201.

13. See D. J. McAllister, D. Kamdar, E. W. Morrison, and D. B. Turban, "Disentangling Role Perceptions: How Perceived Role Breadth, Discretion, Instrumentality, and Efficacy Relate to Helping and Taking Charge," *Journal of Applied Psychology*, September 2007, 1200–1211.

14. See K. D. Benne and P. Sheats, "Functional Roles of Group Members," *Journal of Social Issues*, Spring 1948, 41–49.

15. "B of A's Krawcheck Sets Her Team: The Memo," *The Wall Street Journal Online*, September 29, 2009, http://blogs.wsj.com/deals/2009/09/29/bofas-krawcheck-sets-her-team-the-memo/.

16. See H. J. Klein and P. W. Mulvey, "Two Investigations of the Relationships among Group Goals, Goal Commitment, Cohesion, and Performance," *Organizational Behavior and Human Decision Processes*, January 1995, 44–53; and D. Knight, C. C. Durham, and E. A. Locke, "The Relationship of Team Goals, Incentives, and Efficacy to Strategic Risk, Tactical Implementation, and Performance," *Academy of Management Journal*, April 2001, 326–338.

17. K. Roseman, "Who's Your Office Mom?" *The Wall Street Journal*, March 27, 2013, D1–2.

18. A. Zander, "The Value of Belonging to a Group in Japan," *Small Group Behavior*, February 1983, 7–8. Emphasis added.

19. Adapted from K. Goetz, "How 3M Gave Everyone Days Off and Created an Innovation Dynamo," *Fast Company*, February 1, 2011.

20. World Alliance for Public Safety, "WHO Surgical Safety Checklist," http://who.int/patientsafety/safesurgery/ss_checklist/en/, accessed May 25, 2013.

21. Dean Takahashi, "The DeanBeat: King Overtakes Zynga as the Largest Social Gaming Company," *VentureBeat.com*, April 26, 2013, http://venturebeat.com/2013/04/26/the-deanbeat-king-overtakes-zynga-as-the-largest-social-gaming-company/. See also C. Edwards and A. Levy, "*Candy Crush* Maker King Said to File for U.S. Share Sale," *Bloomberg Technology News*, October 2, 2013, http://www.bloomberg.com/news/2013-10-02/-candy-crush-maker-king-said-to-file-for-u-s-public-offering.html.

22. For an instructive overview of five different theories of group development, see J. P. Wanous, A. E. Reichers, and S. D. Malik, "Organizational Socialization and Group Development: Toward an Integrative Perspective," *Academy of Management Review*, October 1984, 670–683.

23. See B. W. Tuckman, "Developmental Sequence in Small Groups," *Psychological Bulletin*, June 1965, 384–399; and B. W. Tuckman and M. A. C. Jensen, "Stages of Small-Group Development Revisited," *Group & Organization Studies*, December 1977, 419–427.

24. Based on J. L. Farh, C. Lee, and C. I. C. Farh, "Task Conflict and Team Creativity: A Question of How Much and When," *Journal of Applied Psychology*, 2010, 1173–1180.

25. J. McGregor, "Forget Going with Your Gut," *BusinessWeek*, March 20, 2006, 112.

26. S. Clifford, "JC Penney Ousts Chief of 17 Months," *The New York Times,* April 8, 2013, http://www.nytimes.com/2013/04/09/business/ron-johnson-out-as-jc-penney-chief.html?pagewanted=all&_r=0, accessed May 25, 2013; and B. Tuttle, "The 5 Big Mistakes That Led to Ron Johnson's Ouster at JC Penney," *Time,* April 9, 2013, http://business.time.com/2013/04/09/the-5-big-mistakes-that-led-to-ron-johnsons-ouster-at-jc-penney/print/, accessed May 25, 2013.

27. For related research, see M. Van Vugt and C. M. Hart, "Social Identity as Social Glue: The Origins of Group Loyalty," *Journal of Personality and Social Psychology,* April 2004, 585–598.

28. A. Efrati, "Page Shakes Up Google Leadership Team Further," *The Wall Street Journal,* March 15, 2013, B4.

29. J. P. de Jong, P. L. Curseu, and R. T. A. J. Leenders, "When Do Bad Apples Not Spoil the Barrel? Negative Relationships in Teams, Team Performance, and Buffering Mechanisms," *Journal of Applied Psychology,* 2014, doi: 10.1037/a0036284.

30. "Top 10 Leadership Tips from Jeff Immelt," *Fast Company,* April 2004, 96.

31. As quoted in A. Sellers, "Jamie Dimon's Full Disclosure," *Fortune,* April 13, 2010.

32. J. Dixon, C. Belnap, C. Albrecht, and K. Lee, "The Importance of Soft Skills," *Corporate Finance Review,* May–June 2010, 35–38.

33. "How Three Bosses Got to the Top," *The Arizona Republic,* August 5, 2007, D5.

34. Condensed and adapted from ibid., 214. See also R. Rico, M. Sánchez-Manzanares, F. Gil, and C. Gibson, "Team Implicit Coordination Processes: A Team Knowledge-Based Approach," *Academy of Management Review,* January 2008, 163–184.

35. "Company Is a Team, Not a Family," *HR Magazine,* April 2007, 18.

36. J. R. Katzenbach and D. K. Smith, "The Discipline of Teams," *Harvard Business Review,* March–April 1993, 112.

37. M. Hoegl, "Smaller Teams—Better Teamwork: How to Keep Project Teams Small," *Business Horizons,* 2005, 209–214.

38. L. Buchanan, "The Chief Recruiter: Kevin P. Ryan of AlleyCorp," *Inc. Magazine,* March 1, 2010, http://www.inc.com/magazine/20100301/the-chief-recruiter-kevin-p-ryan-alleycorp.html, accessed May 20, 2013.

39. Excerpted from *Harvard Business Essentials: Creating Teams with an Edge* (Boston, MA: Harvard Business School Press, 2004).

40. Based on discussion in B. Latane, K. Williams, and S. Harkins, "Many Hands Make Light the Work: The Causes and Consequences of Social Loafing," *Journal of Personality and Social Psychology,* June 1979, 822–832.

41. A. Jassawalla, H. Sashittal, and A. Malshe, "Student's Perception of Social Loafing: Its Antecedents and Consequences in Undergraduate Business Classroom Teams," *Academy of Management Learning & Education,* 2009, 42–54.

42. Ibid.

43. Data from J. A. Wagner III, "Studies of Individualism-Collectivism: Effects on Cooperation in Groups," *Academy of Management Journal,* February 1995, 152–172. See also P. W. Mulvey, L. Bowes-Sperry, and H. J. Klein, "The Effects of Perceived Loafing and Defensive Impression Management on Group Effectiveness," *Small Group Research,* June 1998, 394–415.

44. M. Ridley, "Are You Wasting Money on L&D?" *Training Journal,* February 2011, http://www.trainingjournal.com/feature/2011-02-01-are-you-wasting-money-on-ld/.

45. Ibid.

46. A. Leigh, "Prove It! Making Sense of the ROI from Developing People," *Training & Management Development Methods,* 2009, 1–7.

47. Adapted from J. Garfield and K. Stanton, "Building Effective Teams in Real Time," *Harvard Business Review,* November 2005, http://cb.hbsp.harvard.edu/cb/web/he/product_view.seam?R=U0511A-PDF=ENG&T=EC&C=PRODUCT_DETAIL&CS=36e0cf4e0ce7cc9a90fd5aa6a5cb96d0, accessed May 28, 2013.

48. F. Aime, S. Humphrey, D. S. DeRue, and J. B. Paul, "The Riddle of Heterarch: Power Transitions in Cross-Functional Teams," *The Academy of Management Journal,* 2014, 327–352.

49. Data from J. P. Millikin, P. W. Hom, and C. C. Manz, "Self-Management Competencies in Self-Managing Teams: Their Impact on Multi-Team System Productivity," *The Leadership Quarterly,* 2010, 687–702.

50. B. Stone, "Inside Google's Secret Lab," *Bloomberg BusinessWeek,* May 22, 2013, 56–61.

51. As quoted in K. Pattison, "How Herman Miller Has Designed Employee Loyalty," *Fast Company,* September 2010.

52. Millikin, Hom, and Manz, "Self-Management Competencies in Self-Managing Teams."

53. See P. S. Goodman, R. Devadas, and T. L. Griffith Hughson, "Groups and Productivity: Analyzing the Effectiveness of Self-Managing Teams," in *Productivity in Organizations,* ed. J. P. Campbell, R. J. Campbell and Associates (San Francisco: Jossey-Bass, 1988), 295–327; see also S. Kauffeld, "Self-Directed Work Groups and Team Competence," *Journal of Occupational and Organizational Psychology,* March 2006, 1–21.

54. S. E. Humphrey, J. R. Hollenbeck, C. J. Meyer, and D. R. Ilgen, "Personality Configurations in Self-Managed Teams: A Natural Experiment on the Effects of Maximizing and Minimizing Variance in Traits," *Journal of Applied Social Psychology,* 2011, 1701–1732.

55. Adapted from G. Colvin, "The Art of the Self-Managing Team," *Fortune,* December 3, 2012, 22–23.

56. M. Moskowitz and R. Levering, "Fortune's 100 Best Companies to Work For," *Fortune,* February 4, 2013, 88.

57. J. E. Hoch and S. W. Kozlowski, "Leading Virtual Teams: Hierarchical Leadership, Structural Supports, and Shared Team Leadership," *Journal of Applied Psychology,* 2012, 1–13.

58. See C. Saunders, C. Van Slyke, and D. R. Vogel, "My Time or Yours? Managing Time Visions in Global Virtual Teams," *Academy of Management Executive,* February 2004, 19–31.

59. Hoch and Kozlowski, "Leading Virtual Teams."

60. "Virtual Teams," SHRM Report, July 13, 2012, http://www.shrm.org/research/surveyfindings/articles/pages/virtualteams.aspx, accessed May 29, 2013.

61. Adapted from F. Siebdrat, M. Hoegl, and J. Ernst, "How to Manage Virtual Teams," *MIT Sloan Management Review,* Summer 2009, 63–68; see also B. L. Kirkman, B. Rosen, C. B. Gibson, P. E. Tesluk, and S. O. McPherson, "Five Challenges to Virtual Team Success: Lessons from Sabre, Inc.," *Academy of Management Executive,* August 2002, 67–79.

62. "Virtual Teams."

63. Hoch and Kozlowski, "Leading Virtual Teams."

64. "The Challenges of Working in Virtual Teams," *RW3 Culture Wizard,* http://rw-3.com/VTSReportv7.pdf.

65. "Virtual Teams."

66. Hoch and Kozlowski, "Leading Virtual Teams."

67. Adapted from A. Bruzzese, "Keep Remote Workers in the Loop," *The Arizona Republic,* March 2, 2011; and D. Clemons and M. Kroth, *Managing the Mobile Workforce* (New York: McGraw-Hill, 2010).

68. Bruzzese, "Keep Remote Workers in the Loop."

69. Ibid.

70. B. Leonard, "Managing Virtual Teams," *HR Magazine,* June 1, 2011. See also N. Lockwood, "Successfully Transitioning to a Virtual Organization: Challenges, Impact, and Technology," *Society of Human Resource Management—Research Quarterly,* First Quarter 2010.

71. E. Martinez-Mareno, A. Zornoza, P. Gonzalez-Navarro, and L. F. Thompson, "Investigating Face-to-Face and Virtual Teamwork over Time: When Does Early Task Conflict Trigger Relationship Conflict?" *Group Dynamics: Theory, Research, and Practice,* 2012, 159–171; and, T. D. Golden, J. F. Veiga, and R. N. Dino. "The Impact of Professional Isolation on Teleworker Job Performance in Turnover Intentions: Does Time Spent Teleworking, Interacting Face to

Face, or Having Access to Communication-Enhancing Technology Matter?" *Journal of Applied Psychology,* 2008, 1412–1421.

72. W. Turmel, "Face to Face Still Rules—Tell Your Boss and the Bean Counters," *CBSNews.com,* March 18, 2011, http://www.cbsnews.com/8301-505125_162-44241198/face-to-face-still-rules--tell-your-boss-and-the-bean-counters/?tag=bnetdomain, accessed May 30, 2013.

73. J. Lehrer, "The Steve Jobs Approach to Teamwork," *Wired,* October 10, 2011, http://www.wired.com/wiredscience/2011/10/the-steve-jobs-approach-to-teamwork/.

74. E. Meyer, "The Four Keys to Success with Virtual Teams," *Forbes.com,* August 19, 2010, http://www.forbes.com/2010/08/19/virtual-teams-meetings-leadership-managing-cooperation_print.html; see also R. F. Maruca, "How Do You Manage an Off-Site Team?," *BusinessWeek,* September 30, 2007, http://www.businessweek.com.

75. J. Schuitema, "Trust in Government, Business Still in Crisis," *MoneyWeb,* January 29, 2013, http://www.moneyweb.co.za/moneyweb-corporate-governance/trust-in-government-business-still-in-crisis, accessed May 30, 2013.

76. G. Brown, C. Crossley, and S. L. Robinson, "Psychological Ownership, Territorial Behavior, and Being Perceived as a Team Contributor: The Critical Role of Trust in the Work Environment," *Personnel Psychology,* 2014, 463–485.

77. From R. Hastings, "Broken Trust Is Bad for Business," *Society of Human Resource Management,* March 7, 2011.

78. See R. Zemke, "Little Lies," *Training,* February 2004, 8.

79. Adapted from F. Bartolomé, "Nobody Trusts the Boss Completely—Now What?" *Harvard Business Review,* March–April 1989, 135–142.

80. S. Buchold and T. Roth, *Creating the High-Performance Team* (New York: John Wiley & Sons, 1987).

81. Based on J. E. Mathieu and T. L. Ra, "Laying the Foundation for Successful Team Performance Trajectories: The Roles of Team Charters and Performance Strategies," *Journal of Applied Psychology,* 2009, 90–103.

82. C. Cheng, R. Y. J. Chua, M. W. Morris, and L. Lee, "Finding the Right Mix: How the Composition of Self-Managing Multicultural Teams' Cultural Value Orientation Influences Performance over Time," *Journal of Organizational Behavior,* 2012, 389–411.

83. B. H. Bradley, A. C. Klotz, B. E. Postlethwaite, and K. G. Brown, "Ready to Rumble: How Team Personality Composition and Task Conflict Interact to Improve Performance," *Journal of Applied Psychology,* 2013, 385–392.

84. Derived from K. R. Randall, C. J. Resick, and L. A. DeChurch, "Building Team Adaptive Capacity: The Roles of Sensegiving and Team Composition," *Journal of Applied Psychology,* February 14, 2011.

85. M. Mankins, A. Bird, and J. Root, "Making Star Teams Out of Star Players," *Harvard Business Review,* January–February 2013, 74–78.

86. J. Mackey and R. Sisodia, "Want to Hire Great People? Hire Consciously," *CNNMoney,* January 17, 2013, http://management.fortune.cnn.com/2013/01/17/best-companies-whole-foods-mackey/, accessed June 4, 2013.

87. K. E. Keeton, L. L. Schmidt, K. J. Slack, and A. A. Malka, "The Rocket Science of Teams," *Industrial and Organizational Psychology,* March 2012, 32–35.

88. "A Team's-Eye View of Teams," *Training,* November 1995, 16; and L. Gratton and T. J. Erickson, "Eight Ways to Build Collaborative Teams," *Harvard Business Review,* November 2007, 101–109.

89. D. Coutu, "Why Teams Don't Work," *Harvard Business Review,* May 2009.

90. M. Hoegl, "Smaller Teams—Better Teamwork."

91. M. Langley and J. D. Rockoff, "Drug Companies Join NIH in Study of Alzheimer's, Diabetes, Rheumatoid Arthritis, Lupus," *The Wall Street Journal,* February 3, 2014.

92. Ibid.

93. M. Harper, "The Cost of Creating a New Drug Now $5 Billion, Pushing Big Pharma to Change," *Forbes,* August 7, 2013, http://www.forbes.com/sites/matthewherper/2013/08/11/how-the-staggering-cost-of-inventing-new-drugs-is-shaping-the-future-of-medicine/print/.

94. "Accelerating Medicines Partnership," *National Institutes of Health,* http://www.nih.gov/science/amp/index.htm, accessed April 22, 2014, unless otherwise referenced.

95. G. Kolata, "An Unusual Partnership to Tackle Stubborn Diseases," *The New York Times,* February 4, 2014, http://www.nytimes.com/2014/02/05/health/nih-joins-drug-makers-and-nonprofits-on-stubborn-diseases.html.

96. Ibid.

97. "Accelerating Medicines Partnership."

98. The final paragraph is based loosely on J. Eisinger, "Postcrisis, A Struggle over Mortgage Bond Ratings," *The New York Times,* January 5, 2011.

Chapter 9

1. Adapted from M. Civiello, "Communication Counts in Landing a Job," *Training & Development,* February 2009, 82–83.

2. See B. Kowitt, "Building the (Workplace) Ties That Bind," *Fortune,* December 6, 2010, 78.

3. "AHRQ's Patient Safety Initiative: Building Foundations, Reducing Risk," U.S. Department of Health & Human Services, Agency for Healthcare Research and Quality, http://www.ahrq.gov/research/findings/final-reports/pscongrpt/psini2.html, accessed September 7, 2013.

4. J. T. James, "A New, Evidence-Based Estimate of Patient Harms Associated with Hospital Care," *Journal of Patient Safety,* September 2013, 122–128, http://journals.lww.com/journalpatientsafety/Fulltext/2013/09000/A_New,_Evidence_based_Estimate_of_Patient_Harms.2.aspx.

5. J. L. Bowditch and A. F. Buono, *A Primer on Organizational Behavior,* 4th ed. (New York: John Wiley & Sons, 1997), 120. For an alternative perspective, see U. Hasson, "I Can Make Your Brain Look Like Mine," *Harvard Business Review,* December 2010, 32–33.

6. "3Rs or 4 Cs?," *Training,* July–August 2010, 8.

7. How to lay off employees is discussed in L. Rubis, "Laying Off Employees Still Best Done Face-to-Face," *Society of Human Resource Management,* June 30, 2009.

8. G. A. Fowler, "In China's Offices, Foreign Colleagues Might Get an Earful," *The Wall Street Journal,* February 13, 2007, B1.

9. S. Shellenbarger, "The Biggest Distraction in the Office Is Sitting Next to You," *The Wall Street Journal,* September 11, 2013, D1, D3.

10. F. Hassan, "The Frontline Advantage," *Harvard Business Review,* May 2011, 106–114.

11. R. L. Daft and R. H. Lengel, "Information Richness: A New Approach to Managerial Behavior and Organizational Design," in *Research in Organizational Behavior,* ed. B. M. Staw and L. L. Cummings (Greenwich, CT: JAI Press, 1984), 196.

12. R. Fisman and T. Sullivan, "In Defense of the CEO," *The Wall Street Journal,* January 12–13, 2013, C1.

13. For a good discussion, see A. M. Kaplan and M. Haenlein, "Users of the World, Unite! The Challenges and Opportunities of Social Media," *Business Horizons,* January–February 2010, 59–68.

14. J. Pollack and J. Neff, "Notebook: Krugman a Downer, Few Practicing What They Tweet," *Advertising Age,* October 18, 2010, 22.

15. "Managing Organizational Communication," *Society of Human Resource Management,* March 26, 2010.

16. A. R. Sanchez, A. Pico, and L. B. Comer, "Salespeople's Communication Competence: A Study of the Mexican Market," *Journal of Business & Economic Studies,* Spring 2010 1–19.

17. J. A. Waters, "Managerial Assertiveness," *Business Horizons,* September–October 1982, 27.

18. Sanchez, Pico, and Comer, "Salespeople's Communication Competence," 37.

19. See A. Bruzzese, "Beware of Workplace Liars," *The Arizona Republic,* June 26, 2013, CL1.

20. Ibid.

21. G. Billikopf, "Communicating Correctly Is Key for Family Ranches," *Beef,* April 19, 2012, http://beefmagazine.com/estate-planning/communicating-correctly-key-family-ranches.

22. L. Talley, "Body Language: Read It or Weep," *HR Magazine*, July 2010, 64–65, http://www.shrm.org/Publications/hrmagazine/EditorialContent/2010/0710/Pages/0710talley.aspx. See also D. B. Rane, "Effective Body Language for Organizational Success," *Journal of Soft Skills,* 2010, 17–26.

23. Related research is summarized by J. A. Hall, "Male and Female Nonverbal Behavior," in *Multichannel Integrations of Nonverbal Behavior,* ed. A. W. Siegman and S. Feldstein (Hillsdale, NJ: Lawrence Erlbaum, 1985), 195–226.

24. Data found in L. Fitzpatrick, "Are Hugs the New *Handshakes?,*" *Time,* February 12, 2009.

25. Rane, "Effective Body Language for Organizational Success," 17–26.

26. N. O. Rule, N. Ambady, R. B. Adams, H. Ozono, S. Nakashima, S. Yoshikawa, and M. Watabe, "Polling the Face: Prediction and Consensus across Cultures," *Journal of Personality and Social Psychology,* 2010, 1–15.

27. Norms for cross-cultural eye contact are discussed by C. Engholm, *When Business East Meets Business West: The Guide to Practice and Protocol in the Pacific Rim* (New York: John Wiley & Sons, 1991).

28. See D. Knight, "Perks Keeping Workers out of Revolving Door," *The Wall Street Journal,* April 30, 2005, D3; and G. Rooper, "Managing Employee Relations," *HR Magazine,* May 2005, 101–104.

29. J. Beeson, "Why You Didn't Get That Promotion," *Harvard Business Review,* June 2009.

30. "CarMax," Wikipedia entry, last modified September 2013, http://en.wikipedia.org/wiki/CarMax.

31. E. Fry, "How CarMax Cares," *Fortune,* April 8, 2013, 21.

32. See J. Keyser, "Active Listening Leads to Business Success," *T+D,* July 2013, 26–28.

33. This discussion is based on C. G. Pearce, I. W. Johnson, and R. T. Barker, "Assessment of the Listening Styles Inventory: Progress in Establishing Reliability and Validity," *Journal of Business and Technical Communication,* January 2003, 84–113.

34. J. R. Gibb, "Defensive Communication," *Journal of Communication,* 1961, 141–148.

35. D. Tannen, "The Power of Talk: Who Gets Heard and Why," *Harvard Business Review,* September–October 1995, 139. Emphasis added.

36. K. Coussement and D. Van den Poel, "Improving Customer Complaint Management by Automatic Email Classification Using Linguistic Style," *Decision Support Systems,* March 2008.

37. See D. Tannen, "The Power of Talk: Who Gets Heard and Why," in R. J. Lewicki and D. M. Saunders, eds., *Negotiation: Readings, Exercises, and Cases,* 3rd ed. (Boston, MA: Irwin/McGraw-Hill, 1999), 160–173.

38. For a thorough review of the evolutionary explanation of sex differences in communication, see A. H. Eagly and W. Wood, "The Origins of Sex Differences in Human Behavior," *American Psychologist,* June 1999, 408–423.

39. See E. Bernstein, "The Perils of Giving Advice," *The Wall Street Journal,* June 25, 2013, D1, D2; and M. Dainton and E. D. Zelley, *Applying Communication Theory for Professional Life: A Practical Introduction* (Thousand Oaks, CA: Sage, 2005).

40. E. Melero, "Are Workplaces with Many Women in Management Run Differently?," *Journal of Business Research,* 2011, 385–393.

41. J. R. Fine, "Enhancing Gen Y Communication Skills," *Society for Human Resource Management,* March 13, 2009.

42. Ibid. For an excellent, detailed description of generational differences and implications at work, see J. C. Meister and K. Willyerd, *The 2020 Workplace* (New York: HarperCollins, 2010).

43. Based on C. Houck, "Multigenerational and Virtual: How Do We Build a Mentoring Program for Today's Workforce?" *Performance Improvement,* February 2011, 25–30.

44. A. Hofschneider, "That Thing with the Buttons and Receiver? Pick It Up," *The Wall Street Journal,* August 28, 2013, D1, D2.

45. Ibid.

46. Adapted from J. Goudreau, "How to Communicate in the New Multigenerational Office," *Forbes,* February 14, 2013, http://www.forbes.com/sites/jennagoudreau/2013/02/14/how-to-communicate-in-the-new-multigenerational office/, accessed August 21, 2014.

47. Data from "The Real Generation Gap: How Adults and Teens Use Social Media Differently," Entrepreneur.com, August 26, 2013, http://www.entrepreneur.com/article/228029.

48. R. E. Ployhart, "Social Media in the Workplace: Issues and Strategic Questions," *SHRM Executive Briefing,* November 2011, http://www.shrm.org/about/foundation/products/documents/social%20media%20briefing%20final.pdf, accessed October 2, 2013.

49. Meister and Willyerd, *The 2020 Workplace,* 31–32.

50. B. A. Lautsch and E. E. Kossek, "Managing a Blended Workforce: Telecommuters and Non-Telecommuters," *Organizational Dynamics,* 2011, 10–17.

51. J. Meister, "Want to Be a More Productive Employee? Get on Social Networks," *Forbes,* April 18, 2013, http://www.forbes.com/sites/jeannemeister/2013/04/18/want-to-be-a-more-productive-employee-get-on-social-networks/, accessed October 3, 2013.

52. Ibid.

53. Ibid.

54. Ibid.

55. Ibid.

56. S. Ng and S. Vranica, "P&G Shifting Ad Dollars to Digital," *The Wall Street Journal,* August 2, 2013, B7.

57. K. Gustafsson, "Who Ya Gonna Call? Lego Dials Fans," *Bloomberg-Businessweek,* April 7–13, 2014, 27–28.

58. T. Wasserman, "Pepsi Snafu Illustrates Dangers of Crowd Sourcing," *Crowdsourcing.org,* January 7, 2011, http://www.crowdsourcing.org/document/pepsico-snafu-illustrates-dangers-of-crowd-sourcing/2249.

59. A. Schneider, "Fantasy Football Expected to Cost $8 Billion in Lost Work Time This NFL Season," *KUHF Public Radio,* September 3, 2013, http://app1.kuhf.org/articles/1377884091-Fantasy-Football-Expected-To-Cost-$8-Billion-In-Lost-Work-Time-This-NFL-Season.html, accessed October 3, 2013.

60. S. Vozza, "Why Banning Facebook at Work Is a Stupid Move," *Business Insider,* October 2, 2013, http://www.businessinsider.com/why-banning-facebook-at-work-is-a-stupid-move-2013-10, accessed October 4, 2013.

61. Schneider, "Fantasy Football Expected to Cost $8 Billion in Lost Work Time This NFL Season."

62. Vozza, "Why Banning Facebook at Work Is a Stupid Move."

63. Ibid.

64. J. Deschenaux, "Seven States Protect Social Media Privacy," *HR Magazine,* June 2013, 16.

65. Ployhart, "Social Media in the Workplace."

66. Adapted from ibid.

67. J. Oravec, "Deconstructing 'Personal Privacy' in an Age of Social Media: Information Control and Reputation Management Dimensions," *International Journal of the Academic Business World 6,* Spring 2012, 95–101.

68. Ibid.

69. M. Meece, "Who's the Boss, You or Your Gadget?," *The New York Times,* February 5, 2011.

70. A. Akitunde, "Employees Gone Wild: Eight Reasons You Need a Social Media Policy TODAY," *Open Forum,* August 15, 2013, https://www.openforum.com/articles/employee-social-media-policy/, accessed September 9, 2013.

71. C. Anderson, "How to Give a Killer Presentation," *Harvard Business Review,* June 2013, 121–125.

72. K. Patterson, J. Grenny, R. McMillan, and A. Switzler, *Crucial Conversations: Tools for Talking When Stakes Are High* (New York: McGraw Hill, 2012).

73. Ibid., 9.

74. Ibid., 5.

75. Adapted from ibid., 154.

76. Adapted from M. Rosenthal, "Constructive Criticism for Managers," *Training Magazine,* July/August 2013, 64; and C. Patton, "Coaching Up," *Training Magazine,* July/August 2013, 29–31.

77. Ibid.

78. E. J. Fox, "Worker Wages: Wendy's vs. Wal-Mart vs. Costco," *CNNMoney,* August 6, 2013, http://money.cnn.com/2013/08/06/news/economy/costco-fast-food-strikes/.

79. A. Zimmerman, "Costco's Dilemma: Be Kind to Its Workers, or Wall Street?," *The Wall Street Journal,* March 26, 2004, B1.

80. M. E. Belicove, "NLRB Slams Costco on Social Media Use Policy: What It Means for Your Business," *Forbes,* September 28, 2012, http://www.forbes.com/sites/mikalbelicove/2012/09/28/nlrb-slams-costco-on-social-media-use-policy-what-it-means-for-your-business/.

81. M. A. Sands, S. L. M. Riley, and S. J. Ghassemi-Vanni, "Social Media Policies and the NLRB: What Employers Need to Know," position paper, Fenwick & West LLP, http://www.fenwick.com/publications/Pages/Social-Media-Policies-And-The-NLRB-What-Employers-Need-To-Know.aspx.

82. N. Hayes, "Five Common Legal and Regulatory Challenges with Social Media," *Forrester,* July 31, 2013, http://blogs.forrester.com/nick_hayes/13-07-31-five_common_legal_regulatory_challenges_with_social_media.

83. E. Sherman, "Waitress Fired for Facebook Post Complaining about Bad Tippers," September 11, 2013, http://jobs.aol.com/articles/2013,09/11/daves-bbq-waitress-complains-bad-tips-facebook/.

Chapter 10

1. K. Gurchiek, "Managed Right, Conflict Can Help Organizations," *SHRM.org,* December 10, 2008, http://www.shrm.org/Publications/HRNews/Pages/ManagedRightConflict.aspx, accessed June 12, 2013.

2. P. E. Spector, "Introduction: Conflict in Organizations," *Journal of Organizational Behavior,* January 2008, 3.

3. J. A. Wall Jr. and R. Robert Callister, "Conflict and Its Management," *Journal of Management 3,* 1995, 517.

4. E. Mystal, "At Top Law Firms, a Class Conflict during Bonus Season," *Bloomberg Businessweek,* December 6, 2012, http://www.businessweek.com/articles/2012-12-06/at-top-law-firms-a-class-conflict-during-bonus-season, accessed June 12, 2013.

5. S. Stellin, "In the Air, Minor Tiffs Can Escalate Fast," *The New York Times,* January 29, 2013, http://www.nytimes.com/2013/01/29/business/passenger-vs-airline-policy-stand-offs-in-the-air.html?_r=0.

6. "General Information on Escalation," *International Online Training Program on Intractable Conflict,* Conflict Research Consortium, University of Colorado, http://www.colorado.edu/conflict/peace/problem/escalation.htm, accessed June 12, 2013.

7. Ibid.

8. K. Duncum, "Turning Conflict into Cooperation," *Bloomberg Businessweek,* October 15, 2010.

9. G. R. Massey and P. L. Dawes, "The Antecedents and Consequence of Functional and Dysfunctional Conflict between Marketing Managers and Sales Managers," *Industrial Marketing Management,* 2007, 1118–1129. See also S. Alper, D. Tjosvold, and K. S. Law, "Interdependence and Controversy in Group Decision Making: Antecedents to Effective Self-Managing Teams," *Organizational Behavior and Human Decision Processes,* April 1998, 33–52.

10. C. G. Donald, J. D. Ralston, and S. F. Webb, "Arbitral Views of Fighting: An Analysis of Arbitration Cases, 1989–2003," *Journal of Academic and Business Ethics,* July 2009, 1–19.

11. "Exhibit 99.1: Scotts Miracle-Gro Announces Resignation of Board Members," press release, June 3, 2013, SEC, http://www.sec.gov/Archives/edgar/data/825542/000144398413000025/smg2013-06x038xkex991.htm. See also D. Bukszpan, "Rude Executive Outbursts," *CNBC.com,* updated June 4, 2013, http://www.cnbc.com/id/43013036/page/2.

12. K. Cloke and J. Goldsmith, *Resolving Conflicts at Work: A Complete Guide for Everyone on the Job* (San Francisco, CA: Jossey-Bass, 2000), 31–32.

13. Excerpted and adapted from K. Sulkowicz, "Analyze This," *BusinessWeek,* September 29, 2008, 19. Also see S. A. Joni and D. Beyer, "How to Pick a Good Fight," *Harvard Business Review,* December 2009, 48–57.

14. Cloke and Goldsmith, *Resolving Conflicts at Work,* 25, 27, 29. See also R. Lipsyte, "'Jock Culture' Permeates Life," *USA Today,* April 10, 2008, 11A.

15. D. Brady, "It's All Donald, All the Time," *BusinessWeek,* January 22, 2007, 51.

16. Cloke and Goldsmith, *Resolving Conflicts at Work,* 31–32.

17. Excerpted from T. Ursiny, *The Coward's Guide to Conflict: Empowering Solutions for Those Who Would Rather Run Than Fight* (Naperville, IL: Sourcebooks, 2003), 27.

18. Excerpted and adapted from Duncum, "Turning Conflict into Cooperation."

19. Adapted from discussion in D. Tjosvold, *Learning to Manage Conflict: Getting People eto Work Together Productively* (Lanham, MD: Lexington Books, 2000), 12–13.

20. Data from "Do I Have It?," *BusinessWeek,* July 7, 2003, 14.

21. Data from D. Stamps, "Yes, Your Boss Is Crazy," *Training,* July 1998, 35–39. See also S. S. Wang, "Mental Illness, Redefined," *The Wall Street Journal,* February 10, 2010, A3; A. Andors, "Dispel the Stigma of Mental Illness," *HR Magazine,* October 2010, 83–86; and M. Harvey, M. Moeller, H. Sloan III, and A. Williams, "Impaired Employees: Lessons Learned from *The Wonderful Wizard of Oz,*" *Business Horizons,* November–December 2010, 561–570.

22. See L. P. Postol, "ADAAA Will Result in Renewed Emphasis on Reasonable Accommodations," *SHRM Legal Report,* January 2009, 1–6; R. J. Grossman, "What to Do about Substance Abuse," *HR Magazine,* November 2010, 32–38; and D. Cadrain, "The Marijuana Exception," *HR Magazine,* November 2010, 40–42.

23. Q. Hardy and N. Bilton, "Personality and Change Inflamed Mozilla Crisis," *The New York Times,* April 4, 2014.

24. L. M. Cortina and V. J. Magley, "Patterns and Profiles of Responses to Incivility in the Workplace," *Journal of Occupational Health Psychology,* 2009, 272–288.

25. "The New Teamwork," *Fortune,* April 28, 2014, 82.

26. J. Battista, "N.F.L. Reaches Labor Deal with Referees," *The New York Times,* September 26, 2012.

27. L. A. DeChurch, J. R. Mesmer-Magnus, and D. Doty, "Moving Beyond Relationship and Task Conflict: Toward a Process-State Perspective," *Journal of Applied Psychology,* 2013.

28. Ibid.

29. Ibid., abstract.

30. T. Reed. "Three Unions Say American Airlines Merger Gains Passed Them By," *TheStreet.Com,* March 31, 2014.

31. Based on discussion in G. Labianca, D. J. Brass, and B. Gray, "Social Networks and Perceptions of Intergroup Conflict: The Role of Negative Relationships and Third Parties," *Academy of Management Journal,* February 1998, 55–67.

32. J. Binder, H. Zagefka, R. Brown, R. Funke, T. Kessler, A. Mummendey, A. Maquil, S. Demoulin, and J. P. Leyens, "Does Contact Reduce Prejudice or Does Prejudice Reduce Contact? A Longitudinal Test of the Contact Hypothesis among Majority and Minority Groups in Three European Countries," *Journal of Personality and Social Psychology,* 2009, 843–856.

33. For example, see S. C. Wright, A. Aron, T. McLaughlin-Volpe, and S. A. Ropp, "The Extended Contact Effect: Knowledge of Cross-Group Friendships and Prejudice," *Journal of Personality and Social Psychology,* July 1997, 73–90.

34. Based on and adapted from research evidence in G. Labianca, D. J. Brass, and B. Gray, "Social Networks and Perceptions of Intergroup Conflict: The Role of Negative Relationships and Third Parties," *Academy of Management Journal,* February 1998, 55–67; C. D. Batson et al., "Empathy and Attitudes: Can Feeling for a Member of a Stigmatized Group Improve Feelings toward the Group?," *Journal of Personality and Social Psychology,* January 1997, 105–118; and S. C. Wright et al., "The Extended Contact Effect: Knowledge of Cross-Group Friendships and Prejudice," *Journal of Personality and Social Psychology,* July 1997, 73–90.

35. B. H. Bradley, B. E. Postlethwaite, A. C. Klotz, and M. R. Hamdani, "Reaping the Benefits of Task Conflict in Teams: The Critical Role of Team Psychological Safety," *Journal of Applied Psychology 97,* 2012, 152.

36. J. Wang, K. Lueng, and F. Zhou, "Dispositional Approach to Psychological Climate: Relationships between Interpersonal Harmony Motives and Psychological Climate for Communication Safety," *Human Relations,* 2014, 489–515.

37. Ibid.

38. T. D. Allen, R. C. Johnson, K. M. Kiburz, and K. M. Shockley, "Work-Family Conflict and Flexible Work Arrangements: Deconstructing Flexibility," *Personnel Psychology 66,* 2013, 345–376.

39. "Flexible Work Plans Key to Retention," *HR Magazine,* December 2010, 105.

40. See J. M. Hoobler, J. Hu, and M. Wilson, "Do Workers Who Experience Conflict between the Work and Family Domains Hit a 'Glass Ceiling?' A Meta-Analytic Examination," *Journal of Vocational Behavior,* December 2010, 481–494; and G. N. Powell and J. H. Greenhaus, "Sex, Gender, and the Work-to-Family Interface: Exploring Negative and Positive Interdependencies," *Academy of Management Journal,* June 2010, 513–534.

41. S. C. Paustian-Underdahl and J. R. B. Halbesleben, "Examining the Influence of Climate, Supervisor Guidance, and Behavioral Integrity on Work-Family Conflict: A Demands and Resources Approach," *Journal of Organizational Behavior,* 2014, 447–463.

42. M. Houshmand, J. O'Reilly, S. Robinson, and A. Wolff, "Escaping Bullying: The Simultaneous Impact of Individual and Unit-Level Bullying on Turnover Intentions," *Human Relations 65,* 2012, 901–918.

43. C. Porath and C. Pearson, "The Price of Incivility—Lack of Respect Hurts Morale and the Bottom Line," *Harvard Business Review,* January–February 2013, 115–121.

44. Ibid.

45. Ibid.

46. Houshmand et al., "Escaping Bullying."

47. Ibid.

48. R. M. Kowalski, G.W. Giumetti, A. N. Schroder, and M. R Lattaner, "Bullying in the Digital Age: A Critical Review and Meta-Analysis of Cyberbullying Research Among Youth," *Psychological Bulletin,* 2014, 1–66.

49. D. P. Ford, "Virtual Harassment: Media Characteristics' Role in Psychological Health," *Journal of Managerial Psychology 28,* 2013, 408–428.

50. M. McGoldrick, "Dynamics of Email Conflict in the Workplace," US Department of Homeland Security, July 20, 2010, http://www.adr .gov/events/2010/july20-2010-materials-dynamics-email-conflict .pdf, acccessed June 10, 2013.

51. Adapted from N. J. Goldstein, I. S. Vezich, and J. R. Shapiro, "Perceived Perspective Taking: When Others Walk in Our Shoes," *Journal of Personality and Social Psychology 106,* 2014, 941–960.

52. T. A. Daniel, "Managing Workplace Conflict," *SHRM,* December 27, 2012, http://www.shrm.org/templatestools/toolkits/pages/ managingworkplaceconflict.aspx, accessed June 6, 2013.

53. R. A. Cosier and C. R. Schwenk, "Agreement and Thinking Alike: Ingredients for Poor Decisions," *Academy of Management Executive,* February 1990, 71.

54. See G. Katzenstein, "The Debate on Structured Debate: Toward a Unified Theory," *Organizational Behavior and Human Decision Processes,* June 1996, 316–332.

55. See J. S. Valacich and C. Schwenk, "Devil's Advocacy and Dialectical Inquiry Effects on Face-to-Face and Computer-Mediated Group Decision Making," *Organizational Behavior and Human Decision Processes,* August 1995, 158–173.

56. See D. M. Schweiger, W. R. Sandberg, and P. L. Rechner, "Experiential Effects of Dialectical Inquiry, Devil's Advocacy, and Consensus Approaches to Strategic Decision Making," *Academy of Management Journal,* December 1989, 745–772.

57. A statistical validation for this model can be found in M. A. Rahim and N. R. Magner, "Confirmatory Factor Analysis of the Styles of Handling Interpersonal Conflict: First-Order Factor Model and Its Invariance across Groups," *Journal of Applied Psychology,* February 1995, 122–132. See also N. M. Atteya, "The Conflict Management Grid: A Selection and Development Tool to Resolve the Conflict between the Marketing and Sales Organizations," *International Journal of Business and Management 7,* 2012, 28–37.

58. P. K. Lam and K. S. Chin, "Managing Conflict in Collaborative New Product Development: A Supplier Perspective," *International Journal of Quality and Reliability Management 24,* 2007, 891–907.

59. J. Morrison, "The Relationship between Emotional Intelligence Competencies and Preferred Conflict Handling Styles," *Journal of Nursing Management,* August 2008, 974–983.

60. F. Aquila, "Taming the Litigation Beast," *Bloomberg Businessweek,* April 6, 2010.

61. B. Morrow and L. M. Bernardi, "Resolving Workplace Disputes," *Canadian Manager,* Spring 1999, 17. For related research, see J. M. Brett, M. Olekalns, R. Friedman, N. Goates, C. Anderson, and C. Cherry Lisco, "Sticks and Stones: Language, Face, and Online Dispute Resolution," *Academy of Management Journal,* February 2007, 85–99.

62. Adapted from the discussion in K. O. Wilburn, "Employment Disputes: Solving Them out of Court," *Management Review,* March 1998, 17–21; and Morrow and Bernardi, "Resolving Workplace Disputes," 17–19, 27.

63. For more, see M. M. Clark, "A Jury of Their Peers," *HR Magazine,* January 2004, 54–59.

64. Wilburn, "Employment Disputes," 19.

65. For an excellent description of the pros and cons from both employee and employer perspectives, see C. D. Coleman, "Is Mandatory Employment Arbitration Living Up to Its Expectations? A View from the Employer's Perspective," *ABA Journal of Labor & Employment Law,* Winter 2010, 227–239. The EEOC website also has excellent additional information on ADR techniques: http://www .eeoc.gov/federal/adr/typesofadr.cfm.

66. Aquila, "Taming the Litigation Beast."

67. B. Uzzi and S. Dunlap, "Make Your Enemies Your Allies," *Harvard Business Review,* May 2012, 133–137.

68. This real example comes from the consulting work of one of the authors.

69. P. L. Stockli and C. Tanner, "Are Integrative or Distributive Outcomes More Satisfactory? The Effects of Interest-Based versus Value-Based Issues on Negotiator Satisfaction," *European Journal of Social Psychology,* 2014, 202–208.

70. A. Zerres, J. Huffmeier, P. A. Freund, and K. Backhaus. "Does It Take Two to Tango? Longitudinal Effects of Unilateral and Bilateral Integrative Negotiation Training," *Journal of Applied Psychology,* 2013, 478–491.

71. B. Schulte, "Teaming Up with the Enemy," *U.S. News & World Report,* November 19, 2007, 54, 56.

72. N. Dimotakis, D. E. Conlon, and R. Ilies, "The Mind and Heart (Literally) of the Negotiator: Personality and Contextual Determinants

of Experiential Reactions in Economic Outcomes in Negotiation," *Journal of Applied Psychology* 97, 2012, 183–193.

73. L. Schiff, "Revisiting 'Win-Win' Negotiation: It's Still a Losing Game," *Forbes*, March 13, 2013, http://www.forbes.com/sites/jimcamp/2013/03/11/revisiting-win-win-negotiation-its-still-a-losing-game/, accessed August 19, 2013.

74. "Win-Win Negotiations: Managing Your Counterpart's Satisfaction," Harvard Law School Program on Negotiation, May 23, 2013, http://www.pon.harvard.edu/category/daily/business-negotiations/, accessed August 20, 2013.

75. Ibid.

76. Ibid.

77. N. A. Welsh, "The Reputational Advantages of Demonstrating Trustworthiness: Using the Reputation Index with Law Students," *Negotiation Journal*, January 2012, 117–141.

78. Adapted from K. Albrecht and S. Albrecht, "Added Value Negotiating," *Training*, April 1993, 26–29.

79. Adapted from K. Leary, J. Pillemer, and M. Wheeler, "Negotiating with Emotion," *Harvard Business Review*, January–February 2013, 96–103.

80. S. DuBois, "Men's Wearhouse Founder Firing: What Happened?," *Fortune*, June 19, 2013, http://management.fortune.cnn.com/2013/06/19/mens-wearhouse-george-zimmer/.

81. S. Schaefer, "George Zimmer Fires Back in Men's Wearhouse War of Words," *Forbes*, June 26, 2013, http://www.forbes.com/sites/steveschaefer/2013/06/26/mens-wearhouse-war-of-words-continues-zimmer-fires-back/.

82. K. Stock, "Men's Wearhouse Keeps Fraying after Ousting Its Bearded Pitchman," *Bloomberg Businessweek*, September 12, 2013, http://www.businessweek.com/articles/2013-09-12/mens-wearhouse-keeps-fraying-after-ousting-its-bearded-pitchman.

83. L. Stampler, "Men's Wearhouse's First New Ad without George Zimmer Is Really Sleazy," *Business Insider*, August 13, 2013, http://www.businessinsider.com/mens-wearhouse-released-its-first-new-ad-without-george-zimmer--and-its-really-sleazy-2013-8.

84. Associated Press, "Women's Wear Daily Report Says Zimmer Eyeing Men's Wearhouse," August 22, 2013, http://www.newsdaily.com/article/c6bdad19d6805c062c70ce450e3c12dc/wwd-report-says-zimmer-eyeing-mens-wearhouse.

85. Schaefer, "George Zimmer Fires Back."

86. Stock, "Men's Wearhouse Keeps Fraying."

Chapter 11

1. J. M. Kraushaar and D. C. Novak, "Examining the Effects of Student Multitasking with Laptops during the Lecture," *Journal of Information Systems Education*, Summer 2010, 241–251.

2. "The Multitasking Paradox," *Harvard Business Review*, March 2013, 30–31; and K. Tyler, "Dropping the Ball," *HR Magazine*, July 2013, 42–43.

3. A. C. van der Horst, U.-C. Klehe, and L. van Leeuwen, "Doing It All at Once: Multitasking as a Predictor of Call Center Agents' Performance and Performance-Based Dismissal," *International Journal of Selection and Assessment*, December 2012, 434–441.

4. M. Beck, "What Cocktail Parties Teach Us," *The Wall Street Journal*, April 24, 2012, D1.

5. A. Saadia, aka *learner365*, "Is Multitasking Good or Bad: Practical Tips and Tricks of Multitasking," on *Hub Pages: Education and Science*, November 15, 2012, http://learner365.hubpages.com/hub/Is-Multitasking-Good-Or-Bad-Practical-Tips-And-Tricks-Of-Multitasking.

6. P. Davidson, "Watch Interview Behavior," *The Arizona Republic*, May 15, 2013, CL1.

7. "All-Around Leadership," *Training*, May/June 2013, 32–36.

8. M. Beck, "Squeeze Looms for Doctors," *The Wall Street Journal*, March 14, 2013, A3.

9. This study was conducted by P. C. Nutt, "Expanding the Search for Alternatives during Strategic Decision Making," *Academy of Management Executive*, November 2004, 13–28.

10. "London Whale to Haunt J.P. Morgan Chase, Jamie Dimon for Months," *Huffington Post*, August 31, 2012, http://www.huffingtonpost.com/2012/08/31/london-whale-jp-morgan-jamie-dimon_n_184...

11. D. Fitzpatrick, "Dimon, Showing Old Swagger, Ponders Wake of the 'Whale,'" *The Wall Street Journal*, June 12, 2013, C2.

12. H. A. Simon, "Rational Decision Making in Business Organizations," *American Economic Review*, September 1979, 510.

13. These conclusions were proposed by R. Brown, *Rational Choice and Judgment* (Hoboken, NJ: John Wiley & Sons, 2005), 9.

14. Results can be found in J. P. Byrnes, D. C. Miller, and W. D. Schafer, "Gender Differences in Risk Taking: A Meta-Analysis," *Psychological Bulletin*, May 1999, 367–383.

15. Bounded rationality is discussed by A. R. Memati, A. M. Bhatti, M. Maqsal, I. Mansoor, and F. Naveed, "Impact of Resource Based View and Resource Dependence Theory on Strategic Decision Making," *International Journal of Business Management*, December 2010, 110–115; and H. A. Simon, *Administrative Behavior*, 2nd ed. (New York: Free Press, 1957).

16. J. W. Miller, A. MacDonald, and R. M. Stewart, "Miner Rio Tinto Ousts CEO as Bad Bets Cost Billions," *The Wall Street Journal*, January 18, 2013, A1, A2.

17. Excerpted from C. C. Miller and R. D. Ireland, "Intuition in Strategic Decision Making: Friend or Foe in the Fast-Paced 21st Century?," *Academy of Management Executive*, February 2005, 20.

18. D. Kahneman and G. Klein, "Conditions for Intuitive Expertise: A Failure to Disagree," *American Psychologist*, September 2009, 519.

19. See E. Dane and M. G. Pratt, "Exploring Intuition and Its Role in Managerial Decision Making," *Academy of Management Review*, January 2007, 33–54.

20. K. C. Williams, "Business Intuition: The Mortar among the Bricks of Analysis," *Journal of Management Policy and Practice*, December 2012, 48–65.

21. See D. J. Snowden and M. E. Boone, "A Leader's Framework for Decision Making," *Harvard Business Review*, November 2007, 69–76.

22. S. Elbanna, J. Child, and M. Dayan, "A Model of Antecedents and Consequences of Intuition in Strategic Decision-Making: Evidence from Egypt," *Long Range Planning*, February 2013, 149–176.

23. Biases associated with using shortcuts in decision making are discussed by A. Tversky and D. Kahneman, "Judgment under Uncertainty: Heuristics and Biases," *Science*, September 1974, 1124–1131.

24. J. Nordqvist, "Diagnostic Errors Cause Up to 160,000 Deaths Annually, USA," *Medical News Today*, April 24, 2013, http:www.medicalnewstoday.com/articles/259550.php.

25. G. Çaliki and A. B. Bener, "Influence of Confirmation Bias of Developers on Software Quality: An Empirical Study," *Software Quality Journal*, 2013, 377–416.

26. M. J. Mauboussin, "The True Measures of Success," *Harvard Business Review*, October 2012, 46–56.

27. D. Maxey, "The Downside of Entrepreneurial Success," *The Wall Street Journal*, June 10, 2013, R3; and F. B. Zaidi and M. Z. Tauni, "Influence of Investor's Personality Traits and Demographics on Overconfidence Bias," *Interdisciplinary Journal of Contemporary Research in Business*, October 2012, 730–746.

28. M. Smith, "Coast Guard, BP End Gulf Cleanup in Three States," *CNN*, June 11, 2013, http://www.cnn.com/2013/06/10/us/gulf-oil-spill/index.html?iref=allsearch.

29. Excerpted from S. Borenstein, "Disasters Often Stem from Hubris," *The Arizona Republic*, July 12, 2010, A4.

30. H. Shefrin and E. M. Cervellati, "BP's Failure to Debias: Underscoring the Importance of Behavioral Corporate Finance," *Quarterly Journal of Finance*, March 2011, 127–168, http://post.nyssa.org/nyssa-news/2011/05/bps-failure-to-debias-underscoring-the-importance-of-behavioral-corporate-finance.html.

31. "Deepwater Horizon Oil Spill," *Wikipedia*, http://en.wikipedia.org/wiki/Deepwater_Horizon_oil_spill, accessed February 25, 2014.

32. T. Pachur, R. Hertwig, and F. Hertwig, "How Do People Judge Risks: Availability Heuristic, Affect Heuristic, or Both?," *Journal of Experimental Psychology: Applied,* September 2012, 314–330.

33. See S. Nestler, B. Egloff, A. C. P. Küfner, and M. D. Back, "An Integrative Lens Model Approach to Bias and Accuracy in Human Inferences: Hindsight Effects and Knowledge Updating in Personality Judgments," *Journal of Personality and Social Psychology,* October 2012, 689–717.

34. "Insights from Our Online Panel," *The Wall Street Journal,* June 10, 2013, R5.

35. S. Li, Y. Sun, and Y. Wang, "50% Off or Buy One, Get One Free? Frame Preference as a Function of Consumable Nature in Dairy Products," *Journal of Social Psychology,* 2007, 413–21.

36. D. A. Kaplan, "Hostess Is Bankrupt . . . Again," *Fortune,* August 13, 2012, 66.

37. See J. Ross and B. M. Staw, "Organizational Escalation and Exit: Lessons from the Shoreham Nuclear Power Plant," *Academy of Management Journal,* August 1993, 701–732.

38. V. V. Baba and F. HakemZadeh, "Toward a Theory of Evidence-Based Decision Making," *Management Decision 5,* 2012, 832–867.

39. S. Grobart, "Big Dairy Enters the Era of Big Data," *Bloomberg Businessweek,* October 22–28, 2012, 41–42.

40. P. Coro, "NBA's Sabermetrics?," *The Arizona Republic,* January 18, 2013, C7.

41. These definitions come from P. M. Tingling and M. J. Brydon, "Is Decision-Based Evidence Making Necessarily Bad?," *MIT Sloan Management Review,* Summer 2010, 72–74.

42. H. Weinzierl, "New Digital Universe Study Reveals Big Data Gap: Less Than 1% of World's Data Is Analyzed; Less Than 20% Is Protected," *EMC Newsroom,* http://www.emc.com/about/news/press/2012/20121211-.htm, accessed June 19, 2013. The press release summarizes findings in EMC's December 2012 IDC Digital Universe Study.

43. M. Buchanan, "Speak Softly and Carry Big Data," *The New Yorker* "Elements" science blog, June 7, 2013, http://www.newyorker.com/online/blogs/elements/2013/06/nsa-prism-big-data-national-security.html.

44. G. Dutton, "What's the Big Deal About Big Data?," *Training,* March/April 2014, 16–20.

45. These recommendations derive from J. Manyika, M. Chui, B. Brown, J. Bughin, R. Dobbs, C. Roxburgh, and A. H Byers, "Big Data: The Next Frontier for Innovation, Competition, and Productivity," McKinsey Global Institute, May 2011, http://www.mckinsey.com/insights/business_technology/big_data_the_next_frontier_for_innovation.

46. A. Mouton, "Commentary: Is NSA Showing Real Cost of 'Big Data'?," *USA Today,* June 18, 2013, http://www.usatoday.com/story/tech/2013/06/17/nsa-big-data-yahoo-facebook-microsoft/2431295/.

47. Excerpted from J. Jargon, "Kroger's New Weapon: Infrared Cameras," *The Wall Street Journal,* May 2, 2013, B4.

48. Definition derived from A. J. Rowe and R. O. Mason, *Managing with Style: A Guide to Understanding, Assessing, and Improving Decision Making* (San Francisco, CA: Jossey-Bass, 1987).

49. Ibid.

50. Excerpted from B. Gimbel, "Keeping Planes Apart," *Fortune,* June 27, 2005, 112.

51. B. Bremner and D. Roberts, "A Billion Tough Sells," *BusinessWeek,* March 20, 2006, 44.

52. See M. Gupta, A. Brantley, and V. P. Jackson, "Product Involvement as a Predictor of Generation Y Consumer Decision Making Styles," *The Business Review,* Summer 2010, 28–33; and S. S. Wang, "Why So Many People Can't Make Decisions," *The Wall Street Journal,* September 28, 2010, D1, D2.

53. "Ethics and Employee Engagement," *Ethics Resource Center,* 2010, http://www.ethics.org/nbes, accessed March 5, 2011.

54. The decision tree and resulting discussion are based on C. E. Bagley, "The Ethical Leader's Decision Tree," *Harvard Business Review,* February 2003, 18–19.

55. M. Kimes, "Bad to the Bone," *Fortune,* October 8, 2012, 140–154.

56. S. Z. Al-Mahmood, "Doomed Factories Raced to Fill Orders," *The Wall Street Journal,* April 30, 2013, A1, A9.

57. See M. B. Curtis, T. L. Conover, and L. C. Chui, "A Cross-Cultural Study of the Influence of Country of Origin, Justice, Power Distance, and Gender on Ethical Decision Making," *Journal of International Accounting Research,* 2012, 5–34; and L. Langlois and C. Lapointe, "Can Ethics Be Learned?," *Journal of Educational Administration,* November 2010, 147–163.

58. G. W. Hill, "Group versus Individual Performance: Are N + 1 Heads Better Than 1?," *Psychological Bulletin,* May 1982, 517–539.

59. T. Connolly, L. Ordóñez, and S. Barker, "Judgment and Decision Making," in N. W. Schmitt and S. Highhouse, eds., *Handbook of Psychology,* 2nd ed., vol. 12 (Hoboken, NJ: Wiley, 2013), 493–522.

60. These advantages are based on N. R. F. Maier, "Assets and Liabilities in Group Problem Solving: The Need for an Integrative Function," *Psychological Review,* July 1967, 239–249.

61. Ibid.

62. I. L. Janis, *Groupthink,* 2nd ed. (Boston: Houghton Mifflin, 1982), 9. Alternative models are discussed in K. Granstrom and D. Stiwne, "A Bipolar Model of Groupthink: An Expansion of Janis's Concept," *Small Group Research,* February 1998, 32–56.

63. R. Bénabou, "Groupthink: Collective Delusions in Organizations and Markets," *Review of Economic Studies,* April 2013, 429–462.

64. Adapted from Janis, *Groupthink,* 174–175. Also see J. M. Wellen and M. Neale, "Deviance, Self-Typicality, and Group Cohesion: The Corrosive Effects of the Bad Ales on the Barrel," *Small Group Research,* April 2006, 165–186.

65. See C. K. W. De Dreu and M. A. West, "Minority Dissent and Team Innovation: The Importance of Participation in Decision Making," *Journal of Applied Psychology,* December 2001, 1191–1201; and G. Park and R. P. DeShon, "A Multilevel Model of Minority Opinion Expression and Team Decision-Making Effectiveness," *Journal of Applied Psychology,* September 2010, 824–833.

66. G. M. Parker, *Team Players and Teamwork: The New Competitive Business Strategy* (San Francisco, CA: Jossey-Bass, 1990).

67. A. F. Osborn, *Applied Imagination: Principles and Procedures of Creative Thinking,* 3rd ed. (New York: Scribners, 1979).

68. See R. L. Keeney, "Value-Focused Brainstorming," *Decision Analysis,* December 2012, 303–313.

69. R. Tartell, "Power Up Your Brainstorming," *Training,* November/December 2012, 14.

70. See N. C. Dalkey, D. L. Rourke, R. Lewis, and D. Snyder, *Studies in the Quality of Life: Delphi and Decision Making* (Lexington, MA: Lexington Books, 1972).

71. An application of the Delphi technique can be found in A. Graefe and J. S. Armstrong, "Comparing Face-to-Face Meetings, Nominal Groups, Delphi and Prediction Markets on an Estimating Task," *International Journal of Forecasting,* January–March 2011, 183–195.

72. A.-M. Suduc, M. Bîzoi, M. Cioca, and F. G. Filip, "Evolution of Decision Support Systems Research Field in Numbers," *Informatica Economică,* 2010, 78.

73. See P. Dvorak, "Best Buy Taps 'Prediction Market'; Imaginary Stocks Let Workers Forecast Whether Retailer's Plans Will Meet Goals," *The Wall Street Journal,* September 16, 2008, B1.

74. E. Turban, T.-P. Liang, and S. P. J. Wu, "A Framework for Adopting Collaboration 2.0 Tools for Virtual Group Decision Making," *Group Decision Negotiations,* March 2011, 137–154.

75. The case is based on S. M. Latta, "Save Your Staff, Improve Your Business," *HR Magazine,* January 2012, 30–32.

76. J. Zhou and C. E. Shalley, "Deepening Our Understanding of Creativity in the Workplace: A Review of Different Approaches to

Creativity Research," in S. Zedeck, ed., *Handbook of Industrial and Organizational Psychology* (Washington, DC: American Psychological Association, 2011), 275–302.

77. T. Montag, C. P. Maertz Jr., and M. Baer, "A Critical Analysis of the Workplace Creativity Criterion Space," *Journal of Management,* July 2012, 1369.

78. This discussion is based on T. Montag, C. P. Maertz Jr., and M. Baer, "A Critical Analysis of the Workplace Creativity Criterion Space," *Journal of Management,* July 2012, 1362–1386.

79. D. Coutu, "Creativity Step by Step," *Harvard Business Review,* April 2008, 48–49 (interview with Twyla Tharp).

80. See S. Shellenbarger, "Tactics to Spark Creativity," *The Wall Street Journal,* April 3, 2013, D1, D2.

81. See Zhou and Shalley, "Deepening Our Understanding of Creativity in the Workplace"; and Y. Gong, S.-Y. Cheung, M. Wang, and J.-C. Huang, "Unfolding the Proactive Process for Creativity: Integration of the Employee Proactivity, Information Exchange, and Psychological Safety Perspectives," *Journal of Management,* September 2012, 1611–1633.

82. Zhou and Shalley, "Deepening Our Understanding of Creativity in the Workplace"; and C. E. Shalley, J. Zhou, and G. R. Oldham, "The Effects of Personal and Contextual Characteristics on Creativity: Where Should We Go from Here?," *Journal of Management,* December 2004, 933–958.

83. R. E. Silverman, "The Science of Serendipity in the Workplace," *The Wall Street Journal,* May 1, 2013, B6.

84. See B. Comstock, "Figure It Out," *Harvard Business Review,* May 2013, 42; and C. A. Hartnell, A. Y. Ou, and A. Kinicki, "Organizational Culture and Organizational Effectiveness: A Meta-Analytic Investigation of the Competing Values Framework's Theoretical Suppositions," *Journal of Applied Psychology,* 2011, 677–694.

85. Derived from E. Catmull, "How Pixar Fosters Collective Creativity," *Harvard Business Review,* September 2008, 65–72; "Keeping Creatives Happy," *Fortune,* March 16, 2009, 40 (interview with Jeffrey Katzenberg); and L. Tischler, "A Designer Takes on His Biggest Challenge Ever," *Fast Company,* February 2009, 78–83.

86. See A. Oke, N. Munshi, and F. O. Walumbwa, "The Influence of Leadership on Innovation Processes and Activities," *Organizational Dynamics,* January–March 2009, 64–72.

87. D. A. Peluso, "Preserving Employee Know-How," *HR Magazine,* May 2010, 99.

88. B. Ortutay, "Groupon Ousts CEO Andrew Mason, Still Faces Underlying Problems," *Associated Press,* February 28, 2013.

89. L. Etter, "Groupon Therapy," *Vanity Fair,* August 2011, http://www.vanityfair.com/business/features/2011/08/groupon-201108.

90. S. Basak, "Andrew Mason: Groupon's Shooting Star," *Medill Reports,* Chicago, Northwestern University, May 15, 2013, http://news.medill.northwestern.edu/chicago/news.aspx?id=221426.

91. J. Pepitone, "Groupon IPO Prices at $20 a Share," *CNN/Money,* November 4, 2011, http://money.cnn.com/2011/11/04/technology/groupon_IPO_price/index.htm. In August 2011 regulators made Groupon refile for its IPO with financials following standard practices. The first reissue restated what had erroneously been shown as operating profits as operating losses, under generally accepted accounting principles. A second filing recategorized monies first shown as cash instead as outstanding liabilities (for money yet to be paid to merchants).

92. A. Cessna, "Groupon Can't Shake This Lawsuit," *Wall Street Cheatsheet,* September 22, 2013, http://wallstcheatsheet.com/stocks/groupon-cant-shake-this-lawsuit.html/?a=viewall.

93. A. Hartung, "Groupon Needs a New CEO—NOW!!," *Forbes,* August 15, 2012, http://www.forbes.com/sites/adamhartung/2012/08/15/groupon-needs-a-new-ceo-now/.

94. Excerpted from A. W. Mathews, "Hospitals Prescribe Big Data to Track Doctors at Work," *The Wall Street Journal,* July 12, 2013, A1, A10.

Chapter 12

1. A. Buzzese, "Make Your Meetings Work for You," *The Arizona Republic,* May 5, 2013, D6.

2. S. Shellenbarger, "Meet the Meeting Killers," *The Wall Street Journal,* May 15, 2012.

3. R. E. Silverman, "Where's the Boss? Trapped in a Meeting," *The Wall Street Journal,* February 14, 2012.

4. Buzzese, "Make Your Meetings Work for You."

5. See A. D. Wright, "Survey: Nonprofits Fall Short on Ethics," *HR Magazine,* May 2008, 24; and R. Riney, "Heal Leadership Disorders," *HR Magazine,* May 2008, 62–66.

6. B. Worthen and J. S. Lublin, "Hurd Deal Inflamed Directors," *The Wall Street Journal,* August 16, 2010.

7. S. Forbes, "Deficit Size Egos," *Forbes,* April 11, 2011.

8. P. Brinkley and E. Glazer, "Exide Files for Bankruptcy," *The Wall Street Journal,* June 10, 2013, http://online.wsj.com/article/SB10001424127887324904004578537414297602332.html, accessed June 11, 2013.

9. S. Berfield, "A Pistachio Farmer, Pom Wonderful, and the FTC," *Bloomberg Businessweek,* November 11, 2010. See also Federal Trade Commission press release, "FTC Commissioners Uphold Trial Judge Decision," January 16, 2013, http://www.ftc.gov/opa/2013/01/pom.shtm, accessed September 6, 2013.

10. B. Protess and J. Silver-Greenberg, "Former Regulators Find a Home with Powerful Firm," *The New York Times,* April 9, 2013, http://dealbook.nytimes.com/2013/04/09/for-former-regulators-a-home-on-wall-street/, accessed April 10, 2013.

11. Editorial Board, "The Capitol's Spinning Door Accelerates," *The New York Times,* Februrary 2, 2014, http://www.nytimes.com/2014/02/03/opinion/the-capitols-spinning-door-accelerates.html.

12. Adapted from D. Cardwell, "Solar Industry Borrows a Page, and a Party, from Tupperware," *The New York Times,* November 30, 2012, http://www.nytimes.com/2012/12/01/business/energy-environment/solar-industry-borrows-a-page-and-a-party-from-tupperware.html?_r=0, accessed December 4, 2012.

13. S. E. Ante and J. S. Lublin, "New Microsoft CEO Shapes His Team," *The Wall Street Journal,* March 3, 2014, http://online.wsj.com/news/articles/SB10001424052702304585004579417562352185026?KEYWORDS=new+microsoft+CEO&mg=reno64-wsj, accessed March 7, 2014.

14. Based on E. Garone, "Managing Your Former Peers Takes Extra Effort," *The Wall Street Journal,* March 10, 2008, http://online.wsj.com/news/articles/SB120490121314719429.

15. W. Clark, "The Potency of Persuasion," *Fortune,* November 12, 2007, 48.

16. M. Kimes, "Why J&J's Headache Won't Go Away," *Fortune,* September 6, 2010, 104–106.

17. See B. Gupta and N. K. Sharma, "Compliance with Bases of Power and Subordinates' Perception of Superiors: Moderating Effect of Quality of Interaction," *Singapore Management Review,* 2008, 1–24; and P. M. Podsakoff and C. A. Schriesheim, "Field Studies of French and Raven's Bases of Power: Critique, Reanalysis, and Suggestions for Future Research," *Psychological Bulletin,* May 1985, 388.

18. M. T. Maynard, L. L. Gilson, and J. E. Mathieu, "Empowerment—Fad or Fab? A Multilevel Review of the Past Two Decades of Research," *Journal of Management 20,* 2012, 1–51.

19. S. E. Seibert, G. Wang, and S. H. Courtright, "Antecedents and Consequences of Psychological and Team Empowerment in Organizations: A Meta-Analytic Review," *Journal of Applied Psychology 5,* 2011, 981–1003.

20. L. Shaper Walters, "A Leader Redefines Management," *Christian Science Monitor*, September 22, 1992, 14. Also see A. D. Amar, C. Hentrich, and V. Hlupic, "To Be a Better Leader, Give Up Authority," *Harvard Business Review*, December 2009, 22–24; and L. Wiseman and G. McKeown, "Bringing Out the Best in Your People," *Harvard Business Review*, May 2010, 117–121.

21. A. Fox, "Raising Engagement," *HR Magazine*, May 2010, 39. See also "How May We Help You?," *Inc*, March 2011, 63.

22. Maynard et al., "Empowerment—Fad or Fab?" See also X. Zhang and K. M. Bartol, "Linking Empowering Leadership and Employee Creativity: The Influence of Psychological Empowerment, Intrinsic Motivation, and Reactive Process Engagement," *Academy of Management Journal* 53, 2010, 107–128.

23. Maynard et al., "Empowerment—Fad or Fab?," 4.

24. M. T. Maynard, J. E. Mathieu, L. L. Gilson, E. H. O'Boyle, and K. P. Cigularov, "Drivers and Outcomes of Team Psychological Empowerment: A Meta-Analytic Review and Model Test," *Organizational Psychological Review* 3, 2012, 101–137.

25. M. M Luciano, J. E. Mathieu, and T. M. Ruddy, "Leading Multiple Teams: Average and Relative External Leadership Influences on Team Empowerment and Effectiveness," *Journal of Applied Psychology* 2014, 322–331.

26. Ibid.

27. M. Macphee, V. S. Dahinten, S. Hejazi, H. Lachinger, A. Kazanjian, A. McCutcheon, J. Skelton-Green, and L. O'Brien-Pallas, "Testing the Effects of an Empowerment-Based Leadership Development Programme: Part 1—Leader Outcomes," *Journal of Nursing Management*, 2014, 4–15.

28. Ibid.

29. K. Bhasin, "Bill Ackman's Costly Defeat Marks the End of an Era for J.C. Penney," *Huffington Post*, August 26, 2013, http://www.huffingtonpost.com/2013/08/26/bill-ackman-jcpenney-stake_n_3818817.html.

30. For related reading, see K. D. Elsbach, "How to Pitch a Brilliant Idea," *Harvard Business Review*, September 2003, 117–123.

31. Excerpted and adapted from "Increasing Your Influence—The Seven Traits of Influential People," *Manager*, Winter 2010.

32. "The Uses (and Abuses) of Influence," *Harvard Business Review*, July–August 2013, 76–81. Also adapted from R. B. Cialdini, "Harnessing the Science of Persuasion," *Harvard Business Review*, October 2001, 72–79.

33. "The Uses (and Abuses) of Influence," 77.

34. G. N. Gotsis and Z. Kortezi, "Ethical Considerations in Organizational Politics: Expanding the Perspective," *Journal of Business Ethics*, 2010, 497–517.

35. G. Atinc, M. Darrat, B. Fuller, and B. W. Parker, "Perceptions of Organizational Politics: A Meta-Analysis of Theoretical Antecedents," *Journal of Managerial Issues*, Winter 2010, 494–513.

36. E. Chasan, "Arthur Levitt Backs Auditor Term Limits," *The Wall Street Journal*, October 19, 2011, http://blogs.wsj.com/cfo/2011/10/19/arthur-levitt-backs-auditor-term-limits/tab/print/, accessed September 8, 2013.

37. Atinc et al., "Perceptions of Organizational Politics." See also discussion in D. R. Beeman and T. W. Sharkey, "The Use and Abuse of Corporate Politics," *Business Horizons*, March–April 1987, 26–30.

38. Quote and data from "The Big Picture: Reasons for Raises," *Business Week*, May 29, 2006, 11.

39. A. Raia, "Power, Politics, and the Human Resource Professional," *Human Resource Planning*, no. 4, 1985, 203.

40. B. Dattner and R. Hogan, "Can You Handle Failure?" *Harvard Business Review*, April 2011.

41. This three-level distinction comes from A. T. Cobb, "Political Diagnosis: Applications in Organizational Development," *Academy of Management Review*, July 1986, 482–496.

42. An excellent historical and theoretical perspective of coalitions can be found in W. B. Stevenson, J. L. Pearce, and L. W. Porter, "The Concept of 'Coalition' in Organization Theory and Research," *Academy of Management Review*, April 1985, 256–268.

43. M. Gordon, "Farmers, Airlines Exempt from Derivatives Rules," *Bloomberg Businessweek*, April 12, 2011.

44. D. Faber, "Goldman Sachs—Power and Peril," *CNBC*, October 6, 2010. For more on networks and influence, see J. Pfeffer, *Power—Why Some People Have It and Others Don't* (New York: Harper-Collins, 2010).

45. B. K. Miller, M. A. Rutherford, and R. W. Kolodinsky, "Perceptions of Organizational Politics: A Meta-Analysis of Outcomes," *Journal of Business and Psychology*, March 2008, 209–223.

46. H. H. Hsiung, C. W. Lin, and C. S. Lin, "Nourishing or Suppressing? The Contradictory Influences of Perception of Organizational Politics on Organizational Citizenship Behavior," *Journal of Occupational and Organizational Psychology* 85, 2012, 258–276.

47. A. Zaleznik, "Real Work," *Harvard Business Review*, January–February 1989, 60.

48. C. M. Koen Jr. and S. M. Crow, "Human Relations and Political Skills," *HR Focus*, December 1995, 11.

49. Excerpted and adapted from "Best Practices for Managing Organizational Politics," *Nonprofit World*, July–August 2010.

50. H. Zhao and R. C. Liden, "Internship: A Recruitment and Selection Perspective," *Journal of Applied Psychology*, 2011, 221–229.

51. M. S. Kim, D. T. Kim, and J. I. Kim, "CSR for Sustainable Development: CSR Beneficiary Positioning and Impression Management Motivation," *Corporate Social Responsibility and Environmental Management*, 2014, 14–27.

52. M. R. Barrick, B. W. Swider, and G. L. Stewart, "Initial Evaluations in the Interview: Relationships with Subsequent Interviewer Evaluations and Employment Offers," *Journal of Applied Psychology*, 2010, 1163–1172.

53. "Craig Newmark," Biographical Note, *The Huffington Post*, http://www.huffingtonpost.com/craig-newmark/, accessed March 5, 2014.

54. Adapted from "5 Ways to Make a Killer First Impression," *Forbes*, November 2, 2011, http://www.forbes.com/sites/yec/2011/11/02/5-ways-to-make-a-killer-first-impression/, accessed June 13, 2013.

55. J. D. Westphal, S. Hyun, M. L. McDonald, and M. L. A. Hayward, "Helping Other CEOs Avoid Bad Press: Social Exchange and Impression Management Support among CEOs in Communications with Journalists," *Administrative Science Quarterly*, June 2012, 217–268.

56. J. D. Westphal and M. E. Graebner, "A Matter of Appearances: How Corporate Leaders Manage the Impressions of Financial Analysts about the Conduct of Their Boards," *Academy of Management Journal*, 2010, 15–43.

57. S. Friedman, "What Do You Really Care About? What Are You Most Interested in?," *Fast Company*, March 1999, 90.

58. N. Perlroth, "Venture Capital Firms, Once Discreet, Learn the Promotional Game," *The New York Times*, July 22, 2013, http://www.nytimes.com/2012/07/23/business/venture-capital-firms-once-discreet-learn-the-promotional-game.html?pagewanted=all&_r=0, accessed July 23, 2013.

59. See S. J. Wayne and G. R. Ferris, "Influence Tactics, Affect, and Exchange Quality in Supervisor-Subordinate Interactions: A Laboratory Experiment and Field Study," *Journal of Applied Psychology*, October 1990, 487–499. For another version, see Table 1 (246) in S. J. Wayne and R. C. Liden, "Effects of Impression Management on Performance Ratings: A Longitudinal Study," *Academy of Management Journal*, February 1995, 232–260.

60. See R. A. Gordon, "Impact of Ingratiation on Judgments and Evaluations: A Meta-Analytic Investigation," *Journal of Personality and Social Psychology*, July 1996, 54–70.

61. See Y.-Y. Chen and W. Fang, "The Moderating Effect of Impression Management on the Organizational Politics-Performance Relationship," *Journal of Business Ethics*, May 2008, 263–277.

62. See, for example, D. C. Treadway, G. R. Ferris, A. B. Duke, G. L. Adams, and J. B. Thatcher, "The Moderating Role of Subordinate

Political Skill on Supervisors' Impressions of Subordinate Ingratiation and Ratings of Subordinate Interpersonal Facilitation," *Journal of Applied Psychology,* May 2007, 848–855.

63. Excerpted and adapted from R. Hosking, "Poor Behaviors: Could You Be Making a Bad Impression with Your Boss?," *OfficePro,* August–September 2010, 5.

64. P. S. Goodman, "In Case of Emergency: What Not to Do," *The New York Times,* August 21, 2010.

65. Ibid.

66. Ibid.

67. Ibid. (adapted).

68. K. T. Dirks, P. H. Kim, D. L. Ferrin, and C. D. Cooper, "Understanding the Effects of Substantive Responses on Trust Following Transgression," *Organizational Behavior and Decision Processes,* 2011, 87–103.

69. Ibid.

70. L. A. Helmchen, M. R. Richards, and T. B. McDonald, "Successful Remediation of Patient Safety Incidents: A Tale of Two Medication Errors," *Health Care Management Review,* 2011, 114–123.

71. D. Streitfield, "The Best Book Reviews Money Can Buy," *The New York Times,* August 25, 2012, BU1.

72. B. Liu, "Opinion Spam Detection: Detecting Fake Reviews and Reviewers," University of Illinois at Chicago, Faculty Website, http://www.cs.uic.edu/~liub/FBS/fake-reviews.html, accessed October 25, 2013.

73. "R. J. Ellory, Author, Caught Writing Fake Amazon Reviews for Books," *The Huffington Post,* September 4, 2012, http://www.huffingtonpost.com/2012/09/04/rj-ellory-fake-amazon-reviews-caught_n_1854713.html.

74. A. Hoy, "Karma! Man Who Sold Book Reviews Is Shamed Online," *Writers Weekly,* September 12, 2012, http://writersweekly.com/the_latest_from_angelahoycom/007557_09122012.html.

75. B. R. Schlenker and T. W. Britt, "Beneficial Impression Management: Strategically Controlling Information to Help Friends," *Journal of Personality and Social Psychology,* April 1999, 559.

Chapter 13

1. B. Avolio, J. J. Sosik, and Y. Berson, "Leadership Models, Methods, and Applications: Progress and Remaining Blind Spots," in N. W. Schmitt and S. Highhouse, eds., *Handbook of Psychology* (Vol. 12), 2nd ed. (Hoboken, NJ: Wiley, 2013), 367–389.

2. M. Buckingham, "Leadership Development in the Age of the Algorithm," *Harvard Business Review,* June 2012, 86–94.

3. R. Saunderson, "Trying to Follow the Leader," *Training,* May/June 2012, 79.

4. The following steps are based on S. J. Ashford and D. S. DeRue, "Developing as a Leader: The Power of Mindful Engagement," *Organizational Dynamics,* April–June 2012, 146–154.

5. D. S. DeRue, J. D. Nahrgang, J. R. Hollenbeck, and K. Workman, "A Quasi-Experimental Study of After-Event Reviews and Leadership Development," *Journal of Applied Psychology,* September 2012, 997–1015.

6. P. G. Northouse, *Leadership: Theory and Practice,* 6th ed. (Thousand Oaks, CA: Sage, 2012), 3.

7. "State of the American Workplace: Employee Engagement Insights for U.S. Business Leaders," Washington, DC: Gallup, 2013, http://www.gallup.com/strategicconsulting/163007/state-american-workplace.aspx, accessed March 12, 2014.

8. See J. Hogan, R. Hogan, and R. B. Kaiser, "Management Derailment," in S. Zedeck, ed., *APA Handbook of Industrial and Organizational Psychology* (Washington, DC: American Psychological Association, 2011), 555–575.

9. See D. S. DeRue, J. D. Nahrgang, N. Wellman, and S. E. Humphrey, "Trait and Behavioral Theories of Leadership: An Integration and Meta-Analytic Test of Their Relative Validity," *Personnel Psychology,*

2011, 7–52; and N. J. Hiller, L. A. DeChurch, T. Murase, and D. Doty, "Searching for Outcomes of Leadership: A 25-Year Review," *Journal of Management,* July 2011, 1137–1177.

10. See A. Kinicki, K. Jacobson, S. Peterson, and G. Prussia, "The Development and Validation of the Performance Management Behavior Questionnaire," *Personnel Psychology,* 2013, 1–46.

11. B. M. Bass and R. Bass, *The Bass Handbook of Leadership: Theory, Research, and Managerial Applications,* 4th ed. (New York: Free Press, 2008), 654.

12. See P. Sellers, "The Next JetBlue," *Fortune,* July 26, 2010, 97–100.

13. See B. Stone and P. Burrows, "Opening Remarks: The Essence of Apple," *Bloomberg Businessweek,* January 24–30, 2011, 6–8; and P. Ingrassia, "Ford's Renaissance Man," *The Wall Street Journal,* February 27–28, 2010, A13.

14. Bass and Bass, *The Bass Handbook of Leadership,* 103–135.

15. These results are based on E. H. O'Boyle Jr., D. F. Forsyth, G. C. Banks, and M. A. McDaniel, "A Meta-Analysis of the Dark Triad and Work Behavior: A Social Exchange Perspective," *Journal of Applied Psychology,* May 2012, 557–579; and DeRue, Nahrgang, Wellman, and Humphrey, "Trait and Behavioral Theories of Leadership."

16. See S. M. Spain, P. Harms, and J. M. Lebreton, "The Dark Side of Personality at Work," *Journal of Organizational Behavior,* February 2014, S41–S60.

17. B. M. Galvin, D. A. Waldman, and P. Balthazard, "Visionary Communication Qualities as Mediators of the Relationship between Narcissism and Attributions of Leader Charisma," *Personnel Psychology,* Autumn 2010, 510.

18. Ibid., 509–537; and O'Boyle Jr., Forsyth, Banks, and McDaniel, "A Meta-Analysis of the Dark Triad and Work Behavior."

19. T. A. Judge, A. E. Colbert, and R. Ilies, "Intelligence and Leadership: A Quantitative Review and Test of Theoretical Propositions," *Journal of Applied Psychology,* June 2004, 542–552.

20. Hogan, Hogan, and Kaiser, "Management Derailment." Also see M. F. R. Kets de Vries, "Coaching the Toxic Leader," *Harvard Business Review,* April 2014, 101–09.

21. R. S. Nadler, *Leading with Emotional Intelligence* (New York: McGraw-Hill, 2011).

22. See D. S. Whitman, "Emotional Intelligence and Leadership in Organizations: A Meta-Analytic Test of Process Mechanisms," dissertation submitted for Doctor of Philosophy, Florida International University, 2009; and F. Walter, R. H. Humphrey, and M. S. Cole, "Unleashing Leadership Potential: Toward an Evidence-Based Management of Emotional Intelligence," *Organizational Dynamics,* July–September 2012, 212–219.

23. Gender and the emergence of leaders was examined by A. H. Eagly and S. J. Karau, "Gender and the Emergence of Leaders: A Meta-Analysis," *Journal of Personality and Social Psychology,* May 1991, 685–710; and R. Ayman and K. Korabik, "Leadership: Why Gender and Culture Matter," *American Psychologist,* April 2010, 157–170.

24. See A. H. Eagly, S. J. Karau, and B. T. Johnson, "Gender and Leadership Style among School Principals: A Meta-Analysis," *Educational Administration Quarterly,* February 1992, 76–102.

25. Supportive findings are contained in J. M. Twenge, "Changes in Women's Assertiveness in Response to Status and Roles: A Cross-Temporal Meta-Analysis, 1931–1993," *Journal of Personality and Social Psychology,* July 2001, 133–145.

26. For a summary of this research, see H. Ibarra and O. Obodaru, "Women and the Vision Thing," *Harvard Business Review,* January 2009, 62–70.

27. Implicit leadership theory is discussed by Bass and Bass, *The Bass Handbook of Leadership,* 46–78; and J. S. Mueller, J. A. Goncalo, and D. Kamdar, "Recognizing Creative Leadership: Can Creative Idea Expression Negatively Relate to Perceptions of Leadership Potential?," *Journal of Experimental Social Psychology 47,* 2011, 494–498, https://1318d3f964915c29847671207924

aec761817d4b6cf4d3ee8ac05a.ssl.cf2.rackcdn.com/or-mueller_
goncalo_kamdar_201_jesp_creativity-and-leadership.pdf.

28. Results can be found in R. G. Lord, C. L. De Vader, and G. M. Al-
liger, "A Meta-Analysis of the Relation between Personality Traits
and Leadership Perceptions: An Application of Validity General-
ization Procedures," *Journal of Applied Psychology*, August
1986, 402–410.

29. See S. Melwani, J. S. Mueller, and J. R. Overbeck, "Looking
Down: The Influence of Contempt and Compassion on Emergent
Leadership Categorizations," *Journal of Applied Psychology*,
November 2012, 1171–1185; and A. H. Eagly and J. L. Chin, "Diversity
and Leadership in a Changing World," *American Psychologist*,
April 2010, 216–224.

30. M. Buck and M. Martin, "Leaders Teaching Leaders," *HR Magazine*,
September 2012, 60–62.

31. D. Zielinski, "Effective Assessments," *HR Magazine*, January
2011, 61–64.

32. Abstracted from M. Weinstein, "World-Class Leaders," *Training*,
May/June 2012, 18–21.

33. G. Yukl, "Effective Leadership Behavior: What We Know and
What Questions Need More Attention," *Academy of Management Perspectives*, November 2012, 69.

34. DeRue, Nahrgang, Wellman, and Humphrey, "Trait and Behavioral Theories of Leadership."

35. T. A. Judge, R. F. Piccolo, and R. Ilies, "The Forgotten Ones? The
Validity of Consideration and Initiating Structure in Leadership
Research," *Journal of Applied Psychology*, February 2004, 36–51.

36. An addition and description of transactional leadership is provided
by Bass and Bass, *The Bass Handbook of Leadership*, 618–648.

37. Excerpted from D. McGinn, "Battling Back from Betrayal," *Harvard
Business Review*, December 2010, 131.

38. DeRue, Nahrgang, Wellman, and Humphrey, "Trait and Behavioral
Theories of Leadership."

39. Excerpted from B. O'Keefe, "Leader of the Crimson Tide," *Fortune*,
September 24, 2012, 151–160.

40. Yukl, "Effective Leadership Behavior."

41. Judge, Piccolo, and Ilies, "The Forgotten Ones?"

42. M. T. Maynard, L. L. Gilson, and J. E. Mathieu, "Empowerment—
Fad or Fab? A Multilevel Review of the Past Two Decades of Research," *Journal of Management*, July 2012, 1231–1281.

43. M. Moskowitz and R. Levering, "The 100 Best Companies to
Work For," *Fortune*, February 4, 2013, 88.

44. M. Littman, "Best Bosses Tell All," *Working Woman*, October
2000, 55.

45. See Maynard, Gilson, and Mathieu, "Empowerment—Fad or Fab?";
and X. Zhang and K. M. Bartol, "Linking Empowering Leadership
and Employee Creativity: The Influence of Psychological Empowerment, Intrinsic Motivation, and Creative Process Engagement,"
Academy of Management Journal, February 2010, 107–128.

46. An overall summary of servant-leadership is provided by L. C.
Spears, *Reflections on Leadership: How Robert K. Greenleaf's
Theory of Servant-Leadership Influenced Today's Top Manage-
ment Thinkers* (New York: Wiley, 1995).

47. M. Weinstein, "The Secret Sauce for a Better Boss," *Training*,
May/June 2013, 41.

48. See S. J. Peterson, B. M. Galvin, and D. Lange, "CEO Servant
Leadership: Exploring Executive Characteristics and Firm Performance," *Personnel Psychology*, 2012, 565–596; and F. O. Walumbwa, C. A. Hartnell, and A. Oke, "Servant Leadership,
Procedural Justice Climate, Service Climate, Employee Attitudes,
and Organizational Citizenship Behavior: A Cross-Level Investigation," *Journal of Applied Psychology*, May 2010, 517–529.

49. "The Best Advice I Ever Got," *Fortune*, May 12, 2008, 74.

50. See DeRue, Nahrgang, Wellman, and Humphrey, "Trait and Behavioral Theories of Leadership."

51. Results can be found in A. H. Eagly, M. C. Johannesen-Schmidt,
and M. L. van Engen, "Transformational, Transactional, and

52. See DeRue, Nahrgang, Wellman, and Humphrey, "Trait and Behavioral Theories of Leadership."

53. See S. T. Hannah and B. J. Avolio, "Ready or Not: How Do We
Accelerate the Developmental Readiness of Leaders?" *Journal
of Organizational Behavior*, November 2010, 1181–1187; and
J. M. Leigh, E. R. Shapiro, and S. H. Penney, "Developing Diverse,
Collaborative Leaders: An Empirical Program Evaluation," *Journal of Leadership & Organizational Studies*, November 2010,
370–379.

54. For more on this theory, see F. E. Fiedler, "A Contingency Model
of Leadership Effectiveness," in *Advances in Experimental Social
Psychology*, vol. 1, ed. L. Berkowitz (New York: Academic Press,
1964); and F. E. Fiedler, *A Theory of Leadership Effectiveness*
(New York: McGraw-Hill, 1967).

55. See L. H. Peters, D. D. Hartke, and J. T. Pohlmann, "Fiedler's Contin-
gency Theory of Leadership: An Application of the Meta-Analysis
Procedures of Schmidt and Hunter," *Psychological Bulletin*,
March 1985, 274–285; and C. A. Schriesheim, B. J. Tepper, and
L. A. Tetrault, "Least Preferred Co-worker Score, Situational Control,
and Leadership Effectiveness: A Meta-Analysis of Contingency
Model Performance Predictions," *Journal of Applied Psychology*,
August 1994, 561–573.

56. B. Groysberg, A. N. McLean, and N. Nohria, "Are Leaders Portable?," *Harvard Business Review*, May 2006, 95, 97.

57. See L. S. Lambert, B. J. Tepper, J. C. Carr, T. Holt, and A. J.
Barelka, "Forgotten but Not Gone: An Examination of Fit Between
Leader Consideration and Initiating Structure Needed and Re-
ceived," *Journal of Applied Psychology*, September 2012, 913–930.

58. Excerpted from B. Marriott, "How I Did It . . . Marriott's Executive
Chairman on Choosing the First Nonfamily CEO," *Harvard Business Review*, May 2013, 45–48.

59. See R. Siklos, "Bob Iger Rocks Disney," *Fortune*, January 19,
2009, 80–86.

60. Results can be found in P. M. Podskoff, S. B. MacKenzie,
M. Ahearne, and W. H. Bommer, "Searching for a Needle in a
Haystack: Trying to Identify the Illusive Moderators of Leadership
Behaviors," *Journal of Management*, 1995, 422–470.

61. The steps were developed by H. P. Sims Jr., S. Faraj, and S. Yun,
"When Should a Leader Be Directive or Empowering? How to
Develop Your Own Situational Theory of Leadership," *Business
Horizons*, March–April 2009, 149–158.

62. See J. B. Wu, A. S. Tsui, and A. J. Kinicki, "Consequences of Dif-
ferentiated Leadership in Groups," *Academy of Management
Journal*, February 2010, 90–106.

63. M. Weber, *The Theory of Social and Economic Organization*
(New York: Oxford University Press, 1947).

64. A historical review of transformational leadership is provided by
D. V. Knippenberg and S. B. Sitkin, "A Critical Assessment of
Charismatic–Transformational Leadership Research: Back to the
Drawing Board?," *The Academy of Management Annals*, 2013, 1–60.

65. B. Nanus, *Visionary Leadership* (San Francisco, CA: Jossey-Bass,
1992), 8.

66. Moskowitz and Levering, "The 100 Best Companies to Work For."

67. See "We Should Never Cut, Ration, or Restrict Humanity," *The
Wall Street Journal*, June 20, 2013, A7.

68. "Yvon Chouinard," Wikipedia, http://en.wikipedia.org/wiki/Yvon_
Chouinard, accessed March 12, 2014, and S. Stevenson, "Ameri-
ca's Most Unlikely Corporate Guru," *The Wall Street Journal
Magazine*, May 2012, 86–89.

69. D. Brady, "Can GE Still Manage?" *Bloomberg Businessweek*,
April 25, 2010, 28.

70. M. A. Tucker, "Make Managers Responsible," *HR Magazine*,
March 2012, 75–78.

71. Supportive results can be found in P. D. Harms and M. Credé,
"Emotional Intelligence and Transformational and Transactional

72. See Eagly, Johannesen-Schmidt, and van Engen, "Transformational, Transactional, and Laissez-Faire Leadership Styles."

73. See S. Clarke, "Safety Leadership: A Meta-Analytic Review of Transformational and Transactional Leadership Styles as Antecedents of Safety Behaviors," Journal of Occupational and Organizational Psychology, March 2013, 22–49; and G. Wang, I.-S. Oh, S. H. Courtright, and A. E. Colbert, "Transformational Leadership and Performance across Criteria and Levels: A Meta-Analytic Review of 25 Years of Research," Group & Organization Management, 2011, 223–270.

74. Knippenberg and Sitkin, "A Critical Assessment of Charismatic–Transformational Leadership Research."

75. Visionary leadership is studied by C. A. Hartnell and F. O. Walumbwa, "Transformational Leadership and Organizational Culture," in N. M. Ashkanasy, C. P. M. Wilderom, and M. F. Peterson, eds., The Handbook of Organizational Culture and Climate, 2nd ed. (Thousand Oaks, CA: Sage, 2011), 225–248; and M. A. Griffin, S. K. Parker, and C. M. Mason, "Leader Vision and the Development of Adaptive and Proactive Performance: A Longitudinal Study," Journal of Applied Psychology, January 2010, 174–182.

76. Supportive results can be found in T. A. Judge and R. F. Piccolo, "Transformational and Transactional Leadership: A Meta-Analytic Test of Their Relative Validity," Journal of Applied Psychology, October 2004, 755–768.

77. X.-H. Wang and J. M. Howell, "Exploring the Dual-Level Effects of Transformational Leadership on Followers," Journal of Applied Psychology, November 2010, 1134–1144.

78. T. Whitford and S. A. Moss, "Transformational Leadership in Distributed Work Groups: The Moderating Role of Follower Regulatory Focus and Goal Orientation," Communication Research, December 2009, 810–837.

79. See F. Dansereau Jr., G. Graen, and W. Haga, "A Vertical Dyad Linkage Approach to Leadership within Formal Organizations," Organizational Behavior and Human Performance, February 1975, 46–78; and J. H. Dulebohn, W. H. Bommer, R. C. Liden, R. L. Brouer, and G. R. Ferris, "A Meta-Analysis of Antecedents and Consequences of Leader-Member Exchange: Integrating the Past with an Eye toward the Future," Journal of Management, November 2012, 1715–1759.

80. Based on Dulebohn, Bommer, Liden, Brouer, and Ferris, "A Meta-Analysis of Antecedents and Consequences of Leader-Member Exchange."

81. Ibid.

82. W. V. Breukelen, R. V. D. Leeden, W. Wesselius, and M. Hoes, "Differential Treatment within Sports Teams, Leader-Member (Coach-Player) Exchange Quality, Team Atmosphere, and Team Performance," Journal of Organizational Behavior, January 2012, 43–63.

83. T. Rockstuhl, J. H. Dulebohn, S. Ang, and L. M. Shore, "Leader-Member Exchange (LMX) and Culture: A Meta-Analysis of Correlates of LMX across 23 Countries," Journal of Applied Psychology, November 2012, 1097–1130.

84. From Dulebohn, Bommer, Liden, Brouer, and Ferris, "A Meta-Analysis of Antecedents and Consequences of Leader-Member Exchange."

85. Unless otherwise noted, from G. C. Mage, "Leading Despite Your Boss," HR Magazine, September 2003, 139–144, http://www.shrm.org/Publications/hrmagazine/EditorialContent/Pages/0903mage.aspx.

86. J. S. Lublin, "How to Prove Your Worth to the New CEO," The Wall Street Journal, March 6, 2013, B8. http://online.wsj.com/news/articles/SB20001424127887323494504578342492648887964.

87. Bass and Bass, The Bass Handbook of Leadership, 408.

88. See L. Bossidy, "What Your Leader Expects of You and What You Should Expect in Return," Harvard Business Review, April 2007, 58–65.

89. See R. Goffee and G. Jones, "Followership: It's Personal, Too," Harvard Business Review, December 2001, 148.

90. This checklist was proposed by J. J. Gabarro and J. P. Kotter, "Managing Your Boss," Harvard Business Review, January 2005, 92–99.

91. Partially based on B. Dattner, "Forewarned Is Forearmed," BusinessWeek, September 1, 2008, 50; and P. Drucker, "Managing Oneself," Harvard Business Review, January 2005, 2–11.

92. As discussed by Gabarro and Kotter, "Managing Your Boss." See also J. Banks and D. Coutu, "How to Protect Your Job in a Recession," Harvard Business Review, September 2008, 113–116.

93. See A. Bruzzese, "New Boss, New Rules," The Arizona Republic, February 3, 2013, D6.

94. D. A. Kaplan, "Lloyd Dean: The Medicine Man of Dignity Health," Fortune, January 14, 2013, http://management.fortune.cnn.com/2013/01/09/lloyd-dean-dignity-health/.

95. C. Roades and E. Larsen, "Lessons from the C-suite: Lloyd Dean, CEO of Dignity Health," Advisory.com Daily Briefing, June 21, 2013, http://www.advisory.com/Daily-Briefing/2013/06/21/Lessons-from-C-suite-Lloyd-Dean-Dignity-Health/.

96. Ibid.

97. J. C. Robinson and S. Dratler, "Corporate Structure and Capital Strategy at Catholic Healthcare West," Health Affairs 25(1), January 2006, 134–147.

98. Ibid.

99. Abstracted from C. M. Matthews, J. Hodgson, and L. Burkitt, "Glaxo Probes Tactics Used to Sell Botox in China," The Wall Street Journal, July 8, 2013, B1, B6.

Chapter 14

1. L. Hill, "Only BFFs Need Apply," Bloomberg Businessweek, January 7–13, 2013, 63–65.

2. See L. Rivera, "Hiring as Cultural Matching: The Case of Elite Professional Service Firms," American Sociological Review, December 2012, 999–1022.

3. A. L. Kristof-Brown, R. D. Zimmerman, and E. C. Johnson, "Consequences of Individuals' Fit at Work: A Meta-Analysis of Person-Job, Person-Organization, Person-Group, and Person-Supervisor Fit," Personnel Psychology, Summer 2005, 281.

4. Ibid., 281–342. See also J. P Meyer, T. D. Hecht, H. Gill, and L. Toplonytsky, "Person-Organization (Culture) Fit and Employee Commitment under Conditions of Change: A Longitudinal Study," Journal of Vocational Behavior, June 2010, 458–473.

5. See J. Bennett and M. Ramsey, "Ford Boss Reinvented Himself," The Wall Street Journal, April 22, 2014, B6; and M. Ramsey, "Ford Boss Mulally to Exit Early," The Wall Street Journal, April 22, 2014, A1, A7.

6. See G. D. Klein, "Creating Cultures That Lead to Success: Lincoln Electric, Southwest Airlines, and SAS Institute," Organizational Dynamics, January–March 2012, 32–43.

7. E. H. Schein, "Culture: The Missing Concept in Organization Studies," Administrative Science Quarterly, June 1996, 236.

8. R. Kehoe and R. M. Wright, "The Impact of High-Performance Human Resource Practices on Employees' Attitudes and Behaviors," Journal of Management, February 2013, 366–391.

9. See B. Schneider, M. G. Ehrhart, and W. H. Macey, "Organizational Climate and Culture," Annual Review of Psychology, 2013, 361–388.

10. M. Helft and J. Hempel, "Inside Facebook," Fortune, March 19, 2012, 113–122.

11. C. Suddath, "Inside the Elephant Room," Bloomberg Businessweek, December 16, 2012, 84–85.

12. "Purpose, Values, and Principles," Procter & Gamble corporate website, http://www.pg.com/en_US/company/purpose_people/pvp.shtml, accessed March 27, 2014.

13. See G. Colvin, "Who's to Blame at BP?," *Fortune,* July 26, 2010, 60; and "U.S. Sues BP, 8 Other Companies in Gulf Oil Spill," http://news.yahoo.com/s/ap/ us_golf_oil_spill, accessed January 3, 2011.

14. Results are discussed in "Executing Ethics," *Training,* March 2007, 8.

15. See M. Cording, J. S. Harrison, R. E. Hoskisson, and K. Jonsen, "Walking the Talk: A Multistakeholder Exploration of Organizational Authenticity, Employee Productivity, and Post-Merger Performance," *Academy of Management Perspectives,* February 2014, 38–56.

16. B. Roberts, "Values-Driven HR," *HR Magazine,* March 2012, 45–48.

17. A. Fox, "Get in the Business of Being Green," *HR Magazine,* June 2008, 45–46.

18. See T. L. Friedman, *Hot Flat and Crowded: Why We Need a Green Revolution—and How It Can Renew America, Release 2.0* (New York: Picador, 2009), especially "Outgreening al-Qaeda," 373–398. Also see K. Kuehn and L. McIntire, "Sustainability a CFO Can Love," *Harvard Business Review,* April 2014, 66–74.

19. Excerpted from M. Gunther, "Unilever's CEO Has a Green Thumb," *Fortune,* June 10, 2013, 125–130.

20. "Southwest Corporate Fact Sheet," http://swamedia.com, accessed July 2013.

21. "Southwest Airlines Careers," http://www.southwest.com/html/about-southwest/careers/index.html, accessed March 2014.

22. Southwest's mission statement can be found in "The Mission of Southwest Airlines," http://www.southwest.com/html/about-southwest/index.html?tab=5, accessed March 2014.

23. M. Woodward, "Why Employee Ownership Matters," *Fox Business Network,* February 25, 2013, http://www.foxbusiness.com/personal-finance/2013/02/25/why-employee-ownership-matters/.

24. See C. Ostroff, A. J. Kinicki, and R. S. Muhammad, "Organizational Culture and Climate," in I. B. Weiner, N. W. Schmitt, and S. Highhouse, eds., *Handbook of Psychology,* vol. 12, 2nd ed. (Hoboken, NJ: Wiley, 2012), 643–676.

25. A thorough description of the CVF is provided in K. S. Cameron, R. E. Quinn, J. Degraff, and A. V. Thakor, *Competing Values Leadership* (Northampton, MA: Edward Elgar, 2006).

26. See M. Moskowitz and R. Levering, "The 100 Best Companies to Work For," *Fortune,* February 3, 2014, 109.

27. A. Lashinsky, "The *Fortune* Interview: Larry Page," *Fortune,* February 6, 2012, 99.

28. See Moskowitz and Levering, "The 100 Best Companies to Work For," 110.

29. B. Casselman, "Risk-Averse Culture Infects U.S. Workers, Entrepreneurs," *The Wall Street Journal,* June 3, 2013, A1, A14.

30. T. Kelley and M. F. Cortez, "AstraZeneca's Risky Bet on Drug Discovery," *Bloomberg Businessweek,* January 3–9, 2011, 21.

31. See M. Arndt and B. Einhorn, "The 50 Most Innovative Companies," *Bloomberg Businessweek,* April 25, 2010, 39; and Arundhuti Gasrupta, "The Heart of the Meter," *Tata.com,* March 2010, http://www.tata.com/company/articlesinside/1pPYF0M8Bc4=/TLYVr3YPkMU=.

32. Excerpted from M. F. Guillén and E. García-Canal, "Execution as Strategy," *Harvard Business Review,* October 2012, 103–107.

33. B. Simpson, "'Flying People, Not Planes': The CEO of Bombardier on Building a World-Class Culture," *McKinsey Quarterly,* March 2011, http://www.mckinsey.com/insights/organization/and_8220flying_people_not_planes_and_8221_the_ceo_of_bombardier_on_building_a_world-class_culture.

34. See A. Srinivasan and B. Kurey, "Creating a Culture of Quality," *Harvard Business Review,* April 2014, 23–26.

35. Excerpted from T. Higgins, "The Contender," *Bloomberg Businessweek,* June 17–23, 2013, 64–67.

36. Excerpted from S. Thomke, "Mumbai's Models of Service Excellence," *Harvard Business Review,* November 2012, 121–126.

37. M. Gunther, "3M's Innovation Revival," *Fortune,* September 27, 2010, 73–76.

38. Results can be found in C. Hartnell, Y. Ou, and A. Kinicki, "Organizational Culture and Organizational Effectiveness: A Meta-Analytic Investigation of the Competing Values Framework's Theoretical Suppositions," *Journal of Applied Psychology,* 2011, 677–694.

39. E. H. Schein, *Organizational Culture and Leadership* (San Francisco, CA: Jossey-Bass, 2010).

40. J. Reingold, "Still Crazy after All These Years," *Fortune,* January 14, 2012, 96.

41. D. W. Young, "The Six Levers for Managing Organizational Culture," in J. A. Wagner III and J. R. Hollenbeck, eds., *Readings in Organizational Behavior* (New York: Routledge, 2010), 533–546.

42. W. Disney, quoted in B. Nanus, *Visionary Leadership: Creating a Compelling Sense of Direction for Your Organization* (San Francisco, CA: Jossey-Bass, 1992), 28; reprinted from B. Thomas, *Walt Disney: An American Tradition* (New York: Simon & Schuster, 1976), 247.

43. The 12 mechanisms were based on material contained in E. H. Schein, "The Role of the Founder in Creating Organizational Culture," *Organizational Dynamics,* Summer 1983, 13–28.

44. J. Collins, "The Secret of Enduring Greatness," *Fortune,* May 5, 2008, 73–76.

45. A. Fox, "Don't Let Silos Stand in the Way," *HR Magazine,* May 2010, 51.

46. J. R. Katzenbach, I. Steffan, and C. Kronley, "Cultural Change That Sticks," *Harvard Business Review,* July–August 2012, 111.

47. M. Weinstein, "Cultivating Culture," *Training,* May/June 2013, 17.

48. D. Moss, "Triage: Methodically Developing Its Employees," *HR Magazine,* July 2007, 45.

49. M. T. Hansen, H. Ibarra, and U. Peyer, "The Best-Performing CEOs in the World," *Harvard Business Review,* January–February 2013, 84.

50. A. Grant, "How Customers Can Rally Your Troops," *Harvard Business Review,* June 2011, 99.

51. Moskowitz and Levering, "The 100 Best Companies to Work For," 92.

52. C. Hymowitz, "New CEOs May Spur Resistance if They Try to Alter Firm's Culture," *The Wall Street Journal,* August 13, 2007, B1.

53. See W. J. Becker and R. Cropanzano, "Organizational Neuroscience: The Promise and Prospects of an Emerging Discipline," *Journal of Organizational Behavior,* October 2010, 1055–1059.

54. G. Chazan and D. Mattioli, "BP Links Pay to Safety in 4th Quarter," *The Wall Street Journal,* October 19, 2010, B5.

55. R. E. Silverman, "Bringing Happy Hour to the Office," *The Wall Street Journal,* June 26, 2013, B8.

56. Excerpted from S. Shellenbarger, "Believers in the 'Project Beard' and Other Office Rituals," *The Wall Street Journal,* June 26, 2013, D1, D2.

57. Fox, "Don't Let Silos Stand in the Way," 51.

58. See J. Palazzolo, "Is It a Bribe . . . or Not?," *The Wall Street Journal,* July 22, 2013, R3.

59. A. Jones, "The Costs of Compliance Grow," *The Wall Street Journal,* October 2, 2012, B14.

60. See C. Palmeri and B. Faries, "Big Mickey Is Watching," *Bloomberg Businessweek,* March 7, 2014, 22–23.

61. D. Zielinski, "Giving Praise," *HR Magazine,* October 2012, 77.

62. R. E. Silverman and L. Kwoh, "Performance Reviews, Facebook Style," *The Wall Street Journal,* August 1, 2012, B6.

63. D. Zielinski, "Group Learning," *HR Magazine,* May 2012, 49.

64. Excerpted from J. Larrere, "Develop Great Leaders," *Leadership Excellence,* April 2010, 12.

65. See J. S. Lublin, "Making Sure the Boss Is the Right Fit," *The Wall Street Journal,* April 16, 2014, B7.

66. J. Van Maanen, "Breaking In: Socialization to Work," in R. Dubin, ed., *Handbook of Work, Organization, and Society* (Chicago: Rand-McNally, 1976), 67.

67. "Best Practices & Outstanding Initiatives: PricewaterhouseCoopers: 101: PwC Internship Experience," *Training,* February 2010, 104.

68. M. A. Tucker, "Show and Tell," *HR Magazine,* January 2012, 51–53.

69. Ibid.

70. Ibid.

71. See J. M. Phillips, "Effects of Realistic Job Previews on Multiple Organizational Outcomes: A Meta-Analysis," *Academy of Management Journal,* December 1998, 673–690.

72. Onboarding programs are discussed in T. Arnold, "Ramping Up Onboarding," *HR Magazine,* May 2010, 75–76; and K. Fritz, M. Kaestner, and M. Bergman, "Coca-Cola Enterprises Invests in On-Boarding at the Front Lines to Benefit the Bottom Line," *Global Business and Organizational Excellence,* May–June 2010, 15–22.

73. See M. P. Savitt, "Welcome!," *Training,* March/April 2012, 34–37.

74. M. Helft and J. Hempel, "Inside Facebook," *Fortune,* March 19, 2012, 117.

75. R. E. Silverman, "First Day on Job: Not Just Paperwork," *The Wall Street Journal,* May 29, 2013, B10.

76. A. Lashinsky, "The Secrets Apple Keeps," *Fortune,* February 6, 2012, 88.

77. M. Weinstein, "Cultivating Culture," *Training,* May/June 2013, 17.

78. H. R. Rafferty, "Social Media Etiquette: Communicate Behavioral Expectations," *SHRM,* March 24, 2010, http://www.shrm.org .hrdisciplines/technology/Articles/Pages/SocialMediaEtiquette .aspx.

79. M. Weinstein, "Miami Children's Hospital Puts People First," *Training,* January/February 2012, 43–48.

80. See M. M. Smith, "Recognition ROI . . . Now More Than Ever," *HR Magazine: Special Advertisement Supplement—The Power of Incentives,* 2008, 87–94.

81. See J. Wang and T.-Y. Kim, "Proactive Socialization Behavior in China: The Mediating Role of Perceived Insider Status and the Moderating Role of Supervisors' Traditionality," *Journal of Organizational Behavior,* April 2013, 389–406.

82. See J. D. Kammeyer-Mueller, L. S. Simon, and B. L. Rich, "The Psychic Cost of Doing Wrong: Ethical Conflict, Divestiture Socialization, and Emotional Exhaustion," *Journal of Management,* May 2012, 784–808.

83. J. Fan and J. P. Wanous, "Organizational and Cultural Entry: A New Type of Orientation Program for Multiple Boundary Crossings," *Journal of Applied Psychology,* November 2008, 1390–1400.

84. R. Levering and M. Moskowitz, "The 100 Best Companies to Work For: And the Winners Are . . .," *Fortune,* January 23, 2006, 94.

85. A review of stage model research can be found in B. E. Ashforth, *Role Transitions in Organizational Life: An Identity-Based Perspective* (Mahwah, NJ: Lawrence Erlbaum Associates, 2001).

86. For a thorough review of research on the socialization of diverse employees with disabilities, see A. Colella, "Organizational Socialization of Newcomers with Disabilities: A Framework for Future Research," in G. R. Ferris, ed., *Research in Personnel and Human Resources Management* (Greenwich, CT: JAI Press, 1996), 351–417.

87. This definition is based on the network perspective of mentoring proposed by M. Higgins and K. Kram, "Reconceptualizing Mentoring at Work: A Developmental Network Perspective," *Academy of Management Review,* April 2001, 264–288.

88. See T. D. Allen, L. T. Eby, M. L. Poteet, and E. Lentz, "Career Benefits Associated with Mentoring for Protégés: A Meta-Analysis," *Journal of Applied Psychology,* February 2004, 127–136; and J. U. Chun,

J. J. Sosik, and N. Y. Yun, "A Longitudinal Study of Mentor and Protégé Outcomes in Formal Mentoring Relationships," *Journal of Organizational Behavior,* November 2012, 1071–1094.

89. Career functions are discussed in detail in K. Kram, *Mentoring of Work: Developmental Relationships in Organizational Life* (Glenview, IL: Scott, Foresman, 1985).

90. T. J. DeLong, J. J. Gabarro, and R. J. Lees, "Why Mentoring Matters in a Hypercompetitive World," *Harvard Business Review,* January 2008, 115–121.

91. This discussion is based on Higgins and Kram, "Reconceptualizing Mentoring at Work," 264–288.

92. R. Hoffman and B. Casnocha, "The Real Way to Build a Network," *Fortune,* February 6, 2012, 23–30.

93. Ibid., 30.

94. See L. T. Eby, J. R. Durley, S. C. Evans, and B. R. Ragins, "Mentors' Perceptions of Negative Mentoring Experiences: Sale Development and Nomological Validation," *Journal of Applied Psychology,* March 2008, 358–373.

95. See S. Wang, E. D. Tomlinson, and R. A. Noe, "The Role of Mentor Trust and Protégé Internal Locus of Control in Formal Mentoring Relationships," *Journal of Applied Psychology,* March 2010, 358–367.

96. See A. D. Wright, "Your Social Media Is Showing," *HR Magazine,* March 2012, 16.

97. See T. Gutner, "Finding Anchors in the Storm: Mentors," *The Wall Street Journal,* January 27, 2009, D4.

98. G. Dutton, "Leadership Incubator Lessons," *Training,* May/June 2013, 38–39.

99. B. Womach, "Yahoo's Profit Tops Estimates as Mayer's Turnaround Gains Steam," *Bloomberg,* October 15, 2013, http://www .bloomberg.com/news/2013-10-15/yahoo-s-profit-tops-estimates-as-mayer-s-turnaround-gains-steam.html.

100. R. Needleman, "Five Things Marissa Mayer Will Change about Yahoo," *CNet News,* July 16, 2012, Google-cached version at http://webcache.googleusercontent.com/search?q=cache:M0tj1 o3JPRAJ:news.cnet.com/8301-1023_3-57473319-93/5-things-marissa-mayer-will-change-about-yahoo/ +&cd=1&hl=en&ct=clnk&gl=us, accessed November 12, 2013.

101. S. Hansell, "In the Race with Google, It's Consistency vs. 'Wow,'" *The New York Times,* July 24, 2006, http://www.nytimes .com/2006/07/24/technology/24yahoo.html?_r=0.

102. "Yahoo Memo: The 'Peanut Butter Manifesto,'" *The Wall Street Journal,* November 18, 2006, http://online.wsj.com/news/articles/ SB116379821933826657. See also P. May, "Lack of Corporate Focus Leaves Yahoos [Sic] in Limbo," *San Jose Mercury News,* September 16, 2011, http://www.mercurynews.com/ci_18912191; and R. Pendola, "Yahoo's Lack of Focus: Certainly a Downer," *Seeking Alpha* Blog, August 2, 2011, http://seekingalpha.com/ article/283844-yahoos-lack-of-focus-certainly-a-downer.

103. K. Swisher, "Yahoo Gets Googley Q&A Tool at Friday FYI and Uses It to Ask about Exec Accountability and Leaks," *All Things D,* August 6, 2012, http://allthingsd.com/20120806/yahoo-gets-googley-qa-tool-at-friday-fyi-and-uses-it-to-ask-about-exec-accountability-and-leaks/.

104. R. Hof, "Grading Marissa Mayer's First Year as Yahoo CEO," *Forbes,* July 24, 2013; and "Yahoo CEO Marissa Mayer's Mixed Marks for Her First Year," *Forbes,* August 12, 2013, http://www .forbes.com/sites/roberthof/2013/07/24/grading-marissa-mayers-first-year-as-yahoo-ceo/; http://www.forbes.com/sites/ roberthof/2013/07/24/yahoo-ceo-marissa-mayers-mixed-marks-for-her-first-year-2/.

105. R. McMillan, "Marissa Mayer's Biggest Win So Far? Keeping Yahoo's Engineers Optimistic," *Wired,* October 24, 2013, http:// www.wired.com/wiredenterprise/2013/10/engineeer_outlook/.

106. Announcement of acquisition on Mayer's Tumblr account, http:// marissamayr.tumblr.com/post/50902274591/im-delighted-to-announce-that-weve-reached-an.

107. D. Guthrie, "Marissa Mayer: Choosing Corporate Culture over Worker Independence," *Forbes,* March 8, 2013, http://www.forbes.com/sites/dougguthrie/2013/03/08/marissa-mayer-choosing-corporate-culture-over-worker-independence/.

108. N. Perlrot, "The Latest Change to Yahoo Mail Angers Its Users," *The New York Times,* October 21, 2013, B6, http://bits.blogs.ny-times.com/2013/10/16/furor-over-yahoo-mail-changes/?_r=0.

109. B. Womack, "Yahoo CEO Mayer Dismisses Operating Chief Castro," *Bloomberg.com,* January 16, 2014, http://www.bloomberg.com/news/2014-01-15/yahoo-chief-operating-officer-de-castro-to-leave-web-portal.html.

110. B. P. Eha, "In the Latest Move to Revamp Yahoo's Culture, Marissa Mayer Expands Parental Leave," *Entrepreneur,* May 1, 2013, http://www.entrepreneur.com/article/226542.

111. P. M. Barrett, "Bad Sports," *Bloomberg Businessweek,* March 3–9, 2014, 51.

112. P. M. Barrett, "UNC Officials Apologize for a Huge Sports Scandal, While Attacking the Woman Who Brought It to Light," *Bloomberg Businessweek,* February 3–9, 2014, 26.

113. Barrett, "Bad Sports."

Chapter 15

1. R. E. Silverman, "Step into the Office-Less Company," *The Wall Street Journal,* September 5, 2012, B6; and K. Piombino, "Infographic: 20 Percent of Global Workforce Telecommutes," http://www.ragan.com/Main/Articles?inforgraphic_20_percent_of_global_workforce_teleco…, June 18, 2013.

2. These tips were based in part on "Freelancing Professionally," *The Arizona Republic,* July 10, 2013, CL1; and M. Stanger, "10 Tips for Working Effectively at Home," http://www.businessinsider.com/how-to-be-more-productive-working-from-home-2012-9?…, September 29, 2012.

3. C. I. Barnard, *The Functions of the Executive* (Cambridge, MA: Harvard University Press, 1938), 73.

4. Drawn from E. H. Schein, *Organizational Psychology,* 3rd ed. (Englewood Cliffs, NJ: Prentice Hall, 1980), 12–15.

5. See V. Smeets and F. Warzynski, "Too Many Theories, Too Few Facts: What the Data Tell Us about the Link between Span of Control, Compensation, and Career Dynamics," *Labour Economics,* August 2008, 688–704.

6. See G. L. Neilson and J. Wulf, "How Many Direct Reports," *Harvard Business Review,* April 2012, 112–119.

7. This discussion is based on P. Graves, "What Kinds of Factors Should Determine How Many Direct Reports a Manager Supervises?," *HR Magazine,* July 2013, 19.

8. A management-oriented discussion of general systems theory can be found in K. E. Boulding, "General Systems Theory—The Skeleton of Science," *Management Science,* April 1956, 197–208. For more recent systems-related ideas, see A. J. Kinicki, K. J. L. Jacobson, B. M. Galvin, and G. E. Prussia, "A Multi-Systems Model of Leadership," *Journal of Leadership & Organizational Studies,* May 2011, 133–149.

9. R. M. Fulmer and J. B. Keys, "A Conversation with Peter Senge: New Development in Organizational Learning," *Organizational Dynamics,* Autumn 1998, 35.

10. This definition was based on D. A. Garvin, "Building a Learning Organization," *Harvard Business Review,* July–August 1993, 78–91.

11. L. G. Flores, W. Zheng, D. Rau, and C. H. Thomas, "Organizational Learning: Subprocess Identification, Construct Validation, and an Empirical Test of Cultural Antecedents," *Journal of Management,* March 2012, 640–667.

12. Ibid., 643.

13. R. Biswas-Diener, "Embracing Errors," *HR Magazine,* January 2012, 67.

14. Flores et al., "Organizational Learning," 644.

15. K. Dillon, "'I Think of My Failures as a Gift,'" *Harvard Business Review,* April 2011, 86.

16. A. G. Lafley, *Wikipedia,* http://en.wikipedia.org/wiki/A._G._Lafley, accessed April 7, 2014.

17. S. Ng and P. Ziobro, "At P&G, Lafley's Return Engagement," *The Wall Street Journal,* July 29, 2013, B2.

18. R. Greenwood and D. Miller, "Tackling Design Anew: Getting Back to the Heart of Organizational Theory," *Academy of Management Perspectives,* November 2010, 78.

19. M. C. Mankins and P. Rogers, "The Decision-Driven Organization," *Harvard Business Review,* June 2010, 56–57.

20. See ibid.; and "Full Speed Ahead," *HR Magazine,* March 2011, 18.

21. The following discussion is based on N. Anand and R. L. Daft, "What Is the Right Organization Design?," *Organizational Dynamics,* 2007, 329–344.

22. "Boundaryless Organization," http://www.businessdictionary.com/definition/boundaryless-organizatino.html, accessed August 2, 2013.

23. "Characteristics of a Boundaryless Organization," http://wiki.answers.com/Q/Characteristics-of-a-boundaryless_organization_structure, accessed August 2, 2013.

24. See J. McGregor, "Zappos Says Goodbye to Bosses," http://www.washingtonpost.com/blogs/on-leadership/wp/2014/01/03/zappos-gets-rid-of-all…, updated January 3, 2014.

25. "General Electric," http://en.wikipedia.org/wiki/General_Electric, last modified July 23, 2013.

26. M. Dervan, "Managing the Matrix in the New Normal," *T + D,* July 2010, 43–45.

27. J. R. Galbraith, *Designing Matrix Organizations That Actually Work* (San Francisco, CA: Jossey-Bass, 2009), ix.

28. "Who We Are: Working in Our Unique Culture," http://www.gore.com/en_xx/careers/whoweare/ourculture/gore-company-culture.html, accessed August 2, 2013.

29. "Who We Are: What We Believe," http://www.gore.com/en_xx/careers/whoweare/ourculture/gore-company-culture.html, accessed August 2, 2013.

30. "Who We Are: Working in Our Unique Culture."

31. "Our Culture: A Team-Based, Flat Lattice Organization," http://www.gore.com/en_xx/aboutus/culture/index.html, accessed August 2, 2013.

32. P. Lawrence, "Herman Miller's Creative Network," interview with Brian Walker, *BusinessWeek,* February 15, 2008, http://www.businessweek.com/stories/2008-02-15/herman-millers-creative-networkbusinessweek-business-news-stock-market-and-financial-advice.

33. C. Cuomo, B. Adhikari, and M. Patrick, "TaskRabbit: Putting Americans Back to Work, One Odd Job at a Time," September 29, 2011, http://abcnews.go.com/US/taskrabbit-putting-americans-back-work-odd-job-time/story?id=14626495.

34. G. A. Fowler and B. Cronin, "Freelancers Get Jobs via Web Services," *The Wall Street Journal,* May 29, 2013, B5.

35. Silverman, "Step into the Office-Less Company." See also "Automattic," http://en.wikipedia.org/wiki/Automattic, accessed August 2, 2013.

36. The following discussion is based on K. Reimer and N. Vehring, "Virtual or Vague? A Literature Review Exposing Conceptual Differences in Defining Virtual Organizations in IS Research," *Electron Markets,* 2012, 267–282.

37. Silverman, "Step into the Office-Less Company."

38. L. A. Clark, S. J. Karau, and M. D. Michalisin, "Telecommuting Attitudes and the 'Big Five' Personality Dimensions," *Journal of Management Policy and Practice,* June 2012, 31–46.

39. Material on Emma was derived from S. Bruzzese, "Working Remotely Poses Challenges," *The Arizona Republic,* May 9, 2012, CL1.

40. A. Taylor III, "How Toyota Lost Its Way," *Fortune,* July 26, 2010, 110.

41. See "Whole Foods Market," http://en.wikipedia.org/wiki/Whole_Foods_Market; and the corporate website's FAQ section, http://media.wholefoodsmarket.com/faq/, both accessed April 5, 2014.

42. C. Fishman, "Whole Foods Is All Teams," http://www.fastcompany.com/26671/whole-foods-all-teams, accessed August 2, 2013.

43. "We Support Team Member Happiness and Excellence," http://www.wholefoodsmarket.com/mission-values/core-values/we-support-team-member-..., accessed August 31, 2013.

44. See B. Tuttle, "The 5 Big Mistakes That Led to Ron Johnson's Ouster at JC Penney," *Time,* April 9, 2013, http://business.time.com/2013/04/09/the-5-big-mistakes-that-led-to-ron-johnsons-ouster-at-jc-penney/.

45. P. Kaestle, "A New Rationale for Organizational Structure," *Planning Review,* July–August 1990, 22.

46. Details of this study can be found in T. Burns and G. M. Stalker, *The Management of Innovation* (London: Tavistock, 1961).

47. J. D. Sherman and H. L. Smith, "The Influence of Organizational Structure on Intrinsic versus Extrinsic Motivation," *Academy of Management Journal,* December 1984, 883.

48. See J. A. Courtright, G. T. Fairhurst, and L. E. Rogers, "Interaction Patterns in Organic and Mechanistic Systems," *Academy of Management Journal,* December 1989, 773–802.

49. This discussion is based on L. Galetić, I. Marić, and A. Aleksić, "How Contingency Factors Determine Organization: Re-Examining Their Influence in Building Organizational Structure," *An Enterprise Odyssey, International Conference Proceedings,* University of Zagreb, Faculty of Economics and Business, 2012.

50. A. Taylor III, "Can This Car Save Ford?," *Fortune,* April 22, 2008, http://money.cnn.com/2008/04/21/news/companies/saving_ford.fortune/index.htm.

51. P. Gumbel, "Big Mac's Local Flavor," *Fortune,* May 2, 2008, http://money.cnn.com/2008/04/29/news/companies/big_macs_local.fortune/index.htm.

52. See Galbraith, *Designing Matrix Organizations That Actually Work,* 115–125.

53. Anand and Daft, "What Is the Right Organization Design?," 331–333.

54. B. Gruley and J. McCracken, "Best Guy?," *Bloomberg Businessweek,* October 22–28, 2012, 75.

55. Anand and Daft, "What Is the Right Organization Design?," 333–340.

56. See T. Johns and L. Gratton, "The Third Wave of Virtual Work," *Harvard Business Review,* January–February 2013, 66–72.

57. K. Cameron, "Critical Questions in Assessing Organizational Effectiveness," *Organizational Dynamics,* Autumn 1980, 70.

58. B. E. A. Oghojafor, F. I. Muo, and S. A. Aduloju, "Organizational Effectiveness: Whom and What Do We Believe?," *Advances in Management and Applied Economics,* 2012, 81–108.

59. See S. C. Voelpel and C. K. Streb, "A Balanced Scorecard for Managing the Aging Workforce," *Organizational Dynamics,* January–March 2010, 84–90.

60. J. Jargon, "McDonald's Says 'Service Is Broken,' Tries a Fix," *The Wall Street Journal,* April 11, 2013, B1, B2.

61. See R. S. Kaplan and D. P. Norton, "Having Trouble with Your Strategy? Then Map It," *Harvard Business Review,* September–October 2000, 167–176.

62. B. H. Moss, "How to Build a Workforce, One Person at a Time," *HR Magazine,* June 2012, 66–68.

63. Cameron, "Critical Questions in Assessing Organizational Effectiveness," 67.

64. A. Taylor III, "How Volkswagen Shucked Off Its Provincial Ways and Became a Global Powerhouse," *Fortune,* July 23, 2012, 154.

65. P. Dvorak, "How Irdeto Split Headquarters," *The Wall Street Journal,* January 7, 2008, B3; and at http://online.wsj.com/news/articles/SB119967570698371545.

66. K. S. Cameron, "Effectiveness as Paradox: Consensus and Conflict in Conceptions of Organizational Effectiveness," *Management Science,* May 1986, 542.

67. See B. Christie, "Southwest Finds Jet Cracks," *The Arizona Republic,* April 4, 2011, B4, B5; and A. Pasztor and T. W. Martin, "Mystery Still Surrounds Cause of Rupture Aboard Southwest Jet," *The Wall Street Journal,* April 4, 2011, B1, B4.

68. J. Mullich, "Investing in Innovation," *The Wall Street Journal,* June 12, 2013, B5.

69. A. Fisher, "America's Most Admired Companies," *Fortune,* March 17, 2008, 66.

70. "How P&G Plans to Clean Up," *BusinessWeek,* April 13, 2009, 44.

71. J. I. Cash Jr., M. J. Earl, and R. Morison, "Teaming Up to Crack Innovation Enterprise Integration," *Harvard Business Review,* November 2008, 90–100.

72. This discussion is based on B. Nagji and G. Tuff, "Managing Your Innovation Portfolio," *Harvard Business Review,* May 2012, 67–72.

73. E. Yoon and L. Deeken, "Why It Pays to Be a Category Creator," *Harvard Business Review,* March 2013, 21–23.

74. J. Welch and S. Welch, "Finding Innovation Where It Lives," *BusinessWeek,* April 21, 2008, 84.

75. Source quoted in S. Berkum, *The Myths of Innovation* (Sebastopol, CA: O'Reilly Media, 2007), 44.

76. This discussion is based on Berkum, *The Myths of Innovation.*

77. Curiosity is examined by S. H. Harrison, D. M. Sluss, and B. E. Ashforth, "Curiosity Adapted the Cat: The Role of Trait Curiosity in Newcomer Adaptation," *Journal of Applied Psychology,* January 2011, 211–220.

78. See L. Kwoh, "Memo to Staff: Take More Risks," *The Wall Street Journal,* March 20, 2013, B8.

79. Ibid.

80. M. Boyle, "Unilever: Taking on the World, One Stall at a Time," *Bloomberg Businessweek,* January 7–13, 2013, 18–20.

81. R. Jana, "Inspiration from Emerging Economies," *BusinessWeek,* March 23 and 30, 2009, 41.

82. Ibid.

83. R. Saunderson, "Oops! Learning from Our Mistakes," *Training,* December 2012, 62–63.

84. Ibid., 63.

85. R. Biswas-Diener, "Embracing Errors," *HR Magazine,* January 2012, 67.

86. See P. M. Madsen and V. Desai, "Failing to Learn? The Effects of Failure and Success on Organizational Learning in the Global Orbital Launch Vehicle Industry," *Academy of Management Journal,* June 2010, 451–476.

87. J. R. Immelt, "How We Did It . . .," *Harvard Business Review,* March 2012, 45.

88. D. Eng, "StubHub: The Anatomy of a Game-Changing Idea," *Fortune,* July 23, 2012, 60.

89. See C. A. Hartnell, A. Y. Ou, and A. Kinicki, "Organizational Culture and Organizational Effectiveness: A Meta-Analytic Investigation of the Competing Values Framework's Theoretical Suppositions," *Journal of Applied Psychology,* July 2011, 677–694.

90. See S. Prokesch, "How GE Teaches Teams to Lead Change," *Harvard Business Review,* January 2009, 99–106.

91. See J. N. Choi and J. Y. Chang, "Innovation Implementation in the Public Sector: An Integration of Institutional and Collective Dynamics," *Journal of Applied Psychology,* January 2009, 245–253; and F. Yuon and R. W. Woodman, "Innovative Behavior in the Workplace: The Role of Performance and Image Outcome Expectations," *Academy of Management Journal,* April 2010, 323–342.

92. D. Meinert, "Wings of Change," *HR Magazine,* November 2012, 30–36.

93. M. Helft, "Larry Page Looks Ahead," *Fortune,* January 14, 2013, 54.

94. "Crowdsourcing," *Wikipedia,* http://en.wikipedia.org/wiki/Crowdsourcing, accessed April 7, 2014.

95. K. J. Boudreau and K. R. Lakhani, "Using the Crowd as an Innovation Partner," *Harvard Business Review,* April 2013, 69.

96. Taken from company web page, http://www.ideo.com/about/; and "IDEO CEO Tim Brown on the Future of Design Thinking," January 6, 2013, http://www.cbsnews.com/video/watch/?id=50138337n.

97. "IDEO," http://en.wikipedia.org/wiki/IDEO; and "Contact" page of the IDEO website, http://www.ideo.com/contact/, both accessed April 7, 2014.

98. Frank Dobbin, "High Commitment Practices," lecture, Harvard University, October 10, 2012, as referenced in *Wikipedia* article, "IDEO."

99. M. Kimes, "At Sears, Lampert's Warring Divisions Model Adds to the Troubles," *Bloomberg Businessweek*, July 11, 2013, http://www.businessweek.com/articles/2013-07-11/at-sears-eddie-lamperts-warring-divisions-model-adds-to-the-troubles. Kimes serves as the primary source for this case unless otherwise noted.

100. D. Mattioli, "Lampert to Assume CEO Role at Spears," *The Wall Street Journal,* January 7, 2013, http://online.wsj.com/news/articles/SB10001424127887323706704578228230474184530.

101. Kimes, "At Sears, Lampert's Warring Divisions Model Adds to the Troubles."

102. R. Cyran and L. Silva, "Mr. Lampert, Fire Thyself," *The Wall Street Journal, Breaking Views–U.S.,* August 29, 2008, http://online.wsj.com/news/articles/SB121996631827281475.

103. Kimes, "At Sears, Lampert's Warring Divisions Model Adds to the Troubles," in reader comments following online version, posted shortly after publication. See also comments posted by TE, http://www.businessweek.com/articles/2013-07-11/at-sears-eddie-lamperts-warring-divisions-model-adds-to-the-troubles, accessed January 4, 2014.

104. Bob Sutton, "Dysfunctional Competition, the Knowing-Doing Gap, and Sears Holdings," *Work Matters Blog,* August 21, 2013, http://bobsutton.typepad.com/my_weblog/2013/08/dysfunctional-competition-the-knowing-doing-gap-and-sears-holdings-a-compelling-and-instructive-story-on-sears-holdings-ap.html.

105. K. Stock, "The Plan to Make Sears Shoppers Go Digital," *Bloomberg Businessweek*, May 29, 2013, http://www.businessweek.com/articles/2013-05-29/the-plan-to-make-sears-shoppers-go-digital.

106. See Kimes, "At Sears, Lampert's Warring Divisions Model Adds to the Troubles"; Mattioli, "Lampert to Assume CEO Role at Spears"; former Head of Sears Canada, Mark Cohen, as quoted in interview on *Bloomberg TV*, "Sears in 'Death Spiral' Under Lampert, Cohen Says," June 18, 2013, http://www.bloomberg.com/video/sears-in-death-spiral-under-lampert-cohen-says-Y~K9HiLBTO2kWNnM8dmv4g.html; S. Tobak, "The Worst CEO of 2013," *Fox Business News*, December 30, 2013, in which Lampert ranked seventh, http://www.foxbusiness.com/business-leaders/2013/12/30/worst-ceo-2013/; B. Napach, "The Worst CEOs of 2013," *Yahoo! Finance*, December 16, 2013, interviewing Sydney Finkelstein, http://finance.yahoo.com/blogs/daily-ticker/the-worst-ceos-of-2013--according-to-dartmouth-business-professor-sydney-finkelstein-145035471.html; and A. Hartung, "Oops! Five CEOs Who Should Have Already Been Fired," *Forbes*, May 12, 2012, in which Lampert ranked second, and in which Lampert was not yet technically the CEO, http://www.forbes.com/sites/adamhartung/2012/05/12/oops-5-ceos-that-should-have-already-been-fired-cisco-ge-walmart-sears-microsoft/3/.

107. Excerpted from J. Angwin, "The Web's New Gold Mine: Your Secrets," *The Wall Street Journal*, July 31–August 1, 2010, W1.

Chapter 16

1. S. Melnick, *Success under Stress* (New York: AMACOM Press, 2013).

2. E. Byron, "How to Market to an Aging Boomer: Flattery, Subterfuge and Euphemism," *The Wall Street Journal*, February 2, 2011, A1, A12, http://online.wsj.com/news/articles/SB2000142405274870401360457610439420906299.6.

3. P. Coy, "A Message from the Street," *Bloomberg Businessweek,* February 7–February 13, 2011, 58–65.

4. J. Cifuentes, "Infographic: LinkedIn Transforms Job Recruiting," *PCMag.com,* May 4, 2013, http://www.pcmag.com/article2/0,2817,2418403,00.asp, accessed September 17, 2013.

5. S. Adams, "New Survey, LinkedIn More Dominant Than Ever among Job Seekers and Recruiters, but Facebook Poised to Gain," *Forbes*, February 5, 2013, http://www.forbes.com/sites/susanadams/2013/02/05/new-survey-linked-in-more-dominant-than-ever-among-job-seekers-and-recruiters-but-facebook-poised-to-gain/, accessed March 29, 2014.

6. B. Brown, J. Sikes, and P. Willmott, "Bullish on Digital: McKinsey Global Survey Results," *McKinsey Highlights*, August 2013, http://www.mckinsey.com/insights/business_technology/bullish_on_digital_mckinsey_global_survey_results?cid=other-eml-nsl-mip-mck-oth-1309, accessed September 17, 2013.

7. Ibid.

8. N. Minow, "More Shareholders Are Just Saying No on Executive Pay," *Bloomberg View*, July 19, 2012, http://www.bloomberg.com/news/2012-07-19/more-shareholders-are-just-saying-no-on-executive-pay.html, accessed September 19, 2013; and Steven Hall Partners, "List of Companies That Have Failed Say on Pay in 2013," December 31, 2013, *Steven Hall Partners White Papers*, http://www.shallpartners.com/our-thinking/short-takes/2013-say-on-pay-fails/, accessed March 29, 2014.

9. L. McCrea, "16 Brands Leading the Way with Exemplary Social Media Customer Service," *Ignite Social Media*, November 7, 2012, http://www.ignitesocialmedia.com/social-media-examples/top-brands-social-media-customer-service-facebook-twitter/, accessed September 18, 2013.

10. Ibid.

11. H. L. Lee, "Don't Tweak Your Supply Chain—Rethink It End to End," *Harvard Business Review,* October 2010, 64–65, http://hbr.org/2010/10/dont-tweak-your-supply-chain-rethink-it-end-to-end/ar/1.

12. M. Spencer and J. Whalen, "Change France? Sanofi Finds It Can't," *The Wall Street Journal*, April 11, 2013, B1, B5, http://online.wsj.com/news/articles/SB10001424127887324010704578414624186895676.

13. J. Pepitone, "Foxconn Workers Strike over iPhone 5 Demands, Labour Group Says," *CNNMoney*, October 7, 2012, http://money.cnn.com/2012/10/05/technology/mobile/foxconn-iphone-5-strike/index.html, accessed September 18, 2013.

14. M. Maxwell, "New Bosses Often Clean House," *The Wall Street Journal*, September 17, 2013, http://blogs.wsj.com/riskandcompliance/2013/09/17/new-bosses-often-clean-house/, accessed September 17, 2013.

15. E. M. Rusli, G. A. Fowler, and J. Letzing, "Struggling Groupon Ousts Its Quirky CEO," *The Wall Street Journal*, February 28, 2013, http://online.wsj.com/news/articles/SB10001424127887324662404578332084043537590.

16. C. T. Carley, "BP Works toward Culture of Safety after 2010 Oil Spill," *Hattiesburg American*, August 21, 2013, http://www.hattiesburgamerican.com/article/20130823/OPINION02/308230001/BP-works-toward-culture-safety-after-2010-oil-spill, accessed September 19, 2013.

17. T. Ray, "Intel: Building on Otellini's Legacy," *Barrons.com*, November 24, 2012, http://online.barrons.com/article/SB50001424052748703961304578131031470913730.html, accessed February 9, 2013.

18. For a thorough discussion of the model, see K. Lewin, *Field Theory in Social Science* (New York: Harper & Row, 1951); and J. Helms, K. Dye, and A. J. Mills, *Understanding Organizational Change* (New York: Routledge, 2009), 39–55.

19. These assumptions are discussed in E. H. Schein, *Organizational Psychology,* 3rd ed. (Englewood Cliffs, NJ: Prentice Hall, 1980).

20. E. M. Rusli, "Even Facebook Must Change," *The Wall Street Journal,* January 30, 2013, B1, B7, http://online.wsj.com/news/articles/SB10001424127887323829504578272233666653120.

21. Ibid.

22. Adapted from J. Zhiguo, "Tsingtao's Chairman on Jump-Starting a Sluggish Company," *Harvard Business Review*, April 2012, 41–44,

http://hbr.org/2012/04/tsingtaos-chairman-on-jump-starting-a-sluggish-company/ar/1.

23. D. Meinert, "Wings of Change," *SHRM*, November 1, 2012, http://www.shrm.org/Publications/hrmagazine/EditorialContent/2012/1112/Pages/1112-change-management.aspx, accessed September 19, 2013.

24. L. R. Hearld and J. A. Alexander, "Governance Processes and Change within Organizational Participants of Multi-Sectoral Community Health Care Alliances: The Mediating Role of Vision, Mission, Strategy Agreement and Perceived Alliance Value," *American Journal of Community Psychology*, 2014, 185–197.

25. E. M. Rusli, "Instagram Pictures Itself Making Money," *The Wall Street Journal*, September 8, 2013, http://online.wsj.com/article/SB10001424127887324577304579059230069305894.html, accessed September 20, 2013.

26. Adapted from J. Mackey and R. Sisodia, *Conscious Capitalism* (Boston, MA: Harvard Business School Publishing, 2013), 46.

27. Interface company website: http://www.interfaceglobal.com/.

28. A. E. Rafferty, N. L. Jimmieson, and A. A. Armenakis, "Change Readiness: A Multilevel Review," *Journal of Management 39*, 2013, 110–135.

29. B. Burnes and B. Cooke, "The Past, Present, and Future of Organization Development: Taking the Long View," *Human Relations*, 2012, 1295–1429.

30. Ibid., 1400.

31. See R. Rodgers, J. E. Hunter, and D. L. Rogers, "Influence of Top Management Commitment on Management Program Success," *Journal of Applied Psychology*, February 1993, 151–155.

32. Results can be found in P. J. Robertson, D. R. Roberts, and J. I. Porras, "Dynamics of Planned Organizational Change: Assessing Empirical Support for a Theoretical Model," *Academy of Management Journal*, June 1993, 619–634.

33. Results from the meta-analysis can be found in G. A. Neuman, J. E. Edwards, and N. S. Raju, "Organizational Development Interventions: A Meta-Analysis of Their Effects on Satisfaction and Other Attitudes," *Personnel Psychology*, Autumn 1989, 461–490.

34. Results can be found in C.-M. Lau and H.-Y. Ngo, "Organization Development and Firm Performance: A Comparison of Multinational and Local Firms," *Journal of International Business Studies*, First Quarter 2001, 95–114.

35. J. Hagel, "Take the Shift Index Organizational Self-Assessment: Weekend Reading," *The Wall Street Journal*, July 18, 2014, http://deloitte.wsj.com/riskandcompliance/2014/07/18/take-the-shift-index-organizational-self-assessment-weekend-reading/tab/print, accessed September 2, 2014.

36. Adapted from R. J. Marshak, *Covert Processes at Work* (San Francisco, CA: Berrett-Koehler Publishers, 2006); and A. S. Judson, *Changing Behavior in Organizations: Minimizing Resistance to Change* (Cambridge, MA: Blackwell, 1991).

37. S. Oreg et al., "Dispositional Resistance to Change: Measurement Equivalence and Link to Personal Values across 17 Nations," *Journal of Applied Psychology*, 2008, 935–944.

38. See R. H. Schaffer, "Mistakes Leaders Keep Making," *Harvard Business Review*, September 2010, 86–91.

39. L. Goering, "Land of Plenty No Longer," *Chicago Tribune*, May 20, 2008, sec. 1, 8.

40. See D. M. Harold, D. B. Fedor, S. Caldwell, and Y. Liu, "The Effects of Transformational and Change Leadership on Employees' Commitment to Change: A Multilevel Study," *Journal of Applied Psychology*, March 2008, 346–357.

41. See R. H. Miles, "Accelerating Corporate Transformations (Don't Lose Your Nerve!)," *Harvard Business Review*, January–February 2010, 69–75, http://hbr.org/2010/01/accelerating-corporate-transformations-dont-lose-your-nerve/ar/1.

42. See S. A. Furst and D. M. Cable, "Employee Resistance to Organizational Change: Managerial Influence Tactics and Leader-Member Exchange," *Journal of Applied Psychology*, March 2008, 453–462.

43. J. Bennett, "GM's New Chief to Accelerate Profit Push," *The Wall Street Journal*, January 23, 2014, http://online.wsj.com/news/articles/SB10001424052702304632204579338751924201992?KEYWORDS=mary+barra&mg=reno64-wsj, accessed March 31, 2014.

44. J. B. White and J. Bennett, "Letter from GM CEO: 'Deeply Regret' Need to Recall 1.6 Million Cars," *The Wall Street Journal*, March 4, 2014, http://blogs.wsj.com/corporate-intelligence/2014/03/04/letter-from-gm-ceo-deeply-regret-need-to-recall-1-6-million-cars/tab/print/?KEYWORDS=mary+barra, accessed March 31, 2014.

45. D. C. Ganster and C. C. Rosen, "Work Stress and Employee Health: A Multidisciplinary Review," *Journal of Management 39*, July 2013, 1085–1122; and T. A. Wright, "The Role of Psychological Well-Being in Job Performance, Employee Retention and Cardiovascular Health," *Organizational Dynamics*, January–March 2010, 13–23.

46. See Hans Selye, *Stress without Distress* (Philadelphia, PA: Lippincott, 1974).

47. See J. D. Nahrgang, F. P. Morgeson, and D. A. Hoffman, "Safety at Work: A Meta-Analytic Investigation of the Link between Job Demands, Job Resources, Burnout, Engagement, and Safety Outcomes," *Journal of Applied Psychology*, January 2011, 71–94; and S. Ohly and C. Fritz, "Work Characteristics, Challenge Appraisal, Creativity, and Proactive Behavior: A Multi-Level Study," *Journal of Organizational Behavior*, May 2010, 543–565.

48. D. Meinert, "Sleepless in Seattle . . . and Cincinnati and Syracuse," *HR Magazine*, October 2012, 55–58.

49. C. K. Goodman, "Survey: Most Americans Stressed Out about Work," *Dallas Morning News*, April 21, 2013, D2.

50. Meinert, "Sleepless in Seattle."

51. "Too Much Information," *HR Magazine*, January 2011, 19.

52. See R. A. Clay, "Stressed in America," *Monitor on Psychology*, January 2011, 60–61.

53. Adapted from Meinert, "Sleepless in Seattle."

54. Results are presented in J. A. Penley, J. Tomaka, and J. S. Wiebe, "The Association of Coping to Physical and Psychological Health Outcomes: A Meta-Analytic Review," *Journal of Behavioral Medicine*, December 2002, 551–609.

55. See J. D. Kammeyer-Mueller, T. A. Judge, and B. A. Scott, "The Role of Core Self-Evaluations in the Coping Process," *Journal of Applied Psychology*, January 2009, 177–195.

56. M. F. Dollard and J. A. Gordon, "Evaluation of a Participatory Risk Management Work Stress Intervention," *International Journal of Stress Management*, 2014, 27–42.

57. Supportive results can be found in R. Ilies, N. Dimotakis, and I. E. De Pater, "Psychological and Physiological Reactions to High Workloads: Implications for Well-Being," *Personnel Psychology*, Summer 2010, 407–436; and E. R. Crawford, J. A. LePine, and B. L. Rich, "Linking Job Demands and Resources to Employee Engagement and Burnout: A Theoretical Extension and Meta-Analytic Test," *Journal of Applied Psychology*, September 2010, 834–848.

58. See M. R. Frone, "Are Work Stressors Related to Employee Substance Use? The Importance of Temporal Context in Assessments of Alcohol and Illicit Drug Use," *Journal of Applied Psychology*, January 2008, 199–206.

59. Supportive results can be found in Wright, "The Role of Psychological Well-Being in Job Performance, Employee Retention and Cardiovascular Health"; P. Steel, J. Schmidt, and J. Shultz, "Refining the Relationship between Personality and Subjective Well-Being," *Psychological Bulletin*, January 2008, 138–161; and G. E. Miller, E. Chen, and E. S. Zhou, "If It Goes Up, Must It Come Down? Chronic Stress and the Hypothalamic-Pituitary-Adrenocortical Axis in Humans," *Psychological Bulletin*, January 2007, 25–45.

60. B. Huppert, "Ad Agency Gives Workers 500 Paid Hours to Pursue Passions," August 20, 2013, http://bdd.us/news.php.

61. Details of this example can be found in D. Kesmodel, "How 'Chief Beer Taster' Blended Molson, Coors," *The Wall Street Journal,* October 1, 2007, B1, B5.

62. 60 Minutes, video from CBS News. March 25, 2012. Downloaded from: http://www.cbs.com/shows/60_minutes/video/2215220708/sergio-marchionne-resurrecting-chrysler/

63. Dollard and Gordon, "Evaluation of a Participatory Risk Management Work Stress Intervention."

64. J. P. Kotter, "Leading Change: Why Transformation Efforts Fail," *Harvard Business Review,* 1995, 64.

65. J. Martin, "Stress at Work Is Bunk for Business," *Forbes,* August 2, 2012, http://www.forbes.com/sites/work-in-progress/2012/08/02/stress-at-work-is-bunk-for-business/.

66. L. L. ten Bummelhuis and J. P. Trougakos, "The Recovery Potential of Intrinsically versus Extrinsically Motivated Off-Job Activities," *Journal of Organizational and Occupational Psychology,* 2014, 177–199.

67. Results are presented in K. M. Richardson and H. R. Rothstein, "Effects of Occupational Stress Management Intervention Programs: A Meta-Analysis," *Journal of Occupational Health Psychology,* January 2008, 69–93.

68. These steps were based on a discussion in L. Dzubow, "Optimism 101," *The Oprah Magazine,* April 2011, 130.

69. V. Lipman, "New Study Explores Why Change Management Fails—and How to (Perhaps) Succeed," *Forbes,* September 4, 2013, http://www.forbes.com/sites/victorlipman/2013/09/04/new-study-explores-why-change-management-fails-and-how-to-perhaps-succeed/, accessed September 16, 2013.

70. J. Kahn, "Report: Texas Football in for Major Culture Change under Charlie Strong," *The Bleacher Report,* January 14, 2014, http://bleacherreport.com/articles/1923429-texasl-football-in-for-major-culture-change-under-charlie-strong, accessed September 2, 2014.

71. B. Parks, "Continuum Redesigns Audi's Car Dealership Experience," *Bloomberg Businessweek,* February 14, 2013, http://www.businessweek.com/articles/2013-02-14/continuum-redesigns-audis-car-dealership-experience. Quotations and information in the case come from this article unless otherwise noted.

72. "Sales and Share of Total Market by Manufacturer," Auto Sales, *Wall Street Journal Online,* January 3, 2014, http://online.wsj.com/mdc/public/page/2_3022-autosales.html. See also "BMW Group Outsells Fiat in Europe as Small Luxury Gains Traction," *Automotive News Europe,* September 19, 2013, http://europe.autonews.com/article/20130919/ANE/309199984/bmw-group-outsells-fiat-in-europe-as-small-luxury-gains-traction.

73. G. Nelson, "Audi Says iPads Will Be Used throughout Dealership," *Automotive News,* January 25, 2014, http://www.autonews.com/article/20140125/RETAIL06/140129863/audi-says-ipads-will-be-used-throughout-dealership#axzz2rS4tNKbq.

74. H. Touryalai, "Wall Street Profits Hit Record Levels, So Why Are Banks Still Killing Jobs?," *The Wall Street Journal,* August 9, 2013, http://www.forbes.com/sites/halahtouryalai/2013/08/09/wall-street-profits-hit-record-levels-so-why-are-banks-still-killing-jobs/, accessed April 1, 2014.

75. S. Raice and J. Steinberg, "Goldman CEO's Pay Is Back on Top," *The Wall Street Journal,* March 18, 2014, http://online.wsj.com/news/articles/SB10001424052702304017604579447631180090114.

76. J. Silver-Greenberg and S. Craig, "Fined Billions, JPMorgan Chase Will Give Dimon a Raise," *The New York Times,* January 23, 2014, http://dealbook.nytimes.com/2014/01/23/fined-billions-bank-approves-raise-for-chief/.

77. Ibid.

bias
  anchoring, 378–379
  availability, 378
  confirmation, 376
  in decision making, 376–379
  escalation of commitment, **379**
  in feedback perception, 198
  framing, 379
  fundamental attribution, **121**, 198
  hindsight, 379
  overconfidence, 376–377
  in performance evaluation, 192–193, *193*
  representativeness, 378
  self-serving, **121**
Big data Reflects the vast quantity of data available for decision making. **382**–383, 392, 400, 499–500
Big Five Personality Dimensions Five basic dimensions that simplify more complex models of personality: extraversion, agreeableness, conscientiousness, emotional stability, and openness to experience. *81*, **81**–82, 84
biofeedback, 587, *587*
blame, and politics, 423
blindness
  indirect, *17*
  motivated, *17*
blind spots, 89
bodily-kinesthetic intelligence, *78*
body language, 299–301, 427
body movements and gestures, 300
bonuses, 210
book reviews, questionable, 435–436
Botox, rewards for prescribing, 474–475
bottom-up job design, 168, 172–174, *173*
boundaries
  task, 172, *173*
  team, 255
Boundaryless organization An organization where management has largely succeeded in breaking down barriers between internal levels, job functions and departments, as well as reducing external barriers between the organization and those with whom it does business. **528**
Bounded rationality Represents the notion that decision makers are "bounded" or restricted by a variety of constraints when making decisions. **371**–372
Brainstorming A method used to help groups generate multiple ideas and alternatives for solving problems. 369, **392**, *393*
brainwriting, 392
brand reinforcement, social media and, 314
brand reputation, social media and, 314–315, 324–325
breathing meditation, 233
Buddhism, 229
Buffering effect The buffering or reduction of the impact of negative events and stressors. **220**

Bullying The repeated mistreatment of an individual or individuals by aggressive or unreasonable behavior, including persistent abuse and humiliation by verbal, nonverbal, psychological, or physical means. **39,** 62, 342, 345–347
  anti-bullying strategies for, 346, *346*
  cyber bullying, 346–347
  Legal/Ethical Challenge on, 363
  Self-Assessment of, 347
  taking perspective of target, 347
bureaucracy, 537
business skills, of leaders, *446*

C

capital
  human and social, 9–12, *11,* 547–548
  psychological, 220, 235–238
career labyrinth, 128
career planning, 131
careful, slow decision making, 385–386
categorization, and stereotyping, 117
Causal attributions Suspected or inferred causes of behavior. **119**–121
"celebrations," as reinforcement, 210
Centralized decision making Key decisions are made by top management. **536**
central tendency, in performance evaluation, *193*
CEOs. *See* chief executive officers
chain of command, 520
change, 556–595
  adaptive, *563,* 563–564
  changing stage of, *565,* 565–566
  customers and, 560–561
  demographics and, 559
  external forces for, 558–561, *559*
  force-field analysis and, 594–595
  general types of, *563,* 563–564
  human resources and, 561–562
  innovative, *563,* 564
  internal forces for, *559,* 561–562
  Kotter's eight steps for leading, 570–571, *571*
  Lewin's model of, 564–566, *565*
  managerial behaviors/decisions and, 562
  motivation for, 564–565
  organizational development and, 571–573
  radically innovative, *563,* 564
  readiness for, **569**
  refreezing stage of, *565,* 566
  resistance to, 564, **574**–578, 585–586
  Self-Assessment of attitudes toward, 558
  shareholders and, 560
  social and political pressures for, 561
  systems model of, 566–570, *567,* 584
  target elements of, 569–570
  technology and, 560
  unfreezing stage of, 564–565, *565*
Change agent Someone who is a catalyst in helping organizations to deal with old problems in new ways. **574**

characteristics of, 577
  effective, tools of, 578
  relationship with recipient, 577–578, 585
Change and acquisition phase Requires employees to master important tasks and roles and to adjust to their work group's values and norms. **505**–506
change management, 584–589
  applying systems model in, 584–585
  contingency approach in, 586
  improving change agent–employee relationships in, 585
  Integrative Framework for, 556, 590, *591*
  managerial strategies in, *586*
  organizational processes and practices in, 585–586
  overcoming resistance in, 585–586
  Problem-Solving Application Case on, 592–593
  tips for managers, 588–589
  W.I.N. at Change approach in, 557
channel, communication, 298
Charisma A form of interpersonal attraction that inspires acceptance, devotion, and enthusiasm. 406, **462**
cheating, 13–14, 17
chief executive officers (CEOs)
  "clean house" approach of, 562
  female, 127
  impression management by, 428
  pay for performance of, 163, 204–205, 560
  rewards despite hardships, 179, 593
  successful, traits of, 73
citizenship behavior, organizational, 63–64, 92–93, 147
Clan culture One that values internal focus and flexibility rather than stability and control. **488**, *488,* 492
"clean house" approach, 562
Climate Represents employees' shared perceptions of policies, practices, and procedures. **341**
  creativity, 395–396
  diversity, **131**–132
  justice, 161
  organizational, **239**, *240,* 395–396, 548
  positive organizational behavior, 239–241
  psychological safety, **341**
Closed system A self-sufficient entity. **522**–523
Coaching A customized process between two or more people with the intent of enhancing learning and motivating change. **199**, 451
coalition tactics, 415
Coalition An informal group bound together by the active pursuit of a single issue. **423**–424
Coercive power Power to make threats of punishment and deliver actual punishment. **405**
  compliance with, 409
  outcomes of, 410, *410*
cognition
  implicit, **115**
  social, 115

glossary/subject index

characteristics of U.S., 127–130
customer, responding to changes in, 135
as force for change, 559
Integrative Framework for, 110, 139, *139*
denial, in diversity management, 133
derivatives trading, 436
design, organizational. *See* organizational design
design thinking, 549
detached listening, 302
develop stage presence, 317
developers (mentors), 509
developmental networks, *509,* 509–510
receptive, 510
traditional, 510
Developmental relationship strength The quality of relationships among the individual and those involved in his or her developmental network. **510**
Devil's advocacy Involves assigning someone the role of critic. **348**–350, *349*
diagnosis, 572
Diagnostic and Statistical Manual of Mental Disorders, 337
Dialectic method A method managers use to foster a structured debate of opposing viewpoints prior to making a decision. **349**
diplomats, followers as, 469
directive style, of decision making, 384–385, *385*
Discrimination Occurs when employment decisions about an individual are due to reasons not associated with performance or are not related to the job. **124,** 128, 140–141, 337
Disneyland, 495
Dispositional resistance to change An individual difference characterized by a laick of willingness to voluntarily initiate changes and increased likelihood to form negative attitudes toward the changes [they] encounter. **576**
dispositions, 59
dissolving, 30
Distinctiveness Compares a person's behavior on one task with his or her behavior on other tasks. **119,** *120*
distractions, from negativity, 227–228
distributed workers, 276
distribution criteria, for rewards, *201,* 201–202
Distributive justice The perceived fairness of how resources and rewards are distributed or allocated. **158,** *160*
Distributive negotiation Usually involves a single issue—a "fixed pie"—in which one person gains at the expense of another. **356**
Diversity The multitude of individual differences and similarities that exist among people. **122**–143
deep-level characteristics in, *123,* **124**
discrimination and, **124,** 128, 140–141

Integrative Framework for, 110, 139, *139*
layers of, 122–124, *123*
leader–member exchange theory and, 468
organizational dimensions of, *123,* 124
as organizational priority, 132
organizational socialization and, 507
surface-level characteristics in, *123,* **123**
workplace, trends in, 127–130
Diversity climate A subcomponent of an organization's overall climate and is defined as the employees' aggregate perceptions about the organization's diversity-related formal structure characteristics and informal values. **131**
diversity management
action options in, 133–135
affirmative action *versus,* 124–125
barriers and challenges to, 131–132
business rationale for, 126–130
company responses in, 135–137
Group Exercise on, 142–143
maximizing potential in, 125, 136
organizational practices for, 133–137
resistance to change in, 132
Self-Assessments of, 132, 137
Diversity of developmental relationships The variety of people within the network an individual uses for developmental assistance. **509**
Divisional structure Employees are segregated into organization groups based on similar products or services, customers or clients, or geographic regions. **528,** *533,* 538
division of labor, 520, 521–522
Dodd–Frank Act, 560, *560*
doing well and doing good, 221–222
Dominating style Exhibiting a high concern for self and low concern for others. **350,** *350, 352*
domination, 412
dopamine, 186
dress, and first impression, 426–427
DSS. *See* decision support systems
dyad, vertical, 466
Dysfunctional conflict Conflict that threatens an organization's interests. **333**

Ecomagination Challenge, 310
effect, law of, **206**–207
effectiveness. *See* organizational effectiveness; *specific topics*
efficacy, 87–89, 235, 237, 238
effort, goal setting and, 167
Electronic brainstorming (also called brainwriting) Allows participants to submit their ideas and alternatives over a computer network. **392**
email, 311, *311*
Emotions Complex, relatively brief responses aimed at a particular target, such as a person, information, experience, event, or nonevent. They

also change psychological and/or physiological states. **98**–101
beyond good *versus* bad, 224–225
in crucial conversations, 320
goal attainment and, 98–99
managing, 217
mixed, 99
negative, 98–101, *101,* 224–225, 252
in negotiations, 358
past *versus* future, 99
positive, 98–99, 224–228, 242, 243
practical implications for managers, 99
ratio of positive to negative, 227, 228
workplace management of, 99–101, *101,* 108–109
Emotional intelligence (EI) The ability to monitor your own emotions and those of others, to discriminate among them, and to use this information to guide your thinking and actions. 78, **95**–97
benefits of, 95–96
developing, 96, *97*
of leaders, 96, 445
Emotional stability Being relaxed, secure, unworried, and less likely to experience negative emotions under pressure. *81,* **92**–93
Emotion display norms Rules that dictate which types of emotions are expected and appropriate for their members to show. **99**–100
empathy, 334, 417
Employee engagement The harnessing of organization members' selves to their work roles; in engagement, people employ and express themselves physically, cognitively, and emotionally during role performance. **52**–55
alternative rewards and, 203–204
empowerment and, 412
feelings in, 52
increasing, 54
motivation and, 147
outcomes of, 53
Problem-Solving Application on, 54–55
Self-Assessment of, 53–54
in U.S. workforce, 52–53
employee turnover, 65
employee voice, **159**–160, 203–204
Empowering leadership The extent to which a leader creates perceptions of psychological empowerment in others. **451**
Empowerment Efforts to enhance employee performance, well-being, and positive attitudes. **411**–415
evolution of, 412, *412*
inputs in, 413–414, *414*
organizational development and, 571
outputs in, 414, *414*
and performance, 412
process of, 413–414, *414*
psychological, 412–413, 451
structural, 411–412
team and organizational level, 413

glossary/subject index

glossary/subject index

glossary/subject index

glossary/subject index

Opportunity Represents a situation in which there are possibilities to do things that lead to results that exceed goals and expectations. **369**
in conflict, 335
in decision making, 369

Optimism Making a positive attribution (optimism) about succeeding now and in the future. **235**, 238

Optimists People who view successes as due to their "personal, permanent, and pervasive causes, and negative events to external, temporary, and situation-specific ones. **237**

Organic organizations Flexible networks of multitalented individuals who perform a variety of tasks. **535**–537

Organization A system of consciously coordinated activities or forces of two or more persons. **520**
aligned goals of, 520
boundaryless, **528**
closed system of, **522**–523
coordination in, 520
division of labor in, 520, 521–522
foundation of, 520–525
goals and strategies of, 520, 537
hierarchy of authority in, 520, 521, *521*
human resources of, 537–538
learning, *524*, **524**–525
line and staff positions in, 522
mechanistic *versus* organic, 535–537
open system of, **522**–524, *523*
size of, 537
span of control in, **522**

Organizational behavior (OB) Describes an interdisciplinary field dedicated to understanding and managing people at work. **4** *See also specific topics*
contingency perspective on, 4–6
Integrative Framework for, *27*, 27–32
interactional perspective on, 24–25
levels of, individual, group/team, and organization, 25
person and environmental factors in, 23–26
problem solving in, 20–22

Organizational citizenship behavior (OCB) Individual behavior that is discretionary, not directly or explicitly recognized by the formal reward system, and that in the aggregate promotes the effective functioning of the organization. **63**–64
emotional stability and, 92–93
motivation and, 147

Organizational climate Employees' perceptions of formal and informal organizational policies, practices, procedures, and routines. **239**, *240*, 395–396, 548

Organizational commitment The extent to which an individual identifies with an organization and commits to its goals. **50**–52
best practices to increase, 51–52
personal values and, 50–51
psychological contracts and, 51

Organizational culture The set of shared, taken-for-granted implicit assumptions that a group holds and that determines how it perceives, thinks about, and reacts to its various environments. **480**, 395–396, 478–517
adhocracy, *488*, 488–489, 492
basic underlying assumptions of, **483**–484, 494–495
characteristics of, 480–481
clan, 488, *488*, 492
competing values framework and, 487–492, *488*
drivers and flow of, 481, *481*
enacted values of, **482**–483
espoused values of, **482**–483, 494–495
fit and, 479, 500–501
foundation of, 480–486
functions of, *484*, 484–486
hierarchy, *488*, 490–491
and innovation, 548
Integrative Framework for, 478, 513, *513*
levels of, 481–484
market, *488*, 489–490, 492, 499
mentoring and, 508–511
observable artifacts of, 481–482, *482*, 494–495
outcomes associated with, 492–493, *493*
Self-Assessment of, 492, 501
socialization and, 502–507
and span of control, 522
types of, 487–492, *488*
organizational culture change, 494–501
employee cycle in, *496*, 500
explicit rewards, status symbols, and promotion criteria in, *496*, 497
formal statements in, 495, *496*
leader reactions to critical incidents and crises in, *496*, 498
leadership in, 494
mechanisms for, 495–500, *496*
organizational activities, processes, or outcomes in, *496*, 498
organizational systems and procedures in, *496*, 499–500
Problem-Solving Application Case on, 514–515
rites and rituals in, *496*, **498**–499
role modeling and training in, *496*, 496–497
slogans, language, acronyms, and sayings in, *496*, *496*
stories, legends, or myths in, *496*, *497*, 497–498
structured approach to, 495
vision in, 495
workflow and organizational structure in, *496*, 499
workplace design in, 495–496, *496*

Organizational design The structures of accountability and responsibility used to develop and implement strategies, and the human resource practices and information and business processes that activate those structures. **526**–534
categories and eras of, *527*, 527–528
contingency approach to, 535–539
divisional, 528, *533*, 538
fit of, 537–539
functional, 528, *533*, 538
hollow, 530–531, *533*, 539
horizontal, 527, *527*, 529–530, *533*, 539
and innovation, 549
Integrative Framework for, 518, 551, *551*
matrix, 528–529, *533*, 538–539
modular, 531–532, *533*, 539
open, *527*, 527–528
organizational culture and, 481, *496*, 499
Problem-Solving Application Case on, 552–553
traditional, 527, *527*
types of, 528–534, *533*
virtual, 519, 532–534, *533*, 539
organizational development (OD), 571–573, *572*
diagnosis in, 572, *572*
evaluation in, *572*, 573
feedback in, *572*, 573
history and philosophy of, 572
and Integrative Framework, 573
intervention in, *572*, 572–573
process of, *572*, 572–573
organizational effectiveness, 540–543, *541*
goal accomplishment in, 540–541, 543
internal processes in, 541–542, 543
practical guidelines for, 542–543
resource acquisition in, 542, 543
satisfaction of strategic constituencies in, 542, 543
organizational functions, 257
organizational identity, 485
organizational innovation, 544
organizational justice, 158
organizational learning, 524
organizational levels, 25–26
organizational memory, 525

Organizational politics Intentional acts of influence to enhance or protect the self-interest of individuals or groups that are not endorsed by or aligned with those of the organization. **420**–422. *See also* politics

Organizational practices Refer to a host of procedures, policies, practices, routines, and rules that organizations use to get things done. **240**, *240*

Organizational socialization The process by which a person learns the values, norms, and required behaviors expected in order to participate as a member of the organization. **502**–507
anticipatory phase of, *503*, 503–504
change and acquisition phase of, 505–506
encounter phase of, *503*, 504–505
model of, 502–506, *503*

glossary/subject index

glossary/subject index

Sustainability culture A company's ability to make a profit without sacrificing the resources of its people, the community, and the planet. **483**–484

SWOT analysis, 569

Symptom management strategies Methods focusing on reducing the symptoms of stress. **582**

Systems Approach, 27

systems model of change, 566–570, *567*

  applying, 584–585

  inputs in, *567*, 567–569

  outputs in, 570

T

Tacit knowledge Information gained through experience that is difficult to express and formalize. **374**

tactics

  influence, **415**–417

  political, *422*, 422–423

  socialization, 506, *507*

Take-Away Applications (TAAPs), 22

talent, practice *versus*, 103

Talent Is Overrated: What Really Separates Performers from Everybody Else (Colvin), 103

talent recruitment, via social media, 314

target elements of change, 569

task boundaries, 172, *173*

task identity, 171

task-oriented leadership, 441, 448–450, 454–457, *455*

Task roles Roles that enable the work group to define, clarify, and pursue a common purpose. 258–**260**

  types and descriptions of, *259*

task significance, 171

task strategies, 167

task structure, *455*, 455–457, 459–460

Team(s) A small number of people with complementary skills who are committed to a common purpose, performance goals, and approach for which they hold themselves mutually accountable. **267**–278

  conflict on, 338–341

  criteria for, 268

  effectiveness of, 268, 282–284

  empowerment of, 413

  versus group, 267–269

  in group development terms, 268–269

  high-performing, characteristics of, 282

  horizontal design and, 527, 529–530, 539

  Integrative Framework for, 253, 254, 285, *286*

  NASA example of, 283–284

  rewards, competition, and collaboration on, 283

  self-managed, 274–276

  size of, 284

  3Cs of, 282–283

  virtual, 276–278

Team adaptive capacity The ability of a team to meet changing demands and to effectively transition members in and out. **283**

Team building A catchall term for a host of techniques aimed at improving the internal functioning of work groups. **272**–274

  accelerated process of, 273–274

  return on investment, 272–273

Team charters Descriptions of how the team will operate, such as processes for sharing information and decision making (teamwork). 255, **282**–283

Team composition The collection of jobs, personalities, knowledge, skills, abilities, and experience of team members. **283**

team identity, 255

Team performance strategies Deliberate plans that outline what exactly the team is to do, such as goal setting and defining particular member roles, tasks, and responsibilities. **282**–283

team players, 269–272

  social loafers (free riders) *versus*, 271–272

  3Cs of, 271

team vision, 255

teamwork competencies, 269–272, *270*

technological advancements, 560

technology

  advantages *versus* disadvantages of, 24

  conflict intensification by, 342–348

  as force for change, 560

  and organizational design, 537

  virtual teams via, 276–278

TED (Technology, Education, Design) talks, 317–319

Telecommuting Allows employees to do all or some of their work from home, using advanced telecommunications technology and Internet tools to send work electronically from home to the office, and vice versa. **60**, 344, 530

telephone communication, 295, 298, 307

Temperance A shared belief in showing restraint and control when faced with temptation and provocation. It promotes self-control, humility, and prudence. **239**

10,000-hour rule, for practice, 102

Theory X A pessimistic view of employees: that they dislike work, must be monitored, and can only be motivated with rewards and punishment ("carrots and sticks"). **148**

Theory Y A modern and positive set of assumptions about people at work: that they are selfengaged, committed, responsible, and creative. **148**

thesis, 349

third-party intervention, in conflict, 353–355

3Cs

  of team players, 271

  of teams, 282–283

3-Stop Problem Solving Approach, 6, 21–22, 29, 31–32

360-degree feedback Individuals compare perceptions of their own performance with behaviorally specific (and usually anonymous) performance information from their manager, subordinates, and peers. **192**–193

time bound, 188

timeliness, and performance, 192

tobacco-free hiring, 108

tolerance for ambiguity, 384, *385*

toleration, in diversity management, 134

top-down job design, 168–172

Total rewards Rewards not only involving compensation and benefits, but also personal and professional growth opportunities and a motivating work environment that includes recognition, job design, and work–life balance. **203**

touch, 300

tracking, of consumers, 553–554

tracking sensors, 251–252

traditional designs, 527, *527*

traditionalists (generation), 129, *130*, 136

training

  core self-evaluations and, 94

  in cultural change, *496*, 496–497

  in diversity management, 136

traits, 74–75, *75*, 102

  generational differences in, 129, *130*

trait theories of leadership, 443–447, *444*

Trait approach Attempts to identify personality characteristics or interpersonal attributes that can be used to differentiate leaders from followers. **443**

Transactional leadership Focuses on clarifying employees' role and task requirements and providing followers with positive and negative rewards contingent on performance. **448**–449

Transformational innovations Targeted at creating new markets and customers that rely on developing breakthroughs and inventing things that don't currently exist. **545**

Transformational leadership Leaders that transform followers to pursue organizational goals over self-interests. 441, 445, **462**–465, *463*

  ethics in, 465

  idealized influence in, *463*, 463–464

  implications for managers, 465

  individualized consideration in, *463*, 464

  inspirational motivation in, **462**–463, *463*, 465

  intellectual stimulation in, *463*, 464

  process of, *463*, 464–465

  Self-Assessment of, 465

  virtual, 465

name index

company index

company index

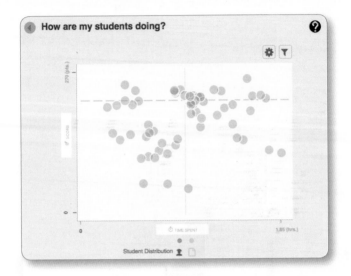

How are my students doing?

Connect Insight

The first and only analytics tool of its kind, Connect Insight is a series of visual data displays, each of which is framed by an intuitive question and provides at-a-glance information regarding how an instructor's class is performing. Connect Insight is available through Connect titles.

EASY TO USE

Learning Management System Integration

McGraw-Hill Campus is a one-stop teaching and learning experience available to use with any learning management system. McGraw-Hill Campus provides single sign-on to faculty and students for all McGraw-Hill material and technology from within the school website. McGraw-Hill Campus also allows instructors instant access to all supplements and teaching materials for all McGraw-Hill products.

Blackboard users also benefit from McGraw-Hill's industry-leading integration, providing single sign-on to access all Connect assignments and automatic feeding of assignment results to the Blackboard grade book.

The **Best** of
Both Worlds

POWERFUL REPORTING

Connect generates comprehensive reports and graphs that provide instructors with an instant view of the performance of individual students, a specific section, or multiple sections. Since all content is mapped to learning objectives, Connect reporting is ideal for accreditation or other administrative documentation.

CONNECT FEATURES

Interactive Applications

Interactive Applications offer a variety of automatically graded exercises that require students to **apply** key concepts. Whether the assignment includes a *click and drag*, *video case*, or *decision generator*, these applications provide instant feedback and progress tracking for students and detailed results for the instructor.

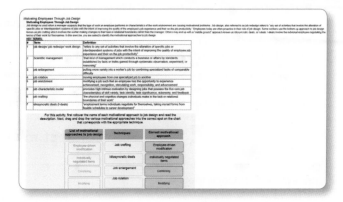

Self-Assessments

Self-awareness is a fundamental aspect of personal or professional development. With 95 researched-based self-assessments, students will have frequent opportunities to make the chapter concepts come to life by seeing how they apply to them personally.

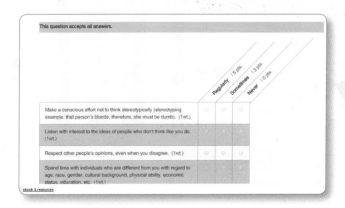

Manager's Hot Seat Videos

The Manager's Hot Seat is an interactive online video program that allows students to watch real managers apply their years of experience in confronting issues. Students assume the role of the manager as they watch the video and answer multiple-choice questions that pop up during the segment, forcing them to make decisions on the spot. Students learn from the manager's mistakes and successes, and then do a report critiquing the manager's approach by defending their reasoning.

McGraw Hill Education

connect®

LEARN WITHOUT LIMITS

Continually evolving, McGraw-Hill Connect® has been redesigned to provide the only true adaptive learning experience delivered within a simple and easy-to-navigate environment, placing students at the very center.

- **Performance Analytics** – Now available for both instructors and students, easy-to-decipher data illuminates course performance. Students always know how they're doing in class, while instructors can view student and section performance at-a-glance.

- **Mobile** – Available on tablets, students can now access assignments, quizzes, and results on-the-go, while instructors can assess student and section performance anytime, anywhere.

- **Personalized Learning** – Squeezing the most out of study time, the adaptive engine within Connect creates a highly personalized learning path for each student by identifying areas of weakness and providing learning resources to assist in the moment of need. This seamless integration of reading, practice, and assessment ensures that the focus is on the most important content for that individual.

connect.mheducation.com

Connect Performance Metrics

- ■ Without Connect
- ■ With Connect

Data compiled from independent research studies at higher education institutions.

Exam Scores: 74.7% / 80.4%
Pass Rates: 72.9% / 83.7%
Attendance Rates: 74.5% / 92.5%
Retention Rates: 71.1% / 87.5%

Average Grade Distribution

With Connect: A B C D F
Without Connect: A B C D F

Base: Seven control/test groups from six institutions.
Data compiled from independent research studies at higher education institutions.

Grade Distribution

Without LearnSmart: A 19.3%, B 38.6%, C 28.0%
With LearnSmart: A 30.5%, B 33.5%, C 22.6%

58% more A's with LearnSmart

Student Retention Rate

Without LearnSmart: Dropout Rate 31%
With LearnSmart: Dropout Rate 20%

35% fewer dropouts with LearnSmart

Student Pass Rate

Without LearnSmart: 57% / 43%
With LearnSmart: 30% / 70%

23% more students passed with LearnSmart

Connect reduces time spent on administrative tasks...

Reviewing Homework: 60 minutes without Connect → 15 minutes with Connect

Giving Tests or Quizzes: 60 minutes without Connect → 0 minutes with Connect

Grading: 60 minutes without Connect → 12 minutes with Connect

...allowing for more time to focus on concept application and other learning.

Without Connect
Time spent giving tests or quizzes: 20%
Time spent reviewing homework: 40%
Time spent on concept application and/or active learning: 40%

With Connect
Time spent giving tests or quizzes: 0%
Time spent reviewing homework: 10%
Time spent on concept application and/or active learning: 90%

SmartBook Achieve

Accelerate student success with SmartBook Achieve™, the first and only adaptive study experience that pinpoints individual student knowledge gaps and provides targeted, interactive help at the moment of need.